Microsoft®

Access® 2010
IN DEPTH

Roger Jennings

Middlesbrough College

00088917

MICROSOFT® ACCESS® 2010 IN DEPTH

Library of Congress Cataloging-in-Publication Data
Jennings, Roger.
 Microsoft Access 2010 in depth / Roger Jennings. -- 1st ed.
     p. cm.
 Includes index.
 ISBN 978-0-7897-4307-7
 1. Database management. 2. Microsoft Access. I. Title.
 QA76.9.D3J4683 2011
 005.75'65--dc22

                             2010048411

ISBN-13: 978-0-7897-4307-7

ISBN-10: 0-7897-4307-8

Printed in the United States of America

First Printing: December 2010

Trademarks

All terms mentioned in this book that are known to be trademarks or service marks have been appropriately capitalized. Que Publishing cannot attest to the accuracy of this information. Use of a term in this book should not be regarded as affecting the validity of any trademark or service mark.

Warning and Disclaimer

Every effort has been made to make this book as complete and as accurate as possible, but no warranty or fitness is implied. The information provided is on an "as is" basis. The author and the publisher shall have neither liability nor responsibility to any person or entity with respect to any loss or damages arising from the information contained in this book.

Bulk Sales

Que Publishing offers excellent discounts on this book when ordered in quantity for bulk purchases or special sales. For more information, please contact

U.S. Corporate and Government Sales
1-800-382-3419
corpsales@pearsontechgroup.com

For sales outside of the U.S., please contact

International Sales
international@pearson.com

Associate Publisher
Greg Wiegand

Acquisitions Editor
Loretta Yates

Development Editor
Charlotte Kughen

Technical Editor
Scott Diamond

Managing Editor
Sandra Schroeder

Project Editor
Mandie Frank

Copy Editor
Barbara Hacha

Indexer
Tim Wright

Production
Bronkella Publishing LLC

Designer
Anne Jones

Editorial Coordinator
Cindy Teeters

CONTENTS AT A GLANCE

Introduction

I Getting Acquainted with Access 2010

1 Access 2010 for Access 2007 Users: What's New   17
2 Building Simple Tracking Applications   45
3 Navigating the Fluent User Interface   95

II Learning the Fundamentals of Access Databases

4 Exploring Relational Database Theory and Practice   155
5 Working with Access Databases and Tables   179
6 Entering, Editing, and Validating Access Table Data   245
7 Sorting, Finding, and Filtering Data   267
8 Linking, Importing, and Exporting Data   297

III Transforming Data with Queries and PivotTables

9   Designing Queries for Access Databases   347
10 Understanding Access Query Operators and Expressions   381
11 Creating Multitable and Crosstab Queries   421
12 Working with PivotTable and PivotChart Views   505
13 Creating and Updating Access Tables with Action Queries   535

IV Designing Forms and Reports

14 Creating and Using Access Forms   565
15 Designing Custom Multitable Forms   607
16 Working with Simple Reports and Mailing Labels   683
17 Preparing Advanced Reports   729
18 Adding Graphs, PivotCharts, and PivotTables   755

V Programming Databases with Macros

19 Automating Access Applications with Macros and Procedures   797
20 Emulating Table Triggers with Access Data Macros   821

VI Collaborating with Access Data

21 Linking Access Front Ends to Access and Client/Server Tables   859
22 Collaborating with Windows SharePoint Foundation 2010   917
23 Sharing Web Databases with SharePoint Server 2010   975

VII Working with HTML and XML Documents

24 Importing and Exporting Web Pages   1007 (Online)
25 Integrating with XML and InfoPath 2010   1053 (Online)

VIII Creating Access Front Ends to SQL Server Databases

26 Exploring Access Data Projects and SQL Server 2008   1089 (Online)
27 Moving from Access Queries to Transact-SQL   1137 (Online)
28 Upsizing Access Applications to Access Data Projects and SQL Azure   1171 (Online)

IX Programming and Converting Access Applications

29 Learning Visual Basic for Applications   1239 (Online)
30 Handling Events with VBA and Macros   1279 (Online)
31 Programming Combo and List Boxes   1317 (Online)
32 Understanding Data Access Objects, OLE DB, and ADO   1349 (Online)
33 Upgrading Access 2003 and Earlier Applications to Access 2010   1403 (Online)

X Appendix

A What Was New in Access 2007 for Users of Access 2003 and Earlier   1423 (Online)
B Glossary   1475 (Online)
   Index   1505

CONTENTS

Introduction

Who Should Read This Book   2

How This Book Is Organized   4
  Printed Parts and Chapters   5
  Online-Only Parts and Chapters   8
  Part IX: Programming and Converting
  Access Applications   10
  Appendixes   10
  The Downloadable Sample Files   11

How This Book Is Designed   11

Typographic Conventions Used in This
Book   12
  Key Combinations, Menu Choices, and
  Filenames   12
  SQL Statements and Keywords in Other
  Languages   12
  Typographic Conventions Used for
  VBA   13
  Typographic Conventions Used for
  VBScript   14

System Requirements for Access 2010   14

Other Sources of Information for Access   15
  Books   15
  Internet   16

I Getting Acquainted with Access 2010

**1 Access 2010 for Access 2007 Users:
What's New   17**

What's New in Microsoft Office Access
2010: An Overview   18

Changes to the Office 2007 Ribbon User
Interface   22
  Access 2007's Main Ribbons   22
  Contextual Ribbons for Access
  Databases and Projects   24

  The Quick Access Toolbar   26
  The File Tab's Backstage View   26

Security, Trusted Locations, Packages, and
Certificates   29
  Specifying Trusted Locations   31
  Packaging and Code-Signing
  Databases   31
  Enabling Non-trusted Application
  Automation with Macros   31

Access Web Databases and SharePoint
Lists   32

Application Development by Templates   32

Access Macros Redux   33

SQL Server 2008 [R2] Express Edition
Setup   35
  Downloading and Installing SSX   35
  Managing SSX   40

**2 Building Simple Tracking
Applications   45**

Creating Access Applications from
Downloaded Templates   46
  Using the Getting Started Window to
  Download Templates   46
  Changing the Default Folder for New
  Databases and Projects   48
  Creating a Database from a Getting
  Started Window Template   48
  Designating the Default Database Folder
  as a Trusted Location   53
  Creating a Database from Any Access
  Template on Microsoft Office Online   55
  Changing Forms from Overlapping
  Windows to Tabbed Documents   58

Touring the Modified Tasks
Application   59
  Understanding the Role of the
  Navigation Pane   59

Opening Forms and Reports with Macros **66**

Importing and Exporting Data from and to Outlook 2010 **70**
Importing Contacts from an Outlook Contacts Folder **70**
Exporting Contacts to Outlook **72**
Using Outlook to Email Lists and Detail Items **74**
Collecting Data by Email with Outlook HTML Forms **78**

Integrating Objects from Other Template Databases **79**
Import Missing Objects **80**
Alter Inappropriate Field Names **83**
Conform MVLF Combo Boxes of List and Details Forms **86**
Add Approved By and Assigned To Employee Lookup Fields **90**
Add Approved By and Assigned To Combo Boxes to Lists and Details Forms **93**

3 Navigating the Fluent User Interface 95

Defining Access Functions **95**

Defining Access Operating Modes **98**

Opening the Northwind.accdb Sample Database **100**

Understanding Access's Table Windows **102**

Navigating the Home and Create Ribbons **106**
The Home Ribbon **106**
Context-Specific Table Tools Ribbons **110**
The Create Ribbon **118**

Using the Function Keys **121**
Global Function Keys **121**

Function-Key Assignments and Shortcut Keys for Fields, Grids, and Text Boxes **121**

Setting Default Options **122**
The General Page **123**
The Current Database Page **124**
The Datasheet Page **126**
The Object Designers Page **126**
The Proofing Page **128**
The Language Page **129**
The Client Settings Page **129**
The Customize Ribbon Page **132**
The Quick Access Toolbar Page **132**
The Add-Ins Page **134**
The Trust Center Pages **134**

Creating a Customized Template File **137**

Using Access Online Help **138**
Searching for a Phrase **139**
Searching Other Sources **141**

Spelunking the Database Utilities **141**
Compacting and Repairing Databases **142**
Converting Earlier Database Formats to Access 2007 Format **143**
Compile Errors in the Convert Database Process **143**
Creating .accde Files **143**
Creating .accdr Runtime Files **144**

Packaging, Signing, and Distributing an Access 2007 Database **144**
Generate and Install a Self-Certified Digital Certificate **145**
Creating a Signed Package File (*.accdc) **148**
Testing a Signed Package File (*.accdc) **148**
Creating and Testing a Packaged Solution Installer File (*.msi) **150**

II Learning the Fundamentals of Access Databases

4 Exploring Relational Database Theory and Practice 155

Moving from Spreadsheets to Databases 155

Reliving Database History 156
The Early History of Databases 156
The Relational Database Model 157
Client/Server and Desktop RDBMSs 158

Defining the Structure of Relational Databases 159
Removing Data Redundancy with Relationships 160

Conforming to Table Design Rules 164
First Normal Form 164
Second Normal Form 166
Third Normal Form 167
Fourth Normal Form 168
Fifth Normal Form 169

Choosing Primary Key Codes 169

Maintaining Data Integrity and Accuracy 170
Referential Integrity 171
Entity Integrity and Indexes 172
Data Validation Rules and Check Constraints 172
Transactions 173

Displaying Data with Queries and Views 174

5 Working with Access Databases and Tables 179

Understanding Access Database Files 179
Upgrading from Jet .mdb to Access .accdb Database Files 179
Migrating from Access Applications to SQL Server Data Projects 180

Access Record-Locking Information Files 180
Access Add-In (Library) Databases 181

Creating a New Access Database from Scratch 181

Exploring the Properties of Tables and Fields 183
Table Properties for Subdatasheets 185
Field Properties 186

Choosing Field Data Types, Sizes, and Formats 191
Choosing Field Sizes for Numeric and Text Data 193
Selecting a Display Format 196
Using Input Masks 202

Preparing to Add a Table Related to the Employees Table 204
Determining What Information the Table Should Include 206
Assigning Information to Fields 207
Creating the HRActions Table in Design View 208
Creating Tables from Templates 212
Creating a Table Directly in Datasheet View 213

Setting Default Values of Fields 213

Working with Relations, Key Fields, and Indexes 215
Establishing Relationships Between Tables 215
Cascading Updates and Deletions 220
Selecting a Primary Key 221
Adding Indexes to Tables 222

Altering Fields and Relationships 224
Rearranging the Sequence of Fields in a Table 225
Changing Field Data Types and Sizes 226
Changing Relationships Between Tables 227

Working with Object Dependencies and
Access Smart Tags **228**
  Enabling and Viewing Object
  Dependencies **228**
  Activating the Access Property Options
  Smart Tag **229**
  Adding an Internet-Based Smart Tag to a
  Field **231**

Copying and Pasting Tables **232**

Using the Table Analyzer Wizard **235**

Generating a Data Dictionary with the
Database Documenter **240**

**6 Entering, Editing, and Validating
Access Table Data 245**

Using Keyboard Operations for Entering and
Editing Data **246**
  Creating a Working Copy of Northwind.
  accdb **246**
  Setting Data Entry Options **246**
  Using Data Entry and Editing Keys **248**
  Using Key Combinations for Windows
  Clipboard Operations **250**
  Using Shortcut Keys for Fields and Text
  Boxes **252**

Adding Records to a Table **252**

Selecting, Appending, Replacing, and
Deleting Table Records **254**

Validating Data Entry **254**
  Adding Field-Level Validation Rules **255**
  Adding Table-Level Validation Rules
  with the Expression Builder **257**
  Adding a Simple Lookup List to the
  ActionType Field **258**

Adding Records to the HRActions
Table **261**

Testing Field and Table Validation
Rules **264**

**7 Sorting, Finding, and Filtering
Data 267**

Sorting Table Data **267**
  Freezing Display of a Table Field **268**
  Sorting Data on a Single Field **268**
  Sorting Data on Multiple Fields **269**
  Removing a Table Sort Order and
  Thawing Columns **270**

Finding Matching Records in a Table **271**

Replacing Matched Field Values
Automatically **274**

Filtering Table Data **274**
  Filtering by Selection **275**
  Using the Text Filters Option **277**
  Filtering by Form **278**
  Applying Menu-based Filters and Sort
  Orders **284**

Applying Advanced Filters and Sort
Orders **285**
  Adding Multifield Sort and Compound
  Filter Criteria **286**
  Using Composite Criteria **288**
  Saving Your Filter as a Query and
  Loading a Filter **291**
  Applying a Saved Query as a Filter **292**

Customizing Table Datasheet View **292**

Copying, Exporting, and Mailing Sorted and
Filtered Data **295**

**8 Linking, Importing, and Exporting
Data 297**

Importing and Linking Spreadsheet
Files **298**
  Creating a Table by Importing an Excel
  Worksheet **299**
  Linking Excel Worksheets **307**

Working with Microsoft Outlook and
Exchange Folders   **308**
   Importing and Exporting Access Tables
   with Outlook 2010   **308**
   Linking with the Exchange/Outlook
   Wizard   **311**

Importing Text Files   **313**
   Using the Import Text Wizard   **314**
   Setting the Import Text Wizard's
   Advanced Options   **318**

Working with Tables in Other Database File
Formats   **321**
   Dealing with PC Database Files   **324**
   Linking and Importing External ISAM
   Tables   **324**
   Dealing with Images in External
   Database Files   **326**
   Converting Field Data Types to Access
   Data Types   **328**

Using the Linked Table Manager Add-in to
Relink Tables   **330**

Using the Access Mail Merge Wizard   **331**
   Creating and Previewing a New Form
   Letter   **332**
   Using an Existing Mail Merge Document
   with a New Data Source   **339**

Exporting Tables to Word, Excel, PDF, and
XPS Files   **341**

Exporting Table Data as Text Files   **344**

Exporting Data in Other File Formats   **345**

**III Transforming Data with Queries and
      PivotTables**

**9 Designing Queries for Access
    Databases   347**

Trying the Simple Query Wizard   **348**
   Creating a Simple SELECT Query   **348**

Using the Query Design Window   **355**
   Selecting Fields for Your Query   **356**
   Selecting Records by Criteria and Sorting
   the Display   **360**
   Preventing Updates to the Query
   Resultset   **362**
   Creating More Complex Criteria   **364**
   Changing the Names of Query Column
   Headers   **365**
   Printing Your Query as a Report   **367**

Testing the Other Query Wizards   **369**
   Finding Duplicate Values in a Field   **371**
   Finding Values in One Table with No
   Matching Values in a Related Table   **372**

Creating Other Types of Queries   **373**
   Creating and Using a Simple Make-Table
   Action Query   **374**
   Adding a Parameter to Your Make-Table
   Query   **375**

**10 Understanding Access Query
     Operators and Expressions   381**

Understanding the Elements of
Expressions   **382**

Operators   **384**
   Arithmetic Operators   **385**
   Assignment and Comparison
   Operators   **386**
   Logical Operators   **386**
   Concatenation Operators   **387**
   Identifier Operators   **387**
   Other Operators   **388**

Literals   **389**

Identifiers   **390**

Functions   **391**
   Using the Immediate Window   **391**
   Getting Help as You Write Queries   **392**
   The Variant Data Type in VBA   **394**
   The TempVars Collection   **396**
   Functions for Date and Time   **396**

Text Manipulation Functions   398
Numeric, Logical, Date/Time, and String
Data-Type Conversion Functions   402

Intrinsic and Named Constants   403

Creating Access Expressions   404
Expressions for Creating Default
Values   404
Expressions for Validating Data   405
Expressions for Query Criteria   405
The SQL Server Version of a Query   414
Expressions for Calculating Query Field
Values   418

**11 Creating Multitable and Crosstab
Queries   421**

Joining Tables to Create Multitable
Queries   422
Creating Conventional Single-Column
Inner Joins   424
Specifying a Sort Order and Top Values
Limit   426
Designing Nested Queries   430
Creating Queries from Tables with
Indirect Relationships   433
Creating Multicolumn Inner Joins and
Selecting Unique Values   438

Using Lookup Fields in Tables   442
Adding a Foreign Key Drop-down List
with the Lookup Wizard   443
Adding a Fixed-Value Lookup List to a
Table   447
Creating Multivalued Lookup
Fields   450

Adding Subdatasheets to a Table or
Query   456
Table Subdatasheets   458
Query Subdatasheets   459

Outer, Self, and Theta Joins   463
Creating Outer Joins   463
Creating Self-Joins   466

Creating Not-Equal (Theta) Joins with
Criteria   467

Updating Table Data with Queries   469
Characteristics That Determine Whether
You Can Update a Query   469
Taking Advantage of Access's Row
Fix-up Feature   471
Formatting Data with the Query Field
Property Sheet   472

Making All Fields of Tables Accessible   474

Making Calculations on Multiple
Records   475
Using the SQL Aggregate Functions   476
Making Calculations Based on All
Records of a Table   476
Making Calculations Based on Selected
Sets of Rows or Records   479

Designing Parameter Queries   481
Adding a Parameter to the Monthly Sales
Query   482
Specifying the Parameter's Data
Type   484

Creating Crosstab Queries   485
Using the Wizard to Generate a Quarterly
Product Sales Crosstab Query   486
Designing a Monthly Product Sales
Crosstab Query   492
Using Fixed Column Headings with
Crosstab Queries   493

Writing UNION Queries and Subqueries   496
Using UNION Queries to Combine
Multiple Resultsets   496
Implementing Subqueries   499

Creating Queries from Tables in Other
Databases   500

12 Working with PivotTable and PivotChart Views   505

Slicing and Dicing Data with PivotTables   506
Creating the Query for a Sample PivotTable View   506
Designing the PivotTable View of the Sample Query   507
Generating the Initial PivotTable   509
Reducing the Level of Detail and Adding Grand Totals   512
Filtering PivotTable Category Values   515
Increasing the Level of Detail for Drill-Down   517
Changing Fill/Background and Text Colors   519
Exchanging PivotTable Axes and Category Hierarchies   519

Setting PivotTable Property Values   520

Exporting the PivotTable to Excel   523

Optimizing Performance of PivotTables   524

Formatting and Manipulating PivotCharts   528
Adding Legends, Axis Titles, and Filters   529
Altering Category Presentation   530
Changing the Chart Type   532

13 Creating and Updating Access Tables with Action Queries   535

Creating New Tables with Make-Table Queries   536
Designing and Testing the Select Query   537
Converting the Select Query to a Make-Table Query   537
Establishing Relationships for the New Table   540
Using the New tblShipAddresses Table   543

Creating Action Queries to Append Records to a Table   543

Deleting Records from a Table with an Action Query   546

Updating Values of Multiple Records in a Table   549
Adding a ShipToID Field to the tblOrders Table   549
Adding a ShipToID Field and Composite Primary Key to the tblShipAddresses Table   550
Writing Update Queries to Update Foreign Key Values in the tblOrders Table   551
Using the tblShipAddress Table in a Query   554
Using the tblShipAddress Table with UNION Queries   555

Testing Cascading Deletion and Cascading Updates   559
Creating the Test Tables and Establishing Relationships   559
Testing Cascading Deletions   562
Testing Cascading Updates   562

IV Designing Forms and Reports

14 Creating and Using Access Forms   565

Autogenerating a Basic Transaction-Processing Form   566
Creating a Master/Child Form from Related Tables   567
Exploring the frmHRActions Form in Layout View   567

Form Layout View's Contextual Ribbons   568
The Form Layout Tools—Format Ribbon   568
The Form Layout Tools—Arrange Ribbon   572

Rearranging the Default Form Layout **573**

Changing Form View from a Tabbed
Document to a Modal Pop-up Window **575**
  Setting Form Appearance
  Properties **577**
  Default Values for Forms **577**
  Changing the Office Theme **579**
  Changing an Object's Colors Without
  Changing the Theme **585**
  Using the Windows Clipboard and
  Deleting Controls **592**
  Changing the Content of Text
  Controls **592**
  Using the Format Painter **592**

Creating a Master/Child Form with the Form
Wizard **594**
  Refining the Wizard-Generated Form's
  Layout **596**
  Setting Subform Properties **598**
  Using HTML to Format Memo Data as
  Rich Text **600**

Generating Multiple Items and Split
Forms **601**

Using Transaction-Processing Forms **602**
  Appending New Records to the
  HRActions Table **603**

Modifying the Properties of a Form or
Control After Testing **605**
  Removing Fields from the Tab
  Order **605**
  Disabling Editing of Specific
  Controls **606**

**15 Designing Custom Multitable
Forms 607**

Getting Acquainted with Form Design
View's Contextual Ribbons **608**
  The Form Design Tools—Design
  Ribbon **608**
  Control Categories **611**
  The Form Design Tools—Arrange
  Ribbon **612**

Working in Form Design View **613**
  Selecting Form Elements and
  Controls **613**
  Changing the Size of the Form and Its
  Sections **615**
  Selecting, Moving, and Sizing a Single
  Control or Label/Control Pair **615**
  Aligning Controls to the Grid **617**
  Selecting and Moving Multiple
  Controls **617**
  Aligning a Group of Controls **619**

Adding Label and Text Box Controls to a
Blank Form **620**
  Creating the Query Data Source for the
  Main Form **620**
  Creating a Blank Form with a Header and
  Footer **621**
  Adding a Label to the Form Header **624**
  Formatting Text and Adjusting Text
  Control Sizes **625**
  Creating Bound and Calculated Text
  Boxes **626**
  Accepting or Declining Control Error
  Correction **630**
  Changing the Default View and
  Obtaining Help for Properties **631**

Adding Group Boxes with the Wizard **632**
  Changing One Control Type to
  Another **637**

Using the Clipboard to Copy Controls to
Another Form **637**

Adding Combo and List Boxes **639**
  Using the Combo Box Wizard **640**
  Using the Query Builder to Populate a
  Combo Box **645**
  Creating a Combo Box with a List of
  Static Values **648**
  Creating a Combo Box to Find Specific
  Records **651**

Adding an Attachment Control for
Images **656**

Working with Tab Controls **659**
  Adding the Tab Control to a Form **659**
  Adding Tab Control Pages **660**
  Changing the Page Order **661**
  Deleting a Tab Control Page **662**
  Setting the Tab Control's
  Properties **662**
  Placing Other Controls on Tab
  Pages **664**

Optimizing the Form's Design **665**

Adding a History Subform to a Tab Control
Page **667**
  Creating a Modified HRActions
  Subform **667**
  Adding the sbfHRActionsTab Subform
  with the Wizard **669**
  Modifying the Design of Continuous
  Forms **672**

Adding New Records in the HRActionEntry
Form **673**

Using the New Navigation Control and
Application Parts **676**

Using the Web Browser Control **679**

Overriding the Field Properties of
Tables **680**

Adding Page Headers and Footers for
Printing Forms **681**

**16 Working with Simple Reports and
Mailing Labels 683**

Categorizing Types of Access Reports **685**

Autogenerating a Simple Tabular
Report **686**

Creating a Grouped Report with the Report
Wizard **688**

Using Access's Report Ribbons **695**
  The Report Design and Layout Tools—
  Design Ribbons **695**
  The Report Layout and Design Tools—
  Arrange Ribbon **697**
  The Report Design and Layout Tools—
  Format Ribbon **698**
  The Report Layout and Design Tools—
  Page Setup Ribbon **698**

The Print Preview Ribbon **699**

Modifying a Basic Wizard Report **701**
  Deleting, Relocating, and Editing
  Existing Controls **701**
  Printing the Lookup Fields of a
  Table **703**
  Completing the Initial Report
  Modifications **704**
  Adding the Calculated Controls **709**
  Aligning and Formatting Controls and
  Adjusting Line Spacing **713**
  Aligning Controls Horizontally and
  Vertically **714**
  Formatting Controls **714**
  Adjusting Line Spacing **715**

Adjusting Margins and Printing
Conventional Reports **717**

Preventing Widowed Records with the
Group Keep Together Property **720**

Printing Multicolumn Reports as Mailing
Labels **721**
  Creating a Mailing Label with the Label
  Wizard **721**
  Modifying an Existing Mailing Label
  Report **725**

17 Preparing Advanced Reports 729

Grouping and Sorting Report Data **730**
  Grouping Data **731**
  Sorting Data Groups **735**

Working from a Blank Report   737
   Using a Report as a Subreport   737
   Creating the Monthly Sales by Category
   Report   739

Incorporating Subreports   744
   Adding a Linked Subreport to a Bound
   Report   744
   Using Unlinked Subreports and Unbound
   Reports   748

Customizing De Novo Reports   749
   Adding and Deleting Sections of Your
   Report   749
   Controlling Page Breaks and Printing
   Page Headers and Footers   750
   Adding Other Controls to Reports   751
   Reducing the Length of Reports   752

Mailing Reports as Attachments   752
   Sending a Report with an Outlook
   Message   752

**18 Adding Graphs, PivotCharts, and
   PivotTables   755**

Generating Graphs and Charts with
Microsoft Graph   755
   Creating the Query Data Source for the
   Graph   756
   Using the Chart Wizard to Create an
   Unlinked Graph   759
   Modifying the Design Features of Your
   Graph   764
   Changing the Graph to a Chart   768

Printing Graphs or Charts in Reports   771

Creating a Linked Graph from an Access
Crosstab Query   775
   Designing the Crosstab Query for the
   Graph   776
   Assigning the Crosstab Query as the
   Graph's Row Source   778
   Linking the Graph to a Single Record of a
   Table or Query   779

Working with PivotChart Forms   783
   Creating a PivotChart Form from a
   Query   784
   Using the PivotChart Form as a
   Subform   787
   Linking the PivotChart to the Main
   Form's Current Record   790
   Cloning a Linked PivotChart Form/
   Subform Pair   791
   Tweaking the Design of the PivotChart
   Subform   792
   Persisting Linked PivotChart Properties
   with VBA Code   794

Substituting or Adding a PivotTable in a
Form   795

V Programming Databases with Macros

**19 Automating Access Applications with
   Macros and Procedures   797**

What Are Access Macros?   798

How Do I View a Macro's Actions?   799

Why Use Macros Instead of VBA?   801

Exploring Access 2010's Event
Repertoire   801

Generating Embedded Macros with the
Command Button Wizard   804

Responding to Events from Combo and List
Boxes   810
   Create a Category Combo Box with the
   Wizard   810
   Write and Test an Embedded ApplyFilter
   Macro   812

Exploring Access 2010's Macro-based
Switchboard Manager   816

20 Emulating Table Triggers with Access Data Macros   821

Designing Simple Event-Driven Data Macros   823
   Writing a Simple Data Macro to Handle After Update Events   825
   Eliminating Macro Recursion Errors   834
   Logging Table Updates   836

Writing and Invoking Named Data Macros   841
   Writing a Parameterized Named Data Macro for Creating and Setting Custom Log Records   842

VI Collaborating with Access Data

21 Linking Access Front Ends to Access and Client/Server Tables   859

Separating Tables from Access Front-End Objects   860
   Creating Linked Access Tables with the Database Splitter   861
   Establishing Network Share, Folder, and File Security for the Back End   864
   Verifying Back-End Database Network Security   868

Evaluating the Benefits of Migrating to Client/Server Databases   870
   Client/Server Reliability and Scalability Benefits   871
   SQL Server 2008 R2 Express Edition Features and Limitations   871

Choosing a Client/Server Migration Strategy   873
   Migrating Access Applications to SQL Server with the Upsizing Wizard   873
   Exporting Tables to Other RDBMSs   874

Upsizing a Single-File Application to SQL Server 2005 or Later   875
   Modifying Table Properties to Ensure Successful Upsizing   876
   Running the Upsizing Wizard   877
   Verifying the Upsizing and Linking Process   881
   Upsizing an Application with Linked Tables   884
   Examining the ODBC Table Connection String   885

Moving the Upsized Database to Another Server   886
   Moving or Copying the SQL Server Database Files   886
   Changing the Link Connection String with a VBA Subprocedure   887

Linking Client/Server Tables Manually   890
   Creating the ODBC Data Source   890
   Exporting Access Table Data to the RDBMS   893
   Attaching the Exported Tables   895

Writing and Executing Pass-through Queries   897

Adding SQL Server User Logins with SQL Server Management Studio   900
   Understanding Server and Database Roles   901
   Creating the NWReader and NWWriter Logins with SSMSX   902
   Granting Execute Rights to Stored Procedures   907
   Verifying Database Securables Protection   910

Password-Protecting and Encrypting Access Front Ends   911
   Adding a Database Password   912
   Password-Protecting VBA Code   914
   Creating and Testing an .accde Front End   915

22 Collaborating with Windows SharePoint Foundation 2010 917

Installing SPF 2010 Under 64-Bit Windows Server 2008 919

Getting Acquainted with SPF 2010 920
   Standard SPF 2010 Site Types 921
   Add a New SPF 2010 Subsite 921
   SPF 2010 Users and Security Groups 930

Managing Data with Access and SharePoint 2010 934

Saving an Existing Access Database in a SharePoint Document Library 935

Moving Tables and Saving an Existing Database to SharePoint 940
   SharePoint List Data Types 940
   Customize SharePoint List Views 941
   Moving and Saving the Northwind Database to SPF 2010 948
   Fixing Up Lists to Resemble Source Tables 951
   Checking Out and Checking In a Database from a Document Library 954

Working Offline and Synchronizing Lists 964

Exporting Tables or Queries to a SharePoint List 967

Linking a SharePoint List to an Access Table 970
   Link or Export SharePoint Lists to Access Tables from Sharepoint 970
   Link Access Tables to Sharepoint Lists from Access 971

23 Sharing Web Databases with SharePoint Server 2010 975

Licensing SharePoint Server 2010 976
   Server, External Connector, and Client Access Licenses 976
   Hosted SharePoint 2010 Enterprise Sites 977
   SharePoint Trial Software 978

Understanding the Role of Access Services 978
   The Reporting Services 2008 R2 for SharePoint 2010 Add-in 979
   Access Services Limitations and Restrictions 979

Installing SharePoint Server 2010 980
   Hardware and Software Requirements 980
   Starting Installation from a DVD 981
   Installing the SQL Server 2008 R2 Reporting Services Add-In 982
   Continuing the SharePoint Setup Process 983

Creating a Web Database from a Template 985
   Fixing the Session State Issue with the SharePoint 2010 Management Shell 989

Making Design Changes to Web Databases 992
   Deleting the Getting Started Form from the Contacts Web Database 992
   Investigating and Correcting Web Database Incompatibilities 996

Working with a Hosted SharePoint Site 998

Signing Up for and Testing a Trial Access Hosting Account 999
   Publishing a Web Database to an Access Hosting Subsite 1000
   Working Around Time Zone Conflicts 1003
   Publishing Web Databases to Office 365 SharePoint Servers 1004

VII Working with HTML and XML Documents

24 Importing and Exporting Web Pages   1007 (Online)

Importing or Linking Data from HTML Tables   **1008**

Analyzing an HTML Table's Structure   **1009**

Importing HTML Tables from Web Pages   **1009**

Counting Duplicate Rows with the Find Duplicates Query Wizard   **1016**

Removing Duplicate Rows with an Append Query   **1018**

Linking HTML Documents to Access Tables   **1020**

Importing HTML Lists to Access Tables   **1020**

Fixing Source Content Before Importing with HTML Tidy   **1025**

Downloading and Running HTML Tidy   **1026**

Running tidy.exe from the Command Prompt   **1027**

Using HTML Tidy Configuration Files   **1028**

Exporting Access Tables to HTML Files   **1028**

Exporting Reports to HTML Tables   **1031**

Modifying Page Layout with HTML Templates   **1035**

Upgrading Access HTML Documents to HTML 4.01 and CSS   **1038**

Using HTML Tidy's Clean Option   **1038**

Fixing Tidy-Generated CSS Code   **1041**

Linking Documents to a CSS File   **1042**

Converting HTML 4.01 Files to XHTML 1.0 with Tidy   **1043**

Gathering Data by Email with HTML Forms   **1044**

Creating an HTML Form for the CustomersUpdate Table   **1045**

Emulating the Recipient by Editing the Form(s)   **1048**

Creating a Message to Add a Record to a Table   **1051**

25 Integrating with XML and InfoPath 2010   1053 (Online)

Gaining an XML Vocabulary   **1054**

Exporting Tables and Queries to XML and HTML   **1058**

Analyzing the Exported XML Schema and Data   **1059**

Spelunking the vwUnion.xsl File   **1064**

Reformatting HTML Tables and Adding Page Elements   **1065**

Applying CSS Rules to Table and Text Elements   **1065**

Adding a Table Header and Caption   **1067**

Deploying Exported XML File Sets to a Web Server   **1069**

Exporting Static Reports as XML and Web Pages   **1070**

Importing XML Data to Tables   **1073**

Importing a Flat XML Data Document   **1074**

Importing Data with an XML Schema   **1077**

Exporting and Importing Data in Related Tables   **1077**

Exporting Related Tables and Their Schema   **1078**

Re-creating and Populating Related Tables   **1079**

Gathering Data by Email with InfoPath 2010
Forms   **1080**

Creating an InfoPath Form for the
SuppliersUpdate Table   **1081**
Editing Existing Table Data and Adding
a New Record   **1084**

**VIII Creating Access Front Ends to SQL
Server Databases**

**26 Exploring Access Data Projects and
SQL Server 2008   1089 (Online)**

Understanding the Role of SQL Server and
ADP   **1091**

SQL Server Editions, Licensing, and
Features   **1092**
Benefits and Drawbacks of Access Data
Projects   **1092**

Exploring the NorthwindSQL Sample
Project   **1093**

Working with SQL Server Tables in the
Project Designer   **1096**

Project Designer's Table Design
View   **1097**
The Table Properties Dialog   **1099**
The Relationships Page   **1101**

Exploring SQL Server Views   **1106**

Taking Advantage of Inline Functions   **1113**

Creating a Parameterized Table-Valued
Function   **1113**
Adding Default Values for the Input
Parameters   **1115**

Examining Stored Procedures   **1116**

Creating and Executing Make-Table and
Update Stored Procedures   **1117**
Adding Records with Append Stored
Procedures   **1119**
Dealing with Identity Fields   **1119**
Updating Records   **1124**
Deleting Records   **1124**

Diagramming Table Relationships   **1125**

Backing Up and Restoring Databases   **1127**

Transferring the Project's Database to a
Server   **1131**

Connecting to a Remote SQL Server
Database   **1133**

Designing Forms and Reports with SQL
Server Data Sources   **1134**

Securing Your Project as an .ade File   **1134**

**27 Moving from Access Queries to
Transact-SQL   1137 (Online)**

Understanding SQL Grammar   **1138**

Writing SELECT Queries in SQL   **1140**

Using SQL Punctuation and
Symbols   **1142**
Translating SQL Statements into QBE
Designs   **1143**
Using the SQL Aggregate Functions and
Writing Inline Functions   **1148**
Creating Joins with SQL   **1152**
Writing UNION Queries   **1155**
Implementing Subqueries   **1158**

Writing Action Queries and Stored
Procedures   **1160**

Specifying Parameters for Criteria and
Update Values   **1162**
Taking Advantage of Transactions in
Stored Procedures   **1163**

Working with Tables in Another
Database   **1165**

Creating Tables with ANSI-SQL92
DDL   **1167**

Using SQL Statements with Forms, Reports,
and Controls   **1169**

28 Upsizing Access Applications to Access Data Projects and SQL Azure 1171 (Online)

Preparing to Upsize Your Access Applications **1172**

Upsizing with the Trial-and-Error Approach **1173**
Performing an Initial Test of the Upsizing Process **1173**
Running a Second Upsizing Pass **1179**
Correcting Wizard Errors **1180**
Conforming Computed Columns to the ANSI SQL Standard **1183**
Upsizing Access SQL Statements Executed by Forms, Reports, and Controls **1195**

Comparing ANSI-92 SQL, T-SQL, and Access SQL **1197**
ANSI-92 SQL Reserved Words in Access SQL **1198**
Access SQL Reserved Words, Operators, and Functions Not in ANSI SQL **1200**
Access's DISTINCTROW and ANSI SQL's DISTINCT Keywords **1202**
Access and Corresponding SQL Server Data Types **1202**
VBA Functions That Upsize to SQL Server Functions **1203**
VBA Functions That You Must Manually Convert to Related SQL Server Functions **1204**

Emulating Access Crosstab Queries with T-SQL **1205**
The Pragmatic Approach for Static Data—Cheat **1206**
The Better Approach for Dynamic and Static Data—PIVOT Views or Stored Procedures **1212**

Crossfooting Crosstab Queries **1221**

Securing Upsized Projects and Their Data **1225**

Linking Access Applications to SQL Azure Cloud Databases **1227**
Opening a SQL Azure Account **1228**
Using the SQL Server Migration Assistant with Access Applications **1230**
Linking SQL Azure Tables to a Sample Access Front End **1231**

IX Programming and Converting Access Applications

29 Learning Visual Basic for Applications 1239 (Online)

Getting Acquainted with VBA 6.0 **1240**
Where You Use VBA Code **1240**
Security Issues with VBA Code **1241**
Typographic and Naming Conventions Used for VBA **1241**
Modules, Functions, and Subprocedures **1242**
Elements of Modules **1244**
References to VBA and Access Libraries **1246**
The Object Browser **1247**
Data Types and Database Objects in VBA **1248**
Variables and Naming Conventions **1250**
Symbolic Constants **1257**
VBA Named and Optional Arguments **1259**

Controlling Program Flow **1260**
Branching and Labels **1260**
Conditional Statements **1261**
Repetitive Operations: Looping **1264**

Handling Runtime Errors **1266**
  Detecting the Type of Error with the Err
  Object **1268**
  Using the Error Event in Form and Report
  Modules **1268**

Exploring the VBA Editor **1269**
  The Toolbar of the Module
  Window **1269**
  Module Shortcut Keys **1271**
  The VBA Help System **1271**

Examining the Utility Functions
Module **1273**
  Adding a Breakpoint to the IsLoaded()
  Function **1273**
  Printing to the Immediate Window with
  the Debug Object **1275**

Using Text Comparison Options **1278**

**30 Handling Events with VBA and
     Macros 1279 (Online)**

Understanding the Role of Class
Modules **1280**
  Creating a Switchboard Class Module
  with the Macro-to-VBA Converter **1280**
  Testing and Fixing Converted
  Code **1283**

Examining Project Class Module Members in
Object Browser and Project Explorer **1287**

Using Functions to Respond to Events **1289**

Working with Access 2010's DoCmd
Methods **1291**
  DoCmd Methods by Task **1292**
  Arguments of DoCmd Methods **1293**

Customizing Applications with Ribbon
Objects **1294**
  Creating New RibbonX Objects **1295**
  Obtaining RibbonX Documentation and
  Sample Code **1296**
  Editing RibbonX Documents with Visual
  Studio 2005 or Later **1299**

Editing RibbonX Documents with XML
Notepad 2007 **1300**
  Converting Macros to VBA Callback
  Functions **1303**

Referring to Access Objects with
VBA **1307**
  Referring to Open Forms or Reports and
  Their Properties **1307**
  Referring to Controls and Their
  Properties **1309**
  Referring to Controls on a Subform or the
  Main Form **1310**
  Using Alternative Collection
  Syntax **1311**

Responding to Data Events Triggered by
Forms and Controls **1311**
  Validating Data Entry in a
  BeforeUpdate Event Handler **1311**
  Using the On Current Event to Set
  Linked PivotChart Properties **1312**

**31 Programming Combo and List
     Boxes 1317 (Online)**

Constraining Query Choices with Combo
Boxes **1317**
  Designing the Decision-Support
  Query **1318**
  Creating the Form and Adding a List
  Box **1318**
  Adding the Query Combo Boxes to the
  Form **1321**

Adding Code to Create the Query's SQL
Statement **1326**

Drilling Down from a List Box
Selection **1330**
  Creating the Drill-Down Query and
  Adding the List Box **1330**
  Programming the Drill-Down List
  Box **1331**

Adding New Features to List and Combo Boxes   **1334**

Iterating List Box Items and Selecting an Item   **1334**

Adding an Option to Select All Countries or Products   **1336**

Converting Your Combo Box Form to an Access Data Project   **1340**

Importing and Testing the Combo Box Forms   **1341**

Replacing the Access qryCombo1 Query with an SQL Server View   **1343**

Conforming the Access SQL of qryDrill-Down to T-SQL Syntax   **1344**

32 Understanding Data Access Objects, OLE DB, and ADO   1349 (Online)

Comparing DAO and ADO Objects   **1350**

Creating DAO.Recordset2 and ADODB.Recordset Objects   **1352**

Creating a DAO.Recordset2 Object with Code and Binding a Form and Controls to It   **1353**

Creating the Recordset from an SQL Server Express Database   **1356**

Binding a Form to ADODB.Recordset Objects   **1357**

Using the Object Browser to Display DAO and ADODB Properties, Methods, and Events   **1360**

Working with the ADODB.Connection Object   **1363**

Connection Properties   **1363**

Errors Collection and Error Objects   **1367**

Connection Methods   **1370**

Connection Events   **1373**

Using the ADODB.Command Object   **1374**

Command Properties   **1374**

Command Methods   **1379**

Understanding the ADODB.Recordset Object   **1383**

Recordset Properties   **1384**

Fields Collection and Field Objects   **1389**

Recordset Methods   **1392**

Events   **1397**

Exploring the AddOrders.adp Sample Project   **1398**

33 Upgrading Access 2003 and Earlier Applications to Access 2010   1403 (Online)

Reviewing Upgrade Pros and Cons   **1404**

Converting Unsecured Files from Access 9x to 200x   **1404**

Upgrading on First Opening the File in Access 200x   **1405**

Upgrading After Opening the File in Access 200x   **1407**

Fixing Missing VBA References in Access 9x Upgrades   **1408**

Converting Secure Access 9x Files to 200x   **1410**

Upgrading in a Mixed Access 97 and 200x Environment   **1410**

Upgrading the Back-End Database and Workgroup File   **1411**

Upgrading Access 200x Files to Access 2010   **1412**

Upgrading Unsecured Access 200x Files   **1412**

Upgrading Secured Access 200x Files   **1412**

Moving from MSDE to the SQL Server 2005 or Later Express Edition   **1415**

Upgrading from MSDE 1.0 to SQL Server 2005   **1415**

Removing MSDE and Installing SQL Server 2000   **1416**

Attaching and Upgrading MSDE Databases **1417**

Changing the Database Owner and Setting Database Compatibility Level **1419**

X Appendix

A What Was New in Access 2007 for Users of Access 2003 and Earlier **1423 (Online)**

What Was New in Microsoft Office Access 2007: An Overview **1424**

The Office 2007 Ribbon User Interface **1427**
Access 2007's Main Ribbons **1429**
Contextual Ribbons for Access Databases **1432**
Contextual Ribbons for Access Data Projects **1437**
Customizing Ribbons for Specific Applications **1438**
The Quick Access Toolbar **1439**
The Office Button and Its Gallery **1442**

Security, Trusted Locations, Packages, and Certificates **1446**
Specifying Trusted Locations **1447**
Packaging and Code-Signing Databases **1447**
Enabling Nontrusted Application Automation with Macros **1447**

The Navigation Pane **1447**
Customizing the Custom Category **1449**
Hiding Prebuilt Categories and Locking the Navigation Pane **1452**
Searching, Filtering, and Sorting the Navigation Pane **1452**

Changes to Tables and the Access Database Engine **1453**
Taking Advantage of New or Upgraded Data Types **1453**
Enhancing Datasheet View **1454**

Application Development by Templates **1458**

New Form and Report Features **1458**
Tabbed Documents and Modal Dialogs **1458**
Form and Report Layout View **1459**
Default Form and Report Layouts **1459**
Control Grouping, Anchoring, Margins, and Padding **1461**
Publish to PDF or XPS Documents **1461**

Access Macros Redux **1462**

Collaboration with SharePoint **1463**

Features Missing from Access 2007 **1464**

SQL Server 2005 Express Edition SP2 Setup **1465**
Downloading and Installing SSX **1465**
Managing SSX **1470**

B Glossary **1475 (Online)**

Index **1505**

ABOUT THE AUTHOR

Roger Jennings is an author and consultant specializing in Microsoft .NET, SQL Server, and Access database applications, as well as Windows Azure and SQL Azure cloud computing projects. He was a technical beta tester for all 10 editions of Microsoft Access; SQL Server 6.5, 7.0, 2000, 2005, 2008, and 2008 R2; every release of Visual Basic since version 2.0 and Windows 3.1; and all subsequent Microsoft Windows operating systems. He also was one of the founding members of Microsoft's former Access Insiders group.

Roger's books have more than 1.25 million English copies in print and have been translated into more than 20 languages. He is the author of Que's *Special Edition Using Microsoft Access* titles for Access versions 1.0, 1.1, 2.0, 95, 97 (first and second editions), 2000, 2002, and 2003, 2007, and *Platinum Edition Using Access 97*. He also wrote Que's *Special Edition Using Windows NT Server 4*, *Special Edition Using Windows 2000 Server*, *Unveiling Windows 95*, *Access Hot Tips*, and *Discover Windows 3.1 Multimedia*. For Pearson Education's Sams imprint, he has written two editions of *Access Developer's Guide* and three editions of *Database Developers Guide with Visual Basic*. Additionally, he was the series editor for the *Roger Jennings' Database Workshop* titles.

Roger is a contributing editor for the Redmond Media Group's *Visual Studio Magazine* and an occasional contributor to the group's .NET *Insight* and Redmond Developer News newsletters. Roger coauthored with Microsoft's Greg Nelson "A Client/Server Application: From Concept to Reality," a 1995 Tech*Ed presentation and whitepaper on Access 2.0 that was featured in the *Microsoft Developer Network News*.

Roger has more than 30 years of computer-related experience, beginning with his work on the Wang 700 desktop calculator/computer. He is a principal of OakLeaf Systems, a Northern California software consulting firm, and is the curator of the OakLeaf Systems blog (http://oakleafblog.blogspot.com), which specializes in the Windows Azure Platform, and the OakLeaf Mobile blog (http://oakleafmobiblogspot.com), which covers Windows Phone 7 and Windows Azure. He is also the author of Roger Jennings' Access Blog (http://accessindepth.blogspot.com). His OakLeaf U.S. Code of Federal Regulations (CFR) XML Web services demonstration project won the 2001 Microsoft .NET Best Award for horizontal solutions. You can contact Roger at Roger_Jennings@compuserve.com.

Dedication

This book is dedicated to my wife, Alexandra.

ACKNOWLEDGMENTS

Loretta Yates, senior acquisitions editor, made sure that I didn't fall too far behind the manuscript submission and author review schedule. Barbara Hacha, copy editor, fixed my typos and grammatical errors. Charlotte Kughen was this edition's development editor. Mandie Frank, project editor, worked hard to make sure that all components of this edition flowed through the editing process and got to their final destination on time. Tim Wright indexed the print and online editions. Media developer Dan Scherf handled production of the downloadable sample databases and code.

Technical Editor Scott B. Diamond is an Access Most Valuable Professional (MVP, http://bit.ly/acbdnd) and seasoned database designer. During the past 20+ years, he has designed databases on a wide range of platforms, including dBASE, FoxPro, SQL/DS, Lotus Approach, Lotus Notes and, for the past 10 years, Microsoft Access. Scott has worked as an in-house and freelance consultant and support professional at firms that are among the leaders of their industries. Scott spends some of his free time answering questions at the premier site for Access support: www.utteraccess.com. Scott's sharp eyes alerted me to technical issues and inconsistencies in my manuscript. However, any technical errors that remain are entirely my responsibility.

Steven Gray and Rick Lievano, authors of *Roger Jennings' Database Workshop: Microsoft Transaction Server 2.0*, created the original version of the CD-ROM's Oakmont.accdb Access and Oakmont.mdf SQL Server database.

TELL US WHAT YOU THINK!

As the reader of this book, you are our most important critic and commentator. We value your opinion and want to know what we're doing right, what we could do better, what areas you'd like to see us publish in, and any other words of wisdom you're willing to pass our way.

As an associate publisher for Que, I welcome your comments. You can fax, e-mail, or write me directly to let me know what you did or didn't like about this book—as well as what we can do to make our books stronger.

Please note that I cannot help you with technical problems related to the topic of this book, and that due to the high volume of mail I receive, I might not be able to reply to every message.

When you write, please be sure to include this book's title and author as well as your name and phone or fax number. I will carefully review your comments and share them with the author and editors who worked on the book.

E-mail: feedback@quepublishing.com

Mail: Greg Wiegand

          Que Publishing

          800 East 96th Street

          Indianapolis, IN 46240 USA

Reader Services

Visit our website and register this book at informit.com/title/9780789743077 for convenient access to any updates, downloads, or errata that might be available for this book.

Introduction

Microsoft Office Access 2010 (version 14, called Access 2010 in this book) is a powerful, robust, and mature 32-bit and, finally, 64-bit relational database management system (RDBMS) for creating desktop and client/server database applications that run under Windows 7/Vista/XP/2000+. As a component of the Professional and higher editions of the 2010 Microsoft Office suite, Access 2010 has an updated user interface that's consistent with the Fluent user interface (UI) of other Office 2010 members.

Access has vanquished all desktop RDBMS rivals except FileMaker Pro and Microsoft's Visual FoxPro. However, in March 2007, Microsoft announced that Visual FoxPro (VFP) v9.0 would be the last version. In April 2007, Microsoft representative Yair Alan Griver announced that VFP v9.0 would be supported through 2015. Thus FileMaker Pro is the only likely long-term competition for Access.

The primary reasons for Access's success are its inclusion in the Microsoft Office productivity suite and its prowess as a rapid application development (RAD) environment for creating industrial-strength database applications. Another contributor to Access's market share is the capability to duplicate on the PC desktop the features of client/server relational database systems, also called *SQL databases*. Client/server RDBMSs have led the way in transferring database applications from costly mainframes and UNIX servers to modestly priced networked PCs and mobile devices. Despite Access's power—and the claims of its erstwhile competitors—this desktop RDBMS is easy for nonprogrammers to use.

note

Microsoft's Visual Studio Team introduced a beta version of Visual Studio LightSwitch (VSLS), a commercial product that shares similar rapid application development (RAD) features with Access, in August 2010. On its release, VSLS Silverlight applications will be able to connect to SQL Server, SQL Azure, Access, SharePoint, and several other popular data sources, and will be able to create new SQL Server databases by modeling them in the UI. VSLS offers form templates similar to those of Access 2010, built-in data validation, extensibility with VB.NET or C# code, and add-ins. VSLS applications can be deployed to desktops or the Web without changing code. For more information about VSLS and a trial edition, see http://bit.ly/bgTU8a, http://www.microsoft.com/visualstudio/en-us/lightswitch.

Microsoft's top priority for Access 2010 is to broaden the base of new users by focusing on typical tracking applications generated by a bevy of out-of-the box templates and more templates from Office Online that take maximum advantage of Access 2010's new navigation features and tabbed document presentation. Many potential Access customers view Access as difficult to master. The new Access templates enable information workers to create and begin using simple database applications in a few minutes.

2010 NEW The Access team devoted substantial resources to integrating Access 2010 with Microsoft SharePoint Foundation (SPF) 2010, formerly Windows SharePoint Services (WSS) 3.0, and Windows SharePoint Services (SPS) 2010, formerly Microsoft Office SharePoint Server (MOSS) 2007. WPF is a no-charge add-on to 64-bit Windows Server 2003 or 2008 [R2] that lets you share Access 2010 applications from document libraries and use Access to create or edit SharePoint lists. WPF ease of use lets workgroup members manage their own SharePoint website. SPS 2010 builds on WPF 2010 to create complete document management systems. SPS and SPF (collectively called SharePoint in this book) are Microsoft's primary workgroup and enterprise-level collaboration tools for knowledge workers. Access 2010 supports browser-based web databases published to Access Services running in SPS; Access web databases replace Data Access Pages (DAP), which Access 2007 discontinued.

Near the top of the feature list is support for Microsoft SQL Server 2005, 2008, and 2008 R2, and their freely distributable Express Editions (SQLX). SQLX Graphic table and query designers make creating and modifying SQL Server tables, views, functions, and stored procedures almost as easy as working with Access tables and queries. Extended properties add lookup fields, subdatasheets, input masks, and other Access accoutrements to SQL Server databases.

Microsoft's rallying cry for Windows 7/Vista/XP/2003+ Server and Office 2010 is total cost of ownership (TCO). Ease of use is one of the primary requisites for reducing TCO; Access 2010 includes many wizards and other aids designed for first-time database users. If you're still using Access 97 or 2000, Access 2010 and SQLX alone justify the cost of upgrading to Office 2010. If your team has a SharePoint site, make upgrading from Access 2000 or earlier to 2010 your first priority.

Who Should Read This Book

Microsoft Access 2010 In Depth takes an approach that's different from most books about database management applications. This book doesn't begin with the creation of a database for Widgets, Inc., nor does it require you to type a list of fictional customers for the company's new WidgetPlus product line to learn the basics of Access. Instead, this book makes the following basic assumptions about your interest in Microsoft's relational database management system:

- You aren't starting from "ground zero." You now have or will have access via your computer, network, the Internet (or all three) to much of the data that you want to process with a Windows database manager. You've acquired Access and want to learn to use it more quickly and effectively. Or, you might be considering using Access as the database manager for yourself, your department or division, or your entire organization.

- Your existing data is in the form of databases, spreadsheets, mailing lists, web pages, or even plain-text files that you want to manipulate with a relational database management system. Access 2010 can process the most common varieties of these file types, as well as HTML tables, element-centric XML files, Outlook contact lists, SPF lists, and other tabular data sources.

- If you're planning to use Access 2010 as a front end to a client/server RDBMS, you'll use SQL Server 2005 Express Edition (SSX) or SQL Server 2005 or later as the back-end database. Access 2010 lets you replicate data between a local or workgroup copy of SSX and SQL Server 2005+ on a network server.

- If your data is on a mainframe computer, you're connected to that computer by a local area network and a database gateway, or through terminal-emulation software and an adapter card. Alternatively, you download text files from the mainframe to create Access or SQL Server tables.

If some or all of your data is in the form of ASCII/ANSI text files, or files from a spreadsheet application, you need to know how to create an Access database from the beginning and import the data into Access's new .accdb file structure. If your data is in the form of dBASE, FoxPro, or Paradox files, you can import it directly to Access tables. Access 2010 also lets you link Excel workbook and conventional text files, as well as Outlook and SharePoint lists to Access databases. The capability to link files in their native format lets you synchronize the contents of your database tables with the original source documents. All these subjects receive thorough coverage in this book.

Learning relational database design and management with Access 2010 as the training tool is the quickest and easiest way to upgrade your professional skills. If you're a web designer, the expertise in client/server database techniques that you gain by working with Access data projects, SQL Server, and Access Web databases greatly enhances your future employment prospects. Despite the prolonged downturn in the dot-com sector, there's no slack in the demand for unlocking islands of data stored in client/server databases and making the data available as usable business information on corporate intranets.

Access 2010 is a great first step in gaining XML, XML schema (XSD), and XSL transform (XSLT) skills. Most XML-related books and other training materials use trivial examples to illustrate XML and XSL(T) methodology. Access 2010 lets you dynamically generate real-world XML data and provides a standard transform to render data in HTML format. Working with the resulting .xsl files and their embedded VBScript is the fastest way to learn practical XSLT techniques for delivering XML data as fully formatted web pages.

How This Book Is Organized

In the spirit of conservation, *Microsoft Access 2010 In Depth* is a hybrid book. The print version consists of six printed parts totaling approximately 1,000 pages and four electronic book (ebook) sections of about 600 pages arranged in increasing levels of detail and complexity. Electronic versions of the book for Kindle (Mobi format); Sony Reader, iPad, iPhone, Android and other mobile devices (ePub format), and PDF readers contain this introduction, all chapters, and the appendixes.

Each division after Part I, "Getting Acquainted with Access 2010," follows the normal course of database application design, which involves the following initial steps:

- **Create tables to hold the data and establish relationships between the tables**—After you've defined the purpose of your database application and have found and organized the data it will process, you design a table for each *entity* (also called an *object* or *subject*). For example, contacts, tasks, orders, line items, and invoices are entities. In many cases, table data will be available in files that have another format. Part II, "Learning the Fundamentals of Access Databases," covers table design and importing or linking data to tables.

- **Design queries to filter, format, sort, and display data contained in one or more tables**—Relational databases use queries for turning raw data into useful information. Part III, "Transforming Data with Queries and PivotTables," shows you how to master Access's graphic query designer and generate PivotCharts and PivotTables.

- **Prepare forms for data entry and visualization**—Although you can enter data into tables directly, providing one or more forms simplifies data entry and minimizes the potential for entering bad data. Forms with graphs, PivotTables, and PivotCharts make data understandable to your supervisors and managers. Three of the chapters in Part IV, "Designing Forms and Reports," cover this topic.

- **Lay out reports to summarize data**—Access is famous for its report designer, which lets you quickly design fully formatted reports with group subtotals and grand totals, or generate mailing labels. Part IV's remaining two chapters show you how to take best advantage of Access reports.

Parts II, III, IV, V, and VI draw on the knowledge and experience that you've gained in the previous parts, so use of the book in a linear, front-to-back manner through Part IV, "Designing Forms and Reports," is recommended during the initial learning process. After you absorb the basics of working with Access databases, you progress through using Access macros to automate database operations, changing from single-user to multiuser database applications and linking access front ends to SSX, SQL Server 2005 or later tables, or SharePoint Foundation lists, as well as creating new Access web databases that depend on SharePoint Server's Access services.

The electronic-only chapters cover Access's HTML and XML features and show you how to upsize Access databases to Access Data Projects with SQLX, SQL Server, or SQL Azure back ends. Finally, you learn how to automate your applications with Visual Basic for Applications (VBA) code.

As you progress through the chapters in this book, you create a model of an Access application called Human Resources Actions. In Chapter 5, "Working with Access Databases and Tables," you create the HR Actions table. In the following chapters, you add new features to the HR Actions application. Be sure to perform the sample exercises for the HR Actions application each time you encounter them because succeeding examples build on your previous work. The ten parts of *Microsoft Access 2010 In Depth* and the topics that they cover are described in the following sections for the printed and electronic-only sections.

Printed Parts and Chapters

The printed book includes this Introduction and Parts I through VI:

Part I: Getting Acquainted with Access 2010

The chapters in Part I introduce you to Access and many of the unique features that make Access 2010 the premier desktop database management system.

 note

Appendix A, "What Was New in Access 2010 for Users of Access 2003 and Earlier" contains content that's of interest primarily to readers who now use Access 2000, 2002, or 2003 because there were major changes between these versions and Access 2007. Readers new to Access, however, benefit from the explanations of why many of these new features are significant in everyday Access 2010 use.

■ Chapter 1, "Access 2010 for Access 2007 Users: What's New," provides a summary of the most important new features of Access 2010 and a detailed description of each addition and improvement. Chapter 1 includes detailed instructions for installing SQL Server 2008 R2 Express and SQL Server Management Studio 2008 R2.

■ In Chapter 2, "Building Simple Tracking Applications," you create a database from an out-of-the-box database template included with Access 2010. You gain a basic understanding of the standard data-related objects of Access, including tables, queries, forms, reports, and macros. Chapter 2 also introduces you to automating Access operations with Access macros.

■ Chapter 3, "Navigating the Fluent User Interface," shows you how to take best advantage of Access 2010's "Fluent" ribbon user interface by explaining its command button, menu, and context menu choices and then showing how they relate to the structure of the Access object model. Chapter 3 also shows you how to use Access 2010's online help system.

Part II: Learning the Fundamentals of Access Databases

Part II is devoted to understanding the design principles of relational databases, creating new Access tables, adding and editing table data, and integrating Access tables with other sources of data. Most of the techniques that you learn in Part II also apply to SQL Server tables.

■ Chapter 4, "Exploring Relational Database Theory and Practice," describes the process that you use to create relational database tables from real-world data—a technique called *normalizing the database structure*. The chapter also introduces you to the concepts of key fields, primary keys, data integrity, and views of tables that contain related data.

■ Chapter 5, "Working with Access Databases and Tables," delves into the details of Access desktop database tables, shows you how to create tables, and explains how to choose the optimum data types from the many new types that Access offers. Chapter 5 explains how to use subdatasheets and lookup tables to display and edit records in related tables. The chapter also explains how to use the Database Documentor tool included with Access 2010 to create a data dictionary that fully identifies each object in your database.

- Chapter 6, "Entering, Editing, and Validating Access Table Data," describes how to add new records to tables, enter data in the new records, and edit data in existing records. Using keyboard shortcuts instead of the mouse for editing speeds manual data entry. Adding input masks and data validation rules minimizes the chance for typographic errors when entering new data.

- Chapter 7, "Sorting, Finding, and Filtering Data," shows you how to arrange the data in tables to suit your needs and to limit the data displayed to only that information you want. You learn how to use Find and Replace to search for and alter multiple instances of data in the fields of tables. Chapter 7 further describes how to make best use of the Filter by Form and Filter by Selection features of Access 2010.

- Chapter 8, "Linking, Importing, and Exporting Data," explains how to import and export files of other database managers, spreadsheet applications, and text files downloaded from mainframe or UNIX database servers or the Internet. You also learn how use the Access Mail Merge Wizard to create form letters from data stored in Access tables.

Part III: Transforming Data with Queries and PivotTables

The chapters in Part III explain how to create Access queries to select the way that you view data contained in tables and how to take advantage of Access's relational database structure to link multiple tables with joins. Part III also covers Access 2010's PivotTable and PivotChart views of query resultsets.

- Chapter 9, "Designing Queries for Access Databases," starts with simple queries you create with Access's graphical Query Design window. You learn how to choose the fields of the tables included in your query and return query resultsets from these tables. Examples of Access SQL generated by the queries you design let you learn SQL "by osmosis." Chapter 9 shows you how to use the Simple Query Wizard to simplify the design process.

 note

Chapter 28, "Upsizing Access Applications to Access Data Projects and SQL Azure," describes how to migrate Access database tables to SQL Azure tables deployed in Microsoft data centers. The chapter also explains how to link access front ends to SQL Azure databases.

- Chapter 10, "Understanding Access Query Operators and Expressions," introduces you to the operators and expressions that you need to create queries that provide a meaningful result. Most Access operators and expressions are the same as those that you use in VBA programs. You use the Immediate window of the Office 2010 VBA editor to evaluate the expressions you write.

- In Chapter 11, "Creating Multitable and Crosstab Queries," you create relations between tables, called *joins*, and learn how to add criteria to queries so that the query resultset includes only records that you want. Chapter 11 also takes you through the process of designing powerful crosstab queries to summarize data and to present information in a format similar to that of worksheets.

- Chapter 12, "Working with PivotTable and PivotChart Views," shows you how to manipulate data from multitable queries in the OWC's PivotTable control and then display the results in PivotChart controls. The query design and PivotTable/PivotChart techniques that you learn here also apply to PivotTables and PivotCharts that you embed in Access forms.

- Chapter 13, "Creating and Updating Access Tables with Action Queries," shows you how to develop action queries that update the tables underlying append, delete, update, and make-table queries. Chapter 13 also covers Access 2010's advanced referential integrity features, including cascading updates and cascading deletions.

Part IV: Designing Forms and Reports

The chapters in Part IV introduce you to the primary application objects of Access. (Tables and queries are considered database objects.) Forms make your Access applications come alive with the control objects that you add from the Form Tools, Design ribbon and the Report Tools, Design ribbon. Access's full-featured report generator lets you print fully formatted reports, export or mail reports as PDF or XPS (XML Paper Specification) files, and save reports to files that you can process in Excel 2010 or Word 2010 or earlier.

- Chapter 14, "Creating and Using Basic Access Forms," shows you how to use Access's Form Wizards to create simple forms and subforms that you can modify to suit your particular needs. Chapter 14 introduces you to the Subform Builder Wizard that uses drag-and-drop techniques to automatically create subforms for you.

- Chapter 15, "Designing Custom Multitable Forms," shows you how to design custom forms for viewing and entering your own data with Access's advanced form design tools.

- Chapter 16, "Working with Simple Reports and Mailing Labels," describes how to design and print basic reports with Access's Report Wizard, and how to print preformatted mailing labels by using the Mailing Label Wizard.

- Chapter 17, "Preparing Advanced Reports," describes how to use more sophisticated sorting and grouping techniques, as well as subreports, to obtain a result that exactly meets your detail and summary data-reporting requirements. Chapter 17 also covers the technology that lets you distribute Access reports as Outlook email attachments.

- In Chapter 18, "Adding Graphs, PivotCharts, and PivotTables," you first learn to use the OLE-based Chart Wizard to create data-bound graphs and charts based on Access crosstab queries. PivotCharts are destined to replace conventional Access Charts, so Chapter 18 builds on Chapter 12 by showing you how to add bound PivotTables and PivotCharts whose data is supplied by the form's data source.

Part V: Programming Databases with Macros

- Chapter 19, "Automating Access Applications with Macros," is an introduction to Access macros, which Microsoft resurrected from their previously deprecated status in Access 97 and later. You learn how to write simple standalone or embedded macros to run a query and open a form or report when you click a button on a form.

- **2010 NEW** Chapter 20, "Emulating Table Triggers with Access Data Macros," explains that data macros are a new feature of Access 2010 that lets you extend the range of containers for embedded macros from forms and reports only to include Access tables. Data macros respond to events generated by Data Manipulation Language (DML) instructions, such as Access SQL INSERT, DELETE, and UPDATE commands. In this respect, data macros are similar to SQL Server triggers, which are a special type of stored procedure.

Part VI: Collaborating with Access Data

- Chapter 21, "Linking Access Front Ends to Access and Client/Server Tables," explains how to use the Upsizing Wizard to migrate from single-file or split (front-end/back-end) Access applications to SQL Server back-end databases. Retaining the front-end queries and application objects in an Access (.accdb) file, and using the SQL Server ODBC driver to connect to the server database, minimizes application changes required to take advantage of client/server technology. This chapter also explains how to secure Access databases with file system Access Control Lists (ACLs), because Access 2010 supports workgroup information (.mdw) files only for Access 2003 and earlier .mdb files.

- Chapter 22, "Collaborating with SharePoint Foundation 2010," introduces you to SPF 2010 and its data-related features. You learn to export Access or SQL Server tables to SPF lists, and how to link the lists to Access tables (and vice versa). You also learn to take linked SharePoint lists offline, modify them while disconnected, reconnect to SharePoint, and synchronize your and others' changes. Finally, the chapter shows you how to publish Access applications to SharePoint document libraries and share the published .accdb files with multiple collaborators.

- **2010 NEW** Chapter 23, "Sharing Web Databases with SharePointServer 2010" explains how to take advantage of SPS 2010's Access Services and the replacement for earlier versions of Access Data Pages (ADP). Like Access, SharePoint emphasizes self-service design of sharable objects by teams or groups within small businesses to large enterprises. Publishing Access business applications as web databases to a SharePoint website enables IT management to secure and audit them, as well ensure availability by backing them up on a regular schedule.

Online-Only Parts and Chapters

The online-only section contains Parts VII through X.

Part VII: Working with HTML and XML Documents

The chapters in Part VII explain how to take advantage of Access's HTML and XML export/import features:.

- Chapter 24, "Importing and Exporting Web Pages," shows you how to generate Access tables from HTML tables and lists in web pages, optimize HTML files to ensure proper importation, and export static or dynamic HTML pages. The chapter also explains how to gather data by email with Outlook 2010 HTML forms and automatically add the data acquired to the appropriate table.

- Chapter 25, "Integrating with XML and InfoPath 2010," explains the role of XML in database applications and how Access 2010's ReportML XML schema describes Access objects as an XML data document. The chapter shows you how to take advantage of the Report2HTML4.xsl XML transform to generate HTML pages from tables and queries with the Save As XML option. You learn how to modify Access's standard XSLT files to format the resulting tables and add images to the tables. Exporting conventional Access reports as fully formatted static and live web reports also receives detailed coverage. The chapter also explains the role of InfoPath 2010 as an alternative to Outlook 2010 HTML forms for gathering data.

Part VIII: Creating Access Front Ends to SQL Server Databases

From Access 2000 on, SQL Server [Express] has been the preferred back-end data source for secure, robust, and reliable Access multiuser applications. You can link SQL Server tables to a conventional Access .accdb front-end file, but a direct connection to an Access data project (.adp) front end is the better approach. This is especially true because Access 2010 no longer supports user-level (also called *workgroup*) security. If you're new to client/server RDBMSs, Access 2010 is the ideal learning tool for upgrading your database design and management skills to the requirements of today's job market.

- Chapter 26, "Exploring Access Data Projects and SQL Server 2008," introduces you to Access data projects and SSX. The chapter shows you how to use Access 2010's built-in project designer to create and modify SQL Server tables, views, functions, and stored procedures. Backing up, restoring, copying, and moving SQL Server databases is covered in detail. You also learn how to link other databases, including Access .accdb files, with OLE DB data providers and how to secure ADP front ends as .ade files.

- Chapter 27, "Moving from Access Queries to Transact-SQL," provides a formal introduction to ANSI-92 SQL and explains how the Access and Transact-SQL dialects differ. Special emphasis is given to queries that you can't create in the graphical project designer—such as UNION queries and subqueries—and enabling transactions in stored procedures that update two or more tables.

- Chapter 28, "Upsizing Access Applications to Access Data Projects and SQL Azure," explains how to use the Upsizing Wizard to convert existing Access applications directly to Access data project front ends and SQL Server tables, views, functions, and stored procedures. The wizard can't upsize Access crosstab queries, so the chapter explains how to write T-SQL PIVOT queries to emulate Access crosstab queries. When this book was written, Access 2010 was capable of linking—but not upsizing—to SQL Azure "databases in the cloud;" ultimately, it's likely that the Access Upsizing Wizard will also accommodate SQL Azure back ends.

Part IX: Programming and Converting Access Applications

The chapters in Part IX assume that you have no programming experience in any language. These chapters explain the principles of writing Access macros and VBA programming code. They also show you how to apply these principles to automate Access applications and use VBA to work directly with ADO Recordset objects. Part VII also supplies tips for converting Access 97 and 200x applications to Access 2010.

- Chapter 29, "Learning Visual Basic for Applications," introduces you to the VBA language with emphasis on using VBA to automate your Access front ends. The chapter describes how to write VBA code to create user-defined functions stored in modules and to write simple procedures that you activate directly from events.

- Chapter 30, "Handling Events with Macros and Procedures," describes how to use embedded macros and VBA event-handling subprocedures in class modules. This chapter explains the events triggered by Access form, report, and control objects, and tells you how to use macro actions or methods of the DoCmd object to respond to events, such as loading or activating a form.

- Chapter 31, "Programming Combo and List Boxes," shows you how to take maximum advantage of Access 2010's unique databound combo and list boxes in decision-support applications. This chapter explains the VBA coding techniques for loading combo box lists and populating text and list boxes based on your combo box selections.

- Chapter 32, "Understanding Data Access Objects, OLE DB, and ADO," explains Microsoft's approach to Access and SQL Server data connectivity in Office applications, and describes how to program Data Access Objects (DAO) and ActiveX Data Objects (DAO), as well as tells how to decide on DAO or ADO for your new Access 2010 projects.

- Chapter 33, "Upgrading 2003 and Earlier Applications to Access 2010," tells you what changes you need to make when you convert your current 32-bit Access database applications and data access pages to 32-bit or 64-bit Access 2010.

Appendixes

The book's two appendixes are

- Appendix A, "What Was New in Access 2007 for Users of Access 2003 and Earlier," is intended to ease the transition of Access 2003 and earlier users to the Fluent user interface and the other dramatic changes to navigation with the Access UI. It is a verbatim copy of *Special Edition Using Microsoft Office Access 2007*'s Chapter 1, "Access 2007 for Access 200x Users: What's New."

- Appendix B, "Glossary," presents a descriptive list of the terms, abbreviations, and acronyms used in this book that you might not be familiar with and that can't be found in commonly used dictionaries.

The Downloadable Sample Files

 The sample database files that you can download after registering at http://www.quepublishing.com/title/0789743078 contain sample databases for each chapter that deals with hands-on development. Extracting the individual files from the archive creates ...\Access2010\Chaptr## folders (## is the chapter number) containing the *.accdb and other related files.

The sample database files contain tables, queries, forms, reports, HTML pages, VBA, and special files to complement design examples, and show you the expected result. An icon identifies sections that point to chapter files included in the downloadable samples.

A very large (20MB) database named Oakmont.accdb is included for optional use with some of the examples in this book. Oakmont University is a fictitious institution in Texas with 30,000 students and 2,300 employees. Databases with a large number of records in their tables are useful when designing applications to optimize performance, so the downloadable files also include a version of the Northwind.accdb database, NwindXL19.accdb, that has 21,096 records in the Orders table and about 193,280 Order Details records.

Installing the downloadable sample files to your \Access2010 folder requires about 200MB of free disk space.

 caution

Cautions are provided when an action can lead to an unexpected or unpredictable result, including loss of data; the text provides an explanation of how you can avoid such a result.

tip

Tips describe shortcuts and alternative approaches to gaining an objective. These tips are based on the experience the author has gained during more than seven years of testing successive alpha and beta versions of Access and Microsoft Office Developer (MOD).

How This Book Is Designed

The following special features are included in this book to assist readers.

If you've never used a database management application, you're provided with quick-start examples to gain confidence and experience while using Access with the Northwind Traders sample database. Like Access, this book uses the *tabula rasa* approach: Each major topic begins with the assumption that you have no prior experience with the subject. Therefore, when a command button on a ribbon, such as Design view, is used, its icon is displayed in the margin.

Access SQL

The book provides numerous examples of Access SQL statements for queries and Transact-SQL statements for views, functions, and stored procedures.

XML

Part VI of this book includes sample XML, XSL, and XML Schema documents (XSD) and examples of altering XSL Transforms (XSLT) to modify the presentation of HTML documents.

2010 NEW Features that are new or that have been modified in Access 2010 are indicated by the 2010 icon in the margin, unless the change is only cosmetic. Where the changes are extensive and apply to an entire section of a chapter, the icon appears to the left or right of the section head.

2007 NEW Features that were new in Access 2007 are indicated by this marginal icon.

References to resources available on the Internet—such as World Wide Web Consortium (W3C) Recommendations—are identified by the Web icon.

Cross-references to specific sections in other chapters follow the material that they pertain to, as in the following sample reference:

 For more information, **see** *"A Section in Another Chapter,"* **p. XXX.**

Most chapters include "Troubleshooting" sections. The elements of these sections help you solve specific problems—common and uncommon—that you might run into when creating applications that use specific Access features or techniques.

Typographic Conventions Used in This Book

This book uses various typesetting styles to distinguish between explanatory and instructional text, text that you enter in dialogs (set in **bold**), and text that you enter in code-editing windows (set in monospace type).

Key Combinations, Menu Choices, and Filenames

Key combinations that you use to perform Windows operations are indicated by joining the keys with a plus sign: Alt+F4, for example. In cases when you must press and release a key and then press another key, such as Alt, to activate KeyTips, the keys are separated by a comma without an intervening space: Alt, H. Conventional shortcut key combinations appear as Ctrl+*Key*.

> **note**
>
> Notes offer advice to help you use Access, describe differences between various versions of Access, and explain the few remaining anomalies that you find in Access 2010.

Sequences of individual menu items are separated by a comma: Edit, Cut.

Most file and folder names are initial-letter-capitalized in the text and headings of this book to conform with 32-bit Windows filenaming conventions and the appearance of filenames in Windows Explorer.

SQL Statements and Keywords in Other Languages

SQL statements and code examples are set in a special monospace font. Keywords of SQL statements, such as SELECT, are set in all uppercase. Ellipses (. . .) indicate intervening programming code that isn't shown in the text or examples.

Square brackets in monospace type ([ ]) that appear within Access SQL statements don't indicate optional items, as they do in syntax descriptions. In this case, the square brackets are used instead of quotation marks to frame a literal string or to allow use of a table and field names, such as

[Order Details], that include embedded spaces or special punctuation, or field names that are identical to reserved words in VBA.

Typographic Conventions Used for VBA

This book uses a special set of typographic conventions for references to Visual Basic for Applications keywords in the presentation of VBA examples:

- Monospace type is used for all examples of VBA code, as in the following statement:

  ```
  Dim NewArray ( ) As Long
  ```

  ```
  ReDim NewArray (9, 9, 9)
  ```

- Monospace type also is used when referring to names of properties of Access database objects, such as *FormName*.Width. The captions for text boxes and drop-down lists in which you enter values of properties, such as Source Connect String, are set in this book's regular textual font.

- **Bold monospace** type is used for all VBA reserved words and type-declaration symbols, as shown in the preceding example. Standard function names in VBA also are set in **bold monospace** type so that reserved words, standard function names, and reserved symbols stand out from variable and function names and values that you assign to variables.

- *Italic monospace* type indicates a replaceable item, as in

  ```
  Dim DataItem As String
  ```

- ***Bold italic monospace*** type indicates a replaceable reserved word, such as a data type, as in

  ```
  Dim DataItem As DataType
  ```

  DataItem is replaced by a keyword corresponding to the desired VBA data type, such as **String** or **Variant**.

- An ellipsis (...) substitutes for code not shown in syntax and code examples, as in

  ```
  If... Then... Else... End If
  ```

- Braces ({}) enclosing two or more identifiers separated by the pipe symbol (¦) indicate that you must choose one of these identifiers, as in

  ```
  Do {While¦Until}... Loop
  ```

  In this case, you must use the **While** or **Until** reserved word in your statement, but not the braces or the pipe character.

- Three-letter prefixes to variable names indicate the VBA data type of the variable, such as bln for **Boolean**, str for **String**, and lng for **Long** (integer).

- Square brackets ([ ]) enclosing an identifier indicate that the identifier is optional, as in

  Set tbl*Name* = db*Name*.OpenTable(str*TableName*[, blnExclusive])

  Here, the blnExclusive flag, if set to **True**, opens the table specified by str*TableName* for exclusive use. blnExclusive is an optional argument. Don't include the brackets in any code that you type.

Typographic Conventions Used for VBScript

The few Visual Basic Scripting Edition (VBScript) examples in this book use lowercase monospace type for reserved words, a practice that originated in ECMAScript (JavaScript or Microsoft JScript). Variables are in mixed case with a data type prefix, despite the lack of VBScript support for data types other than **Variant**. Object, property, and method names included in the World Wide Web Consortium (W3C) Document Object Model (DOM) standard also are in lowercase. Most non-DOM objects, such as MSODSC.RecordsetDefs(), use mixed case.

System Requirements for Access 2010

Access 2010 is a very resource-intensive application, as are all other Office 2010 members, including InfoPath 2010. You'll find execution of Access applications on Pentium PCs slower than 1GHz running Windows XP SP2 to be impaired, at best. The Windows Vista Capable PC minimum—"A modern processor (at least 800MHz)"—isn't likely to provide generally accepted performance standards.

Microsoft's somewhat optimistic minimum RAM recommendations for Microsoft Office Professional 2010 running under Windows 7 or XP (SP2) is 256MB. However, the Windows Vista Capable PC minimum is 512MB.

The preceding recommendations don't take into account the RAM required to run SQL Server 2005 [Express] or later. Double the realistic RAM recommendations to 1GB to achieve acceptable performance with SSX. All the examples of this book were created and tested under virtual 64-bit Windows 7 or Windows Server 2008 R2 guest operating systems running on a 64-bit 2.83GHz Core2 Quad CPU with 8GB RAM. 3GB of RAM was assigned to each of the two guest OSes.

The Microsoft Access team recommends that you install 64-bit Access 2010 only if you need more than 2GB of RAM to cache very large databases in memory. The 32-bit version incurs no performance hit from running under 64-bit Windows 7's or Vista's WOW64 (Windows-on-Windows64) feature.

Standard installation of Microsoft Office Professional 2010—without SQL Server 2005 Express or later, SQL Server Management Studio, or SQL Server Books Online—requires about 1GB of free disk space. Add another 100MB for SQL Server and 50MB each for InfoPath and Windows SharePoint Services. From a practical standpoint, you need 1.5GB or more of free disk space to use Office 2010 effectively. Add another 200MB for the downloadable sample files.

Other Sources of Information for Access

Relational database design and SQL, discussed in Chapters 4 and 27, are the subject of myriad guides and texts covering one or both of these topics. Articles in database-related periodicals in print form or on the Internet provide up-to-date assistance in using Access 2010. The following sections provide a bibliography of database-related books and periodicals, as well as a brief description of websites and newsgroups of interest to Access users.

Books

The following books complement the content of this book by providing detailed coverage of database design techniques, Structured Query Language, VBA database programming, SQL Server 2000, XML, and HTML:

- *Database Design for Mere Mortals, Second Edition,* by Michael J. Hernandez (Addison-Wesley, ISBN 0-201-75284-0), is a comprehensive guide to sound relational database design techniques for developing productive desktop and client/server databases. The book is platform agnostic, but the methods that you learn are especially effective for Access and SQL Server database design.

- *Understanding the New SQL: A Complete Guide*, by Jim Melton and Alan R. Simpson (Morgan Kaufmann Publishers, ISBN 1-55860-245-3), describes the history and implementation of the American National Standards Institute's X3.135.1-1992 standard for Structured Query Language, SQL-92, on which Access SQL is based. Melton was the editor of the ANSI SQL-92 standard, which consists of more than 500 pages of fine print.

 note

SQL: 1999—Understanding Relational Language Components, by Jim Melton and Alan R. Simpson (Morgan Kaufmann Publishers, ISBN 1-55860-456-1, 2001), is a newer book that covers SQL-99. However, neither Access nor SQLX supports the elements added to SQL-92 by SQL-99.

- *SQL Queries for Mere Mortals*, by Michael J. Hernandez and John L. Viescas (Addison-Wesley, ISBN 0-201-43336-2), is your best source for learning to write effective SELECT queries in any SQL dialect. The book includes detailed coverage of JOIN, UNION, GROUP BY, HAVING, and subquery syntax.

- *Special Edition Using XML, Second Edition*, by David Gulbrandsen, et al. (Que, ISBN 0-7897-2748-X), describes the technologies and standards that make up XML. It includes chapters that cover modeling with XML Schema, managing namespaces, using XSL transformations, and applying styles with XSL Formatting Objects and Cascading Style Sheets.

- *Special Edition Using HTML and XHTML*, by Molly E. Holzschlag (Que, ISBN 0-7897-2713-5), is an indispensable tutorial and reference for learning the basics of HTML and gaining a full understanding of Dynamic HTML (DHTML), Cascading Style Sheets (CSS), and XHTML.

Internet

Microsoft's Office Online and Access Developer Portal websites now are the primary source of new and updated information for Access users and developers. Following are the primary websites and newsgroups for Access 2007 users and developers:

■ Microsoft's Access page, http://office.microsoft.com/en-us/access/default.aspx, is the jumping-off point for U.S. Access users. It includes links to all related Access 2007 and earlier pages on the Microsoft website.

■ Microsoft's Access Developer Portal page, http://msdn2.microsoft.com/en-us/office/aa905400. aspx, provides links to information of particular interest to the Access developer community.

■ The Access Team blog (http://blogs.msdn.com/b/access/), subtitled "The official blog of the Microsoft Access product development group," is a running source of information on the new features in Access 2010.

■ Microsoft's online support page for Office 2007 and 2010, http://support.microsoft.com/gp/gp_off_main#tab0, provides links to Microsoft Knowledge Base pages for all its products. For other support options, go to www.microsoft.com/support/.

■ The Access for Developers forum at http://social.msdn.microsoft.com/Forums/en-US/accessdev/threads is "for developer discussions and questions."

ACCESS 2010 FOR ACCESS 2007 USERS: WHAT'S NEW

Access 1.0, 1.1, and 2.0 were very successful standalone desktop database platforms. The first Access team consisted of highly skilled development, marketing, and management personnel who were devoted entirely to making Access the premier desktop relational database management system (RDBMS) for Windows. Access, which reports say cost $60 million to develop, sold for US$99 and, according to Jim Gray of Microsoft Research, was generating revenue of about US$300 million per year by February 1994 or earlier.

Microsoft created Office 95 Professional by adding Access to Office 95 Standard's Word, Excel, PowerPoint, and Schedule+ applications and adding US$100 to the retail price. Access gained a few new features with each subsequent release, but generally suffered from not-so-benign neglect by Office management. Access 2003, for example, delivered only minor, incremental improvements over Access 2002.

Access 2007 represented a sea change to the traditional incremental improve-

 note

2007 NEW Access 2007 ceased supporting many less widely used Access features, such as Data Access Pages (DAP) and user-level security for the new .accdb and .accde file formats. Access 2010 introduces Access Services and web databases to replace DAP for browser-based database front ends.

ments in version upgrades. The Office team grafted what became known as the Fluent user interface (UI) to Access 2007, which caused consternation among access veterans. According to Erik Rucker, then Group Program Manager for Access, the development team for Access 2007 was about seven times as large as that for Access 2003. The overwhelming changes to its UI represented only a fraction of the new and mostly improved features of Access 2007.

➥ *To learn more about elements of earlier versions that Access 2007 dropped,* **see** *"Features Missing from Access 2007,"* **p. 1464.**

What's New in Microsoft Office Access 2010: An Overview

2010 NEW Microsoft's primary goals for Access 2010 are to improve usability for new users and increase productivity for experienced users and developers. Following are brief descriptions of the most important new features of Access 2010:

- **File tab and Backstage View**—Access 2010 replaces Access 2007's Office button with a File tab that opens what the Access team calls the Backstage View. The Backstage View contains command buttons that execute operations on entire databases, such as Open, which displays a list of recently used databases, or New, which opens a collection of templates on which to base new databases. (See Figure 1.1.) Chapter 3, "Navigating the Fluent Access User Interface," covers the Fluent UI and Backstage View in detail.

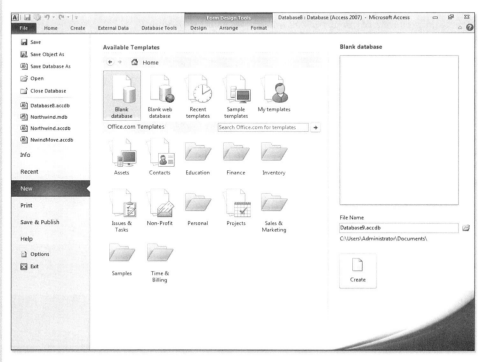

Figure 1.1
Clicking the new File tab opens the Backstage View of command buttons for opening a recently used database or selecting a template for creating a new database.

- **Calculated table fields**—Earlier Access versions required using Access queries to create computed columns. Access 2010 enables defining fields whose values are derived from other fields in the same table. Chapter 5, "Working with Access Databases and Tables," shows you how to define calculated fields.

- 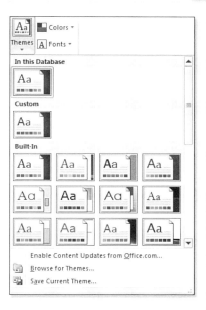 **Office Themes for forms and reports**—Office Themes enable applying a standardized set of colors and fonts to all custom Office applications; they replace the Autoformat feature of earlier Access versions (see Figure 1.2).

Figure 1.2
Office Themes let you apply preset complementary colors and font families to all Access and Office 2010 applications.

- **Conditional formatting with data bars**—Data bars convey the relative value of numeric cells with a color gradient, which emulates similar Excel 2010 formatting styles (see Figure 1.3). Chapter 15, "Designing Custom Multitable Forms," describes applying conditional formatting to databound text boxes to let users quickly spot data trends.

- **Navigation control**—A specialized hierarchical Navigation tab control, which Chapter 15 describes, enables point-and-click navigation between forms. Dragging a form from the Navigation pane to an [Add New] drop zone creates a tab named for the form. This new control is intended to replace earlier Access versions' Switchboard form (see Figure 1.4).

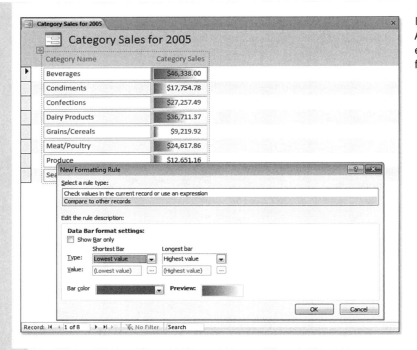

Figure 1.3
Access 2010 Data Bars let you emulate Excel formatting styles for numeric values.

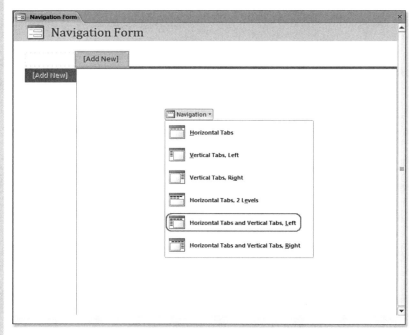

Figure 1.4
Drag a form icon from the Navigation pane to a horizontal or vertical drop zone tab of the Navigation control to create a new tab.

- 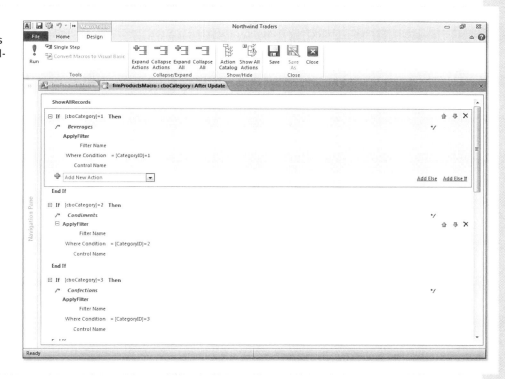 **Web Browser control**—Access 2010's new Web Browser control lets you create web mashups and display web content in your Access applications.

- **Access Macro Builder**—Microsoft deprecated Access macros in favor of VBA programming code beginning with Access 97. Macros enable limited application automation without requiring the .accdb file to be placed in a trusted location or having a signed .accde file from a package. The new Macro Builder offers IntelliSense and aids understanding of multiple macro actions (see Figure 1.5), which is likely to increase use of macros. You must use Access macros to automate web databases because Access Services don't support VBA. Chapter 19, "Automating Access Applications with Macros," shows you how to respond to events with macros.

Figure 1.5
Access 2010's new drag-and-drop Macro Builder with IntelliSense simplifies authoring macros.

- **Data Macros**—Access 2007 and earlier macros handle events triggered by forms and reports, as well as their controls. Access 2010 introduces Data Macros that handle table-generated events, such as Before Update, Before Delete, After Update, After Insert or After Delete of a row. Access 2010 Data Macros correspond to SQL Server's triggers. Chapter 20, "Emulating Table Triggers with Access Data Macros," teaches you how to take advantage of Data Macros.

- **Collaboration with SharePoint**—Microsoft downplays Access 2010/SQL Server projects for client/server applications in favor of linking Access tables from SharePoint lists and sharing .accdb files from SharePoint Document Libraries. Manipulating relational data in Sharepoint's nonrelational, web-based environment probably will interest only organizations that have a substantial commitment to an SPF 3.0 or SPS 2010 infrastructure. Chapter 22, "Collaborating with SharePoint Foundation 2010," introduces you to linking or moving tables to SPF or SPS.

- **Web databases**—Data Access Pages authored in Access 2003 were suited to private intranets but not the public Internet. Access 2010's new web databases and SPS's Access Services enable publishing browser-based applications to intranets and the Internet. Web databases substitute SharePoint lists for Access tables. Chapter 23, "Sharing Web Databases with SharePoint Server 2010," shows you how to publish a standard Access front end to an interactive web application.

> **tip**
>
> The remainder of this chapter assumes familiarity with Access 2007. If you're migrating from Access 2003 or earlier, Appendix A, "What Was New in Access 2007 for Users of Access 2003 and Earlier," introduces the many new features added—and a few removed—by Access 2007.
>
> If you haven't used an earlier Access version, you might want to skip to the "SQL Server 2008 R2 Express Edition Setup" section near the end of this chapter. The succeeding chapters of this book cover in detail all the material presented in this chapter, with the exception of initial SQL Server 2008 R2 Express Edition installation.

The sections that follow expand on the brief descriptions in the preceding list and provide cross-references to detailed coverage of new features in later chapters.

Changes to the Office 2007 Ribbon User Interface

Other than replacing the Office button with the File tab and its Backstage View, Access 2010 made mostly cosmetic changes to Access 2007 Fluent UI. Access 2010 adds an improved UI in the Options dialog for creating new and customizing what Microsoft calls command tabs and groups. Optionally, click the New Tab to create a new command tab. With a new or existing ribbon selected in the right list, click the New Group button to add a new group, select a command icon in the left list, and, with the new group selected, click the Add button to add the new command icon.

Access 2007's Main Ribbons

Access 2010 has five main command tabs and ribbons. Press Alt to display the shortcut keys (called *KeyTips*) for each main ribbon, the Office button, and Quick Access Toolbar (1...*n*), as shown in Figure 1.7 (top). Press Alt+*Key* to display the second-level shortcut keys (see Figure 1.7 center and bottom). Many Access 2010 KeyTips differ from those of Access 2007, and group names and their members have changed.

Following are brief descriptions of the primary purposes of each main ribbon, which are largely unchanged:

Figure 1.6
Adding a new command tab, group, or icon is a select-and-click operation in Access 2010.

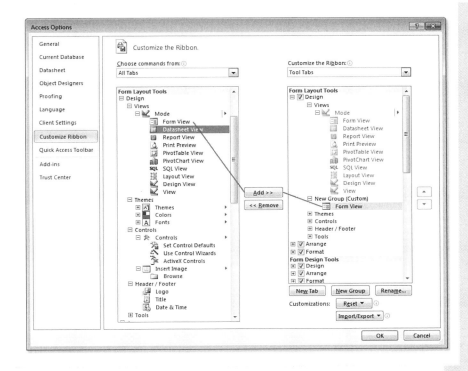

Figure 1.7
The top Home half-ribbon shows shortcut-key combinations to activate one of the five main ribbons (File, Home, Create, External Data, and Database Tools) or the Quick Access Toolbar (QAT).

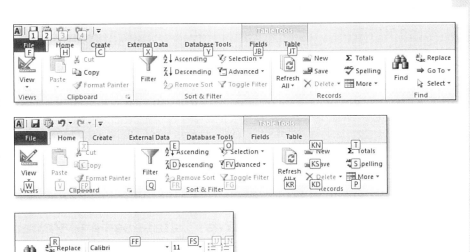

- **Home**—Lets you select Datasheet, Form, Report, Layout, or Design view; perform Clipboard operations; specify font properties; format memo fields with HTML; and refresh, add, delete, save, sort, filter, find, and spell check records (refer to Figure 1.7).

- **Create**—Lets you create a new empty table or a table from a template in Datasheet view, or an empty table in Design view; create a SharePoint list and a table that links to the list; create a form or report bound to a table or query that's selected in the Navigation pane; and create a new query, macro, module, or class module (see Figure 1.8).

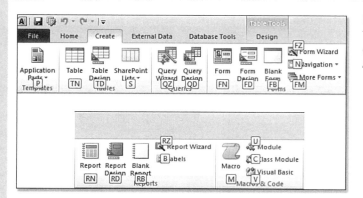

Figure 1.8
The Create ribbon's buttons and drop-down galleries enable adding new Access objects to your database.

- **External Data**—Lets you import, link, or export external data in a variety of formats; collect or update data via emailed HTML forms; save import or export specifications; work with SharePoint lists while offline; and move select objects or the entire database to a SharePoint site (see Figure 1.9).

- **Database Tools**—Lets you open the VBA editor for a module or Class Module; run a macro, create a shortcut menu from a macro, or convert a macro to VBA; open the Relationships window to create or edit table relationships; show or hide the Object Dependencies pane, property sheet for an object, or message bar; run the Database Documenter, Performance Analyzer, or Table Analyzer Wizard; move tables to a back-end Access database or upsize tables and queries to SQL Server 2005 or later [Express]; run the Linked Table Manager for linked Access tables; create or edit a switchboard with the Switchboard Manager; encrypt the database and set a database password; manage Access add-ins; and make an execute-only database by stripping out VBA source code (see Figure 1.10).

Contextual Ribbons for Access Databases and Projects

Access 2010 has 16 different contextual ribbons, which contain buttons for commands that are appropriate to specific Access object contexts. With the exception of the Print Preview ribbon, all contextual ribbon tabs appear to the right of the Database Tools tab. Most of the contextual ribbons have minor changes to group names and command icon placements. Chapter 3 provides detailed descriptions of these ribbons and illustrates galleries, when applicable.

Figure 1.9
The External Data ribbon has galleries for choosing the Import and Export data types.

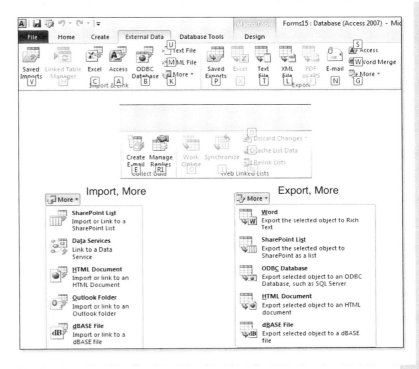

Figure 1.10
The Database Tools ribbon's buttons perform their actions without the need for gallery choices.

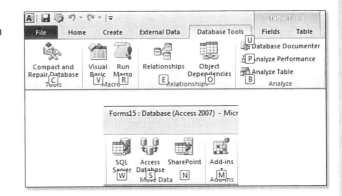

The Quick Access Toolbar

The Quick Access Toolbar (QAT) lets you create custom shortcuts to frequently used commands. By default, the QAT has three command buttons: Save, Undo, and Redo. The Undo and Redo buttons usually are disabled and sport Can't Undo and Can't Redo ToolTips.

Clicking the drop-down button to the right of the Can't Redo button opens a gallery of popular command buttons that you can add to the QAT (see Figure 1.11).

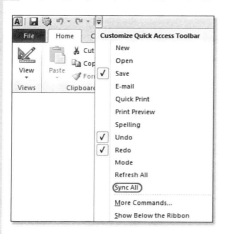

Figure 1.11
You can add popular command buttons to the QAT and specify its location—above or below the ribbon—from its drop-down gallery. The Sync All command is new in Access 2010.

The File Tab's Backstage View

There's no conventional File or Tools menu, so the Backstage view that opens when you click the File tab handles many of those two menu's former tasks. If you've opened a database or project file, the gallery opens with an Info[rmation] pane. Click the View and Edit Database Properties list to open the *Filename* Properties dialog (see Figure 1.12).

Here's what happens when you click one of the gallery's following eight links and command buttons with an .accdb file open:

- ▪ **2010 NEW Info**—Opens the Information About *DatabaseFile* pane (refer to Figure 1.12).

- ▪ **2010 NEW Recent**—Opens a Recent Databases (MRU) list.

Figure 1.12
The Office gallery's default view is the Info page if you have a database or project file open; otherwise, it's a most recently used (MRU) file list.

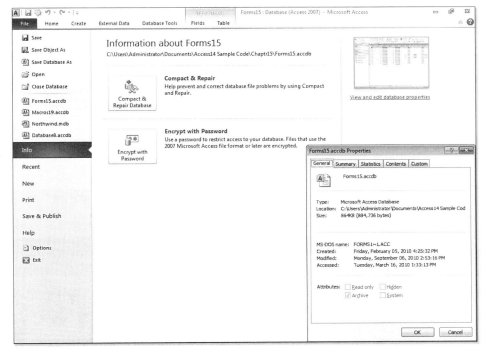

- **New**—Opens the Getting Started with Microsoft Office Access dialog, which lets you create a database from a local or downloaded template, open an empty database, or open a new ADP (refer to Figure 1.3).

- 2010 NEW **Print**—Opens the Print pane that offers Quick Print, Print, and Print Preview buttons.

- 2010 NEW **Save & Publish**—Opens a pane with options to save the current database or object as a new database or object; publish to as a web database to Access Services, save the database file in Access 2007, 2002–3, or 2000 format or as an Access Template (*.accdt file); package and distribute the database, package and digitally sign the database, make an execute-only database (*.accde file) with design mode disabled; back up the database; or save it to a SharePoint Document Library (see Figure 1.13).

- 2010 NEW **Help**—Opens a pane to access Microsoft Office Help, Getting Started help topics, links to Office Support pages, the Options dialog, and online Updates (see Figure 1.14).

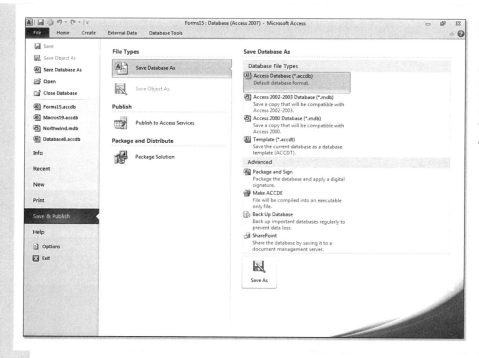

Figure 1.13
The Save & Publish pane offers a variety of options for saving the database in various formats or publishing it as a web database with Access Services.

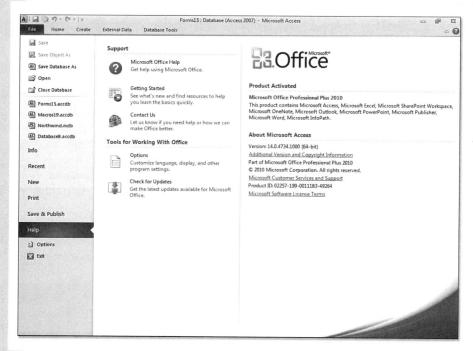

Figure 1.14
The Help page contains links to obtain answers to users' questions. You can also open the Options dialog and check for updated Access 2010 files.

- ■ **2010 NEW** **Options**—Opens the Access Options dialog, which lets you specify settings for Access 2010 and the current database (see Figure 1.15).

Figure 1.15
The Options dialog's General page lets you specify optional settings for all Access databases you open.

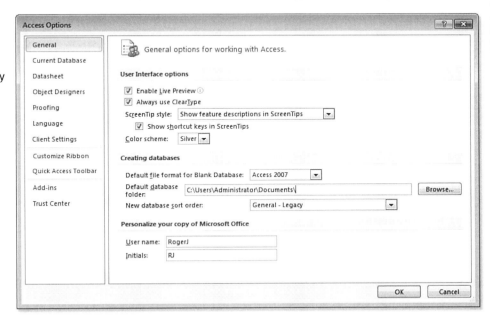

Security, Trusted Locations, Packages, and Certificates

Access 2010's approach to system and database security is very similar to that of Access 2007. System security attempts to prevent—or at least dissuade—users from opening database or project files that might contain *harmful code* in macros or VBA modules. The term *harmful code* generally means code that can access local computer or network resources and (potentially) install malware, bots, or viruses.

2010 NEW When you open any database from a location that you haven't designated as trusted or that hasn't been signed with a digital signature from a publisher you trust, Access opens with a Security Warning bar. Clicking the bar's Click for More Details link (look ahead to Figure 1.17), opens the Info pane with a Security Warning button added. Opening the button's gallery gives you two choices for enabling potentially dangerous content (see Figure 1.16).

Selecting Advanced Options closes the Info pane and opens a Security Alert dialog that's identical to the Access 2007 version (see Figure 1.17).

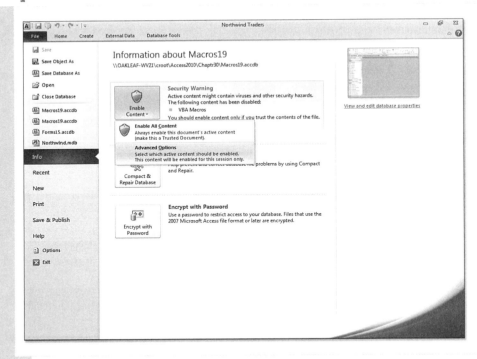

Figure 1.16
You can enable all content or open the Security Alert dialog to select the content to trust in the Security Warning gallery.

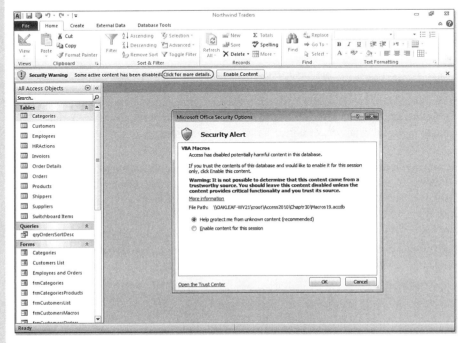

Figure 1.17
Access 2010's Security Warning message differs slightly from Access 2007's. Select the Enable the Content option if you trust the database's source.

Specifying Trusted Locations

You can prevent the Security Warning bar from appearing by storing the .accdb or .adp file in a *trusted location* (folder). You specify trusted location(s) in the Trusted Locations dialog of the Access Options dialog's Trust Center page.

 For an example of creating a trusted location, **see** *"Designating the Default Database Folder as a Trusted Location,"* **p. 53.**

Packaging and Code-Signing Databases

An alternative to requiring users of your Access application to create a trusted location for the database is to create a Microsoft Office Access Signed Package (.accdc file) from the .accdb file. Creating a Signed Package code-signs all objects in the database and compresses the file by a factor of about five to reduce download time.

To sign a package, you must have a code-signing (Class 3) certificate from a commercial certificate authority (CA), such as Comodo, Thawte, or VeriSign, or create a self-signed certificate with Office 2007's Digital Certificate for VBA Projects application (SelfCert.exe). Code-signing certificates from a commercial CA cost from $99 to $199 per year.

Self-signed certificates usually are limited to personal or small workgroup use. By default, self-signed certificates work only for packages you extract on the same machine that created and signed them. Use trusted locations to avoid security warnings unless you have a compelling reason to do otherwise.

Enabling Non-trusted Application Automation with Macros

Access 2010 users in organizations with highly secure computer operations might be prevented from enabling "potentially harmful content" by a group policy setting. In this case, you can take advantage of the default "safe" subset of Access macro actions that will run without enabling VBA code by trusting the database. To enable unsafe macro actions, you must click the Macro Tools, Design ribbon's Show All Actions button, which toggles between displaying a list of all and safe-only actions.

 For more information on Access macros, **see** *"Access Macros Redux,"* **p. 33.**

 note

The primary difference between the Access 2010 and 2007 security warning is the detour to the Info pane. With the example shown here, the Info Pane's Enable All Content button and the Security Alert dialog's Enable the Content option accomplish the same thing.

When you create a new empty (blank) database in the Getting Started with Microsoft Office Access dialog, the Security Warning bar doesn't appear until you reopen the database.

 note

Access 2010 doesn't support GEOMETRY, GEOGRAPHY, or HIERARCHYID data types, nor will it open SQL Server 2008 [R2] database diagrams.

 note

SharePoint Foundation and SharePoint Server 2010 are designed to run on the 64-bit version of Windows Server 2008 [R2] and require a 64-bit CPU/motherboard. They will install and run under 64-bit Windows 7 also, but only for test and development purposes.

 note

Microsoft touts the capability of macro actions to execute in non-trusted applications as one of the reasons for the resurrection of Access macros as a recommended programming technology.

Access Web Databases and SharePoint Lists

2010 NEW Access 2010's changes to Access 2007 tables and database engine are relatively minor, unless you publish Access databases to SharePoint Server 2010 to enable browser-based intranet or Internet access with web databases. Web databases, which store tables as SharePoint Server 2010 lists and don't support VBA, serve as the replacement for Data Access Pages, which Access 2007 dropped. Chapter 23 is devoted to Web Databases.

The Access and SharePoint teams devoted substantial development and testing resources to improving the performance of tables linked to SharePoint lists by optimizing client-side and server-side caching. Chapter 22 explains how to link or move tables to SharePoint Foundation 2010, which is available to licensees of 64-bit Windows Server 2008 or 2008 R2 at no charge.

2010 NEW Access 2010 also supports linking tables to Data Services, which can be conventional SOAP Web services with Web Service Definition Language (WSDL) files or SharePoint Business Connectivity Services (BCS) entities with Application Definition XML files that contain External Content Type metadata. Linking to Data Services is beyond the scope of this book.

Application Development by Templates

Access 2010 includes 12 built-in templates: seven for conventional Access databases (Events, Faculty, Marketing Projects, Northwind, Sales Pipeline, Students, and Tasks) and five for web databases (Assets, Charitable Contributions, Contacts, Issues, and Projects). In Backstage view, click New and Sample Templates to open the Available Templates gallery (see Figure 1.18).

The Access 2007 team commissioned a complete makeover of the original 25 Access 2003 templates available from Office Online. These templates were popular; for example, the Access 2003 Contact Management template had close to 600,000 downloads before it was converted to Access 2007. This template has four related tables and manages detailed contact information *and* call history. A benefit of Access 2003 and earlier templates is that most have a few rows of sample data.

The new templates page at http://office.microsoft.com/en-us/templates/CT010214400.aspx has Access 2010, Access 2007, and Previous Versions categories.

 To learn how to create an Access 2010 application from earlier versions of templates, **see** *"Creating a Database from Any Access Template on Microsoft Office Online,"* **p. 55.**

Figure 1.18
The Available Templates gallery exposes buttons for Access 2010's 12 built-in templates. (Scroll down to display Sales Pipeline, Students and Tasks template buttons).

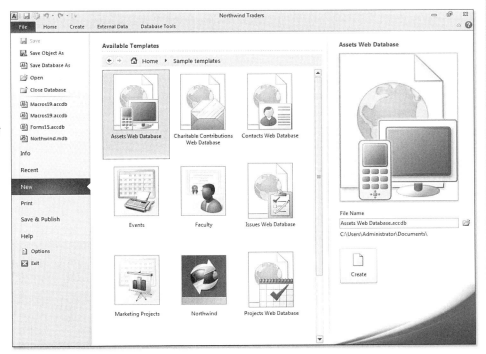

Access Macros Redux

Access 2010 treats macros as full-fledged objects, and the Access team encourages their use by new users and seasoned developers alike. As of Office 97, which replaced Access Basic with VBA, macros were deprecated. VBA was designated the strategic programming language for automating Access applications, and Office 97 included a macro-to-VBA converter to ease the upgrade effort. (The Database Tools ribbon's Macro group includes a Convert Form's Macros to Visual Basic button.)

Original Access macros had two basic defects: no error-handling capability and the lack of an equivalent to form and report Class Modules (also called *code behind forms*, or CBF). Access 2007 overcame the first limitation with the new On Error macro action, which lets you specify how errors are handled with one of the following values of the Go To argument:

- **Next** disregards the error, and execution proceeds to the next macro action.

- **MacroName** stops executing the current macro and jumps to the named macro.

- **Fail** stops execution and displays an error message.

Embedded macros handle the missing CBF equivalent. Each form or report event has a builder button that opens a Choose Builder dialog that lets you select a Macro Builder, Expression Builder, or Code Builder.

As an example, an embedded macro in the \Access2010\Chaptr01\NavPane.accdb database's Form1 (Customers List) hides the prebuilt Object Type, Tables and Related Views, Modified Date, and Created Date categories and locks the NavPane when you open the form (see Figure 1.19). Ordinarily, the AutoExec macro would execute these actions.

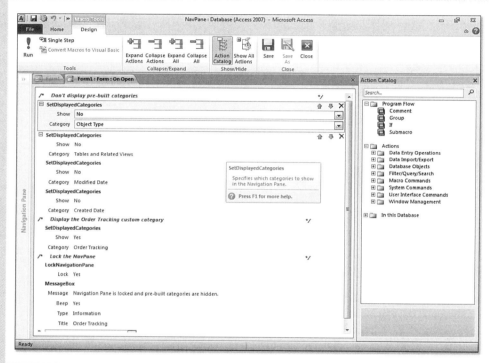

Figure 1.19
This embedded macro in Access 2010's new Macro Builder prevents users from seeing tables and queries in the NavPane's prebuilt categories.

A similar macro that enables the prebuilt categories and unlocks the NavPane executes when you open Form2 (Orders List).

Chapter 19, "Automating Access Applications with Macros," and Chapter 30, "Handling Events with Macros and Procedures," show you how to write Access macros to handle simple tasks. VBA is better used for complex application automation chores, but web databases don't support VBA. Therefore, the Access team added Data Macros to handle events associated with adding, deleting and updating rows of Access tables.

SQL Server 2008 [R2] Express Edition Setup

SQL Server 2005 Express replaced Access 2000's Microsoft Data Engine (MSDE) 1.0 (based on SQL Server 7.0) and Access 2002 and 2003's Microsoft SQL Server Desktop Engine (MSDE) 2000 (based on SQL Server 2000). SQL Server 2005 Express was a major upgrade to MSDE 2000 and took Microsoft almost five years to finish. SQL Server 2005 Express was the first free SQL Server version to include a management tool—SQL Server Management Studio Express (SSMS). SQL Server 2005 Express removed MSDE's performance throttle, which limited query execution to five simultaneously running queries.

Microsoft released SQL Server 2008 [Express] on August 6, 2008. SQL Server 2008 added spatial (GEOMETRY and GEOGRAPHY), HIERARCHYID and specialized date/time data types, as well as Transparent Data Encryption (TDE) and improved data compression features. SQL Server 2008 R2 (called *SSX* in this book) released to manufacturing on April 21, 2010, six days after Office 2010 RTMed. The R2 upgrade added new features, including PowerPivot for Excel and SharePoint, Master Data Services, StreamInsight, ReportBuilder 3.0, and Reporting Services Add-in for SharePoint.

Office 2000–2003 included installation code for MSDE 1.0 and 2000; the Office 2010 CD-ROM images don't include SQL Server 2008 R2 Express Edition and Management Tools, which is the recommended version for Access users who don't have a network connection to SQL Server 2005 Workgroup Edition or later.

 note

Access 2010 doesn't support GEOMETRY, GEOGRAPHY, or HIERARCHYID data types, nor will it open SQL Server 2008 [R2] database diagrams.

 tip

If you're creating multiuser database applications for an organization or team and loss or corruption of data would have serious economic or social consequences, consider substituting Access data projects and SSX for .accdb databases. SSX is a much more robust, secure, and reliable data engine than Access's. The only downside of moving to SSX is loss of new SharePoint-specific features, such as the Attachment field data type, MVLFs, and append-only Memo fields.

Downloading and Installing SSX

If you intend to develop or just explore Access 2010 data projects (ADP) or Access front-ends linked to SQL Server 2008 R2 or SQL Azure tables, do the following to install SSX on your client PC or a network server:

1. Download and save the SQL Server 2008 R2 Express Edition and Management Tools installer (SQLEXPRWT_x86.exe, 32-bit: 235MB or SQLEXPRWT_x64.exe, 64-bit: 247MB) from http://www.microsoft.com/express/database/ to a temporary folder, usually \Users*UserName*\Downloads.

 note

32-bit or 64-bit SSX (R2) is recommended because it has a maximum database size of 10 GB, while SQL Server 2008 Express is limited to 4 GB. SQL Server 2008 R2 Management Studio Express, which is included in the Management Tools, is required to connect to SQL Azure cloud databases, which are one of the topics of Chapter 28. SQL Azure is a customized version of SQL Server 2008. The Management Tools also include SQL Server 2008 Reporting Services and Full-Text Search.

2. Run SQLEXPRWT_x??.exe with an administrative account, accept the End User License Agreement, click Next, and then click Install to extract the setup files and open the SQL Server Installation Center dialog (see Figure 1.20).

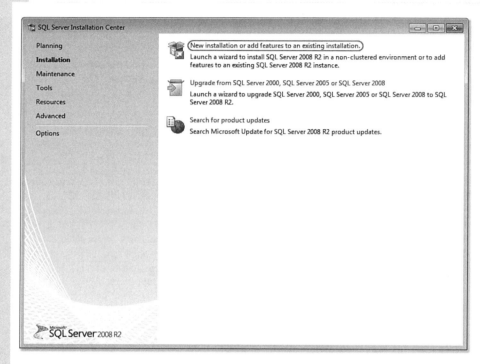

Figure 1.20
The SQL Server Installation Center dialog opens a few seconds after the installer extracts the setup files.

3. Click the New Installation or Add Features to an Existing Installation link to open the License Terms dialog.

4. Mark the I Accept the License terms check box, optionally mark the Send Feature Usage Data to Microsoft check box, and click Next to open the Setup Support Files dialog.

5. After the Setup Support Files install and the system configuration check completes, the Feature Selection dialog opens (see Figure 1.21).

6. Accept the default features and click Next to perform another System Configuration Check, and click Next to open the Instance Configuration dialog.

Figure 1.21
The Feature
Selection
dialog opens
with all avail-
able features
selected by
default.

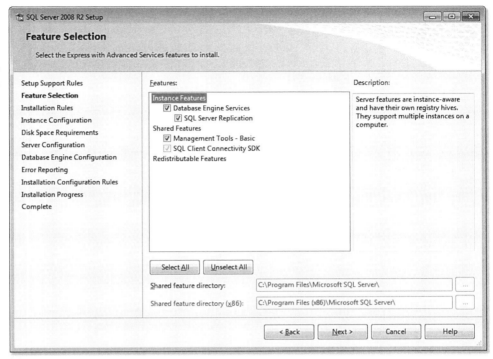

7. Accept the default Named Instance option and, optionally, change the Instance ID value from SQLExpress to SQLEXPRESS (see Figure 1.22).

8. Click Next to open the Instance Configuration dialog (see Figure 1.23).

note

SQL Server instance names aren't case sensitive.

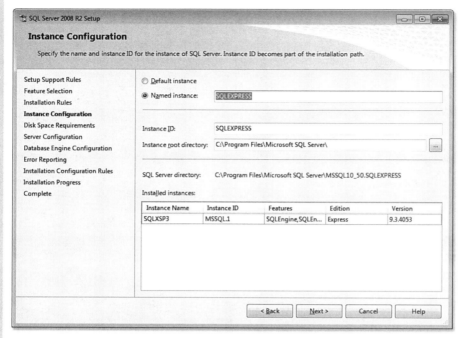

Figure 1.22
The default instance name for SQL Server Express databases is SQLEXPRESS. Other SQL Server instances, for example an SQL Server 2005 SP3 Express instance named SQLXSP3, appear in the Installed Instances list.

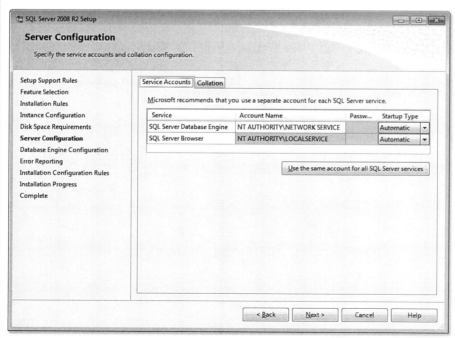

Figure 1.23
The Instance Configuration dialog lets you specify an Account Name and Password for the SQL Server Database Engine and SQL Server Browser. The default values shown here usually are satisfactory.

9. Accept the default Service Accounts and Collation and click Next to open the Database Engine Configuration dialog. Mark the Mixed Mode check box to enable logon with SQL Server's System Administrator (sa) account. Type and confirm a complex (upper- and lower-case letters, numeral(s) and symbol) password, and click Add Current User if you aren't logged in as the local machine administrator (see Figure 1.24).

Figure 1.24
The Account Provisioning dialog lets you add an sa login with SQL Server security in addition to the required integrated Windows security login for the local machine Administrator account.

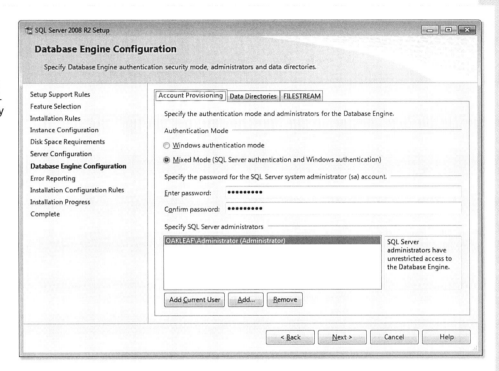

10. Review the Data Directories and FILESTREAM pages, and click Next to open the Error Reporting dialog.

11. If you want to share error information with the SQL Server team, mark the Send Windows and SQL Server Error Reports to Microsoft check box. Click Next to open the Installation Progress dialog and start installation.

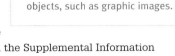 **note**
The FILESTREAM feature, which isn't enabled by default, gives SQL Server access to the local file system for storage of large objects, such as graphic images.

12. After a few minutes, the Complete dialog opens with a message that the installation completed successfully and added details in the Supplemental Information text box (see Figure 1.25).

13. After you've read the Supplemental Information, click Close to close the Complete dialog.

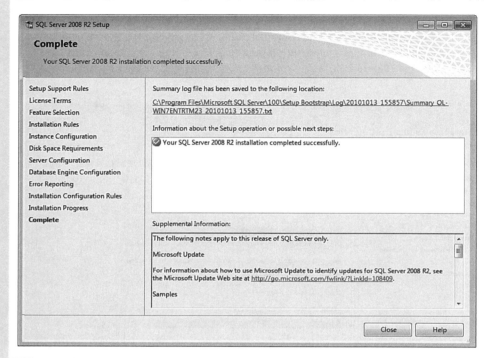

Figure 1.25
The Complete dialog's supplemental information text box contains details for downloading the SQL Server 2008 R2 Books Online (help) file and sample databases.

Setup installs a Programs, Microsoft SQL Server 2008 R2 submenu with Import and Export Data (32-bit), Import, Export Data (64-bit), and SQL Server Management Studio choices, plus Configuration Tools and Integration Services folders. Installing Books Online adds its choice to the Documentation and Tutorials submenu.

  To learn more about SQL Server Management Studio Express (SSMSX), **see** *"Adding SQL Server User Logins with SQL,"* **p. 900** *and "Moving from MSDE to the SQL Server 2005 or Later Express Edition,"* **p. 1415**.

Managing SSX

If you run SSX on the same machine as your Access front end, you don't need to do anything after installation. SSX will start as a service automatically when you boot your computer. If you want to make the instance of SSX you install accessible to remote networked users, you must perform some minimal management tasks. You must set the SQL Server Browser Service to start automatically and enable at least the TCP/IP protocol for SSX. The Browser Service enables clients to locate SQL Server 2005

> **note**
>
> The Configuration Tools folder contains Reporting Services Configuration, SQL Server Configuration Manager, SQL Server Error and Usage Reporting, and SQL Server Installation Center (##-bit) choices. The default configuration is for local (shared memory) access of SQL Server 2008 R2.

instances on remote computers. If you're running the Windows Firewall and Install doesn't establish exceptions for SQL Server and SQL Server Browser, you must create an exception for SQL Server and Browser connections also.

Making SSX Accessible to Remote Users

To make a local SSX instance accessible to other networked computers, do the following:

1. Choose Programs, Microsoft SQL Server 2008 R2, Configuration Tools, SQL Server Configuration Manager to open the dialog of the same name.

2. Double-click the SQL Server Configuration Manager (Local) node to display the nodes SQL Server 2008 Services, SQL Server 2008 Network Configuration, and SQL Native Client Configuration.

3. Double-click the SQL Server 2008 Services node to display the SQL Server Browser and SQL Server (SQLEXPRESS) service items in the right pane (see Figure 1.26). If you installed other services, they will appear also.

Figure 1.26
Installing the SSX database engine installs but doesn't start the SQL Server Browser service automatically.

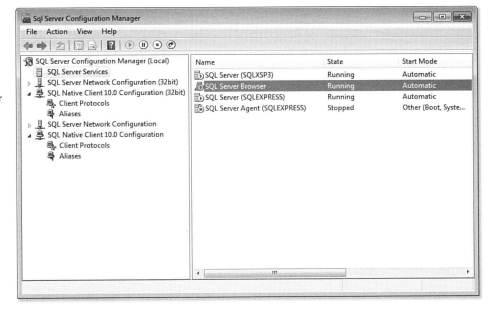

4. Right-click the SQL Server Browser item and choose Properties to open the SQL Server Browser Properties dialog. Click the Service tab, open the Start Mode list box, and choose Automatic (see Figure 1.27). Click OK to close the Properties dialog.

Figure 1.27
Change the SQL Server Browser's Start Mode setting to Automatic, if it's currently Disabled or Manual.

5. If you changed the setting to Automatic, right-click the SQL Server Browser item and choose Start to start the service for the first time.

6. Double-click to expand the SQL Server 2008 Network Configuration item, select the Protocols for SQL Express node, right-click the TCP/IP item in the right pane's Protocol Name list, and choose Enabled (see Figure 1.28). Acknowledge the message that states you must stop and restart SSX for the change to become effective.

7. Repeat step 6 for the SQL Server Network Configuration (32-bit) node, if you installed the 64-bit version.

8. If you want to communicate with remote SSX or SQL Server instances, expand the SQL Native Client 10.0 Configuration node, select Client Protocols, and enable the TCP/IP protocol.

9. Repeat step 8 for the SQL Server Native Client Configuration (32-bit) node, if you installed the 64-bit version.

10. Select SQL Services, right-click SQL Server (SQLEXPRESS), choose Stop, wait for the service to stop, and then choose Start.

11. Close SQL Server Configuration Manager.

Alternatively, you can access SQL Server Configuration manager from the Computer Management dialog's Services and Applications node.

Figure 1.28
Enable the
TCP/IP protocol
for SSX to com-
municate with
remote clients.

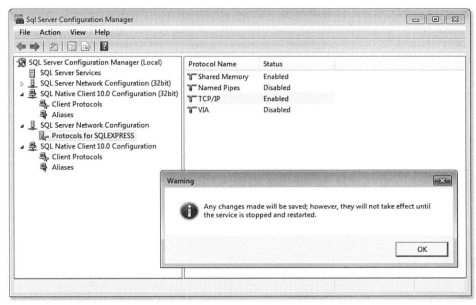

BUILDING SIMPLE TRACKING APPLICATIONS

Unlike other members of Microsoft Office 2010, Access 2010 requires that you build an application to take advantage of the product's power as a database development platform. It's up to you to design and implement the Access applications you need for most database projects.

A full-scale Access application involves at least the following four basic Access object types:

- Tables that store the data you or others add to the database

- Queries to filter and sort table data as well as to combine data in related tables

- Forms for displaying and entering data, controlling the opening and closing of other forms, and printing reports

- Reports to print detail data, summary information, or both in tables

Many Access applications include modules to store Visual Basic for Applications (VBA) code. Word 2010 and Excel 2010 let you automate simple repetitive operations by recording VBA macros. Access 2010 also supports a set of *macro commands* (also called *macro actions*) primarily for compatibility with previous versions and to support web databases, but Access macros don't use VBA. Access doesn't capture your mouse clicks or keystrokes and turn them into a series of macro commands or VBA code. You define Access macros by selecting the macro command you want from a list in the new Macro Builder window and customizing its action.

Access forms can (and often do) contain VBA code in a special type of module, called a *Class Module*. Access 2010 forms also can contain a special type of macro, called an *embedded macro*, which corresponds to a Class Module. Bear in mind that you can create many useful Access applications without writing a single macro or a line of VBA code.

All objects that make up your application are stored in a container called a *Database object*, which is a single file with an .accdb extension, such as the Northwind.accdb sample database downloadable sample files stored in your \Access2010\Nwind folder. Access is unique among desktop databases in that it can store an entire database application in a single file. Other desktop databases, such as Microsoft Visual FoxPro, require multiple files to store their objects.

Creating Access Applications from Downloaded Templates

New Access users often find it difficult to "get a grip" on how to start developing a self-contained database application. Dealing with an unfamiliar set of objects tends to intimidate first-time database developers. Fortunately, Microsoft Office Online offers a set of templates that create typical Access 2010 "starter" applications automatically.

In this chapter, you download templates to create a relatively simple but useful data compilation and tracking application. Then you explore the objects generated by the templates to gain perspective on the relationship of Access objects and learn how they're integrated within a typical Access database application.

 tip

All versions of Access have offered macros as an alternative to writing programming code. Starting with Access 97, Microsoft recommended abandoning the use of macros in favor of VBA code in modules and Class Modules. Access 97 and later include a Macro to Module Converter that automates replacing macro commands with VBA code. The implication was that macros would disappear in future Access versions.

Now Microsoft is resurrecting macros in the belief that writing macros presents a lesser challenge for new Access users than writing VBA code. The downside of adopting macros is that eventually you'll find that you need VBA code to accomplish many tasks for which there are no macro commands. In this case, you would need to learn *two* programming methodologies and languages. However, if you need to automate web databases, Access 2010 macros are the only option because web databases don't support VBA.

Using the Getting Started Window to Download Templates

When you launch Access 2010 from the Start, [All] Programs, Microsoft Office menu, the Backstage view's New pane opens by default with an Available Templates gallery open (see Figure 2.1).

The New pane offers the following options:

- Open a blank (empty) database with no Access objects other than a starter table. You can type data into the starter table's initial column and as many more columns as you need. (The starter table disappears if you don't modify its design and save your changes.) You then add table, query, form, and report objects with the Create ribbon's button.

- Open a blank Access data project (ADP or project). A project substitutes an SQL Server database for Access's built-in table and query objects. Chapter 26, "Exploring Access Data Projects and

SQL Server 2008," through Chapter 28, "Upsizing Access Applications to Access Data Projects and SQL Azure," cover projects.

Figure 2.1
The Backstage view's New pane is the entry point to creating a new Access database application.

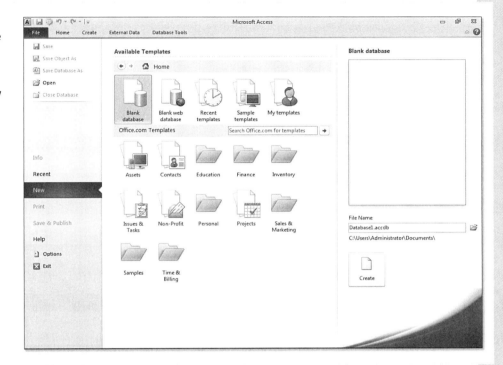

- Open a blank (empty) web database, which uses SharePoint Server 2010's Access Services to store tables, queries, forms, and macros in an on-premises or hosted instance of SharePoint Server 2010.

- Open a gallery of icons for templates that you have used recently.

- Open one of 12 sample templates installed by running the Access setup program (see Figure 2.2).

- Open a template that you saved in the My Templates folder.

- Select a template from 10 Access template categories available for download from the Microsoft Office Online website at http://office.microsoft.com/en-us/templates/.

- Search the Microsoft Office Online website for and then browse a collection of templates for Access 2000 and later.

To open the Getting Started window if you have a database open, click the File tab in the upper-left corner of Access's main window to open the Backstage view and then click the New link.

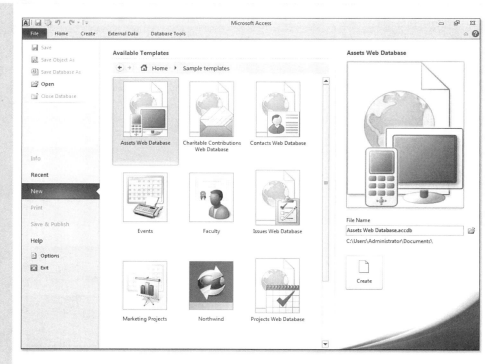

Figure 2.2
Click the Sample Templates button to open a gallery of 12 Access 2010 templates installed by the setup program. (The Sales Pipeline, Students, and Tasks template icons aren't visible in the screen capture.)

Changing the Default Folder for New Databases and Projects

Access stores all new databases and projects that you create in the C:\Documents and Settings*UserName*\My Documents folder (Windows XP and Server 2003) or C:\Users*UserName*\Documents folder (Windows 7, Vista and Server 2008 [R2]) by default.

You can change the default database location by doing the following:

1. Click the File tab in the upper-left corner of Access's main window to open the File gallery (refer to Figure 2.1).

2. [icon] Click the Access Options button to open the Access Options dialog.

3. On the default General page's Default Database Folder text box, type or browse to the path to the new default database location (see Figure 2.3).

Creating a Database from a Getting Started Window Template

The Sample Templates gallery contains icons for templates that are designed specifically for Access 2010's Fluent user interface (UI). The gallery contains seven templates for conventional Access databases (*.accdb files) and five for creating web databases.

Figure 2.3
Specify the default
database folder in the
default page of the
Access Options dialog.

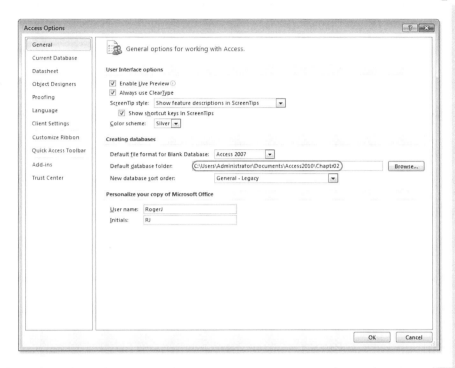

---

note

Access 2010 Web Database templates create conventional *.accdb databases in Access 2007 format that meet web database design requirements and require users to authenticate themselves by logging in with a username selected from a list. Publishing an *.accdb database to a web database requires that you have access to an on-premises or hosted SharePoint Server 2010 instance. Chapter 23, "Sharing Web Databases with SharePoint Server 2010," explains the requirements for an on-premises SharePoint 2010 server and provides an example of publishing a web database to a hosted SharePoint 2010 server instance.

Reviewing the Sample Templates

Following are the names and brief descriptions of templates whose icons appear in the Sample Templates gallery:

- **Assets Web Database**—Contains the Assets and Users tables, Assets Extended, AssetsOpen and AssetsRetired queries, 16 forms, and three reports that relate to tracking and valuing business assets.

- **Charitable Contributions Web Database**—Contains Campaigns, Donations, Donors, Event Attendees, Events, Settings, Tasks and Users tables, 13 queries, 35 forms, and 11 reports.

- **Contacts Web Database**—Contains Contacts and Comments tables, a Contacts Extended query, 13 forms, and six reports.

- **Events**—Contains an Events table, Current Events query, Event Details and Event List forms, and five reports classified by date and time.

- **Faculty**—Contains a modified version of Contacts that includes the capability to classify a faculty member by selections from Faculty Type and Department combo boxes. Although you can edit the combo box lists, it's a better database design technique to populate combo and list boxes from entries in tables. The Faculty List form includes Collect Data via E-mail, Add [Faculty Members] from Outlook, and E-mail [Faculty] List buttons.

- **Issues Web Database**—Contains Issues, Related Issues, Comments and Users tables, five queries, 20 forms, and five reports. Issues is a starting point for a help desk, customer service, or bug reports database.

- **Marketing Projects**—An expanded version of Projects that contains Projects, Deliverables, Common Deliverables, Employees, and Vendors tables, nine queries, 16 forms (one of which is a PivotChart form for budgets), and 11 reports.

> **note**
>
> Faculty also has Emergency Contact, Physician Name, Physician Phone, Medications and Emergency information incorporated as fields of the Students table, which violates relational database design rules. As you'll learn in Chapter 4, "Exploring Relational Database Theory and Practice," Emergency Contact and physician/medical information should be contained in separate, related tables.

- **Northwind**—Is a complete rework of the traditional Northwind Traders sample database with 20 tables, 27 queries, 34 forms, 15 reports. All tables have a few sample records. Northwind is the most complex of the databases generated from the Sample Templates.

- **Projects Web Database**—A basic project management database with Projects, Project History, Customers, Tasks and Users tables, nine queries, 25 forms, eight reports, two macros, and eight VBA modules.

- **Sales Pipeline**—A mini customer relationship management (CRM) application with Customers, Opportunities, and Employees tables, five queries, 13 forms, nine reports, and a standalone macro group. Sales Pipeline offers PivotChart and PivotTable forms for forecasting.

- **Students**—A simplification of the Faculty database that has a defective table design.

- **Tasks**—A variation on the Issues theme with Contacts and Tasks tables, Contacts Extended and Open Tasks queries, five forms, and seven reports.

The Assets, Contacts, Events, Issues, and Tasks templates create database tables that have the same structure as the same-named WSS 3.0 and MOSS 2007 lists.

Embedding Macros in Featured Templates

Forms in many of the databases that you create from Sample Templates have buttons that execute embedded macros to perform actions, such as the following:

- **New or Add** *Item*—Opens an empty *Item* Details form for the item type, such as Contact or Event, to add a new row to the table. Some *Item* Details forms are unnecessarily obese modal dialogs, not tabbed documents.

- **Edit Item**—Opens an *Item* Details form for the item you have selected in a datasheet view to let you change the record.

- **Collect Data via E-Mail**—Opens a multistep Collect Data Through E-Mail Messages Wizard that uses Outlook 2010 and an HTML form to let recipients update existing or add new rows to the form's underlying table.

- **E-Mail List**—Lets you send the content of the *Item* table as an email enclosure in one of nine standard or proprietary formats.

- **2007 NEW Reports List**—Lets you open each of the database reports in Report view, which Access 2007 introduced to complement Print Preview view.

Some templates, such as Marketing Projects, also include standalone macro groups. Standalone macro groups aren't limited to execution from a particular form.

Spelunking Specialized Templates for Business and Personal Use

The following are Access 2007 templates for more specialized use that you can search for by typing their name in the Search Office.com for Templates list box and clicking the right-pointing arrow:

- **Business Account Ledger**—A simple, single-entry application that can generate a profit and loss statement. A Categories table represents a simple chart of accounts for income and expenses.

- **Customer Service**—Contains Customers, Cases, Calls, Employees, and Knowledge Base tables, seven queries, 16 forms, 11 reports, and a standalone Report Center macro group. The most interesting feature of this database is the Report Center form with a Tab control to display Overdue, Days Active, Status, and Category PivotCharts.

- **Lending Library**—Intended for a book or equipment rental service with Assets (for rent), Contacts (customers), and Transactions tables, three queries, eight forms (including Check Out and Check In), 13 reports, and a standalone Transactions macro group.

- **Home Inventory**—A single-table database for creating a home inventory list, presumably for insurance purposes.

- **Nutrition**—A very complex application with eight tables, nine queries, a start-up screen, 18 other forms, and eight standalone macro groups.

- **Personal Account Ledger**—A version of the Business Account Ledger with a Categories table that has accounts more suited to personal income and expenses.

 note

Copies of all the preceding template-generated databases are in the \Access2010\Chaptr02 folder, if you downloaded the sample files from the QUE Publishing site.

Downloading Templates to Generate Sample Databases

To download a template and create the corresponding *TemplateName*.accdb database, do the following:

1. Click one of the templates or folders in the Office.com Templates gallery. Alternatively, type the template's name or a search term in the Search Office.com for Templates list box and click the right-pointing arrow.

2. If more than one template matches your choice, click the template to download in the second gallery level.

3. Open the database after the template creates it. If the Navigation pane isn't open, click the Open Shutter Bar button to display it.

4. If all the Navigation pane's headers don't display items below them, click their Category Items Show buttons to expand them.

5. Click Ctrl+F1 to hide the ribbon, if necessary, to add depth to the Navigation pane so it shows all or most items.

Figure 2.4 shows the Tasks.accdb database's empty Tasks List form open in Form view. The default Tasks Navigation, Show All navigation options are selected in the Navigation pane at the left of the Contact List. This chapter's later "Understanding the Role of the Navigation Pane" section describes Navigation pane options.

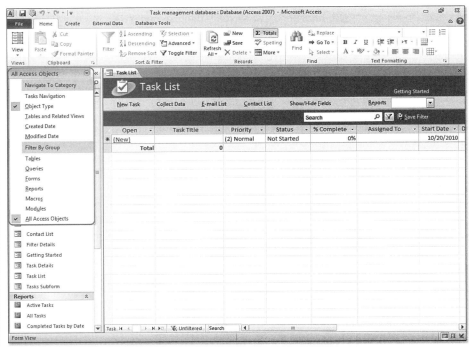

Figure 2.4
The Tasks template creates the Tasks.accdb database with table, query, form, and report objects and opens its default Tasks List form. Tables don't appear by default in the Navigation pane's Tasks Navigation display, so click the down-pointing arrow in the top navigation bar and select display by Object Type, as shown here.

Designating the Default Database Folder as a Trusted Location

If the template contains VBA code, a "Security Warning: Certain content in the database has been disabled" message bar appears at the top of the form window. Clicking the message bar's Click for More Details link opens the Info pane with a Security Warning button (see Figure 2.5). You can choose to Enable Content or click the Trust Center Settings link to open the Option dialog with the Trust Center page active.

Figure 2.5
Clicking the message bar's More Details link opens the Information pane with a button that offers an Enable Content operation for this session only.

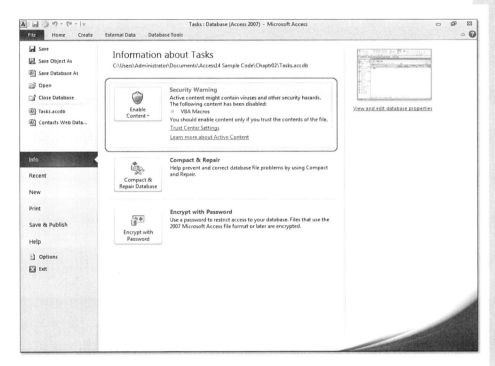

VBA code and certain Access macro commands (actions) can access your computer's resources, such as disk drives or, for VBA, network interface cards. This means that a database with malicious code or macros could plant a virus or worm on your disk that might infect your network.

You can click the Options button and select the Enable Content option each time you open any Access database, or specify one or more folders on your local machine or networked computers as *trusted locations*. Databases opened from trusted locations don't display the message bar.

To specify a folder—C:\Access2010 for this example—and its subfolders as trusted locations, do the following:

1. Click the File button to open the Backstage view, and click the Options button to open the Access Options dialog.

2. Click the Trust Center button to open the Trust Center page, and click the Trust Center Settings button to open the Trusted Locations page, which has by default a single trusted C:\Program Files\Microsoft Office\Office 14\ACCWIZ\ folder for Access's wizards.

3. Click the Add New Location button to open the Microsoft Office Trusted Location dialog. Then type the folder's path into the Path text box, mark the Subfolders of This Location Are Also Trusted check box, and type a brief description of the folder in the Description text box (see Figure 2.6).

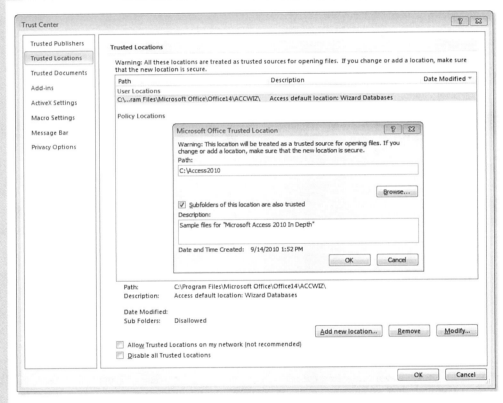

Figure 2.6
The Microsoft Office Trusted Location dialog lets you specify that Access is to trust any databases stored in the specified location and, optionally, its subfolders.

4. Click OK to add the location to the User Locations list (see Figure 2.7). Mark the Allow Trusted Locations on My Network check box if you want. Click OK twice to close the dialogs and gallery, and trust the new location.

The next time you open a database from the C:\Access2010\ folder or its subfolders, the Security Warning message box won't appear.

Figure 2.7
The User
Locations
list has an
item for each
location on
your local
computer
and, option-
ally, your
intranet.

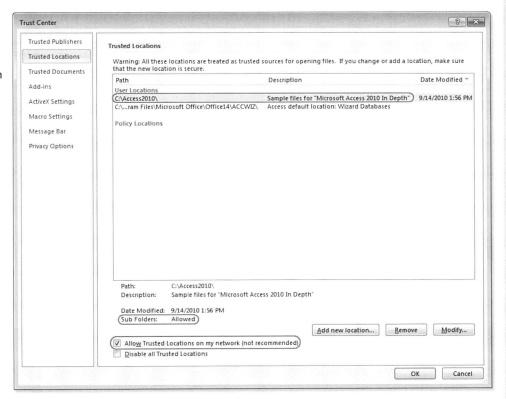

Creating a Database from Any Access Template on Microsoft Office Online

The Microsoft Office Online website's Templates page offers many Access templates for versions 2007 and earlier. You can generate Access 2010 databases from these templates, but you might need to modify their forms somewhat to accommodate the Access 2010 UI. Many Access 2010 templates have roots in those earlier Access versions.

To view the full list of available Access templates and give one of the templates a test drive, open the File gallery and click Close to close any open database, and then follow these steps:

1. Click the File button to open the Backstage view, and click the New tab..

2. Type **Access** into the Office.com Templates text box, and click the adjacent arrow button to display a list of available templates in the Search Results pane below.

3. Click one of the template icons, such as Contact Management, to open its primary form in the Preview pane on the right (see Figure 2.8).

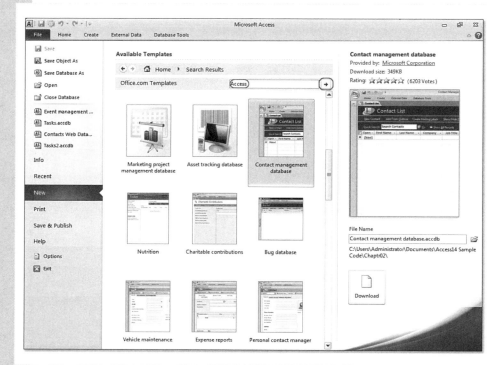

4. Double-click the template icon or click the Download Now button to retrieve the template file, create the database, and display a modal Getting Started with Contacts dialog (see Figure 2.9).

5. Close the Getting Started with Contacts window to display the Contacts datasheet form (see Figure 2.10).

Figure 2.9
This dialog opens each time you open the Contacts Management database, unless you clear the Show Getting Started When This Database Is Opened check box.

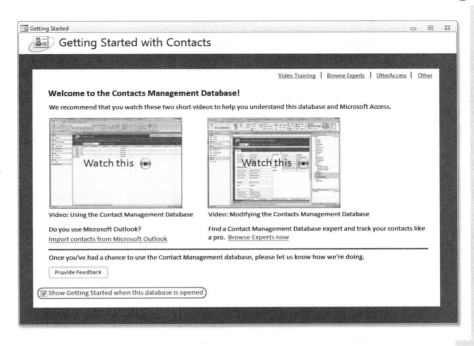

Figure 2.10
The Contacts Management template was upgraded from Access 2003 to 2007, so it doesn't share the look and feel of the native Access 2010 templates in the Sample Templates gallery.

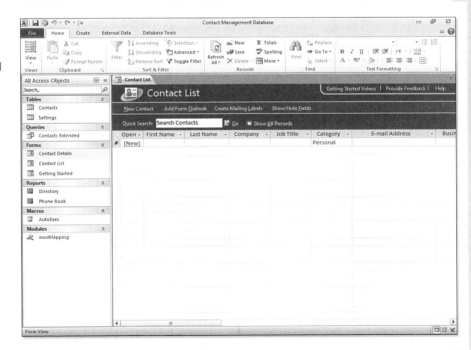

Changing Forms from Overlapping Windows to Tabbed Documents

Tabbed Documents is most users' preferred display format option, but some older templates use overlapping, resizeable windows. Figure 2.11 shows the Contacts Management database's Contact List and Contact Details forms open as overlapping windows.

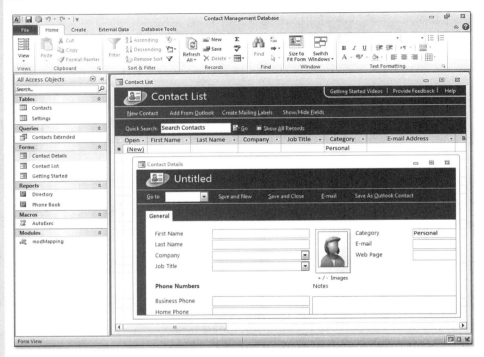

Figure 2.11
Overlapping, resizable windows are common in templates designed for Access 2003 and earlier databases, which have a Database window for navigation.

To change from Overlapping Windows to Tabbed Document style, do the following:

1. Click the File tab and Options button to open the Access Options dialog.

2. Click the Current Database button to open the page of the same name.

3. In the Document Window Options group, select the Tabbed Documents option (see Figure 2.12).

4. Click OK to accept the change. Then click OK to acknowledge the message that the change won't take place until you close and reopen the database.

5. Close and reopen the database to display the default form in its new display format (refer to Figure 2.10).

Figure 2.12
Change the display mode of the current database from Overlapping Windows to Tabbed Documents on the Access Options dialog's Current Database page.

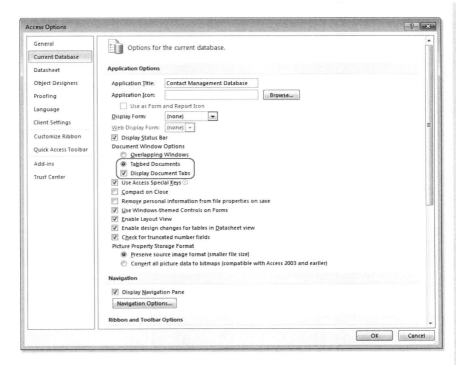

Forms generated by many Access 2003 sample templates have a Tasks pane on the right. The Tasks pane buttons execute macro commands from macro groups instead of Access 2007 and later embedded macros. Clicking the Dial Contacts button opens the Access Autodialer accessory that uses a modem to dial the contact's number.

Touring the Modified Tasks Application

Most databases generated from Access 2007 templates use *pop-up modal dialogs* instead of tabbed documents for *Items* Details data entry forms. Pop-up modal dialogs are forms that overlay all other open windows, can't be minimized, and must be closed before the application's user can proceed to other tasks. The remainder of this chapter's examples assume use of the \Access2010\Chaptr02\Tasks.accdb database.

Understanding the Role of the Navigation Pane

2007 NEW The Outlook-like Navigation pane at the left of the main window is an important feature introduced by Access 2007. The Navigation pane—called *NavPane* from this point for brevity—replaces the Database Window of Access 2003 and earlier. The primary purpose of the NavPane is to let you select, open, lay out, design, export copy, classify, and delete Access objects. Figure 2.13 shows the context menu that opens when you right-click a NavPane's table object.

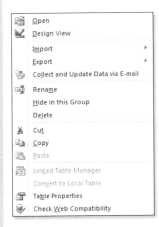

Figure 2.13
The context menu for a NavPane's table item in the NavPane requires only one or two mouse clicks to perform the most common operations for the selected object type (tables in this case).

Template-generated databases default the NavPane's navigation category to *Items* Navigation, Show All, where *Items* represents the database name, such as Tasks, or the name of the main table, such as Projects for Marketing Projects.

Choosing the Object Classification Method

 You can select the NavPane's object classification method (Navigate To category) by clicking the Navigation Options button and selecting one of the five Navigate To options and one of the two to five Filter by Group options shown in Figure 2.14.

Figure 2.15 shows the Tasks database's NavPane for Figure 2.14's four Navigate To selections.

Large-scale Access applications can involve hundreds or even thousands of objects, which require assignment to many custom groups to make navigation manageable. Access assigns each new object you create to the Unclassified Object category. Items in this category have an Add to Group context menu choice with custom categories, Supporting Objects, and New Group submenu choices.

> **note**
>
> A copy of the ContactManagement.accdb database with the Overlapping Windows option selected is in the \Access2010\Chapt02 folder of the downloadable sample files.

Figure 2.14
Each Navigate To category you choose has a set of Filter By Group options. For this example, the application was created and modified the same day this figure was captured, so the Created Data and Modified Date categories have only Today and All Dates options under Filter By Group.

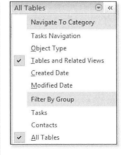

Figure 2.15
This is the appearance of the Tasks application NavPane for the four object classification methods shown in Figure 2.14.

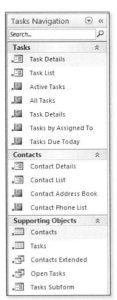
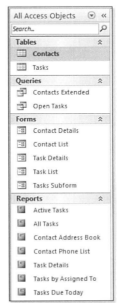
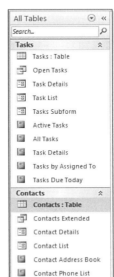
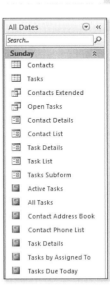

Opening Forms from the Navigation Pane and Adding Records

It's a generally accepted database application design practice (GADBADP) to require ordinary users to use forms to add or edit records in tables. The alternative—entering data directly in a table—is prone to typographic and other data entry errors.

To open—and add an entry to—the Contacts table, do the following:

1. Double-click a NavPane form item (Contact Details for this example) to open the form as a modal dialog in Form view. If the Home ribbon isn't visible, toggle it with Ctrl+F1.

2. Type an entry for a first fictitious customer as the first contact. (Look ahead to Figure 2.18 for a suggestion).

3. If you have a photo of the customer in a file format that's supported by the Attachment data type introduced by Access 2007, right-click the temporary image, and choose Manage Attachments to open the Attachments dialog. (If you don't have a photo, skip to step 7.)

4. Click the Add button to open the Choose File dialog and select the image file to add (see Figure 2.16).

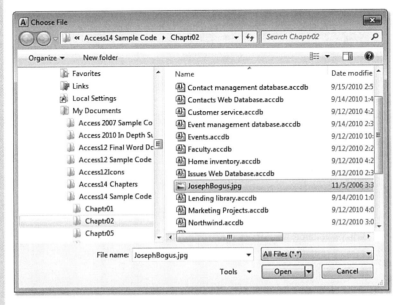

> **note**
>
> Access 2010 creates the NavPane's Supporting Objects, Unclassified Objects, Tables, Queries, Forms, Reports, Macros, and Modules categories and Filter By Group options. (Macros and Modules appear if the database contains these objects.) Tasks and Contacts are custom (user-created) groups.

> **note**
>
> The Attachment data type supports .bmp, .gif, .jpg, .png, .tif, and other image formats. You also can attach Word, Excel, or PDF files, as well as other common Multipurpose Internet Mail Extensions (MIME) documents.

Figure 2.16
Select the image file(s) for a field of the Attachments data type in the Choose File dialog.

5. Click OK to close the dialog and add the filename to the Attachments dialog (see Figure 2.17).

6. Click OK to close the Attachments dialog and return to the Contact Details form (see Figure 2.18).

Figure 2.17
The Attachments dialog lets you add multiple MIME attachments to a single record.

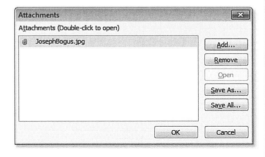

Figure 2.18
The completed Contact Details form for the first contact is ready for addition to the Contacts table.

7. When you're satisfied with the entry, click the Save and New link button to add the record to the Contacts table, and click Close to dismiss the dialog.

8. Double-click the NavPane's Contact List item to open the Contact List form, which displays the newly added record with an ID value of 1 and a second record with an ID value of (New).

9. Click the Shutter Bar Close button to devote more room to the Contact List (see Figure 2.19). Notice that the Contact List is missing 11 of the 17 fields for which you entered data in the Contact Details form.

 The type of the Contact Details and Contacts List's forms is a *split form*, which is one of the three new form types Access 2007 introduced. A split form lets you display multiple records in row/column (Datasheet) format above the split. You also can type data for the selected record in the text boxes of a panel below the split. The Contacts List's panel below the split is hidden, so only the Datasheet panel is visible. The Contact Details' panel above the split is hidden, so only the data entry form is visible. You can select other orientations, such as the Datasheet panel below the data entry panel.

> ### 🔍 note
> This book calls the empty (New) record the *tentative append record*, because this record isn't saved in the table until you take a deliberate action to save the record, such as adding another record or clicking the ...Details form's Save and New button. Until you save the record, you can return the tentative row to its original empty condition by closing the form or, in the ...List form, pressing Esc twice.

Adding a Task Record

The Task Details form also is a pop-up modal dialog. To create an initial task, do the following:

1. Click the New link in the Task List dataset's ID column to open an empty Task Details form as a modal dialog.

2. Type a task title, select a contact from the Assigned To combo box (Joseph Bogus is the only choice at this point), accept the default Not Started value in the Status combo box, accept 0% as % Complete, select a Priority value other than Normal, if you want, and accept today's date as the Start date.

3. Tab to the Due Date text box to activate the Date Picker icon, and click it to open the new Date Picker control (see Figure 2.20). Click a day of the month to set the Due Date value and close the Date Picker.

4. Type a description of the task in the Description text box, click the Save and New link button to save the first Tasks record, and click Close.

> ### 🔍 note
> Chapter 14, "Creating and Using Basic Access Forms," provides examples of Access 2010's conventional data entry and editing forms.
>
> Chapter 18, "Adding Graphs, PivotCharts, and PivotTables," describes how to take advantage of special-purpose, read-only forms.

Figure 2.19
The Contact
List form has
only seven
data columns.
Access gen-
erates the
numeric ID
column's incre-
mental value
automatically.

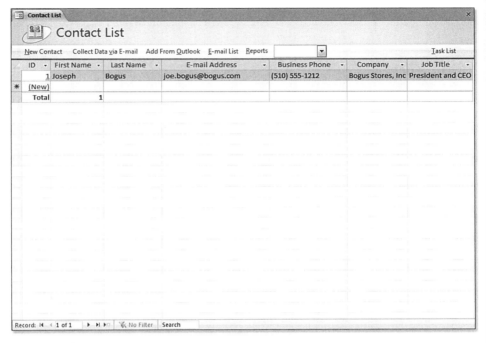

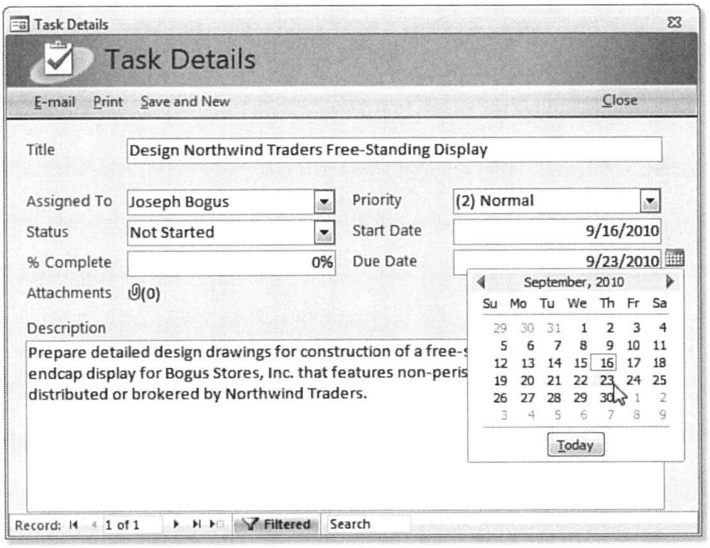

Figure 2.20
The new Date Picker control lets you
select a date by scrolling months and
clicking a day of the month.

5. Verify the presence of the new record in the Task List form (see Figure 2.21).

Unlike the Contact List, the Task List includes all columns (fields) of the Tasks table.

Opening Forms and Reports with Macros

The Contact List and Task List forms' ID field is formatted as a hyperlink. Clicking the (New) or serially numbered ID cell of a particular row, or clicking the New *Item* link button, opens the corresponding Contact or Task table record in the dialog version of the Details form (see Figure 2.22).

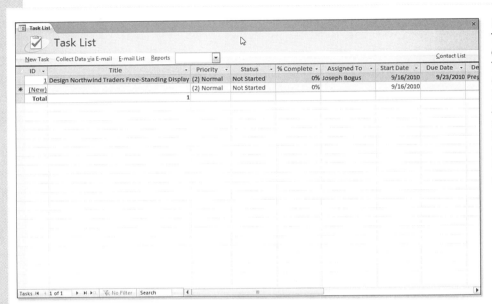

Figure 2.21
The Task List displays all Task table columns (including the Attachments column, which isn't visible at the right of the Description column).

Clicking a text box or a link button fires an On Click event. You can select Event Procedure (VBA code) or Embedded Macro as the *event handler* to respond to the event. All template-generated Access 2010 applications use embedded macro event handlers.

To inspect the macro that handles the ID column's OnClick event, do the following:

1. Right-click the Contact List or Task List form's NavPane item and choose Layout View to open the form in Access's Layout view, which Access 2007 introduced.

2. Right-click the Contact List label, choose Properties to open the Property Sheet, click the ID column's Total cell, or open the drop-down list and choose ID, and click the Event tab to display the On Click event in the first row (see Figure 2.23).

Figure 2.22
Clicking a ...List form's (New) cell, an ID column number, or the New *Item* button opens a ...Details dialog, unless the ... Details form is open. If the ... Details form is open, Access activates the form.

Figure 2.23
All template-based applications handle On Click and other events with embedded macros.

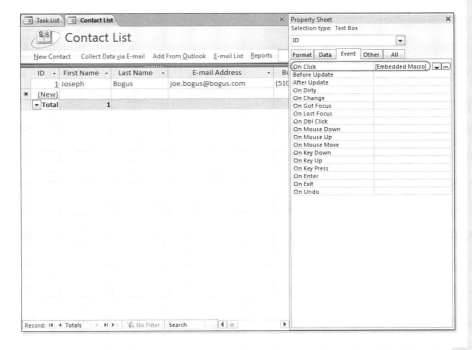

3. 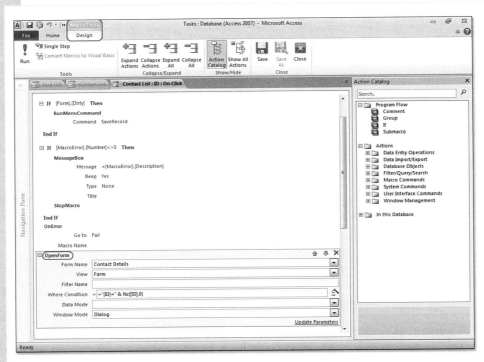 Click the builder button to the right of the drop-down list arrow to open the embedded macro in Access 2010's new Macro Designer with the Macro Tools, Design ribbon activated (see Figure 2.24). The selected OpenForm macro action opens the ... Details form in Dialog mode.

4. **X** Click the Close box to close the Macro Builder.

The Task Details form has a Print link button whose On Click event runs an embedded macro to open the Windows Print dialog over a Report view tabbed document (see Figure 2.25). Report view is an Access 2007 and later alternative to Print Preview for reports.

Figure 2.24
Macro Design view displays the set of sequential actions to take when responding to an event—in this case the ...List ID column's On Click event.

Figure 2.26 shows the Task Details report in Report view. The Title text box and Assigned To combo box links have On Click embedded macros that open the Task Details and Contact Details forms as dialogs.

The Tasks application has seven prebuilt reports, but reports other than Task Details are of little interest without more task or contact entries.

Figure 2.25
Substituting the OpenReport and Print actions for the OpenForm action lets you print a report from the ...Details data and displays it in Report view.

Figure 2.26
Access 2010's Report view shows details for the first added task and an overlaid Print dialog.

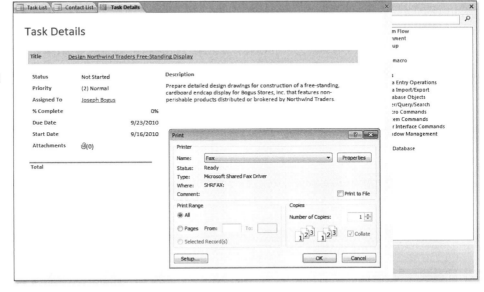

Importing and Exporting Data from and to Outlook 2010

One of Microsoft's primary sales pitches for Office 2010 is application interaction and Office server integration. The primary integration points for Access are SharePoint, Outlook, Excel, and Word. Template-generated Access 2010 applications include forms that import and export contact data from and to Outlook Contact folders, collect data with Outlook-generated forms, as well as send lists as email attachments and detail items as messages.

 note

If you have Outlook contacts that are suited to the role of customers in the Tasks application, you can add them to the \Access2010\Chaptr02\Tasks.accdb application. Otherwise, open the \Access2010\Chaptr02\TasksWithData.accdb database, which has contacts added from the \Access2010\Nwind\Northwind.accdb sample database's Customers table.

Importing Contacts from an Outlook Contacts Folder

2007 NEW The Contact List form has an Add From Outlook link button that executes the AddFromOutlook macro action. This feature lets you search for and import Contact items from Outlook Contacts folders into the Contacts table. The Contacts table and Contact List form have fields whose contents correspond to fields of the same name in Outlook contact records.

To add contacts from an Outlook Customers contacts folder, do the following:

1. Open the Contact List form and click the Add from Outlook link button to open the Select Names to Add dialog.

2. Open the Address List drop-down list, and select the Contacts folder to open (Customers for this example; see Figure 2.27).

3. Select as many contacts as you want in the list, and click Add to add their names to the text box below the list (see Figure 2.28).

Figure 2.27
For this example, the Select Names to Add: Customers dialog lists Outlook contacts that are contained in a Customers folder.

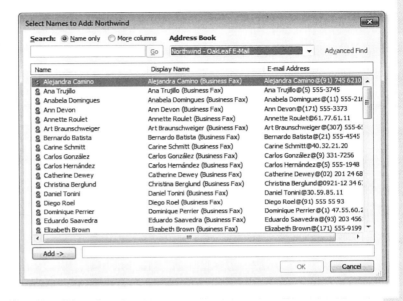

Figure 2.28
Clicking the Add button copies the selected names to a text box for addition. The purpose of the (Business Fax) suffix isn't known.

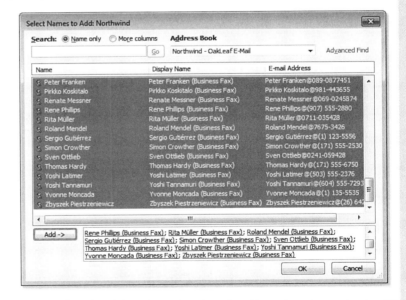

4. Click OK, wait for a few seconds, and then verify that the number of names that you specified have been added to the Contacts list (see Figure 2.29).

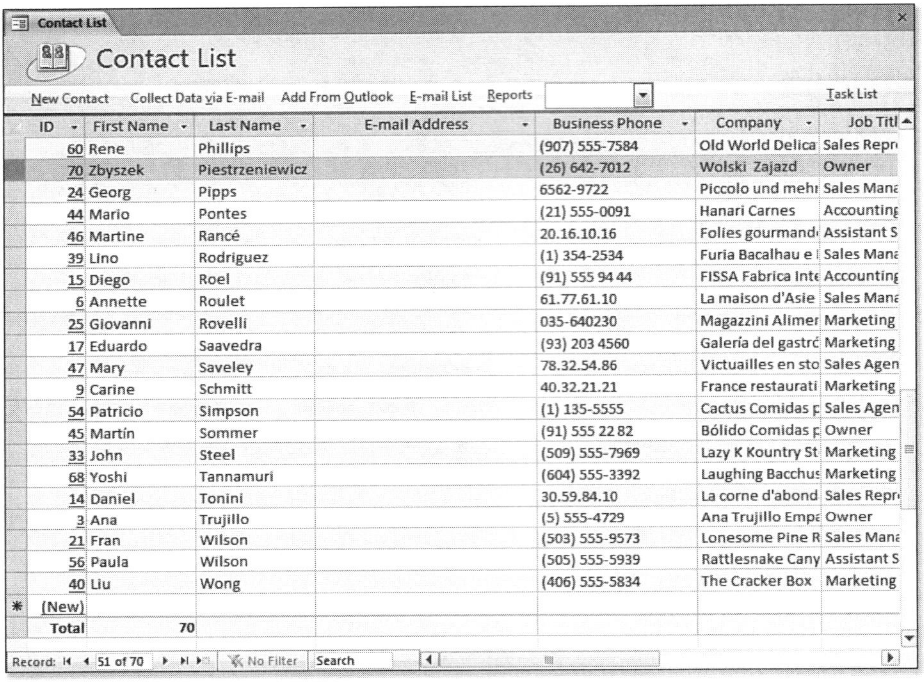

Figure 2.29
The 69 contacts from the Outlook Customers folder are added to the Contact List, which contained one earlier contact (Joseph Bogus).

 Σ The built-in Totals row at the bottom of a form's datasheet is a feature introduced by Access 2007. Record count is your only choice for columns containing ID (Autonumber) or text values. Numeric columns can display total, count, sum, average, maximum, minimum, standard deviation, and variance. Date/Time columns can have count, average, maximum, and minimum values. Click the Home ribbon's Records button and select Totals to toggle the visibility of the Total row.

➥ *To learn more about creating an Access table linked to an Outlook Contacts folder,* **see** *"Linking with the Exchange/Outlook Wizard,"* **p. 311.**

> **tip**
>
> An alternative to importing Contact items from Outlook is to substitute an Access table that's linked to a Contacts folder. This permits users of multiple application copies to share a common Outlook Contacts list. In this case, it isn't necessary to import or export Contact items.

Exporting Contacts to Outlook

The Contact Details form has a Create Outlook Contact link button that exports a Contacts table record to Outlook by executing the SaveAsOutlookContact macro action. To test-drive this feature introduced in Access 2007, do the following:

1. Open the Contact List form, select the contact to export, and click its ID column link to open the Contact Details form for the selected contact.

2. Click the Create Outlook Contact link button to open Outlook's Contact entry form filled with data from the Contact Details form.

3. If you have a photo file, click the Picture button, navigate to the picture's folder, and double-click the file item to add it to the contact (see Figure 2.30). Outlook doesn't add images from the Attachments fields. The storage format of Access and Outlook images differs.

Figure 2.30
Access can export a fully compatible Outlook contact to Outlook's Contacts folder.

4. Click the Save & Close button to add the contact to Outlook's default Contacts folder. There's no option to select an alternate folder.

5. Drag the added contact from the Contacts folder to another folder of your choice (Northwind for this example; see Figure 2.31).

For a different approach to exporting and importing Access data to and from Outlook folders, **see** "Importing and Exporting Access Tables with Outlook 2010," **p. 308.**

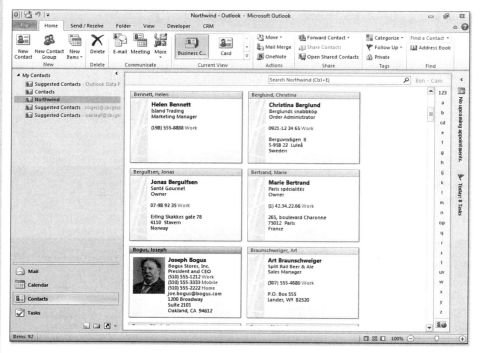

Using Outlook to Email Lists and Detail Items

Automating communication between participants in a process, such as tracking tasks for customers, is an important element of all tracking applications. Integration with SharePoint Foundation or SharePoint Server 2010 on an intranet is one approach to facilitating collaboration, but email is a much more universal communication method than SharePoint.

The Contact List and Task List forms have E-mail List buttons that execute the SendObject macro action to create a message with the Contact List or Task List as an attachment. Clicking the E-mail List button executes the SendObject macro action, which opens a Send Object As dialog for selecting the attachment's MIME type (see Figure 2.32).

> **note**
>
> The ability to include HTML-formatted text in table Memo fields was new in Access 2007. Memo fields can store up to 65,535 characters when you enter them from a text box or one billion characters if you create the text with VBA code.

Figure 2.32
The SendObject macro action's arguments require specifying the list attachment's format, recipients, subject line, and message. You specify the format in the Send Object As dialog.

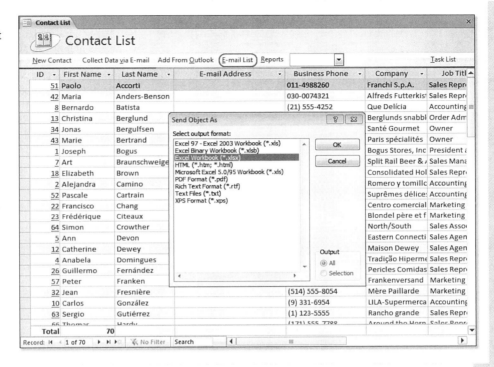

When you click the Contact List's E-mail List button, the Outlook message window opens. Figure 2.33 is how the window might look after you add a pair of recipients, type a title, and compose a message.

The worksheet generated by the Send action includes an empty cboReport column (A) that you can delete before sending the message (see Figure 2.34).

Figure 2.33
Selecting *.xlsx in Figure 2.32's Send Object As dialog and adding a pair of recipients creates this message and Contact List.xlsx attachment. The lower Microsoft Dynamics CRM pane appears only if you have synchronized the Outlook Client for Dynamics CRM 2011 with the server.

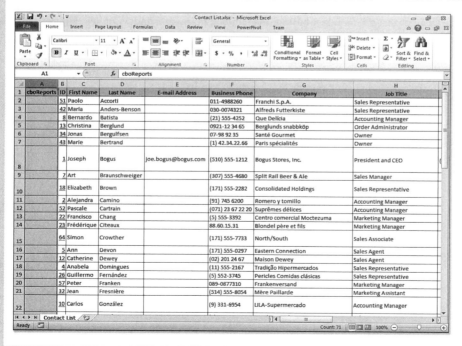

Figure 2.34
The list worksheet attachment might need editing before sending. The worksheet shown here has auto-adjusted column width and has an empty cboReport column that you can delete.

2010
NEW Confirming task creation and sending periodic task status information is an important tracking application capability. The Task Details and Contact Details forms have E-mail buttons that execute the new EMailDatabaseObject macro action with complex functions to provide the email address, subject line, and, for Task Details, description. Figure 2.35 shows the macro sheet for the On Click event of the Task Details form's E-mail button.

Figure 2.35
The EMail
DatabaseObject
macro action
that handles the
On Click event
of the E-mail
button uses
functions to sup-
ply argument
values.

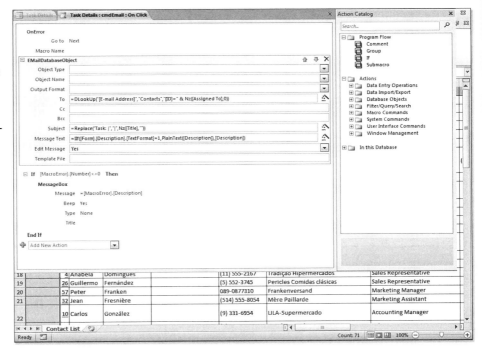

Following are the complete function text values for the EMailDatabaseObject macro action's To, Subject, and Message Text arguments:

- To =DLookUp("[E-mail Address]", "Contacts", "[ID]=" & Nz([Assigned To], 0)) looks up the email address of the selected contact.

- Subject =Replace("Task: |", " | ", Nz([Title]," ")) prefixes the form title with "Task:"

- **2007**
  NEW Message Text =IIf([Form].[Description].[TextFormat]=1, PlainText([Description]), [Description]) converts HTML-formatted text in Memo fields to plain ASCII text.

Access 2010's EMailDatabaseObject macro action replaces the SendObject macro action for selected items that have an email address value.

Figure 2.36 is the starting text of a message to Joe Bogus that his requested task has been initiated.

Figure 2.36
The default message for a Task Details email needs editing to be meaningful to the recipient.

It's obvious from the preceding function list that writing macros isn't always a piece of cake. In fact, VBA code to supply argument values to and execute the SendObject macro action is probably simpler to write and certainly much easier to debug than an embedded macro. VBA code also lets you add other field values to and format the default message.

Collecting Data by Email with Outlook HTML Forms

2007 NEW Access 2007 introduced the capability to autogenerate Outlook 2007 HTML forms that enable message recipients to edit existing data in or add new records to Access tables. You click the Collect Data via E-mail button to start a wizardlike process that defines the fields to edit, specifies the recipients, and determines how replies are handled.

> For an example of collecting data with an Outlook HTML form, **see** *"Gathering Data by Email with HTML Forms,"*
> **p. 1044.**

 note

2010 NEW Access 2010's EMailDatabaseObject macro action replaces the SendObject macro action for selected items than have an e-mail address value.

2007 NEW The ability to include HTML-formatted text in table Memo fields was new in Access 2007. Memo fields can store up to 65,535 characters when you enter them from a text box or one billion characters if you create the text with VBA code.

 tip

Template-based databases are an excellent source of special-purpose embedded macros that you can copy and paste into empty macro sheets in the application that you're developing.

The process for creating the HTML form is complex and beyond the scope of this chapter. Figure 2.37 shows the upper 10 percent of the HTML form for editing Joe Bogus's contact data.

Figure 2.37
The recipient can edit and submit the HTML data collection form sent by Outlook. The CRM group appears if you have synchronized the Outlook Client for Dynamics CRM 2011 with the server.

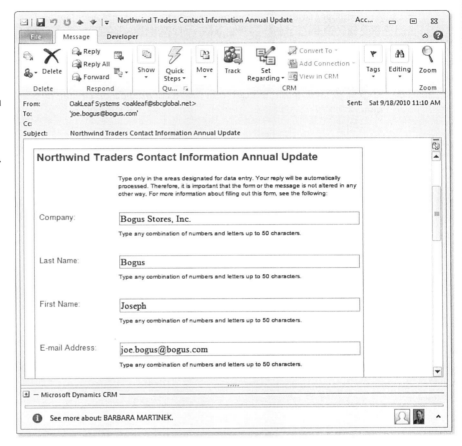

Integrating Objects from Other Template Databases

As mentioned earlier in the chapter, template-based applications are "starter kits" for real-world tracking applications. The Tasks application for a marketing team, for example, would involve customer-related tasks that are assigned to an employee to perform or manage. A task might benefit a few or many customers (contacts).

 tip
The following sections cover advanced Access topics and introduce many new terms. If you don't feel up to performing the steps of this example, scan the instructions with the \Access2010\Chaptr02\ TasksWithEmployees.accdb database open. This database has all objects from the \Access2010\ Chaptr02\ProductsWithData.accdb database fully integrated.

Import Missing Objects

Supplier (Northwind) employees—not customer contacts—are responsible for completing tasks, so for this example, the Tasks application needs a set of employee-related objects similar to that for contacts: Employees table, Employees Extended query, Employee List and Employee Details forms, and Employee Address Book and Employee Phone List reports. These objects are available from the Project.accdb database, but for this example, you import the objects from the \Access2010\ Chaptr02\ProjectsWithData.accdb database. That database has an Employee Details form that's similar to the Contact Details form, except that it's a tabbed document instead of a modal dialog (see Figure 2.38) and data imported from the Northwind.accdb sample database's Employees table (see Figure 2.39).

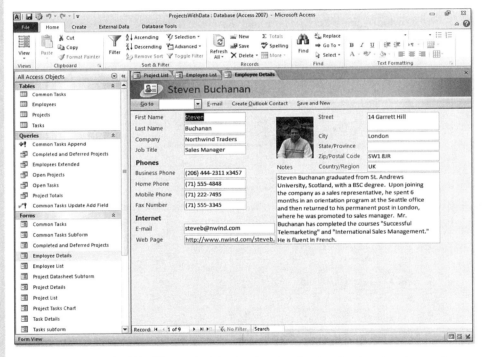

Figure 2.38
The ProjectWithData application's Employee Details form is modeled on the TasksWithData database's modified Contact Details form.

Figure 2.39
The layout of the ProjectWithData application's Employee List form is very similar to that of the Contact List.

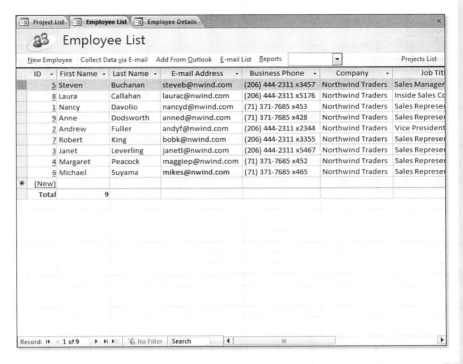

ID	First Name	Last Name	E-mail Address	Business Phone	Company	Job Tit
5	Steven	Buchanan	steveb@nwind.com	(206) 444-2311 x3457	Northwind Traders	Sales Manager
8	Laura	Callahan	laurac@nwind.com	(206) 444-2311 x5176	Northwind Traders	Inside Sales Co
1	Nancy	Davolio	nancyd@nwind.com	(71) 371-7685 x453	Northwind Traders	Sales Represer
9	Anne	Dodsworth	anned@nwind.com	(71) 371-7685 x428	Northwind Traders	Sales Represer
2	Andrew	Fuller	andyf@nwind.com	(206) 444-2311 x2344	Northwind Traders	Vice President
7	Robert	King	bobk@nwind.com	(206) 444-2311 x3355	Northwind Traders	Sales Represer
3	Janet	Leverling	janetl@nwind.com	(206) 444-2311 x5467	Northwind Traders	Sales Represer
4	Margaret	Peacock	maggiep@nwind.com	(71) 371-7685 x452	Northwind Traders	Sales Represer
6	Michael	Suyama	mikes@nwind.com	(71) 371-7685 x465	Northwind Traders	Sales Represer

To import the preceding objects into the \Access2010\Chaptr02\TasksWithData.accdb database, which has 70 Contacts List items and 12 Tasks List items, do the following:

1. Open \Access2010\Chaptr02\TasksWithData.accdb, if it isn't already open, click the External Data tab, and click the Import & Link group's Access button to open the Get External Data – Access Database dialog.

2. Click Browse to open the File Open dialog, navigate to the \Access2010\Chaptr02 folder, double-click the ProjectsWithData.accdb file to return to the Get External Data dialog, and, with the default Import Tables, Queries, Forms … option selected, click OK to open the Import Objects dialog.

3. On the default Tables page, select Employees (see Figure 2.40).

4. Click the Queries tab, select Employees Extended.

5. Click the Forms tab, select Employee Details and Employee List, click the Reports tab, and select Employee Address Book and Employee Phone List.

6. Click OK to import all objects to the TasksWithEmployees database and close the dialog.

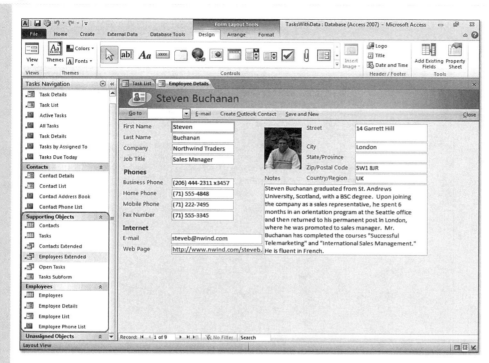

Figure 2.40
The Import Objects dialog lets you import all the objects you select on its six pages in a single operation. In case of duplicate names, the import object names gain a 1 suffix.

The Access objects you import into a database create items in the NavPane's Unassigned Objects group. To assign these objects to a new Employees navigation group, do the following:

1. Select Tasks Navigation in the top navigation bar, right-click the Employee Details form item, and choose Add to Group.

2. Right-click the Employee List form item and choose Add to Group, New Group to add a new Custom Group 1 bar to the NavPane Employees.

3. Rename the Custom Group 1 bar to Employees.

4. Repeat step 2 for the Employee Address Book and Employee Phone list reports, but add these objects to the Employees group.

5. Right-click the Employees table, and choose Add to Group, Supporting Objects.

6. Right-click the Employees Extended query, and choose Add to Group, Supporting Objects.

See Figure 2.41 for an example of the correct contents of the Employees group.

Figure 2.41
Objects
imported from
the Projects
with Data.
accdb database
are assigned
to Employees
and Supporting
Objects naviga-
tion groups.

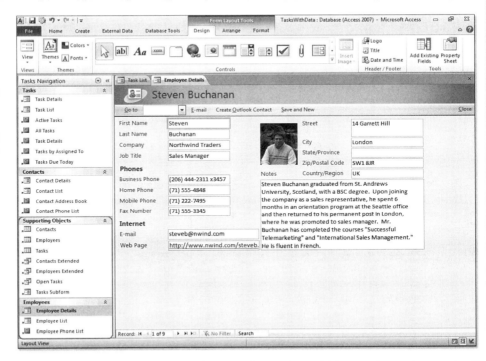

Alter Inappropriate Field Names

The Task table's Assigned To field, which you'll change shortly to Requested For, has a combo box
with a *lookup list* that displays values from the Contact Name field and sets values from the ID field
of the Contacts table. Doing this requires a query with the following Row Source property, which is
an SQL query statement:

```
SELECT [Contacts Extended].ID, [Contacts Extended].[Contact Name]
FROM [Contacts Extended]
ORDER BY [Contacts Extended].[Contact Name];
```

When you change the name of the Assigned To field to Requested For, displaying the company
name before the contact name and sorting the combo box list by company name makes choosing the
right contact easier for users. Here's the revised version of the Row Source SQL statement to create
the example that follows:

```
SELECT [Contacts Extended].ID, [Contacts Extended].[Company],
    [Contacts Extended].[Contact Name]
FROM [Contacts Extended]
ORDER BY [Contacts Extended].[Company];
```

Here's a simpler version that accomplishes the same result:

```
SELECT ID, Company, [Contact Name]
FROM [Contacts Extended]
ORDER BY Company;
```

Chapter 9, "Designing Queries for Access Databases," shows you how to create queries graphically and with Access SQL statements.

➡ *To learn more about MVLFs,* **see** *"Creating Multivalued Lookup Fields,"* **p. 450.**

To change the name of the Assigned To field to Requested For and establish a many-to-many relationship between the Contacts and Tasks tables with an MVLF, do the following:

1. ⌨ Click the Database Tools tab and click the Relationships button to open the Relationships window. Select the line between the Contacts and Tasks field lists (see Figure 2.42), press Delete, and click Yes to confirm that you want to remove the relationship. You can't create an MVLF until you remove all relationships that rely on the field. Close the Relationships window.

> **🔍 note**
>
> 2007 NEW Access 2007 introduced lookup fields as a convenience for creating many-to-many relationships between tables and to support relationships by Access tables exported or linked to SharePoint 2010. For example, many tasks can be requested for different contacts. Relational database purists consider lookup fields and, especially, multivalued lookup fields (MVLFs) for creating many-to-many relationships to be an abomination.

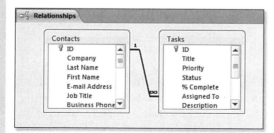

Figure 2.42
Selecting the relationship line with the mouse thickens it. You must select the relationship line to delete the relationship between the Contacts and Tasks tables.

2. 🖼 Close all open forms, right-click the Tasks table item in the NavPane's Supporting Objects group, and choose Design View.

3. Scroll down, if necessary, to the Assigned To field and change its Field Name to **Requested For**.

4. A task can be requested for multiple customers, so click the Lookup tab and change the Allow Multiple Values property from No to Yes. Click Yes to acknowledge the message that warns you can't undo this change, and set the Yes property value (see Figure 2.43).

5. Right-click the Row Source text box, and choose Zoom to open the Zoom dialog with the Row Source's SQL statement. (Click the Font button to increase the font size, if necessary.)

Figure 2.43
Setting the
Multiple Values
for a lookup field
to Yes opens a
message box
that warns you
that Undo can't
reverse this
operation.

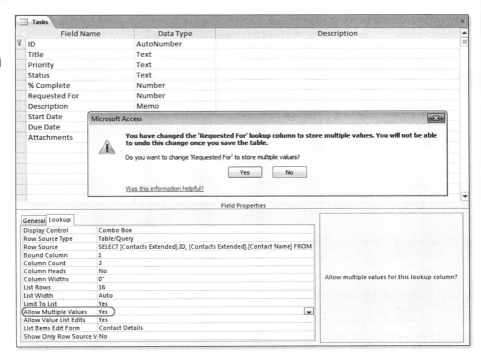

6. Type **[Contacts Extended].[Company]**, after ....ID, to add the company name prefix to the combo box list and change ORDER BY [Contacts Extended].[Contact Name]; to ORDER BY [Contacts Extended].[Company]; to sort the list by company name (see Figure 2.44).

Figure 2.44
This SQL statement for the Row Source property delivers a two-column list of Company and Contact Name values.

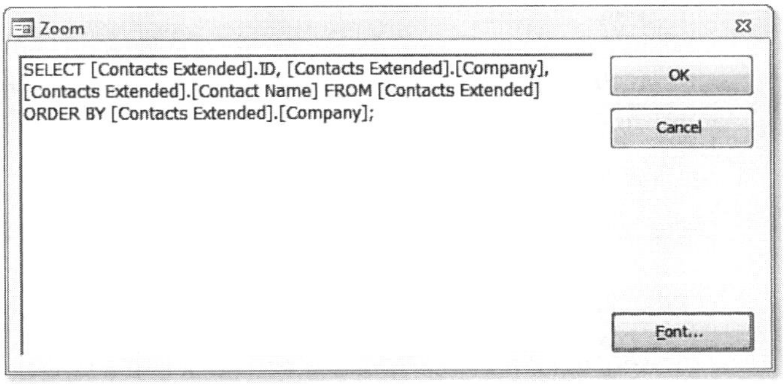

SELECT [Contacts Extended].ID, [Contacts Extended].[Company],
[Contacts Extended].[Contact Name] FROM [Contacts Extended]
ORDER BY [Contacts Extended].[Company];

7. Change the Column Count property value from 2 to **3**, change the Allow Value List Edits from Yes to No, delete Contact Details from the List Items Edit Form property, and change Show Only Row Source Values from No to Yes (see Figure 2.45).

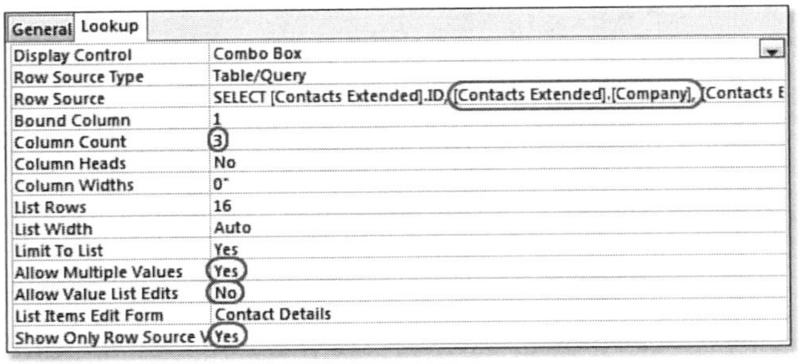

Figure 2.45
The Lookup page's property values reflect the changes in the preceding steps and prevent users from editing the combo box list. (The change to the Row Source property's ORDER BY clause isn't visible.)

8. Click the Datasheet View button and click Yes to save your changes.

Test the MVLF's Requested For combo box list and verify that the Task Details form's Assigned To combo box needs fixing by doing the following:

1. In the Tasks table's Datasheet view, scroll to the right until the Requested For column is visible, and then expand the width of the column by dragging the right column head border to the right.

2. Place the cursor in the first row, and click the arrow button to display the combo list with check boxes (see Figure 2.46). Notice that the check box adjacent to Bogus Stores, Inc. | Joe Bogus is marked.

3. Close the Tasks table's window and save your layout changes.

4. Open the Task Details form in Form view and open the Assigned To combo box. The list is unchanged by the modifications to the underlying table.

Conform MVLF Combo Boxes of List and Details Forms

The Task List and Task Details forms aren't modified by the changes you made to the former Assigned To table field, so you must create the Requested For combo box on both forms.

To create the Task List form's Requested For combo box, do the following:

1. Right-click the Task List form item in the NavPane and choose Design View to open the form in Design view.

2. Click the Add Existing Fields button to open the Field List pane.

Figure 2.46
The list element of a combo box for an MVLF has a column of list boxes to make the multiple selections required by a many-to-many relationship (in this case between Contacts and Tasks).

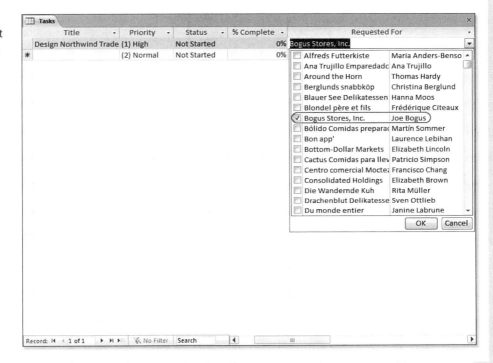

3. There's no longer an Assigned To field, so select and delete the Assigned To label and combo box.

4. Drag the Requested For item from the Field List and drop it immediately in the space previously occupied by the Assigned To field, as shown in Figure 2.47.

5. Place the cursor in a Requested For cell, press F4 to open the Property Sheet, click the Data tab, and then change the value of the Allow Value List Edits property from Yes to No, delete the Contact Form from the List Items Edit Form property, and change Show Only Row Source Values from No to Yes.

6. Click the Form View button and scroll to the right to expose the Requested For field. Select the field header, drag the field to the right of the Title field, and open the combo box list (see Figure 2.48).

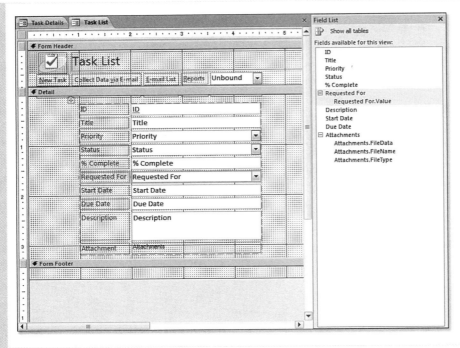

Figure 2.47
Dragging a field from the Field List to the Design view of a form adds a label and combo box for a single-valued or multivalued table lookup field.

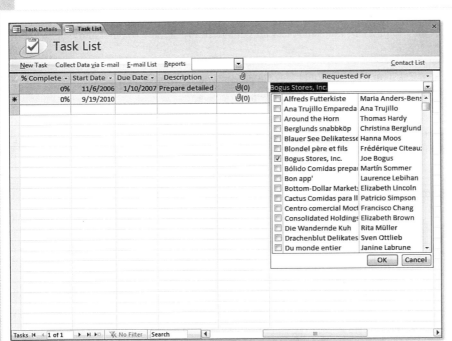

Figure 2.48
Combo box lists for MVLFs contained in forms open to the right of the associated column.

7. Close the Task List form and save your design changes.

To create the Task Details form's Requested For combo box, do the following:

1. Open the Task Details form in Design view and click the Add Existing Fields button.

2. Delete the Assigned To label and the adjacent combo box, and drag the Requested For field from the Field List to the location of the deleted controls.

3. Select the new Requested For combo box, open the Property Sheet, and click the Format tab. Then change the Border Style property value from Transparent to Solid, change Column Widths from 0" to **0";2";2"**, and change List Width from Auto to **4"**.

4. Click the Data tab and make the same changes as you did in step 5 of the preceding example.

5. Click the Form View button and test the combo list (see Figure 2.49).

Figure 2.49
The Task
Details form's
Requested For
combo box
emulates that
of the Task List
form.

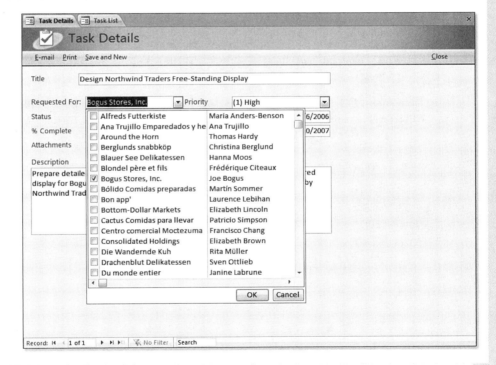

Add Approved By and Assigned To Employee Lookup Fields

Customers can make requests to any marketing department employee to initiate a task on their behalf. However, an employee with a title of Manager or higher must approve the task and then assign one or more employees to complete the task. This business rule means you must add, for starters, an Approved By single-valued lookup field and an Assigned To MVLF to the Tasks table.

To add the Approved By field to the Tasks table, do this:

1. Close all forms and open the Tasks table in Design view.

2. Select the Description field and press Insert to add an empty field above.

3. Type **Approved By** as the field name, tab to the Data Type column, and select Number from the list. The Field Size property value is Long Integer by default, which matches the field size of the Employees table's ID field.

4. Click the Lookup tab and change the Display Control property value from the default Text Box to Combo Box.

5. Type **SELECT ID, [First Name] & " " & [Last Name] FROM Employees WHERE [Job Title] IN("Sales Manager", "Vice President, Sales", "President") ORDER BY [Last Name];** as the Row Source property value. Press Shift+F2 to use the Zoom box if you want.

   ➡ *To learn more about lookup fields in general,* **see** *"Using Lookup Fields in Tables,"* **p. 442.**

6. Change the Column Count property value from 1 to **2**, Column Widths from empty to **0";2.0"**, Allow Value List Edits from Yes to No, and Show Only Row Source Values from No to Yes (see Figure 2.50).

> 🔍 **note**
>
> SELECT ID, [First Name] & " " & [Last Name] returns the employee ID number and first and last names separated by a space. The WHERE [Job Title] IN("Sales Manager", "Vice President, Sales", "President") SQL clause limits the list to employees with those titles.

Figure 2.50
Design view of the Approved By single-valued lookup field is identical to that of the Requested For MVLF except for the Row Source, Column Count, Column Widths, and Allow Multiple Values property values.

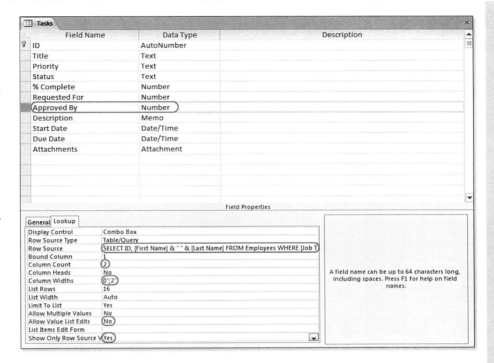

7. Change to Form view, save your changes, scroll to the Approved By field, and test your work so far (see Figure 2.51).

To add an Assigned To MVLF to the Tasks table, repeat the preceding steps, except

1. In step 3, type **Assigned To** as the field name.

2. In step 5, omit the WHERE [Job Title] IN("Sales Manager", "Vice President, Sales", "President") clause.

3. In step 6, change the Allow Multiple Values property value from No to Yes.

When you change to Form view, the Assigned To combo box appears as shown in Figure 2.52.

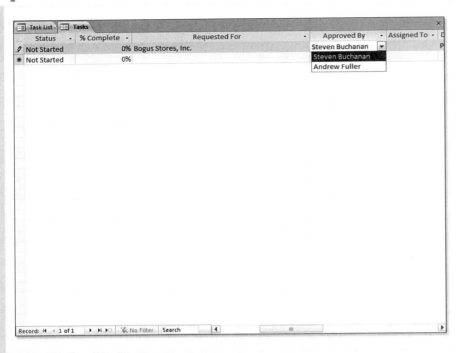

Figure 2.51
Only Andrew Fuller, Vice President, Sales, and Steven Buchanan, Sales Manager, can approve requests for marketing tasks.

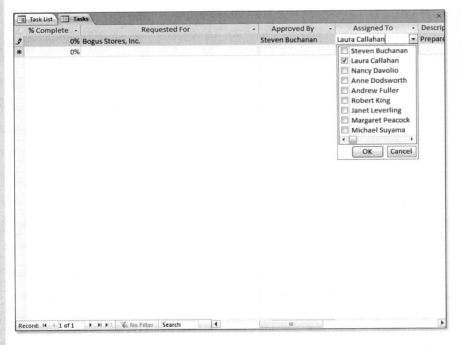

Figure 2.52
This combo box for an MVLF has only a single column for the full employee name.

Add Approved By and Assigned To Combo Boxes to Lists and Details Forms

The final step in the initial application modification is to add the Approved By and Assigned To fields' combo boxes to the Task List and Task Details form by the same technique that you used to add the Requested For combo boxes. Figure 2.53 shows the Task Details form with the two added combo boxes. Note that when you add multiple values, the values appear (separated by commas) in the combo box's text box.

Figure 2.53
The Approved By and Assigned To combo boxes have been added to the Task Details form.

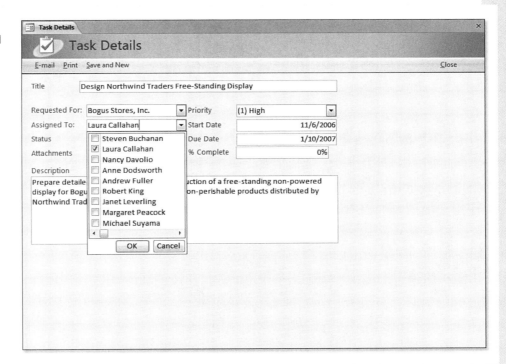

At this point you've created a working three-table application that has a many-to-many relationship between customer contacts and marketing tasks. Many tasks can be requested for a specific contact, and the result of a specific task, such as the translation of a catalog, can be useful to multiple contacts or companies.

You've also added a one-to-many relationship between employees who have approval authority and tasks. Only one manager is needed to approve a task, and a manager can approve many tasks.

Finally, you added another many-to-many relationship between tasks and the employees whom management assigns to complete them. It might take a team of employees to complete a task, and one employee might be assigned to several tasks simultaneously.

 note
The completed version of the TasksWithData.accdb project is \Access2010\Chaptro2\ TasksWithEmployees.accdb, which is used for examples in other chapters as well.

3

NAVIGATING THE FLUENT USER INTERFACE

Access, unlike word processing and spreadsheet applications, is a truly multifunctional program. Although word processing applications, for example, have many sophisticated capabilities, their basic purpose is to support text entry, page layout, and formatted printing. The primary functions and supporting features of all word processing applications are directed to these ends. You perform all word processing operations with views that represent a sheet of paper. Most spreadsheet applications use the row-column metaphor for all their functions. In contrast, Access consists of a multitude of related tools for generating, organizing, segregating, displaying, printing, and publishing data. The following sections describe Access's basic functions and operating modes.

Defining Access Functions

To qualify as a full-fledged relational database management system (RDBMS), an application must perform the following four basic but distinct functions, each with its own presentation to the user:

- *Data organization* involves creating and manipulating tables that contain data in conventional tabular (row-column or spreadsheet) format, called *Datasheet view* by Access.

- *List management* substitutes Access tables linked to SharePoint lists. SharePoint lists behave similarly to Access tables, but don't maintain referential integrity with foreign key constraints.

➡️ *For an explanation of the benefits of referential integrity,* **see** *"Maintaining Data Integrity and Accuracy,"* **p. 170.**

- *Table joining and data extraction* use queries to connect multiple tables by data relationships and create virtual (temporary) tables, called *Recordsets*, stored in your computer's RAM or temporary disk files. Expressions are used to calculate values from data (for example, you can calculate an extended amount by multiplying unit price and quantity) and display the calculated values as though they were a field in one of the tables.

- *Data entry and editing* require design and implementation of data viewing, entry, and editing forms as an alternative to tabular presentation. A form lets you, rather than the application, control how the data is presented. Most users find forms much easier to use for data entry than tabular format, especially when many fields are involved.

- *Data presentation* requires the creation of reports that you can view, print, or publish on the Internet or an intranet (the last step in the process). Charts and graphs summarize the data for those officials who take the "broad brush" approach.

> **note**
>
> You can base forms and reports on data from Access, SQL Server or SQL Azure tables, or linked SharePoint Lists, but it's more common to use a query as the data source for forms and reports. An SQL Server or SQL Azure view is the direct counterpart of an Access SELECT query. You also can use SQL Server or SQL Azure inline functions and stored procedures as data sources for forms and reports.

The basic functions of Access are organized into the application structure shown in Figure 3.1. If you're creating a new database, you use the basic functions of Access in the top-down sequence shown in Figure 3.1.

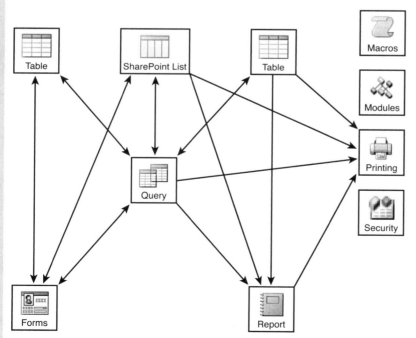

Figure 3.1
This diagram shows the relationship of the basic and supporting functions of Access. Reports have a one-way relationship with other functions because you can't use a report to modify data.

Four supporting functions apply to all basic functions of Access:

- Macros are sequences of actions that automate repetitive database operations. In Access 97 and earlier versions, macros were the most common means of automating database operations. In versions 2000 through 2003, macros were supported for backward compatibility only and Microsoft recommended Visual Basic for Applications (VBA) to automate Access applications.

---

tip

New in Access 2010 icon Microsoft now recommends using macros wherever possible because macros will run under more restrictive security settings than VBA. Access Web Databases don't support VBA, so macros are necessary to automate Access Web Databases. Microsoft also raises the dubious contention that macros are simpler for new users to write than VBA code. In an attempt to make macros more palatable to application developers, the Access team created new Data macros and Macro Builder in Access 2010; Access 2007 introduced embedded macros and added event-handling actions.

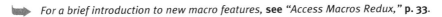 *For a brief introduction to new macro features,* **see** *"Access Macros Redux,"* **p. 33.**

- Modules are containers for functions and procedures written in the VBA programming language. You use VBA functions to make calculations that are more complex than those that can be expressed easily by a series of conventional mathematical symbols. You run a VBA subprocedure by attaching it to particular event, such as clicking a command button with the mouse when a form or page is the active object.

- **2010 NEW** Security features for Access 2010 (and 2007) applications have been downgraded dramatically. You no longer can grant access to user groups and individuals with user-level security. Nor can you restrict users' ability to view or modify objects in the database except by creating an encrypted .accde file, which corresponds to earlier versions' .mde file.

- **2007 NEW** *Printing* lets you print virtually anything you can view in Access's run mode. Printing is the most common form of distributing reports. Access 2007 enabled exporting reports to web pages or to Portable Document Format (Adobe .pdf), Microsoft XML Paper Specification (.xps), or Report Snapshot (.snp) files. Access 2010 doesn't support the Report Snapshot format.

note

Access 2010 supports user-level (also called *workgroup*) security for Access 2000 through 2003 .mdb files and Access 2000 through 2007 .adp (data project) files. However, using older file formats disables Access 2007 and later .accdb features, such as the Attachment data type, multivalued lookup columns, and append-only memo fields.

The terms *open* and *close* have the same basic usage in Access as in other Windows applications but usually involve more than one basic function:

- Opening a database makes its content available to the application through the Navigation pane, which replaces earlier versions' Database window. You can open only one database at a time in the Access user interface, but you can link tables from Access, client/server, and other desktop databases, as well as Windows SharePoint Services (WSS) 3.0 or Microsoft Office SharePoint Services (MOSS) 2007 lists. You also can open multiple databases with VBA code.

- Opening a table displays a Datasheet view of its contents. Access automatically creates the first table of a new database and defines its structure by the data you enter in it.

- Opening a SELECT query, the most common query type, opens one or more tables and displays the data specified by the query in Datasheet view. You can change data in the tables associated with the query if the query's *Recordset is updatable* (write-enabled).

- Opening a form or report automatically opens the table or query that's associated with it. As mentioned earlier, forms and reports usually are associated with (called *bound to*) queries rather than tables.

- Closing a query closes the associated tables.

- Closing a form or report closes the associated query and its tables or the table to which it's bound.

You open existing database objects by double-clicking the corresponding item in the Navigation pane. Closing a query, form, or report doesn't close its associated objects (table, query, or both) if you've opened them independently.

Defining Access Operating Modes

Access has four basic operating modes:

- Startup mode occurs after you launch Access 2007 but before you open an existing database or create a new one. By default, Startup mode displays the Backstage window's New view, which gives you the options of creating a new blank (empty) database or creating an Access application from one of several local (also called out-of-the-box) template files or online templates in many categories (see Figure 3.2).

After you've opened one or more databases, links to the last few databases you've opened appear in the most recently used list below the Close Database icon when you launch Access.

- 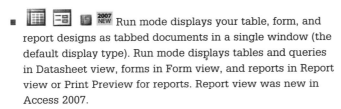 Run mode displays your table, form, and report designs as tabbed documents in a single window (the default display type). Run mode displays tables and queries in Datasheet view, forms in Form view, and reports in Report view or Print Preview for reports. Report view was new in Access 2007.

> **tip**
>
> Only Access uses these macros, so learning to construct them gains you no leverage with the many other Windows applications that use VBA. What's worse, macros have a very limited programming repertoire. If you intend to create Access applications for others to use, learning to write VBA code is highly recommended.

> **note**
>
> Chapter 2, "Building Simple Tracking Applications," shows you how to create a complete Access database application from the Tasks online template in a few minutes.

Figure 3.2
When you
launch Access
2010 for the
first time, the
Backstage win-
dow opens with
the default New
tab selected.
From here you
can create
a new blank
database or
generate a
database from
one of the local
templates or
many online
templates in
several catego-
ries.

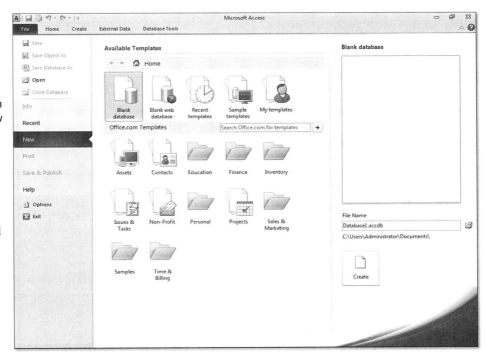

- Design mode lets you create and modify the structure of tables and queries; develop forms to display and edit your data; format reports for printing; design macros; or write VBA code in the separate VBA Editor application. Access calls design mode Design view.

> **note**
>
> Earlier Access versions' .mdb files open by default as conventional overlapping (nonmodal) windows.

- Layout mode lets you alter the layout of the forms and reports that you created in Design mode or generated from a template. The primary advantage of layout mode is that you can adjust the size and location of controls (typically text boxes) with live data visible. Data sources (tables or queries) for your forms or reports have content to gain the most out of layout mode. Layout mode, which Access calls *Layout view*, was new in Access 2007.

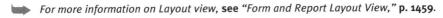

For more information on Layout view, **see** *"Form and Report Layout View,"* **p. 1459.**

For more information on Layout view, **see** *"Form and Report Layout View,"* **p. 1459.**

You can choose Datasheet, Form, Report, Layout, or Design view from the Home ribbon's Views group, or you can press Alt and the appropriate shortcut key. Access's shortcut keys are the same as Access 200x's, despite the dramatic change to Office 2007's and 2010's user interfaces.

Opening the Northwind.accdb Sample Database

Online sample files icon The Northwind Traders sample database (Northwind.accdb) is the primary Access application used in this book's examples. Access 2010 doesn't include a sample database, so the downloadable sample files provide an upgraded and updated version of Northwind.mdb from Access 2003 and earlier. Downloading and saving the CD-ROM's sample chapter files to \UserName\Downloads folder places Northwind.accdb in your \UserName\Downloads\Access2010\Nwind\ folder, which also contains a copy of Access 2003's Northwind.mdb file in Access 2000 format.

After downloading the sample files, open Northwind.accdb and display its Home ribbon and default Navigation pane by doing the following:

> **note**
>
> The default location for Access databases and other application-related files, such as graphics files for images, is Windows 7 and Vista's Documents folder or Windows XP's My Documents folder. The \Program Files [(x86)]\Microsoft Office\ Office##\Samples folder, formerly used to hold the Access sample files, contains only the venerable SOLVSAMP.XLS file.

1.  Launch Microsoft Office Access 2010, if it isn't running.

2. Click the File button to open Backstage view and choose Open to launch the Open dialog. Navigate to your …\Access2010\Nwind folder, which contains three sample files (see Figure 3.3).

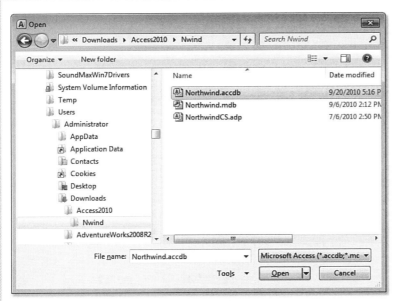

Figure 3.3
The Open dialog lets you open almost all varieties of Access 2000 through 2007 database files.

3. Select Northwind.accdb, and click Open to open the Switchboard form as a tabbed document (see Figure 3.4). The message bar displays a security warning with a Click for More Details link. The content that's been disabled is the VBA code in the Utility Functions module, so click Enable Content.

Figure 3.4
The
Switchboard
form's default
page lets you
select one of
four catego-
ries of sample
forms and
sales reports
to open. The
Navigation
pane displays
all database
objects in an
Outlook-style
sidebar.

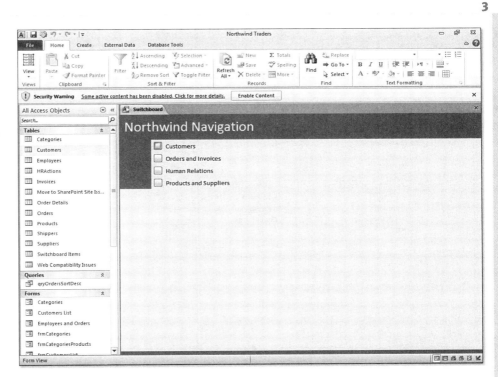

4. Optionally, click the Products and Suppliers button and then click a button to open one of the sample forms or reports. Figure 3.5 shows the Suppliers and Products List in Form view.

➡ *To learn more about enabling VBA code to run,* **see** *"Security, Trusted Locations, Packages and Certificates,"* **p. 29.**

➡ *For more information on the differences between VBA code and embedded Access macros,* **see** *"Converting Macros to VBA Callback,"* **p. 1303.**

After you open Northwind.accdb for the first time, an entry for the database appears in the Office gallery's Recent Documents pane. It's quicker to open Northwind.accdb or any other recently used databases from the Recent Documents pane.

➡ *For the details of setting all Access options for the current and new databases,* **see** *"Setting Default Options,"* **p. 122.**

note

2007 NEW Access 2007 and 2010's Switchboard Manager differs from earlier versions by substi- tuting Access macros for VBA code to open forms or reports and perform other actions. VBA code won't run when the Security Warning message is present, but most macro actions aren't embargoed.

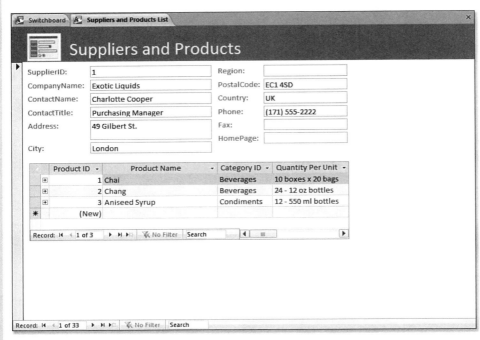

Understanding Access's Table Windows

You're probably familiar with the terms for and behavior of many new components that compose the basic window in which all Office 2010 applications run. Ribbons, groups, command buttons, and the Quick Access Toolbar (QAT) replace conventional hierarchical menus and toolbars. As with other Office 2010 applications, the presentation of Access windows varies with each basic function that Access performs. Because tables are the basic component of relational databases, the examples that follow use Table Datasheet view. Figure 3.6 shows Access 2010's display for run-mode operations with tables; Table 3.1 describes the window's Access-related components.

 tip

To prevent the Switchboard form from appearing each time you open Northwind.accdb, click the File tab and Access Options button to open the Access Options dialog, and then click the Current Database button to open the Options for the Current Database page. Open the Display Form list, select (None), click OK to close the dialog, and click OK again to dismiss the message that you must close and restart Access for the change to take effect.

Figure 3.6
Access uses
the default
document
interface (MDI)
to display
all database
objects except
code in mod-
ules and scripts
for pages. The
VBA editor and
Microsoft Script
editor are sepa-
rate applica-
tions.

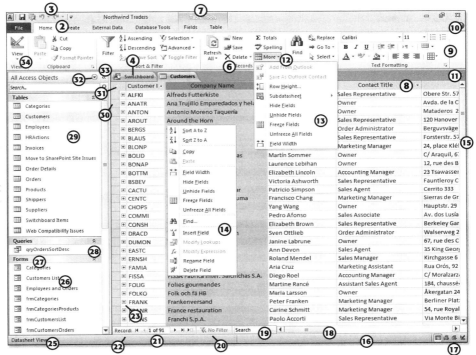

1. Office button
2. Ribbon tab
3. Quick-Access toolbar
4. Tabbed document
5. Selected cell
6. Button group
7. Contextual ribbon
8. Field headers
9. Ribbon
10. Online/Offline help
11. Document Close button
12. Gallery

13. Context menu
14. Context submenu
15. Record scrollbar
16. Status bar
17. View shortcuts
18. Field scrollbar
19. Quick Search textbox
20. Filter status
21. Record indicator
22. Record Navigation bar
23. Open subdatasheet
24. New Record

25. Status message
26. Navigation item
27. Navigation group
28. Show/Hide Navigation items
29. Navigation pane
30. Row Selection button
31. Select All button
32. Show Navigation gallery
33. Navigation pane
    expand/retract
34. Open View or Gallery button

Table 3.1   Components of the Access Display for Tables

Term	Description
Ribbon Tab	Selects the active ribbon from the five standard ribbons—File, Home, Create, External Data, Database Tools—and one or two contextual (Tools) ribbons, such as Table Tools, Datasheet(w) or Table Tools, Design.
Quick Access Toolbar	Lets you add icons that act as shortcuts to command buttons on all ribbons and most galleries. The default choices are Save, Undo, and Redo.

Table 3.1 Continued

Term	Description
Tabbed Document	Access 2010's default window for displaying all database objects in any view.
Selected Cell	The currently selected cell into which you can type data.
Button Group	A collection of a ribbon's command buttons that perform related tasks.
Contextual Ribbon	A ribbon that appears in response to the selected object type (table, query, form, or report) and mode (run or design).
Field Headers	Displays the name of the field and, when clicked, selects all cells of the column. Right-clicking opens a context menu with choices similar to those of the context submenu shown in Figure 3.6.
Ribbon	The standard navigation window for Office 2007 that's customized for each Office application.
⑦	Online/Offline Help — Opens Access's help win dow, which draws from help content on Office Online as well as local help files.
✕	Document Close Button — Closes the active tabbed document.
Gallery	A graphic menu with command button icons that represent choices. Access uses galleries to display buttons that aren't visible in a group.
Context Menu	An extension to a gallery or a floating right-click menu that offers choices that depend on the selected button or object type.
Context Submenu	A second or third menu hierarchy.
Record Scrollbar	Scrolls table records or query rows.
Status Bar	Displays context information or user-specified text.
▦ ▥ ▦ ✑	View Shortcuts — Provides a context-based alternative to selection from the Views group's gallery: Datasheet, PivotChart, PivotTable, Form, Report, Design.
Field Scrollbar	Scrolls table fields or query columns.
Quick Search Text Box	Typing text searches for the first instance of the characters in any field. If a match is found, pressing Enter finds the next occurrence.
Filter Status	Advises the user if all records are visible (No Filter) or a filter has been applied (Filtered).
Record Indicator	Displays the number of the current record and the total number of records displayed.
◀◀ ◀ ▶ ▶▶ ▶✱	Record Navigation Bar — Provides VCR-like buttons (First, Previous, Next, and Last) for selecting the current table record or query row and a New Row button to navigate to the tentative append record, if the table or query is updatable.

Term	Description	
⊞	Open Subdatasheet	Opens a table's sub datasheet that displays records in a related table, if a subdatasheet has been defined.
✳	New Record	The tentative append record that becomes a new record when you type in at least one field.
Status Message	Context information or user-specified text.	
Navigation Item	A shortcut to a database object; double-clicking the item opens it in a tabbed document (the default) or a modal dialog form.	
Navigation Group	A named collection of related navigation items.	
Show/Hide Navigation Items	Expands or collapses the list of a navigation group's items.	
Navigation Pane	An Outlook-style, customizable, shutter-bar list of all database objects, except those that are hidden deliberately.	
▮	Row Selection Button	Click to make the row the current row.
Select All Button	Click to select all rows and columns (the equivalent of pressing Ctrl+A).	
▼	Show Navigation Gallery	Click to open or close the Navigation gallery; right-click to open a context menu with Category, Sort By, View By, Show All Groups, Paste, Navigation Options, and Search Bar choices.
» «	Navigation Pane Expand/ Retract	Expand or retract the Navigation pane. The default state is expanded.
	Open View or Gallery Button	Clicking the icon displays the specified view; clicking View opens a gallery of the available views for the object.

➡ *For a detailed overview of the ribbon UI, Quick Access Toolbar, and Office gallery,* **see** *"The Office 2007 Ribbon User Interface,"* **p. 1427.**

➡ *To learn how to customize the Navigation pane,* **see** *"Customizing the Custom Category,"* **p. 1449.**

➡ *For a brief explanation of Access 2007's tabbed documents and modal dialogs that replace conventional modeless forms,* **see** *"Tabbed Documents and Modal Dialogs,"* **p. 1458.**

 note

This chapter concentrates on the ribbons that apply to Table Datasheet and Table Design views. Chapter 14, "Creating and Using Basic Access Forms," describes the context-specific ribbons for Form Layout and Form Design views. Chapter 16, "Working with Simple Reports and Mailing Labels," explains the elements of the Report Layout Tools, Format, Arrange, and Page Setup; Report Design Tools, Design, Arrange, and Page Setup; and Print Preview ribbons.

Navigating the Home and Create Ribbons

The Home, Create, External Data, and Database Tools ribbons vary only slightly as you change objects, operating modes, screen resolution, or window width. Access enables or disables a few command buttons and gallery items in response to changes of object type and view. Familiarity with the Home and Create ribbons is required to get up to speed with Access 2007, so this chapter covers these ribbons in detail.

For a brief overview of all four primary Access ribbons, **see** *"Access 2007's Main Ribbons,"* **p. 1429.**

The Home Ribbon

Figure 3.7 is a multiple-exposure, split view of the Home ribbon for table Datasheet view in 1,024×768 resolution. The View, Font Color, Text Highlight Color, Refresh, Advanced Filter Options, Selection and Go To galleries are open.

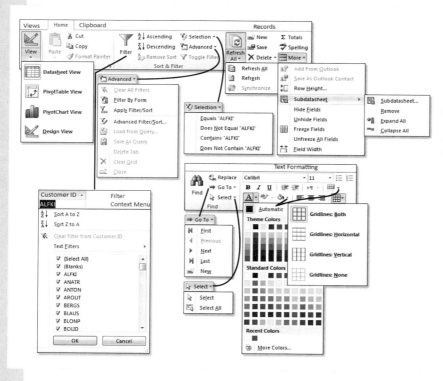

Figure 3.7
Control buttons on ribbons haven't replaced all hierarchical Office menus. Drop-down galleries and context menus substitute icons, lists, or both for earlier Access versions' conventional Windows menu choices.

Table 3.2 lists the Home ribbon's command buttons, keyboard shortcuts (also called *KeyTips*), and actions. Press Alt+H to activate the KeyTips, release the Alt key, and then sequentially press the keys shown in the Shortcut column.

Table 3.2 The Home Ribbon's Command Buttons and Their Actions in Table Datasheet View

Icon	Command Button	Shortcut Alt+H, ...	Command Action
Views Group			
	Datasheet View	W, H	Changes to Datasheet view
	PivotChart View	W, O	Changes to PivotChart view
	PivotTable View	W, V	Changes to PivotTable view
	Design View	W, D	Changes to Design view
Clipboard Group			
	Paste	V, P (Ctrl+V)	Pastes Clipboard content
	Paste, Special	V, S	Pastes Clipboard content in selected format
None	Paste, Append	V, N	Inserts records copied to the Clipboard
	Cut	X (Ctrl+X)	Cuts selected content to the Clipboard
	Copy	C (Ctrl+C)	Copies selected content to the Clipboard
	Format Painter	F, P	Copies the format from one object to another
None	Office Clipboard	F, O	Opens the Office Clipboard task pane
Sort and Filter Group (see Chapter 7)			
	Sort Ascending	E	Sorts the selected field/column in ascending (A–Z) order
	Sort Descending	D	Sorts the selected field/column in descending (Z–A) order
	Remove Sort	F, R	Removes sorts from all fields/columns
	Filter	Q	Opens the filter context menu for the selected field/column
	Selection	O	Opens a context menu that lets you filter records by selection
	Advanced Filter/ Sort	FV	Opens a context menu that lets you choose advanced filter/sort features
	Toggle Filter	J	Alternately applies and removes the current filter

Table 3.2   Continued

Icon	Command Button	Shortcut Alt+H, ...	Command Action
Records Group (see Chapter 6)			
	Refresh All	K, R	Regenerates the Recordset and repaints the Datasheet
	New Record	K, N Ctrl++	Moves to the tentative append record
	Save	K, S Shift+Enter	Saves changes to a record
	Delete	K, D (Del)	Deletes the selected (current) record
Σ	Totals	T	Toggles the appearance of a totals row below the tentative append record
	Spelling	S (F7)	Starts the spelling checker for the selected object and opens the Spelling: *Language* dialog (see Figure 3.9)
	More	P	Opens a context menu with Datasheet formatting choices
Find Group (see Chapter 7)			
	Find	F, D Ctrl+F	Opens the Find and Replace dialog with the Find page active
	Replace	R Ctrl+H	Opens the Find dialog with the Replace page active
	Go To	G	Opens a context menu with First, Previous, Next, Last, and New choices
	Select	H	Opens a context menu with Select and Select All choices
Text Formatting Group			
None	Font, Face	F, F	Sets the focus to the Font Face list box
None	Font, Size	F, S	Sets the focus to the Font Size list box
B	Bold	1 Ctrl+B	Applies bold attribute to selected text
I	Italic	2 Ctrl+I	Applies italic attribute to selected text
U	Underline	3 Ctrl+U	Applies underline attribute to selected text

Icon	Command Button	Shortcut Alt+H, ...	Command Action
▤	Align Left	A, L	Aligns selected text left
▤	Align Center	A, C	Centers selected text
▤	Align Right	A, R	Aligns selected text right
A	Font Color	F, C	Opens font color picker
◈	Fill/Back Color	F, B	Opens fill/background color picker
▦	Gridlines	B	Opens gridlines gallery
▦	Alternate Fill/ Back Color	F, A	Opens fill/background color picker for alternate rows
None	Datasheet Formatting	L	Opens the Datasheet Formatting dialog (see Figure 3.8)

Rich Text Group (for rich-text-enabled Memo fields only)

Icon	Command Button	Shortcut Alt+H, ...	Command Action
⇥	Decrease List Level	A, O	Decreases rich-text indent level
⇤	Increase List Level	A, I	Increases rich-text indent level
▶¶	Left-to-Right	A, F	Enables changing rich-text entry direction
≣	Numbering	N	Starts a rich-text numbered list
≔	Bullets	U	Starts a rich-text unordered list
ab🖉	Text Highlight Color	I	Opens a color picker to highlight selected rich text

note

The QAT and ribbon UI comprise a window that's independent of the Access window that contains the Navigation pane and tabbed documents. When you press Alt once or twice to set focus to the ribbon window and display the KeyTips, pressing the left or right arrow key cycles focus through the primary and context-specific ribbons, QAT, and Office button. Pressing Tab or an arrow key cycles the focus through the selected ribbon's command buttons. You move between ribbon and command button selection with the up- and down-arrow keys. Pressing Enter with a command button selected executes its action.

Figure 3.8
The Datasheet Formatting dialog consolidates most Datasheet appearance settings in a single location.

Figure 3.9
Access's Spelling: Language dialog is common to all Office 2010 applications.

Context-Specific Table Tools Ribbons

Opening any Access object except a module in Design view adds one or more context-specific ObjectType Design Tools ribbons. Similarly, opening a form or report in Layout view adds ObjectType Layout Tools ribbons. Opening a table in Datasheet or Design view adds a Table Tools, Datasheet ribbon. Changing to Design view substitutes a Table Tools, Design ribbon. The following sections describe these two context-sensitive ribbons briefly.

The Table Tools, Datasheet Ribbon

Microsoft encourages Access users to create tables in Datasheet view, type data in the default empty column provided, add new columns as needed, and populate the new columns. As mentioned earlier, opening a new empty database creates an empty starter table. Alternatively, you can add a starter table by clicking the Create ribbon's Table button. In either case, the Table Tools, Datasheet ribbon opens by default.

Figure 3.10 is a split view of the Table Tools, Fields ribbon.

Figure 3.10
The Table Tools, Fields ribbon enables adding new fields or changing the properties of existing fields of the selected table.

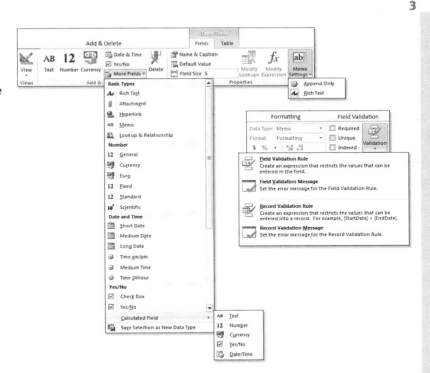

Table 3.3 lists the Table Tools, Fields ribbon's command buttons, shortcut keystrokes, and command actions. Like primary ribbons, you press Alt, release the Alt key, then press J, B and the shortcut key. The Views button behaves identically to the same button on the Home ribbon.

 tip

You can discourage users from making table design changes in Datasheet view by clearing the Enable Design Changes for Tables in Datasheet View check box in the Application Options group of the Access Options dialog's Current Database page, as described in the later section "The Current Database Page."

To prevent users from changing options, you must split the database and secure the front end, as described in Chapter 21, "Linking Access Front Ends to Access and Client/Server Tables."

 note

Microsoft promotes ad-hoc table design by emulating spreadsheet methodology so Access appears easier for neophytes to use. A substantial part of the market for desktop database platforms is replacing spreadsheets that should have been databases from the start. New users' impromptu table structures often don't abide by basic rules for relational database design. This is one of the primary reasons that RDBMSs such as Access have acquired a bad reputation among professional software developers and database administrators (DBAs).

Table 3.3 The Table Tools, Datasheet Ribbon's Command Buttons and Their Actions in Table Datasheet View

Icon	Command Button	Shortcut Alt+J,B, ...	Command Action
Add & Delete Group (disabled for SharePoint lists)			
AB	Text	D, T	Adds a Text field with default 255-character length
12	Number	D, N	Adds a Number field with default Long Integer size
(icon)	Currency	D, C	Adds a Currency field with default unit
(icon)	Date & Time	D, D	Inserts a DateTime field
(icon)	Yes/No	D, Y	Inserts a Yes/No [Boolean] field
(icon)	More Fields	F	Opens a gallery of Basic, Number, Date and Time, Yes/No, and Calculated Field data types
(icon)	Delete	T	Deletes the field you added or the selected field
Properties Group (disabled for SharePoint lists)			
(icon)	Name & Caption	C	Enables typing a field name and optional caption
(icon)	Default Value	V, D	Enables specifying a default value of fields that accept default values
None	Field Size	D, S	Enables setting a size for Number fields or maximum length for Text fields
(icon)	Modify Lookups	L	Opens the Lookup Wizard to modify a Lookup specification
f_x	Modify Expression	E	Opens the Expression Builder dialog to modify the expression for a calculated field
ab|	Memo Settings	G	Enables adding Append Only restriction and Rich Text formatting to Memo Fields
Formatting Group (disabled for SharePoint lists)			
None	Data Type	S	Enables selecting one of the nine basic Access data types
None	Formatting	R	Enables selecting formatting of Number, Date/Time and Currency fields

Icon	Command Button	Shortcut Alt+J,B, ...	Command Action
$	Apply Currency Format	A, N	Formats the Number data with the Windows default currency format
%	Apply Percentage Format	P	Multiplies the Number data by 100 and adds two decimal digits (does not affect the cell value)
,	Apply Comma Number Format	K	Adds comma (or dot) thousands separators and two decimal digits
.00 →.0	Decrease Decimals	0	Reduces the number of decimal digits
←.0 .00	Increase Decimals	9	Increases the number of decimal digits

Field Validation Group (disabled for SharePoint lists)

✓	Required	Q	Prevents NULL values in the field
✓	Unique	U	Requires unique values in the field
✓	Indexed	I	Adds an index to the field
✓	Validation	V, A	Opens a gallery of validation options: Field Validation Rule, Field Validation Message, Record Validation Rule, Record Validation Message

The Table Tools, Table Ribbon

New in Access 2010 icon Clicking the Table Tools, Table tab in Table Datasheet view opens the Table ribbon shown in Figure 3.11. This ribbon primarily handles creating and editing Access 2010's new data macros, as well as displaying the Relationships window and the Object Dependencies task pane. You press Alt, release the Alt key, then press J, T and the shortcut key to activate a button. Table 3.4 lists command buttons, shortcut keystrokes, and command actions.

 note

Chapter 22, "Collaborating with Windows SharePoint Foundation 2010," provides detailed instruction for integrating Access 2010 and SPF or SPS 2010.

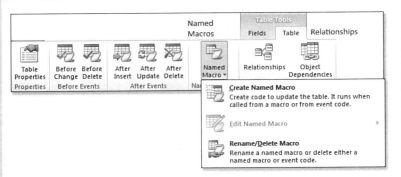

Figure 3.11
The Table Tools, Table ribbon has groups for adding or editing table properties, Data macros, named macros and relationships, as well as viewing objects dependent on the selected table.

Table 3.4   The Table Tools, Table Ribbon's Command Buttons and Their Actions in Table Datasheet View

Icon	Command Button	Shortcut Alt+W, ...	Command Action
Table Properties Group (disabled for SharePoint lists)			
	Table Properties	T	Opens the Table properties dialog shown in Figure 3.12
Before Events Group (see Chapter 20; disabled for SharePoint lists)			
	Before Change	C, 1	Opens the macro builder for the Before Change data macro event
	Before Delete	V	Opens the macro builder for the Before Delete data macro event
After Events Group (see Chapter 20; disabled for SharePoint lists)			
	After Insert	I	Opens the macro builder for the After Insert data macro event
	After Update	U	Opens the macro builder for the After Update data macro event
	After Delete	D	Opens the macro builder for the After Delete data macro event
Named Macros Group (see Chapter 19)			
	Named Macros	C, 2	Opens the macro builder to create or edit a named macro
Relationships Group			
	Relationships	E	Opens the Relationships window
	Object Dependencies	O	Opens the Object Dependencies task pane (see Figure 3.13)

Figure 3.12
The Enter Table Properties dialog lets you specify a default sort order and filter expression, as well as text orientation and whether the table should be read-only when disconnected from its data source.

Figure 3.13
The Object Dependencies task pane for the Northwind.accdb Customer table shows that two tables, eight forms, and one report are dependent on the data it contains.

The Table Tools, Design Ribbon

Changing to Table Design view replaces the Table Tools, Fields ribbon with the Table Tools, Design ribbon shown in Figure 3.14. Table Design view is the better choice for designing tables than typing data items to generate an ad-hoc table structure. Design view and the Table Tools, Design ribbon expose many more field and table properties than Datasheet view and the Table Tools, Datasheet ribbon.

Table 3.5 lists the Table Tools, Design ribbon's command buttons, shortcut keystrokes, and command actions.

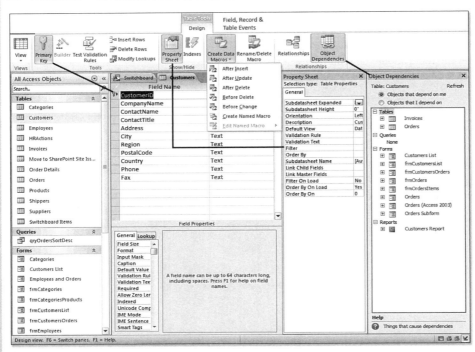

Figure 3.14
The Table Tools, Design ribbon replaces the Fields and Table ribbons in Table Design view. The field design grid and the Field Properties pane set values for individual fields. Property Sheet settings apply to the entire table and the Object Dependencies task pane lists table, forms, and reports that depend on the selected table.

 tip

Almost all nontrivial databases contain more than one table because a single-table database is the functional equivalent of a spreadsheet or a SharePoint list. Before you design a table for a production database that requires two or more related tables, read—or at least skim—Chapter 4, "Exploring Relational Database Theory and Practice," and Chapter 5, "Working with Access Databases and Tables."

Many novice database designers find that the usability or performance of their application deteriorates greatly as the number of table rows increases. Changing table design to overcome deficiencies after users enter large amounts of data is time-consuming, frustrating, and prone to errors. Starting your first database project with one of the many Access database templates, even if you must modify it to suit your application, provides a reasonable degree of assurance that you won't "design yourself into a nonrelational corner."

Table 3.5 The Table Tools, Design Ribbon's Command Buttons and Their Actions in Table Design View

Icon	Command Button	Shortcut Alt+J, D, ...	Command Action
Tools Group			
🔑	Primary Key	P	Toggles the status of the selected column(s) as the primary key for the table
	Builder	B	Opens the Expression Builder dialog when entering Default Value or Validation Rule property values
	Test Validation Rules	V	Tests new or modified validation rules with existing data
	Insert Rows	I	Inserts a new field grid row above the current row
	Delete Rows	R	Deletes the selected field grid row(s)
	Modify Lookups	L	Starts the Lookup Wizard
Show/Hide Group			
	Property Sheet	H, P	Toggles visibility of the Property Sheet pane
	Indexes	X	Opens the Indexes: *TableName* dialog to add indexes on fields other than the primary key field
Field, Record & Table Events Group			
	Create Data Macros	C	Opens a context menu that lets you select a data macro event for the macro builder
	Rename/Delete Macro	M	Opens the Data Macro Manager dialog in which you can rename or delete a data macro
Relationships Group			
	Relationships	E	Opens the Relationships window
	Object Dependencies	O	Opens the Object Dependencies task pane

> For a brief description of primary keys, **see** *"Selecting a Primary Key,"* **p. 221.**

> For more information about the Expression Builder and validation rules, **see** *"Adding Table-Level Validation Rules with the Expression Builder,"* **p. 257.**

> To learn more about the Indexes: TableName dialog, **see** *"Adding Indexes to Tables,"* **p. 222.**

The Create Ribbon

You use the Create ribbon to add new table, query, form, report, macro, and module objects to Access databases (see Figure 3.15).

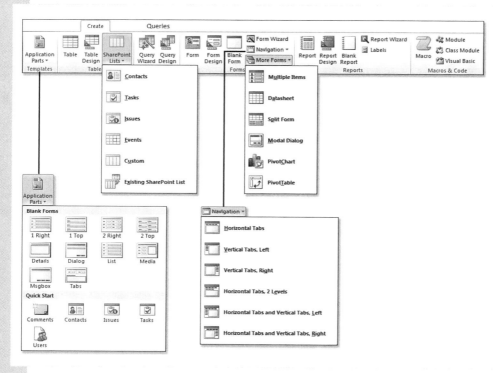

Figure 3.15
The Create ribbon lets you add new Access objects to your database and take advantage of form and SharePoint list templates, when applicable.

Table 3.6 lists the Create ribbon's command buttons, shortcut keystrokes, and command actions.

Table 3.6   The Create Ribbon's Command Buttons and Their Actions in Table Datasheet View

Icon	Command Button	Shortcut Alt+C, ...	Command Action
Templates Group (see Chapters 14 and Chapter 15)			
	Application Parts	P	Opens a gallery of blank and quick-start forms
Tables Group (see Part II of this book)			
	Table	T, N	Adds a new table with a single field in Datasheet view
	Table Design	T, D	Opens a new table in Table Design view
	SharePoint Lists	S	Opens a gallery that contains the following six command buttons

Icon	Command Button	Shortcut Alt+C, ...	Command Action
	Contacts	S, C	Generates a Contacts list in the designated SharePoint site and links it and a User Information List to an Access table
	Tasks	S, T	Does the same for a Tasks list and table
	Issues	S, I	Does the same for an Issues list and table
	Events	S, E	Does the same for an Events list and table
	Custom	S, U	Generates a basic SharePoint list with visible ID (AutoNumber), Title (Text), and Attachments (Attachment) fields, as well as 11 hidden SharePoint-specific fields and links it to an Access table
	Existing SharePoint List	S, X	Lets you import or link the data from a SharePoint list you specify to an Access table

Queries Group *(see Part III of this book)*

Icon	Command Button	Shortcut Alt+C, ...	Command Action
	Query Wizard	Q, Z	Opens the New Query dialog, which lets you select the Simple Query, Crosstab Query, Find Duplicates, or Find Unmatched Query Wizard to help you design a query from one or more tables
	Query Design	Q, D	Opens a new query in Design view and displays the Show Table dialog

Forms Group *(see Chapters 14 and Chapter 15)*

Icon	Command Button	Shortcut Alt+C, ...	Command Action
	Form	F, N	Generates a formatted columnar form from the selected table or query and adds a Datasheet sub-form bound to a related form, if present
	Form Design	F, D	Opens a new blank form in Form Design view
	Blank Form	F, B	Creates an empty (blank) form in Layout view and opens the Field List pane
	Form Wizard	F, Z	Starts the Form Wizard, which lets you create a columnar, tabular, Datasheet, or justified form from table fields or query columns you select with a format from one of 25 predesigned styles
	N		Opens a gallery, which lets you select one of six button options for a Navigation form.
	More Forms	F, M	Opens a gallery with the following five command buttons to create a new form of the specified design

Table 3.6   Continued

Icon	Command Button	Shortcut Alt+C, ...	Command Action
	Multiple Items	F, M, U	Continuous form showing multiple rows
	Datasheet	F, M, D	Creates a form that's indistinguishable from table Datasheet view
	Split Form	F, M, P	Creates a form that combines a details view and a datasheet
	Modal Dialog	F, M, M	Creates an empty modal dialog (overlapping window) in Layout view and opens the Field List pane
	PivotChart	F, M, C	Creates a form that contains a PivotChart control (see Chapter 18)
	PivotTable	F, M, T	Creates a form that contains a PivotTable control (see Chapter 18)

Reports Group (see Chapters 16 and 17)

Icon	Command Button	Shortcut Alt+C, ...	Command Action
	Report	R, N	Generates a simple formatted list from the selected table or query with the same font size as forms and opens it in Report view
	Report Design	R, D	Opens a new blank report for the selected table or query in Design view
	Blank Report	R, B	Opens a blank report in Layout view for the selected table or query and opens the Field List pane
	Report Wizard	R, Z	Starts the Report Wizard, which lets you base the report on a table or query you select, and add grouping, sort order, and format
	Labels	B	Starts the Mailing Label Wizard to print mailing labels standard label sheets you specify

Macros and Code Group (see Parts V and IX of this book)

Icon	Command Button	Shortcut Alt+C, ...	Command Action
	Macro	M	Opens an empty macro builder window
	Module	U	Opens an empty VBA module in the VBA Editor application
	Class Module	C	Opens an empty VBA Class Module in the VBA Editor application
	Visual Basic	V	Opens the VBA Editor application

Using the Function Keys

Access assigns specific purposes to all 12 function keys of the 101-key extended keyboard. Some function-key combinations, such as Shift+F4 (which you press to find the next occurrence of a match with the Find dialog), derive from other Microsoft applications—in this case, Word.

Global Function Keys

Windows, rather than Access, uses global function-key assignments, except for F11, Ctrl+F1, and Alt+F1, to perform identical functions in all Windows applications. Table 3.7 lists the global function-key assignments.

Table 3.7   Global Function-Key Assignments

Key	Function
F1	Displays context-sensitive help related to the present basic function and status of Access. If a context-sensitive help topic isn't available, F1 opens the Microsoft Access Help task pane page, which lets you search online help for a keyword or open its table of contents.
Ctrl+F1	Toggles (alternates) visibility of the ribbon window in all Office 2007 members.
2007 NEW Ctrl+F4	Closes the active window.
Alt+F4	Exits Access or closes a dialog if one is open.
Ctrl+F6	Selects each open window in sequence as the active window.
2007 NEW F11	Toggles Navigation pane visibility.
F12	Opens the selected object's Save As dialog.
Shift+F12	Saves your open database; the equivalent of the File menu's Save command.

Function-Key Assignments and Shortcut Keys for Fields, Grids, and Text Boxes

Access assigns function-key combinations that aren't reserved for global operations to actions specific to the basic function you're performing at the moment. Table 3.8 lists the function-key combinations that apply to fields, grids, and text boxes. (To present complete information, this table repeats some information that appears in the previous tables.)

 note

Chapter 8, "Linking, Importing, and Exporting Data," covers use of the External Data ribbon, and Chapter 5 explains the Database Tools ribbon's command button actions.

 For an extensive list of Access shortcut key assignments, **see** *"Using Keyboard Operations for Entering and Editing Data,"* **p. 246.**

Table 3.8   Function Keys for Fields, Grids, and Text Boxes

Key	Function
F2	Toggles between displaying the caret for editing and selecting the entire field.
Shift+F2	Opens the Zoom box to make typing expressions and other text easier.
F4	Opens a drop-down combo list or list box.
Shift+F4	Finds the next occurrence of a match of the text typed in the Find or Replace dialog, if the dialog is closed.
F5	Moves the caret to the record-number box. Type the number of the record that you want to display.
F6	In Table Design view, cycles between upper and lower parts of the window. In Form Design view, cycles through the header, body (detail section), and footer.
F7	Starts the spelling checker.
F8	Turns on extend mode. Press F8 again to extend the selection to a word, the entire field, the whole record, and then all records.
Shift+F8	Reverses the F8 selection process.
Ctrl+F	Opens the Find and Replace dialog with the Find page active.
Ctrl+H	Opens the Find and Replace dialog with the Replace page active.
Ctrl++ (plus sign)	Adds a new record to the current table or query, if the table or query is updatable.
Shift+Enter	Saves changes to the active record in the table.
Esc	Undoes changes in the current record or field. By pressing Esc twice, you can undo changes in the current field and record. Also cancels extend mode.

Setting Default Options

New in Access 2007 icon You can set about 100 options that establish the default settings for Access. (But you aren't likely to want to change default options until you're more familiar with Access 2010.) This book is a reference as well as a tutorial guide, and options are a basic element of Access's overall structure, so this section explains how to change these settings.

You set defaults by clicking the File tab to open Backstage view and then clicking the Options button to open the Access Options dialog's default General page (see Figure 3.16). The options you set on the General, Datasheet, Object Designers, Proofing, Language, Client Settings, Customize ribbons, Quick Access Toolbar, Add-Ins and Trust Center pages apply to the system as a whole. Settings on the Current Database page apply only to the database that's open when you change the settings.

 note

Ctrl+G opens the VBA editor and sets the focus to the Immediate window (formerly the Debug window), and Ctrl+Break halts execution of VBA code.

Figure 3.16
The default General page of the Access Options properties dialog sets global option values that apply to all databases you open in Access 2010, as do all other pages except Current Database.

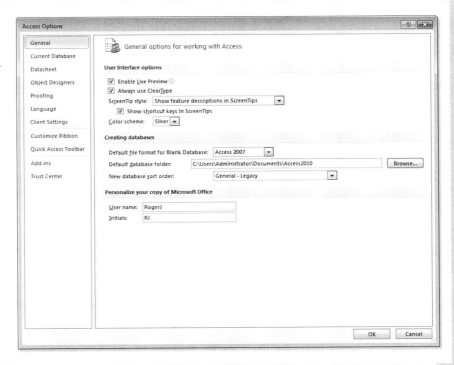

Most settings are option buttons and check boxes, although many other items require multiple-choice entries that you select from drop-down lists. In some cases, you must type a specific value in a text box. After you complete your changes, click OK to close the dialog to save your changes. If you decide not to implement your changes, click Cancel to exit without making any changes. The next few sections and their tables summarize options that affect Access as a whole and those options that affect viewing and printing data in Datasheet view.

The General Page

The General page (refer to Figure 3.16) contains the following control groups to set the most common default option for all Access databases and projects you create:

- **User Interface Options**—Enables Live Preview and ClearType for LCD monitors. Also sets the ScreenTip style and default color scheme: Blue, Silver or Black. (*ScreenTips* are the formatted ToolTips for ribbon command buttons.)

- **Creating Databases**—Sets the default file format for new database files (Access 2007 .accdb, Access 2002–2003 .mdb,

 note

If you're familiar with Access 2003 or earlier versions, you'll notice that the Access Options dialog is a dramatic departure from the tabbed dialog that opened from the Tools, Options menu choice. Most of the individual settings are common to earlier versions, but their organization into pages differs.

or Access 2000 .mdb). Also specifies the default .accdb or .mdb file location (Documents for Windows 7 and Vista; My Documents for Windows XP) and default database sort order (General - Legacy to use the Windows language's sort order).

- **Personalize Your Copy of Microsoft Office**—Lets you change the default username and add or edit initials.

The Current Database Page

The Current Database Page lets you change default properties of the currently open database or project with controls in the following groups:

- **Application Options**—Lets you specify a custom application title and icon; substitute the custom icon for standard form and report icons; name a startup form to open when Access loads; hide the status bar at the bottom of the Access window; replace tabbed documents with nonmodal (overlapping) windows; disable special access keys (F11 for the Navigation pane, Ctrl+G for the VBA Editor's Immediate window, and Ctrl+Break to halt VBA code execution); and automatically compact the database after closing the file (see Figure 3.17).

 note

New in Access 2010 icon Live Preview is a new Office 2010 feature that lets you view content copied to the Office Clipboard before you paste it into a table, form, report or module. After copying content, right-click and hover the mouse pointer over the Paste options, Access 2010 shows a preview of the content's appearance for the selected Paste option before you paste it to the destination.

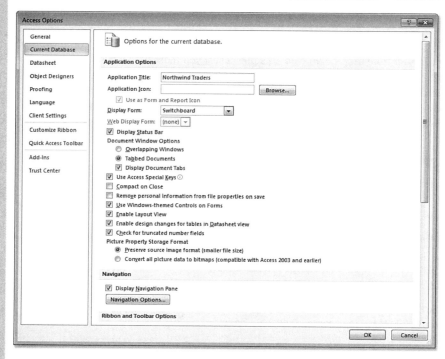

Figure 3.17
The Current Database page's Application Options group includes new option settings for tabbed documents, Layout view, designing tables in Datasheet view, and the Attachments field data type.

- You also can remove personally identifiable information from the .accdb or .mdb file; disable Windows XP or Windows Vista themed controls; disable Layout view; disable making design changes in table Database view; disable testing for truncated numbers when changing number format; and convert all image files to Windows bitmap (.bmp) format for backward compatibility.

- **Navigation**—The Display Navigation Pane check box enables hiding the Navigation pane (see Figure 3.18). The Navigation Options button opens the Navigation Options dialog.

Figure 3.18
The Current Database page's remaining groups are more specialized than Application Options.

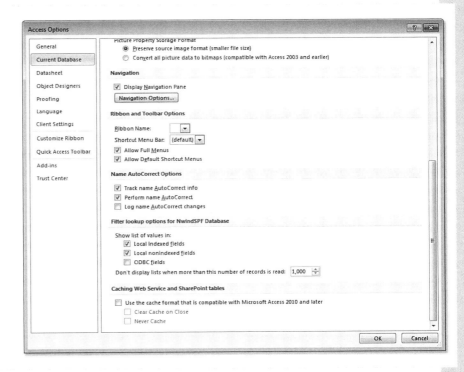

> To find out how to use the Navigation Options dialog, **see** "Customizing the Custom Category,"
> p. 1449.

- **Ribbon and Toolbar Options**—Lets you replace all ribbons and add groups and command buttons to existing ribbons by selecting a stored RibbonX (XML) document, or discourage users from editing objects. For example, you can specify a custom shortcut (context) menu bar; clear the Allow Full Menus check box to hide all ribbons except Home; and clear the Allow Default Shortcut Menu check box to hide noncustom context menus.

> For an introduction to RibbonX documents, **see** "Customizing Ribbons for Specific Applications,"
> p. 1438.

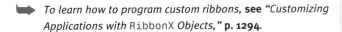 *To learn how to program custom ribbons,* **see** *"Customizing Applications with* `RibbonX` *Objects," p. 1294.*

- **Name AutoCorrect Options**—Enables a controversial process for conforming references to renamed Access objects. If you'd rather do the job yourself, clear the Track Name AutoCorrect Info and Perform Name AutoCorrect check boxes. (Don't bother trying Alt+A; all the check boxes have the same shortcut key combination.)

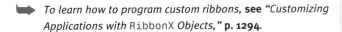 *To learn more about Name AutoCorrect,* **see** *"Altering Fields and Relationships," p. 224.*

- **Filter Lookup Options**—Lets you disable displaying lookup field lists from indexed, non-indexed, or ODBC fields in linked or client/server tables, or where the lists would have more than a specified number of items. As an example, a lookup list of customers in an orders table might have 10,000 or more items from which to choose, which could cause a substantial performance hit.

> ### note
>
> The Name AutoCorrect feature is controversial because of its history of serious problems that occurred with the initial Access 2000 version and several issues that you might encounter with Access 2010. Most Access developers recommend that you disable this feature. To learn more about the feature's problematic history, perform a Bing or Google search on "Name AutoCorrect" problem.

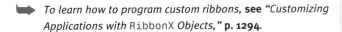 *For more information about lookup fields,* **see** *"Using Lookup Fields in Tables," p. 442.*

The Datasheet Page

The Datasheet page (see Figure 3.19) sets the defaults for table, query, and form Datasheets.

Following are descriptions of the page's two groups:

- **Gridlines and Cell Effects**—Enables customizing visibility of horizontal and vertical gridlines, as well as cell special effects and default column width.

- **Default Font**—Lets you change the size and weight and other attributes of the default 11-point Calibri font. You can't change the default Calibri font family.

The Object Designers Page

The Object Designers page (see Figure 3.20) sets the defaults for table, query, form, and report Design view.

Following are descriptions of the page's four groups:

- **Table Design**—Sets the defaults for new field data types (Text) and default Text field size (255 characters, the maximum) and Number field size (Long Integer). By default, Access adds an index to any field that contains the characters "ID", "key", "code", or "num". You might want to remove the semicolon-separated string from the text box so that you, not Access, determine when to add indexes fields. Clearing the Show Property Update Options Buttons check box hides the drop-down lists for properties (such as Format) on the General page of table Design view's lower pane, which is not a recommended practice.

Figure 3.19
The Datasheet page
sets design defaults
for Datasheet views in
new databases.

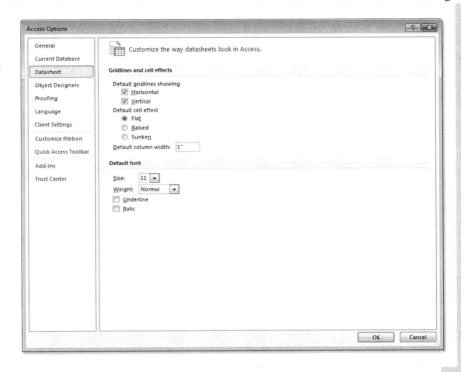

Figure 3.20
The Object
Designers
page's first
two groups set
design defaults
for Table
Design view,
Query Design
view, and SQL
view.

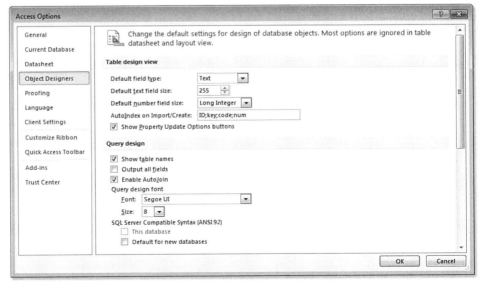

- **Query Design**—Lets you disable auto-addition of table names to all query SQL statements, add an all-fields asterisk (*) to all query field lists, or disable automatically creating join lines between related tables or fields with the same name. You also can change the default design font from Segoe UI to a different family and larger size, and specify SQL Server–compatible syntax based on the ANSI SQL-92 standard. With the exception of font size, departing from the default query Design settings isn't recommended.

- **Forms/Reports**—Enables changing how controls on forms and reports are selected (partial or full enclosure) and the names of form and report templates (see Figure 3.21). You can use an existing form or report as a template or create a form or report specifically as a template for the new objects you create. This book uses forms and reports generated from the default Normal templates. If you mark the Always Use Event Procedures check box, you won't be able to select embedded macros to handle form or report events.

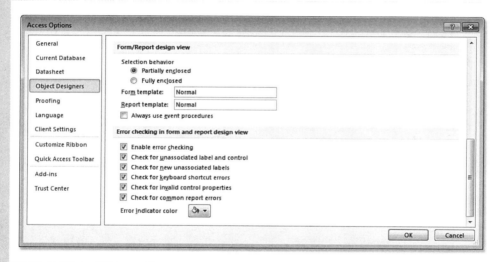

Figure 3.21
The Object Designers page's last two groups specify design defaults for form and report Design view and control design error checking.

- **Error Checking**—Enables or disables Design-mode error checking, selects the types of errors detected, and uses a color picker to select the error indicator smart tag's color.

The Proofing Page

The Proofing page enables customizing the AutoCorrect feature and Office spelling checker for all Access applications (see Figure 3.22).

The Proofing page has these two groups:

- **AutoCorrect Options**—Provides an AutoCorrect Options button to open the Office AutoCorrect dialog.

Figure 3.22
The brief
Proofing
page lets you
modify default
AutoCorrect
and spelling
checker set-
tings.

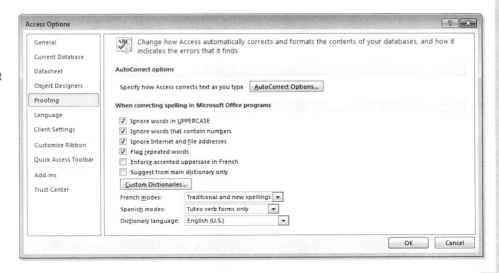

- **When Correcting Spelling in Microsoft Office Programs**—Lets you set spell-checking options, including custom dictionaries in the Custom Dictionaries dialog, and specify a main dictionary language other than the default English (U.S.).

The Language Page

New in Access 2010 icon Access 2010's Language page lets you add additional Office editing languages to the default language specified by your Windows installation by making selections from the Add Additional Editing Languages list and setting their priority in the Display Language list box (see Figure 3.23).

The Client Settings Page

The Client Settings page (see Figure 3.24) contains the following five groups:

- **Editing**—Lets you customize the default cursor, arrow key, find/replace, confirmations, Datasheet IME (Input Method Editor) control, and Hijiri (Islamic or Arabic) lunar calendar options. (Saudi Arabia, Kuwait, and Yemen use the Hijiri calendar officially.)

➡ *For detailed explanations of cursor and arrow-key options,* **see** *"Setting Data Entry Options,"* **p. 246.**

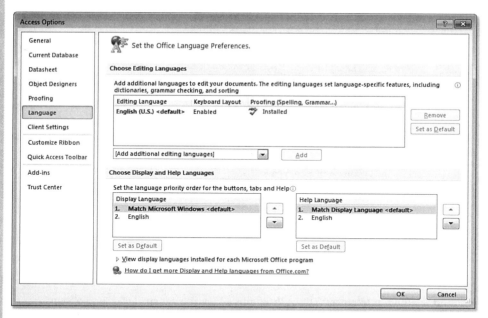

Figure 3.23
The Language page lets you specify multiple editing languages and set their priority.

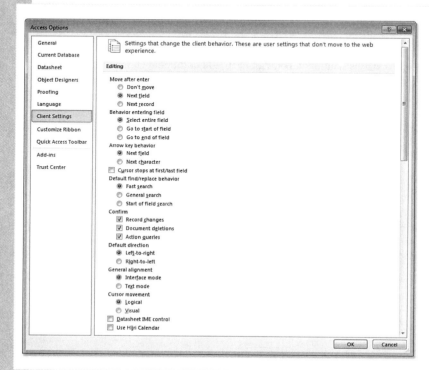

Figure 3.24
The Client Settings page's Editing group enables customizing data entry defaults and use of the Hijiri calendar.

- **Display**—Enables changing the number of most recently used (MRU) databases displayed in the Office button's gallery; hiding the status bar, animations, smart tags on Datasheets, and Smart Tags on form and reports; and showing the Names and Conditions columns when editing stand-alone or embedded macros (see Figure 3.25).

Figure 3.25
The Client Settings page's Display, Printing, and General groups let you customize 13 more properties.

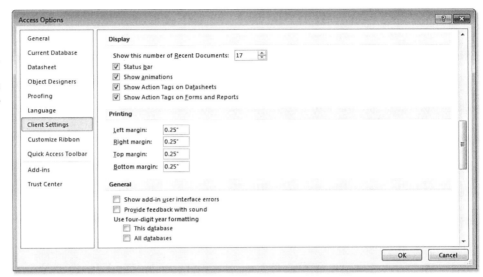

- ![2007 NEW] **Printing**—Lets you change the default printing margins (0.25 inch).

  ![arrow] *For a brief description and screen capture of the Print Preview ribbon,* **see** *"Contextual Ribbons for Access Databases,"* **p. 1432.**

- **General**—Lets Access raise an error if a RibbonX document for a customized ribbon is incorrect, add audio cues to keyboard and other actions, animate cursors for several operations, and require four-character year formatting for the current database, all databases, or both.

- **Advanced**—Enables specifying the last-opened database as the default when opening Access, changing the default open and record-locking mode, setting OLE/DDE and ODBC properties, specifying command arguments to be used when starting Access, and specifying the encryption method for data in tables (see Figure 3.26).

- ![2010 NEW] **Default Theme**—Enables specifying the Office theme file to use as the default for all datasheets, forms, and reports.

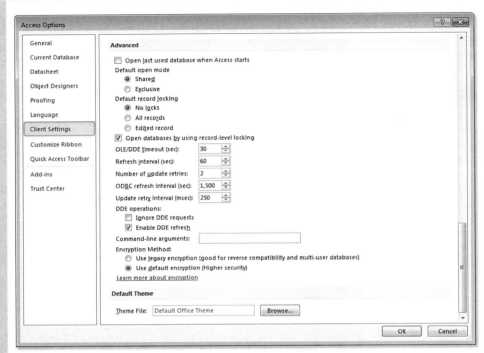

Figure 3.26
The Client Settings page's Advanced group contains controls to set orphaned properties' default values.

The Customize Ribbon Page

New in Access 2010 icon The Customize Ribbon page lets you select a command button from groups, such as Popular Commands, Commands Not in the Ribbon, All Commands, Macros, and so on, and assign it to an existing or new group on any of the seven main ribbons or a new ribbon (see Figure 3.27). You can rename ribbons or groups, reset the ribbon to its original group and command complement, as well as import or export an XML customization file.

The Quick Access Toolbar Page

The Customize Ribbon page lets you add command buttons—represented by 16×16-pixel icons—from any standard ribbon to the Quick Access Toolbar. The Quick Access Toolbar page opens with a list of popular commands and their icons in the left list box and an Add button to move selected commands to the right list box, which contains the default Save, Undo, and Redo commands (see Figure 3.28).

 note

Access 2007 called the Client Settings page the Advanced page.

The only Advanced group change you might want to make is to mark the Open Last Used Database When Access Starts check box.

 note

Access 2010 has more than 1,000 unique icons; this book uses about 400 different icons to identify commonly used command buttons

Figure 3.27
The Customize Ribbon page enables adding a command button from any ribbon to an existing or new group on an existing or new ribbon. The names of existing command buttons appear below their group.

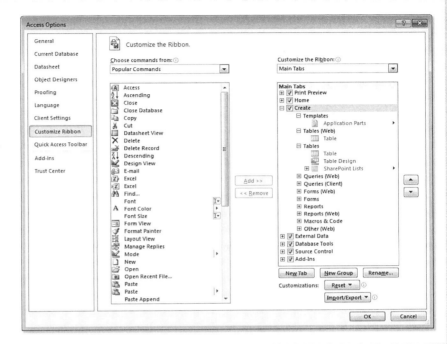

Figure 3.28
The Customize page opens with the three default commands for the QAT and the Popular Commands list for adding QAT commands.

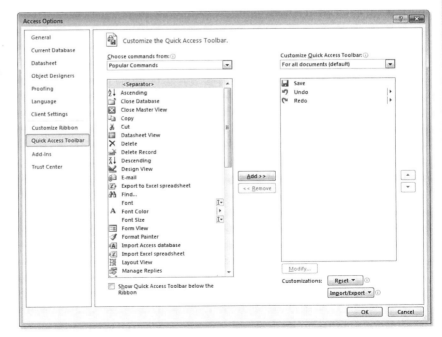

The Choose Commands From list lets you select commands from Access's 28 ribbons (tabs) or five other categories.

You can add the most popular commands to the QAT by clicking the arrow button to the right of the QAT to open the menu shown in Figure 3.29 and clicking the commands to add. Alternatively, right-click any command button in the selected ribbon and choose Add to Quick Access Toolbar from the context menu.

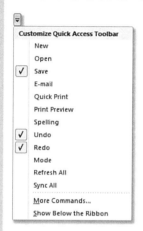

Figure 3.29
Clicking the arrow to the right of the QAT opens this menu, which lets you add the most popular QAT commands quickly.

The Add-Ins Page

The Add-Ins page lets you manage Microsoft and third-party COM (Component Object Model) and Access add-in applications (see Figure 3.30). Microsoft includes a single Microsoft Access Package Solution Wizard COM add-in to aid in packaging customized Access databases for distribution.

Selecting COM Add-Ins in the Manage list and clicking Go opens the COM Add-Ins dialog, which lets you enable, add, or remove COM add-ins. Selecting Access Add-Ins and clicking Go opens the Access Add-In manager dialog, which lets you Add New or Uninstall Access add-in libraries (.accda, .accde, .mda, or .mde files). Third-party add-in suppliers usually include detailed instructions for installing and using their add-ins.

The Trust Center Pages

The opening Trust Center page consists of links to Microsoft privacy statements and Microsoft Trustworthy Computing propaganda. The only feature of interest on this page is the Trust Center Settings button, which opens a second Trust Center page to establish Access-wide security settings.

 note
Office Online's "View, Manage, and Install Add-ins in Office Programs" article at http://bit.ly/c1qmPy describes working with add-ons in detail.

 For a brief overview of new Access 2007 security features, which also apply to Access 2010, **see** *"Security, Trusted Locations, Packages, and Certificates,"* **p. 1446.**

The second Trust Center page offers the following subpages.

Figure 3.30
The Customize page opens with the three default commands for the QAT and the Popular Commands list for adding QAT commands.

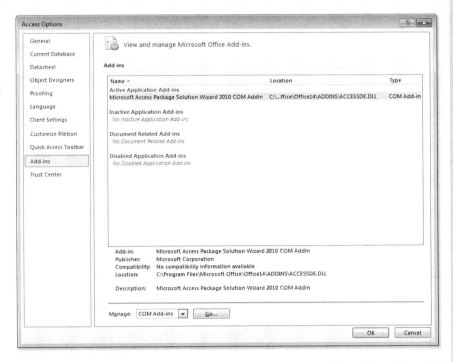

Trusted Publishers

Trusted Publishers can apply digital signatures from a code-signing certificate to Access packages or VBA code and class modules. Signing an Access package certifies that all database objects, not just code, have not been modified since being signed. If the certificate is valid, the database (and its code) is considered trusted when the user extracts it.

 To learn how to create and sign Access packages, **see** *"Packaging, Signing, and Distributing an Access 2010 Database,"* **p. 144**.

 For more information on code-signing certificates, **see** *"Security Issues with VBA Code,"* **p. 1241**.

If you want to test code-signed packages without spending U.S.$99 to U.S.$199 per year, you can create a self-signed certificate with the SelfCert.exe application available at the \Program Files\Microsoft Office\Office14. Figure 3.31 shows the Trusted Publishers page displaying a self-signed certificate for OakLeaf Systems.

> **note**
>
> As mentioned throughout this book, Access 2007 and 2010 have abandoned previous versions' user-level security (also called workgroup security) features in favor of database password security combined with file- and folder-level security. User-level security, which Access 2010 supports for Access 2000 and 2002/2003 .mdb files, provides very granular access conditions to all database objects for individual user and group accounts. Access 2010's security features are rudimentary, at best.

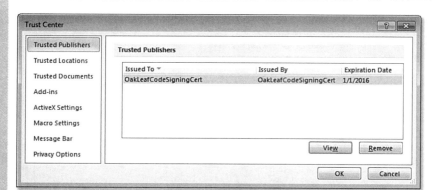

Figure 3.31
A self-signed certificate, such as the OakLeafCode SigningCertificate, can be used to create a package that doesn't generate a security warning upon extracting the database.

Trusted Locations

New in Access 2007 icon Placing .accdb files in a trusted location (folder) is the most practical method to eliminate the need to enable VBA code and potentially dangerous macro actions for each Access 2010 session. By default, Access trusts the \Program Files\Microsoft Office\Office14\ ACCWIZ folder that holds all Access wizard files, as shown in Figure 3.32.

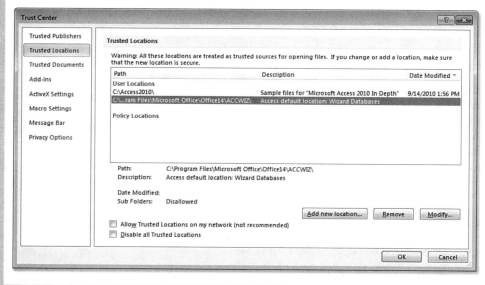

Figure 3.32
Access automatically trusts the \Program Files\ Microsoft Office\ Office14\ACCWIZ folder so that wizards will run without generating a security warning. C:\ Access2010 and its subfolders have been added as a trusted location for this book's downloadable sample files.

You add other folders and their subfolders as trusted documents by clicking the Add New Location button to open the Microsoft Office Trusted Location dialog, browsing to the folder you want to trust, marking the Subfolders of This Location Are Also Trusted check box (if applicable), adding an optional description, and clicking OK. You no longer see the security warning in the message bar when you open the database from the trusted location.

➡ *For an example of creating a trusted location,* **see** *"Designating the Default Database Folder as a Trusted Location,"* **p. 53.**

Add-Ins, Macro Settings, Message Bar, and Privacy Options

New in Access 2007 icon The remaining Trust Center pages resemble groups of other Access Options pages (see Figure 3.33). The option names are sufficiently self-describing as to not warrant relisting here. The default selections shown in Figure 3.33 should be satisfactory for most applications.

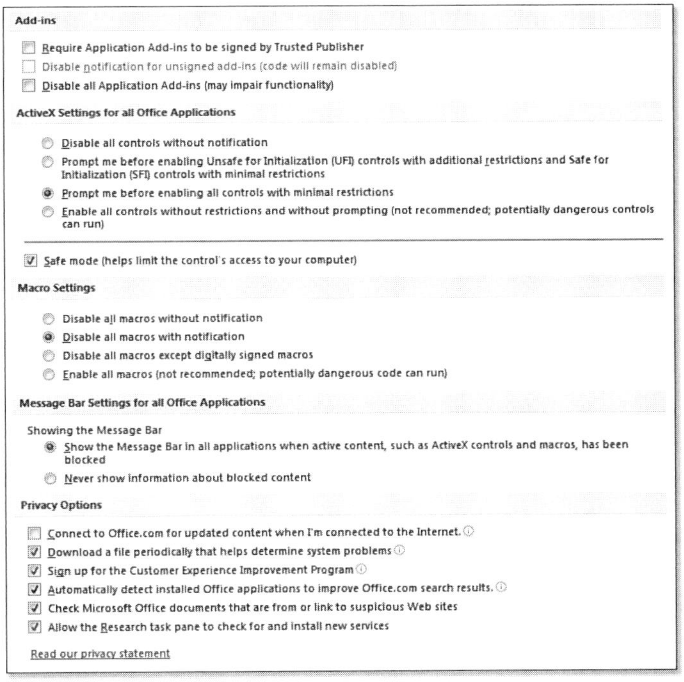

Figure 3.33
The Add-Ins, Macro Settings, Message Bar, and Privacy Options pages might better have been groups on a single page.

Creating a Customized Template File

After you've set the options for all databases and the current database, you might want to use the database as a template for all new databases you create. You can specify the database to use as the template for all new databases you create by saving it as \Program Files\Microsoft Office\ Templates\1033\Access\Blank.accdb. This location is called the *System Template Folder*.

Alternatively, you can save it under Windows 7 or Vista as \Users*UserName*\Documents\
Templates\Blank.accdb, or Windows XP as \Documents and Settings\Application Data\Microsoft\
Templates\Blank.accdb.

Using Access Online Help

Access 2010 and other Office 2010 members share a common online help system that differs
markedly from that of Office 2003 and earlier releases. Access 2010's sizable Access Help window
consists of a Table of Contents pane with a tree view list and, when you first click the Help button,
the default Browse Access Help list in the right (content) pane (see Figure 3.34).

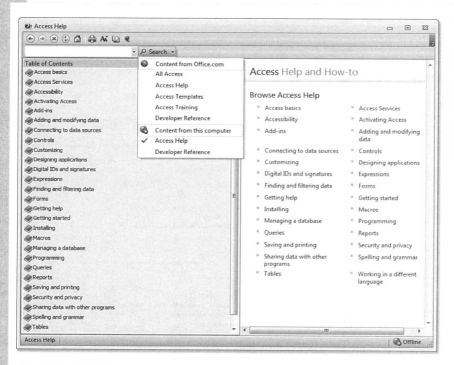

Figure 3.34
The Access Help win-
dow opens in normal
(resizable) window
mode and occupies
the entire display by
default. The Search
menu lets you select
the scope of a key-
word search.

Unless you clear the Search Microsoft Office Online for Help Content When I'm Connected to the
Internet check box on the Trust Center's Privacy Options page, help content from Office Online
supplements the local computer's help files.

Searching for a Phrase

Typing a phrase without enclosing it between double quotes causes the help system to return topics with any of the words present. For example, typing **Attachment data type** in the Search text box and clicking the Search button returns more than 100 topics (see Figure 3.35). Many are obviously unrelated topics, such as "Import or link to data in an Excel Workbook."

Figure 3.35
Searching Help for
multiple words returns
many unrelated topics.

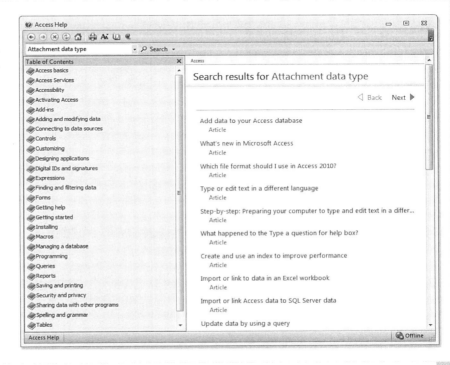

Enclosing the search term in double quotes returns the two topics shown in Figure 3.36, which contain the exact phrase, as shown for the "Which file format should I use in Access 2010?" topic in Figure 3.37.

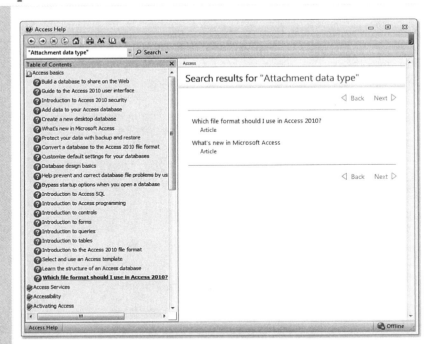

Figure 3.36
Searching for a quoted phrase in the text box requires wrapping the Searched For expression in a pair of double quotes.

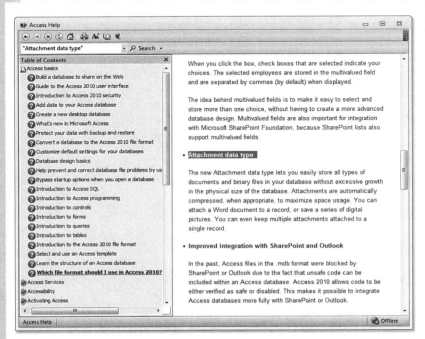

Figure 3.37
The text of the first topic shown in Figure 3.36 contains the expected "Attachment data type" phrase.

Searching Other Sources

Clicking the All Access link under the Content from Office.com item in the results page (refer to Figure 3.34) returns a web page with three topics; the additional topic is "Save an Access 2010 database in an earlier file format."

Spelunking the Database Utilities

Access 200x offered eight utility functions that you could access by choosing Tools, Database Utilities. Following are the locations of these tools in Access 2010:

- Convert Database becomes Backstage, Save Database As, Access 2000 Database, Access 2002–2003 Database, or Access 2007 Database.

- Compact and Repair Database moves to Backstage, Info, Compact and Repair, which checks the database for consistency, repairs problems found, and then compacts it to save disk space. Access automatically replaces the existing database with the compacted or repaired version.

- Back Up Database moves to Backstage, Save & Publish, Save Database As, Back Up Database and opens the Save Backup As dialog and proposes to save your current database file as FileName_YYYY-MM-DD.accdb. Using the backup feature is a bit faster than making a copy with Windows Explorer.

- Linked Table Manager moves to the Linked Table Manager command in the External Data ribbon's Import & Link group. It tests for the existence of linked .accdb or other types of data files and, if the links aren't valid, lets you change the path to the linked files. This choice is disabled if you don't have a database with linked tables open.

- Database Splitter becomes the Access Database command in the Database Tools ribbon's Move Data group. It divides a single-file Access .accdb application with application and data objects into a front-end .accdb file and a back-end Access database. This choice is disabled if you don't have a database open. Chapter 21, "Linking Access Front Ends to Access and Client/Server Tables," covers linking to tables in an Access back-end database.

- Switchboard Manager has moved to "Commands Not in the Ribbon" purgatory, but you can add the command to the QAT, as described in the earlier "The Quick Access Toolbar Page" section. It creates a new Switchboard form if one isn't present in the current database and lets you edit the new or an existing Switchboard form. This choice is disabled if you don't have a database open.

- Upsizing Wizard becomes the SQL Server command in the Database Tools ribbon's Move Data group. It lets you move tables and queries from the current Access database to SQL Server 2005 [Express] and, optionally, change the .accdb file containing application objects to an Access Data Project (.adp) file. Chapter 21 describes how to use the Upsizing Wizard to link an .adddb front end to SQL Server tables. Chapter 28, "Upsizing Access Applications to Access Data Projects and SQL Azure," covers creating ADPs.

- Make MDE File moves to the Backstage, Save & Publish, Save Database As, Advanced, Make ACCDE command. It creates a secure copy of the file, which prevents users from opening objects in Design view and viewing or changing VBA code.

Compacting and Repairing Databases

After you make numerous additions and changes to objects within a database file—especially deletions of large amounts of data in tables—the database file can become disorganized. When you delete a record, you don't automatically regain the space in the file that the deleted data occupied. You must compact the database to optimize its file size and the organization of data within the tables that the file contains. When you compact an Access file, you regain space only in 32KB increments.

> **note**
>
> Access 2010's Switchboard Manager generates Access macro code for switchboards in .accdb files and VBA code for switchboards in .mdb files.

To compact the current database, do the following:

1. Open the database you want to compact.

2. Click the File and Info tabs, and then click the Compact & Repair Database button. Access immediately closes the database and begins compacting it.

When Access finishes compacting the database, it opens the database and returns you to where you were in the application before. Your compacted database is stored with the same name it had before you compacted it.

A database can become corrupted as the result of the following problems:

- Hardware problems that occur when writing to your database file, either locally or on a network server

- Accidentally restarting the computer while Access databases are open

- A power failure that occurs after you make modifications to an Access object but before you save the object

Occasionally, a file might become corrupted without Access detecting the problem. This lack of detection occurs most frequently with corrupted indexes. If Access or your application behaves strangely when you open an existing database and display its contents, try compacting and repairing the database.

Periodically compacting and repairing production database files usually is the duty of the database administrator in a multiuser environment, typically in relation to backup operations. You should back up your existing file on disk or tape before creating a compacted version. When you're developing an Access 2010 database, you should compact and repair the database frequently. Access 2010 databases that are not compacted grow in size much more rapidly during modification than earlier versions.

Converting Earlier Database Formats to Access 2007 Format

To convert earlier Access version .mdb database or .mda library files created with Access 95 through Access 2003 to the Access 2007 database format of Access 2010, open the file in Access 2010 and click the File tab, Save As, Access 2010 Database. Chapter 33, "Upgrading Access 2003 and Earlier Applications to Access 2010," covers this conversion process in detail.

> **tip**
>
> Be sure to save an archive copy of any .accdb file you convert to .accde format on a removable disk, CD-ROM, or DVD-ROM and store the archive copy in a safe place. The copy you make in .accde format is permanently altered; you can't restore an .accdb from an .accde file.

Compile Errors in the Convert Database Process

Sometimes error messages appear when you convert to Access 200x from early Access versions. Access 2.0 and earlier were 16-bit applications. The first error message you might receive is, "There are calls to 16-bit dynamic-link libraries (.dll) in this application." In this case, you must alter the code of Declare statements to call the current 32-bit equivalents of the 16-bit DLLs. For example, you must change calls to functions in User.dll, Kernel.dll, and Gdi.dll to User32.dll, Kernel32.dll, and Gdi32.dll.

A more common error message when converting Access 2.0, 95, and 97 applications is, "There were compilation errors during the enabling or conversion of this database." If you're converting from Access 2.0, many of these errors are likely to arise from Access Basic reserved words and symbol usage that VBA 6.0 doesn't support. Similar problems occur with applications that originated in Access 2.0 or earlier and were converted to Access 9x. In some cases, conversion of earlier application versions to Access 97, and then to Access 2007 format is easier than attempting direct conversion. See Chapter 33 for additional information on conversion issues.

> **tip**
>
> To compact the current database automatically each time you close it, click File, Access Options, Current Database, and mark the Application Group's Compact on Close check box.

Creating .accde Files

An .accde file is a special version of an Access .accdb file. In an .accde file, all VBA code is stored only in compiled format, and the program source code for that database is unavailable. Also, users can no longer modify forms, reports, queries, or tables stored in that database, although those objects can be exported to other databases. Typically, .accde databases are used to create libraries of add-in wizards, deliver custom database applications intended for commercial or in-house distribution, and provide templates for forms, reports, queries, and other objects for use in other databases.

 You can convert any Access 2007 or 2010 .accdb database to an .accde file by opening the file, clicking the Database Tools tab, and clicking the Make ACCDE button to open the Save As dialog. Navigate to the location for the .accde file and click Save to create and save the file. Then close the dialog.

Creating .accdr Runtime Files

New in Access 2007 icon An .accdr file is called a *runtime Access file*. You create a runtime file by changing *FileName*.accde to *FileName*.accdr. The .accdr version hides the ribbon and Navigation pane, so you must provide a switchboard or equivalent to open forms and reports. The QAT is disabled and the Office button's gallery offers Print, Privacy Options, and Exit buttons only. Runtime Access files provide a minimalist UI, as illustrated by Figure 3.38.

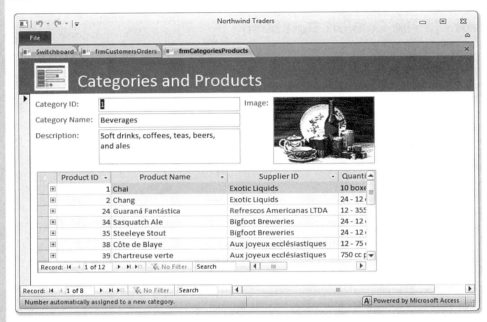

Figure 3.38
Access Runtime (.accdr) files open with the ribbon and Navigation pane hidden and disabled.

The problem with .accdr files is that users quickly discover they can simply change the file extension from .accdr to .accdb to regain lost design and navigation features.

Packaging, Signing, and Distributing an Access 2007 Database

New in Access 2007 icon The Backstage view's Save & Publish menu's Advanced group offers the following two choices that haven't been covered yet:

■ **Package and Sign**—Creates an Access Deployment file (.accdc) whose origin and integrity is certified by a digital signature. You can deploy database copies from an .accdc file published to a SharePoint document library. The sections that follow describe how to generate a self-signed digital certificate and then use the certificate to sign an Access Deployment file.

-  **SharePoint**—Publishes the database to a SharePoint Foundation (SPF) or SharePoint Server (SPS) 2010 site and enables users to open a read-only or read-write copy, depending on their group membership. Chapter 22 shows you how to share databases from a SharePoint document library.

Generate and Install a Self-Certified Digital Certificate

To create a self-signed certificate, do the following:

1. Choose Start, Programs, Microsoft Office, Microsoft Office Tools, Digital Certificate for VBA Projects to open the Create Digital Certificate dialog. Type the name for the certificate in the text box (see Figure 3.39).

Figure 3.39
Type a certificate name in the text box and click OK to add the certificate to the Windows Personal certificate store.

2. Click OK to add the certificate to the Personal category of the Windows certificate store, which is managed by IE.

3. Launch IE. Choose Tools, Internet Options in IE 8 or later to open the paged Internet Options dialog. Click the Content tab and Certificates button to open the Certificates dialog, and click the Personal tab to display the certificate you created in step 2 (see Figure 3.40).

4. Select the certificate, click Export to start the Export Certificate Wizard, and click Next to open the Export Private Key dialog. This option isn't available for self-signed certificates, so click Next to open the Export File Format dialog.

5. Accept the default DER-Encoded Binary X.509 (.CER) option, and click Next to open File to Export dialog.

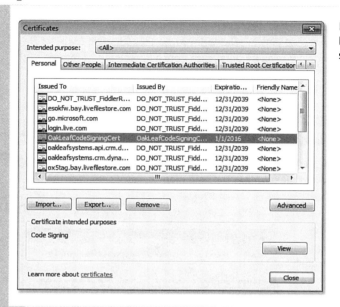

Figure 3.40
IE's Certificates dialog displays the new self-signed certificate on the Personal page.

6. Click Browse to open the Save As dialog, navigate to a folder in which to save the certificate, type a filename (**OakLeafCodeSigningCertificate** for this example), and click Save to save the file with a .cer extension. Click Finish to dismiss the wizard and acknowledge the "Certificate export was successful" message.

7. Click the Certificates dialog's Trusted Root Certificate Authorities tab, click the Import button to start the Certificate Import Wizard, and click Next to open the File to Import dialog.

8. Click Browse to open the Open dialog, navigate to the location you specified in step 6, and double-click the certificate file. Click Next to open the Certificate Store dialog.

 note

The certificate isn't valid at this point because you aren't a trusted root certification authority. You must export the certificate to a file and then import it to the Trusted Root Certification Authority page to enable trust. If you double-click the entry for the certificate, a "This CA Root certificate is not trusted" warning appears on the Certificate dialog's general page.

9. Accept the default Place All Certificates in the Following Store option, verify that the Certificate Store is Trusted Root Certificate Authorities, and click Next and then Finish to display a security warning (see Figure 3.41).

10. Click Yes to add the certificate to the Trusted Root Certificate Authorities group. Double-click the item to verify the certificate (see Figure 3.42).

11. Repeat steps 7 to 9, except substitute Trusted Publishers for Trusted Root Certificate Authorities in each step. In this case, you don't receive the security warning described in step 9.

Figure 3.41
This security warning appears for any certificate you add to the Trusted Root Certificate Authorities list. The default list contains most generally accepted certificate authorities (CAs).

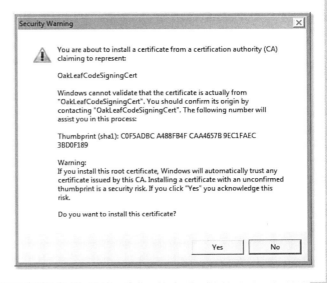

Figure 3.42
A certificate with the purposes "Ensures software came from software publisher" and "Protects software from alteration after publication" is a code-signing certificate.

12. Click the File tab, Options, Trust Center, Trust Center Settings, Trusted Publishers, and then verify that your certificate appears in the Trusted Publishers list (refer to Figure 3.31).

13. Click Macro Settings, and select the Disable All Macros Except Digitally Signed Macros option (refer to Figure 3.33). Click OK twice to save your changes and return to your source database.

Creating a Signed Package File (*.accdc)

To create, sign, and test a Signed Package file with a *.accdc extension, do the following:

1. Open the .accdb file to package (preferably a database with VBA code in a class module or standalone module), and click the File tab, click the Save & Publish tab, and double-click the Package and Sign button in the Advanced group to open the Select Certificate dialog (see Figure 3.43).

> **note**
>
> If you don't make the change in step 13, you'll see a security warning in the message bar when you test the extracted file in the next section.

Figure 3.43
The Select Certificate dialog lets you select the code-signing certificate to use if you have more than one.

2. Click OK to close the dialog and open the Create Microsoft Access Signed Package dialog (see Figure 3.44).

3. Optionally, browse for a different location to save the *.accdc file, and click Create to save the Signed Package and close the dialog.

Testing a Signed Package File (*.accdc)

Creating a Signed Package makes it easier for other users to install and trust databases, especially databases signed with a self-signed certificate. To emulate the user experience with a self-signed certificate, do the following:

1. Copy the *.accdc (Deployment) file to another computer that doesn't have the self-signed certificate in its Trusted Publishers list.

2. Double-click the *.accdc file to start the extraction process. A self-signed certificate opens the Microsoft Access Security Notice dialog, which reports "A potential security concern has been identified" (see Figure 3.45).

Figure 3.44
The default signed package location is the folder containing the original *.accdb database file.

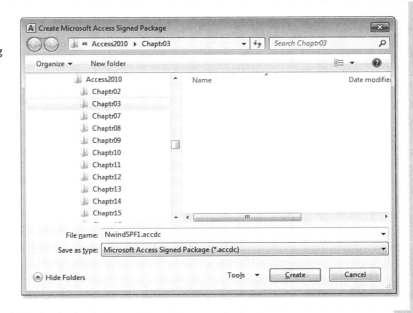

Figure 3.45
This security notice dialog opens when extracting the database from a package whose publisher isn't trusted by the receiving user or computer.

3. Click Open to trust the publisher for this database only, start Access 2010, and open the Extract Database To dialog (see Figure 3.46).

4. Click OK to extract the *.accdb file, close Access, and open the *.accdb file, which indicates it's trusted by not displaying the yellow Security Warning below the ribbon.

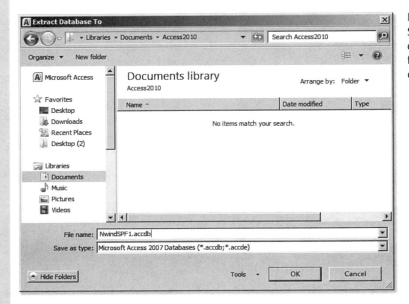

Figure 3.46
Select the location for and, optionally, rename the database file in the Extract Database To dialog.

Creating and Testing a Packaged Solution Installer File (*.msi)

A Packaged Solution is a Windows Installer Package (*.msi file) that installs a database (*.accdb, *.accdc, *.accde or *.accdw file), optional supporting files, and can include the Access 2010 Runtime or prompt the user to download the Access 2010 Runtime. To create a Packaged Solution from the *.accdc file you created and tested in the two preceding sections, do the following:

1. Click the File and Save & Publish tabs to display the Package Solution group.

2. Click the large Package Solution button to start the Package Solution Wizard.

3. Accept the default Destination Folder for the package (see Figure 3.47), unless you have a reason to do otherwise, and click Next to open the Installation Options dialog.

4. Complete the Installation Options dialog, which offers the options to require Access 2010 be installed or use Access 2010 Runtime Support (see Figure 3.48).

 note

The "Package, Sign, and Distribute an Access Database" help topic included the following note when this book was written: "If you use a self-signed certificate to sign a database package and then click Trust All from Publisher when you open that package, packages signed by using your self-signed certificates will always be trusted."

The note is incorrect. The Trust All from Publisher button is disabled for self-signed certificates (refer to Figure 3.45).

Figure 3.47
The first Package
Solution Wizard
dialog specifies
the location for the
installer file(s).

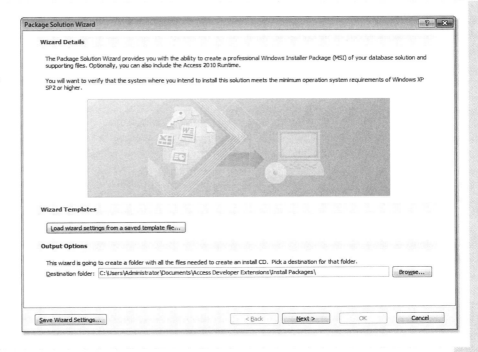

Figure 3.48
Specify the *.accdb
file to package, the
root install folder,
install subfolder,
Access 2010 ver-
sion to use, install
locations, shortcut
name, and icon file.

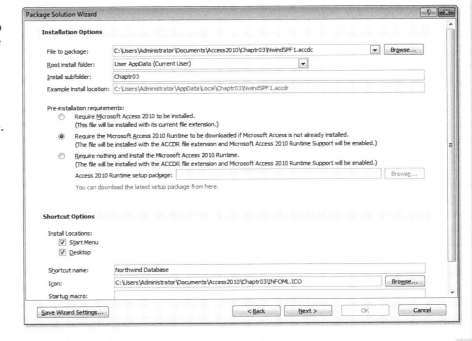

5. Click Next to open the Additional Files dialog, and click the upper Add button to open an Open dialog for adding supporting files, such as a self-signed certificate (see Figure 3.49) or a Readme.txt file.

6. Click the lower Add button to add required Registry keys, if any.

7. Click next to Complete at least the required fields of the General Properties and other categories of information partly shown in Figure 3.50.

note

You might find that the wizard throws an error if you include the *.cer certificate file as a supporting file. In this case, add a note to the Readme.txt supporting file advising users where they can open the *.cer file to add it to their Trusted Publishers list.

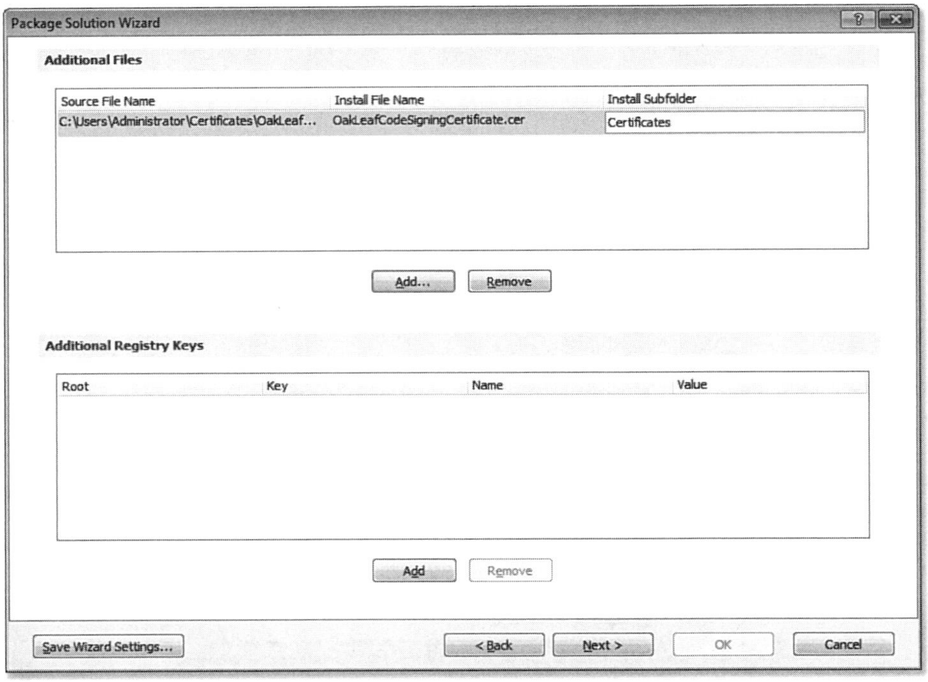

Figure 3.49
Specify supporting files to include in the package and Registry keys to add, if any, in the Additional Files dialog.

8. Click OK to generate the *DatabaseName*.msi file and a Setup folder in your [My] Documents\Access Developer Extensions\ Install Packages*DatabaseName*\Files folder.

9. Burn a distribution CD-R with the contents of the *DatabaseName* folder and its subfolders.

note

Clicking OK also adds standard Autorun.inf and Setup.exe files to the ...\DatabaseName folder, as well as a ...\Files\Setup subfolder with a Setup.ini file.

Figure 3.50
Scroll to
the second
Installation
Options dia-
log's Advanced
Options section,
which is below
the bottom
edge of this
screen capture.

Package Solution Wizard

General Properties

Product Name: Northwind Sample Access 2010 Database

Install Language: English

Microsoft Software License
Terms: Browse...

Feature Information

Users see the feature information when they choose the "Custom" installation mode

Feature Title: Downloadable Sample Database

Feature Description: Created by the Access 2010 Package Solution Wizard

Add/Remove Programs Information

Publisher: OakLeaf Systems

Product Version: Major: 1   Minor: 0   Build: 0

Contact Person: Roger Jennings

Help/Support URL: http://accessindepth.blogspot.com

Product Updates URL: http://accessindepth.blogspot.com

Additional support info:

File Properties for the Windows Installer Package

Title: Northwind Sample Access 2010 Database Installer

Subject:

Save Wizard Settings...   < Back   Next >   OK   Cancel

10. Insert the CD-R in another computer's drive and, if Autorun doesn't start Setup.exe, run Setup.
exe from Windows Explorer to open the Setup dialog, Northwind Sample Access 2010 Database
Setup for this example (see Figure 3.51).

Figure 3.51
The Setup dialog displays the title you specified in step 7.

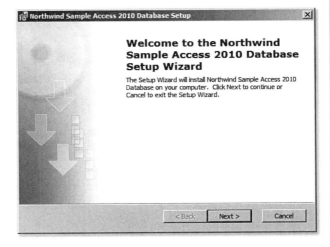

Northwind Sample Access 2010 Database Setup

**Welcome to the Northwind
Sample Access 2010 Database
Setup Wizard**

The Setup Wizard will install Northwind Sample Access 2010
Database on your computer. Click Next to continue or
Cancel to exit the Setup Wizard.

< Back   Next >   Cancel

11. Click Next to open the Customer Information dialog (see Figure 3.52).

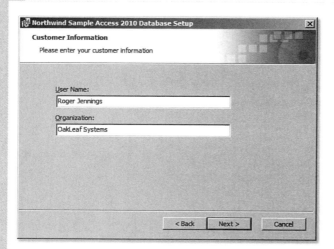

Figure 3.52
The second step displays setup's standard Customer Information dialog.

12. Click Next to open the Choose Setup Type dialog. Clicking Typical automatically extracts the signed *.accdb file to the location you specified in step 7.

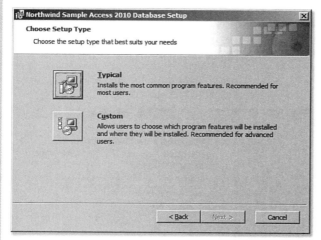

Figure 3.53
The final install step lets users select the default (Typical) or a Custom database file location.

4

EXPLORING RELATIONAL DATABASE THEORY AND PRACTICE

Moving from Spreadsheets to Databases

Word processing and spreadsheet applications were the engines that drove the fledgling personal computer market. In the early PC days, WordPerfect and Lotus 1-2-3 dominated the productivity software business. Today, most office workers use Microsoft Word and Excel on a daily basis. It's probably a safe bet that more data is stored in Excel spreadsheets than in all the world's databases. It's an equally good wager that most new Access users have at least intermediate-level spreadsheet skills, and many qualify as Excel power users.

Excel 2010's Data ribbon offers elementary database features, such as sorting, filtering, validation, and data entry forms. You can quickly import and export data in a variety of formats, including those of database management applications, such as Access. Excel's limitations become apparent as your needs for entering, manipulating, and reporting data grow beyond the spreadsheet's basic row-column metaphor. Basically, spreadsheets are list managers; it's easy to generate a simple name and address list with Excel. If your needs expand to contact management and integrating the contact data with other information generated by your organization, a spreadsheet isn't the optimal approach.

The first problem arises when your contacts list needs additional rows for multiple persons from a single company. You must copy or retype all the company information, which generates redundant data. If the company moves, you must search and replace every entry for your contacts at the firm with the new address. If you want to record a history of dealings with a particular individual, you add pairs of date and text columns for each important contact with the person. Eventually, you find yourself spending more time navigating the spreadsheet's rows and columns than using the data they contain.

Contact lists are only one example of problems that arise when attempting to make spreadsheets do the work of databases. Tracking medical or biological research data, managing consulting time and billings, organizing concert tours, booking artist engagements, and myriad other complex processes are far better suited to database than spreadsheet applications.

Moving to a relational database management system (RDBMS), such as Access, solves data redundancy and navigation problems and greatly simplifies updating existing information. After you understand the basic rules of relational database design, Access makes creating highly efficient databases quick and easy. Access 2010 has a collection of wizards to lead you step-by-step through each process involved in developing and using a production-grade database application. Unfortunately, no "Relational Wizard" exists to design the underlying database structure for you, but you'll find a wealth of pre-built database templates in the Backstage page's New tab. (Click the ribbon's File tab to open the new Backstage page.)

Reliving Database History

Databases form the foundation of world commerce and knowledge distribution. Without databases, there would be no World Wide Web, automatic teller machines, credit/debit cards, or online airline reservation systems. Newsgathering organizations, research institutions, universities, and libraries would be unable to categorize and selectively disseminate their vast store of current and historical information. It's difficult to imagine today a world without a network of enormous databases, many of which probably contain a substantial amount of your personal data that you don't want to be easily available to others.

The Early History of Databases

The forerunner of today's databases consisted of stacks of machine-readable punched cards, which Herman Hollerith used to record the 1890 U.S. census. Hollerith formed the Computing-Tabulating-Recording Company, which later became International Business Machines. From 1900 to the mid-1950s, punched cards were the primary form of business data storage and retrieval, and IBM was the primary supplier of equipment to combine and sort (collate) punched cards, and print reports based on punched-card data.

 tip

If your goal is learning relational database fundamentals, start with Access 2010. Access is by far the first choice of universities, colleges, trade schools, and computer-training firms for courses ranging from introductory data management to advanced client/server database programming. The reason for Access's popularity as a training platform is its unique combination of initial ease of use and support for advanced database application development techniques.

 note

Jim Gray's article, "Data Management: Past, Present, and Future," which is available as a Microsoft Word document at http://research.microsoft.com/~gray/DB_History.doc, offers a more detailed history of data processing systems. Dr. Gray was a senior researcher and the manager of Microsoft's Bay Area Research Center (BARC) until early 2007, when he became lost at sea while sailing off the California coast.

The development of large computer-maintained databases—originally called *databanks*—is a post–World War II phenomenon. Mainframes replaced punched cards with high-capacity magnetic tape drives to store large amounts of data. The first databases were built on the hierarchical and network models, which were well suited to the mainframe computers of the 1950s. Hierarchical databases use parent-child relationships to define data structures, whose diagrams resemble business organization charts or an inverted tree with its root at the top of the hierarchy. Network databases allow relaxation of the rules of hierarchical data structures by defining additional relationships between data items. Hierarchical and network databases ordinarily are self-contained and aren't easy to link with other external databases over a network.

Early databases used batch processing for data entry and retrieval. Keypunch operators typed data from documents, such as incoming orders. At night, other operators collated the day's batch of punched cards, updated the information stored on magnetic tape, and produced reports. Many smaller merchants continue to use batch processing of customer's credit-card purchases, despite the availability of terminals that permit almost instantaneous processing of credit- and debit-card transactions.

The Relational Database Model

 Dr. E. F. Codd, an employee of IBM Corporation, published "A Relational Model of Data for Large Shared Databanks" in a journal of the Association for Computing Machinery (ACM) in June 1970. A partial copy of the paper is available at http://www.acm.org/classics/nov95/. Dr. Codd's specialty was a branch of mathematics called set theory, which includes the concept of *relations.* He defined a relation as a named set of *tuples* (records or rows) that have *attributes* (fields or columns). One of the attributes must contain a unique value to identify each tuple. The common term for relation is a *table* whose presentation to the user is similar to that of a spreadsheet.

> **note**
>
> Hierarchical databases remain alive and well in the twenty-first century. For example, data storage for Windows 2000's Active Directory and Microsoft Exchange Server is derived from the hierarchical version of Access's original relational Jet databases. The name Jet comes from the original Access database engine called *Joint Engine Technology.*
>
> The Internet's Domain Name System (DNS) is a collection of hierarchical databases for translating character-based Internet domain names into numerical Internet Protocol (IP) addresses. The DNS database is called a *distributed database,* because its data is held by a global network of thousands of computers.

Relational databases solve a serious problem associated with earlier database types. Hierarchical and network databases define sets of data and explicit links between each data set as parent-child and owner-member, respectively. To extract information from these databases, programmers had to know the structure of the entire database. Complex programs in COBOL or other mainframe computer languages are needed to navigate through the hierarchy or network and extract information into a format understandable by users.

Dr. Codd's objective was to simplify the process of extracting formatted information and make adding or altering data easier by eliminating complex navigational programming. During the 1970s, Dr. Codd and others developed a comparatively simple language, Structured Query Language (SQL), for creating, manipulating, and retrieving relational data. With a few hours of training, ordinary database users could write SQL statements to define simple information needs and bypass the delays inherent in the database programming process. SQL, which was first standardized in 1985, now is the *lingua franca* of database programming, and all commercial database products support SQL.

Client/Server and Desktop RDBMSs

In the early database era, the most common presentation of data took the form of lengthy reports processed by centralized, high-speed impact printers on fan-folded paper. The next step was to present data to the user on green-screen video terminals, often having small printers attached, which were connected to mainframe databases. As use of personal computers gained momentum, terminal emulator cards enabled PCs to substitute for mainframe terminals. Mainframe-scale relational databases, such as IBM's DB2, began to supplement and later replace hierarchical and network databases, but terminals continued to be the primary means of data entry and retrieval.

Oracle, Ingres, Informix, Sybase, and other software firms developed relational databases for lower-cost minicomputers, most of which ran various flavors of the UNIX operating system. Terminals continued to be the primary data entry and display systems for multiuser UNIX databases.

The next step was the advent of early PC-based flat-file managers and relational database management systems. Early flat-file database managers, typified by Jim Button's PCFile for DOS (1981) and Claris FileMaker for Macintosh (1988) and Windows (1992), used a single table to store data and offered few advantages over storing data in a spreadsheet. The early desktop RDBMSs—such as dBASE, Clipper, FoxBase, and Paradox—ran under DOS and didn't support SQL. These products later became available in multiuser versions, adopted SQL features, and eventually migrated to Windows. Access 1.0, which Microsoft introduced in November 1992, rapidly eclipsed its DOS and Windows competitors by virtue of Access's combination of graphical SQL support, versatility, and overall ease of use.

 note

The most widely used SQL standard, SQL-92, was published by the American National Standards Institute (ANSI) in 1992. Few, if any, commercial relational database management systems (RDBMSs) today fully conform to the entire SQL-92 standard. The later SQL-99 (also called SQL3) and SQL-200n specifications add new features that aren't germane to Access databases.

RDBMS competitors have erected an SQL Tower of Babel by adding nonstandard extensions to the language. For example, Microsoft's Transact-SQL (T-SQL) for SQL Server, which is the subject of Chapter 27, "Moving from Access Queries to Transact-SQL," has many proprietary keywords and features. Oracle Corporation's Oracle:SQL and PL/SQL dialects also have proprietary SQL extensions.

PC-based desktop RDBMSs are classified as shared-file systems because they store their data in conventional files that multiple users can share on a network. One of Access's initial attractions for users and developers was its capability to store all application objects—forms, reports, and programming code—and tables for a database application in a single file, which used the earlier .mdb extension.. FoxPro, dBASE, Clipper, and Paradox require a multitude of individual files to store application and data objects. Today, almost every multiuser Access application is divided (split) into a front-end .accdb file, which contains application objects and links to a back-end database .accdb file that holds the data. Each user has a copy of the front-end .accdb file and shares connections to a single back-end .accdb file on a peer Windows workstation or server.

Client/server RDBMSs have an architecture similar to Access's front-end/back-end shared-file multiuser configuration. What differentiates client/server from shared-file architecture is that the RDBMS on the server handles most of the data-processing activity. The client front end provides a graphical user interface (GUI) for data entry, display, and reporting. Only SQL statements and the specific data requested by the user pass over the network. Client/server databases traditionally run on network operating systems, such as Windows and UNIX, and are much more robust than

note

Prior to Access 2000, Jet was Access's standard database engine, so the terms *Access database* and *Jet database* were interchangeable. Microsoft considered SQL Server to be its *strategic* RDBMS for Access 2000 and 2003. *Strategic* means that SQL Server gets continuing development funds and Jet doesn't. Jet 4.0, which was included with Access 2003 and is a part of the Windows XP and later operating systems, is the final version and is headed toward retirement.

Microsoft's Access team decided to enhance Jet 4.0 with the new features described in Chapter 1, "Access 2010 for Access 2007 Users: What's New," change the file extension from .mdb to .accdb, and drop all references to Jet. To reflect this change, this edition uses the terms *Access database* and *SQL Server database*. Unless otherwise noted, *SQL Server* refers to all SQL Server 2005 editions except the Compact and Mobile editions.

shared-file databases, especially for applications in which many users make simultaneous additions, changes, and deletions to the database. All commercial data-driven Web applications use client/server databases.

Since version 1.0, Access has had the capability to connect to client/server databases by linking their tables to an Access database. Linking lets you treat client/server tables almost as if they were native Access tables. Linking uses Microsoft's widely accepted Open Database Connectivity (ODBC) standard, and Access 2010 includes an ODBC driver for SQL Server and Oracle databases. You can purchase licenses for ODBC drivers that support other UNIX or Windows RDBMSs, such as Sybase or Informix, from the database supplier or third parties. Chapter 21, "Linking Access Front Ends to Access and Client/Server Databases," describes the process of linking Access and Microsoft SQL Server 2008 databases. Although Chapter 19 uses SQL Server for its examples, the linking procedure is the same for—or at least similar to—other client/server RDBMSs.

> **note**
>
> This book uses the terms *field* and *record* when referring to tables, and *columns* and *rows* when discussing data derived from tables, such as the views and query result sets described later in this chapter.

Access data projects (ADP) and the Microsoft SQL Server 2005 Express Edition combine to make Access 2010 a versatile tool for designing and testing client/server databases and creating advanced data entry and reporting applications. You can start with a conventional Access database and later use Access's Upsizing Wizard to convert the .mdb file(s) to an .adp file that holds application objects and an SQL Server 2005 back-end database. Access 2010's Upsizing Wizard has incorporated many improvements to the Access 2000 and earlier wizard versions, but Access 2010's Wizard is the same as 2007's. Despite the upgraded wizardry, you're likely to need to make changes to queries to accommodate differences between Access and SQL Server's SQL dialects.

➡ *For an example of differences between Access and SQL Server SQL syntax that affects the upsizing process,* **see** *"Displaying Data with Queries and Views,"* **p. 174**.

Defining the Structure of Relational Databases

Relational databases consist of a collection of self-contained, related tables. Tables typically represent classes of physical objects, such as customers, sales orders, invoices, checks, products for sale, or employees. Each member object, such as an invoice, has its own record in the invoices table. For invoices, the field that uniquely identifies a record, called a *primary key[field]*, is a serial invoice number.

Figure 4.1 shows Access's Datasheet view of an Invoices table, which is based on the Northwind.mdb sample database's Orders table. The InvoiceNo field is the primary key. Values in the OrderID, CustomerID, EmployeeID, and ShipperID fields relate to primary key values in Northwind's Orders, Customers, Employees, and Shippers tables. A field that contains values equal to those of primary key values in other tables is called a *foreign key [field]*.

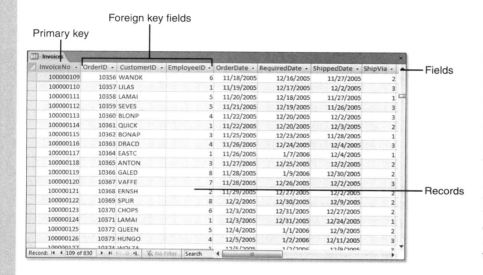

Primary key

Foreign key fields

Fields

Records

Figure 4.1
This simple Invoices table was created from the Northwind Orders table and doesn't take advantage of Access's extended properties, such as the field captions, lookup fields, and sub-datasheets in the Datasheet view of the Orders table.

To learn more about primary keys in Access tables, **see** *"Selecting a Primary Key,"* **p. 221**.

If you need information about a particular invoice or set of invoices, open the Invoices table and search for the invoice(s) by number (InvoiceNo) or another attribute, such as a customer code (CustomerID), date (ShippedDate), or range of dates. Unlike earlier database models, the user can access the Invoices table independently of its related tables. No database navigation programming is needed. A simple, intuitive SQL statement, SELECT * FROM Invoices, returns all the data in the table. The asterisk (*) represents a request to display the contents of all fields of the table.

Removing Data Redundancy with Relationships

The Invoices table of Figure 4.1 is similar to a spreadsheet containing customer billing information. What's missing is the customer name and address information. A five-character customer code (CustomerID) identifies each customer to whom the invoice is directed. The CustomerID values in the Invoices table match CustomerID values in a modified version of Northwind's Customers table (see Figure 4.2). Matching a foreign key with a primary key value often is called a *lookup operation*.

Using a key-based lookup operation eliminates the need to repeatedly enter name, address, and other customer-specific data in the Invoices table. In addition, if you change the customer's address, the change applies to all past and future invoices.

Figure 4.2
Foreign key values in the Invoices table must match primary key values in the Customers table.

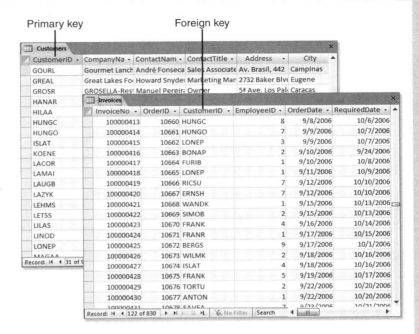

The Invoices table also connects with other tables, which contain information on orders, sales department employees, and the products ordered. Connections between fields of related tables having common values are called *relationships* (not relations). Figure 4.3 shows Access's Relationships window displaying the relationships between the Invoices table and the other tables of the Northwind sample database.

Relationships come in the following three flavors:

- *One-to-many* relationships represent connections between a single primary key value (the "one" side) and multiple instances of the same value in the foreign key field (the "many" side). One-to-many relationships commonly are identified by the number 1 and the infinity (∞) symbol, as in Figure 4.3. All the direct relationships between the tables in Figure 4.3 are one-to-many. One-to-many—also called many-to-one—relationships are by far the most common.

- *One-to-one* relationships connect primary key values in two tables. You might think that the relationship between the Orders and Invoices tables could be one-to-one, but an order requires more than one invoice if one or more items are backordered and then shipped later. One-to-one relationships are uncommon.

tip

Using derived key values, such as alphabetic codes for Customer, is no longer in favor among database designers. Most designers now use automatically generated numerical key values—called Access AutoNumber or SQL Server *identity* fields. The Northwind Orders and Products tables, among others, have primary keys that use the AutoNumber data type. The Employees, Shippers, Products, and Suppliers tables use AutoNumber keys to identify the persons or objects to which the table's records refer. Objects that are inherently sequentially numbered, such as checks, are ideal candidates for an AutoNumber key that corresponds to the check number, as mentioned in "Choosing Primary Key Codes" later in this chapter.

Another method of generating unique keys is by use of Globally Unique Identifiers (GUIDs), which also are called Universally Unique Identifiers (UUIDs). GUIDs are 16-byte computed binary numbers that are guaranteed to be unique locally and universally; no other computer in the world will duplicate a GUID. SQL Server's uniqueidentifier data type is a GUID. Because GUIDs can't represent a property of an object, such as a check number, GUID keys are called *surrogate keys*. You can't select a GUID data type in Access's Table Design mode.

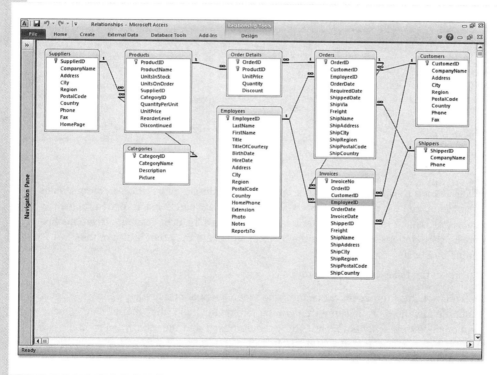

Figure 4.3
Access's Relationships window displays the relationships between the tables of the Northwind sample database, plus the added Invoices table. Every relationship between these tables is one-to-many. The many-to-many relationship between Products and Orders is an indirect relationship.

- *Many-to-many* relationships require three tables, one of which is called a *linking table*. The linking table must have two foreign keys, each of which has a many-to-one relationship with a primary key in two related tables. In the example of Figure 4.3, the Order Details table is the linking table for the many-to-many relationship between the Orders and Products tables. Many-to-many relationships also are called indirect relationships.

There are many other indirect relationships between the tables shown in Figure 4.3. For example, a many-to-many relationship exists between the Suppliers and Orders tables. In this case, Products and Order Details act as linking tables between the Suppliers and Orders tables.

 The Relationships window displays the names of primary key fields in a boldface font. Notice in Figure 4.3 that the OrderID and ProductID field names are preceded by a key symbol. The OrderID and ProductID fields compose a *composite primary key*, which uniquely identifies an order line item. You can't repeat the same combination of OrderID and ProductID; this precaution makes sense for products that have only one stock-keeping unit (SKU), such as for Aniseed Syrup, which comes only in a carton of 12 550ml bottles.

🔍 note

Access 2010's multivalue field feature automatically generates a hidden linking table "under the covers." Access 2007 introduced the multivalued field for compatibility with SharePoint lists.

The Oakmont.accdb sample database file in the \2010Samples\Oakmont folder of the downloadable code has a structure that differs from that of Northwind.accdb, but the design principles of the two databases are similar. OakmontSQL.mdf is an SQL Server 2008 database for use with ADP. ADP uses a special set of tools—called the *project designer* or *da Vinci toolset* in this book—for designing and managing SQL Server databases. The Oakmont files are course enrollment databases for a college. Figure 4.4 shows the Database Diagram window for the OakmontSQL database. The SQL Server Diagram window is similar to the Relationships window for Access's traditional Access databases. The key and infinity symbols at the ends of each line represent the one and many sides, respectively, of the one-to-many relationships between the tables. Access and SQL Server databases store information on table relationships as an object within the database file.

Figure 4.4
The SQL Server Database Diagram window for the OakmontSQL database shows one-to-many relationships between primary key fields (identified by key symbols) and foreign key fields (infinity symbols).

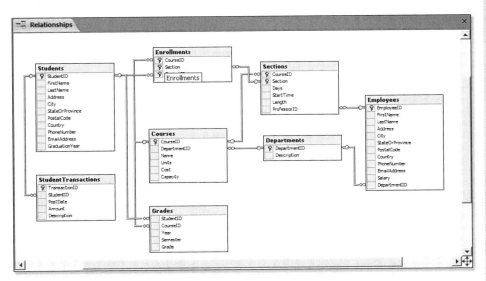

This book uses the Access 2010 and SQL Server 2008 R2 versions of the Northwind and Oakmont sample databases in almost all examples. The tables of the Oakmont database have many more records than the Northwind tables. The large number of records in the Oakmont database makes it better suited than Northwind for predicting the performance of production Access and SQL Server database applications.

 note

The one-product-entry-per-order restriction prevents shared use of the Order Details table as an invoice line items table. If you short-ship an order item on one invoice, you can't add another record to the Order Details table when you ship the remaining quantity of the item. Microsoft didn't add an Invoices table for Northwind Traders, probably because of the complexity of dealing with backorders and drop-shipments.

Conforming to Table Design Rules

Designing tables for relational databases follows a formalized procedure called *normalization*. Dr. Codd described the complete normalization process in his 1972 paper "Further Normalization of the Data Base Relational Model." This paper isn't an easy read; it's steeped in the language of set theory and relational algebra. The sections that follow explain in common English the application of the normalization process to Access's Northwind database.

You normalize tables in a series of steps called *normal forms*. Applying the normalization process is necessary to move spreadsheet-style data to relational tables. You also employ the normalization rules when designing a new database or analyzing existing databases. In specific cases, however, you might need to depart from strict adherence to normalization rules to retain a history of data values that change over time or to improve performance of a large database.

First Normal Form

First normal form requires tables to be flat and have no repeating or potentially repeating fields or groups of fields. A *flat table* is one in which every record has the same number of fields. In addition, a single field cannot contain multiple data values. Repeating fields must be moved to a related table. The first normal form is the most important of the normalization steps. If all your tables don't meet the rules of first normal form, you are in *big* trouble.

Northwind's Customers and Suppliers tables violate the no repeating fields rule. If a customer or supplier has more than one person involved in the ordering process, which is likely, the table would need repeating pairs of fields with different names, such as ContactName2 and ContactTitle2 or the like. To conform the Customers and Suppliers tables to first normal form, you must create two new tables—CustPers(sonel) and SuppPers(sonel), for example—to hold contact records. Including contact names in the Customers and Suppliers tables also violates third normal form, which is the subject of the later "Third Normal Form" section.

The ContactName field also violates the rule against multiple data values in a single field by combining given and family names. This isn't a serious violation of first normal form, but it's a good database design practice always to identify persons by given and family names in separate fields. When you create the new CustPers and SuppPers tables, separate the ContactName field into two fields, such as LastName and GivenName, which can include initials. You can then use a code similar to that for CustomerID for the ContactID field. For this example, the ContactID code is the first character of GivenName and the first four characters of LastName. Alternatively, you could assign an AutoNumber value to ContactID.

Figure 4.5 shows the first 19 of the 91 records of the CustPers table generated from the Customers table. The CustomerID field is required for a many-to-one relationship with the Customers table. Additional fields, such as Suffix, TitleOfCourtesy, Email(Address), Phone, and Fax, make the individual contact records more useful for creating mailing lists and integration with other applications, such as Microsoft Outlook.

Figure 4.5
You extract data for records of the CustPers table from the ContactName and ContactTitle fields of the Customers table. Separating given and last names simplifies generating a ContactID code to identify each record.

ContactID	Custome	LastName	GivenNar	Suff	Title	1
MANDE000	ALFKI	Anders	Maria		Sales Representative	F
ATRUJ000	ANATR	Trujillo	Ana		Owner	
AMORE000	ANTON	Moreno	Antonio		Owner	
THARD000	AROUT	Hardy	Thomas	, Jr.	Sales Representative	N
CBERG000	BERGS	Berglund	Christina		Order Administrator	N
HMOOS000	BLAUS	Moos	Hanna		Sales Representative	F
FCITE000	BLONP	Citeaux	Frédérique		Marketing Manager	N
MSOMM000	BOLID	Sommer	Martín		Owner	N
LLEBI000	BONAP	Lebihan	Laurence		Owner	N
ELINC000	BOTTM	Lincoln	Elizabeth		Accounting Manager	N
VASHW000	BSBEV	Ashworth	Victoria		Sales Representative	N
PSIMP000	CACTU	Simpson	Patricio		Sales Agent	N
FCHAN000	CENTC	Chang	Francisco		Marketing Manager	N
YWANG000	CHOPS	Wang	Yang		Owner	N
PAFON000	COMMI	Afonso	Pedro		Sales Associate	S
EBROW000	CONSH	Brown	Elizabeth		Sales Representative	N
SOTTL000	DRACD	Ottlieb	Sven		Order Administrator	N
JLABR000	DUMON	Labrune	Janine		Owner	N
ADEVO000	EASTC	Devon	Ann		Sales Agent	A

Record: 1 of 91 — No Filter — Search

For more information on importing from Excel, **see** *"Importing and Linking Spreadsheet Files,"* **p. 298.**

To learn how to use Access action queries, **see** *"Creating Action Queries to Append Records to a Table,"* **p. 543.**

Figure 4.6 shows the Relationships window with the CustPers and SuppPers tables added to the Northwind database and their many-to-one relationships with the Customers and Suppliers tables, respectively.

 tip

You don't need to retype the data to populate the CustPers and SuppPers tables. You can use Access to import the data from an Excel worksheet or text file, or use Access action queries (append and update) to handle this chore.

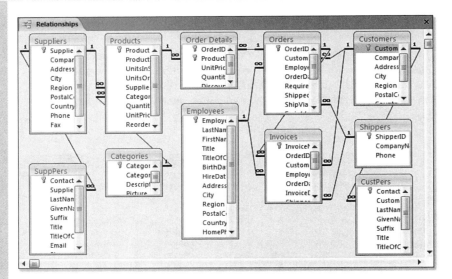

Figure 4.6
The Relationships window displays the many-to-one relationships between the Customers and CustPers tables and the Suppliers and SuppPers tables.

Second Normal Form

Second normal form requires that data in all non-key fields be fully dependent on the value of a primary key. The objective of second normal form is to avoid data redundancy in your tables.

Only Northwind's Order Details linking table (see Figure 4.7) has a composite primary key (OrderID + ProductID). The UnitPrice field appears to violate the second normal form, because UnitPrice is a field of the Products table. UnitPrice values added to the Order Details table are dependent on the ProductID component of the composite primary key and not the OrderID component, so UnitPrice data is not *fully dependent* on the primary key. On first glance, the UnitPrice field appears to be redundant data. If you change the unit price of a product, it would appear that you would need to alter the UnitPrice value in every Order Details record for the product.

The Order Details table is an example of a situation in which you *must* retain what appears to be redundant information to maintain the integrity of historical data. Prices of products vary over time, so the price of a particular product is likely to change for orders placed on different dates. If the price of a product changes between the order and shipping (invoice) dates, the invoice reflects a different amount than the order. Despite the "Prices are subject to change without notice" boilerplate, customers become incensed if the invoice price is greater than the order price.

Eliminating the UnitPrice field from the Order Details table and looking up its value from the current price in the Products table also can cause accounting errors and distortion of historical reports based on bookings and sales data. Removing the UnitPrice data also violates the rules for the fifth normal form, explained later in this chapter.

Figure 4.7
The Order Details linking table has a composite primary key consisting of the OrderID and ProductID fields.

Orde ▾	ProductID ▾	UnitPrice ▾	Quantity ▾	Discount ▾	Add New Field
10248	11	$14.00	12	0%	
10248	42	$9.80	10	0%	
10248	72	$34.80	5	0%	
10249	14	$18.60	9	0%	
10249	51	$42.40	40	0%	
10250	41	$7.70	10	0%	
10250	51	$42.40	35	15%	
10250	65	$16.80	15	15%	
10251	22	$16.80	6	5%	
10251	57	$15.60	15	5%	
10251	65	$16.80	20	0%	
10252	20	$64.80	40	5%	
10252	33	$2.00	25	5%	
10252	60	$27.20	40	0%	
10253	31	$10.00	20	0%	
10253	39	$14.40	42	0%	
10253	49	$16.00	40	0%	
10254	24	$3.60	15	15%	
10254	55	$19.20	21	15%	

Record: ◄ ◄ 1 of 2155 ► ►I ►☒   No Filter   Search

Third Normal Form

Third normal form requires that data in all non-key fields of the table be fully dependent on the value of the primary key and describe only the object that the table represents. In other words, make sure that the table doesn't include non-key fields that relate to some other object or process and includes non-key fields for descriptive data that isn't contained in another related table.

As mentioned in the "First Normal Form" section, including contact information in the Customers and Products table violates third normal form rules. Contacts are persons, not customer or supplier organizations, and deserve their own related table that has attributes related to individuals.

Other examples of a common third normal form violation are the UnitsInStock and UnitsOnOrder fields of the Products table (see Figure 4.8). These fields aren't fully dependent on the primary key value, nor do they describe the object; they describe how many of the product you have now and how many you might have if the supplier decides to ship your latest order. In a production order entry database, these values vary over time and must be updated for each sale of the product, each purchase order issued to the product's supplier, and each receipt of the product. Purchases, receipts, and invoices tables are the most common source of the data on which the calculations are based.

Including UnitsInStock and UnitsOnOrder fields isn't a serious violation of the normalization rules, and it's not uncommon for product-based tables of order entry databases to include calculated values. The problem with calculated inventory values is the need to process a potentially large number of records in other tables to obtain an accurate current value.

Products							
ProductID ▾	ProductName ▾	UnitsInStock ▾	UnitsOnOrder ▾	SupplierID ▾	CategoryID ▾	QuantityPerUnit ▲	
1	Chai	39	0	1	1	10 boxes x 20 bags	
2	Chang	17	40	1	1	24 - 12 oz bottles	
3	Aniseed Syrup	13	70	1	2	12 - 550 ml bottles	
4	Chef Anton's Cajun S	53	0	2	2	48 - 6 oz jars	
5	Chef Anton's Gumbo	0	0	2	2	36 boxes	
6	Grandma's Boysenbe	120	0	3	2	12 - 8 oz jars	
7	Uncle Bob's Organic I	15	0	3	7	12 - 1 lb pkgs.	
8	Northwoods Cranber	6	0	3	2	12 - 12 oz jars	
9	Mishi Kobe Niku	29	0	4	6	18 - 500 g pkgs.	
10	Ikura	31	0	4	8	12 - 200 ml jars	
11	Queso Cabrales	22	30	5	4	1 kg pkg.	
12	Queso Manchego La	86	0	5	4	10 - 500 g pkgs.	
13	Konbu	24	0	6	8	2 kg box	
14	Tofu	35	0	6	7	40 - 100 g pkgs.	
15	Genen Shouyu	39	0	6	2	24 - 250 ml bottles	
16	Pavlova	29	0	7	3	32 - 500 g boxes	
17	Alice Mutton	0	0	7	6	20 - 1 kg tins	
18	Carnarvon Tigers	42	0	7	8	16 kg pkg.	
19	Teatime Chocolate B	25	0	8	3	10 boxes x 12 piece	

Record: I◄ ◄ 1 of 77 ► ►I ►▷ 𝕏 No Filter | Search

Figure 4.8
The Products table's UnitsInStock and UnitsOnOrder values must be calculated from data in tables that record purchases, receipts, and shipments of products.

Fourth Normal Form

Fourth normal form requires that tables not contain fields for two or more independent, multivalued facts. Loosely translated, this rule requires splitting tables that consist of lists of independent attributes. The Northwind and Oakmont databases don't have an example of a fourth normal form violation, so the following is a fabricated example.

One of the objectives of Human Resources departments is to match employee job skills with job openings. A multinational organization is likely to require a combination of specific job skills and language fluency for a particular assignment. A table of job skill types and levels exists with entries such as JP3 for Java Programmer–Intermediate, as well as language/fluency with entries such as TE5 for Telugu–Very Fluent. Therefore, the HR department constructs an EmplSkillLang linking table with the following foreign key fields: EmployeeID, SkillID, and LanguageID.

 tip

If you're designing an order entry database, make sure to take into account committed inventory. Committed inventory consists of products in stock or en route from suppliers for which you have unfulfilled orders. If you decide to include inventory information in a products table, add a UnitsCommitted field.

The problem with the linking table is that job skills and language fluency are independent facts about an employee. The ability to speak French has nothing to do with an employee's ability to write Java code. Therefore, the HR department must split (decompose) the three-field table into two two-field linking tables: EmplSkills and EmplLangs.

Fifth Normal Form

Fifth normal form involves further reducing redundancy by creating multiple two-field tables from tables that have more than two foreign keys. The classic example is identifying independent sales agents who sell multiple products or categories of products for different companies. In this case, you have a table with AgentID, CompanyID, and ProductID or CategoryID. You can reduce redundancy—at the risk of making the database design overly complex—by creating three two-field tables: AgentCompany, CompanyProduct (or CompanyCategory), and AgentProduct (or AgentCategory). Database developers seldom attempt to normalize designs to fifth normal form because doing so requires adding many additional small tables to the database.

 tip

AutoNumber primary key values work well for serially numbered documents if you don't allow records to be deleted. Adding a true-false (Boolean) field named Deleted and setting the value to true is one approach. This technique complicates queries against the tables, so you might consider moving deleted records to another table. Doing this lets you write a query to reconstruct all records for audit purposes.

Choosing Primary Key Codes

All Northwind and Oakmont tables use codes for primary key values, as do almost all production databases. The critical requirement is that the primary key value is unique to each record in the table. Following are some tips, many with online resources, to aid in establishing primary key codes:

- Many types of tables—such as those for storing information on sales orders, invoices, purchase orders, and checks—are based on documents that have consecutive serial numbers, which are obvious choices for unique primary key values. In fact, most database designs begin with collecting and analyzing the paper forms used by an organization. If the table itself or programming code generates the consecutive number, make sure that every serial number is present in the table, even if an order is canceled or voided. Auditors are *very* suspicious of invoice and purchase order registers that skip serial numbers.

- Packaged retail products sold in the United States have a globally unique 10-digit or longer Uniform Product Code (UPC). The UPC identifies both the supplier and the product's SKU. The Uniform Code Council, Inc. (http://www.uc-council.org/) assigns supplier and product ID values, which are combined into linear bar codes for automated identification and data capture (AIDC). The European Article Number (EAN) is coordinated with the UPC to prevent duplication. The UPC/EAN code is a much better choice than Microsoft's serially assigned number for the ProductID field.

- Books have 10-digit and 13-digit International Standard Book Number (ISBN) codes that are unique throughout the world and, in North America, a UPC. ISBNs include a publisher prefix and book number, assigned to U.S. publishers by the U.S. ISBN Agency (http://www.bowker.com/standards/home/isbn/us/isbnus.html). ISBN Group Agencies assign codes for other countries. Canada has separate agencies for English- and French-language books. Either a UPC or ISBN field is suitable for the primary key of a North American books database, but ISBN is preferred if the code is for books only.

- The North American Industry Classification System (NAICS, pronounced *nakes*) is replacing the U.S. Standard Industrial Classification (SIC) for categorizing organizations by their type of business. A six-digit primary key code for 18,000 classifications replaces the four-digit SIC code. Five of the six digits represent codes for classifications common to the United States, Canada, and Mexico. You can view a text file or purchase a CD-ROM of the NAICS codes and their SIC counterparts at http://www.naics.com/.

- The U.S. Postal Service offers Address Information Systems (AIS) files for verifying addresses and corresponding ZIP/ZIP+4 codes. For more information on these files, go to http://www.usps.com and click the Address Quality link.

- Social Security Numbers (SSNs) for U.S. residents are a possible choice for a primary key of an Employees table, but their disclosure compromises employees' privacy. Large numbers of counterfeit Social Security cards having identical numbers circulate in the United States, making SSN even less attractive as a primary key field. The Oakmont database uses fictitious nine-digit SSNs for EmployeeID and StudentID fields. Most organizations assign each employee a sequential serial number. Sequential EmployeeID numbers can do double duty as seniority-level indicators.

Specifying a primary key for tables such as CustPers isn't easy. If you use the five-character code based on first and last names for the primary key, you encounter the problem with potential duplication of CustomerID codes discussed earlier. In this case, however, common last names—Jones, Smith, and Anderson, for example—quickly result in duplicate values. Creating a composite primary key from CustomerID and ContactID is a potential solution; doing this increases the number of new contacts you can add for a company before inevitable duplicates occur. In most cases, it's easier to use an AutoNumber key for all ID values.

Figure 4.9 shows the final design of the modified Northwind database with the added contact details tables. The tables of this database are included on the accompanying CD-ROM as Nwind04. mdb in the \2010Samples\Chaptr04 folder.

The modified Northwind database doesn't qualify as a full-fledged customer relationship management (CRM) system, but the design is sufficiently flexible to serve as the model for a sales and purchasing database for a small-sized wholesale or retail concern.

Maintaining Data Integrity and Accuracy

When you add, modify, or delete table data, it's important that the additions and changes you make to the data don't conflict with the normalization rules that you used to create the database. One of the most vexing problems facing users of large RDBMs is "unclean data." Over time, data entry errors and stray records accumulate to the point where obtaining accurate historical information from the database becomes difficult or impossible. Software vendors and database consultants have created a major-scale "data cleansing" business to solve the problem. You can avoid the time and expense of retroactive corrections to your data by taking advantage of Access and SQL Server features that aid in preventing errors during the data entry process.

 note

You also must avoid changing the primary keys of or deleting one of two tables in a one-to-one relationship.

Figure 4.9
The final design of the expanded Northwind database with customer and supplier contact details tables added.

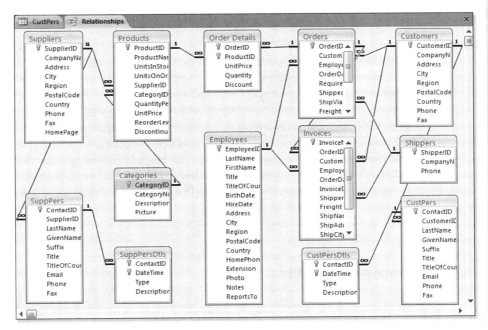

Referential Integrity

Maintaining referential integrity requires strict adherence to a single rule: *Each foreign key value in a related table must correspond with a primary key value in a base (primary) table.* This rule requires that the following types of modifications to data be prevented:

- Adding a record on the many side of a one-to-many relationship without the existence of a related record on the one side of the relationship (for example, adding a record to the Orders table with a CustomerID value of BOGUS when no such customer record exists in the Customers table)

- Deleting a record on the one side of a one-to-many relationship without first deleting all corresponding records on the many side of the relationship (for example, deleting Around the Horn's Customers record when the Orders table contains records with AROUT as the CustomerID value)

- Changing the value of a primary key field of a base table on which records in a related base or linking table depend, such as changing AROUT to ABOUT in the CustomerID field of the Customers table

 note

Keypunch operators kept their eyes on the source documents, which gave rise to the term *heads-down data entry*. The term continues in common use to describe any data entry process in which the operator attention is fully devoted to adding or editing database records as quickly as possible.

- Changing the value of a foreign key field in a linking table to a value that doesn't exist in the primary key field of a base table (for example, changing AROUT to ABOUT in the CustomerID field for OrderID 10355)

A record in a related table that doesn't have a corresponding foreign key value in the primary key of a base table is called an *orphan record*. For example, if the CustomerID value of a record in the Orders table is ABCDE and no ABCDE value exists in the CustomerID primary key field of the Customers table, there's no way to determine which customer placed the order.

Access and SQL Server databases offer the option of automatically enforcing referential integrity when adding or updating data. Cascading updates and deletions are optional. If you specify cascading updates, changing the value of a primary key of a table makes the identical change to the foreign key value in related tables. Cascading deletions delete all related records with a foreign key that corresponds to the primary key of a record in a base table that you want to delete.

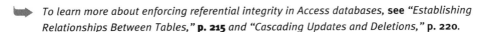 *To learn more about enforcing referential integrity in Access databases,* **see** *"Establishing Relationships Between Tables,"* **p. 215** *and "Cascading Updates and Deletions,"* **p. 220.**

Entity Integrity and Indexes

When you add new records to a base table, entity integrity assures that each primary key value is unique. Access and SQL Server ensure entity integrity by adding a no-duplicates index to the field you specify for the primary key. If duplicate values exist when you attempt to designate a field as the primary key, you receive an error message. You receive a similar error message if you enter a duplicate primary key value in the table.

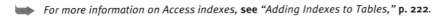 *For more information on Access indexes,* **see** *"Adding Indexes to Tables,"* **p. 222.**

Indexes also speed searches of tables and improve performance when executing SQL statements that return data from fields of base and related tables.

Data Validation Rules and Check Constraints

Data entry errors are another major source of "unclean data." In the days of punched-card data entry, keypunch operators typed the data, and verifiers, who usually worked during the succeeding shift, inserted the cards in a punched-card reader and repeated the keystrokes from the same source document. This process detected typographical errors, which the verifier corrected. Keypunch operators had no visual feedback during data entry, so typos were inevitable; video display terminals didn't arrive until the mainframe era.

Rekeying data leads to low productivity, so most data entry applications support data validation rules designed to detect attempts to enter illegal or unreasonable values in fields. An example of a validation rule is preventing entry of a shipping date that's earlier than the order date. The rule is expressed as an inequality: ShipDate >= OrderDate, which returns False if the rule is violated. Similarly, UnitPrice > 0 prevents accidentally giving away a line item of an order.

Access tables and fields have a Validation Rule property that you set to the inequality expression. SQL Server calls validation rules *check constraints.* Both Access and SQL Server have a Validation Text property for which you specify the text to appear in an error message box when the entry violates the rule or constraint. It's a more common practice when working with client/server databases to validate data in the front-end application before sending the entry to the back-end server. Detecting the error on the server and returning an error message requires a *roundtrip* from the client to the server. Server roundtrips generate quite a bit of network traffic and reduce data entry efficiency. One of the objectives of client/server front-end design is to minimize server round-tripping.

 To learn more about Access's validation methods, **see** *"Validating Data Entry,"* **p. 254.**

Transactions

A database transaction occurs when multiple records in one or more tables must be added, deleted, or modified to complete a data entry operation. Adding an order or invoice that has multiple line items is an example of a transaction. If an order or invoice has five line items, but a network or database problem prevents adding one or more item records, the entire order or invoice is invalid. Maintaining referential integrity prevents adding line item records without a corresponding order or invoice record, but missing item records don't violate integrity rules.

Transaction processing (TP), also called *online transaction processing (OLTP),* solves the missing line item problem. Requiring TP for order entry, invoice processing, and similar multirecord operations enforces an all-or-nothing rule. If every individual update to the tables' records occurs, the transaction succeeds (*commits*); if any update fails, changes made before the failure occurs are reversed (*rolled back*). Transaction processing isn't limited to RDBMSs. Early mainframe databases offered TP and transaction monitors. IBM's Customer Information and Control System (CICS, pronounced *kicks*) was one of the first transaction processing and monitoring systems, and it remains in widespread use today.

Access and SQL Server databases offer built-in TP features. Access has a Use Transactions property that you set to Yes to require TP for updates. SQL Server traditionally requires writing T-SQL statements—BEGIN TRANS, COMMIT TRANS, and ROLLBACK TRANS—to manage transactions, but Access 2010's ADP forms have a new Batch Updates property that lets you enforce transactions without writing complex T-SQL statements.

> ### 🔍 note
>
> As mentioned earlier in the chapter, *fields* become *columns* and *records* become *rows* in a query. This terminology is an arbitrary convention of this book and not related to relational database design theory. The reason for the change in terminology is that a query's rows and columns need not—and often do not—represent data values stored in the underlying tables. Queries can have columns whose values are calculated from multiple fields and rows with aggregated data, such as subtotals and totals.

 For a brief description of the batch update feature introduced by Access 2007, see *"Changes to ADP Features," in Online Appendix B.*

Displaying Data with Queries and Views

So far, this chapter has concentrated on designing relational databases and their tables, and adding or altering data. SQL SELECT queries return data to Access, but you don't need to write SQL statements to display data in forms or print reports from the data. Access has built-in graphical tools to automatically write Access SQL for Access databases and T-SQL for SQL Server databases. Access's query tools use a modern implementation of *query-by-example (QBE)*, an IBM trademark. QBE is a simple method of specifying the tables and columns to view, how the data is sorted, and rows to include or exclude.

Linking related tables by their primary and foreign keys is called *joining* the tables. Early QBE programs required defining joins between tables; specifying table relationships automatically defines joins when you add records from two or more related Access or SQL Server tables.

Figure 4.10 is an example of Access's QBE implementation for Access databases, called Query Design View. You add tables to the query—in this case, Northwind's Customers, Orders, and Employees tables. As you add the tables, join lines indicate the relationships between them. You drag the field names for the query columns from the table lists in the upper pane to the Field row of the lower pane. You also can specify the name of a calculated column (Salesperson) and the expression to create the column values ([FirstName] & "" & [LastName]) in the Field row. The brackets surrounding FirstName and LastName designate that the values are field names.

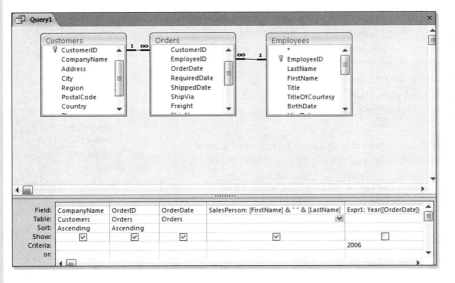

Figure 4.10
Access's Query Design view for Access databases uses graphical QBE to create queries you can store in the database.

Selecting Ascending or Descending in the Sort column orders the rows in left-to-right column priority. You can restrict the display to a particular set of values by adding an expression in the Criteria column.

Running the query returns the resultset, part of which is shown by Figure 4.11. You can save the query for later reuse as a named Access QueryDef(inition) object in the database.

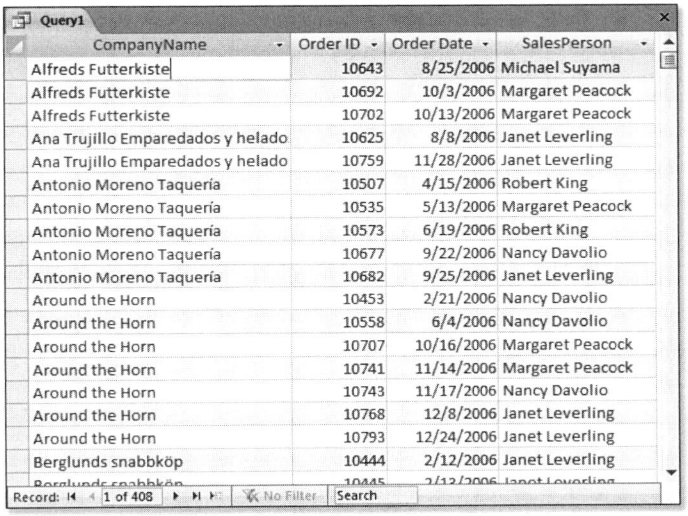

Figure 4.11
These are the first 16 of the 408 rows of the query resultset returned by executing the query design of Figure 4.10.

CompanyName	Order ID	Order Date	SalesPerson
Alfreds Futterkiste	10643	8/25/2006	Michael Suyama
Alfreds Futterkiste	10692	10/3/2006	Margaret Peacock
Alfreds Futterkiste	10702	10/13/2006	Margaret Peacock
Ana Trujillo Emparedados y helado	10625	8/8/2006	Janet Leverling
Ana Trujillo Emparedados y helado	10759	11/28/2006	Janet Leverling
Antonio Moreno Taquería	10507	4/15/2006	Robert King
Antonio Moreno Taquería	10535	5/13/2006	Margaret Peacock
Antonio Moreno Taquería	10573	6/19/2006	Robert King
Antonio Moreno Taquería	10677	9/22/2006	Nancy Davolio
Antonio Moreno Taquería	10682	9/25/2006	Janet Leverling
Around the Horn	10453	2/21/2006	Nancy Davolio
Around the Horn	10558	6/4/2006	Nancy Davolio
Around the Horn	10707	10/16/2006	Margaret Peacock
Around the Horn	10741	11/14/2006	Margaret Peacock
Around the Horn	10743	11/17/2006	Nancy Davolio
Around the Horn	10768	12/8/2006	Janet Leverling
Around the Horn	10793	12/24/2006	Janet Leverling
Berglunds snabbköp	10444	2/12/2006	Janet Leverling
Berglunds snabbköp	10445	2/12/2006	Janet Leverling

Record: 1 of 408   No Filter   Search

Access SQL

Access QBE automatically converts the query design of Figure 4.10 into the following Access SQL statement:

```
SELECT Customers.CompanyName, Orders.OrderID, Orders.OrderDate,
        [FirstName] & "" & [LastName] AS Salesperson
    FROM Employees
        INNER JOIN (Customers
            INNER JOIN Orders
            ON Customers.CustomerID = Orders.CustomerID)
        ON Employees.EmployeeID = Orders.EmployeeID
    WHERE ((Year([OrderDate])=2006))
    ORDER BY Customers.CompanyName, Orders.OrderID;Note
```

It's obvious that using QBE is much simpler than writing SELECT queries to concatenate field values, join tables, establish row selection criteria, and specify sort order. Access's QBE features are powerful; many developers use Access to generate the SQL statements needed by Visual Basic, C++, and Java programs.

The da Vinci QBE tool for creating T-SQL views is similar to the Access Query Design view, but has an additional pane to display the T-SQL statement as you generate it. You add tables to the upper pane and drag field names to the Column cells of the middle pane. An SQL Server view is the client/server equivalent of an Access QueryDef. As with Access QueryDefs, you can execute a query on an SQL Server view.

 note

T-SQL uses + rather than & to concatenate strings, uses a single quote (') as the string delimiter, and requires a numerical instead of a string criterion for the YEAR function. Here's the T-SQL version of the preceding Access SQL statement after the SELECT and WHERE clauses have been tweaked:

The TOP modifier is needed to permit an ORDER BY clause in a view; prior to the addition of the TOP keyword in SQL Server 7.0, creating sorted views wasn't possible. The da Vinci query parser adds the TOP 100 PERCENT modifier if an ORDER BY clause is present. However, TOP 100 PERCENT ... ORDER BY doesn't sort SQL Server 2005 views. Replacing 100 PERCENT with a large integer (⇐= 2147483647) sorts the view.

The dbo. prefix to table and field names is an abbreviation for *database owner*, the default owner for all SQL Server databases you create as a system administrator. Figure 4.12 shows the design of the T-SQL query generated by pasting the preceding statement into the da Vinci query pane.

Despite their common ANSI SQL-92 heritage, SQL Server won't execute most Access SQL statements, and vice versa. Copying the preceding Access SQL statement to the Clipboard and pasting it into the SQL pane of the query designer for the NorthwindCS sample database doesn't work. The da Vinci designer does its best to translate the Access SQL flavor into T-SQL when you paste, but you receive errors when you try to run the query.

```
SELECT TOP (2147483647) dbo.Customers.CompanyName,
       dbo.Orders.OrderID, dbo.Orders.OrderDate,
       dbo.Employees.FirstName + ' ' +
       dbo.Employees.LastName AS Salesperson
  FROM dbo.Employees
     INNER JOIN dbo.Customers
        INNER JOIN dbo.Orders
        ON dbo.Customers.CustomerID = dbo.Orders.CustomerID
     ON dbo.Employees.EmployeeID = dbo.Orders.EmployeeID
  WHERE (YEAR(dbo.Orders.OrderDate) = 2006)
  ORDER BY dbo.Customers.CompanyName, dbo.Orders.OrderID
```

➡ *For more information on the da Vinci toolset,* **see** *"Exploring SQL Server Views," in online Chapter 27.*

➡ *For detailed instructions on installing SQL Server Express and NorthwindCS.adp,* **see** *"SQL Server 2008 [R2] Express Edition,"* **p. 35,** *and "Exploring the NorthwindSQL Sample Project,"* **p. 1093** *.*

The Datasheet view of the SQL Server view generated by the preceding SQL statement is identical to the Access query's Datasheet view shown in Figure 4.11.

Figure 4.12
Pasting an Access SQL statement
into Access's version of the da
Vinci query design tool and mak-
ing a few minor changes to the
T-SQL statement results in an
SQL Server view equivalent to the
Access query of Figure 4.10.

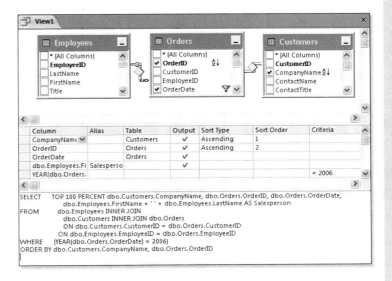

5

WORKING WITH ACCESS DATABASES AND TABLES

Understanding Access Database Files

 Before the arrival of Microsoft Office Access 2007, there was only one extension for Access database files: .mdb. The traditional name for an.mdb file that stores Access application, data objects, or both, has been *Access database* since Microsoft released Access 1.0 in November 1993. As other database programming tools and technologies, such as Visual Basic and ADO.NET, began using .mdb files, *Jet database* became the preferred designation for Access files containing only tables and query definitions. Later versions of Access were only one of many Microsoft applications and programming tools to take advantage of the Jet database engine.

The use of Jet databases in Microsoft products became so widespread that the Windows development group incorporated Jet/Access dynamic link libraries (DLLs) as part of the Windows 2000, XP, 2003, and Vista operating systems. When the Windows team decided to make Jet part of Windows 2000 Professional and Server editions, the SQL Server team took ownership of Jet.

> **tip**
>
> You don't need to upgrade your Access 95–2003 .mdb files to Access 2007 .accdb files unless you require the new SharePoint-specific capabilities or new macro features, such as embedded or data macros.

Upgrading from Jet .mdb to Access .accdb Database Files

Jet 4.0, which Access 2000, 2002, and 2003 use, is the latest *and last* Jet version. The SQL Server team considers its flagship product to be the "strategic database" for Windows applications and is unwilling to invest resources in adding new features to or otherwise improving Jet.

The Access team wanted to increase the compatibility of its database tables with Windows SharePoint Services 3.0 lists. This required new multivalued lookup fields and the Attachment data type. Therefore, the Access team created a new Access-only version of Jet—the *Access Database Engine* (sometimes called the *Access Connectivity Engine,* or *ACE*)—for Access 2007 and later. The upgraded engine requires database files to replace .mdb with an.accdb extension to gain access to the new features. However, Access 2010 also can open, edit, and save.mdb files in Access 2000 and 2002/2003 formats. Access 2010 also lets developers create compiled.accde files that don't allow users to read or modify VBA source code. (Access 2007 .accde files correspond to earlier versions' .mde files.)

> For more information about multivalued lookup fields, **see** *"Creating Multivalued Lookup Fields,"* **p. 450,** and for the Attachment data type, **see** *"Choosing Field Data Types, Sizes, and Formats,"* **p. 191.**

> For more information about embedded macros, **see** *"Generating Embedded Macros with the Command Button Wizard,"* **p. 804.**

Migrating from Access Applications to SQL Server Data Projects

Microsoft's determination to make SQL Server the database engine of choice for Access 2003 and later versions is another reason for changing from Jet to Access terminology for applications that use .accdb and related files. Access 2000 and later versions store application objects—forms, reports, macros, and modules—in a new compound file format called a *DocFile.* Conventional Access applications store the application object DocFile within the .accdb or .mdb file. Access Data Projects (ADP), which now represent the preferred approach to designing Access applications that connect to SQL Server databases, store the DocFile directly on disk as an .adp file. Combining ADP front ends with SQL Server back-end databases eliminates the need to periodically compact .accdb files and occasionally repair corrupted Access databases. The chapters of Part 8, "Creating Access Front Ends to SQL Server Databases," cover designing ADP and SQL Server databases.

 tip

Using ADP and SQL Server databases for simple, single-user Access applications is overkill. You don't need the power of SQL Server 2008 for mailing list, contact management, or similar projects. Creating applications that use Access to store your data is easier than designing and managing SQL Server databases. Therefore, the beginning chapters of this book deal exclusively with Access databases.

> For more information on how to use the Upsizing Wizard, **see** *"Migrating Access Applications to SQL Server with the Upsizing Wizard,"* **p. 873** and *"Upsizing with the Trial-and-Error Approach"* **p. 1173.**

Access Record-Locking Information Files

When you open an .accdb or .mdb file, Access automatically creates a record-locking file having the same name as the database but with an .laccdb or .ldb extension. The purpose of the .laccdb or .ldb file is to maintain for multiuser applications a list of records that each user currently is updating.

The record-locking file prevents data corruption when two or more users simultaneously attempt to change data in the same record. The presence of a record-locking file also prevents two or more users from saving design changes to the same database. If you open a database that another user has open with an object in design mode, you receive a message that you can't save any changes you make. The same restriction applies if you have the same database open in two instances of Access. When all users or instances of Access close the .accdb or .mdb file, Access deletes the .laccdb or .ldb file.

ⓦ tip

If you intend to create multiuser applications, which let several users update the database simultaneously, seriously consider using the no-charge Express Edition of SQL Server 2008 R2 (SSX) to store the data. Consider using SQL Server for any databases whose content is vital to the continued success—or existence—of an organization, such as sales orders, invoices, and accounts receivable. Access 2010 includes an Upsizing Wizard that greatly simplifies moving from Access to SQL Server databases. So, you can start with Access and then move to SQL Server as you become proficient in database application design.

Another reason for migrating your data to SQL Server 2008 R2 is the lack of support for user-level security by the .accdb or .accde file format. Access 2010 does let you edit workgroup files (System.mdw) for changing user-level security settings in existing .mdb or .mde files. The .accdb format offers more secure database password protection than earlier versions, but all users of .accdb or .accde files have Administrator permissions and, as a result, can alter any data and change the design of or delete any object in the database.

Access Add-In (Library) Databases

 Another category of Access database files is *add-ins*, also called *libraries*. Add-ins are Access databases—usually with an .accda, .accde, or .accdu (.mda or .mde for earlier versions) extension to distinguish them from user databases—that you can link to Access by choosing Tools, References in the VBA editor's menu. Alternatively, you can do this through the Add-In Manager, by opening the Add-Ins page of the Access Options dialog. The Add-In Manager also lets you add another class of extensions to Access called *COM Add-ins,* which have a .dll extension, such as Acecnf.dll for the Access Database Engine Conflict Resolver.

When you link an Access add-in, all elements of the library database are available to you after you open Access. The Access 2010 wizards that you use to create forms, reports, graphs, and other application objects are stored in a series of Access add-in database files: Acwzlib.accde, Acwztool.accde, Acwzmain.accde, Utility.accda, Acwzdat14.accdu, and Acwzusr14.accdu. The standard Access wizards don't appear in the Add-In Manager's dialog. Add-in databases are an important and unique feature of Access; third-party firms provide useful libraries to add new features and capabilities to Access.

Creating a New Access Database from Scratch

If you have experience with relational database management systems, you might want to start building your own database as you progress through this book. In this case, you need to create a new database file at this point. If database management systems are new to you, however, you should instead explore the sample databases supplied with Access or ones that you create with templates from the Office Online site and in the book's downloadable online sample files as you progress through the chapters of this book. Before you design your first database, review the principles outlined in Chapter 4, "Exploring Relational Database Theory and Practice." Then return to this section and create your new database file.

 For more information about creating databases from Office Online templates, **see** *"Creating Access Applications from Downloaded Templates,"* **p. 46.**

To create a new Access database in Access 2007 .accdb format, follow these steps:

1. If you aren't already running Access, launch it.

2. If Access doesn't open with the File tab selected, click the File tab and the New button.

3. Optionally, click the folder icon to the right of the File Name text box to open the File New Database dialog (see Figure 5.1).

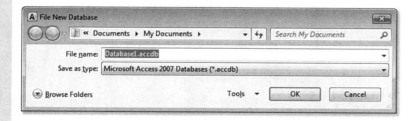

Figure 5.1
Clicking the folder icon of the Getting Started dialog opens the File New Database dialog with Database1.accdb as the default database name, the Documents Library as its location, and Microsoft Access 2010 Databases.

4. In the File Name text box, type a filename for the new database. Use conventional filenaming rules; you can use spaces and punctuation in the name, but doing so isn't a recommended practice. You don't need to include an extension in the filename; Access automatically supplies the .accdb extension.

5. Click OK or press Enter to close the File New Database dialog. Then click Create to close the Getting Started dialog and create the new Access database file (Test.accdb for this example).

If a database was open when you created the new database, Access closes open windows displaying database objects. Then the Navigation pane for the new database opens with a default empty table named Table1.

All Office 2010 applications use DocFiles to store their data and share a similar *FileName* Properties dialog (see Figure 5.2), which opens when you click the File page's View and Edit Database Properties link. Each new .accdb database occupies 340KB of disk space when you create it. Most of the 340KB is space consumed

> **note**
>
> Access supplies the default filename Database1.accdb for new databases and proposes to save the database in your My Documents folder. If you've previously saved a database file as Database1.accdb in the current folder, Access supplies Database2.accdb as the default.

by hidden system tables for adding the information necessary to specify the names and locations of other database elements that the database file contains.

Figure 5.2
The *FileName* Properties dialog for .accdb files has five tabbed pages that contain properties similar to the DocFiles and XML files created by other Office 2007 applications.

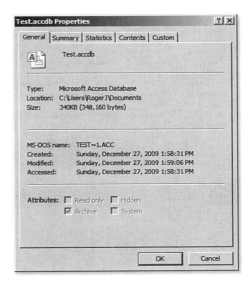

Exploring the Properties of Tables and Fields

Before you add a table to a database that you've created or to one of the sample databases supplied with Access, you need to know the terms and conventions that Access uses to describe the structure of a table and the fields that contain the table's data items. With Access, you specify property values for tables and fields.

Properties of Access tables apply to the table as a whole. You enter properties of tables in text boxes of the Table Properties sheet (see Figure 5.3), which you display by clicking Table Design view, saving Table1, and clicking the Properties button. Setting table property values is optional unless you have a specific reason to override the default values.

Following are brief descriptions of some of the 15 table properties of .accdb databases. The next section details properties related to subdatasheets.

- *Description* is a text explanation of the table's purpose. This description also is useful with a data dictionary, which you use to document databases and database applications.

- *Default View* lets you select from Datasheet, PivotTable, and PivotChart views of a table. The default selection is Datasheet view. PivotTable and PivotChart views of tables seldom are meaningful. Chapter 12, "Working with PivotTable and PivotChart Views," describes how to design queries that optimize the usefulness of these two views.

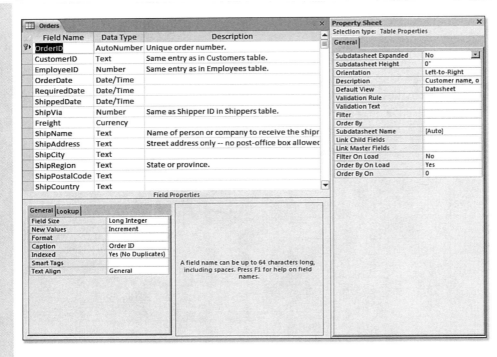

Figure 5.3
The Table
Properties
dialog for
Northwind.
accdb's
Orders table
uses default
values for
all but the
Description
property.

- *Validation Rule* is an expression (formula) that's used to establish domain integrity rules for more than one field of the table. The Validation Rule expression that you enter here applies to the table as a whole, instead of to a single field. Validation rules and domain integrity are two of the subjects covered in Chapter 6, "Entering, Editing, and Validating Access Table Data."

  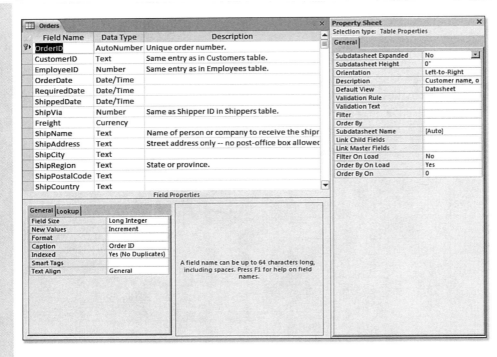 *For more information on validation rules for tables,* **see** *"Adding Table-Level Validation Rules with the Expression Builder,"* **p. 257.**

- *Validation Text* specifies the text of the message box that opens if you violate a table's Validation Rule expression.

- *Filter* specifies a constraint to apply to the table whenever it's applied. Filters restrict the number of records that appear, based on selection criteria you supply. Chapter 7, "Sorting, Finding, and Filtering Data," discusses filters.

  To learn more about filters, **see** *"Filtering Table Data,"* **p. 274.**

- *Order By* specifies a sort(ing) order to apply to the table, by default, whenever you open the table in Datasheet view. Chapter 7 also explains sort orders. If you don't specify a sort order, records display in the order of the primary key, if a primary key exists. (Table1 has a default primary key field named ID.) Otherwise, the records appear in the order in which you enter them. The

"Working with Relations, Key Fields, and Indexes" section, later in this chapter, discusses primary key fields.

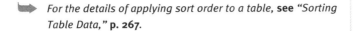 For the details of applying sort order to a table, **see** "Sorting Table Data," **p. 267.**

- *Orientation*, another Access 2002 property, lets you specify right-to-left display of data in languages such as Hebrew and Arabic. Orientation is an Access-only data display property and doesn't affect how Access stores the data. The default value for European languages is Left-to-Right.

- **2007 NEW** *Display Views on SharePoint* determines if forms and reports associated based on this table should appear in the SharePoint View menu if you publish the database to a SharePoint site. The default value is Do Not Display.

- **2007 NEW** *Filter On Load* specifies whether the filter criterion of the Filter property is applied automatically when the table is in use. The default value is No.

- **2007 NEW** *Order By On Load* specifies whether the sort order of the Sort property is applied automatically when the table is in use. The default value is Yes.

 note

In SQL Server 2000 and later, an *extended properties* feature supports special Access and Access table and field properties, such as subdatasheets and lookup fields. The Table Properties dialog differs greatly from Access's version, but Table Design view of SQL Server's da Vinci toolset—also called the *project designer*—is similar to Access Table Design view.

Table Properties for Subdatasheets

Access 2000 introduced subdatasheets to display sets of records of related tables in nested datasheets. You can use subdatasheets in the Datasheet view of tables and queries, and also in forms and subforms. Figure 5.4 illustrates Northwind.accdb's Orders table in Datasheet view with a subdatasheet opened to display related records from the Order Details table. The Orders Details (child) table has a many-to-one relationship with the Orders (master) table. To open a subdatasheet, click the + symbol adjacent to a record selection button.

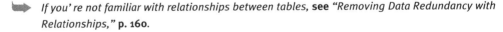 If you're not familiar with relationships between tables, **see** "Removing Data Redundancy with Relationships," **p. 160.**

The following table properties apply to subdatasheets:

- *Subdatasheet Name* determines whether and how subdatasheets display data in related records. The default value is [Auto], which automatically adds subdatasheets for records linked from a related table that has a many-to-one relationship with the open table. You also can select a name from a list of the database's tables and queries. A value of [None] turns off subdatasheets in the master table.

- *Link Child Fields* specifies the name of the linked field of the related (subordinate) table whose records appear in the subdatasheet. You don't need to specify a value if the Subdatasheet Name property value is [Auto] and a many-to-one relationship exists with the master table.

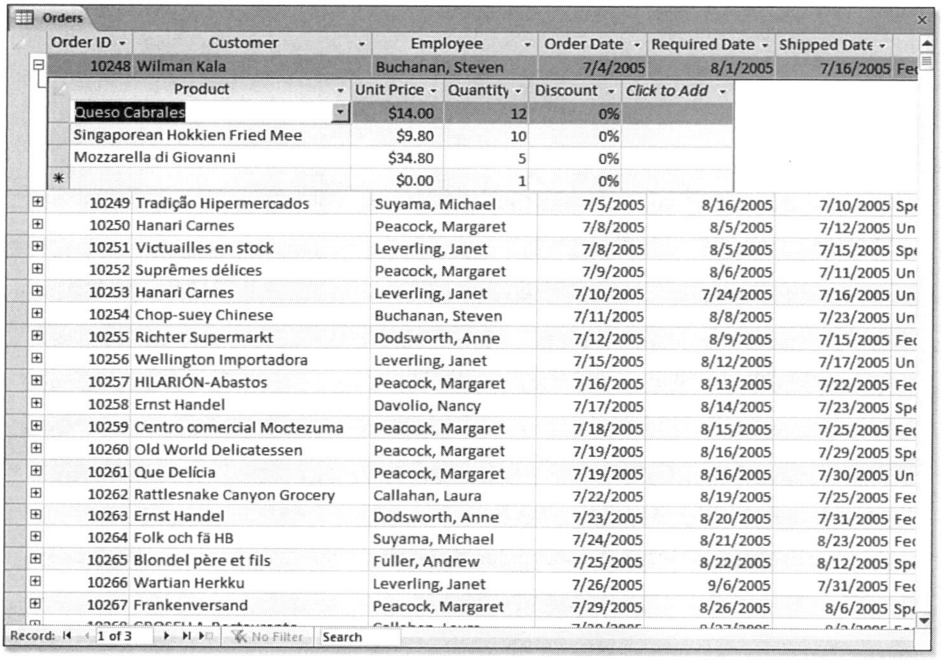

Figure 5.4
Opening a subdata-sheet dis-plays records of the child table (Order Details) that are related to the selected record in the master table (Orders).

- *Link Master Fields* specifies the name of the linking field of the master table, if you specify a Subdatasheet Name value.

- *Subdatasheet Height*, if supplied, specifies the maximum height of the subdatasheet. A value of 0 (the default) allows the subdatasheet to display all related records, limited only by the size of the master datasheet or subdatasheet.

- *Subdatasheet Expanded* controls the initial display of the sub-datasheet. Setting the value to Yes causes the datasheet to open with all subdatasheets expanded (open).

 For information on how to create a subdatasheet for a table, **see** "Adding Subdatasheets to a Table or Query," **p. 456**.

> ### note
>
> You can nest subdatasheets within other subdatasheets. For example, the Northwind data-base's Customers table has an Order table subdatasheet that, in turn, has an Order Details table subdatasheet.

Field Properties

You assign each field of an Access table a set of properties. You specify values for the first three field properties—Field Name, Data Type, and Description—in the Table Design grid, the upper pane of the Table Design window shown in Figure 5.5. As an example, the primary key of

Figure 5.5
Northwind.
accdb's
Customers
table's
CustomerID
field is des-
ignated the
primary key
field. All
fields of the
Customer
table are of
the Text data
type.

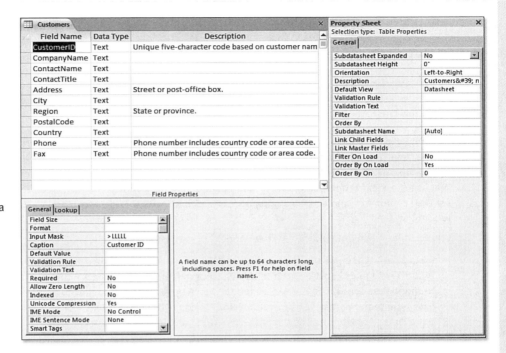

the Customers table is the CustomerID field, indicated by a small key symbol in the field selection button. You set the remaining property values in the Table Design window's lower pane, Field Properties.

➡ If you're not familiar with the term primary key, **see** "Defining the Structure of Relational Databases," **p. 159**.

The following list summarizes the properties you set in the Table Design grid:

- **Field Name**—You type the name of the field in the Table Design grid's first column. Field names can be as long as 64 characters and can include embedded (but not leading) spaces and punctuation—except periods (.), exclamation marks (!), and square brackets ([]). Field names are mandatory, and you can't assign the same field name to more than one field in the same table. It's good database programming practice not to include spaces or punctuation characters in field names. Instead, substitute an underscore (_) for spaces or use uppercase and lowercase letters (CamelCase) to improve the readability of field names. Minimizing the length of field names conserves resources.

- **Data Type**—You select data types from a drop-down list in the Table Design grid's second column. Data types include Text, Memo, Number, Date/Time, Currency, AutoNumber, Yes/No, OLE Object, Hyperlink, Attachment, and Lookup Wizard. (The Lookup Wizard is an Access feature, not a data type.) Choosing a data type is the subject of the next section.

■ **Description**—You can enter an optional description of the field in the text box in the Table Design grid's third column. If you add a description, it appears in the status bar at the lower left of Access's window when you select the field for data entry or editing. Description is a special property of Access and SQL Server 2005 databases and is for informative purposes only.

■ 🔑 **Primary Key**—To choose a field as the primary key field, select the field by clicking the field-selection button to the left of the Field Name column, and then click the Primary Key button on the Table Tools Design ribbon.

Depending on the specific data type that you choose for a field, you can set additional properties for a table field. You set these additional properties on the General page of the Table Design window's Field Properties pane by selecting from drop-down or combo lists or by typing values in text boxes. You use the Field Properties pane's Lookup page to set the control type for lookup fields on forms—list box, combo list, and so on. Chapter 15, "Designing Custom Multitable Forms," describes how to use lookup fields.

The following list summarizes the General field properties of Access tables:

■ **Field Size**—You enter the field size for the Text data type in this text box. (See the "Fixed-Width Text Fields" section later in this chapter to learn how to select a text field size.) For most Numeric data types, you determine the field size by selecting from a drop-down list. The Decimal data type requires that you type values for Precision and Scale. Field size doesn't apply to the Date/Time, Yes/No, Currency, Memo, Hyperlink, or OLE Object data type.

■ **Format**—You can select a standard, predefined format in which to display the values in the field from the drop-down combo list that's applicable to the data type you selected (except Text). Alternatively, you can enter a custom format in the text box (see "Custom Display Formats" later in this chapter). The Format property doesn't affect the data values; it affects only how these values are displayed. The Format property doesn't apply to OLE Object fields.

■ **Precision**—This property appears only when you select Decimal as the data size of the Number data type. Precision defines the total number of digits to represent a numeric value. The default is 18, and the maximum value is 28 for Access .accdb files.

■ **Scale**—Like Precision, this property appears only for the Decimal data size selection. Scale determines the number of decimal digits to the right of the decimal point. The value of Scale must be less than or equal to the Precision value.

■ **Decimal Places**—You can select Auto or a specific number of decimal places from the drop-down combo list, or you can enter a number in the text box. The Decimal Places property applies only to Number and Currency fields. Like the Format property, the Decimal Places property affects only the display, not the data values, of the field.

■ **Input Mask**—Input masks are character strings, similar to the character strings used for the Format property, that determine how to display data during data entry and editing. If you click the Builder button for a field of the Text, Currency, Number, or Date/Time field data type, Access starts the Input Mask Wizard to provide you with a predetermined selection of standard input masks, such as telephone numbers with optional area codes.

- **Caption**—If you want a name (other than the field name) to appear in the field name header button in Table Datasheet view, you can enter an alias for the field name in the Caption list box. The restrictions on field name punctuation symbols don't apply to the Caption property. (You can use periods, exclamation points, and square brackets, if you want.)

- **Default Value**—By entering a value in the Default Value text box, you specify a value that Access automatically enters in the field when you add a new record to the table. The current date is a common default value for a Date/Time field. (See "Setting Default Values of Fields" later in this chapter for more information.) Default values don't apply to fields with the AutoNumber, OLE Object, or Attachment field data type.

- **Validation Rule**—Validation rules test the value entered in a field against criteria that you supply in the form of an Access expression. Unlike table-level validation rules, the field validation expression operates only on a single field. The Validation Rule property isn't available for fields with the AutoNumber, Memo, OLE Object, or Attachment field data type.

    → *For an example of applying field-level validation rules,* **see** *"Adding Field-Level Validation Rules,"* **p. 255.**

- **Validation Text**—You enter the text that is to appear in the status bar if the value entered does not meet the Validation Rule criteria.

- **Required**—If you set the value of the Required property to Yes, you must enter a value in the field. Setting the Required property to Yes is the equivalent of typing **Is Not Null** as a field validation rule. (You don't need to set the value of the Required property to Yes for fields included in the primary key because Access doesn't permit Null values in primary key fields.)

- **Allow Zero Length**—If you set the value of the Allow Zero Length property to No and the Required property to Yes, the field must contain at least one character. The Allow Zero Length property applies to the Text, Memo, and Hyperlink field data types only. A zero-length string ("") and the Null value aren't the same.

- **Indexed**—From the drop-down list, you can select between an index that allows duplicate values and one that requires each value of the field to be unique. You remove an existing index (except from a field that is a single primary key field) by selecting No. The Indexed property is not available for Memo, OLE Object, and Hyperlink fields. (See "Adding Indexes to Tables" later in this chapter for more information on indexes.)

- **New Values**—This property applies only to AutoNumber fields. You select either Increment or Random from a drop-down list. If you set the New Values property to Increment, Access generates new values for the AutoNumber field by adding 1 to the highest existing AutoNumber field value. If you set the property to Random, Access generates new values for the AutoNumber field by producing a pseudo-random long integer.

- **Unicode Compression**—Unicode is a method of encoding characters in multiple alphabets with two bytes, instead of the conventional single-byte ASCII or ANSI representation. Ordinarily, the use of two-byte encoding doubles the space occupied by values typed in Text, Memo, and Hyperlink fields. The first Unicode character of languages using the Latin alphabet is 0. If Unicode compression is set to Yes, the default value, Access stores all Unicode characters with a first-byte value of 0 in a single byte.

Gaps in AutoNumber Field Values

When I accidentally add a new record to a table with an AutoNumber field and then delete it, the next record I add has the wrong AutoNumber value—increment of 2 instead of 1.

That's the major drawback of AutoNumber fields, especially when the AutoNumber field value corresponds to a physical record, such as an invoice or check number. The AutoNumber feature offers no simple method of replacing an incorrect record that you delete from the table. The best approach, which ensures that your table is auditable, is to never delete a record from a table with an AutoNumber field. Instead, type **VOID** in a Status field, and add an explanation (if there's a field available to do so).

- **IME Mode and IME Sentence Mode**—These two properties apply only to fields having the Text, Memo, or Hyperlink data type. IME is an abbreviation for Office 2007+'s Input Method Editor, which governs the method of inputting characters of East Asian languages. IME Sentence Mode is applicable only to the Japanese language. A discussion of IME features is beyond the scope of this book.

- **Smart Tags**—You can add smart tags, which usually link Internet resources to a specific field. For example, you can add a Financial Symbol smart tag to an Access table field containing New York Stock Exchange or NASDAQ stock symbols to let users select from stock quotes, company reports, and recent company news from the MSN Money Central website. Access 2007+ also uses a smart tag to apply changes in a property value to dependent database objects.

- **2007 NEW Text Align**—You can specify the alignment of Text and Memo fields as General, Left, Center, or Distributed (justified). General applies right alignment for numeric values; otherwise, left alignment. The default value is General.

- **2007 NEW Text Format**—Specifying Rich Text enables HTML formatting of Memo fields with text formatting by selections from the Font and Rich Text groups of the Datasheet and Form views. The default value is Plain Text (no formatting).

- **2007 NEW Append Only**—Prevents users from modifying existing text of a Memo field but allows adding new text. This property is useful for version control and change tracking. The default value is No.

For details on Access 2010's use of smart tags to propagate field property value changes to other database objects, **see** *"Working with Object Dependencies and Access Smart Tags,"* **p. 228.**

5

As illustrated later in this chapter, adding the first sample table, HRActions, to the Northwind.accdb database requires you to specify appropriate data types, sizes, and formats for the table's fields.

Choosing Field Data Types, Sizes, and Formats

You must assign a field data type to each field of a table, unless you want to use the Text data type that Access assigns by default. One principle of relational database design is that all data in a single field consists of one data type. Access provides a much wider variety of data types and formats from which to choose than most other PC database managers. In addition to setting the data type, you can set other field properties that determine the format, size, and other characteristics of the data that affect its appearance and the accuracy with which numerical values are stored. Table 5.1 describes the field data types that you can select for data contained in Access tables.

Table 5.1   Field Data Types Available in Access 2010

Information	Data Type	Description of Data Type
Characters	Text	Text fields are most common, so Access assigns Text as the default data type. A Text field can contain as many as 255 characters, and you can designate a maximum length less than or equal to 255. Access assigns a default length of 50 characters.
Characters	Memo	Memo fields ordinarily can contain as many as 65,535 characters. You use them to provide descriptive comments. Access displays the contents of Memo fields in Datasheet view. A Memo field can't be a key field.
Numeric Values	Number	Several numeric data subtypes are avail- able. You choose the appropriate data subtype by selecting one of the Field Size property settings listed in Table 5.2. You specify how to display the number by setting its Format property to one of the formats listed in Table 5.3.
	AutoNumber	An AutoNumber field is a numeric (Long Integer) value that Access automatically fills in for each new record you add to a table. Access can increment the Auto Number field by 1 for each new record, or fill in the field with a randomly gener ated number, depending on the New Val ues property setting that you choose. The maximum number of records in a table that can use the AutoNumber field with the Long Integer size is slightly more than two billion.

Table 5.1 Continued

Information	Data Type	Description of Data Type
2010 NEW	Calculated	A Calculated field displays the result of an expression having other field values in the row as its arguments. For example, you can calculate the Extended value of an Order Details record with this expression: [Quantity]*[UnitPrice]* (1 - [Discount]). Choose the data type of the resulting value in the Result Type list and add formatting, if necessary, from Format list. (The default data type is Double.)
	Yes/No	Logical (Boolean) fields in Access use numeric values: -1 for Yes (True) and 0 for No (False). You use the Format property to display Yes/No fields as Yes or No, True or False, On or Off, or -1 or 0. (You can also use any non-zero number to represent True.) Logical fields can't be key fields but can be indexed.
Number	Currency	Currency is a special fixed format with four decimal places designed to prevent rounding errors that would affect ac- counting operations in which the value must match to the penny.
Dates and Times	Date/Time	Dates and times are stored in a special fixed format. The date is represented by the whole number part of the Date/Time value, which is the number of days from December 30, 1899. Time of day is rep resented by the decimal fraction. For ex ample, 2.25 is 1/1/1900 6:00 a.m. You control how Access displays dates by selecting one of the Date/Time Format properties listed in Table 5.3.
Large Objects	OLE Object	Includes bitmapped and vector-type (Bi nary Data) graphics and other BLOBs (binary large objects), such as waveform audio files and video files. You can't assign an OLE Object field as a key field, nor can you include an OLE Object field in an index. Clicking an OLE Object in Datasheet view opens the object in its editing application.
2007 NEW	Attachment	An alternative to OLE Object for storing multiple large objects in a format com patible with SharePoint lists. Access compresses the attachments for more efficient storage. You can't assign an Attachment field as a key field, nor can it be indexed.
Web Addresses	Hyperlink	Hyperlink fields store web page docu ment addresses. A web address stored in the Hyperlink field can refer to a web page on the Internet or one stored locally on your computer or network. Clicking a Hyperlink field in Datasheet view causes Access to start your web browser and display the referenced web page. Choose Insert, Hyperlink to add a new hyperlink address to a Hyperlink field.

Information	Data Type	Description of Data Type
Related Data	Lookup Wizard	Lookup Wizard isn't a legitimate data type; it's a property of a field. Selecting Lookup Wizard starts the Lookup Wizard to add a lookup feature to the table. Most lookup operations execute a query to obtain data from a field of a related table.

 To learn how to use the Lookup Wizard, **see** *"Using Lookup Fields in Tables,"* **p. 442.**

 note

The OLE Object field data type is unique to Access; other applications that use Access or Jet databases designate the OLE Object field data type as *Binary or Long Binary*. When you add an OLE object, such as a bitmapped graphic from Windows Paint or a Word document, Access adds a special header, which identifies the source application, to the binary graphics data. Other applications can't read data from OLE Object fields you create in Access. OLE Object fields won't upsize to SQL Server 2005+ because SQL Server's `varbinary(max)` and image fields don't support the OLE Object data type.

The Attachment field data type is similar to the OLE Object data type, but it stores any type of data that you can attach to an email message and doesn't depend on a local OLE server to display the attachment's contents. Each Attachment cell can contain any number of attachments, limited only by the 1GB maximum storage capacity of an Access field.

Choosing Field Sizes for Numeric and Text Data

The Field Size property of a field determines which data type a Number field uses or how many characters fixed-length text fields can accept. Field Size properties are called *subtypes* to distinguish them from the data types listed in Table 5.1. For numbers, you select a Field Size property value from the Field Size drop-down list in the Table Design window's Field Properties pane (see Figure 5.6).

 note

Access's default field type is Text with 255 characters as the default Size property value. Long Integer is the default numeric subtype. You can change these defaults in the Tables section of the Access Options dialog's Object Designers page.

Subtypes for Numeric Data

The Number data type of the previously shown Table 5.1 isn't a fully specified data type. You must accept the default subtype (Long Integer) or select one of the subtypes from those listed in Table 5.2 for the Field Size property to define the numeric data type properly. To select a data subtype for a Number field, follow these steps:

 note

These data types are available in Visual Basic for Applications (VBA) 6.0. VBA includes all the data types listed in Table 5.2 as reserved words. You can't use a reserved data type word for any purpose in VBA functions and procedures other than to specify a data type.

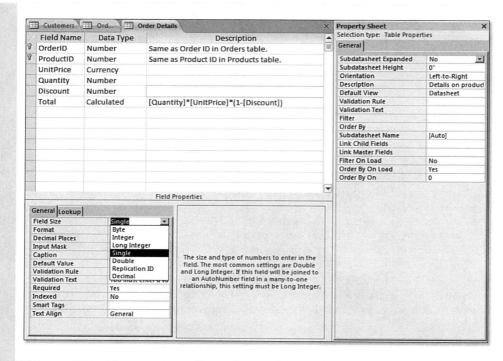

Figure 5.6
You can select one of seven Field Size (data subtype) property values for fields having a Number data type from the drop-down list.

1. Select the Data Type cell of the Number field for which you want to select the subtype.

2. Click the Field Size text box in the Field Properties window. You also can press F6 to switch windows, and then use the arrow keys to position the caret within the Field Size text box.

3. Click the drop-down arrow to open the list of choices shown previously in Figure 5.6.

4. Select the data subtype. (Table 5.2 describes data subtypes.) When you make a selection, the list closes.

After you select a Field Size property, you select a Format property from those listed in Table 5.3 (later in this chapter) to determine how to display the data. Table 5.2 includes the Currency data type because it also can be considered a subtype of the Number data type.

Regardless of how you format your data for display, the number of decimal digits, the range, and the storage requirements remain those specified by the Field Size property.

 tip

Always use the Decimal data type for fractional values—such as percentages—that you intend to use for calculating Currency or other Decimal values. The Order Details table's Discount field uses the Access Single data type, which is notorious for causing rounding errors in decimal calculations.

note

You can apply the Replication ID field size to Number or AutoNumber fields. A replication ID is a specially formatted 32-character (16-byte) hexadecimal number (values 0 through 9 and A through F) surrounded by French braces. The more common name for a replication ID is *globally unique identifier* (*GUID*, pronounced "goo id" or "gwid"). A typical GUID looks like {8AA5F467-3AF5-4669-B4CB-5207CDC79EF4}. GUID values, which Windows calculates for you, supposedly are unique throughout the world. If you apply the Replication ID field size to an AutoNumber field, Access automatically adds a GUID value for each row of the table.

Table 5.2   Subtypes of the Number Data Type Determined by the Field Size Property

Field Size	Decimals	Range of Values	Bytes
Decimal	28 places	-10-28 to 1028 -1	14
Double	15 places	$-1.797 * 10^{308}$ to $+1.797 * 10^{308}$	8
Single	7 places	$-3.4 * 10^{38}$ to $+3.4 * 10^{38}$	4
Long Integer	None	-2,147,483,648 to +2,147,483,647	4
Integer	None	-32,768 to 32,767	2
Byte	None	0 to 255	1
Replication ID	None	Not applicable	16
Currency	4 places	-922337203685477.5808 to +922337203685477.5808	8

   For more information on VBA reserved words for data types, see "Data Types and Database Objects in VBA" (Online Chapter 30).

As a rule, you select the Field Size property that results in the smallest number of bytes that encompasses the range of values you expect and that expresses the value in sufficient precision for your needs. Mathematical operations with Integer and Long Integer proceed more quickly than those with Single and Double data types (called floating-point numbers) or the Currency and Date/Time data types (fixed-point numbers). Microsoft added the Decimal data subtype for conformance with the SQL Server decimal data type.

Fixed-Width Text Fields

You can create a fixed-width Text field by setting the value of the Field Size property, which limits the number of characters the field will store. By default, Access creates a 255-character-wide Text field. Enter the number, from 1 to 255, in the Field Size cell corresponding to the maximum length that you want. Datasheets will not let you enter more than the maximum number of characters. If the data you import to the field is longer than the selected field size, Access truncates the data, so you lose the far-right characters that exceed your specified limit. You should enter a field length value that accommodates the maximum number of characters you expect to enter in the field.

Selecting a Display Format

You establish the Format property for the data types you select so that Access displays them appropriately for your application. You select a format by selecting the field and then clicking the Format text box in the Field Properties window. Figure 5.7 shows the choices that Access offers for formatting the Long Integer data type. You format Number, Date/Time, and Yes/No data types by selecting a standard format or creating your own custom format. The following sections describe these two methods.

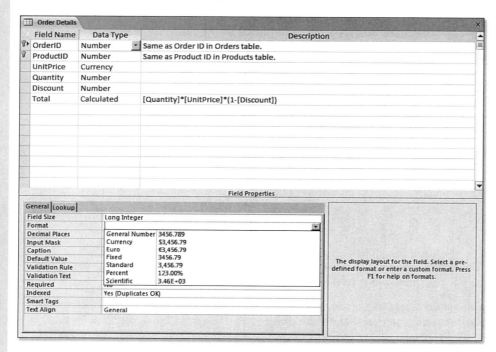

Figure 5.7
You can apply one of seven numeric display formats to fields of the Number data type and the Long Integer subtype. Access 2000 added the Euro format.

 tip

Standard Formats for Number, Date/Time, and Yes/No Data Types

Access provides 18 standard formats that apply to the numeric values in fields of the Number, Date/Time, and Yes/No data types. The standard formats shown in Table 5.3 should meet most of your needs.

Table 5.3   Standard Display Formats for Access's Number, Date/Time, and Yes/No Data Types

Data Type	Format	Appearance
Number	General Number	1234.5
	Currency	$1,234.50
	Euro	€1,234.50
	Fixed	12345 or 12345.00, depending on Decimal Places setting
	Standard	1,234.50
	Percent	0.1234 = 12.34%
	Scientific	1.23E+03
Date/Time	General Date	3/1/99 4:00:00 PM
	Long Date	Thursday, March 1, 2003
	Medium Date	1-Mar-2003
	Short Date	3/1/2003
	Long Time	4:00:00 PM
	Medium Time	04:00 PM
	Short Time	16:00
Yes/No	Yes/No	Yes or No
	True/False	True or False
	On/Off	On or Off
	None	−1 or 0

 note

The terms *fixed width* and *fixed length* have different meanings in Access. Even if you specify a fixed width for a field of the Text field data type, Access stores the data in the field in variable-length format. Therefore, setting the Length value to 255 for all Text fields has no effect on the ultimate size of the database file.

Microsoft's Year 2000 (Y2K) compliance features include the General section of the Advanced page of the Access Options dialog. The Use Four-Digit Year Formatting group has two check boxes: This Database and All Databases. Marking either check box changes Date/Time field formatting as shown in Table 5.4. Long Date and Time formats don't change; the formatting shown in the Access 2010 Default column is based on the standard Windows Short Date format, m/d/yy.

Marking the This Database check box sets a flag in the current database, so the formatting changes apply only to the current database. Marking the All Databases check box adds a Registry entry to your PC, so opening any Access database in Access forces four-digit-year formatting.

Table 5.4   A Comparison of Access 2010 Default and Four-Digit Year Formatting

Date/Time Format	Access 2010 Default	With Four-Digit Year
General Date (default)	1/15/03 10:10 AM	1/15/2003 10:10 AM
Short Date	1/15/03	1/15/2003
Long Date	Friday January 15, 2003	Friday January 15, 2003
Medium Date	15-Jan-03	15-Jan-2003
Medium Time	10:10 AM	10:10 AM
mm/dd/yy	01/15/03	01/15/2003

The Null Value in Access Tables

Fields in Access tables can have a special value, Null, which is a new term for most spreadsheet users. The Null value indicates that the field contains no data at all. Null is similar but not equivalent to an empty string (a string of zero length, "", often called a *null string*). For now, the best synonym for Null is *no entry* or *unknown*.

The Null value is useful for determining whether a value has been entered in a field, especially a numeric field in which zero values are valid. The next section and the later "Setting Default Values of Fields" section use the Null value.

Custom Display Formats

To display a format that's not a standard format in Access, you must create a custom format. You can set a custom display format for any field type, except OLE Object, by creating an image of the format with combinations of a special set of characters called *placeholders* (see Table 5.5). Figure 5.8 shows an example of a custom format for date and time. If you type **mmmm dd, yyyy - hh:nn** as the format, the date 03/01/07 displays as March 1, 2007 - 00:00. Access automatically adds double quotes around the comma when you save the table.

Except as noted, the sample numeric value that Table 5.4 uses is 1234.5. Bold type distinguishes the placeholders that you type from the surrounding text. The resulting display is shown in mono-space type.

Figure 5.8
If one of the standard Format property values doesn't meet your needs, you can type a string to represent a custom format in the Format text box. This format string (dd-mmm-yyyy) substitutes four-digit years for the Medium Date format's two-digit years.

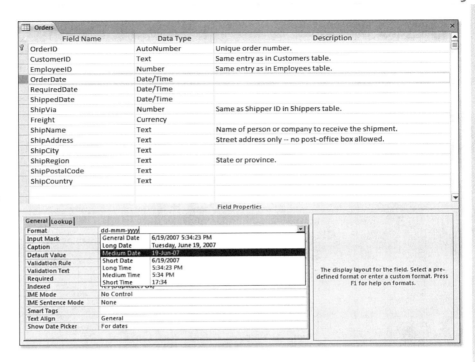

Table 5.5 Placeholders for Creating Custom Display Formats

Placeholder	Function
Empty string	Displays the number with no formatting. Enter an empty string by deleting the value in the Format field of the Field Properties pane.
0	Displays a digit, if one exists in the position, or a zero if not. You can use the 0 placeholder to display leading zeros for whole numbers and trailing zeros in decimal fractions. 00000.000 displays 01234.500.
#	Displays a digit, if one exists in the position. The # placeholder is similar to 0, except that leading and trailing zeros aren't displayed. #####.### displays 1234.5.
$	Displays a dollar sign in the position. $###,###.00 displays $1,234.50.
.	Displays a decimal point at the indicated position in a string of 0 and # placeholders. ##.## displays 1234.5.
%	Multiplies the value by 100 and adds a percent sign in the position shown with 0 and # placeholders. #0.00% displays 0.12345 as 12.35% (12.345 is rounded to 12.35).
,	Adds commas as thousands separators in strings of 0 and # placeholders. ###,###,###.00 displays 1,234.50.

Table 5.5 Continued

Placeholder	Function
E- e-	Displays values in scientific format with the sign of exponent for negative values only. #.####E-00 dis plays 1.2345E03. 0.12345 is displayed as 1.2345E-01.
E+ e+	Displays values in scientific format with the sign of exponent for positive and negative values. #.####E+00 displays 1.2345E+03.
/	Separates the day, month, and year to format date values. Typing mm/dd/yyyy displays 03/06/2003. (You can substitute hyphens for virgules to display 03-06-2003.)
m	Specifies how to display months for dates. m dis plays 1, mm displays 01, mmm displays Jan, and mmmm displays January.
d	Specifies how to display days for dates. d displays 1, dd displays 01, ddd displays Mon, and dddd displays Monday.
y	Specifies how to display years for dates. yy displays 07; yyyy displays 2007.
:	Separates hours, minutes, and seconds in format time values. hh:mm:ss displays 02:02:02.
h	Specifies how to display hours for time. h displays 2; hh displays 02. If you use an AM/PM placeholder, h or hh displays 4 PM for 16:00 hours.
n	Minutes placeholder for time. n displays 1; nn displays 01. hhnn "hours" displays 1600 hours.
s	Seconds placeholder for time. s displays 1; ss displays 01.
AM/PM	Displays time in 12-hour time with AM or PM appended. h:nn AM/PM displays 4:00 PM. Alternative formats include am/pm, A/P, and a/p.
@	Indicates that a character is required in the position in a Text or Memo field. You can use @ to format telephone numbers in a Text field, as in @@@- @@@-@@@@ or (@@@) @@@-@@@@.
&	Indicates that a character in a Text or Memo field is optional.
>	Changes all text characters in the field to uppercase.
<	Changes all text characters in the field to lowercase.
*	Displays the character following the asterisk as a fill character for empty spaces in a field. "**ABCD**"*x in an eight-character field appears as ABCDxxxx.

The Format property is one of the few examples in Access in which you can select from a list of options or type your own entry. Format uses a true drop-down combo list; lists that enable you to select only from the listed options are drop-down lists with the Limit to List property value set to Yes. The comma is a nonstandard formatting symbol for dates (but is standard for number fields). When you create nonstandard formatting characters in the Field Properties window, Access automatically encloses them in double quotation marks.

When you change Format or any other field property value, and then change to Datasheet view to see the result of your work, you must first save the updated table design. The confirmation dialog shown at the top of Figure 5.9 asks you to confirm any design changes. Clicking

No returns you to Table Design view. If you want to discard your changes, close Table Design view and click No when asked if you want to save your changes (see Figure 5.9, bottom).

Figure 5.9
Changing from Table Design to Datasheet view after making changes to the table's design displays the upper message box. If you close the table in Design view, the lower message box gives you the option of saving or discarding changes, or returning to Table Design view.

If you apply the custom format string **mmmm dd", "yyyy** (refer to Figure 5.8) to the BirthDate field of the Employees table, the BirthDate field entries appear as shown in Figure 5.10. For example, Nancy Davolio's birth date appears as December 08, 1968. The original format of the BirthDate field was dd-mmm-yyyy (medium date), the format also used for the HireDate field. The Birth Date caption property value appears in the heading row.

Figure 5.10
The BirthDate field of the modified employees table displays the effect of applying mmmm dd", "yyyy as the custom date/time format. The pop-up calendar for entering or editing data in Date fields was a new in Access 2007.

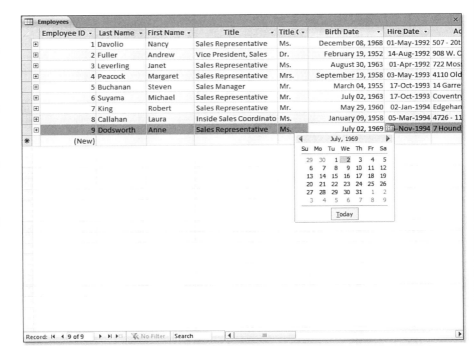

You must expand the width of the BirthDate field to accommodate the additional characters in the Long Date format. You increase the field's width by dragging the field name header's right vertical bar to the right to display the entire field.

Conditional Formatting

Conditional formatting enables applying formatting that depends on the value of numeric data: greater than zero (>0); less than zero (<0); zero (=0); Null. Semicolons separate the format strings for the four value conditions.

The following is an example that formats negative numbers enclosed in parentheses and replaces a Null entry with text:

$###,###,##0.00;$(###,###,##0.00);0.00;"No Entry Here"

The entries 1234567.89, −1234567.89, 0, and a Null default value appear as follows:

```
$1,234,567.89
 $(1,234,567.89)
 0.00
No Entry Here
```

Using Input Masks

Access 2010 lets you restrict entries in Text fields to numbers or to otherwise control the formatting of entered data. Access's Input Mask property is used to format telephone numbers, Social Security numbers, ZIP Codes, and similar data. Table 5.6 lists the placeholders that you can use in character strings for input masks in fields of the Text field data type.

Table 5.6 Placeholders for Creating Input Masks

Placeholder	Function
Empty string	No input mask.
0	Number (0–9) required; sign (+/–) not allowed.
9	Number (0–9) or space optional; sign (+/-) not allowed.
#	Number (0–9) or space optional (a space if nothing is entered).
L	Letter (A–Z) required.
?	Letter (A–Z) not required (a space if nothing is entered).
A	Letter (A–Z) or number (0–9) required.
a	Letter (A–Z) or number (0–9) optional.
&	Any character or a space required.
C	Any character or a space optional.

Placeholder	Function
Password	Displays the characters you type as asterisks (***...) to prevent others from viewing the entry.
.,:; / ( )	Literal decimal, thousands, date, time, and special separators.
>	All characters to the right are converted to upper case.
<	All characters to the right are converted to lower case.
!	Fills the mask from right to left.
\	Precedes the other placeholders to include the lit eral character in a format string.

For example, typing **\(000") "000\-0000** as the value of the Input Mask property results in the appearance of (___) ___ - ____ for a blank telephone number cell of a table. Typing **000\-00\-0000** creates a mask for Social Security numbers, ___ - __ - ____. When you type the telephone number or Social Security number, the digits that you type replace the underscores.

 Access includes an Input Mask Wizard that opens when you move to the Input Mask field for the Text or Date/Time field data type and click the Builder (...) button at the extreme right of the text box. Figure 5.11 shows the opening dialog of the Input Mask Wizard for Text fields, which lets you select from 10 common input mask formats. The Input Mask Wizard offers only Long Time, Short Date, Short Time, Medium Time, and Medium Date masks for Date/Time fields. The wizard works only with Text and Date/Time field data types.

> **note**
>
> The \ characters (often called *escape characters*) that precede parentheses and hyphens specify that the character that follows is a literal, not a formatting character. If the format includes spaces, enclose the spaces and adjacent literal characters in double quotation marks, as shown for the telephone number format.

Figure 5.11
The Input Mask Wizard lets you select one of 10 preset formats to specify a fixed data entry pattern for the selected field. In the second wizard dialog, you can add a custom format.

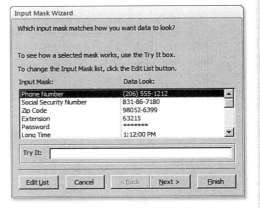

Adding a Table to the Northwind Traders Sample Database

One fundamental problem with books about database management applications is the usual method of demonstrating how to create a "typical" database. You are asked to type fictitious names, addresses, and telephone numbers into a Customers table. Next, you must create additional tables that relate these fictitious customers to their purchases of various widgets in assorted sizes and quantities. This process is unrewarding for readers and authors, and few readers ever complete the exercises.

 Therefore, this book takes a different tack. Earlier Access versions included a comprehensive—but outdated—sample order entry database, Northwind Traders (Northwind.mdb). The Microsoft Office 2010 Professional and higher editions don't include a sample database in the setup program's options. The online sample databases for this book includes several updated versions of the Northwind database in the \Access2010\Nwind folder. If you expanded the sample code from the book's website to the default \Access2010 folder, the \Access2010\Chaptr05 folder holds a Northwind.accdb starter version that contains only updated tables.

Rather than create a new database at this point, you create a new table as an addition to the \Access2010\Chaptr05\Northwind.accdb table. Adding a new table minimizes the amount of typing required and requires just a few entries to make the table functional. The HRActions table you add demonstrates many elements of relational database design.

Preparing to Add a Table Related to the Employees Table

Northwind.accdb in your \2010Samples\Chaptr05 folder includes the Employees table that provides information typical of personnel tables maintained by Human Resources departments 10 or more years ago. The following sections explain how to add a new table to the Northwind database that is related to the Employees table and called HRActions. The HRActions table is a record of hire date, salary, commission rate, bonuses, performance reviews, and other compensation-related events for employees. Because HRActions is based on information in the Employees table, the first step is to review the Employees table's structure. In Chapter 6, you add validation rules to the HRActions table and enter records in the table.

> ### note
>
> Northwind.accdb's Employees table has an added Picture field of the new Attachments data type. Otherwise, this table is identical to the Employees table of earlier Access version.

Figure 5.12 shows the Employees table in Design view. The fields grid in the figure shows property values for only 16 of the 18 fields of the table. Scroll down to display the properties of the remaining two fields.

Figure 5.12
Design view of the Employees table displays most of the table's fields in the upper grid pane. The most important field is the primary key, EmployeeID, on which the new table's relationship depends.

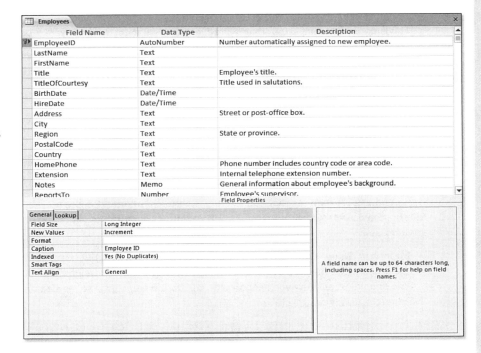

Designing the HRActions Table

Designing the HRActions table is typical of the process you go through when you create a set of relational tables for almost any purpose. Rather than add fields for entries—such as salary, commission rate, and bonuses—to the Employees table, you should place employee performance and remuneration data in a table of its own, for the following reasons:

- Multiple HRActions are taken for individual employees over time. If you add these actions to records in the Employees table, you would need to create many additional fields to hold an arbitrary number of HRActions. If, for example, quarterly performance reviews are entered, you would need to add a new field for every quarter to hold the review information. In this situation, which is an example of a repeating group, spreadsheet applications and flat-file managers encounter serious difficulties. Relational databases use related tables to handle the repeating group problem.

- HRActions usually are considered confidential information and are made accessible only to a limited number of people. Although you can design forms that don't display confidential information, restricting permission to view an entire table is a more secure approach.

- You can identify employees uniquely by their EmployeeID numbers. Therefore, records for entries of HRActions can be related to the Employees table by an EmployeeID field. This feature eliminates the necessity of adding employee names and other constant or slowly changing information to the records in the HRActions table. You link the Employees table to the HRActions table by the EmployeeID field, and the two tables are joined; they act as though they are a single table. Minimizing information duplication to only what is required to link the tables is your reward for choosing a relational, rather than a flat-file, database management system.

- You can categorize HRActions by type so that any action taken can use a common set of field names and field data types. This feature simplifies the design of the HRActions table.

The next step is to start the design of the HRActions table. Chapter 4 discusses the theory of database design and the tables that make up databases. Because the HRActions table has an easily discernible relationship to the Employees table, the theoretical background isn't necessary for this example.

Determining What Information the Table Should Include

Designing a table requires that you identify the type of information the table should contain. Information associated with typical Human Resources department actions might consist of the following items:

- **Important dates**—The date of hire and termination, if applicable, are important dates, but so are the dates when the employer adjusts salaries, changes commission rates, and grants bonuses. You should accompany each action with the date when it was scheduled to occur and the date when it actually occurred.

- **Types of actions**—Less typing is required if HRActions are identified by a code character rather than a full-text description of the action. This feature saves valuable disk space, too. First-letter abbreviations used as codes, such as H for hired, T for terminated, and Q for quarterly review, are easy to remember.

- **Initiation and approval of actions**—As a rule, the employee's supervisor initiates a personnel action, and the supervisor's manager approves it. Therefore, the table should include the supervisor's and manager's EmployeeID number.

- **Amounts involved**—Salaries are assumed to be bimonthly based on a monthly amount, hourly employees are paid weekly, bonuses are quarterly with quarterly performance reviews, and commissions are paid on a percentage of sales made by the employee.

- **Performance rating**—Rating employee performance by a numerical value is a universal, but somewhat arbitrary, practice. Scales of 1 to 9 are common, with exceptional performance ranked as 9 and candidacy for termination as 1.

- **Summaries and comments**—The table should provide for a summary of performance, an explanation of exceptionally high or low ratings, and reasons for adjusting salaries or bonuses.

If you're involved in personnel management, you probably can think of additional information that the table might include, such as accruable sick leave and vacation hours per pay period. The

 note

Fields containing a code for pay type—salary, hourly, commission—and bonus eligibility would be useful additions to the Employees table. You could use such codes to validate amount entries in the HRActions table.

HRActions table is just an example; it isn't meant to add full-scale Human Resources application capabilities to the database. The limited amount of data described so far serves to demonstrate several uses of the new table in this and subsequent chapters.

Assigning Information to Fields

After you determine the types of information—called *data attributes* or just *attributes*—to include in the table, you must assign each data entity to a field of the table. This process involves specifying a field name that must be unique within the table. Table 5.7 lists the candidate fields for the HRActions table. Candidate fields are written descriptions of the fields proposed for the table. Data types are logically derived from the type of value described. Table 5.8 adds specifics for the data types.

Table 5.7 Candidate Fields for the HRActions Table

Field Name	Data Type	Description
EmployeeID	Number	The employee to whom the action applies. EmployeeID numbers are assigned based on the EmployeeID field of the Employee table (to which the HRActions table is related).
ActionType	Text	Code for the type of action taken: H is for hired; Q, quarterly review; Y, yearly re view; S, salary adjustment; R, hourly rate adjustment; B, bonus adjustment; C, commission rate adjustment; and T, terminated.
InitiatedBy	Number	The EmployeeID number of the supervisor who initiates or is responsible for recom mending the action.
ScheduledDate	Date/Time	The date when the action is scheduled to occur.
ApprovedBy	Number	The EmployeeID number of the manager who approves the action proposed by the supervisor.
EffectiveDate	Date/Time	The date when the action occurred. The effective date remains blank (Null value) if the action has not occurred.
HRRating	Number	Performance on a scale of 1–9, with higher numbers indicating better performance. A blank (Null value) indicates no rating; 0 is reserved for terminated employees.
NewSalary	Currency	The new salary per month, as of the effect tive date, for salaried employees.
NewRate	Currency	The new hourly rate for hourly employees.
NewBonus	Currency	The new quarterly bonus amount for eligible employees.
NewCommission	Percent	The new commission rate for commis sioned salespersons, some of whom might also receive a salary.
HRComments	Memo	Abstracts of performance reviews and comments on actions proposed or taken. The comments can be of unlimited length. The supervisor and manager can contribute to the comments.

Creating the HRActions Table in Design View

Now you can put to work what you've learned about field names, data types, and formats by adding the HRActions table to the Northwind Traders database. Table 5.8 shows the field names, taken from Table 5.7, and the set of properties that you assign to the fields. Fields with values required in a new record have an asterisk (*) following the field name. The text in the Caption column substitutes for the Field Name property that is otherwise displayed in the field header buttons.

 tip

Use distinctive names (without spaces or punctuation characters) for each field. This example precedes some field names with the abbreviation HR to associate—or establish relations with—field names in other tables that might be used by the Human Resources department.

 note

You must set the EmployeeID field's Field Size property to the Long Integer data type, although you might not expect Northwind Traders to have more than the 32,767 employees that an integer allows. The Long Integer data type is required because the AutoNumber field data type of the Employees table's EmployeeID field is a Long Integer. Later in this chapter, the "Working with Relations, Key Fields, and Indexes" section explains why EmployeeID's data type must match that of the Employees table's EmployeeID number field.

Table 5.8   Field Properties for the HRActions Table

Field Name	Caption	Data Type	Field Size	Format
EmployeeID*	ID	Number	Long Integer	General Number
ActionType*	Type	Text	1	>@ (all uppercase)
InitiatedBy*	Initiated By	Number	Long Integer	General Number
ScheduledDate*	Scheduled	Date/Time	N/A	mm/dd/yyyy
ApprovedBy	Approved By	Number	Long Integer	General Number
EffectiveDate	Effective	Date/Time	N/A	Short Date
HRRating	Rating	Number	Byte	General Number
NewSalary	Salary	Currency	N/A	Standard
NewRate	Rate	Currency	N/A	Standard
NewBonus	Bonus	Currency	N/A	Standard
NewCommission	% Comm	Number	Single	#0.0
HRComments	**Comments**	**Memo**	**N/A**	**(None)**

To add the new HRActions table to the Northwind database, complete the following steps:

1. Close the Employees table, if it's open.

2. Click the Create tab and then click the Table Design button. Access enters design mode, opens a blank grid, and selects the grid's first cell. The General page of the lower properties pane is empty for a new table with no fields.

3. Type **EmployeeID** as the first field name, and press Tab to accept the field name and move to the Data Type column. Access adds the default field type, Text.

4. Click to open the Data Type list (see Figure 5.13) and select Number. Alternatively, type **N[umber]** in the list. Typing characters that unambiguously match an item in the drop-down list selects the item.

<aside>
note

Another selection alternative in drop-down lists is to use Alt+down arrow to open the list, press the up- or down-arrow key to make the selection, and then press Enter.
</aside>

Figure 5.13
The Data Type list lets you select from one of the nine Access data types or the Lookup Wizard. If you type a text value in a Data Type cell, the value must match the first character or two of one of the entries in the drop-down list.

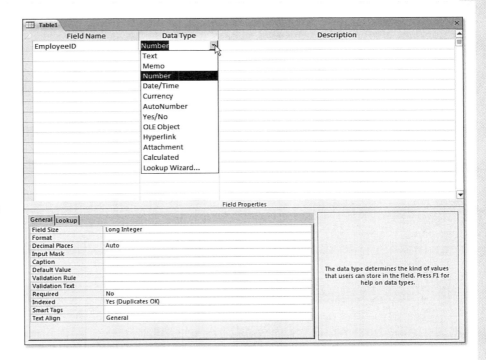

5. Press F6 to move to or click the Field Size text box in the Field Properties window. Access has already entered Long Integer as the value of the default Field Size property for a Number field.

6. For Number data types other than Long Integer, select from
   the list the appropriate Field Size value from Table 5.8, or type
   the first letter of one of the values of the list, such as **B[yte]** or
   S[ingle]. For Text fields, type the maximum number of characters.

7. Press the down-arrow key or click to select the Format text
   box, and type **G[eneral]** or select General Number from the list
   (see Figure 5.14).

note

When entering a Text field with
the Required property set to Yes,
set the Allow Zero Length property value to No.

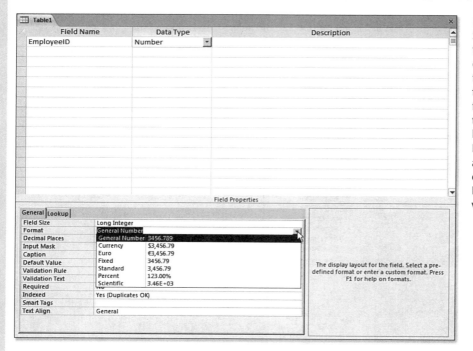

Figure 5.14
Select one of
the seven stan-
dard number
formats from
the list or type a
format string in
the Format text
box. The General
Number format
applies if you
don't set the
Format property
value.

8. Press the down-arrow key, or select the Caption text box,
   and type **ID** as the caption. ID is used as the Caption property to minimize the column width necessary to display the
   EmployeeID number.

9. Press the down-arrow key four times, bypassing the Default
   Value, Validation Rule, and Validation Text properties, and
   type **Y** in the Required text box. Typing **Y[es]** or **N[o]** is an
   alternative to selecting Yes or No in the drop-down list.

10. Press F6 to return to the Table Design grid.

tip

Add descriptions to create
prompts that appear in the status bar when you are adding or
editing records in Run mode's
Datasheet view. Although
descriptions are optional, it's
good database design practice
to enter the field's purpose if its
use isn't obvious from its Field
Name or Caption property.

11. Press Enter to move the caret to the first cell of the next row of the grid.

12. Repeat steps 3 through 11, entering the values shown in Table 5.8 for each of the 11 remaining fields of the HRActions table. N/A (not applicable) means that the entry in Table 5.8 doesn't apply to the field's data type.

Your Table Design grid should now look similar to the one shown in Figure 5.15, with the exception of the optional Description property values. You can double-check your properties' entries by selecting each field name with the arrow keys and reading the values shown in the property text boxes of the Field Properties window.

note

Whenever you create a new Number type field, Access enters Long Integer in the Field Size property as the default. Because the EmployeeID field should be a Long Integer, you don't need to set the Field Size property for this field and can skip to step 8; continue with steps 6 and 7 when you enter the other fields from Table 5.8.

Figure 5.15
The 12 fields of the new HRActions table fully describe any of the eight types of personnel actions defined by the ActionType codes. Adding the Description property, which can be up to 255 characters long, is optional but recommended.

Field Name	Data Type	Description
EmployeeID	Number	Linked to the EmployeeID field of the Employees table
ActionType	Text	H = Hired; Q = Quarterly Review; Y = Yearly Review; T = Terminated
InitiatedBy	Number	EmployeeID of supervisor
ScheduledDate	Date/Time	Proposed date of action
ApprovedBy	Number	EmployeeID of supervisor's manager
EffectiveDate	Date/Time	Date approved action is to take place
HRRating	Number	Performance rating 1 to 8; 0 for termination
New Salary	Currency	New monthly salary
New Rate	Currency	New hourly rate
New Bonus	Currency	New yearly bonus
New Commission	Number	New commission %
HRComments	Memo	Optional comments about the action taken

Field Properties

General | Lookup

Field Size	Long Integer
Format	General Number
Decimal Places	Auto
Input Mask	
Caption	ID
Default Value	
Validation Rule	
Validation Text	
Required	Yes
Indexed	Yes (Duplicates OK)
Smart Tags	
Text Align	General

A field name can be up to 64 characters long, including spaces. Press F1 for help on field names.

Click the Datasheet View button to view the results of your work. Click Yes when the Do You Want to Save the Table Now? message opens (see Figure 5.16, top). The Save As dialog opens, requesting that you give your table a name and suggesting the default table name, Table1. Type **HRActions**, as shown in Figure 5.16 (middle), and press Enter or click OK.

At this point, Access displays a message informing you that the new table does not have a primary key (see Figure 5.16, bottom). You add primary keys to the HRActions table later in this chapter, so click No in this message box.

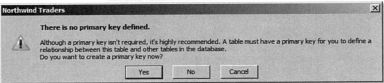

Figure 5.16
When you change the view of a new table that doesn't have a primary key to Datasheet, these three messages appear in sequence.

Your table opens in Datasheet view, with its first default record. To view all the fields of your new table, narrow the field name header buttons by dragging to the left the right vertical bar that separates each header. When you finish adjusting your fields' display widths, the HRActions table appears in Datasheet view. Only the tentative append record (a new record that Access adds to your table only if you enter values in the cells) is present. You have more property values to add to your HRActions table, so don't enter data in the tentative append record at this point. If you close the table, a message asks if you want to save your table layout changes. Click Yes.

Creating Tables from Templates

The Create ribbon's Templates group contains an Application Parts button, which displays a gallery of one table design (Comments) and five combined table and form design templates (Contacts, Issues, Tasks and Users) for tracking applications (see Figure 5.17). Clicking a gallery button adds the table and form, when applicable, to your database.

Microsoft offers Table Templates as the replacement for earlier Access versions' Table Wizard. However, the Table Wizard offered a wider variety of table types, enabled users to select desired fields, and included the capability to easily establish relationships with existing database tables. Users of earlier Access versions probably will miss the Table Wizard.

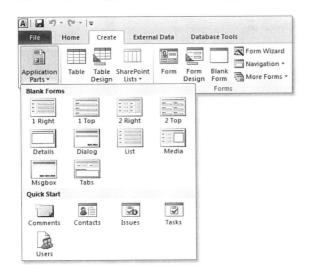

Figure 5.17
The Application Parts template gallery lets you select from common form designs, a Comments table or a Contacts, Issues, Tasks, or Users table with an associated form template.

Creating a Table Directly in Datasheet View

If you're under pressure to create a set of database tables immediately, Access lets you create tables directly in Datasheet view. Clicking the Table button in the Create ribbon's Tables group adds a sequentially numbered Table# starter table with an autoincrementing ID column for the primary key and an empty Add New Field column. The starter table is the same as that described in the "Creating a New Access Database from Scratch" section near the beginning of this chapter.

You can then enter data directly into the Add New Field column, which becomes a sequentially numbered Field# column when you add the first value. As you enter data, Access analyzes the data you entered and attempts to select a data type for each field that matches the entries. If you add an entry that doesn't match the initially determined data type, a smart tag opens and offers you the option to change the data type, cancel the entry, or seek help on data types (see Figure 5.18). You can edit the field names in the header row by double-clicking Field#. Thus, it's possible to create and populate a table without entering Table Design view.

Creating tables in Datasheet view is an ad hoc shortcut that seldom produces a satisfactory result. Adding tables to a database requires advance planning to ensure that the design follows Chapter 4's normalization rules, employs appropriate data types, and establishes specific relationships to existing tables.

Setting Default Values of Fields

Access 2010 doesn't assign Number and Currency fields a default value of 0 as earlier Access versions did; all field types are Null (empty) by default. You can save data entry time by establishing default values for fields. Table 5.9 lists the default values you should enter for the HRActions table's fields.

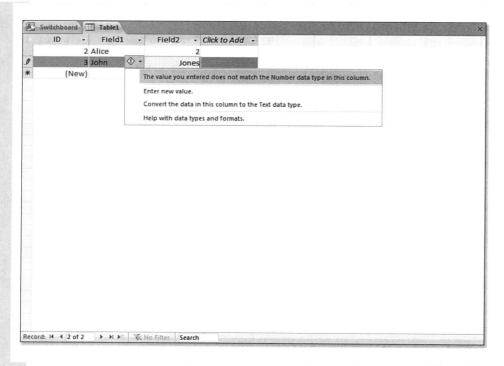

Figure 5.18
Access 2010 lets you create new tables in Datasheet view by typing values in cells of the default table design.

Table 5.9 Default Field Values for the HRActions Table

Field Name	Default Value	Comments
EmployeeID	Null	Accept Access 2010's default.
ActionType	"Q"	Quarterly performance reviews are the most common personnel action.
InitiatedBy	Null	Accept Access 2010's default.
ScheduledDate	=Date()	This expression enters today's date from the computer system's clock.
ApprovedBy	Null	Accept Access 2010's default.
EffectiveDate	=Date()+28	This expression enters today's date plus four weeks.
HRRating	Null	Accept Access 2010's default. A 0 rating is reserved for terminated employees.
NewSalary	Null	Null represents no change.
NewRate	Null	Null represents no change.
NewBonus	Null	Null represents no change.
NewCommission	Null	Null represents no change.
HRComments	Null	Accept Access 2010's default.

If you don't enter anything in the Default Value text box, you create a Null default value. You can use Null values for testing whether a value has been entered into a field. Such a test can ensure that users have entered required data.

You use expressions, such as =Date()+28, to enter values in fields, make calculations, and perform other useful duties, such as validating data entries. Expressions are discussed briefly in the next section and in much greater detail in Chapter 10, "Understanding Access Query Operators and Expressions." An equal sign must precede expressions that establish default values.

To assign the new default values from those of Table 5.9 to the fields of the HRActions table, complete these steps:

1. Click the Home ribbon's Datasheet View button. Access selects the first field of the table.

2. Press F6 to switch to the Field Properties window, move the caret to the Default Value text box, and type **Null** for the default value of the EmployeeID field.

3. Press F6 to switch back to the Table Design grid. Move to the next field and press F6 again.

4. Add the default values for the 10 remaining fields having the default entries shown in Table 5.9, repeating steps 1 through 3. For example, after selecting the Default Value text box for the ActionType field, type **Q** to set the default value; Access automatically surrounds Q with double quotes.

5. After completing your default entries, click the View button of the Table Design toolbar, and click Yes when asked if you want to save the table. The HRActions table appears in Datasheet view with the new default entries you assigned (see Figure 5.19).

The Nwind05.accdb database in the \Access2010\Chaptr05 folder of the online sample databases includes the HRActions table, which you can import into Northwind.accdb.

Working with Relations, Key Fields, and Indexes

Your final tasks before adding records to the HRActions table are to determine the relationship between HRActions and an existing table in the database, assign a primary key field, and add indexes to your table.

Establishing Relationships Between Tables

Many records in the HRActions table apply to a single employee whose record appears in the Employees table. The HR department adds a record in HRActions when the employee is hired, and for each quarterly and yearly performance review. Also, any changes made to bonuses or commissions other than as the result of a performance review are added, and employees might be terminated. Over time, the number of records in the HRActions table is likely to be greater by a factor of 10 or more than the number of records in the Employees table. Therefore, the records in the new Personnel table have a many-to-one relationship with the records in the Employees table. Establishing the relationships between new and existing tables when you create a new table

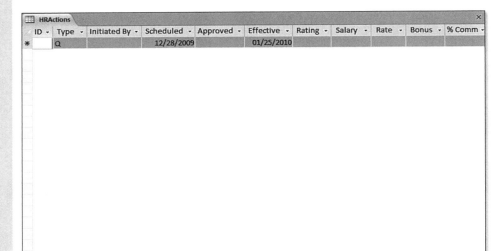

Figure 5.19
Datasheet view of the HRActions table confirms the changes you make to the Default Value property of the fields.

enables Access to enforce the relationship when you use the tables in queries, forms, pages, and reports.

➡ For a description of the three types of relationships between tables, **see** "Removing Data Redundancy with Relationships," **p. 160.**

Access requires that the two fields participating in the relationship have the same data type. In the case of the Number field data type, the Field Size property of the two fields must be identical. You cannot, for example, create a relationship between an AutoNumber type field (which uses a Long Integer data type) and a field containing Byte, Integer, Single, Double, or Currency data. (You *can* create a relationship between fields having AutoNumber and Long Integer data types.) On the other hand, Access lets you relate two tables by text fields of different lengths. Such a relationship, if created, can lead to strange behavior when you create queries, which is the subject of Part III, "Transforming Data with Queries and PivotTables." As a rule, the relationships between text fields should use fields of the same length.

Access uses a graphical Relationships window to display and create the relationships among tables in a database. To establish the relationships between two tables with Access's Relationships window, using the Employees and HRActions tables as an example, follow these steps:

1. Close the Employees and HRActions tables, and click the Relationships button of the Database Tools ribbon to open the Relationships window (see Figure 5.20).

Figure 5.20
The Relationships window for the Northwind. accdb database displays lines representing the one-to-many relationships between the original sample tables. The 1 symbol indicates the "one" side and the infinity (∞) symbol indicates the "many" side of one-to-many relationships. Bold type identifies primary key fields.

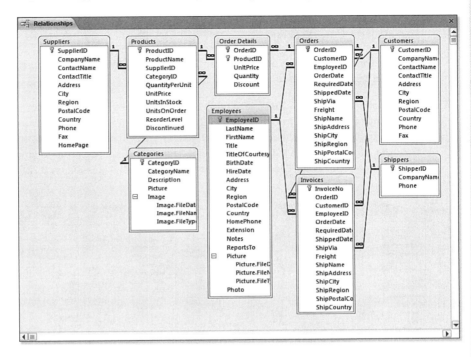

2. 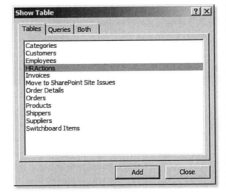 Click the Show Table button of the Relationship Tools, Design ribbon to open the Show Table dialog (see Figure 5.21).

Figure 5.21
The Tables page of the Show Table dialog displays a list of all tables in the database.

3. For this example, add the HRActions table to the Relationships window by double-clicking the HRActions entry in the Tables list, or by clicking the entry to select it and then clicking the Add button. Click the Close button.

4. Move the HRActions table object under the Suppliers table object, and drag the bottom of the HRActions table object to expose all its fields.

5. The relationship of the HRActions table to the Employees table is based on the HRActions table's EmployeeID field (the foreign key) and the Employees table's EmployeeID field (the primary key). Click the Employees table's EmployeeID field and, holding the left mouse button down, drag it to the HRActions table's EmployeeID field. Release the mouse button to drop the field symbol on the EmployeeID field. The Edit Relationships dialog opens (see Figure 5.22).

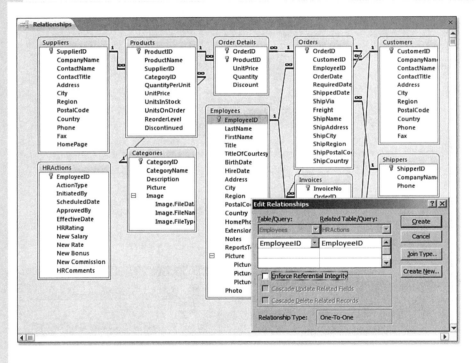

Figure 5.22
Establishing a relationship by dragging a field symbol from one table object to another opens the Edit Relationships dialog. By default, the name of the table with a primary key field appears in the Table/Query list and the other table appears in the Related Table/Query list. In this case, Access automatically detects a one-to-many relationship.

6. Click the Join Type button to display the Join Properties dialog shown in Figure 5.23. You are creating a one-to-many join between the Employees table's EmployeeID field (the one side) and the HRActions table's EmployeeID field (the many side). You want to display all Employee records, even if one or more of these records don't have a corresponding record in HRActions. To do so, select option 2 in the Join Properties dialog. Click OK to close the dialog and return to the Edit Relationships dialog.

Figure 5.23
The Join Properties dialog lets you specify one of three types
of one-to-many joins for the relationship. Option 1 is called
an INNER JOIN by SQL, 2 is a LEFT OUTER JOIN, and 3 is a
RIGHT OUTER JOIN.

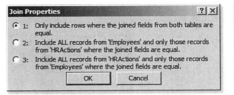

7. The Edit Relationships dialog offers the Enforce Referential Integrity check box so that you can
   specify that Access perform validation testing and accept entries in the EmployeeID field that
   correspond only to values present in the Employees table's EmployeeID field. This process is
   called enforcing (or maintaining) referential integrity. (The following section discusses referential
   integrity.) The relationship between these two tables requires enforcing referential integrity, so
   make sure to select this check box (see Figure 5.24).

Figure 5.24
Marking the Enforce Referential Integrity check box ensures
that values you enter in the HRActions table's EmployeeID
field have corresponding values in the EmployeeID field of
the Employees table.

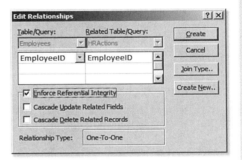

For basic referential integrity principles of relational databases, **see** "Referential Integrity," **p. 171.**

8. Click the Create button to accept the new relationship and display it in the Relationships window (see Figure 5.25).

9. Close the Relationships window, and click Yes when asked
   to confirm that you want to save the layout changes to the
   Relationships diagram.

 Access uses the relationship that you've created when you
design queries and design forms, pages, and reports that use
data in the HRActions table. You can print the contents of the
Relationships window as a report by clicking the Relationship
Tools Design ribbon's Relationship Report button.

> 🔍 **note**
> Access automatically maintains
> referential integrity of tables by
> providing check boxes you can
> mark to cause cascading updates
> to, and cascade deletions of,
> related records when the primary
> table changes. The following
> section discusses cascading
> updates and deletions. Access
> enables the cascade check boxes
> only if you elect to enforce refer-
> ential integrity.

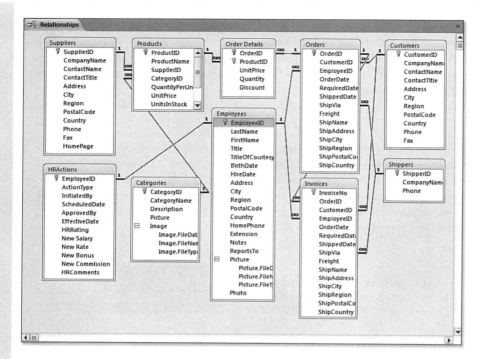

Figure 5.25
The Relationships window displays the newly added one-to-many relationship between the Employees and HRActions table.

 note

Automatically enforcing referential integrity is usually, but not always, good database design practice. An example of where you would not want to employ cascade deletions is between the EmployeeID fields of the Orders and Employee tables. If you terminate an employee and then attempt to delete the employee's record, you might accidentally choose to delete the dependent records in the Orders table. Deleting records in the Orders table could have serious consequences from a marketing and accounting standpoint. (In practice, however, you probably wouldn't delete a terminated employee's record. Instead, you'd change a Status field value to Terminated or the equivalent.)

Cascading Updates and Deletions

Access's cascading deletion and cascading update options for tables with enforced referential integrity makes maintaining referential integrity easy: Just mark the Cascade Update Related Fields and Cascade Delete Related Records check boxes. In this case, marking the Cascade Update Related Fields check box is unnecessary, because you can't change the value of the AutoNumber EmployeeID field of the Employees table. You can delete records in the Employees table, so marking the Cascade Delete Related Records check box prevents orphan records—records without a corresponding record in the Employees table—from appearing in the HRActions table.

Selecting a Primary Key

Using a primary key field is a simple method of preventing the duplication of records in a table. Access requires that you specify a primary key if you want to create a one-to-one relationship or to update records from two or more tables in the same datasheet or form. (Chapter 11, "Creating Multitable and Crosstab Queries," covers this subject.)

Technically, assigning a primary key field to each table isn't an absolute requirement. The ANSI SQL specification doesn't define the term *primary key*; however, relational theory requires that one or more field values identify each record uniquely. Access considers a table without a primary key field an oddity; therefore, when you make changes to the table and return to Design view, you might see a message stating that you haven't created a key field. (Access 2000 and later versions ask only once whether you want to add a primary key field.) Related tables can have primary key fields and usually do. A primary key field based on field values is useful for preventing the accidental addition of duplicate records.

You can create primary keys on more than one field. In the case of the HRActions table, a primary key that prevents duplicate records *must* consist of more than one field. If you establish the rule that no more than one personnel action of a given type for a particular employee can be scheduled for the same date, you can create a primary key that consists of the EmployeeID, ActionType, and ScheduledDate fields. When you create a primary key, Access creates a no-duplicates index based on the primary key.

To create a multiple-field primary key, called a *composite primary key,* and a primary key index for the HRActions table, follow these steps:

1. Open the HRActions table in Design view.

2. Click the selection button for the EmployeeID field.

3. Ctrl+click the selection button for the ActionType field. In most instances, when you Ctrl+click a selection button, you can make multiple selections.

4. Ctrl+click the selection button for the ScheduledDate field.

5. Click the Table Tools Design ribbon's Primary Key button. Symbols of keys appear in each previously selected field, indicating their inclusion in the primary key.

6. To verify the sequence of the fields in the primary key, click the toolbar's Index button to display the Indexes dialog, shown in Figure 5.26.

7. Close the Indexes dialog, and press Ctrl+S to save your table design changes.

You now have a multiple-field primary key and a corresponding index on the HRActions table that precludes the addition of records that duplicate records with the same primary key value.

> **tip**
>
> You should add only indexes you need to improve search performance. Each index you add slows the addition of new records, because adding a new record requires an addition to each index. Similarly, editing indexed fields is slower, because the edit updates the record and the index. When you create relationships between tables, Access automatically creates a hidden index on the related fields, if the index doesn't already exist. Hidden indexes count against the 32-index limit of each table. If an extra index appears in the Indexes dialog, see the "Extra Indexes Added by Access" item in the "Troubleshooting" section near the end of this chapter.

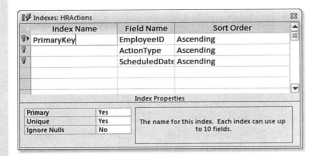

Figure 5.26
The three fields of the HRActions table's composite primary key have indexes.

Adding Indexes to Tables

Although Access creates one or more indexes on the primary key, you might want to create an index on some other field or fields in the table. Indexes speed searches for records that contain specific types of data. For example, you might want to find all HRActions that occurred in a given period and all quarterly reviews for all employees in ScheduledDate sequence. If you have many records in the table, an index speeds up the searching process. A disadvantage of multiple indexes is that data entry operations are slowed by the time it takes to update the additional indexes. You can create as many as 32 indexes for each Access table, and five of those can be of the multiple-field type. Each multiple-field index can include as many as 10 fields.

Extra Indexes Added by Access

After I specified a primary key on a field containing the characters "ID", an additional index appeared for the field.

In many cases, Access automatically specifies a primary key and index on fields whose names contain the characters "ID", "key", "code", and "num" when you create or import tables. This behavior is controlled by the contents of the AutoIndex on Import/Create text box of the Tables/Queries page of the Options dialog (from the Tools menu). When you change the primary key field(s), the old index remains. You can safely delete the automatically added index.

To create a single-field index for the HRActions table based on the EffectiveDate field, and a multiple-field index based on the ActionType and the ScheduledDate fields, follow these steps:

1. Select the EffectiveDate field by clicking its selection button.

2. Select the Indexed text box in the Field Properties window.

3. Open the Indexed drop-down list by clicking the arrow button or pressing Alt+down arrow (see Figure 5.27).

Figure 5.27
You can add
an index on a
single field by
setting the value
of the Indexed
property to Yes
(Duplicates
OK) or Yes (No
Duplicates).

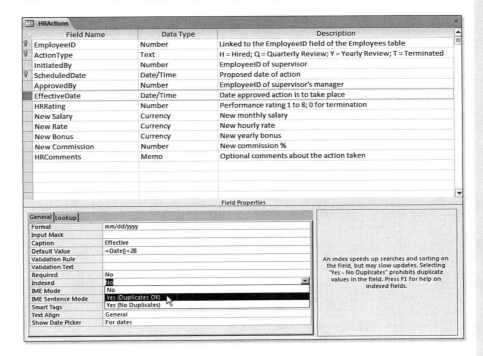

4. In this case, duplicate entries on the same date are likely, so select Yes (Duplicates OK) and close the list. You can create only a single-field index with this method.

5. Click the Indexes button. The Primary Key and EffectiveDate indexes already created appear in the list boxes. Type **ActionTypeEffectiveDate** as the name of the composite index, and then select ActionType in the Field Name drop-down list. Move the caret to the next row of the Field Name column and select ScheduledDate to create a multiple-field index on these two fields (see Figure 5.28).

6. In the Ignore Nulls row of the Index Properties pane for the EffectiveDate field, select Yes so that records without an EffectiveDate value aren't included in the index.

7. Click the Datasheet View button, and click Yes to save your design changes.

You now have three indexes for the Primary Key table: the index automatically created for the primary key, the single-key index on EffectiveDate, and the multiple-key index on ActionType and ScheduledDate.

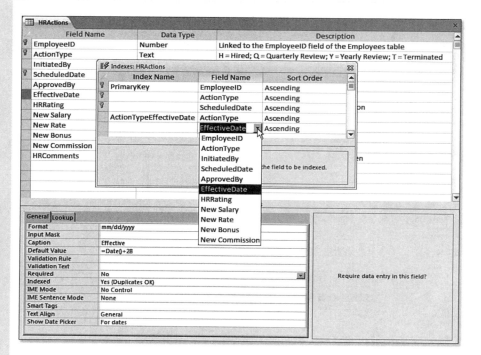

Figure 5.28
You add multiple-field indexes in the Indexes dialog.

Altering Fields and Relationships

When you're designing a database, you often discover that you must alter the original choices you made for the sequence of fields in a table, data types, or relationships between tables. One reason for adding substantial numbers of records to tables during the testing process is to discover any necessary changes before putting the database into daily use.

You can change formats, validation rules and text, lengths of Text fields, and other minor items in the table by changing to design mode, selecting the field to modify, and making the changes in the property boxes. Changing data types can cause a loss of data, however, so be sure to read the later "Changing Field Data Types and Sizes" section before you attempt to make such changes. Changing the data type of a field that participates in a relationship with another table requires that you delete and, if possible, re-create the relationship. Changing relationships between tables is considered a drastic action if you have entered a substantial amount of data, so this subject is also covered in "Changing Relationships Between Tables," also later in this chapter.

 To learn how field property value changes propagate to dependent database objects, **see** *"Working with Object Dependencies and Access Smart Tags,"* **p. 228.**

note

Access 2000 introduced the Name AutoCorrect feature. Renaming a database object in earlier versions required you to search manually through all objects of your database and change all references to the renamed objects. The Name AutoCorrect feature handles the corrections for you; when you open a database object, Access scans and fixes discrepancies.

New databases you create in Access 2010, whether in 2000 or 2002/2003 file format, have this feature turned on by default. Databases you open as .mdb files or convert from previous versions require you to turn on Name AutoCorrect by opening the Access Options dialog's Current Database page, and then marking the Track Name AutoCorrect Info and Perform Name AutoCorrect check boxes in the Name Autocorrect Options group. Marking the Log Name Autocorrect Changes check box creates a Name AutoCorrect Log table in the database that maintains a record of all changes made by the Perform Name Autocorrect feature.

Track Name AutoCorrect must be enabled to view object dependencies and enable table field property change propagation, but Perform Name AutoCorrect isn't required.

Rearranging the Sequence of Fields in a Table

If you're typing historical data in Datasheet view, you might find that the sequence of entries isn't optimum. You might, for example, be entering data from a printed form with a top-to-bottom, left-to-right sequence that doesn't correspond to the left-to-right sequence of the corresponding fields in your table. Access makes rearranging the order of fields in tables a matter of dragging and dropping fields where you want them. You can decide whether to make the revised layout temporary or permanent when you close the table.

To rearrange the fields of the HRActions table, follow these steps:

1. ▦ Click the Datasheet View button. Rearranging the sequence of fields is the only table design change you can implement in Access's Datasheet view.

2. Click the field name button of the field you want to move. This action selects the field name button and all the field's data cells.

3. Hold down the left mouse button while hovering over the field name button. The mouse pointer turns into the drag-and-drop symbol, and a heavy vertical bar marks the field's leftmost position.

4. Move the vertical bar to the new position for the selected field and release the mouse button. The field assumes the new position.

5. When you close the HRActions table, you see the familiar Save Changes message box. To make the field location modification permanent, click Yes; otherwise, click No.

Rearranging the field sequence in Datasheet view doesn't change the order in Design view's fields grid. To reposition fields in Design view, click the select button of the row of the field you want to move and then drag the row vertically to a new location. Changing the position of a table's field doesn't change any of the field's other properties.

Changing Field Data Types and Sizes

You might have to change a field data type as the design of your database develops or if you import tables from another database, a spreadsheet, or a text file. If you import tables, the data type automatically chosen by Access during the importation process probably won't be what you want, especially with Number fields. Chapter 8, "Linking, Importing, and Exporting Data," discusses importing and exporting tables and data from other applications. Another example of altering field properties is changing the number of characters in fixed-length Text fields to accommodate entries that are longer than expected, or converting Text to Memo fields.

 *For details on propagating field property value changes to dependent database objects, **see** "Working with Object Dependencies and Access Smart Tags," **p. 228**.*

Numeric Fields

Changing a data type to one that requires more bytes of storage is, in almost all circumstances, safe; you don't sacrifice your data's accuracy. Changing a numeric data type from Byte to Integer to Long Integer to Single and, finally, to Double doesn't affect your data's value because each change, except for Long Integer to Single, requires more bytes of storage for a data value. Changing from Long Integer to Single and Single to Currency involves the same number of bytes and decreases the accuracy of the data only in exceptional circumstances. The exceptions can occur when you are using very high numbers or extremely small decimal fractions, such as in some scientific and engineering calculations.

On the other hand, if you change to a data type with fewer data bytes required to store it, Access might truncate your data. If you change from a fixed-point format (Currency) or floating-point format (Single or Double) to Byte, Integer, or Long Integer, any decimal fractions in your data are truncated. Truncation means reducing the number of digits in a number to fit the new Field Size property that you choose. If you change a numeric data type from Single to Currency, for example, you might lose your Single data in the fifth, sixth, and seventh decimal places (if any exists) because Single provides as many as seven decimal places and Currency provides only four.

You can't convert any field type to an AutoNumber-type field. You can use the AutoNumber field only as a unique record identifier. The only way you can enter a new value in an AutoNumber field is by appending new records. You can't edit an AutoNumber field. When you delete a record in Access, the AutoNumber values of the higher-numbered records are not reduced by 1.

  caution

Before making changes to the field data types of a table that contains a substantial amount of data, back up the table by copying or exporting it to a backup Access database. If you accidentally lose parts of the data contained in the table (such as decimal fractions) while changing the field data type, you can import the backup table to your current database. Chapter 8 covers the simple and quick process of exporting Access tables. After creating a backup database file, you can copy a table to Windows Clipboard and then paste the table to the backup database. The later section "Copying and Pasting Tables" discusses Clipboard operations.

Text Fields

You can convert Text fields to Memo fields without Access truncating your text. You can't add indexes to Memo fields, so any index(es) on the converted Text field disappear. Access won't let Memo fields participate in relationships.

Converting a Memo field to a Text field truncates characters beyond the 255-character limit of Text fields. Similarly, if you convert a variable-length Text field to a fixed-length field, and some records contain character strings that exceed the length you chose, Access truncates these strings.

Conversion Between Number, Date, and Text Field Data Types

Access makes many conversions between Number, Date, and Text field data types for you. Conversion from Number or Date to Text field data types does not follow the Format property that you assigned to the original data type. Numbers are converted with the General Number format, and dates use the Short Date format. Access is intelligent in the methods it uses to convert suitable Text fields to Number data types. For example, it accepts dollar signs, commas, and decimals during the conversion, but ignores trailing spaces. Access converts dates and times in the following Text formats to internal Date/Time values that you then can format the way you want:

```
1/4/2010 10:00 AM
 04-Jan-10
 January 4
 10:00
10:00:00
```

Changing Relationships Between Tables

Adding new relationships between tables is a straightforward process, but changing relationships might require you to change data types so that the related fields have the same data type. To change a relationship between two tables, complete the following steps:

1. Close the tables involved in the relationship.

2. Display the Relationships window by clicking the Database Tools ribbon's Relationships button.

3. Click the join line that connects to the field whose data type you want to change. When you select the join line, the line becomes darker (wider).

4. Press Delete to clear the existing relationship. Click Yes when the message box asks you to confirm your deletion.

5. If you intend to change the data type of a field that constitutes or is a member field of the primary table's primary key, delete

> **note**
>
> Technically, control objects don't support inheritance as defined by standards for object-oriented programming. Instead, control objects contain a copy of the property values of the source field. The copied properties aren't automatically updated when you change the source field's property values.

> **note**
>
> Access adds the current year when converting January 4 from text to a DateTime value. Converting text time values without a date to a DateTime value sets the date to December 30, 1899.

all other relationships that exist between the primary table and every other table to which it is related.

6. Change the data types of the fields in the tables so that the data types match in the new relationships.

7. Re-create the relationships by using the procedure described earlier in the section "Establishing Relationships Between Tables."

Working with Object Dependencies and Access Smart Tags

In versions of Access earlier than 2003, changing a table field's property value—such as the Format or Input Mask specification—often wreaked havoc on other Access form and report objects that were dependent on the field. Typically, you bind form and report control objects, such as text boxes, to fields of a table or query. In Access terminology, the control objects *inherit* the properties of the underlying table fields.

Enabling and Viewing Object Dependencies

Access 2010 offers a feature called *object dependencies*, which enables field property change propagation to dependent objects, such as queries, forms, and reports. Before you can use change propagation, you must generate dependency data for your database. The version of Northwind.mdb included in the online sample files doesn't have the required hidden object dependency table. To enable the object dependency feature of the Northwind.mdb file in the \2010Samples\Nwind folder, follow these steps:

1. Open \2010Samples\Nwind\Northwind.mdb and close all open Northwind objects except the Navigation pane.

2. Select a table, such as HRActions, in the Navigation pane, and mark the Database Tools' Object Dependencies check box in the Relationships group. If the Name AutoCorrect feature isn't turned on, a message box opens; click OK to enable Name AutoCorrect.

3. Click OK in the message box that asks if you want to update object dependencies (see Figure 5.29, top).

After a few seconds, the Object Dependencies properties sheet displays the dependencies for the selected table (HRActions for this example). The Employees table depends on the HRActions table because of the relationship you created in the earlier "Establishing Relationships Between Tables" section (see Figure 5.30). Some types of objects, such as union queries (Query: Customers and Suppliers by City) and SQL-specific queries (Query: Products Above Average Price) don't support dependency tracking, so they are ignored. When you select the option Objects That I Depend On, the Employees table appears, but the Ignored Objects node disappears from the list.

Figure 5.29
Before you can display object dependency information, you must generate a hidden dependency table for the current database (top). To remove object dependency information, you must close all objects and reset the tables (bottom).

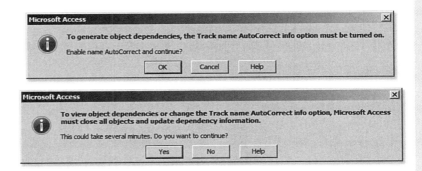

Figure 5.30
The Employees table depends on the HRActions table, and vice versa, because of the one-to-many relationship between the EmployeeID fields of the two tables.

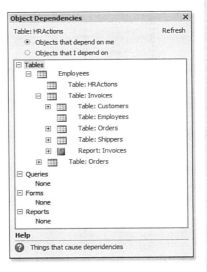

At this point, no queries, forms, or reports depend on the HRActions table. To view multiple object dependencies, select the Customers table and mark the Object Dependencies check box. One table, three queries, five forms, and a report depend on the Customers table (see Figure 5.31). Click the + symbol for a dependent object to display that object's dependencies in a tree view.

Activating the Access Property Options Smart Tag

Access uses a special-purpose Property Options smart tag to propagate altered field property values. To activate this smart tag, open the Customers table in Design view and temporarily change the CustomerID field's Input Mask property value from >LLLLL to >**LLLL**. When you move the cursor to the Caption field, the smart tag icon appears to the left of the property value text box (see Figure 5.32). Moving the mouse pointer over the icon changes its color, exposes a drop-down arrow, and adds a Property Update Options screen tip. Clicking the arrow opens the single active option—

Update Input Mask Everywhere CustomerID Is Used. Don't click the option in this case; return the Input Mask property to its original value, which causes the smart tag option to disappear. Close the table without saving your changes.

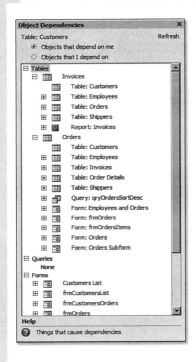

Figure 5.31
Multiple Access objects depend on the Northwind 2003.accdb database's Customers table. The Orders table has even more dependencies than the Customers table. This database includes query, form and report objects.

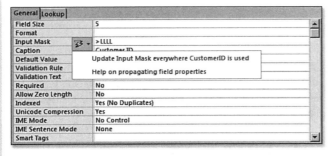

Figure 5.32
Opening the Property Options drop-down list displays the single option that updates dependent objects with the altered property value. The alternative is to get help for the field properties propagation feature.

Adding an Internet-Based Smart Tag to a Field

 Access 2010 also supports smart tags linked to web pages. The only web-based smart tag included with the product is Financial Symbol, which links to stock quotes, company reports, and recent company news from MSN MoneyCentral. To give this smart tag a test drive, do the following:

1. Create a new table with a field named Symbol and, optionally, another field named Company.

2. Select the Symbol field, move the cursor to the Smart Tags property's text box, and click the builder button to open the Smart Tags dialog.

3. Mark the Financial Symbol check box (see Figure 5.33), and click OK to add "urn:schemas-microsoft-com:office:smarttags# stockticker" as the SmartTags property's value.

4. Change to Datasheet view, and add a few NASDAQ and New York Stock Exchange stock symbols to the Symbols field. As you add symbols, a triangular marker is present at the bottom right of the cell, and a smart tag information icon appears adjacent to the cell.

5. ⓘ Move the mouse pointer over the icon, and click the arrow to open the Smart Tag Options list (see Figure 5.34).

6. Select one of the options—Stock Quote on MSN MoneyCentral for this example—to open the specified web page (see Figure 5.35).

> **note**
>
> Field property change propagation doesn't apply to changing the Name property of a field. Access's Name AutoCorrect feature propagates field name changes. As mentioned earlier in the "Altering Fields and Relationships" section, Track Name AutoCorrect must be enabled to generate object dependency data and enable viewing of dependencies in the Object Dependencies properties sheet.

> **tip**
>
> If you click the option, you must repeat the process with ···⁙LLLLL as the Input Mask value to return the objects to their original condition.

> **note**
>
> The object dependencies feature and Property Options smart tags aren't available in Access data projects (ADP).

Figure 5.33
Records in a table with a Smart Tag property value specified for a field have an identifier in the lower-right corner of the field and display a smart tag icon when selected.

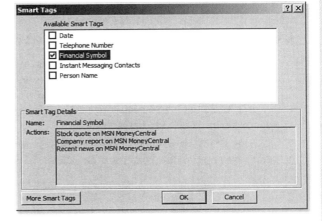

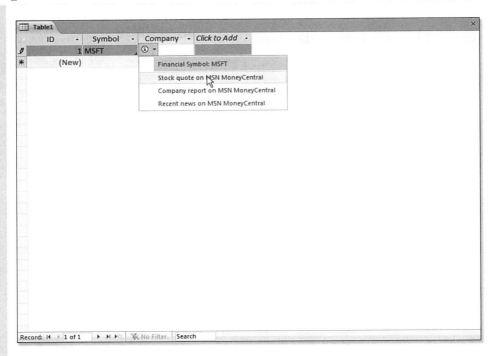

Figure 5.34
Selecting the smart tag icon and opening its drop-down list displays the available smart tag actions.

Custom smart tags, such as Financial Symbol, are defined by XML documents. The `urn:schemas-microsoft-com:office:smarttags#stockticker` property value is the Universal Resource Name (URN) for the custom smart tag `type` attribute value. The corresponding custom smart tag is defined by the Stocks.xml document in the Windows Vista or the Windows 7 \Program Files\ Common Files\Microsoft Shared\Smart Tag\Lists\1033\ folder (for the U.S. English locale). Navigate to and double-click Stocks.xml to open the document in Internet Explorer (see Figure 5.36). The three `<FL:action>` elements define the action options you see when opening the list (refer to Figure 5.36).

Copying and Pasting Tables

To copy a complete table or the records of a table to the Windows Clipboard, use the same methods that apply to most other Windows applications. (Using the Clipboard to paste individual records or sets of records into a table is one of the subjects of Chapter 6, "Entering, Editing, and Validating Access Table Data.") You can copy tables into other databases, such as a general-purpose backup database, by using the Clipboard.

To copy a table to another Access database, a destination database must exist. To create a backup database and copy the contents of the HRActions table to the database, follow these steps:

Figure 5.35
The MSN
Money site
displays
the current
Microsoft
(MSFT) stock
quotation.

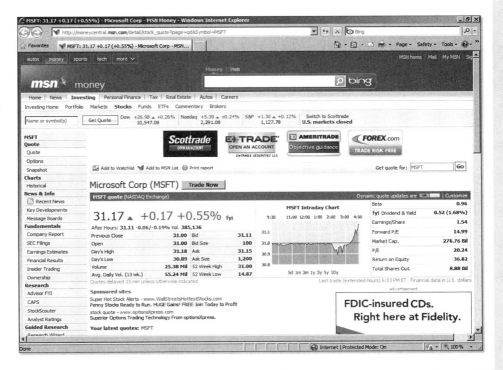

1. Expand the Navigation Pane, if necessary.

2. Click the Tables bar, if necessary, to display the list of tables.

3. Select the table that you want to copy to the new database.

4. Click the Copy button on the Home ribbon or press Ctrl+C.If you plan to copy the table to your current database, skip to step 7.

5. If you've created a destination backup database, click the Office button and click its link in the Recent Documents link, or click Open to open the database; then skip to step 7.

6. To create a backup database, click the Office, Manage, and Back Up Database buttons to open the Save As dialog. Accept the default filename, which appends the current date in YYYY-MM-DD format, or name the new database Backup.accdb or another appropriate filename.

note

Creating custom smart tags is beyond the scope of this book. If you want to learn more about Microsoft smart tag technology, go to http://msdn.microsoft.com and search for "smart tag" with the double-quotes included in the search term.

note

The Access 97 and 2000 versions of the Table Analyzer Wizard had several bugs that resulted in error messages or spurious typographical error entries. The Access 2007 and 2010 versions correct these problems.

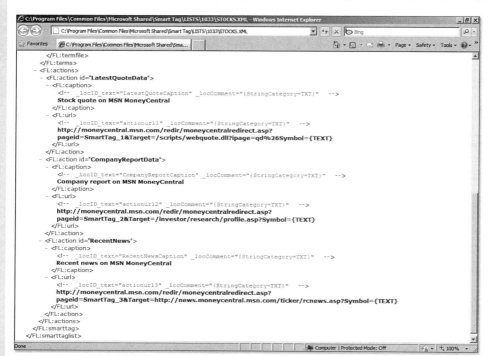

Figure 5.36
These `<FL:action>` elements of the Stocks. xml document generate two of the three fixed list (FL) items for the MSN Money Financial Symbols smart tag.

7. 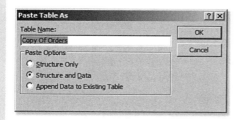 Click the Home ribbon's Paste button, press Ctrl+V, or choose Edit, Paste to open the Paste Table As dialog (see Figure 5.37).

Figure 5.37
The Paste Table As dialog lets you paste a backup copy of a table into the current or another database.

8. You have three options for pasting the backup table to the destination database. The most common choice is Structure and Data, with which you can create a new table or replace the data in a table with the name you enter in the Table Name text box. You can also paste only the structure and then append data to the table later by selecting Structure Only, or append the records to an existing table of the name that you enter. For this example, accept the default: Structure and Data.

9. Your current or backup database now has a copy of the table that you selected, and the name you entered appears in the Navigation pane. You can save multiple copies of the same table under different names if you're making a series of changes to the table that might affect the integrity of the data that it contains.

To delete a table from a database, select the table name in the Navigation pane and then press Delete. A confirmation message appears. Click Yes to delete the table forever. You can't undo deleting a table.

Using the Table Analyzer Wizard

Access 2010's Table Analyzer Wizard detects cells containing repeated data in table columns and proposes to create two new related tables to eliminate the repetition. This wizard uses the Lookup Wizard—described in Chapter 11—to create the relationship between the two new tables. After the wizard creates the new related tables, *NewName* and *Lookup*, your original table is renamed to *TableName*_OLD, and the wizard creates a one-to-many INNER JOIN query named *TableName* to return a resultset that duplicates the Datasheet view of the original table. So, you need not change the references to *TableName* in your Access application objects.

The *Lookup* table must have a valid primary key field to provide unambiguous association of a single record in the lookup table with a foreign key field in the *NewName* table. One of the problems associated with repetitious data is data entry errors, such as occasional misspelling of a company name or an address element in *Lookup*. The Table Analyzer Wizard detects and displays instances of minor mismatches in repeated cell values, such as a missing apostrophe, for correction. If such errors aren't corrected, the *Lookup* table includes spurious, almost-duplicate entries that violate the rules of table normalization.

Northwind.accdb's Orders table has a set of fields for shipping addresses. The data in these fields is the same for every order placed by each customer with three exceptions: order numbers 10248, 10249, and 10260. Shipping addresses compose the bulk of the data in the Orders table, so removal of duplicate shipping information greatly reduces the size of the Orders table. Placing shipping addresses in a lookup table also offers the opportunity to streamline the data entry process.

To demonstrate the use of the Table Analyzer Wizard to eliminate duplicate shipping address information in the Orders table of Northwind.accdb, follow these steps:

1. Use the Clipboard method—described in the preceding section—to create a copy of the Orders table named SalesOrders in the Northwind.accdb database. Working with a copy prevents making changes to Northwind.accdb's sample tables that would affect later examples in this book.

2. Launch the Table Analyzer Wizard by clicking the Analyze Tables button in the Database Tools ribbon's Analyze group.

3. Skip the two introductory dialogs by clicking the Next button twice to reach the Table Selection dialog shown in Figure 5.38.

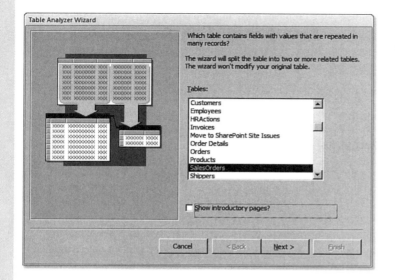

Figure 5.38
Select the table to analyze in the third Table Analyzer Wizard dialog.

4. Select the table with the duplicated data in the Tables list box (the SalesOrders table for this example) and clear the Show Introductory Pages? check box. Click Next to continue.

5. You want to choose the fields for the Lookup table, so select the No, I Want to Decide option, and click Next. The wizard displays a list of fields in the SalesOrders table renamed to Table1.

6. Click to select in the Table1 field list the first of the fields with duplicated information, ShipName; then press Shift and click the last of the fields to move, ShipCountry (see Figure 5.39).

7. Holding the left mouse button down, drag the selected fields from the field list to an empty area to the right of the Table1 list. When you release the mouse button, the wizard creates a new field list for proposed Table1 with a many-to-one relationship between Table1 and Table2. The relationship is based on a lookup field in Table1 and a Generated Unique ID (AutoNumber) field in Table2. An input box opens to rename Table1; type **ShipAddresses** in the Table Name text box (see Figure 5.40). Click OK to close the input box.

8. ![key icon] CustomerID is a better choice than an AutoNumber field for the initial primary key field of ShipAddresses, because there's currently only one correct ShipAddress per customer in the Orders table. Click and drag the CustomerID field from the Table1 field list to the ShipAddresses field list. With the CustomerID field selected in the ShipAddresses field list, click the Set Unique Identifier button (the one with the key icon only). The Generated Unique ID field disappears and the CustomerID field becomes the primary key for the proposed ShipAddress table (see Figure 5.41). Click Next to continue.

Figure 5.39
Select the fields with the duplicate data to move to a new lookup table. For this example, the fields to select begin with "Ship."

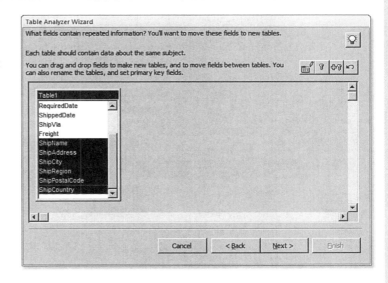

Figure 5.40
The wizard designs a lookup table to contain the fields moved from the source table, and opens an input box in which you assign a name to the lookup table.

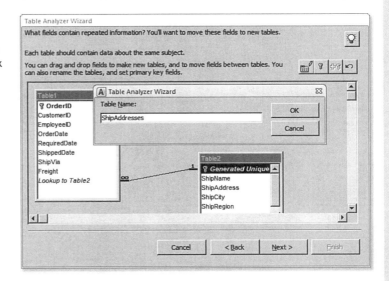

9. If the wizard detects a misspelling of an entry in the lookup table, it opens a Correcting Typographical Errors dialog. The wizard bases the value in the Correction column on the frequency of exact duplication of records. In this case, the wizard has detected two ShipAddress values for Old World Delicatessen (see Figure 5.42). Click the Next Key button.

10. Click the Next Key button three times to view the three additional records (10260 for OLDWO, 10249 for TRADH, and 10248 for WILMK) with different shipping addresses. Shipping information in the three records later reverts to the values selected in the check boxes, because the wizard can't handle multiple shipping addresses for a single primary key value.

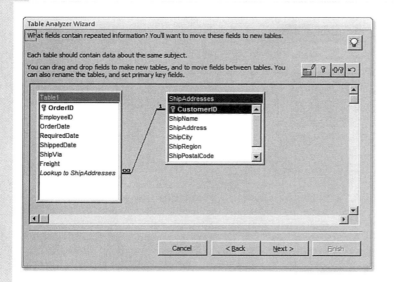

Figure 5.41
Specify the CustomerID field as the primary key for the ShipAddresses lookup table.

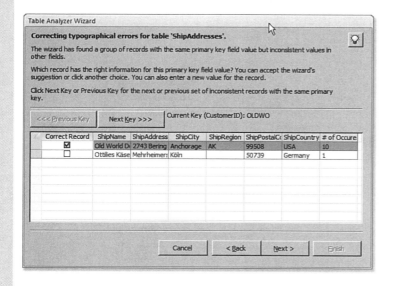

Figure 5.42
The wizard detects and proposes to correct a misspelled shipping address, which actually reflects a second shipping address. Two additional records have different shipping addresses, which call for shipment to a destination other than the customer's billing address.

11. Click Next, and the wizard proposes to create a query, in this case named SalesOrders, that substitutes for the original SalesOrders table. Accept the default option, Yes, Create the Query. Clear the Display Help check box to prevent two wizard Help screens from appearing when you complete the operation.

12. Click Finish to create the SalesOrders query, and then open the SalesOrders query.

13. Select the Lookup to ShipAddresses field and click the down-arrow button to open the lookup list, which displays the shipping addresses extracted from the SalesOrders table (see Figure 5.43). Notice that the list has only one entry for ALKFI, proving that the wizard corrected the spelling error.

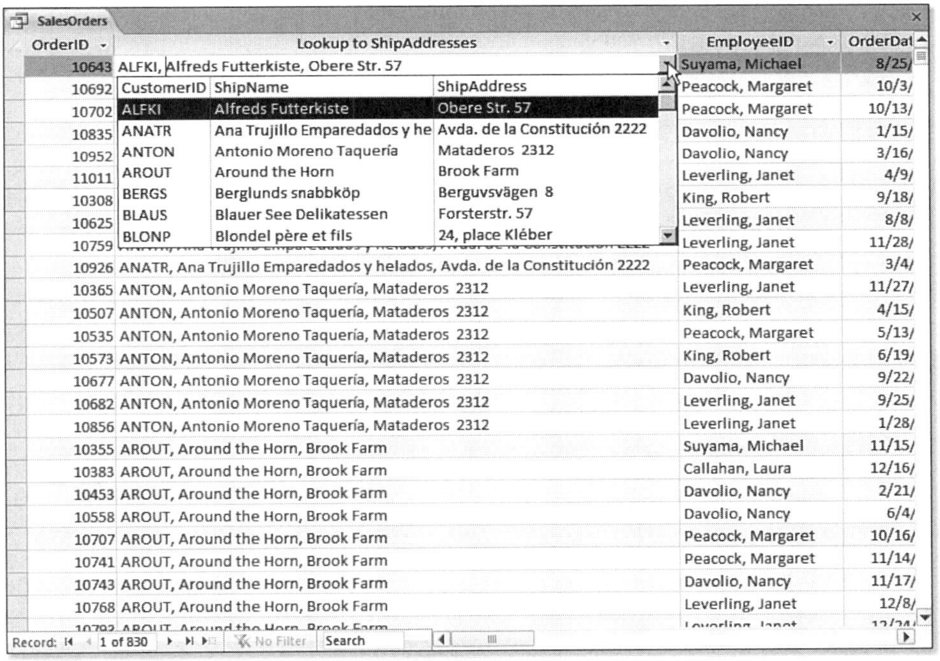

Figure 5.43
The SalesOrders query, which replaces the SalesOrders table, has a lookup field from which you can select a shipping address for the order.

The wizard has renamed the original SalesOrders table as SalesOrders_OLD, and substitutes the SalesOrders query for the SalesOrders table. The Nwind05.accdb database in the \Access2010\ Chaptr05 folder of the accompanying Online includes the tables and query created in the preceding steps.

Generating a Data Dictionary with the Database Documenter

After you've determined the individual data entities that make up the tables of your database and have established the relationships between them, the next step is to prepare a preliminary written description of the database, called a *data dictionary*. Data dictionaries are indispensable to database systems; an undocumented database system is almost impossible to administer and maintain properly. Errors and omissions in database design often are uncovered when you prepare the preliminary data dictionary.

 note

If you want to return Northwind. accdb to its original state, delete the SalesOrders query plus the SalesOrders_OLD, Table1, and ShipAddress tables from the Navigation pane.

When you've completed and tested your database design, you prepare the final detailed version of the data dictionary. As you add new forms and reports to applications or modify existing forms and reports, update the data dictionary to keep it current. Even if you're making a database for your personal use, a simplified version of a data dictionary pays many dividends on the time invested.

Access 2010's Database Documenter creates a report that details the objects and values of the properties of the objects in the current database. You can also export the report to a Word or Excel file.

In many cases, Documenter tells you more than you would ever want to know about your database; the full report for all objects in Northwind.accdb, for example, requires about 400 printed pages. Most often, you only want to document your tables and, perhaps, your queries to create a complete data dictionary. The following steps show you how to create a data dictionary for the table objects (only) of Nwind05.accdb:

1. Open the database you want to document, \2010Samples\Chaptr05\Nwind05.accdb for this example, and click the Database Tools ribbon's Documenter button to open Documenter's tabbed dialog.

2. Click the tab for the type of database object(s) you want to document. Current Database and Tables are the most common data dictionary objects, so click the Current Database tab.

3. Mark the Properties and Relationships check boxes, or click Select All (see Figure 5.44), and then click the Tables tab.

4. Mark the check boxes of the tables to analyze, Employees and HRActions for this example (see Figure 5.45), and click the Options button to open the Print Table Definition dialog.

5. Northwind.accdb isn't a secure database, so clear the Permissions by User and Group check box. The default options for fields and indexes specify the full gamut of information on these objects (see Figure 5.46). Click OK to close the dialog.

6. Click OK to close the Documenter dialog and start the report generation process. After a few seconds, page 1 of a 22-page report opens in Print Preview mode.

Figure 5.44
Mark both the Properties and Relationships check boxes to list database properties and generate simple diagrams of table relationships.

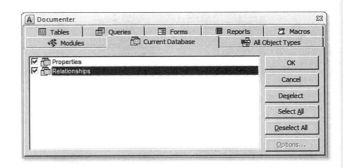

Figure 5.45
Select a couple of tables to give the Documenter a test run.

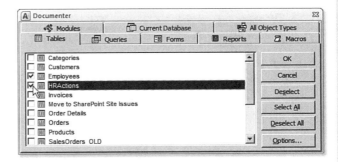

Figure 5.46
The Print Table Definition dialog lets you specify the amount of detail the report contains for tables.

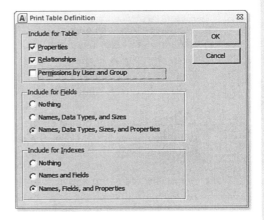

7. Click the Print Preview window to display the report at 100% scale and expand the size of the window to display the full width of the report (see Figure 5.47). For this example, the Employees table is the report's first object.

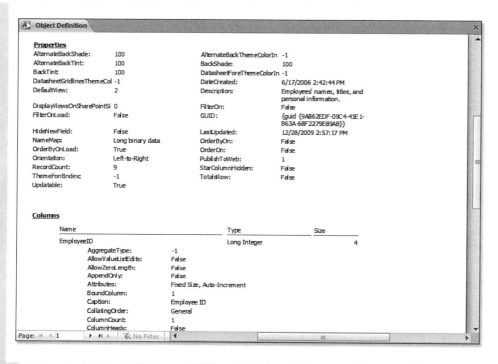

8. Scroll the report to review the remainder of page 1, and then click the next page button to display additional fields of the Employees table and the HRActions table.

9. Database properties appear at the end of the report. Navigate to page 15 to view the first page of the Database section of the report. Pages 18 through 22 of the sample report display simplified entity-relationship (E-R) diagrams for the database's relationships (see Figure 5.48).

> **note**
>
> To email or export Database Documenter reports in Adobe Portable Document Format (PDF) or Microsoft XML Paper Specification (XPS) format, you must download the PDF and XPS converter from the Office Live Website, if you haven't done this previously.

10. Click the Print button on the Quick-Access Toolbar to print the report, or right-click the report and choose Print Preview or Print.

11. Right-click the report and choose Send To, Mail Recipient (as Attachment) to open the Send dialog, where you can choose one of six formats, including HTML, Report Snapshot, and XML. Alternatively, choose Export, to open the Export Report dialog, and save the file in one of the eight supported formats.

Documenting other types of objects in your database follows the same method outlined in the preceding steps. The capability to send Documenter reports by email simplifies keeping others involved in the database design project up to date on changes.

Figure 5.48
Documenter's Current Database, Relationships option generates Spartan entity-relationship diagrams for all tables in the database, regardless of the tables you select to document.

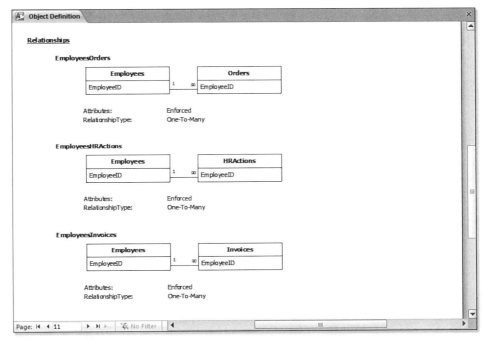

ENTERING, EDITING, AND VALIDATING ACCESS TABLE DATA

Ease of data entry is a primary criterion for an effective database development environment. Most of your Access database applications probably will use forms for data entry. In many instances, however, entering data in Table Datasheet view is quicker than using a form, especially during the database development cycle. For example, it's a good idea to test your proposed database structure before you commit to designing the forms and reports. Although the Name AutoCorrect feature reduces object name discrepancies, changing table and field names or altering relationships between tables after you create a collection of forms and reports can involve a substantial amount of work.

To test the database design, you must enter test data. In this instance, using Table Datasheet view to enter data makes more sense than using a form. Even if you import data from another database type or from a spreadsheet, you probably need to edit the data to make it compatible with your new application. The first part of this chapter concentrates on data entry and editing methods in datasheets.

Another important factor in a database development environment is maintaining the integrity of your data. Entity integrity rules limit the data you enter in fields to a particular range or set of valid values.

Like earlier versions, Access 2010 lets you enforce entity integrity rules (often called *business rules*) at the field and table levels. You enforce entity integrity (also called *domain integrity*) by entering expressions as the value of the Validation Rule property of fields and tables. This chapter shows you how to use simple expressions for domain integrity validation rules. After you master Access/VBA operators and expressions in Chapter 10, "Understanding Access Query Operators and Expressions," you'll be able to write complex validation rules that minimize the possibility of data entry errors in your Access tables.

Using Keyboard Operations for Entering and Editing Data

Access 2010 is more mouse oriented than its 2003 and earlier predecessors, as are the other members of the Office 2010 suite, but keyboard equivalents are available for the most common actions. One reason for providing keyboard commands is that constantly shifting the hand from a keyboard to a mouse and back can reduce data entry rates by more than half. Shifting between a keyboard and mouse can also lead to or aggravate repetitive stress injury (RSI), of which the most common type is carpal tunnel syndrome (CTS).

Keyboard operations are as important or more important in a data entry environment than they are in word processing applications. Consequently, the information concerning key combinations for data entry appears here instead of being relegated to fine print in an appendix. The data entry procedures you learn in the following sections prove useful when you come to the "Testing Field and Table Validation Rules" section near the end of the chapter.

tip

This chapter uses the HRActions table for data entry and validation examples. If you didn't create the HRActions table in the preceding chapter, click the External Data tab, click the Access button, and import the HRActions table from Nwind05. accdb in the location where you saved the CD-ROM files, typically C:\A2010Samples\Chaptr05. After you import the table, open the Relationships window, add the HRActions table, and create a one-to-many relationship between the EmployeeID fields of the Employees and HRActions tables. Nwind05.accdb only contains tables and a single query.

Creating a Working Copy of Northwind.accdb

If you want to experiment with the keyboard operations described in the following sections, work with a copy of the Northwind.accdb sample database. By using a copy, you don't need to worry about making changes that affect the sample database.

Setting Data Entry Options

Most keyboard operations described in the following sections apply to tables and updatable queries in Datasheet view, text boxes on forms, and text boxes used for entering property values in Properties windows and in the Field Properties grid of Table Design view. In the examples, the Arrow Key Behavior property is set to Next Character rather than the default Next Field value.

tip

If you set the Arrow Key Behavior property value to Next Field, you won't be able to select a block of cells in Datasheet View in the later "Using Key Combinations for Windows Clipboard Operations" section. Data entry operators ordinarily don't need to select blocks of cells in the normal course of their work.

When the Arrow Key Behavior property is set to Next Field, the arrow keys move the cursor from field to field. Data entry operators accustomed to mainframe terminals or DOS applications probably prefer to use the Next Character setting.

To modify the behavior of the arrow keys and the Tab and Enter keys, click the File tab to open the gallery, and click Access Options to open the Access Options dialog. Click the Advanced list item to display the Editing options settings (see Figure 6.1). Table 6.1 lists the available options with the default values. These keyboard options let you emulate the behavior of the data entry keys of mainframe and other data entry terminals.

Figure 6.1
The settings you specify on the Advanced page of the Access Options dialog apply to all databases you open, because they're stored in your computer's Registry.

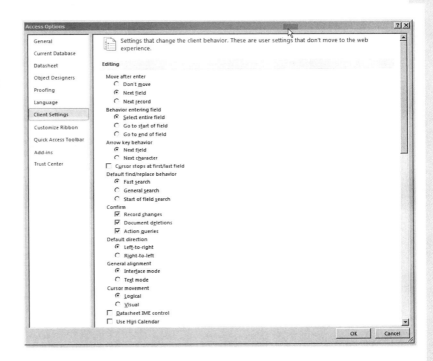

Table 6.1 Keyboard Options for All Access Databases

Option	Function
Move After Enter Group	
Don't Move	When this option is selected, the cursor remains in the current field when you press Enter.
Next Field (default)	When this option is selected, the cursor moves to the next field when you press Enter. Use this setting to duplicate dBASE and its clones' behavior.
Next Record	When this option is selected, the cursor moves down the column to the next record when you press Enter.
Behavior Entering Field Group	
Select Entire Field (default)	When this option is selected, the entire field's contents are selected when you use the arrow keys to move the cursor into the field.

Table 6.1 Continued

Option	Function
Go to Start of Field	Selecting this option causes the cursor to move to the beginning of the field when you use the arrow keys to move the cursor into the field.
Go to End of Field	Selecting this option causes the cursor to move to the end of the field when you use the arrow keys to move the cursor into the field. Use this setting to duplicate mainframe terminal and xBase behavior.
Arrow Key Behavior Group	
Next Field (default)	If this option is selected, pressing the right- or left-arrow key moves the cursor to the next field.
Next Character	If this option is selected, pressing the right- or left-arrow key moves the cursor to the previous or next character in the same field. Use this setting if you want to duplicate the behavior of mainframe terminal or xBase applications.
Individual Settings	
Cursor Stops at First/ Last Field	Marking this check box keeps the cursor from moving to another record when the left- or right-arrow key is pressed and the cursor is in the first or last field of the record.
2007 NEW Use Hijri Calendar	Marking this check box substitutes the Hijri lunar (Islamic) calendar for the Gregorian calendar.
Datasheet IME Control	Marking this check box enables the Input Method Editor (IME) for entering data in East Asian languages (Windows Vista, XP, and 2003 only).
Cursor Movement Group	
2007 NEW Logical (default)	If this option is selected, cursor movement progresses within bidirectional text according to the direction of the language encountered.
2007 NEW Visual	If this option is selected, cursor movement progresses within bidirectional text by moving to the next visually adjacent character.

Using Data Entry and Editing Keys

Arrow keys and key combinations in Access are, for the most part, identical to those used in other Windows applications. The F2 key, used for editing cell contents in Excel, has a different function in Access—F2 toggles between editing and select mode. (*Toggle* means to alternate between two states.) In the editing state, the cursor indicates the insertion point in the field; the key combinations shown in Table 6.2 are active. If the field or any character in the field is selected (indicated by a black background with white type), the editing keys behave as indicated in Table 6.3.

Table 6.2   Keys for Editing Fields, Grids, and Text Boxes

Key	Function
F2	Toggles between displaying the cursor for editing and selecting the entire field. The field must be deselected (black text on a white background) and the cursor must be visible for the keys in this table to operate as described.
End	Moves the cursor to the end of the field in a single- line field or the end of the line in a multiple-line field.
Ctrl+End	Moves the cursor to the end of a multiple-line field.
← (left arrow)	Moves the cursor one character to the left until you reach the first character in the line.
Ctrl+ ← (left arrow)	Moves the cursor one word to the left until you reach the first word in the line.
Home	Moves the cursor to the beginning of the line.
Ctrl+Home	Moves the cursor to the beginning of the field in multiple-line fields.
Backspace	Deletes the entire selection or the character to the left of the cursor.
Delete	Deletes the entire selection or the character to the right of the cursor.
Ctrl+Z or Alt+Backspace	Undoes typing, a replace operation, or any other change to the record since the last time it was saved. An edited record is saved to the database when you move to a new record or close the editing window.
Esc	Undoes changes to the current field. Press Esc twice to undo changes to the current field and to the entire current record, if you edited other fields.

Table 6.3   Keys for Selecting Text in Fields, Grids, and Text Boxes

Key	Function
Text Within a Field	
F2	Toggles between displaying the cursor for editing and selecting the entire field. The field must be selected (white type on a black background) for the keys in this table to operate as described.
Shift+ (left arrow)	Selects or deselects one character to the right.
Ctrl+Shift+	Selects or deselects one word to the right. Includes trailing spaces.
Shift+ (right arrow)	Selects or deselects one character to the left.
Ctrl+Shift+ (left arrow)	Selects or deselects one word to the left.

Table 6.3 Continued

Key	Function
Next Field	
Tab or Enter	Selects the next field if the default Next Field option is selected.
Record	
Shift+spacebar	Selects or deselects the entire current record.
(up arrow)	Selects the first field in the preceding record when a record is selected.
(down arrow)	Selects the first field in the next record when a record is selected.
Column	
Ctrl+spacebar	Toggles selection of the current column.
(right arrow)	Selects the first field in the column to the left (if a column is selected and a column is to the left).
Fields and Records	
F8	Turns on Extend mode. You see EXT in the status bar. In Extend mode, pressing F8 extends the selection to the word, then the field, then the record, and then all the records.
Shift+F8	Reverses the last F8.
Esc	Cancels Extend mode.

Operations that select the entire field or a portion of the field, as listed in Table 6.3, generally are used with Windows Clipboard operations.

Using Key Combinations for Windows Clipboard Operations

In Table Datasheet view, the Clipboard is used primarily for transferring Access data between applications, such as copying data to an Excel worksheet or a Word table. However, you can also use the Clipboard for repetitive data entry. Access lets you select a rectangular block of data cells in a table and copy the block to the Clipboard. To select a block of cells, follow these steps:

1. Position the mouse pointer at the left edge of the top-left cell of the block you want to select. The cursor (a mouse pointer shaped like an I-beam until this point) turns into a cross similar to the mouse pointer for Excel worksheets.

2. Drag the mouse pointer to the right edge of the bottom-right cell of the desired block.

3. The selected block appears in reverse type (white on black, also called *reverse video*). Release the mouse button when the selection meets your requirement.

 tip

To create a new, empty table from the copied block, click the Table button of the Create ribbon's Tables group. With the second column selected, click the Home tab and then click the Paste, Paste Append button to add the block to the table. Pasting the records to the table adds the field names. If you don't want the default AutoNumber primary key, delete the ID column in Table Design view.

4. Press Ctrl+C to copy the selected block to the Clipboard.

Figure 6.2 shows a selected block of data in the Customers table. You can copy data blocks but can't cut them.

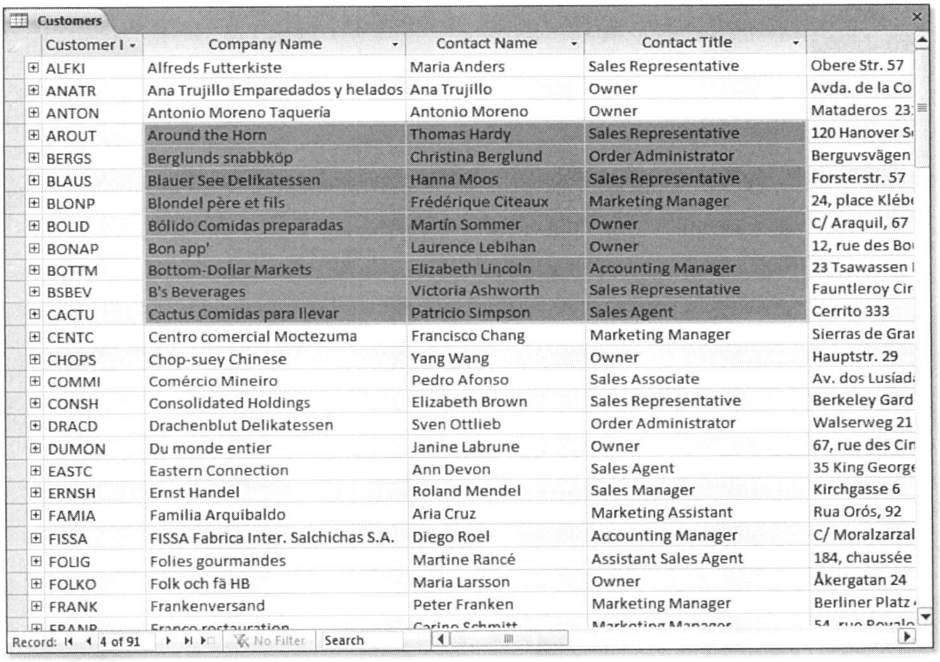

Customers

Customer I	Company Name	Contact Name	Contact Title	
ALFKI	Alfreds Futterkiste	Maria Anders	Sales Representative	Obere Str. 57
ANATR	Ana Trujillo Emparedados y helados	Ana Trujillo	Owner	Avda. de la Co
ANTON	Antonio Moreno Taquería	Antonio Moreno	Owner	Mataderos 23
AROUT	Around the Horn	Thomas Hardy	Sales Representative	120 Hanover S
BERGS	Berglunds snabbköp	Christina Berglund	Order Administrator	Berguvsvägen
BLAUS	Blauer See Delikatessen	Hanna Moos	Sales Representative	Forsterstr. 57
BLONP	Blondel père et fils	Frédérique Citeaux	Marketing Manager	24, place Kléb
BOLID	Bólido Comidas preparadas	Martín Sommer	Owner	C/ Araquil, 67
BONAP	Bon app'	Laurence Lebihan	Owner	12, rue des Bo
BOTTM	Bottom-Dollar Markets	Elizabeth Lincoln	Accounting Manager	23 Tsawassen
BSBEV	B's Beverages	Victoria Ashworth	Sales Representative	Fauntleroy Cir
CACTU	Cactus Comidas para llevar	Patricio Simpson	Sales Agent	Cerrito 333
CENTC	Centro comercial Moctezuma	Francisco Chang	Marketing Manager	Sierras de Gra
CHOPS	Chop-suey Chinese	Yang Wang	Owner	Hauptstr. 29
COMMI	Comércio Mineiro	Pedro Afonso	Sales Associate	Av. dos Lusíad
CONSH	Consolidated Holdings	Elizabeth Brown	Sales Representative	Berkeley Gard
DRACD	Drachenblut Delikatessen	Sven Ottlieb	Order Administrator	Walserweg 21
DUMON	Du monde entier	Janine Labrune	Owner	67, rue des Cin
EASTC	Eastern Connection	Ann Devon	Sales Agent	35 King Georg
ERNSH	Ernst Handel	Roland Mendel	Sales Manager	Kirchgasse 6
FAMIA	Familia Arquibaldo	Aria Cruz	Marketing Assistant	Rua Orós, 92
FISSA	FISSA Fabrica Inter. Salchichas S.A.	Diego Roel	Accounting Manager	C/ Moralzarzal
FOLIG	Folies gourmandes	Martine Rancé	Assistant Sales Agent	184, chaussée
FOLKO	Folk och fä HB	Maria Larsson	Owner	Åkergatan 24
FRANK	Frankenversand	Peter Franken	Marketing Manager	Berliner Platz

Record: 4 of 91 No Filter Search

Figure 6.2 You can select a rectangular block of data to copy to the Clipboard and then paste the block to cells of an Excel worksheet or Word table.

Table 6.4 lists the key combinations for copying or cutting data to and pasting data from the Clipboard.

Table 6.4 Key Combinations for Windows Clipboard Operations

Key	Function
Ctrl+C or Ctrl+Insert	Copies the selection to the Clipboard.
Ctrl+V or Shift+Insert	Pastes the Clipboard's contents at the cursor's location.
Ctrl+X or Shift+Delete	Copies the selection to the Clipboard and then deletes it. This operation also is called a cut. You can cut only the content of a single cell you select with the cursor.
Ctrl+Z or Alt+Backspace	Undoes your last Cut, Delete, or Paste operation.

Using Shortcut Keys for Fields and Text Boxes

Shortcut keys minimize the number of keystrokes required to accomplish common data entry tasks. Most shortcut key combinations use the Ctrl key with other keys. Ctrl+C, Ctrl+V, and Ctrl+X for Clipboard operations are examples of global shortcut keys in Windows. Table 6.5 lists shortcut keys for field and text box entries.

 tip

Ctrl+' or Ctrl+" are the most important of the shortcut keys for entering table data. The ability to copy data from a field of the preceding record into the same field of a new record is a welcome timesaver.

Table 6.5   Shortcut Keys for Text Boxes and Fields in Tables

Key	Function
Ctrl+; (semicolon)	Inserts the current date
Ctrl+: (colon)	Inserts the current time
Ctrl+' (apostrophe) or Ctrl+" (double quote)	Inserts the value from the same field in the preceding record
Ctrl+Enter	Inserts a newline character (carriage return plus line feed, or CRLF) in a text box
Ctrl++ (plus)	Adds a new record to the table
Ctrl+− (minus)	Deletes the current record from the table
Shift+Enter	Saves all changes to the current record

Adding Records to a Table

 tip

Emulating the data entry key behavior of a mainframe terminal or DOS database application can make a major difference in the acceptance of your database applications by data entry operators with years of experience with mainframe and DOS database applications.

When you open an updatable table in Datasheet view, the last row is an empty placeholder for a new record, called the *tentative append record* in this book. (An *updatable table* is one whose data you can add to or edit.) An asterisk in the last record selection button in the datasheet indicates the tentative append record. Record selection buttons are the gray buttons in the leftmost column of Table Datasheet view. If you open a database for read-only access, the tentative append record doesn't appear. Tables attached from other databases can also be read-only. The updatability of attached tables is discussed in Chapter 8, "Linking, Importing, and Exporting Data."

 tip

To go to the tentative append record of a table quickly, press Ctrl++ (plus).

When you press Ctrl++ or place the cursor in a field of the tentative append record, the record selection button's asterisk symbol turns into the selected (current) record symbol. When you add data to a field of the selected tentative append record, the selected record symbol changes to the edit symbol (a pencil), and a new tentative append record appears in the row after your addition. Figure 6.3 shows a new record in the process of being added to the Customers table. The CustomerID field has an Input Mask property value (>LLLLL) that requires you to enter five letters, which are capitalized automatically as you enter them. The input mask changes the cursor from an I-beam to a reverse-video block.

> To review how input masks work, **see** *"Using Input Masks,"* **p. 202.**

To cancel the addition of a new record, press the Esc key twice. Pressing Esc once cancels the changes you made to the current field. You might not need to press Esc twice, but doing so guarantees canceling the record addition.

> **note**
>
> You can cut groups of records to the Clipboard, deleting them from the table, but you can't cut data blocks. A group of records includes all fields of one or more selected records. A data block consists of a selection in a table datasheet that doesn't include all fields of the selected rows. The Edit, Cut command is enabled for groups of records and disabled for data blocks.

Figure 6.3
The CustomerID field of Northwind's Customers table has an input mask that requires exactly five letters and automatically capitalizes the letters as you enter them.

Customer I ▾	Company Name ▾	Contact Name ▾	Contact Title ▾	
⊞ RICSU	Richter Supermarkt	Michael Holz	Sales Manager	Grenzacherwe
⊞ ROMEY	Romero y tomillo	Alejandra Camino	Accounting Manager	Gran Vía, 1
⊞ SANTG	Santé Gourmet	Jonas Bergulfsen	Owner	Erling Skakkes
⊞ SAVEA	Save-a-lot Markets	Jose Pavarotti	Sales Representative	187 Suffolk Ln.
⊞ SEVES	Seven Seas Imports	Hari Kumar	Sales Manager	90 Wadhurst R
⊞ SIMOB	Simons bistro	Jytte Petersen	Owner	Vinbæltet 34
⊞ SPECD	Spécialités du monde	Dominique Perrier	Marketing Manager	25, rue Lauriste
⊞ SPLIR	Split Rail Beer & Ale	Art Braunschweiger	Sales Manager	P.O. Box 555
⊞ SUPRD	Suprêmes délices	Pascale Cartrain	Accounting Manager	Boulevard Tirc
⊞ THEBI	The Big Cheese	Liz Nixon	Marketing Manager	89 Jefferson W
⊞ THECR	The Cracker Box	Liu Wong	Marketing Assistant	55 Grizzly Peak
⊞ TOMSP	Toms Spezialitäten	Karin Josephs	Marketing Manager	Luisenstr. 48
⊞ TORTU	Tortuga Restaurante	Miguel Angel Paolino	Owner	Avda. Azteca 1
⊞ TRADH	Tradição Hipermercados	Anabela Domingues	Sales Representative	Av. Inês de Cas
⊞ TRAIH	Trail's Head Gourmet Provisioners	Helvetius Nagy	Sales Associate	722 DaVinci Blv
⊞ VAFFE	Vaffeljernet	Palle Ibsen	Sales Manager	Smagsløget 45
⊞ VICTE	Victuailles en stock	Mary Saveley	Sales Agent	2, rue du Comr
⊞ VINET	Vins et alcools Chevalier	Paul Henriot	Accounting Manager	59 rue de l'Abb
⊞ WANDK	Die Wandernde Kuh	Rita Müller	Sales Representative	Adenauerallee
⊞ WARTH	Wartian Herkku	Pirkko Koskitalo	Accounting Manager	Torikatu 38
⊞ WELLI	Wellington Importadora	Paula Parente	Sales Manager	Rua do Mercac
⊞ WHITC	White Clover Markets	Karl Jablonski	Owner	305 - 14th Ave.
⊞ WILMK	Wilman Kala	Matti Karttunen	Owner/Marketing Assistant	Keskuskatu 45
⊞ WOLZA	Wolski Zajazd	Zbyszek Piestrzeniewicz	Owner	ul. Filtrowa 68
⊞ XYZ				

Record: I◄ ◄ 92 of 92 ► ►I ►✳ No Filter Search

Selecting, Appending, Replacing, and Deleting Table Records

You can select a single record or a group of records to copy or cut to the Clipboard, or to delete from the table, by the following methods:

- To select a single record, click its record selection button.

- To select a contiguous group of records, click the first record's selection button and then drag the mouse pointer along the record selection buttons to the last record of the group.

- Alternatively, to select a group of records, click the first record's selection button and then Shift+click the last record to include in the group. You can also press Shift+down arrow to select a group of records.

You can't use Ctrl+click to select noncontiguous records.

You can cut or copy and append duplicate records to the same table (if appending the duplicate records doesn't cause a primary key violation) or to another table. You can't cut records from a primary table that has dependent records in a related table if you enforce referential integrity. The following methods apply to appending or replacing the content of records with records stored in the Clipboard:

- To append records from the Clipboard to a table, click Paste, Paste Append.

- To replace the content of a record(s) with data from the Clipboard, select the record(s) whose content you want to replace and then press Ctrl+V. Only the number of records you select or the number of records stored in the Clipboard (whichever is fewer) is replaced.

 note

SQL Server substitutes CHECK constraints for the Validation Rule property. As with Access, CHECK constraints can apply at the table or field level. The Access Expression Service lets you use VBA functions, such as UCase( ), in validation rules. SQL Server requires use of Transact-SQL (T-SQL) functions for CHECK constraints. Chapter 27, "Moving from Access Queries to Transact-SQL," explains how to translate Access/VBA functions into T-SQL functions.

To delete one or more records, select those records and press Delete. If deletion is allowed, a message box asks you to confirm your deletion, if you haven't cleared the Confirm Record Changes text box on the Edit/Find page of the Options dialog. You can't undo deletions of records.

Validating Data Entry

The data entered in tables must be accurate if the database is to be valuable to you or your organization. Even the most experienced data entry operators occasionally enter incorrect information. To add simple tests for the reasonableness of entries, add short expressions as a Validation Rule in the General page of Table Design view's Field Properties pane. If the entered data fails to pass your validation rule, a message box informs the operator that a violation occurred. You can customize the error message by adding the text as the value of the Validation Text property. Validating data maintains the entity integrity of your tables.

Expressions are a core element of computer programming. Access lets you create expressions without requiring that you be a programmer, although some familiarity with a programming language is helpful. Expressions use the familiar arithmetic symbols +, −, * (multiply), and / (divide). These symbols are called operators because they operate on (use) the values that precede and follow them. These operators are reserved symbols in VBA. The values operated on by operators are called *operands*.

You can also use operators to compare two values; the < (less than) and > (greater than) symbols are examples of comparison operators. And, Or, Is, Not, Between, and Like are called logical operators. (Between and Like are Access, not VBA, operators, so they don't appear in bold type). Comparison and logical operators return only True, False, and no value (the Null value). The & operator combines two text entries (character strings or just strings) into a single string. To qualify as an expression, at least one operator must be included. You can construct complex expressions by combining the different operators according to rules that apply to each operator involved. The collection of these rules is called *operator syntax*.

 To learn more about Access operators, **see** *"Understanding the Elements in Expressions,"* **p. 382.**

Data validation rules use expressions that result in one of two values: True or False. Entries in a data cell are accepted if the result of the validation is true and rejected if it's false. If the data is rejected by the validation rule, the text you enter as the Validation Text property value appears in a message box. Chapter 10 explains the syntax of Access validation expressions.

Adding Field-Level Validation Rules

Validation rules that restrict the values entered in a field and are based on only one field are called *field-level validation rules*. Table 6.6 lists the simple field-level validation rules used for some fields in the HRActions table you created in Chapter 5, "Working with Access Databases and Tables."

 note

You must allow ScheduledDate values as early as 2000 to accommodate the hire dates in the first two records of the Employees table. This book's Northwind.accdb sample database has more recent dates than Microsoft's Northwind.mdb in the Employees and Orders tables.

Table 6.6 Validation Criteria for the Fields of the HRActions Table

Field Name	Validation Rule	Validation Text
EmployeeID	>0	Please enter a valid employee ID number.
ActionType	In("H","Q","Y","S","R","B","C","T")	Only H, Q, Y, S, R, B, C, and T codes are valid.
Initiated By	>0	Please enter a valid supervisor ID number.
ScheduledDate	Between Date()-5475 And Date()+365	Scheduled dates can't be more than 15 years ago or more than 1 year from now.
ApprovedBy	>0 Or Is Null	Enter a valid manager ID number or leave blank if not approved.

Field Name	Validation Rule	Validation Text
EffectiveDate	None	
HRRating	Between 0 And 9 Or Is Null	Rating range is 0 for terminated employees, 1 to 9, or blank.
NewSalary	None	None.
NewRate	>8.55 Or Is Null	Hourly rate must be more than the prevailing minimum wage ($8.55 per hour for the state of Washington in 2010).
NewBonus	None	None.
NewCommission	<=0.1 or Is Null	Commission rate can't exceed 10%.
HRComments	None	None.

In their present form, the validation rules for fields that require employee ID numbers can't ensure that a valid ID number is entered. You could enter an employee ID number that isn't present in the Employees table. A validation rule for the EmployeeID field could test the EmployeeID number field of the Employees table to determine whether the employee ID number is present. You don't need to create this test because the rules of referential integrity perform this validation for you automatically. However, validation rules for InitiatedBy and ApprovedBy require tests based on entries in the Employees table.

 tip

The In operator simplifies expressions that otherwise would require multiple Or operators. For example, using the Or operator for the Validation Rule property value of the ActionType field requires typing **"H" Or "Q" Or "Y" Or "S" Or "R" Or "B" Or "C" Or "T"**, which has many more characters.

 To review referential integrity rules, **see** *"Working with Relations, Key Fields, and Indexes,"* **p. 215.**

To add the validation rules of Table 6.6 to the HRActions table, follow these steps:

1. From the Navigation pane, open the HRActions table in Design view, if it isn't already open, by right-clicking the table name and choosing Design View.

2. Press F6 to switch to the Field Properties window, and then move to the Validation Rule text box.

3. Type **>0** and move to the text box labeled Validation Text.

4. Type **Please enter a valid employee ID number.** The text scrolls to the left when it becomes longer than what can be displayed in the text box. To display the beginning of the text, press Home. Press End to position the cursor at the last character. Figure 6.4 shows your entries in the Field Properties text boxes.

5. Enter the validation rule and validation text for the seven remaining fields listed in Table 6.6 that use data entry validation.

You test your validation rule entries later in the "Testing Field and Table Validation Rules" section.

Figure 6.4
The Field
Properties pane
displays the first
Validation Rule
and Validation
Text property
values entered
from the data in
Table 6.6.

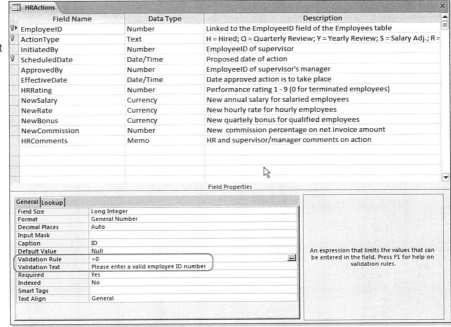

Adding Table-Level Validation Rules with the Expression Builder

One field, EffectiveDate, requires a validation rule that depends on ScheduledDate's value. The effective date of the personnel department's action shouldn't be before the scheduled date for the review that results in the action. You can't refer to other field names in an Access validation rule expression; instead, you add such validation rules in the Table Properties window. Validation rules in which the value of one field depends on a previously entered value in another field of the current record are called *table-level validation rules.*

The following steps add a table description and create a table-level validation rule for the EffectiveDate field:

1. Right-click the upper pane of Table Design view to open the Table Properties sheet.

2. Type **Human Resources Department Actions** in the Description text box (see Figure 6.5).

3. [...] In the Validation Rule text box, click the ellipsis (Builder) button to display the Expression Builder dialog. The current table, HRActions, is selected in the left list, and the fields of the table appear in the center list.

4. Double-click EffectiveDate in the center list to place [EffectiveDate] in the Expression Builder's text box at the top of the dialog. Square brackets surround field names to distinguish them from literal (string) values.

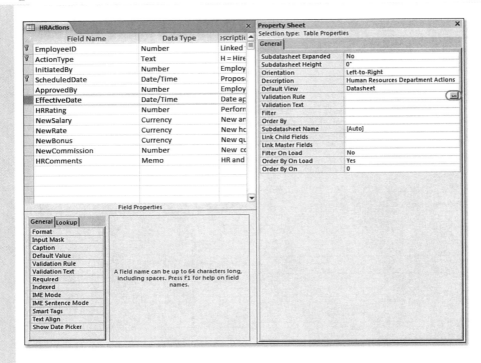

Figure 6.5
When you move the cursor to the Validation Rule row of the Table Properties Sheet, the ellipsis button appears so you can open the Access Expression Builder.

5. Type >= in the text box and double-click ScheduledDate in the center list to add [ScheduledDate] to the expression.

6. To accept a blank entry if the effective date of the personnel action isn't scheduled, add **Or [EffectiveDate] Is Null** to the expression, which appears as shown in Figure 6.6.

7. Click OK to add the table-level validation rule and close the Expression Builder dialog.

8. In the Validation Text text box, type **Effective date must be on or after the scheduled date**. Your Field Properties pane appears as shown in Figure 6.7.

9. Close the Table Properties sheet.

Adding a Simple Lookup List to the ActionType Field

Lookup tables require queries, which are the subject of this book's Part 3, "Transforming Data with Queries and PivotTables." However, you can add a lookup list to the table by adding a set of values that's similar to a validation expression. You create a lookup list by selecting the field the list applies to in Table Design view and specifying property values in the Lookup page of the Field Properties pane.

Figure 6.6
You can use the Access Expression Builder to generate more complex expressions for use as table-level validation rules.

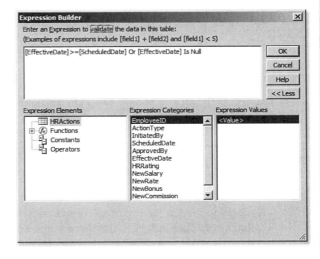

Figure 6.7
Closing the Expression Builder adds the expression of Figure 6.6 as the Validation Rule property value of the table.

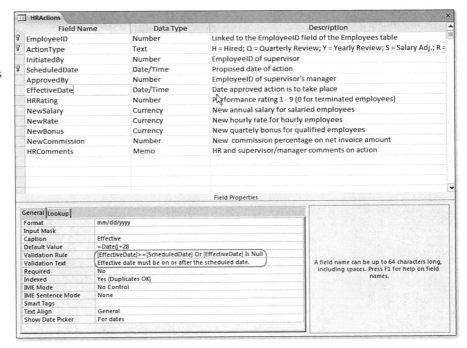

To add a combo box lookup list to the ActionType field of the HRActions table, do this:

1. In Design view, select the ActionType field and click the Lookup tab in the Field Properties pane.

2. Open the Display Control list and select Combo Box or List Box. This example uses a combo box.

3. Open the Row Source Type list and select Value List.

4. Accept the first column (1) default in the Bound Column list, and type **2** in the Column Count text box. The value list needs code and description columns.

5. In the Column Widths text box type **0.3";1.2"**, and in the List Width text box type **1.5"**.

6. Type **Y**(es) in the Limit to List text box. Limiting entries to the list's items is equivalent to the validation rule you added for this field.

7. Return to the Row Source property and type **H;Hired;Q;Quarterly Review;Y;Yearly Review;S;Salary Adj.;R;Hourly Rate Adj.;B;Bonus Adj.;C;Commission Adj.;T;Terminated** in the text box. The semicolons separate the entries you add in pairs to create the list. Your lookup list design appears as shown in Figure 6.8.

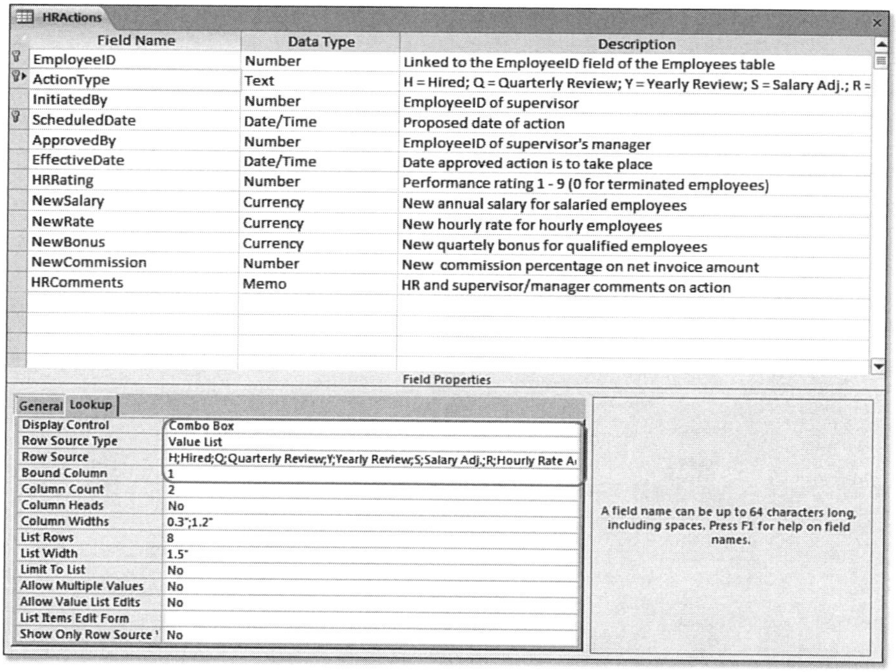

HRActions

Field Name	Data Type	Description
EmployeeID	Number	Linked to the EmployeeID field of the Employees table
ActionType	Text	H = Hired; Q = Quarterly Review; Y = Yearly Review; S = Salary Adj.; R =
InitiatedBy	Number	EmployeeID of supervisor
ScheduledDate	Date/Time	Proposed date of action
ApprovedBy	Number	EmployeeID of supervisor's manager
EffectiveDate	Date/Time	Date approved action is to take place
HRRating	Number	Performance rating 1 - 9 (0 for terminated employees)
NewSalary	Currency	New annual salary for salaried employees
NewRate	Currency	New hourly rate for hourly employees
NewBonus	Currency	New quarterly bonus for qualified employees
NewCommission	Number	New commission percentage on net invoice amount
HRComments	Memo	HR and supervisor/manager comments on action

Field Properties

General | Lookup

Display Control	Combo Box
Row Source Type	Value List
Row Source	H;Hired;Q;Quarterly Review;Y;Yearly Review;S;Salary Adj.;R;Hourly Rate A
Bound Column	1
Column Count	2
Column Heads	No
Column Widths	0.3";1.2"
List Rows	8
List Width	1.5"
Limit To List	No
Allow Multiple Values	No
Allow Value List Edits	No
List Items Edit Form	
Show Only Row Source	No

A field name can be up to 64 characters long, including spaces. Press F1 for help on field names.

Figure 6.8
You create a lookup list by specifying a combo box or list box and setting its properties in the Lookup page of the Field Properties pane.

8. Return to Datasheet view and save your design changes.

9. Press Tab to move to the ActionType field and press F4 to open the lookup list (see Figure 6.9).

Figure 6.9
The lookup list for ActionType codes has a description for each of the eight valid codes.

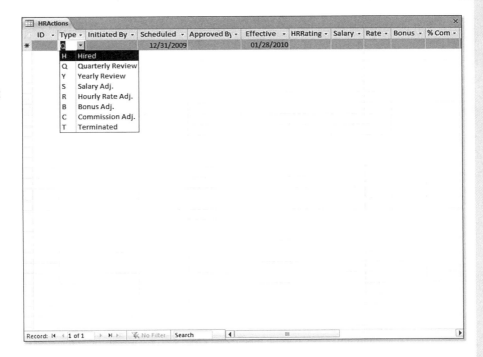

Lookup lists are handy for adding codes and other field values that seldom, if ever, change. When entering data, you can use the lookup list or type the code letter; the latter is considerably faster. You must keep lookup lists up to date. Also, if multiple tables use the same list, you must update each table's list manually. Lookups from tables or queries, which are preferable to lookup lists, are one of the topics of Chapter 11, "Creating Multitable and Crosstab Queries." You can use a single lookup table or query for all fields that need the lookup values.

Adding Records to the HRActions Table

Now you can test your work in creating the HRActions table and check whether Access is enforcing domain integrity. Table 6.7 shows the initial entries for each employee of Northwind Traders. The dates are based on values in the Employees table's HireDate field. No Rating entries appear in Table 6.7 because ratings don't apply to newly hired employees.

Table 6.7   First Nine Entries for the HRActions Table

Employee ID	Action Type	Initiated By	Scheduled Date	Approved By	Effective Date	New Salary	HRComment
1	H	1	05/01/2000	1	05/01/2000	2,000	Hired
2	H	1	08/14/2000	1	08/14/2000	3,500	Hired
3	H	1	04/01/2000	1	04/01/2000	2,250	Hired
4	H	2	05/03/2001	2	05/03/2001	2,250	Hired
5	H	2	10/17/2001	2	10/17/2001	2,500	Hired
6	H	5	10/17/2001	2	10/17/2001	4,000	Hired
7	H	5	01/02/2002	2	01/02/2002	3,000	Hired
8	H	2	05/05/2002	2	05/05/2002	2,500	Hired
9	H	5	11/15/2002	2	11/15/2002	3,000	Hired

Entering historical information in a table in Datasheet view is a relatively fast process for experienced data entry operators. This process also gives you a chance to test your default entries and Format properties for each field. You can enter bogus values that don't comply with your validation rules to verify that your rules are operational.

To add the first nine historical records to the HRActions table with the data from Table 6.7, follow these steps:

1. Click the Datasheet View button to return to Datasheet view, if necessary. The cursor is positioned in the EmployeeID field of the default first record.

2. Enter the EmployeeID of the employee. Press Enter, Tab, or the right-arrow key to move to the next field and to add a new default blank record to the view but not to the table's content.

3. Type **H** in the Type field or select H from the lookup list, and move to the next field.

4. Type the numeric value of 1 or greater for the InitiatedBy field. (You need a value in this field for each employee because of the field's validation rule.) Move to the next field.

5. Type the ScheduledDate entry. You don't need to delete the default date value; typing a new date replaces the default value. Then press Enter, Tab, or the right-arrow key.

6. Type the ApprovedBy value and move to the next field.

7. Type the EffectiveDate entry, and skip the HRRating field.

8. Type the NewSalary of the monthly salary at the time of hiring, and skip the NewRate, NewBonus, and NewCommission fields.

9. Type **Hired** or any other comment you care to make in the HRComments field. Move to the EmployeeID field of the next default blank record.

10. Repeat steps 2 through 9 for eight more employees in Table 6.7.

When you complete your entries, the HRActions table appears as shown in Figure 6.10. If you skipped any of the sample procedures in this chapter, an updated version of the Nwind05.accdb database (Nwind06.accdb) with the data entered for you is in your \\SEUA12\Chaptr06 folder. As mentioned early in the chapter, importing the HRActions table requires adding a one-to-many relationship to the Employees table. If you don't add the relationship, some validation tests in the next section won't behave as expected.

Error Messages from Validation Enforcement

If error messages appear when you enter data in fields with validation rules, edit or reenter the data to conform to the data types and validation rules for the field. Error messages that appear when you enter the data correctly indicate that something is amiss with your validation rules. In this case, change to Design mode and review your validation rules for the offending fields against those listed in Table 6.6. You might want to remove the validation rule temporarily by selecting the entire expression and cutting it to the Clipboard. (You can paste the expression back into the text box later.) Return to Run mode to continue with your entries.

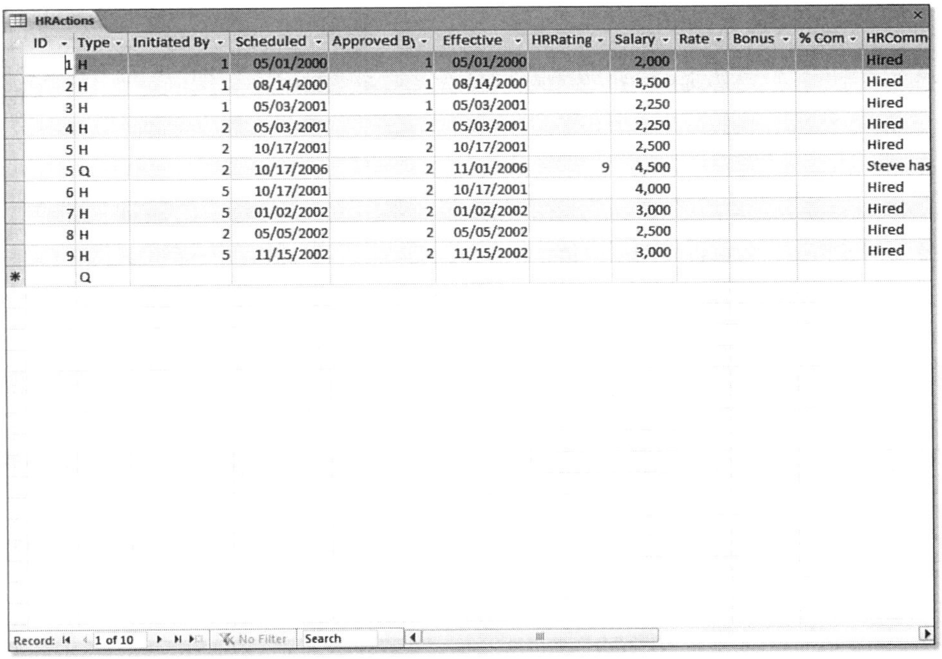

Figure 6.10
The HRActions tables contain initial entries for the nine employees of Northwind Traders.

ID	Type	Initiated By	Scheduled	Approved By	Effective	HRRating	Salary	Rate	Bonus	% Com	HRComm
1	H	1	05/01/2000	1	05/01/2000		2,000				Hired
2	H	1	08/14/2000	1	08/14/2000		3,500				Hired
3	H	1	05/03/2001	1	05/03/2001		2,250				Hired
4	H	2	05/03/2001	2	05/03/2001		2,250				Hired
5	H	2	10/17/2001	2	10/17/2001		2,500				Hired
5	Q	2	10/17/2006	2	11/01/2006	9	4,500				Steve has
6	H	5	10/17/2001	2	10/17/2001		4,000				Hired
7	H	5	01/02/2002	2	01/02/2002		3,000				Hired
8	H	2	05/05/2002	2	05/05/2002		2,500				Hired
9	H	5	11/15/2002	2	11/15/2002		3,000				Hired
*	Q										

Record: I◀ ◀ 1 of 10 ▶ ▶I ▶⁕ No Filter Search

Testing Field and Table Validation Rules

You can experiment with entering table data and testing your validation rules at the same time. Testing database applications often requires much more time and effort than creating them. The following basic tests are required to confirm your validation rules:

- **Referential integrity**—Type **25** in the EmployeeID field, select today's date from the Calendar control in the ScheduledDate field and **2** in the InitiatedBy field of the default blank record (number 10), and then press the up-arrow key. Pressing the up-arrow key tells Access that you're finished with the current record and to move up to the preceding record with the cursor in the same field. Access then tests the primary key integrity before enabling you to leave the current record, and the message box shown in Figure 6.11 appears. Click OK and press Esc to abandon the entry.

- **No duplicates restriction for primary key**—In the tentative append record, attempt to duplicate exactly the entries for the first four fields of record 9, and then press the up-arrow key. You see the message box shown in Figure 6.12. Click OK, but in this case pressing Esc doesn't cancel the entry.

Figure 6.11
If you violate referential integrity rules by typing an EmployeeID value without a corresponding record in the Employees table, this message appears.

- **ActionType validation**—Type **x** in the ActionType field and press the right-arrow key to display the message that appears if you added the lookup list and set the Limit To List property value to Yes (see Figure 6.13, top). Otherwise, the message box with the validation text you entered for the ActionType field appears (see Figure 6.13, bottom). Click OK and press Esc to abandon the entry.

Figure 6.12
If you duplicate the values of another record in the EmployeeID, ActionType, and ScheduledDate fields, you receive an error message because a primary key duplication occurs.

Figure 6.13
The error message for a lookup list with the Limit to List restriction set responds to an entry error with the upper message. If the Limit to List restriction is missing or you didn't add a lookup list, the Validation Text message appears.

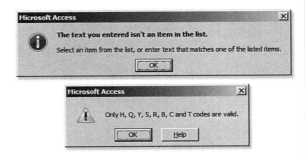

- **Employee ID validation in the InitiatedBy field**—Type **q** and move to the InitiatedBy field. When the cursor leaves the ActionType field, the q changes to Q because of the > format character used. Type **0** (an invalid employee ID number), and press the right-arrow key to display the message box shown in Figure 6.14. Click OK or press Enter.

Figure 6.14
Typing **0** in the InitiatedBy field violates the ····⊱o validation rule and displays the validation text.

Continue with the testing. Type a date, such as **1/31/2001**, for the ScheduledDate, and type a date one day earlier (such as **1/30/2001**) for the EffectiveDate to display the error message boxes with the validation text you entered. (You must move the cursor to a different record to cause the table-level validation rule to be applied.) Enter a valid date after the test. To edit a field, rather than retype it, press F2 to deselect the entire field and display the cursor for editing. F2 toggles selection and editing operations.

When you finish your testing, click the selection button of the last record you added, and then press Delete. The confirmation message shown in Figure 6.15 appears. You can turn off record deletion confirmation messages by clearing the Record Changes text box in the Confirm group of the Access Options dialog's Advanced page.

Figure 6.15
Unless you turn off confirmation of record changes, this message appears when you delete a record.

Field Property Values Cause Paste Failures

If Access beeps when you attempt to paste data into a cell, the Paste operation violates a domain or referential integrity rule, usually the Field Size property value. For instance, if you attempt to paste more than five characters into the CustomerID field of the Customers table, the Paste operation fails without an error message. Make sure that the cells or blocks of cells you paste conform to Field Size and other data validation rules.

Multiple Record Selection Causes Silent Paste Failures

If nothing happens when you try to paste data in a cell, a likely cause is that you've selected multiple records, then attempted to paste the records into a single cell, even the first cell of the tentative append record, which results in a silent paste failure. Access limits multiple-record insert operations to the Edit, Paste Append command.

7

SORTING, FINDING, AND FILTERING DATA

Microsoft Access 2010 provides a variety of sorting and filtering features that make customizing the display data in Table Datasheet view a quick and simple process. Sorting and filtering records in tables is especially useful when you use the data to create a mailing list or print a particular set of records.

Access also includes versatile search-and-replace facilities that let you locate every record with a value that matches a value you specify and then, optionally, change that value. Using the Search features, you can quickly locate values even in large tables. Search and replace often is needed when you import data from another database or a worksheet, which is the primary subject of the next chapter.

Access's sorting, filtering, searching, and replacing features actually are implemented "behind the scenes" by queries that Access creates for you. When you reach Part III, "Transforming Data with Queries and PivotTables," you'll probably choose to implement these features in Access's graphical Query Design window. Learning the fundamentals of these operations with tables, however, makes queries easier to understand. You also can apply filters to query resultsets, use the Find feature with queries in Datasheet view, and use search and replace on the resultsets of updatable queries.

Sorting Table Data

By default, Access displays records in the order of the primary key. If your table doesn't have a primary key, the records display in the order in which you enter them. Access uses sorting methods to display records in the desired order. If an index exists on the field in which you sort the records, the sorting process for large tables is quicker. Access automatically uses indexes, if indexes exist, to speed the sort in a process called *query optimization*.

The following sections show how to use Access's sorting methods to display records in the sequence you want. The Customers table of Northwind.accdb is used for most examples in this chapter because it's typical of a table whose data you might want to sort.

Freezing Display of a Table Field

If the table you're sorting contains more fields than you can display in Access's Table Datasheet view, you can freeze one or more fields to make viewing the sorted data easier. Freezing a field makes the field visible at all times, regardless of which other fields you display by manipulating the horizontal scrollbar.

To freeze the CustomerID and CompanyName fields of the Customers table, follow these steps:

1. Open the Customers table in Datasheet view.

2. Click the field header button of the CustomerID field to select the first field.

3. Shift+click the CompanyName field header button. Alternatively, you can drag the mouse from the CustomerID field header to the CompanyName field header to select the first and second fields.

4. Right-click the Datasheet and choose Freeze Fields.

When you scroll to fields to the right of the frozen columns, your Datasheet view of the Customers table appears as shown in Figure 7.1. There are no visual elements to indicate that columns are frozen.

Sorting Data on a Single Field

 Access provides an easy way to sort data in the Datasheet view: Right-click the field you want to use to sort the table's data to open the context menu, and click either the Sort A to Z or the Sort Z to A icon of the context menu. In mailing lists, a standard practice in the United States is to sort the records in ascending ZIP Code order. This practice often is observed in other countries that use postal codes. To quickly sort the Customers table in the order of the Postal Code field, follow these steps:

note

You can use the \ Access2010\Chaptr07\Nwind07. accdb database that you install from the online sample code as the working file for this database.

You also can use the 15MB Oakmont.accdb database, which has a 30,000-record Students table, to evaluate sorting operations on large tables. If you haven't installed all the sample files from the online sample code, copy Oakmont.accdb from the \Access2010\Oakmont folder to your working folder. Right-click the Explorer entry for the copy of Oakmont.accdb, choose Properties, and clear the Read-Only check box in the Attributes group if it's marked.

note

This example and those that follow use field names, rather than column header names (captions). The Microsoft developers added spaces to the table's caption property when two nouns make up a field name, such as Company and Name. Caption is an extended—and, in this case, superficial—property of fields.

Figure 7.1 The CustomerID and CompanyName fields of this Datasheet view of the Customers table are frozen.

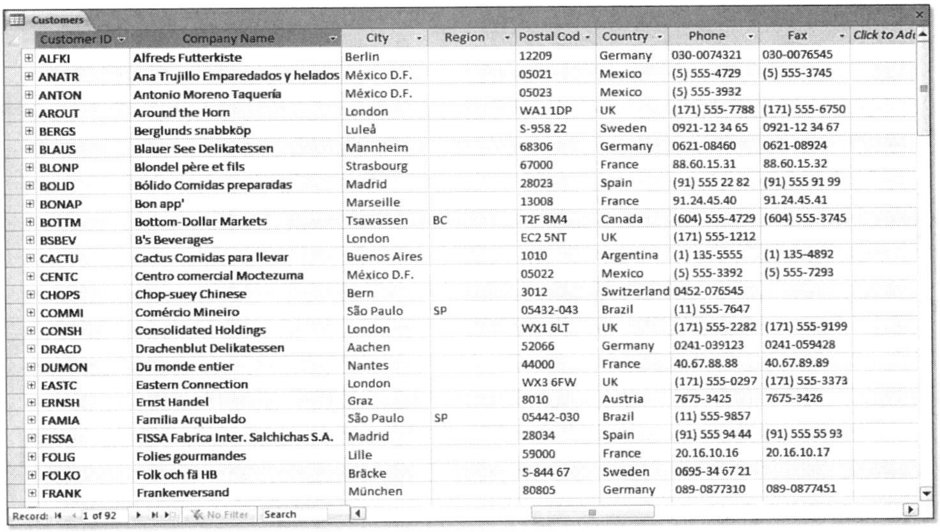

Customer ID	Company Name	City	Region	Postal Cod	Country	Phone	Fax	Click to Add
ALFKI	Alfreds Futterkiste	Berlin		12209	Germany	030-0074321	030-0076545	
ANATR	Ana Trujillo Emparedados y helados	México D.F.		05021	Mexico	(5) 555-4729	(5) 555-3745	
ANTON	Antonio Moreno Taquería	México D.F.		05023	Mexico	(5) 555-3932		
AROUT	Around the Horn	London		WA1 1DP	UK	(171) 555-7788	(171) 555-6750	
BERGS	Berglunds snabbköp	Luleå		S-958 22	Sweden	0921-12 34 65	0921-12 34 67	
BLAUS	Blauer See Delikatessen	Mannheim		68306	Germany	0621-08460	0621-08924	
BLONP	Blondel père et fils	Strasbourg		67000	France	88.60.15.31	88.60.15.32	
BOLID	Bólido Comidas preparadas	Madrid		28023	Spain	(91) 555 22 82	(91) 555 91 99	
BONAP	Bon app'	Marseille		13008	France	91.24.45.40	91.24.45.41	
BOTTM	Bottom-Dollar Markets	Tsawassen	BC	T2F 8M4	Canada	(604) 555-4729	(604) 555-3745	
BSBEV	B's Beverages	London		EC2 5NT	UK	(171) 555-1212		
CACTU	Cactus Comidas para llevar	Buenos Aires		1010	Argentina	(1) 135-5555	(1) 135-4892	
CENTC	Centro comercial Moctezuma	México D.F.		05022	Mexico	(5) 555-3392	(5) 555-7293	
CHOPS	Chop-suey Chinese	Bern		3012	Switzerland	0452-076545		
COMMI	Comércio Mineiro	São Paulo	SP	05432-043	Brazil	(11) 555-7647		
CONSH	Consolidated Holdings	London		WX1 6LT	UK	(171) 555-2282	(171) 555-9199	
DRACD	Drachenblut Delikatessen	Aachen		52066	Germany	0241-039123	0241-059428	
DUMON	Du monde entier	Nantes		44000	France	40.67.88.88	40.67.89.89	
EASTC	Eastern Connection	London		WX3 6FW	UK	(171) 555-0297	(171) 555-3373	
ERNSH	Ernst Handel	Graz		8010	Austria	7675-3425	7675-3426	
FAMIA	Familia Arquibaldo	São Paulo	SP	05442-030	Brazil	(11) 555-9857		
FISSA	FISSA Fabrica Inter. Salchichas S.A.	Madrid		28034	Spain	(91) 555 94 44	(91) 555 55 93	
FOLIG	Folies gourmandes	Lille		59000	France	20.16.10.16	20.16.10.17	
FOLKO	Folk och fä HB	Bräcke		S-844 67	Sweden	0695-34 67 21		
FRANK	Frankenversand	München		80805	Germany	089-0877310	089-0877451	

1. Open the PostalCode field's context menu by right-clicking anywhere in the field's column.

2. Click the context menu's Sort A to Z button.

Your Customers table quickly is sorted into the order shown in Figure 7.2.

Sorting Data on Multiple Fields

Although the sort operation in the preceding section accomplishes exactly what you specify, the result is less than useful because of the variants of postal code formats used in different countries. What's needed here is a multiple-field sort: first on the Country field and then on the PostalCode field. You can select the Country and the PostalCode fields to perform the multicolumn sort. The Quick Sort technique, however, automatically applies the sorting priority to the leftmost field you select, PostalCode. Access offers two methods of handling this problem: Reorder the field display or specify the sort order in a Filter window. Follow these steps to use the reordering process:

Filters are discussed later in this chapter; **see** *"Filtering Table Data ,"* **p. 274.**

1. Select the Country field by clicking its field header button.

2. Hold down the left mouse button and drag the Country field to the left of the PostalCode field. Release the left mouse button to drop the field in its new location.

3. Shift+click the header button of the PostalCode field to select the Country and PostalCode fields.

4. Right-click in either selected column and then click the context menu's Sort A to Z button.

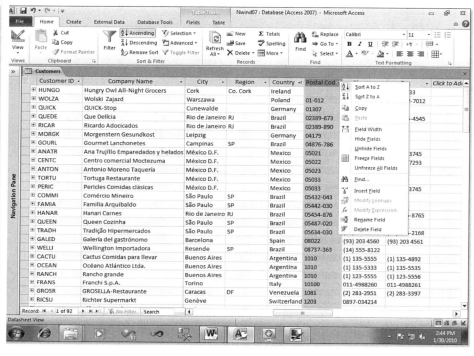

Figure 7.2
Access's Sort feature works on a single field or multiple fields in left-to-right sequence. This Datasheet is sorted on the PostalCode field.

The sorted table, shown in Figure 7.3, now makes much more sense. A multiple-field sort on a table sometimes is called a *composite sort*.

Removing a Table Sort Order and Thawing Columns

After you freeze columns and apply sort orders to a table, you might want to return the table to its original condition. To do so, Access offers you the following choices:

- To return the Datasheet view of an Access table with a primary key to its original sort order, select the field(s) that compose the primary key (in the order of the primary key fields), and click the Sort Ascending button.

- To return to the original order when the table has no primary key field, close the table without saving the changes and then reopen the table.

- To thaw your frozen columns, right-click the datasheet and choose Unfreeze All Fields.

- To return the sequence of fields to its original state, drag the fields you moved back to their prior positions or close the table without saving your changes.

If you make substantial changes to the layout of the table and apply a sort order, it's usually quicker to close and reopen the table. (Don't save your changes to the table layout.)

Figure 7.3
Rearrange
the fields to
sort on mul-
tiple fields in
left-to-right
sequence.
Changing
the
sequence
of fields in
Datasheet
view affects
the dis-
play—but
not the
design—of
the table.

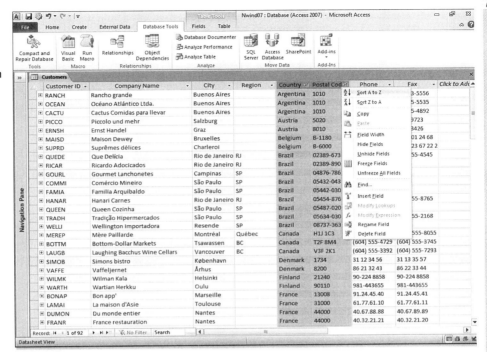

Finding Matching Records in a Table

To search for and select records with field values that match (or partially match) a particular value, use Access's Find feature. To find Luleå (a relatively large city in northern Sweden close to the Arctic Circle) in the City field, follow these steps:

1. In the Customers table, select the field (City) you want to search for by clicking its header button or by placing the cursor in that field.

2. Click the Home ribbon's Find button or press Ctrl+F to display the Find and Replace dialog (see Figure 7.4). The dialog opens with the Find page active and the Search Fields as Formatted check box marked by default.

3. Type the name of the city (**Lulea**) in the Find What text box (see Figure 7.5). The Find Next command button is enabled. The default values of the Match and Search lists are satisfactory at this point. Matching case or format isn't important here, so clear the Search Fields as Formatted check box.

4. Click the Find Next button. If you don't have a Scandinavian keyboard, Access displays the message box shown in Figure 7.6. Click OK to dismiss the message box.

Figure 7.4
The Find and Replace dialog opens with Current Field (the selected field) in the Look In list of the Find page. The Find Next button is disabled until you type an entry in the Find What text box.

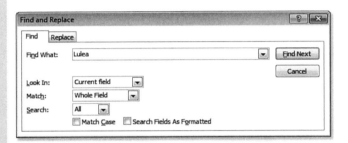

Figure 7.5
A Whole Field match is selected by default, so type the entire value (Lulea, for this example) to find in the Find What text box.

Figure 7.6
If the Find feature doesn't find a match for your entry, you receive a "not found" message.

 tip

2007 NEW You can do a quick search for the first instance of Luleå by typing **lule, ule,** or **lulea** into the small Search Box at the bottom of the Datasheet to the left of the horizontal scrollbar (refer to Figure 7.7). As you type characters into the Search Box, focus moves to the first cell of any field that contains the characters. After you locate the first instance of the value you want, press Enter to move to subsequent instances, if any. Ctrl+Shift+F sets the focus to the Search Box and Esc sets the focus to the found instance.

The "not found" message indicates that the Find feature didn't locate a match in the City field of the entire table. Access missed your entry because the Scandinavian diacritical º is missing over the letter *a* in Lulea. In the ANSI character set, "a" has a value of 97, and "å" has a value of 229.

If the letters preceding an extended character are sufficient to define your search parameter, follow these steps to find Luleå:

1. Type **Lule**, omitting the *a*, in the Find What text box.

2. Select Start of Field from the Match drop-down list.

3. Click the Find Next button. Access finds and highlights Luleå in the City field (see Figure 7.7).

Figure 7.7
Omitting the special Scandinavian character from the search and using the Start of Field search option finds Luleå.

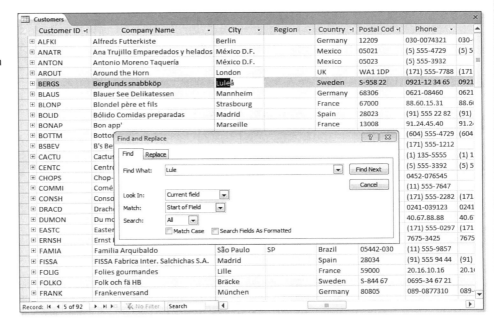

You also can find entries in any part of the field. If you type **ule** in the Find What text box and choose Any Part of Field from the Match drop-down list, you get a match on Luleå. However, you could also match Thule, the location of the Bluie West One airfield (also known as Thule Air Force Base) in Greenland. (There's no actual entry for Thule in the Customers table.)

Following is a list of the options available in the Find dialog:

- To specify a case-sensitive search, mark the Match Case check box.

- To search by using the field's format, mark the Search Fields as Formatted check box. This way you can enter a search term that matches the formatted appearance of the field, such as (510) 555-1212, rather than the native (unformatted) value (5105551212), if you applied a Format property value to the field. Using the Search Fields as Formatted option slows the search operation because indexes aren't used.

- To find additional matches, if any, click the Find Next button. If the Search option is set to Down, clicking the Find Next button starts the search at the current position of the record pointer and searches to the end of the table.

- To start the search at the last record of the table, select Up in the Search drop-down list.

Replacing Matched Field Values Automatically

The Find and Replace dialog's Replace page lets you replace values selectively in fields that match the entry in the Find What text box. To open the dialog with the Replace page active, click the Home ribbon's Find button, then the Replace button, or press Ctrl+H. The shortcut key combination for the Edit menu's Replace command is Ctrl+H, which is the same for Microsoft Word and most other Office members.

 The entries to search for Luleå and replace with Lulea appear in Figure 7.8. If you performed the search in the preceding section, select Customers:Table from the Look In drop-down list, click the Find Next button, and then click the Replace button for those records in which you want to replace the value. You can do a bulk replace in all matching records by clicking the Replace All button. Unlike in Word and Excel, you can't undo search-and-replace operations in Access (or SQL Server) tables. Before replacements are made, a message box opens to request that you confirm the pending changes.

Filtering Table Data

Access lets you apply a filter to specify the records that appear in the Datasheet view of a table or a query resultset. For example, if you want to view only those customers located in Germany, you use a filter to limit the displayed records to only those whose

 tip

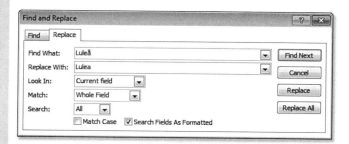 To enter international (extended) characters in the Find What text box, type the English letters and then use the Windows 7, Vista or XP Character Map applet to find and copy the extended character to the Clipboard. In Windows 7, type Character Map in the Search Programs and Files Text box. (Don't worry about choosing the correct font.) Paste the character into the Find What text box at the appropriate location.

tip

You can search all fields of the table for a match by opening the Look In list and selecting *Tablename*: Table. Searching all fields in a table for a matching entry is usually much slower than searching a single field, especially if you have an index on the field being searched. Unless you specify the Any Part of Field Match option, Access uses the index to speed the searching operation.

Figure 7.8
Click the Replace tab, if necessary; type a replacement value in the Replace With text box, and then click Find Next and Replace for each match; or click Replace All for all occurrences of the Find What value.

Country field contains the text Germany. Access gives you four ways to apply filters to the data in a table:

- *Filter by Selection* is the fastest and simplest way to apply a filter. You establish the filter criteria by selecting all or part of the data in one of the table's fields; Access displays only records that match the selected sample. With Filter by Selection, you can filter records based only on criteria in a single field of the table.

- *Filter by Form* is the second fastest way to apply a filter. You enter the filter criteria into a blank datasheet form of the table; Access displays records that match the combined criteria in each field. Use Filter by Form to quickly filter records based on criteria in more than one field.

- *Menu-based Filter/Sort* uses a context menu to apply ascending or descending sorts, a Text Filters choice that, for Text fields, lets you select Equals, Does Not Equal, Begins With, Does Not Begin With, Contains, Does Not Contain, Ends With, or Does Not End With comparison operators against characters you type in a Custom Filter input box. You also can filter for individual values by clearing or marking check boxes; this option is similar to Excel 2007's Filter menu.

- *Advanced Filter/Sort* is the most powerful—but least speedy—type of filter. With an advanced filter/sort, you can make an Access filter do double duty because you can also add a sort order on one or more fields.

 note

For Number and Currency fields, the comparison operators are Equals, Less Than, Greater Than, and Between.

The comparison operators for Date/Time fields are more interesting: the preceding numeric operators as well as Tomorrow, Today, Yesterday, {Next | This | Last}{Week | Month | Quarter | Year}, Past, and Future. Date Filters have a total of 24 operators, including All Dates in Period.

Filtering by Selection

Creating a Filter by Selection is as easy as selecting text in a field. When you apply the filter, Access uses the selected text to determine which records to display. Table 7.1 summarizes which records are displayed, depending on how you select text in the field. In all cases, Access applies the filter criteria only to the field in which you have selected text. Filter by selection lets you establish filter criteria for only a single field at one time.

Table 7.1 Selected Text Affects Filter by Selection

Selected Text	Filter Effect
Entire field	Displays only records whose fields contain exactly matching values
Beginning of field	Displays records in which the text at the beginning of the field matches the selected text
End of field	Displays records in which the text at the end of the field matches the selected text
Characters anywhere in field	Displays records in which any part of the field matches the selected text

To create a Filter by Selection on the Customers table (displaying only those customers located in Germany), follow these steps:

1. If necessary, open the Customers table in Datasheet view and use the scrollbars to make the Country field visible in the Table window.

2. Place the cursor in the Country field of the first record in the Customers table and, optionally, select all the text. (This entry should be Germany.)

3. Click the Home ribbon's Selection button in the Sort & Filter group, and choose Equals "Germany." Access applies the filter, as shown in Figure 7.9.

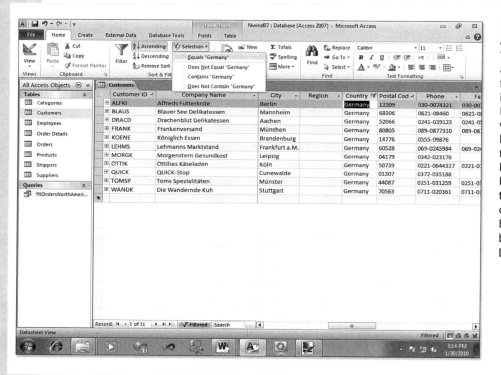

Figure 7.9
Applying "Germany" as a selection filter results in the filtered Datasheet view shown here. Notice the highlighted Filtered button to the left of the Search Box at the bottom of the Datasheet.

Notice that the Selection button is now displayed in active status (a contrasting background color), indicating that a filter is being applied to the table, and its ToolTip changes to Remove Filter. The legend (Filtered) also is added to the record selection and status bar at the bottom of the Table window. A small filter icon appears to the right of the field name, and the Filtered button at the bottom of the Datasheet is highlighted. (The Filtered button was new in Access 2007). To remove the filter, click the Home Ribbon's Toggle Filter button or the Datasheet's Filtered button.

As mentioned previously, you can also apply a Filter by Selection based on partially selected text in a field. Figure 7.10 shows the Customers table with a different Filter by Selection applied—this time, only the letters "er" in the Country field and Equals "er" were selected. You must remove the previous filter before applying a new filter to the entire table, rather than the filtered records.

Figure 7.10
Selecting only a part of the field—in this case the letters "er"—displays records containing the partial selection in any part of the field.

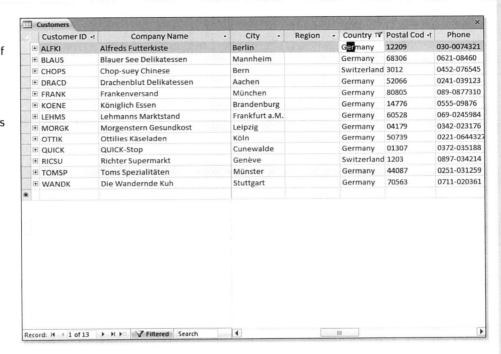

Customer ID	Company Name	City	Region	Country	Postal Cod	Phone
ALFKI	Alfreds Futterkiste	Berlin		Germany	12209	030-0074321
BLAUS	Blauer See Delikatessen	Mannheim		Germany	68306	0621-08460
CHOPS	Chop-suey Chinese	Bern		Switzerland	3012	0452-076545
DRACD	Drachenblut Delikatessen	Aachen		Germany	52066	0241-039123
FRANK	Frankenversand	München		Germany	80805	089-0877310
KOENE	Königlich Essen	Brandenburg		Germany	14776	0555-09876
LEHMS	Lehmanns Marktstand	Frankfurt a.M.		Germany	60528	069-0245984
MORGK	Morgenstern Gesundkost	Leipzig		Germany	04179	0342-023176
OTTIK	Ottilies Käseladen	Köln		Germany	50739	0221-0644327
QUICK	QUICK-Stop	Cunewalde		Germany	01307	0372-035188
RICSU	Richter Supermarkt	Genève		Switzerland	1203	0897-034214
TOMSP	Toms Spezialitäten	Münster		Germany	44087	0251-031259
WANDK	Die Wandernde Kuh	Stuttgart		Germany	70563	0711-020361

Record: 1 of 13 ▶ ▶▶ ▼ Filtered   Search

 tip

You can apply a Filter by Selection to more than one field at a time. For example, after applying a Filter by Selection to display only those customers in Germany, you could then move to the City field and apply a second Filter by Selection for Berlin. The resulting table would include only those customers in Berlin, Germany. An easier way to apply filters based on more than one field value is to use a Filter by Form, described in the "Filtering by Form" section coming up.

Using the Text Filters Option

The Text Filters option is a quick method for applying a filter to a single field. To use the Text Filters feature, do this:

1. Right-click the field on which you want to filter the table, and choose Text Filters, Equals in the context menu to open the Custom Filter input box.

2. In the text box, type the value you want to filter on, such as **USA** for the Country field of the Customers table, and press Enter to apply the filter.

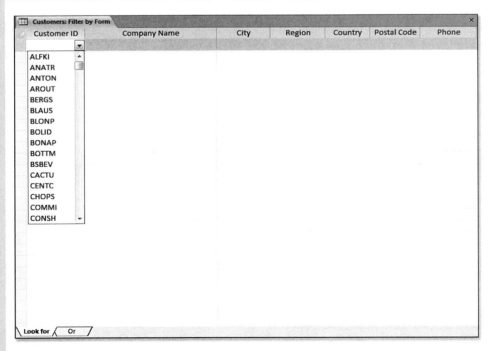 To remove the filter, click the Filtered button or right-click anywhere in the Datasheet window and choose Clear Filter from *FieldName*. Alternatively, click the Home ribbon's Advanced Filter Options button and choose Clear All Filters. Use this shortcut to remove all filters you've applied to the table.

Filtering by Form

Filtering by form is slightly more complex than filtering by selection because it lets you filter records based on criteria in more than one field at a time. For example, you saw in the preceding section how to use a Filter by Selection to view only those customers in Germany. To further limit the displayed records to those customers located in Berlin, Germany (and not Berlin, New Hampshire), use a Filter by Form.

In a Filter by Form, Access displays a blank form for the table (see Figure 7.11). This window is called a form to distinguish it from the Table Datasheet window, although it's not the same as the data entry forms discussed later in this book. You can combine criteria in a Filter by Form with a logical **Or** operator or a logical **And** operator. For example, you can filter the Customers table to display only those customers in the United States or Canada. As another example, you could filter the Customers table to display only those customers in the United States with ZIP Codes beginning with the digit 9 (such as 94609 or 90807).

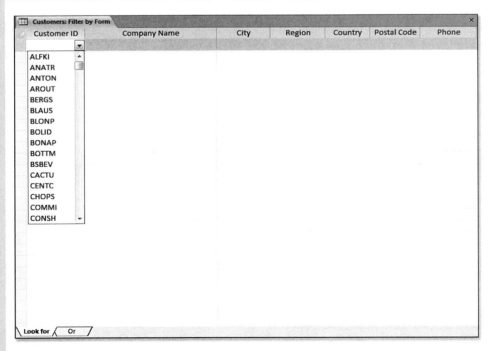

Figure 7.11
The Filter by Form variation of Datasheet view has a single row in which you add filter criteria. Each field has a drop-down list of values you can choose for the filter.

To create a Filter by Form on the Customers table to display only those customers in the United States or Canada, follow these steps:

1. If necessary, open the Customers table in Datasheet view.

2. Click the Home ribbon's Sort & Filter Options group's Advanced button and choose Filter by Form to display the Filter by Form window (refer to Figure 7.11).

3. Make the Country field visible in the Filter by Form window, if necessary. (The CustomerID and CompanyName fields in the figures have been frozen, as described previously in this chapter.)

4. Click inside the Country field and open the Country list box, or press F4. The drop-down list contains all the unique values in the Country field.

5. Select Canada in the list box, as shown in Figure 7.12. Access automatically adds the quotation marks around the value you select and enters it into the Country field form box.

 tip

Verify that all the fields of the filter form are empty before designing a new filter. The last filter expression you apply appears in the filter form when you open it if the Filter on Load property value is Yes. For instance, the Country field contains Like "*er*" if you tested the partial selection example in the preceding section and set Filter on Load to Yes.

Figure 7.12
The drop-down list in the Filter by Form data-sheet lets you select a single criterion on which to filter the field.

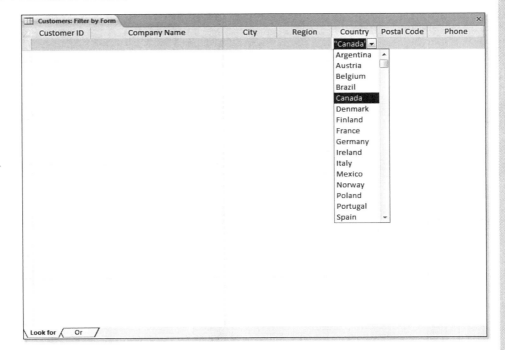

6. Click the Or tab at the bottom of the Filter by Form window. Access combines criteria that you enter on separate tabs in the Filter by Form window with a logical **Or** operator. When you add an **Or** operator, a tab for another **Or** operator appears.

7. Click the arrow to open the Country list box or press F4. Select USA from the drop-down list (see Figure 7.13).

Figure 7.13
Clicking the Or tab of the Filter by Form window opens another empty row in which you can select another criterion. Each time you add an Or criterion, an additional disabled Or tab appears at the bottom of the window.

8. Click the Toggle Filter button. Access applies the new filter to the table, displaying the records shown in Figure 7.14.

You can also combine filter criteria in a logical **And** operator by entering criteria in more than one field on the same tab of the Form window. For example, you want to filter the Orders table to find all orders handled by Nancy Davolio and shipped to France. You easily can use a Filter by Form to do so, as the following example shows:

1. Open the Orders table and freeze the OrderID, Customer, and Employee fields. Then position the ShipCountry field so that it's visible (see Figure 7.15). Freezing the fields isn't an essential step, but it makes setting up the filter and viewing the filtered data easier.

2. Click the Advanced Filter & Sort button and choose Filter by Form to display the Filter by Form window.

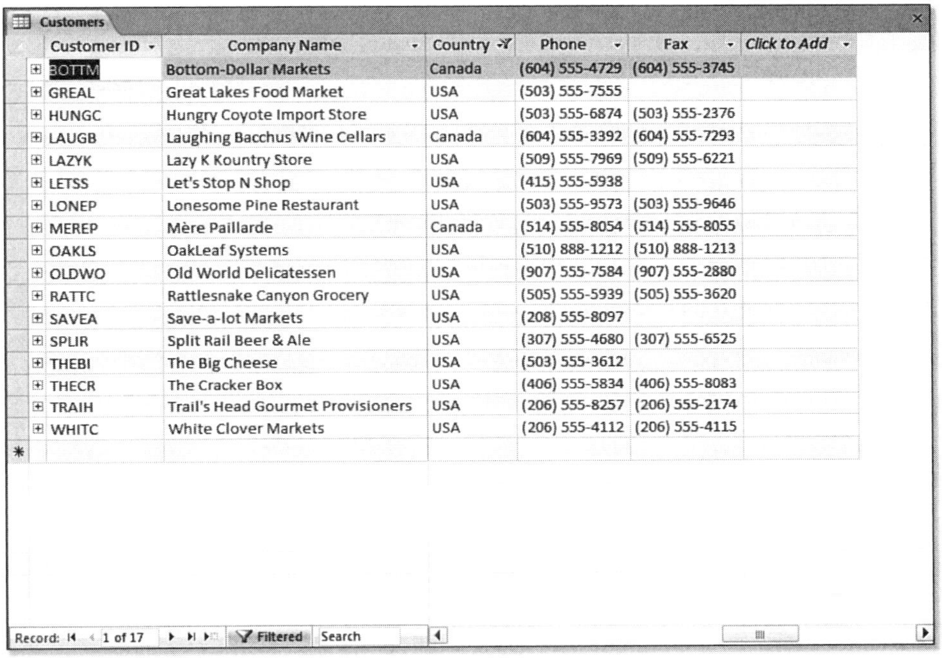

Figure 7.14
The
Customers
table in
Datasheet
view displays
the result of
applying the
"Canada" or
"USA" filter.

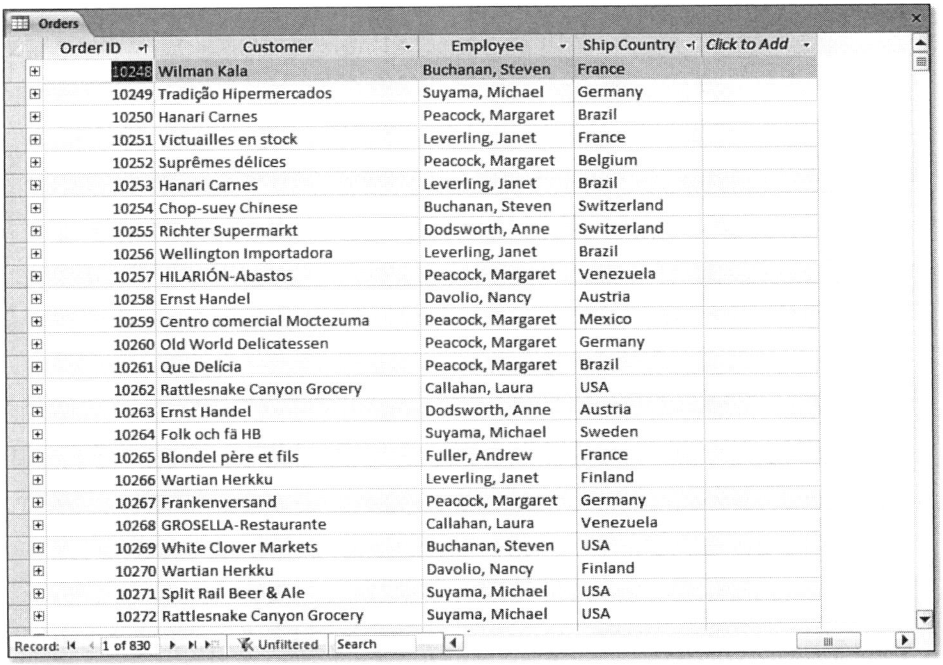

Customers					
Customer ID ▾	Company Name ▾	Country ▾	Phone ▾	Fax ▾	Click to Add ▾
⊞ BOTTM	Bottom-Dollar Markets	Canada	(604) 555-4729	(604) 555-3745	
⊞ GREAL	Great Lakes Food Market	USA	(503) 555-7555		
⊞ HUNGC	Hungry Coyote Import Store	USA	(503) 555-6874	(503) 555-2376	
⊞ LAUGB	Laughing Bacchus Wine Cellars	Canada	(604) 555-3392	(604) 555-7293	
⊞ LAZYK	Lazy K Kountry Store	USA	(509) 555-7969	(509) 555-6221	
⊞ LETSS	Let's Stop N Shop	USA	(415) 555-5938		
⊞ LONEP	Lonesome Pine Restaurant	USA	(503) 555-9573	(503) 555-9646	
⊞ MEREP	Mère Paillarde	Canada	(514) 555-8054	(514) 555-8055	
⊞ OAKLS	OakLeaf Systems	USA	(510) 888-1212	(510) 888-1213	
⊞ OLDWO	Old World Delicatessen	USA	(907) 555-7584	(907) 555-2880	
⊞ RATTC	Rattlesnake Canyon Grocery	USA	(505) 555-5939	(505) 555-3620	
⊞ SAVEA	Save-a-lot Markets	USA	(208) 555-8097		
⊞ SPLIR	Split Rail Beer & Ale	USA	(307) 555-4680	(307) 555-6525	
⊞ THEBI	The Big Cheese	USA	(503) 555-3612		
⊞ THECR	The Cracker Box	USA	(406) 555-5834	(406) 555-8083	
⊞ TRAIH	Trail's Head Gourmet Provisioners	USA	(206) 555-8257	(206) 555-2174	
⊞ WHITC	White Clover Markets	USA	(206) 555-4112	(206) 555-4115	

Record: I◄ ◄ 1 of 17 ► ►I ►❑ ▼ Filtered Search

Figure 7.15
Simplify
the filtering
process by
freezing the
first three
fields of the
Orders table.

Orders				
Order ID ◄|	Customer ▾	Employee ▾	Ship Country ◄|	Click to Add ▾
⊞	10248 Wilman Kala	Buchanan, Steven	France	
⊞	10249 Tradição Hipermercados	Suyama, Michael	Germany	
⊞	10250 Hanari Carnes	Peacock, Margaret	Brazil	
⊞	10251 Victuailles en stock	Leverling, Janet	France	
⊞	10252 Suprêmes délices	Peacock, Margaret	Belgium	
⊞	10253 Hanari Carnes	Leverling, Janet	Brazil	
⊞	10254 Chop-suey Chinese	Buchanan, Steven	Switzerland	
⊞	10255 Richter Supermarkt	Dodsworth, Anne	Switzerland	
⊞	10256 Wellington Importadora	Leverling, Janet	Brazil	
⊞	10257 HILARIÓN-Abastos	Peacock, Margaret	Venezuela	
⊞	10258 Ernst Handel	Davolio, Nancy	Austria	
⊞	10259 Centro comercial Moctezuma	Peacock, Margaret	Mexico	
⊞	10260 Old World Delicatessen	Peacock, Margaret	Germany	
⊞	10261 Que Delícia	Peacock, Margaret	Brazil	
⊞	10262 Rattlesnake Canyon Grocery	Callahan, Laura	USA	
⊞	10263 Ernst Handel	Dodsworth, Anne	Austria	
⊞	10264 Folk och fä HB	Suyama, Michael	Sweden	
⊞	10265 Blondel père et fils	Fuller, Andrew	France	
⊞	10266 Wartian Herkku	Leverling, Janet	Finland	
⊞	10267 Frankenversand	Peacock, Margaret	Germany	
⊞	10268 GROSELLA-Restaurante	Callahan, Laura	Venezuela	
⊞	10269 White Clover Markets	Buchanan, Steven	USA	
⊞	10270 Wartian Herkku	Davolio, Nancy	Finland	
⊞	10271 Split Rail Beer & Ale	Suyama, Michael	USA	
⊞	10272 Rattlesnake Canyon Grocery	Suyama, Michael	USA	

Record: I◄ ◄ 1 of 830 ► ►I ►❑ ☒ Unfiltered Search

3. Click the Advanced Filter & Sort button again and choose Clear All Filters to clear any previous filter criteria from the Filter by Form grid. (This choice is disabled if no filters are applied.)

4. Use the drop-down list in the EmployeeID field to select Davolio, Nancy, and then use the drop-down list in the ShipCountry field to select France. You must manually add quotes around a text criterion that includes a comma (see Figure 7.16).

5. Click the Toggle Filter button. Access applies the new filter to the table, displaying the records shown in Figure 7.17. This filter shows only those records for orders that were handled by Nancy Davolio and shipped to France.

note

Access stores the last filter you applied as the value of the table's Filter property. To view the filter value, change to Table Design view and click the Property Sheet button to open the Property Sheet for the table. For the preceding example, the filter value is ((Customers.Country="Canada")) OR ((Customers.Country="USA")). The parenthesis pairs are superfluous for this filter.

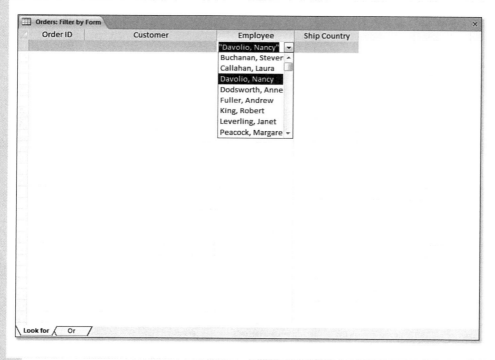

Figure 7.16
The criterion in the EmployeeID field is based on the lookup field that displays the LastName and FirstName values from the Employees tables, separated by a comma and space. Matching a composite criterion requires surrounding the value with quotes.

Figure 7.17
The EmployeeID and Country filter criteria shown in Figure 7.16 result in the following Datasheet view of the Orders table.

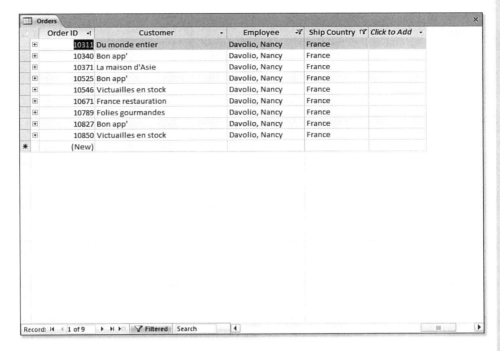

 note

For this example, the value of the table's Filter property is ((Lookup_EmployeeID.Name="Davolio, Nancy") AND (Orders. ShipCountry="France")), because the Lookup Row Source property for EmployeeID is SELECT DISTINCTROW Employees. EmployeeID, [LastName] & "," & [FirstName] AS Name FROM Employees ORDER BY Employees.LastName, Employees. FirstName;.

The Lookup_FieldName.Alias expression enables comparison with the lookup value instead of the numeric EmployeeID value.

Filter by Form Doesn't Find the Expected Records

Access keeps your last filter settings for a table until you close the table. If you've applied a different filter—whether through Filter by Selection or Filter by Form earlier in your current work session—Access might be applying additional filter criteria that you're not expecting. Right-click the datasheet, and choose Remove Filter/Sort to clear all previous filter criteria and ensure that the new filter criteria you enter are the only ones in effect. Alternatively, choose Records, Remove Filter/Sort from the main Access menu.

Applying Menu-based Filters and Sort Orders

Access 2010's menu-based filter and sort order feature, which Access 2007 introduced, emulates Excel's approach to the process but isn't very efficient, especially for fields that store a large number of different values. To display the menu, select the field to filter, sort, or both, and then click the Home ribbon's large Filter button. Alternatively, click the small arrow to the right of the field name to open the menu.

Working with menu-based filters is easy, if the feature is capable of accomplishing your task. To apply a menu-based filter for orders received in 2006 and a descending (newest to oldest) sort order to the OrderDate field of the orders table, do the following:

1. Open the Orders table, if necessary, select the OrderDate field and click the Filter button to open the filter and sort context menu.

2. Choose Date Filters to open the Date Filters context menu (see Figure 7.18).

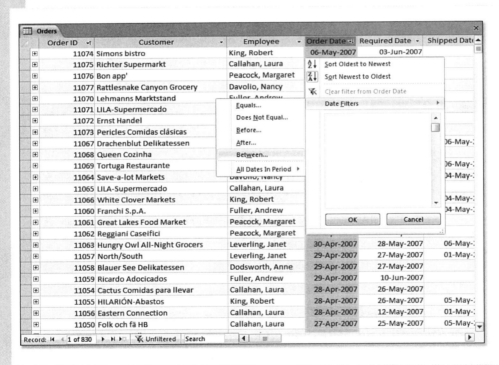

Figure 7.18
The menu-based Date Filters for the Orders table's OrderDate field provide a range of dynamic date and date range choices.

3. Select Between to open the Between Dates dialog. Type **1/1/2006** in the Oldest and **12/31/2006** in the Newest text box (see Figure 7.19) and then click OK to apply the filter.

4. Reopen the filter and sort context menu and select Sort Newest to Oldest. The Orders table window appears, as shown in Figure 7.20.

Figure 7.19
The Between Dates dialog offers Date Pickers for Oldest and Newest values, but typing the dates usually is faster than navigating the Date Pickers.

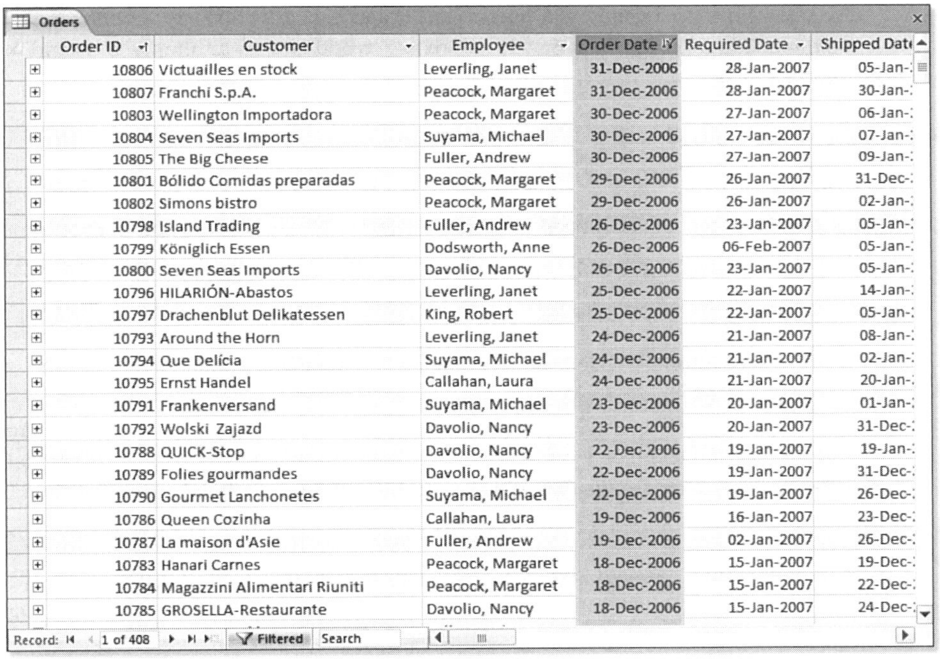

Figure 7.20
Orders rows for the year 2006 are sorted in reverse chronological order.

	Order ID	Customer	Employee	Order Date	Required Date	Shipped Date
⊞	10806	Victuailles en stock	Leverling, Janet	31-Dec-2006	28-Jan-2007	05-Jan-2
⊞	10807	Franchi S.p.A.	Peacock, Margaret	31-Dec-2006	28-Jan-2007	30-Jan-2
⊞	10803	Wellington Importadora	Peacock, Margaret	30-Dec-2006	27-Jan-2007	06-Jan-2
⊞	10804	Seven Seas Imports	Suyama, Michael	30-Dec-2006	27-Jan-2007	07-Jan-2
⊞	10805	The Big Cheese	Fuller, Andrew	30-Dec-2006	27-Jan-2007	09-Jan-2
⊞	10801	Bólido Comidas preparadas	Peacock, Margaret	29-Dec-2006	26-Jan-2007	31-Dec-
⊞	10802	Simons bistro	Peacock, Margaret	29-Dec-2006	26-Jan-2007	02-Jan-2
⊞	10798	Island Trading	Fuller, Andrew	26-Dec-2006	23-Jan-2007	05-Jan-2
⊞	10799	Königlich Essen	Dodsworth, Anne	26-Dec-2006	06-Feb-2007	05-Jan-2
⊞	10800	Seven Seas Imports	Davolio, Nancy	26-Dec-2006	23-Jan-2007	05-Jan-2
⊞	10796	HILARIÓN-Abastos	Leverling, Janet	25-Dec-2006	22-Jan-2007	14-Jan-2
⊞	10797	Drachenblut Delikatessen	King, Robert	25-Dec-2006	22-Jan-2007	05-Jan-2
⊞	10793	Around the Horn	Leverling, Janet	24-Dec-2006	21-Jan-2007	08-Jan-2
⊞	10794	Que Delícia	Suyama, Michael	24-Dec-2006	21-Jan-2007	02-Jan-2
⊞	10795	Ernst Handel	Callahan, Laura	24-Dec-2006	21-Jan-2007	20-Jan-2
⊞	10791	Frankenversand	Suyama, Michael	23-Dec-2006	20-Jan-2007	01-Jan-2
⊞	10792	Wolski Zajazd	Davolio, Nancy	23-Dec-2006	20-Jan-2007	31-Dec-
⊞	10788	QUICK-Stop	Davolio, Nancy	22-Dec-2006	19-Jan-2007	19-Jan-2
⊞	10789	Folies gourmandes	Davolio, Nancy	22-Dec-2006	19-Jan-2007	31-Dec-
⊞	10790	Gourmet Lanchonetes	Suyama, Michael	22-Dec-2006	19-Jan-2007	26-Dec-
⊞	10786	Queen Cozinha	Callahan, Laura	19-Dec-2006	16-Jan-2007	23-Dec-
⊞	10787	La maison d'Asie	Fuller, Andrew	19-Dec-2006	02-Jan-2007	26-Dec-
⊞	10783	Hanari Carnes	Peacock, Margaret	18-Dec-2006	15-Jan-2007	19-Dec-
⊞	10784	Magazzini Alimentari Riuniti	Peacock, Margaret	18-Dec-2006	15-Jan-2007	22-Dec-
⊞	10785	GROSELLA-Restaurante	Davolio, Nancy	18-Dec-2006	15-Jan-2007	24-Dec-

Record: I◀ ◀ 1 of 408 ▶ ▶I ▶ ▼ Filtered Search

5. Click the Home ribbon's Toggle Filter and Remove Sort buttons to clear the filter and sort order you applied.

Applying Advanced Filters and Sort Orders

Filters in Access, as mentioned previously, are queries in disguise, and they provide a useful introduction to single-table Access queries, the subject of Chapter 9, "Designing Queries for Access Databases." Creating an advanced filter/sort is much like creating a query, with some basic differences, as follows:

- The Show Table dialog doesn't appear.

- The SQL button is missing from the toolbar, so you can't display the underlying SQL statement.

- The Show row is missing from the Filter Design grid.

> **note**
>
> SQL Server tables opened in ADP don't support Access's advanced filter/sort function.

Filters are limited to using one table or query that Access automatically specifies when you enter Filter Design view. You can save a filter you create as a query or load a filter from a query, but Access has no provision for saving a filter as a separate filter object. The table saves (persists) the filter and sort order you add if you save your changes when closing the table. The following sections describe how to add criteria to filter records and to add a sort order in the Filter Design window.

Adding Multifield Sort and Compound Filter Criteria

In its default configuration, the Datasheet toolbar doesn't have an Advanced Filter/Sort button. Instead, you start the advanced filter/sort operation by clicking the Sort & Filter group's Advanced button and choosing Advanced Filter/Sort. To create a filter on the Orders table (which provides more records to filter than the Customers table), follow these steps:

1. Open the Orders table, if necessary. Click the Toggle Filter and Remove Sort buttons to clear filter or sort criteria. These buttons are enabled only if you applied either or both previously.

2. ⚡ Click the Filter & Sort group's Advanced button and choose Advanced Filter/Sort to display the Filter window (see Figure 7.21). The default filter name, Filter1, is concatenated with the table name to create the default name of the first filter, OrdersFilter1. The Field List window for the Orders table appears in the upper pane of the Filter window.

3. One field that you might want to use to sort or limit displayed records is OrderID. Click it in the field list in the upper pane and drag it to the first column of the Field row of the Filter Design grid in the lower pane. (When your mouse pointer reaches the lower pane, the pointer turns into a field symbol.) Alternatively, double-click the OrderID field to add it to the grid.

4. Repeat step 3 for other fields on which you might want to sort or establish criteria. Candidates are CustomerID, ShipCountry, ShipPostalCode, OrderDate, and ShippedDate.

5. To check the sorting capabilities of your first advanced filter, add an ascending sort to the ShipCountry and ShipPostalCode fields by selecting Ascending from those fields' Sort cell. Your Filter Design window appears as shown in Figure 7.22.

6. Click the Toggle Filter toolbar button or right-click in the table pane and choose Filter, Apply Filter/Sort.

7. Freeze the OrderID and columns and use the horizontal scrollbar of the datasheet to reveal the ShipCountry and ShipPostalCode fields. Your sorted table appears as shown in Figure 7.23.

Figure 7.21
The Filter
window is
similar to the
Query Design
window, but
it doesn't
have Table
or Show
rows in the
lower pane's
grid.

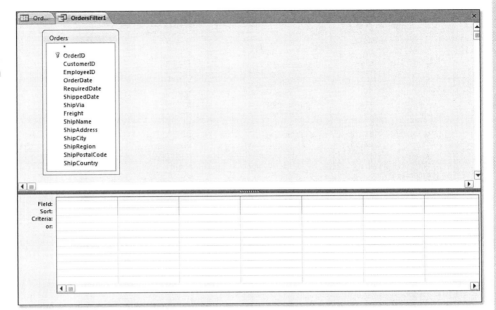

Figure 7.22
The grid of
the Filter
Design
window has
ascending
sorts speci-
fied for the
ShipCountry
and
ShipPostal
Code fields.

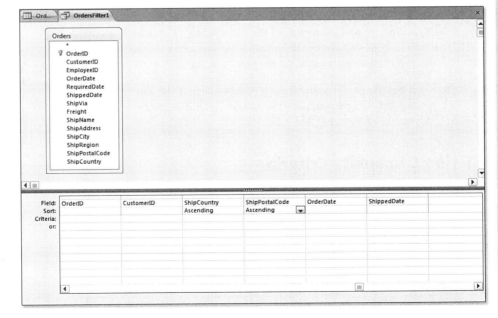

Order ID ⚬	Customer	Ship City ⚬	Ship Region ⚬	Ship Postal Code ⚬	Ship Country ⚬	Click to ⚬
10898	Océano Atlántico Ltda.	Buenos Aires		1010	Argentina	
11019	Rancho grande	Buenos Aires		1010	Argentina	
10986	Océano Atlántico Ltda.	Buenos Aires		1010	Argentina	
10958	Océano Atlántico Ltda.	Buenos Aires		1010	Argentina	
10937	Cactus Comidas para llevar	Buenos Aires		1010	Argentina	
10716	Rancho grande	Buenos Aires		1010	Argentina	
10409	Océano Atlántico Ltda.	Buenos Aires		1010	Argentina	
10916	Rancho grande	Buenos Aires		1010	Argentina	
11054	Cactus Comidas para llevar	Buenos Aires		1010	Argentina	
10881	Cactus Comidas para llevar	Buenos Aires		1010	Argentina	
10448	Rancho grande	Buenos Aires		1010	Argentina	
10828	Rancho grande	Buenos Aires		1010	Argentina	
10782	Cactus Comidas para llevar	Buenos Aires		1010	Argentina	
10819	Cactus Comidas para llevar	Buenos Aires		1010	Argentina	
10521	Cactus Comidas para llevar	Buenos Aires		1010	Argentina	
10531	Océano Atlántico Ltda.	Buenos Aires		1010	Argentina	
10686	Piccolo und mehr	Salzburg		5020	Austria	
10353	Piccolo und mehr	Salzburg		5020	Austria	
10597	Piccolo und mehr	Salzburg		5020	Austria	
10392	Piccolo und mehr	Salzburg		5020	Austria	
10489	Piccolo und mehr	Salzburg		5020	Austria	
11053	Piccolo und mehr	Salzburg		5020	Austria	
10530	Piccolo und mehr	Salzburg		5020	Austria	
10427	Piccolo und mehr	Salzburg		5020	Austria	
10844	Piccolo und mehr	Salzburg		5020	Austria	

Record: I◀ ◀ 1 of 830 ▶ ▶I ▶* No Filter Search

Figure 7.23
The sorted ShipCountry field is to the left of the sorted ShipPostalCode field in Query Design view, so the table is sorted first by country and then by postal code. Applying an Advanced Filter/Sort doesn't require repositioning the fields in Datasheet view.

8. Click the Advanced Filter Options button and choose Advanced Filter/Sort to edit the filter criteria.

9. Type **USA** in the Criteria row of the ShipCountry field to limit records to those orders shipped to an address in the United States. Access automatically adds quotes around "USA".

10. Click the Toggle Filter button and scroll to display the sorted fields. Only records with destinations in the United States appear, as shown in Figure 7.24.

 note
You must repeat the date criterion for each country criterion because of a limitation in constructing SQL statements from Access query grids, which is discussed shortly.

Using Composite Criteria

You can apply composite criteria to expand or further limit the records that Access displays. Composite criteria are applied to more than one field. To display all orders from the Orders table that were received on or after 1/1/2006 with destinations in North America, extend the exercise in the preceding section and try the following:

1. Click Advanced and choose Advanced Filter/Sort to display the Filter Design window.

2. Type **Canada** in the second criteria row of the ShipCountry field and **Mexico** in the third row; then move the cursor to a different cell. When you add criteria under one another, the effect is to make the criteria alternative—that is, combined by a logical **Or** operator.

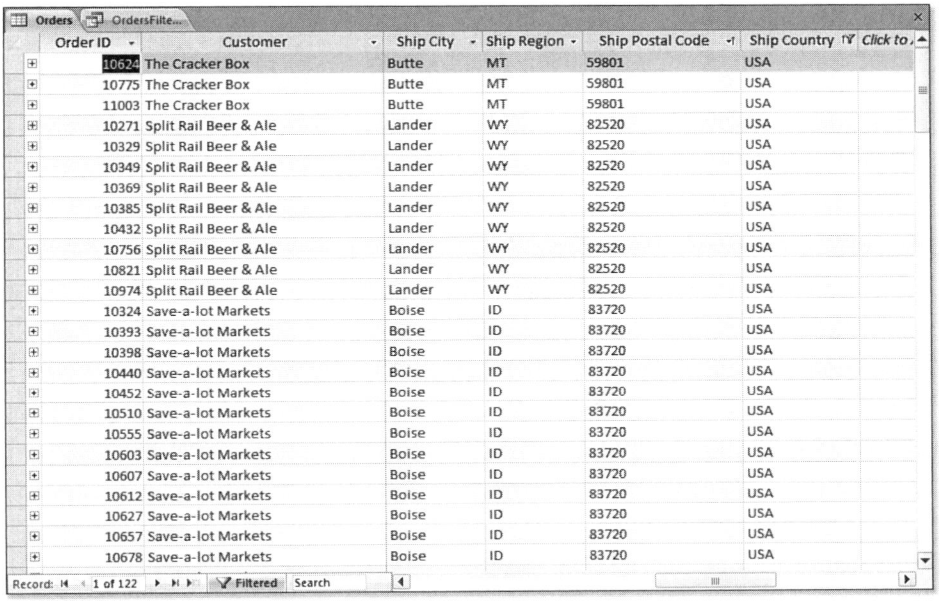

Order ID	Customer	Ship City	Ship Region	Ship Postal Code	Ship Country	Click to...
10624	The Cracker Box	Butte	MT	59801	USA	
10775	The Cracker Box	Butte	MT	59801	USA	
11003	The Cracker Box	Butte	MT	59801	USA	
10271	Split Rail Beer & Ale	Lander	WY	82520	USA	
10329	Split Rail Beer & Ale	Lander	WY	82520	USA	
10349	Split Rail Beer & Ale	Lander	WY	82520	USA	
10369	Split Rail Beer & Ale	Lander	WY	82520	USA	
10385	Split Rail Beer & Ale	Lander	WY	82520	USA	
10432	Split Rail Beer & Ale	Lander	WY	82520	USA	
10756	Split Rail Beer & Ale	Lander	WY	82520	USA	
10821	Split Rail Beer & Ale	Lander	WY	82520	USA	
10974	Split Rail Beer & Ale	Lander	WY	82520	USA	
10324	Save-a-lot Markets	Boise	ID	83720	USA	
10393	Save-a-lot Markets	Boise	ID	83720	USA	
10398	Save-a-lot Markets	Boise	ID	83720	USA	
10440	Save-a-lot Markets	Boise	ID	83720	USA	
10452	Save-a-lot Markets	Boise	ID	83720	USA	
10510	Save-a-lot Markets	Boise	ID	83720	USA	
10555	Save-a-lot Markets	Boise	ID	83720	USA	
10603	Save-a-lot Markets	Boise	ID	83720	USA	
10607	Save-a-lot Markets	Boise	ID	83720	USA	
10612	Save-a-lot Markets	Boise	ID	83720	USA	
10627	Save-a-lot Markets	Boise	ID	83720	USA	
10657	Save-a-lot Markets	Boise	ID	83720	USA	
10678	Save-a-lot Markets	Boise	ID	83720	USA	

Figure 7.24 Adding "USA" in the Criteria row under the ShipCountry field filters the Datasheet view to display orders destined for the United States only.

3. Open the Sort list for the PostalCode field and select (not sorted) to remove the sort. Open the Sort list for the OrderDate field and select Ascending.

4. Type **>=#1/1/2006#** in the first criteria line of the OrderDate field. When you add criteria on the same line as another criterion, the criteria is additive (a logical **And** operator)—that is, orders placed on or after 1/1/2006. The # symbols indicate to Access that the enclosed value is of the Date/Time data type; Access adds the symbols if you don't.

5. Press F2 to select the date entry you made in step 3 and then press Ctrl+C to copy the expression to the Clipboard. Position the cursor in the second row of the OrderDate field and press Ctrl+V to add the same expression for Canada. Repeat this process to add the date criterion for Mexican orders. Your Filter Design grid now appears as shown in Figure 7.25.

6. Click the Toggle Filter button to display your newly filtered datasheet (see Figure 7.26, which has the field sequence rearranged and is scrolled to show the three countries).

To become more familiar with the power of selecting data with criteria, **see** *"Using the Query Design Window,"* **p. 355**.

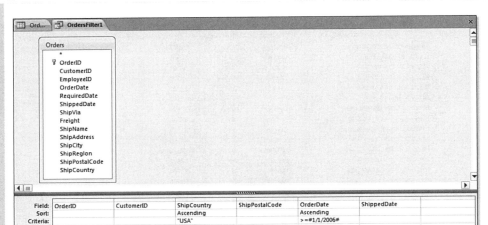

Figure 7.25
The design of this composite filter restricts the display to orders received in 2006 and later destined for North America.

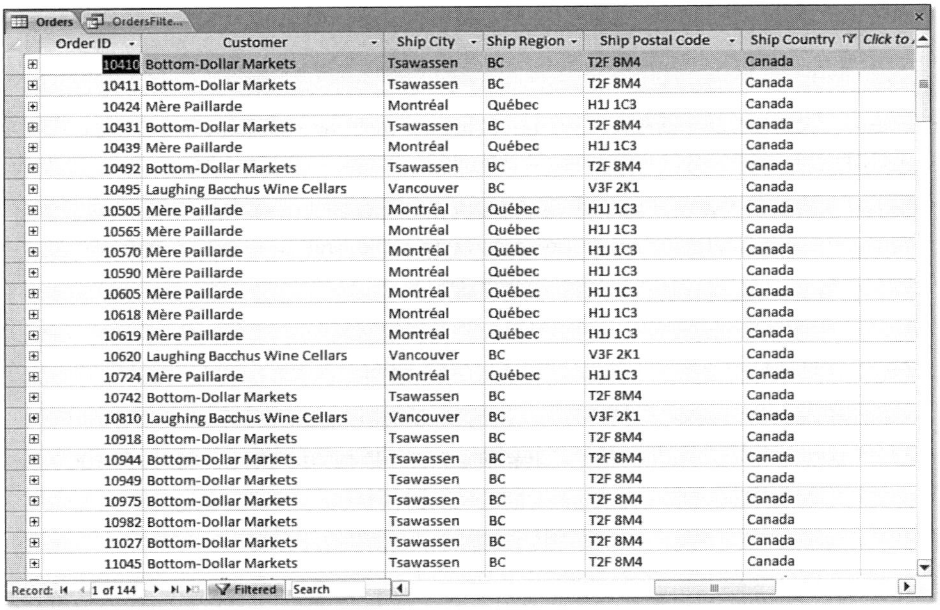

Figure 7.26
This Datasheet view of the Orders table has the filter of Figure 7.25 applied. The field sequence has been rearranged to permit viewing the OrderDate and ShipCountry fields.

Saving Your Filter as a Query and Loading a Filter

As mentioned earlier, Access doesn't have a persistent Filter object. A persistent database object is one you create that's stored as a component of your database's .accdb file. Persistent database objects appear as items in one of the list views of the Navigation pane. A filter is equivalent to a single-table query, so Access lets you save your filter as a `QueryDef` (query definition) object. Access saves the names of the filters associated with each table in the system tables of your database when you save a filter as a query. This feature is the principal advantage of using a filter rather than a query when only a single table is involved.

To save your filter and remove the filter from the Orders table, follow these steps:

1. Click the Advanced button and choose Advanced Filter/Sort to display the Filter Design window if it isn't already displayed.

2. Right-click the upper pane and choose Save as Query to display the Save as Query input box.

3. Enter a descriptive name—such as **fltOrdersNorthAmerica2006+**—for your filter in the Query Name text box. Using the flt prefix distinguishes the filters you save from conventional queries (see Figure 7.27).

Figure 7.27
Use a descriptive name when saving the filter as a `QueryDef` object.

4. Click OK to save the filter, close the Filter window, add a Queries category to the Navigation pane, and add fltOrdersNorthAmerica2006 as a member of the Queries category.

5. Click the Advanced Filter Options button and choose Clear All Filters to remove the filter from the Orders datasheet.

6. Close the Orders table, and save the changes.

Reapplying a filter from the filter you saved as a query requires the following steps:

1. Reopen the Orders table in Datasheet view.

2. Click the Advanced button and choose Advanced Filter/Sort to open the Filter Design window with the default OrdersFilter1 filter.

3. Click Advanced again and choose Load from Query to open the Applicable Filter dialog (see Figure 7.28). You use the Applicable Filter dialog to select the filter you want if you've saved more than one filter for the table.

Figure 7.28
Clicking the Load from Query toolbar button opens the Applicable Filter dialog from which you can select the filter to apply to the table.

4. Double-click the fltOrdersNorthAmerica2006+ filter item to load the saved query into the Filter window.

5. Click the Toggle Filter toolbar button to display the resulting filtered set in the Orders datasheet.

Applying a Saved Query as a Filter

An alternative to the preceding steps is to execute the saved filter as query. You execute a query the same way you open a table:

1. Close the Orders table.

2. Double-click the fltOrdersNorthAmerica2006 item under the Queries category. The Datasheet of the fltOrdersNorthAmerica window that opens is similar to the Datasheet you created in step 5 of the preceding operation, except that the fields appear in the original order of the table design.

3. Click the Design View button to display the query design (see Figure 7.29). Fields in which no selection criteria or sort order are entered don't appear in the Query Design grid.

 tip

To remove a filter saved as a query so it doesn't appear in the Applicable Filters list, delete the query from the Navigation Pane's Queries group.

Customizing Table Datasheet View

To customize the appearance of Table Datasheet view, you can hide the fields you don't want to appear in your datasheet, change the height of the record rows, eliminate the gridlines, and select a different font for your display. The following list describes each option for customizing Table and Query Datasheet views:

- To hide a field, select it by clicking its header or placing the cursor in the column for the field. Then choose Format, Hide Columns.

Figure 7.29
The Query Design view of a filter is similar to the Filter Design view, but adds Table and Show rows to the grid.

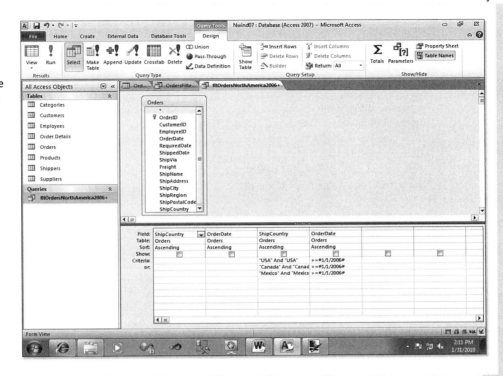

- To show a hidden field, right-click the field and choose Unhide Columns to display the Unhide Columns dialog (see Figure 7.30). A mark next to the field name in the Column list indicates fields appearing in Datasheet view. Click the check box to the left of the field name to toggle between hiding and showing the field.

Figure 7.30
The Unhide Columns dialog lets you specify the fields that appear in Table Datasheet view.

- To change the font used to display and print the datasheet, use the Font drop-down list in the Home ribbon's Font group.

- To remove gridlines from the display and printed versions of the datasheet, open the Font group's Gridlines drop-down list. Access displays a gallery of four gridline display choices: Both, Horizontal, Vertical, and None; click the button corresponding to the gridline display you want.

- To change the height of the rows as displayed and printed, position the mouse pointer at the bottom edge of one of the record selector buttons. The pointer turns into a double-headed arrow (see Figure 7.31). Drag the bottom edge of the button to adjust the height of all the rows. Alternatively, choose Format, Row Height and set the height in points in the Row Height dialog. (Multiply the size of your font by about 1.25 to obtain normal row spacing; printers call 10-point type with 12-point spacing "10 on 12.")

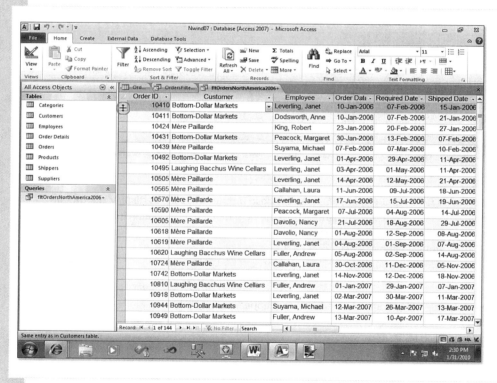

Figure 7.31
This cus-tomized Datasheet view uses a 9-point Verdana type and no gridlines. You adjust line spacing, shown here between the second and third record selection buttons, by dragging the double-headed arrow up or down.

- To change the width of the field columns to accommodate a larger font, right-click the column and choose Field Width and then click the Best Fit button to let Access determine the size of your columns. You might need to adjust individual column widths by dragging the right edge of the field header with the mouse.

Copying, Exporting, and Mailing Sorted and Filtered Data

A common use for filters and customized datasheets is to export the filtered and sorted records to another application, such as Microsoft Excel or Word. Several methods for exporting filtered and custom-formatted records are available on the External Data ribbon.

The next chapter provides complete descriptions of Access's traditional data export features, including exporting filtered and sorted tables to Microsoft Excel workbooks and Word mail-merge documents. Chapter 23, "Collaborating with SharePoint Foundation 2010," Chapter 24, "Sharing Web Databases with SharePoint Server 2010 ," and Chapter 26, "Integrating with XML and InfoPath" describe other Access 2010 data export/import features.

8

LINKING, IMPORTING, AND EXPORTING DATA

Undoubtedly, every personal computer user has data that can be processed through database-management techniques. Any data that a computer can arrange in tabular form—even tables in word processing files—can be converted to database tables. The strength of a relational database management system (RDBMS) lies in its capability to handle large numbers of individual pieces of data stored in tables and to relate the pieces of data in a meaningful way.

PC users turn to RDBMSs when the amount of data created exceeds a conventional productivity application's capability to manipulate the data effectively. A common example is a large mailing list created in Microsoft Excel or Word. As the number of names in the list increases, using Excel or Word to make selective mailings and maintain histories of responses to mailings becomes increasingly difficult. An RDBMS is the most effective type of application for manipulating large lists.

One strong point of Access is its capability to transform existing spreadsheets, database tables, and text files created by other Windows and even DOS applications into the Access .accdb format—a process known as importing a file. Access can export (create) table files in any format in which it can import the files, including HTML and Extensible Markup Language (XML) documents. You also can import/export SharePoint Foundation (SPF) 2010 or Microsoft SharePoint Server (SPS) 2010 lists.

Access can link a database table file created by Access or another RDBMS, an Excel worksheet, or a SharePoint list to your current Access database. Access then acts as

 note

This chapter doesn't include use of Access 2010's HTML, XML, and SharePoint import/ export features for intranet- and Internet-based database applications. The chapters of Part VI, "Collaborating with Access Data," and Part VII, "Working with HTML and XML Documents," cover these topics.

a data-entry front end for the linked object. This capability is far less common in other desktop and client/server RDBMSs. When you link a table from a different RDBMS, spreadsheet, or list, you can display and, in many cases, update the linked table as though it were an Access table contained in your .accdb file. If the file containing the table is shared on a network, in some cases others can use the file with their applications while it's linked to your database.

The capability to link files is important for two reasons: It lets you connect to multiple Access databases, and you can create new applications in Access that can coexist with applications created by other database managers and applications. Access 2010 also can link Outlook contacts, tasks, and calendar folders, as well as Enterprise Services web services. Outlook 2010 also lets you import and export folders to and from Access 2010 and earlier tables.

The External Data ribbon displays Excel, Access, ODBC Database, Text File, XML File, and More buttons in the Import group. Clicking the More button opens a rogue's gallery of buttons for SharePoint List, and less popular formats—Data (Web) Services, HTML Document, Outlook Folder, and dBASE File (see Figure 8.1).

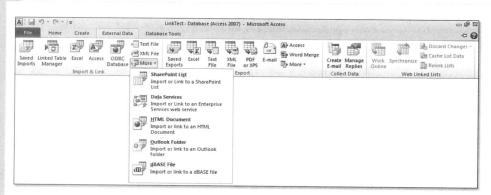

Figure 8.1
The External Data ribbon's Import group has a button for each database or file type that Access can import, link, or both.

Importing and Linking Spreadsheet Files

Moving spreadsheets to relational database tables is one of the more common applications for Microsoft Access. Access 2010 can import files created by spreadsheet and related applications, such as project management systems, in the following formats:

- Excel 3, 4, 5, 7, 9x, and 200x .xls files, as well as task and resource files created by Microsoft Project in .xls format.

- Excel 2007 and 2010 .xlsb, .xlsm, and .xlsx Open XML Format files.

- A single code library handles the import of all Excel formats.

Creating a Table by Importing an Excel Worksheet

Figure 8.2 illustrates the preferred format for Excel and other spreadsheet applications for importing to Access and other RDBMS tables. The names of the fields are typed in the first row and the remainder of the database range consists of data. The type of data in each column must be consistent within the database range you select.

To prepare the data in an Excel spreadsheet for importation into an Access table, follow these steps:

1. Launch Excel and then open the .xls, .xlsx, .xlsb, or .xlsm file that contains the data you want to import.

2. Add field names above the first row of the data you plan to export (if you haven't done so). Field names can't include periods (.), exclamation points (!), or square brackets ([]). You can't have duplicate field names. If you include improper characters in field names or use duplicate field names, you see an error message when you attempt to import the worksheet.

> **note**
>
> **2010 NEW** The Data Services (Import or Link to Enterprise Services or Web Service) choice enables importing Business Connectivity Services (formerly Business Data Catalog, BDC) to read-only Access 2010 tables.
>
> The Access development team deprecated Lotus 1-2-3 worksheet, Paradox 3, 4, 5, 6, and 7 database, and Access 1.0 and 2.0 (also called Jet 2 or Red 2) database files in Access 2010. You must have Access 2007 or earlier to import, link or export these file types.

Figure 8.2
This Excel 2010 worksheet was created by exporting the Orders table to a workbook file. The worksheet serves as an example for importing a worksheet to an Access table.

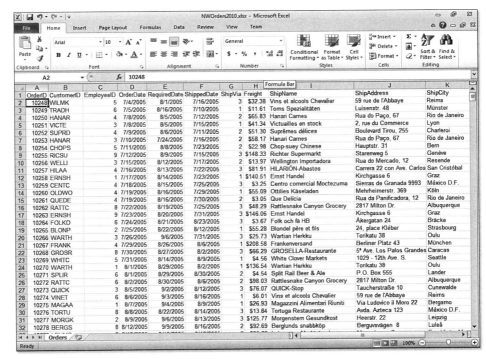

3. If your worksheet contains cells with data you don't want to include in the imported table, select the range that contains the field names row and all the rows of data needed for the table. In Excel, choose Insert, Name, Define and then name the range.

4. Save the Excel file (use a different filename if you froze values) and exit Excel.

 Now you're ready to import worksheets from the Excel workbook file, \Access2010\Chaptr08\\NWOrders2010.xlsx, for this example. To import the prepared data from an Excel spreadsheet into an Access table, follow these steps:

1. Open the database you want to add the new table to.

2. Click the External Data tab and the Import group's Excel button to open the Get External Data – Excel Data dialog, accept the default Import the Source Data into a New Table option, click the Browse button to open the File Open dialog, and navigate to the folder that contains the .xlsx, .xlsb, or .xlsm file with the worksheet to import (NWOrders2010.xlsx for this example; see Figure 8.3).

> **note**
> You can use OLE to embed or link charts created by Microsoft Excel and stored in files with an .xlc extension. Copy the contents of the file to the Windows Clipboard from Excel. Choose Edit, Paste to embed or link (via OLE) the chart in a field of the OLE Object type; then display the chart on a form or print it on a report as an unbound object. Similarly, you can embed or link most views displayed in Microsoft Project, which also uses the Microsoft Graph applet; the exceptions are task and resource forms and the Task PERT chart.

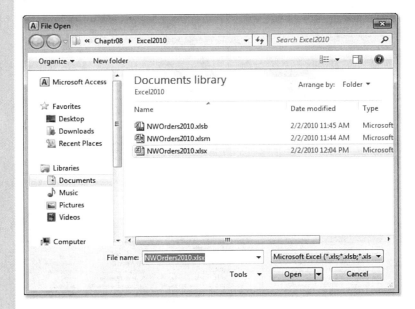

Figure 8.3
Navigate to the folder, select Microsoft Excel (*.xls; *.xlsb; *.xlsm, *.xlsx) in the Files of Type list, and select the worksheet to import.

3. Double-click the name of the Excel workbook that contains the spreadsheet you want to import to return to the Get External Data – Excel Spreadsheet dialog. Alternatively, click the filename to select it and then click Open (see Figure 8.4). If you want to append rows to an existing table having the same structure and data types as the spreadsheet, select the Append a Copy of the Records to the Table option and select the table from the adjacent list. Otherwise, accept the default Import the Source Data into a New Table in the Current Database option.

Figure 8.4
Accept the default Import the Source Data into a New Table in the Current Database option to create an Access table from the worksheet you specify in the File Name text box.

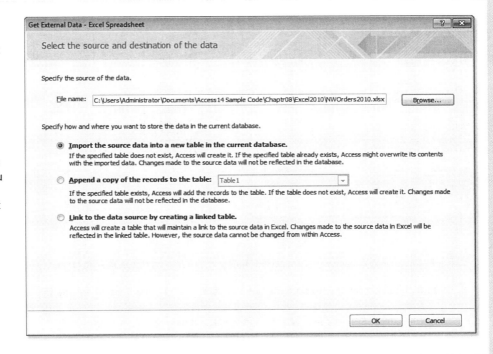

4. Click OK to close the Get External Data – Excel Spreadsheet dialog and invoke the Import Spreadsheet Wizard (see Figure 8.5).

5. If you're importing an entire worksheet, select the Show Worksheets option; if you're importing a named range, select the Show Named Ranges option. The Import Spreadsheet Wizard lists the worksheets or named data ranges, depending on the option you select in the list box in the upper-right corner of the wizard's opening dialog.

6. Select the worksheet or the named data range that you want to import in the list box. The Import Spreadsheet Wizard shows a sample view of the data in the worksheet (Orders in the NWOrders2010.xlsx workbook for this example) or the named range at the bottom of the dialog.

💡 tip
You get an opportunity to assign field names to the columns in the worksheet during the importation process, although the process is easier if you add field names as column headings first.

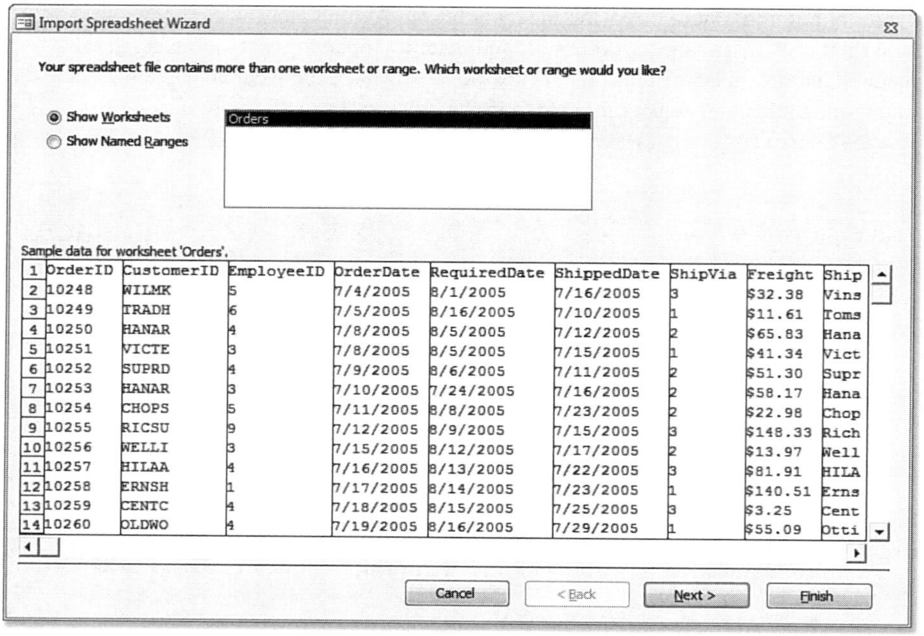

Figure 8.5
The first dialog of the Import Spreadsheet Wizard lets you select a specific worksheet or named range to import as a table.

7. Click Next to move to the second dialog of the Import Spreadsheet Wizard, shown in Figure 8.6.

8. If the first row of your spreadsheet data contains the field names for the imported table, select the First Row Contains Column Headings check box. Click Next to continue with the third step; the Import Spreadsheet Wizard displays the dialog shown in Figure 8.7.

9. If you want to exclude a column from the imported database, select the column by clicking it, select the Do Not Import Field (Skip) check box, and skip to step 12.

10. The Import Spreadsheet Wizard lets you edit or add the field names for the spreadsheet columns; click the column whose name you want to edit or add and then type the name in the Field Name text box.

11. If you want Access to index this field, choose the appropriate index type in the Indexed list box; you can choose No, Yes (Duplicates OK), or Yes (No Duplicates).

12. Repeat steps 9, 10, and 11 for each column in the worksheet or data range that you import. When you're satisfied with your options for each column, click Next to move to the fifth dialog.

> **note**
>
> If you elect to add the imported data to an existing table, the Import Spreadsheet Wizard skips over all intervening steps and goes immediately to its final dialog, described in step 14.

Figure 8.6
The wizard's
second dialog
lets you spec-
ify whether
the first row of
the worksheet
or named
range contains
column head-
ings.

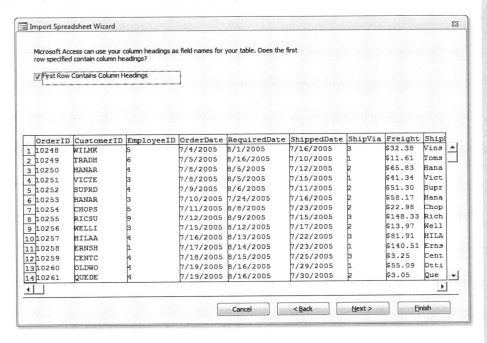

Figure 8.7
The third wiz-
ard dialog lets
you edit the
field name,
specify an
index, or skip
a field.

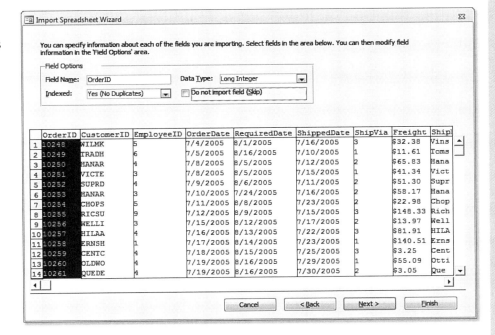

13. Select the Let Access Add Primary Key option to have Access add an AutoNumber field to the imported table; Access fills in a unique number for each existing row in the worksheet that you're importing. Select the Choose My Own Primary Key option and select the primary key field in the drop-down list if you know you can use a column in the worksheet or data range as a primary key for the imported table. The OrderID column is the primary key field for this example (see Figure 8.8). If this imported table doesn't need a primary key, select the No Primary Key option.

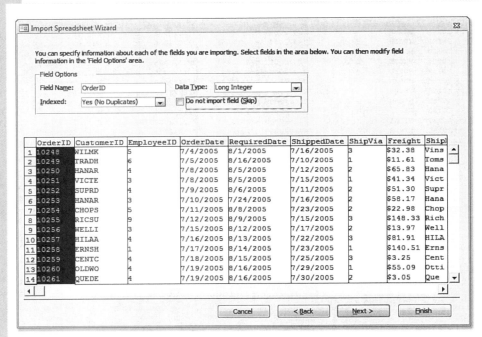

Figure 8.8
If the data you're importing contains a column with a unique value to identify each row, select the Choose My Own Primary Key option and the column name with the unique data.

14. Click Next to move to the final dialog of the Import Spreadsheet Wizard (see Figure 8.9). Type the name of the new table (**Orders**, for this example) in the Import to Table text box; Access uses the name of the worksheet or data range as the default table name. If you want to use the Table Analyzer Wizard to split the imported table into two or more related tables, select the I Would Like a Wizard to Analyze My Table After Importing the Data check box.

 tip

You can use the Table Analyzer Wizard at any time on any table by clicking the Analyze Tables button of the Database Tools ribbon's Analyze group.

 To review use of the Table Analyzer Wizard to move duplicate data to a related table, **see** *"Using the Table Analyzer Wizard,"* **p. 235.**

Figure 8.9
The final wizard dialog lets you rename the table and, optionally, run the Table Analyzer Wizard on the table data after the import operation completes, open the help window, or both.

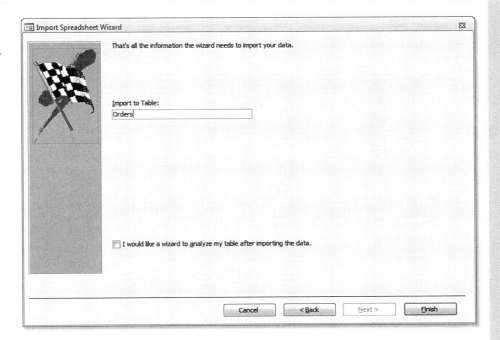

15. Click Finish to dismiss the wizard and open the Save Import Steps dialog. If you want to save the preceding steps in an import workflow specification, mark the Save Import Steps check box and, optionally, add a description, mark the Create Outlook Task for repetitive operations, or both (see Figure 8.10).

16. Click the Save Import or Cancel button to complete the importing process. Access closes the Import Spreadsheet Wizard and imports the data. If you mark the Create Outlook Task check box, Outlook should display a detailed task message. Set the recurrence parameters, if you want, and then click the Save & Close button. However, the initial Release to Manufacturing (RTM) version of Access 2010 displays the message shown in Figure 8.11 when attempting to create the task. This problem probably will be fixed in an early Office 2011 service pack.

 tip
Use scheduled repetitive import operations only for appending data to an existing table. If the import operation creates a new table, manual intervention is required to enable overwriting the existing table.

The Import Spreadsheet Wizard analyzes approximately the first 20 rows of the spreadsheet you are importing and assigns data types to the imported fields based on this analysis. If every cell in a column has a numeric or date value, the columns convert to the Number or Date/Time field data type, respectively. If a column contains mixed text and numbers, the wizard converts the column as a text field. If, however, a column contains numeric data in the first 20 or so rows (the rows that the wizard analyzes) and then has one or more text entries, the wizard doesn't convert these rows.

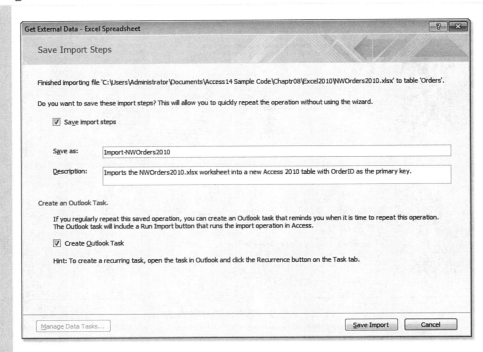

Figure 8.10
You can auto-
mate repeated
spreadsheet
importation
by saving the
import steps.

If the wizard encounters cell values that it can't convert to the data type that it assigned to the imported field, Access creates an Import Errors table with one record for each error. You can review this table, select the records in which the errors are reported, and fix them. A better approach, however, is to correct the cells in the spreadsheet, resave the file, and import the corrected data.

The Navigation Pane now contains a new table with the name you accepted or edited in the final dialog of the Import Spreadsheet Wizard. If you import another file with the same name as your worksheet or named range, the wizard asks if you want to overwrite the existing table.

The wizard applies the Access Double data type to all numeric fields except Currency (this includes the OrderID, EmployeeID, and ShipVia fields of the Order table), which you should change to the Long Integer data type. The wizard will correctly detect the Date/Time data type for the OrderDate, RequiredDate, and ShippedDate fields, and the Currency data type for the Freight field (because a dollar sign prefixes data in the worksheet column).

tip

The Import Spreadsheet Wizard doesn't display an error message when it encounters inconsistent field data types; it just creates the Import Errors table. You must look in the Navigation Pane to see whether the Import Errors table is present. After you resolve the import errors, make sure that you delete the Import Errors table so that you can more easily detect errors the next time you import a spreadsheet or other external file.

Figure 8.11
This Outlook message occurs when the RTM release of Access 2010 can't create an Outlook task.

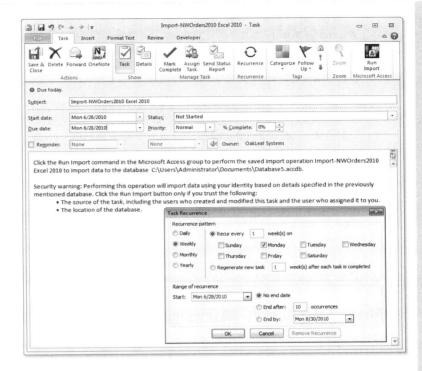

Linking Excel Worksheets

The advantages of linking an Excel worksheet are that you always work with the latest version of the worksheet; changes made to the Excel data appear in the linked table. However, you can't alter worksheet cell values from within Access, nor can you change field data types. You can assign a primary key, but Access doesn't enforce unique values in the key field(s).

Linking an Excel spreadsheet uses a truncated version of the Import Spreadsheet Wizard renamed to the Link Spreadsheet Wizard. To link an Excel worksheet to an Access 2010 table, do the following:

1. Follow the first three steps of the preceding Excel import process, but select the Link to the Data Source by Creating a Linked Table option in the Get External Data – Excel Spreadsheet dialog.

2. Click OK to start the Link Spreadsheet Wizard.

 tip

Don't use the Double (or Single) data type for primary key fields. These data types require floating-point arithmetic to determine their values, which is subject to rounding errors. Relationships based on floating-point values might fail because of these rounding errors. In addition, multitable queries having relationships based on Double (or Single) fields usually exhibit very poor performance.

3. Select the worksheet or named range to link (the Orders sample worksheet in NWOrdersLink.xls for this example) and then click the Next button.

4. Mark the First Row Contains Column Headings check box, if applicable. Click Next to continue.

5. The wizard proposes the name of the worksheet as the table name. Change the table name if you want, click Finish, and then click OK to link the table. The linked table is identified in the Navigation pane by an Excel icon and an arrow.

6. Open the linked table in Design view, clicking OK to acknowledge that you can't change the design of a linked table. Unfortunately, the wizard again makes the wrong data type choice (Double) for the OrderID, EmployeeID, and ShipVia columns.

 note

According to Microsoft Knowledge Base article 904953 (http://support.microsoft.com/kb/904953/), "legal issues" were responsible for making linked worksheets read-only for Access 2002 and later. The "legal issue" was an $8.9-million award in 2005 to the holder of a patent on the software to create a read/write link between Excel and Access.

The Linked Table Manager, which is the subject of the "Using the Linked Table Manager Add-in to Relink Tables" section later in the chapter, lets you fix broken links to worksheets.

Working with Microsoft Outlook and Exchange Folders

Microsoft Outlook 2010 lets you import data from and export data to a wide range of file types, including Access 2007 databases. For example, you can export data to a variety of file types and import OPML, vCard, iCalendar, or vCalendar files. Outlook's import capability is far more eclectic than that of Access; you can import from the ACT! 3.x, 4.x, and 2000 Contact Manager, and Lotus Organizer 4.x and 5.x files.

 tip

Excel users must save their worksheet to the .xls* file, and Access users must close and reopen the table to see changes to the linked data.

Access 2000 added the Exchange/Outlook Wizard for linking to the contents of Outlook's private and Exchange's public folders. The following two sections show you how to export, import, and link Contacts folders. The Contacts folder is most commonly used with databases; working with other folders follows a similar course.

Importing and Exporting Access Tables with Outlook 2010

To use Outlook to import an Access table to an Outlook 2010 Contacts folder, do the following:

1. Open Outlook and select the folder you want to import to. (Create a new empty Contacts subfolder, Northwind for this example, in the My Contacts folder when you're testing import and export operations.)

 tip

If you want to put data from vCard, ACT! or Lotus Organizer into Access 2010, importing to Outlook and exporting to Access is the best alternative unless you have versions of these applications that handle exporting to Access databases.

2. Choose File, Open, Import to start the Import and Export Wizard. Select Import from Another Program or File in the Choose an Action to Perform list shown in Figure 8.12, and click Next.

Figure 8.12
Select Import from Another Program or File in the first dialog of Outlook's Import and Export Wizard.

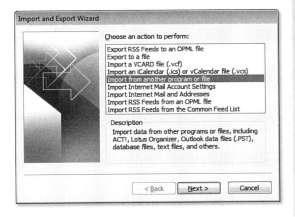

3. Select Microsoft Access (2000 – 2003) in the Import a File dialog shown in Figure 8.13, and click Next.

Figure 8.13
Select Microsoft Access in the second wizard dialog.

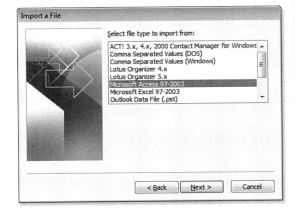

4. In the second Import a File dialog, click Browse to open the Browse dialog, and then navigate to and select the .mdb file that contains the table you want to import. This example uses Northwind.mdb's Customers table. Select an option for handling duplicates, and then click Next (see Figure 8.14).

Make sure the .accdb file you intend to import the data from is closed at this point. If the .mdb file is open, you might receive an error message when you attempt to complete the next step.

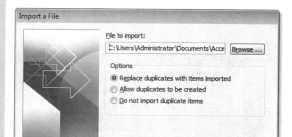

Figure 8.14
Navigate to the database you want to import the contact data from, and select Replace Duplicates with Items Imported to ensure your Outlook contact information is up to date.

5. The destination folder you specified in step 1 is selected in the Import a File dialog (see Figure 8.15). If you didn't select a folder, you must do so at this point. Click Next.

6. Mark the Import *TableName* into the *FolderName* option for the table to import (Customers into Northwind, for this example).

 tip

Outlook 2010 doesn't support importing contacts from Access 2007+ .accdb or Excel 2007+ .xslx files. Therefore, you're better off exporting table data from Access 2010 to Outlook 2010.

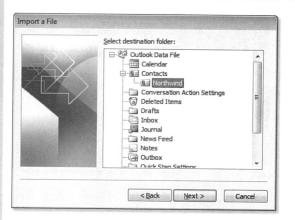

Figure 8.15
Verify the destination folder in the fourth wizard dialog. In this case, the folder is created in the Contacts folder of your Personal Folders.

7. Click Map Custom Fields to open the Map Custom Fields dialog, and drag the fields you want to include in the Northwind list from the left list (the From category) to the appropriate Outlook field name in the right list (the To category), as shown in Figure 8.16. Fields that you don't drag to the right list aren't included in the new Contacts folder.

Figure 8.16
Drag field names from the Access source table to the corresponding Outlook fields.

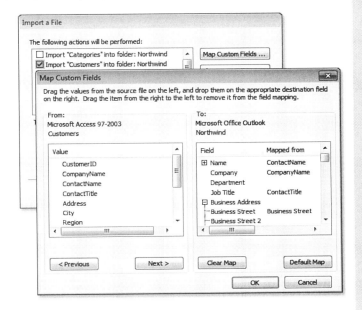

8. Click OK to close the Map Custom Fields dialog; then click Finish to close the Import File dialog and complete the import process. When the records are imported, Outlook automatically displays them (see Figure 8.17).

Exporting Contacts or other Outlook records to an Access table with the Outlook Import and Export Wizard follows the pattern of the preceding steps. Select the folder to export, choose File, Options, Advanced, click Export to open the Import and Export Wizard, select Export to a File, Microsoft Access 97 – 2003, and confirm the folder selection. Then specify the destination .mdb file, and export the records to a table with the name of the folder or a name you specify.

Linking with the Exchange/Outlook Wizard

The Exchange/Outlook Wizard provides the capability of linking records in Outlook or Exchange folders to an Access table (or tables). Linking is a better option than importing because your Access table is always up to date with information entered in Outlook, and vice versa. Unlike with linked Excel worksheets, Access can update data linked to Outlook folders.

 tip

The better approach is to use Access's Import Exchange/Outlook version of Outlook's Export Wizard. The Access wizard's method of selecting the fields to import is simpler than Outlook's Export Wizard.

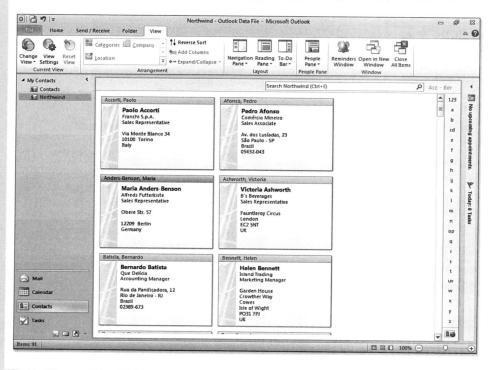

Figure 8.17
Outlook's Contacts folder by default displays the contact name and company address in Business Card view.

To link a Contacts folder to an Access table, follow these steps:

1. Open the database to which you want to link the Outlook folder, click the External Data tab, click the Import section's More button to open the gallery, and click the Outlook Folder button to open the Get External Data – Outlook Folder dialog.

2. Select the Link to the Data Source by Creating a Linked Table option, and click OK to open the Link Exchange/Outlook Wizard. This example uses Outlook.

3. Expand the nodes as necessary to open the folder to link. This example uses the Contacts subfolder (Northwind) you created in the preceding section (see Figure 8.18).

4. Click Next to open the second (and last) wizard dialog, in which you accept the folder name as the table name or change it to your liking (NorthwindContacts for this example). Accept the default I Would Like the Wizard to Store My MAPI Profile with My Linked Table option if Outlook is using Exchange rather than Outlook to store contact data.

5. Click Finish to link the table, and acknowledge the Finished Linking message. Your linked table appears in the Navigation pane, identified by an envelope icon with an adjacent arrow.

 tip

Exchange 2000+ uses Active Directory to store recipient data, so you can link to the Global Address List. If all users on a Windows 200x Server network are mailbox-enabled (not just mail-enabled), a link to the Global Address List provides a link to information about every network user.

Figure 8.18
Select the
folder to link
in the Link
Exchange/
Outlook
Wizard's first
dialog.

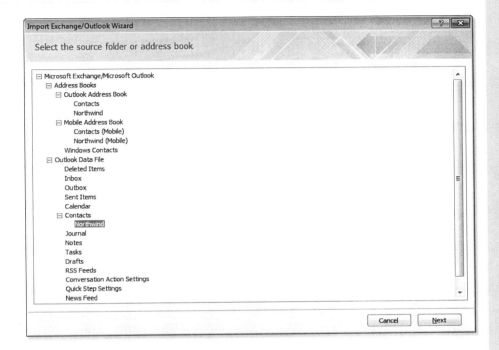

6. Open the linked table in Datasheet view. The rows appear in company name order, and many Contacts fields are empty. Right-click each empty column and choose Hide Columns, and rearrange the field's sequence to improve readability (see Figure 8.19). Tables linked to Exchange address lists aren't updatable. Tables linked to personal and public folders are updatable, even without a primary key field, but your account must have permissions to make changes to Exchange public folders.

 note

Text files in three of these formats (CSV, TAB, and TXT) derived from Northwind.accdb's Orders table are located in the \ Samples2010\Chaptro8\TextFile folder of the downloadable sample files.

The response of linked Exchange public folders to changes, sorts, and other operations is slower than linked Access database tables because a local temporary link table (ACCESS*xxxx*.tmp) acts as an intermediary between Access and Exchange.

Importing Text Files

If the data you want to import into an Access table was developed in a database management system, word processor, or other application that can't export the data as a .dbf or .xls file, you must create a text file in one of the text formats supported by Access. Most DOS- and Windows-compatible data files created from data stored by mainframes and minicomputers, as well as files generated from nine-track magnetic tapes, are text files.

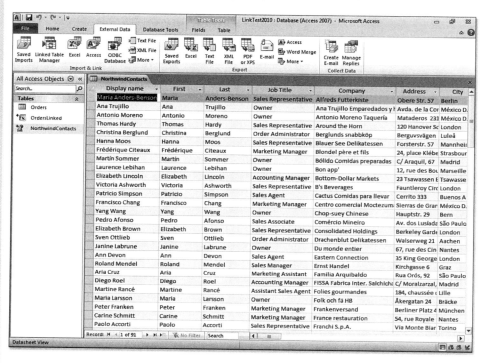

Figure 8.19
The linked Northwind Contacts table contains fields whose data is stored in an Outlook Contacts folder. Empty fields are hidden, and the Job Title field is relocated from near the end of the field list.

Access refers to the characters that separate fields as *delimiters* or *separators*. In this book, the term *delimiter* refers to characters that identify the end of a field; the term *text identifiers* refers to the single or double quotation marks that you can use to distinguish text from numeric data.

Table 8.1 details the text formats that Access supports for import and export operations.

> **note**
>
> A copy of the data imported from the Exchange Global Address List folder of the sample oakmont.edu domain is included in the LinkTest.accdb database in the \Samples2010\Chaptro8 folder of the downloadable sample data. Fields with no data have been skipped in the table.

Using the Import Text Wizard

To import any of the text file types listed in Table 8.1, you follow a procedure similar to the procedure for importing any external data into Access. To import a text file, follow these steps:

1. Open the database you want to import the text file into, click the External Data tab, and click the Text File button to open the External Data – Text File dialog.

2. Accept the default Import the Source Data into a New Table in the Current Database option, and click Browse to open the File Open dialog with Text Files (*.txt; *.csv; *.tab; *.asc) selected in the Files of Type list.

Table 8.1 Text File Formats Supported by Access 2010

Format	Description
Comma-delimited text files (also called CSV files)	Commas separate (delimit) fields. The newline pair, carriage-return (ASCII character 13), and line feed (ASCII character 10) separate records. Some applications enclose all values within double quotation marks, a format often called *mail merge*, to prevent commas in a field value from erroneously specifying the end of the field. Other applications enclose only text (strings) in quotation marks to differentiate between text and numeric values, the standard format for files created by the xBase command COPY TO FILENAME DELIMITED.
Tab-delimited text files (also called TAB files)	These files treat all values as text and separate fields with tabs. Records are separated by newline pairs. Most word processing applications use this format to export tabular text.
Space-delimited files	Some text files use spaces to separate fields in a line of text. The use of spaces as delimiter characters is uncommon because it can cause what should be single fields, such as street addresses, to be divided inconsistently into different fields.
Fixed-width text files (usually called TXT or ASCII files)	Access separates (parses) the individual records into fields based on the position of the data items in a line of text. Newline pairs separate records, and every record must have exactly the same length. Spaces pad the fields to a specified fixed width. Fixed width is the most common format for data exported by mainframes and minicomputers on nine-track tape.

3. Navigate to the folder that contains the text file you want to import (\Samples2010\Chaptr08\TextFiles\Orders.csv for the initial example) and double-click the text file's name. Access starts the Import Text Wizard, shown in Figure 8.20, which is similar to Excel's wizard of the same name.

4. Select the Delimited option to import a delimited text file or select Fixed Width to import a fixed-width text file. The Import Text Wizard displays a sample of the text file's contents in the lower portion of the dialog to help you determine the correct file type. Figure 8.20 shows a comma-delimited text file (\Access2010\Chaptr08\TextFilesOrders.csv) being imported. Click Next to proceed to the next step in the Import Text Wizard.If you selected Delimited as the file type for the Orders.csv file, the Import Text Wizard displays the dialog shown in Figure 8.21; if you selected the Fixed Width option for the Orders.txt file, the wizard displays the dialog in Figure 8.22.

5. If you're importing a delimited text file, accept the default or select the delimiter character that separates fields in the table (most delimited files use the tab separator). If the text file you're importing uses a text qualifier other than double quotation marks, type it in the Text Qualifier text box. If the first line in the text file contains field names (such as the column headings in a spreadsheet file), select the First Row Contains Field Names check box. Click Next to move to the next step of the Import Text Wizard.

 note

The wizard doesn't detect the EmployeeID field, so you must add a break after the five-character CustomerID field. You also must add a break before the RequiredDate, ShipVia and Region fields and remove two breaks from the ShipAddress field.

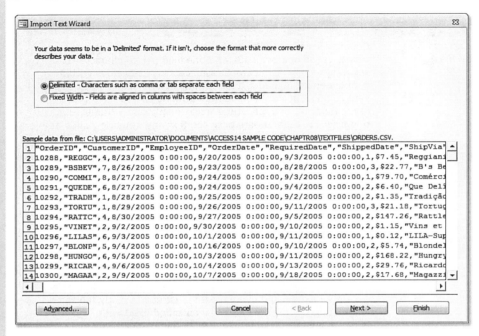

Figure 8.20
The first dialog of the Import Text Wizard lets you select between delimited (the default) or fixed-width files, and displays sample data from the file.

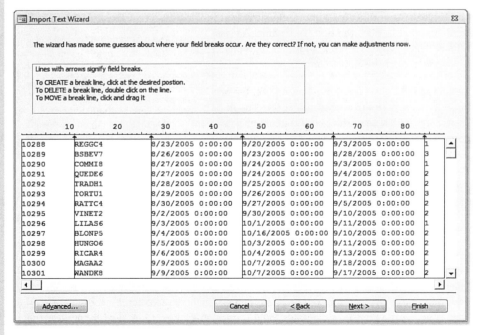

Figure 8.21
The wizard's second dialog gives a preview of the table to be created upon importing the Orders.csv text file.

Figure 8.22
If you import
from the
fixed-width
Orders.txt, the
second dia-
log lets you
define field
boundaries.

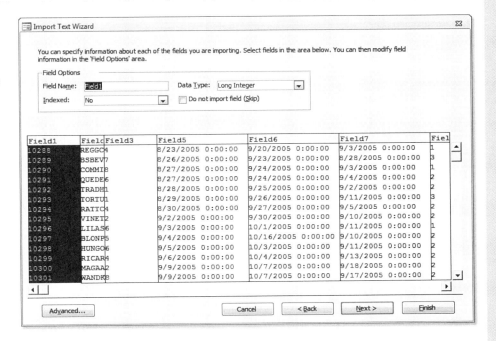

6. If you're importing a fixed-width text file, the Import Text Wizard analyzes the columns and makes an approximation about where the field breaks lie. Scan through the sample data at the bottom of the dialog; if the field breaks aren't in the right place, or if there are too many or too few field breaks, you can add, delete, or move the field breaks that the Import Text Wizard suggests. To move a field break, drag it with the mouse. To remove a field break, double-click it. To add a field break, click at the desired location. When you're satisfied with the field break arrangement, click Next to continue.

7. The third wizard dialog lets you edit field names, choose whether to use an index and what kind to use for each field, and set each field's data type (see Figure 8.23). To set the options for a field, click the field column at the bottom of the dialog to select it; you then can edit the field name, select an index method in the Indexed drop-down list, and select the data type for the field in the Data Type drop-down list. Select the Do Not Import Field (Skip) check box if you don't want to import the selected field column. The OrderID, EmployeeID, and ShipVia columns require the Long Integer data type to conform to the original table design, and a No Duplicates index selection is appropriate for the OrderID primary key field. When you're satisfied with your field settings, click Next.

8. The wizard displays the dialog in Figure 8.24. Choose the appropriate option for the primary key: Allow Access to add a new field with an automatically generated primary key, select an existing field to use as a primary key yourself, or import the table without a primary key. For this example, OrderID is the primary key. Click Next.

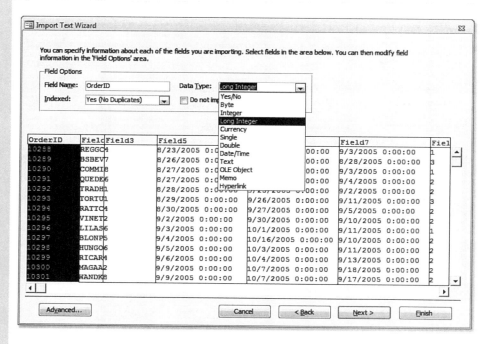

Figure 8.23
The third dialog lets you change or assign field names, alter data types, specify indexes, and skip fields.

9. The wizard displays its final dialog with the filename of the text file or the existing table you specified in step 7 as the default table name. Edit the table name, or type a different table name, if you want. Click Finish to open the Get External Data – Text dialog.

10. If you want to save an import specification, mark the Save Import Steps check box, specify the name and a description, and, optionally, mark the Create Outlook Task check box. Click OK to close the dialog, and then open the new table.

As with other import operations, Access creates an Import Errors table to document any errors that occurred during the import process and displays a message informing you that errors occurred.

Setting the Import Text Wizard's Advanced Options

You're likely to find that you import text data from the same text file more than once or that you have several text files with the same format. A typical situation in many corporations is that data from the company's mainframe computer system is provided to desktop computer users in the form of a text file report.

 caution

The wizard matches fields from left to right when you import a text file into an existing table. You must make sure that the data types of the fields in the imported text file match those in the Access table; otherwise, the added data values aren't inserted into the correct fields. In most cases, you end up with many import errors in the Import Errors table. If you're not certain that the format of your input data exactly matches the format of the desired table, you can choose the In a New Table option and then place your data in the existing table with an append query, as discussed in Chapter 13, "Creating and Updating Access Tables with Action Queries."

Figure 8.24
The fourth dialog offers three primary key choices. For the Orders table, select Choose My Own Primary Key option and the OrderID field as the primary key.

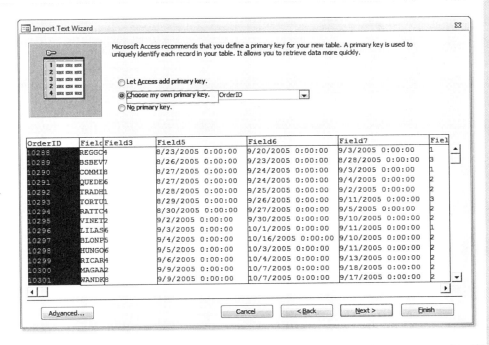

Frequently, reports are delivered over the network in a text file, using the same name for the text file each time. You can use the Import Text Wizard's advanced options to configure Access to import a text file with a specific set of options and save the option values so that you don't have to go through every step in the wizard every time you import the text file.

Every dialog of the Import Text Wizard has an Advanced button. Clicking this button displays the *TableName* Import Specification dialog that shows all the Import Text Wizard settings in a single dialog and allows you to select a few options, such as date formatting, that don't appear in the regular Import Text Wizard dialogs. If you select the Delimited option and the text file includes field names, the Customers Import Specification dialog has the options and field grid shown in Figure 8.25. Settings in the Data Type and Indexed columns reflect the changes suggested in Figure 8.23.

If you select the Fixed-Width option for a file without field names in the first record, the dialog has the options and field grid shown in Figure 8.26. For the Orders.txt sample file, type the field names, specify the data types, and set the indexes.

You can select the following options in the *TableName* Import Specification dialog:

■ **File Format**—Use these option buttons to choose which type of text file format you're importing: delimited or fixed width. The file format you select determines which additional options are available.

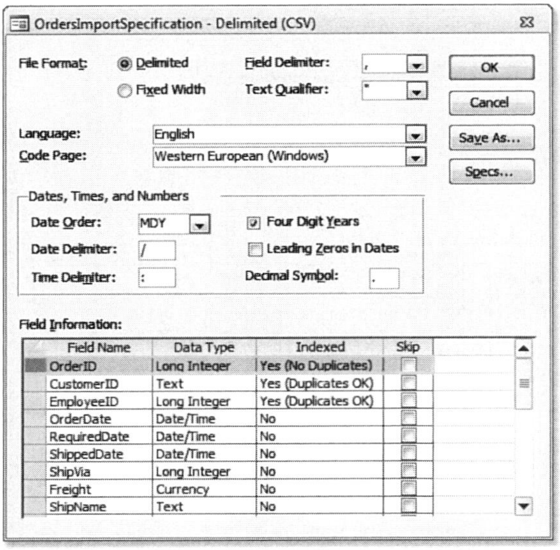

Figure 8.25
The Orders Import Specification dialog for the sample Orders.csv text file lets you fine-tune field properties and indexes, as well as create a template for future import of text files in the same format.

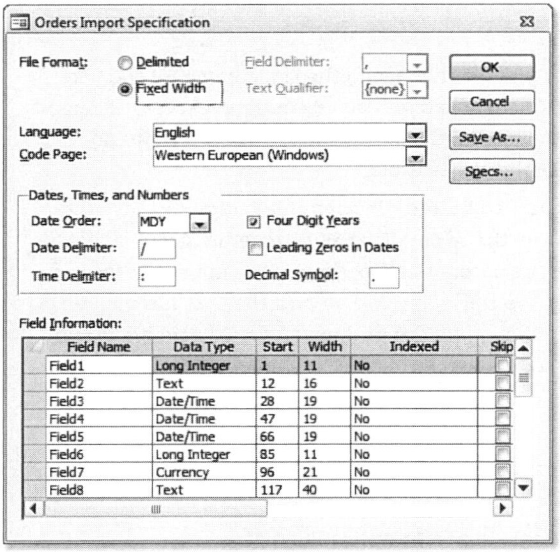

Figure 8.26
The Orders Import Specification dialog for a fixed-width table without field names in the first row assigns default Field# field names.

- **Field Delimiter**—Use this drop-down list to select the symbol that delimits fields in the text file. This option is disabled for fixed-width text files.

- **Text Qualifier**—Use this drop-down list to select the symbol that marks the beginning and end of text strings in the text file. This option is disabled for fixed-width text files.

- **Language and Code Page**—Use these lists to handle localized text files.

- **Date Order**—If the data in the text file uses a European or other date format that varies from the month-day-year format typical in the United States, select the appropriate date order in the Date Order drop-down list.

- **Date Delimiter and Time Delimiter**—Type the symbol used to separate the month, day, and year in a date in the Date Delimiter text box; type the symbol used to separate hours, minutes, and seconds in the Time Delimiter text box. For example, in the United States, the date delimiter is the virgule (/) character, and the time delimiter is the colon (:).

- **Four Digit Years**—Mark this check box if the dates in the text file use four digits for the year, such as 8/28/2006.

- **Leading Zeros in Dates**—Mark this check box if the dates in the text file have leading zeros, such as 08/09/2006.

- **Decimal Symbol**—Type the symbol used for the decimal separator in numeric values in the text box. In the United States, the decimal symbol is the period (.), but many European nations use a comma (,).

- **Field Information**—The appearance of this grid depends on the file format you select. For a delimited text file, the Field Information grid lets you edit field names, select the field's data type and indexing, and specify whether to skip the field in importing (refer to Figure 8.25). For a fixed-width text file, the Field Information grid lets you perform the same operations but adds specifications for the starting column and width of each field (refer to Figure 8.26).

- **Save As**—Click this button to display the Save Import/Export Specification dialog. By typing a name for the specification and clicking OK, you can save the file import settings for later use (see Figure 8.27).

- **Specs**—Click this button to display the Import/Export Specifications dialog. Select a previously saved specification and click OK to use import settings that you defined previously.

Saving the export specification from the wizard's Orders Import Specification dialog accomplishes the same objective as marking the Save Import Steps check box in the External Data – Text File dialog. To use a saved import specification created by marking the Save Import Steps check box, click the External Data ribbon's Saved Imports button to open the Manage Data Tasks dialog's Imports page (see Figure 8.28).

The LinkTest.accdb sample database in the \Access2010\Chaptr08 folder of the downloadable sample files includes several import and export specifications.

Working with Tables in Other Database File Formats

Access and other Microsoft programming platforms, such as Visual Studio 2005 and later, dominate today's database front-end development market. Thus, the importance of Access's import/link sup-

Figure 8.27
The Save Import/Export Specification dialog lets you save or select a set of saved import specifications to apply when importing a text file. This figure illustrates saving the import specification for the sample Orders.csv comma-separated-values file.

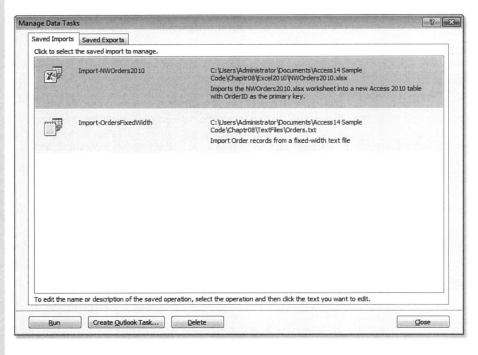

Figure 8.28
The Manage Data Tasks dialog's Imports page lists the import specifications you save by marking the Save Import Steps check box. The list does not include specifications you save with the wizard's *FileName* Import Specification dialog's Save As input box.

port for legacy desktop database files has decreased as use of Paradox, dBASE, and FoxPro have declined, especially for new projects. Paradox, dBASE, Clipper, and FoxPro now qualify as *legacy* data formats, although today's diehard Visual FoxPro programmers certainly would argue this point.

 As noted earlier, the Access development team deprecated Paradox 3, 4, 5, 6, and 7, and Access 1.0 and 2.0 (also called Jet 2 or Red 2) database files in Access 2010. You must have Access 2007 or earlier to import, link, or export these file types.

Conventional desktop database development applications maintain each table in an individual file. Each file contains a header followed by the data. A *header* is a group of bytes that provides information on the file's structure, such as the names and types of fields, number of records in the table, and file length. This information usually is called *metadata* (data about data). When you create a table file in dBASE, Visual FoxPro, or Paradox, for example, the file contains only a header. As you add records to the file, the file size increases by the number of bytes required for one record, and the header is updated to reflect the new file size and record count.

Desktop RDBMSs create a variety of supplemental files, some of which are required to import, link, or export RDBMSs:

- dBASE .dbf files store memo-type data in a separate .dbt file. If a dBASE table file contains a memo field, the .dbt file must be available. If the .dbt file is missing, you can't import or link dBASE tables that contain a memo field.

- Access doesn't support dBASE 7 or later file formats.

- Use of .ndx (dBASE III) or .mdx (dBASE IV+) index files is optional. You always should use index files when you have them. If you don't link the index files when you link an indexed .dbf table file, modifications you make to the linked tables aren't reflected in the index, which causes errors to occur when you try to use the indexed tables with dBASE. Linking an indexed dBASE table requires the Borland Database Engine (BDE) described in the following Note.

- You must have exclusive access to the dBASE file when you first create the link; multiuser (shared) access is supported thereafter. For more information see the "Using dBASE Data with Access and Jet" Knowledge Base topic at http://support. microsoft.com/kb/230125/, which describes the BDE and how to obtain it.

All supplemental files must be in the same folder as the related database file to be used by Access.

 note

If you even suspect that you'll need to import the same or a similar text file, save the import specification in your database by marking the Save Export Steps check box and adding a descriptive name and detailed description. You can edit the specification in the wizard and resave it with the Save Export Steps check box, if necessary.

 note

Microsoft supports the 32-bit Visual FoxPro (VFP) ODBC driver only under Windows 2000. Access doesn't support the replacement 32-bit OLE DB driver. Microsoft doesn't supply a 64-bit VFP ODBC driver and plans no further investment in VFP. Therefore, this book doesn't include instructions for importing, exporting or linking VFP database files.

 note

If you work in a multiuser environment, you must have exclusive access to the file you intend to import. No one else can have this file open when you initiate the importing process, and everyone else is denied access to the file until you close the Import dialog.

Dealing with PC Database Files

Access can import and export, subject to the preceding limitations, the following types of database table files used by the most common PC da tabase managers:

- *dBASE .dbf table* and *.dbt memo files*—dBASE III+ files are a common denominator of the PC RDBMS industry. Most PC RDBMSs and all common spreadsheet applications can import and export .dbf files; the most popular formats are dBASE III and IV.

- *dBASE III .ndx* and *dBASE IV* and *5.0 .mdx* index files—Some PC RDBMSs can update existing .ndx and .mdx index files, and a few RDBMSs can create these index files. Access 2010 links and exports .ndx and .mdx indexes only if you have the BDE installed. When this book was written, the current BDE version was 5.2.

Linking and Importing External ISAM Tables

ISAM is an acronym for indexed sequential access method, the architecture used for all desktop RDBMS tables. To link or import a dBASE file as a table in Access 2010 (.accdb) file format, follow these steps:

> **tip**
>
> Create a new folder to store the tables you import or export. The default folder for exporting and importing files is \My Documents in all current Windows operating systems. If you intend to import or export a large number of files, change the Default Database Folder entry in the Personalize page of the Access Options dialog (click the Office and Access Options buttons).

1. If you have a test database that you can use for this procedure, open it, and skip to step 4.

2. If you don't have a test database, create a sample to use throughout this chapter. Click the File tab to expose the Blank Database pane..

3. Navigate to the folder in which to store the new database, type a name (such as LinkTest.accdb) in the File Name text box, and click Create. Access creates and tests the new database. Delete the default Table1.

4. In this example, you link an external table to the database. Click the ribbon's External Data tab, and click the Import group's More button to open the secondary file-type gallery.

5. Click the dBASE File to open the Get External Data – dBASE File dialog (see Figure 8.29).

6. Click Browse to open the File Open dialog, navigate to the location of the file to link, and open the Files of Type drop-down list to select the file version, as shown in Figure 8.30.

7. Double-click the name of the table you want to link or import (or click the name to select it and then click the Link button). Access supplies the standard .dbf extension for dBASE table files.

8. Verify that you've selected the Link to the Data Source by Creating a Linked Table option, and click OK to close the Get Extended Data – *DBType* File dialog. If a memo or other related file is missing, you receive an error message at this point.

Figure 8.29
Each file type has its own Get External Data dialog that lets you choose between importing data from or linking to the file you select in the File Name text box.

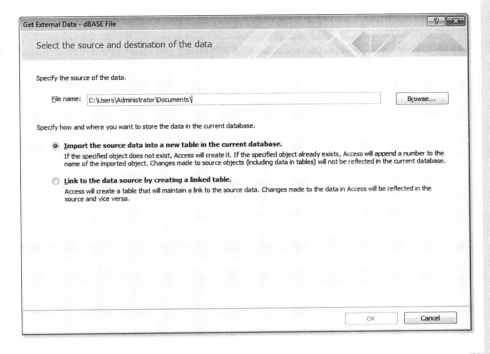

Figure 8.30
Navigate to the folder that holds the database file to link and select the type of database file in the drop-down list.

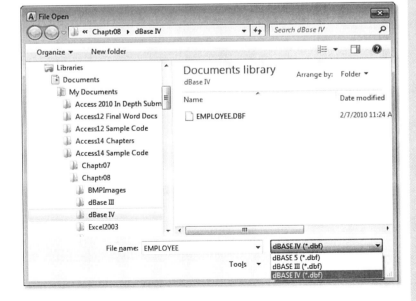

The table(s) you linked or imported now are listed in the Navigation pane. If you linked a file, Access adds an icon that shows the type of database table and an arrow to indicate the table is linked. Figure 8.31 illustrates an imported dBASE III CUSTOMER and linked dBASE IV EMPLOYEE tables. Scroll to the right in the linked EMPLOYEE datasheet to verify that the content of the EMPLOYEE.DBT file appears in the Notes field, which has been moved in Figure 8.31.

After you link an external file as a table, you can use it almost as though it were a table in your own database. If you don't have the BDE installed, linked dBASE 5 and later tables are read-only. A general limitation is that you can't change the structure of a linked table: field names, field data types, and the Field Size properties. There is no limitation on changing the structure or properties of an imported table.

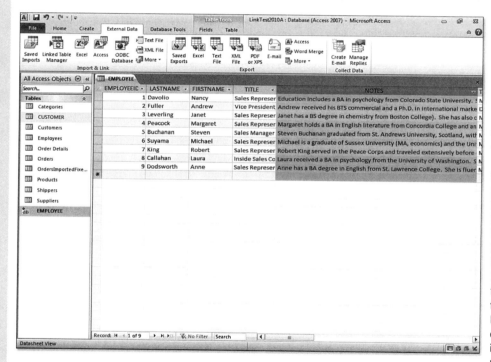

Figure 8.31
Linked tables are identified in the Navigation pane by an icon for the file type (dB for dBASE) with an arrow to represent the link. The EMPLOYEE table is linked from a pair of dBASE IV tables— EMPLOYEE. DBF and EMPLPLOYEE. DBT. The EMPLOYEE.DBT file contains the data for the Notes field and doesn't appear in the Navigation pane.

Dealing with Images in External Database Files

Most database managers designed for Windows include some form of graphics field data type. Early versions of Paradox, for example, provide a special field data type for graphics; later versions support OLE objects. Although early versions of dBASE lack a field data type for graphics, third-party software firms publish applications that let you store images in dBASE memo fields. Various add-on applications for desktop RDBMSs let programmers display and edit graphic images. The images usually are in individual files, but a few third-party applications continue to place images in memo files.

When you try to import or link desktop database files containing images or other binary data, you might receive an error message that the memo file is corrupted or that you can't import the .dbf file that contains the offending memo field. In rare cases—usually involving tiny images—you can import the .dbf and .dbt files, but you see random characters in the Access memo field.

The simplest approach to dealing with graphics files missing from imported tables is to convert the individual files to Graphic Interchange Format (.gif) or Joint Photographic Experts Group (.jpg) format, and then use Windows Paint to import the images into an OLE Object field. The following procedure uses the employees table imported from the dBASE IV database of the preceding section, and the nine JPEG files, EMPID1.JPG-EMPID9.JPG, in the \Access2010\Chaptr08\JPEGImages folder.

To add an OLE Object field and images from files to an imported (or new) table, do this:

1. Open the table in Design view, select the field below the location for the new OLE Object field, and press Insert to add an empty field.This example uses the EMPLOYEE table imported from the dBASE IV EMPLOYEE table, which has a PHOTO field of the Text data type containing the names of bitmap files of employee photos; delete and re-create the field. (If you linked an EMPLOYEE table earlier in the chapter, the table will be named EMPLOYEE1.)

2. Name the new field **PHOTO** and select OLE Object as the Data Type setting (see Figure 8.32).

3. Return to Datasheet view, save the design changes, right-click the OLE Object cell in the first row and choose Insert Object to open the Microsoft Office Access (formerly Insert Object) dialog.

4. Select the Create from File option, click Browse to open the Browse dialog, and navigate to the folder that contains your image files (\Samples2010\Chaptr08\JPEGImages for this example).

5. Double-click the image file you want to embed in the field (EMPID1.JPG for the first image), which adds the well-formed path to the file in the text box (see Figure 8.33).

6. Click OK to embed or link the image, which adds a Bitmap Image (for .bmp files) or Package (for other image types) value to the cell. Double-click the cell to open the image in Windows Photo

 tip

Although you can't change field properties for linked tables, you can change the name of the attached table within this database only. Select the link, press F2, and type the new name for the table. The name for the table (called an alias) is changed only in the current Access database and not in the native database.

 tip

An alternative is to add a field of the new Attachment data type instead of OLE Object. Attachment fields consume less disk space and memory than corresponding OLE Object fields, but aren't backward compatible with the traditional .mdb format.

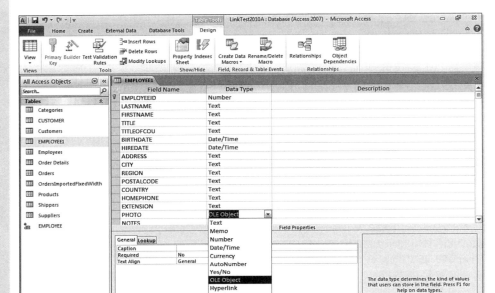

Figure 8.32
Add an OLE Object field to the imported table to hold image data in OLE 2.0 format or to create a link to external image files.

Viewer (see Figure 8.34). You can edit the image in Paint; Access automatically saves your changes when you close Paint and return to the table.

7. Repeat steps 4, 5, and 6 for each image to add, selecting the row appropriate to the image file.

The EMPLOYEES1 table of the LinkTest2010.accdb database in the \Samples2010\Chaptr08 folder of the downloadable sample files includes several embedded bitmap images. Subfolders contain sets of images in .bmp, .png, and .jpg formats.

tip

Instead of embedding the image in the database, you can create a link to the image's source file by selecting the Link check box. Linking reduces the size of the .accdb file, but requires a permanent path to the source image files. If a network server stores the image files, the path might change. If this happens, you receive an error when attempting to open the linked image file.

Converting Field Data Types to Access Data Types

When you import or link a file, Access reads the header of the file and converts the field data types to Access data types. Access usually is successful in this conversion because it offers a greater variety of data types than most of the other widely used PC RDBMSs. Table 8.2 shows the correspondence of field data types between dBASE, Paradox, and Access files.

Figure 8.33
By default, the bitmap data is included in the OLE Object field. Select the Link check box to maintain the image data in the source .png, .gif, .jpg, or .bmp files.

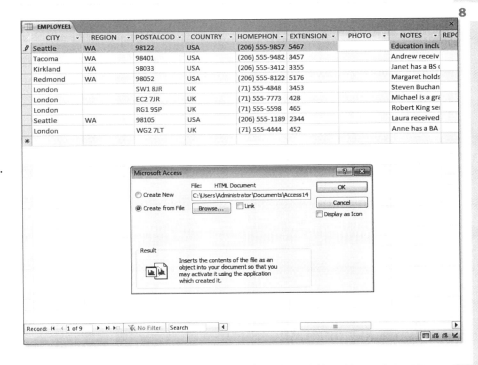

Figure 8.34
Double-clicking a Bitmap Image cell opens the image for editing in Windows Paint, if Paint is associated in Windows Explorer with the image's file type. If Windows has associated a different OLE 2.0–compliant application to the file type, such as Windows Photo Viewer for Portable Network Graphic (.PNG) files, the image opens in that application.

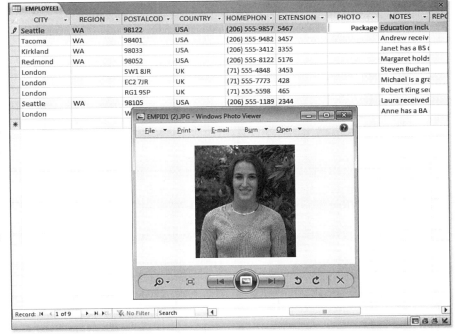

Table 8.2 Field Data Type Conversion Between Access and Other RDBMSs

dBASE III/IV/5	Access
Character	Text (Specify Size property)
Numeric, Float*	Number (Double)
Logical	Yes/No
Date	Date/Time
Memo	Memo

*Sometimes two types of field data, separated by commas, are shown within a single column in Table 8.2. When Access exports a table that contains a data type that corresponds with one of the two field data types, the first data type is assigned to the field in the exported table. The Float data type is available only in dBASE IV and 5.

 To review field properties of Access databases, **see** *"Choosing Field Data Types, Sizes, and Formats,"* **p. 191.**

Using the Linked Table Manager Add-in to Relink Tables

Moving linked files to another folder or logical drive causes the existing links to break. Access provides an add-in assistant known as the Linked Table Manager to simplify relinking tables.

If you move a file that provides a linked table to an Access database, right-click the table in the Navigation pane, and select Linked Table Manager. The list displays the path to the database or file containing the linked table(s) at the time the link was created, with the exception of the path to files or databases linked by ODBC. Click the check box of the file(s) whose location(s) might have changed (see Figure 8.35).

Click OK to display the Select New Location of *TableName* dialog shown in Figure 8.36. (If your linked files haven't moved, mark the Always Prompt for New Location check box to open the dialog.) Navigate to the folder where the table or database is located; then double-click the new link file's name and close the dialog. If Access successfully refreshes the table links, it displays a dialog saying so; click OK to close the success message dialog. Click the Close button of the Linked Table Manager to close the add-in.

 tip

If you're importing tables, you can change the field data type and the Field Size property to make them more suitable to the type of information contained in the field. When you change a data type or the Field Size property, however, follow the precautions noted in Chapter 5, "Working with Access Databases and Tables."

Remember that you can't change the field data type or Field Size property of linked tables. You can, however, use the Format property with imported or linked tables to display the data in any format compatible with the field data type of imported or linked files. You can change any remaining properties that are applicable to the field data type, such as validation rules and text. By using the Caption property, you can give the field a new and more descriptive name.

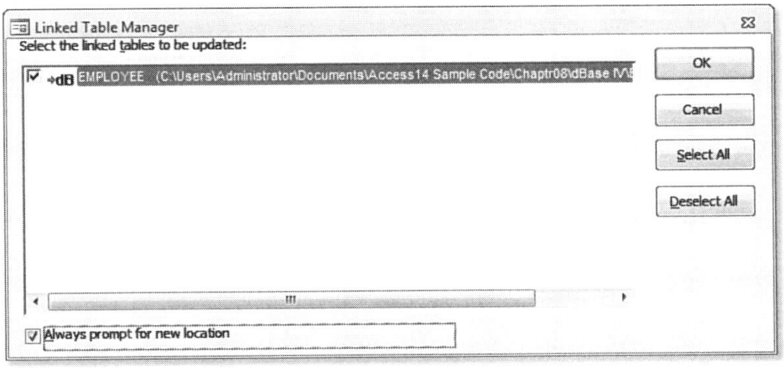

Figure 8.35
The Linked Table Manager handles re-creating links to tables or databases that have moved since you created the original links to an Access database.

Figure 8.36
The Select New Location of *TableName* dialog lets you substitute another folder or database file for the broken link.

Using the Access Mail Merge Wizard

Access 2010's Mail Merge Wizard can help you create a new mail merge document or employ an existing mail merge document from which to create form letters. The Mail Merge Wizard uses a table or a query as the data source for the merge data file. The sections that follow describe two methods of creating a form letter:

 tip
You also can view the path to the folder containing a linked table by opening the linked table in Design view, opening the Table Properties window, and scrolling through the contents of the Description text box.

- Using the Mail Merge Wizard to create a new mail merge document whose merge data source is an Access table

- Using an existing mail merge document with a merge data source from an Access table with a filter or a select query

Access 2000 and earlier used Dynamic Data Exchange (DDE) to send mail merge data to Word. Access 2010 uses an OLE DB data source to generate mail merge documents. OLE DB and Automation is a much more reliable method of interapplication communication than DDE. Using OLE DB also lets you take advantage of Word's filter and sort features, which were unavailable from documents created with earlier versions of the Mail Merge Wizard.

note

If you select a table linked by ODBC, the ODBC Manager's Select Data Source dialog opens so you can re-create the data source for the linked table or database.

Creating and Previewing a New Form Letter

When you first try a new wizard, it's customary to create a new object rather than use the wizard to modify an existing object, such as a mail merge document. The following steps use the Mail Merge Wizard to create a new mail merge document from records in the Customers table of Northwind.accdb:

note

The Linked Table Manager can refresh links only for a table that has been moved to another disk or folder—the table must have the same name. If the linked table's file was renamed, you must delete the table link from your Access database and relink the table under its new name.

1. Open Northwind.accdb, if necessary, click the External Data tab, and select the Customers table in the Navigation pane.

2. Click the Export group's Word Merge icon to launch the Microsoft Word Mail Merge Wizard.

3. Select the Create a New Document and Then Link the Data to It option (see Figure 8.37) to create a new mail merge document using fields from the Customers table.

4. Click OK to launch Word 2010, if it isn't running. Word opens a new mail merge main document, Document1, and displays the Mailings ribbon and the Mail Merge page of the task pane.

5. Click the Write & Insert Fields group's Insert Merge Fields button to verify the available database fields from the NorthwindContacts table in the Insert Merge Field dialog, as shown in Figure 8.38. Click Cancel to close the dialog, and close the task pane.

6. Click the Insert Merge Field dialog's Match Fields button to open the dialog of the same name. Open the lists to match standard Word Address Block field names to the database names (see Figure 8.39), and then click OK and Cancel to close both dialogs.

7. With the cursor at the top of the document, click the Insert tab, and then click the Date and Time button to display the Date and Time dialog. Choose any date format you want, mark the Update Automatically check box, and click OK to add a date field to the main document.

Figure 8.37
The Mail Merge Wizard's only dialog lets you use an existing merge document (the default) or create a new document.

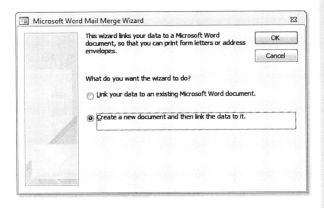

Figure 8.38
When you start the mail merge process, the Insert Merge Field dialog confirms that you selected the correct table as the merge data source.

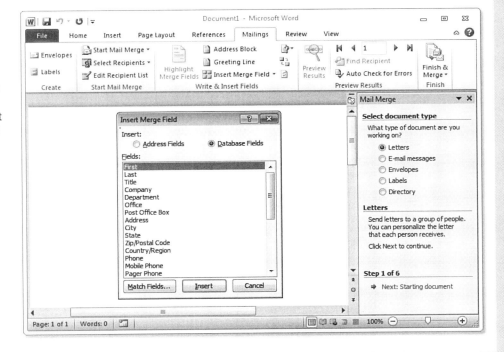

8. Add two blank lines, click the Mailings tab, and click the Address Block button to open the Address Block dialog for inserting the CompanyName, Address, City, Region, PostalCode, and Country fields from the Customers table to create the Address Block section of the main document (see Figure 8.40). Click OK to add the AddressBlock field, and press Enter.

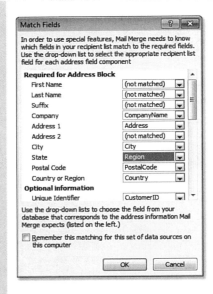

Figure 8.39
The match Fields dialog lets you select from dropdown lists the fields that correspond to values of standard elements of Word's Address Block.

9. Type **Att:**, press Tab, click the Insert Merge Field button, select the Database Names option and ContactName field, and click Insert to add to add the ContactName under the Address Block.

10. Press Shift+Return, press Tab, open the Insert Merge Field dialog, select the ContactTitle field, and click Insert to add the ContactTitle field (see Figure 8.41.)

11. Click the Preview Results button of the Mail Merge toolbar to preview the appearance of the first of your form letters.

12. The form letters go only to customers in the United States, so you should check the address format for United States addresses. Click the Find Recipient button to open the Find Entry dialog, type **USA** in the Find text box, and select Country from the This Field list. Click Find Next to find the first U.S. record. The preview of the form letter for Great Lakes Food Market appears, as shown in Figure 8.42.

> ### tip
> ¶ Click File, Options to open the Word Options dialog and mark the options on the Display page to show paragraph marks and tab characters, which are usually hidden. All figures of Word 2010 in these sections were captured in Draft view with the preceding Display options.

Figure 8.40
Arrange merge fields
in the Address Block.

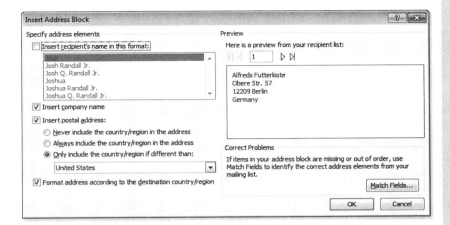

Figure 8.41
Add to the
letter the
AddressBlock,
ContactName,
and
ContactTitle
fields..

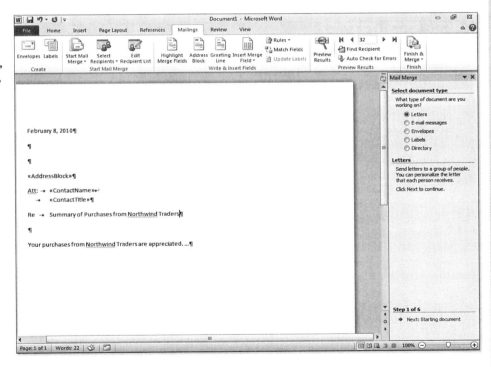

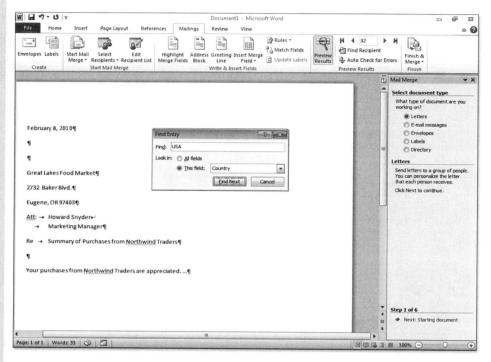

Figure 8.42
After clicking the Preview Results button, use the Find in Field dialog to locate the record for the first U.S. customer.

13. To send letters to U.S. customers only, click the Edit Recipient List button to open the Mail Merge Recipients dialog with the current record selected. Open the Country field's list and choose (Advanced), as shown in Figure 8.43, to specify a Word filter on the Country field.

14. In the Filter and Sort dialog, select the Country field, if necessary; accept the default Equal To comparison, and type **USA** in the Compare To text box (see Figure 8.44). You can create complex filters by adding additional criteria and selecting And or Or to determine the filter logic. Click the Sort tab, select PostalCode in the Sort By list, and click OK to close the dialog.

Figure 8.43
Word 2010's Mail Merge
Recipients dialog lets you
choose how to filter and
sort the data source for mail
merge documents.

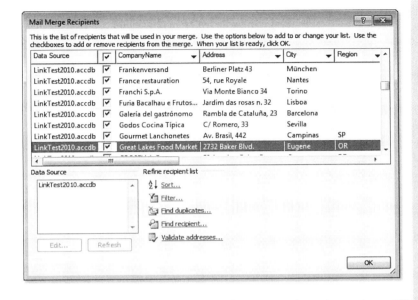

Figure 8.44
The Filter page of the Filter
and Sort dialog lets you
specify expressions and
criteria on which to filter the
data source.

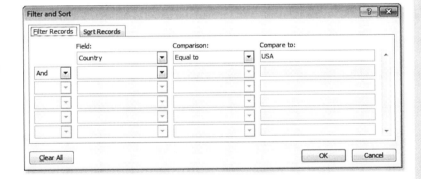

15. Applying a filter marks for inclusion only those records that meet the filter criterion (see Figure 8.45). Click OK to close the dialog.

16. The filtered list is applied to the mail merge document. Click the Next Record button to display only the U.S. records in sequence.

17. Click the Finish & Merge and Edit Individual Documents button to open the Merge to New Document dialog. Accept the All (records) option, and click OK to generate the Letters1 document that contains the 13 letters to U.S. customers (see Figure 8.46).

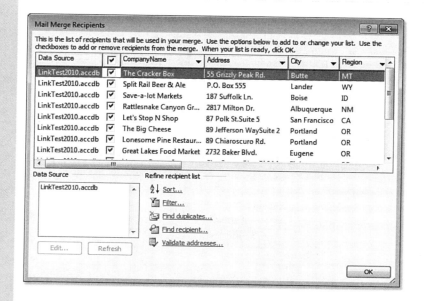

Figure 8.45
The wizard marks and sorts the set of filtered records in preparation for generating the mail merge documents.

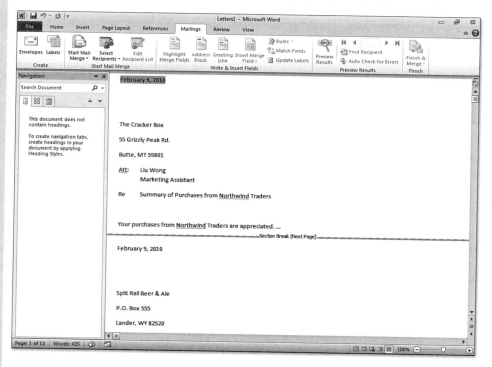

Figure 8.46
The merge document contains a letter for each of the 13 U.S. customers in the filtered list.

18. Close Letters1 and save it with a descriptive name, such as USCustomersLetters.docx, and do the same for Document1, the mail merge document (USCustomersMerge.docx).

The two documents created in the preceding steps are located in the \Access2010\Chaptr08\ MailMerge folder of the downloadable sample files. The merge document doesn't save the filter, so you must reestablish the filter when opening the mail merge document.

Using an Existing Mail Merge Document with a New Data Source

After you create a standard mail merge document, the most common practice is to use different data sources to create form letters by addressee category. Word mail merge documents store database and table connection data as well as retain filter settings. Using Access filters or queries to restrict the recipient list usually is more convenient than performing the same operation in Word.

Take the following steps to use the main mail merge document you created in the preceding section, USCustomersMerge.docx, with a data source based on a filter for the Customers table:

1. In Access, open the Customers table in Datasheet view, click the Home tab, if necessary, and then click the Filter & Sort group's Advanced button and choose Filter by Form.

2. Scroll to the Country field, open the field list, and select USA.

3. Click the Toggle Filter button to filter the table data and display only U.S. customers.

4. Click the Advanced button again and select Advanced Filter/Sort to open the Filter Design window, which displays the filter criterion you applied in step 2. Drag the PostalCode field to the second column, and select an Ascending sort (see Figure 8.47).

> To review use of Access's Advanced Filter/Sort feature, **see** "Applying Advanced Filters and Sort Orders," **p. 285** (Chapter 7).

5. Right-click the upper pane of the CustomerFilter1 window, choose Save as Query, give your filter a descriptive name (such as **fltUSCustomers**), and click OK.

6. Close the Filter window and the Customers table, and don't save your changes.

7. Double-click the filter item (fltUSCustomers, for this example) to open the query resultset and test the filter. Close the Query Datasheet window.

8. With fltUSCustomers selected in the Navigation pane, click the Word Merge button to launch the Mail Merge Wizard. With the Link Your Data to an Existing Microsoft Word Document option marked (the default), click OK to open the Select Microsoft Word Document dialog.

9. Navigate to and double-click the mail merge document you created in the preceding section (USCustomersMerge.doc for this example) in the file list to open the document in Word.

tip

If you attempt to connect to an open document, you might receive a File in Use error message. Click Cancel, and then click OK when the Command Failed error message appears. Close the merge document and try again.

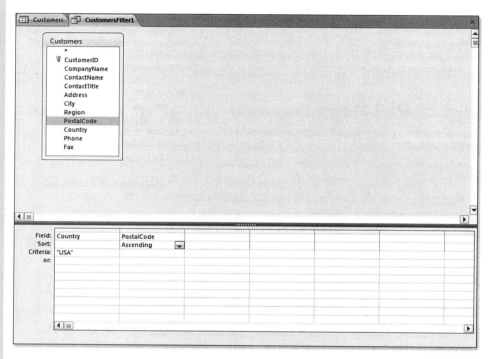

Figure 8.47
The Filter Design window opened by the Advanced Filter Sort command displays the filter for the Customers table with an ascending sort on the PostalCode field.

10. If Word can't resolve the data source type, the Confirm Data Source dialog opens to verify the use of an OLE DB data source for the Access query. Accept the default, OLE DB Database Files, and click OK to continue in Word.

11. Confirm that the filter is the new merge data source—[fltUS-Customers] in "LinkTest2010.accdb"—in the task pane's Mail Merge page (see Figure 8.48). Double-check the list by clicking the Mail Merge Recipients button. Only the filtered records appear in the list. Click OK to close the list.

12. You can merge the main document and data source directly to the printer, spam the customers via email, send faxes, or create a series of form letters in a new document, which is identical to the sample document you created in the preceding section.

If you close Word at this point, be sure to save your changes to the main mail merge document.

 tip

If you want to export a subset of a table's records without writing a query, open the table in Datasheet view, select the records to export, and then open the Export – RTF File dialog. This will enable the Export Only the Selected Records text box and let you export the selected subset to Word.

Figure 8.48
The Mail
Merge task
pane page
confirms
that the
document
is using the
fltUSCus-
tomers filter.

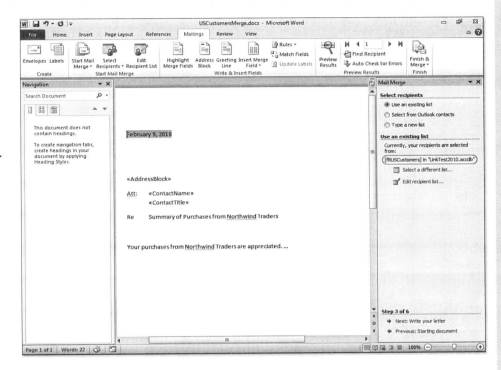

Exporting Tables to Word, Excel, PDF, and XPS Files

You can select the table or query to save in the Navigation pane, click the External Data tab, and then do one or more of the following:

- Click the More button in the Export group and select Word to open the Export – RTF File dialog, which lets you generate a Rich Text Format (.rtf) file named for the table or query and, if you marked the Open the Destination File After the Export Operation Is Complete check box, display the table in Word (see Figure 8.49). The .rtf format embeds formatting instructions and data for text, images, and other objects. Most word processing applications, including WordPad, can open .rtf files.

- Click the Excel button in the Export group to open the Export – Excel Spreadsheet dialog. Then mark the Export Data with Formatting and Layout and Open the Destination File After the Export Operation Is Complete check boxes to generate a workbook (.xlsx) file named for the table or query and display the worksheet in Excel (see Figure 8.50).

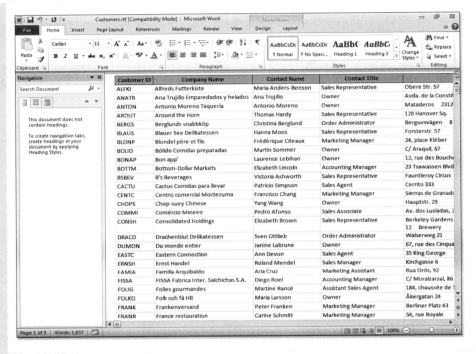

Figure 8.49
Clicking the More button and selecting Word lets you export a TableOr QueryName.rtf file of the selected table or query object and open it in Word.

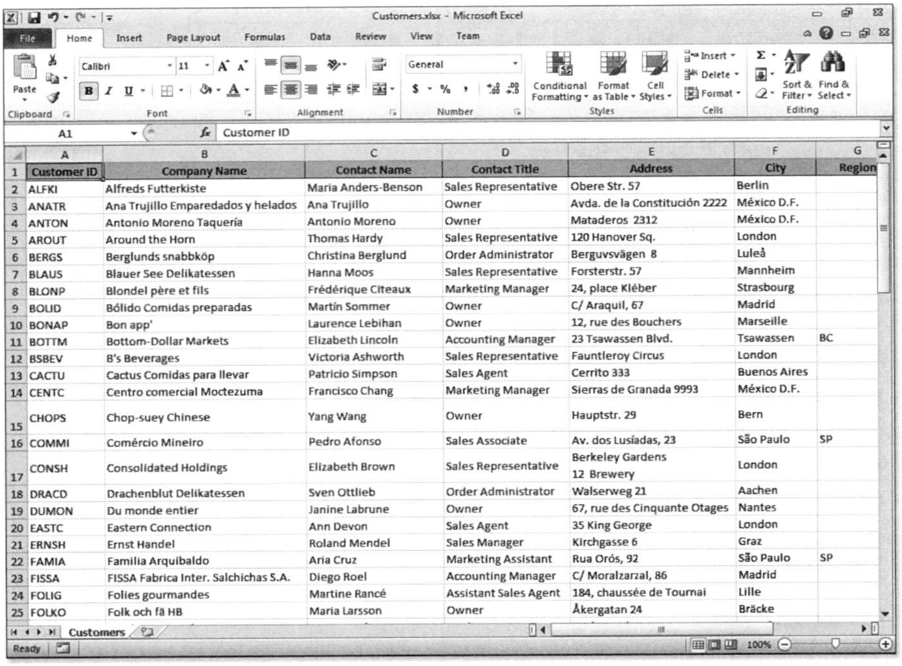

Figure 8.50
Not surprisingly, clicking the Excel button exports an .xlsx file of the object and opens the worksheet in Excel.

- Click the PDF or XPS button in the Export group to generate an Adobe Portable Document Format (.pdf) file named for the table or query and display the file in Adobe Reader(see Figure 8.51). The Publish as PDF or XPS dialog includes options to optimize the file for print or online publishing. PDF is the default file type in the Publish as PDF or XPS dialog's Save as Type list.

 tip

If the Publish as PDF or XPS dialog's Open File after Publishing check box is disabled, you must download the free Adobe Reader from http://www.adobe.com.

Figure 8.51
As you'd expect by now, clicking the PDF button exports a *TableName*.pdf file of the object and, if you've installed the Adobe Reader, opens the document in Adobe Reader.

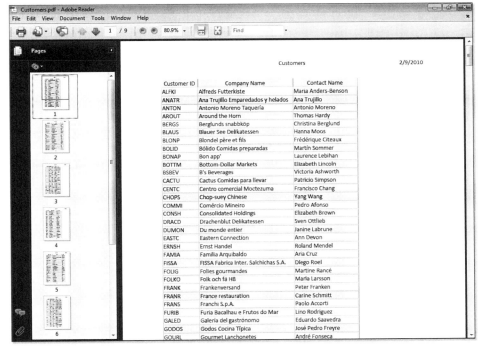

- Alternatively, select XPS in the Files of Type list to export the table in Microsoft XML Paper Specification format (see Figure 8.52). Viewing XPS files requires your computer to have the WinFX API installed. Windows Vista provides WinFX natively; you must install Microsoft .NET Framework 3.0 to obtain the WinFX API if you're not running Windows Vista.

In all cases, Access stores the exported files in your My Documents folder or Documents library by default. You can change the file's name and path in the Export – *FileType* File dialog's File Name text box.

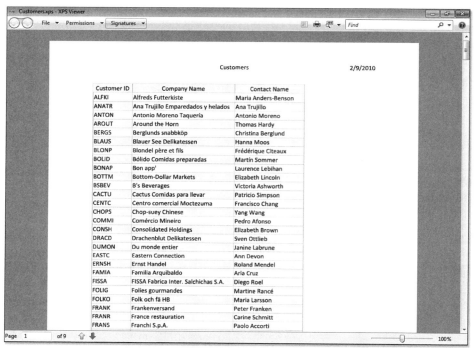

Figure 8.52
Finally, clicking the XPS button exports a *TableName*.xps file of the object and opens the document in the XPS Viewer, if you have WinFX installed by Windows Vista or Microsoft .NET Framework 3.0.

Exporting Table Data as Text Files

Exporting a table involves a sequence of operations similar to importing a file with the same format. To export a table as a comma- or tab-delimited file that you can use as a merge file with a variety of word processing applications, complete these steps:

1. Select the table you want to export in the Navigation pane (Customers, for this example), click the External Data tab, and click the Export group's Text File button to open the Export – Text File dialog.

2. Click Browse to open the File Save dialog, navigate to the location for the text file, and accept the default or edit the *TableName*.txt filename. (This example uses Customers.tab.) Click Save to return to the Export – Text File dialog.

3. Accept the Export Data with Formatting and Layout check box's default (not marked), and click OK to start the Text Export Wizard.

4. Follow the procedures as though you were importing a text file. Figure 8.53 shows the Customers table exported as a tab-separated text file from the Northwind.accdb database and displayed in Windows Notepad.

note

Using the Text Export Wizard, including its advanced options, is the same as using the Import Text Wizard described in the "Importing Text Files" section earlier in the chapter, except that the result is an external text file instead of an Access table. You save and reuse export specifications by the method described for import specs.

When exporting a text file, the Text Export Wizard doesn't have a step to edit field names or select field data types; these options aren't relevant when exporting data.

The records in files created by Access are exported in the order of the primary key. Any other order you might have created is ignored. If you don't assign primary key fields, the records are exported in the sequence in which you entered them into the table.

Figure 8.53
The two highlighted records of the tab-separated text file demonstrate the problem that arises when fields contain newline pairs to, for instance, create a multi-line display of address data.

Exporting Data in Other File Formats

In addition to Microsoft Word and text files, you can export data to any other file format that Access can import. Access supports exports to the following file formats:

- Excel 5.0, 95, and 97 through 2003 Workbook (.xls) files

- Excel 2007 and 2010 Binary Workbook (.xlsb) files

- dBASE III/III+, IV, and 5.0 files.

- Any format supported by an installed ODBC driver, including client/server databases

 caution

The two highlighted lines in Figure 8.53 are a single record from the Access table that was split into two text records during the export process. A newline pair is included in the Address field of the record for Consolidated Holdings. The purpose of the newline pair is to separate a single field into two lines: Berkeley Gardens and 12 Brewery. Use of newline pairs within fields causes many problems with exported files. Use of embedded newline pairs in text fields is a bad database design practice. Use two address fields if you need secondary address lines.

DESIGNING QUERIES FOR ACCESS DATABASES

Queries are an essential tool in any database management system. You use queries to select records as well as add, update, and delete records in tables. Most often you use queries to select specific groups of records that meet criteria you specify. You can also use queries to combine information from different tables, providing a unified view of related data items. In this chapter, you learn the basics of creating your own select queries, including specifying selection criteria and using the results of your queries to generate reports and create new tables. You create queries using more than one table in Chapter 11, "Creating Multitable and Crosstab Queries," after you learn the details of how to use operators and create expressions in Chapter 10, "Understanding Access Query Operators and Expressions."

This chapter covers queries that apply to Access databases and to client/server databases, such as SQL Server, that you link to a conventional Access front-end .accdb file. When you link client/server tables to an Access front end, your application uses the Access query engine to process the back-end data. Access has its own dialect of SQL, called Access SQL, which, for the most part, conforms to the ANSI SQL-92 standard but has several extensions that aren't included in SQL-92. All query techniques you learn in Part III, "Transforming Data with Queries and PivotTables," apply to Access databases and client/server tables linked to an Access front end that stores application objects—queries, forms, reports, and modules—in an .accdb file.

 note

The chapters of Part III include examples and brief explanations of the SQL statements the Access query engine generates from your graphical query designs. The objective of these examples is to encourage learning "SQL by osmosis," a process similar to learning a foreign language by immersion rather than from a grammar textbook. By the time you complete Chapter 13, "Creating and Updating Access Tables with Action Queries," you'll have a working knowledge of basic SQL syntax.

In contrast, Access data projects (ADPs) use SQL Server's query engine. An ADP offers three types of queries—views, functions, and stored procedures—and uses the SQL Server design tools, called the *da Vinci toolset* in this book, for designing queries. (Microsoft used the da Vinci codename for the toolset during its beta cycle, and it stuck). SQL Server uses Transact-SQL (T-SQL), another flavor of SQL-92 that has many proprietary extensions to the language. Most of the Access SQL SELECT query examples in this chapter also work for creating ADP views. Chapter 27, "Moving from Access Queries to Transact-SQL," provides detailed coverage of SQL-92 topics and explains the differences between Access SQL and T-SQL.

Trying the Simple Query Wizard

The Simple Query Wizard is aptly named; it's capable of generating only trivial select queries. If you don't have a numeric or date field in the table on which you base the query, the wizard has only two dialogs—one to select the table(s) and fields to include and the other to name the query. After you create the basic query with the wizard, you can embellish it in Design view.

Following are the characteristics of the Simple Query Wizard:

 tip

Use crosstab queries for grouping records with numeric values, especially when you're interested in returning a time series, such as multiple monthly, quarterly, or yearly totals or averages. Crosstab queries deliver greatly enhanced grouping capability and show the query resultset in a much more readable format compared to that delivered by the Simple Query Wizard. Chapter 11 shows you how to take maximum advantage of Access SQL's powerful crosstab queries.

- You can't use the wizard to add selection criteria or specify the sort order of the query.

- You can't use the wizard to change the order of the fields in the query; fields always appear in the sequence in which you add them in the first wizard dialog.

- If one or more of your selected fields is numeric, the wizard lets you produce a summary query that shows the total, average, minimum, or maximum value of the numeric field(s). You also can include a count of the number of records in the query resultset.

- If one or more of your selected fields is of the Date/Time data type, you can specify a summary query grouping by date range—day, month, quarter, or year.

Creating a Simple SELECT Query

The queries in this chapter—like the examples in preceding chapters—use the Northwind.accdb sample database tables from the book's downloadable sample files. The \Access2010\Chaptr09\ Nwind09.accdb file contains the query and table objects you create in this chapter's examples.

Northwind.accdb's Orders table has a Currency field and several Date/Time fields, so it's the best choice for demonstrating the Simple Query Wizard. To give the wizard a test drive with the Orders table, do the following:

1. Open Northwind.accdb, if necessary, and click the Create tab and the Query Wizard button to open the New Query dialog.

2. Double-click the Simple Query Wizard item to open the Simple Query Wizard's first dialog.

3. Select Table: Orders in the Tables/Queries list. All fields of the Orders table appear in the Available Fields list.

4. Select the OrderID field in the Available Fields list and click the right-arrow (>) button to add OrderID to the Selected Fields list and remove it from the Available Fields list. Alternatively, you can double-click the field to add it to the query.

5. Repeat step 4 for the CustomerID, OrderDate, and Freight fields. The first wizard dialog appears as shown in Figure 9.1.

Figure 9.1
You select the source of the query—either a table or a query—in the first dialog of the Simple Query Wizard.

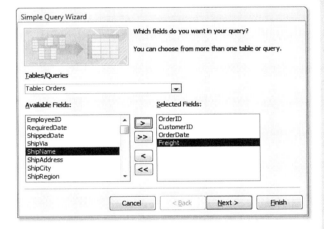

6. Click Next to open the second wizard dialog, which lets you select between detail and summary queries. Accept the default Detail option (see Figure 9.2).

7. Click Next to open the final dialog (see Figure 9.3). Rename the query to **qryOrders1** or the like, and click Finish to display the query resultset in Datasheet view (see Figure 9.4).

8. Click the Home tab and the View button caption to open the query View list, and choose SQL View to open the SQL window, which displays the Access SQL version of the query. Click the Query Tools, Design ribbon's Property Sheet button to open the Property Sheet pane for the query (see Figure 9.5).

9. Close the SQL window and save your changes if you altered the query's layout.

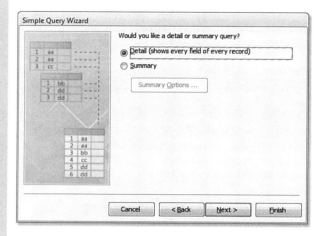

Figure 9.2
The second wizard dialog, which appears only for data sources with numeric or date fields, gives you the option of displaying all records or generating a summary query.

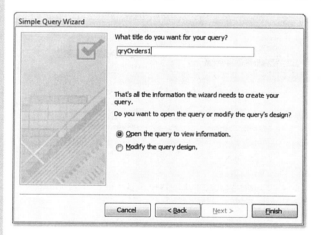

Figure 9.3
The final wizard dialog lets you name the query. This book uses a naming convention called Hungarian notation, which adds a two- or three-letter prefix (qry for queries) to Access object names, except names of tables.

 note

The `SELECT Orders.OrderID, Orders.CustomerID, Orders.OrderDate, Orders.Freight FROM Orders;` statement generated by the wizard is an example of a simple SQL `SELECT` query. The `Orders.` prefixes specify the query's source table name.

The `SELECT` keyword indicates that the query returns records; by tradition, SQL keywords in Access and T-SQL are capitalized. Field lists contain field names, separated by commas. The `FROM` clause, `FROM tablename`, specifies the query's data source. Access SQL uses the semicolon to indicate the end of a query; like the square brackets, the semicolon isn't necessary if the query includes only one complete SQL statement.

Figure 9.4
The wiz-
ard's query
resultset
substitutes
captions
for the field
names you
selected in
steps 4 and
5, and the
customer
name for the
CustomerID
lookup field.
Queries
inherit table
properties,
such as cap-
tions and
lookup fields,
from the data
source.

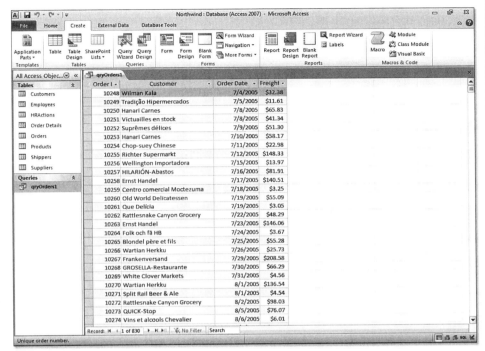

If you want to test the Simple Query Wizard's capability to base a query on another query and check the wizard's summary query capabilities, do the following:

1. Return to the Create ribbon, click the Query Wizard button, and start the Simple Query Wizard. Select Query: qryOrders1 Tables/Queries list.

2. Add only the OrderDate and Freight fields to the Selected Fields list.

3. Click Next to open the second wizard dialog (refer to Figure 9.2). Select the Summary option and then click Summary Options to open the identically named dialog. Mark the Avg check box to cal-culate the average freight cost, and mark the Count Records in qryOrders1 check box to add a column with the record count for the group (see Figure 9.6).

4. Click OK to return to the second wizard dialog, and then click Next to move to the third wizard dialog. The wizard has detected the OrderDate Date/Time field and offers you the choice of date grouping; select Quarter (see Figure 9.7).

> **note**
> Access calls a query whose source is a query, rather than a table, a *nested query*. You some-times see the term *subquery* incorrectly applied to a nested query. A subquery is a single SQL statement for a query within a query.

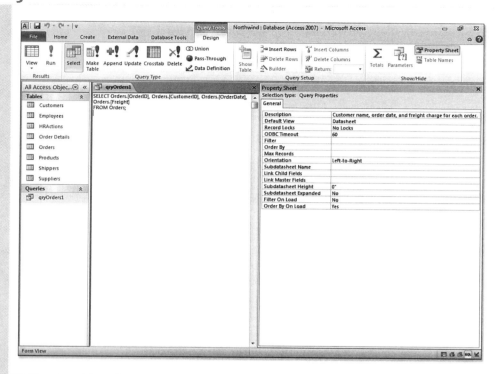

Figure 9.5
The SQL window displays the Access SQL statement that the Simple Query Wizard generated from your selections in steps 4–6.

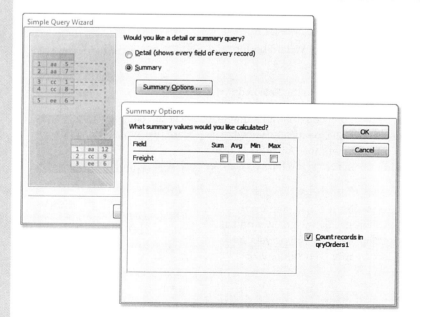

Figure 9.6
If you select a summary query, you must specify one of the functions in the Summary Options dialog.

Figure 9.7
Summary queries with a field of the Date/Time data type open an additional wizard dialog that lets you group the resultset by a date interval.

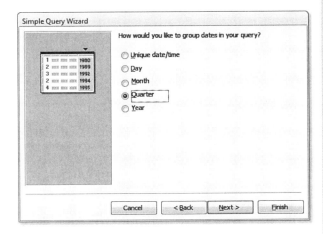

5. Click Next to open the last wizard dialog and replace the default query name, qryOrders1 Query, with a more descriptive name, such as **qryFreightQuarterlyAverage**.

6. Accept the default Open the Query to View Information option and click Finish to execute the summary query. The query resultset appears as shown in Figure 9.8. Open the SQL window to display the SQL statement that generates this considerably more complex query (see Figure 9.9).

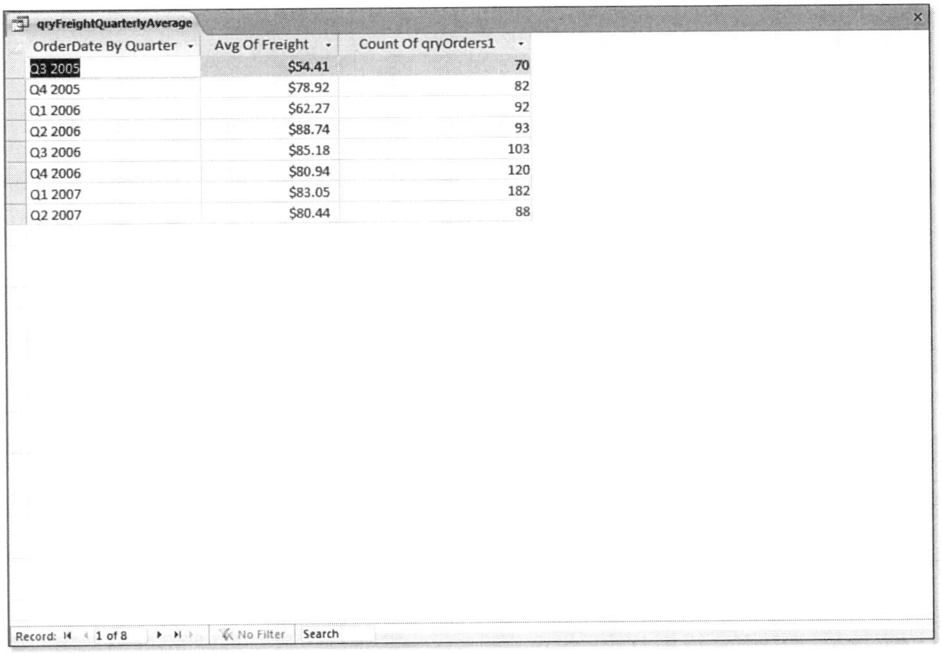

Figure 9.8
The query resultset displays the average freight charge and number of orders for each quarter within the range of dates for which data is available.

qryFreightQuarterlyAverage			
OrderDate By Quarter ▾	Avg Of Freight ▾	Count Of qryOrders1 ▾	
Q3 2005	$54.41	70	
Q4 2005	$78.92	82	
Q1 2006	$62.27	92	
Q2 2006	$88.74	93	
Q3 2006	$85.18	103	
Q4 2006	$80.94	120	
Q1 2007	$83.05	182	
Q2 2007	$80.44	88	

Record: I◄ ◄ 1 of 8 ► ►I ► 🦆 No Filter | Search

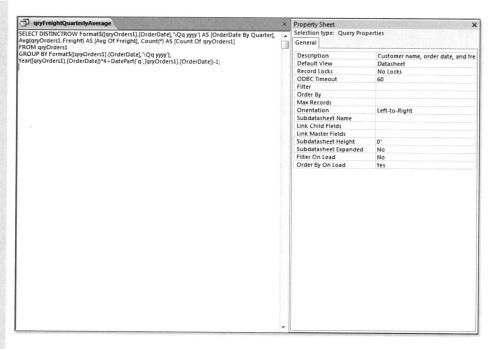

Figure 9.9
The SQL statement for the wizard's summary query belies the simplicity of the steps required to create the query.

Non-updatable Summary Queries

The reason you can't update data in your summary query is because summary queries aggregate data, so there's no direct relationship between the content of a query row and records in the underlying table(s). This means that there's no way for changes to aggregate values (dates, totals, averages, and the like) to propagate back to the table records. If you want to fudge the figures, change your select summary query to a make-table summary query, and then alter the data in the new table.

```
SELECT DISTINCTROW
    Format$([qryOrders1].[OrderDate],'\Qq yyyy')
        AS [OrderDate By Quarter],
    Avg(qryOrders1.Freight) AS [Avg Of Freight],
    Count(*) AS [Count Of qryOrders1]
  FROM qryOrders1
  GROUP BY Format$([qryOrders1].[OrderDate],'\Qq yyyy'),
    Year([qryOrders1].[OrderDate])*4+
   DatePart('q',[qryOrders1].[OrderDate])-1;
```

Summary queries—more commonly called *aggregate queries*—are a common element of decision-support applications that deliver time-based trend data to management. Aggregate queries also are the foundation for graphical data analysis, which is one of the subjects of Chapter 12, "Working with PivotTable and PivotChart Views." PivotTables and PivotCharts must be based on queries to present meaningful information. PivotTables have built-in aggregation features, so you can use detail queries as PivotTable data sources.

 note

The SQL statement for the summary query, which is a bit advanced for this point in your SQL learning curve, requires formatting for better readability:

Using the Query Design Window

The Simple Query Wizard has limited usefulness, so the better approach is to design your queries from scratch in Access's graphical Query Design window. The Query Design window is one of Access's most powerful features and has changed very little from the original Access 1.0 version that appeared in late 1992.

 note

DISTINCTROW is an Access SQL keyword that isn't required in this query. The Format$ function determines the appearance of the first column ('\Qq yyyy'). AS specifies the caption (alias) for the column. Avg is the aggregate function you selected in step 3. Count(*) adds the third column to the result set. Access treats queries as if they were tables, so the FROM clause specifies the source query. GROUP BY is the clause that specifies the date grouping range you chose in step 4 to calculate the values in the second column.

Square brackets ([ ]) surround query column names—such as OrderDate by Quarter—that have spaces or punctuation symbols, which aren't permitted by the SQL-92 specification. In some cases, the Access query processor adds square brackets where they're not needed, as in [qryOrders1].[OrderDate].

Avg, Year, DatePart, and Format$ are VBA functions executed by the Access expression service. The next chapter shows you how to apply these functions to queries. SQL-92 and T-SQL don't include DISTINCTROW and VBA functions, but do support the COUNT function.

To devise a simple query that lets you customize mailing lists for selected customers of Northwind Traders, for example, follow these steps:

1. Click the Create tab's Query Design button to open the Query Design window. The Show Table dialog is superimposed on the Query Design window, as shown in Figure 9.10. The tabbed lists in the Show Table dialog let you select from all existing tables, all saved queries, or a combination of all tables and queries. You can base a new query on one or more existing tables or queries.

2. This example uses only tables in the query, so accept the default selection of Tables. Click (or use the down-arrow key to select) Customers in the Show Table list to select the Customers table and then click the Add button. Alternatively, double-click Customers to add the table to the query. You can use more than one table in a query by choosing another related table from the list and choosing Add again. This example, however, uses only one table. After selecting the tables that you want to use, click Close.

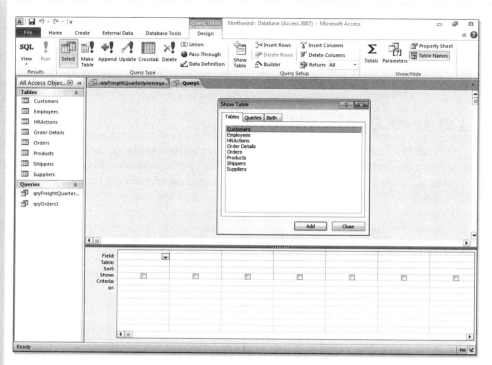

Figure 9.10
When you open a new query in Design view, the Show Table dialog lets you select from lists of tables, queries, or both, to designate the new query's data source.

The Fields list for the Customers table appears at the left in the upper pane of the Query Design window, and a blank Query Design grid appears in the lower pane. The Fields list displays all the names of the fields of the Customers table, but you must scroll to display more than five entries with the default Fields list size. The asterisk (*) item at the top of the list is a shortcut symbol for adding all table fields to the query.

Selecting Fields for Your Query

After you add a table from the Show Table dialog, the next step is to decide which of the table's fields to include in your query. Because you plan to use this query to create a customer mailing list, you need the fields that make up a personalized mailing address.

To select the fields to include in the Query Design grid, do this:

1. When you open the Query Design window, the cursor is located in the Field row of the first column. Click the List Box button that appears in the right corner of the first column or press Alt+down arrow to open the Field Names list (see Figure 9.11).

 note

Access adds the five fields to your query, in sequence, starting with the column in which you drop the symbol. When the mouse pointer is in an area where you can't drop the fields, it becomes the international Do Not Enter symbol shown in the upper pane of the Query Design window of Figure 9.12.

Table or Query Fields list   Upper (Table or Query) pane

Figure 9.11
One way to
add a field to
your query
is to select it
in the drop-
down query
fields list of
the Query
Design grid.

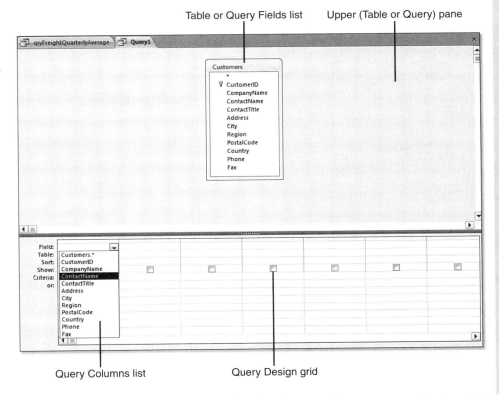

Query Columns list   Query Design grid

2. Select the ContactName field as the first field header of the query or use the down-arrow key to highlight the name and press Enter. The Field list in the lower pane closes.

3. Move the cursor to the second column by using the right-arrow key or Tab key. Double-click CompanyName in the Customers Field list in the upper pane to add CompanyName as the second field of your query. Double-clicking entries in the upper pane's list is the second method that Access provides to add fields to a query.

4. Access offers a third method of adding fields to your query: the drag-and-drop method. To use the drag-and-drop method to add the Address, City, Region, PostalCode, and Country fields to columns 3 through 7, first select the fields. In the Customers Field list of the upper pane's Query Design window, click Address, and then Shift+click Country. Alternatively, select Address with the down-arrow key, hold down the Shift or Ctrl key, and press the down-arrow key four more times. You've selected the Address, City, Region, PostalCode, and Country fields, as shown in the Customers field list of Figure 9.12.

5. Position the mouse pointer over the selected fields and click the left mouse button. Your mouse pointer turns into a symbol representing the multiple field names (after you drag the mouse a bit). Drag the symbol for the multiple fields to the third column of your query's Field row, as shown in Figure 9.12, and release the left mouse button.

International Do Not Enter cursor

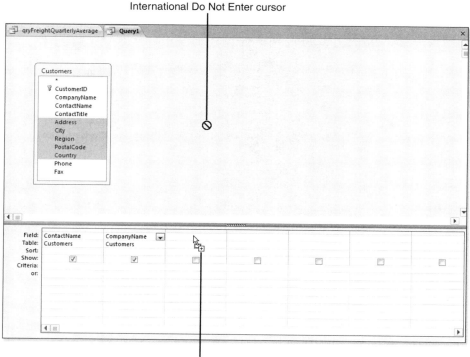

Figure 9.12
You also can select multiple fields in the table fields list and drag them to the Fields row of the Query Design grid.

6. To reduce the columns' width, drag the divider of the grid's header bars to the left. Click the scroll-right button (on the horizontal scroll bar at the bottom of the window) or drag the scrollbar slider button to the right to expose the remaining fields. Your Query Design window appears as shown in Figure 9.13.

7. Click the Datasheet view or Run button to execute the query.

You haven't yet entered any selection criteria in the Criteria row of the Query Design grid, so your query resultset in the Customers table displays all records. These records appear in the order of the primary key index on the CustomerID field because you haven't specified a sorting order in the Sort row of the Query Design grid. (The values in the CustomerID field are alphabetic codes derived from the CompanyName field.) Figure 9.14 shows the result of your first query after the width of the fields have been adjusted.

Figure 9.13 Reduce the width of the columns so Design view displays all columns in your current display resolution (1,024x768 for most figures in this book).

Contact Name	Company Name	Address	City	Regi	Postal Co	Country
Maria Anders	Alfreds Futterkiste	Obere Str. 57	Berlin		12209	Germany
Ana Trujillo	Ana Trujillo Emparedados y helados	Avda. de la Constitución 2222	México D.F.		05021	Mexico
Antonio Moreno	Antonio Moreno Taquería	Mataderos 2312	México D.F.		05023	Mexico
Thomas Hardy	Around the Horn	120 Hanover Sq.	London		WA1 1DP	UK
Christina Berglund	Berglunds snabbköp	Berguvsvägen 8	Luleå		S-958 22	Sweden
Hanna Moos	Blauer See Delikatessen	Forsterstr. 57	Mannheim		68306	Germany
Frédérique Citeaux	Blondel père et fils	24, place Kléber	Strasbourg		67000	France
Martín Sommer	Bólido Comidas preparadas	C/ Araquil, 67	Madrid		28023	Spain
Laurence Lebihan	Bon app'	12, rue des Bouchers	Marseille		13008	France
Elizabeth Lincoln	Bottom-Dollar Markets	23 Tsawassen Blvd.	Tsawassen	BC	T2F 8M4	Canada
Victoria Ashworth	B's Beverages	Fauntleroy Circus	London		EC2 5NT	UK
Patricio Simpson	Cactus Comidas para llevar	Cerrito 333	Buenos Aires		1010	Argentina
Francisco Chang	Centro comercial Moctezuma	Sierras de Granada 9993	México D.F.		05022	Mexico
Yang Wang	Chop-suey Chinese	Hauptstr. 29	Bern		3012	Switzerlanc
Pedro Afonso	Comércio Mineiro	Av. dos Lusíadas, 23	São Paulo	SP	05432-043	Brazil
Elizabeth Brown	Consolidated Holdings	Berkeley Gardens	London		WX1 6LT	UK
Sven Ottlieb	Drachenblut Delikatessen	Walserweg 21	Aachen		52066	Germany
Janine Labrune	Du monde entier	67, rue des Cinquante Otages	Nantes		44000	France
Ann Devon	Eastern Connection	35 King George	London		WX3 6FW	UK
Roland Mendel	Ernst Handel	Kirchgasse 6	Graz		8010	Austria
Aria Cruz	Familia Arquibaldo	Rua Orós, 92	São Paulo	SP	05442-030	Brazil
Diego Roel	FISSA Fabrica Inter. Salchichas S.A.	C/ Moralzarzal, 86	Madrid		28034	Spain
Martine Rancé	Folies gourmandes	184, chaussée de Tournai	Lille		59000	France
Maria Larsson	Folk och fä HB	Åkergatan 24	Bräcke		S-844 67	Sweden
Peter Franken	Frankenversand	Berliner Platz 43	München		80805	Germany
Carine Schmitt	France restauration	54, rue Royale	Nantes		44000	France
Paolo Accorti	Franchi S.p.A.	Via Monte Bianco 34	Torino		10100	Italy

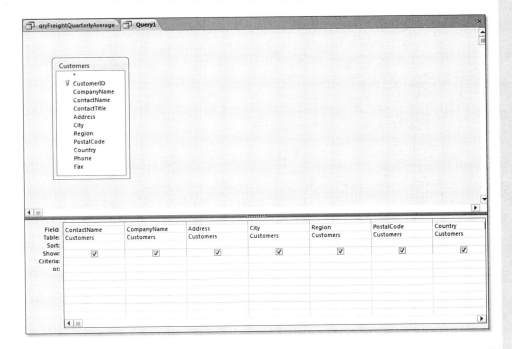

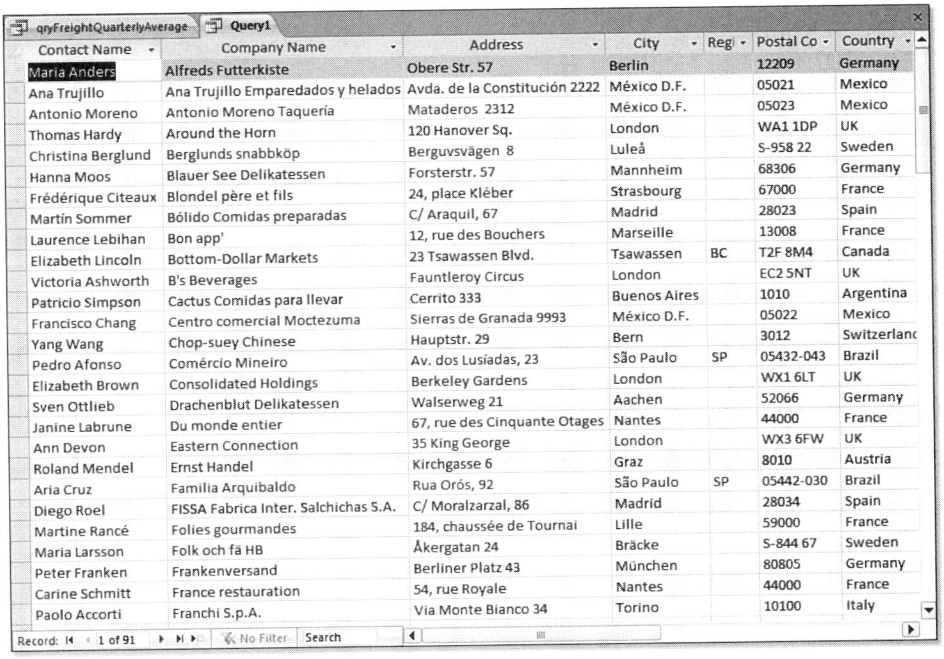

Figure 9.14 The initial query design in Datasheet view displays the seven selected fields of all records in the Customers table.

Selecting Records by Criteria and Sorting the Display

The mailing for which you're creating a list with your sample query is to be sent to U.S. customers only, so you want to include in your query only those records that have USA in the Country field. Selecting records based on the values of fields—that is, establishing the criteria for the records to be returned (displayed) by the query—is the heart of the query process.

Take the following steps to establish criteria for selecting the records to make up your mailing list:

1. Click the Design View button.

2. To restrict the result of your query to firms in the United States, type **USA** in the Criteria row of the Country column. Entering a criterion's value without preceding the value with an operator, such as = or >, indicates that the value of the field must match the value you type. You don't need to add quotation marks to the expression; Access adds them for you (see the Country column in Figure 9.15).

3. Click the Show check box in the Country column to clear the check mark that appeared when you added the column. After you clear the Show check box, the Country field doesn't appear when you run your query. If you don't clear a Show check box, that field in the query appears in the query's result by default.

4. Move the cursor to the PostalCode column's Sort row and press Alt+down arrow to display the sorting options for that field: Ascending, Descending, and (Not Sorted). Select the Ascending option to sort the query by postal code from low codes to high. At this point, the Query Design grid appears as shown in Figure 9.15.

5. Click the Datasheet View or Run button to display the result of the criterion and sorting order.

Figure 9.16 shows the query resultset that Access refers to as an *updatable Recordset* (also called an Access *Dynaset*), which is indicated by the tentative append (*) in the last (empty) row of the query resultset's leftmost selection column. A `Recordset` object is a temporary table stored in your computer's memory; it's not a permanent component of the database file. You can edit the data in any visible fields of the underlying table(s) in Query Datasheet view if your `Recordset` is updatable.

> **note**
> The SQL statement for a sorted SELECT query with a criterion is much simpler than the statement of the preceding example.

```
SELECT Customers.ContactName, Customers.CompanyName,
     Customers.Address, Customers.City, Customers.Region,
     Customers.PostalCode
  FROM Customers
  WHERE (((Customers.Country)="USA"))
ORDER BY Customers.PostalCode;
```

Figure 9.15
Add the USA criterion, hide the Country column, and apply an ascending sort order to the PostalCode column to complete the mailing list query.

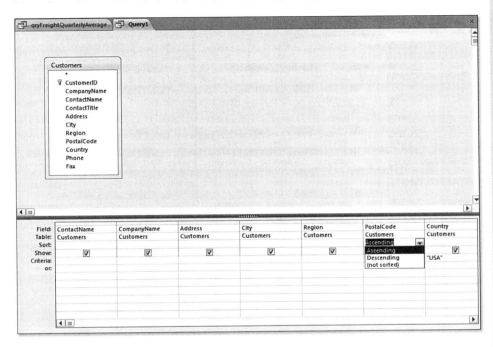

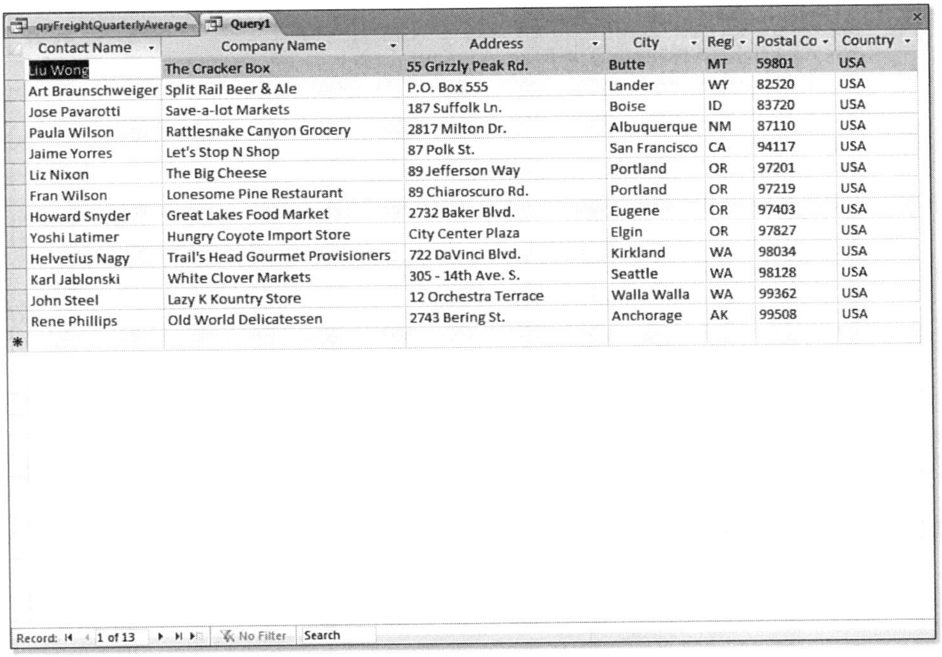

Figure 9.16
Datasheet view displays the mailing list query's updatable resultset (Recordset).

Contact Name	Company Name	Address	City	Regi	Postal Co	Country
Liu Wong	The Cracker Box	55 Grizzly Peak Rd.	Butte	MT	59801	USA
Art Braunschweiger	Split Rail Beer & Ale	P.O. Box 555	Lander	WY	82520	USA
Jose Pavarotti	Save-a-lot Markets	187 Suffolk Ln.	Boise	ID	83720	USA
Paula Wilson	Rattlesnake Canyon Grocery	2817 Milton Dr.	Albuquerque	NM	87110	USA
Jaime Yorres	Let's Stop N Shop	87 Polk St.	San Francisco	CA	94117	USA
Liz Nixon	The Big Cheese	89 Jefferson Way	Portland	OR	97201	USA
Fran Wilson	Lonesome Pine Restaurant	89 Chiaroscuro Rd.	Portland	OR	97219	USA
Howard Snyder	Great Lakes Food Market	2732 Baker Blvd.	Eugene	OR	97403	USA
Yoshi Latimer	Hungry Coyote Import Store	City Center Plaza	Elgin	OR	97827	USA
Helvetius Nagy	Trail's Head Gourmet Provisioners	722 DaVinci Blvd.	Kirkland	WA	98034	USA
Karl Jablonski	White Clover Markets	305 - 14th Ave. S.	Seattle	WA	98128	USA
John Steel	Lazy K Kountry Store	12 Orchestra Terrace	Walla Walla	WA	99362	USA
Rene Phillips	Old World Delicatessen	2743 Bering St.	Anchorage	AK	99508	USA

Record: 1 of 13   No Filter   Search

Missing Required Fields

If you have a situation in which you created a query that shows the tentative append record, but you receive a "The field 'FieldName' can't contain a Null value because the Required property is set to True" error message when you try to add a new record, you must include in your query resultset all columns whose Required property value is set to Yes. This means, of course, that each of these fields must have a value typed in it. A unique primary key value is required to add a new record to any table with a primary key. For example, attempting to add a new record to a query on the Customers table that doesn't include CustomerID and CustomerName columns fails because CustomerID is the primary key and CustomerName is a required field of the table.

Preventing Updates to the Query Resultset

▶★ You can edit any of the values in the seven columns of the preceding query and, theoretically, add new records because the tentative append record appears in the last row of the query and the new record navigation button is enabled. You can't add a new record, however, because the query doesn't include the primary key field (CustomerID). If you attempt to add a new record by moving to a different record, you receive the message shown in Figure 9.17. You must press Esc to delete all characters you typed in any field of the tentative append record.

 note

The WHERE clause specifies the selection criterion and the ORDER BY clause determines the sort order. ASC[ENDING] is the default sort order; DESC[ENDING] performs a reverse sort. SQL-92 permits abbreviation of the directional keywords. Access adds multiple sets of unneeded parentheses to the WHERE clause; if you remove them all, the query executes correctly.

The message that appears to a user of your query who attempts to add a new record is confusing, because most database users don't know what "primary key" and "Null value" mean. It's good database design practice to prevent users from attempting operations they can't complete, so you should designate the query as not updatable by changing the query type to an Access *Snapshot*. The terms *Dynaset* and *Snapshot* refer to the cursor type of the query; a Dynaset has a *read-write* (*updatable*) *cursor* and a Snapshot has a *read-only* (*non-updatable*) *cursor*. A *cursor* is what RDBMSs use to navigate, read, and—if the cursor is updatable—update the rows returned by the query, add a new row, or delete a row.

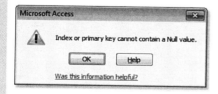

Figure 9.17
If you attempt to add a new record to the query, you receive the message shown here because you can't add a value for the primary key field, CustomerID.

To change the type of cursor, which doesn't affect the SQL statement for the query, do this:

1. 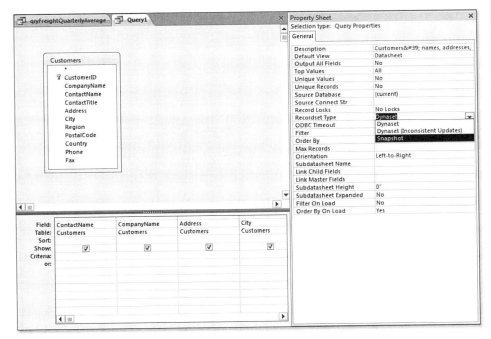 Click the Design View button to return to Query Design view.

2. Click the Properties toggle button or right-click in an empty area in the upper Query Design pane and then choose Properties to open the Query Properties dialog.

3. Select the Recordset Type text box, open the drop-down list, and choose Snapshot (see Figure 9.18).

Figure 9.18
Open the Query Properties dialog and select Snapshot as the value of the Recordset Type property to create a read-only query resultset.

4. Return to Datasheet view to verify that the tentative append record is missing and the new record navigation button is disabled (see Figure 9.19).

5. Press Ctrl+S, choose File, Save, or close the query. Then type a name for the query in the text box (**qryCustomersUSA** for this example) and click OK to save the query.

When you save the query, the Northwind.accdb file saves only the design specifications of the query, not the values that the query contains. The query design specification is called a QueryDef (query definition) object. When you open the query, Access executes the query and displays the resultset in Datasheet view.

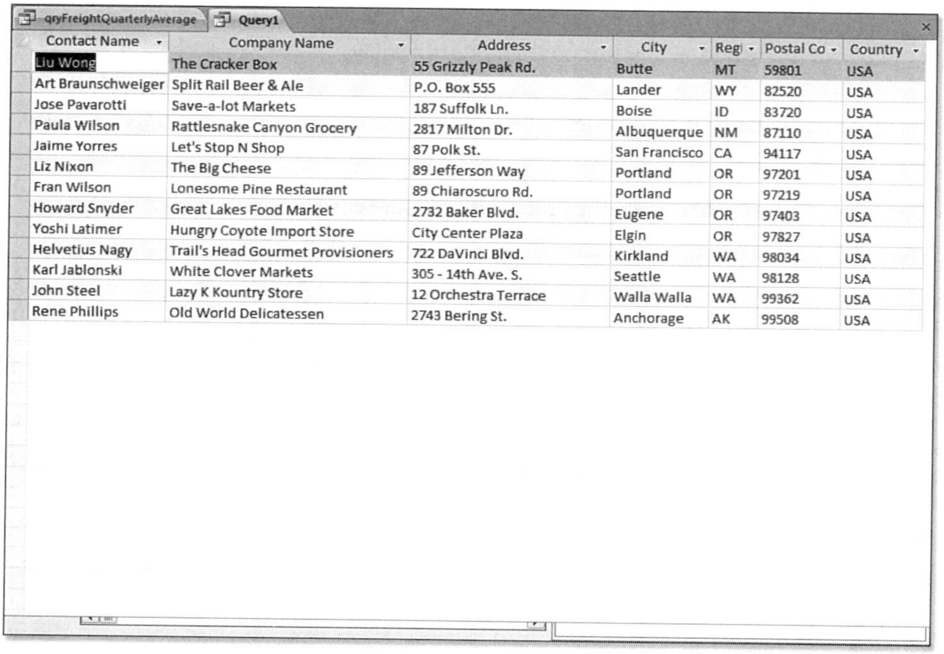

Contact Name	Company Name	Address	City	Regi	Postal Co	Country
Liu Wong	The Cracker Box	55 Grizzly Peak Rd.	Butte	MT	59801	USA
Art Braunschweiger	Split Rail Beer & Ale	P.O. Box 555	Lander	WY	82520	USA
Jose Pavarotti	Save-a-lot Markets	187 Suffolk Ln.	Boise	ID	83720	USA
Paula Wilson	Rattlesnake Canyon Grocery	2817 Milton Dr.	Albuquerque	NM	87110	USA
Jaime Yorres	Let's Stop N Shop	87 Polk St.	San Francisco	CA	94117	USA
Liz Nixon	The Big Cheese	89 Jefferson Way	Portland	OR	97201	USA
Fran Wilson	Lonesome Pine Restaurant	89 Chiaroscuro Rd.	Portland	OR	97219	USA
Howard Snyder	Great Lakes Food Market	2732 Baker Blvd.	Eugene	OR	97403	USA
Yoshi Latimer	Hungry Coyote Import Store	City Center Plaza	Elgin	OR	97827	USA
Helvetius Nagy	Trail's Head Gourmet Provisioners	722 DaVinci Blvd.	Kirkland	WA	98034	USA
Karl Jablonski	White Clover Markets	305 - 14th Ave. S.	Seattle	WA	98128	USA
John Steel	Lazy K Kountry Store	12 Orchestra Terrace	Walla Walla	WA	99362	USA
Rene Phillips	Old World Delicatessen	2743 Bering St.	Anchorage	AK	99508	USA

Figure 9.19 The read-only Snapshot query doesn't have a tentative append record, and the new record button is disabled.

Creating More Complex Criteria

To limit your mailing to customers in a particular state or group of states, you can add a Criteria expression to the Region or PostalCode field. To restrict the mailing to customers in California, Oregon, and Washington, for example, you can specify that the value of the PostalCode field must be equal to or greater than 90000. Alternatively, you can specify that Region values must be CA, OR, and WA.

Follow these steps to restrict your mailing to customers in California, Oregon, and Washington:

1. Open the query and click the Design View button.

2. Move to the Region column and type **CA** in the first criterion row of the Region column. Access adds the quotation marks around CA (as it did when you restricted your mailing to U.S. locations with the USA criterion).

3. Press the down-arrow key to move to the next criterion row in the Region column. Type **OR** and then move to the third criterion row and type **WA**. Your query design now appears as shown in Figure 9.20. Access also adds the required quotation marks to these criteria.

4.   Click the Datasheet View or Run toolbar button. The query resultset appears as shown in Figure 9.21.

Figure 9.20
You can further restrict records returned by the query with additional criteria in the Region field.

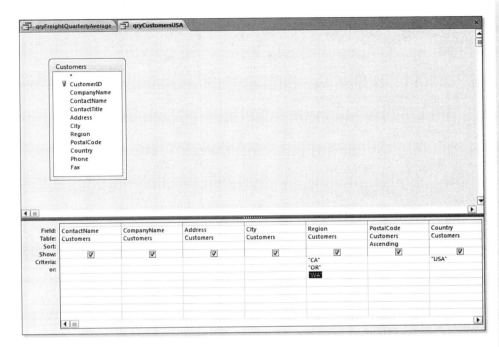

After you type a criterion on the same line as a previously entered criterion in another field, only those records that meet both criteria are selected for display. In the preceding example, therefore, records with Region values equal to CA and Country values equal to USA, and records with Region values of OR and WA, are displayed.

The SQL statement that includes the additional criteria is

tip

If you already have a main document for mail merge operations, substitute the main merge document's merge field names for the table's field header names in your query.

```
SELECT Customers.ContactName, Customers.CompanyName,
    Customers.Address, Customers.City, Customers.Region,
    Customers.PostalCode
FROM Customers
WHERE (((Customers.Region)="CA") AND ((Customers.Country)="USA"))
    OR (((Customers.Region)="OR")) OR (((Customers.Region)="WA"))
ORDER BY Customers.PostalCode;
```

Changing the Names of Query Column Headers

You can substitute a query's field header names with column header names of your choice—a process called *aliasing*—but only if the header name hasn't been changed by an entry in the Caption

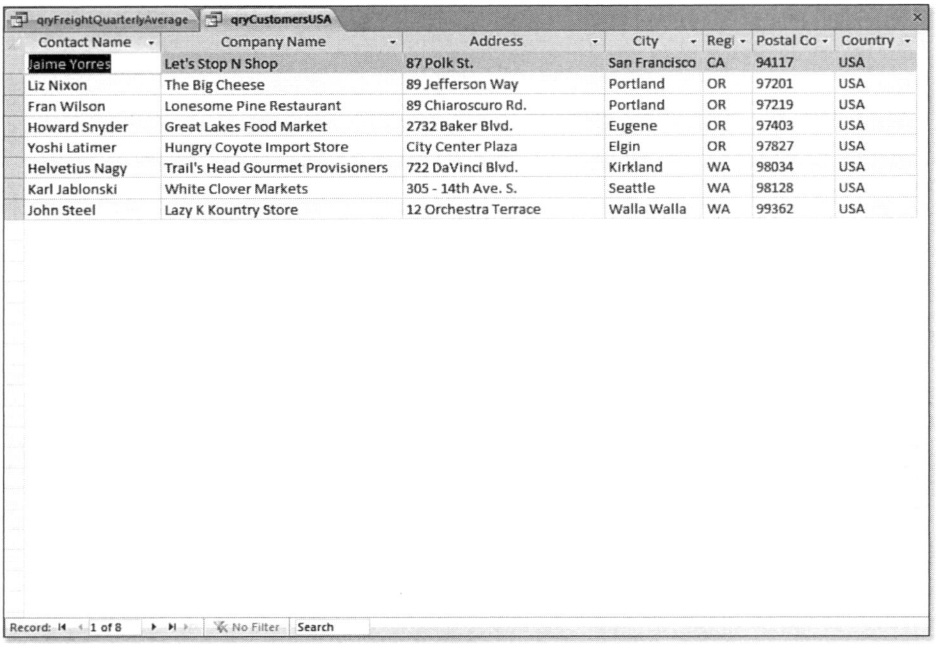

Contact Name	Company Name	Address	City	Regi	Postal Co	Country
Jaime Yorres	Let's Stop N Shop	87 Polk St.	San Francisco	CA	94117	USA
Liz Nixon	The Big Cheese	89 Jefferson Way	Portland	OR	97201	USA
Fran Wilson	Lonesome Pine Restaurant	89 Chiaroscuro Rd.	Portland	OR	97219	USA
Howard Snyder	Great Lakes Food Market	2732 Baker Blvd.	Eugene	OR	97403	USA
Yoshi Latimer	Hungry Coyote Import Store	City Center Plaza	Elgin	OR	97827	USA
Helvetius Nagy	Trail's Head Gourmet Provisioners	722 DaVinci Blvd.	Kirkland	WA	98034	USA
Karl Jablonski	White Clover Markets	305 - 14th Ave. S.	Seattle	WA	98128	USA
John Steel	Lazy K Kountry Store	12 Orchestra Terrace	Walla Walla	WA	99362	USA

Record: I◄ ◄ 1 of 8 ► ►I ► No Filter   Search

Figure 9.21
The query resultset with the additional criteria includes only records for the three West Coast states.

property of the table's field. If yours is a U.S. firm, for example, you might want to change Region to State and PostalCode to ZIP. (Canadian firms might want to change only Region to Province.)

As demonstrated in the following example, you can't change the PostalCode field for queries based on the Customers table because the PostalCode field previously has been changed (aliased) to Postal Code by the Caption property for the field. You can, however, make the change to the Region field because this field isn't aliased at the table level.

➡ *For more information on merging data with documents,* **see** *"Using the Access Mail Merge Wizard,"* **p. 331.**

To change the query column header names, perform the following steps:

1. Click the Design View button. Then place the cursor in the Field column containing the field header name that you want to change—in this case, the Region column.

2. Press F2 to deselect the field; then press Home to move the cursor to the first character position.

🔍 note

Field names in queries that have been altered by use of the Caption property in the source table can't be aliased, so don't use the Caption property of table fields. If you want to display different field headers, use a query for this purpose. In a client/server RDBMS, such a query is called an SQL VIEW. Aliasing field names in tables rather than in queries isn't considered a generally accepted database design practice.

3. Type the new name for the column and follow the name with a colon (with no spaces), as in **State:**. The colon separates the new column name that you type from the existing table field name, which shifts to the right to make room for your addition. The result, in this example, is State: Region.

4. Use the arrow key to move to the PostalCode field and repeat steps 2 and 3, typing **ZIP:** as that header's new name. The result is ZIP: PostalCode.

5. Change the column header for the ContactName field to **Contact**; change the column header for the CompanyName field to **Company**.

6. Delete the three criteria (the "CA" Or "OR" Or "WA" criterion you added to the SQL statement described in the preceding section) from the State: Region column so that all records for the United States appear (see Figure 9.22). If you altered the SQL statement, add the Country field to the grid, clear the Show check box, and add **USA** as the criterion.

7. Click the Run or Datasheet View button to execute the query. Observe that only the Region column header is changed to State; the other columns are unaffected by the alias entry (see Figure 9.23).

8. Choose File, Save As, and save your query with the name **qry-USMailList**.

The SQL statement that attempts to rename all query columns is

```
SELECT Customers.ContactName AS Contact,
    Customers.CompanyName AS Company,
    Customers.Address, Customers.City,
    Customers.Region AS State,
    Customers.PostalCode AS ZIP
  FROM Customers
  WHERE (((Customers.Country)="USA"))
ORDER BY Customers.PostalCode;
```

note

Again, Access adds many superfluous parentheses, but the first element of the WHERE clause requires a single pair in the (Customers.Region ="CA" AND Customers.Country)="USA") expression.

To be displayed, records for Region values OR and WA need not have Country values equal to USA, because the USA criterion is missing from the OR and WA rows. This omission doesn't affect the selection of records in this case, because all OR and WA records also are USA records. Therefore, the WHERE clause can be simplified to WHERE Customers.Region="CA" OR Customers.Region="OR" OR Customers.Region="WA". If you edit the SQL statement accordingly, the query resultset is the same.

tip

To make field aliasing in queries operable, in Table Design view delete the entry in the Caption field for each aliased field of the table. Deleting these entries makes the aliases you entered in the preceding example work as expected.

Printing Your Query as a Report

You often use queries to print quick, ad hoc reports. Access 2010's Print Preview ribbon lets you print your report to a printer or to an Adobe Portable Document Format (.pdf) or Microsoft XML Paper Specification (.xps) file. You also can export the data to a Microsoft Word .rtf (rich-text format) file, an Excel worksheet .xlsx file, a DOS .txt (text) file, an XML document, a SharePoint list, one of

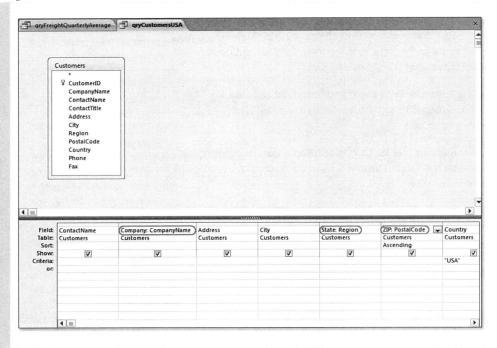

Figure 9.22
This query
design
attempts
to assign
aliases to
field names
that have
Caption
property
values
assigned
at the table
level.

Figure 9.23
The table's
Caption
property
value over-
rides alias
names
assigned by
the query.
Only the
Region
field, which
doesn't have
a caption,
is aliased to
State in this
example.

several database formats, or a Microsoft Word merge data source. You also can publish a query as an HTML file to a web server. The table export procedures described in the preceding chapter also apply to queries.

Previewing your query table's appearance to see how the table will appear when printed is usually a good idea. After you determine from the preview that everything in the table is correct, you can print the finished query resultset in various formats.

To preview a query resultset before printing it, follow these steps:

1. In Query Datasheet view, click the File tab and click Print, Print Preview. A miniature version of the query table opens in Report Print Preview mode.

2. Position the Zoom pointer (the magnifying glass cursor) anywhere on the query table and click the left mouse button to view the report at approximately the scale at which it will print.

3. Use the vertical and horizontal scrollbar buttons to position the preview in the window (see Figure 9.24).

4. Right-click the Print Preview window and choose Page Setup to open the Page Setup dialog shown in Figure 9.25. If necessary, click the Print Options tab to display the Margins settings.

5. Enter any changes that you want to make to the margins; mark the Print Headings check box if you want to print the field header names. Click the Page tab to change the print orientation, paper size or source, or printer. Then click OK to return to Print Preview.

6. Click the Print button to print your query report, and then click the Close Print Preview button to return to Datasheet view.

> **note**
>
> Although the SQL statement renames four fields, only the `Customer.Region` field receives a renamed column.

> **note**
>
> Field width in the query table is based on the column width that you last established in Run mode. You might have to drag the right edge of the field header buttons to the right to increase the columns' width so that the printed report doesn't truncate the data. If the query data's width exceeds the available printing width (the paper width minus the width of the left and right margins), Access prints two or more sheets for each page of the report.

Testing the Other Query Wizards

In addition to the Simple Query Wizard that you tried early in the chapter, the New Query dialog lets you choose one of the following three specialized Query wizards:

- **Crosstab Query Wizard**—This wizard helps you create queries that calculate and report the sum, average, or other aggregate value for the data grouped by rows and columns. As an example, a crosstab query can calculate total sales for product categories (in rows) and quarters or years (in columns) in a format similar to an Excel Pivot Table. Chapter 11 shows you how to use the Crosstab Query Wizard.

- **Find Duplicates Query Wizard**—This wizard finds duplicate values in one or more columns of a single table.

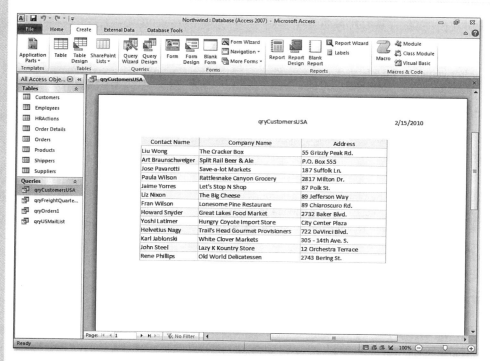

Figure 9.24
You can quickly print a query by opening it in the Print Preview window and clicking the image to zoom it to approximately the print scale.

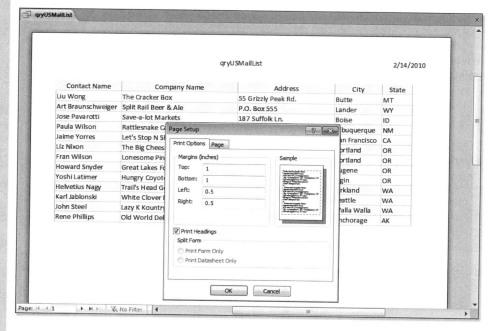

Figure 9.25
The Print Options tab of the Print Setup dialog lets you change printing margins from the default 1-inch values. The Page tab has orientation, paper size and source, and printer selection options.

■ **Find Unmatched Query Wizard**—This wizard lists values from a column in one table that have no matching values in the corresponding column of a related table.

The following two sections show you how to use the Find Duplicates and Find Unmatched Query Wizards.

Finding Duplicate Values in a Field

The most common use for the Find Duplicates Query Wizard is to eliminate duplicate values in the field that you want to be the primary key for a table. A primary key that's based on a custom identifying code for or the actual name of an object or person is called a *natural primary key* because it's based on naturally occurring data. The Customers table's CustomerID field, which has values derived from the CompanyName field, is an example of a natural primary key. (A key that's not based on naturally occurring data, such as an Access AutoNumber or SQL Server identity column or uniqueidentifier (rowguid) datatype, is called a *surrogate primary key*.) If you select the candidate field for a natural primary key in table Design view and click the Primary Key button, you receive an error message if the field contains duplicate values.

To test-drive the Find Duplicates Query Wizard with the CustomersWithDups table in the \Access2010\Chapter09 folder, do the following:

1. Open Nwind09.accdb, if necessary; click the Create tab and the Query group's Query Wizard tab to open the New Query dialog, and double-click the Find Duplicates Query Wizard item to open the first dialog.

2. With Tables selected in the View group, select the CustomersWithDups table, and click Next.

3. CustomerID is the candidate primary key field, so select it in the Available Fields list, click the right-arrow button, and click Next.

4. Click the Company Name in the Available Fields list, click the right-arrow button to add it to the query resultset, and click Next (see Figure 9.26).

5. Replace the default Find Duplicates for CustomersWithDups title with qryFindDups1 and, with the View the Results option selected, click Finish to save the query and display its data sheet with duplicate records for Blondel père et fils (BLONP) and The Big Cheese (THEBI).

The simplified Access SQL statement for the preceding query provides an example of using the GROUP BY and HAVING clauses with the COUNT function in a subquery to find more than one occurrence of a value:

```
SELECT CustomerID, CompanyName FROM CustomersWithDups
    WHERE CustomerID IN
        (SELECT CustomerID FROM Customers with Dups as Tmp
            GROUP BY CustomerID HAVING Count(*) > 1)
    ORDER BY CustomerID;
```

 note

Chapter 11 covers multitable queries.

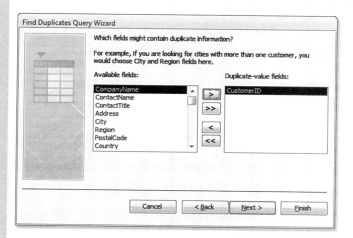

Figure 9.26
Select the field(s) to test for duplicate values in the second Find Duplicates Query Wizard dialog.

For an example of using the Find Duplicates Query Wizard with an Access table created by importing a large HTML table, **see** "Counting Duplicate Rows with the Find Duplicates Query Wizard," **p. 1016**.

Finding Values in One Table with No Matching Values in a Related Table

The Find Unmatched Query Wizard has these two primary applications:

- Finding parent records with no child records in a related table, such as finding records for Customers that have no related Orders records.

- Finding child records without parent records in a related table; child records without parent records are called *orphan records*.

To demonstrate the Find Unmatched Query Wizard with the Customers and Orders tables of the \ Samples2010\Ch09\Nwind09.accb sample database, do the following:

1. Open Nwind09.accdb, if necessary; click the Create tab and the Queries group's Query Wizard item to open the New Query dialog, and double-click the Find Unmatched Query Wizard item to open the first dialog.

2. With Tables selected in the View group, select Customers as the parent table, and click Next.

3. With Tables selected in the View group, select Orders as the child table, and click Next.

4. Accept the default CustomerID field as the primary key in the Fields in 'Customers' list and foreign key in the Fields in 'Orders' list. The Matching Fields text box displays CustomerID <=> CustomerID (see Figure 9.27). Click Next.

Figure 9.27
Select the field to test for missing values in the third Find Unmatched Query Wizard dialog.

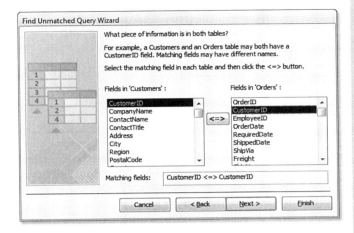

5. Select the CustomerIDfield, click the right-arrow button, select CompanyName, click the right-arrow to display these two fields for unmatched records, and click Next.

6. Replace the default Customers Without Matching Orders name with **qryUnmatched** and click Finish to display in the Datasheet FISSA (FISSA Fabrica Inter. Salchicas, S.A.) and PARIS (Paris spècialitès) as the two Northwind customers with no Orders records.

Following is the simplified Access SQL statement for the preceding query:

```
SELECT Customers.CustomerID, Customers.CompanyName
    FROM Customers LEFT JOIN Orders
        ON Customers.CustomerID = Orders.CustomerID
    WHERE Orders.CustomerID Is Null
```

To learn more about LEFT JOIN SQL syntax, **see** *"Creating Outer Joins,"* **p. 463.**

Creating Other Types of Queries

Access lets you create the following five basic types of queries to achieve different objectives:

- *Select* queries extract data from one or more tables and display the data in tabular form. A *union query* is a special type of select query that combines records from two or more tables in a common set of columns.

- *Crosstab* queries summarize data from one or more tables in the form of a spreadsheet. Such queries are useful for analyzing data and creating graphs or charts based on the sum of the numeric field values of many records.

- *Action* queries create new database tables from query tables or make major alterations to a table. Such queries let you add or delete records from a table or make changes to records based on expressions that you enter in a query design. The action query category includes *append*, *update*, *delete*, and *make-table*.

- *Pass-through* queries bypass the Access query processor and send SQL statements directly to the query processor of a back-end database, which returns rows or messages to Access objects. You can't open a pass-through query in Design view; only SQL and Datasheet views are available.

- *Parameter* queries repeatedly use a query and make only simple changes to its criteria. The mailing list query that you created earlier is an excellent candidate for a parameter query because you can change the criterion of the Region field for mailings to different groups of customers. When you run a parameter query, Access displays a dialog to prompt you for the new criterion. Parameter queries aren't actually a separate query type because you can add the parameter function to select, crosstab, and action queries.

Chapter 11 and Chapter 13 explain how to create each of the five query types. Creating a table from the mailing list query to export to a mail merge file is an example of a make-table action query. In fact, this is the simplest example of an action query and also the safest because make-table queries don't modify data in existing tables. A make-table query creates a new table from your query result-set.

➡️ *To review the use of tables for Word mail merge operations,* **see** *"Using the Access Mail Merge Wizard,"* **p. 331.**

Creating and Using a Simple Make-Table Action Query

To create a table from your mailing list query, you first must convert the query from a select to an action query. Follow these steps to make this change:

1. Open your mailing list query in Query Design view, click the Design tab, and click the Query Type group's Query Type: Make Table button to open the Make Table dialog.

2. In the Table Name text box, type a descriptive table name for your query table, such as **tblUS-MailList** (see Figure 9.28).

Figure 9.28
Specify the table name for your make-table query. When creating a table with a query, it's a good practice to use the tbl prefix to identify the table as one created by a query.

3. Click OK. Access converts your select query to the make-table type of action query.

4. Save your make-table query with a new name and close it. An exclamation point prefixes the query's icon in the Navigation Pane, which indicates that the query is an action query.

The SQL statement for the make-table query is

```
SELECT Customers.ContactName AS Contact,
     Customers.CompanyName AS Company,
     Customers.Address, Customers.City,
     Customers.Region AS State, Customers.PostalCode AS ZIP
  INTO tblUSMailList
  FROM Customers
  WHERE (((Customers.Country)="USA"))
ORDER BY Customers.PostalCode;
```

Now that you've converted your query from a select query to an action query, you can create a new U.S. mailing list table. To create the table, follow these steps:

1. Run the newly converted action query table to create your mailing list by double-clicking its name in the Navigation Pane's Queries group. Acknowledge the messages that ask if you want to run the make-table query, confirm that the table, if it exists, will be overwritten, and acknowledge the number of rows to be "pasted" to the new table (see Figure 9.29). Access adds the new tblUSMailList table to the list of tables in the Northwind database.

 note

The Make Table dialog lets you define your query table's properties further in two ways. You can add the table to the Northwind database by choosing the Current Database option (the default). You also can pick the Another Database option to add the table to a different database that you specify in the File Name text box.

2. Double-click the tblUSMailList item in the Navigation Pane's Tables group to open the table. Its contents are identical to the contents of the Datasheet view of the make-table query.

After you create the new table, you can export its data to any of the other file formats supported by Access. To do so, use any of the methods described in Chapter 8, "Linking, Importing, and Exporting Data."

Adding a Parameter to Your Make-Table Query

A simple modification to your mailing list query lets you enter a selection criterion, called a parameter, from a prompt generated by Access. Parameterized queries are very useful for generating custom tables for Word mail-merge operations. You can use the same merge specifications with different tables to generate multiple lists for selected regions or types of recipients.

 note

The clause that differentiates the make-table query from the select query from which it's derived is INTO tblUSMailList. The INTO clause lets you specify the table name.

 For more information on parameterized queries, **see** *"Designing Parameter Queries,"* **p. 481.**

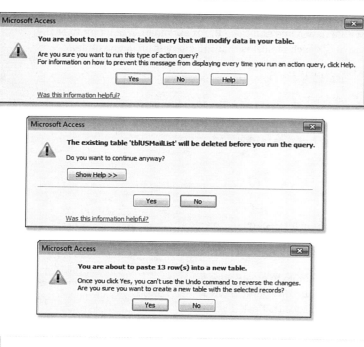

Figure 9.29
Access displays two or three warning messages before your make-table query creates the table, if you haven't cleared the Action Queries and Record Changes text boxes in the Confirm section on the Advanced page of the Access Options dialog.

To create a parameterized SELECT query, follow these steps:

1. Close the tblUSMailList table, and then expand the Navigation pane, if necessary.

2. Right-click the item for the make-table query that you created in the preceding section, and choose Design View.

3. Type **[Enter the state code:]** in the first criterion row of the State: Region column, as shown in Figure 9.30. The enclosing square brackets indicate that the entry is a prompt for a parameter when you run the action query.

4. Press Ctrl+S to save the query. (You must save the query to re-create the table.)

5. Change to Datasheet view. Access opens the first two warning messages, and then the Enter Parameter Value dialog, which contains the prompt for you to enter the state criterion. Type **WA** for this example (see Figure 9.31), and click OK to open the third warning message and replace the tblUSMailList table (see Figure 9.32).

The Access SQL statement for the parameterized make-table query is

 note

The first Customers. Region)=[Enter the state code:] criterion of the WHERE clause specifies the prompt and opens the Enter Parameter Value dialog. This syntax is Access-specific and isn't supported by SQL-92 or T-SQL. ADP use SQL Server functions to return parameterized query resultsets.

Figure 9.30
Adding a criterion enclosed in square brackets creates a prompt for a parameter value to filter the query resultset.

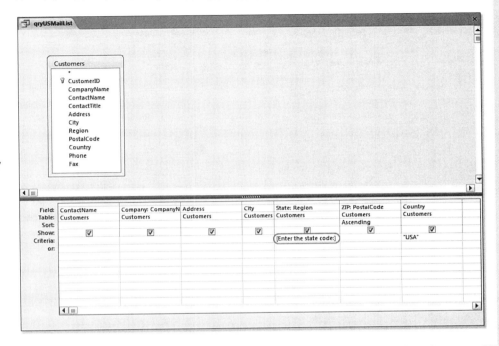

Figure 9.31
The Enter Parameter Value dialog includes the prompt you added as the criterion of the field for which a value is required.

```
SELECT Customers.ContactName AS Contact,
    Customers.CompanyName AS Company,
    Customers.Address, Customers.City,
    Customers.Region AS State, Customers.PostalCode AS ZIP
 INTO tblUSMailList
 FROM Customers
 WHERE (((Customers.Region)=[Enter the state code:]))
    AND ((Customers.Country)="USA")))
ORDER BY Customers.PostalCode;
```

Access doesn't limit you to using a single parameter. For example, you can replace the "USA" criterion for the Country field with [Enter the country name:], and drag the Country column to the left of the Region column so the country prompt occurs first. In the case of the Orders table, however, you

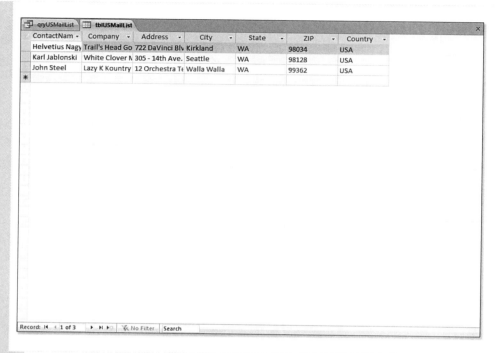

Figure 9.32
This replace-
ment table
illustrates
the effect of
applying a
parameter
to the WHERE
clause of a
make-table
query.

encounter a problem with countries such as Germany and the UK that don't have entries in Region columns. See the "Problems with Null Values in Parameter Fields" of the next section for more information on this issue.

Problems with Null Values in Parameter Fields

When you enter an empty parameter value to return records without an entry in the specified field and the query returns no records, you need to edit the Access SQL statement for the query to include an OR FieldName IS NULL expression to the WHERE clause. For example, in a query against the Orders table with Region and Country parameters, you must add OR Customers.Region IS NULL to return records for Germany and other countries whose Region values are missing. Following is the SQL statement that corrects the missing records for Germany problem:

```
SELECT Customers.ContactName AS Contact,
    Customers.CompanyName AS Company,
    Customers.Address, Customers.City,
    Customers.Region AS State,
    Customers.PostalCode AS ZIP
```

 note

The Access website's "The Evils of Lookup Fields in Tables" page (at http://www.mvps.org/ access/lookupfields.htm) offers eight good reasons why you shouldn't use lookup fields in production databases.

```
  INTO tblUSMailList
  FROM Customers
  WHERE Customers.Country=[Enter the country name:]
     AND (Customers.Region=[Enter the state code:]
     OR Customers.Region IS NULL)
ORDER BY Customers.PostalCode;
```

In the preceding SQL statement, nonessential parentheses added by the Access query designer have been removed. The parentheses surrounding the (`Customers.Region=[Enter the state code:]` `OR Customers.Region IS NULL`) expression are required to group the two condition expressions into a single criterion. This issue exemplifies the importance of learning SQL while you're gaining experience with query design.

10

UNDERSTANDING ACCESS QUERY OPERATORS AND EXPRESSIONS

2010 NEW Chapter 5, "Working with Access Databases and Tables," described how to use expressions to define values in calculated fields, which are new in Access 2010. Chapter 6, "Entering, Editing, and Validating Access Table Data," briefly introduced you to operators and the expressions that use them when you added validation rules to table fields. Chapter 9, "Designing Queries for Access Databases," touched on expressions again when you devised selection criteria for the query that you created. Expressions play an important role in all the chapters that follow.

Much of this chapter is devoted to describing the VBA functions available to you for dealing with data of the Numeric, Date/Time, and Text field data types. Functions play important roles in every element of Access—from query criteria, to validation rules for tables and fields of tables, to the control of program flow with Access macros and VBA. You use functions when creating queries, forms, reports, writing macros, and even more extensively when writing VBA and VBScript code.

To use Access 2010 effectively, you must know what functions are available to you and how to use functions and operators effectively.

An Access 2010 macro security feature—called sandbox mode—proscribes the use of unsafe VBA expressions. Here's how Microsoft describes unsafe expressions: "Unsafe expressions contain methods or functions that could be exploited by malicious users to access drives, files, or other resources for which they do not have authorization." None of the functions of this chapter are blocked unless they are used to supply the default value of

note

As mentioned in earlier chapters, the Access expression service enables Access to take advantage of most VBA functions in validation rules for Access tables. You can use VBA-specific functions to set criteria and format fields of queries against Access databases and client/server databases attached to Access front-end .accdb and .mdb files.

Access data projects (ADP), which use the SQL Server query processor, don't support any VBA-specific functions and use different characters for some operators. You must use corresponding Transact-SQL (T-SQL) built-in functions, where available, for CHECK constraints, VIEW column formatting, WHERE clause criteria, and elsewhere. T-SQL built-in functions aren't the same as SQL Server functions, which are more properly called *user-defined functions*. Chapter 27, "Moving from Access Queries to Transact-SQL," covers differences between Access and T-SQL operators, expressions and functions.

Access web databases (AWB) don't support some elements of the Access expression service or any VBA-specific functions because of limitations of SharePoint Server 2010's Access Services feature and SharePoint lists. Chapters 23, "Collaborating with SharePoint Foundation 2010," and 24, "Sharing Web Databases with SharePoint Server 2010," describe differences between Access and Web-compatible operators, expressions and functions.

a text box control on a form, report, or data access page. However, this and other chapters that make use of the VBA Editor require that the \Access2010 folder and its subfolders be designated as Trusted Locations by doing the following:

1. Click the File tab, and click the Options link to open the Access Options dialog.

2. Click the Trust Center link and the dialog's Trust Center button to open the Trusted Center page; then click the Trusted Locations link to open the Trusted Locations dialog.

3. Click the Add New Location button to open the Microsoft Office Trusted Location dialog, type the full path to the \Access2010 folder (usually C:\Access2010\ or \[My] Documents\Access2010).

4. Mark the Subfolders of This Location Are Also Trusted check box (see Figure 10.1), and click OK three times to return to the File page.

tip

This chapter provides brief descriptions of the SQL Server Transact-SQL (T-SQL) substitutes for VBA operators and functions, where equivalent or similar operators and functions exist. Chapter 21 provides more detailed information on differences between T-SQL and Access query syntax.

Understanding the Elements of Expressions

An *expression* is a statement of intent. If you want an action to occur after meeting a specific condition, your expression must specify that condition. To select records in a query that contains ZIP field values of 90000 or higher, for example, you use the expression

```
ZIP >= 90000
```

if the ZIP field has a numeric data type.

Figure 10.1
Eliminate the need to allow VBA execution in each sample Access 2010 database by designating the ...\Access2010 folder and its subfolders as Trusted Locations.

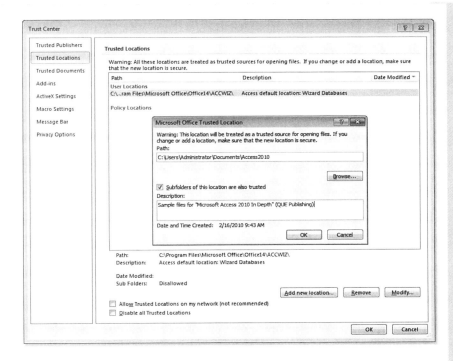

Arithmetic calculations also are expressions. If you need an ExtendedAmount field in a query, for example, use

```
ExtendedAmount: Quantity * UnitPrice
```

Alternatively, for a calculated column with a discounted value, use

```
[UnitPrice]*[Quantity]*(1-[Discount])
```

as the expression to create calculated values in the data cells of the ExtendedAmount column.

To qualify as an expression, a statement must have at least one operator and at least one literal, identifier, or function. In some cases, such as simple query criteria and field-validation rules, the equals operator (=) is inferred. The following list describes these elements:

 note

Expressions in this book appear in `monospace` type to distinguish expressions from the explanatory text. Operators, including symbolic operators, built-in functions, and other reserved words and symbols of VBA, are set in `monospace` **bold** type. (VBA reserved words appear in blue color in the Code-Editing window of modules.) SQL operators and names of Access objects are set in `monospace` type; by convention, SQL-92 reserved words are capitalized.

■ *Operators* include the familiar arithmetic symbols +, –, * (multiply), and / (divide), as well as many other symbols and abbreviations. Some operators are specific to Access or SQL, such as the Between, In, Is, and Like operators.

■ *Literals* consist of values that you type, such as **12345** or **ABCDE**. Literals are used most often to create default values and, in combination with field identifiers, to compare values in table fields and query columns.

■ *Identifiers* are the names of objects in Access (such as forms and reports) or fields in tables that return distinct numeric or text values. The term *return*, when used with expressions, means that the present value of the identifier is substituted for its name in the expression. For example, the field name identifier CompanyName in an expression returns the value (a firm name) of the CompanyName field for the currently selected record. Access has five predefined named constants that also serve as identifiers: True, False, Yes, No, and Null. Named constants and variables that you create in Access VBA also are identifiers.

■ *Functions* return a value in place of the function name in the expression, such as the Date... and Format... functions, which are used in the examples in Chapter 9. Unlike identifiers, most functions require you to supply an identifier or value as an argument enclosed by parentheses. Later in this chapter, the "Functions" section explains functions and their arguments.

When literals, identifiers, or functions are used with operators, these combinations are called *operands*. The following sections explain these four elements of expressions more thoroughly.

Operators

Access and VBA provide six categories of operators that you can use to create expressions:

■ *Arithmetic* operators perform addition, subtraction, multiplication, and division.

■ *Assignment* and *comparison* operators set values and compare values.

■ *Logical* operators deal with values that can only be true or false.

■ *Concatenation* operators combine strings of characters.

■ *Identifier* operators create unambiguous names for database objects so that you can assign the same field name, for example, in several tables and queries.

■ Other operators, such as the Like, Is, In, and Between operators, simplify the creation of expressions for selecting records with queries.

 tip

SQL Server supports all Access/ VBA operators, except ^ (exponentiation). T-SQL substitutes % for Mod.

Operators in the first four categories are available in almost all programming languages. Identifier operators are specific to Access; the other operators of the last category are provided only in RDBMSs that create queries based on SQL. The following sections explain how to use each of the operators in these categories.

Arithmetic Operators

Arithmetic operators operate only on numeric values and must have two numeric operands, with the following exceptions:

- When the minus sign (–) changes the sign (negates the value) of an operand. In this case, the minus sign is called the *unary minus*.

- When the equal sign (=) assigns a value to an Access object, property value, or a VBA variable identifier.

Table 10.1 lists the arithmetic operators that you can use in Access expressions.

Table 10.1 Arithmetic Operators

Operator	Description	Example
+	Adds two operands	Subtotal + Tax
–	Subtracts two operands	Date - 30
– (unary)	Changes the sign of an operand	-12345
*	Multiplies two operands	Units * UnitPrice
/	Divides one operand by another	Quantity / 12.55
\	Divides one integer operand by another	Units \ 2
Mod	Returns the remainder of division by an integer	Units **Mod** 12
^	Raises an operand to a power (exponent)	Value ^ Exponent

VBA operators are identical to operators used by all current versions of BASIC. If you aren't familiar with BASIC programming, the following operators need further explanation:

Operator	Description
\	The integer division symbol is the equivalent of "goes into," as used in the litany of elementary school arithmetic: 3 goes into 13 four times, with 1 left over. When you use integer division, operators with decimal fractions are rounded to integers, but any decimal fraction in the result is truncated.
Mod	An abbreviation for modulus, this operator returns the leftover value of integer division. Therefore, 13 Mod 4, for example, returns 1.
^	The exponentiation operator raises the first operand to the power of the second. For example, 2 ^ 4, or two to the fourth power, returns 16 (2*2*2*2).

These three operators seldom are used in queries for business applications but often occur in VBA program code.

Assignment and Comparison Operators

Table 10.1 omits the equal sign associated with arithmetic expressions because in Access you use it in two ways—neither of which falls under the arithmetic category. The most common use of the equal sign is as an assignment operator; = assigns the value of a single operand to an Access object, property value, or to a variable or constant. When you use the expression = "Q" to assign a default value to a field, the equal sign acts as an assignment operator. Otherwise, = is a comparison operator that determines whether one of two operands is equal to the other.

 tip

T-SQL has conventional AND, OR, and NOT logical operators. Xor is supported by the ^ bitwise comparison operator. Other T-SQL bitwise operators are & (bitwise and) and ¦ (bitwise or).

Comparison operators compare the values of two operands and return a logical value (**True** or **False**) depending on the relationship between the two operands and the operator. An exception is when one of the operands has the **Null** value. In this case, any comparison returns a value of **Null**. Because **Null** represents an unknown value, you cannot compare an unknown value with a known value and come to a valid **True** or **False** conclusion.

Table 10.2 lists the comparison operators available in Access.

Table 10.2 Comparison Operators

Operator	Description	Example	Result
<	Less than	123 < 1000	True
<=	Less than or equal to	15 <= 15	True
=	Equal to	2 = 4	False
>=	Greater than or equal to	1234 >= 456	True
>	Greater than	123 > 123	False
<>	Not equal	123 <> 456	True

The principal uses of comparison operators are to create data entry validation rules, to establish criteria for selecting records in queries, to determine actions taken by macros, to create joins using the SQL-89 WHERE and SQL-92 JOIN clauses, and to control program flow in VBA.

Logical Operators

Logical operators (also called *Boolean* operators) are used most often to combine the results of two or more comparison expressions into a single result. Logical operators can combine only expressions that return the logical values **True**, **False**, and **Null**. With the exception of **Not**, which is the logical equivalent of the unary minus, logical operators always require two operands.

Table 10.3 lists the Access logical operators.

Table 10.3 Logical Operators

Operator	Description	Example 1 / Example 2	Result 1 / Result 2
And	Logical and	True And True	True
		True And False	False
Or	Inclusive or	True Or False	True
		False Or False	False
Not	Logical not	Not True	False
		Not False	True
Xor	Exclusive or	True Xor False	True
		True Xor True	False

The logical operators **And**, **Or**, and **Not** are used extensively in Access expressions and SQL statements; in SQL statements these operators are uppercase, as in AND, OR, and NOT. Xor is seldom used in queries or VBA. **Eqv** (equivalent) and Imp (implication) are rarely seen, even in programming code, so Table 10.3 omits these two operators.

Concatenation Operators

Concatenation operators combine two text values into a single string of characters. If you concatenate ABC with DEF, for example, the result is ABCDEF. The ampersand (&) is the preferred concatenation operator in VBA and Access. Concatenation is one of the subjects of "The **Variant** Data Type in VBA" section later in the chapter.

Identifier Operators

Earlier versions of Access used identifier operators, ! (the exclamation point, often called the *bang* operator) and . (the period, called the *dot* operator in VBA). As of Access 2000, the period replaced the bang operator, which Access 2007 continues to support for backward compatibility. The period operator performs the following operations:

- Combines the names of object classes and object names to select a specific object or property of an object. For example, the following expression identifies the Personnel Actions form:

 tip

Don't use the + symbol to concatenate strings in queries or Access SQL. In Access SQL and VBA, + is reserved for the addition of numbers; & concatenates literals and variables of any field data type. The & operator performs implicit type conversion from numbers to text; the & operator treats all variables as character strings. Thus, 1234 & 5678 returns 12345678, not 6912.

 tip

T-SQL uses the + symbol for string concatenation. The SQL-92 specification, however, designates two vertical bars (pipe symbols) as the official concatenation operator, as in 'String1' ¦¦ 'String2'. The string concatenation symbol is one of the least consistent elements of common flavors of SQL.

```
Forms.HRActions
```

This identification is necessary because you might also have a table called HRActions.

- Separates object names from property names. Consider the following expression:

```
TextBox1.FontSize = 8
```

`TextBox1` is a control object, and `FontSize` is a property.

- Identifies specific fields in tables, as in the following expression, which specifies the CompanyName field of the Customers table:

```
Customers.CompanyName
```

Other Operators

The remaining operators are related to the comparison operators. These operators return **True** or **False**, depending on whether the value in a field meets the chosen operator's specification when used in a WHERE clause criterion. A **True** value causes a record to be included in a query; a **False** value rejects the record. When you use these operators in validation rules, entries are accepted or rejected based on the logical value returned by the expression.

Table 10.4 lists the four other operators used in Access queries and validation rules.

Table 10.4   Other Operators

Operator	Description	Example
Is	Used with **Null** to determine whether a value is **Null** or **Not Null**.	Is **Null** Is **Not Null**
Like	Determines whether a string value begins with one or more characters. (For Like to work properly, you must add a wildcard character, * or one or more ? characters.)	Like "Jon*" Like "FILE????"
In	Determines whether a string value is a member of a list of values.	In("CA", "OR", "WA")
Between	Determines whether a numeric or date value lies within a specified range of values.	Between 1 **And** 5

You use the wildcard characters * and ? with the Like operator the same way that you use them in the Search tool or Command Window. The * (often called *star* or *splat*) takes the place of any number of characters. The ? takes the place of a single character. For example, Like "Jon*" returns **True** for values such as Jones or Jonathan. Like "*on*" returns **True** for any value that contains "on". Like "FILE????" returns **True** for FILENAME, but not for FILE000 or FILENUMBER. Wildcard characters can precede the characters that you want to match, as in Like "*son" or Like "????NAME".

Except for Is, the operators in this other category are equivalent to the SQL reserved words LIKE, IN, and BETWEEN. Access includes these operators to promote compatibility with SQL. You can create each of these operators by combining other VBA operators or functions. Like "Jon*" is the equivalent of VBA's **InStr(Left**(FieldName, 3), "Jon"); In("CA", "OR", "WA") is similar to InStr("CAORWA", FieldName), except that matches would occur for the ambiguous AO and RW combinations. Between 1 **And** 5 is the equivalent of >= 1 **And** <= 5.

 tip

T-SQL supports the IS, LIKE, IN, and BETWEEN logical operators, as described in Table 10.4. However, T-SQL uses the single quote (') as the string identifier, rather than Access's default double quote (").

Literals

VBA provides three types of literals that you can combine with operators to create expressions. The following list describes these types of literals:

- *Numeric* literals are typed as a series of digits, including the arithmetic sign and decimal point if applicable. You don't have to prefix positive numbers with the plus sign; Access assumes positive values unless the minus sign is present. Numeric literals can include E or e and the sign of the exponent to indicate an exponent in scientific notation—for example, -1.23E-02.

- *Text* (or *string*) literals can include any printable character, plus unprintable characters returned by the Chr function. The Chr function returns the characters specified by a numeric value from the ANSI character table (similar to the ASCII character table) that Windows uses. For example, Chr(9) returns the Tab character. Printable characters include the letters A through Z, numbers 0 through 9, punctuation symbols, and other special keyboard symbols such as the tilde (~). VBA expressions require that you enclose string literals within double quotation marks (""). Combinations of printable and unprintable characters are concatenated with &. For example, the following expression separates two strings with a newline pair:

```
"First line" & Chr(13) & Chr(10) & "Second line"
```

 tip

Always use Between...And, not the ⟶>= and ⟨⟶= comparison operators, to specify a range of dates. You must repeat the field name when using the comparison operators, as in DateValue ⟶>= #1/1/2006# And DateValue ⟨⟶= #12/31/2006#. The Between syntax is shorter and easier to understand, as demonstrated by DateValue Between #1/1/2006# And #12/31/2006#.

 tip

T-SQL numeric literals are identical to Access's, but, as mentioned earlier, string (character) literals are enclosed between single quotes ('string'). T-SQL doesn't have a Date/Time identifier; you must supply date values as quoted strings in one of the standard formats that T-SQL recognizes, such as '3/15/2007'.

Chr(13) is the carriage return (CR), and Chr(10) is the line-feed (LF) character; together they form the newline pair. VBA has a string constant, vbCrLf, which you can substitute for Chr(13) & Chr(10).

When you enter string literals in the cells of tables and Query Design grids, Access adds the quotation marks to literal strings for you. In other places, you must enter the quotation marks yourself.

- *Date/Time* VBA/Access literals are enclosed within number or pound signs (#), as in the expressions #1-Jan-1980# and #10:20:30#. If Access detects that you're typing a date or time in one of the standard Access Date/Time formats into a Design grid, it adds the enclosing pound signs for you. Otherwise, you must type the # signs.

Identifiers

An identifier usually is the name of an object; databases, tables, fields, queries, forms, and reports are objects in Access. Each object has a name that uniquely identifies that object. Sometimes, to identify a subobject, an identifier name consists of a family name (object class) separated from a given name (object name) by a bang symbol or a period (an identifier operator). The family name of the identifier comes first, followed by the separator and then the given name. SQL uses the period as an object separator. An example of an identifier in an SQL statement is the following:

Customers.Address

In this example, the identifier for the Address field object is contained in the Customers table object. Customers is the family name of the object (the table), and Address is the given name of the subobject (the field). In VBA, however, you use the . symbol to separate table names and field names. (The period separates objects and their properties.) If an identifier contains a space or other punctuation, enclose the identifier within square brackets, as in this example:

 tip

T-SQL uses the period to separate table and field names, but adds an **ownername** prefix (dbo for database owner, by default) to the table name, as in dbo. **Customers.Address**. SQL Server queries also enclose table names having spaces or other SQL-illegal punctuation with square brackets [ ], as in SELECT * FROM [Order Details].

[Order Details].Quantity

You can't include periods or exclamation points within the names of identifiers; [Unit.Price], for example, isn't allowed.

In simple queries that use only one table, you can omit the TableName. prefix. You use identifiers to return the values of fields in form and report objects. Chapters 14 through 18 cover the specific method of identifying objects within forms and reports.

Functions

Functions return values to their names; functions can take the place of identifiers in expressions. One of the most common functions used in VBA/Access expressions is **Now**, which returns to its name the date and time from your computer's system clock. If you type **Now** as the Default Value property of a table's Date/Time field, for example, 12/15/2006 9:00 appears in the field when you change to Datasheet view (at 9:00 a.m. on December 15, 2006).

VBA defines about 150 individual functions. The following list groups functions by purpose:

- *Date and time* functions manipulate date/time values in fields or Date/Time values that you enter as literals. You can extract parts of dates (such as the year or day of the month) and parts of times (such as hours and minutes) with date and time functions.

- *Text-manipulation* functions are used for working with strings of characters.

- *Data-type conversion* functions enable you to specify the data type of values in numeric fields instead of depending on Access to pick the most appropriate data type.

- *Mathematic and trigonometric* functions perform on numeric values operations that are beyond the capability of the standard Access arithmetic operators. You can use simple trigonometric functions, for example, to calculate the length of the sides of a right triangle (if you know the length of one side and the included angle).

- *Financial* functions are similar to functions provided by Lotus 1-2-3 and Microsoft Excel. They calculate depreciation, values of annuities, and rates of return on investments. To determine the present value of a lottery prize paid out in 25 equal yearly installments, for example, you can use the PV function.

- *General-purpose* functions don't fit any of the preceding classifications; you use these functions to create Access queries, forms, and reports.

- *Other* functions include Access domain aggregate functions, SQL aggregate functions, and functions used primarily in VBA programming.

Only the first three groups of functions and SQL aggregate functions commonly are used in Access queries; Chapters 30 through 33 offer examples of the use of some of the members of the last four function groups.

Using the Immediate Window

When you write VBA programming code in a module, the Immediate window is available to assist you in debugging your code. You also can use the module's Immediate window to demonstrate the use and syntax of functions.

To experiment with some of the functions described in the following sections, open the Northwind. accdb database and perform these steps:

1. Press Ctrl+G to open the VBA Editor and its Immediate window. (You don't need an open database to launch the VBA Editor.)

2. Type **? Now** in the Immediate window (see Figure 10.2) and press Enter. The date and time from your computer's clock appear on the next line. The **?** is shorthand for the VBA **Print** statement (which displays the value of a function or variable) and must be added to the **Now** function call to display the function's value.

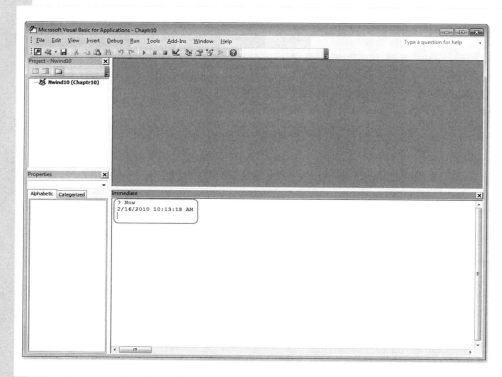

Figure 10.2
The VBA editor's Immediate window lets you quickly test the return values of VBA functions.

3. To reposition the Immediate window more easily, click its title bar and drag the window to a central area of your display where it remains undocked.

Getting Help as You Write Queries

As you type in your functions in the Immediate window, Access displays an Autocompletion ScreenTip, showing the function's name and its complete argument list. You must type a space or opening parenthesis after the function name to make the Autocompletion ScreenTip appear. An argument list is the list of information that you specify for the function to work on—for example, if you use the Sqr function to compute the square root of a number, you must supply a number inside the function's

 tip

If you neglected to precede the function entry with ? or Print, an error message appears, indicating that the VBA editor expected you to type a statement or an equal sign. Click OK and type ? before the function name in the Immediate window. Press End to return the cursor to the end of the line and then press Enter to retry the test.

parentheses. Figure 10.3 shows the ScreenTip for the Sqr function. You can turn this feature on and off by choosing Tools, Options and marking or clearing the Auto Quick Info option on the Editor page.

Figure 10.3
Typing a function in the Immediate window displays the VBA Autocompletion ScreenTip before you add required arguments for the function.

Figure 10.4
Positioning the cursor within the name of a function and pressing F1 opens the Microsoft Visual Basic Help window and displays the online help topic for the function.

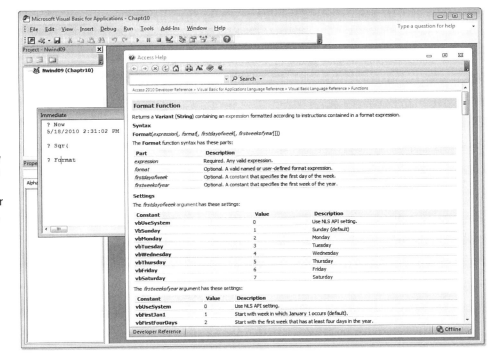

If you click an enabled Example link in any function Help window, the window displays an example of the function used in Access VBA code. Alternatively, scroll to find examples below the function definition. These examples show the syntax of the functions and appropriate arguments. The examples, however, usually aren't applicable to the function's use in an Access query or validation rule. Figure 10.5 illustrates VBA code examples for the VBA `Format` function, which commonly is used in queries.

The `Variant` Data Type in VBA

`Variant` is a special data type unique to Visual Basic dialects. The `Variant` data type enables you to concatenate values that ordinarily have different data types, such as an integer and a character string, which otherwise would result in an error. The capability to concatenate different data types is called *turning off datatype checking* or *evil type coercion (ETC)*. The `Variant` data type also lets you use operands with data of different types, such as adding `Integer` and `Double` values. Internally, Access handles all data in tables and queries as `Variant` data.

The `Variant` data type enables you to concatenate field values of tables and queries that have dissimilar data types without using VBA's data-type conversion functions, such as `Str`. (`Str` converts numeric values to the `String` data type.) The `Variant` data type simplifies expressions that combine field values to create concatenated indexes. The `Variant` data type also enables you to use the `&` symbol to concatenate values of different data types.

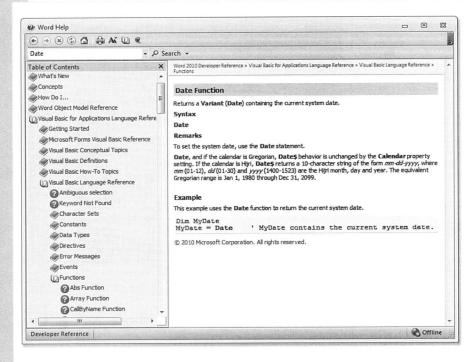

Figure 10.5
Most examples of VBA function syntax apply to writing VBA code, not formatting the columns of Access query resultsets.

Table 10.5 lists the 16 common subtypes of the **Variant** data type of VBA 6.0, along with the names of the intrinsic Visual Basic constants, vbConstant, corresponding to the **Variant** subtype value. In addition to the Access intrinsic constants, VBA provides its own set of intrinsic constants, which are prefixed with vb. Access intrinsic constants are prefixed with ac. Intrinsic constants, which you use primarily when writing VBA code, are one of the subjects of Chapter 32, "Understanding Universal Data Access, OLE DB, and ADO."

Table 10.5   Subtypes of the Variant Data Type

Subtype	Constant	Corresponds To	Stored As
0	(None)	Empty	Not applicable (uninitialized)
1	vbNull	Null	Not applicable (no valid data)
2	vbInteger	Integer	2-byte integer
3	vbLong	Long	4-byte long integer
4	vbSingle	Single	4-byte single-precision floating point
5	vbDouble	Double	8-byte double-precision floating point
6	vbCurrency	Currency	4-byte fixed point
7	vbDate	Date/Time	8-byte double-precision floating point
8	vbString	String	Conventional string variable
9	vbObject	Object	Automation object
10	vbError	**Error**	Error data type (error number)
11	**vbBoolean**	**Boolean**	True or False values only
12	**vbVariant**	**Variant**	Used with Variant arrays
13	vbDataObject	**Special**	Non-Automation object
17	vbByte	Byte	Numeric value from 0 255
8192	**vbArray**	**Array**	Used with Variant arrays

You can concatenate **Variant** values with **Variant** subtypes 1 through 8 listed in Table 10.5. You can concatenate a subtype 8 **Variant** (**String**) with a subtype 5 **Variant** (**Double**), for example, without receiving the Type Mismatch error message displayed when you attempt this concatenation with conventional **String** (text) and **Double** data types. Access returns a value with the **Variant** subtype corresponding to the highest subtype number of the concatenated values. This example, therefore, returns a subtype 8 (**String**) **Variant** because 8 is greater than 5, the subtype number for the **Double** value. If you concatenate a subtype 2 (**Integer**) value with a subtype 3 (**Long**) value, Access returns subtype 3 **Variant** data.

Distinguishing between the empty and **Null** subtypes of **Variant** is important. Empty indicates that a variable you created with VBA code has a name but doesn't have an initial value. Empty applies only to VBA variables (see Chapter 30, "Learning Visual Basic for Applications"). **Null** indicates that a data cell doesn't contain an entry. You can assign the **Null** value to a variable, in which case the variable is initialized to the **Null** value, **Variant** subtype 1.

The TempVars **Collection**

 Access 2007 added a new TempVars collection that lets you define temporary **Variant** text or numeric variables and set and retrieve the variable values with VBA code or macro actions. You set a TempVars member's value with a VBA expression such as TempVars("tvOne").Value = 3 or TempVars!tvTwo.Value = "CA". Alternatively, you can create and set the value of a TempVar member with the SetTempVar macro action.

You can use the value in a query expression, such as SELECT * FROM Customers WHERE Region = TempVars!tvTwo.Value. Chapter 19, "Automating Access Applications with Macros," and Chapter 30, "Learning Visual Basic for Applications," provide more information on the use of the TempVars collection.

> **🅦 tip**
>
> SQL Server 2005 supports the sql_variant data type, which can store any SQL Server data type except text (Memo), ntext (Unicode or national text), image (long binary), timestamp, and sql_variant data. Concatenation rules for sql_variant values differ from Access/VBA Variants. The sql_variant data type seldom is used.

Functions for Date and Time

Access offers a variety of functions for dealing with dates and times. If you've used Visual Basic, you probably recognize most of the functions applicable to the Date/Time field data types shown in Table 10.6. VBA has several Date/Time functions, such as **DateAdd** and **DateDiff**, to simplify the calculation of date values. **MonthName** and **WeekdayName** functions are new to VBA 6.0.

Table 10.6 Access Functions for Date and Time

Function	Description	Example	Returns
Date	Returns the current system date and time as a subtype 7 date **Variant** or a standard date **String** subtype 8.	**Date**	3/15/20100 3-15-2010
DateAdd	Returns a subtype 7 date with a specified number of days ("d"), weeks ("ww"), months ("m"), or years ("y") added to the date.	**DateAdd**("d",31, #3/15/2010#)	4/15/2010
DateDiff	Returns an **Integer** representing the difference between two dates using the d/w/m/y specification.	**DateDiff** ("d", Date, #3/15/2009#)	116 (assuming Date = 11/19/2009)

Function	Description	Example	Returns
DatePart	Returns the specified part of a date such as day, month, year, day of week ("w"), and so on, as an **Integer**.	**DatePart** ("w", #3/19/2010#)	6 (Friday)
DateSerial	Returns a subtype 7 **Variant** from year, month, and day arguments.	**DateSerial** (2010, 3,15)	3/15/2010
DateValue	Returns a subtype 7 **Variant** that corresponds to a date argument in a character format.	**DateValue** ("15-Mar-2010")	3/15/2010
Day	Returns an **Integer** between 1 and 31 (inclusive) that represents a day of the month from a Date/Time value.	**Day(Date)**	15 (assuming that the date is the 15th of the month)
Hour	Returns an **Integer** between 0 and 23 (inclusive) that represents the hour of the Date/Time value.	**Hour** (#2:30 PM#)	14
Minute	Returns an **Integer** between 0 and 59 (inclusive) that represents the minute of a Date/Time value.	**Minute** (#2:30 PM#)	30
Month	Returns an **Integer** between 1 and 12 (inclusive) that represents the month of a Date/Time value.	**Month** (#15-Jul-10#)	7
MonthName	Returns the full or abbreviated name of a month from the month number (1 to 12). If you omit the second argument, the function returns the full name.	**MonthName** (10, False) **MonthName** (10, True)	October Oct
Now	Returns the date and time of a computer's system clock as a **Variant** of subtype 7.	**Now**	3/15/2010 11:57:28 AM
Second	Returns an **Integer** between 0 and 59 (inclusive) that represents the second of a Date/Time value.	**Second(Now)**	28
Time	Returns the time portion of a Date/Time value from the system clock.	**Time**	11:57:20 AM

Table 10.6 Continued

Function	Description	Example	Returns
TimeSerial	Returns the time serial value of the time expressed in hours, minutes, and seconds.	**TimeSerial** (11, 57, 20)	11:57:20 AM
TimeValue	Returns the time serial value of the time (entered as the **String** value) as a subtype 7 **Variant**.	**TimeValue** ("11:57")	11:57
Weekday	Returns the day of the week (Sunday = 1) corresponding to the date as an **Integer**.	**Weekday** (#3/15/2010#)	2
Weekday Name	Returns the full or abbreviated name of the day from the day number (0 to 7). Setting the second argument to **True** abbreviates the name. A third optional argument lets you specify the first day of the week.	**WeekdayName** (4, False) **WeekdayName** (4, True)	Wednesday Wed
Year	Returns the year of a Date/Time value as an **Integer**.	**Year** (#3/15/2010#)	2010

Access/VBA Function	SQL Server Function
Date	CONVERT(datetime, CONVERT(varchar, GETDATE( ))
DateAdd( )	DATEADD( )
DateDiff( )	DATEDIFF( )
DatePart( )	DATEPART( )
Day( )	DATEPART(dd, date)
Hour( )	DATEPART(hh, time)
Minute( )	DATEPART(mi, time)
Now	GETDATE( )
Second( )	DATEPART(ss, time)
Weekday( )	DATEPART(dw, date)
Year( )	DATEPART(yy, date)

tip

When you use the Upsizing Wizard to convert a conventional Access application with an Access .accdb database to an Access data project with an SQL Server database, the wizard converts the following Access/VBA Date/Time functions to their T-SQL equivalents:

Text Manipulation Functions

Table 10.7 lists the functions that deal with the Text field data type, corresponding to the **String** VBA data type. Most of these functions are modeled on BASIC string functions.

tip

The Wizard doesn't convert Access/VBA functions that aren't included in the preceding list. You must manually correct conversion failures.

Table 10.7 Functions for the `String` Data Type

Function	Description	Example	Returns
Asc	Returns the ANSI numeric value of a character as an Integer	`Asc ("C")`	67
Chr	Returns a character corresponding to the numeric ANSI value as a String	`Chr (67)` `Chr (10)`	C (line feed)
Format	Formats an expression in accordance with appropriate format strings	`Format (Date, "dd-mmm-yyyy")`	15-Mar-2007
InStr	Returns the position of one string within another as a **Long**	`InStr ("ABCD", "C")`	3
InStrRev	Returns the position of one string within another as a **Long**, starting at the end of the string but counting from the start of the string	`InStrRev ("ABCD", "C")`	3
Join	Generates a String from a one-dimension array consisting of strings (spaces separate the array strings)	`Join (astrArray)`	Depends on the array's contents
LCase	Returns the lowercase version of a string	`LCase ("ABCD")`	abcd
Left	Returns the leftmost characters of a string	`Left ("ABCDEF", 3)`	ABC
Len	Returns the number of characters in a string as a Long	`Len ("ABCDE")`	5
LTrim	Removes leading spaces from a string	`LTrim (" ABC")`	ABC
Mid	Returns a part of a string, beginning at the character position specified by the second argument	`Mid("ABCDE", 2, 3)`	BCD
?PlainText	Strips HTML formatting tags from Memo fields with Rich Text as the Text Format property value	`PlainText("<b>Hello</b>")`	Hello

Table 10.7 Continued

Function	Description	Example	Returns
Replace	Replaces occurrences of a specified substring in a string	Replace("ABCDE", "BC", "YZ")	AYZDE
Right	Returns the rightmost characters of a string	Right("ABCDEF", 3)	DEF
RTrim	Removes trailing spaces from a string	RTrim("ABC ")	ABC
Space	Returns a string consisting of a specified number of spaces	Space(5)	
Split	Returns an array of substrings based on a separator character (the default is a space)	Split("ABC DEF")	(0)ABC(1)DEF
Str	Converts the numeric value of any data type to a string	Str(123.45)	123.45
StrComp	Compares two strings for equivalence and returns the integer result of the comparison	StrComp("ABC", "abc")	0
String	Returns a string consisting of specified repeated characters	String(5, "A")	AAAAA
StrReverse	Returns a string whose characters are reversed	StrReverse("ABCDE")	EDCBA
Trim	Removes leading and trailing spaces from a string	Trim(" ABC ")	ABC
UCase	Returns the uppercase version of a string	UCase("abc")	ABC
Val	Returns the numeric value of a string in a data type appropriate to the argument's format	Val("123.45")	123.45

Access/VBA Function	SQL Server Function
Asc( )	ASCII( )
Chr( )	CHAR( )
LCase( )	LOWER( )
Len( )	DATALENGTH( )
LTrim( )	LTRIM( )

Mid( )	SUBSTRING( )
Right( )	RIGHT( )
RTrim( )	RTRIM( )
Space( )	SPACE( )
Str( )	STR( )
UCase( )	UCASE( )

Figure 10.6 shows Immediate window examples of common string manipulation functions. The Immediate window is particularly valuable for learning exactly how these functions behave with different types of literal values.

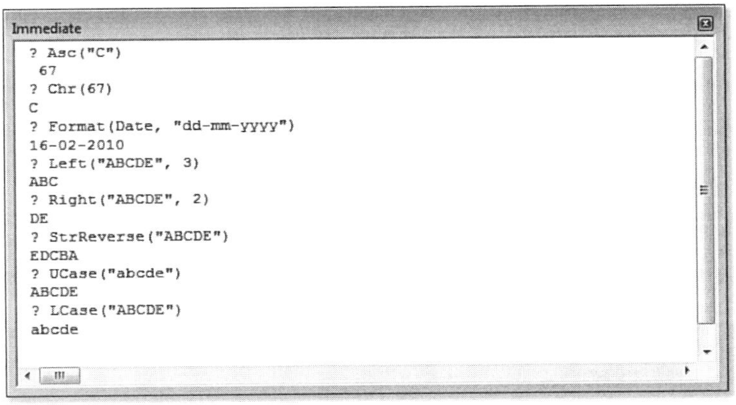

Figure 10.6
Use the Immediate window to verify the syntax of the VBA functions you plan to include in Access queries or validation rules.

```
Immediate
? Asc("C")
 67
? Chr(67)
C
? Format(Date, "dd-mm-yyyy")
16-02-2010
? Left("ABCDE", 3)
ABC
? Right("ABCDE", 2)
DE
? StrReverse("ABCDE")
EDCBA
? UCase("abcde")
ABCDE
? LCase("ABCDE")
abcde
```

You can use the localized **Format...** functions of VBA 6.0 in Access queries, if you provide numeric values for the functions' arguments. For example, you must substitute the numeric values shown for the vb... constants of the **FormatDateTime** function. Following is the syntax for the **Format...** functions:

tip

The Upsizing Wizard converts the following Access/VBA text manipulation functions to their T-SQL equivalents:

Functions included in Table 10.7 but not in this list cause conversion errors. T-SQL doesn't support the Access/VBA Format and Format... functions.

- **FormatCurrency***(NumericValue[, DigitsAfterDecimal [, IncludeLeadingDigit [, ParensForNegativeNumbers [, GroupDigits]]]])* returns a value formatted with the localized currency symbol, including the Euro. With the exception of *NumericValue*, the arguments are optional. If *IncludeLeadingDigit* is **True**, fractional values are prefixed with $0 in North America. Setting *GroupDigits* to **True** applies the group delimiter, which is a comma (as in $1,000) for North America.

- **FormatDateTime**(DateValue [, NamedFormat]) returns a date string whose format depends on the value of NamedFormat. Valid values of NamedFormat are vbGeneralDate (0), vbLong-Date (1), vbShortDate (2), vbLongTime (3), and vbShortTime (4). Figure 10.7 illustrates the use of the **FormatDateTime** and other **Format...** functions.

- FormatNumber(*NumericValue[,DigitsAfterDecimal [,IncludeLeadingDigit [,ParensForNegativeNumbers [,GroupDigits]]]]*) returns the same values as **FormatCurrency**, but without the currency symbol.

- **FormatPercent**(*NumericValue[, DigitsAfterDecimal [,IncludeLeadingDigit [,ParensForNegativeNumbers [,GroupDigits]]]]*) returns the same values as **FormatNumber**, but multiplies *NumericValue* by 100 and adds a trailing % symbol.

Numeric, Logical, Date/Time, and String Data-Type Conversion Functions

You can assign a particular data type to a numeric value with any of the data-type conversion functions. After you freeze (or coerce) a data type with one of the numeric data-type conversion functions, you cannot concatenate that data type with the **String** data type.

Table 10.8 lists VBA's 11 numeric data-type conversion functions. The NumValue argument in the Syntax column can be any numeric or **String** value. However, if you use a String value as the argument of a numeric-type conversion function, the first character of the argument's value must be a digit, a dollar sign, a plus symbol, or a minus symbol. The most commonly used conversion function in queries is **CCur**.

Table 10.8 Data-Type Conversion Functions for Numeric, Time/Date, and String Values

Function	Syntax	Description
CBool	**CBool**(*NumValue*)	Converts a numeric value to the Boolean (True or False) data type
CByte	**CByte** (*NumValue*)	Converts a numeric value to the Byte (0 255) data type
CCur	**CCur**(*NumValue*)	Converts a numeric value to the Currency data type
CDate	**CDate**(*NumValue*)	Converts a numeric value to a Date value (CDate replaces CVDate, which is obsolete)
CDbl	**CDbl**(*NumValue*)	Converts a numeric value to the Double data type

Function	Syntax	Description
CInt	**CInt**(*NumValue*)	Converts a numeric value to the Integer data type
CLng	**CLng**(*NumValue*)	Converts a numeric value to the Long integer data type
CSng	**CSng**(*NumValue*)	Converts a numeric value to the Single data type
CStr	**CStr**(*varValue*)	Converts a Variant value to the String data type
CVar	**CVar**(*NumValue*)	Converts a numeric value to a Variant data type
CVErr	**CVErr**(*NumValue*)	Converts a valid error number to create user-defined errors
Nz	Nz(varFieldVa lue[,ReturnVa lue]	Converts a Null value to 0 or a zero-length string, depending on the context of use

Access/VBA Function	SQL Server Function
CCur(NumValue)	CONVERT(money, NumValue)
CDbl(NumValue)	CONVERT(float, NumValue)
CInt(NumValue)	CONVERT(smallint, NumValue)
CLng(NumValue)	CONVERT(int, NumValue)
CSng(NumValue)	CONVERT(real, NumValue)
CStr(NumValue)	CONVERT(varchar, NumValue)
CDate(NumValue)	CONVERT(datetime, NumValue)
CVDate(NumValue)	CONVERT(datetime, NumValue)

The Nz (Null-to-zero) function accepts only a **Variant** *varFieldValue* argument. Nz returns non-**Null Variant** argument values unchanged. When used in an Access query, Nz returns an empty string (" ") for **Null** argument values, unless you specify 0 or another literal, such as "Null" as the value of the optional ReturnValue argument. The Access expression service supplies the Nz function; it's not a VBA reserved word, so it doesn't appear in bold type.

Intrinsic and Named Constants

As noted earlier in this chapter, VBA and Access have many predefined intrinsic constants. The names of these constants are considered keywords because you cannot use these names for any purpose other than returning the value represented by the names, such as - 1 for **True** and Yes, and 0 for **False** and No. (True and Yes are Access synonyms, as are False and No, so you can use these pairs of values interchangeably in Access, but not in VBA.) As noted throughout the chapter, **Null** indicates a field without a valid entry. **True**, **False**, and **Null** are the most commonly used VBA intrinsic constants.

 tip

The Upsizing Wizard converts the following Access/VBA data-type conversion functions to their T-SQL equivalents:

Functions included in Table 10.8 but not in this list cause conversion errors.

Symbolic constants, which you define, return a single, predetermined value for the entire Access session. You can create named constants for use with forms and reports by defining them in the declarations section of an Access VBA module. Chapter 30 describes how to create and use symbolic (named) constants.

 To find the constants that are built into Access, **see** *"Symbolic Constants,"* **p. 1257.**

Creating Access Expressions

Chapter 6 uses several functions to validate data entry for most fields in the HRActions table. Chapter 9 uses an expression to select the country and states to be included in a mailing-list query. These examples provide the foundation on which to build more complex expressions that define more precisely the validation rules and query criteria for real-world database applications.

 To review examples using functions to restrict data entry values, **see** *"Validating Data Entry,"* **p. 254.**

 For information on how to enter expressions in a query, **see** *"Selecting Records by Criteria and Sorting the Display,"* **p. 360.**

 tip

Use Nz to format the result sets of your crosstab queries, replacing Null values with 0. (Crosstab queries are one of the subjects of Chapter 11, "Creating Multitable and Crosstab Queries.") When you execute a crosstab query—such as quarterly product sales by region—cells for products with no sales in a region for the quarter are empty. Empty cells might mislead management into believing information is missing. Applying the Nz function puts a 0 in empty cells, which eliminates the ambiguity.

The sections that follow provide a few examples of typical expressions for creating default values for fields, validating data entry, creating query criteria, and calculating field values. The examples demonstrate the similarity of syntax for expressions with different purposes. Part IV of this book, "Designing Forms and Reports," provides additional examples of expressions designed for use in forms and reports; Part 7, "Programming and Converting Access Applications," explains the use of expressions with Access VBA code.

Expressions for Creating Default Values

Expressions that create default field values can speed the entry of new records. Assigning values ordinarily requires you to use the assignment operator (=). When entering a default value in the Properties pane for a table in design mode, however, you can enter a simple literal. An example is the Q default value assigned to the ActionType field of the HRActions table in Chapter 5, "Working with Access Databases and Tables." In this case, Access infers the = assignment operator and the quotation marks surrounding the Q. You often can use shorthand techniques when typing expressions because Access infers the missing characters. If you type **= "Q"**, you achieve the same result.

You can use complex expressions for default values if the result of the expression conforms to or can be converted by Access to the proper field data type. You can type **= 1** as the default value for the ActionType field, for example, although 1 is a numeric

 tip

The Upsizing Wizard converts Access default values to SQL Server default values, if the expression for the default value contains functions that have T-SQL equivalents.

value and ActionType has the Text data type. The **Variant** data type used for all Access data operations permits this action.

 To review using the assignment operator to assign a default value, **see** *"Setting Default Values of Fields,"* **p. 213.**

Expressions for Validating Data

 tip

The Upsizing Wizard converts Access default values to SQL Server default values, if the expression for the default value contains functions that have T-SQL equivalents.

The HRActions table uses several expressions to validate data entry. The validation rule for the EmployeeID field is > 0; the rule for the ApprovedBy field is > 0 **Or** Is **Null**. The validation rule for the EmployeeID field is equivalent to the following imaginary inline VBA IIf function:

```
IIf(DataEntry > 0, EmployeeID = DataEntry,
    MsgBox("Please enter a valid employee ID number."))
```

 tip

T-SQL uses 1 for TRUE and 0 for FALSE. Conversion between -1 for True and 1 for TRUE succeeds because True accepts any non-zero number as Not False. The Upsizing Wizard converts Access Boolean fields to the SQL Server **bit** data type.

Access tests DataEntry in the validation rule expression. If the validation expression returns **True**, the value of DataEntry replaces the value in the current record's field. If the expression returns **False**, a message box displays the validation text that you added. **MsgBox** is a function used in VBA programming to display a message box onscreen. You can't type the imaginary validation rule just described as a property value; Access infers the equivalent of the imaginary **IIf** expression after you add the Validation Rule and Validation Text property values with entries in the two text boxes for the EmployeeID field.

You might want to change the validation expression "H" **Or** "Q" **Or** "Y" **Or** "S" **Or** "R" **Or** "B" **Or** "C" **Or** "T", which you use to test the ActionType field, to a function. The Access In function provides a simpler expression that accomplishes the same objective:

```
In("H", "Q", "Y", "S", "R", "B", "C", "T")
```

Alternatively, you can use the following table-level VBA validation expression:

```
InStr("HQYSRBCT",[ActionType]) > 0
```

Instr returns the position of the second argument's character(s) within the first argument's characters. If ActionType is Q, the preceding example returns 2. Both **In** and **Instr** expressions give the same result, but you can use **InStr** only for table-level validation because one of its arguments refers to a field name. Therefore, the In function provides the better solution.

Expressions for Query Criteria

When creating Chapter 9's qryStateMailList query to select records from the states of California, Oregon, and Washington, you type **CA**, **OR**, and **WA** on separate lines; Access adds the equal sign and double quotes around the literals for you. A better expression is In ("CA", "OR", "WA"), entered on the same line as the ="USA" criterion for the Country field. This expression corrects the query's failure to test the Country field for a value equal to USA for the OR and WA entries.

➡ *If you're not sure how multiple criteria should look in the grid,* **see** *"Creating More Complex Criteria,"* **p. 364.**

You can use a wide range of other functions to select specific records to be returned to a query table. Table 10.9 shows some typical functions used as query criteria applicable to the Northwind Traders tables. (Table 10.9 uses 2006 as the year value, because 2006 has a full calendar year of data in the Northwind.accdb tables.)

Table 10.9 Typical Expressions Used as Query Criteria

Field	Expression	Records Returned
Customers Table		
Country	**Not** "USA" **And Not** "Canada"	Firms other than those in the United States and Canada.
Country	**Not** ("USA" **Or** "Canada")	Firms other than those in the United States and Canada; the parentheses apply the condition to both literals.
CompanyName	Like "[N-S]*"	Firms with names beginning with N through S.
CompanyName	Like S* **Or** Like V*	Firms with names beginning with S or V (Access adds quotation marks for you).
CompanyName	Like "*shop*"	Firms with shop, Shop, Shoppe, or SHOPPING in the firm name.
PostalCode	>=90000	Firms with postal codes greater than or equal to 90000, including codes that begin with alphabetic characters.
Orders Table		
OrderDate	**Year**([OrderDate]) = 2006	Orders received in 2006.
OrderDate	Like "*/*/2006"	Orders received in 2006; using wildcards simplifies expressions.
OrderDate	Like "1/*/2006"	Orders received in the month of January 2006.
OrderDate	Like "1/?/2006"	Orders received from the 1st to the 9th of January 2006.
OrderDate 2006	**Year**([OrderDate]) = 2006 **And** **DatePart**("q", [OrderDate]) = 1	Orders received in the first quarter of 2006.

Field	Expression	Records Returned
OrderDate	Between #1/1/2006# **And** #3/31/2006#	Orders received in the first quarter of 2006. 2006
OrderDate	**Year**([OrderDate]) = 2006 **And** **DatePart**("ww", [OrderDate])= 10	Orders received in the 10th 2006. 2006
OrderDate	>= **DateValue** ("1/15/2006")	Orders received on or after 1/15/2006.
ShippedDate	Is **Null**	Orders not yet shipped.
Order Subtotals Query		
Subtotal	>= 5000	Orders with values greater than or equal to $5,000.
Subtotal	Between 5000 **And** 10000	Orders with values greater than or equal to $5,000 and less than or equal to $10,000.
Subtotal	< 1000	Orders less than $1,000.

The wildcard characters used in Like expressions simplify the creation of criteria for selecting names and dates. As in the Windows Search dialog, the asterisk (*) substitutes for any legal number of characters, and the question mark (?) substitutes for a single character. When a wildcard character prefixes or appends a string, the matching process loses case sensitivity, if case sensitivity is specified.

If you want to match a string without regard to case, use the following expression:

`UCase`(FieldName) = `"FIELDNAME"`

 note

The Order Details table, which has Quantity, UnitPrice, and Discount fields, is required to calculate the total amount of each order.

Entering a Query Criterion and Adding a Calculated Field

To experiment with query criteria expressions with tables from the Northwind.accdb sample database and add a calculated field value, follow these steps:

1. Click the Create tab, and click the Query Design button to open the Query Design window and the Add Tables dialog.

2. Double-click the Customers, Orders, and Order Details tables in the Tables list of the Show Table dialog, and then click Close, which activates the Query Tools, Design ribbon. The CustomerID fields of the Customers and Orders tables and the OrderID fields of the Orders and Order Details tables are joined; joins are indicated by a line between the fields of the two tables. (Chapter 11, "Creating Multitable and Crosstab Queries," covers joining multiple tables.)

3. Add the CompanyName, PostalCode, and Country fields of the Customers table to the query. You can add fields by selecting them from the Field drop-down list in the Query Design grid, by

clicking a field in the Customers field list above the grid and dragging the field to the desired Field cell in the grid, or by double-clicking a field in the Customers field list above the grid.

4. Add to the query the OrderID, ShippedDate, and Freight fields of the Orders table. Use the horizontal scrollbar slider under the Query Design grid to expose additional field columns as necessary. Place the cursor in the Sort row of the OrderID field, open the Sort list box, and select Ascending Sort. Type an **Is Not Null** criterion for the ShippedDate column to return only orders that have shipped.

5. Click the ribbon's Totals button to add the Total row to the Query Design grid. The default value, Group By, is added to the Total cell for each field of your query. The Query Design view appears, as shown in Figure 10.8.

 note

The query requires Group By because the Order Details table has multiple rows for most orders. If you don't specify Totals, the query returns a row for each Order Details record.

 note

As mentioned earlier in the chapter, T-SQL substitutes % for * and _ (underscore) for ?. Both % and _ comply with ANSI SQL-92.

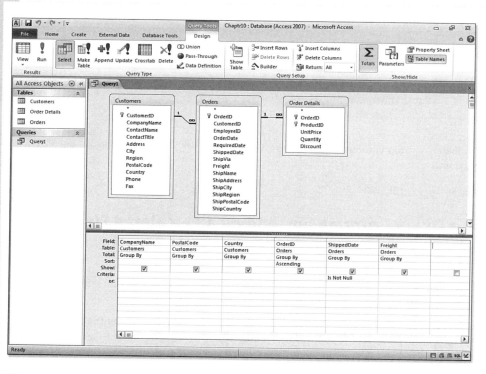

Figure 10.8
This multi-table summary query has one-to-many joins between the Customer and Orders tables, and the Orders and Order Details tables.

6. Click the Query Tools, Design ribbon's Run button to test the result of the interim query design, which returns 809 rows (see Figure 10.9).

Figure 10.9
Datasheet
view of the
interim query
design of
Figure 10.8
verifies
that only
one record
appears for
each order
because of
the addition of
the Group By
expression in
the Total row.

Company Name	Postal Code	Country	Order	Shipped Date	Freight
Wilman Kala	21240	Finland	10248	7/16/2005	$32.38
Tradição Hipermercados	05634-030	Brazil	10249	7/10/2005	$11.61
Hanari Carnes	05454-876	Brazil	10250	7/12/2005	$65.83
Victuailles en stock	69004	France	10251	7/15/2005	$41.34
Suprêmes délices	B-6000	Belgium	10252	7/11/2005	$51.30
Hanari Carnes	05454-876	Brazil	10253	7/16/2005	$58.17
Chop-suey Chinese	3012	Switzerland	10254	7/23/2005	$22.98
Richter Supermarkt	1203	Switzerland	10255	7/15/2005	$148.33
Wellington Importadora	08737-363	Brazil	10256	7/17/2005	$13.97
HILARIÓN-Abastos	5022	Venezuela	10257	7/22/2005	$81.91
Ernst Handel	8010	Austria	10258	7/23/2005	$140.51
Centro comercial Moctezuma	05022	Mexico	10259	7/25/2005	$3.25
Old World Delicatessen	99508	USA	10260	7/29/2005	$55.09
Que Delicia	02389-673	Brazil	10261	7/30/2005	$3.05
Rattlesnake Canyon Grocery	87110	USA	10262	7/25/2005	$48.29
Ernst Handel	8010	Austria	10263	7/31/2005	$146.06
Folk och fä HB	S-844 67	Sweden	10264	8/23/2005	$3.67
Blondel père et fils	67000	France	10265	8/12/2005	$55.28
Wartian Herkku	90110	Finland	10266	7/31/2005	$25.73
Frankenversand	80805	Germany	10267	8/6/2005	$208.58
GROSELLA-Restaurante	1081	Venezuela	10268	8/2/2005	$66.29
White Clover Markets	98128	USA	10269	8/9/2005	$4.56
Wartian Herkku	90110	Finland	10270	8/2/2005	$136.54
Split Rail Beer & Ale	82520	USA	10271	8/30/2005	$4.54
Rattlesnake Canyon Grocery	87110	USA	10272	8/6/2005	$98.03
QUICK-Stop	01307	Germany	10273	8/12/2005	$76.07
Vins et alcools Chevalier	51100	France	10274	8/16/2005	$6.01

Record: 14 ‹ 1 of 809 ▸ ▸I ▸ No Filter Search

7. Return to Design view by clicking the View button, and scroll the grid so that the Freight column appears. Click the selection bar above the Field row to select the Freight column, and press the Insert key to add a new column.

8. Type **Amount: CCur([UnitPrice]*[Quantity]*(1–[Discount])/100)*100** in the new column's Field cell. This expression calculates the net amount of each line item in the Order Details table, formats the column as if the field data type were Currency, and rounds the amount to the nearest cent. The next section discusses how to use expressions to create calculated columns.

9. Move the cursor to the Total row of the new column and open the drop-down list. Select Sum from the list (see Figure 10.10). The Sum option totals the net amount for all line items of each order in the Orders table. In the next chapter, you learn the details of how to create queries that group data.

 For other ways you can manipulate results from queries, **see** *"Making Calculations on Multiple Records,"* **p. 475.**

10. Click the Query Tools, Design ribbon's Run button to run your new query. Your query appears as shown in Figure 10.11. The Amount column contains the total amount of each order, which is net of any discounts.

note

The Total row for all other columns of the query shows Group By. Make sure that you mark the Show check box so that your new query column appears when you run the query.

Don't make an entry in the Table row of your new calculated query column; if you do, you receive an error message when you run the query.

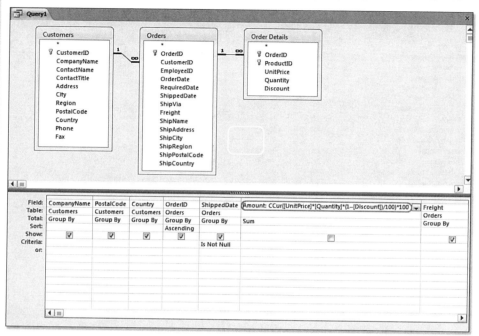

Figure 10.10
The calculated Amount column supplies the total net amount of the line items of the Order Details records for each order.

Figure 10.11
Datasheet view confirms that the Amount column totals the net amount of each line item for an order.

Company Name	Postal Code	Country	Order	Shipped Date	Amount	Freight
Wilman Kala	21240	Finland	10248	7/16/2005	$440.00	$32.38
Tradição Hipermercados	05634-030	Brazil	10249	7/10/2005	$1,863.40	$11.61
Hanari Carnes	05454-876	Brazil	10250	7/12/2005	$1,552.60	$65.83
Victuailles en stock	69004	France	10251	7/15/2005	$654.06	$41.34
Suprêmes délices	B-6000	Belgium	10252	7/11/2005	$3,597.90	$51.30
Hanari Carnes	05454-876	Brazil	10253	7/16/2005	$1,444.80	$58.17
Chop-suey Chinese	3012	Switzerland	10254	7/23/2005	$556.62	$22.98
Richter Supermarkt	1203	Switzerland	10255	7/15/2005	$2,490.50	$148.33
Wellington Importadora	08737-363	Brazil	10256	7/17/2005	$517.80	$13.97
HILARIÓN-Abastos	5022	Venezuela	10257	7/22/2005	$1,119.90	$81.91
Ernst Handel	8010	Austria	10258	7/23/2005	$1,614.88	$140.51
Centro comercial Moctezuma	05022	Mexico	10259	7/25/2005	$100.80	$3.25
Old World Delicatessen	99508	USA	10260	7/29/2005	$1,504.65	$55.09
Que Delícia	02389-673	Brazil	10261	7/30/2005	$448.00	$3.05
Rattlesnake Canyon Grocery	87110	USA	10262	7/25/2005	$584.00	$48.29
Ernst Handel	8010	Austria	10263	7/31/2005	$1,873.80	$146.06
Folk och fä HB	S-844 67	Sweden	10264	8/23/2005	$695.62	$3.67
Blondel père et fils	67000	France	10265	8/12/2005	$1,176.00	$55.28
Wartian Herkku	90110	Finland	10266	7/31/2005	$346.56	$25.73
Frankenversand	80805	Germany	10267	8/6/2005	$3,536.60	$208.58
GROSELLA-Restaurante	1081	Venezuela	10268	8/2/2005	$1,101.20	$66.29
White Clover Markets	98128	USA	10269	8/9/2005	$642.20	$4.56
Wartian Herkku	90110	Finland	10270	8/2/2005	$1,376.00	$136.54
Split Rail Beer & Ale	82520	USA	10271	8/30/2005	$48.00	$4.54
Rattlesnake Canyon Grocery	87110	USA	10272	8/6/2005	$1,456.00	$98.03
QUICK-Stop	01307	Germany	10273	8/12/2005	$2,037.28	$76.07
Vins et alcools Chevalier	51100	France	10274	8/16/2005	$538.60	$6.01

Record: 1 of 809 | No Filter | Search

Using the Expression Builder to Add Query Criteria

After creating and testing your query, you can apply criteria to limit the number of records that the query returns. You can use Access's Expression Builder to simplify the process of adding record-selection criteria to your query. To test some of the expressions listed in Table 10.9, follow these steps:

1. Click the Design View button to change to Query Design mode.

2. Place the cursor in the Criteria row of the field for which you want to establish a record-selection criterion.

3. Click the Query Setup group's Build button to display the Expression Builder's window. Alternatively, you can right-click the Criteria row and then choose Build from the context menu.

4. In the Expression text box at the top of Expression Builder's window, type one of the expressions from Table 10.9. Figure 10.12 shows the sample expression `Like "*shop*"` that applies to the Criteria row of the Company Name column. You can use the Like button under the expression text box as a shortcut for entering `Like`.

5. Click OK to return to the Query Design grid. The Expression Builder places the expression that you built in the field where the cursor is located (see Figure 10.13).

Access SQL

The Access SQL statement for the qryInvoiceAmount query is

```
SELECT Customers.CompanyName, Customers.PostalCode,
    Customers.Country, Orders.OrderID, Orders.ShippedDate,
    Sum(CCur([UnitPrice]*[Quantity]*(1-[Discount])/100)*100) AS Amount,
    Orders.Freight
FROM (Customers
    INNER JOIN Orders
        ON Customers.CustomerID = Orders.CustomerID)
    INNER JOIN [Order Details]
        ON Orders.OrderID = [Order Details].OrderID
GROUP BY Customers.CompanyName, Customers.PostalCode, Customers.Country,
    Orders.OrderID, Orders. ShippedDate, Orders.Freight
    HAVING (((Customers.CompanyName) Like "*shop*") AND
        ((Orders.ShippedDate) Is Not Null))
ORDER BY Orders.OrderID;
```

The Sum(CCur([UnitPrice]*[Quantity]*(1-[Discount])/100)*100) AS Amount expression combines the Sum aggregate operation you specified (refer to Figure 10.10) with the expression you typed to define the calculated Amount column.

Each INNER JOIN...ON clause defines the joins between two tables; JOIN clauses are discussed in the next chapter.

You might think that the GROUP BY clause includes more fields than required and only the Orders.OrderID field is required for grouping. One of the Total aggregate functions must appear in each column of a grouped query.

The HAVING clause for grouped rows is the equivalent of the WHERE clause for individual rows.

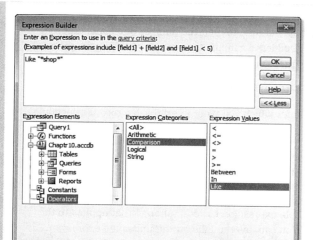

Figure 10.12
You can use the Expression Builder to add simple or complex expressions as WHERE clause criteria.

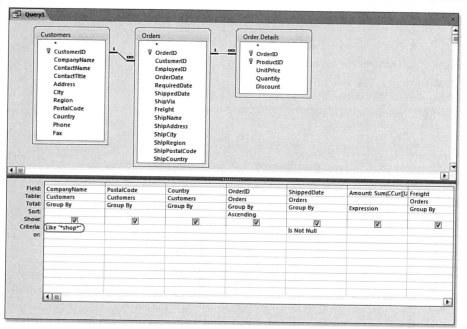

Figure 10.13
The expression you create in the Expression Builder applies to the field you selected when opening the Builder.

6. Click the Run button on the ribbon to test the expression. The query result for the example in Figure 10.13 appears as shown in Figure 10.14.

7. Return to Query Design mode; then select and delete the added expression by pressing the Delete key.

8. Repeat steps 2 through 7 for each expression that you want to test. When you test expressions using Date/Time functions, sort the OrderDate field in ascending order. Similarly, sort on the Amount field when queries are based on amount criteria. You can alter the expressions and try combinations with the implied **And** condition by entering criteria for other fields in the same row. Access warns you with an error message if you make a mistake in an expression's syntax.

9. After you finish experimenting, save your query with a descriptive name, such as qryInvoiceAmount.

The preceding query and its underlying tables are included in the Chaptr10.accdb sample file, located in the \Access2010\Chaptr10 folder of the downloadable sample files.

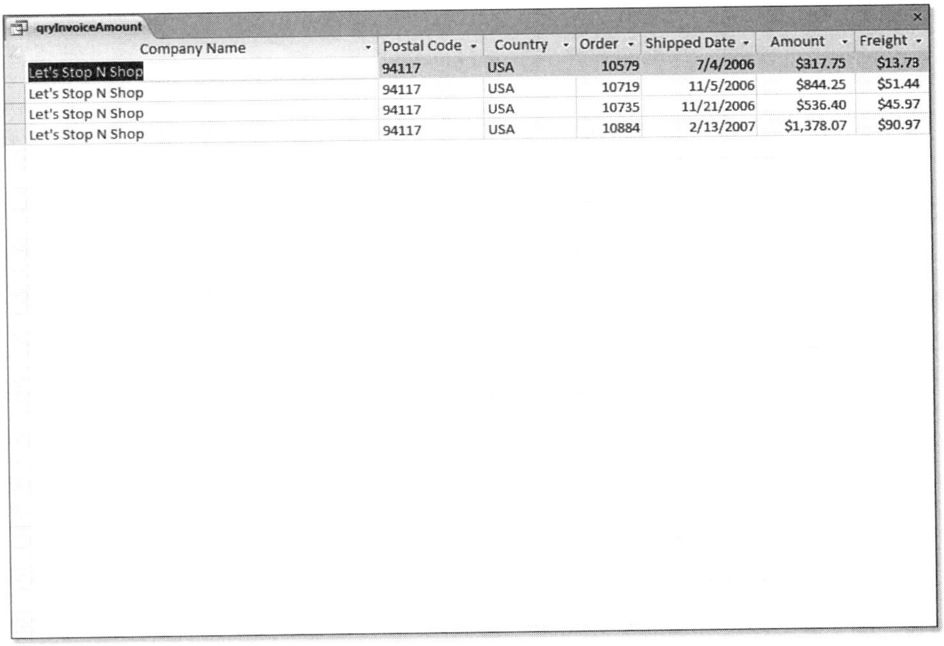

Figure 10.14
The Like "*shop*" expression displays records only for customers whose names contain "shop", "Shop", or "SHOP".

Company Name	Postal Code	Country	Order	Shipped Date	Amount	Freight
Let's Stop N Shop	94117	USA	10579	7/4/2006	$317.75	$13.73
Let's Stop N Shop	94117	USA	10719	11/5/2006	$844.25	$51.44
Let's Stop N Shop	94117	USA	10735	11/21/2006	$536.40	$45.97
Let's Stop N Shop	94117	USA	10884	2/13/2007	$1,378.07	$90.97

qryInvoiceAmount

Aggregate Queries Throw Errors

When you receive a "You tried to execute a query that does not include the specified expression 'ExpressionName' as part of an aggregate function" message when you attempt to run an aggregate query, an aggregate function is missing from the Totals row of one of the columns. You must select Group By, Expression, or an aggregate function—such as Sum, Avg, Min, Max, or Where—for each column of your query. For T-SQL Queries, the da Vinci toolset's "ADO Error: Column 'dbo.TableName. ColumnName' is invalid in the select list because it is not contained in either an aggregate function or the GROUP BY clause" error message is more explicit.

The SQL Server Version of a Query

If you've installed SQL Server 2008 [R2] Express to support ADP, you can run the Upsizing Wizard on the Chaptr10.accdb database to create the SQL Server version of the tables and qryOrderAmount query. Chapter 28, "Upsizing Access Applications to Access Data Projects," provides detailed examples of the upsizing process.

 For instructions on how to install SQL Server 2008 R2 Express from the Microsoft website, **see** *"SQL Server 2008 [R2] Express Edition,"* **p. 35.**

The Chaptr10.accdb database \Access2010\Chaptr10 folder contains the Customers, Orders, and Order Details tables and the qryInvoiceAmount query that you created in the preceding section. To upsize the Chaptr10.accdb database to an SQL Server Chaptr10SQL database and a Chaptr10CS.adp project, do this:

1. Open the Chaptr10.accdb file, if necessary, remove the Like "*shop*" criterion from the qryInvoiceAmount query's CompanyName field, press Ctrl+S to save your changes, and close all open objects.

2. Click the Database Tools tab, and click the Move Data group's SQL Server button to start the upsizing process.

3. Accept the default Create New Database option in the first wizard dialog. Click Next.

4. In the second dialog, accept (local) as the server name, add **\SQLEXPRESS** and mark the Use Trusted Connection to use your Administrator logon account with Windows authentication for SQL Express (see Figure 10.15). Click Next.

5. In the third dialog, click the >> button to add all three tables to the SQL Server database. Click Next.

Figure 10.15
Create a connection to your local instance of SQL Server Express 2008 R2 with the Upsizing Wizard.

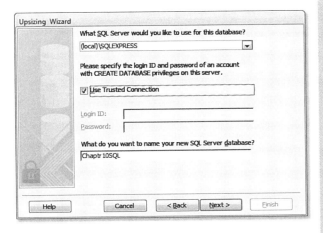

6. In the fourth dialog, mart the Indexes, Validation Rules, Defaults, and Table Relationships check boxes, accept the Use DRI (Declarative Referential Integrity) option and No, Never Add Timestamp Fields to Tables (see Figure 10.16). Click Next.

7. In the fifth dialog, select the Create a New Access Client/Server Project and accept the default project name (usually C:\Users\Administrator\Documents\Access2010\Chaptr10\Chaptr10CS. adp) and mark the Save Password and UserID check box. Click Next and acknowledge the warning about your password being saved in clear text to a file.

8. In the sixth and last dialog, accept the default Open the New ADP File option and click Finish to upsize the database.

9. After a minute or so, depending on the speed of your computer, the Chaptr10CS.adp project opens and displays a seven-page Upsizing Wizard report. Page seven shows the T-SQL statement that the wizard generated from the Access SQL statement (see Figure 10.17).

10. Close the report and, in the Navigation Pane, double-click the qryInvoiceAmount query, which the wizard upsizes to an SQL Express (user defined) function. The Datasheet view of the query is identical to that of the Access version of the query (refer to Figure 10.11).

11. Click the Design button to open the da Vinci Filter Design window. The three tables and the joins between them appear in the upper pane. Field definitions, including the calculated Amount field definition, appear in the lower pane.

 note

The SQL statement is similar to that of the Access query, but substitutes CONVERT(money —) for Access's CCur function. The TOP 100 PERCENT prefix is required to permit an ORDER BY clause in a view or function. The dbo. prefix identifies the default database owner.

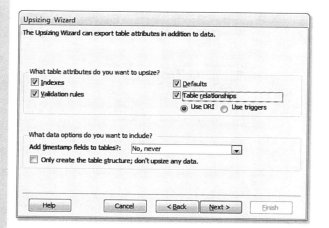

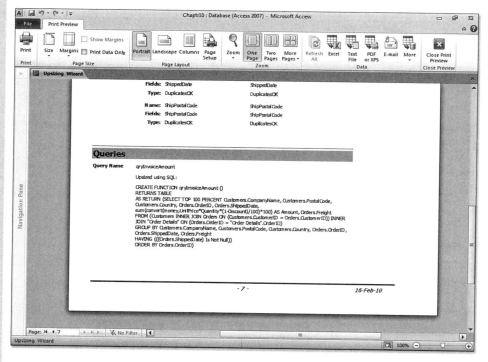

12. Click the small SQL button to display the filter's T-SQL statement. Adjust the position of the table windows and the depths of the three panes as shown in Figure 10.18.

Figure 10.18
The da Vinci
Design view
of a filter,
one of SQL
Server's
three choices
for generat-
ing query
resultsets,
has a three-
pane win-
dow.

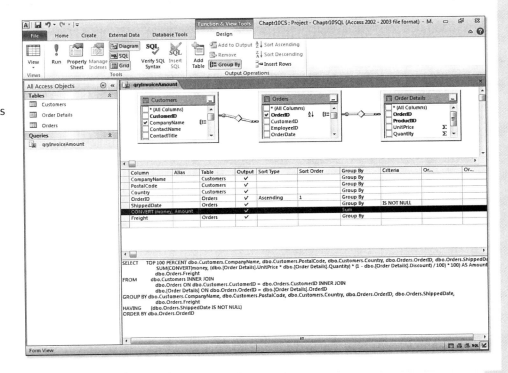

T-SQL

The T-SQL statement for the qryInvoiceAmount function (without a WHERE criterion on the Customers column) is

```
SELECT TOP 100 PERCENT dbo.Customers.CompanyName, dbo.Customers.PostalCode,
    dbo.Customers.Country, dbo.Orders.OrderID, dbo.Orders. ShippedDate,
    SUM(CONVERT(money, (dbo.[Order Details].UnitPrice * dbo.[Order Details].Quantity) *
       (1 - dbo.[Order Details].Discount)/100)*100) AS Amount, dbo.Orders.Freight
FROM  dbo.Customers
    INNER JOIN dbo.Orders
       ON dbo.Customers.CustomerID = dbo.Orders.CustomerID
    INNER JOIN dbo.[Order Details]
       ON dbo.Orders.OrderID = dbo.[Order Details].OrderID
GROUP BY dbo.Customers.CompanyName, dbo.Customers.PostalCode,
    dbo.Customers.Country, dbo.Orders.OrderID, dbo.Orders.OrderDate,
    dbo.Orders.Freight
HAVING (dbo.Orders.ShippedDate IS NOT NULL)
ORDER BY dbo.Orders.OrderID
```

Expressions for Calculating Query Field Values

The three preceding sections demonstrate that you can use expressions to create new, calculated fields in query tables. Calculated fields display data computed based on the values of other fields in the same row of the query table. Table 10.10 shows some representative expressions that you can use to create calculated query fields. Notice that Access field names must be enclosed with square brackets when typed in the Query Design window.

Table 10.10   Typical Expressions to Create Calculated Query Fields

Column Name	Expression	Values Calculated
TotalAmount	`[Amount] + [Freight]`	Sum of the OrderAmount and Freight fields
FreightPercent	`100 * [Freight]/[Amount]`	Freight charges as a percentage of the order amount
FreightPct	**Format**`([Freight]/[Amount], "Percent")`	Freight charges as a percentage of the order amount, but with formatting applied
SalesTax	**Format** `([Amount] * 0.08, "$#,###.00")`	Sales tax of 8 percent of the amount of the order added with a display that's similar to the **Currency** data type

To create a query containing calculated fields in Chaptr10.accdb, follow these steps:

1. In Query Design view, move to the first blank column of the qryInvoiceAmount query. Type the column name shown in Table 10.10, followed by a colon and then the expression:

`TotalInvoice: [Amount]+[Freight]`

2. Place the cursor in the Total cell of the calculated field, select Expression from the drop-down list, and mark the Show check box.If you don't select Expression, your query opens a Parameters dialog or returns an error message when you attempt to execute it.

3. Move to the next empty column, type the following expression, and add the Expression aggregate (see Figure 10.19):

`FreightPct: Format([Freight]/[Amount],"Percent")`

 note

T-SQL doesn't support the VBA Format or Format... functions, and the Upsizing Wizard won't generate views or functions from Access queries that use these functions.

 note

If you don't type the field name and colon, Access provides the default `Expr1` as the calculated field name.

Figure 10.19
Type one of
the expres-
sions of
Table 10.10
to add an
additional
calculated
column. The
example
shown here
calculates
Total Invoice
and Freight
Pct column
values from
another
calculated
column,
Amount, and
a table field,
Freight.

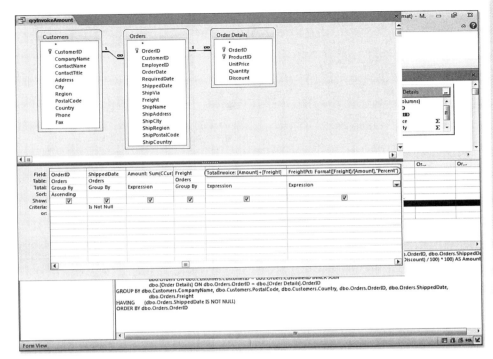

4. Remove the `Like "*shop*"` criterion from the CompanyName column.

5. Run the query. The resultset for the query with the added calculated fields appears as shown in Figure 10.20.

6. Repeat steps 3 through 5 for the remaining examples in Table 10.10.

You use the **Format** function with your expression as its first argument to display the calculated values in a more readable form. When you add the percent symbol (%) to a format expression or specify "Percent" as the format, the value of the expression argument multiplies by 100 and the percent symbol preceded by a space appends to the displayed value.

Query Expressions Fail to Execute

When you're attempting to execute a query that contains an expression and a Can't Evaluate Expression or Wrong Data Type message box appears, it usually indicates a typographical error in naming a function or an object. Depending on the use of the function, an Enter Parameter Value dialog might appear if the named object does not exist. The Wrong Data Type message is most likely to occur as a result of attempting to use mathematic or trigonometric operators with values of the Text or Date/Time field data types. If your expression refers to a control contained in a form or report, the form or report must be open when you execute the function.

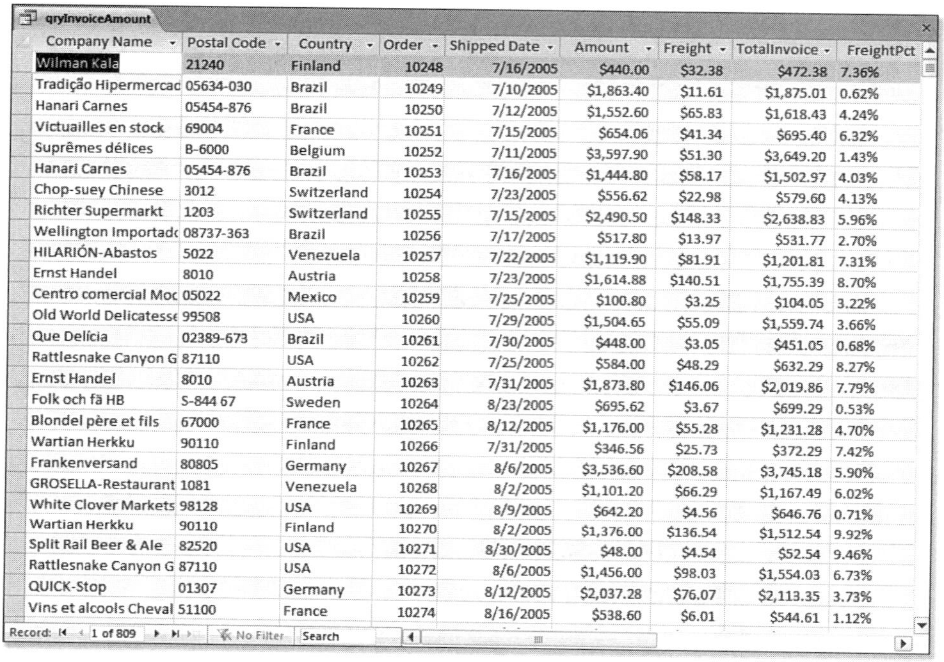

Company Name	Postal Code	Country	Order	Shipped Date	Amount	Freight	TotalInvoice	FreightPct
Wilman Kala	21240	Finland	10248	7/16/2005	$440.00	$32.38	$472.38	7.36%
Tradição Hipermercac	05634-030	Brazil	10249	7/10/2005	$1,863.40	$11.61	$1,875.01	0.62%
Hanari Carnes	05454-876	Brazil	10250	7/12/2005	$1,552.60	$65.83	$1,618.43	4.24%
Victuailles en stock	69004	France	10251	7/15/2005	$654.06	$41.34	$695.40	6.32%
Suprêmes délices	B-6000	Belgium	10252	7/11/2005	$3,597.90	$51.30	$3,649.20	1.43%
Hanari Carnes	05454-876	Brazil	10253	7/16/2005	$1,444.80	$58.17	$1,502.97	4.03%
Chop-suey Chinese	3012	Switzerland	10254	7/23/2005	$556.62	$22.98	$579.60	4.13%
Richter Supermarkt	1203	Switzerland	10255	7/15/2005	$2,490.50	$148.33	$2,638.83	5.96%
Wellington Importadc	08737-363	Brazil	10256	7/17/2005	$517.80	$13.97	$531.77	2.70%
HILARIÓN-Abastos	5022	Venezuela	10257	7/22/2005	$1,119.90	$81.91	$1,201.81	7.31%
Ernst Handel	8010	Austria	10258	7/23/2005	$1,614.88	$140.51	$1,755.39	8.70%
Centro comercial Moc	05022	Mexico	10259	7/25/2005	$100.80	$3.25	$104.05	3.22%
Old World Delicatesse	99508	USA	10260	7/29/2005	$1,504.65	$55.09	$1,559.74	3.66%
Que Delícia	02389-673	Brazil	10261	7/30/2005	$448.00	$3.05	$451.05	0.68%
Rattlesnake Canyon G	87110	USA	10262	7/25/2005	$584.00	$48.29	$632.29	8.27%
Ernst Handel	8010	Austria	10263	7/31/2005	$1,873.80	$146.06	$2,019.86	7.79%
Folk och fä HB	S-844 67	Sweden	10264	8/23/2005	$695.62	$3.67	$699.29	0.53%
Blondel père et fils	67000	France	10265	8/12/2005	$1,176.00	$55.28	$1,231.28	4.70%
Wartian Herkku	90110	Finland	10266	7/31/2005	$346.56	$25.73	$372.29	7.42%
Frankenversand	80805	Germany	10267	8/6/2005	$3,536.60	$208.58	$3,745.18	5.90%
GROSELLA-Restaurant	1081	Venezuela	10268	8/2/2005	$1,101.20	$66.29	$1,167.49	6.02%
White Clover Markets	98128	USA	10269	8/9/2005	$642.20	$4.56	$646.76	0.71%
Wartian Herkku	90110	Finland	10270	8/2/2005	$1,376.00	$136.54	$1,512.54	9.92%
Split Rail Beer & Ale	82520	USA	10271	8/30/2005	$48.00	$4.54	$52.54	9.46%
Rattlesnake Canyon G	87110	USA	10272	8/6/2005	$1,456.00	$98.03	$1,554.03	6.73%
QUICK-Stop	01307	Germany	10273	8/12/2005	$2,037.28	$76.07	$2,113.35	3.73%
Vins et alcools Cheval	51100	France	10274	8/16/2005	$538.60	$6.01	$544.61	1.12%

Record: 1 of 809   No Filter   Search

Figure 10.20
Datasheet view displays the query resultset of the design shown in Figure 10.19.

11

CREATING MULTITABLE AND CROSSTAB QUERIES

You'll only gain a return on your investment in this book and the time you devote to learning about Access if you take full advantage of Access's relational database management capabilities. To do so, you must be able to link related tables based on key fields that have values in common—a process called *joining tables*. Chapter 9, "Designing Queries for Access Databases," and Chapter 10, "Understanding Access Query Operators and Expressions," showed you how to create simple queries based on a single table. If you tried the examples in Chapter 10, you generated a multiple-table query when you joined the Order Details table to the Orders table and the Customers table to create the query for testing expressions. The first part of this chapter deals exclusively with queries created from multiple tables that you relate through joins.

This chapter provides examples of queries that use each of the four basic types of joins that you can create in Access's Query Design view: inner joins, outer joins, self-joins, and theta joins. It also shows you how to take advantage of UNION queries that you can't create in Access's Query Designer. The chapter also briefly covers subqueries, which you can substitute for nested Access queries. Chapter 13, "Creating and Updating Access Tables with Action Queries," presents typical applications for and examples of four types of action queries: update, append, delete, and make-table.

 tip

Read this chapter and create the sample queries sequentially, as the queries appear in text. The sample queries of this chapter build on queries that you create in earlier sections.

Some of the sample queries in this chapter use the HRActions table that you created in Chapter 5, "Working with Access Databases and Tables." If you didn't create the HRActions table and have downloaded and installed the sample databases, click the External Data tab and the Import group's Access button, and import the HRActions table from \Access2010\Chaptr06\Nwind06.accdb to your working database. Alternatively, open \Access2010\Chaptr11\Joins11.accdb, which includes all the examples of this chapter.

➡ *For a detailed description of the HRActions table,* **see** *"Creating the HRActions Table in Design View,"* **p. 208.**

Joining Tables to Create Multitable Queries

Before you can create joins between tables, you must know which fields are related by common values. As mentioned in Chapter 5, assigning identical names to primary key and foreign key fields in different tables that contain related data is a common practice. This approach, used by Microsoft when creating the original Northwind sample database, makes determining relationships and creating joins between tables easier. The CustomerID primary-key field in the Customers table and the CustomerID foreign-key field in the Orders table, for example, are used to join sets of orders with specific customers. A join between tables requires that one field in each table have a common set of values—CustomerID codes for this example.

Figure 11.1 shows the structure of the Northwind.accdb database with a graphical display of the relationships between the tables. Access indicates relationships with lines between field names of different tables. Bold type indicates primary key fields. Each relationship usually involves at least one primary key field. Relationships define *potential* joins between tables, but it's not necessary to have a predefined relationship to create a join.

You can display the structure of the joins between the tables in the Northwind database by clicking the Database Tools tab and then the Relationship button. Click the Relationship Tools, Design tab to create or edit relationships.

tip

To show relationships for only one table, click the Clear Layout button, click the Show Table button to display the Show Table dialog, select the table to display in the Tables list, and then click Add and Close. Click the Show Direct Relationships button to display the relationships for the selected table. Clearing the layout of the Relationships window doesn't affect the underlying relationships between the tables. The Show Direct Relationships feature is useful primarily with databases that contain many related tables. Close the Relationships window and don't save the changes.

You can choose between displaying only the direct relationships for a single table (the Show Direct Relationships button on the toolbar) or all relationships for all tables in a database (the Show All Relationships button). All tables appear by default when you open the Relationships window of the Northwind sample database. In this case, clicking the Show Direct Relationships button has no effect.

Access supports four types of joins in the Query Design window:

Figure 11.1
The Relationships window displays the relationships between primary keys and foreign keys in the Northwind database with the HRActions table added. The 1 above the line that shows the join between two tables indicates the "one" side of a one-to-many relationship; the infinity symbol (∞) indicates the "many" side.

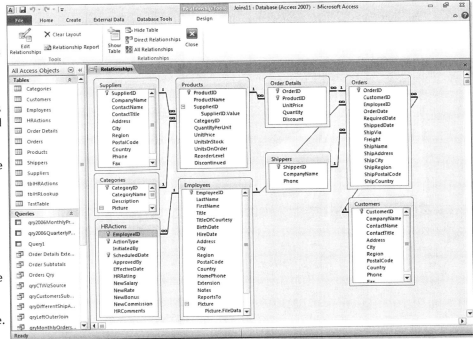

- *Inner joins* are the most common join for creating select queries. The most common type of an inner join is a *natural join* (also called an *equi-join*), which displays all the records in one table that have corresponding records in another table. The correspondence between records is determined by identical values (WHERE `field1` = `field2` in SQL dialects earlier than SQL-89) in the fields that join the tables. In most cases, joins are based on a unique primary key field in one table and a foreign key field in the other table in a one-to-many relationship. If any records in the table that act as the many side of the relationship have field values that don't correspond to a record in the table of the one side, the noncorresponding records on the one side don't appear in the query result.

- *Outer joins* display records in one member of the join, regardless of whether corresponding records exist on the other side of the join.

- *Self-joins* relate data within a single table. You create a self-join in Access by adding to the query a duplicate of the table (Access provides an alias for the duplicate), and then you create a join to the field(s) of the duplicate table.

- *Theta joins* relate data by using comparison operators other than =. Theta joins include not-equal joins (<>) used in queries

 note

Access automatically creates natural joins between tables in Query Design view if there's a relationship defined between the tables or the tables share a common field name that's a primary key of one of the tables.

designed to return records that don't have corresponding values. It's easier to implement theta joins by WHERE criteria rather than by the SQL JOIN reserved word. The Query Design window doesn't indicate theta joins by drawing lines between field names.

The 15.5MB Oakmont.accdb database, in the \Access2010\Oakmont folder of the accompanying CD-ROM, has a circular set of relationships. Open Oakmont.accdb and then click the Database Tools tab and the Relationships button to open the Relationships window (see Figure 11.2). Courses are one-to-many related to Courses; Departments are one-to-many related to Courses; and Employees are one-to-many related to Sections. You also can see a circular relationship between Courses, Enrollments, Students, Grades, and Courses. Oakmont.accdb is useful when you want to test the performance of queries with a large number of records. The fictitious Oakmont University in Navasota, Texas, has about 30,000 students, 2,320 employees, and offers 1,770 sections of 590 courses in 14 academic departments.

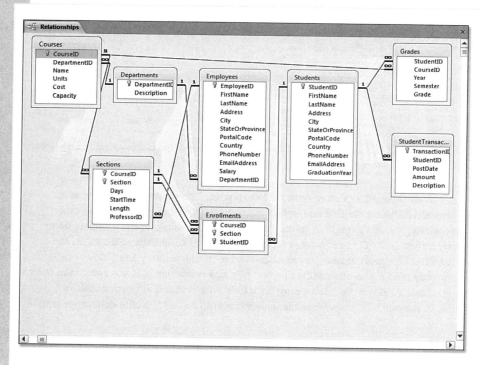

Figure 11.2
The Oakmont. accdb database has a circular set of relationships between the Courses, Enrollments, Students, Grades, and Course tables.

Creating Conventional Single-Column Inner Joins

Joins based on one column in each table are known as *single-column inner equi-joins* and are the most common by far of all join types. The following list, which is based on Northwind.accdb, details the basic rules for designing a database that lets you use simple single-column inner equi-join for all queries:

- Each table on the one side of the relationship must have a primary key with a No Duplicates index to maintain referential integrity. Access automatically creates a No Duplicates index on the primary key field(s) of a table.

- Many-to-many relationships, such as the relationship of Orders to Products, are implemented by an intermediary table (in this case, Order Details) having a one-to-many relationship (Orders to Order Details) with one table and a many-to-one relationship (Order Details to Products) with another.

 note

2007 NEW Access 2007 introduced multivalue lookup fields, which have a many-to-many relationship with a lookup table and have a hidden intermediary table that Access creates for you.

- Duplicated data in tables, where applicable, is extracted to a new table that has a primary key, no-duplicates, one-to-many relationship with the table from which the duplicate data is extracted. Using a multicolumn primary key to identify extracted data uniquely often is necessary because individual key fields might contain duplicate data. The combination (also known as *concatenation*) of the values of the key fields, however, must be unique. Access 2010's Table Analyzer Wizard locates and extracts most duplicate data automatically.

> *For more information on make-table queries,* **see** *"Creating New Tables with Make-Table Queries,"* **p. 536.**

> *If you're not sure how to create relationships,* **see** *"Establishing Relationships Between Tables,"* **p. 215.**

All joins in the Northwind database, shown earlier by the lines that connect field names of related tables in Figure 11.1, are single-column inner joins between tables with one-to-many relationships. Figure 11.2 illustrates the two-column relationship between the CourseID and SectionID fields of the Sections and Enrollments tables. Access uses the ANSI SQL-92 reserved words `INNER JOIN` to identify conventional inner joins and `LEFT JOIN` or `RIGHT JOIN` to specify outer joins.

Among the most common uses for queries based on inner joins is matching customer names and addresses with orders received. You might want to create a simple report, for example, that lists the customer name, order number, order date, and amount. To create a conventional one-to-many, single-column inner join query that relates Northwind's customers to their orders, sorted by company and order date, follow these steps:

1. With Northwind.accdb open, close all open database objects.

2. Click the Create tab and Query Design button. Access displays the Show Table dialog superimposed on an empty Query Design window.

3. Select the Customers table from the Show Table list and click the Add button. Alternatively, you can double-click the Customers table name to add the table to the query. Access adds the Field Names list for Customers to the Query Design window.

4. Double-click the Orders table in the Show Table list and then click the Close button. Access adds to the window the Field Names list for Orders, plus a line that indicates a join between the

CustomerID fields of the two tables. Access creates the join automatically because Access found the relationship with the CustomerID field (a foreign key) in the Orders table.

5. To identify each order with the customer's name, select the CompanyName field of the Customers table and drag the field symbol to the Field row of the Query Design grid's first column.

6. Select the OrderID field of the Orders table and drag the field symbol to the second column's Field row. Drag the OrderDate field to the third column. Your query design appears as shown in Figure 11.3.

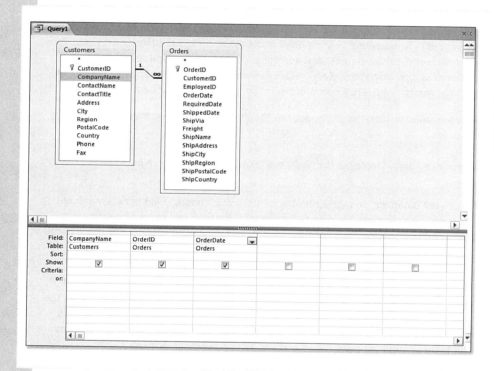

Figure 11.3
Access automatically creates the inner join on the CustomerID field between the Customers and Orders table.

7. Click the Run or Datasheet View button to display the result of the query, the Recordset shown in Figure 11.4. Notice that the field headers of the query resultset show the captions for the table fields, which include spaces, rather than the actual field names, which don't have spaces.

Specifying a Sort Order and Top Values Limit

Access displays query resultsets in the order of the index on the primary key field of the table that represents the one side of the topmost one-to-many relationship of query tables, unless you specify sorting on another field, a different sort direction, or both. If the primary key consists of more than

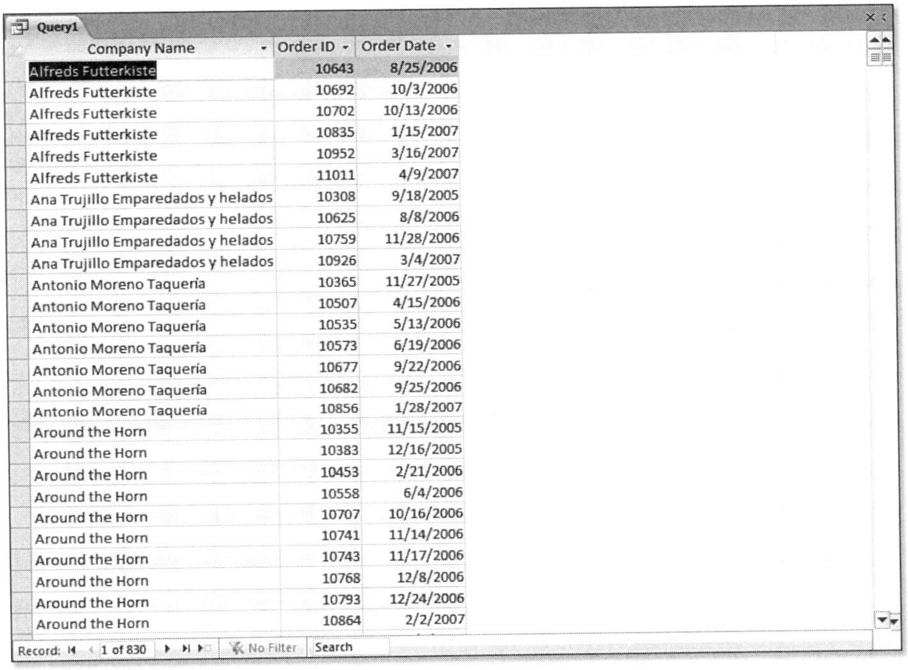

Figure 11.4
The Datasheet view of the query design of Figure 11.3 displays the three fields added to the grid.

Company Name	Order ID	Order Date
Alfreds Futterkiste	10643	8/25/2006
Alfreds Futterkiste	10692	10/3/2006
Alfreds Futterkiste	10702	10/13/2006
Alfreds Futterkiste	10835	1/15/2007
Alfreds Futterkiste	10952	3/16/2007
Alfreds Futterkiste	11011	4/9/2007
Ana Trujillo Emparedados y helados	10308	9/18/2005
Ana Trujillo Emparedados y helados	10625	8/8/2006
Ana Trujillo Emparedados y helados	10759	11/28/2006
Ana Trujillo Emparedados y helados	10926	3/4/2007
Antonio Moreno Taquería	10365	11/27/2005
Antonio Moreno Taquería	10507	4/15/2006
Antonio Moreno Taquería	10535	5/13/2006
Antonio Moreno Taquería	10573	6/19/2006
Antonio Moreno Taquería	10677	9/22/2006
Antonio Moreno Taquería	10682	9/25/2006
Antonio Moreno Taquería	10856	1/28/2007
Around the Horn	10355	11/15/2005
Around the Horn	10383	12/16/2005
Around the Horn	10453	2/21/2006
Around the Horn	10558	6/4/2006
Around the Horn	10707	10/16/2006
Around the Horn	10741	11/14/2006
Around the Horn	10743	11/17/2006
Around the Horn	10768	12/8/2006
Around the Horn	10793	12/24/2006
Around the Horn	10864	2/2/2007

Record: 1 of 830   No Filter   Search

one column, Access sorts query resultsets in left-to-right key-field column precedence. Because Customers is the topmost one member of the preceding query's Customers-Orders relationship, the query resultset displays all orders in CompanyID, OrderID sequence. A query with Orders, Order Details, and Products tables displays rows in ProductID sequence, because Products has a one-to-many relationship with OrderDetails and, indirectly, with Orders. You can override the topmost table's primary key display order by adding a sort order to the query. For example, if you want to see the most recent orders first, you can specify a descending sort by the order date.

➡ *For more information on primary key indexes,* **see** *"Adding Indexes to Tables,"* **p. 222.**

You can use the Top Values option to limit the number of rows returned by the query to those that are likely to be of most interest. For this example with a descending sort, only the most recent orders are relevant. Minimizing the number of rows returned by a query is especially important with client/server queries against large tables or when creating networked applications for remote users having slow dial-up connections.

To add this sort sequence and row limit to your query, follow these steps:

1. Click the Design View button and click the Query Tools, Design tab.

2. Place the cursor in the Sort row of the Order Date column of the Query Design grid and click the arrow or press Alt+down arrow ( ) to open the drop-down list.

3. Select Descending from the drop-down list to specify a descending sort on date—latest orders first (look ahead to Figure 11.5).

4. Open the Return list of the Query Tools Design ribbon's Query Setup group and select 5%. Adding a Top Values constraint doesn't affect the Query Design grid (see Figure 11.5).

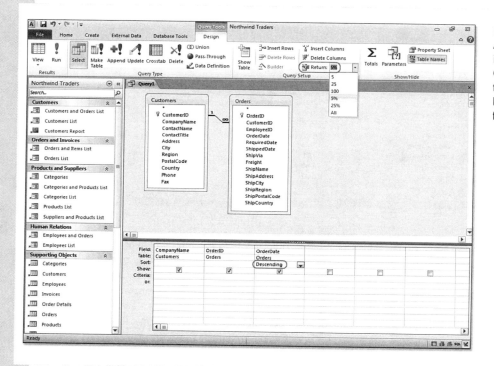

Figure 11.5
Add a descending sort on the OrderDate field to display the latest orders first.

5. Click the Run or Datasheet View button to display the query resultset with the new sort order and row limit (see Figure 11.6).

6. Open the View list button on the toolbar, and choose SQL View to open the SQL window, which displays the Access SQL statement for the query.

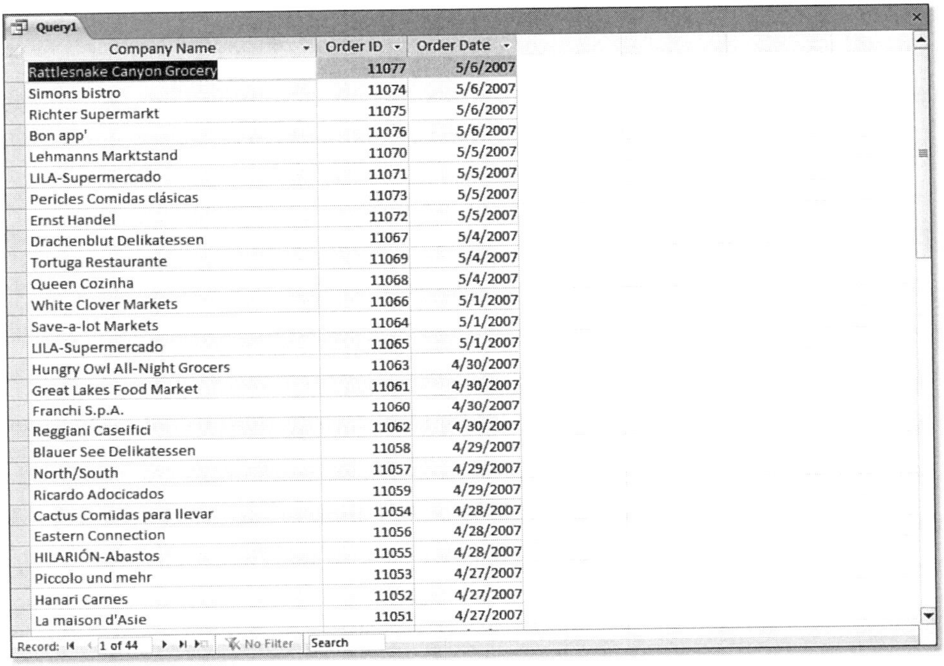

Figure 11.6
Orders appear in descending date sequence in this Datasheet view. With 5% set in the Top Values list, the query returns only 44 rows.

Company Name	Order ID	Order Date
Rattlesnake Canyon Grocery	11077	5/6/2007
Simons bistro	11074	5/6/2007
Richter Supermarkt	11075	5/6/2007
Bon app'	11076	5/6/2007
Lehmanns Marktstand	11070	5/5/2007
LILA-Supermercado	11071	5/5/2007
Pericles Comidas clásicas	11073	5/5/2007
Ernst Handel	11072	5/5/2007
Drachenblut Delikatessen	11067	5/4/2007
Tortuga Restaurante	11069	5/4/2007
Queen Cozinha	11068	5/4/2007
White Clover Markets	11066	5/1/2007
Save-a-lot Markets	11064	5/1/2007
LILA-Supermercado	11065	5/1/2007
Hungry Owl All-Night Grocers	11063	4/30/2007
Great Lakes Food Market	11061	4/30/2007
Franchi S.p.A.	11060	4/30/2007
Reggiani Caseifici	11062	4/30/2007
Blauer See Delikatessen	11058	4/29/2007
North/South	11057	4/29/2007
Ricardo Adocicados	11059	4/29/2007
Cactus Comidas para llevar	11054	4/28/2007
Eastern Connection	11056	4/28/2007
HILARIÓN-Abastos	11055	4/28/2007
Piccolo und mehr	11053	4/27/2007
Hanari Carnes	11052	4/27/2007
La maison d'Asie	11051	4/27/2007

Record: 1 of 44   No Filter   Search

Access SQL

The Access SQL statement for the sorted query with the Top Values limit is

```
SELECT TOP 5 PERCENT Customers.CompanyName,
    Orders.OrderID, Orders.OrderDate
FROM Customers
INNER JOIN Orders
ON Customers.CustomerID=Orders.CustomerID
ORDER BY Orders.OrderDate DESC;
```

The INNER JOIN Orders clause specifies a join with the Customers table, and the ON Customers.CustomerID=Orders.CustomerID qualifier names the joined fields.

A pre-SQL-89 alternative method for creating joins is to use the WHERE clause to specify a join. If you edit the SQL statement as follows, you achieve the same result:

```
SELECT TOP 5 PERCENT Customers.CompanyName,
    Orders.OrderID, Orders.OrderDate
FROM Customers, Orders
WHERE Customers.CustomerID=Orders.CustomerID
ORDER BY Orders.OrderDate DESC;
```

Using WHERE clauses to specify INNER, LEFT, and RIGHT JOINs no longer is common practice, because resultsets created by WHERE clauses aren't updatable.

Designing Nested Queries

Access lets you use a saved query (QueryDef object) in lieu of that query's tables (TableDef objects) in other queries. The only significant difference between these two objects from a query design standpoint is that queries don't have primary keys. Prior to executing the top-level query, Access executes the QueryDef objects of lower-level (nested) queries and then creates the join with other tables.

To add a saved query (Northwind.accdb's sample Order Subtotals query for this example) as a nested query in the customer/orders query you created in the preceding section, follow these steps:

1. Return to Query Design view and click the Show Table button to open the dialog.

2. Click the Queries tab of the Show Tables dialog, double-click the Order Subtotals entry in the list, and click Close.

3. Double-click the Subtotal column of the Order Subtotals query to add it to the grid. Double-click the Freight field of the Orders table to add a Freight column to the query (see Figure 11.7). The join line represents a one-to-one relationship between the OrderID fields of the Orders table and the Order Subtotals query, which the Query Designer detects by field name.

4. Add a calculated Total field by typing **Total: [Subtotal] + [Freight]** in the grid's Field cell to the right of the Freight field.

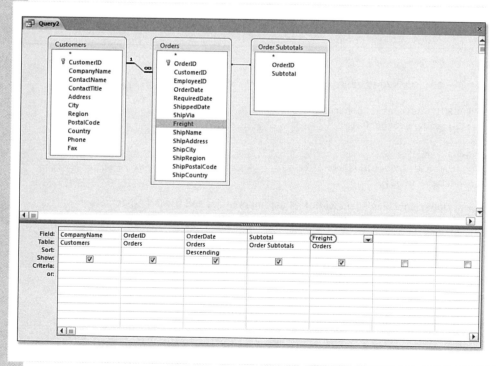

Figure 11.7
Adding a query instead of a table as a query data source adds a relationship between columns and fields of the same name. In this case, the relationship is one-to-one.

5. Click the Run button to display the resultset (see Figure 11.8).

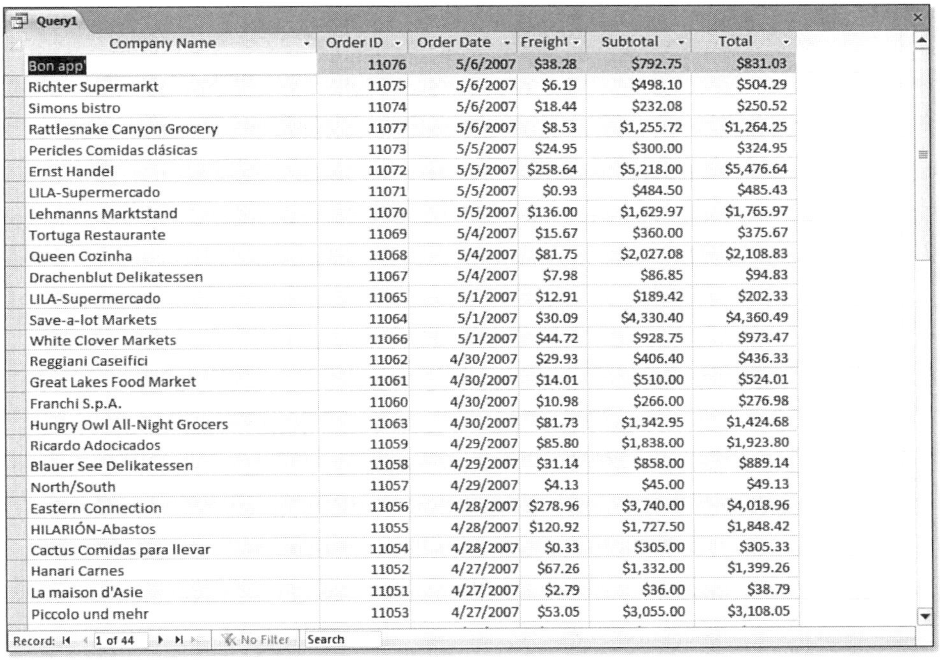

Figure 11.8
The query design of Figure 11.7 adds the Order Subtotals' Subtotal column, the Freight field of the Orders table, and a calculated Totals column.

Company Name	Order ID	Order Date	Freight	Subtotal	Total
Bon app'	11076	5/6/2007	$38.28	$792.75	$831.03
Richter Supermarkt	11075	5/6/2007	$6.19	$498.10	$504.29
Simons bistro	11074	5/6/2007	$18.44	$232.08	$250.52
Rattlesnake Canyon Grocery	11077	5/6/2007	$8.53	$1,255.72	$1,264.25
Pericles Comidas clásicas	11073	5/5/2007	$24.95	$300.00	$324.95
Ernst Handel	11072	5/5/2007	$258.64	$5,218.00	$5,476.64
LILA-Supermercado	11071	5/5/2007	$0.93	$484.50	$485.43
Lehmanns Marktstand	11070	5/5/2007	$136.00	$1,629.97	$1,765.97
Tortuga Restaurante	11069	5/4/2007	$15.67	$360.00	$375.67
Queen Cozinha	11068	5/4/2007	$81.75	$2,027.08	$2,108.83
Drachenblut Delikatessen	11067	5/4/2007	$7.98	$86.85	$94.83
LILA-Supermercado	11065	5/1/2007	$12.91	$189.42	$202.33
Save-a-lot Markets	11064	5/1/2007	$30.09	$4,330.40	$4,360.49
White Clover Markets	11066	5/1/2007	$44.72	$928.75	$973.47
Reggiani Caseifici	11062	4/30/2007	$29.93	$406.40	$436.33
Great Lakes Food Market	11061	4/30/2007	$14.01	$510.00	$524.01
Franchi S.p.A.	11060	4/30/2007	$10.98	$266.00	$276.98
Hungry Owl All-Night Grocers	11063	4/30/2007	$81.73	$1,342.95	$1,424.68
Ricardo Adocicados	11059	4/29/2007	$85.80	$1,838.00	$1,923.80
Blauer See Delikatessen	11058	4/29/2007	$31.14	$858.00	$889.14
North/South	11057	4/29/2007	$4.13	$45.00	$49.13
Eastern Connection	11056	4/28/2007	$278.96	$3,740.00	$4,018.96
HILARIÓN-Abastos	11055	4/28/2007	$120.92	$1,727.50	$1,848.42
Cactus Comidas para llevar	11054	4/28/2007	$0.33	$305.00	$305.33
Hanari Carnes	11052	4/27/2007	$67.62	$1,332.00	$1,399.26
La maison d'Asie	11051	4/27/2007	$2.79	$36.00	$38.79
Piccolo und mehr	11053	4/27/2007	$53.05	$3,055.00	$3,108.05

Record: 1 of 44   No Filter   Search

6. Click the Database Tools tab and the Relationships button to open the Relationships window, click the Show Tables button, click the Queries tab, double-click the Orders Subtotals item in the list, and click Close. Unlike the Query Design process, Access doesn't automatically display the relationship between queries and tables.

7. Drag the OrderID field from the Orders table and drop it on the OrderID column of the Orders Subtotals column to display the Edit Relationships dialog (see Figure 11.9). You can't enforce referential integrity between tables and queries. Click OK to close the dialog.

8. Close the Relationships window, and save the layout changes. Then close your query and save it with a descriptive name, such as **qryOrderAmountsRecentTop5%**.

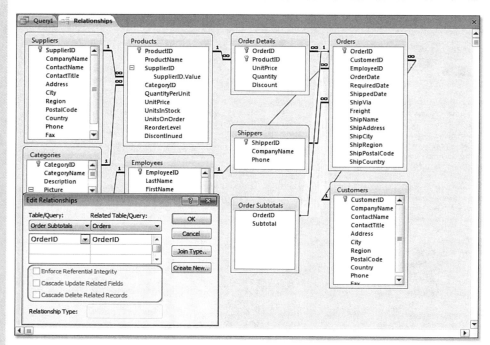

Figure 11.9
Creating a join between a query and a table disables the referential integrity options of the Edit Relationships dialog.

Access SQL

The Access SQL statement for the nested query is

```
SELECT TOP 5 PERCENT Customers.CompanyName, Orders.OrderID,
    Orders.OrderDate, [Order Subtotals].Subtotal, Orders.Freight,
    [Subtotal]+[Freight] AS Total
FROM Customers
    INNER JOIN (Orders
        INNER JOIN [Order Subtotals]
        ON Orders.OrderID = [Order Subtotals].OrderID)
    ON Customers.CustomerID = Orders.CustomerID
ORDER BY Orders.OrderDate DESC;
```

Square bracket pairs ([ ]) surround table or query names having spaces or SQL-illegal punctuation. It's also a common practice to surround field names in expressions for computed columns with square brackets. Indenting the INNER JOIN statements at the same level as the ON prepositions makes the syntax easier to understand

Creating Queries from Tables with Indirect Relationships

You can create queries that return indirectly related records, such as the categories of products purchased by each customer. You must include in the queries each table that serves as a link in the chain of joins. If you're designing queries to display the categories of products purchased by each customer, for example, include each of the tables that link the chain of joins between the Customers and Categories tables. This chain includes the Customers, Orders, Order Details, Products, and Categories tables. You often need indirect relationships for data analysis queries.

To create a query that you can use to analyze customers' purchases by category, which requires specifying fields of indirectly related records, follow these steps:

 tip

As you add tables to the Query Design window, the table field lists might not appear in the upper pane. Use the upper pane's vertical scrollbar to display the "hidden" tables. You can drag the table field lists to the top of the upper pane and then rearrange the field lists to match the appearance of the upper pane of Figure 11.10.

1. Click the Create tab and Query Design button to open the Show Table dialog.

2. Add the Customers, Orders, Order Details, Products, and Categories tables to the query, in sequence; then click the Close button of the Add Table dialog. Access automatically creates a chain of joins between Customers and Categories based on relationships between the primary key field of each intervening table and the identically named foreign key field in the adjacent table.

 tip

Queries with indirect relationships are especially useful to create PivotTable and PivotChart views of data. Several of the next chapter's PivotTable and PivotChart examples use this and related queries as data sources.

3. Double-click the CompanyName and CategoryName fields from the Customers and Categories tables to add them to the first two columns of the grid.

4. In the Field row of the third column, type **Amount: CCur([Order Details]. [UnitPrice]*[Quantity]*(1-[Discount]))** to calculate the net amount of the purchase of each line item in the Orders Details table (see Figure 11.10).

> *For an explanation of the expression that calculates the Amount column values,* **see** *"Entering a Query Criterion and Adding a Calculated Field,"* **p. 407**.

5. Click the Run button to test the query at this intermediate point of the design (see Figure 11.11). The query returns 2,155 rows, which is the number of records in the Order Details table.

6. Return to Design view, click the Query Tools Design tab, and click the Totals button to group the data by CategoryName and CustomerName and to generate total sales by category for each customer. Apply an ascending sort to the CategoryName column, and select Sum from the drop-down list in the Group By row of the Amount column (see Figure 11.12).

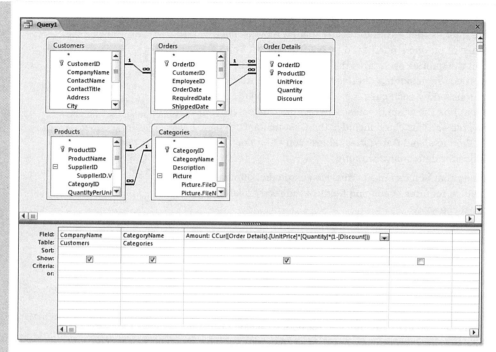

Figure 11.10
The query design shown here calculates the net purchases of each product by every customer.

Figure 11.11
The Datasheet view of the query design of Figure 11.10 has too much detail to be usable for sales analysis of product categories.

Company Name	Category Nam	Amount
QUICK-Stop	Beverages	$518.40
Rattlesnake Canyon Grocery	Beverages	$259.20
Lonesome Pine Restaurant	Beverages	$288.00
Die Wandernde Kuh	Beverages	$183.60
Pericles Comidas clásicas	Beverages	$172.80
Chop-suey Chinese	Beverages	$183.60
Queen Cozinha	Beverages	$144.00
La maison d'Asie	Beverages	$345.60
Princesa Isabel Vinhos	Beverages	$216.00
Lehmanns Marktstand	Beverages	$576.00
Wartian Herkku	Beverages	$122.40
Tortuga Restaurante	Beverages	$180.00
Mère Paillarde	Beverages	$360.00
Du monde entier	Beverages	$54.00
Wolski Zajazd	Beverages	$108.00
Blondel père et fils	Beverages	$450.00
Hungry Owl All-Night Grocers	Beverages	$202.50
Berglunds snabbköp	Beverages	$472.50
QUICK-Stop	Beverages	$540.00
Save-a-lot Markets	Beverages	$72.00
LINO-Delicateses	Beverages	$900.00
North/South	Beverages	$144.00
LINO-Delicateses	Beverages	$54.00
Save-a-lot Markets	Beverages	$1,152.00
HILARIÓN-Abastos	Beverages	$306.00
Seven Seas Imports	Beverages	$720.00
Wellington Importadora	Beverages	$342.00

Record: 1 of 2155   No Filter   Search

Figure 11.12
To reduce the amount of detail, group the records by the CustomerName and CategoryName fields and calculate the sum of the Amount column.

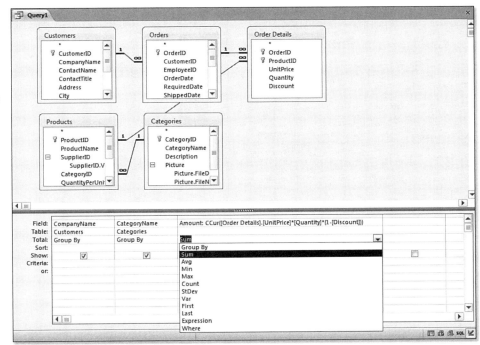

7. Run the query to display the summary (aggregated) resultset, which now contains 598 records.

8. In the Home ribbon, click the Records group's Totals button to add a totals row to the Datasheet. Open the Amount column's Totals list and select Sum (see Figure 11.13).

9. The number of records (598) is still too many for most people to analyze by inspection, so return to Query Design view, open the Field list of the first column, substitute **Country** for CustomerName to reduce the number of records to 165, and rerun the query (see Figure 11.14).

10. Close the query and save it as **qryOrderAmountsByCountryAndCategory**.

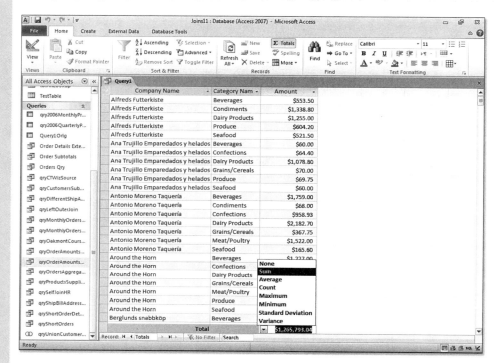

Figure 11.13
This summary query resultset totals product sales by category and customer to reduce the number of rows from 2,155 to 598.

Access SQL

The Access SQL statement for the aggregate query is

```
SELECT Customers.Country, Categories.CategoryName,
    Sum(CCur([Order Details].[UnitPrice]*
    [Quantity]*(1-[Discount]))) AS Amount
FROM (Categories
    INNER JOIN Products
        ON Categories.CategoryID = Products.CategoryID)
    INNER JOIN ((Customers INNER JOIN Orders
        ON Customers.CustomerID = Orders.CustomerID)
    INNER JOIN [Order Details]
        ON Orders.OrderID = [Order Details].OrderID)
        ON Products.ProductID = [Order Details].ProductID
GROUP BY Customers.Country, Categories.CategoryName
ORDER BY Categories.CategoryName;
```

If you write SQL statements for queries with several joins instead of using Access's graphical query design window, it's easier to use a pre-SQL-92 WHERE clause to define the joins, as in:

```
SELECT Customers.Country, Categories.CategoryName,
    Sum(CCur([Order Details].UnitPrice*
    [Quantity]*(1-[Discount]))) AS Amount
 FROM Customers, Orders, [Order Details], Products, Categories
 WHERE Categories.CategoryID=Products.CategoryID
    AND Customers.CustomerID=Orders.CustomerID
    AND Orders.OrderID=[Order Details].OrderID
    AND Products.ProductID=[Order Details].ProductID
GROUP BY Customers.Country, Categories.CategoryName
ORDER BY Categories.CategoryName;
```

The two preceding SQL statements produce the same resultset, but using the WHERE clause causes the join lines to disappear from the Query Design pane. Notice that the WHERE clause elements are identical to the ON elements. Updatability isn't a factor in this case, because aggregate queries aren't updatable.

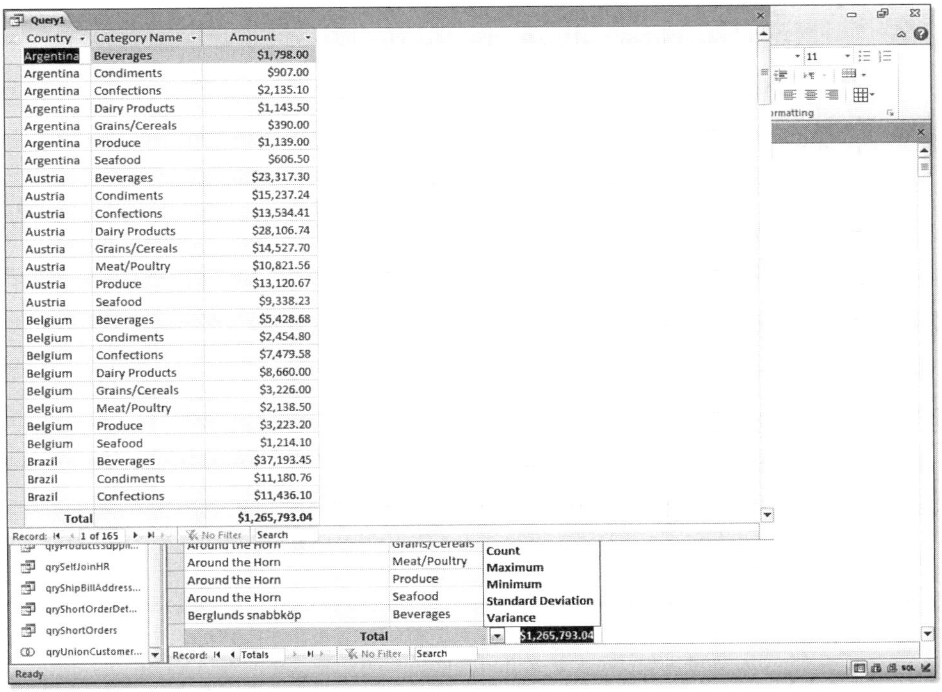

Figure 11.14
Aggregating sales by country and category displays 165 records. If customers in all 21 countries had made purchases in all eight categories, the resultset would have 168 records.

Queries that use SQL aggregate functions are the foundation of Access crosstab queries. Prior to the release of SQL Server 2005, Access data projects (ADP) didn't support crosstab queries, because T-SQL lacked the Access SQL reserved words needed to create crosstabs directly. T-SQL now has the PIVOT (and UNPIVOT) keywords, but not TRANSFORM. It remains more common for ADP to use PivotTables to display aggregate query resultsets in crosstab format.

 tip

Access's graphical Query Design features are much more comprehensive than those included with Windows programming platforms, such as Visual Studio or Visual Basic Express. If you're a Visual Basic programmer (or plan to learn Visual Basic to create database front ends for Jet/Access databases), use Access to write your programs' Jet/Access SQL statements. SQL Server is the production back end preferred by most Visual Basic programmers, but Jet/Access remains an effective database engine for storing and manipulating local data on Windows clients.

> *For more information on summary queries,* **see** *"Using the SQL Aggregate Functions,"* **p. 476.**

> *To learn more about crosstab queries,* **see** *"Creating Crosstab Queries,"* **p. 485.**

Creating Multicolumn Inner Joins and Selecting Unique Values

You can't have more than one join that enforces referential integrity between a pair of tables, but you can have joins on multiple fields. You might, for example, want to create a query that returns the names of customers who have the same billing and shipping addresses. The billing address is the Address field of the Customers table, and the shipping address is the ShipAddress field of the Orders table. Therefore, you need to match the CustomerID fields in the two tables and Customers.Address with Orders.ShipAddress. This task requires a multicolumn inner join.

To create this example of an address-matching, multicolumn inner join, follow these steps:

1. Open a new query in Design view.

2. Add the Customers and Orders tables to the query and close the Add Tables dialog. Access creates the join on the CustomerID fields.

3. Click and drag the Address field of the Customers table's Field List box to the ShipAddress field of the Orders table's Field List box. This creates another join criterion, indicated by the new line between Address and ShipAddress (see the top pane of Figure 11.15). The new join line between Address and ShipAddress has dots at both ends, indicating that the join is between a pair of fields that doesn't have a specified relationship, the same field name, or a primary key index.

4. Drag the Customers table's CompanyName and Address fields to the Field row of the first and second query columns and then drop the fields. Drag the Orders table's ShipAddress field to the query's third column and drop the field in the Field row (refer to the lower pane of Figure 11.15).

Manually Added Join criterion

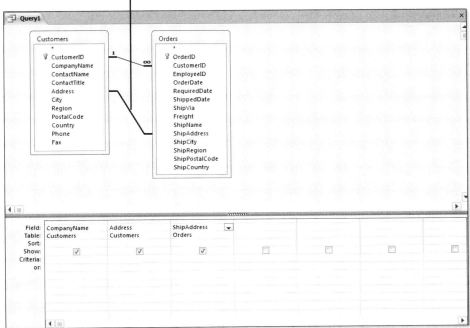

Figure 11.15
This query
has an inner
join on two
fields. You
must manu-
ally add
join criteria
between
fields with
dissimilar
names.

5.   Click the Run button. Figure 11.16 shows the query's
    resultset.

6. To eliminate the duplicate rows, you must use the Unique
    Values option of the Query Property Sheet. To display the Query
    Property Sheet, click the Design View button, right-click an
    empty region of the upper pane, and select Properties from the
    context menu.

7. By default, both the Unique Records query property and the
    Unique Values property are set to No. Open the Unique Values
    list and select Yes (see Figure 11.17). Setting the Unique Values
    property to Yes adds the ANSI SQL reserved word DISTINCT to the query. Close the Query
    Property Sheet.

---

tip

Alternatively, you can change the
property settings for the Unique
Records and Unique Values
properties by double-clicking
their text boxes in the Property
Sheet. All properties with Yes/No
values let you toggle their value
by double-clicking.

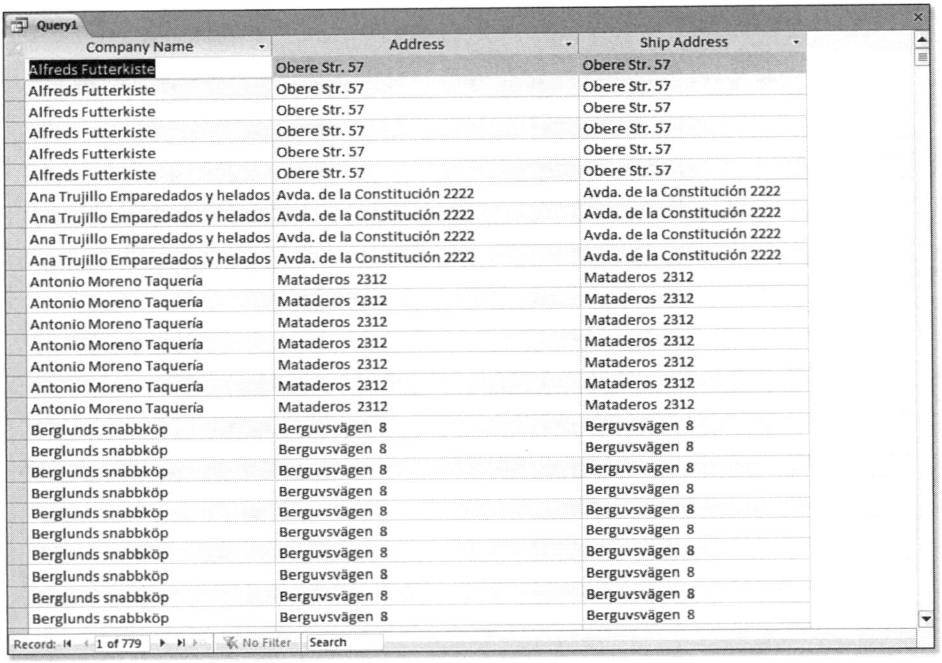

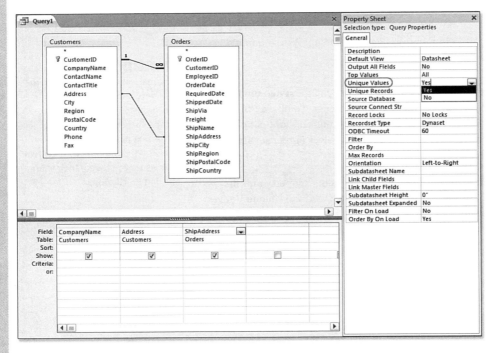

Figure 11.16
The resultset displays records for all orders in which billing and shipping addresses are the same.

Figure 11.17
Setting the Unique Values property to Yes adds the DISTINCT qualifier to the query to display only rows that have different contents.

8. Click the Run button. The resultset no longer contains duplicate rows, as shown by Figure 11.18.

9. Click the Close Window button to close the query and then save it as **qryShipBillAddresses** for use later in the chapter.

Because most of the orders have the same billing and shipping addresses, a more useful query is to find the orders for which the customer's billing and shipping addresses differ. You can create a not-equal join for this purpose by changing the (`Customers.Address = Orders.ShipAddress`) criterion to (`Customers.Address <> Orders.ShipAddress`). If you make this change, Access displays an error message in Query Design view.

Figure 11.18
This result-set demon-strates the effect of adding the DISTINCT qualifier to a query.

Company Name	Address	Ship Address
Alfreds Futterkiste	Obere Str. 57	Obere Str. 57
Ana Trujillo Emparedados y helados	Avda. de la Constitución 2222	Avda. de la Constitución 2222
Antonio Moreno Taquería	Mataderos 2312	Mataderos 2312
Berglunds snabbköp	Berguvsvägen 8	Berguvsvägen 8
Blauer See Delikatessen	Forsterstr. 57	Forsterstr. 57
Blondel père et fils	24, place Kléber	24, place Kléber
Bólido Comidas preparadas	C/ Araquil, 67	C/ Araquil, 67
Bon app'	12, rue des Bouchers	12, rue des Bouchers
Bottom-Dollar Markets	23 Tsawassen Blvd.	23 Tsawassen Blvd.
B's Beverages	Fauntleroy Circus	Fauntleroy Circus
Cactus Comidas para llevar	Cerrito 333	Cerrito 333
Centro comercial Moctezuma	Sierras de Granada 9993	Sierras de Granada 9993
Comércio Mineiro	Av. dos Lusíadas, 23	Av. dos Lusíadas, 23
Consolidated Holdings	Berkeley Gardens	Berkeley Gardens
Die Wandernde Kuh	Adenauerallee 900	Adenauerallee 900
Drachenblut Delikatessen	Walserweg 21	Walserweg 21
Du monde entier	67, rue des Cinquante Otages	67, rue des Cinquante Otages
Eastern Connection	35 King George	35 King George
Ernst Handel	Kirchgasse 6	Kirchgasse 6
Familia Arquibaldo	Rua Orós, 92	Rua Orós, 92
Folies gourmandes	184, chaussée de Tournai	184, chaussée de Tournai
Folk och fä HB	Åkergatan 24	Åkergatan 24
France restauration	54, rue Royale	54, rue Royale
Franchi S.p.A.	Via Monte Bianco 34	Via Monte Bianco 34
Frankenversand	Berliner Platz 43	Berliner Platz 43
Furia Bacalhau e Frutos do Mar	Jardim das rosas n. 32	Jardim das rosas n. 32
Galería del gastrónomo	Rambla de Cataluña, 23	Rambla de Cataluña, 23

Record: 1 of 84 · No Filter · Search

Missing Objects in Queries

When you run a query and an Enter Parameter Value dialog appears that asks you to enter a value even though you didn't specify a parameter for the query, the Access engine's query parser can't identify an object specified in the query or evaluate an expression. Usually, the Enter Parameter Value dialog appears because of a typographic error. Intentionally creating parameter queries is the subject of this chapter's "Designing Parameter Queries" section.

Using Lookup Fields in Tables

Access's lookup feature for table fields lets you substitute drop-down list boxes or list boxes for conventional field text boxes. The lookup feature is a one-to-many query that the Access Lookup Wizard automatically creates for you. The lookup feature lets you provide a list of acceptable values for a particular field. When you select the value from the list, the lookup feature automatically enters the value in the field of the current record. You can specify either of the following two types of lookup field:

- **In a field that contains foreign key values, a list of values from one or more fields of a related base table**—The purpose of this type of lookup field is to add or alter foreign key values, preserving relational integrity by assuring that foreign key values match a primary key value. A relationship must exist in the Relationships window between the tables to define a field as containing a foreign key.

As an example, the Products table of Northwind.accdb has two foreign key fields: SupplierID and CategoryID. The lookup feature of the SupplierID field displays the SupplierID and CompanyName field values from the Suppliers table in a drop-down list (see Figure 11.19).

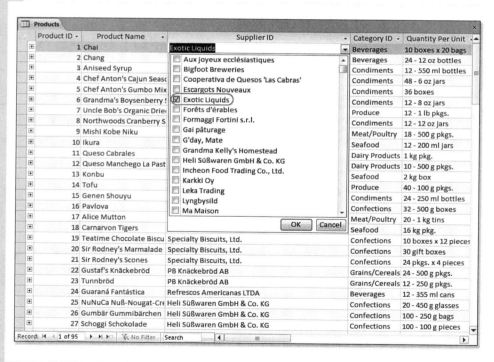

Figure 11.19
The Datasheet view of a query against the Suppliers table generates the lookup list of the Products table's SupplierID field.

- **In any field except a single primary key field, a list of fixed values from which to select**—Field lists are equivalent to validation rules that specify allowable field values, so a fixed lookup list isn't appropriate in this case.

2007 NEW Access 2007 added a Lookup property value, Allow Multiple Values, which lets you add lists with check boxes to enable selecting multiple values. As an example, some Northwind products might have multiple suppliers. Setting the Allow Multiple Values property to Yes, which causes a permanent modification to the table that can't be undone, enables specifying more than one supplier for a product. You also can specify multiple-value lookups for fixed values.

You can add a new lookup field in either Table Design or Table Datasheet view; however, in Design view you can add the lookup feature only to an existing field. In Datasheet view, only the combo box control is displayed, even if you specify a list box control. You can display a combo box or a list box on a form that is bound to a table with lookup fields. In practice, the drop-down list (a combo box with the Limit to List property set to Yes) is the most common type of lookup field control. The following sections describe how to add foreign key and fixed-list lookup features to table fields.

Adding a Foreign Key Drop-down List with the Lookup Wizard

The HRActions table you created in earlier chapters of this book is a candidate for a lookup field that uses a foreign key drop-down list of LastName and FirstName values from the Employees table. If you didn't create and populate the HRActions table, you'll find it in the \Access2010\Chaptr06\ Nwind06.accdb database on the accompanying CD-ROM. Import the HRActions table into your working copy of Northwind.accdb.

Follow these steps to use the Lookup Wizard to change two fields of the HRActions table to lookup fields:

1. In the Database window, select the HRActions table and press Ctrl+C to copy the table to the Clipboard.

2. Press Ctrl+V to display the Paste Table As dialog. Type a name for the copy, such as **tblHRLookup**, and click the OK button to create the copy with the structure and data.

3. Open the table copy in Design view and select the InitiatedBy field. Click the Lookup tab to display the current lookup properties; a text box control has no lookup properties. Open the Data Type drop-down list and select Lookup Wizard (see Figure 11.20) to open the first dialog of the Lookup Wizard.

4. You want the field to look up values in another table (Employees), so accept the first (default) option (see Figure 11.21). Click Next to open the Lookup Wizard's second dialog.

> **tip**
>
> Before using the imported HRActions table, open it in Design view, select the InitiatedBy field, and set the Text Align property value on the General property page to Left. Alternatively, you can make this change after completing the following example. Otherwise, lookup fields with text values are right-justified, which is inconsistent with the justification of other text fields.

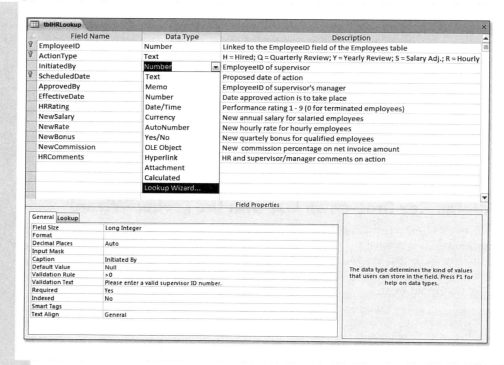

Figure 11.20
You start the Lookup Wizard from the Data Type field of the Table Design grid, despite the fact that Lookup Wizard isn't an Access data type.

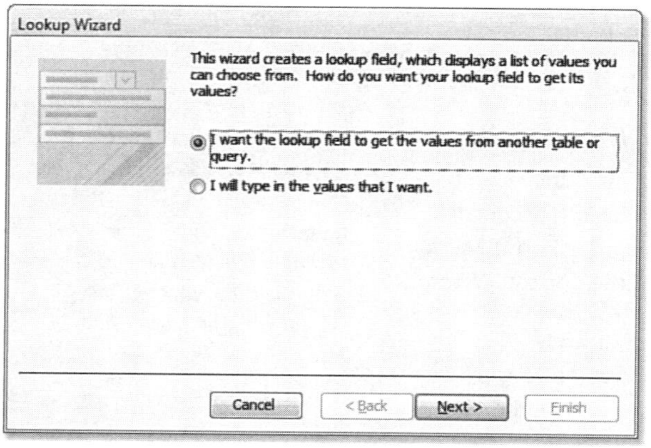

Figure 11.21
The first Lookup Wizard dialog has options for the two types of lookup fields.

5. With the View Tables option enabled, select the Employees table to which the InitiatedBy field is related (see Figure 11.22). Click Next to display the third dialog.

Figure 11.22
The second wizard dialog asks you to select the table to provide data for the lookup columns.

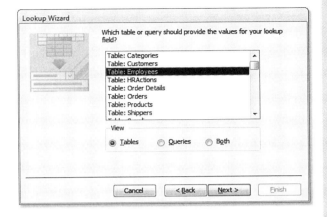

6. Click the > button three times to add the EmployeeID, LastName, and FirstName fields to your lookup list (see Figure 11.23). You must include the base table's primary key field that's related to your foreign key field. Click Next for the fourth dialog.

Figure 11.23
The third dialog requests you to specify the fields to include in the lookup list. You must include the table's primary key field.

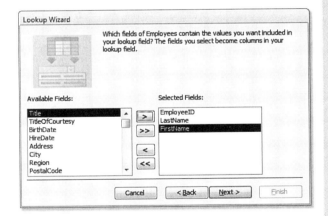

7. The fourth dialog lets you sort the list by up to four fields. In this case, you don't need to apply a sort order, so click Next to open the fifth dialog.

8. Adjust the widths of the columns to display the first and last names without excessive trailing whitespace. The wizard determines that EmployeeID is the key column and recommends hiding the key column by marking the check box (see Figure 11.24). Accept the recommendation, and click Next to display the fifth and final dialog.

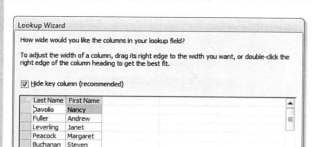

Figure 11.24
Verify the fields to appear in the lookup list and adjust the column widths to suit the data.

9. Accept the default InitiatedBy as the label for the lookup field in the text box of the final wizard dialog. The label you specify doesn't overwrite an existing Caption property value. More than one person can't initiate an action, so don't mark the Allow Multiple Values check box. Click Finish to complete the wizard's work.

10. Click Yes when the message asks whether you want to save the table design and create the relationships. Your new lookup field properties appear as shown in Figure 11.25. The simple Access SQL query statement created by the wizard as the Row Source property is

```
SELECT [Employees].[EmployeeID], [Employees].[Last-
Name], [Employees].[FirstName] FROM [Employees];.
```

 tip

The preceding step 6 adds fields in their table order, but you can add fields with the Lookup Wizard in any order you prefer. Alternatively, you can rearrange columns by editing the Row Source property's SQL statement after you create the lookup list.

11. Click the Datasheet View button. Only the first visible column of the list appears in the Initiated By column. With the cursor in the Initiated By column, open the drop-down list to display the wizard's work (see Figure 11.26).

12. To change the SQL statement to open a single-column, alphabetized LastName, FirstName list, return to Design view, select the Row Source property of the InitiatedBy field in the Lookup page, and press Shift+F2 to open the Zoom dialog. Edit the SQL statement as follows:

```
SELECT Employees.EmployeeID,

   Employees.LastName & ", " & Employees.FirstName

FROM Employees

ORDER BY LastName, FirstName;
```

Click OK to close the Zoom dialog.

Figure 11.25
The Lookup page of the InitiatedBy field displays the lookup list property values added by the wizard.

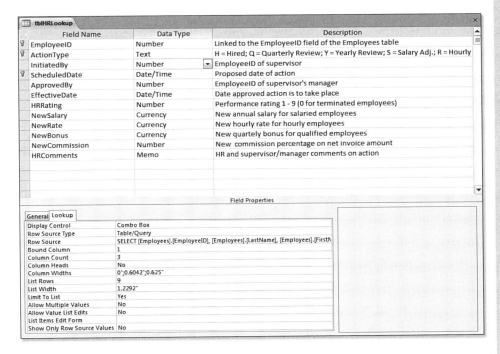

13. Change the value of the Column Count property to **2** and the Column Widths property to **0";1.3"**. Optionally, change the List Rows value to **9** to accommodate Northwind's nine employees without a vertical scrollbar. Click View and then click Yes to save your changes. Then open the lookup list to verify your changes (see Figure 11.27).

 If you need a list of the properties of the combo box control created by the wizard, **see** *"Adding Combo and List Boxes"* **p. 639.**

Adding a Fixed-Value Lookup List to a Table

You add the alternative lookup feature—a fixed list of values—using the Lookup Wizard in much the same way as you created the foreign key lookup list in the preceding section. To add a fixed-list lookup feature to the ActionType field of your copy of the HRActions table, follow these steps:

1. In Design view, select the ActionType field, open the Data Type list, and select Lookup Wizard to launch the wizard.

> **tip**
>
> Make sure to correct the lookup field's name to the original value if the Lookup Wizard changes it. The wizard might change the field name if it isn't the same as the base table's field name. Although Name AutoCorrect can handle field name changes, it's a much better database design practice to freeze the names of tables and fields. Change table and field names during the development process only if absolutely necessary.

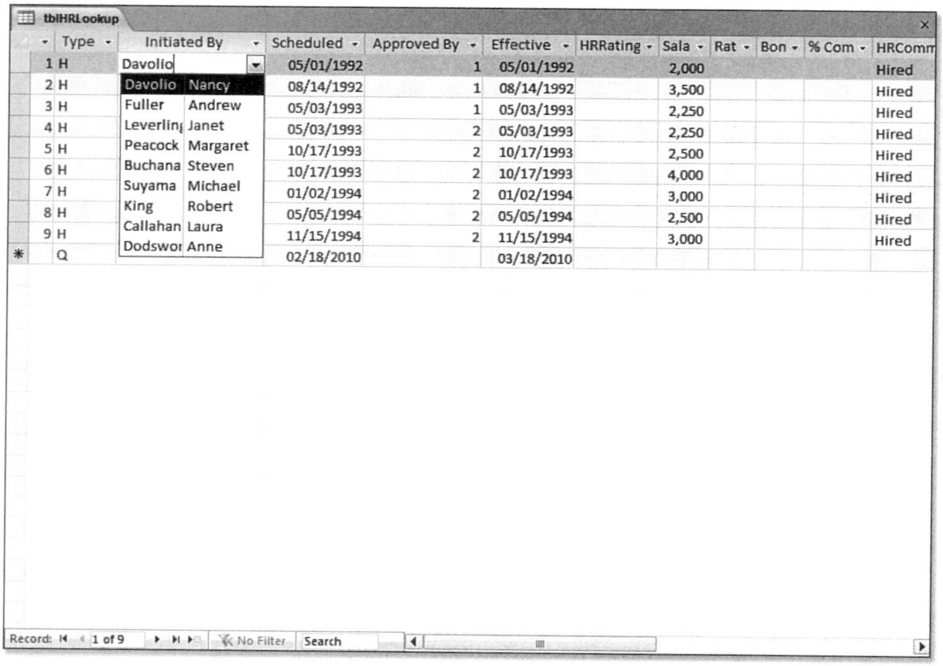

Figure 11.26
The lookup list of the InitiatedBy field has LastName and FirstName columns. Some FirstName values are truncated because the column width setting didn't compensate for the width of the vertical scrollbar. The last names in the InitiatedBy field are right-justified if you don't remove the Format property value from the field.

2. In the first Lookup Wizard dialog, select the I Will Type in the Values That I Want option and click the Next button.

3. In the second Lookup Wizard dialog, type **2** in the Number of Columns text box and press the Tab key to create the second list column.

4. Type **H**, **Hired**; **Q**, **Quarterly Review**; **Y**, **Yearly Review**; **S**, **Salary Adj.**; **R**, **Hourly Rate Adj.**; **B**, **Bonus Adj.**; **C**, **Commission Adj.**; **T**, **Terminated** in the Col1 and Col2 columns of eight rows. (Don't include the commas and semicolons.) Adjust the width of the columns to suit the entries (see Figure 11.28). Click the Next button to display the wizard's third dialog.

5. The ActionType field uses single-character abbreviations for the type of HRActions, so select Col1 as the "field that uniquely identifies the row." (The ActionType field doesn't uniquely identify the row; Col1 contains the single-character value that you want to insert into the field.) Click the Next button to display the fourth and final wizard dialog.

6. Accept ActionType as the label for your column and the Limit to List selection, and click the Finish button. The lookup properties for the ActionType field appear as shown in Figure 11.29. The Row Source Type is Value List. The Row Source contains the following values:

Figure 11.27
A single-col-
umn lookup
list, like that
used for the
EmployeeID
of the Orders
table, is bet-
ter suited
to selecting
peoples'
names.

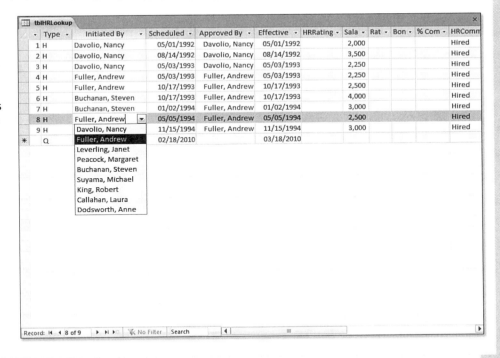

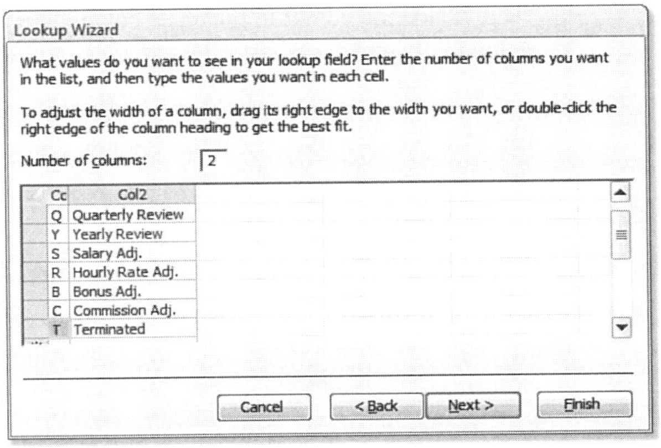

Figure 11.28
Specify the number of columns and type values in the second wizard dialog for a lookup
value list.

```
"H";"Hired";"Q";"Quarterly Review";"Y";"Yearly Review";

"S";"Salary Adj.";"R";"Hourly Rate Adj.";"B";

"Bonus Adj.";"C";"Commission Adj.";"T";"Terminated"
```

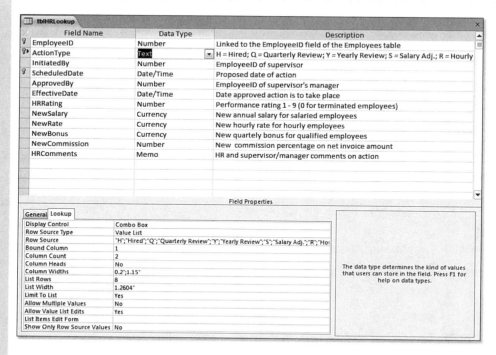

Figure 11.29
Compare the Lookup properties page for a lookup value list with that for a lookup list based on a related table (refer to Figure 11.25).

7. Click the Datasheet View button and save the changes to your table. Place the cursor in the Type column, and open the fixed value list to check the wizard's work (see Figure 11.30).

8. If you don't want the abbreviation to appear in the drop-down list, change the first entry of the Column Widths property value to 0.

Creating Multivalued Lookup Fields

 Access 2007 introduced multivalued lookup fields, a feature that lets you emulate a many-to-many relationship between foreign and primary keys of related tables. As an example, each stock-keeping unit in the original Northwind Products table has a single supplier. This book's version of the Products table has 18 generic (not trademarked) Korean and Chinese food products added, and the Suppliers table has two Korean and two Chinese suppliers added. The new Korean suppliers provide nonbranded kimchi and bean pastes, and the Chinese suppliers do the same for traditional sauces. Therefore, the Products table's SupplierID column is a good candidate for conversion to a multivalued lookup field.

> **note**
>
> Another reason for using the SupplierID column is to illustrate issues with displaying multiple items that have lengthy text. Supplier names include commas, which also are the item separator character, so the display can become ambiguous and difficult to read.

Figure 11.30
Datasheet
view displays
the fixed-
value lookup
list for the
ActionType
field.

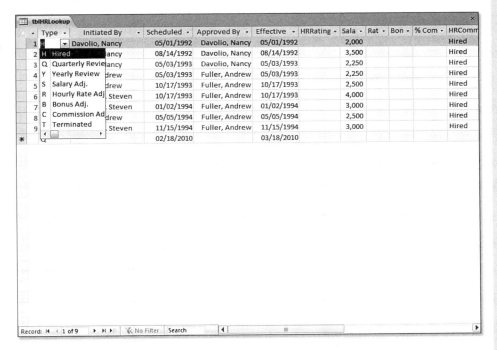

You first create a foreign-key or value-list lookup field by the procedures illustrated in the two preceding sections, and then set the
Allow Multiple Values property value to Yes. This is an irreversible
process, so it's a good practice to make a backup copy of the table
to be modified—Products for this example—before making the
change.

To change the SupplierID column's single-value lookup list to a
multivalued lookup list and generate the intermediary table for the
underlying many-to-many relationship between the Products and
Suppliers table, do the following:

1. Open the Relationships window and temporarily delete the relationship between the Suppliers and Products tables. You can't
   change the data type of the SupplierID field when it has a relationship defined.

2. Open the Products table in Design view and select the
   SupplierID column, which has a single-value lookup combo box.

3. In the Lookup properties sheet, change the value of the Allow
   Multiple Values property to Yes (see Figure 11.31).

 tip

To remove the lookup feature
from a field, select the field, click
the Lookup tab, and choose Text
Box from the Display Control
drop-down list.

 note

Access 2010 has an Edit List
Items dialog that you can use
to edit the value list of single-
column lookup lists. If you use
a single-column combo list, a
builder button appears in the
Row Source property value text
box, and the context menu for
the field in Datasheet View has
an Edit List Items choice.

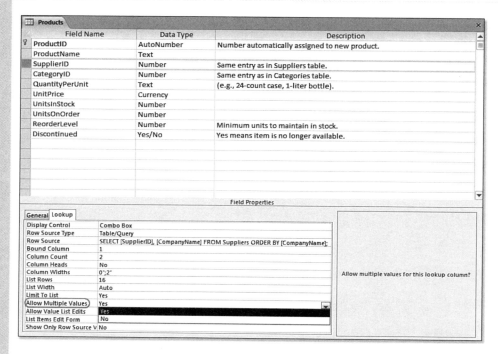

Figure 11.31
Changing the Allow Multiple Values property value to Yes adds check boxes to the conventional lookup combo box list.

4. Click the Datasheet View button, click Yes to save the table, and click Yes again to acknowledge that making this change is irreversible.

5. Open the SupplierID lookup list for one of the kimchi products, such as Hot Cabbage Kimchi (Jar), whose current supplier is Incheon Food Trading Co., Ltd., as indicated by the marked check box.

6. Scroll the list to the other kimchi supplier, Seoul Kimchi Co., Ltd., and mark the adjacent check box (see Figure 11.32). Click OK to close the list and save the selection.

7. Increase the width of the SupplierID datasheet column to display the two suppliers' CompanyName values (see Figure 11.33). Add second suppliers for a few other Asian food products.

8. Click the Relationships tab and notice that the Products field list's SupplierID field has changed to a node with a SupplierID.Value property.

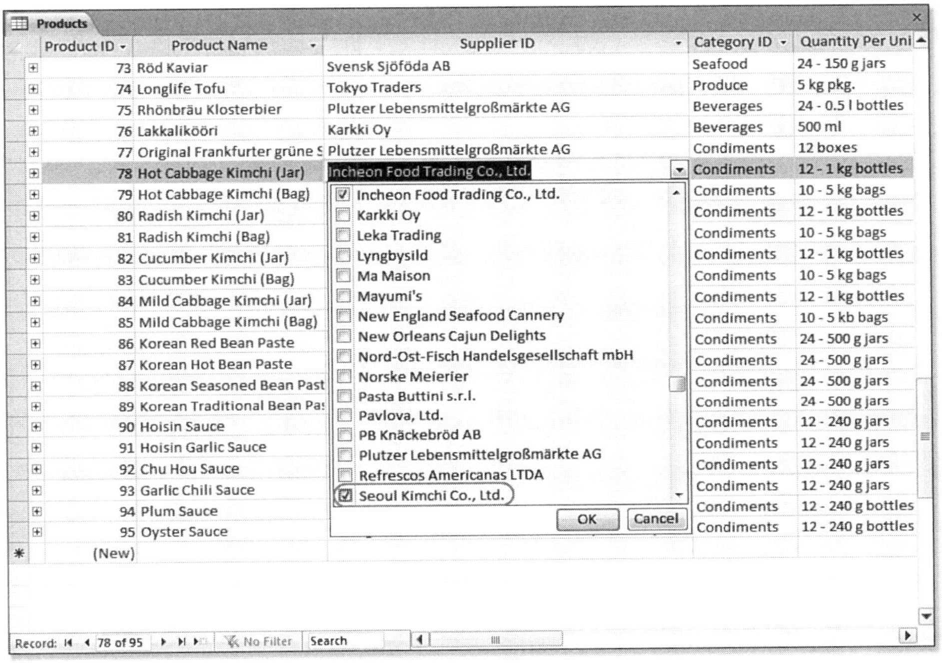

Figure 11.32
Add suppliers of the selected product by marking the check boxes in the multiple-values combo box list.

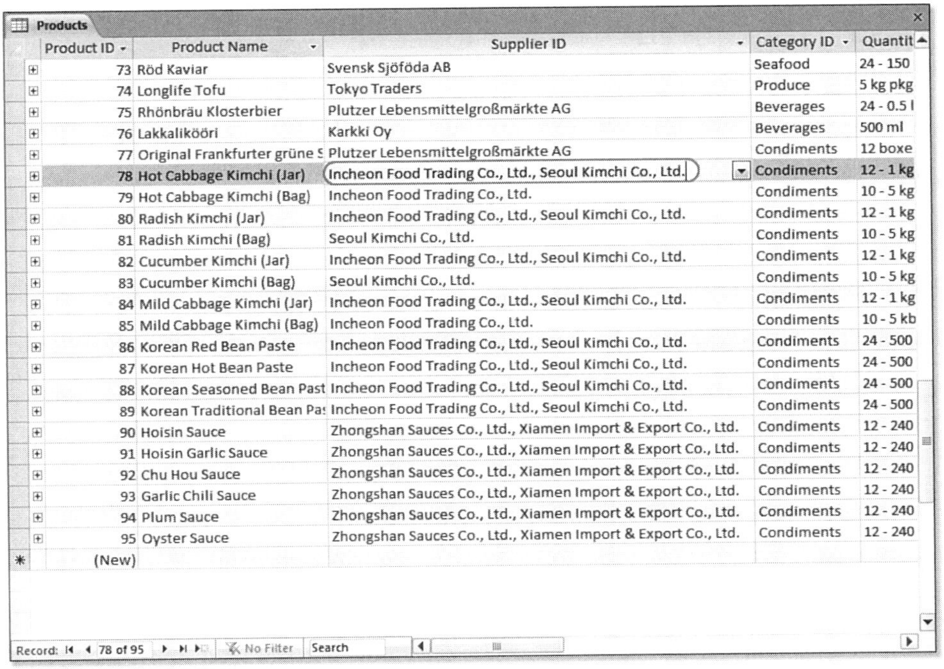

Figure 11.33
Displaying two or more suppliers in a multivalued lookup field requires increasing the field's display width greatly.

9. Attempt to create a relationship by dragging the SupplierID.Value property to the Suppliers tables' SupplierID field, marking the Edit Relationship dialog's Enforce Referential Integrity check box, and clicking OK. If the Products table is open, you receive the error message shown in Figure 11.34 when you click Create.

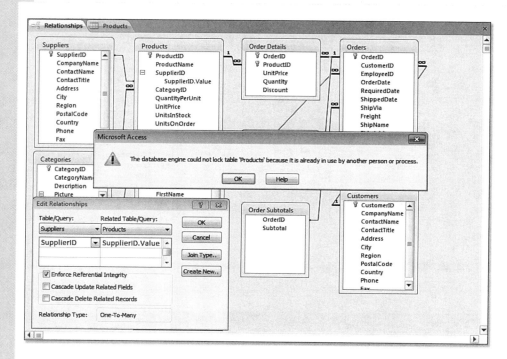

Figure 11.34
This message box displays the name of the hidden intermediary table to support the many-to-many relationship: 'f_<----GUID---->_ TempField*o'.

10. Click OK and Cancel to return to the Relationships window, close the Products window, save the layout, and re-create the relationship between the Products and Suppliers tables with referential integrity supported (see Figure 11.35).

11. Close the Relationships window and save the layout changes.

Specifying multivalued fields in queries requires a two- or three-part name, such as [Products]. SupplierID.Value. To create a query that displays multiple rows for products with multiple suppliers, follow these steps:

1. Create a new query in Design view. Add the Products and Suppliers tables.

2. Add the ProductID, ProductName, and SupplierID.Value fields from the Products table as well as the CompanyName field from the Suppliers table to the query (see Figure 11.36).

Figure 11.35
Creating a relationship that maintains referential integrity requires that neither table be opened in Design or Datasheet view.

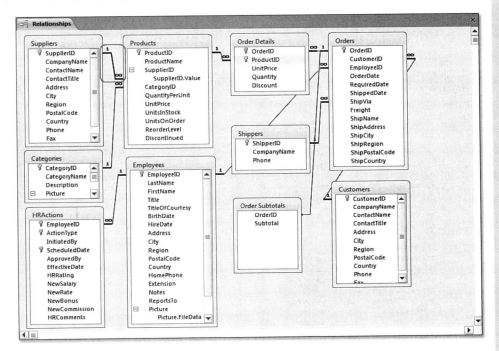

Figure 11.36
Use the Value property of multivalued fields in queries.

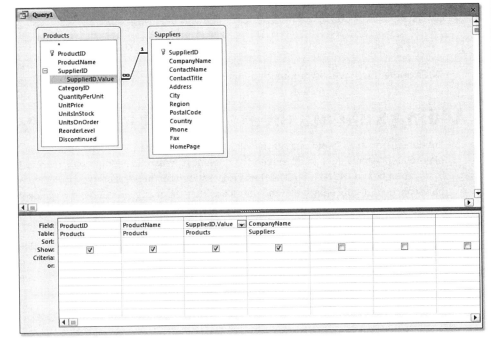

3. 🔔 Click the Run button and verify that the query returns a row for each product-supplier combination, as shown in Figure 11.37, for Korean food products.

Product ID ▾	Product Name ▾	Products.SupplierID.Value ▾	Suppliers.CompanyName ▾
78	Hot Cabbage Kimchi (Jar)	Incheon Food Trading Co., Ltd.	Incheon Food Trading Co., Ltd.
78	Hot Cabbage Kimchi (Jar)	Seoul Kimchi Co., Ltd.	Seoul Kimchi Co., Ltd.
79	Hot Cabbage Kimchi (Bag)	Incheon Food Trading Co., Ltd.	Incheon Food Trading Co., Ltd.
80	Radish Kimchi (Jar)	Seoul Kimchi Co., Ltd.	Seoul Kimchi Co., Ltd.
80	Radish Kimchi (Jar)	Incheon Food Trading Co., Ltd.	Incheon Food Trading Co., Ltd.
81	Radish Kimchi (Bag)	Seoul Kimchi Co., Ltd.	Seoul Kimchi Co., Ltd.
82	Cucumber Kimchi (Jar)	Seoul Kimchi Co., Ltd.	Seoul Kimchi Co., Ltd.
82	Cucumber Kimchi (Jar)	Incheon Food Trading Co., Ltd.	Incheon Food Trading Co., Ltd.
83	Cucumber Kimchi (Bag)	Seoul Kimchi Co., Ltd.	Seoul Kimchi Co., Ltd.
84	Mild Cabbage Kimchi (Jar)	Incheon Food Trading Co., Ltd.	Incheon Food Trading Co., Ltd.
84	Mild Cabbage Kimchi (Jar)	Seoul Kimchi Co., Ltd.	Seoul Kimchi Co., Ltd.
85	Mild Cabbage Kimchi (Bag)	Incheon Food Trading Co., Ltd.	Incheon Food Trading Co., Ltd.
86	Korean Red Bean Paste	Incheon Food Trading Co., Ltd.	Incheon Food Trading Co., Ltd.
86	Korean Red Bean Paste	Seoul Kimchi Co., Ltd.	Seoul Kimchi Co., Ltd.
87	Korean Hot Bean Paste	Incheon Food Trading Co., Ltd.	Incheon Food Trading Co., Ltd.
87	Korean Hot Bean Paste	Seoul Kimchi Co., Ltd.	Seoul Kimchi Co., Ltd.
88	Korean Seasoned Bean Past	Seoul Kimchi Co., Ltd.	Seoul Kimchi Co., Ltd.
88	Korean Seasoned Bean Past	Incheon Food Trading Co., Ltd.	Incheon Food Trading Co., Ltd.
89	Korean Traditional Bean Pas	Seoul Kimchi Co., Ltd.	Seoul Kimchi Co., Ltd.
89	Korean Traditional Bean Pas	Incheon Food Trading Co., Ltd.	Incheon Food Trading Co., Ltd.
90	Hoisin Sauce	Xiamen Import & Export Co., Ltd.	Xiamen Import & Export Co., Ltd.
90	Hoisin Sauce	Zhongshan Sauces Co., Ltd.	Zhongshan Sauces Co., Ltd.
91	Hoisin Garlic Sauce	Zhongshan Sauces Co., Ltd.	Zhongshan Sauces Co., Ltd.
91	Hoisin Garlic Sauce	Xiamen Import & Export Co., Ltd.	Xiamen Import & Export Co., Ltd.
92	Chu Hou Sauce	Zhongshan Sauces Co., Ltd.	Zhongshan Sauces Co., Ltd.
92	Chu Hou Sauce	Xiamen Import & Export Co., Ltd.	Xiamen Import & Export Co., Ltd.
93	Garlic Chili Sauce	Zhongshan Sauces Co., Ltd.	Zhongshan Sauces Co., Ltd.

Record: I◄ ◄ 1 of 109 ► ►I ►I   No Filter   Search

Figure 11.37
The Products. SupplierID. Value property returns a row for each product-supplier combination.

4. Save the query with an appropriate name, such as **qryProductsSuppliersMV**.

Adding Subdatasheets to a Table or Query

Subdatasheets are closely related to lookup fields, but serve a different purpose. *Subdatasheets* display related table values in an embedded datasheet, whereas lookup fields display base table values in a combo box or list box. Both of these Access features depend on the equivalent of one-to-many queries; the difference between the queries is that the many side of a subdatasheet usually is a related table, whereas a lookup field uses a query against a related table to supply the many side values.

You also can cascade subdatasheets to display related data of multiple joined tables or queries, a feature not applicable to lookup fields, but a table or query can't have more than one subdatasheet. Figure 11.38 illustrates the Customers table displaying the Orders subdatasheet for Alfreds Futterkiste with embedded sub-subdatasheets that display Order Details records.

Figure 11.38
The
Customers
table has
a two-level
subdata-
sheet
hierarchy.
Note the +
and - column
at the left
of both the
Customers
and Orders
subdata-
sheets.

Customers									
Customer I ▾	Company Name ▾		Contact Name ▾		Contact Title ▾			Addr ▲	
⊟ ALFKI	Alfreds Futterkiste		Maria Anders		Sales Representative		Obere Str. 57		

		Order I ▾	Employee ▾	Order Date ▾	Required Dat ▾	Shipped Dat ▾	Ship Via ▾	Freight ▾	Shi
	⊞	10643	Suyama, Michael	8/25/2006	9/22/2006	9/2/2006	Speedy Express	$29.46	Alfreds Futt
	⊞	10692	Peacock, Margaret	10/3/2006	10/31/2006	10/13/2006	United Package	$61.02	Alfreds Futt
	⊞	10702	Peacock, Margaret	10/13/2006	11/24/2006	10/21/2006	Speedy Express	$23.94	Alfreds Futt
	⊞	10835	Davolio, Nancy	1/15/2007	2/12/2007	1/21/2007	Federal Shipping	$69.53	Alfreds Futt
	⊞	10952	Davolio, Nancy	3/16/2007	4/27/2007	3/24/2007	Speedy Express	$40.42	Alfreds Futt
	⊟	11011	Leverling, Janet	4/9/2007	5/7/2007	4/13/2007	Speedy Express	$1.21	Alfreds Futt

	Product ▾	Unit Price ▾	Quantity ▾	Discount ▾	Click to Add ▾
	Escargots de Bourgogne	$13.25	40	5%	
	Flotemysost	$21.50	20	0%	
✱		$0.00	1	0%	

						$0.00	
✱	(New)						

⊞ ANATR	Ana Trujillo Emparedados y helados	Ana Trujillo	Owner	Avda. de la Constituci
⊞ ANTON	Antonio Moreno Taquería	Antonio Moreno	Owner	Mataderos 2312
⊞ AROUT	Around the Horn	Thomas Hardy	Sales Representative	120 Hanover Sq.
⊞ BERGS	Berglunds snabbköp	Christina Berglund	Order Administrator	Berguvsvägen 8
⊞ BLAUS	Blauer See Delikatessen	Hanna Moos	Sales Representative	Forsterstr. 57
⊞ BLONP	Blondel père et fils	Frédérique Citeaux	Marketing Manager	24, place Kléber
⊞ BOLID	Bólido Comidas preparadas	Martín Sommer	Owner	C/ Araquil, 67
⊞ BONAP	Bon app'	Laurence Lebihan	Owner	12, rue des Bouchers
⊞ BOTTM	Bottom-Dollar Markets	Elizabeth Lincoln	Accounting Manager	23 Tsawassen Blvd.
⊞ BSBEV	B's Beverages	Victoria Ashworth	Sales Representative	Fauntleroy Circus
⊞ CACTU	Cactus Comidas para llevar	Patricio Simpson	Sales Agent	Cerrito 333
⊞ CENTC	Centro comercial Moctezuma	Francisco Chang	Marketing Manager	Sierras de Granada 999
⊞ CHOPS	Chop-suey Chinese	Yang Wang	Owner	Hauptstr. 29
⊞ COMMI	Comércio Mineiro	Pedro Afonso	Sales Associate	Av. dos Lusíadas, 23 ▾

Record: I◄ ◄ 1 of 2 ► ►I ►✱ 🔻 No Filter Search

For more information on subdatasheets, **see** *"Table Properties for Subdatasheets,"* **p. 185.**

🔍 note

The lookup feature has generated controversy among seasoned database developers. Relational database purists object to embedding queries as table properties. Another objection to the use of foreign key drop-down lists is that it is easy for uninitiated users to inadvertently change data in a table after opening the list. If you're developing Access applications for others to use, user access to tables should be limited to forms, and lookup operations should use combo or list boxes on forms. Access 2010's lookup feature, however, is a useful tool, especially for new database users creating applications for their own use or for web databases to be processed by SharePoint Server 2010's Access Services.

Multivalued fields are even more controversial than lookup fields. Displaying multiple entity values in a single field, even if an intermediary table generates the values, gives users the impression that storing multiple entity values, such as foreign key values, in a single field is an acceptable practice for relational databases. Microsoft added this feature as an accommodation for SharePoint lists, which aren't relational tables. Use multivalue fields sparingly—if at all— because they won't upsize to SQL Server tables correctly.

Table Subdatasheets

Some of the tables of Northwind.accdb already have subdatasheets; Employees doesn't. To add an HRActions subdatasheet to the Employees table, follow these steps:

1. Verify in the Relationships window that a relationship exists between the EmployeeID fields of the HRActions and Employees tables.

2. Open the Employees table in Datasheet view.

3. Click one of the + symbols in the first column of the Employees datasheet to open the Insert Subdatasheet dialog.

4. Select the HRActions table in the list. The EmployeeID foreign key field of the HRActions table appears in the Link Child Fields drop-down list, and the EmployeeID field of the Employees table appears in the Link Master Fields list (see Figure 11.39). The HRAction table is included in the Relationships window; the relationship supplies the default values for the two drop-down lists.

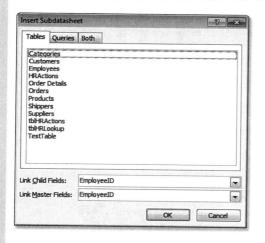

Figure 11.39
Clicking the + symbol in a row of a table that doesn't have a subdatasheet opens the Insert Subdatasheet dialog.

5. Click OK to add the subdatasheet and close the dialog. The subdatasheet for the selected record opens automatically. If the Subdatasheet Expanded property value is Yes, subdatasheets for all records open automatically.

> ⚡ **caution**
>
> Editing data in subdatasheets can lead to serious data entry errors. For example, if you use the Order Details subdatasheet to change an entry in the Product field, the UnitPrice value doesn't change to correspond to the price for the new product. Subdatasheets are dangerous; if you decide to use them, they should be used only to view, not edit, vital business data.

6. Click one or two of the + symbols in the Employees datasheet to display the newly added subdatasheets (see Figure 11.40).

7. Change to Table Design view, right-click the design grid (upper pane), and choose Properties to display the Table Property Sheet. The selections you make in the Insert Subdatasheet dialog appear in the subdatasheet-related properties of the table (see Figure 11.41).

note

The Link Master Fields and Link Child Fields values create a one-to-many join on the specified fields.

Figure 11.40
Only one HRActions record exists for each employee at this point.

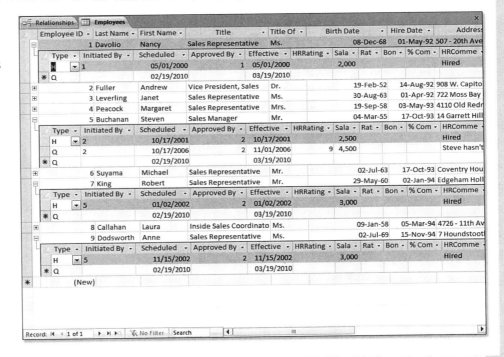

Query Subdatasheets

If you don't want your subdatasheet to display all the related table's columns, you must design a simple select query with only the desired fields and then use the query to populate the subdatasheet. As an example, you can minimize the width of the Orders subdatasheet of the Customers table by doing the following:

1. In Design view, create a simple SELECT query that includes only the OrderID, CustomerID (required for the master-child join), OrderDate, ShippedDate, and ShippedVia fields of the Orders table.

2. Click the empty area of the top pane to open the Query Properties sheet, and set the Recordset Type property to Snapshot. Selecting Snapshot creates a read-only subdatasheet to prevent editing. Close the query and save it as **qryShortOrders**.

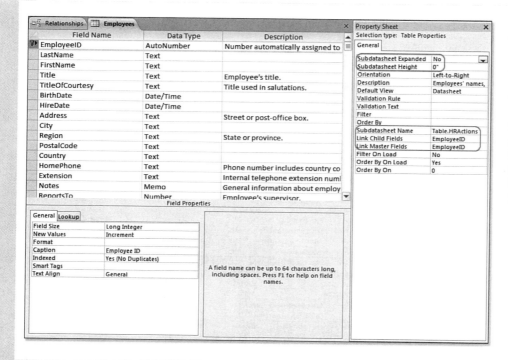

Figure 11.41
You also can add a sub-datasheet by opening the Table Property Sheet and selecting a table or query from the Subdatasheet name list.

3. Open the Customers table in Design view, open the Table Property Sheet, and select Query.qryShortOrders from the Subdatasheet Name list. CustomerID remains the value of the linked fields.

4. Return to Datasheet view, saving your changes. The expanded subdatasheet appears as shown in Figure 11.42, without the + sign column. The query is read-only, so the subdatasheet has no tentative append record and you can't edit the data.

5. In Design view, create another select query that includes all fields (*) of the Order Details table. Open the Query Property Sheet, set the Recordset Type property value to Snapshot, close the windows, and save the query as **qryShort-OrderDetails**.

tip

The default value of the Subdatasheet Name property for new tables you create is [Auto], which adds the column of boxed + symbols to a new table datasheet. To open the Add Subdatasheet dialog for a new table, choose Insert, Subdatasheet. Alternatively, you can set the subdatasheet properties directly in the Table Properties sheet. To remove a subdatasheet, set the Subdatasheet Name property value to [None]. If you remove a subdatasheet from a table, setting Subdatasheet Name to [Auto] displays the boxed + symbols and lets you open a new subdatasheet in Datasheet view.

Figure 11.42
Use a
Snapshot
query to
create a
read-only
subdata-
sheet.

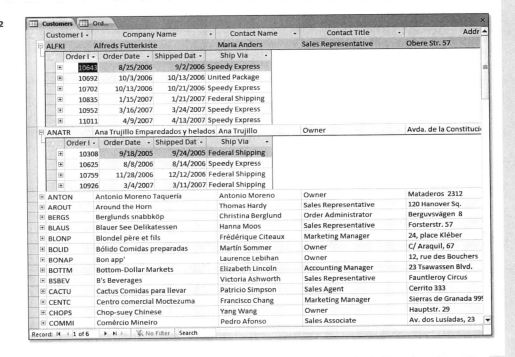

6. Close the Customers table, open qryShortOrders in Design view, click an empty area of the upper pane, and choose Properties to open the Query Property Sheet.

7. Select Query.qryShortOrderDetails in the Subdatasheet Name field and then type **OrderID** in the two Link...Fields text boxes (see Figure 11.43). You must type the field names because you haven't established a relationship between the query and table in the Relationships window.

8. Run the query and then expand one or more of the sub-datasheets to test your work (see Figure 11.44).

9. Close qryShortOrders, save your changes, open the Customers table, and display the subdatasheets. The new version of the Customers table appears as shown in Figure 11.45. You can open the Products list, but you can't change the value of the Product column.

tip

The default value of the Subdatasheet Name property for new tables you create is [Auto], which adds the column of boxed + symbols to a new table datasheet. To open the Add Subdatasheet dialog for a new table, choose Insert, Subdatasheet. Alternatively, you can set the subdatasheet properties directly in the Table Properties sheet. To remove a subdatasheet, set the Subdatasheet Name property value to [None]. If you remove a subdatasheet from a table, setting Subdatasheet Name to [Auto] displays the boxed + symbols and lets you open a new subdatasheet in Datasheet view.

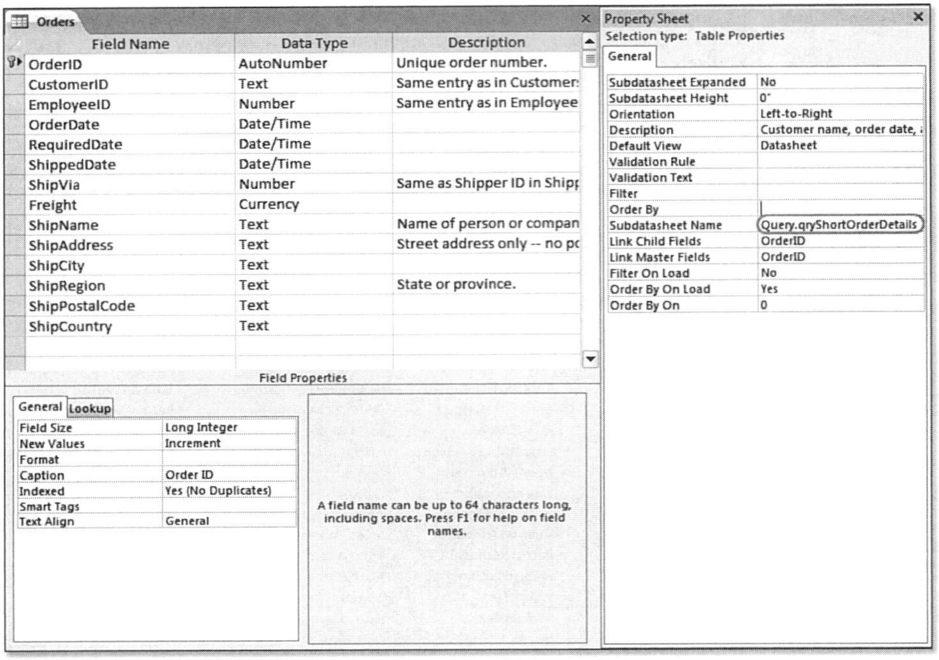

Figure 11.43
After adding Query.qryOrderDetails as the value of the Subdatasheet Name property, you manually set the Link Child Fields and Link Master Fields property values.

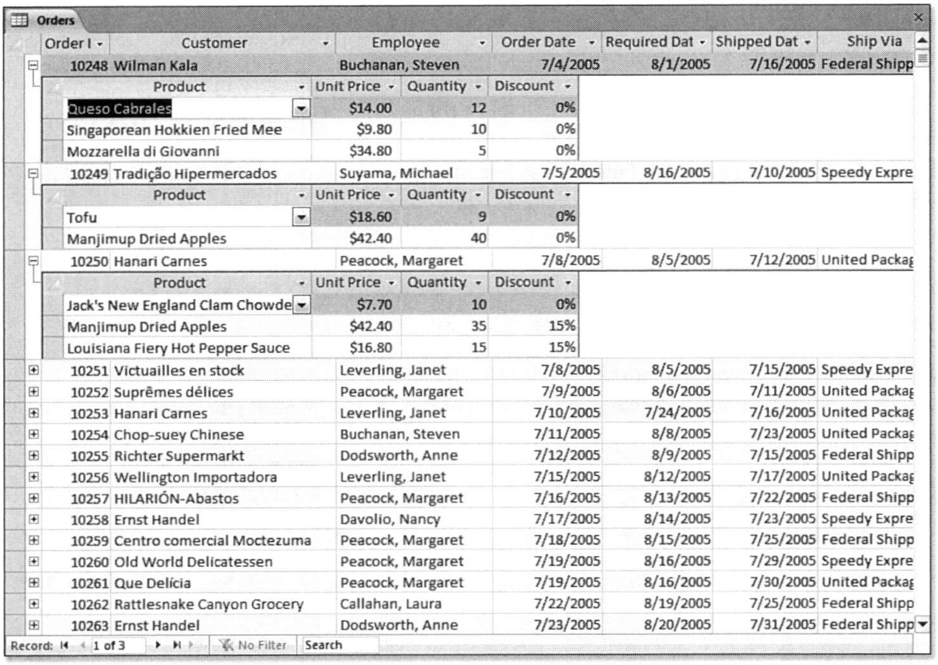

Figure 11.44
The read-only qryShortOrders query has a read-only query subdatasheet based on qryShortOrderDetails.

Figure 11.45
The subdata-sheet and sub-subdata-sheet are read-only, but the Customers table continues to have read-write attributes, as indicated by its tentative append record.

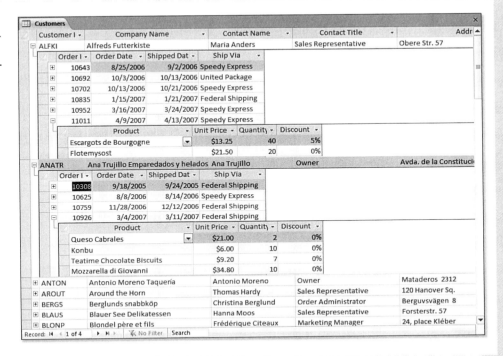

Outer, Self, and Theta Joins

The preceding sections of this chapter described the inner join, which is the most common type of join in database applications. Access also lets you create three other joins: outer, self, and theta. The following sections describe these three less-common types of joins, which also apply to SQL Server views, table-returning functions, and stored procedures.

Creating Outer Joins

Outer joins let you display the fields of all records in a table participating in a query, regardless of whether corresponding records exist in the joined table. Access lets you choose between left and right outer joins.

A left outer join query displays all records in the first table you specify, regardless of whether matching records exist in the second table. For example, *Table1* LEFT JOIN *Table2* displays all records in *Table2*. Conversely, a right outer join query displays all records in the second table, regardless of a record's existence in the first table. Records in the second table without corresponding records in the first table usually, but not necessarily, are orphan records; these kinds of records can have a many-to-one relationship to another table.

To practice creating a left outer join to detect whether records are missing for an employee in the HRActions table, follow these steps:

1. Open the Employees table and add a record for a new (bogus) employee. You need only add values for the LastName and FirstName fields.

2. Open a new query and add the Employees and HRActions tables.

3. Drag the EmployeeID field symbol to the EmployeeID field of HRActions to create an inner join between these fields if Access doesn't create the join automatically.

4. Select and drag the LastName and FirstName fields of the Employees table to columns 1 and 2 of the Query Design grid. Select and drag the ActionType and ScheduledDate fields of the HRActions table to columns 3 and 4.

5. Click the line joining EmployeeID with EmployeeID to select it, as shown in Figure 11.46. The thickness of the center part of the line increases to indicate the selection. (In Figure 11.46, the two Field List boxes are separated so that the thin section of the join line is apparent.)

6. Double-click the thin section of the join line to open the Join Properties dialog. (Double-clicking either of the line's thick sections displays the Query Property Sheet.) Type 1 is a conventional inner join, type 2 is a left join, and type 3 is a right join.

> **note**
>
> Access adds an arrowhead to the line that joins EmployeeID and EmployeeID. The direction of the arrow, left to right, indicates that you've created a left join between the tables, assuming that you haven't moved the field lists from their original position in the table.

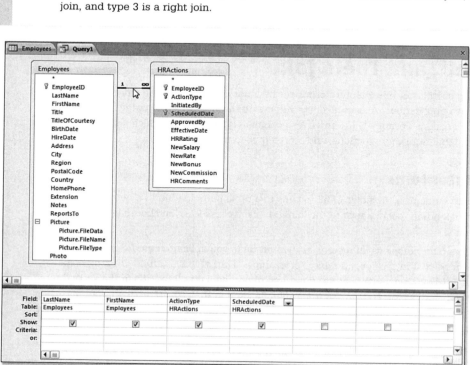

Figure 11.46
Double-clicking the thin region of the join line opens the Join Properties dialog.

7. Select a type 2 join—a left join—by selecting option 2 (see Figure 11.47). Click OK to close the dialog.

8. Click the Run button to display the result of the left join query. In Figure 11.48, the employee you added without a record in the HRActions table appears in the result table's last active row. (Your query resultset might differ, depending on the number of entries that you made when creating the HRActions table.)

Figure 11.47
Select the option for a type 2 join, which includes all records in the left table and only those records of the right table where the two column values match.

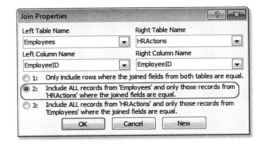

Figure 11.48
A record for EmployeeID 10 with no HRActions record(s) appears in this left outer join.

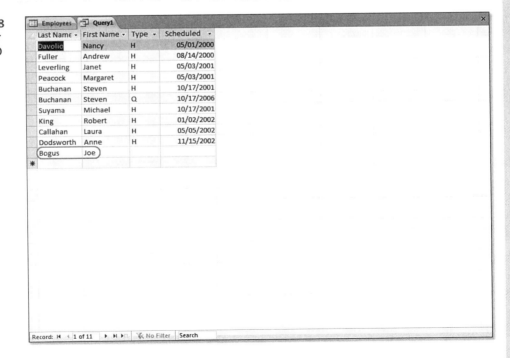

9. Close, but don't save, the query, and then delete the bogus record in the Employees table.

If you could add an HR department action for a nonexistent EmployeeID (referential integrity rules for HRActions table prevent you from doing so), a right join would show the invalid entry with blank employee name fields.

Creating Self-Joins

Self-joins relate values in a single table. Creating a self-join requires that you add a copy of the table to the query and then add a join between the related fields. An example of self-join use is to determine whether supervisors have approved HRActions that they initiated, which is prohibited by the fictitious personnel manual for Northwind Traders.

To create this kind of self-join for the HRActions table, follow these steps:

1. Open a new query and add the HRActions table.

2. Add another copy of the HRActions table to the query by clicking the Add button again. Access names the copy HRActions_1. Close the Show Tables dialog.

3. Drag the original table's InitiatedBy field to the copied table's ApprovedBy field (look ahead to the top pane of Figure 11.49).

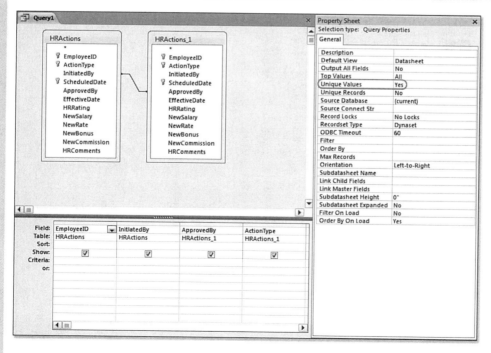

Figure 11.49
A self-join returns rows for which values of two fields in the same table are equal.

4. Drag the EmployeeID and InitiatedBy fields of the original table, and the ApprovedBy and ActionType fields of the copy of the HRActions table, to the Field row of columns 1–4, respectively, of the Query Design grid (see Figure 11.49).

5. With self-joins, you must specify that only unique values are included. (If you don't specify unique values, the query returns every row.) Right-click an empty area in the Query Design window's upper pane, choose Properties, set the value of the Query Property Sheet's Unique Values property to Yes, and close the Query Property Sheet.

6. Click the Run button to display the records in which the same employee initiated and approved an HR department action, as shown in Figure 11.50. In this case, EmployeeID 1 (Nancy Davolio) was the first employee; EmployeeID 2 (Andrew Fuller) is a vice-president and can override personnel policy. (Your results might differ, depending on the entries you made in the HRActions table.)

Figure 11.50
This data-
sheet dis-
plays the
resultset of
the design
of Figure
11.49. If you
don't set
the Unique
Values prop-
erty to Yes,
the resultset
has 27 rows.

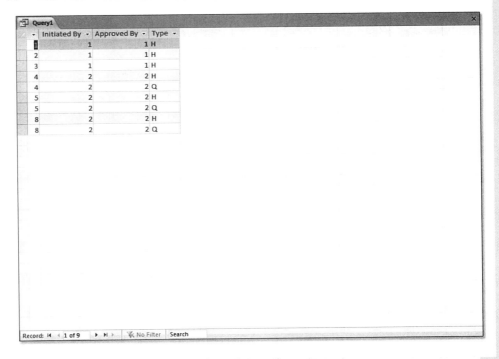

Creating Not-Equal (Theta) Joins with Criteria

Most joins are based on fields with equal values, but sometimes you need to create a join on unequal fields. Joins that you create graphically in Access are restricted to conventional equi-joins and outer joins. You can create the equivalent of a not-equal theta join by applying a criterion to one of the two fields you want to test for not-equal values.

Finding customers that have different billing and shipping addresses, as mentioned previously, is an example in which a not-equal theta join is useful. To create such a join, follow these steps:

1. Create a new query and add the Customers and Orders tables.

2. Select the Customers table's CompanyName and Address fields and the Orders table's ShipAddress field. Drag them to the Query Design grid's first three columns.

3. Type <>**Customers.Address** in the Criteria row of the ShipAddress column. The Query Design window appears as shown in Figure 11.51.

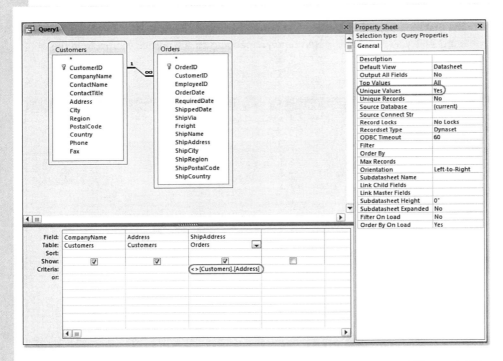

Figure 11.51
Not-equal joins require a not-equal (⟨⋯⋯⟩) WHERE clause criterion to establish the join.

4. Right-click an empty area in the Query Design window's upper pane and choose Properties to open the Query Property Sheet and set the value of the Unique Values property to Yes. Otherwise, the query returns a record for every order with a different ship address.

5. Run the query. Only the records for customers that placed orders with different billing and shipping addresses appear, as shown in Figure 11.52.

6. Click the Close Window button and save your query if you want.

 note

Typing ⟨⋯⋯⟩Orders.ShipAddress in the Address column gives the same result as ⟨⋯⋯⟩Customers.Address in the ShipAddress column.

Figure 11.52
The result-set of the not-equal join displays customers with differ-ent shipping and billing addresses. If you don't set the Unique Values prop-erty to Yes, the query returns 51 rows.

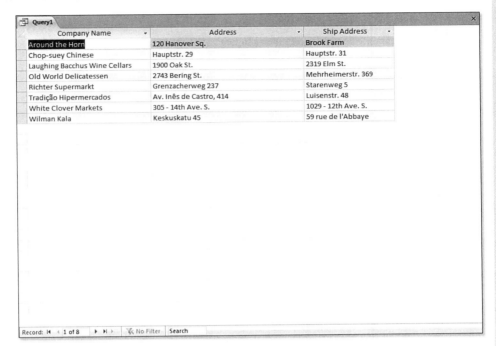

Updating Table Data with Queries

Queries you create with the Unique Values property set to Yes to add the ANSI SQL `DISTINCT` modifier to the SQL statement aren't updatable. If you set the Unique Records property, instead of the Unique Values property, to Yes, some queries are updatable because Unique Records substitutes Access SQL's `DISTINCTROW` modifier for `DISTINCT`.

 note

As mentioned in the earlier "Creating Multicolumn Inner Joins and Selecting Unique Values" section, you can cre-ate a theta join by changing the operator of an equi-join criterion from = to ⟨·······⟩. If you do this, you receive an error message every time you open the query in Design view.

Unique Records queries create Recordset objects of the updatable Dynaset type. You can't update table data with a query unless you see the tentative (blank) append record (with the asterisk in the select button) at the end of the query result table. The next few sections describe the conditions under which you can update a record of a table included in a query. The following sections also discuss how to use the Output Field Property Sheet to format query-data display and editing.

Characteristics That Determine Whether You Can Update a Query

Adding new records to tables or updating existing data in tables included in a query is a definite advantage in some circumstances. Correcting data errors that appear when you run the query is especially tempting. Unfortunately, you can't append or update records in many queries that you create. The following properties of a query prevent you from appending and updating records:

- The Unique Values property is set to Yes in the Query Property Sheet.

- The Recordset Type property is set to Snapshot in the Query Property Sheet.

- Self-joins are used in the query.

- Access SQL aggregate functions, such as Sum( ), are employed in the query. Crosstab queries, for example, use SQL aggregate functions.

- The query has three or more tables with many-to-one-to-many relationships. Most queries with indirect relationships fall in this category.

note

T-SQL doesn't support Access SQL's DISTINCTROW modifier, and the rules that determine the updatability of SQL Server views and table-returning, user-defined functions differ from those of Access. Chapter 27, "Moving from Access Queries to Transact-SQL," covers updatability issues with SQL Server views and functions. Recordsets returned by SQL Server stored procedures aren't updatable.

- No primary key field(s) with a unique (No Duplicates) index exist for the one table in a one-to-many relationship.

When designing a query to use as the basis of a form for data entry or editing, make sure that none of the preceding properties apply to the query.

If none of the preceding properties apply to the query or any table within the query, you can append records to and update fields of queries in the following:

- A single-table query

- Both tables in a one-to-one relationship

- The many table in a one-to-many relationship or the most-many table in a one-to-many-to-many relationship

- The one table in a one-to-many relationship if none of the fields of the many table appear in the query

Updating the one table in a one-to-many query is a special case in Access. To enable updates to this table, follow these steps:

1. Add to the query the primary key field or fields of the one table and additional fields to update. You don't need to add the primary key field if its Access data type is AutoNumber.

2. Add the foreign key field or fields of the many table that correspond to the key field or fields of the one table; this step is required to select the appropriate records for updating.

3. Add the criteria to select the records for updating to the fields chosen in step 2.

4. Click the Show box so that the many table fields don't appear in the query.

After following these steps, you can edit the non-key fields of the one table. You can't, however, alter the values of key fields that have relationships with records in the many table, unless you specify Cascade Update Related Fields in the Relationships window's Edit Relationships dialog for the join. Otherwise, such a modification violates referential integrity.

By adding lookup fields to tables, you often can avoid writing one-to-many queries and precisely following the preceding rules to make such queries updatable. For example, the Orders table, which includes three lookup fields (CustomerID, EmployeeID, and ShipVia) is updatable. If you want to allow updates in Datasheet view (called *browse updating*), using lookup fields is a simpler approach than creating an updatable query. Most database developers, however, consider simple browse updating to be a poor practice because of the potential for inadvertent data entry errors. As mentioned earlier, browse updating with lookup fields is especially prone to data entry errors.

 note

You can't set both the Unique Values and Unique Records properties to Yes. These choices are mutually exclusive. In Access 2010, the default setting of both the Unique Values and Unique Records properties is No.

Taking Advantage of Access's Row Fix-up Feature

Access queries and SQL Server views have a row fix-up feature (called AutoLookup by Access) that fills in query data when you add a new record or change the value of the foreign key of a many-side record. To take advantage of row fix-up, your query must include the foreign key value, not the primary key value of the join.

Northwind Traders' Orders Qry is an example of a query that uses row fix-up. Orders Qry includes every field of the Customers and Orders tables, *except* the CustomerID field of the Customers table. To demonstrate row fix-up, do the following:

1. Open the Orders Qry in Datasheet view, and scroll to the tentative append record. Alternatively, press Ctrl+End, Home, and the down arrow (↓) to avoid the scrolling exercise.

2. Tab to the Customer column, open the lookup list, which is bound to the CustomerID field of the Customers table, and select a customer for a new order. The edited record symbol replaces the asterisk, and the datasheet adds a new tentative append row.

3. Scroll the columns to the right until you reach the Address column, which displays the Address field of the Customers table. Row fix-up automatically enters data from the Customer table's record for the selected customer (see Figure 11.53).

4. Press Esc to cancel the new record addition.

Row fix-up is more useful for forms that are bound to a query than for queries that update data in Datasheet view. Orders Qry is the data source for the sample Orders form. When you add a new order with this form, row fix-up automatically updates its customer data.

 tip

You can't edit data returned by a query with three or more tables in Query Datasheet view, unless the query is one-to-many-to-many, but you can update values in other types of three-table queries in forms that are bound to the query. To make the query updatable with forms, set the Recordset Type property value to Dynaset (Inconsistent Updates).

 note

The format symbol for month in the [Customize] Regional Options dialog is "M", not "m", which is the systemwide symbol for minutes. Access and VBA use "n" for minutes.

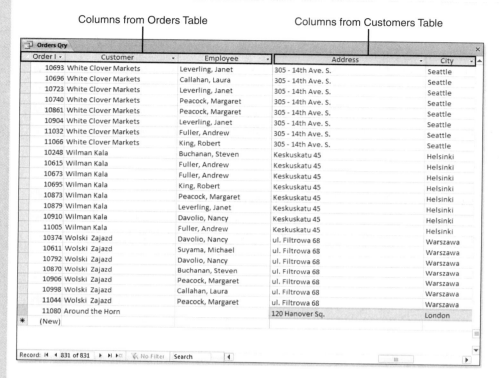

Columns from Orders Table | Columns from Customers Table

Figure 11.53
Row fix-up automatically adds data from the table on the one side of a one-to-many relationship when you add a new row. The first three columns of the datasheet are frozen to demonstrate row fix-up when adding a new record to the Orders table.

Formatting Data with the Query Field Property Sheet

The display format of data in queries is inherited from the format of the data in the tables that underlie the query. You can override the table format by using the **Format** (*ColumnName, FormatString*) function to create a calculated field. In this case, however, the column isn't updatable.

Access provides an easier query column formatting method—the Field Property Sheet, which you can use to format the display of query data. You also can create an input mask to aid in updating the query data. To open the Field Property Sheet, place the cursor in the Field cell of the query column that you want to format and then click the Properties button of the toolbar. Figure 11.54 shows the Field Property Sheet for the OrderDate column of the Orders Qry. Specifying formats in queries lets you alter the column's display format without affecting the display of table fields.

By default, Access 2010's General Date, Long Date, and Short Date formats display four-digit years, which is required for Year 2000 (Y2K) conformance. (Four-digit years is the default for Windows 7, Vista, XP, and 2000.) You can alter the default Short Date or Long Date format in text boxes of the Date page of Control

tip

Add captions to queries, not tables. Table Datasheet view should display field names rather than captions to conform to good database design principles. Unfortunately, the tables in Northwind.accdb don't conform to this recommendation.

Figure 11.54
Access's
Medium
Date format
(dd-mmm-
yy) doesn't
comply with
Y2K require-
ments. To
specify a
four-year
Medium Date
format for
all Windows
operating
systems,
assign the
dd-mmm-
yyyy format.

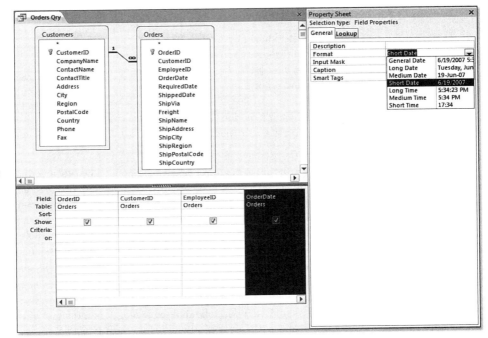

Panel's Customize Regional Options dialog. (Windows 2000's tool is called Regional Options.) Systemwide settings specify the General Date, Long Date, and Short Date formats, but don't affect the Medium Date style. To obtain a four-digit year display with Medium Date format, you must type the Format descriptor string—**dd-mmm-yyyy**—in the Format text box. Most sample tables in Northwind.accdb have the custom dd-mmm-yyyy format applied.

The Field Property Sheet displays the following subset of the properties that apply to a query's fields:

- *Description* lets you enter the text to appear in the status bar when the user selects the field in Datasheet view.

- *Format* lets you control the appearance of the data in Datasheet view, such as Short Date.

- *Input Mask* lets you specify the format for entering data, such as 99/99/0000. (To create an input mask that is appropriate for the field data type, click the ellipsis (builder) button to open the Input Mask Wizard.)

For more information on the Input Mask Wizard and a listing of placeholders, **see** *"Using Input Masks,"* **p. 202.**

- *Caption* lets you change the query column heading, such as Received, for the Order Date column.

- *Smart Tags* are a feature introduced by Access 2007 that enable links to web-based resources and perform other operations, such as propagating changes to field or column properties to dependent forms and reports.

   To learn more about smart tags, **see** *"Working with Object Dependencies and Access Smart Tags,"* **p. 228.**

 tip

Always use the default Short Date and Long Date systemwide formats. Don't depend on users to change their default formats. If you want to specify two-digit day and month values, for example, use a custom date format, such as mm/dd/yyyy.

Each of the preceding query properties follows the rules described in Chapter 5 for setting table field properties. Adding a value (Received) for the Caption property of a query against the Orders table is the equivalent of adding a column alias by typing **Received:** as a prefix in the OrderDate column's Field cell. Adding a Caption property value, however, doesn't change the SQL statement for the query. The value of the Input Mask property need not correspond exactly to the value of the Format property, but input mask characters don't appear if you try to use a Short Date mask with a Medium Date format you apply in the query.

For example, the Received (OrderDate) column in Figure 11.55, which shows the effect of setting the property values shown in the preceding list, has a single-digit (no leading zero) month and day for the Short Date display format, which overrides the mm/dd/yyyy format of the table field. The input mask (99/99/0000;0;_) permits updating with one-digit or two-digit months and days. Adding or editing a single-digit or two-digit entry gives the same result. Most typists prefer to enter a consistent number of digits in a date field.

Making All Fields of Tables Accessible

Most queries you create include only the fields you specifically choose. To choose these fields, you either select them from or type them into the drop-down combo list in the Query Design grid's Field row, or you drag the field names from the field lists to the appropriate cells in the Field row. You can, however, quickly include all fields of a table in a query. Access provides the following three methods for including all fields of a table in a query:

Queries with Linked Tables Aren't Updatable

Unless you specify (or create) primary key indexes for each dBASE table that participates in the query, you can't create an updatable one-to-many query with your linked dBASE tables even if your query displays only fields from the many side of the relationship. The field or fields that you choose must uniquely identify a record; the index doesn't allow duplicate values. Delete the attachment to the dBASE tables and then reattach the table with the primary key indexes. Make sure that you specify which index is the primary key index in the Select Unique Record Identifier dialog that appears after you attach each table.

Also, make sure that you don't include the field of the many-side table on which the join is created in the query. If you add the joined field to the field list, your query isn't updatable.

Figure 11.55
This query uses m/d/yyyy display format and a 99/99/0000 input mask to allow month and date entries as single- or two-digit values.

Order I ▾	Customer	▾	Employee	▾	Order Date ▾	Required Dat ▾	Shipped Dat ▾	Ship Vi: ▲
10643	Alfreds Futterkiste		Suyama, Michael		8/25/2006	9/22/2006	9/2/2006	Speedy Exp
10692	Alfreds Futterkiste		Peacock, Margaret		10/3/2006	10/31/2006	10/13/2006	United Pacl
10702	Alfreds Futterkiste		Peacock, Margaret		10/13/2006	11/24/2006	10/21/2006	Speedy Exp
10835	Alfreds Futterkiste		Davolio, Nancy		1/15/2007	2/12/2007	1/21/2007	Federal Shi
10952	Alfreds Futterkiste		Davolio, Nancy		3/16/2007	4/27/2007	3/24/2007	Speedy Exp
11011	Alfreds Futterkiste		Leverling, Janet		4/9/2007	5/7/2007	4/13/2007	Speedy Exp
10308	Ana Trujillo Emparedados y hela(		King, Robert		9/18/2005	10/16/2005	9/24/2005	Federal Shi
10625	Ana Trujillo Emparedados y hela(		Leverling, Janet		8/8/2006	9/5/2006	8/14/2006	Speedy Exp
10759	Ana Trujillo Emparedados y hela(		Leverling, Janet		11/28/2006	12/26/2006	12/12/2006	Federal Shi
10926	Ana Trujillo Emparedados y hela(		Peacock, Margaret		3/4/2007	4/1/2007	3/11/2007	Federal Shi
10365	Antonio Moreno Taquería		Leverling, Janet		11/27/2005	12/25/2005	12/2/2005	United Pacl
10507	Antonio Moreno Taquería		King, Robert		4/15/2006	5/13/2006	4/22/2006	Speedy Exp
10535	Antonio Moreno Taquería		Peacock, Margaret		5/13/2006	6/10/2006	5/21/2006	Speedy Exp
10573	Antonio Moreno Taquería		King, Robert		6/19/2006	7/17/2006	6/20/2006	Federal Shi
10677	Antonio Moreno Taquería		Davolio, Nancy		9/22/2006	10/20/2006	9/26/2006	Federal Shi
10682	Antonio Moreno Taquería		Leverling, Janet		9/25/2006	10/23/2006	10/1/2006	United Pacl
10856	Antonio Moreno Taquería		Leverling, Janet		1/28/2007	2/25/2007	2/10/2007	United Pacl
10355	Around the Horn		Suyama, Michael		11/15/2005	12/13/2005	11/20/2005	Speedy Exp
10383	Around the Horn		Callahan, Laura		12/16/2005	1/13/2006	12/18/2005	Federal Shi
10453	Around the Horn		Davolio, Nancy		2/21/2006	3/21/2006	2/26/2006	United Pacl
10558	Around the Horn		Davolio, Nancy		6/4/2006	7/2/2006	6/10/2006	United Pacl
10707	Around the Horn		Peacock, Margaret		10/16/2006	10/30/2006	10/23/2006	Federal Shi
10741	Around the Horn		Peacock, Margaret		11/14/2006	11/28/2006	11/18/2006	Federal Shi
10743	Around the Horn		Davolio, Nancy		11/17/2006	12/15/2006	11/21/2006	United Pacl
10768	Around the Horn		Leverling, Janet		12/8/2006	1/5/2007	12/15/2006	United Pacl
10793	Around the Horn		Leverling, Janet		12/24/2006	1/21/2007	1/8/2007	Federal Shi
10864	Around the Horn		Peacock, Margaret		2/2/2007	3/2/2007	2/9/2007	United Pacl ▾

Record: I◄ ◄ 1 of 830 ► ►I ►☰ 🦋 No Filter | Search

- Double-click the field list title bar of the table to select all fields in the field list, and then drag the field list to the Query Design grid. Each field appears in a column of the grid.

- Drag the asterisk (*) to a single Query Design grid column. To sort on or apply selection criteria to a field, drag the field to the Query Design grid and clear the Show check box for the field.

- Set the Output All Fields property value in the Query Properties sheet to Yes to add with asterisks all fields of all tables to the grid.

 note

ANSI SQL and most SQL (client/server) databases support the equivalent of Access SQL's Avg(), Count(), First(), Last(), Max(), Min(), and Sum() aggregate functions as AVG(), COUNT(), FIRST(), LAST(), MAX(), MIN(), and SUM(), respectively. T-SQL also provides equivalents of Access's StdDev(), StdDevP(), Var(), and VarP() functions with the same names.

Making Calculations on Multiple Records

One of SQL's most powerful capabilities is obtaining summary information almost instantly from specified sets of records in tables. Summarized information from databases is the basis for virtually all management information systems (MIS) and business intelligence (BI) projects. These systems or projects usually answer questions: What are our sales to date for this month? How did last month's sales compare with the same month last year? To answer these questions, you must create queries that make calculations on field values from all or selected sets of records in a table. To make calculations on table values, you must create a query that uses the table and employ Access's SQL aggregate functions to perform the calculations.

Using the SQL Aggregate Functions

Summary calculations on fields of tables included in query result tables use the SQL aggregate functions listed in Table 11.1. These are called aggregate functions because they apply to groups (aggregations) of data cells. The SQL aggregate functions satisfy the requirements of most queries needed for business applications.

Σ StDev() and Var() evaluate population samples. You can choose these functions from the drop-down list in the Query Design grid's Total row. (The Total row appears when you click the Totals button on the toolbar or choose View, Totals.) StDevP() and VarP() evaluate populations and must be entered as expressions. If you're familiar with statistical principles, you recognize the difference in the calculation methods of standard deviation and variance for populations and samples of populations. The following section explains the method of choosing the SQL aggregate function for the column of a query.

 tip

Some examples of this chapter use Access Like "{m¦*}/{d¦*}/yyyy" expressions as shorthand for Between #mm/dd/yyyy# And #mm/dd/yyyy# WHERE clause date constraints. Current versions of the Microsoft Data Access Components and the Access OLE DB driver don't recognize Like "*/*/yyyy" and similar Like expressions. If you plan to copy Access SQL statements to Visual Basic .NET programs, use the Between...And operator, not Like for dates.

Making Calculations Based on All Records of a Table

Managers, especially sales and marketing managers, are most often concerned with information about orders received and shipments made during specific periods of time. Financial managers are interested in calculated values, such as the total amount of unpaid invoices and the average number

Table 11.1 SQL Aggregate Functions

Function	Description	Field Types
Avg()	Average of values	All types except Text, Memo, in a field and OLE Object
Count()	Number of Not Null	All field types values in a field
First()	Value of a field of	All field types the first record
Last()	Value of a field of	All field types the last record
Max()	Greatest value in	All numeric data types and Text a field
Min()	Least value in	All numeric data types and Text a field
StDev() StDevP(),	Statistical standard	All numeric data types deviation of values in a field
Sum()	Total of values	All numeric data types in a field
Var(), VarP()	Statistical variation	All numeric data types of values in a field

of days between the invoice and payment dates. Occasionally, you might want to make calculations on all records of a table, such as finding the historical average value of all invoices issued by a firm. Usually, however, you apply criteria to the query to select specific records that you want to total.

Σ Access considers all SQL aggregate functions to be members of the Totals class of functions. You create queries that return any or all SQL aggregate functions by clicking the Totals button (with the Greek sigma, **Σ**, which represents summation) in the Show/Hide group of the Query Tools Design ribbon.

Follow these steps to apply the five most commonly used SQL aggregate functions to the sample Order Subtotals query:

1. Open a new query and add the Order Subtotals query.

2. Drag the OrderID column to the first new query column and then drag the Subtotal column four times to the adjacent column to create four Subtotal columns.

3. Click the Totals button to add the Totals row.

4. Move to the Total row of the OrderID column and press Alt+down arrow (↓) to display the drop-down list of SQL aggregate functions. Choose Count as the function for the OrderID column, as shown in Figure 11.56.

Figure 11.56
You apply the Count() function to one of the rows of the query that has a value in every row to obtain the total number of rows returned by the query. The OrderID column is the logical choice for counting.

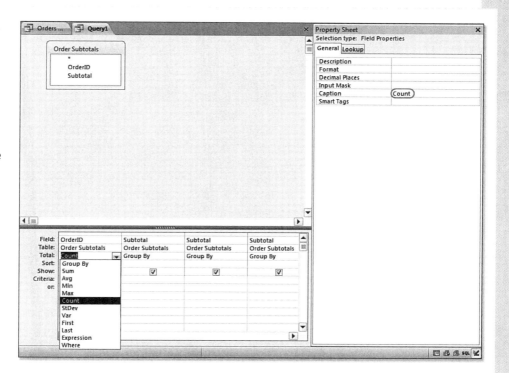

5. Move to the first Subtotal column, open the list, and choose Sum from the Total drop-down list. Repeat the process, choosing Avg for the second Subtotal column, Min for the third, and Max for the fourth.

6. Place the cursor in the OrderID field and click the Properties button on the toolbar (or right-click in the Count field and then click Properties in the pop-up menu) to display the Field Property Sheet. Type **Count** as the value of the Caption property.

7. Repeat step 6 for the four Subtotal columns, typing **Sum**, **Average**, **Minimum**, and **Maximum** as the values of the Caption property for the four columns, respectively. (You don't need to set the Format property, because the Subtotal column is formatted as Currency.)

8. Click Run to display the query's result. The query design doesn't have fields suitable for row-restriction criteria, so the result shown in Figure 11.57 is for the whole table.

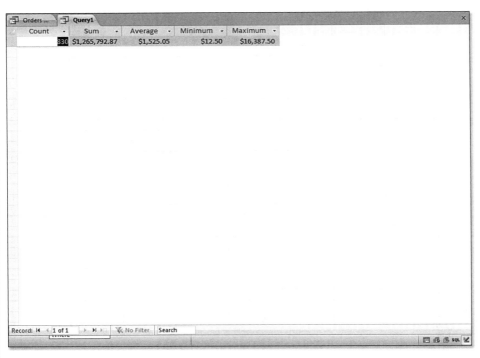

Figure 11.57
The data-sheet displays five SQL aggregate values for all records of the Orders table.

9. Save your query with a descriptive name, such as **qryOrdersAggregates**, because you'll use this query in the two sections that follow.

Making Calculations Based on Selected Sets of Rows or Records

The preceding sample query performed calculations on all orders received by Northwind Traders that were entered in the Orders table. Usually, you are interested in a specific set of records—a range of dates, for example—from which to calculate aggregate values. To restrict the calculation to orders that Northwind received in March 2006, follow these steps:

1. 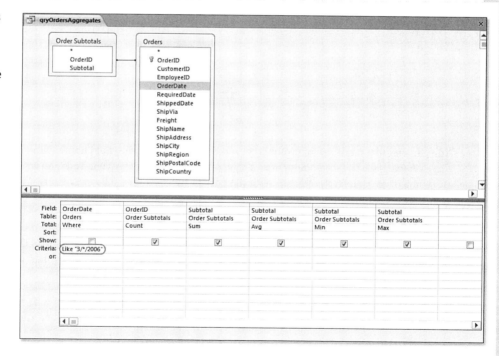 Return to Query Design view and add the Orders table to the qryOrdersAggregates query. Access automatically creates the join on the OrderID fields. If you didn't create this query, you can import it from the Join11.accdb sample database.

2. Drag the OrderDate field onto the OrderID column to add OrderDate as the first column of the query. You need the OrderDate field to restrict the data to a range of dates.

3. Open the Total drop-down list in the OrderDate column and choose Where to replace the default Group By. Access deselects the Show box of the OrderDate column.

4. In the OrderDate column's Criteria row, type **Like "3/*/2006"** to restrict the totals to orders received in the month of March 2006 (see Figure 11.58). When you use the Like operator as a criterion, Access adds the quotation marks if you forget to type them.

Figure 11.58
The OrderDate field of the Orders table is needed to restrict the aggregate data to orders received within a specified period, March 2006 in this case.

5. 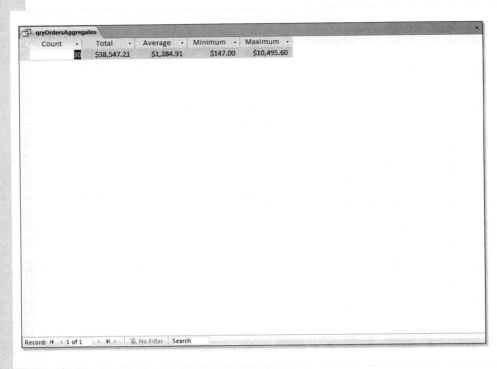 Click the Run button to display the result for orders received during the month of March 2006 (see Figure 11.59).

Figure 11.59
This datasheet shows the effect of adding a date criterion (in this case, orders received in March 2006).

You can create a more useful grouping of records by replacing the field name with an expression. For example, you can group aggregates by the year and month (or year and quarter) by grouping on the value of an expression created with the Format function. The following steps produce a sales summary record for each month of 2006, the most recent year for which 12 months of data are available in the Orders table:

1. Return to Query Design view, and then click the header bar of the query's OrderDate column to select the first column. Press the Insert key to add a new, empty column to the query.

2. Type **Month: Format([OrderDate],"yyyy-mm")** in the first (empty) column's Field row. (You use the "yyyy-mm" format so that the records group in date order. For a single year, you also can use "m" or "mm", but not "mmm", because "mmm" sorts in alphabetic sequence starting with Apr.)

3. Change the Where criterion of the OrderDate column to **Year([OrderDate])=2006** to return a full year of data. Your query design appears as shown in Figure 11.60.

Figure 11.60
This query design returns a row containing aggregate values of orders received in each month of 2006. The Access query parser changes the Year–([OrderDate])=2006 Criteria expression into a Year–([OrderDate]) Field expression with 2006 as the criterion value.

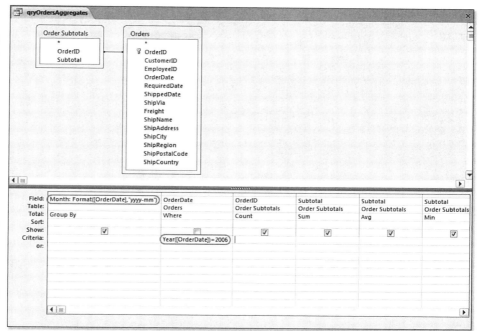

4. ⚲ Click Run to display the result of your query (see Figure 11.61). The query creates sales summary data for each month of 2006.

5. Choose File, Save As and save the query under a different name, such as **qryMonthlyOrders2006**, because you modify the query in the next section.

Designing Parameter Queries

If you expect to run a summary or another type of query repeatedly with changes to the criteria, you can convert the query to a parameter query. Parameter queries—which Chapter 9 explained briefly—enable you to enter criteria with the Enter Parameter Value dialog. Access prompts you for each parameter. For the qryMonthlyOrders2006 query that you created in the preceding section, the only parameter likely to change is the range of dates for which you want to generate the product sales data. The two sections that follow show you how to add a parameter to a query and specify the data type of the parameter.

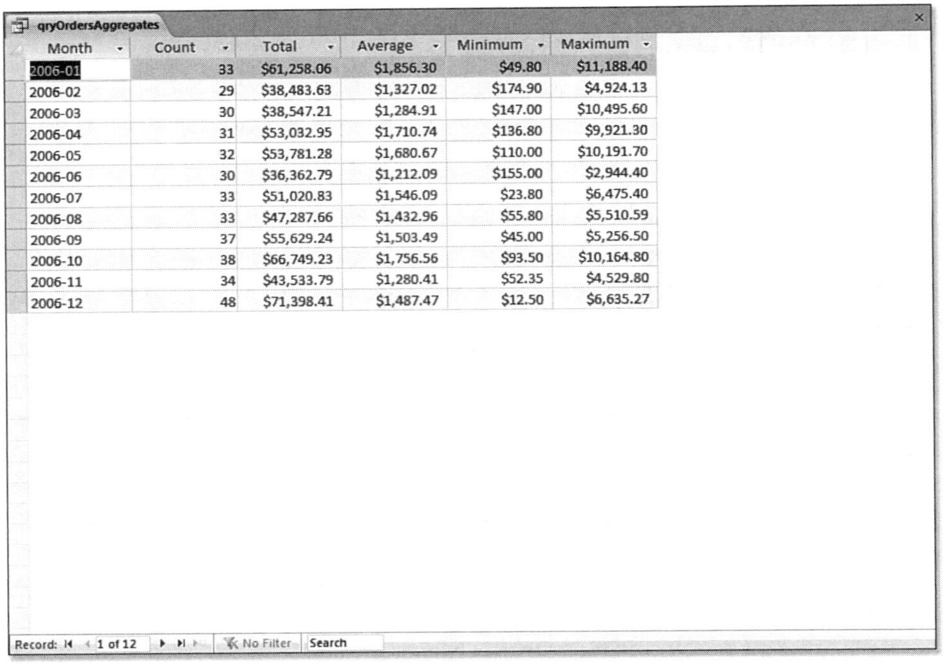

Month	Count	Total	Average	Minimum	Maximum
2006-01	33	$61,258.06	$1,856.30	$49.80	$11,188.40
2006-02	29	$38,483.63	$1,327.02	$174.90	$4,924.13
2006-03	30	$38,547.21	$1,284.91	$147.00	$10,495.60
2006-04	31	$53,032.95	$1,710.74	$136.80	$9,921.30
2006-05	32	$53,781.28	$1,680.67	$110.00	$10,191.70
2006-06	30	$36,362.79	$1,212.09	$155.00	$2,944.40
2006-07	33	$51,020.83	$1,546.09	$23.80	$6,475.40
2006-08	33	$47,287.66	$1,432.96	$55.80	$5,510.59
2006-09	37	$55,629.24	$1,503.49	$45.00	$5,256.50
2006-10	38	$66,749.23	$1,756.56	$93.50	$10,164.80
2006-11	34	$43,533.79	$1,280.41	$52.35	$4,529.80
2006-12	48	$71,398.41	$1,487.47	$12.50	$6,635.27

Record: 1 of 12   No Filter   Search

Figure 11.61
The datasheet displays aggregate rows for each month of 2006.

Adding a Parameter to the Monthly Sales Query

To convert the qryMonthlyOrders2006 summary query to a parameter query, you first create prompts for the Enter Parameter Value dialog that appears when the query runs. You create parameter queries by substituting the text with which to prompt the user, enclosed within square brackets, for actual values. Follow these steps:

1. Open in Design view the qryMonthlyOrders2006 query that you created in the preceding section.

2. With the cursor in the Month column's Field row, press F2 to select the expression in the Field cell. Then press Ctrl+C to copy the expression to the Clipboard.

3. Move the cursor to the OrderDate column's Field row and press F2 to select OrderDate. Then press Ctrl+V to replace OrderDate with the expression used for the first column.

4. Move to the OrderDate column's Criteria cell and replace Year([OrderDate])=2006 with **[Enter the year and month in YYYY-MM format:]** (see Figure 11.62).

5. Click the Office button, choose Save As, and save the query as **qryMonthlyOrdersParam**.

6. Click the Run button. The Enter Parameter Value dialog opens with the label that you assigned as the value of the criterion in step 4.

Figure 11.62
Specify the same format for the parameter column as that of the grouping column, and add the prompt for the Enter Parameter dialog.

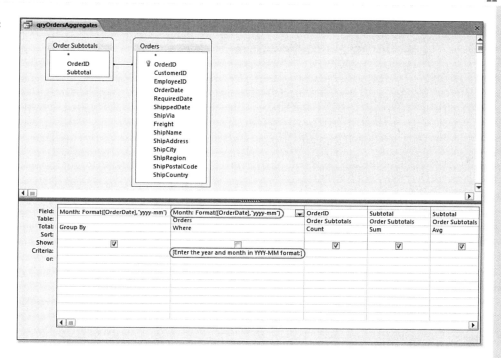

7. Type **2006-03** in the text box to display the data for March 2006, as shown in Figure 11.63.

Figure 11.63
You must type the parameter exactly as shown in the Enter Parameter Value dialog's prompt to return rows.

8. Click OK to run the query. The result appears as shown in Figure 11.64.

 tip

Complete your query design and testing before you convert any type of query to a parameter query. Using fixed criteria with the query maintains consistency during the testing process. Furthermore, you can make repeated changes between Design and Run view more quickly if you don't have to enter one or more parameters in the process. After you finish testing the query, edit the criteria to add the prompt for the Enter Parameter Value dialog.

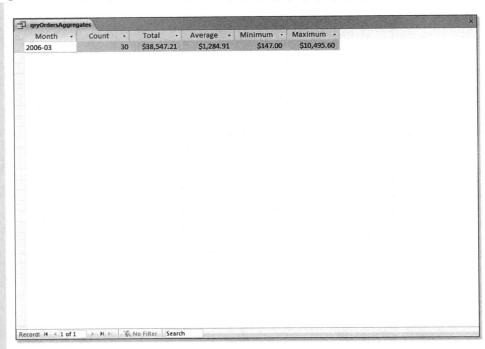

Specifying the Parameter's Data Type

The default field data type for parameters of Access queries is Text. If the parameter creates a crite-rion for a query column of the Date/Time or Number field data type, you must assign a data type to each entry that is made through an Enter Parameter Value dialog. Data types for values entered as parameters are established in the Query Parameters dialog. If you have more than one parameter, you can establish the same or a different data type for each parameter.

Follow these steps to demonstrate adding an optional data type specification to a parameter:

1. Return to Design view, click the Query Tools, Design tab, use the mouse to select the prompt text only in the Month column's Criteria cell (omit the square brackets and colon character), and copy the text of the prompt to the Clipboard by pressing Ctrl+C.

2. Click the Parameters button to display the Query Parameters dialog.

3. To insert the prompt in the Parameter column of the dialog, place the cursor in the column and press Ctrl+V. The prompt entry in the Parameter column must match the prompt entry in the Criteria field exactly; copying and pasting the prompt text ensures an exact match. Don't include the square brackets in the Parameter column.

4. Press Tab to move to the Data Type column, press Alt+down arrow ( ) to open the Data Type drop-down list, and select Date/Time (see Figure 11.65). Close the dialog without clicking OK to prevent adding the Date/Time data type, because it isn't applicable to this query.

Figure 11.65
Select the data type for the parameter's prompt from the Data Type list in
the Query Parameters dialog.

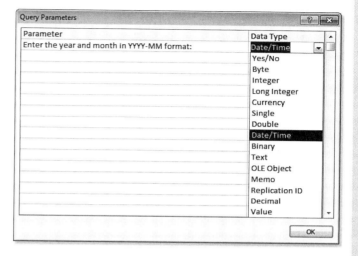

5. If you applied the Date/Time data type to the qryMonthly-
   OrdersParam query, reopen the Query Parameters dialog and
   delete the prompt text, which also deletes the data type entry.

The parameter-conversion process described in this section applies
to all types of queries that you create if one or more of the query
columns includes a criterion expression. The advantage of the
parameter query is that you or a user of the database can run a
query for any range of values—in this case, dates—such as the
current month to date, a particular fiscal quarter, or an entire fiscal
year.

> **note**
> The data type for the prompt
> of the qryMonthlyOrdersParam
> query's parameter is Text
> (the default), not Date/Time.
> Therefore, you don't need to
> apply a data type specification
> for the query.

Creating Crosstab Queries

Crosstab queries are summary queries that let you determine exactly how the summary data
appears onscreen. Crosstab queries rotate the axis of the datasheet and display the equivalent
of repeating fields (often called *buckets*) in columns. Thus, the datasheet displayed by a crosstab
query doesn't conform to first normal form. Crosstab queries are closely related to Access and Excel
PivotTables. PivotTable and PivotChart views of queries are the subject of the next chapter.

 For more information on PivotTables, **see** *"Slicing and Dicing Data with PivotTables,"* **p. 506.**

With crosstab queries, you can perform the following operations:

- Specify the field that creates labels (headings) for rows by using the Group By instruction.

- Determine the fields that create column headers and the criteria that determine the values
  appearing under the headers.

■ Assign calculated data values to the cells of the resulting row-column grid.

The following list details the advantages of using crosstab queries:

■ You can display a substantial amount of summary data in a compact datasheet that's familiar to anyone who uses a spreadsheet application or columnar accounting form.

■ The summary data is presented in a datasheet that's ideally suited for creating graphs and charts automatically with the Access Chart Wizard.

■ Designing queries to create multiple levels of detail is quick and easy. Queries with identical columns but fewer rows can represent increasingly summarized data. Highly summarized queries are ideal to begin a drill-down procedure by instructing the user, for example, to click a Details button to display sales by product.

Using crosstab queries imposes only one restriction: You can't sort your result table on calculated values in columns. You can't, therefore, create a crosstab query that ranks products by increasing sales volume in ascending rows. Columns are likely to have values that cause conflicts in the sorting order of the row. You can choose an ascending sort, a descending sort, or no sort on the *row label values* in the GROUP BY field, which usually is the first column.

Using the Wizard to Generate a Quarterly Product Sales Crosstab Query

Access's Crosstab Query Wizard can generate a crosstab query from a single table, but an individual table seldom contains data suitable as the data source for a crosstab query. If you need more than one table to get the result you want from the wizard, which is almost always the case, you must design a query specifically for crosstab presentation.

Follow these steps to create a query and then use the Crosstab Query Wizard to generate a resultset that shows quarterly sales by product for the year 2006:

1. Create a new query in Design view and add the Orders table and Order Details Extended query. Drag the OrderDate field of the Orders table and the ProductID, ProductName, and ExtendedPrice fields of the Order Details Extended query to the grid. Add **Year([OrderDate])=2006** as the criterion of the OrderDate field to restrict the data to a single year (see Figure 11.66).

2. Right-click the ProductID field in the grid and choose Properties to open the Properties sheet. Click the Lookup tab, and select Text Box in the Display Control to revert from the ProductName lookup to the numeric ProductID value. Click Run to verify your design (see Figure 11.67).

3. Close and save the query as **qryCTWizSource**.

4. Click the Create ribbon's Query Wizard button to open the New Query dialog and double-click the Crosstab Query Wizard to open the wizard's first dialog.

Figure 11.66 The source query for the first crosstab query is based on the sample Orders table and Order Details Extended query.

Order Date	Product	Product Name	Extended Price
1/1/2006	29	Thüringer Rostbratwurst	$2,079.00
1/1/2006	35	Steeleye Stout	$504.00
1/1/2006	49	Maxilaku	$480.00
1/1/2006	30	Nord-Ost Matjeshering	$372.60
1/1/2006	56	Gnocchi di nonna Alice	$2,128.00
1/1/2006	65	Louisiana Fiery Hot Pepper	$336.00
1/1/2006	71	Flotemysost	$1,032.00
1/2/2006	23	Tunnbröd	$432.00
1/2/2006	63	Vegie-spread	$2,281.50
1/3/2006	16	Pavlova	$248.11
1/3/2006	48	Chocolade	$606.90
1/3/2006	26	Gumbär Gummibärchen	$709.65
1/3/2006	42	Singaporean Hokkien Fried	$425.60
1/3/2006	49	Maxilaku	$456.00
1/6/2006	3	Aniseed Syrup	$400.00
1/7/2006	1	Chai	$144.00
1/7/2006	21	Sir Rodney's Scones	$216.00
1/7/2006	28	Rössle Sauerkraut	$1,375.92
1/7/2006	36	Inlagd Sill	$68.40
1/7/2006	40	Boston Crab Meat	$26.46
1/7/2006	11	Queso Cabrales	$504.00
1/7/2006	69	Gudbrandsdalsost	$432.00
1/7/2006	71	Flotemysost	$258.00
1/8/2006	37	Gravad lax	$208.00
1/8/2006	54	Tourtière	$35.40
1/8/2006	62	Tarte au sucre	$1,379.00
1/9/2006	14	Tofu	$223.20

Record: 1 of 1059 No Filter Search

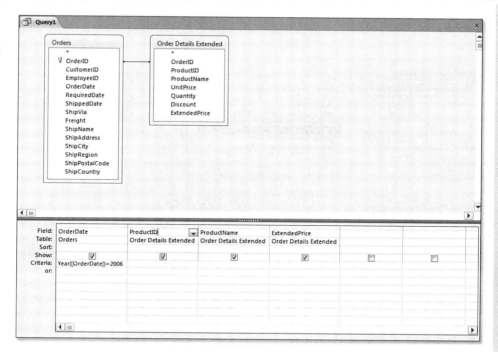

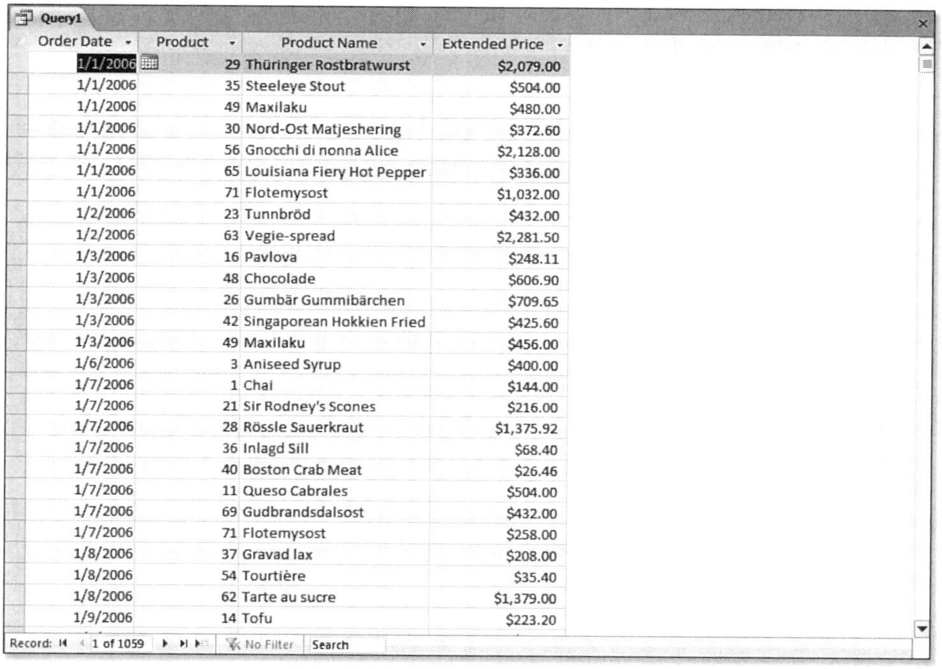

Figure 11.67 This datasheet displays the first few rows of the resultset from the design of Figure 11.66, which has a row for each Order Details item for orders received in 2006.

5. Select the Queries option and then select qryCTWizSource from the list (see Figure 11.68). Click Next.

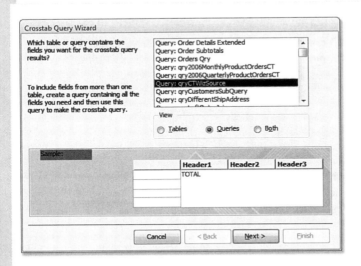

Figure 11.68
Select the data source, usually a query, in the first Crosstab Query Wizard dialog.

6. Double-click the ProductID column to move ProductID from the Available Fields to the Selected Fields list. Do the same for the ProductName column. The second wizard dialog appears as shown in Figure 11.69. Click Next.

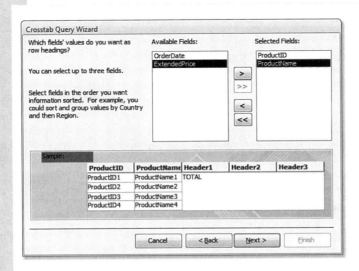

Figure 11.69
Select the query columns to appear as row headers in the second wizard dialog.

7. Accept the default OrderDate field for the column headings (see Figure 11.70). Click Next.

8. Select Quarter as the date interval for the columns (see Figure 11.71). Click Next.

9. Select Sum as the aggregate function to total the ExtendedPrice value (sales) for each quarter. Leave the Yes, Include Row Sums check box marked to include a column that shows the total sales for the four quarters (see Figure 11.72). Click Next.

10. In the final wizard dialog, type **qry2006QuarterlyProductOrdersCrosstab** as the name of the query; then click Finish to display the crosstab query resultset (see Figure 11.73).

Figure 11.70
Specify the query column that provides the column headers in the third wizard dialog.

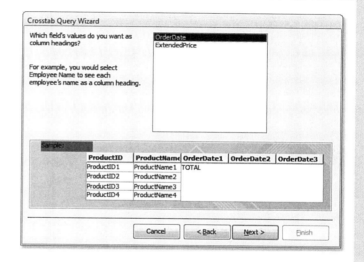

Figure 11.71
Specify the date interval in the fourth dialog's list. This dialog appears only if you specify a date field for row or column headings.

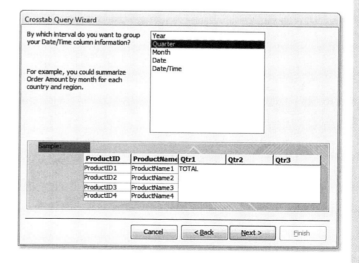

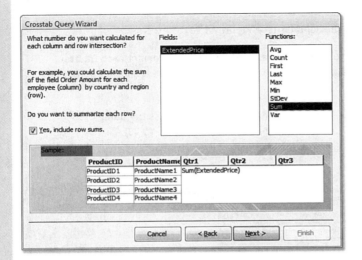

Figure 11.72
You can specify any aggregate function to summarize the numeric data for the crosstab query, but Sum is the most common.

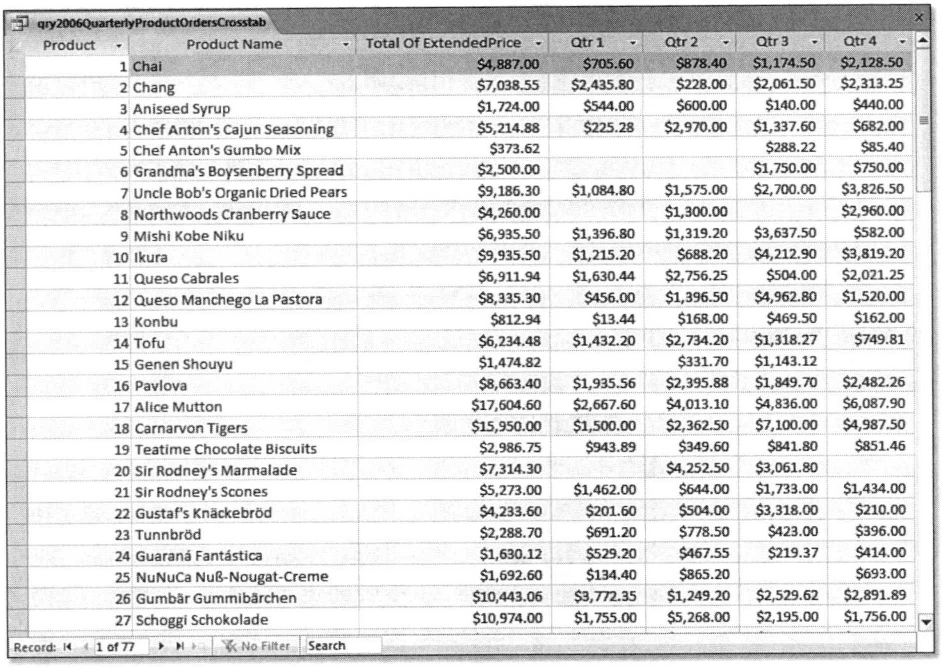

Product	Product Name	Total Of ExtendedPrice	Qtr 1	Qtr 2	Qtr 3	Qtr 4
1	Chai	$4,887.00	$705.60	$878.40	$1,174.50	$2,128.50
2	Chang	$7,038.55	$2,435.80	$228.00	$2,061.50	$2,313.25
3	Aniseed Syrup	$1,724.00	$544.00	$600.00	$140.00	$440.00
4	Chef Anton's Cajun Seasoning	$5,214.88	$225.28	$2,970.00	$1,337.60	$682.00
5	Chef Anton's Gumbo Mix	$373.62			$288.22	$85.40
6	Grandma's Boysenberry Spread	$2,500.00			$1,750.00	$750.00
7	Uncle Bob's Organic Dried Pears	$9,186.30	$1,084.80	$1,575.00	$2,700.00	$3,826.50
8	Northwoods Cranberry Sauce	$4,260.00		$1,300.00		$2,960.00
9	Mishi Kobe Niku	$6,935.50	$1,396.80	$1,319.20	$3,637.50	$582.00
10	Ikura	$9,935.50	$1,215.20	$688.20	$4,212.90	$3,819.20
11	Queso Cabrales	$6,911.94	$1,630.44	$2,756.25	$504.00	$2,021.25
12	Queso Manchego La Pastora	$8,335.30	$456.00	$1,396.50	$4,962.80	$1,520.00
13	Konbu	$812.94	$13.44	$168.00	$469.50	$162.00
14	Tofu	$6,234.48	$1,432.20	$2,734.20	$1,318.27	$749.81
15	Genen Shouyu	$1,474.82		$331.70	$1,143.12	
16	Pavlova	$8,663.40	$1,935.56	$2,395.88	$1,849.70	$2,482.26
17	Alice Mutton	$17,604.60	$2,667.60	$4,013.10	$4,836.00	$6,087.90
18	Carnarvon Tigers	$15,950.00	$1,500.00	$2,362.50	$7,100.00	$4,987.50
19	Teatime Chocolate Biscuits	$2,986.75	$943.89	$349.60	$841.80	$851.46
20	Sir Rodney's Marmalade	$7,314.30		$4,252.50	$3,061.80	
21	Sir Rodney's Scones	$5,273.00	$1,462.00	$644.00	$1,733.00	$1,434.00
22	Gustaf's Knäckebröd	$4,233.60	$201.60	$504.00	$3,318.00	$210.00
23	Tunnbröd	$2,288.70	$691.20	$778.50	$423.00	$396.00
24	Guaraná Fantástica	$1,630.12	$529.20	$467.55	$219.37	$414.00
25	NuNuCa Nuß-Nougat-Creme	$1,692.60	$134.40	$865.20		$693.00
26	Gumbär Gummibärchen	$10,443.06	$3,772.35	$1,249.20	$2,529.62	$2,891.89
27	Schoggi Schokolade	$10,974.00	$1,755.00	$5,268.00	$2,195.00	$1,756.00

Record: 1 of 77   No Filter   Search

Figure 11.73
The crosstab query has rows for each of the 77 products sold by Northwind Traders in 2006. The new Korean and Chinese products were introduced in 2007.

11. 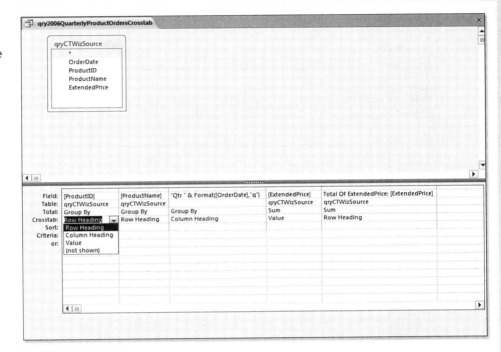 Change to Design view to check the query the Query Wizard based on the original qryC-TWizSource query. Open the list in one of the cells of the added Crosstab row to view the choices for each field of the query (see Figure 11.74).

The Crosstab row choices—Row Heading, Column Heading, Value, and (Not Shown)—determine the location of field values in the crosstab datasheet.

Figure 11.74
Crosstab queries have an additional row, Crosstab, in the grid.

Access SQL

The Access SQL statement for the crosstab query is

```
TRANSFORM Sum(qryCTWizSource.ExtendedPrice) AS SumOfExtendedPrice
  SELECT qryCTWizSource.ProductID, qryCTWizSource.ProductName,
     Sum(qryCTWizSource.ExtendedPrice) AS [Total Of ExtendedPrice]
  FROM qryCTWizSource
  GROUP BY qryCTWizSource.ProductID, qryCTWizSource.ProductName
  PIVOT "Qtr " & Format([OrderDate],"q");
```

The Access SQL PIVOT and TRANSFORM reserved words generate the crosstab query resultset. The expression following TRANSFORM defines the numeric values for the matrix. The SELECT field list supplies the row headings and values. The PIVOT expression defines the column headings and acts as an extension to the GROUP BY expression. The "q" format string specifies a quarterly date interval.

Designing a Monthly Product Sales Crosstab Query

You can bypass the Query Wizard by manually designing a crosstab query from scratch with related tables, rather than a query, as the data source. To create a typical crosstab query in Query Design view that displays products in rows and the monthly sales volume for each product in the corresponding columns, follow these steps:

1. Open a new query in Design view and add the Products, Order Details, and Orders tables to the query.

2. Drag the ProductID and ProductName fields from the Products table to the query's first two columns, and then drag the OrderDate field of the Orders table to the third column.

3. Click the Query Design Tools ribbon's Crosstab button to add the Crosstab row to the Query Design grid.

4. Open the drop-down list of the ProductID column's Crosstab row and select Row Heading. Repeat this process for the ProductName column. These two columns provide the required row headings for your crosstab. A crosstab query must have at least one row heading.

5. Open the Total drop-down list of the OrderDate column and select Where. Type **Year([OrderDate])=2006** in this column's Criteria row to restrict the query to orders received in 2006. Leave the Crosstab cell empty or choose (not shown) from the list.

6. Move to the next (empty) column's Field row and type the following:

```
Sales: Sum([Order Details].[Quantity]*[Order Details].[UnitPrice]*
(1-[Order Details].[Discount]))
```

Move to the Total row, choose Expression from the drop-down list, and then choose Value from the Crosstab row. The expression calculates the net amount of the orders received for each product that populates your crosstab query's data cells. (You must specify the Orders Detail table name; if you don't, you receive an Ambiguous Field Reference error message. Alternatively, you can set Order Details as the Table cell value.)

7. Right-click the Sales column, choose Properties to open the Field Properties sheet for the Sales column, and select Currency as the Format property of the column.

8. In the next (empty) column's Field row, type **Format([OrderDate], "mmm")**. Access adds a default field name, Expr1:. Accept the default because the Format function that you added creates the column names, the three-letter abbreviation for the months of the year ("mmm" format), when you run the query. Accept the default Group By value in the Totals cell. The months of the year (Jan through Dec) are your column headings, so move to the Crosstab row and choose Column Heading from the drop-down list. The design of your crosstab query appears as shown in Figure 11.75.

Figure 11.75
This cross-
tab query
design dis-
plays order
amounts for
products by
month.

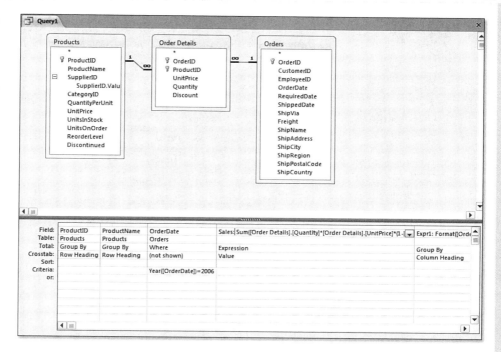

9. Click Run to execute the query (see Figure 11.76).

Notice that the crosstab query result contains a major defect: The columns are arranged alphabetically by month name rather than in calendar order. You can solve this problem by using fixed column headings, which you learn about in the following section.

Using Fixed Column Headings with Crosstab Queries

Access uses an alphabetical or numerical sort on row and column headings to establish the
sequence of appearance in the crosstab query result table. For this reason, if you use short or full
names for months, the sequence is in alphabetic rather than calendar order. You can correct this
problem by assigning fixed column headings to the crosstab query. Follow these steps to modify
and rerun the query:

➥ *To review the ways Access lets you manipulate dates and time,* **see** *"Functions for Date and
Time,"* **p. 396.**

1. Return to Query Design view, right-click the upper pane, and choose Properties. The Query
Properties sheet contains an option that appears only for crosstab queries: Column Headings.

Product ID	Product Name	Apr	Aug	Dec	Feb	Jan	Jul	Jun
1	Chai	$576.00	$652.50			$489.60	$522.00	$180.00
2	Chang	$228.00	$1,871.50	$1,505.75	$733.40	$912.00	$190.00	
3	Aniseed Syrup			$180.00		$400.00	$140.00	
4	Chef Anton's Cajun Seasoning	$935.00	$748.00				$352.00	
5	Chef Anton's Gumbo Mix		$288.22					
6	Grandma's Boysenberry Spread		$1,750.00					
7	Uncle Bob's Organic Dried Pears	$1,275.00	$1,050.00	$1,126.50	$364.80		$1,650.00	
8	Northwoods Cranberry Sauce	$1,300.00		$960.00				
9	Mishi Kobe Niku	$1,319.20				$1,396.80		
10	Ikura	$471.20	$418.50	$1,612.00	$744.00		$2,480.00	$155.00
11	Queso Cabrales		$210.00	$1,601.25	$685.44	$504.00	$294.00	$924.00
12	Queso Manchego La Pastora		$1,162.80		$456.00			
13	Konbu	$60.00	$66.30	$102.00		$8.64	$403.20	
14	Tofu	$1,627.50	$558.00	$279.00		$1,209.00		$1,106.70
15	Genen Shouyu	$176.70					$368.12	$155.00
16	Pavlova	$872.50		$1,483.25	$1,023.73	$248.11	$497.32	$188.46
17	Alice Mutton			$3,480.75	$312.00	$2,355.60	$3,900.00	$1,294.80
18	Carnarvon Tigers	$1,406.25	$5,100.00	$1,875.00			$2,000.00	$956.25
19	Teatime Chocolate Biscuits		$446.20	$646.76	$458.44	$295.65		$257.60
20	Sir Rodney's Marmalade	$3,159.00					$1,360.80	
21	Sir Rodney's Scones	$440.00	$885.00	$400.00	$512.00	$712.00	$140.00	
22	Gustaf's Knäckebröd		$1,995.00	$210.00	$201.60		$1,008.00	
23	Tunnbröd	$72.00		$90.00		$432.00		
24	Guaraná Fantástica	$159.75	$93.37	$166.50	$64.80		$126.00	$166.05
25	NuNuCa Nuß-Nougat-Creme	$865.20		$693.00				
26	Gumbär Gummibärchen		$929.09	$524.66	$1,269.90	$1,755.45	$335.72	
27	Schoggi Schokolade	$5,268.00		$1,756.00	$1,755.00		$2,195.00	

Record: I◄ ◄ 1 ► ►I ► No Filter | Search

Figure 11.76
The "mmm"
format string
for months
sorts the
columns by
month name,
not month
number.

2. In the Column Headings text box, type the three-letter abbreviations of all 12 months of the year. You must spell the abbreviations of the months correctly; data for months with spelling mistakes doesn't appear. You can separate entries with commas or semicolons, and you don't need to type quotation marks because Access adds them (see Figure 11.77). Spaces are unnecessary between the Column Headings values. After you complete all 12 entries, close the Query Property Sheet.

3. Click Run. Now the result table, shown in Figure 11.78, sorts the months in numeric order, although you can see only January through May in the figure. (Scroll to the right to see the remaining months.)

⊛ tip

If your crosstab datasheet differs from that of Figure 11.78, check whether you properly entered the fixed column headings in the Query Property Sheet. A misspelled month causes Access to omit the month from the query resultset; if you specified "mmmm" instead of "mmm", only May appears.

 tip

You might want to use fixed column headings if you use the Group By instruction with country names. Users in the United States will probably place USA first, and Canadian firms will undoubtedly choose Canada as the first entry. If you add a record with a new country, you must remember to update the list of fixed column headings with the new country value. Fixed column headings have another hidden benefit: They often make crosstab queries execute more quickly.

Figure 11.77
Add month names separated by semi-colons or commas to the Column Headings property of crosstab queries.

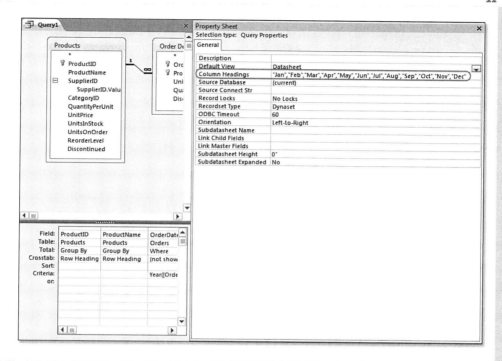

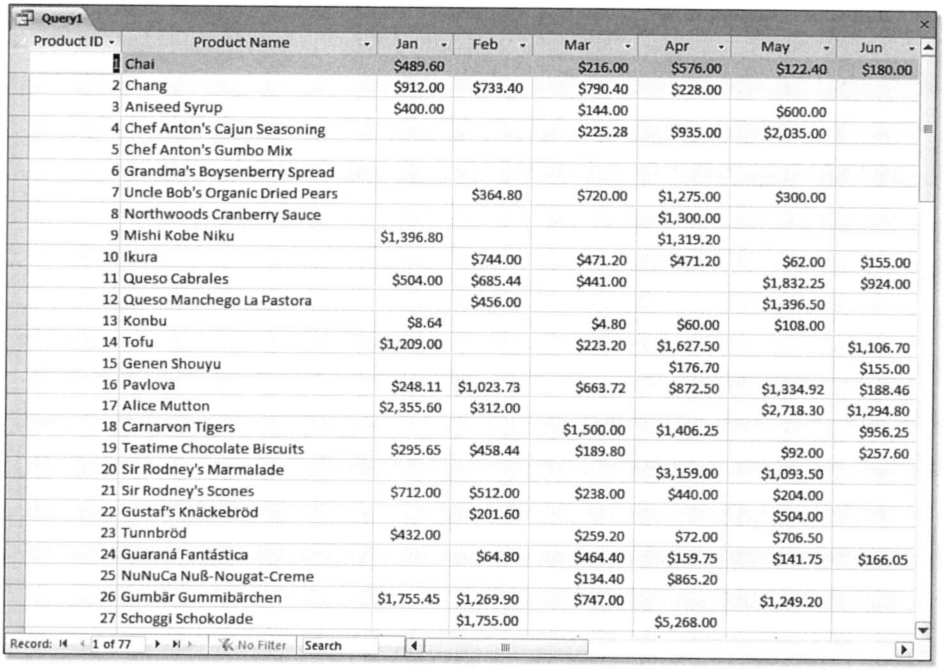

Figure 11.78
Adding the fixed column headers eliminates the sorting problem with the month columns.

Product ID	Product Name	Jan	Feb	Mar	Apr	May	Jun
1	Chai	$489.60		$216.00	$576.00	$122.40	$180.00
2	Chang	$912.00	$733.40	$790.40	$228.00		
3	Aniseed Syrup	$400.00		$144.00		$600.00	
4	Chef Anton's Cajun Seasoning			$225.28	$935.00	$2,035.00	
5	Chef Anton's Gumbo Mix						
6	Grandma's Boysenberry Spread						
7	Uncle Bob's Organic Dried Pears		$364.80	$720.00	$1,275.00	$300.00	
8	Northwoods Cranberry Sauce				$1,300.00		
9	Mishi Kobe Niku	$1,396.80			$1,319.20		
10	Ikura		$744.00	$471.20	$471.20	$62.00	$155.00
11	Queso Cabrales	$504.00	$685.44	$441.00		$1,832.25	$924.00
12	Queso Manchego La Pastora		$456.00			$1,396.50	
13	Konbu	$8.64		$4.80	$60.00	$108.00	
14	Tofu	$1,209.00		$223.20	$1,627.50		$1,106.70
15	Genen Shouyu				$176.70		$155.00
16	Pavlova	$248.11	$1,023.73	$663.72	$872.50	$1,334.92	$188.46
17	Alice Mutton	$2,355.60	$312.00			$2,718.30	$1,294.80
18	Carnarvon Tigers			$1,500.00	$1,406.25		$956.25
19	Teatime Chocolate Biscuits	$295.65	$458.44	$189.80		$92.00	$257.60
20	Sir Rodney's Marmalade				$3,159.00	$1,093.50	
21	Sir Rodney's Scones	$712.00	$512.00	$238.00	$440.00	$204.00	
22	Gustaf's Knäckebröd		$201.60			$504.00	
23	Tunnbröd	$432.00		$259.20	$72.00	$706.50	
24	Guaraná Fantástica		$64.80	$464.40	$159.75	$141.75	$166.05
25	NuNuCa Nuß-Nougat-Creme			$134.40	$865.20		
26	Gumbär Gummibärchen	$1,755.45	$1,269.90	$747.00		$1,249.20	
27	Schoggi Schokolade		$1,755.00		$5,268.00		

Record: ◄ ◄ 1 of 77 ► ►I ►✳ ⚓ No Filter Search

4. Save the query with an appropriate name, such as **qry2006MonthlyProductOrdersCT**.

You can produce a printed report quickly from the query by clicking Quick Access Toolbar's Print button. Alternatively, click the Office button, select Print, Print Preview, set the orientation and margins, and then click the Print button.

Access SQL

The Access SQL statement for the crosstab query with fixed column headings is

```
TRANSFORM Sum([Order Details].[Quantity]*[Order Details].[UnitPrice]*
    (1-[Order Details].[Discount])) AS Sales
SELECT Products.ProductID, Products.ProductName
FROM Orders
    INNER JOIN (Products
        INNER JOIN [Order Details]
        ON Products.ProductID = [Order Details].ProductID)
    ON Orders.OrderID = [Order Details].OrderID
WHERE Year([OrderDate])=2006
GROUP BY Products.ProductID, Products.ProductName
PIVOT Format([OrderDate],"mmm")
    In("Jan","Feb","Mar","Apr","May","Jun",
    "Jul","Aug","Sep","Oct","Nov","Dec");
```

The only significant differences between the preceding SQL statement and that for the quarterly crosstab query is the lack of a grand total column for each product, the change of the date interval ("mmm" instead of "q"), and the addition of the In( ) function with the fixed column names list as its argument.

If you want to add a grand totals column, add to the field list of the SELECT statement, Sum(Sales) AS [Total Orders], return to Design view, select the Total Orders column, and set its Format property to Currency. The added column appears in Figure 11.79.

Writing UNION Queries and Subqueries

UNION queries and queries that include subqueries require you to write Access SQL statements. Union is one of the three buttons in the group on the right in the Query Design Tools ribbon's Query Type group: Union, Passthrough, and Data Definition. There is no button for subquery. The following sections provide general syntax examples for writing UNION and subqueries, and they provide simple Access SQL examples. The general syntax examples use the same format as those of Chapter 27, "Moving from Access Queries to Transact-SQL," for T-SQL statements.

Using UNION Queries to Combine Multiple Resultsets

UNION queries let you combine the resultset of two or more SELECT queries into a single resultset. Northwind.accdb includes an example of a UNION query, which has the special symbol of two overlapping circles, in the Database window. You can create UNION queries only with SQL statements; if you add the UNION keyword to a query, the Query Design Mode button on the toolbar and the query design choices of the View menu are disabled.

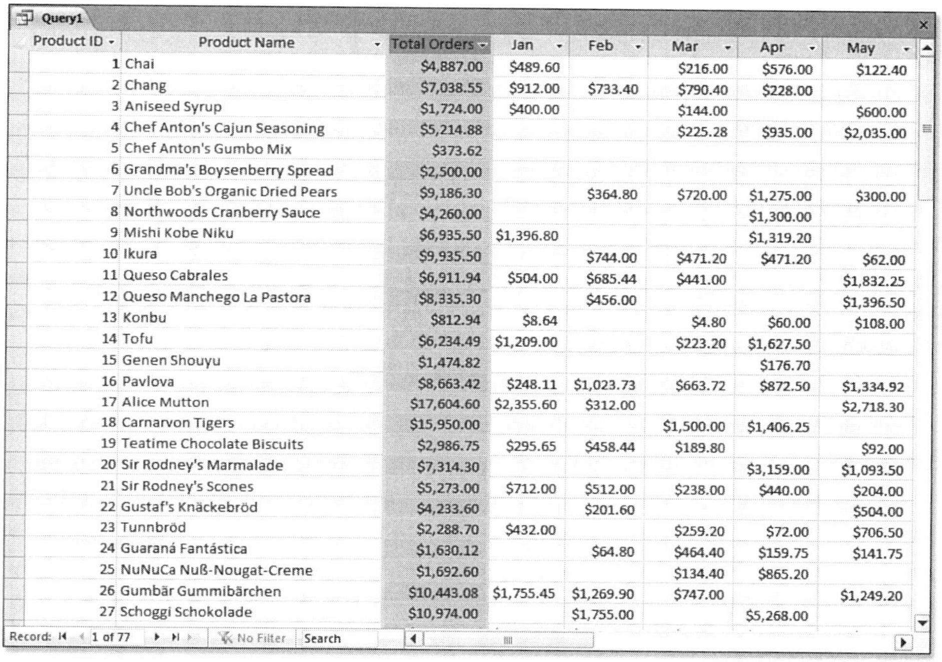

Figure 11.79
You can
add a Total
Orders
column
by adding
Sum(Sales)
AS [Total
Orders] to
the column
list of the
SELECT
statement.
You must
specify the
Currency
format of
the column
in the Field
Property
Sheet.

Product ID	Product Name	Total Orders	Jan	Feb	Mar	Apr	May
1	Chai	$4,887.00	$489.60		$216.00	$576.00	$122.40
2	Chang	$7,038.55	$912.00	$733.40	$790.40	$228.00	
3	Aniseed Syrup	$1,724.00	$400.00		$144.00		$600.00
4	Chef Anton's Cajun Seasoning	$5,214.88			$225.28	$935.00	$2,035.00
5	Chef Anton's Gumbo Mix	$373.62					
6	Grandma's Boysenberry Spread	$2,500.00					
7	Uncle Bob's Organic Dried Pears	$9,186.30		$364.80	$720.00	$1,275.00	$300.00
8	Northwoods Cranberry Sauce	$4,260.00				$1,300.00	
9	Mishi Kobe Niku	$6,935.50	$1,396.80			$1,319.20	
10	Ikura	$9,935.50		$744.00	$471.20	$471.20	$62.00
11	Queso Cabrales	$6,911.94	$504.00	$685.44	$441.00		$1,832.25
12	Queso Manchego La Pastora	$8,335.30		$456.00			$1,396.50
13	Konbu	$812.94	$8.64		$4.80	$60.00	$108.00
14	Tofu	$6,234.49	$1,209.00		$223.20	$1,627.50	
15	Genen Shouyu	$1,474.82				$176.70	
16	Pavlova	$8,663.42	$248.11	$1,023.73	$663.72	$872.50	$1,334.92
17	Alice Mutton	$17,604.60	$2,355.60	$312.00			$2,718.30
18	Carnarvon Tigers	$15,950.00			$1,500.00	$1,406.25	
19	Teatime Chocolate Biscuits	$2,986.75	$295.65	$458.44	$189.80		$92.00
20	Sir Rodney's Marmalade	$7,314.30				$3,159.00	$1,093.50
21	Sir Rodney's Scones	$5,273.00	$712.00	$512.00	$238.00	$440.00	$204.00
22	Gustaf's Knäckebröd	$4,233.60		$201.60			$504.00
23	Tunnbröd	$2,288.70	$432.00		$259.20	$72.00	$706.50
24	Guaraná Fantástica	$1,630.12		$64.80	$464.40	$159.75	$141.75
25	NuNuCa Nuß-Nougat-Creme	$1,692.60			$134.40	$865.20	
26	Gumbär Gummibärchen	$10,443.08	$1,755.45	$1,269.90	$747.00		$1,249.20
27	Schoggi Schokolade	$10,974.00		$1,755.00		$5,268.00	

Record: 1 of 77   No Filter   Search

The general syntax of UNION queries is as follows:

```
SELECT select_statement
    UNION SELECT select_statement
       [GROUP BY group_criteria]
       [HAVING aggregate criteria]
    [UNION SELECT select_statement
       [GROUP BY group_criteria]
       [HAVING aggregate criteria]
    [UNION. . .]
    [ORDER BY column_criteria]
```

The restrictions on statements that create UNION queries are the following:

- The number of fields in the field_list of each SELECT and UNION SELECT query must be the same. You receive an error message if the number of fields is not the same.

- The sequence of the field names in each field_list must correspond to similar entities. You don't receive an error message for dissimilar entities, but the resultset is likely to be unfathomable. The field data types in a single column need not correspond; however, if the column of the result-set contains both numeric and Access Text data types, the data type of the column is set to Text.

- Only one ORDER BY clause is allowed, and it must follow the last UNION SELECT statement. You can add GROUP BY and HAVING clauses to each SELECT and UNION SELECT statement if needed.

The sample Customers and Suppliers by City query is a UNION query that combines rows from the Customers and Suppliers tables. When you open a UNION query, Query Design view is disabled.

To create a new UNION query, create a new query in Design view, close the Show Table dialog, click the Query Design Tools tab, click the Union query button to open the SQL window, and type the SQL statement.

Access SQL

The Access SQL statement for a slightly modified version of the Customers and Suppliers by City query is

```
SELECT City, CompanyName, ContactName,
    CustomerID AS Code, "Customer" AS Relationship
  FROM Customers
  UNION SELECT City, CompanyName, ContactName,
    SupplierID, "Supplier"
  FROM Suppliers
ORDER BY City, CompanyName;
```

The syntax of the preceding SQL statement illustrates the capability of UNION queries to include values from two different field data types, Text (CustomerID) and Long Integer (SupplierID), in the single, aliased Code column (see Figure 11.80).

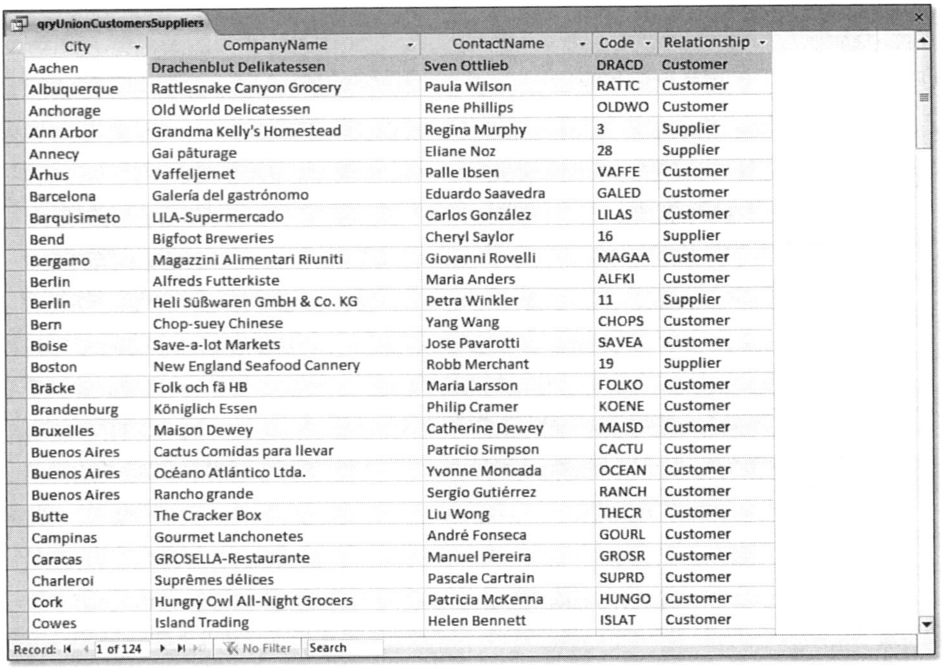

---

qryUnionCustomersSuppliers

City	CompanyName	ContactName	Code	Relationship
Aachen	Drachenblut Delikatessen	Sven Ottlieb	DRACD	Customer
Albuquerque	Rattlesnake Canyon Grocery	Paula Wilson	RATTC	Customer
Anchorage	Old World Delicatessen	Rene Phillips	OLDWO	Customer
Ann Arbor	Grandma Kelly's Homestead	Regina Murphy	3	Supplier
Annecy	Gai pâturage	Eliane Noz	28	Supplier
Århus	Vaffeljernet	Palle Ibsen	VAFFE	Customer
Barcelona	Galería del gastrónomo	Eduardo Saavedra	GALED	Customer
Barquisimeto	LILA-Supermercado	Carlos González	LILAS	Customer
Bend	Bigfoot Breweries	Cheryl Saylor	16	Supplier
Bergamo	Magazzini Alimentari Riuniti	Giovanni Rovelli	MAGAA	Customer
Berlin	Alfreds Futterkiste	Maria Anders	ALFKI	Customer
Berlin	Heli Süßwaren GmbH & Co. KG	Petra Winkler	11	Supplier
Bern	Chop-suey Chinese	Yang Wang	CHOPS	Customer
Boise	Save-a-lot Markets	Jose Pavarotti	SAVEA	Customer
Boston	New England Seafood Cannery	Robb Merchant	19	Supplier
Bräcke	Folk och fä HB	Maria Larsson	FOLKO	Customer
Brandenburg	Königlich Essen	Philip Cramer	KOENE	Customer
Bruxelles	Maison Dewey	Catherine Dewey	MAISD	Customer
Buenos Aires	Cactus Comidas para llevar	Patricio Simpson	CACTU	Customer
Buenos Aires	Océano Atlántico Ltda.	Yvonne Moncada	OCEAN	Customer
Buenos Aires	Rancho grande	Sergio Gutiérrez	RANCH	Customer
Butte	The Cracker Box	Liu Wong	THECR	Customer
Campinas	Gourmet Lanchonetes	André Fonseca	GOURL	Customer
Caracas	GROSELLA-Restaurante	Manuel Pereira	GROSR	Customer
Charleroi	Suprêmes délices	Pascale Cartrain	SUPRD	Customer
Cork	Hungry Owl All-Night Grocers	Patricia McKenna	HUNGO	Customer
Cowes	Island Trading	Helen Bennett	ISLAT	Customer

Record: 1 of 124   No Filter   Search

Figure 11.80
The Code column of this UNION query demonstrates Access's capability to combine values of two different data types. T-SQL UNION queries require compatible data types in a column.

You also can use UNION queries to add (All) or other explicit options to a query resultset when populating combo and list boxes. As an example, the following SQL statement adds (All) to the query resultset for a combo box used to select orders from a particular country or all countries:

```
SELECT Country FROM Customers
    UNION SELECT "(All)" FROM Customers
ORDER BY Country;
```

The parentheses around (All) causes it to sort at the beginning of the list; the ASCII value of "(" is 40 and "A" is 65. Automatic sorting of combo and list box items uses the ASCII value returned by the VBA Asc function.

➡️ *To create a query that returns all rows from joined tables,* **see** *"Using the tblShipAddress Table in a Query,"* **p. 554.**

➡️ *To update a table by substituting a string for a specified value,* **see** *"Using the tblShipAddress Table with UNION Queries,"* **p. 555.**

➡️ *For examples of using a UNION query to add an (All) item to a drop-down list,* **see** *"Adding an Option to Select All Countries or Products,"* **p. 1336.**

Implementing Subqueries

Access traditionally has used nested queries to emulate the subquery capability of ANSI SQL, because early Access versions didn't support subqueries. Access 2007 lets you write a SELECT query that uses another SELECT query to supply the criteria for the WHERE clause. Depending on the complexity of your query, using a subquery instead of nested queries often improves performance. The general syntax of subqueries is as follows:

```
SELECT field_list
    FROM table_list
    WHERE [table_name.]field_name
        IN (SELECT select_statement
    [GROUP BY group_criteria]
        [HAVING aggregate_criteria]
    [ORDER BY sort_criteria]);
```

Access SQL

Following is the Access SQL statement for a subquery that returns names and addresses of Northwind Traders customers who placed orders between January 1, 2006, and June 30, 2006:

```
SELECT CompanyName, ContactName, ContactTitle, Phone
  FROM Customers
  WHERE CustomerID IN
      (SELECT CustomerID FROM Orders
      WHERE OrderDate BETWEEN #1/1/2006# AND #6/30/2006#);
```

The SELECT subquery that begins after the IN predicate returns the CustomerID values from the Orders table against which the CustomerID values of the Customers table are compared. Be sure to surround the subquery with parentheses.

Unlike UNION queries, you can create a subquery in Query Design view. You type **IN**, followed by the SELECT statement, as the criterion of the appropriate column, enclosing the SELECT statement within the parentheses required by the IN predicate. Figure 11.81 shows the query design with part of the IN (SELECT...) statement in the Criteria row of the Customer ID column. Figure 11.82 shows the resultset returned by the SQL statement and the query design.

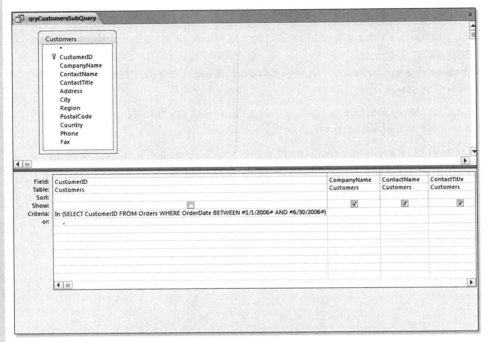

Figure 11.81
You can create the base query in Access's Query Design view, but you must type the IN predicate and the subquery's SELECT statement in the Criteria row of the grid.

Creating Queries from Tables in Other Databases

Access's Query Properties Sheet includes two properties that let you create a query based on tables contained in a database other than the current database. The database that you open after you launch Access is called the *current database*. Databases other than the current database commonly are called *external databases*. The use of these two properties is as follows:

- The value of the Source Database property for desktop databases is the path to the external database and, for Access databases, the name of the database file. To run a query against tables contained in the Oakmont.accdb sample database from the downloadable sample files installed into a C:\Access2010 folder, replace (current) in the Source Database text box with the following, as shown in Figure 11.83:C:\Access2010\Oakmont\Oakmont.accdb

Figure 11.82
This data-
sheet dis-
plays the
resultset of
the subquery
design of
Figure 11.81.

qryCustomersSubQuery			
Company Name ▾	**Contact Name** ▾	**Contact Title** ▾	**Phone** ▾
Antonio Moreno Taqueria	Antonio Moreno	Owner	(5) 555-3932
Around the Horn	Thomas Hardy	Sales Representative	(171) 555-7788
Berglunds snabbköp	Christina Berglund	Order Administrator	0921-12 34 65
Blauer See Delikatessen	Hanna Moos	Sales Representative	0621-08460
Blondel père et fils	Frédérique Citeaux	Marketing Manager	88.60.15.31
Bon app'	Laurence Lebihan	Owner	91.24.45.40
Bottom-Dollar Markets	Elizabeth Lincoln	Accounting Manager	(604) 555-4729
B's Beverages	Victoria Ashworth	Sales Representative	(171) 555-1212
Cactus Comidas para llevar	Patricio Simpson	Sales Agent	(1) 135-5555
Chop-suey Chinese	Yang Wang	Owner	0452-076545
Comércio Mineiro	Pedro Afonso	Sales Associate	(11) 555-7647
Consolidated Holdings	Elizabeth Brown	Sales Representative	(171) 555-2282
Eastern Connection	Ann Devon	Sales Agent	(171) 555-0297
Ernst Handel	Roland Mendel	Sales Manager	7675-3425
Familia Arquibaldo	Aria Cruz	Marketing Assistant	(11) 555-9857
Folies gourmandes	Martine Rancé	Assistant Sales Agent	20.16.10.16
Folk och fä HB	Maria Larsson	Owner	0695-34 67 21
Frankenversand	Peter Franken	Marketing Manager	089-0877310
Franchi S.p.A.	Paolo Accorti	Sales Representative	011-4988260
Furia Bacalhau e Frutos do Mar	Lino Rodriguez	Sales Manager	(1) 354-2534
Galería del gastrónomo	Eduardo Saavedra	Marketing Manager	(93) 203 4560
Godos Cocina Típica	José Pedro Freyre	Sales Manager	(95) 555 82 82
Gourmet Lanchonetes	André Fonseca	Sales Associate	(11) 555-9482
Great Lakes Food Market	Howard Snyder	Marketing Manager	(503) 555-7555
Hanari Carnes	Mario Pontes	Accounting Manager	(21) 555-0091
HILARIÓN-Abastos	Carlos Hernández	Sales Representative	(5) 555-1340
Hungry Coyote Import Store	Yoshi Latimer	Sales Representative	(503) 555-6874

Record: I◀ ◀ 1 of 73 ▶ ▶I ▶❋   No Filter   Search

Figure 11.83
Specify the full path to the external database as the value of the
Source Database property.

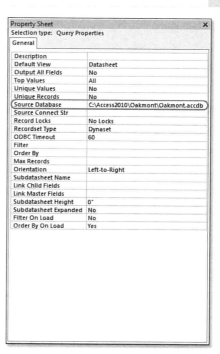

Property Sheet	
Selection type: Query Properties	
General	
Description	
Default View	Datasheet
Output All Fields	No
Top Values	All
Unique Values	No
Unique Records	No
Source Database	C:\Access2010\Oakmont\Oakmont.accdb
Source Connect Str	
Record Locks	No Locks
Recordset Type	Dynaset
ODBC Timeout	60
Filter	
Order By	
Max Records	
Orientation	Left-to-Right
Subdatasheet Name	
Link Child Fields	
Link Master Fields	
Subdatasheet Height	0"
Subdatasheet Expanded	No
Filter On Load	No
Order By On Load	Yes

- The value of the Source Connect Str property depends on the type of external database being used. If your external Access database isn't secure, leave the Source Connect Str text box empty; otherwise, type **UID=**_UserID_**;PWD=**_Password_ to specify the user ID and password needed to open the external database. For other desktop databases, you type the product name, such as **dBASE IV**. ODBC data sources require the complete ODBC connect string.

> **note**
>
> The Joins11.accdb database installed in your \Access2010\ Chaptr11 folder from the online sample code includes all the sample queries of this chapter.

Running a query against an external database is related to running a query against linked tables. When you link tables, the data in the tables is available at any time that your application is running. When you run a query against an external database, the connection to the external database is open only while your query is open in Design or Datasheet view. A slight performance penalty exists for running queries against an external database—each time that you run the query, Access must make a connection to open the database. The connection is closed when you close the query.

After you specify the external database, its tables appear in the Show Table dialog's list. Figure 11.84 illustrates a query design based on tables in the external Oakmont.accdb sample database. Figure 11.85 shows the result of executing the query design of Figure 11.84.

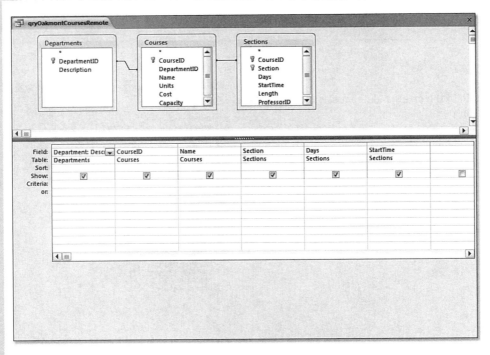

Figure 11.84
Design view of a query in an external Access database is the same as for a query against tables in the current database. You can create joins between external and current database tables, but you can't enforce referential integrity.

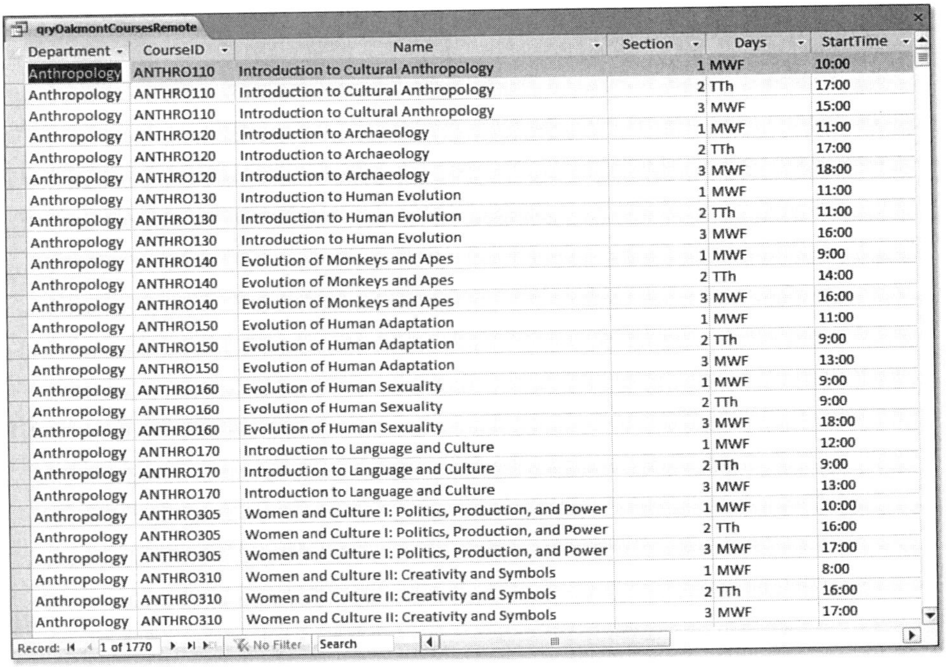

qryOakmontCoursesRemote

Department	CourseID	Name	Section	Days	StartTime
Anthropology	ANTHRO110	Introduction to Cultural Anthropology	1	MWF	10:00
Anthropology	ANTHRO110	Introduction to Cultural Anthropology	2	TTh	17:00
Anthropology	ANTHRO110	Introduction to Cultural Anthropology	3	MWF	15:00
Anthropology	ANTHRO120	Introduction to Archaeology	1	MWF	11:00
Anthropology	ANTHRO120	Introduction to Archaeology	2	TTh	17:00
Anthropology	ANTHRO120	Introduction to Archaeology	3	MWF	18:00
Anthropology	ANTHRO130	Introduction to Human Evolution	1	MWF	11:00
Anthropology	ANTHRO130	Introduction to Human Evolution	2	TTh	11:00
Anthropology	ANTHRO130	Introduction to Human Evolution	3	MWF	16:00
Anthropology	ANTHRO140	Evolution of Monkeys and Apes	1	MWF	9:00
Anthropology	ANTHRO140	Evolution of Monkeys and Apes	2	TTh	14:00
Anthropology	ANTHRO140	Evolution of Monkeys and Apes	3	MWF	16:00
Anthropology	ANTHRO150	Evolution of Human Adaptation	1	MWF	11:00
Anthropology	ANTHRO150	Evolution of Human Adaptation	2	TTh	9:00
Anthropology	ANTHRO150	Evolution of Human Adaptation	3	MWF	13:00
Anthropology	ANTHRO160	Evolution of Human Sexuality	1	MWF	9:00
Anthropology	ANTHRO160	Evolution of Human Sexuality	2	TTh	9:00
Anthropology	ANTHRO160	Evolution of Human Sexuality	3	MWF	18:00
Anthropology	ANTHRO170	Introduction to Language and Culture	1	MWF	12:00
Anthropology	ANTHRO170	Introduction to Language and Culture	2	TTh	9:00
Anthropology	ANTHRO170	Introduction to Language and Culture	3	MWF	13:00
Anthropology	ANTHRO305	Women and Culture I: Politics, Production, and Power	1	MWF	10:00
Anthropology	ANTHRO305	Women and Culture I: Politics, Production, and Power	2	TTh	16:00
Anthropology	ANTHRO305	Women and Culture I: Politics, Production, and Power	3	MWF	17:00
Anthropology	ANTHRO310	Women and Culture II: Creativity and Symbols	1	MWF	8:00
Anthropology	ANTHRO310	Women and Culture II: Creativity and Symbols	2	TTh	16:00
Anthropology	ANTHRO310	Women and Culture II: Creativity and Symbols	3	MWF	17:00

Record: 1 of 1770 No Filter Search

Figure 11.85 This datasheet displays the resultset of the query of Figure 11.85 against the external Oakmont.accdb database.

WORKING WITH PIVOTTABLE AND PIVOTCHART VIEWS

PivotTables and PivotCharts are powerful tools for summarizing detailed data stored in Access or SQL Server databases. Like crosstab queries, PivotTables present data generated by aggregate queries in a spreadsheet-like format that's familiar to all accounting and management personnel. PivotTable views deliver to Access users the benefits of Excel worksheets without having to launch Excel to manipulate the data. PivotChart views automatically render PivotTable views as line, bar, or area charts. PivotTables and PivotCharts accomplish the primary objective of decision-support front ends—converting online transaction processing (OLTP) data to usable business information (BI).

PivotTables replace embedded Excel PivotTables, and PivotCharts supplement or replace Access charts embedded by the Chart Wizard. Excel PivotTables require a local copy of Excel.exe, and the Chart Wizard needs Office 14s Graph.exe to act as Object Linking and Embedding (OLE) 2+ servers. Many Access developers believe that original Excel PivotTables and OLE-based charts are obsolete. Office PivotTables outperform their earlier Excel counterparts, but conventional Access charts you create with the Chart Wizard have several features that PivotCharts don't offer.

> *To add charts or graphs to forms with the Chart Wizard,* **see** *"Using the Chart Wizard to Create an Unlinked Graph,"* **p. 759.**

Access 2002 added two new views to tables, queries, and forms: PivotTable and PivotChart. These views are available in conventional Access 2002+ applications and Access data projects (ADP) in Access 2002 and Access 2003, and Access 2010 Client Databases, but not in Access 2010 Web Databases. PivotTables and PivotCharts are interdependent; when you design a PivotChart view, you create a corresponding

PivotTable view, and vice versa. You can't restrict tables and queries to specific views—such as PivotTable, PivotChart, or both—but you can set the default view. You can set the default view and limit views of forms to include or exclude Pivot... views.

The behavior of the PivotTable and PivotChart views of forms is identical to those of tables or queries. You can use the AutoForm: PivotTable and AutoForm: PivotChart Wizards to create these views of forms from a table or query you specify. Northwind.mdb's sample Sales Analysis form, for example, alternatively displays PivotChart and PivotTable form views of a query in a subform.

Forms and reports can contain PivotTable and PivotCharts as conventional ActiveX control objects. You can set the properties of these controls in forms and reports with Visual Basic for Applications (VBA). You can't, however, program these two controls in PivotTable or PivotChart views of tables or queries.

Slicing and Dicing Data with PivotTables

PivotTables closely resemble Access crosstab query datasheets, which are one of the main topics of Chapter 11, "Creating Multitable and Crosstab Queries." Both PivotTables and crosstab queries employ aggregate functions—sum, average, count, standard deviation, variance, and the like—to summarize data, but PivotTables can handle the entire aggregation process. This enables PivotTables to selectively display the detail data behind subtotals and grand totals.

Crosstab queries are limited to creating row-by-row subtotals, with optional row (but not column) totals. PivotTables not only provide subtotals but also supply grand totals for rows and columns, plus crossfoot totals. *Crossfooting* is an accounting term for testing the accuracy of a set of numerical values by verifying that the grand totals calculated by row and by column are the same. One of the primary advantages of PivotTables over crosstab datasheets is that the Access application's user, not just the database developer who designed the query, can control data presentation.

PivotTables let you swap axes and apply filters to the underlying data. Like filters for tables and queries, you can use PivotTable filters to remove extraneous or unneeded data from the current view.

 note

The limitations of PivotTable and PivotChart views might cause you to wonder why this chapter is in Part 3, "Transforming Data with Queries and PivotTables," rather than in Part 4, "Designing Forms and Reports." The reason is that well-designed queries—usually based on multiple tables—are fundamental to generating meaningful data for presentation in PivotTables and Pi- votCharts. The query and view design techniques you learn in this chapter apply to PivotTables and PivotCharts contained in conventional Access forms, which are the subject of Part IV's Chapter 18, "Adding Graphs, PivotCharts, and PivotTables."

Creating the Query for a Sample PivotTable View

Queries designed for users who are accustomed to using Excel PivotTables should offer a high degree of flexibility for slicing and dicing the data. For example, sales and marketing managers are likely to want to explore the total value of orders received each month or quarter by salesperson, customer, product, country, or any combination of these selection criteria. Therefore, your query must supply more than the ordinary amount of data to the PivotTable.

For more information on the Caption property issue, **see** "Changing the Names of Query Column Headers," **p. 365.**

One of the most common forms of PivotTables displays time-series data, such as orders or sales by quarter for one or more years. To design a time-series query that supplies the underlying data for a PivotTable to display the quarterly value of orders by salesperson and country, do the following:

> **tip**
> Substitute PivotTables for crosstab queries when your data presentation needs crossfooting or you want to apply sophisticated report formatting to the presentation. It's usually much faster to use PivotTable features to generate row totals, subtotals, and grand totals than it is to use crosstab queries. Another advantage of PivotTables is that users can set the amount of detail information that appears in the report and then generate their own graphs or charts from the data.

1. Open a new query in Design view in \Access2010\ Chaptr12\PivotNW.accdb, \Access2010\Northwind\Northwind. accdb, or your working copy of the sample database.

2. Add the Employees and Orders tables as well as the Order Subtotals query, to the new query.

3. Drag the LastName field of the Employees table to the query grid, followed in order by the ShipCountry and OrderDate fields of the Orders table, and the Subtotal field of the Order Subtotals query.

4. Add a **Between #1/1/2006# And #12/31/2006#** criterion to the OrderDate column to restrict the data to the last full year for which order data exists in Northwind.accdb. Clear the Show check box for this column.

5. Drag the OrderDate field from the Orders table to create a new column to the left of the existing OrderDate field. Replace the content of the Field cell of this column with **2006 Quarter: Format([OrderDate],"q")** to create a calculated column to display the number of the calendar quarter in which the order was received.

6. Place the cursor at the beginning of the LastName field, and replace LastName with **Name: Trim(LastName)** to add an alias to the field. Replace ShipCountry with **Country: Trim(ShipCountry)** and add an **Orders:** alias to the Subtotals field. Your query design appears as shown in Figure 12.1.

7. Run the query to check your work, and save the query as **qry2006OrdersByCountryPT** (see Figure 12.2).

Designing the PivotTable View of the Sample Query

Select the PivotTable View button in the ribbon's Views group; the PivotTable Design ribbon activates. An empty PivotTable view opens with the PivotTable Field List window active and empty Filter Fields, Column Fields, Row Fields, and Totals or Detail Fields drop zones (see Figure 12.3).

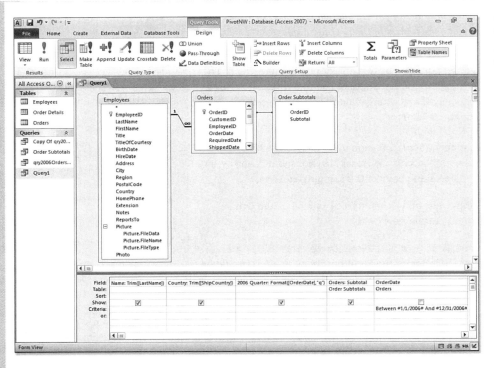

Figure 12.1
This query design provides detail data suitable for analyzing employee sales by country.

You drag fields from the PivotTable Field List to the appropriate drop zone, as follows:

- *Column Fields*—Usually hold date-based fields to create a left-to-right time series. If you're not creating a time-series PivotTable, you can select any appropriate field of the table or query. As a rule, the field having the fewest number of rows belongs in columns.

- *Row Fields*—Hold one or more fields that display data by attribute(s). Adding row fields lets you increase the degree of detail displayed by the PivotTable. Increasing the amount of detail data shown is called *drilling down* or *drill-down*.

- *Totals or Detail Fields*—As the central area of the empty PivotTable, these fields display the crosstabulated data. This drop area accepts only fields having numeric values or fields for which you only want to display a count of records.

- *Filter Fields*—One or more optional fields that let you restrict the number of fields that appear in columns, rows, or both. In most cases, you filter data by column or row fields, not fields dropped in the Filter Fields zone. (A field can appear only in one drop zone of a PivotTable.)

> **tip**
> If the PivotTable Field List isn't visible, click the Field List button in the ribbon's Show/Hide group.

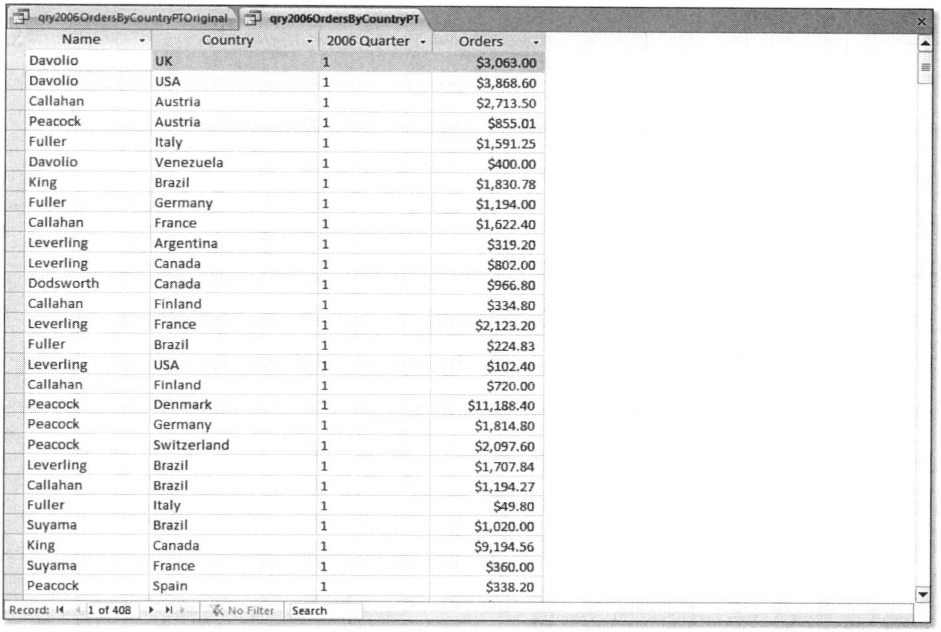

Figure 12.2
The
Datasheet
view of
the query
design of
Figure 12.1
shows the
altered field
captions
and lists the
408 orders
received by
Northwind
Traders in
2006.

Name	Country	2006 Quarter	Orders
Davolio	UK	1	$3,063.00
Davolio	USA	1	$3,868.60
Callahan	Austria	1	$2,713.50
Peacock	Austria	1	$855.01
Fuller	Italy	1	$1,591.25
Davolio	Venezuela	1	$400.00
King	Brazil	1	$1,830.78
Fuller	Germany	1	$1,194.00
Callahan	France	1	$1,622.40
Leverling	Argentina	1	$319.20
Leverling	Canada	1	$802.00
Dodsworth	Canada	1	$966.80
Callahan	Finland	1	$334.80
Leverling	France	1	$2,123.20
Fuller	Brazil	1	$224.83
Leverling	USA	1	$102.40
Callahan	Finland	1	$720.00
Peacock	Denmark	1	$11,188.40
Peacock	Germany	1	$1,814.80
Peacock	Switzerland	1	$2,097.60
Leverling	Brazil	1	$1,707.84
Callahan	Brazil	1	$1,194.27
Fuller	Italy	1	$49.80
Suyama	Brazil	1	$1,020.00
King	Canada	1	$9,194.56
Suyama	France	1	$360.00
Peacock	Spain	1	$338.20

Record: 1 of 408   No Filter   Search

Generating the Initial PivotTable

To create the initial PivotTable view of the qry2006OrdersByCountryPT query, do the following:

1. Drag the 2006 Quarter field to the Column Fields drop zone. As the field symbol enters the drop zone, a blue border appears (see Figure 12.4). When you drop the field by releasing the mouse button, a 2006 Quarter filter button appears on the first row, and four columns display quarter numbers 1 through 4. PivotTables automatically add a Grand Total column to the right of the last column you add from the field list.

2. Drag the Name field to the Row Fields drop zone, the Orders field to the Totals or Detail Fields drop zone, and the Country field to the Filter Fields drop zone. The PivotTable appears with the rows displaying detail values, as shown in Figure 12.5.

3. You can't identify the countries for the orders in the columns, so drag the Country field from the Filter Fields drop zone to the Name button's right side to group the orders by country. Close the PivotTable Field list.

4. Click the Name button to select it, and click the Bold button on the Home tab to increase the contrast of the selected column (see Figure 12.6).

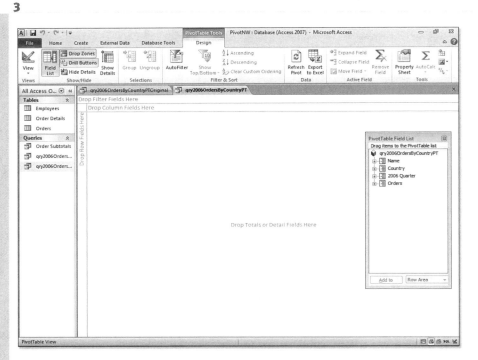

Figure 12.3
When you open a new PivotTable view of a table or query, the field list of the source table or query has the focus.

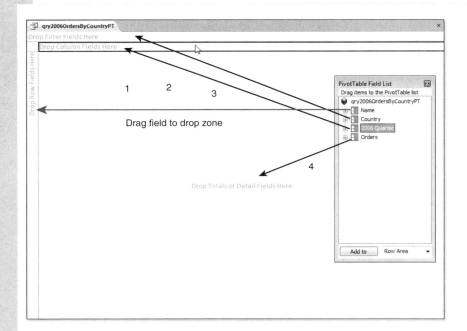

Figure 12.4
When you drag a field from the PivotTable Field List to a drop zone, the drop zone gains a thicker blue border.

Figure 12.5
After you've dragged the four fields to the locations shown here, the default PivotTable view includes detail values for rows. In this case, the amount of each order obtained by the salesperson appears in the expanded quarter columns.

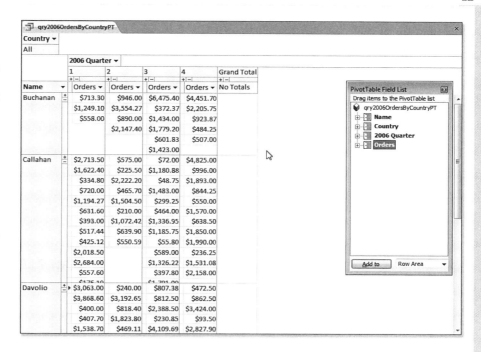

Figure 12.6
Moving the Country field from the Filter Fields to the right of the Name field displays the orders for each country.

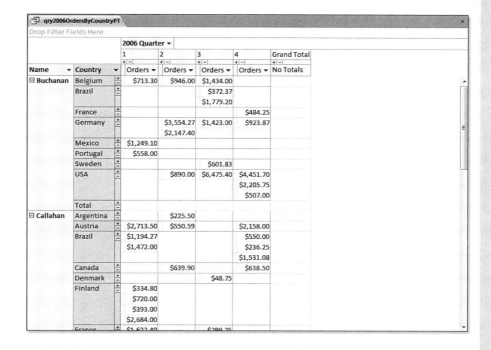

Reducing the Level of Detail and Adding Grand Totals

Including amounts for each order in the PivotTable shows excessive detail. One approach for this example is to alter the query design to an aggregate (summary) query and group the individual orders by salesperson, country, and quarter.

To modify the query, regenerate the PivotTable data, and add grand totals, do this:

1. Change to Design view.

2. Σ Click the Totals button to group the query data by LastName, ShipCountry, and 2006 Quarter.

3. Open the Total cell for the Orders: Subtotal column and choose Sum as the SQL aggregate function. Open the OrderDate field and select Where. Your modified aggregate query design appears as shown in Figure 12.7.

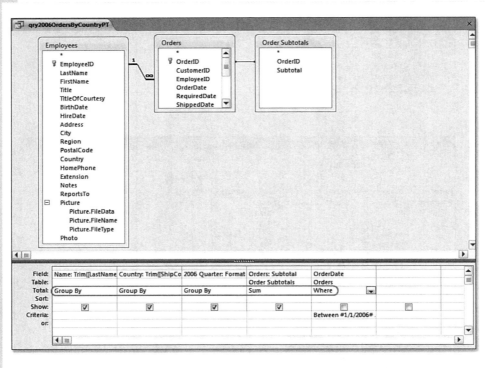

Figure 12.7
Change the query design to an aggregate query to sum individual orders by LastName, ShipCountry, and 2006 Quarter columns.

4. Run the query to verify the design (see Figure 12.8).

5. Return to PivotTable view, which now displays the summary data (see Figure 12.9).

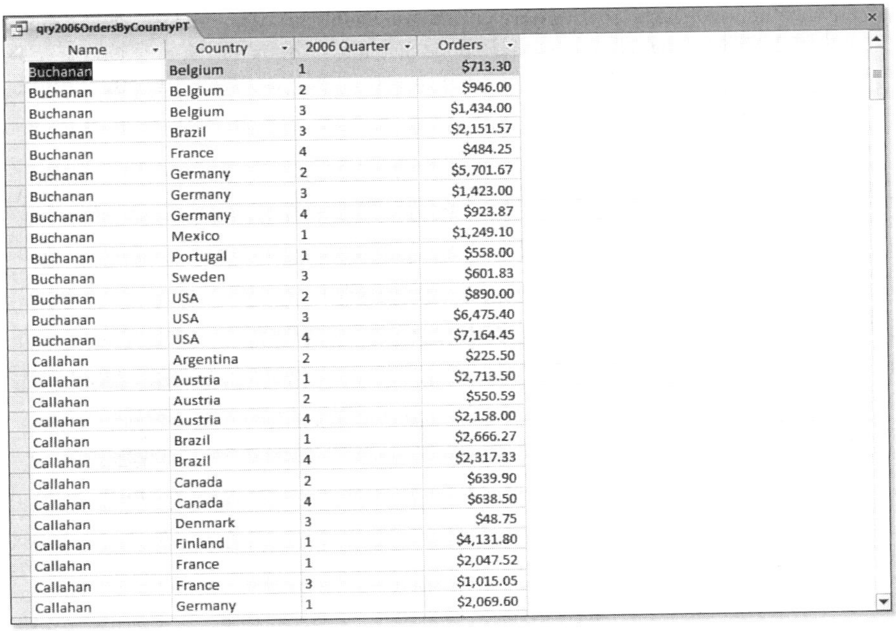

qry2006OrdersByCountryPT

Name	Country	2006 Quarter	Orders
Buchanan	Belgium	1	$713.30
Buchanan	Belgium	2	$946.00
Buchanan	Belgium	3	$1,434.00
Buchanan	Brazil	3	$2,151.57
Buchanan	France	4	$484.25
Buchanan	Germany	2	$5,701.67
Buchanan	Germany	3	$1,423.00
Buchanan	Germany	4	$923.87
Buchanan	Mexico	1	$1,249.10
Buchanan	Portugal	1	$558.00
Buchanan	Sweden	3	$601.83
Buchanan	USA	2	$890.00
Buchanan	USA	3	$6,475.40
Buchanan	USA	4	$7,164.45
Callahan	Argentina	2	$225.50
Callahan	Austria	1	$2,713.50
Callahan	Austria	2	$550.59
Callahan	Austria	4	$2,158.00
Callahan	Brazil	1	$2,666.27
Callahan	Brazil	4	$2,317.33
Callahan	Canada	2	$639.90
Callahan	Canada	4	$638.50
Callahan	Denmark	3	$48.75
Callahan	Finland	1	$4,131.80
Callahan	France	1	$2,047.52
Callahan	France	3	$1,015.05
Callahan	Germany	1	$2,069.60

Figure 12.8 The resultset of the query design has 251 records; the original query had 408 records (refer to Figure 12.2).

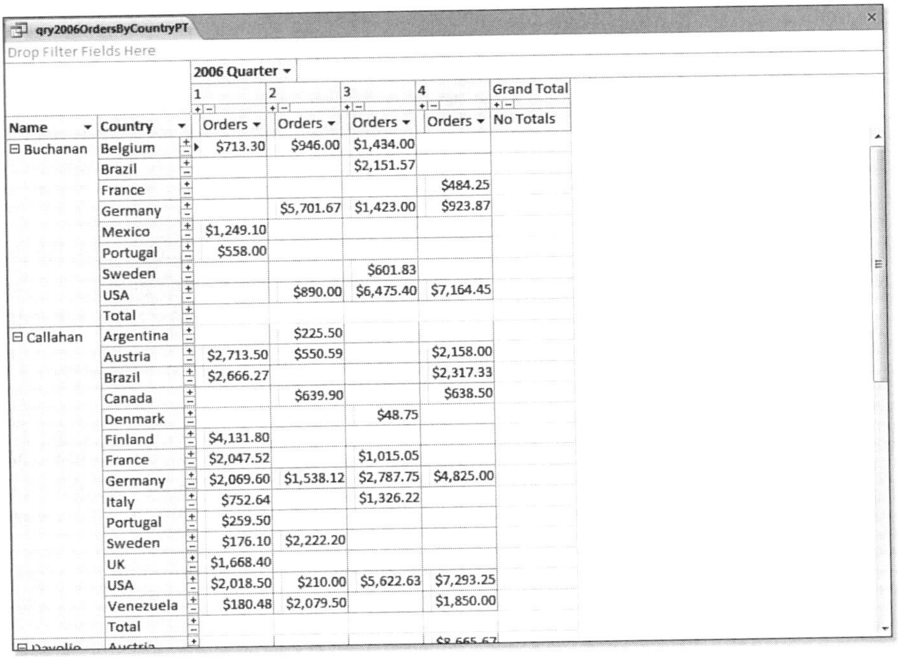

qry2006OrdersByCountryPT

Drop Filter Fields Here

		2006 Quarter				
		1	2	3	4	Grand Total
Name	Country	Orders	Orders	Orders	Orders	No Totals
⊟ Buchanan	Belgium	$713.30	$946.00	$1,434.00		
	Brazil			$2,151.57		
	France				$484.25	
	Germany		$5,701.67	$1,423.00	$923.87	
	Mexico	$1,249.10				
	Portugal	$558.00				
	Sweden			$601.83		
	USA		$890.00	$6,475.40	$7,164.45	
	Total					
⊟ Callahan	Argentina		$225.50			
	Austria	$2,713.50	$550.59		$2,158.00	
	Brazil	$2,666.27			$2,317.33	
	Canada		$639.90		$638.50	
	Denmark			$48.75		
	Finland	$4,131.80				
	France	$2,047.52		$1,015.05		
	Germany	$2,069.60	$1,538.12	$2,787.75	$4,825.00	
	Italy	$752.64		$1,326.22		
	Portugal	$259.50				
	Sweden	$176.10	$2,222.20			
	UK	$1,668.40				
	USA	$2,018.50	$210.00	$5,622.63	$7,293.25	
	Venezuela	$180.48	$2,079.50		$1,850.00	
	Total					

Figure 12.9 Converting the PivotTable source query to an aggregate query results in a PivotTable with a single value for the total amount of orders from each country.

6. To add Grand Total values, click one of the Orders buttons to select all the Quarter columns, click the PivotTable Tools, Design tab's AutoCalc button, and select Sum from the AutoCalc aggregate functions list. Adding Grand Totals also adds Totals and Sum of Orders items to the PivotTable Field List and totals rows to each Country entry (see Figure 12.10). Close the PivotTable Field List, if it's open.

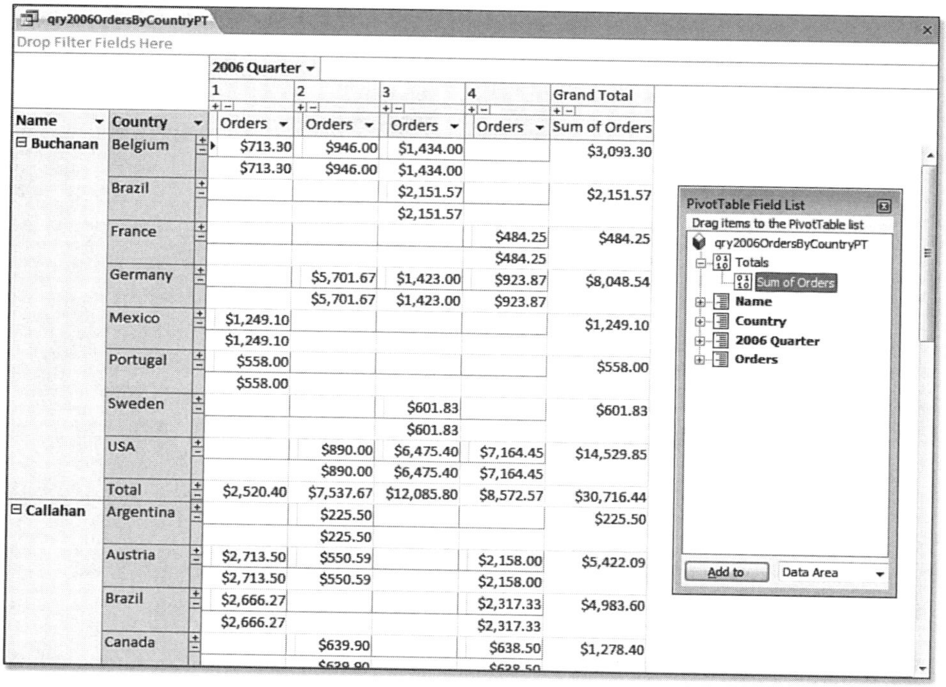

Figure 12.10
Adding Grand Totals to the PivotTable also adds Sum of Orders totals to the Country entries.

7. Click the Country button and click Hide Details to display only a single Sum of Orders value for each employee and country. The PivotTable now displays only a single row per country for each employee. Countries from which the employee obtained no orders during the year don't appear.

8. With the Country field selected, click the Subtotals button to add a Totals row for each employee (see Figure 12.11).

9. Click the Name button to select the column, and click the Active Field group's Collapse button to remove Country values for the employees and display the summary entries for all employees without scrolling (see Figure 12.12). Clicking the adjacent Expand and Collapse buttons toggles display of detail columns.

Figure 12.11
Hiding
detail rows
and adding
subtotals
for each
employee
results in
a more
meaningful
PivotTable
presenta-
tion of your
data. Bold
formatting
is applied
to the Total
label for
emphasis.

| Name | Country | 2006 Quarter ▾ | | | | Grand Total |
		1 Sum of Orders	2 Sum of Orders	3 Sum of Orders	4 Sum of Orders	Sum of Orders
⊟ Buchanan	Belgium	$713.30	$946.00	$1,434.00		$3,093.30
	Brazil			$2,151.57		$2,151.57
	France				$484.25	$484.25
	Germany		$5,701.67	$1,423.00	$923.87	$8,048.54
	Mexico	$1,249.10				$1,249.10
	Portugal	$558.00				$558.00
	Sweden			$601.83		$601.83
	USA		$890.00	$6,475.40	$7,164.45	$14,529.85
	Total	$2,520.40	$7,537.67	$12,085.80	$8,572.57	$30,716.44
⊟ Callahan	Argentina		$225.50			$225.50
	Austria	$2,713.50	$550.59		$2,158.00	$5,422.09
	Brazil	$2,666.27			$2,317.33	$4,983.60
	Canada		$639.90		$638.50	$1,278.40
	Denmark			$48.75		$48.75
	Finland	$4,131.80				$4,131.80
	France	$2,047.52		$1,015.05		$3,062.57
	Germany	$2,069.60	$1,538.12	$2,787.75	$4,825.00	$11,220.47
	Italy	$752.64		$1,326.22		$2,078.86
	Portugal	$259.50				$259.50
	Sweden	$176.10	$2,222.20			$2,398.30
	UK	$1,668.40				$1,668.40
	USA	$2,018.50	$210.00	$5,622.63	$7,293.25	$15,144.38
	Venezuela	$180.48	$2,079.50		$1,850.00	$4,109.98
	Total	$18,684.31	$7,465.81	$10,800.40	$19,082.08	$56,032.60
⊟ Davolio	Austria				$8,665.67	$8,665.67

qry2006OrdersByCountryPT
Drop Filter Fields Here

Filtering PivotTable Category Values

Worldwide sales data probably satisfies top management, but regional managers might want to
display only orders received from a particular area, such as North America, Europe, or Scandinavia.
By default, all field values appear in PivotTable rows or columns and are included in all calculated
values, such as totals.

You can filter the PivotTable to display only selected values of a
category field, such as Country, by following these steps:

1. Expand the PivotTable display to include the field on which you
   want to filter. For this example, select the Name field and click
   the Expand button to display the Countries column.

2. Click the arrow of the field button to filter (Country, for this
   example) to open the field value list. The list contains an item
   for each field value.

3. Click the (All) check box to deselect all fields.

4. Mark the check boxes of the field values you want to include—Canada, Mexico, and USA, for this
   example.

 tip

Use the Filter and Sort group's
AutoFilter button to toggle
quickly between filtered and
unfiltered display.

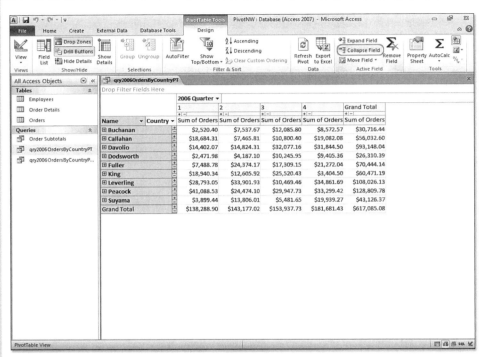

Figure 12.12
Collapsing the Name column eliminates the Country field detail and displays summary data only. Bold formatting is applied to the two Grand Totals labels.

5. Click OK to close the list and apply the filter.

Figure 12.13 illustrates the sample PivotTable with only the Canada, Mexico, and USA fields selected.

You also can filter data by rank, such as the top- or bottom-performing salesperson, or the countries with the highest or lowest sales. To test the PivotTable's Top/Bottom Items feature with the sample query and North America filter, do the following:

1. Select the Name column, click the Filter and Sort group's Show Top/Bottom Items button, choose Show Only the Top, and choose 1 from the submenu. The PivotTable displays data only for Janet Leverling, the top salesperson for North America orders.

2. Click the Show Top/Bottom Items button, choose Show Only the Bottom, and choose 1 from the submenu. The PivotTable shows that Anne Dodsworth occupies the lowest rung on the North America sales ladder.

3. Remove the filter on the Names column by clicking the Show Top/Bottom Items button and choosing Show All.

 tip

You can expand the display for a single employee by clicking the small Show/Hide Details (+) button to the left of the employee's name. The Show/Hide Details button toggles the + and - states.

Figure 12.13
This filtered
PivotTable
view restricts
the vis-
ible values
to orders
received
from Canada,
Mexico, and
the USA.

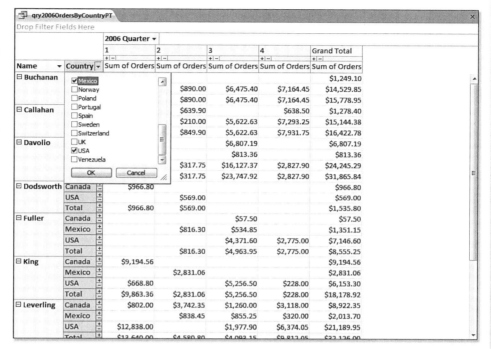

4. Select the Country column, click the Show Top/Bottom Items button, choose Show Only the Top, and choose 2 from the submenu. The PivotTable displays data for Germany and the USA for all employees (see Figure 12.14).

5. Remove the filter on the Country column by clicking the Show Top/Bottom Items button and choosing Show All.

If you select Other in the list of values, the Properties dialog opens to the Filter and Group page, where you can set custom filtering options by numeric or percentage rank.

Increasing the Level of Detail for Drill-Down

The preceding section demonstrates the capability to reduce to a manageable level the amount of detail information displayed by the PivotTable. Total amounts of the orders obtained by employees for each country might satisfy the vice president of sales, but sales managers and salespersons might want to review values of individual orders. Commissioned salespersons want order number and date information to ensure that all orders they book are assigned to them.

Providing additional drill-down information requires you to modify the underlying sample query and regenerate the value data in the PivotTable, as follows:

qry2006OrdersByCountryPT							×
Drop Filter Fields Here							
		2006 Quarter ▾					
		1 ⊞⊟	2 ⊞⊟	3 ⊞⊟	4 ⊞⊟	Grand Total ⊞⊟	
Name ▾	Country ▾	Sum of Orders	Sum of Orders	Sum of Orders	Sum of Orders	Sum of Orders	
⊟ Buchanan	Germany		$5,701.67	$1,423.00	$923.87	$8,048.54	
	USA		$890.00	$6,475.40	$7,164.45	$14,529.85	
	Total		$6,591.67	$7,898.40	$8,088.32	$22,578.39	
⊟ Callahan	Germany	$2,069.60	$1,538.12	$2,787.75	$4,825.00	$11,220.47	
	USA	$2,018.50	$210.00	$5,622.63	$7,293.25	$15,144.38	
	Total	$4,088.10	$1,748.12	$8,410.38	$12,118.25	$26,364.85	
⊟ Davolio	Germany		$709.11	$2,612.02	$5,465.25	$8,786.38	
	USA	$4,972.27	$317.75	$16,127.37	$2,827.90	$24,245.29	
	Total	$4,972.27	$1,026.86	$18,739.39	$8,293.15	$33,031.67	
⊟ Dodsworth	Germany		$1,717.30		$6,083.30	$7,800.60	
	USA		$569.00			$569.00	
	Total		$2,286.30		$6,083.30	$8,369.60	
⊟ Fuller	Germany	$2,778.00	$9,921.30	$3,120.00	$10,164.80	$25,984.10	
	USA			$4,371.60	$2,775.00	$7,146.60	
	Total	$2,778.00	$9,921.30	$7,491.60	$12,939.80	$33,130.70	
⊟ King	Germany		$4,825.60	$1,994.40	$420.00	$7,240.00	
	USA	$668.80		$5,256.50	$228.00	$6,153.30	
	Total	$668.80	$4,825.60	$7,250.90	$648.00	$13,393.30	
⊟ Leverling	Germany	$1,171.60	$12,406.80	$2,284.46	$6,567.82	$22,430.68	
	USA	$12,838.00		$1,977.90	$6,374.05	$21,189.95	
	Total	$14,009.60	$12,406.80	$4,262.36	$12,941.87	$43,620.63	
⊟ Peacock	Germany	$5,664.46	$5,197.30	$8,539.10	$3,518.00	$22,918.86	
	USA	$4,924.13	$3,804.05	$3,275.54	$1,416.00	$13,419.72	
	Total	$10,588.59	$9,001.35	$11,814.64	$4,934.00	$36,338.58	
⊟ Suyama	Germany	$246.24		$814.50	$1,829.76	$2,890.50	

Figure 12.14
The PivotTable's Top/Bottom Items feature lets you filter items by the value rank. Germany and the USA rank by order amount as the top two countries.

1. Return to Query Design view.

2. **Σ** Click the Totals button to remove the Totals row and eliminate data grouping.

3. Drag the OrderID and OrderDate fields of the Orders table field list to the right of the Country field. (The column sequence isn't important.)

4. Return to PivotTable view, click the Show Details button, and click the Field List button to display the PivotTable Field List, which now has Order ID, Order Date, Order Date by Week, and Order Date by Month items added.

5. Right-click the Sum of Orders item in the Field List, and choose Delete to replace the Sum of Orders labels with Orders.

6. Drag the Order ID field to the immediate left of the Orders button. Drag the Order Date field to the immediate right of the Order ID button. Select the Orders button, click the AutoCalc button, and select Sum to add a Sum of Orders row rather than a column (see Figure 12.15), and then close the PivotTable Field List. If the various Order fields aren't in the correct sequence, drag their buttons to the proper relative position.

7. Click the Hide Details button to reduce the PivotTable's level of detail.

> **tip**
>
> Be judicious when increasing the detail level of PivotTables by eliminating grouping in your query. The later "Optimizing Performance of PivotTables" section describes performance problems that result from large query resultsets.

Figure 12.15
The PivotTable now displays Order ID and Order Date values for each order.

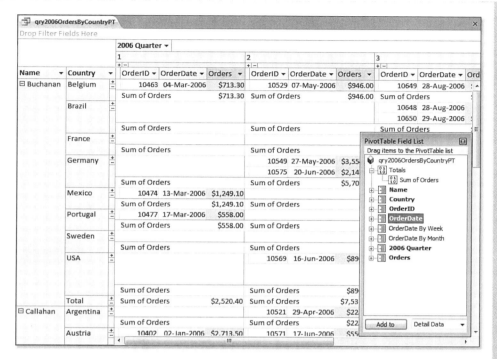

Changing Fill/Background and Text Colors

You can increase the contrast of the PivotTable's display or emphasize elements by changing their color with the Fill Color tool of the Home tab's Text Formatting group. For example, you can remove the gray tint from the Name, Country, Quarter, and Grand Total labels by selecting each field in sequence, clicking the Fill/Back Color tool, and choosing white in the color picker (see Figure 12.16). Alternatively, you can apply a new color scheme to the display by choosing appropriate Office Theme colors.

Exchanging PivotTable Axes and Category Hierarchies

The term PivotTable derives from the capability to exchange (pivot) the x (horizontal) and y (vertical) axes of the table. PivotTables also let you exchange the hierarchy of category columns, which often is more useful than pivoting the table. If you're more interested in sales by country than by employee, drag the sample PivotTable's Country button to the left of the Name button. The All Orders values now represent quarterly sales by country (see Figure 12.17).

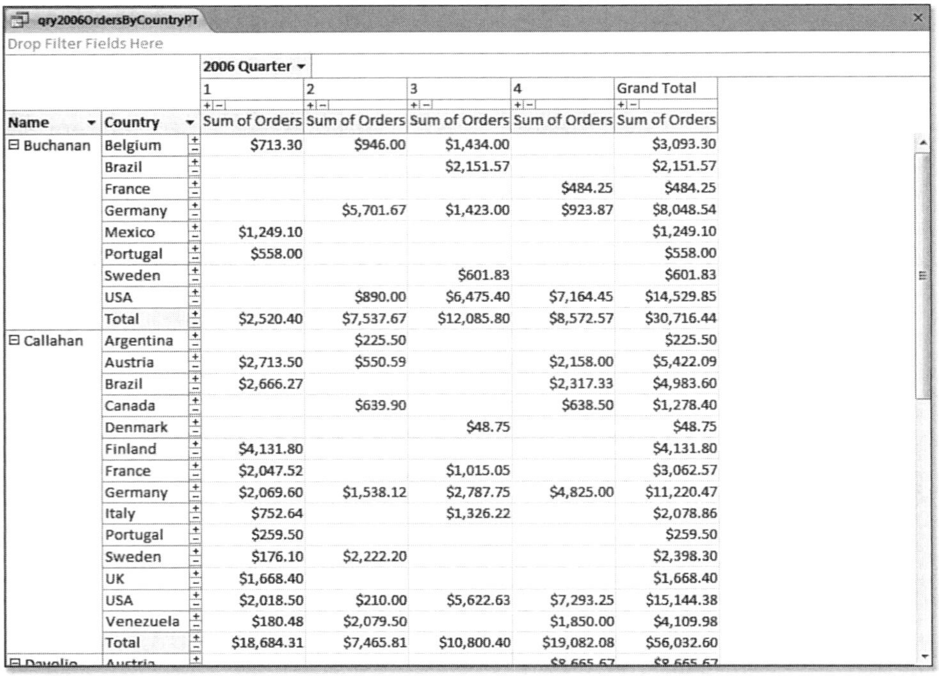

qry2006OrdersByCountryPT

Drop Filter Fields Here

		2006 Quarter				
		1	2	3	4	Grand Total
Name	Country	Sum of Orders	Sum of Orders	Sum of Orders	Sum of Orders	Sum of Orders
Buchanan	Belgium	$713.30	$946.00	$1,434.00		$3,093.30
	Brazil			$2,151.57		$2,151.57
	France				$484.25	$484.25
	Germany		$5,701.67	$1,423.00	$923.87	$8,048.54
	Mexico	$1,249.10				$1,249.10
	Portugal	$558.00				$558.00
	Sweden			$601.83		$601.83
	USA		$890.00	$6,475.40	$7,164.45	$14,529.85
	Total	$2,520.40	$7,537.67	$12,085.80	$8,572.57	$30,716.44
Callahan	Argentina		$225.50			$225.50
	Austria	$2,713.50	$550.59		$2,158.00	$5,422.09
	Brazil	$2,666.27			$2,317.33	$4,983.60
	Canada		$639.90		$638.50	$1,278.40
	Denmark			$48.75		$48.75
	Finland	$4,131.80				$4,131.80
	France	$2,047.52		$1,015.05		$3,062.57
	Germany	$2,069.60	$1,538.12	$2,787.75	$4,825.00	$11,220.47
	Italy	$752.64		$1,326.22		$2,078.86
	Portugal	$259.50				$259.50
	Sweden	$176.10	$2,222.20			$2,398.30
	UK	$1,668.40				$1,668.40
	USA	$2,018.50	$210.00	$5,622.63	$7,293.25	$15,144.38
	Venezuela	$180.48	$2,079.50		$1,850.00	$4,109.98
	Total	$18,684.31	$7,465.81	$10,800.40	$19,082.08	$56,032.60
Davolio	Austria				$8,665.67	$8,665.67

Figure 12.16 Substituting a white background for the default gray color of the Name, Country, Quarter, and Grand Total field labels increases the contrast of the PivotTable.

Interchanging the axes lets you view the data from a different perspective. In many cases, users want data presented in a familiar format. For example, the sales manager might be accustomed to comparing the quarter-by-quarter performance of his or her salespeople with quarterly data in rows, not columns. To exchange the Name and 2006 Quarter axes, drag the Name button to its original position (left of the Country button), drag the 2006 Quarter button to the left of the Name button, and then drag the Name button to the empty Column Fields drop zone. Optionally, drag the Country field to the Filter Fields drop zone (see Figure 12.18).

Setting PivotTable Property Values

The Properties dialog has four pages of PivotTable property settings for active elements. Right-click a field and choose Properties to open the dialog. Following are brief descriptions of the purpose of each page:

- *Format*—Lets you select a field name and select the font name, size, color, attributes (bold, italic, underlined), and justification (left, right, and centered). You also can set the background color, column width, and sort the column or row in ascending (default) or descending order. The value in the Select list determines the field to which properties you set in the Filter and Group and Captions pages apply (see Figure 12.19, left).

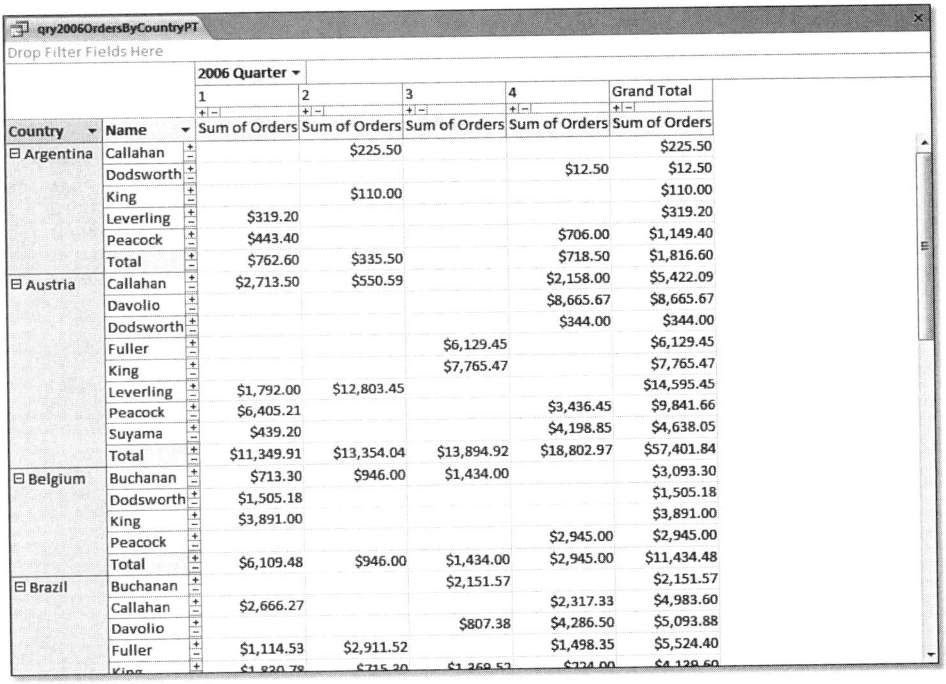

Figure 12.17
Interchanging the Country and Names fields recalculates the PivotTable to display values for quarterly sales by country. Details are hidden with the Hide Details button in this example.

Country ▼	Name ▼	2006 Quarter ▼				
		1	2	3	4	Grand Total
		Sum of Orders	Sum of Orders	Sum of Orders	Sum of Orders	Sum of Orders
⊟ Argentina	Callahan		$225.50			$225.50
	Dodsworth				$12.50	$12.50
	King		$110.00			$110.00
	Leverling	$319.20				$319.20
	Peacock	$443.40			$706.00	$1,149.40
	Total	$762.60	$335.50		$718.50	$1,816.60
⊟ Austria	Callahan	$2,713.50	$550.59		$2,158.00	$5,422.09
	Davolio				$8,665.67	$8,665.67
	Dodsworth				$344.00	$344.00
	Fuller			$6,129.45		$6,129.45
	King			$7,765.47		$7,765.47
	Leverling	$1,792.00	$12,803.45			$14,595.45
	Peacock	$6,405.21			$3,436.45	$9,841.66
	Suyama	$439.20			$4,198.85	$4,638.05
	Total	$11,349.91	$13,354.04	$13,894.92	$18,802.97	$57,401.84
⊟ Belgium	Buchanan	$713.30	$946.00	$1,434.00		$3,093.30
	Dodsworth	$1,505.18				$1,505.18
	King	$3,891.00				$3,891.00
	Peacock				$2,945.00	$2,945.00
	Total	$6,109.48	$946.00	$1,434.00	$2,945.00	$11,434.48
⊟ Brazil	Buchanan			$2,151.57		$2,151.57
	Callahan	$2,666.27			$2,317.33	$4,983.60
	Davolio			$807.38	$4,286.50	$5,093.88
	Fuller	$1,114.53	$2,911.52		$1,498.35	$5,524.40
	King	$1,820.78	$715.30	$1,369.52	$324.00	$4,139.60

- *Filter and Group*—Enables customer top/bottom value filtering of the field you select on the Format page. If you have ungrouped items in a field, you can use the Grouping controls to aggregate them (see Figure 12.19, right).

- *Captions*—Lets you change the caption for the field you selected in the Format page. For example, you can change Sum of Orders caption to All Orders, Order ID to Number, or Order Date to Date. The captions page also has a list of uninteresting property values (see Figure 12.20, left).

- *Behavior*—Options apply to the entire PivotTable. You can hide the Show/Hide Details buttons of fields and the drop zones. In the case of the PivotTable of the sample query, you can hide the Filter Fields drop zone, because there is no suitable field available to drop in the zone. PivotTable views of tables and queries don't have a title bar or built-in toolbar, so two of the check boxes are disabled (see Figure 12.20, right). The PivotTable view of forms have a title bar.

- *Report*—These options also apply to the entire PivotTable. The Report page appears only when you right-click an empty region of the PivotTable. The most important options are Always Display Empty Rows and Empty Columns. Marking either of these check boxes generates a row or column, regardless of whether a value is present. Accept the default options, unless you have a good reason to do otherwise.

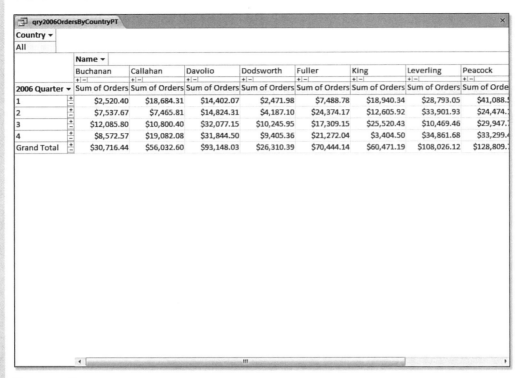

		Buchanan	Callahan	Davolio	Dodsworth	Fuller	King	Leverling	Peacock
2006 Quarter ▾		Sum of Orders	Sum of Orders	Sum of Orders	Sum of Orders	Sum of Orders	Sum of Orders	Sum of Orders	Sum of Orde
1		$2,520.40	$18,684.31	$14,402.07	$2,471.98	$7,488.78	$18,940.34	$28,793.05	$41,088.5
2		$7,537.67	$7,465.81	$14,824.31	$4,187.10	$24,374.17	$12,605.92	$33,901.93	$24,474.1
3		$12,085.80	$10,800.40	$32,077.15	$10,245.95	$17,309.15	$25,520.43	$10,469.46	$29,947.7
4		$8,572.57	$19,082.08	$31,844.50	$9,405.36	$21,272.04	$3,404.50	$34,861.68	$33,299.4
Grand Total		$30,716.44	$56,032.60	$93,148.03	$26,310.39	$70,444.14	$60,471.19	$108,026.12	$128,809.7

Figure 12.18
Rotating the axes of a PivotTable lets you conform data presentation to the users' preference. In this example, only the first eight columns of the Employees field are visible without scrolling horizontally.

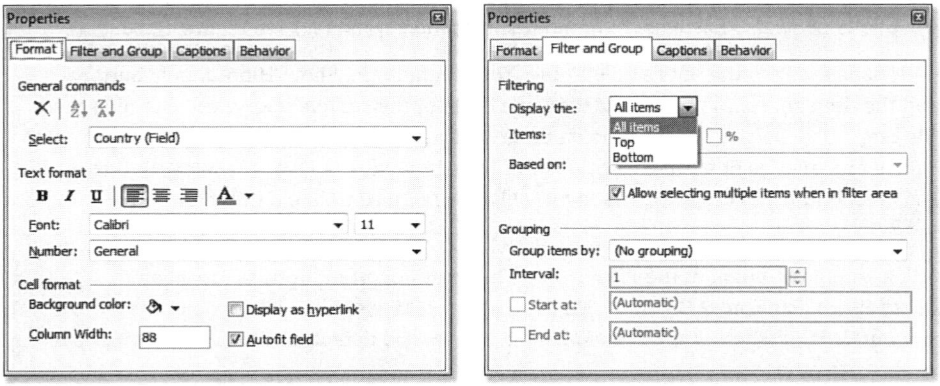

Figure 12.19
The Format (left) page's Select value determines the field to which the settings of the Filter and Group (right) and Captions pages apply.

Figure 12.20
The most important feature of the Captions page (left) is the capability to change the caption of any PivotTable field. The options you set in the Behavior page (right) apply to all fields.

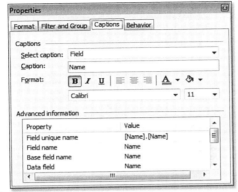
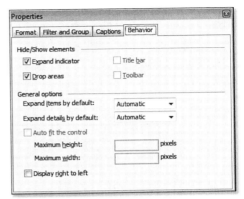

If you right-click an empty area of the PivotTable and choose Properties, only the Captions, Report, and Behavior pages appear. In this case, the Captions page lets you change captions for the four drop zones and the title bar.

Exporting the PivotTable to Excel

You can export the PivotTable as a *FileName*.html file containing a table of data values, and an XPS or PDF representation. This isn't a very exciting feature, because the process exports static tabular data.

Click the External Data ribbon's (Export to Microsoft) Excel button in the Export group to generate the PivotTable workbook. Figure 12.21 shows the default view of the PivotTable exported to Sheet1 of a workbook with the Excel PivotTable Tools, Design tab and PivotTable Field List pane active. You must click the Insert ribbon's PivotTable button and drag the fields to the appropriate box below the Field List to complete the PivotTable import. The qry2006OrdersByCountryPT sheet contains data exported by the source query of the PivotTable, which Excel translates from the Cachedata.xml file. Formatting numeric data as currency requires selecting all Orders and Totals cells and clicking the Home ribbon's $ button in the Numbers group.

 tip

To make PivotTable view the default for your query, change to design mode, open the Query Properties dialog, and change the Default View property value to PivotTable.

To print a PivotTable, choose File, Print in PivotTable view. You might need to widen the columns slightly to print Grand Total columns correctly.

Clicking the Insert tab's Column button in the Charts Group opens a gallery of columnar chart types. For this example, clicking the Stacked Column chart type button automatically generates a PivotChart from the PivotTable. To create a readable chart, clear the Country check box in the PivotTable Field List pane to eliminate the Country detail data before you click the Chart Wizard button. Otherwise, the chart is impossible to decipher. Figure 12.22 shows the PivotChart created from the collapsed PivotTable.

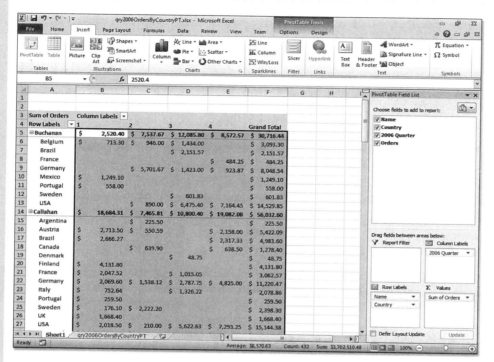

Figure 12.21 This Excel workbook was created by exporting the sample PivotTable from the earlier "Increasing the Level of Detail for Drill-Down" section.

Optimizing Performance of PivotTables

The first and most important rule of PivotTables is, *Minimize the number of rows returned by queries that you intend to use as the data source for PivotTable views.* Access returns only the first 100 rows of the query resultset to the initial Datasheet view, so response is almost instantaneous for a default Dynaset-type query without GROUP BY or other operations that require operations on the entire resultset. The Access database engine retrieves additional rows as you scroll the datasheet. Unfortunately, PivotTables don't take advantage of Access's incremental row retrieval feature.

The Oakmont.mdb sample database has a sufficient number of records to bring a PivotTable view to its knees with a simple query. For example, you might want to analyze tuition revenue by student graduation year and course. The average Oakmont student is enrolled in only two courses, so the query returns 59,996 rows. The objective of the query is to return total revenue and an enrollment count for all sections of each of the 590 courses offered by the college, and to summarize the data by academic department. In theory, the PivotTable's AutoCalc feature should be able to total the revenue and count the number of enrollment records. Figure 12.23 shows the initial design of a query that's capable of providing the required data.

note

The files required to create the Excel workbook described in this section are included in the \Access2010\Chaptr12 folder of the downloadable samples files. Double-click the 2006OrdersByCountryPT.html file to open a static table in IE 8 or the 2006OrdersByCountryPT.pdf to display a static PivotTable image.

Figure 12.22
The Excel
Chart Wizard
displays
in another
worksheet
a PivotChart
based on
each row
and column
displayed
in the
PivotTable.

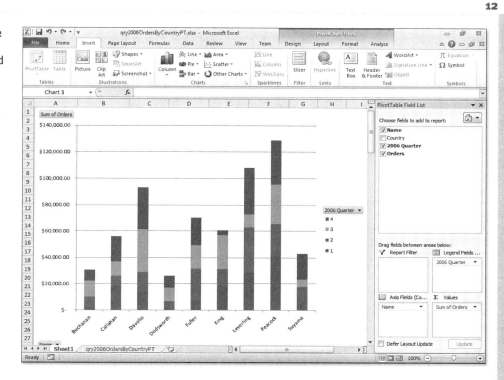

 To review how to use the Linked Table Manager, **see** *"Using the Linked Table Manager Add-in to Relink Tables,"* **p. 330.**

Opening the 60,000-row query design of Figure 12.23 in PivotTable view takes about 5 seconds on a fast computer (a 2.83GHz Intel Core 2 Quad CPU system with 2GB RAM and a fast Serial-ATA (SATA) 2 drive running Windows 7 Professional). This delay occurs every time you move from Query Datasheet or Design view to PivotTable view, because all rows of the query must be loaded into the PivotTable to compute totals. An equal delay occurs between PivotTable and PivotChart views. If the Oakmont.accdb file is on a network server, opening the PivotTable view can take up to 30 seconds and consume a large part (or all) of the network's available bandwidth. Clicking Show Details requires about 5 seconds to regenerate the local PivotTable view.

> 🔍 **note**
>
> 🔗 The three qryOakmontPTTest sample queries (60,000, 2,350, and 52 rows) discussed in this section are included in the PivotOM.accdb database in the \Access2010\Chaptr12 folder of the accompanying CD-ROM. You must install the Oakmont.accdb database from the CD-ROM to its default location, C:\Access2010\Oakmont, for these queries to execute from the default linked tables. If you've installed Oakmont.accdb to another location, click the Database Tools tab's Linked Table Manager button and then change the links to the correct path before attempting to open a table or query.

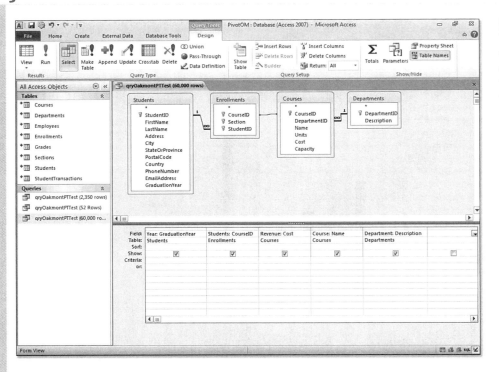

Figure 12.23
This sample query against four tables of the Oakmont.mdb database returns 59,996 rows.

If the opening delay doesn't sufficiently deter you, dropping fields of this query to rows or columns can consume 100% of your CPU cycles and take even longer. If you don't select Hide Details beforehand, dropping the Year field on the Column Fields zone takes a minute or two for the four year (2003 through 2006) columns to appear. Clicking Hide Details and dropping the Year field takes only a few seconds to display the columns. With details hidden, dropping Department on the Row Fields zone and Revenue and Students on the Totals and Detail Fields zones takes only about a second to regenerate totals (see Figure 12.24).

The solution to the preceding performance hit is to use Access's Totals (Group By) feature to reduce the number of query rows. Grouping by year, course, and department; counting Enrollments records; and summing the Cost field of the Courses table lets the Access query engine—instead of the PivotTable—handle the initial aggregation (see Figure 12.25).

The PivotTable—identical to that shown earlier in Figure 12.24—better digests the resultset of the aggregate query, which now contains 2,348 rows. Access takes only about 2 seconds to execute this query from a local database, and the same PivotTable view opens in a bit more than 3 seconds. The detail data is consolidated by the query, so the Show Detail/Hide Detail toggle operation is almost instantaneous. Reducing the number of rows of the local query resultset, however, doesn't reduce network traffic if you're connected to a remote database.

PivotTable Performance Problems with Networked Tables

Sometimes when you link large back-end tables on a network server as the data source for PivotTables you might experience serious deterioration in performance. Opening PivotTables based on aggregate queries against remote Access tables requires moving all affected rows of the underlying tables across the network, because the query that performs the aggregation runs on your local computer. In a lightly loaded 100-bps, the added opening time for a PivotTable isn't a serious issue. If you're connected to a hub (not a switch), and the network has a substantial amount of traffic, aggregate queries against large tables can slow dramatically. For historical (static) data, consider converting the aggregate query to a make-table query and changing the data source to the table. Using a table with fewer rows also helps solve performance problems that result from overtaxed server disk drives.

If you upsize your application to SQL Server, queries run as views, functions, or stored procedures on the server, not the client PC. One of the primary advantages of client/server RDBMSs, such as SQL Server, is that only query resultsets move across the network.

Figure 12.24
This PivotTable performs grouping and aggregation operations on a 60,000-row query resultset. Performing these operations in the PivotTable can take a long time.

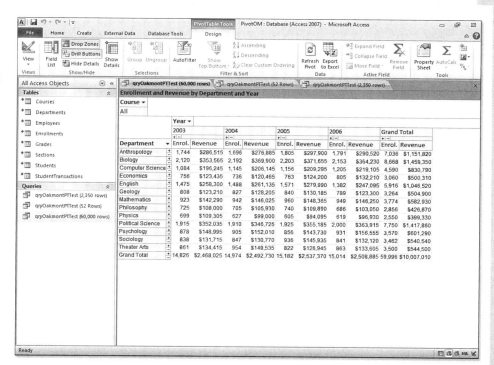

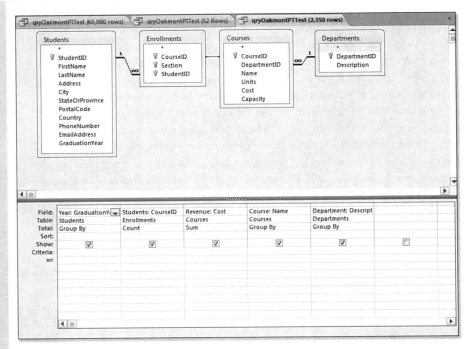

Figure 12.25
Adding a GROUP
BY expression
to the query and
summing the
enrollment count
and tuition reve-
nue in the Access
query reduces
the number of
query rows from
59,996 to 2,348.

If you don't need detail enrollment and revenue data for each course, you can speed PivotTable operations by removing the Course: Name field from the query design of Figure 12.25 to return only 52 rows. Execution of the Access query with 52 rows takes about the same time as for 2,348 rows, but PivotTable operations are almost instantaneous.

Formatting and Manipulating PivotCharts

When you define a PivotTable view, you also automatically generate a corresponding PivotChart view of tables, queries, and forms. Access links PivotTable and PivotChart views, so there's no need for a Chart Wizard to specify the initial design. For example, open the PivotTable view of the qry2006OrdersByCountryPT sample query you created in the "Creating the Query for a Sample PivotTable View" section near the beginning of the chapter. Choose PivotChart view to open the chart, and drag the Country button to the Filter region at the upper left of the chart area to eliminate country from the X-axis, as shown in Figure 12.26.

Figure 12.26
The PivotTable automatically creates a PivotChart view of the qry2006OrdersByCountryPT sample query. Be sure to minimize the amount of category detail in the PivotTable before opening a PivotChart.

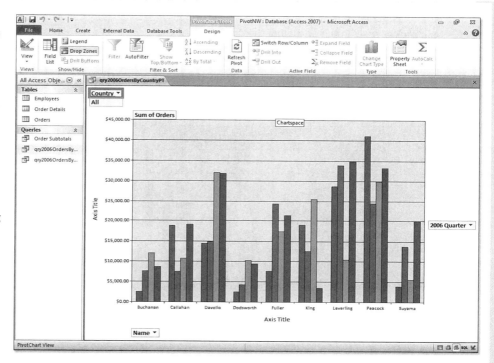

Adding Legends, Axis Titles, and Filters

Following are some of the PivotChart property values you can alter to change the format of PivotCharts and filter the data presented:

- *Legends*—The default PivotChart style is Clustered Column; each column of each category—quarterly sales columns for the Name category for this example—is color coded. Clicking the Show Legend button on the toolbar toggles the legend below the 2006 Quarters field button.

- *Axis titles*—Titles for the x- and y-axes of the sample chart are missing. To add axis titles, right-click the axis title, choose Properties to open the Properties dialog, and click the Format page. You can change the font, size, and attributes, and type the title in the Caption text box.

- *Category filters*—Filters on category fields limit the chart's display to selected values. As you change filter values, the chart automatically reformats the display and changes the scale of the y-axis to optimize the display. Adding filters to category fields also affects the PivotTable view.

 tip

Remove filters applied to category fields as soon as you no longer need them. The only visible feedback that a filter is applied is a change to the color of the small arrows from black to blue, which isn't readily apparent. Accidentally leaving a filter in place when changing the chart's layout can lead to interpretation errors.

Figure 12.27 shows the legend and axis titles added and filters applied to the Name and Country categories. Axis totals and a legend have been added. X-axis category values rotate 90 degrees counterclockwise if their width fits the divisions.

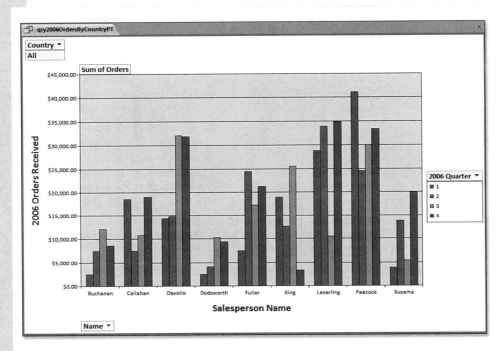

Figure 12.27
The sample PivotChart displays totals of North American orders for the nine employees.

Altering Category Presentation

PivotCharts have Filter Fields and Category Fields drop zones similar to those of PivotTables, and field buttons corresponding to those of the source PivotTable. An additional field button (All Orders for this example) represents the PivotTable's values displayed by the chart, called a *series*. You can change category presentation by dragging category fields to the Filter Fields drop zone and changing the chart's display as follows:

- *Coalesce clusters to totals*—To display total sales for each employee for the year 2006, drag the 2006 Quarter button to the Filter Fields drop zone (see Figure 12.28). The y-axis scale changes to reflect the larger totals.

 tip

If you accidentally drag a field button outside the PivotChart's window and remove it from the PivotChart (and the PivotTable), open the Field List and drag the field to the appropriate drop zone.

Figure 12.28
Dragging
a category
field button
to the Filter
Fields drop
zone changes
the clustered
columns to a
single total
column for
each cat-
egory.

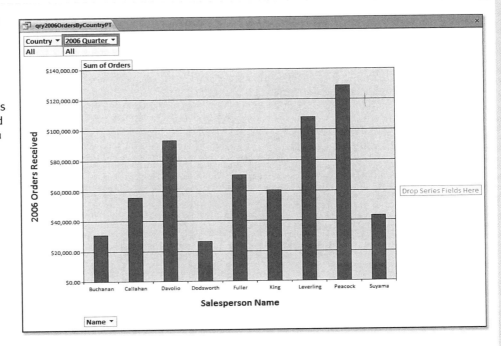

- *Replace categories*—Drag the Name button to the Filter Fields drop zone and Country to the Filter Fields drop zone to display total 2006 sales for each country (see Figure 12.29). Passing the mouse pointer over the chart's bars opens a ScreenTip, which displays detail data.

- *Remove excessive detail*—When you return the Name and 2006 Quarter fields to their original locations—the Category and Series Fields drop zones, respectively—the category axis of the chart becomes an unreadable jumble. To remove the Country bars from the chart, select the Name button and click the Collapse button on the toolbar, or right-click the chart and choose Collapse from the context menu.

> **note**
> Filter Field buttons indicate that a filter is applied by changing the All label to the filter selection. If you select more than one filter criterion, the label displays "(multiple items)."

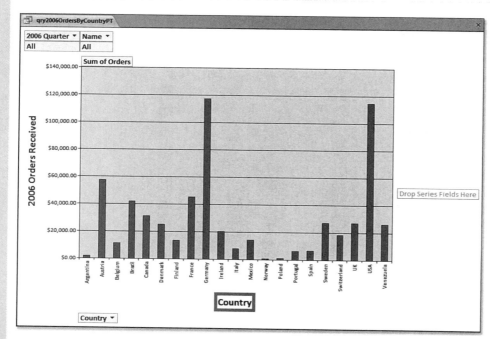

Figure 12.29
Dragging the leftmost (primary) category field button to the Filter Fields drop zone displays data for the remaining category button.

- *Drill down into a category*—The Drill Into toolbar button or context menu choice lets you display the second (or lower) level of detail for a category. To display sales by country for a single salesperson, right-click the name in the category axis and choose Drill Into to display sales by country and quarter for the person (see Figure 12.30). To return to the original chart format, right-click the name and choose Drill Out. The Drill Into and Drill Out ribbon buttons of the Active Field group are enabled only when you select a category item.

Changing the Chart Type

PivotCharts come in a remarkable variety of types and styles, ranging from the default Clustered Column to Radar, which displays values relative to a centerpoint (as in the radar display of an airport approach control facility). To change the chart's style, click outside the chart area and then click the Chart Type button on the ribbon to open the Properties dialog to the Type page. Click one of the styles to preview the chart's appearance. Figure 12.31 shows the sample chart type changed from Clustered to Stacked Column. Choosing a 100% Stacked Column style changes the y-axis units to percent.

 tip

Don't change to a 100% Stacked Column—or any other 100%... style—unless you specifically need this style. When you return to another style, the format of the y-axis values change to General Number. You then must select the values, click the Format tab, and reset the numeric format.

Figure 12.30
Selecting a primary category item in the x-axis, such as Peacock, and clicking the toolbar's Drill Into button displays secondary category values—in this case, sales for Margaret Peacock by country and quarter.

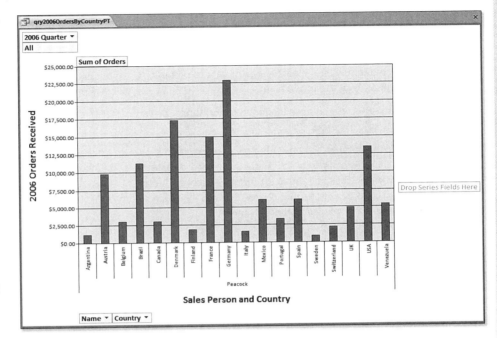

Figure 12.31
Column charts are one of 12 types you can select from the Types page of the Properties dialog. Each type has between 2 and 10 styles, and most types offer 3D versions.

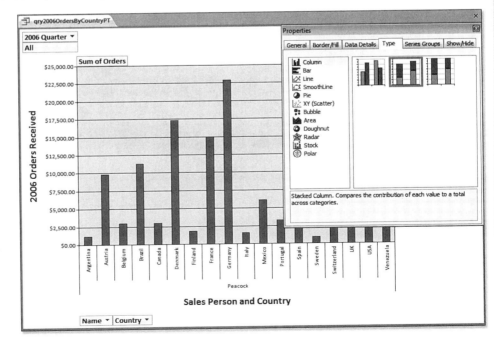

The most useful formats for conventional PivotCharts are as follows:

- *Stacked Column charts*—Display contribution of series elements, such as quarters, to a total value. ScreenTips display the numeric value of each element of the column but, unfortunately, not the total value.

- *Bar charts*—Rotate the axes 90 degrees counterclockwise; offer the same styles as Column charts.

- *Stacked Area charts*—Better suited to time-series data, such as monthly, quarterly, or yearly categories. Figure 12.32 shows a Stacked Area chart from the sample query. Unlike Stacked Bar or Column charts, ScreenTips of stacked area charts don't display numeric values.

note

The qry2006OrdersByCountryPT sample query and the completed PivotChart and PivotTable are included in the PivotNW. accdb sample database located in the \Access2010\Chaptr12 folder of the downloadable sample files. The Oakmont queries are in the PivotOM.accdb database.

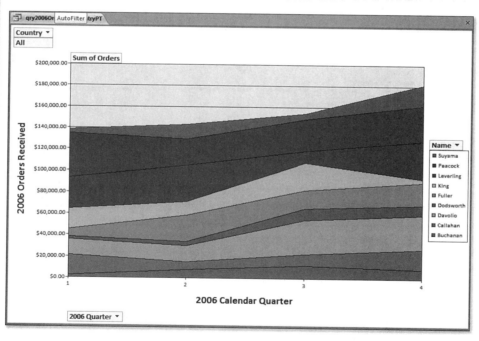

Figure 12.32
This Stacked Area chart displays the quarterly trend of each employee's contribution to total sales order value.

CREATING AND UPDATING ACCESS TABLES WITH ACTION QUERIES

Action queries create new tables or modify the data in existing tables. Access offers the following four types of action queries:

- *Make-table* queries create new tables from the data contained in query resultsets. One of the most common applications for make-table queries is to create tables that you can export to other applications or that summarize data from other tables. A make-table query provides a convenient way to copy a table to another database. In some cases, you can use make-table queries to speed the generation of multiple forms and reports based on a single, complex query.

- *Append* queries add new records to tables from the query's resultset.

- *Delete* queries delete records from tables that correspond to the rows of the query resultset.

- *Update* queries change the existing values of fields of table records that correspond to rows of the query resultset.

By default, new queries you create are select queries. After opening a new or existing query in Design view, you can change its type to one of the four action queries by clicking the Query Tools, Design tab's corresponding Query Type: Make Table, Query Type: Append, Query Type: Delete, and Query Type: Update buttons.

This chapter shows you how to create each of the four types of Access action queries and how to use Access's cascading deletions and cascading updates of related records. Cascading deletions and cascading updates are covered here because these referential-integrity features are related to delete and update action queries, respectively.

Creating New Tables with Make-Table Queries

In the following sections, you learn how to use a make-table query to create a new table, tblShipAddresses, for customers that have different shipping and billing addresses. This process enables the deletion of the tblShipAddresses data that, in most of the records in the Orders table, duplicates the address data in the Customers table. Removing duplicated data to new tables is an important step when you're converting data contained in a flat (nonrelational) database to a relational database structure.

You can use the Table Analyzer Wizard, described in Chapter 5, "Working with Access Database and Tables," to perform an operation similar to that described in the following sections. Removing duplicated data manually, however, is one of the best methods of demonstrating how to design make-table queries.

 To use a wizard to remove duplicate data, **see** *"Using the Table Analyzer Wizard,"* **p. 235.**

A modification of the query that you wrote in the "Creating Not-Equal Theta Joins with Criteria" section of Chapter 11, "Creating Multitable and Crosstab Queries," generates the data for the new tblShipAddresses table. Make-table queries are especially useful in converting flat-file tables that contain duplicated data, including tables created by spreadsheet applications, to relational form.

 note

 Access data projects (ADP) offer similar Query menu choices for action queries when you create a new stored-procedure query. Stored procedures have an additional type of append query, called an Append Values procedure, which lets you add a new record with values you type in the da Vinci Query Design grid. SQL Server functions and views don't support make-table queries.

 tip

Always make a backup copy of a table that you intend to modify with an action query. This is especially important when using the Northwind.accdb sample database from \Acccess2010\ Nwind folder in this chapter's examples. Changes made to table data with action queries are permanent; an error can render a table or an entire database useless. Invalid changes made to a table with an action query containing a design error often are difficult to detect.

 note

 Completed versions of most sample queries in this chapter are included in the Action13. accdb database located in the \Access2010\Chaptr13 folder of the downloadable sample files.

Designing and Testing the Select Query

To create the new tblShipAddresses table from the data in the Orders table, you first must build the following SELECT query:

1. Open your working copy of Northwind.accdb, create a new select query, and add the Customers and Orders tables to it.

2. Drag the CustomerID field from the Customers table and drop it in the query's first column. The CustomerID field links the tblShipAddresses table to the Orders table.

3. Drag the ShipName, ShipAddress, ShipCity, ShipRegion, ShipPostalCode, and ShipCountry fields from the Orders table and drop them in columns 2–7, respectively. You use these fields, in addition to CustomerID, to create the new tblShipAddresses table.

To add criteria to select only those records of the Orders table in which the ShipName doesn't match the CompanyName or the ShipAddress doesn't match the Customers table's address, do this:

1. In the ShipName column's first Criteria row, type the following:

   <>[Customers].[CompanyName]

2. In the next row of the ShipAddress column, type the following:

   <>[Customers].[Address]

3. To ensure against the slight possibility that the same address might occur in two different cities, in the third row of the ShipCity column, type this:

   <>[Customers].[City]

4. Right-click an empty area in the Query Design window's upper pane and choose Properties to open the Query Properties window. Open the Unique Values drop-down list, select Yes, and close the Query Properties window. The query design appears as shown in Figure 13.1.

5. Click Run to execute the select query and test the result (see Figure 13.2).

Converting the Select Query to a Make-Table Query

Now that you've tested the select query to make sure that it creates the necessary data, create the table from the query by following these steps:

1. Return to Query Design view, click the Design tab, and click Query Type: Make Table to open the Make Table dialog. Type the name of the table, tblShipAddresses, in the Table Name text box (see Figure 13.3) and click OK.

2. Click Run. A message confirms the number of records that you are about to add to the new table. Click Yes to create the new table, whose icon and name appear in the Navigation pane's Tables group.

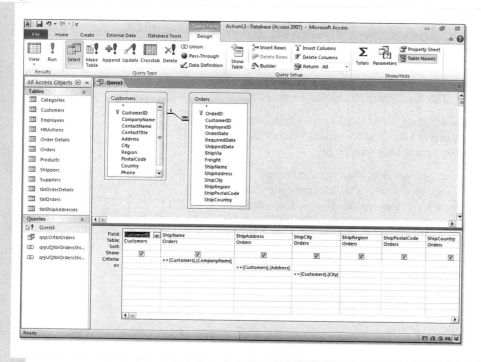

Figure 13.1
The design of the qryMakeShip-Addresses make-table query requires that the not-equal criteria be added on separate rows of the grid.

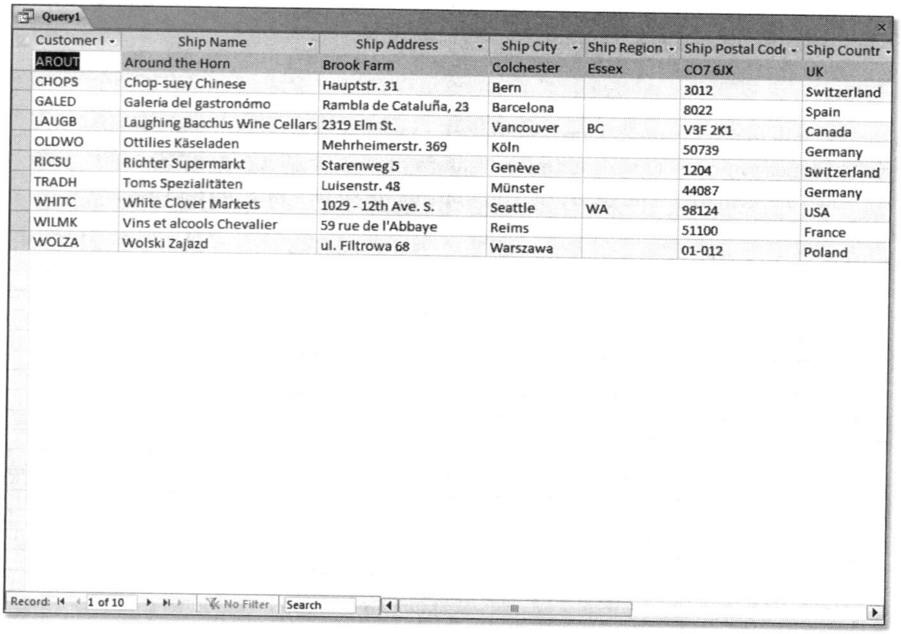

Figure 13.2
The query design of Figure 13.1 returns 9 rows of shipping addresses that differ from the customers' billing addresses.

Figure 13.3
The Make Table dialog lets you type a new name for the table or select an existing table to replace with new data.

3. Close and save your query with an appropriate name, such as **qryMTtblShipAddresses**.

4. Double-click the tblShipAddresses table item in the Navigation pane. The records appear as shown in Figure 13.4.

Figure 13.4
Caption property values of a make-table query don't propagate to the newly created table. Compare the field names of this table with the query result-set of Figure 13.2.

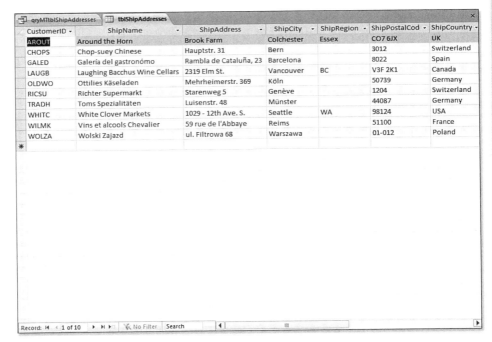

CustomerID	ShipName	ShipAddress	ShipCity	ShipRegion	ShipPostalCod	ShipCountry
AROUT	Around the Horn	Brook Farm	Colchester	Essex	CO7 6JX	UK
CHOPS	Chop-suey Chinese	Hauptstr. 31	Bern		3012	Switzerland
GALED	Galería del gastronómo	Rambla de Cataluña, 23	Barcelona		8022	Spain
LAUGB	Laughing Bacchus Wine Cellars	2319 Elm St.	Vancouver	BC	V3F 2K1	Canada
OLDWO	Ottilies Käseladen	Mehrheimerstr. 369	Köln		50739	Germany
RICSU	Richter Supermarkt	Starenweg 5	Genève		1204	Switzerland
TRADH	Toms Spezialitäten	Luisenstr. 48	Münster		44087	Germany
WHITC	White Clover Markets	1029 - 12th Ave. S.	Seattle	WA	98124	USA
WILMK	Vins et alcools Chevalier	59 rue de l'Abbaye	Reims		51100	France
WOLZA	Wolski Zajazd	ul. Filtrowa 68	Warszawa		01-012	Poland

Record: 1 of 10

Now complete the design of the new tblShipAddresses table by following these steps:

1. Change to Table Design view. The table's basic design is inherited from the Field Name and Data Type properties of the fields of the tables used to create the new table. The tblShipAddresses table doesn't inherit the primary key assignment from the Customers table's CustomerID field.

2. Choose the CustomerID field, open the Indexed property drop-down list, and choose the Yes (Duplicates OK) value. Indexing improves the performance of queries when you have multiple ShipAddresses for customers.

3. The CustomerID, ShipName, ShipAddress, ShipCity, and ShipCountry fields are required, so set the value for each of these fields' Required property to Yes and set the Allow Zero Length property to No.

4. Many countries don't have values for the ShipRegion field, and a few countries don't use postal codes for some or all locations, so verify that the Allow Zero Length property is set to Yes for the ShipRegion and ShipPostalCode fields.

➡ *For more information on using the da Vinci toolset to create T-SQL stored procedures,* **see** *"Examining Stored Procedures,"* **p. 116.**

Access SQL

The only difference between the select and make-table queries is the addition of the INTO tablename clause that specifies the name of the new table to create. Following is the Access SQL statement for the sample make-table query:

```
SELECT DISTINCT Customers.CustomerID, Orders.ShipName,
    Orders.ShipAddress, Order's.ShipCity, Orders.ShipRegion,
    Orders.ShipPostalCode, Orders.ShipCountry
 INTO tblShipAddresses
 FROM Customers
    INNER JOIN Orders
    ON Customers.CustomerID = Orders.CustomerID
WHERE Orders.ShipName<>Customers.CompanyName
   OR Orders.ShipAddress<>Customers.Address
  OR Orders.ShipCity<>Customers.City;
```

This query and the preceding query are SQL-92 and T-SQL compliant. You can copy and paste either query into the SQL pane of the da Vinci stored procedure design window, save the stored procedure, and execute it. The da Vinci toolset, also called the Project Designer, adds SQL Server's dbo. (database owner) prefix to each table name before creating the stored procedure.

Establishing Relationships for the New Table

Now you must complete the process of adding the new table to your database by establishing default relationships and enforcing referential integrity so that all records in the tblShipAddresses table have a corresponding record in the Customers table. Access's graphical Relationships window makes this process simple and intuitive. To establish the relationship of tblShipAddresses and the Customers table, follow these steps:

1. Close the tblShipAddresses table. Answer Yes when asked whether you want to save changes to the table's design, and answer Yes again if asked whether you want to apply the new data integrity rules to the table.

2. 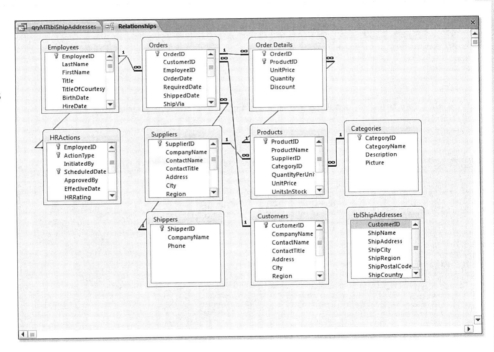 Click the Database Tools tab and then the Relationships button to open the Relationships window.

3. Click the Show Table button and double-click the tblShipAddresses table to add the table to the Relationships window; then close the Show Table dialog. Move the tblShipAddresses field list to the lower-right position shown in Figure 13.5.

4. Click the Customers table's CustomerID field, drag the field symbol to the tblShipAddresses

Figure 13.5
Add the new tblShipAddresses table to the Relationships window.

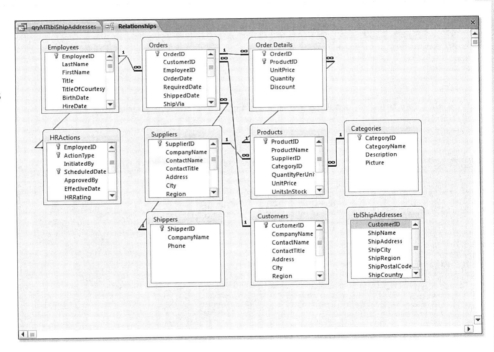

table's CustomerID field, and drop the symbol to open the Edit Relationships dialog.

5. Mark the Enforce Referential Integrity check box. Access sets the default relation type, One-to-Many, which is the correct choice for this relation, if the relationship isn't between two single-field primary keys of the same name (CustomerID isn't tblShipAddresses' primary key at this point). Access also establishes a conventional INNER JOIN as the default join type, so in this case you don't need to click the Join Type button to display the Join Properties window.

6. Mark the Cascade Update Related Fields and Cascade Delete Related Records check boxes to maintain referential integrity automatically (see Figure 13.6).

7. Click the Create button in the Edit Relationships dialog to close it. Your Relationships window appears as shown in Figure 13.7.

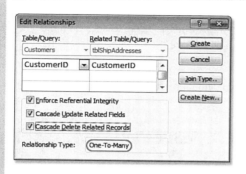

Figure 13.6
Establish a one-to-many relationship between the Orders and tblShipAddresses tables, and specify cascade updates and deletions to maintain referential integrity of the tblShipAddresses table.

8. Close the Relationships window and click Yes to save your changes.

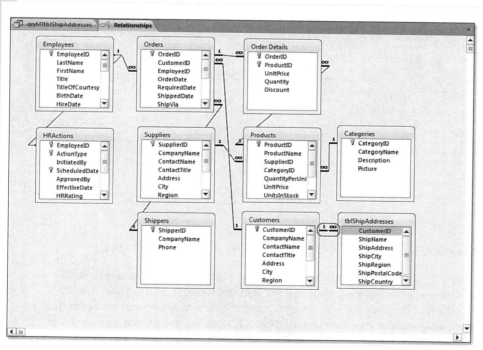

Figure 13.7
An infinity (∞) symbol indicates the many-to-one relationship of the tblShipAddress table with the Customers table.

Using the New tblShipAddresses Table

The purpose of creating the new tblShipAddresses table is to eliminate the data in the Orders table that duplicates information in the Customers table. The additional steps that you must take to use the new table include the following:

- You need a new Number (Long Integer) field, ShipToID for this example, for the tblShipAddresses and Orders tables to indicate which ship-to address to use. In the Orders table's ShipToID field, you can use a default 0 value to indicate that the shipping and billing addresses are the same. You then assign a sequential number to each tblShipAddresses record for each customer. (In this case, the value of the ShipToID field is 1 for all records in tblShipAddresses, which you must add manually before creating the primary key.) By adding the ShipToID field to the tblShipAddresses table, you can create a composite primary key on the CustomerID and ShipToID fields. The composite primary key for tblShipAddresses enables you to retain the One-to-Many relationship with the Orders table.

- Set the Default Value of the tblShipAddresses' ShipToID field to **1** to enable appending records with an Append action query in the next section. Failure to add a value to one of the composite primary key fields causes an error when attempting to append records.

- Don't delete fields that contain duplicated data extracted to a new table until you confirm that the extracted data is correct and modify all the queries, forms, and reports that use the table. You use the update query described later in this chapter to assign the correct ShipToID field value for each record in the Orders table. After you verify that you've assigned the correct value of the ShipToID field, you can delete the duplicate fields.

- Add the new table to any queries, forms, reports, or VBA procedures that require the extracted information.

- Change references to fields in the original table in all database objects that refer to fields in the new table.

During this process, you have the opportunity to test the modification before deleting the duplicated fields from the original table. Making a backup copy of the table before you delete the fields also is a low-cost insurance policy.

Creating Action Queries to Append Records to a Table

A make-table query creates the new table structure from the structure of the records that underlie the query. Only the fields of the records that appear in the Datasheet view of the query are added to the new table's structure. If you design and save a tblShipAddresses table before extracting the duplicated data from the Orders table, you can use an append query to add the extracted data to the new table.

To remove and then append records to the tblShipAddresses table, for example, follow these steps:

 tip

Take extra care when designing action queries not to execute the query prematurely. If you double-click the query in the Navigation pane or open the query in Datasheet view and click OK to acknowledge the warning message, you run the make-table query.

1. 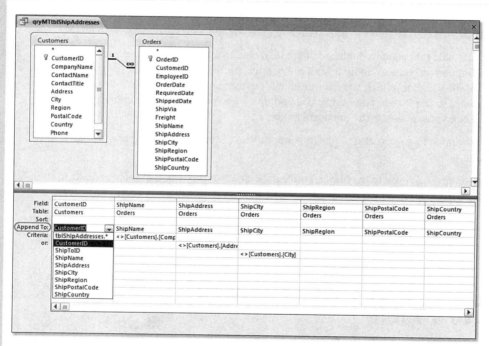 Open the tblShipAddresses table in Datasheet view, press Ctrl+A to select all records, and then press the Delete key to delete all records from the table. Click Yes when asked to confirm the deletion, and then close the table.

2. Open your make-table query, qryMTtblShipAddresses, from the Navigation pane in Design view.

3. Click the Query Tools, Design tab's Query Type: Append button. The Append dialog—a renamed version of the Make Table dialog—opens with tblShipAddresses as the default value in the Table Name drop-down list.

4. Click OK to close the Append dialog and add the Append To row to the Query Design grid (see Figure 13.8).

Figure 13.8
Changing a select or make-table query adds an Append To row to the grid. You can specify appending values to a field by opening the Append To list for the query field and selecting the field name.

5. Click Run to execute the append query. A message box displays the number of records that the query will append to the table. Click Yes to append the records, and then save the query.

6. Open the tblShipAddresses table to verify that you've added the 10 records. If the table was open when you appended the records, you must close and reopen it to view the added records.

7. Close the query without saving the changes, and then close the table.

tip

2010 NEW This Append query works for setting initial values, but appending records for multiple ship addresses will fail because of a duplicate primary key error as a result of using 1 as the default ShipToID value. You can use Access 2010's Data Macros, which emulate SQL Server triggers, to handle this problem. Chapter 21, "Emulating Table Triggers with Access Data Macros," explains how to handle this problem.

 ## Appending Records Causes Primary Key Problems

If you can't create a primary key on the table after appending records to an existing table remember that the Unique Values Only test that you specify in the Query Properties window applies only to the query, not to the table to which you append the records. If possible, create a primary key for the destination table before appending records. For example, if you want to preclude the possibility of appending duplicate records to the tblShipAddresses table, you must first create the composite primary key, discussed in the "Using the New tblShipAddresses Table" section, which creates a No Duplicates index on the primary key, and then append the records.

 tip

Append queries—more commonly called INSERT queries—add an INSERT INTO *tablename*(*field list*) clause to the SELECT statement. The field list argument is what lets you append data to a field with a different name. Following is the SQL statement for the INSERT version of the make-table query:

```
INSERT INTO tblShipAddresses ( CustomerID, ShipName,
    ShipAddress, ShipCity, ShipRegion, ShipPostalCode, ShipCountry )
SELECT DISTINCT Customers.CustomerID, Orders.ShipName,
    Orders.ShipAddress, Orders.ShipCity, Orders.ShipRegion,
        Orders.ShipPostalCode, Orders.ShipCountry
FROM Customers
    INNER JOIN Orders
    ON Customers.CustomerID = Orders.CustomerID
WHERE Orders.ShipName<>Customers.CompanyName
    OR Orders.ShipAddress<>Customers.Address
    OR Orders.ShipCity<>Customers.City;
```

Like the select and make-table versions, the Access SQL statement is SQL-92 compliant, so the preceding statement also executes as an SQL Server stored procedure.

You can't append records containing values that duplicate those of the primary key fields or other fields with a no-duplicates index in existing records. If you try to do so, a message box indicates the number of records that cause key-field violations. Unlike with the paste append operation, however, Access doesn't create a Paste Errors table that contains the unappended records.

Deleting Records from a Table with an Action Query

Often you need to delete a specific set of records from a table. For example, you might want to delete records for canceled orders or for customers that have made no purchases for several years. Deleting records from a table with a delete query is the reverse of the append process. You create a select query with all fields (using the * choice from the field list) and then add the individual fields to be used to specify the criteria for deleting specific records. If you don't specify any criteria, Access deletes all the table's records when you convert the select query into a delete query and run it against the table.

To give you some practice at deleting records—you stop short of actual deletion in this case—suppose that Northwind Traders' credit manager has advised you that Austrian authorities have declared Ernst Handel (CustomerID ERNSH) insolvent and that you are to cancel and delete any orders from Ernst Handel not yet shipped. To design the query that selects all of Ernst Handel's open orders, follow these steps:

1. Open a new query in Design view and add the Orders table to it.

2. Drag the * (all fields) item from the field list to the Field cell of the query's first column.

3. Drag the CustomerID field to the second column's Field cell. You need this field to select a specific customer's record. The fields that make up the query must be exactly those of the Orders table, so clear the Show box to prevent the CustomerID field from appearing in the query's result twice. This field is already included in the first column's * indicator.

4. In the CustomerID field's Criteria cell, type **ERNSH** to represent Ernst Handel's ID.

5. A Null value in the ShippedDate field indicates orders that have not shipped. Drag the ShippedDate field from the field list to the third column's Field cell. Click the Show box to prevent the ShippedDate field from appearing in the select query's result twice, because the * in the first column also includes that field.

6. In the ShippedDate field's Criteria cell, type **Is Null**. To ensure that you delete only records for Ernst Handel *and* only those that have not been shipped, you must place this criterion on the same line as that of the CustomerID field (see Figure 13.9).

7. Run the select query to display the records to delete when the delete query runs (see Figure 13.10).

To proceed with the simulated deletion, which would delete the Order Details records for the two orders, follow these steps:

1. Create a copy of the Orders table by selecting the Orders table item in the Navigation pane and pressing Ctrl+C to copy the table to the Clipboard. Press Ctrl+V to open the Paste Table As dialog. Type **tblOrders** as the name of the new table copy, and press Enter.

Figure 13.9
The test
select query
design
returns all
unshipped
orders for
CustomerID
equal to
ERNSH.

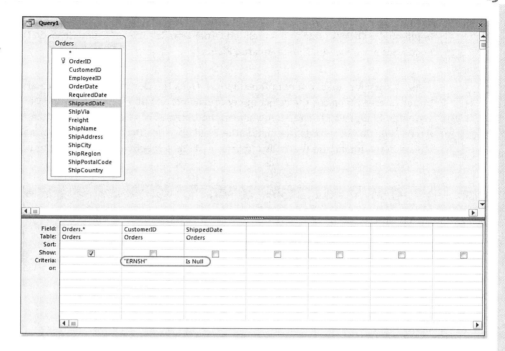

Figure 13.10
The select
query dis-
plays the
two orders
for Ernst
Handel that
haven't been
shipped.

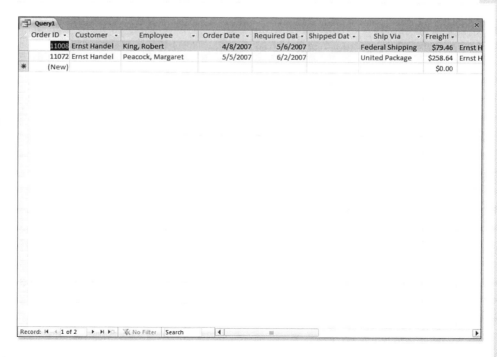

2. Repeat step 1 for the Order Details table, naming it **tblOrderDetails**. These two tables are backup tables in case you actually delete the two records for Ernst Handel. The relationship between the Orders table and its related Order Details table specifies Cascade Delete Related Fields but not Cascade Update Related Fields.

3. Open your select query in Design view. Click the Design tab and the Query Type: Delete button. Access replaces the select query grid's Sort and Show rows with the Delete row, as shown in Figure 13.11. The From value in the Delete row's first column, Orders.*, indicates that Access will delete records that match the Field specification from the Orders table. The Where values in the remaining two cells indicate fields that specify the deletion criteria.

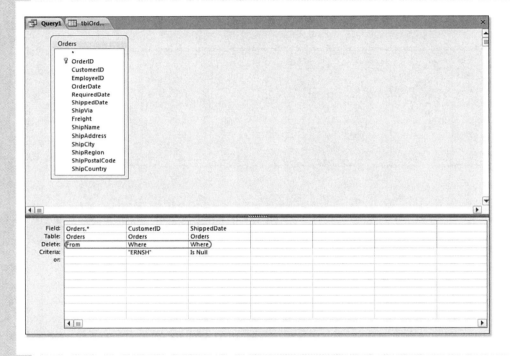

Figure 13.11
Specifying a delete query adds a Delete row to the grid that identifies From and Where fields.

4. Click the Run button. A message box asks you to confirm the deletion of the rows. Click No to prevent the deletion.

5. Close and then save your query if you want.

If you accidentally delete records for Ernst Handel, reverse the process that you used to make the backup tables: Copy the backup tables—tblOrders and tblOrderDetails—to Orders and Order Details, respectively. You use the tblOrders table in the following section.

Updating Values of Multiple Records in a Table

Update queries change the values of data in a table. Such queries are useful when you must update field values for many records with a common expression. For example, you might need to increase or decrease the unit prices of all products or products within a particular category by a fixed percentage.

To see how an update query works, you perform some of the housekeeping chores discussed earlier in the chapter that are associated with using the tblShipAddresses table. To implement this example, you must have created the tblShipAddresses table, as described in the "Creating New Tables with Make-Table Queries" section earlier in this chapter.

Adding a ShipToID Field to the tblOrders Table

You must modify the tblOrders and tblShipAddresses tables to include a field for the ShipToID code that relates the two tables by a composite foreign key. To add the ShipToID field to the tblOrders table, do this:

1. Open the tblOrders table in design mode. If you didn't create the tblOrders table as a backup table for the example of the preceding section, do so now.

2. Select the ShipVia field by clicking its selection button; then press Insert to add a new field between ShippedDate and ShipVia. (Access inserts fields in tables above the selected field.)

3. Type **ShipToID** as the field name, select Number as the field data type, and accept the default Long Integer as the field's Field Size. Set the Default Value property to 0 and the Required property value to Yes. Access automatically adds a Duplicates OK index to fields whose names end with "ID". You don't need an index on this field, so set the Indexed property value to No. The table design pane appears as in Figure 13.12, which shows the new ShipToID field selected.

4. Close the tblOrders table and save the changes to your design. You changed the domain integrity rules when you added the Required property, so a message box asks whether you want to test domain integrity. Click No to avoid the test, which would fail because no values have been added to the ShipToID field. (Default values don't replace Null values in newly added fields.)

> **note**
>
> Following is the Access SQL statement for the sample delete query:
>
> ```
> DELETE Orders.*,
>     Orders.CustomerID,
>     Orders.ShippedDate
>     FROM Orders
> WHERE
>     Orders.
> CustomerID="ERNSH"
>     AND Orders.ShippedDate)
>     Is Null;
> ```
>
> The field list is optional for delete queries, but you must have at least one field in the field list to satisfy the Access query designer. If you delete the field list in SQL view, the query executes, but won't open in Query Design view.
>
> Like all other Access action queries, the Access SQL and T-SQL statements are identical.

> **note**
>
> If you didn't create the tblShipAddresses table and you've downloaded the sample files, you can import this table from the \Access2010\Chaptr13\ Action13.accdb database.

Adding a ShipToID Field and Composite Primary Key to the tblShipAddresses Table

If you didn't do this in the earlier "Creating Action Queries to Append Records to a Table" section, add the ShipToID field and establish a composite primary key for the tblShipAddresses table by doing the following:

1. 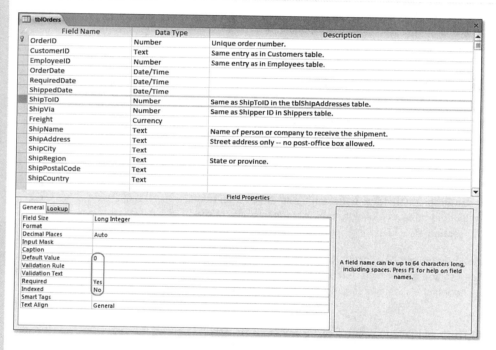 Open the tblShipAddresses table in Datasheet view.

2. Click the ShipName field header and choose Insert, Column to add a Field1 field between the CustomerID and the ShipName fields.

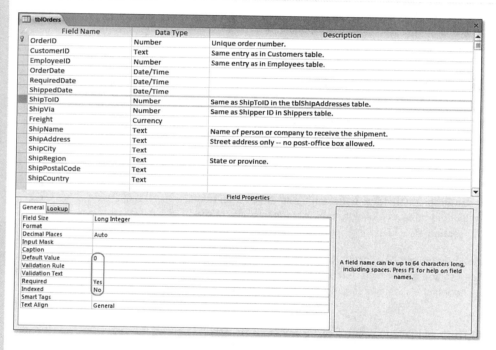

Figure 13.12 Add the ShipToID field as the foreign key for a relationship with the ShipToID field you add to the tblShipAddress table.

3. Type **1** in the Field1 cell for each record of the tblShipAddresses table.

4. Change to design mode and change the name of Field1 to **ShipToID**. Access detects from your data entries that the field should be a Number field and assigns Long Integer as the default Field Size property value. Change the value of the Required property to Yes.

5. Click the CustomerID field and Shift+click the ShipToID field to select both fields.

6. 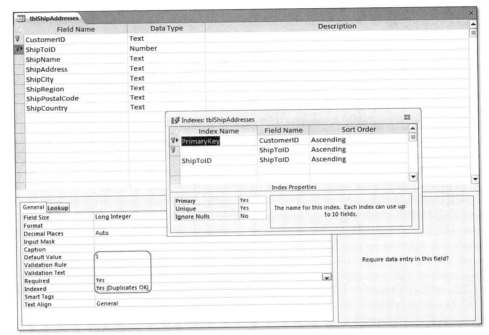 Click the Design Tools' Primary Key button to create a composite primary key on the CustomerID and ShipToID fields. Optionally, click the Indexes button to display the indexes added to the table. Your table design appears as shown in Figure 13.13.

7. Close the tblShipAddresses table. This time you test the changes that you made to the table, so click Yes when the Data Integrity Rules message box opens.

Figure 13.13
The ShipToID and CustomerID fields compose a composite primary key of the tblShipAddresses table. Access adds the indexes automatically.

tblShipAddresses		
Field Name	Data Type	Description
CustomerID	Text	
ShipToID	Number	
ShipName	Text	
ShipAddress	Text	
ShipCity	Text	
ShipRegion	Text	
ShipPostalCode	Text	
ShipCountry	Text	

Indexes: tblShipAddresses

Index Name	Field Name	Sort Order
PrimaryKey	CustomerID	Ascending
	ShipToID	Ascending
ShipToID	ShipToID	Ascending

Index Properties

Primary	Yes	The name for this index. Each index can use up to 10 fields.
Unique	Yes	
Ignore Nulls	No	

General	Lookup	
Field Size	Long Integer	
Format		
Decimal Places	Auto	
Input Mask		
Caption		
Default Value	1	
Validation Rule		
Validation Text		
Required	Yes	
Indexed	Yes (Duplicates OK)	
Smart Tags		
Text Align	General	

Require data entry in this field?

Writing Update Queries to Update Foreign Key Values in the tblOrders Table

To indicate where the orders were shipped, you must update the ShipToID field in tblShipAddresses. The value 1 (or greater) indicates a shipping address other than the customer's address; the value 0 indicates the order is shipped to the customer's billing address. You can accomplish this by running an update query:

1. Close all open tables, create a new query, and add the Customers and tblOrders tables to it. Relationships haven't been specified between the two tables, so the join line between the tables doesn't have one-to-many symbols.

2. Drag the tblOrders table's ShipName and ShipAddress fields to the first two columns of the Query Design grid.

3. Type **<>[Customers].[CompanyName]** in the first Criteria row of the ShipName column and **<>[Customers].[Address]** in the second Criteria row of the ShipAddress column. (Prior tests show that you don't need to test the City, PostalCode, and Country fields.) Your query design appears as shown in Figure 13.14.

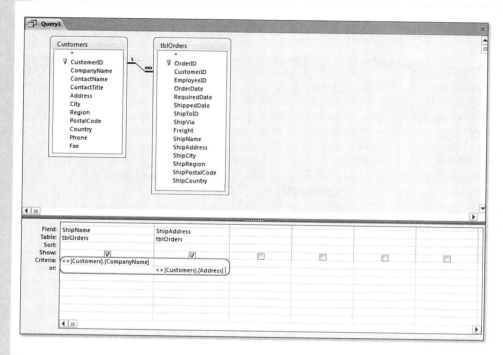

Figure 13.14
This query design, which is similar to qryMTShip-Addresses, returns all orders for which the ship-to name or ship-to address differs from the billing data.

4. Run the query to verify that you have correctly selected the set of records to be updated. In this case, you *don't* specify Unique Values, because you must change every tblOrders record that meets the query criteria.

After ensuring that you've selected the appropriate records of the tblOrders table for updating, 62 rows for the sample query, you're ready to convert the select query to an update query by following these steps:

1. Return to Query Design mode and drag the tblOrders table's ShipToID field to the query's first column.

2. Click the Query Type: Update button. A new Update To row replaces the Sort and Show rows of the select Query Design grid.

3. In the ShipToID column's Update To cell, type **1** to set ShipToID's value to 1 for orders that require the use of a record from the tblShipAddresses table. The Update Query Design grid

appears as shown in Figure 13.15. The Update To cells of the remaining fields are blank, indicating that Access is not to update values in these fields.

Figure 13.15
Type the value (1) for the update to the ShipToID field of records that require a join to a record in the tblShip-Addresses table.

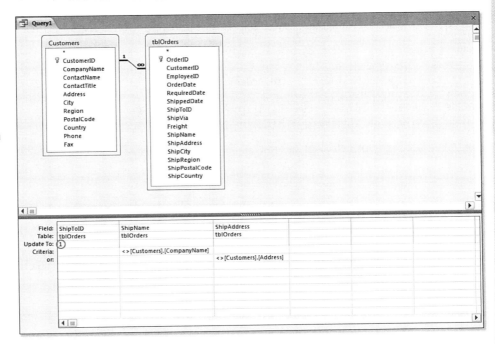

4. Save and run the update query. A message box indicates the number of records to be updated (62 for this example). Click Yes to continue.

5. Click to open the tblOrders table in the Navigation pane. Check a few records to see that you correctly added the ShipToID value of 1.

6. Close the update query.

Finally, you must add 0 values to the ShipToID cells of records that have the same shipping and billing address, if you haven't done this previously, by following these steps:

1. Create a new query, and add only the tblOrders table.

2. Drag the ShipToID field to the query's first column and Query Type: Update button.

3. Type **0** in the Update To row and **Is Null** in the Criteria row. Before running the query, check it in Datasheet view; all fields should be empty.

tip

Update queries substitute UPDATE for SELECT as well as a SET list for the SELECT field list. An update query can set multiple field values by additional, comma-separated *TableName.FieldName = Value* statements. Following is the Access SQL statement for the sample update query:

```
UPDATE Customers
    INNER JOIN tblOrders
        ON Customers.CustomerID = tblOrders.CustomerID
    SET tblOrders.ShipToID = 1
WHERE tblOrders.ShipName<>[Customers].[CompanyName]
    OR tblOrders.ShipAddress<>[Customers].[Address];
```

The Access SQL and T-SQL statements are identical.

4. When you're sure the query is correct, click Run to replace Null values in the ShipToID column with 0. Close and don't save the query.

After you check the tblOrders table to verify the result of your second update query, you can change to Table Design view and safely delete the ShipName, ShipAddress, ShipCity, ShipRegion, ShipPostalCode, and ShipCountry fields from the table.

Using the tblShipAddress Table in a Query

When you join the tblOrders and tblShipAddresses tables in a query to regenerate the appearance of the original Orders table, you must specify a LEFT OUTER JOIN on the CustomerID and ShipToID fields of the tables to return all tblOrders records, not just those with records in the tblShipAddresses table.

To create a query that returns all rows of the tblOrders table with empty Ship...fields for records with 0 ShipToID values, do the following:

1. Open a new query and add the tblOrders and tblShipAddresses tables.

2. Click the OrderID field and Shift+click the Freight field of the tblOrders field list in the upper pane to select the first nine fields; then drag the selected fields to the grid. Add an ascending sort to the OrderID column.

3. Click the ShipName field in the tblShipAddresses field list, Shift+click the ShipCountry field, and drag the six selected fields to the right of the Freight field in the grid.

4. In the upper pane, drag the CustomerID field of tblOrders and drop it on the CustomerID field of tblShipAddresses to create an INNER JOIN. Do the same for the ShipToID fields. The direction in which you drag the field symbol (the same direction as the other join, left-to-right) is important.

Your query design appears as shown in Figure 13.16. The query grid is scrolled to the right to show the first two fields from the tblShipAddresses table.

Figure 13.16
This query
design has
INNER JOINS
between
tblOrders
and tblShip-
Addresses,
so the query
returns
only rows
for which
records
exist in the
tblShip-
Addresses
table.

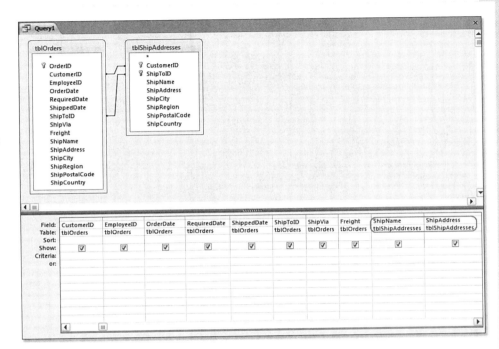

5. Select and then double-click the join line between the CustomerID fields to open the Join Properties dialog. Select option 2, a LEFT OUTER JOIN, and click OK. Specifying this join adds a right-pointing arrow to the join line.

6. Repeat step 5 for the ShipToID field (see Figure 13.17). Both joins must be LEFT OUTER JOINs to return all tblOrders records.

7. 🔔 Run the query to verify that records for orders with and without ship addresses appear (see Figure 13.18). Save the query as **qryLOJtblOrders** or a similar name, but don't close it.

Using the tblShipAddress Table with UNION Queries

If you want to substitute "Same as Bill To" or the like as the Ship To address on invoices for those orders in which the value of the ShipToID field is 0, you can either write VBA code or a UNION query to accomplish this task; however, the latter approach is much simpler.

➡️ *To review creating UNION queries,* **see** *"Using UNION Queries to Combine Multiple Resultsets,"* p. 496.

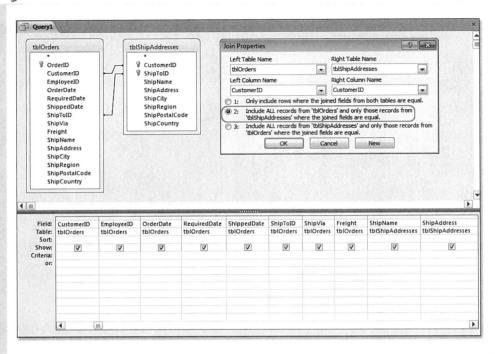

Figure 13.17
Specifying a LEFT (OUTER) JOIN (option 2) in the Join Properties dialog adds an arrow to the join line.

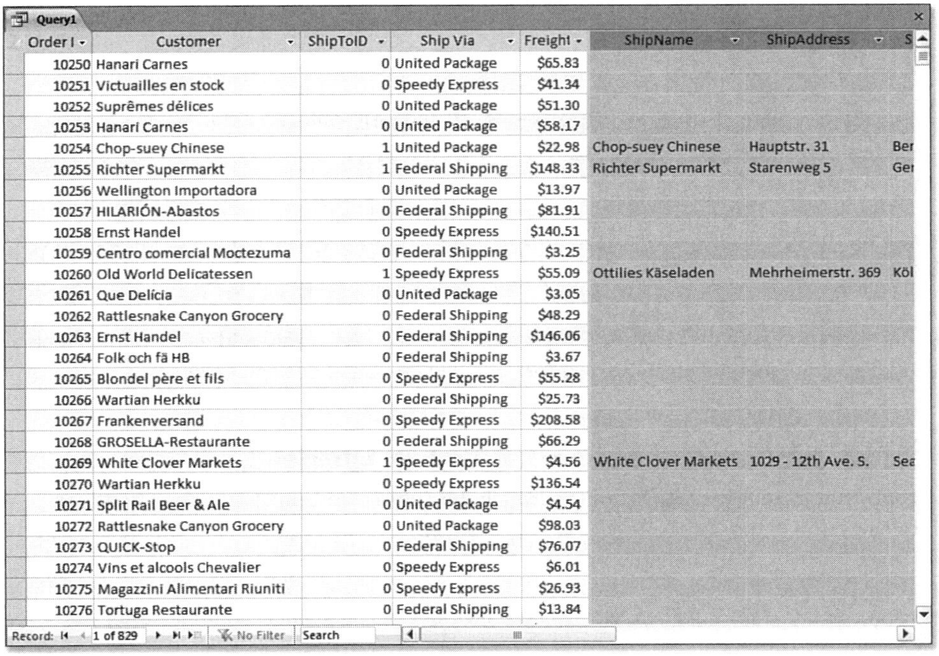

Figure 13.18
This Datasheet view of the query result-set from the design of Figure 13.17 returns all orders. The first two columns are frozen.

To quickly write the SQL statement for a UNION query that adds a text value—Same as Bill To—to the ShipName field for 0 ShipToID values, follow these steps:

1. **SQL** Open the SQL view of qryLOJtblOrders, select the entire SQL statement, and press Ctrl+C to copy it the Clipboard. Close the query.

2. **SQL** Open a new query, close the Show Table dialog, and click the Union Query button to open the SQL window.

3. Press Ctrl+V to paste the SQL statement to the window.

4. Replace LEFT in LEFT JOIN with INNER to return only the rows with values in the tblShipAddresses table.

5. Delete the trailing semicolon of the pasted text, press Enter twice, and type the following UNION SELECT statement as shown here:

```
UNION SELECT tblOrders.OrderID, tblOrders.CustomerID,
    tblOrders.EmployeeID, tblOrders.OrderDate, tblOrders.RequiredDate,
    tblOrders.ShippedDate, tblOrders.ShipToID, tblOrders.ShipVia, tblOrders.Freight,
    "Same as Bill To", " ", " ", " ", " ", " "
FROM tblOrders
WHERE tblOrders.ShipToID = 0;
```

Your SQL window appears as shown in Figure 13.19. The five space values (" ",) in the added statement are required because both components of the UNION query resultset must have the same number of columns.

> **tip**
> You can save some typing by copying the tblOrders...elements of the field list after the UNION SELECT statement.

6. Run the query to verify that the resultset contains the Same as Bill To values in the ShipName column (see Figure 13.20). Save the query as **qryUQtblOrdersShipTo**.

The Query Datasheet view of an Access query you generate from an SQL statement differs from queries you create in the Access query designer. Queries based on SQL statements that Access can't display in Query Design view don't inherit table properties, such as captions and lookup fields.

After you've verified that you can reproduce the data in the original Orders table with a union query, it's safe to delete the ShipName through ShipCountry fields of the tblOrders table.

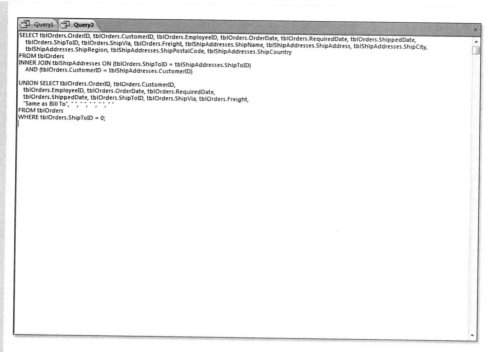

Figure 13.19
This SQL statement consists of a copy of the SELECT query of the preceding example with an INNER JOIN instead of a LEFT JOIN and a UNION SELECT statement to add the rows with the 0 ShipToID values.

```
SELECT tblOrders.OrderID, tblOrders.CustomerID, tblOrders.EmployeeID, tblOrders.OrderDate, tblOrders.RequiredDate, tblOrders.ShippedDate,
    tblOrders.ShipToID, tblOrders.ShipVia, tblOrders.Freight, tblShipAddresses.ShipName, tblShipAddresses.ShipAddress, tblShipAddresses.ShipCity,
    tblShipAddresses.ShipRegion, tblShipAddresses.ShipPostalCode, tblShipAddresses.ShipCountry
FROM tblOrders
INNER JOIN tblShipAddresses ON (tblOrders.ShipToID = tblShipAddresses.ShipToID)
    AND (tblOrders.CustomerID = tblShipAddresses.CustomerID)

UNION SELECT tblOrders.OrderID, tblOrders.CustomerID,
    tblOrders.EmployeeID, tblOrders.OrderDate, tblOrders.RequiredDate,
    tblOrders.ShippedDate, tblOrders.ShipToID, tblOrders.ShipVia, tblOrders.Freight,
    "Same as Bill To", '', '', '', '', ''
FROM tblOrders
WHERE tblOrders.ShipToID = 0;
```

Figure 13.20
The UNION query Access SQL statement of Figure 13.18 returns the expected resultset. (The first two columns are frozen.)

OrderID	CustomerID	ShipToID	ShipVia	Freight	ShipName	ShipAddress	ShipCity
10250	HANAR	0	2	$65.83	Same as Bill To		
10251	VICTE	0	1	$41.34	Same as Bill To		
10252	SUPRD	0	2	$51.30	Same as Bill To		
10253	HANAR	0	2	$58.17	Same as Bill To		
10254	CHOPS	1	2	$22.98	Chop-suey Chinese	Hauptstr. 31	Bern
10255	RICSU	1	3	$148.33	Richter Supermarkt	Starenweg 5	Genève
10256	WELLI	0	2	$13.97	Same as Bill To		
10257	HILAA	0	3	$81.91	Same as Bill To		
10258	ERNSH	0	1	$140.51	Same as Bill To		
10259	CENTC	0	3	$3.25	Same as Bill To		
10260	OLDWO	1	1	$55.09	Ottilies Käseladen	Mehrheimerstr. 369	Köln
10261	QUEDE	0	2	$3.05	Same as Bill To		
10262	RATTC	0	3	$48.29	Same as Bill To		
10263	ERNSH	0	3	$146.06	Same as Bill To		
10264	FOLKO	0	3	$3.67	Same as Bill To		
10265	BLONP	0	1	$55.28	Same as Bill To		
10266	WARTH	0	3	$25.73	Same as Bill To		
10267	FRANK	0	1	$208.58	Same as Bill To		
10268	GROSR	0	3	$66.29	Same as Bill To		
10269	WHITC	1	1	$4.56	White Clover Market	1029 - 12th Ave. S.	Seattle
10270	WARTH	0	1	$136.54	Same as Bill To		
10271	SPLIR	0	2	$4.54	Same as Bill To		
10272	RATTC	0	2	$98.03	Same as Bill To		
10273	QUICK	0	3	$76.07	Same as Bill To		
10274	VINET	0	1	$6.01	Same as Bill To		
10275	MAGAA	0	1	$26.93	Same as Bill To		
10276	TORTU	0	3	$13.84	Same as Bill To		

Record: I◀ ◀ 1 of 829 ▶ ▶I ▶ No Filter Search

tip

You can regenerate an exact duplicate of the original Orders table that has ship-to addresses for each order with the following lengthy SQL statement:

```
SELECT tblOrders.OrderID, tblOrders.CustomerID, tblOrders.EmployeeID,
       tblOrders.OrderDate, tblOrders.RequiredDate, tblOrders.ShippedDate,
       tblOrders.ShipToID, tblOrders.ShipVia, tblOrders.Freight, tblShipAddresses.ShipName,
       tblShipAddresses.ShipAddress, tblShipAddresses.ShipCity,
       tblShipAddresses.ShipRegion, tblShipAddresses.ShipPostalCode,
    tblShipAddresses.ShipCountry
FROM tblOrders
    INNER JOIN tblShipAddresses
        ON (tblOrders.ShipToID = tblShipAddresses.ShipToID)
            AND (tblOrders.CustomerID = tblShipAddresses.CustomerID)

UNION SELECT tblOrders.OrderID, tblOrders.CustomerID, tblOrders.EmployeeID,
       tblOrders.OrderDate, tblOrders.RequiredDate, tblOrders.ShippedDate,
       tblOrders.ShipToID, tblOrders.ShipVia, tblOrders.Freight,
```

Testing Cascading Deletion and Cascading Updates

When you delete a record in a primary or base table on which records in a related table depend, cascading deletions automatically delete the dependent records. Similarly, if you modify the value of a table's primary key field and a related table has records related by the primary key field's value, cascading updates change the value of the related foreign key field for the related records to the new primary key field value.

Cascading deletions and cascading updates are special types of action queries that the Access engine executes for you. The following three sections show you how to use Access's cascading deletions and cascading updates features with a set of test tables copied from the Orders and Order Details tables of Northwind.accdb.

Creating the Test Tables and Establishing Relationships

When experimenting with database features, you should work with test tables rather than live data. As mentioned in the note at the beginning of this chapter, using copied test tables is particularly advisable when the tables are participants in action queries. The remaining sections of this chapter use the two test tables, tblOrders and tblOrderDetails, that you created in preceding sections:

1. Open the tblOrders table in Table Design view.

2. Change the field data type of the OrderID field from AutoNumber to Number and make sure that the Field Size property is set to Long Integer. (This change is necessary to test cascading updates in the next section.)

3. Close tblOrders and save your changes.

tip

```
Customers.CompanyName, Customers.Address, Customers.City, Customers.Region,
     Customers.PostalCode, Customers.Country
FROM tblOrders
   INNER JOIN Customers
      ON (Customers.CustomerID = tblOrders.CustomerID)
WHERE tblOrders.ShipToID = 0;
```

You can save time by copying the basic structure of the first SELECT statement to the UNION SELECT statement, changing tblShipAddresses... field names to corresponding Customers... field names, and altering the INNER JOIN statement to join the Customers and tblOrders tables on the CustomerID field. (The name of this query is qryUQtblOrdersShipTo; Figure 13.21 shows its query resultset.)

Figure 13.21
You can produce a query resultset that's an exact duplicate of the original Orders table with a UNION query that returns Bill To addresses from the Customers table.

OrderID	CustomerID	ShipVia	Freight	ShipName	ShipAddress	ShipCit
10250	HANAR	2	$65.83	Hanari Carnes	Rua do Paço, 67	Rio de Jane
10251	VICTE	1	$41.34	Victuailles en stock	2, rue du Commerce	Lyon
10252	SUPRD	2	$51.30	Suprêmes délices	Boulevard Tirou, 255	Charleroi
10253	HANAR	2	$58.17	Hanari Carnes	Rua do Paço, 67	Rio de Jane
10254	CHOPS	2	$22.98	Chop-suey Chinese	Hauptstr. 31	Bern
10255	RICSU	3	$148.33	Richter Supermarkt	Starenweg 5	Genève
10256	WELLI	2	$13.97	Wellington Importadora	Rua do Mercado, 12	Resende
10257	HILAA	3	$81.91	HILARIÓN-Abastos	Carrera 22 con Ave. Carlos	San Cristóba
10258	ERNSH	1	$140.51	Ernst Handel	Kirchgasse 6	Graz
10259	CENTC	3	$3.25	Centro comercial Moctezuma	Sierras de Granada 9993	México D.F.
10260	OLDWO	1	$55.09	Ottilies Käseladen	Mehrheimerstr. 369	Köln
10261	QUEDE	2	$3.05	Que Delícia	Rua da Panificadora, 12	Rio de Jane
10262	RATTC	3	$48.29	Rattlesnake Canyon Grocery	2817 Milton Dr.	Albuquerqu
10263	ERNSH	3	$146.06	Ernst Handel	Kirchgasse 6	Graz
10264	FOLKO	3	$3.67	Folk och fä HB	Åkergatan 24	Bräcke
10265	BLONP	1	$55.28	Blondel père et fils	24, place Kléber	Strasbourg
10266	WARTH	3	$25.73	Wartian Herkku	Torikatu 38	Oulu
10267	FRANK	1	$208.58	Frankenversand	Berliner Platz 43	München
10268	GROSR	3	$66.29	GROSELLA-Restaurante	5ª Ave. Los Palos Grandes	Caracas
10269	WHITC	1	$4.56	White Clover Markets	1029 - 12th Ave. S.	Seattle
10270	WARTH	1	$136.54	Wartian Herkku	Torikatu 38	Oulu
10271	SPLIR	2	$4.54	Split Rail Beer & Ale	P.O. Box 555	Lander
10272	RATTC	2	$98.03	Rattlesnake Canyon Grocery	2817 Milton Dr.	Albuquerqu
10273	QUICK	3	$76.07	QUICK-Stop	Taucherstraße 10	Cunewalde
10274	VINET	1	$6.01	Vins et alcools Chevalier	59 rue de l'Abbaye	Reims
10275	MAGAA	1	$26.93	Magazzini Alimentari Riuniti	Via Ludovico il Moro 22	Bergamo
10276	TORTU	3	$13.84	Tortuga Restaurante	Avda. Azteca 123	México D.F.

Record: 1 of 829 | No Filter | Search

Cascading deletions and updates require that you establish a default relationship between the primary and related tables as well as enforce referential integrity. To add both cascading deletions and updates to the tblOrderDetails table, follow these steps:

1. If you haven't created tblOrderDetails, use the Clipboard to copy the Order Details table to tblOrderDetails.

2. 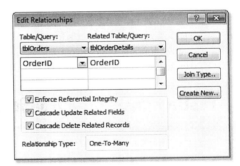 Click the Database Tools tab and the Relationships button to display the Relationships window.

3. Scroll right to an empty area of the Relationships window.

4. Click the Show Table button to display the Add Table dialog.

5. Double-click the tblOrders and tblOrderDetails items in the list, and then close the Show Table dialog.

6. Click and drag the OrderID field of tblOrders to the tblOrderDetails table's OrderID field to establish a one-to-many join on the OrderID field and open the Relationships dialog.

7. Mark the Enforce Referential Integrity check box, which enables the two cascade check boxes.

8. Mark the Cascade Update Related Fields and Cascade Delete Related Records check boxes, as shown in Figure 13.22.

Figure 13.22
Add Access's Cascade Update Related Fields and Cascade Delete Related Records features to automatically maintain the tblOrderDetails table's referential integrity.

9. Click OK to make your changes to the join effective and close the Relationships window. Click Yes when Access asks if you want to save your changes to the window's layout.

Access Won't Create a Relationship to a New Table

When you get a "Can't create relationship to enforce referential integrity" message when you try to enforce referential integrity it's because you dragged the field symbols in the wrong direction when you created the relationship. The related (to-many) table is in the Table/Query list and the primary (one-to) table is in the Related Table/Query list. Close the Edit Relationships dialog, click the thin area of the join line to select the join, and then press the Delete key to delete the join. Make sure that you drag the field name that you want from the primary table to the related table. Alternatively, you can make these changes in the Edit Relationships dialog.

Testing Cascading Deletions

To try cascading deletions with the test tables, follow these steps:

1. Open the tblOrders and tblOrderDetails tables in Datasheet view.

2. Click the tblOrders datasheet's tab to make it the active window and then click a record-selection button to pick an order in tblOrders to delete.

3. Press the Delete key to tentatively delete the selected records and the related order's line-item records in tblOrderDetails.

4. A message asks you to confirm the deletion. Click Yes to delete the records.

To verify that you've deleted the related records, click the tblOrderDetails tab and scroll to the related record or records for the order that you deleted in the tblOrderDetails table. The data cell values for the deleted related records are replaced with #Deleted. (These values aren't saved with the table.) Press F5 to refresh the Datasheet and remove the #Deleted rows.

Testing Cascading Updates

Cascading updates to the foreign key field of records that depend on a primary key value that you want to change in a primary table are a valuable Access feature. Performing updates of primary key values while enforcing referential integrity is not a simple process; Chapter 5 briefly discusses the problems associated with performing such updates manually. To see how Access takes the complexity out of cascading updates, follow these steps:

1. Click the tblOrders tab, and change the value of the OrderID cell of the first record to the order number that you deleted in the preceding section. Alternatively, change the value of the OrderID cell to a value such as **20000**, which is outside the range of the values of the test table.

2. Move the cursor to another record to cause the cascading update to occur. You immediately see the changes in the OrderID foreign key field of the related dependent records (see Figure 13.23).

Figure 13.23
Changing
the OrderID
value in
the base
table auto-
matically
changes
the OrderID
values of
related
records, if
you specify
cascading
updates.

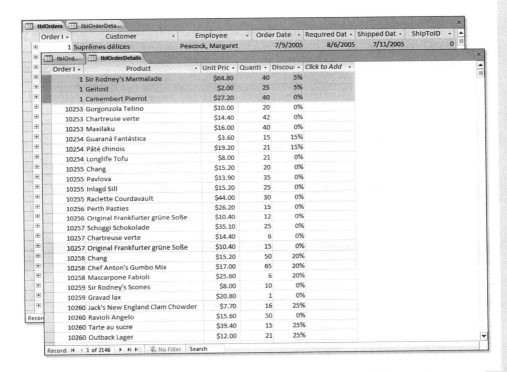

No confirmation message appears when you execute a cascading update, because the effect is reversible. If you make an erroneous entry that causes an undesired cascading update, you can change the entry to its original value by reentering the original or the correct value manually.

14

CREATING AND USING ACCESS FORMS

Access forms create the user interface to your tables. Although you can use Table view and Query view to perform many of the same functions as forms, forms offer the advantage of presenting data in an organized and attractive manner. You can arrange the location of fields on a form so that data entry or editing operations for a single record follow a natural left-to-right, top-to-bottom sequence. You can limit the number of fields that appear on the form, and allow or prevent editing of specific field values. A properly designed form speeds data entry and minimizes operator keying errors.

Forms are constructed from a collection of individual design elements called *controls* or *control objects*. An Access form consists of a window in which you place the following classes of Access controls:

- *Bound controls* display the data from the table or query that serves as the data source of the form. Access's native bound controls include text boxes, combo and list boxes, subforms, and object frames for graphics. You can bind many Microsoft and third-party ActiveX controls to a form's data source. For example, you can bind the PivotTable, PivotChart, and Spreadsheet controls of the Office Web Components (OWC) to the data source of your form.

- *Unbound dynamic controls*, also called *calculated controls*, can display data from sources other than the table or query that serves as the data source for the form. For example, you can use an unbound text box to display the current date and time.

- *Unbound static controls* display, for example, fixed-text labels and logo graphics.

In most cases, you base an Access form on a table or query, which you specify during the initial form design step, to serve as the master data source for your form. Connecting a form to a table or query is called data binding. This chapter concentrates on creating bound forms with dynamic text-based controls and subforms. A *subform* is another bound form contained within a form. You usually link the subform with the main form to synchronize the subform's content with the record selected by the main form. The primary use of subforms is to display detail data from a table or query that has a many-to-one relationship with the form's master data source.

> ➡ *For an example of an unbound Switchboard form with embedded macros,* **see** *"Exploring Access 2010's Macro-based Switchboard Manager,"* **p. 816.**

> ➡ *For a similar example with VBA code,* **see** *"Creating a Switchboard Class Module with the Macro-to-VBA Converter,"* **p. 1280.**

 note

The form design techniques you learn in this chapter also apply to designing forms of Access data projects (ADP), one of the subjects of Chapter 26, "Exploring Access Data Projects and SQL Server 2008." Forms for ADP are identical in almost all respects to forms that use Access tables or queries as data sources. The primary differences are ADP's connection to the SQL Server data source (instead of a native Access connection) and Access's method of storing the forms in an .adp file (rather than in an .accdb file).

Chapter 31, "Programming Combo and List Boxes," provides examples of unbound forms that don't have a data source.

Autogenerating a Basic Transaction-Processing Form

The content and appearance of your form depend on its use in your database application. Database applications fall into two basic categories:

- *Transaction-processing* applications add new records to tables, or edit or delete existing records. Transaction-processing applications require write access to (permissions for) the tables that are linked to the form.

- *Decision-support applications* supply information as graphs, tables, or individual data elements but don't allow the user to add or edit data. Decision-support applications require only read access to the tables that are linked to the form.

The form that you create in this example is typical of transaction-processing forms used to add new records to the many side of a *one-to-many* relationship. Adding line items to an invoice is an example of when a form of this kind—called a *one-to-many* or *master/child* form—is necessary. The objective of the HRActions form is to add new records to the HRActions table or let you edit the existing records.

Maintaining a record of employee performance reviews and actions resulting from the reviews is one of the primary responsibilities of personnel departments. For organizations with more than a few employees, a database is an effective tool for recording dates on which employees were hired, promoted, demoted, or terminated, and the justification for actions taken. This information often is critical in the defense of wrongful termination or other litigation brought by disgruntled former (or even current) employees. Human resources (HR) databases—the more politically correct term for personnel databases—also can handle scheduling of periodic reviews and aid in ensuring that managers or supervisors handle their HR responsibilities in a timely manner.

Creating a Master/Child Form from Related Tables

The "Default Form and Report Layouts" section of Chapter 1, "Access 2010 for Access 2007 Users: What's New," mentions that clicking the Create ribbon's form button with a table or query selected creates a form with Access 2010's default format, which has one or two columns of stacked controls, depending on the number of table fields or query columns. If the selected table has a single one-to-many relationship with another table, the form-generation process adds a Datasheet-style subform. The subform is bound to the related table, which in turn links to the main or master form.

 note

This book uses the term *master/child* to describe the form/subform relationship because the property names for the linkage are Link Master Fields and Link Child Fields.

You can't use the Northwind.accdb sample database to autogenerate the master/child form because the Employees table has relationships with the Orders table as well as the HRActions table. Ordinarily, you would start with a new database, import the Employees and HRActions tables into it, and then establish a many-to-one relationship between them on the EmployeeID field. To save time, you'll find a pre-built HRActions14.accdb database with the two related tables in the \Access2010\Chaptr14 folder.

To autogenerate the master/child form with the HRActions.accdb database, do the following:

1. Open the \Access2010\Chaptr14\HRActions.accdb database.

2. Select the Employees table in the Navigation pane, click the Create tab, and click the Forms group's Form button to create and open the Employees master/child form in the form Layout view (see Figure 14.1).

3. Press Ctrl+S to open the Save As dialog, type **frmHRActions** as the form name, and click OK to save the form.

Exploring the frmHRActions Form in Layout View

The master (main) form consists of two columns of text boxes—each with an associated label—for entering or editing data values in all but the EmployeeID and Picture fields of the Employees table. The subform contains all fields from the HRActions table (except the EmployeeID foreign key field) arranged in a tabular layout. Access uses the fields' Caption property values as default text box labels and also as column headings for the tabular subform.

In Figure 14.1, notice that a horizontal scrollbar appears in the subform area. The subform is larger than the area created for it in the main form, so Access automatically adds one or two scrollbars to let you access all data displayed in the subform. The subform's record navigation buttons let you scroll all records related to the current record of the main form.

The basic form needs many cosmetic adjustments to the layout of the main form and the subform. The remaining discussions and exercises in this chapter show you how to modify autogenerated forms and those created with the Form Wizard; you can apply these form-editing skills when you create your own forms from scratch, as described in the next chapter.

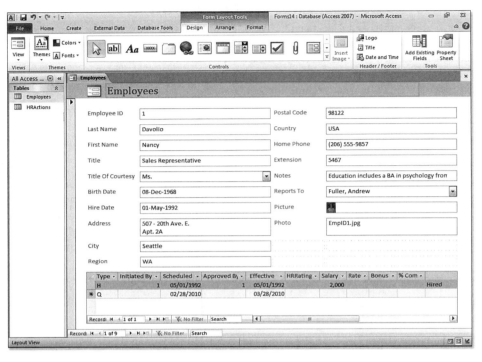

Figure 14.1
The basic Employees form autogenerated from the Employees and HRActions tables is the starting point of the final form layout process. Some of the form's text boxes have been resized to make all controls visible in the window.

Form Layout View's Contextual Ribbons

 Access 2010's updated Layout view for forms and reports speeds the design process by enabling grouped controls in stacked or tabular styles and letting you manipulate controls or groups of controls with live data visible. Selecting Layout or Design view in the Home ribbon's View gallery adds three contextual ribbons to the UI grouped under the heading Form Layout Tools: Design, Arrange (see Figure 14.2, bottom) and Format (see Figure 14.2, top). The following two sections describe the Arrange and Format ribbons in detail.

> **⚡ tip**
>
> No matter how adept you become at designing Access forms, auto-generating them or using the Form Wizard to create the basic form design saves you time.

The Form Layout Tools—Format Ribbon

The Format contextual ribbon has control button groups for specifying the view, formatting text and numbers, modifying Datasheet gridlines, setting control properties, and applying AutoFormats to forms. Table 14.1 lists the icon, name, KeyTips, and a brief description of each command button of the Form Layout Tools—Format ribbon. The keyboard shortcut to display KeyTips is Alt+JF.

Figure 14.2
Form Layout
view adds
Form Layout
Tools—Format
(top) and Form
Layout Tools—
Arrange con-
textual ribbons
(bottom).

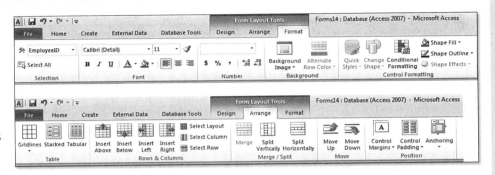

Table 14.1 Icons, Command Buttons, KeyTip Shortcuts, and Command Button Actions for the
Form Layout Tools—Format Ribbon.

Icon	Command Button	Shortcut	Command Action
		Selection Group	
⚒ CustomerID ▼	Object	B	Selects control to format from list
▤	Select All	CA	Selects all controls for formatting
		Font Group	
Calibri ▼	Font	FF	Sets font family from list
11 ▼	Font Size	FS	Sets font size from list
B	Bold	1	Sets selected text bold
I	Italic	2	Sets selected text italic
U̲	Underline	3	Underlines selected text
☰	Align Left	AL	Aligns selected text left
☰	Center	AC	Centers selected text
☰	Align Right	AR	Aligns selected text right
🖌	Format Painter	FP	Applies selected format to other con-trols

Table 14.1   Continued

Icon	Command Button	Shortcut	Command Action
A	Font Color	FC	Opens color picker to apply color to selected text
		Number Group	
Formatting ▾	Formatting	R	Sets number format from list
$	Currency	AN	Applies currency format
%	Percent	P	Multiplies display value by 100 and adds % symbol
,	Comma Format	K	Applies commas as thousands separators
←.0 .00	Increase Decimals	0	Adds decimal digits
.00 →.0	Decrease Decimals	9	Reduces decimal digits
		Background Group	
	Background Image	G	Opens an Insert Picture dialog to select a background graphic
	Alternate Row Color	FA	Opens a color picker to select a color to shade controls in alternate rows
		Control Formatting Group	
	Quick Styles	SS	Opens a gallery styles and colors for buttons
	Change Shape	I	Opens a gallery of rounded corners for buttons and tab control tabs
	Conditional Formatting	O	Opens the Conditional Formatting dialog to enable formatting a control based on the result of an expression or the control receiving the focus (see Figure 14.3)
	Shape Fill	SF	
	Shape Outline	L	

> **tip**
>
> **2010 NEW** Chapter 15, "Designing Custom Multitable Forms," describes how to use the new Quick Styles, Change Shape, Shape Fill and Shape Outline features.

Applying Conditional Formatting

The Conditional Formatting dialog lets you specifiy one or more conditions that format the text and background color of a control in response to changes in the value of the control, the value of a Boolean expression (True), or the control receiving the focus (see Figure 14.3). You select the target control, click the Conditional Formatting button, and then click New Rule to open the New Formatting Rule dialog (see Figure 14.4). Then select the condition type—Field Value Is, Expression Is, or Field Has Focus—in the leftmost drop-down list, type the value or expression in the right text box, and click OK to return to the Conditional Formatting dialog.

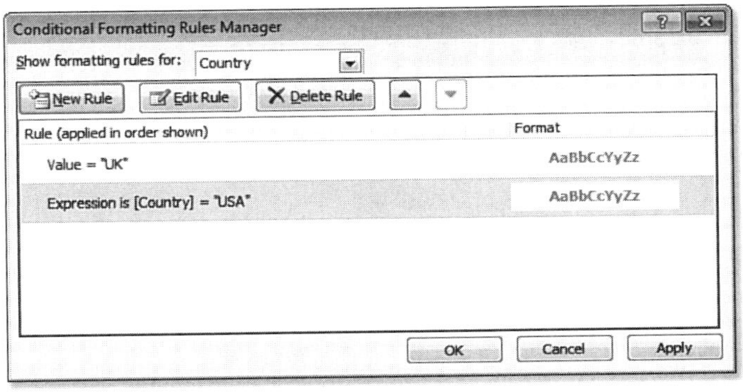

Figure 14.3
These two condiitional formatting expressions set the Country text box's value bold for UK and USA addresses, and color the text red for USA or Green for UK addresses.

Condition 1 creates an expression based on the control's numeric or alphabetic value. You can select from equal to (=), not equal to (<>), greater than (>), less than (<), greater than or equal to (>=), and less than or equal to (<=) conditions. Condition 2 requires typing in the text box a VBA expression that evaluates to True or False. Chapter 10, "Understanding Access Query Operators and Expressions," describes expressions that return Boolean values.

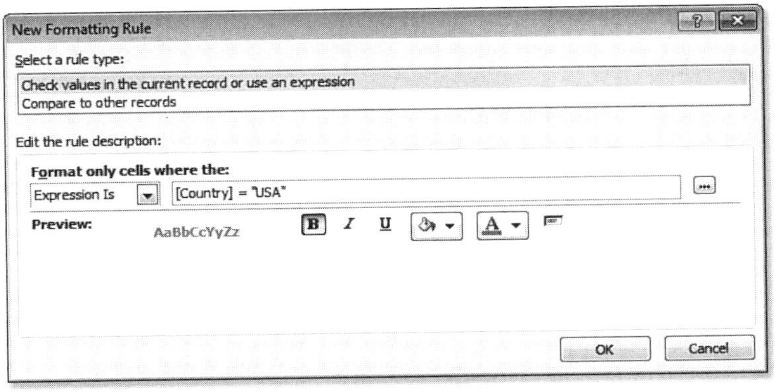

Figure 14.4
The New Formatting Rule dialog lets you add multiple formatting conditions to a control. This example is the expression for bolding USA and coloring the text red.

The Form Layout Tools—Arrange Ribbon

The Arrange contextual ribbon has groups for managing control groups, setting text margins and padding for controls, toggling the Snap to Grid layout feature, setting tab order, aligning and positioning controls, and displaying the Property Sheet. Table 14.2 lists the icon, name, KeyTips, and a brief description of each command button of the Form Layout Tools—Arrange ribbon. The keyboard shortcut to display KeyTips is Alt+JL.

Table 14.2 Icons, Command Buttons, KeyTip Shortcuts and Command Button Actions for the Form Layout Tools—Arrange Ribbon.

Icon	Command Button	Shortcut	Command Action
		Table Group	
	Gridlines	B	
	Stacked	SU	Adds the selected controls to a stacked control group
	Tabular	O	Adds the selected controls to a tabular control group
		Rows & Columns Group	
	Insert Above	A	Inserts space for a control above the selected control
	Insert Below	B	Inserts space for a control below the selected control
	Insert Left	L	Inserts space for a control to the left of the selected control
	Insert Right	R	Inserts space for a control to the right of the selected control
	Select Layout	SL	Selects all controls in the layout
	Select Column	SC	Selects all controls in the selected column
	Select Row	SR	Selects all controls in the selected row
		Merge/Split Group	
	Merge	M	Merges cells
	Split Vertically	SP	Splits the selected row into two rows

Icon	Command Button	Shortcut	Command Action
	Split Horizontally	SP	Splits the selected column into two columns
	Move Group		
	Move Up	U	Moves the selected control up one row
	Move Down	D	Moves the selected control down one row
	Position Group		
	Control Margins	G	Opens a gallery from which you can select the space between control borders and text: None, Narrow, Medium, or Wide
	Control Padding	P	Opens a gallery from which you can select the space between adjacent controls: None, Narrow, Medium, or Wide
	Anchoring	C	Opens a gallery of nine options for positioning a control when resizing the form's window

Rearranging the Default Form Layout

You can rearrange a form's layout in traditional Design view or the new Layout view, but Layout view accompanies the layout process with live data in the form's controls. Some form and control property values can be changed only in Design view. The procedure that follows explains how to resize form controls in a layout independent of controls in adjacent columns.

The sample main form has two stacked control groups; the HRActions Datasheet at the bottom of the form is a single Subform control. The most obvious problems with the default form layout are, from top to bottom:

- The label (Auto_Header0) in the form's Header section needs to be changed to reflect the form's purpose.

- The width of the two stacked control groups is excessive for all fields except Notes.

- Including Birth Date data on a data entry form is not politically correct and might violate government regulations.

- The size of the Picture field's Attachment control is too small and its aspect ratio is incorrect.

> **tip**
>
> Select Normal windows mode for Access with a window size of 1,024×768 pixels to make the instructions example easier to follow and the figures more representative. This book's screen captures use 1,024×768-pixel resolution for readability.

■ The Photo field's TextBox and Label controls (inherited from earlier Northwind versions) isn't needed.

■ The HRActions subform (Child36) has more depth than necessary.

To start the form rearrangement process and learn how to work with grouped (stacked) controls, do the following:

1. Navigate through the nine Employees records to verify the approximate width of the content in each text box.

2. Select the Employee ID text box (not the label) and drag its right edge to the left to reduce the width of all text boxes in the group (see Figure 14.5). When you release the mouse, the third and fourth columns move to the left.

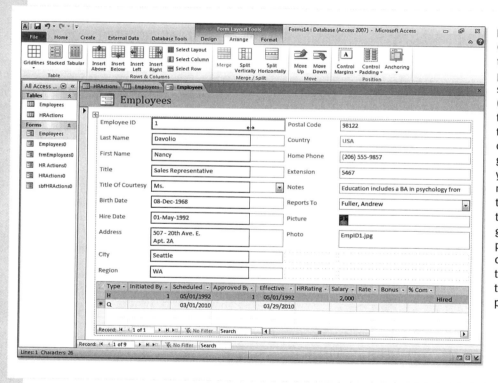

Figure 14.5
Changing the width (or position) of a single grouped (stacked) control changes the width of all controls in the group. When you release the mouse button, the outline of the original group disappears and other columns move to maintain their relative position.

3. Select and then click to activate the Employees label. Replace Employees with **Northwind Human Resources Actions** as the label's caption, and then change the font from Cambria (serif) to Calibri (sans serif).

4. Select the Birth Date label and text box, and press Delete to remove them.

5. Select the Hire Date, Address, City, and Region labels and text boxes and click the Move Up button to move them up one row.

6. Repeat step 4 for the Photo label and text box.

7. Drag the bottom of the City text box up to make its depth equal to the other text boxes above it.

8. Select the Country label and text box, and drag them together from the top of the right group to the bottom of the left group.

9. Select the Home Phone, Extension, Notes labels and text boxes and click the Move Up button until Home Phone aligns horizontally with Employee ID.

10. Shift+click to select the Notes text box and the empty space below it, and then click the Merge button to increase the depth of the Notes text box (look ahead to Figure 14.6).

11. Shift+click to select the Picture Attachment control and the five empty text box locations below it, and then click the Merge button to increase the depth of the control (look ahead to Figure 14.6).

12. Select the Picture Attachment control, click the Format ribbon's Shape Outline button, and mark the Transparent check box to remove the border.

13. Drag the two control groups closer to the top of the Details section, and then drag the subform closer to the bottom of the Country text box.

14. Drag the subform's right border to the left and align it with the right group's right border, and, optionally, drag the bottom of the subform up to reduce its depth.

15. Click the Form Layout Tools—Format tab or the Home tab and change to Design view. Drag the form's right border to within about 0.25 inch of the right control group's right border.

16. Change to Form view. Figure 14.6 shows the redesigned form in Form view.

17. Optionally, right-click the Navigation pane's Employees form item, choose Rename, and change the name of the form to **frmHRActions**.

18. Press Ctrl+S to save your changes so far.

Changing Form View from a Tabbed Document to a Modal Pop-up Window

The alternative to tabbed documents for displaying forms is a modal pop-up window that's the default display mode for *TableName* Details forms generated from Access 2007 templates.

To change frmHRActions' display mode to a modal pop-up window, do the following:

1. Open frmHRActions, if necessary.

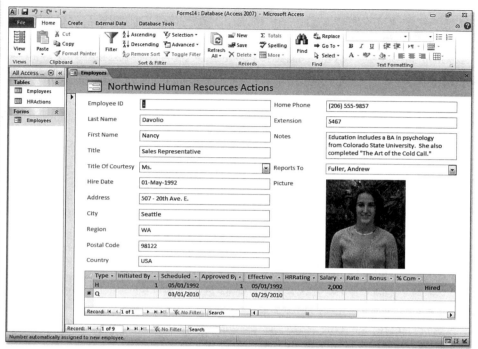

Figure 14.6
A few minutes of redesign reduces the form's obesity greatly. Form size isn't a major issue when viewed as a tabbed document, but minimizing bloat is a good policy for forms you want to display in modal or nonmodal pop-up windows.

2. In Design View, press Alt+Enter to open the Property Sheet, and click the vertical Record Selector button at the left of the form to specify Form as the selected object.

3. Click the Other tab, and change the Pop-Up and Modal property values from No to Yes.

4. Close the Property Sheet and frmHRActions, and click Yes when asked if you want to save your changes.

5. Double-click the Navigation pane item for the form to open it as a modal pop-up window (see Figure 14.7).

6. To experiment with a nonmodal pop-up form, close the form, open it in Design view, open the Property Sheet for the form, click the Other tab, and set the Modal property value to No.

7. Close the form, save your changes, then double-click the item to open the form. With a nonmodal form, you can change the focus to the Access UI or any other window while the form is open. However, the True Pop-Up property causes the window to remain on top of all other windows, even when minimized.

8. To return to the default tabbed document mode, open the Property Sheet for the form, click the Other tab, set the Pop-Up property value to No, close the form, and save your changes.

It's a common practice to add a Close button, Save & Close button, or both, to the Header or Details section of pop-up forms.

Figure 14.7
Users can mini-mize or maxi-mize a modal pop-up form, but can't shift the focus to Access or another win-dow without closing the form.

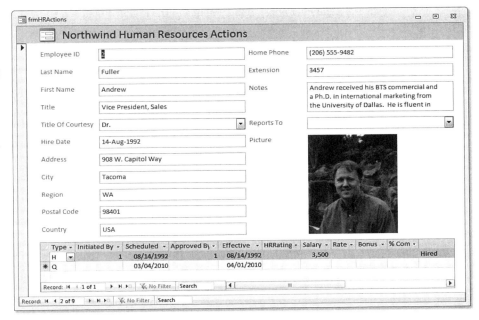

Setting Form Appearance Properties

Access offers several formatting properties that you can use to customize the appearance of your forms and the control objects they contain. You also can apply many of the property settings described in the following sections to subforms that you open in separate windows.

Default Values for Forms

You can change a few default values used in the creation of all forms by clicking the File tab and Options button to open the Access Options dialog, clicking the Object Designers button, and scroll-ing to the Forms/Reports section (see Figure 14.8). The Selection Behavior options determine how you select control objects with the mouse. You can create a form to use as a template and replace the standard (Normal) template, and then mark the Always Use Event Procedures check box to per-mit only VBA code for automating applications and prevent embedding Access macros in forms.

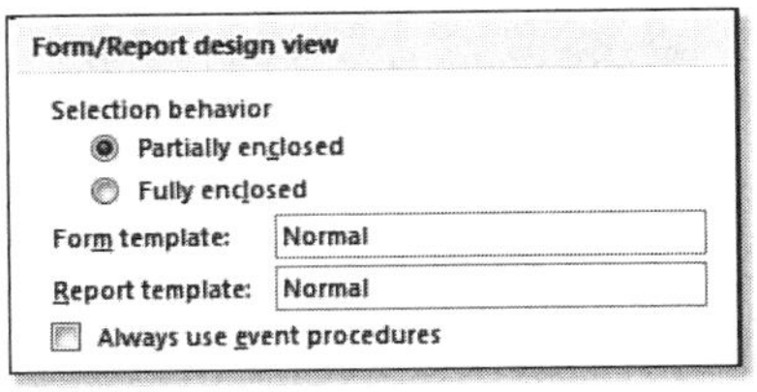

Figure 14.8
You can change a few default form values that apply to all data-bases you create in the Forms/Reports section of the Access Option dialog's Object Designers page.

Form/Report design view

Selection behavior
- ● Partially enclosed
- ○ Fully enclosed

Form template: Normal

Report template: Normal

☐ Always use event procedures

The Application Options section of the Access Options dialog's Current Database page (see Figure 14.9) has several items that apply default values to the forms of the current database.

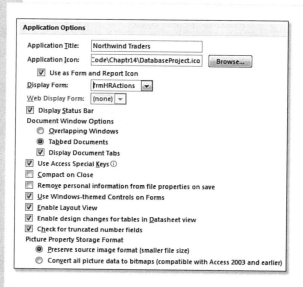

Figure 14.9
Six items under the Application Options section of the Access Options dialog's Current Database page apply default values to forms and controls.

Following are the application options that apply to forms and their controls:

- *Application Icon*—Specify the path and filename of a desktop and toolbar icon to replace Access's icon.

- *Use as Form and Report Icon*—Mark to replace the Access icon with the small version of the icon on a form or report's tabbed document or window.

- *Display Form*—Select the form to open automatically when the user launches the database.

- *Document Window Options*—Select the Overlapping Windows option to replace tabbed documents with modal pop-up forms. Clear Display Document Tabs to hide the tabs of tabbed documents, which requires users to employ the Navigation pane to select the active form.

- *Use Windows-themed Controls on Forms*—Clearing this check box removes Windows XP or Vista themes from form controls.

- *Enable Layout View*—Clearing this check box prevents users from opening forms in Layout view.

 tip

Check the Selection Type and object name of the Property Sheet before you change property values to make sure the selected object is the one whose properties you want to change. It's a common practice to leave the Property Sheet open as you alter the form design, and the selected object might not be the object you intend.

All form, form section, and control properties have default values. You can change the default values for the current form, section, or controls by choosing the object and then changing the default values displayed in the Properties window for that object.

You can also use the AutoFormat feature to quickly apply a predefined format to all controls in the form. The next section describes using AutoFormat to change a form's appearance, and subsequent sections describe ways to change the format of text or controls manually on a form.

> **note**
>
> Office Themes replace the AutoFormat feature and wizard of Access 2007 and earlier. Office Themes apply to all Office 2010 members, so you can style your Access datasheets and forms with the same colors and fonts as your Excel worksheets or other Office documents.

Changing the Office Theme

Office Themes let you apply a predefined font and set of colors to an entire form with only a few mouse clicks. Office 2010 comes with 40 predefined (built-in) themes, and you also can create or customize your own theme colors and fonts.

Applying a Nondefault Office Theme from the Gallery

To apply a theme to a form with one of Access 2010's 40 standard AutoFormats, follow these steps:

1. Click the Form Layout Tools—Format tab and then the Themes group's Themes button to open the AutoFormat gallery shown in Figure 14.10. Access default's theme is the first (upper left) in the gallery.

2. Pass the mouse over a theme in the gallery to apply the format to the form temporarily. Figure 14.11 shows the frmHRActions form after the Apex format has been applied.

Figure 14.10
A theme that you select from the gallery applies a predefined format to the entire form.

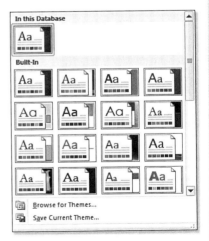

3. Press Ctrl+Z to return to the original format you selected when creating the form, if you want.

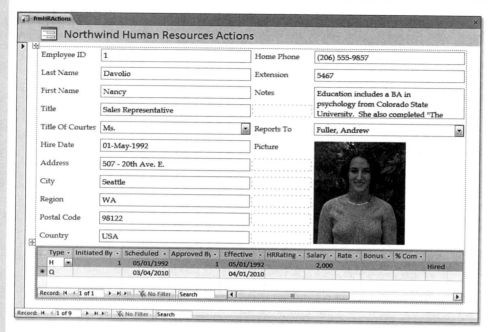

Figure 14.11
The frmHRAc-
tions form
shown here has
the Apex theme
applied to the
main form.

Customizing Theme Fonts

The predefined fonts and colors might not suit your tastes, or you might want to create Theme Fonts specific to your organization or application.

To create and apply a new Font Theme, do the following:

1. In the Form Layout Tools—Design ribbon, click the Fonts button to open the Fonts gallery (see Figure 14.12).

2. Click the Create New Theme Fonts link to open the dialog of the same name.

3. Select the Heading Font and Body Font from the drop-down lists and type a name for the Theme Font: **OakLeaf** for this example (see Figure 14.13).

> **note**
>
> The Apex theme uses the sans serif Lucida Sans font for header/footer titles and the serif Book Antigua font for labels and text boxes. You replaced the default Office theme's Cambria title font with Calibri, so applying the Apex theme affects only the body of the form shown in Figure 14.11. Changing the theme of the main form doesn't affect the subform.

Figure 14.12
The Fonts gallery offers 40 built-in Theme Fonts, which correspond to the same-named built-in Office Themes.

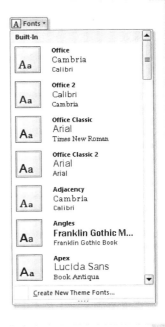

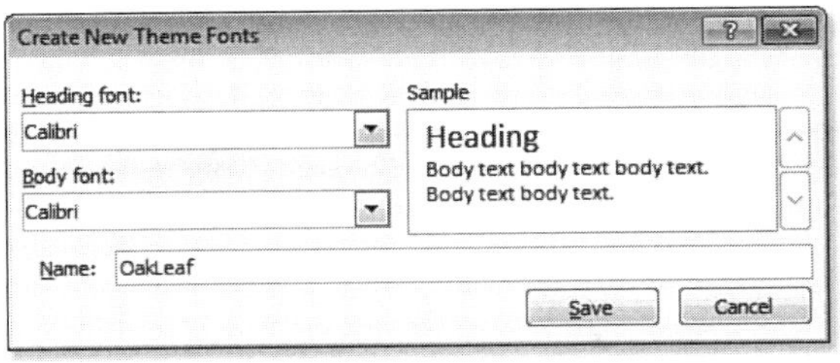

Figure 14.13
The Create New Theme Fonts dialog lets you define a Theme Font from any one or two fonts installed on your computer.

4. Click the Save button to apply the Theme Font to your currently open form, add it to the Custom section of the Fonts gallery (see Figure 14.14), save it as **\Users\UserName\AppData\ Roaming\Microsoft\Templates\Document Themes\Fonts\FontName.xml**, and close the dialog.

Figure 14.14
Saving a new Theme Font applies it to forms in the current database and adds it to the Font gallery's Custom group.

Double-clicking the *FontName*.xml file opens it in Internet Explorer (see Figure 14.15).

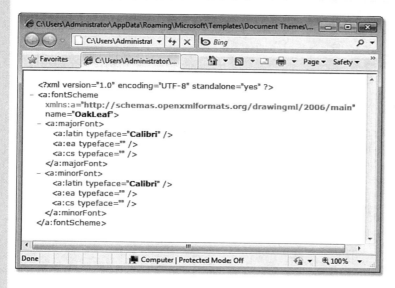

Figure 14.15
FontName.xml is a readable XML file containing `majorFont` (title) and `minorFont` (body) font names. (`ea` is an abbreviation of "east Asian" and `cs` is an abbreviation of complex script).

Customizing Theme Colors

The process for customizing Theme Colors is similar to that for customizing Theme Fonts:

1. Click the Color button of the Form Layout Tools—Design ribbon's Themes section to open the Theme Colors gallery (see Figure 14.16).

Figure 14.16
The Theme Colors gallery includes sets of eight standard UI component colors for each built-in Office Theme.

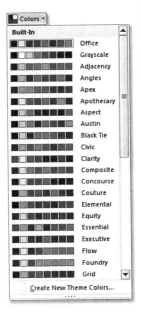

2. Click the Create New Theme Colors link to open the dialog of the same name.

3. Give the new Theme Colors a name, **OakLeaf** for this example, and click the color button for the color you want to change (see Figure 14.17). Alternatively, click the More Colors link to open the Colors dialog, which the "Creating Custom Colors with the Color Builder" section describes later in this chapter.

4. Click the Save button to apply the Theme Colors to your currently open form, add it to the Custom section of the Theme Colors gallery (see Figure 14.18), save it as **\Users\UserName\ AppData\Roaming\Microsoft\Templates\Document Themes\Colors\ColorsName.xml**, and close the dialog.

5. Double-click the *FontName*.xml file to open it in Internet Explorer (see Figure 14.18).

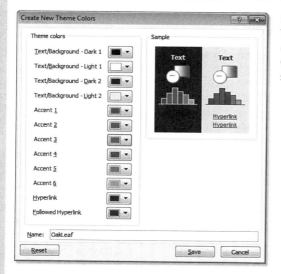

Figure 14.17
You can select different Theme Colors from the default or selected Office Theme for the database, as well as the Colors dialog. In this case a darker shade of chartreuse is selected for Accent 3.

Saving a New or Customized Theme

After you add or change Theme Fonts, Colors, or both, for your current database, you can save the changes to a new Office Theme by clicking the Theme gallery's Save Current Theme link to open the dialog of the same name, naming the theme (**OakLeaf,** see Figure 14.19) and clicking Save.

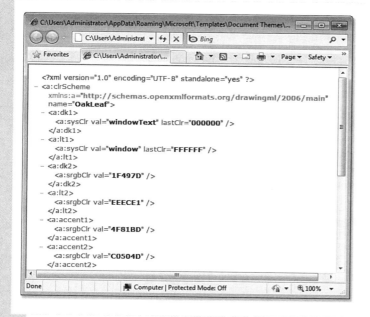

Figure 14.18
Colors.xml is a readable XML file that contains six-character, hexadecimal RGB (red, green blue) values for each color, of which the first six are shown here.

Figure 14.19
User-specific Office Theme files have a *.thmx format and aren't readable directly.

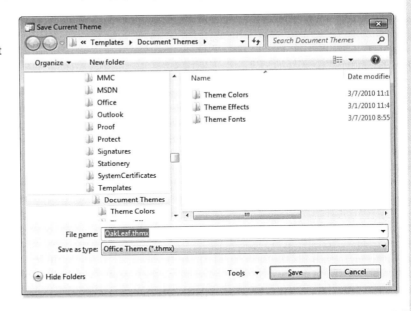

Access creates a user-specific file, \Users*UserName*\AppData\Roaming\Microsoft\Templates\ Document ThemesFilename.thmx (Windows 7). Double-clicking a *.thmx file opens an empty PowerPoint 2010 slide with the theme's color(s) and fonts. *.thmx files aren't XML files, so you can't read them with Internet Explorer or Notepad.

Changing an Object's Colors Without Changing the Theme

You select object colors with color pickers, as well as by setting form and control property values in the Property Sheet. When you change an object's color(s), the change overrides colors defined by the current Office Theme or Theme Colors setting, but doesn't change these themes. The following sections describe how to use the Formatting toolbar controls and the Property Sheet to change background and foreground colors of form sections and control objects, as well as border properties of control objects.

The Access Color Palette

The Access color palette consists of 10 Theme Colors, which the current or default Office Theme specifies, 5 variations of the 10 theme colors with different luminance values, 70 standard (named) colors, and up to 10 recent colors. The theme colors are divided into 10 colors for specific objects, such as White, Background 1, Tan, Background 2, Black, Text 1, and Lighter or Darker variations.

Figure 14.20 shows the color picker that opens when you click the drop-down button of the Form Layout Tools—Format ribbon's Font Color, Fill/Back Color, or Alternate Fill/Back Color button in the Font group; or the Gridlines gallery's Color button. The color picker is the same for all buttons, and each color button has a ToolTip to display the color name. The color picker doesn't include Windows System colors, which depend on the user's Windows theme; you select Windows System colors in the Property Sheet for the object.

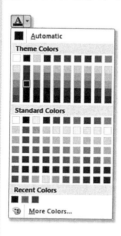

Figure 14.20
Access's standard color picker offers a total of 130 predefined colors, up to 10 recently used colors, and a More Colors link to open a Colors dialog with additional color selection options.

Following are the color names for the first row of the color picker's buttons, from left to right, with the OakLeaf theme applied:

White, Background 1   Red, Accent 2

Black, Text 1   Olive Green, Accent 3

Tan, Background 2   Purple, Accent 4

Dark Blue, Text 2   Aqua, Accent 5

Blue, Accent 1   Orange, Accent 6

Background Colors

The background color (Back Color property) of a form section (Header, Detail, or Footer) applies to all areas of that section except areas occupied by control objects that don't have a transparent background. The default background color of form Detail and Footer sections is White, Background 1; the form Header section is Text 2, Lighter 80%.

If you're creating a form that you intend to print, a dark or deeply textured background will not only be distracting but will also consume substantial amounts of printer toner. Data entry operators often prefer a white or light gray background rather than a colored or textured background. Colored and textured backgrounds tend to distract users.

There's no command button to format a section's background color. To change the background color of a section of a form in Layout view, follow these steps:

1. Click an empty area within the section of the form (Header, Detail, or Footer) whose background color you want to change. (In Design view, you can click the section's header bar.) This step selects the appropriate section.

2. Press Alt+Enter to open the Property Sheet. Verify that the section you want is selected, and click the Format tab.

3. Click the builder button to open the color picker (see Figure 14.21).

Figure 14.21
Use the Property Sheet's color property builder buttons to open the color picker.

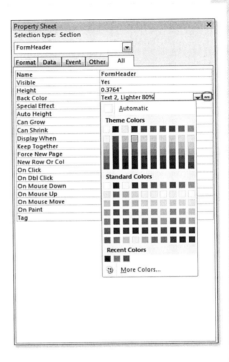

4. Click the button for the color you want to use.

Because the background color of each form section is independent, you must repeat the process if you want to change the color for other sections of your form. Clicking the Automatic button sets the Back Color property to white (#FFFFFF).

You choose the background color for a control object, such as a label, by selecting the control and clicking the Form Layout Tools—Format button and the Fill/Back Color drop-down button to open the color picker. Alternatively, use the Home ribbon's Font buttons. The default value of the Back Color property of text boxes is white so that text boxes (and the data they contain) contrast with the form's background color.

 tip

In most cases, the preferred background color of labels is the same as that of the form. Set labels' Back Style color to transparent so the background color shows.

Background Images and Logos

You can use a bitmap or vector image as the background for a form. Unlike background colors that you assign to form sections, you select a single bitmap picture for the entire form. Access 2007 came with a few .gif bitmaps that you could tile as form backgrounds, plus the Globe.wmf metafile from an AutoFormat of an earlier Access version. Access 2007 stored these images in the Program Files\Microsoft Office\Office12\Bitmaps\Styles folder as the background for the form. Office 2010 doesn't include a ...\Microsoft Office\Office14\Bitmaps folders, so the \Access2010\Chaptr14\Bitmaps folder holds copies of these files. You can use any .bmp, .dib, .emf, .gif, .ico, .jpg, .pcx, .png, or .wmf graphics file as a background for a form.

tip

Forms with background logos can look dramatic and, therefore, are best suited for decision-support forms intended for management personnel. (Management types are known to prefer form over substance.) For accurate, high-speed data entry, keep your transaction-processing forms visually simple so that users can easily distinguish data fields on the form and easily read text labels.

You set or remove a form's background image through the form's Property Sheet; you can also specify several viewing and formatting properties for the background picture. Follow these steps to set the background image properties of a form:

1. Open the form in Layout view if necessary.

2. Click the Form (Record) Select button.

3. If the Property Sheet isn't already open, press Ctrl+Enter.

4. Click the Format tab in the Property Sheet to display the various Picture properties: Picture, Picture Tiling, Picture Alignment, Picture Type, and Picture Size Mode. These properties and their effects are described in the list following these numbered steps.

5. Specify the path and filename for the graphics file in the Picture text box, and set the various Picture properties until you're satisfied with the appearance of the form. As you change each property, results of the change become immediately visible on the form. Figure 14.22 illustrates use of a tiled Acbluprt.gif image to create a simple grid pattern.

6. Optionally, close the Property Sheet.

The following list summarizes form properties related to the background picture, available choices for each property, and the effects of each choice:

- The Picture property contains the folder path and filename of the graphics file that Access uses as the form's background. You can either type the folder path and filename directly in the Picture property text box or use the Builder to help you select the background graphics file. To use the Builder, click the Picture property field to select that field, and then click the Build button that appears next to the text box. Access opens the Insert Picture dialog; navigate to the location and select the graphics file to use, as shown in Figure 14.23.

Figure 14.22
A tiled bitmap
can create a
uniform pat-
tern or texture
for the form's
background.

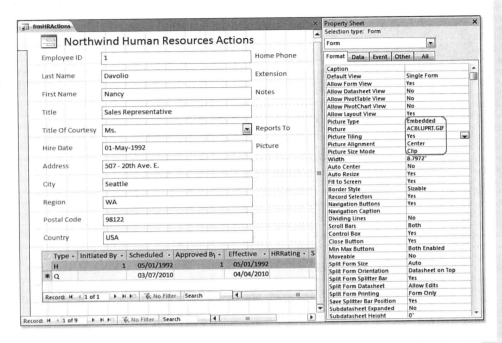

Figure 14.23
Use the Insert
Picture dialog to
select a graphics
file for a form's
background.

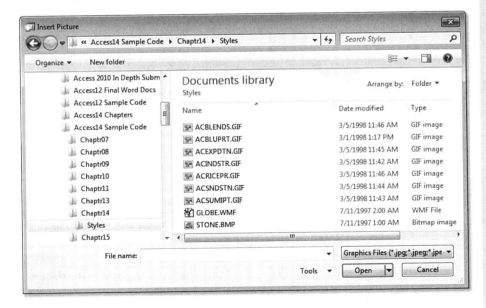

- The Picture Type property specifies the method that Access uses to attach the background picture to the form. You can select either Embedded or Linked as the picture type. Use the Embedded picture type, especially if you intend to distribute your database application; the resulting form is self-contained and doesn't rely on the presence of external files that might be moved or deleted. If you have many forms that use the same background bitmap graphic, linking the background picture can save some disk space.

 tip

To remove a background picture, delete the entry in the Picture text box and click Yes when asked if you want to remove the picture from the form.

- The Picture Size Mode property controls how Access sizes the background picture. The available choices are Clip, Stretch, and Zoom. Clip causes Access to display the picture at its full size behind the form. If the picture is larger than the form, the picture is clipped to fit the form. If the picture is smaller than the form, the form's own background color shows in any part of the form background not covered by the picture. Stretch causes Access to stretch the picture vertically and horizontally to match the size of the form; the Stretch option permits distortions in the picture. Zoom causes Access to magnify the picture, without distortion, to fit the size of the form.

 tip

To ensure that a background picture is displayed relative to the form, rather than the form's window, select Form Center as the value for the Picture Alignment property.

- The Picture Alignment property controls where Access positions the background picture. The available choices are Top-left (aligns the upper-left corner of the picture with the upper-left corner of the form window), Top-right (aligns the upper-right corner of the picture with the upper-right corner of the form window), Center (places the picture in the center of the form window), Bottom-left (aligns the lower-left corner of the picture with the lower-left corner of the form), Bottom-right (aligns the lower-right corner of the picture with the lower-right corner of the form), and Form Center (centers the picture on the form).

- The Picture Tiling property has two permissible values: Yes and No. Tiling means that the picture is repeatedly displayed to fill the entire form or form window (if the Picture Alignment property is set to Form Center, the tiling fills just the form).

Now that you know how to adjust the background picture and colors of a form, the next section describes how to adjust the foreground colors and border properties of the form and objects on the form.

Font Color, Border Color, and Border Style

You can set the font color, border color, and border width with buttons on the Form Layout Tools—Format ribbon or directly in the Property Sheet for a selected control.

Font color (the Fore Color property) is applicable only to control objects. (The Font Color ribbon button is disabled when you select a form section.) Font color specifies the color for the text in labels and text boxes. The default value of the Fore Color property is black. You choose border colors, pattern, and thickness for control objects that have borders by clicking the appropriate Controls group button.

To set a control's foreground color, border width, or border color by using the Font or Controls group's buttons, first click the control whose properties you want to change and then click the command button for the property you want to change: Font Color, Line Thickness.

To set a control's foreground color, border width, border color, or border style in the Properties window, first select the control whose properties you want to change by clicking it. Click the Format tab in the Property Sheet and then scroll to the text box for the property you want to change. Most of the border properties are selected from drop-down lists; color properties require you to select a named color or open the color picker and click one of the standard color buttons. Alternatively, you can use the Color Builder described in the following section.

Creating Custom Colors with the Color Builder

If you aren't satisfied with one of the predefined colors for your form sections or control objects, you can specify your own custom colors by following these steps:

1. Place the cursor in the Back/Fill Color, Fore Color, or Border Color text box of the Properties window for a form section or control.

2. Click the Builder button to open the color picker, and then click More Colors to open the Colors dialog (see Figure 14.24, left). If one of the colors of the hexagonal palette suits your taste, select the color button, click OK to assign that color as the value of the property, and then close the dialog. If you want a more customized color, proceed to step 3.

3. Click the Custom tab and accept the default RGB (red, green, blue) color model, as shown in Figure 14.18 (right), or choose HSL (hue, saturation, luminance) if you prefer.

4. Click and drag the cursor within the square Hue/Saturation area to choose the color you want.

5. Click and drag the arrow at the right of the rectangular luminance area while observing the Color block; release the mouse button when the Color block has the luminance (brightness) value you want.

6. Click OK to add this color value to the property, and close the Color dialog.

Figure 14.24
Choose a custom color from the Color dialog's Standard (left) or Custom page (right). The Custom page lets you choose the RGB (red, green, blue) or HSL (hue, saturation, luminance) color model.

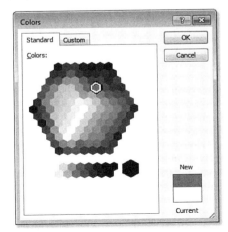
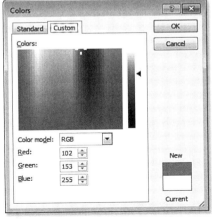

Using the Windows Clipboard and Deleting Controls

All conventional Windows Clipboard commands apply to control objects. You can cut or copy a selected control or group of controls to the Clipboard. After that, you can paste the control or group to the form with the Windows keyboard shortcut keys: Ctrl+X to cut, Ctrl+C to copy selected controls to the Clipboard, and Ctrl+V to paste the Clipboard contents.

You can delete a control by selecting it and then pressing Delete. If you accidentally delete a label associated with a control, and pressing Ctrl+Z or clicking the Quick Access Toolbar's Undo button doesn't solve the problem, do the following: Select another label, copy it to the Clipboard, select the control the label needs to be associated with, and paste the label to the control.

Changing the Content of Text Controls

You can edit the content of text controls by using conventional Windows text-editing techniques. When you place the mouse pointer within the confines of a text control and click the mouse button, the mouse pointer becomes the Windows text-editing cursor that you use to insert or delete text. You can select text by dragging the mouse over it or by holding down Shift and moving the cursor with the arrow keys. All Windows Clipboard operations are applicable to text within controls. Keyboard text selection and editing techniques using the arrow keys in combination with Shift are available as well.

Most Access text boxes are bound to table or query fields. If you change the name of a field in a text box and make an error naming the field, you receive a "#Name?" error message in the offending text box when you select Run mode. Following is a better method of changing a text box with an associated label:

1. Delete the existing field control by clicking to select it and then pressing Delete.

2. Click the Controls group's Add Existing Fields button in the Form Layout Tools—Format ribbon to display the Field List dialog.

3. Scroll through the entries in the list until you find the table or query field name you want.

4. Click the field name to select it; then drag the field name to the location of the deleted control. Release the mouse button to drop the new name.

5. Close the Field List dialog when you're finished.

You can relocate and resize the new field caption and text box (or edit the caption) as necessary. If you drag the field name inside a Tabular or Stacked control group, the caption and text box resize automatically.

Using the Format Painter

The Format Painter lets you quickly copy the format of any control on the form to any other control on the form. The Format Painter copies only those formatting properties that are relevant to the control on which you apply the Format Painter. To use the Format Painter, follow these steps:

1. Select the control with the formatting you want to copy.

2. Click or double-click the Format Painter button on the toolbar; the mouse cursor changes to a pointing arrow with a paintbrush icon attached to it. (Double-clicking "locks" the Format Painter on. Double-click the Format Painter button only if you want to copy the formatting to more than one control.)

3. Click any control that you want to copy the formatting to; the Format Painter copies all relevant formatting properties to this control. If you didn't double-click the Format Painter button, the Format Painter turns itself off after copying the formatting properties to one control.

4. If you locked the Format Painter on by double-clicking its button, you can repeat step 3 as many times as you want. Click the Format Painter button again to turn off the Format Painter.

Typically, you use the Format Painter to quickly set the formatting properties for field text labels, or in any situation where selecting several controls by dragging a selection rectangle seems undesirable. By locking the Format Painter, it's easy to format several controls one after another.

Form Problems

When you can't add a new record to a form or subform that's bound to an Access query, the most likely cause of this problem is that the query you're using as the record source for the form or subform isn't updatable. Run the query and verify that the tentative append record appears after the last record with data. If the tentative append record is present in the datasheet and not in the form or subform, you might have accidentally set the Allow Additions property value to No.

If you ever run into a situation where the text boxes on your form are empty, the Next and Previous record navigation buttons are disabled, and the First and Last record buttons don't work, you accidentally set the Data Entry property value of the form to Yes. Setting the Data Entry property permits adding new records, but prevents the user from seeing existing records. Why the First and Last buttons are enabled is a mystery. This problem also occurs with subforms and often results from selecting the form instead of the subform when setting the Data Entry property value.

When no controls appear on your form in Form view, you've set the Allow Additions property to No, and accidentally set the Data Entry property value of the form to Yes. In this case, subforms don't appear on the form. There have been many requests by Access users and developers to display an error message when these mutually exclusive property values are specified. (New Access users have been known to panic after having spent several hours designing a form and then seeing their work disappear in Form view.) The problem also applies to subforms but isn't as dramatic.

Creating a Master/Child Form with the Form Wizard

An alternative to autogenerating a master/child form by clicking the Create ribbon's Form button is to use the Form Wizard to generate the master form and its child subform. The advantage to using the Form Wizard is that you can use the wizard to customize the form design and create a subform that you can further customize in the form Design view. You don't need to select a table or query prior to running the Form Wizard. However, forms created by the Form Wizard require much effort to create a layout that optimizes data entry efficiency.

To use the Form Wizard to create a frmEmployees form similar to frmHRActions, do the following:

1. Close frmHRActions if it's open, and click the Create tab to open the gallery. Click the Form Wizard button to launch the Form Wizard.

2. In the first wizard dialog, select the Employees table for the master form and click the >> button to add all fields. Select the BirthDate field and click < to remove it. Then do the same for the Photo field.

3. Select the HRActions table for the child subform, click the >> button to move all fields. Select the HRActions.EmployeeID field and click < to remove it. Do the same for New Rate and New Commission because Northwind doesn't have hourly employees or commissioned salespeople (see Figure 14.25).

4. Click Next and accept the default setting By Employees (as the way to view data) and the Form with Subform(s) option (see Figure 14.26). (You can add more than one subform in step 3.)

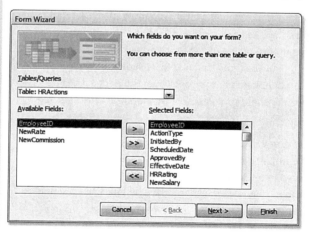

Figure 14.25
Select the tables to act as the record sources for the master and child forms and fields to display in the first Form Wizard dialog.

Figure 14.26
Specify Employees as the record source for the master form and use a subform (rather than a linked form) for the child form.

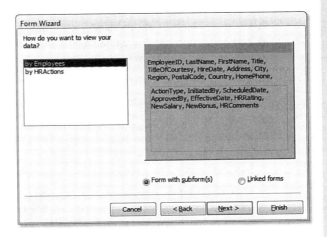

5. Click Next and select Tabular as the default layout for the subform. (You can change the layout Datasheet view later, if you want.)

6. Click Next and change the form name to **frmEmployees** and the subform name to **sbfHRActions**. Also, accept the option Open the Form to View or Enter Information (see Figure 14.27), and click Finish to generate the new master/child form.

Figure 14.27
The final Form Wizard dialog lets you name the master and child forms.

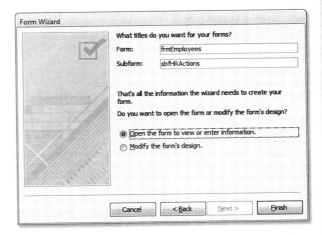

Figure 14.28 shows the initial master/child form in Form view. Four stacked control group columns contain the master form's label/text box control pairs. The form's layout obviously needs substantial modification, including regrouping the label and text box controls and making substantial changes to the tabular subform.

Refining the Wizard-Generated Form's Layout

The primary objective of this section is to emulate the layout of the master/child form you created early in the chapter, taking advantage of grouped controls where practical. Another goal is to demonstrate how to manipulate grouped control stacks.

To adjust the layout while minimizing the use of form Design view, do the following:

1. Change to the form Layout view, select the frmEmployees label, and reduce its height to about 0.5 inch.

2. Move the sbfHRActions subform and its label down about 2 inches to make room for three more label/text box pairs in the first column.

3. Click and drag the Region label and text box in the second column to the bottom of the first control stack. Do the same for the Postal Code and Country fields.

4. Shift+click to select all labels and text boxes in the left column and click the Stacked button of the Form Layout Tools—Arrange ribbon's Tables group to create a stacked control group.

5. Increase the width of the new stacked group's labels column to accommodate the longest line of text (Title of Courtesy).

 note

You can drag controls from one stacked control group to another stacked control group or a tabular control to another tabular control group. However, you can't drag a control from a stacked control group to a tabular control group, and vice versa. You can't drag an ungrouped control into another control group, but you can create a control group by selecting a single control and clicking the Stacked or Tabular button.

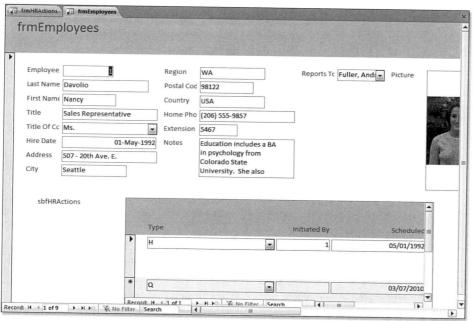

Figure 14.28
The Form Wizard creates the necessary Access objects, but the initial layout won't win any design awards.

6. Click and drag the Reports To field below the Notes field, and the Picture field below the Notes field. Shift+click to select all labels, text boxes, and picture in the right column and click the Stacked button to create a second stacked control group.

7. Scroll to the right and delete the six Picture.Fill labels and text boxes.

8. Drag the right edge of each group to the right to increase the label and text box width, then align the two stacked control groups to emulate the frmHRActions form. Optionally, drag the bottom up one grid notch to reduce the stacks' height (look ahead to Figure 14.29).

9. Replace the frmEmployees label text with **Northwind Human Resources Data Entry**.

10. Select and delete the sbfHRActions label, reposition the subform (see Figure 14.29), and save your changes.

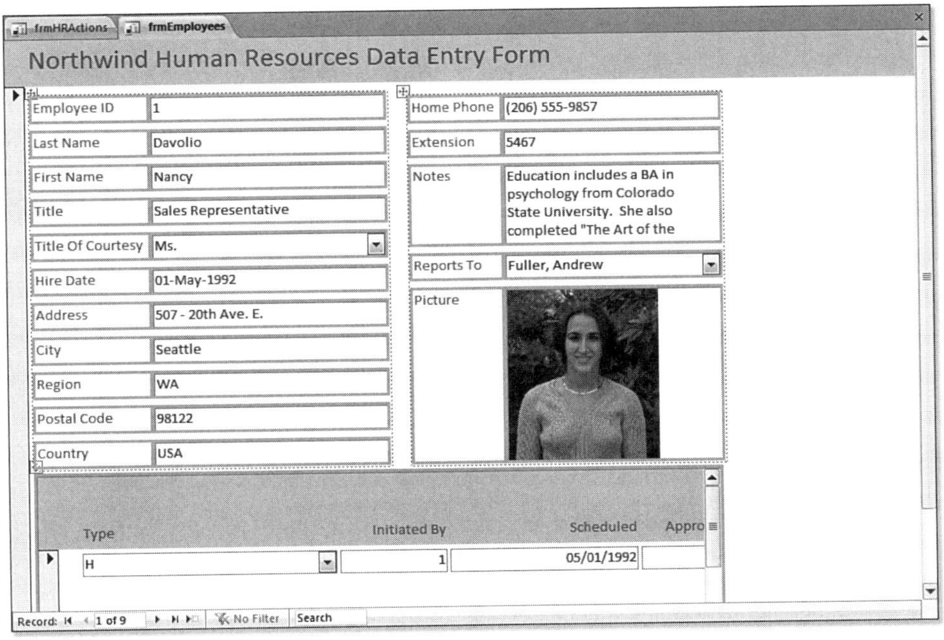

tip

Although you can use the in-situ subform-editing feature to alter the design of a subform, in most cases it's easier to use the traditional method of subform design modification. In-situ editing is better suited for changing subform property values than for altering subform dimensions.

Figure 14.29
The rearranged main form is now ready for subform redesign.

Setting Subform Properties

You can learn about modifying the properties of a subform by working with the subform that's used to create the history of prior HRActions for an employee. In this example, editing or deleting entries using the subform isn't allowed, but you can add new entries. The subform needs to be modified so that all its columns are readable without horizontal scrolling. When you complete the following steps, the sbfHRActions subform appears as shown in Figure 14.30.

tip

Click and drag controls vertically within the stacked control group to relocate them. You also can drag controls horizontally within a tabular control group.

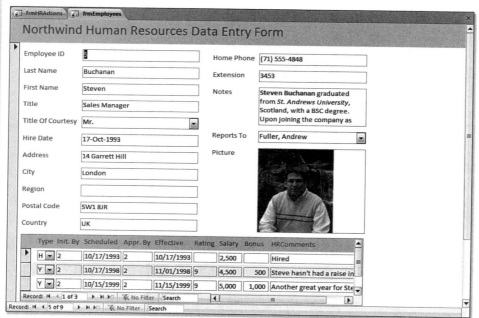

Figure 14.30
The sbfHRActions subform in the frmHRActions form appears as shown here after its field sizes and overall dimensions have been modified.

To change the properties of the sbfHRActions subform, follow these steps:

1. Open frmEmployees in Design view, right-click the sbfHRActions subform, and choose Subform in New Window from the context menu. Alternatively, click the Form Design Tools—Design tab, and click the Tools group's Subform in New Window button. The new subform window replaces the in-situ subform.

2. Open the Property Sheet, set the Height to 0.20 inch, and set Text Align to Left. Drag the Form Footer bar up to within one grid division of the Detail section's text boxes.

3. Click the Details bar to select the Details section and set the Alternate Back Color property value to Alternate Row.

tip

When you close a subform that's been opened in its own window, the in-situ subform disappears from Form Design view. To regain the in-situ version, click Form view and then Form Design view.

4. Close the Property Sheet and drag the mouse pointer over all the labels to select them, drag the group to the top of the form Header section, and then drag the Details bar to the bottom of the labels.

5. Press Ctrl+A to select all controls and click the Tabular button to create a Tabular control group. Creating the control group lets you change the widths of labels and text boxes simultaneously.

> **tip**
>
> As you make changes to the subform, press Ctrl+S to save them. It's frustrating to spend several minutes adjusting the positions and formatting of fields, and then lose your changes by an inadvertent error.

6. Change to Layout view, select each column in sequence, abbreviate the field name, and adjust the widths of the columns (except the Comments column) to accommodate their data. Set the format of the Salary and Bonus fields to Currency with 0 decimal places (see Figure 14.31).

Figure 14.31
Choosing New Window from the context menu opens the subform in a separate window. Change the field names and adjust the widths of the subform's labels and fields as shown here.

Type	Init. By	Scheduled	Appr. By	Effective	Rating	Salary	Bonus	HRComments
H	1	05/01/1992	1	05/01/1992		2,000		Hired
H	1	08/14/1992	1	08/14/1992		3,500		Hired
H	1	05/03/1993	1	05/03/1993		2,250		Hired
H	2	05/03/1993	2	05/03/1993		2,250		Hired
H	2	10/17/1993	2	10/17/1993		2,500		Hired
Y	2	10/17/1998	2	11/01/1998	9	4,500	500	Steve hasn't had a raise in five years
Y	2	10/15/1999	2	11/15/1999	9	5,000	1,000	Another great year for Steve
H	5	10/17/1993	2	10/17/1993		4,000		Hired
H	5	01/02/1994	2	01/02/1994		3,000		Hired
H	2	05/05/1994	2	05/05/1994		2,500		Hired
H	5	11/15/1994	2	11/15/1994		3,000		Hired
Q		03/08/2010		04/05/2010				

Record: 1 of 11   No Filter   Search

7. Return to the form Design view, and drag the right edge of the form to the left until the form is slightly wider than the fields (about 7 ½ inches). Then drag the form Footer section upward so that the Detail section is about ⅝ inches high.

8. With the subform window active, open the Property Sheet, select Form in the selection type list, and click the Data tab.

> **note**
>
> You can set the Data Entry property to Yes to achieve a result that is similar to setting the Allow Edits and Allow Deletions property to No and the Allow Additions property to Yes. When you set the Data Entry property to Yes, however, only the tentative new record appears—no previous entries appear in the subform.

9. Set the Allow Edits and Allow Deletions property values to No (to prevent modifying previous actions) and set Allow Additions to Yes.

10. Save your changes, close the sbfHRActions subform, and close and reopen the frmEmployees form in Design view.

11. Save your changes and then close and reopen the frmEmployees form in Form view. Your form appears as shown in earlier Figure 14.30.

 tip

You must close and reopen the main form to make changes you apply to a subform in the window appear in Form view. The form embeds a copy of the subform; the embedded copy doesn't change until you close and reopen the form.

 Subform Problems

If the subform you added to the main form doesn't change its data when you move the main form's record pointer with the navigation buttons, you didn't create the required link between the main form and the subform in the Data page of the main form's Properties window, or the link is broken as the result of changing a table or query name.

Select the subform container of the main form (not the subform itself) by clicking the edge of the subform in the form Design view, open the Properties window, and click the Data tab. Click the Builder button to open the Subform Field Linker dialog, and add or correct the field names of the linked tables or queries.

Using HTML to Format Memo Data as Rich Text

 note

The meaning of "Rich Text" format in this context isn't the same as that of Microsoft's Rich Text Format (*.rtf) files, which use formatting tags that differ from HTML.

Access 2007 introduced the Text Format property to enable use of HTML tags to format Memo field content as Rich Text. If you examine the Notes field of Figure 14.30, you can see that "Steven Buchanan" is in boldface (as the result of enclosing the text between a `<strong>...</strong>` tag pair) and "St. Andrews University" is italic (because of `<i>...</i>` tags).

Enabling HTML formatting of a table's Memo field requires changing the field's Text Format property value from Plain Text to Rich Text, which opens the message shown in Figure 14.32.

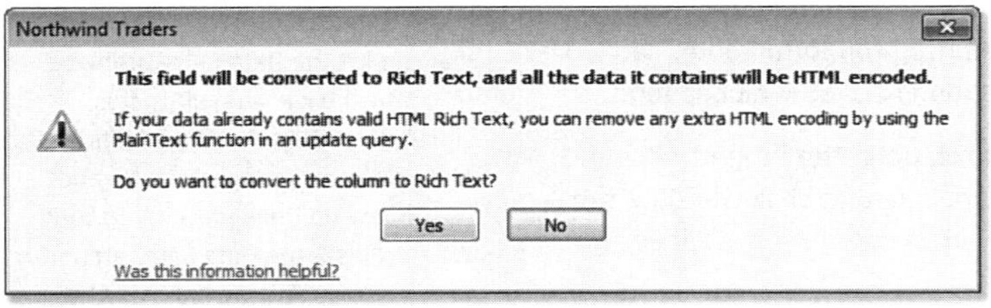

Northwind Traders

⚠ **This field will be converted to Rich Text, and all the data it contains will be HTML encoded.**

If your data already contains valid HTML Rich Text, you can remove any extra HTML encoding by using the PlainText function in an update query.

Do you want to convert the column to Rich Text?

[Yes]   [No]

Was this information helpful?

Figure 14.32
You receive this message when changing a Memo field's Text Format property from Plain Text to Rich Text and a similar message when reverting to Plain Text.

If other objects bind to the field, you might receive a message asking if you want to change the bound controls Text Format property to Rich Text. If you don't make this change on the Data page of their properties sheet, text boxes will display the HTML tags instead of the desired formatting.

Generating Multiple Items and Split Forms

Selecting a table or query and clicking the Multiple Items choice of the More Forms gallery in the Create Ribbon's Forms group generates a Datasheet-style tabular list of all table fields and records or query columns and rows. This form style is very similar to that which the Form Wizard creates for subforms if you choose the Datasheet instead of the Tabular style with the Default AutoFormat. The primary differences are in the Header section: the addition of a logo and minor changes to the column header format. Figure 14.33 shows a multiple-items form generated from the HRActions table.

 tip

You can use the Multiple Items button to create a Datasheet-style form for a subform with a style similar to the default main form, but using the Form Wizard to do this is faster and offers more flexibility.

Chapter 2, "Building Simple Tracking Applications," introduced you to the split form design, which you create by choosing Split Form instead of Continuous Form. A split form lets you display multiple records in Datasheet format above the split. You also can type data for the selected record in the text boxes of a panel below the split. The idea behind the split form is the ability to quickly select the record of interest from a large number of records in the Datasheet and edit the record more efficiently in stacked text boxes. A vertically adjustable splitter bar divides the main form with stacked text boxes and an Attachment control from the lower datasheet section (see Figure 14.34).

Figure 14.33
The HRActions multiple-items form appears as shown here after the column widths and row height have been adjusted.

HRActions

ID	Type	Initiated By	Scheduled	Approved By	Effective	HRRating	Salary	Rate	Bonus	% Comm	HRComment
1	H	1	05/01/1992	1	05/01/1992		2,000				Hired
2	H	1	08/14/1992	1	08/14/1992		3,500				Hired
3	H	1	05/03/1993	1	05/03/1993		2,250				Hired
4	H	2	05/03/1993	2	05/03/1993		2,250				Hired
5	H	2	10/17/1993	2	10/17/1993		2,500				Hired
5	Y	2	10/17/1998	2	11/01/1998	9	4,500		500.00		Steve hasn't
5	Y	2	10/15/1999	2	11/15/1999	9	5,000		1,000.00		Another gre
6	H	5	10/17/1993	2	10/17/1993		4,000				Hired
7	H	5	01/02/1994	2	01/02/1994		3,000				Hired
8	H	2	05/05/1994	2	05/05/1994		2,500				Hired
9	H	5	11/15/1994	2	11/15/1994		3,000				Hired
*	Q		03/08/2010		04/05/2010						

Record: ◄ ◄ 1 of 11 ► ►► ►* No Filter Search

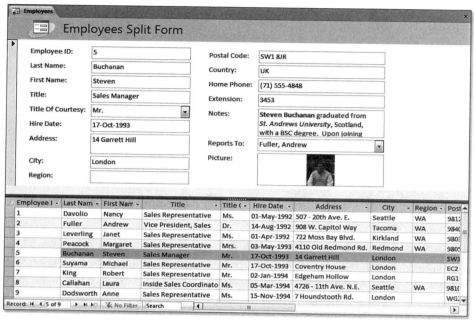

Using Transaction-Processing Forms

As noted near the beginning of this chapter, the purpose of transaction-processing forms is to add new records to, delete records from, or edit data in one or more tables that underlie the form. The sections that follow describe how to add new records to the HRActions table with the frmHRActions form.

Forms you create with the Create ribbon's Form button and the Form Wizard use the standard record-navigation buttons located at the bottom of the form. The record-navigation buttons perform the same functions with forms as they do with tables and queries. You can select the first or last records in the table or query that is the source of data for your main form, or you can select the next or previous record. Subforms include their own set of record-selection buttons that operate independently of the set for the main form.

Navigation between the text boxes used for entering or editing data in the form is similar to navigation in queries and tables in Datasheet view, except that the up-arrow and down-arrow keys cause the cursor to move between fields rather than between records. Accept the values you've entered by pressing Enter or Tab.

Appending New Records to the HRActions Table

 In Datasheet view of a table or query, the last record in the datasheet is provided as a tentative append record (indicated by an asterisk on the record-selection button). If you enter data in this record, the data automatically is appended to the table, and Access starts a new tentative append record. Forms also provide a tentative append record, unless you set the Allow Additions property value for the form to No.

The following comments apply to adding HRAction records with the frmEmployees form:

 note

If you didn't create the frmHRActions form in the preceding sections of this chapter, the forms, subforms, and Employees and HRActions objects are included in the Forms14.accdb database in the downloadable sample files' \Access2010\Chaptr14 folder.

- Because data from the Employees table is included in the main form, the ID number, name, and title of the employee appear in the text boxes on the main form. Your form design lets you edit the LastName, FirstName, and Title data, although these fields are incorporated in the table (Employees) on the one side of a one-to-many relationship. The editing capability of a form is the same as that for the underlying table or query that serves as its source unless you change the form's editing capabilities by setting the form's Allow Editing property and other related properties.

tip

When experimenting with adding records to the HRActions table, temporarily set the subform's Allow Edits and Allow Deletions property values to Yes.

- After you add a new record to the HRActions table, you can't delete or edit it, because the Allow Edits and Allow Deletions property values are set to No.

- If you added an entry for the chosen employee ID when you created the HRActions table in Chapter 5, "Working with Access Databases and Tables," the entry appears in the subform's fields. The subform's data display is linked to the data in the main form through the one-to-many relationship between the Employees table and the HRActions table. The subform displays only records from the HRActions table whose EmployeeID fields match the value of the EmployeeID field of the record currently displayed by the main form.

To append a new record to the HRActions table and enter the required data, follow these steps:

1. Open the frmEmployees form if it isn't already open, or click the Form View button if you're in Design view. Data for the first record of the Employees table—with the matching data from the corresponding record(s) in the HRActions table—appears in the text-box controls of your form.

2. Access places the cursor in the first text box of the main form, the ID text box. The first example uses Nancy Davolio, whose employee ID is 1.

3. Click in the Type field of the tentative append record in the subform. If the tentative append record in the subform isn't visible, click the New Record button of the subform's navigation control to move to the tentative append record at the end of the existing HRActions table entries for Steven Buchanan.

4. Type a valid HRAction type (**H**, **Q**, **Y**, **S**, **R**, **B**, **C**, or **T** because of the field's validation rule) in the Type text box. (If you added the lookup list to the Action field, you can select the type code from the list.) Default date values appear in the Scheduled and Effective date fields. In this example, you bring Steven Buchanan's HRActions records up to date for 1998 by adding yearly performance review information. Type **Y** and then press Tab or Enter to accept the default Type value and move the cursor to the next data-entry text box, Initiated By.

5. Mr. Buchanan reports to the vice president of sales, Andrew Fuller, whose employee ID is 2. Type **2** in the Initiated By text box and press Enter.

6. Mr. Buchanan was hired on 10/17/1993, but Northwind Traders had no Human Resources (HR) department to maintain HR data until mid-1998, so type **10/17/1998** in the Scheduled field if you didn't add this entry earlier. If there is a 10/17/1998 entry, type **10/17/1999**.

7. Because Mr. Fuller is a vice president, he has the authority to approve salary increases. Type Mr. Fuller's employee ID, **2**, in the Approved By text box and then press Enter to move the cursor to the next field.

8. The effective date for salary adjustments for Northwind Traders is the 1st or 15th day of the month in which the performance review is scheduled. Type the appropriate date in the Effective text box.

9. You can type any number from **0** (terminated) to **9** (excellent) in the Rating text box, which reflects the employee's performance.

10. You can be as generous as you want with the salary and bonus that you enter in the Salary and Bonus text boxes. The value of the Salary field is a new monthly salary, not an incremental value.

11. In the Comments multiline text box to the right of the New Amount field, add any comments you care to make concerning how generous or stingy you were with this salary increase. The multiline text box includes a scrollbar that appears when the cursor is within the text box, but the text box shows only one line.

12. When you complete your entries, Access stores them in a memory buffer but doesn't add the new record to the HRActions table. You can add the record to the table by clicking the New Record button or changing the position of the record pointer with the Previous or Next record selector button. If you want to cancel the addition of a record, press Esc twice.

13. Repeat steps 3 through 12 to add a few additional records.

> **tip**
>
> If you click the Next Record selector button to select the tentative append record, and then decide that you don't want to add any more data, click the Previous Record button to make sure this new record isn't added to the table. If the table has required fields without default values, however, you must enter a value for each required field, and then delete the added record. Deleting records requires setting the subform's Allow Deletions property value to Yes.

When you add a record, your form appears like the one shown in Figure 14.35. Each record for an employee appears in the subform datasheet in the order of the primary key fields of the HRActions table.

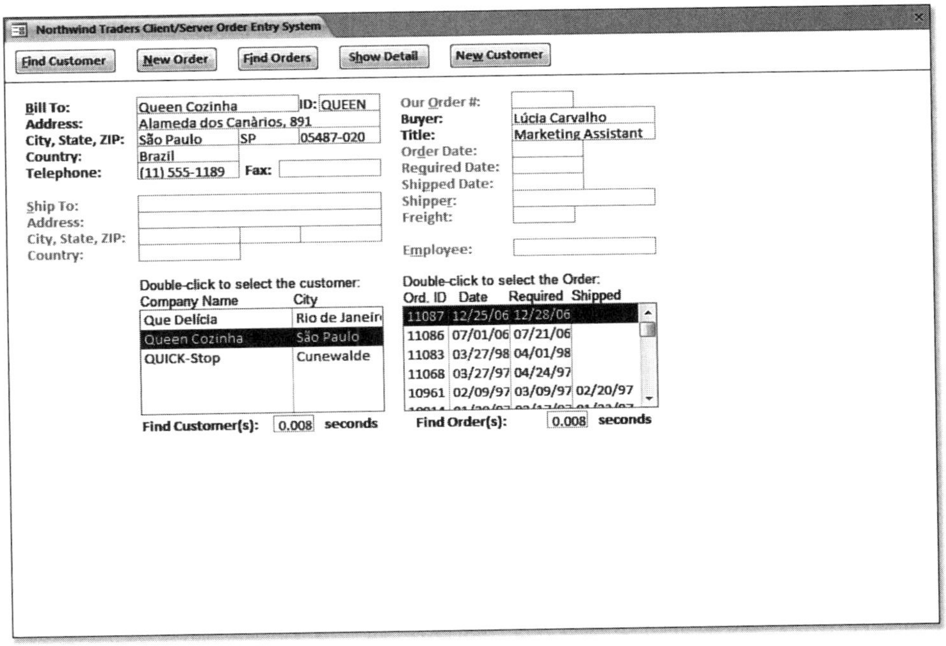

Figure 14.35 The frmEmployees form appears as shown here after a new subform record has been appended for an employee.

Modifying the Properties of a Form or Control After Testing

The entries you added and edited gave you an opportunity to test your form. Testing a form to ensure that it accomplishes the objectives you have in mind usually takes much longer than creating the form and the query that underlies it. During the testing process, you might notice that the order of the fields isn't what you want or that records in the subform aren't displayed in an appropriate sequence. The following two sections deal with modifying the properties of the form and subform control.

> **note**
>
> The pencil symbol, which indicates that you're editing a record, replaces the triangle at the top of the Record Selector bar to the left of the record that you are entering. The Description property you entered for the field in the table underlying this query appears in the status bar and changes as you move the cursor to the next field. (To change a previous entry, press Shift+Tab, or use the up- and down-arrow keys to maneuver to whichever text box contains a value you want to change.)

Removing Fields from the Tab Order

Access lets you set the value of the Tab Stop property to No to prevent controls from receiving the focus in the tab order. To remove a control from the tab order, select the control, open the Properties window, select Other, and change the value of the Tab Stop property to No. You can't edit the EmployeeID field, so set the Tab Stop property to No for this control.

Disabling Editing of Specific Controls

It's a common practice to disable controls that users can't or shouldn't edit. For example, the Employee ID text box is read-only because it's bound to an AutoNumber EmployeeID field. It's tempting to disable this field by setting its Enabled property value to No, but doing this grays the label and text box text, and displays an unattractive text box background color. Therefore, the better choice, along with removing disabled controls from the tab order, is to set the control's Locked property value to Yes. When the user opens the form, focus is on the next control in the tab order.

15

DESIGNING CUSTOM MULTITABLE FORMS

This chapter emphasizes use of Form Design mode and shows you how to get the most out of those form controls that aren't covered in other chapters. Chapter 18, "Adding Graphs, PivotCharts, and PivotTables" covers the Chart control, as well as PivotChart and PivotTable forms. The "Opening Forms from the Navigation Pane and Adding Records" section of Chapter 2, "Building Simple Tracking Applications," describes how to use the Attachments dialog to add images to Attachment fields.

When you work in form Layout view, the primary subject of the preceding chapter, you can customize the design of forms that you autogenerate with the Create ribbon's Form, Split Form, or Multiple Items button, or with the Form Wizard. Layout view limits the types of controls that you can add to a form to text boxes, combo boxes, attachments, check boxes, and subforms. These controls must be bound to table fields or query columns and have an attached label. You can add new controls only by dragging them from the Field List dialog or by clicking the Logo, Title, or Date & Time button. The benefit you gain from this abridgement of your form design freedom by Layout view is the ability to relocate and resize controls with live data visible.

 note

The form-design techniques you learn in this chapter also apply to Access data projects (ADP). ADP forms are identical to conventional Access forms, except that the forms and controls bind to objects in SQL Server 2005 or later databases—not Access databases.

Form Design mode, on the other hand, offers virtually unbridled freedom to add any of Access's 20 native control types or hundreds—perhaps thousands—of Access-compatible ActiveX controls to the form. (The term *native controls* means those that Access 2010 provides in its Form Design Tool—Design contextual ribbon.) Several native controls have associated wizards to guide you in their usage. You aren't restricted to adding controls bound to table fields or query columns; unbound controls can supply values to VBA code or Access macros.

Getting Acquainted with Form Design View's Contextual Ribbons

Form Design view replaces Layout view's Form Layout Tools—Format ribbon with the Form Design Tools—Design ribbon, and it replaces Form Layout Tools—Arrange with the identical Form Design Tools—Arrange ribbon, which has an additional Remove Layout button in the Tables group and an added Sizing & Ordering group. The following two sections include tables that describe all the buttons of both ribbons for completeness.

The Form Design Tools—Design Ribbon

The Design contextual ribbon has control button groups for specifying the view, adding native Access controls, setting control properties, opening Field List and Property Sheet dialogs, opening the VBA code editor, and opening a subform in a new window (see Figure 15.1).

Figure 15.1
The Form Design Tools—Design contextual ribbon includes buttons to add 23 Access native controls, as well as Logo, Title, and Time and Date elements, to forms.

Table 15.1 lists the icon, name, KeyTips, and a brief description of each command button of the Form Design Tools—Design ribbon. The keyboard shortcut to display KeyTips for the 23 native controls in the Control gallery is Alt+JD, C.

Table 15.1 Icons, Command Buttons, KeyTip Shortcuts, and Command Button Actions for the Form Design Tools—Design Contextual Ribbon

Icon	Command Button	Shortcut Alt+JD,	Command Action
		Views Group, W+	
	Form View	F	Displays selected form in Form view
	Layout View	Y	Displays selected form in Layout view
	Design View	D	Displays selected form in Design view
		Themes Group, T+	
	Themes	H	Opens a gallery of 40 predefined Office Themes, as well as In This Database and Custom buttons
	Colors	C	Opens a gallery of one Custom and 40 built-in color schemes of 10 Theme Colors each
	Fonts	F	Opens a gallery of one custom and 40 pairs of built-in Theme Fonts
		Controls Group, C+	
	Select	S	Selects an object
	Text Box	T	Enables drawing a text box with an associated label on the form
	Label	L	Enables drawing a standalone label on the form
	Button	B	Enables drawing a control button on the form and starts the Command Button Wizard*
	Tab Control	R	Enables drawing a tabbed container for other controls on a form
	Hyperlink	I	Opens the Insert Hyperlink dialog to add a button that opens an existing file or web page, a database object, or Outlook to author an email to the recipient
	Web Browser Control	W	Displays web content and enables Web 2.0-style mash-ups
	Navigation Control	V	Adds tab-based form or report navigation in a subform control with one of six built-in layouts
	Combo Box	C	Enables drawing a combo box on the form and starts the Combo Box Wizard*

Table 15.1   Continued

Icon	Command Button	Shortcut Alt+JD,	Command Action
	List Box	I	Enables drawing a list box on the form and starts the List Box Wizard*
	Subform/ Subreport	F	Enables drawing a subform on the form and starts the Subform Wizard*
	Line	L	Enables drawing a line on the form
	Rectangle	C, E	Enables drawing a rectangular box on the form
	Bound Object Frame	C, D	Enables drawing a rectangle to dis play the contents of an OLE Object field on the form (obsolescent, use an Attachment control)Option GroupOEnables drawing a container for option buttons, check boxes, com mand buttons, or toggle buttons on the form and starts the Option Group Wizard*
	Check Box	K	Enables drawing a check box on the form to represent Boolean (Yes/No) values
	Option Button	U	Enables drawing an option button on the form to repre-sent Boolean (Yes/No) values
	Toggle Button	CT	Enables drawing a button that changes from a Yes to No to Yes value when clicked repeatedly
	Chart	C	Enables drawing a rectangle to hold a graph or chart and starts the Chart Wizard (see Chapter 18)
	Unbound Object Frame	D	Enables drawing a rectangle to display a static OLE Object (obsolescent, use an Image control)
	Image	M	Enables drawing a rectangle to display a static image from a variety of bitmap and vector image files
	Insert or Remove Page Break	P	Toggles a page break in a form section (for printing)
	Attachment	A	Opens the Attachments dialog to add, modify, or delete a MIME attachment
	Use Control Wizards	W	Specifies using wizards to design command buttons, combo boxes, list boxes, option groups, subforms, and charts
	ActiveX Control	O	Opens the Insert ActiveX Control dialog, which lets you select any ActiveX control registered on the local com-puter

Table 15.1   Continued

Icon	Command Button	Shortcut Alt+JD,	Command Action
			Header/Footer Group
	Logo	L	Opens an Insert Picture dialog to select a graphic for a Image control in the form's Header section
	Title	T	Inserts a Title label in the form's Header section
	Date and Time	D	Opens a Date and Time dialog to insert a date or time value, or both, in the form's Header section
			Tools Group
	Add Existing Fields	X	Opens the Field List dialog from which to drag additional master and child fields to the form
	Property Sheet	H, P	Opens the Property Sheet dialog for the selected form, section, or control
	Tab Order	A, T	Opens the Tab Order dialog to set the sequence in which controls gain the focus
	View Code	V, 1	Opens the VBA Editor
	Convert Form's Macros to Visual Basic	V, 2	Opens the Convert from Macros: *FormName* dialog

*Wizards start only if the Use Control Wizards toggle button is active.

To add a control to the form, click to set the command button for the control you want, place the mouse cursor in the section and at the location where you want the upper-left corner of the control, press the left mouse button, and draw a rectangle to specify the control's size. When you release the mouse button, the control materializes or a wizard starts, depending on the control type and the state of the Use Control Wizards toggle button.

 note

2010 NEW Access 2010 introduces the Web Browser and Navigation controls.

Control Categories

Three control object categories apply to Access forms and reports:

- *Bound controls* are associated with a field in the data source for the form or subform. *Binding a control* means connecting the control to a data source, such as a field of a table or a column of a query that supplies the current value to or accepts an updated value from a control. Bound controls display and update values of the data cell in the associated field of the currently selected record. Text boxes are the most common bound control. You can display the content of graphic objects or play audio files embedded in a table with a bound OLE object. You can bind toggle buttons and check boxes to Yes/No fields. Option button groups bind to fields with numeric values. All bound controls have associated labels that display the Caption property of the field; you can edit or delete these labels without affecting the bound control.

- *Unbound controls* display data you provide that is independent of the form's or subform's data source. You use the image or unbound OLE object control to add a drawing or bitmapped image to a form. You can use lines and rectangles to divide a form into logical groups or simulate boxes used on the paper form. Unbound text boxes are used to enter data that isn't intended to update a field in the data source but is intended for other purposes, such as establishing a value used in an expression. Some unbound controls, such as unbound text boxes, include labels; others, such as unbound OLE objects, don't have labels. Labels also are unbound controls.

- *Calculated controls* use expressions as their source of data. Usually, the data source expression includes the value of a field, but you also can use values created by unbound text boxes in calculated control expressions.

The Form Design Tools—Arrange Ribbon

The Form Design Tools—Arrange contextual ribbon's Table, Rows & Columns, Merge/Split, Move and Position groups are the same as those of the Form Layout Tools—Arrange ribbon (see Figure 14.2 of Chapter 14, "Creating and Using Basic Access Forms"), except as follows:

- The Table ribbon gains a Remove Layout button to delete a layout, if one is applied to the form. The Gridlines button is enabled only when you select a datasheet.

- The Rows & Columns Merge/Split and Move groups' buttons are disabled because these buttons apply only to controls in layouts.

- The added Sizing & Ordering group's Size/Space, Align, Bring to Front and Send to Back buttons format controls you add in Design view.

Figure 15.2 shows the Form Design Tools—Arrange ribbon in Design view with a text box control selected.

> **note**
>
> You must select at least one control to enable most control buttons except Snap to Grid and Tab Order. You must select two or more controls to enable the Align button.

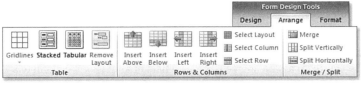

Figure 15.2
The Form Design Tools—Arrange contextual ribbon has sets of command buttons that are similar to the Form Layout Tools—Arrange ribbon.

Table 15.2 lists the icon, name, KeyTips, and a brief description of each command button added to the Form Design Tools—Arrange ribbon. The keyboard shortcut to display KeyTips is Alt+J, A, which is the same as that for the Form Layout Tools—Arrange ribbon.

Table 15.2   Icons, Command Buttons, KeyTip Shortcuts, and Command Button Actions for the Form Design Tools—Arrange Contextual Ribbon

Icon	Command Button	Shortcut Alt+J, A +	Command Action
		Table Group	
	Remove Layout	N	Removes the selected layout from the form
		Sizing and Ordering	
	Size/Space	S, S	Opens a gallery of command buttons in grouped by Size, Spacing, Grid and Grouping functions
	Align	S, A	Opens a gallery of To Grid, Left, Right, Top and Bottom control alignment buttons
	Bring to Front	I	Sets the Z-order of the control in front of other controls
	Send to Back	K	Sets the Z-order of the control in front of other controls

➡ *To review how to set the tab order,* **see** *"Removing Fields from the Tab Order,"* **p. 605.**

Working in Form Design View

◻ It's a common practice to start with a blank form in design mode, but you'll probably find it more efficient to start with one of the Create ribbon's three default forms. Figure 15.3 is an abbreviated version of the HRActions form that you created in Chapter 14, which is open in Form Design view. Clicking the form context menu's Page Header/Footer choice adds Page Header and Footer sections, which only appear when you print the form.

Selecting Form Elements and Controls

The following list describes how to select and display the properties of form sections and control objects:

- **Entire form**—To select the entire form, which includes all the following elements, click the Select Form button. The Property Sheet displays properties that apply to the form as a whole.

- **Header section only**—To select a Header section, click the Form Header or Page Header bar. The Property Sheet has items for the Form Header or Page Header section only.

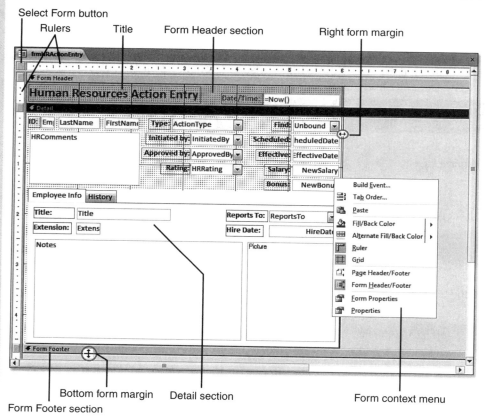

Select Form button
Rulers   Title   Form Header section   Right form margin

Bottom form margin   Detail section   Form context menu
Form Footer section

Figure 15.3
A form and tabbed sub-form in Design view with Page Header and Page Footer sections added and the form context menu activated (multiple exposure).

- **Detail section only**—To select the Detail section, click the Detail bar. The properties are similar to those of the Form Header section, but all apply to the Detail section.

- **Footer section only**—To select a Footer section, click the Form Footer or Page Footer bar. A set of properties identical to the header properties is available for the footer sections. A Form Footer appears only if a Form Header has been added. The same applies to Page Headers and Footers, which appear only when you print the form.

- **Control object (or both elements of a control with an associated label)**—Click the surface of the control to select the control. A thick orange border with a solid square anchor handle at the upper-left corner identifies a selected individual control. If the control has a grouped label, the control/label pair replaces the solid anchor handles with a handle that contains a cross-cursor symbol. Each control type has its own set of properties.

Changing the Size of the Form and Its Sections

 You can change the height of a form section by dragging the Form Header, Page Header, Detail, Page Footer, or Form Footer bar vertically with the mouse. When you position the mouse pointer at the top edge of a section divider bar, it turns into a line with two vertical arrows (refer to Figure 15.3). You drag the pointer with the mouse to adjust the size of the section above the mouse pointer.

The height of the Detail section is determined by the vertical size of the window in which the form is displayed, less the combined heights of all header and footer sections. When you move the vertical scrollbar, only the Detail section scrolls.

Selecting, Moving, and Sizing a Single Control or Label/Control Pair

When you select a single control object by clicking its surface, the control is enclosed by an orange rectangle with an anchor rectangle at its upper-left corner and seven smaller, rectangular sizing handles (see Figure 15.4). This section's examples use text boxes, but the techniques you learn apply to most other controls except the Line, Insert Page, and Page Break controls. Some controls, such as Button, Toggle Button, Hyperlink, and Tab controls, don't have associated labels.

Selecting and deselecting controls is a toggling process. *Toggling* means repeating an action with the effect of alternating between On and Off conditions. The Property Sheet, for example, appears and disappears if you repeatedly click the Form Design Tools—Design ribbon's Property Sheet button.

The following choices are available for moving or changing the size of a control object (the numbers correspond to the numbers in Figure 15.4):

1. *To select a control* (and activate or select its associated or grouped label, if any), click anywhere on its surface.

2. *To move the control* (and its associated label, if any) to a new position, click to select the control. If the control has an associated label, press Shift and click the label to select it. Press and hold down the left mouse button while dragging either control anchor to the new location for the control(s). If the control has a grouped label, drag the grouped control anchor to the new location. An outline of the control indicates its position as you move the mouse. When the control is where you want it to be, release the mouse button to drop the control in its new position.

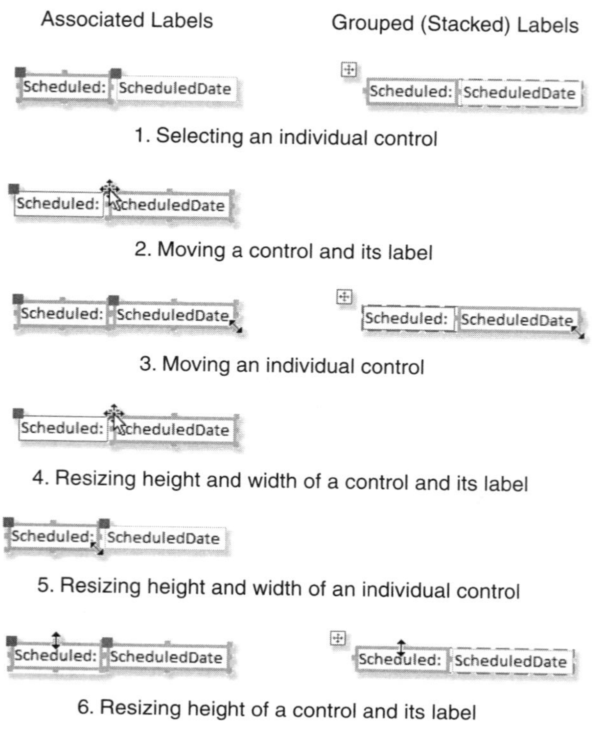

Associated Labels   Grouped (Stacked) Labels

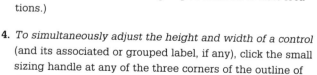

1. Selecting an individual control

2. Moving a control and its label

3. Moving an individual control

4. Resizing height and width of a control and its label

5. Resizing height and width of an individual control

6. Resizing height of a control and its label

Figure 15.4
The appearance of selection or sizing handles and the mouse pointer depend on the moving or sizing operation in progress and whether the control is associated or grouped with another control. A missing example in the Grouped Label column indicates that the operation isn't supported.

3. *To separately move the elements of a control that has an associated label,* position the mouse pointer on the anchor handle in the upper-left corner of the control that you want to move. Click and drag the individual element to its new position and then release the mouse button. (You can't drag individual elements of grouped controls to new locations.)

4. *To simultaneously adjust the height and width of a control* (and its associated or grouped label, if any), click the small sizing handle at any of the three corners of the outline of the selected control(s) or the corners of a grouped control pair. The mouse pointer becomes a diagonal two-headed arrow. Click and drag this arrow to a new position and then release the mouse button.

5. *To simultaneously adjust the height and width of an individual control,* click and drag one of the three corner sizing handles. (You can't resize individual elements of grouped controls.)

> **tip**
> You can use the arrow keys to move the selected control(s) to a new location in default increments of 1/24 inch. When using the arrow keys to move a control with an associated label, you don't need to select the label to move the pair in unison.

6. *To adjust only the height or width of the control,* click the sizing handle on one of the horizontal or vertical surfaces of the outline or the center of the control for a grouped control pair. The mouse pointer becomes a vertical or horizontal two-headed arrow. Click and drag this arrow to a new position and then release the mouse button.

 tip

If you have trouble selecting a small control, such as a thin line (particularly one that is adjacent to a section bar), you can select the control from the drop-down list at the top of the Property Sheet.

Aligning Controls to the Grid

The Form Design window includes a grid that consists of one-pixel dots with a default spacing of 24 to the inch both horizontally and vertically. When the grid is visible, you can use the grid dots to assist in maintaining the horizontal and vertical alignment of rows and columns of controls. Even if the grid isn't visible, you can cause controls to "snap to the grid" by clicking the Form Design Tools—Arrange ribbon's Snap to Grid button in the Size/Space group's gallery. This command is a toggle, and when Snap to Grid is active, the button is activated. Whenever you move a control while Snap to Grid is activated, the upper-left corner of the object jumps to the closest grid dot.

 tip

If Snap to Grid is on and you want to locate or size a control without reference to the grid, press and hold the Ctrl key while you move or resize the control.

You can cause the size of control objects to conform to grid spacing by right-clicking the control and choosing To Grid in the Size/Space group's gallery. You also can make the size of the control fit its content by choosing To Fit.

Toggling the Form Design Tools—Arrange ribbon's Grid command button (refer to Figure 15.3's Form Context Menu) controls the visibility of the grid; by default, the grid is hidden for all new forms. If the grid spacing is set to more than 24 per inch or 10 per centimeter, the dots aren't visible. For "nonmetrified" users, better values are 16 per inch for Grid X and 12 per inch for Grid Y. To change the grid spacing for a form, follow these steps:

1. Click the Form Select button or press Ctrl+R to select the entire form.

2. Click the toolbar's Properties button to open the Property Sheet.

3. Click the Format tab, and then scroll through the list until the Grid X and Grid Y properties are visible.

4. Change the value of Grid X and Grid Y to 16 dots if you want controls to align with inch ruler ticks. Metrified users are likely to prefer a value of 10 or 20 for Grid X and Grid Y.

Selecting and Moving Multiple Controls

You can select and move several objects at a time by using one of the following methods:

- *Enclose the objects with a selection rectangle.* Begin by clicking the surface of the form outside the outline of a control object. Press and hold down the mouse button while dragging the mouse pointer to create an enclosing rectangle that includes each of the objects you want to select (see Figure 15.5, top left). Release the mouse button to select the objects. You can now move the selected objects (see Figure 15.5, top right) by clicking and dragging the anchor handle of any one of them.

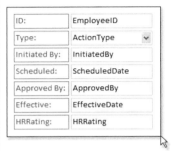

Controls selected by enclosing

Selected controls

Figure 15.5
Selecting a group of objects by dragging a selection rectangle (top left) or holding the Shift key down and clicking to select the individual controls (top right). You can group the controls so they act in unison (bottom left), or add them to a control stack.

Grouped controls

Stacked controls

- *Click to select one object; then hold down the Shift key while you click to select the next object.* You can repeat this step as many times as necessary to select all the objects you want (see Figure 15.5, top right).

- *To remove a selected object from a group,* hold down the Shift key and click the object with the mouse to deselect it. To deselect an entire group, click any inactive area of the form. An inactive area is an area outside the outline of a control.

- *To create a tabular layout group of the multiselected objects,* click the Form Design Tools—Arrange ribbon's Tabular command button. A tabular layout encloses the objects. Click the Remove Layout button to remove the

 note

The selection rectangle selects a control if any part of the control is included within the rectangle. This behavior is unlike many drawing applications in which the entire object must be enclosed to be selected. You can change the behavior of Access's selection rectangle to require full enclosure of the object by clicking the File tab, opening the Access Options dialog, selecting the Object Designers page, and changing the value of the Selection Behavior option from Partially Enclosed to Fully Enclosed.

layout attribute from the enclosed objects. Alternatively, right-click the group and choose Layout, Tabular or Layout, Remove Layout.

- *To create a control stack from multiselected objects,* click the Form Design Tools—Arrange ribbon's Stacked command button. To remove a control from the stack, select it and click the ribbon's Remove button. Alternatively, right-click the group and choose Layout, Stacked or Layout, Remove Layout.

If you select or deselect a control with an associated label, the label is selected or deselected along with the control. You can change some property values—such as the font size or family and the foreground or background color—of all multiple-selected controls.

Aligning a Group of Controls

You can align selected individual controls, or groups of controls, to the grid or each other by completing the following actions in Form Design view:

- To fine-adjust the position of a control by the width of a single pixel, select the control and press Ctrl+arrow key.

- To align a selected control (or group of controls) to the grid, right-click the group and choose Align, To Grid from the context menu.

- To adjust the positions of controls within a selected columnar group so that their left edges fall into vertical alignment with the leftmost control, choose Align, Left from the context menu.

- To adjust the positions of controls within a selected columnar group so that their right edges fall into vertical alignment with the right edge of the rightmost control, choose Align, Right from the context menu.

- To align rows of controls at their top edges, choose Align, Top from the context menu.

- To align rows of controls at their bottom edges, choose Align, Bottom from the context menu.

Your forms have a more professional appearance if you take the time to align groups of controls vertically and horizontally.

 tip

To quickly select a group of controls in a column or row, click within the horizontal or vertical ruler. This shortcut selects all controls intersected by the vertical or horizontal projection of the arrow that appears when you move the mouse within the ruler.

 note

Alternatively, you can click the Sizing & Ordering group's Align button and click the gallery's To Grid, Left, Right, Top, or Bottom button.

Almost all control management techniques you learn in this chapter apply to Access reports. Using controls in the design of reports is discussed in Chapter 16, "Working with Simple Reports and Mailing Labels," and Chapter 17, "Preparing Advanced Reports."

Adding Label and Text Box Controls to a Blank Form

Using one of the Create ribbon's Forms group buttons or the Form Wizard simplifies the generation of standard forms for displaying and updating data in tables. Creating forms from scratch in Form Design view by adding controls from the toolbox provides much greater design flexibility than automated form generation. The examples in this chapter use the HRActions table you created in Chapter 5, "Working with Access Databases and Tables," and used with Layout mode in Chapter 14, as well as a query called qryHRActions, which you create in the next section.

 For more information on creating the data source for this chapter and establishing the correct relationships, **see** *"Creating the HRActions Table,"* p. 208.

Creating the Query Data Source for the Main Form

The HRActions table identifies employees uniquely by their sequential ID numbers, located in the EmployeeID field. As before, you should display the employee's name and title on the form to avoid entering records for the wrong person. The form design example in this chapter uses a one-to-many query to provide a single source of data for the new, custom HRActions form.

To create the HRActions query that serves as the data source for your main form, follow these steps:

1. If Northwind.accdb or your working database is open, close all open objects; otherwise, open the database.

2. Click the Create tab and the Query Design button to open Query1 and the Show Table dialog. Select the HRActions table and click Add. (Don't worry if your query's name contains a different number.)

3. Select the Employees table in the Show Table dialog, and click Add to add the Employees table to your query. Click the Close button to close the Show Table dialog.

4. If you defined relationships for the HRActions table as described in Chapter 5, the line connecting the two tables indicates that a many-to-one relationship exists between the EmployeeID field in the HRActions table and the EmployeeID field of the Employees table.

5. Click the * field of the HRActions table, and then drag and drop it in the first column of the Query Design grid. This adds all the fields of the HRActions table to your query.

 tip

If you haven't created the HRActions table, you can import it from the Forms15.accdb database in the online sample code's \\Access2010\Chaptr15 folder.

 tip

If you didn't define any relationships, the join line doesn't appear. In this case, you must drag the EmployeeID field from the HRActions field list to the EmployeeID field of the Employees field list to create a join between these two fields.

6. From the Employees table, click and drag the LastName, FirstName, Title, HireDate, Extension, ReportsTo, Notes, and Picture fields to columns 2 through 9 of the Query grid, respectively, as shown in Figure 15.6.

Figure 15.6
The query includes all fields (*) from the HRActions table and eight fields from the Employees table.

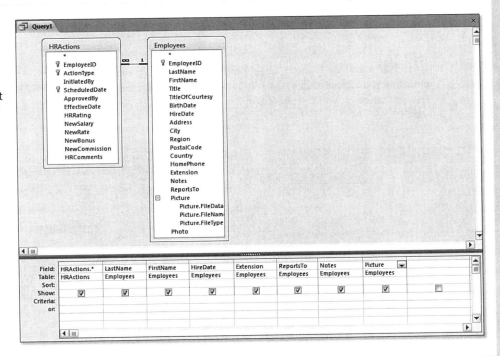

7. To simplify finding an employee, click the Sort row of the LastName column and select an Ascending sort.

8. Click the Run button to check your work, and then close the new query. Click Yes when the message box asks if you want to save the query.

9. In the Save As dialog, name the query **qryHRActions** and click OK.

Now that you've created the query that provides a unified data source for the main form, you're ready to begin creating your custom multitable form.

Creating a Blank Form with a Header and Footer

Understanding the entire form design process requires starting from a *tabula rasa* (blank slate). To open a blank form, assign qryHRActions as its data source, and add Form Header and Footer sections to emulate a simplified version of the form you autogenerated in Layout view and created with the Form Wizard in Chapter 14, do the following:

1. 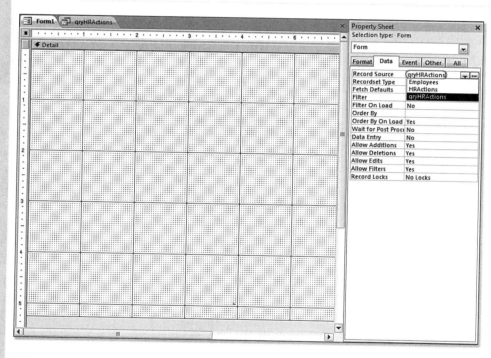 Click the Create tab and the Blank Form button to open a new, empty form (Form1) with an empty field list in Layout view. Right-click the form and choose Design View. Choosing Design View adds the Form Design Tools—Design and Layout contextual ribbon tabs with Design selected.

2. Click the Property Sheet button to open the Property Sheet. Click the Form Select button at the intersection of the two rulers, click the Data tab, and select qryHRActions in the Record Source property's drop-down list (see Figure 15.7). Accept the remaining defaults and click OK.

Figure 15.7
Select qryHRActions as the record source for the new form in the Property Sheet.

3. Click the Add Existing Fields button to open the Field List dialog, which displays all fields of the Employees and HRActions tables by default. Click the Show All Fields button (link) at the bottom of the dialog to display columns of the qryHRActions query. (The link changes to Show All Fields in the Current Record Source.)

tip

If the grid dots aren't visible, right-click the form's Detail area and choose Grid from the context menu.

4. Right-click the form's Detail section and choose Form Header/Footer to add a header and footer to the form.

The default width of blank forms is about 6.12 inches. The default height of the Form Header and Footer sections is 0.25 inch, and the height of the Detail section is 5.25 inches. To adjust the height of the form's Detail section and the width of the form, do the following:

1. Place the mouse pointer on the top line of the Form Footer bar. The mouse pointer becomes a double-headed arrow with a line between the heads. Hold down the left mouse button and drag the bar to create a Detail section height of about 4.75 inches, measured by the left vertical ruler. The active surface of the form, which displays the default 24x24 grid dots, shrinks vertically as you move the Form Footer bar upward.

2. Minimize the Form Footer section by dragging the bottom margin of the form to the bottom of the Form Footer bar.

3. Drag the right margin of the form to 6 inches, as measured by the horizontal ruler at the top of the form, as shown in Figure 15.8.

Figure 15.8
Create a starting form that has a Detail section of approximately 6x3.5 inches with Form Header and minimized Form Footer sections.

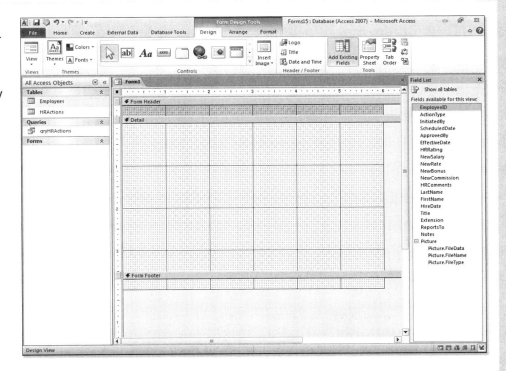

Adding a Label to the Form Header

The label is the simplest Access control to use. By default, labels are unbound and static, and they display only the text you enter. Static means that the label retains the value you originally assigned as long as the form is displayed, unless you change the Caption property value with VBA code or an Access macro. To add a label to the Form Header section, complete the following steps:

1. **_Aa_** Click the Form Design Tools—Design ribbon's Label button in the Controls group. When you move the mouse pointer to the form's active area, the pointer becomes the symbol for the Label button, combined with a crosshair. The center point of the crosshair defines the position of the control's upper-left corner.

2. Locate the crosshair at the upper-left of the Form Header section. Press and hold down the left mouse button while you drag the crosshair to the position for the lower-right corner of the label (see Figure 15.9).

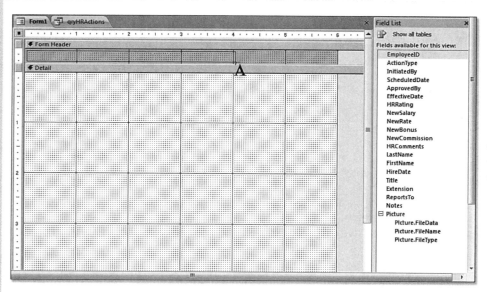

Figure 15.9
Drag the symbol for the control (a label in this example) from the upper left to the lower right to define a rectangle that represents the size of the control.

3. If you move the crosshair beyond the bottom of the Form Header section, the Form Header bar moves to accommodate the size of the label after you release the left mouse button. When the label is the size you want, release the mouse button.

4. The mouse pointer becomes the text-editing cursor inside the outline of the label. Type **Human Resources Action Entry** as the text for the label, and click anywhere outside

 note

As you drag the crosshair, the outline of the container for the label follows your movement. The number of lines and characters that the text box can display in the currently selected font appears in the status bar.

the label to finish its creation. If you don't type at least one text character in a label after creating it, the box disappears the next time you click the mouse.

5. Press Ctrl+S and type the name **frmHRActionEntry** in the Form Name text box of the Save As dialog. Click OK.

> ➥ *For tips on manipulating elements of a form,* **see** *"Selecting, Moving, and Sizing a Single Control or Label/Control Pair,"* **p. 615.**

You use the basic process described in the preceding steps to add most of the other types of controls to a form. (Some control command buttons, such as the Combo Box, List Box, and Insert Chart buttons, launch a Control Wizard to help you create the control if the Use Control Wizards button is activated.)

After you add the control, you use the anchor and sizing handles described earlier in this chapter to move the control to the desired position and to size the control to accommodate the content. The location of the anchor handle determines the Left (horizontal) and Top (vertical) properties of the control. The sizing handles establish the control's Width and Height property values.

Formatting Text and Adjusting Text Control Sizes

Calibri ▾ | 11 ▾ | When you select a control that accepts text as the value, the typeface and font size combo boxes appear in the Form Layout Tools—Format ribbon's Font Group. The default is 11-point Calibri, the same font used by Datasheets, with a Fore Color property value of Text 1—Lighter 50%. To format the text that appears in a label or text box for a title, follow these steps:

1. Click the Human Resources Action Entry label you created in the preceding section to select it. If the Property Sheet isn't open, click the ribbon's Property Sheet button.

2. Calibri ▾ | Open the Font list in the Fonts group and select the typeface family you want.

3. 11 ▾ | Open the Font Size list and select 18 points.

4. **B** Click the Bold attribute button on the toolbar.

5. Open the Fore Color properties list and choose Text Black to make the text darker.

6. The size of the label you created probably isn't large enough to display the larger font. To adjust the size of the label to accommodate the content of the label, right-click the label and choose Size, To Fit. Access resizes the label's text box to display the entire label; if necessary, Access also increases the size of the Form Header section.

When you change the properties of a control, the new values are reflected in the Property Sheet for the control, as shown in Figure 15.10. If you move or resize the label, you see the label's Left, Top, Width, and Height property values change in the Property Sheet's Format page. You usually use the Property Sheet to change the property values of a control only if a ribbon command button or context-menu choice isn't available.

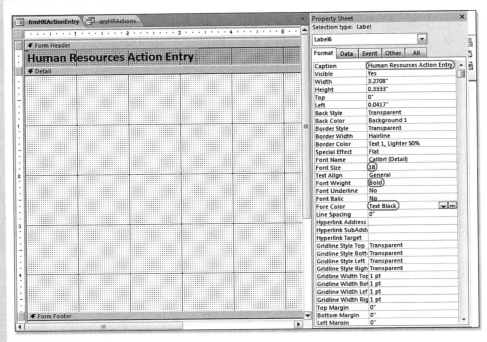

Figure 15.10
The Property Sheet reflects changes you make to the property values of a control with ribbon controls, which are highlighted.

Creating Bound and Calculated Text Boxes

Following are the most common attributes of Access text boxes:

- *Single-line text boxes* usually are bound to Text or numeric fields of a table or columns of a query.

- *Multiline text boxes* usually are bound to fields of the Memo type and include a vertical scrollbar to allow access to text that doesn't fit within the box's dimensions.

- *Calculated text boxes* obtain values from expressions that begin with an equal sign (=) and are usually a single line. Most calculated text boxes get their values from expressions that manipulate table field or query column values; but the =Now expression to supply the current date and time also is common. Calculated text boxes are unbound and read-only. You can't edit the value displayed by a calculated text box.

- *Unbound text boxes* can be used to supply values—such as limiting dates—to Access VBA procedures. As a rule, an unbound text box that doesn't contain a calculation expression can be edited. (An unbound text box control can be set to inhibit editing, but doing so negates the control's purpose in most cases.)

> **note**
>
> You can select different fonts and the Bold, Italic, and Underline attributes (or a combination) for any label or caption for a control. Good design practices dictate use of a single font family, such as Calibri, for all controls on a form. If the PC running your Access application doesn't have the font family you specified, Windows selects the closest available match— usually Arial for sans serif fonts. Changes you make to the formatting of data in controls don't affect the data's display in Datasheet view.

The following sections show you how to create the first three types of text boxes.

Adding Bound Text Box/Label Pairs

The most common text box used in Access forms is the single-line bound Text Box control, which makes up the majority of the controls for the frmHRActions form of Chapter 14. Access associates a label with the field or column name with bound text boxes. To add a bound text box and an associated label in Design view, do the following:

1. 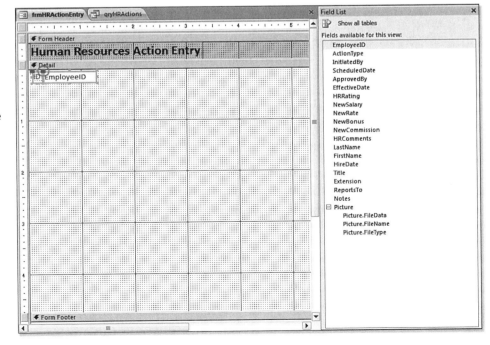 If necessary, click the ribbon's Add Existing Fields button to redisplay the Field List dialog and click the Show Only Fields in the Current Record Source link to display the qryHRActions query's columns.

2. Click and drag the EmployeeID field from the Field List dialog to the upper-left corner of the form's Detail section. When you move the mouse pointer to the active area of the form, the pointer becomes a field symbol, but no crosshair appears. The position of the field symbol indicates the upper-left corner of the text box, not the label, so drop the symbol in the approximate position of the text box anchor handle, as shown in Figure 15.11.

3. Drag the text box by the anchor handle closer to the ID label, and decrease the box's width to accommodate two or three characters.

4. **B** Small type sizes outside a field text box are more readable when you turn the Bold attribute on. Select the ID label and press Ctrl+B.

Figure 15.11
Add a bound text box with an associated label by dragging the field name to the position where you want the text box to appear.

5. Drag the HRComments field from the Field List to the form about 0.75 inch below the ID label, delete the label, and resize the text box to about 1x2.5 inches deep and 3 inches wide, as shown later in Figure 15.12. When you add a text box bound to a Memo field, Access automatically sets the Scroll Bars property to Vertical, and the scrollbar appears when the memo text is longer than the text box space or when you place the cursor in the text box.

6. Press Ctrl+S to save your work.

When you drag fields from the Field list in this manner, you automatically create a bound control. By default, however, all controls you add from the Ribbon's Controls group are *unbound* controls. You can bind a control to a field by creating an unbound control with a tool and selecting a field in the Control Source property drop-down list (reach the Control Source list by clicking the Data tab in the Property Sheet for the control).

Adding a Calculated Text Box and Formatting Date/Time Values

You can display the result of all valid Access expressions in a calculated text box. An expression must begin with = and can use VBA functions to return values. To create a calculated text box that displays the current date and time, do the following:

1. **ab|** Close the Property Sheet, click the Text Box button on the ribbon, and draw an unbound text box at the right of the Form Header section of the form.

2. **Aa** Edit the label of the new text box to read **Date/Time**, and relocate the label so that it's adjacent to the text box. Apply the Bold attribute to the label.

3. Type **=Now** in the text box to display the current date and time from your computer's system clock; Access adds a trailing parentheses pair for you. Adjust the width of the label and the text box to accommodate the approximate length of the text.

4. Change to Form Layout view and inspect the default date format (MM/DD/YYYY HH:MM:SS AM/PM for North America).

5. Multiselect all labels and text boxes, and set the Fore Color property value to Text Black.

6. To delete the seconds value, open the Property Sheet for the text box and click the Format tab. Select the Format property and type **mm/dd/yyyy hh:nn ampm** in the text box.

Your reformatted Date/Time text box appears as shown below the ID label/text box in Figure 15.12. Access lets you alter properties of text boxes and other controls in the form Layout *and* Form Design views. When you change the focus to another control, the format string (mm/dd/yyyy hh:nn ampm for this example) properly reformats the text box.

Figure 15.12
A copy of the Form Header section's Date/ Time control, which you create in the next section, demonstrates the formatted unbound text box value. (The Property Sheet obscures the original control). Multiline text boxes don't display vertical scroll-bars in Layout view.

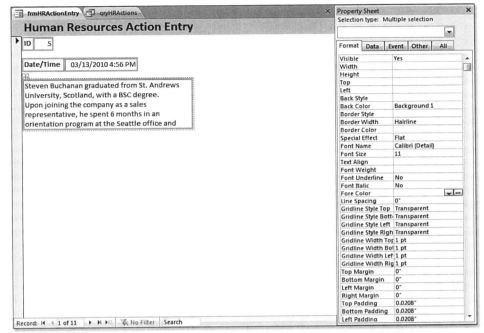

Using the Clipboard with Controls

You can use the Windows Clipboard to make copies of controls and their properties. As an example, create a copy of the Date/ Time control, as shown in Figure 15.12, with the Clipboard by performing the following steps:

tip

2010 NEW Access 2010 lets you drag selected controls between form sections, such as from Detail to Header. This wasn't possible in Access 2007 and earlier.

1. Return to Form Design view and select the unbound Date/Time control and its label by clicking the text box. Both the label and the text box are selected, as indicated by the selection handles on both controls.

2. Copy the selected control to the Clipboard by pressing Ctrl+C.

3. Click the Detail bar to select the Detail section, and paste the copy of the control below the original version by pressing Ctrl+V. (Access pastes the control into the top-left corner of the Detail section, so you'll need to reposition it.)

4. Click the Format property in the Property Sheet for the copied control, and select Long Date from the drop-down list.

5. To check the appearance of the controls you've created, right-click the form and choose Form View.

6. Return to Design view and delete the added Date/Time text box and label. To do so, enclose both with a selection boundary created by dragging the mouse pointer across the text boxes from the upper-left to the lower-right corner. Press Delete. (You need the Date/Time text box only in the Form Header section for this form.)

Accepting or Declining Control Error Correction

(i) If you add a text box control without a label to the Form Header section, and then add a new label from the Controls gallery, Access 2010's control error-correction feature becomes evident in Form Design view. The new label sports a green flag in its upper-left corner. When you select a control with an error flag, the error-checking smart tag icon—a diamond-shaped sign with an exclamation point—appears to the right of the control.

When you pass the mouse pointer over the icon, an error message screen tip describing the problem appears (in this case, "This is a new label and is not associated with a control"). Clicking the icon's arrow opens the following list (see Figure 15.13):

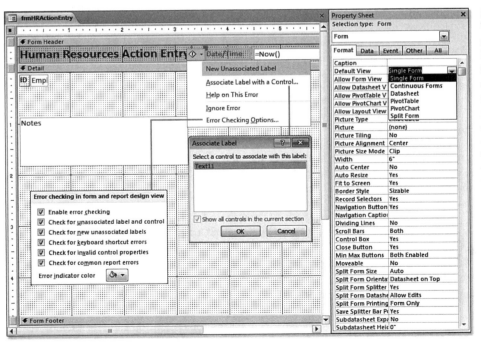

Figure 15.13
When you add an unbound label control that's not associated with a text box, Access 2010 flags the control for error correction and offers these selections to ignore or correct the purported error. The Associate Label dialog and Error Checking choices are pasted into the original screen capture.

- **New Unassociated Label**—Error description, not a menu choice.

- **Associate Label with Control**—Opens an Associate Label dialog with a list of text box(es) in the section to which the label can be associated.

- **Help on This Item**—Opens a Microsoft Access Help window, which should (but doesn't) display the topic relating to the error.

- **Ignore Error**—Removes the flag from the selected control.

- **Error Checking Options**—Opens the Access Options dialog's Object Designers page, which has an Error Checking group at the bottom to let you specify the errors to be flagged or turn off error checking. Clearing the Check for Unassociated Label and Control check box and clicking OK removes the flag from the selected control. Clicking OK with a check box cleared prevents further error checking for the selection.

Adding new unassociated labels is a common task, so consider removing this error check. Changes you make in the error checking Options dialog apply to all databases.

Changing the Default View and Obtaining Help for Properties

A form that fills Access's Design window might not necessarily fill the window in Run mode. Run mode might allow the beginning of a second copy of the form to appear. A second copy appears if the Default View property has a value of Continuous Forms. Forms have the following six Default View property values from which you can choose (refer to Figure 15.13):

- *Single Form* displays one record at a time in one form.

- *Continuous Forms* displays multiple records, each record having a copy of the form's Detail section. You can use the vertical scrollbar or the record selection buttons to select which record to display. Continuous Forms view is the default value for subforms created by the Form Wizard.

- *Datasheet* displays the form fields arranged in rows and columns.

- *PivotTable* displays an empty PivotTable design form, unless you've previously designed the PivotTable.

- *PivotChart* displays an empty PivotChart design form, unless you've previously designed the PivotChart.

- *Split Form* adds a Datasheet to the top of the form with a column for each field assigned to a control on the form.

 note

PivotTable and PivotChart views of the data source for a data entry form seldom are useful. These views require aggregate values, which are uncommon except in decision-support forms. Rather than use a PivotTable or PivotChart view of the data, add these views as controls to a form. Chapter 18 describes how to add PivotTable and PivotChart controls to forms.

note

The vertical scrollbar disappears from the form in Form view if a single form fits within its tabbed document or overlapping window.

To change the form's Default View property, do the following:

1. Return to Form Design view, if necessary.

2. Right-click the form and choose Properties.

3. Click the Form Select button to display formwide properties, and then click the Format tab.

4. Click the Default View property and open the list.

5. Select the value you want for this property for the current form. For this exercise, select Single Form (the default) from the list (refer to Figure 15.13).

Adding Group Boxes with the Wizard

Option buttons, toggle buttons, and check boxes ordinarily return only Yes/No (–1/0 or True/False) values when used by themselves on a form. These three controls also can return Null values if you change the TripleState property value to Yes. Individual bound option button controls are limited to providing values to Yes/No fields of a table or query. When you place any of these controls within an option group, however, the buttons or check boxes can return a number you specify for the value of the control's Option Value property.

The capability to assign numbers to the Option Value property lets you use one of the preceding three control types inside an option group frame for assigning values to the HRRating field of the HRActions table. Option buttons are most commonly used in Windows applications to select one value from a limited number of values.

> **note**
>
> Access's toggled ribbon command buttons indicate the On (True) state by a border with a colored background under Windows Vista and XP. This differs from toggle buttons on forms, which use a very light gray background and a sunken effect to indicate the On (pressed) state. Background colors differ if you've applied a nondefault Windows desktop theme.

The Option Group Wizard is one of three Control Wizards that take you step-by-step through the creation of complex controls. To create an option group for the HRRating field of the HRActions table with the Option Group Wizard, follow these steps:

1. Click the Use Control Wizards button to turn on the wizards if the toggle button isn't On (the default value).

2. Click the Option Group tool, position the pointer where you want the upper-left corner of the option group, and click the mouse button to display the first dialog of the Option Group Wizard.

3. For this example, type five of the nine ratings in the Label Names datasheet (pressing Tab, not Enter, to separate them): **Excellent**, **Good**, **Acceptable**, **Fair**, and **Poor** (see Figure 15.14). Click Next.

> **tip**
>
> You can specify accelerator keys in the captions of your option buttons by placing an ampersand (**&**) before the letter to be used as an accelerator key. Thereafter, pressing Alt in combination with that letter key selects the option when your form is in Run mode. To include an ampersand in your caption, type **&&**.

Figure 15.14
Type the caption for each option button of the option group in the first dialog of the Option Group Wizard.

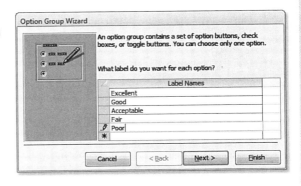

4. The second dialog lets you set an optional default value for the option group. Select the option named Yes, the Default Choice Is, and open the drop-down list. Select Good, as shown in Figure 15.15, and click Next. If you need to, you can return to any previous step by clicking Back one or more times.

Figure 15.15
Select a default value in the second Option Group Wizard dialog.

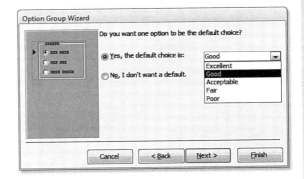

5. The third dialog of the Option Group Wizard lets you assign option values to each option button of the group. The default value is the numbered sequence of the buttons. Type **9**, **7**, **5**, **3**, and **1** in the five text boxes, as illustrated in Figure 15.16, and click Next.

 note

Check boxes are an inappropriate choice for controls in an option group. Windows programming standards reserve multiple check boxes for situations in which more than one option choice is permissible.

The sunken and raised styles of option groups, option buttons, and check boxes are applicable only to control objects on forms or option groups with a Back Color property other than white.

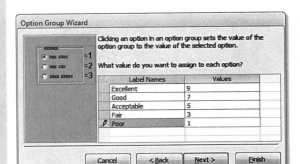

Figure 15.16
Assign a numeric value to each option button in the group. In Form view, clicking an option button assigns its value to the option frame.

6. The fourth wizard dialog lets you bind the option group to a field of a table or a column of a query that you specified as the Record Source property value of the bound form. Select the HRRating column of the qryHRActions query to which your form is bound (see Figure 15.17). Click Next.

note

The domain integrity rule for the HRRating field provides for nine different ratings. Nine option buttons, however, occupy too much space on a form, so this example uses only five of the nine ratings. (In the real world, you wouldn't just eliminate options because there are too many; you would substitute a combo box control.)

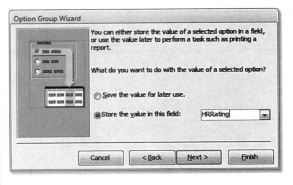

Figure 15.17
Bind the option group value to a numeric field (HRRating for this example).

7. The fifth dialog lets you determine the style of the option group, as well as the type of controls (option buttons, check boxes, or toggle buttons) to add to the option group. You can preview the appearance of your option group and button style choices in the Sample pane. For this example, select Option Buttons and Flat (see Figure 15.18). The flat effect matches the default effect applied to all controls by Access 2007.

Figure 15.18
The fifth wizard dialog lets you choose the option frame's control type and appearance.

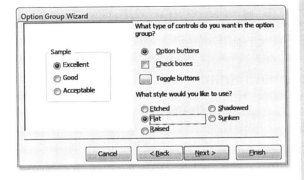

8. The last dialog provides a text box for entering the Caption property value of the label for the option group. Type **Rating**, as shown in Figure 15.19, and click Finish to let the wizard complete its work.

Figure 15.19
Add the caption for the option group in the last wizard dialog.

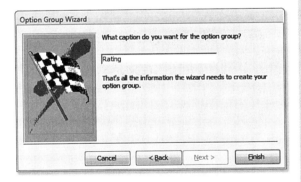

9. Open the Properties dialog for the option group, and assign the control a name (**grpRating** for this example), select the caption and five option buttons, press Ctrl+B to apply the bold font attribute, and set the Fore Color property value to Text Black. Figure 15.20 shows the completed Rating option group and its Property Sheet in Form Design view.

➡ *For more information on Access and VBA naming conventions,* **see** *"Typographic and Naming Conventions Used for VBA,"* **p. 1241.**

To test your new bound option group, select the Text Box tool and drag the HRRating field from the field list to the form to add a text box that's bound to the HRRating column. Figure 15.21 shows the option group in Form view with a HRRating label and text box added, and the Bold attribute and the Text Black Fore Color property applied to the option group and text box labels. Click the option buttons to display the rating value in the text box. Although your entry on the form tentatively updates the value onscreen, the value in the table doesn't change until you move the record pointer or change the view of the form. Press Ctrl+S to save your form.

tip

Name the controls you add to identify their use, rather than accepting the Access default value for the Name property. This book uses object-naming conventions that consist of a three-letter, lowercase abbreviation of the object type—*grp* for option groups, *opt* for option buttons, *txt* for text boxes, *frm* for forms, and the like—followed by a descriptive name for the control. Using a consistent object-naming convention makes it much easier to write (and later interpret) VBA code for automating your application.

2007 NEW   Access 2000 added the capability to change property values in Form view; Access 2007and later no longer support displaying the Property Sheet in Form view, but compensates by adding Layout view. However, you can change the Name property value of an object only in Form Design view.

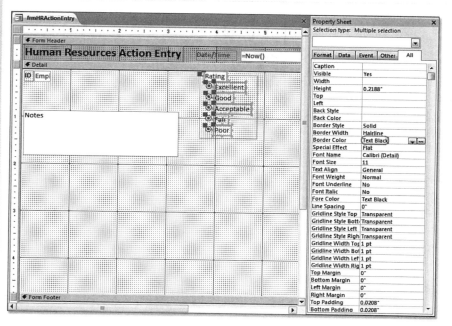

Figure 15.20
The Properties dialog for the grpRating option group (originally called an *option frame*) displays the property values assigned by the wizard.

Figure 15.21
Clicking an option button displays its value in the HRRating text box and makes a tentative change to the HRRating field of the current record of the HRActions table.

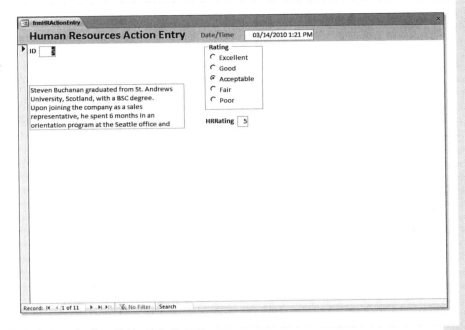

Changing One Control Type to Another

Access lets you "morph" a control of one type to become a control of a compatible type. You can change an option button to a check box, for example, or you can change a toggle button to an option button. You can't, however, change a text box to an object frame or other control with a different field data type. To change a control to a different type, follow these steps:

1. In the form's Design or Layout view, right-click the control whose type you want to change.

2. Choose Change To to see a submenu of form control types. Only the submenu choices for control types that are compatible with the selected control are enabled.

3. Choose the control type you want from the submenu's active choices. Access changes the control type.

 note

2010 NEW Using the Clipboard to copy controls from one form to another is a more granular design approach than using built-in or creating new Application Part templates to generate all or part of a new form (or report). Built-in Application Parts have styles that probably won't complement designs you've created previously.

Using the Clipboard to Copy Controls to Another Form

Access's capability of copying controls and their properties to the Windows Clipboard lets you create controls on one form and copy them to another. You can copy the controls in the header of a previously designed form to a new form and edit the content as necessary. The form that contains the controls to be copied need not be in the same database as the destination form in which the copy is pasted. This feature lets you create a library of standard controls in a dedicated form that is used only for holding standard controls. If your library includes bound controls, you can copy them to the form, and then change the field or column to which they're bound.

The Date/Time calculated text box is a candidate to add to Chapter 14's frmHRActions form. You might want to add a Time/Date text box to the Form Header or Detail section of all your transaction forms. To add the Date/Time control to the frmHRActions form, assuming both forms are in the same database, Forms15.accdb for this example, do the following:

1. With the frmHRActionEntry form open, click the Design View button, and select the Date/Time control and its label by clicking the text box.

2. Press Ctrl+C to copy the selected control(s) to the Clipboard.

3. Open the HR Actions (see Chapter 14) form from the Navigation pane and change to Design view. Reduce the title's font size to 16 points and move the title label to the left to make room for the date/time text box.

4. Click the Header section selection bar, and press Ctrl+V. A copy of the control appears in the upper-left corner of the form header.

5. Deselect the text box and press Delete to remove the Date/Time label.

6. Hold down the mouse button and drag the text box to a position to the right of the Title label. Optionally change the Back Style and Border Style property values to Transparent to allow the header background color to show through.

7. Click Form view to display the modified HR Actions form (see Figure 15.22).

8. Return to Form Design view, press Ctrl+S to save your changes, and close the HR Actions form.

Error Messages on Copied Controls

When you copy a control from one form to another, the copied control throws error messages whenever that control gets the focus.

This occurs because when you copy a control to a form that uses a data source different from the one used to create the original control, you need to change the Control Source property to correspond with the field the new control is to be bound to. Changing the Control Source property doesn't change the Status Bar Text, Validation Rule, and Validation Text properties for the new control source. You must enter the appropriate values manually.

Figure 15.22
Copying a previously formatted control from one form to another saves design time.

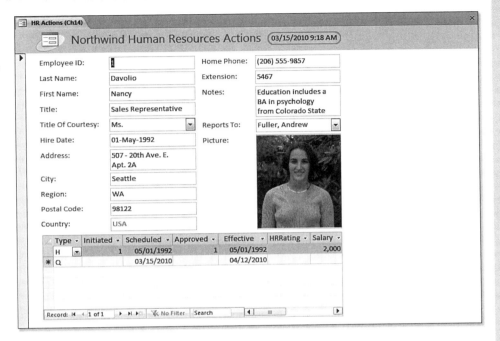

Adding Combo and List Boxes

Combo and list boxes both serve the same basic purpose by letting you pick a value from a list, rather than type the value in a text box. These two kinds of lists are especially useful when you need to enter a code that represents the name of a person, firm, or product. You don't need to refer to a paper list of the codes and names to make the entry. The following list describes the differences between combo and list boxes:

- *Combo boxes* consume less space than list boxes in the form, but you must open these controls to select a value. You can allow the user to enter a value in the text box element of the drop-down combo list or limit the selection to just the members in the drop-down list. If you limit the choice to members of the drop-down list (sometimes called a *pick list*), the user can still use the text box to type the beginning of the list value—Access searches for a matching entry. This feature reduces the time needed to locate a choice in a long list.

- *List boxes* don't need to be opened to display their content; the portion of the list that fits within the size of the list box you assign is visible at all times. Your choices are limited to values included in the list.

In most cases, you bind the combo or list box to a field so that the choice updates the value of this field. Two-column controls often are the most common. The first column contains the code that updates the value of the bound field, and the second column contains the name associated with the code. A multiple-column list is most useful when assigning supervisor and manager employee ID numbers to the InitiatedBy and ApprovedBy fields in the frmHRActionEntry form, for example.

Using the Combo Box Wizard

Designing combo boxes is a more complex process than creating an option group, so you're likely to use the Combo Box Wizard for every combo box you add to forms. Follow these steps to use the Combo Box Wizard to create the cboInitiatedBy drop-down list, which lets you select from a list of Northwind Traders' employees:

1. Open the frmHRActionEntry form (which you created and saved earlier in this chapter) from the Navigation pane in Form Design view if it isn't presently open.

2. Click the Controls gallery's Use Control Wizards button, if necessary, to turn on the wizards.

3. Click the Combo Box button. The mouse pointer turns into a combo box symbol while on the active surface of the form.

4. Click the Add Existing Fields button to display the Field List dialog.

5. Drag the InitiatedBy field to an empty region form's Detail section. The first Combo Box Wizard dialog opens.

6. You want the combo box to look up values in the Employees table, so accept the default option (see Figure 15.23). Your selection specifies Table/Query as the value of the Row Source Type property of the combo box. Click Next.

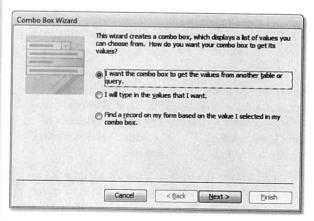

Figure 15.23
The first Combo Box Wizard dialog lets you select the type of combo box to create. This example uses a lookup-type combo box.

7. In the second wizard dialog, select Employees from the list of tables (see Figure 15.24) and click Next.

Figure 15.24
Select the table or query to provide the list items of the combo box in the Combo Box Wizard's second dialog. Use a base table (Employees for this example) to ensure that the list doesn't contain multiple entries for a single lookup value.

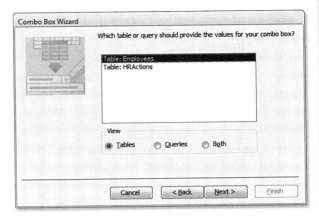

8. For this example, the combo box needs the EmployeeID and LastName fields of the Employees table. EmployeeID is the field that provides the value to the bound column of the query, and your combo box displays the LastName field. EmployeeID is selected in the Available Fields list by default, so click the > button to move EmployeeID to the Selected Fields list. LastName is then selected automatically, so click the > button again to move LastName to the Selected Fields list. Your Combo Box Wizard dialog appears as shown in Figure 15.25. This selection generates the Access SQL SELECT query that serves as the value of the combo box's Row Source property and populates its list. Click Next.

> **tip**
>
> If two or more employees have the same last name, add the FirstName field to the combo list. Unlike conventional combo and list boxes, Access controls can display multiple columns.

Figure 15.25
In the third Combo Box Wizard dialog, add the bound column and one or more additional columns to display in the combo box list.

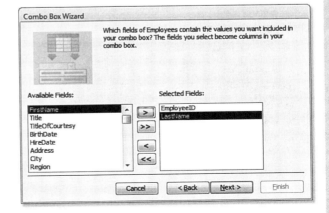

9. To sort the list by last name, open the first list and select the LastName field (see Figure 15.26). Selecting a sort on one or more fields adds an ORDER BY clause to the combo box's SELECT query.

10. The fifth dialog displays the list items for the combo box. Access has successfully determined that the EmployeeID field is the key field of the Employees table and has assumed (correctly) that the EmployeeID field binds the combo box.

11. Resize the LastName column by dragging the right edge of the column to the left—you want the column wide enough to display everyone's last name but not any wider than absolutely necessary (see Figure 15.27). Click Next.

 note

The Hide Key Column check box is selected by default; this option causes Access to hide the bound column of the combo box. You've selected two columns for the combo box, but only one column (the LastName field) displays in the combo box's list. The EmployeeID column is hidden and used only to supply the data value for the InitiatedBy field.

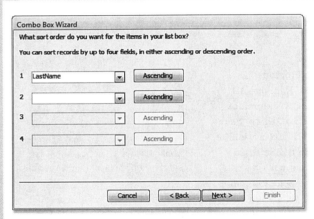

Figure 15.26
In the new Combo Box Wizard sorting dialog, select the field(s) on which to apply an ascending or descending sort. Clicking an Ascending button toggles a descending or ascending sort.

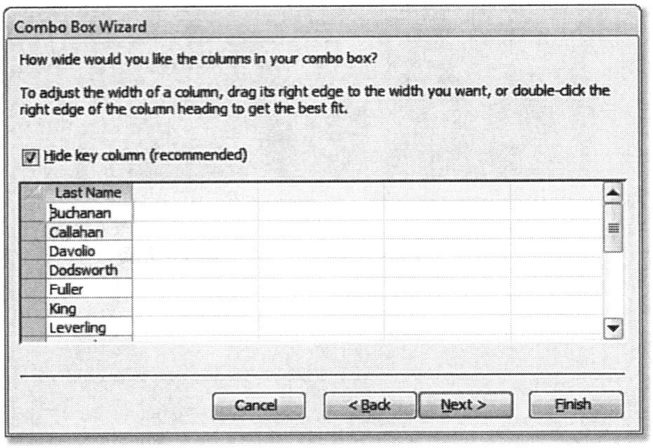

Figure 15.27
The Combo Box Wizard queries the combo box's data source (the Employees table) and displays the control's list items. Double-click the right edge of the list to size the list's width to fit the list items.

12. Your combo box updates the InitiatedBy field with the
EmployeeID value corresponding to the name you select.
You previously specified that the Control Source property
is the InitiatedBy column when you dragged the field symbol to the form in step 5. The Combo Box Wizard uses your
previous selection as the default value of the Control Source
property (see Figure 15.28), so accept the default by clicking
the Next button to display the sixth and final dialog.

 note

Resizing the list width doesn't
accomplish its objective. The Combo
Box Wizard adds a combo box of the
size you created when dragging the
tool on the form, regardless of the
width you specify at this point.

Figure 15.28
The fifth Combo Box Wizard dialog specifies the
column of the query to be updated by the combo
box selection.

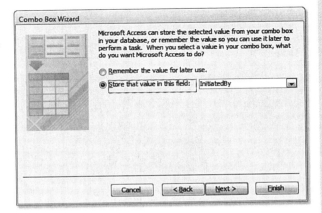

13. The last dialog lets you edit the label associated with the combo box (see Figure 15.29). Type
Initiated by and click Finish to add the combo box to your form.

Figure 15.29
Type the label caption for the combo box in the
sixth and last Combo Box Wizard dialog.

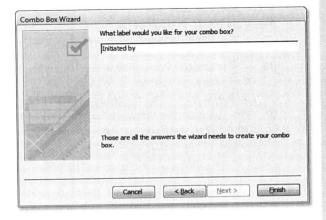

14. **B** Press Ctrl+B to apply the bold attribute to the combo box label, set the label's and text box's Fore Color property to Text Black, set the Text Align property to Left, and adjust the width and position of the label. Open the Property Sheet for the combo box, and change its name to **cboInitiatedBy**. Figure 15.30 shows the new combo box in Form Design view.

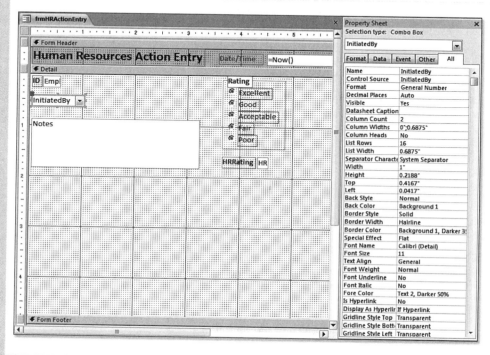

Figure 15.30
The Combo Box Wizard sets the property values for the combo box, but leaves it up to you to specify a meaningful control name.

15. Close the Property Sheet and drag the combo box and its label to the top of the right side of the form.

16. Change to Form view to test your combo box. Change the Initiated By value to another person, and then use the navigation buttons to move the record pointer and make the change permanent. Return to the original record, and verify that the combo box is bound to the InitiatedBy field (see Figure 15.31).

> **note**
>
> The Row Source property is the SQL SELECT statement that fills the combo box's list. Specifying a Column Width value of 0 hides the first column. The Description property of the EmployeeID field provides the default Status Bar Text property value.

Figure 15.31
The combo box in Form view displays a list with the default maximum of eight items. The default Text Align property value is General, so the text box is aligned right because the InitiatedBy field is numeric.

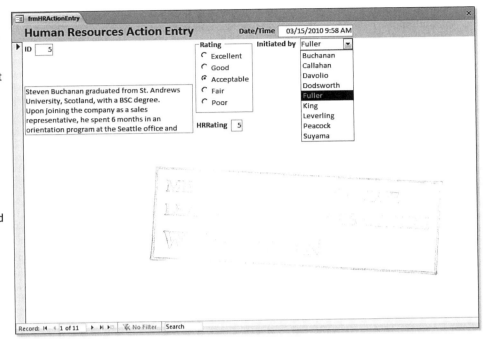

The Access SQL statement generated by the Combo Box Wizard for cboInitiatedBy is

```
SELECT Employees.EmployeeID, Employees.LastName
  FROM Employees
ORDER BY [LastName];
```

Using the Query Builder to Populate a Combo Box

If the Row Source Type property for a combo box is Table/Query, you can substitute a custom SQL statement for a named table or query as the value of the Row Source property. For either tables or queries, you can choose only the fields or columns you want for the text box, eliminating the need to hide columns. In addition, you can specify a sort order for the list element of your combo box and specify criteria to limit the list.

> **tip**
>
> If you don't use the Combo Box Wizard to generate the combo box, you can select an existing table or query to serve as the Row Source for the combo box.

To invoke Access's Query Builder and create an SQL statement for populating a manually added Approved By combo box, follow these steps:

1. Return to or open frmHRActionEntry in Design view, and click to disable the ribbon's Use Control Wizards button to add the combo box manually. Click the Add Existing Fields button, if necessary, to display the Field List dialog.

2. 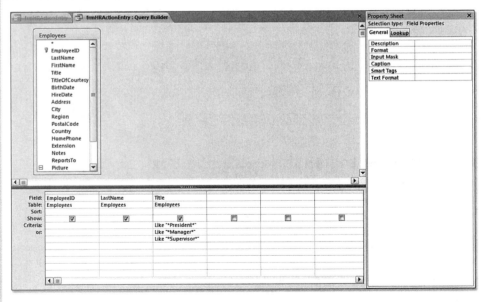 Click the Combo Box button in the toolbox, and then drag the ApprovedBy field to add a new combo box in the original position of the Initiated By combo box you added in the preceding section. Select the new control and open the Property Sheet if necessary.

3. Select the Data tab's Row Source property, and click the Builder button to launch the Query Builder with the Show Table dialog open. The Query Builder window is identical in most respects to the Query Design window, but its title and behavior differ.

> **tip**
>
> Test the results of your query by clicking the Query Tools—Design ribbon's Run button. Access executes the query and displays a Datasheet view of the query's results. For this example, only Mr. Buchanan and Dr. Fuller meet the criteria.

4. Add the Employees table to the query, and then close the Show Table dialog. Drag the EmployeeID, LastName, and Title fields to the Query Design grid.

5. You want an ascending sort on the LastName field, so select Ascending in the Sort check box. Only presidents, vice presidents, managers, and supervisors can approve HR actions, so type **Like *President*** in the first Criteria row of the grid's Title column, **Like *Manager*** in the second, and **Like *Supervisor*** in the third. Access adds the quotation marks surrounding the Like argument for you. Clear the Show check box of the Title column. Your query design appears as shown in Figure 15.32.

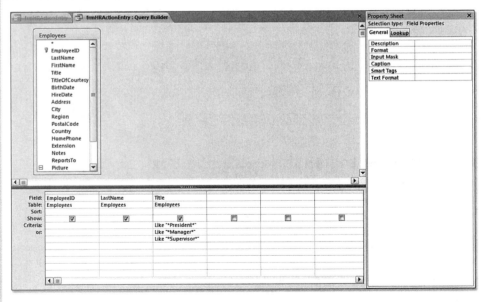

Figure 15.32
This query design limits approval to employees whose titles include President, Manager, or Supervisor.

6. Close the Query Builder. The message box shown in Figure 15.33 appears to confirm your change to the Row Source property value, instead of asking if you want to save your query. Click Yes, and the SQL statement derived from the graphical Query Design grid becomes the value of the Row Source property.

Figure 15.33
This query design supplies the corresponding Access SQL statement as the value of the combo box's Row Source property.

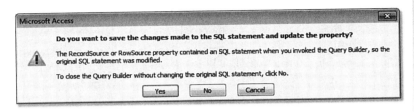

7. In the combo box's Property Sheet, change the name of the combo box to **cboApprovedBy**. Change the Column Count property value to **2** and type **0.2;0.8** in the Column Widths text box. You specify column widths in inches, separated by semicolons, and Access adds the units for inches ('') to the widths. (Metrified users specify column widths in cm.) Finally, change the Limit to List value to **Yes**, and set the Fore Color of the label and text box to Text Black.

 tip

You can display only the LastName field in the combo box, making the combo box similar in appearance to that for the InitiatedBy field, by setting the first Column Width value to **0**.

8. **B** Change the label caption to **Approved by** and apply the Bold attribute, and move the combo box and its label below the Initiated By control/label pair.

9. ⊞ Switch to Form view to test the effect of adding the sort (the ORDER BY clause) and criteria (the WHERE clause) to the query (see Figure 15.34). Press Ctrl+S to save your form changes.

The Access SQL statement generated by the Query Builder is

```
SELECT Employees.EmployeeID, Employees.LastName
  FROM Employees
  WHERE (((Employees.Title) Like "*President*")) OR
        (Employees.Title)   Like "*Manager*") OR
        (Employees.Title)   Like "*Supervisor*"))
ORDER BY Employees.LastName;
```

Access SQL uses the DOS and UNIX * and ? wildcards for all characters and a single character, respectively. T-SQL requires the ANSI SQL wildcards % and _, and surrounds character strings with single quotes rather than double quotes. The table name prefixes aren't needed, and the parentheses in the WHERE clause are superfluous.

The simplified T-SQL equivalent of the preceding Access SQL statement for an ADP is

```
SELECT EmployeeID, LastName
  FROM dbo.Employees
  WHERE Title LIKE '%President%' OR
        Title LIKE    '%Manager%' OR
        Title LIKE    '%Supervisor%'
ORDER BY LastName
```

Continued...

The dbo. prefix—called the *schema* component of the table name—in the preceding statement is optional, but is a common practice in T-SQL statements.

It's a more common practice for ADP to use SQL Server 2005 views, stored procedures, or table-returning functions to provide the Row Source for forms, combo boxes, and list boxes.

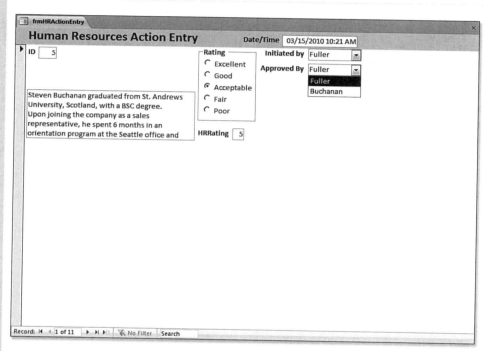

Figure 15.34
The combo box list contains items for employees whose titles comply with the Like criteria.

Creating a Combo Box with a List of Static Values

Another application for list boxes and combo boxes is picking values from a static list of options that you create. A drop-down list to choose a Rating value saves space in a form compared with the equivalent control created with option buttons within an option group. As you design more complex forms, you find that display "real estate" becomes increasingly valuable.

The option group you added to the frmHRActionEntry form provides a choice of only five of the possible 10 ratings. To add a drop-down list with the Combo Box Wizard to allow entry of all possible values, do the following:

1.  Change to Form Design view, and click the Use Control Wizards button to enable the Combo Box Wizard.

2. 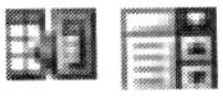 Open the Add Existing Fields dialog, and then click the Combo Box tool in the toolbox. Drag the HRRating field symbol to the original position of the cboApprovedBy combo box you added previously.

3. In the first wizard dialog, select the I Will Type in the Values That I Want option (refer to Figure 15.23), and then click Next to open the second dialog.

4. The Rating combo box requires two columns: The first column contains the allowable values of HRRating, 0 through 9, and the second column contains the corresponding description of each rating code. Type **2** as the number of columns.

5. Access assigns value-list Row Source property values in column-row sequence; you enter each of the values for the columns in the first row and then do the same for the remaining rows. Type **9 Excellent, 8 Very Good, 7 Good, 6 Average, 5 Acceptable, 4 Marginal, 3 Fair, 2 Sub-par, 1 Poor, 0 Terminated** (use the Tab key to separate the value sets; don't type the commas).

6. Set the widths of the columns you want by dragging the edge of each column header button to the left, as shown in Figure 15.35. If you don't want the rating number to appear, drag the left edge of column 1 fully to the left to reduce its width to 0. When you've adjusted the column widths, click Next to open the third dialog.

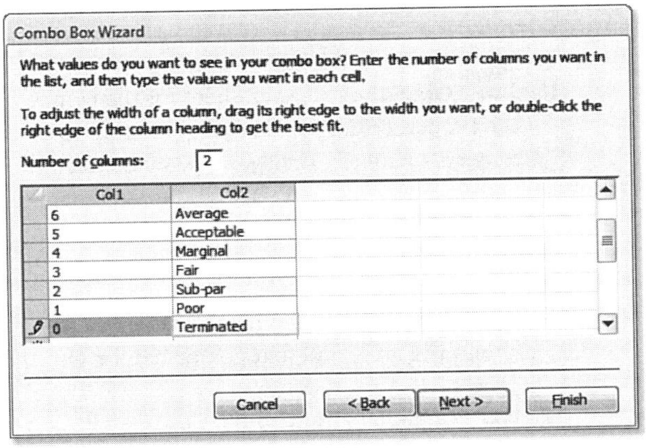

Figure 15.35
Type the values for the two columns in the list, and then adjust the column widths to suit the list's contents.

7. Select Col1, the HRRating code, as the bound column for your value list—that is, the column containing the value you want to store or use later (see Figure 15.36); this column must contain unique values. Click Next to open the fourth dialog.

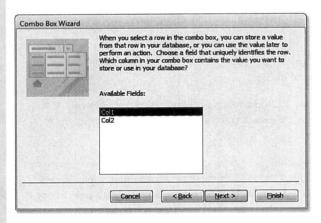

Figure 15.36
Select the column that contains the unique value to identify the rows of the list (in most cases, Col1).

8. Accept the default value (the HRRating column) in the fourth dialog, and click Next to open the final dialog of the Combo Box Wizard.

9. **B** Type **Rating** as the label for the new combo box control, apply the Bold attribute to the label, and then click Finish to complete the combo box specification and return to Form Design view.

10. Open the Property Sheet for the combo box, change the Name to **cboRating**, and then click the Property Sheet's Data tab. Set Limit to List to Yes to convert the drop-down combo to a drop-down list. Quickly review the Row Source property. Notice that the wizard has added semicolons between the row entries, and quotation marks to surround the text values in the Row Source property. You use this format when you enter list values manually.

11. Click the Property Sheet's Format tab, replace the Column Width property value with **0;0.8,** which forces the rating names to replace the numeric values, type **Auto** or **0.8** as the List Width, format the label and text box as before, and then set Text Align to Left.

12. Change to Form view. The open Rating static-value combo box and its Property Sheet appear as shown in Figure 15.37.

Another opportunity to use a static-value combo box is as a substitute for the Type text box. Several kinds of performance reviews exist: Quarterly, Yearly, Bonus, Salary, Commission, and so on, each represented by an initial letter code.

Figure 15.37
The value-list
version of
the cboRat-
ing combo
box closely
resembles the
cboApprovedBy
combo box.

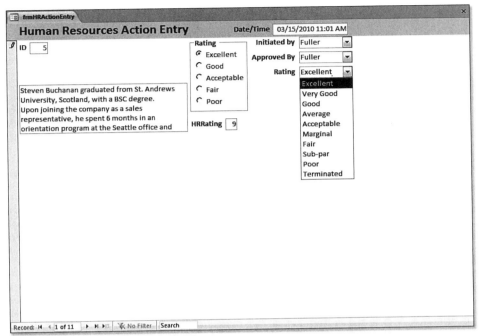

Creating a Combo Box to Find Specific Records

The Combo Box Wizard includes a third type of combo list box
that you can create—a combo list that locates a record on the
form based on a value you select from the list. You can use this
type of combo box, for example, to create a Find box on the
frmHRActionEntry form that contains a drop-down list of all last
names from the Employees table. Thus, you can quickly find
HRActions records for employees.

To create a combo box that finds records on the form based on a
value you select from a drop-down list, follow these steps:

1. Change to Design view, and click the Use Control
   Wizards button in the toolbox, if necessary, to enable the
   Combo Box Wizard.

> **tip**
>
> You can improve the
> appearance of columns of labels
> and associated text, list, and combo
> boxes by right-aligning the text of
> the labels and left-aligning the text
> of the boxes. Select all the labels in
> a column with the mouse, and click
> the Align Right button on the tool-
> bar. Then select all the boxes and
> click the Align Left button.

2. Click the Combo Box tool in the toolbox, and then click and drag on the surface of the form's Detail section to create the new combo box in a position underneath the cboRating combo box you created previously. Release the mouse, and the first Combo Box Wizard dialog appears. When you don't drag a column name to the form, you create an unbound combo box.

3. Select the Find a Record on My Form Based on the Value I Selected in My Combo Box option, and click Next (refer to Figure 15.23).

4. In the second wizard dialog, scroll the Available Fields list until the LastName field is visible. Click to select this field, and then click the > button to move it to the Selected Fields list (see Figure 15.38). Click Next to open the third dialog.

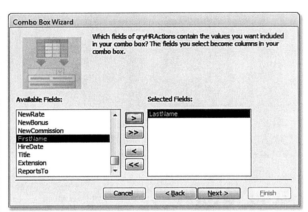

Figure 15.38
Select the name of the field to search in the Available Fields list, and click ····➔ to add the entry to the Selected Fields list.

5. The Combo Box Wizard now displays a list of the field values from the column you just selected. Double-click the right edge of the LastName column to get the best column-width fit for the data values in the column, and then click Next to go to the fourth and final step of the wizard.

6. **B** Type **Find** as the label for the new combo box, and then click Finish to complete the new combo box control. After applying the bold attribute to the label, aligning its text right, and adjusting its size, your form appears in Design view as shown in Figure 15.39.

> **tip**
>
> When creating a combo box to find records, select only one field. The combo box won't work for finding records if you select more than one field for the combo box's lists.
>
> If the record source contains more than one person with the same last name, you must add a calculated FullName query column to use the find-record combo box version. For this example, the expression to create a FullName query column is FullName: [LastName] & ", " & [FirstName].

Figure 15.39
The record-finding version of the combo box uses an event procedure to move the record pointer to the first record matching the combo box selection.

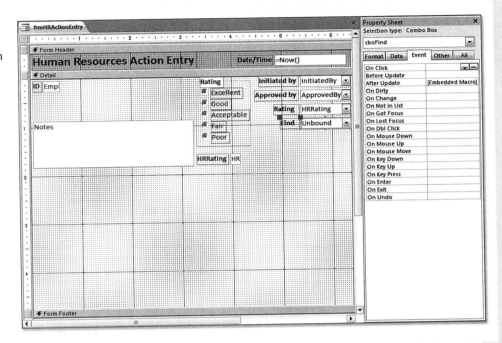

7. Click the Form View button on the toolbar to display the form. Type **s** in the text box to select Michael Suyama, then click the arrow to open the list and replace the text box's suyama value with Suyama. The open Find: combo box appears as shown in Figure 15.40.

8. Press Ctrl+S to save your work so far.

2007 NEW When you create this type of combo box, the Combo Box Wizard automatically creates an embedded macro for the After Update property of the combo box (refer to the Property window in Figure 15.39). Access automatically executes the assigned embedded macro whenever a particular event occurs—in this case, updating the combo box. Chapter 19, "Automating Access Applications with Macros," describes embedded and standalone Access macros, and Chapter 30, "Handling Events with Macros and Procedures," describes how to write event-handling macros and VBA subprocedures.

2010 NEW To view the embedded macro sheet that the wizard created for your new combo box, change to Design view, open the Property Sheet for the Find: combo box, click the Events tab in the window, select the After Update property text box, and then click the Builder button. Access 2010 opens its new macro sheet designer tabbed document for the cboFind:After Update event and its Macro Tools—Design contextual ribbon shown in Figure 15.41. Close the macro sheet designer and return to Design view.

> **tip**
> Always use unbound combo box controls for record selection. If you bind a record-selection combo box to a field, the combo box updates field values with its value.

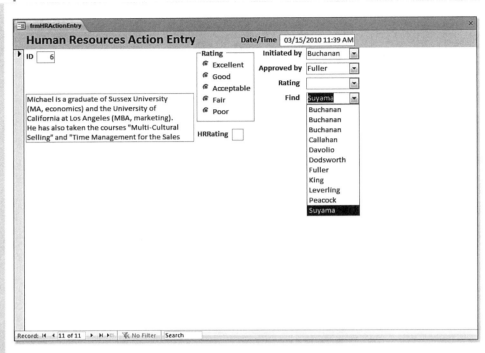

To use a combo box of this type, select a value from the list. As soon as you select the new value, Access updates the combo box's text box, which then invokes the embedded macro for the After Update event. The Search for Record macro action finds the first record in the form's Recordset with a matching value and displays it.

Because the field on the form is based on the LastName column of the form's underlying query, you see an entry in the list for every last name entry in the Recordset produced by the qryHRActions query. If, for instance, more than one HRActions records exist for Steve Buchanan, Buchanan appears in the combo list as many times as there are records for him. If all employees have at least one record, you can change the Record Source's Access SQL Statement to the following:

```
SELECT DISTINCT [qryHRActions].[LastName] FROM [qryHRActions];
```

If an employee doesn't have a record in the qryHRActions query resultset, the name doesn't appear in the list. To display a unique list of all employee last names, change the Row Source property to obtain the LastName field values for the combo box list with an SQL statement based on a query from the Employees table.

Figure 15.41
The Combo
Box Wizard
generates the
cboFind:After
Update embed-
ded macro to
find the first
record con-
taining the
selected last
name.

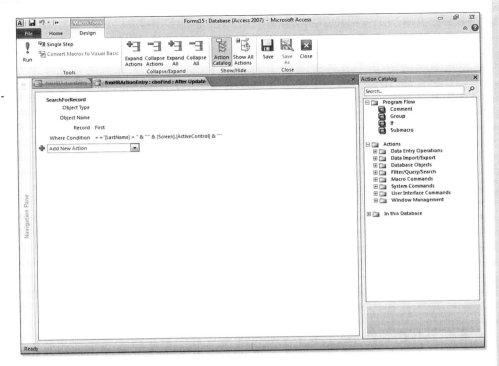

To change the Row Source property, follow the procedure you learned in the "Using the Query Builder to Populate a Combo Box" section, earlier in this chapter: Open the Property Sheet of the cboFind combo box, click the Data tab, select the Row Source text box, and then open the Query Builder. Change the query so that it uses the LastName field of the Employees table, add an ascending sort, as shown in Figure 15.42, and change the query's Unique Values and combo box's Limit to List property values to Yes.

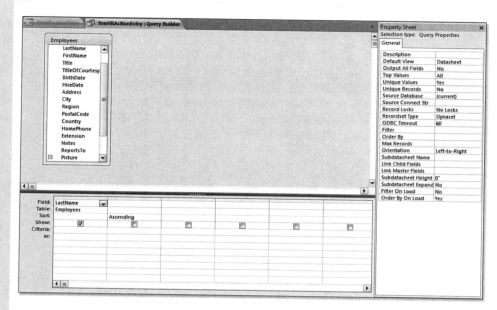

Figure 15.42
Changing the
Row Source
of the combo
box to a query
against the
Employees
table elimi-
nates duplicate
items in the
cboFind combo
box.

Adding an Attachment Control for Images

Previous versions of Access used OLE Object fields to store images, sounds, or other nontextual content and Bound Object Frame controls to display or play back the content. Bound Object Frame controls relied on OLE 2.0 full servers, such as Windows Paintbrush, Paint, or Sound Recorder, as an editing intermediary between the in OLE Object fields' content and the form's user. The choice of content data type was limited to those from the set of OLE 2.0 servers installed on users' computers.

2007 NEW As noted in earlier chapters, the Attachment data type introduced by Access 2007 lets users store a variety of file-based content in Access tables. A unique feature of the Attachment data type is the capability to store multiple images or the contents of other file types in a single table cell. By default, the control displays the first image (or icons for nongraphics items) from an internal list that's sorted by source filename.

Table 15.3 lists the graphics file extensions and format names that the Attachment control renders natively. The Compressed column indicates whether adding the content type to the column compresses the data to save space.

Table 15.3 Graphics Formats Rendered by the Attachment Control

Extension Graphics	Format	Compressed
.bmp	Windows Bitmap	Yes
.dib	Device Independent Bitmap	Yes
.emf	Enhanced Metafile	Yes

Extension Graphics	Format	Compressed
.exif	Exchangeable File Format	Yes
.gif	Graphics Interchange Format	No
.ico, .icon	Icon	Yes
.jpg, .jpeg, .jpe	Joint Photographic Experts Group	No
.rle	Run Length Encoded Bitmap	Yes
.png	Portable Network Graphics	No
.tif, .tiff	Tagged Image File Format	Yes
.wmf	Windows Metafile	Yes

To manage attachments, including opening content added from nongraphics files, do one of the following to open the Attachments dialog:

- Double-click the Attachment control's surface.
- [paperclip icon] Click the Attachment symbol (a paperclip) on the floating mini-toolbar that appears when you hover the mouse over the control.
- Right-click the Attachment control and choose Manage Attachments.

➡ *To review an early example of working with the Attachment data type and Attachments control,* **see** *"Opening Forms from the Navigation Pane and Adding Records,"* **p. 62.**

The Attachments dialog lets you add files of almost any type, except those that have the following extensions:

.ade	.csh	.lnk	.mda	.pif	.vb
.adp	.exe	.mad	.mdb	.prf	.vbe
.app	.fxp	.maf	.mde	.prg	.vbs
.asp	.hlp	.mag	.mdt	.pst	.vsmacros
.bas	.hta	.mam	.mdw	.reg	.vss
.bat	.inf	.maq	.mdz	.scf	.vst
.cer	.ins	.mar	.msc	.scr	.vsw
.chm	.isp	.mas	.msi	.sct	.ws
.cmd	.its	.mat	.msp	.shb	.wsc
.com	.js	.mau	.mst	.shs	.wsf
.cpl	.jse	.mav	.ops	.tmp	.wsh
.crt	.ksh	.maw	.pcd	.url	

The Attachment control embargoes the preceding extensions because files of these types might contain executable content and thus have the potential to be malicious.

The qryHRActions query includes the Picture Attachment field. To experiment with the Attachment data type and control's Attachments dialog, do the following:

1. With the frmHRActionEntry form open in Layout view, delete the Rating option frame, the Rating text box, and the two Rating labels.

2. Click the Form Layout Tools—Design ribbon's Add Existing Fields button to open the Field List, click the Show Only Fields in the Current Record Source link, and drag the Picture field to the form at the right of the Notes text box.

3. Adjust the height of the control to that of the Notes text box and the width of the control to match that of the image. Pass the mouse over the image to activate the mini-toolbar (see Figure 15.43).

> **note**
>
> The Attachment control embargoes file extensions for earlier Access versions (.ade, .adp, .mda, .mdb, .mde, .mdt, .mdw, .mdz) but not their Access 2007 and 2010 equivalents (.accdb, .accde, and so on).

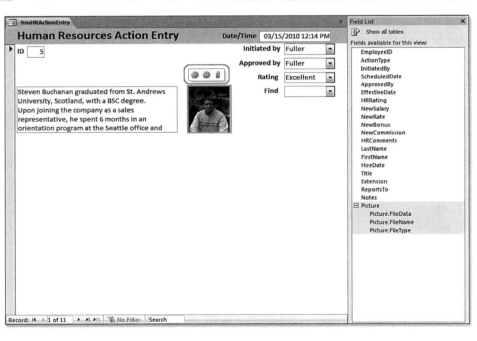

Figure 15.43
A mini-toolbar lets you scan multiple images or other content in the selected Attachment cell. Clicking the paperclip icon opens the Attachments dialog.

4. You can't add or remove content in Layout view, so change to Form view, change the Picture control's Locked property to No, and double-click the control to open the Attachments dialog and display the content imported from one of the EMPID1.JPG through EMPID9.JPG files in the downloadable sample file's \Access2010\Nwind folder.

5. Click the Add button to open the Choose File dialog, navigate to a source of media files to add to the selected Attachment table cell, select a file, and then click Open to close the Choose File dialog and add the file to the Attachments dialog's list (see Figure 15.44).

6. Verify that you can open the added content in its default application by double-clicking the list item or selecting the item and clicking Open. You can save an individual item with the Save button or save all items to a specified folder by clicking the Save All button.

7. Select each item you added in steps 5 and 6 and click Remove to set it for deletion from the list. Click OK to remove the items and close the dialog.

Figure 15.44
The Attachments dialog displays the contents of a table cell with JPEG images of Steven Buchanan and an album cover, three Windows Media Audio (.wma) files, and two MP3 music files.

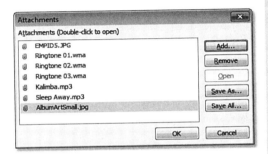

Working with Tab Controls

The tab control lets you easily create multipage forms in a single tabbed dialog, similar to Access 2010's tabbed documents. The tab control is a very efficient alternative to creating multipage forms with the Page Break control. You can use the tab control to conserve space onscreen and show information from one or more tables. The sections that follow show you how to add images to a new OLE object field of the Employees table, add a tab control to a form, and display images in a bound image control on a tab control page. You also learn to set the important properties of the tab control as a whole, as well as the properties of individual pages of the tab control.

> **tip**
>
> Use the Image control—not an Unbound Object Frame control—to display static images, such as logos and background bitmaps. The Image control accepts an even wider range of graphics formats than the Attachment control.

Adding the Tab Control to a Form

To add a tab control to the frmHRActionEntry form, follow these steps:

1. Click the Design View button if the frmHRActionEntry form isn't already in Design view. No wizard for the tab control exists, so the status of the Use Control Wizards button doesn't matter.

2. 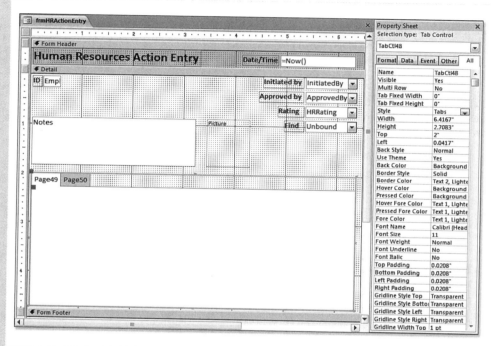 Click the Tab Control button on the Form Design Tools—Design ribbon; the mouse cursor changes to the Tab Control icon while it's over the active surface of the form.

3. Click and drag on the surface of the form's Detail section to create the new tab control near the bottom center of the form (see Figure 15.45).

Figure 15.45
Access's default tab control has two pages.

By default, Access creates a tab control with two pages. Each page's tab displays the name of the page combined with a sequential number corresponding to the number of controls you placed on your form in this work session. The next few sections describe how to change the page tab's caption, add or delete pages in the tab control, add controls to the pages, and set the page and tab control properties.

Adding Tab Control Pages

Depending on the data you want to display and how you want to organize that data, you might want to include more than two pages in your tab control. To add a page to a tab control, follow these steps:

1. In Design view, right-click the tab control to open the context menu.

2. Choose Insert Page; Access inserts a new page in the tab control to the right of the last page.

Changing the Page Order

Because Access adds a new page only after the last page, it isn't possible to add a new page at the beginning or middle of the existing tab pages. As a result, if you want the new tab control page to appear in another location in the tab control, you must change the order of pages in the tab control. You might also want to change the order of tab control pages as you work with and test your forms—in general, you should place the most frequently used (or most important) page at the front of the tab control.

To change the order of pages in a tab control, follow these steps:

1. Right-click one of the tabs and choose Page Order to open the Page Order dialog shown in Figure 15.46.

Figure 15.46
Change the left-to-right sequence of the tabs with the Page Order dialog.

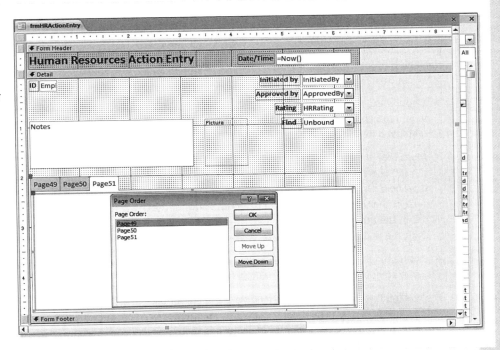

2. In the Page Order list, select the page whose position you want to change.

3. Click the Move Up or Move Down buttons, as appropriate, until the page is in the position you want.

4. Repeat steps 3 and 4 until you have arranged the tab control pages in the order you want, and then click OK to close the Page Order dialog and apply the new page order to the tab control.

4

Deleting a Tab Control Page

At some point, you might decide that you don't want or need a page in a tab control. The frmHRActionEntry form needs only two pages in its tab control. If you added a page to the tab control by following the steps at the beginning of this section, you can delete a page from the tab control by following this procedure:

1. Right-click the page tab of the page you want to delete; Access brings that page to the front of the tab control.

2. Choose Delete Page; Access deletes the currently selected tab control page.

Setting the Tab Control's Properties

Two sets of properties govern the appearance and behavior of a tab control. A set of properties exists for the entire tab control, and a separate set of properties applies to each page in the tab control. The following list summarizes the important properties of the tab control and its pages; the remaining property settings for the tab control and its pages are similar to those you've seen for other controls (height, width, color, and so on):

- *Caption* is a text property. It controls the text that appears on the page's tab and applies to individual tab control pages only. If this property is empty (the default), the page's Name property is displayed on the page's tab.

- *MultiRow* is a Yes/No property. It applies to the tab control as a whole and determines whether the tab control can display more than one row of tabs. (The Options dialog, reached by choosing Tools, Options, is an example of a multirow tabbed dialog.) The default setting is No. In this case, if there are more tabs than fit in the width of the tab control, Access displays a scroll button in the tab control. If you change this property to Yes and there are more page tabs than will fit in the width of the tab control, Access displays multiple rows of tabs.

- *Picture* displays an icon in any or all the page tabs. You can use any of Access's built-in icons or insert any bitmapped (.bmp) graphics file as the page's tab icon.

- *Style* applies to the tab control as a whole and controls the style in which the tab control's page tabs are displayed. The default setting, Tabs, produces the standard page tabs you're accustomed to seeing in the Property Sheet and in various dialogs in Access and Windows. Two other settings are available: Buttons and None. The Buttons setting causes the page tabs to be displayed as command buttons in a row across the top of the tab control. The None setting causes the tab control to omit the page tabs altogether. Use the None setting if you want to control which page of the tab control has the focus with command buttons or option buttons located outside the tab control. However, using command buttons external to the tab control to change pages requires writing Access VBA program code. You should use the default Tabs setting unless you have a specific reason for doing otherwise—using the Tabs setting ensures that the appearance of your tab controls is consistent with other portions of the Access user interface. Using this setting also saves you the effort of writing VBA program code.

- *Tab Fixed Height* and *Tab Fixed Width* apply to the tab control as a whole and govern the height and width of the page tabs in the control, respectively. The default setting for these properties is 0. When these properties are set to 0, the tab control sizes the page tabs to accommodate the size of the Caption for the page. If you want all the page tabs to have the same height or width, enter a value (in inches or centimeters, depending on your specific version of Access) in the corresponding property text box.

- *Tab Shape* is adjustable by selecting the entire Tab control (see the following paragraph), which enables the Form Design Tools—Format ribbon's Change Shape button. Clicking the Change Shape button opens a gallery of tab shapes, including rounded top corners of different radii, rectangular, rounded rectangular and oval buttons. (The Tab control is one of the few controls that enables the Change Shape button.)

To display the Property Sheet for the entire Tab control, right-click the edge of the tab control, and choose Properties from the resulting context menu. Alternatively, click the edge of the tab control to select it (clicking the blank area to the right of the page tabs is easiest), and then click the Properties button on the toolbar to display the Property Sheet.

To display the Property Sheet for an individual page in the tab control, click the page's tab to select it, and then click the Properties button on the toolbar to display the page's Property Sheet.

The tab control in the frmHRActionEntry form uses one page to display current information about an employee: the employee's job title, supervisor, company telephone extension, hire date, and photo. The second tab control page displays a history of that employee's HRActions in a subform you add later in the chapter.

Follow these steps to set the Caption property for the frmHRActionEntry form's Tab control:

1. Open the frmHRActionEntry form, and change to Form Design view, if necessary.

2. Click the first page of the tab control to select it, and then click the Properties button on the toolbar to display that page's Property Sheet.

3. Click the Format tab, if necessary, to display the Format properties for the tab control page.

4. Type **Employee Info** in the Caption property's text box.

5. Click the Other tab and change the Name property value to **pagEmployeeInfo**.

6. Click the second page of the tab control to select it; the contents of the Property dialog change to show the properties of the second tab control page. Click the Format tab.

7. Type **History** in the Caption property text box for the second page of the Tab control, type **pagHistory** in the Name property of the Other page, and close the Property Sheet.

8. Click outside the tabbed region to select the entire tab control, and type **tabHRAction** as the name of the control.

Figure 15.47 shows the tab control with both page captions set and the first page of the tab control selected. Notice that the sizing handles visible in the tab control are inside the control—this position indicates that the page, not the entire control, is currently selected. When the entire tab control is selected, the sizing handles appear on the edges of the tab control.

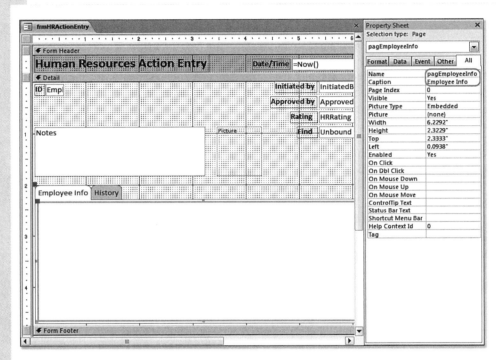

Figure 15.47
Set the Page properties by clicking the tab of one of the pages. Click the empty area to the right of the tabs to set the properties of the entire tab control.

Placing Other Controls on Tab Pages

You can place any of Access's other types of controls on the pages of aTab control—labels, text boxes, list boxes, even subforms. To add a control of any type to a tab control's page, follow this procedure:

1. In Design view, click the page tab you want to add the control to; Access selects the page and brings it to the front of the tab control.

2. Add the desired control to the Tab control's page using the techniques presented earlier in this chapter for creating controls on the main form.

2010 NEW Alternatively, you can copy controls from the same or another form and paste them into the tab control's pages by using the same techniques you learned for copying and pasting controls on a form's Detail and Header/Footer sections. Access 2010 lets you drag controls from the form's Detail or Header/Footer sections onto the tab control's page, and vice versa, which wasn't possible in Access 2007 and earlier.

As you proceed with the examples in this chapter and complete the frmHRActionEntry form, you place various bound and unbound controls on the pages of the tab control.

Optimizing the Form's Design

The preceding sections of this chapter have shown you how to use Toolbox controls without regard to positioning the controls to optimize data entry operations. In this section, you add more controls from the qryHRActions query's field list to the main form's Detail section and the Company Info page of the tab control. You place new controls for adding or editing fields of the HRActions table on the main form, and relocate the controls you added earlier into a logical data entry sequence. The Employee Info page of the tab control displays reference data from the Employees table. Multipage tab controls are especially effective for displaying data that's related to the entries you make on the main form.

To add and rearrange the form's controls to optimize data entry, follow these steps (look ahead to Figure 15.48 for control placement and formatting):

1. Return to Design view, if necessary, and delete the Picture Attachment control and Notes text box. You add these controls to the tab control in later steps.

2. Click the Add Existing Fields button to open the Field List dialog if it isn't already open.

3. Drag the LastName field from the Field List to a position to the right of the ID field text box; delete the field's label.

4. Drag the FirstName field from the Field List to a position to the right of the LastName field; delete the FirstName field's label.

5. Drag the ActionType field from the Field List to a position at the right of the FirstName field to add a combo box.

6. Repeat step 4 for the ScheduledDate, EffectiveDate, NewSalary, and NewBonus fields (see Figure 15.48 for field positioning and sizing). You must move the InitiatedBy, ApprovedBy, HRRating, and Name text boxes that you placed on the form earlier in this chapter.

7. Resize the HRComments field so that it's underneath the EmployeeID and name fields (look ahead to Figure 15.48). Next, resize the tab control so that it fills the width of the form and extends from an area below the HRComments field to the bottom of the form. The tab control needs to be as large as possible to display as much data as possible in the subform that you add later to its second page.

8. Click the first tab of the tab control to bring it to the front, and then drag the Title field from the Field List to a position near the top-left corner of the Company Info page.

> **tip**
>
> Use the Format Painter to format the text labels of the fields.

9. Repeat step 8 for the ReportsTo, Extension, and HireDate fields (see Figure 15.48 for field placement).

10. Drag the Picture field onto the right side of the tab control's first page, and delete its label. (The fact that this field displays a photo of the employee is enough to identify the field.) Size and position the Photo field at the right edge of the tab control's page; you might need to resize the tab control and the form after inserting the Photo field.

11. Drag the Notes field to the bottom-left corner of the tab control's first page and delete its label.

12. Use the techniques you learned in Chapter 14 to move, rearrange, and change the label formats to match the appearance of Figure 15.48. (All labels are bold, sized to fit, and right-aligned.)

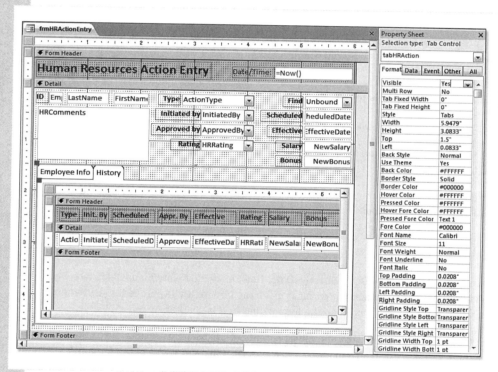

Figure 15.48
Here's the final design of the form with new controls and formatting.

➡ *For more information on creating a uniform appearance with the Format Painter,* **see** *"Using the Format Painter,"* **p. 592.**

13. Change the Format property value of the ScheduledDate and EffectiveDate text boxes to **mm/dd/ yyyy** to ensure Y2K compliance, and change the Format property value of the Salary and Bonus text boxes to Currency to add a dollar sign and change the Decimal Places property value to 0.

14. To replace the letter code or number with text in the Type, ApprovedBy, and Rating combo boxes, change the Column Widths property value of the Type control to **0";1.2** and ApprovedBy and Rating to **0";0.65"**.

15. 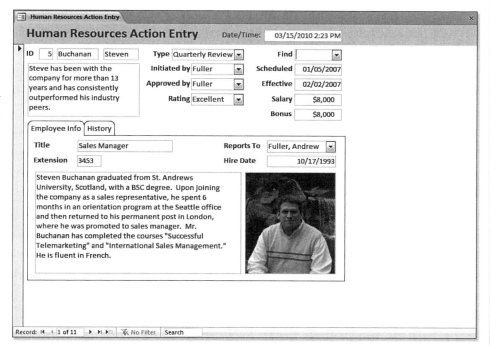 Click the Select Form button, and set the Caption property value of the form to **Human Resources Action Entry**.

16. Press Ctrl+S to save your changes, and test your new and modified controls by changing to Form view (see Figure 15.49).

Figure 15.49
The form is now complete, except for the addition of a subform to the History page of the tab control.

Adding a History Subform to a Tab Control Page

The frmHRActionEntry form needs a subform to display the history of HRActions for the employee displayed in the main part of the form. The HRActions table provides the data source for the subform. Access's Subform/Subreport control offers the Subform Wizard, which lets you quickly add an existing form as a new subform, as described in the following sections.

Creating a Modified HRActions Subform

If you didn't create the sbfHRActions subform in the preceding chapter, import the sbfHRActions subform from your \Program Files\Seua11\Chaptr14\Forms14.accdb database.

Follow these steps to adapt the sbfHRActions subform for use on the History page of the tab control:

1. Select sbfHRActions in the Navigation pane, and press Ctrl+C and Ctrl+V to create a copy of the subform named sbfHRActionsTab and open it in Design view.

2. Delete the HRComments column's header and text box.

3. Right-click the ActionType combo box, and choose Change To, Text Box.

4. ≣ Shift+click to select the ActionType, InitiatedBy, ApprovedBy, and HRRating text boxes, and click the toolbar's Center button to center the text and labels.

5. Select all labels and drag them to the middle of the Form header section. Click the Bold button of the Formatting toolbar to apply the bold attribute to all labels. Drag the Detail section bar up to the bottom of the labels.

6. Select all text boxes and drag them to the bottom of the Detail bar. Drag the Form Footer bar up to the bottom of the text boxes.

7. Reduce the width of the subform to about 5.38 inches, and save your changes (see Figure 15.50).

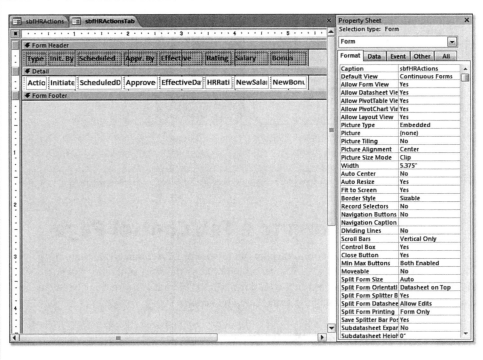

Figure 15.50
Form Design view shows the changes you make to the layout for the sbfHRActionsTab subform for addition to the History tab page.

8. Change to Form Design view to check your work (see Figure 15.51) and close the subform.

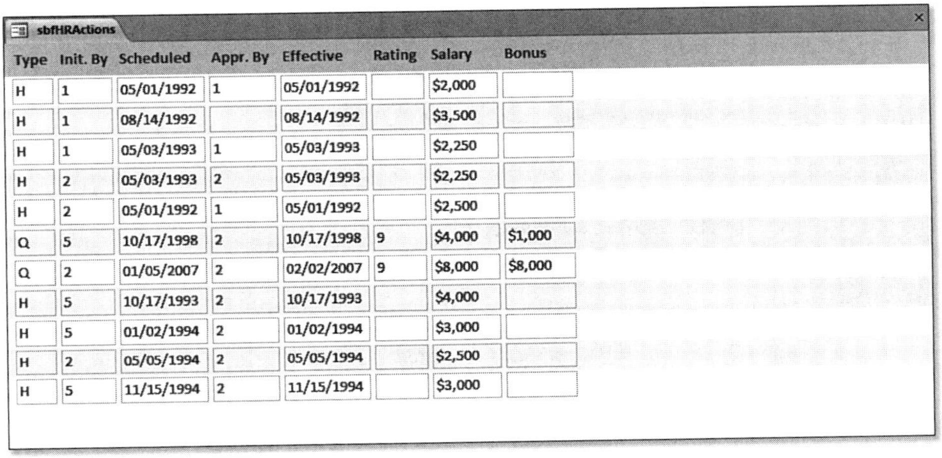

Figure 15.51
The final version of the read-only subform to be added to the History tab page.

Type	Init. By	Scheduled	Appr. By	Effective	Rating	Salary	Bonus
H	1	05/01/1992	1	05/01/1992		$2,000	
H	1	08/14/1992		08/14/1992		$3,500	
H	1	05/03/1993	1	05/03/1993		$2,250	
H	2	05/03/1993	2	05/03/1993		$2,250	
H	2	05/01/1992	1	05/01/1992		$2,500	
Q	5	10/17/1998	2	10/17/1998	9	$4,000	$1,000
Q	2	01/05/2007	2	02/02/2007	9	$8,000	$8,000
H	5	10/17/1993	2	10/17/1993		$4,000	
H	5	01/02/1994	2	01/02/1994		$3,000	
H	2	05/05/1994	2	05/05/1994		$2,500	
H	5	11/15/1994	2	11/15/1994		$3,000	

Adding the sbfHRActionsTab Subform with the Wizard

To add the sbfActionsTab subform to the History page of the tab control with the Subform Wizard, do the following:

1.  With the wizard activated, open frmHRActionEntry in Design view, click the History tab of the tab control, and select the Subform/Subreport tool in the toolbox.

2. Drag the mouse pointer icon, which assumes the shape of the Subform/Subreport tool, to the History page. The icon changes to a pointer when you reach the active region of the History page, which changes from white to black.

3. Release the mouse to open the Subform Wizard's first dialog.

4. Select the Use an Existing Form option and select sbfHRActionEntryTab in the list (see Figure 15.52). Click Next.

5. In the second wizard dialog, accept the Choose from a List option and then select Show HRActions for Each Record in qryHRActions Using Employee[ID] (see Figure 15.53). Click Next.

6. Accept sbfHRActionEntryTab as the name of the subform, and click Finish to dismiss the wizard.

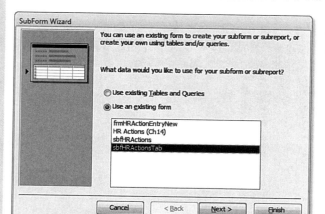

Figure 15.52
The Subform Wizard's first dialog lets you select the existing form to use as a subform.

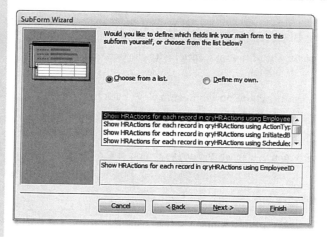

Figure 15.53
In the second dialog you specify the value of the LinkChildFields and LinkMasterFields properties (EmployeeID for this example).

7. Delete the label and adjust the size of the subform to occupy most of the available area of the History page (see Figure 15.54).

8. Change to Form view, select Buchanan in the Find list, and click the History tab to display the hired entry for Steven Buchanan and a tentative append record (see Figure 15.55).

Figure 15.54
After the wizard adds the subform, adjust its dimensions to suit the active area of the tab control's page.

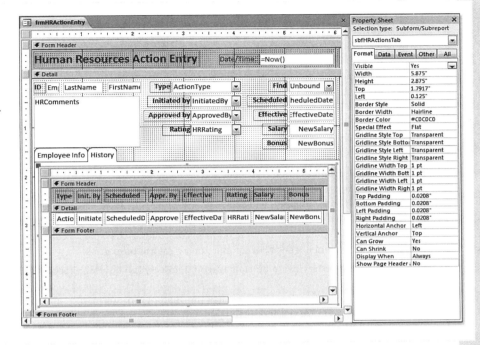

Figure 15.55
Form view with the History page selected displays HRActions record(s) for the employee selected in the Find combo box.

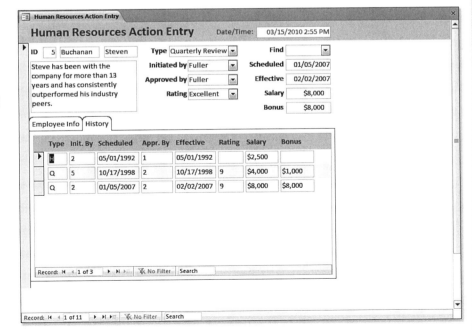

Modifying the Design of Continuous Forms

The default design of the History page's subform as created by the Subform Wizard lets you edit records of the HRActions table. The term *History* implies read-only access to the table in the tab control. Therefore, you should alter the properties of the subform to make the form read-only and remove unnecessary controls. For example, the vertical scrollbar lets you display any HRActions record for the employee, so you don't need record navigation buttons, nor do you need record selectors.

Access's in-situ subform editing feature lets you change many of the properties of subforms with the main form open in Design view. Unfortunately, you can't change property values, such as Record Selectors and Navigation Buttons, that affect the structure of the subform. Therefore, you must change the design of the subform independently of its main form container. Access has a command—Subform in New Window—that provides a shortcut for changing subform properties.

To further optimize the design of the sbfHRActionEntryTab subform, follow these steps:

1. Return to Design view, click the History tab, select and right-click the subform, and choose Subform in New Window to open sbfHRActionEntryTab in Design view. Then click the Properties button to display the Property Sheet for the subform.

2. In the Format page of the Property Sheet, set Scrollbars to Vertical Only, Record Selectors to No, and Navigation Buttons to No.

3. In the Data page, set the Recordset Type to Snapshot. Doing so has the same effect as setting Allow Edits, Allow Deletions, and Allow Additions to No. Your subform is now read-only because all snapshot-type Recordsets are read-only.

4. Select all text boxes and set the Tab Stop property to No for the group. Close the subform and save your changes.

5. In the now-empty History page, reduce the width of the subform and the tab control by about 1/8-inch to reflect removal of the Record Selector buttons. You can reduce the width of the subform container only when the subform isn't open for in-situ editing.

6. In the main form, select the tab control, and set its Tab Stop property to No. Do the same for the EmployeeID, LastName, and FirstName text boxes.

7. Set the tab order by clicking the Form Design Tools—Arrange tab and the Tab Stop button to open the Tab Order dialog. Click Auto Order to set the tab order of the controls for which the Tab Order property is Yes. Select and move the cboFind combo box to the top of the tab order. The default control tab order is top-to-bottom, left-to-right. Click OK to close this dialog.

8. Return to Form view and click the History tab to verify your changes to the subform (see Figure 15.56).

Figure 15.56
Form view
reflects sub-
form linking on
the EmployeeID
field and the
changes you
made to the
design and
dimensions of
the subform.

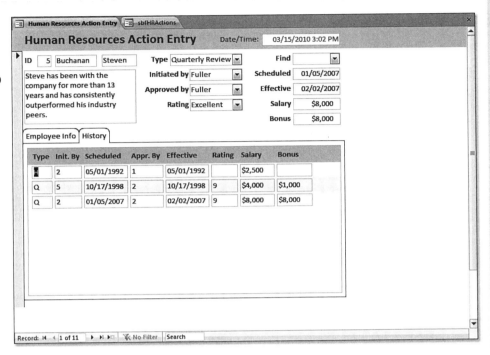

Adding New Records in the HRActionEntry Form

Unlike Chapter 14's frmHRActions form, the Record Source for
the main frmHrActionEntry form is a query. The query design
takes advantage of Access' row fix-up feature when you add
a new record to the HRActions table in the form. Row fix-up
works in this case because the source of the qryHRActions
query's EmployeeID column is a field of the HRActions table,
not the Employees table.

> *For a review of row fix-up in one-to-many queries,* **see**
> *"Taking Advantage of Access' s Row Fix-up Feature,"*
> **p. 471.**

To add a new record to the HRActions table, do the following:

1. Open frmHRActionEntry in Form view, and click
   the tentative append (new) record button to add a new record. All data disappears from the form.

> ## tip
> Removing text boxes and other con-
> trols from the tab order that you sel-
> dom or can't edit speeds data entry.
> To further optimize data entry, set
> the Tab Stop property of all controls
> on both pages of the tab control to
> No. Labels don't have a tab stop
> control; if you multiselect all con-
> trols on a page, use Shift+click to
> deselect the labels to set Tab Stop
> to No for all other controls.

2. Type a number in the [Employee]ID text box; for this example type **5** for Steven Buchanan. Press Tab or Enter to add data for the selected employee in the query columns from the Employees table and default values from the HRActions table to the form's controls (see Figure 15.57).

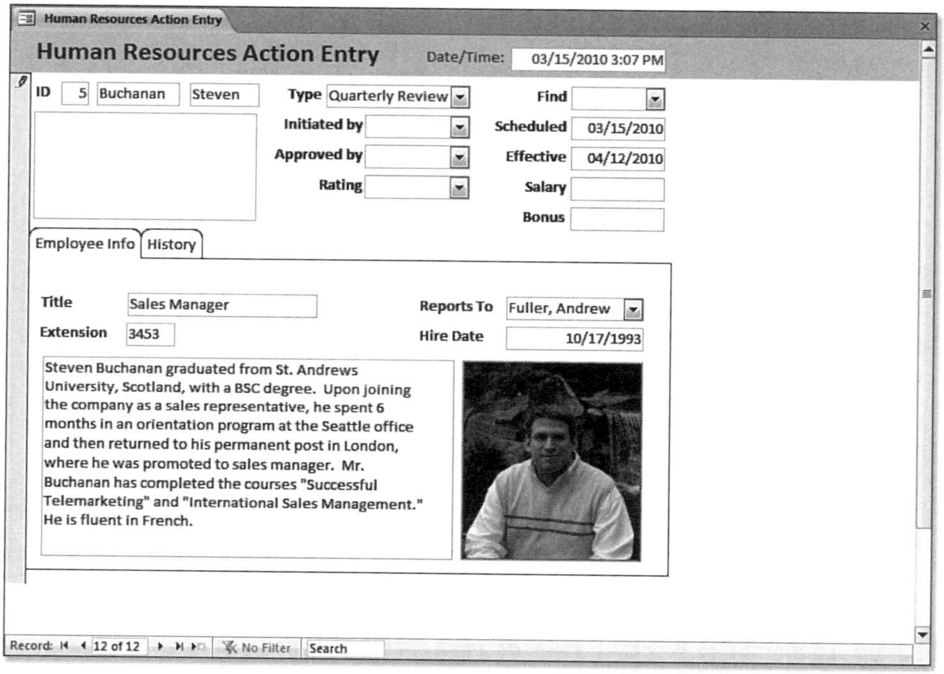

Figure 15.57
Adding a new record and typing an employee ID in the ID text box fills the form with employee data and default values from the qryHRActions query.

3. Make selections in the combo boxes, change the default dates, if necessary, and add a note regarding the action. If your cursor isn't in the Notes multiline text box, press Shift+Enter to save the record (see Figure 15.58). Shift+Enter in a multiline text box adds a newline character and doesn't save the record.

4. Verify that you added the record correctly by selecting the employee for whom you added the action—in this case Steven Buchanan—in the Find combo box. Click the History tab to display the employee's entries (see Figure 15.59). The History subform's snapshot Recordset must be refreshed to display the added record.

At this point in its development, frmHRActionEntry would be dangerous to release for use by data entry operators. For example, all fields in the main form are updatable. Thus, an operator could change the FirstName, LastName, and other values of the Employees table, as well as the EmployeeID for an existing HRActions record. You can set the Locked property to Yes for all controls linked to the Employees table, but you can't lock the EmployeeID text box that's required to specify the EmployeeID of a new record. You can control the locked status of form controls by adding VBA event-handling code for the form's Before Insert and After Insert events.

Figure 15.58
Completing the record addition requires only a few combo box selections, changes to dates, and an optional note.

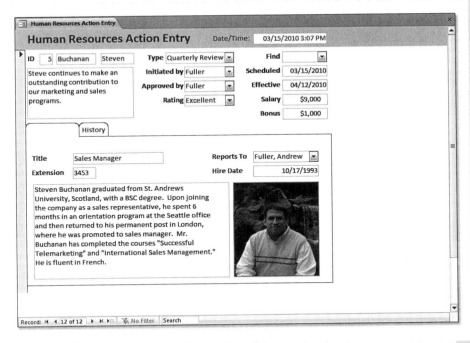

Figure 15.59
After you refresh the History subform by selecting the employee in the Find combo box, the newly added record appears.

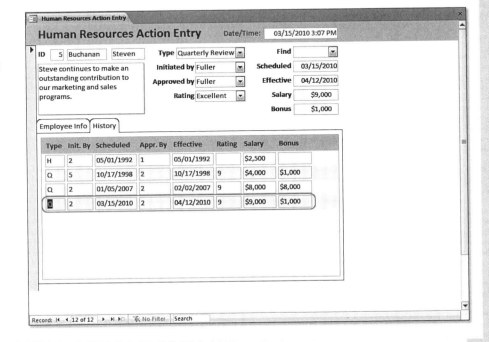

Using the New Navigation Control and Application Parts

 Access 2010's new Navigation control offers a more weblike alternative to Access's traditional switchboard navigation between forms and reports. The Navigation control consists of a form containing a subform that you fill by dragging multiple forms or reports from the Navigation page to an Add New tab at the top, side or both of the Navigation form's Design view.

Clicking the Navigation button of the Create ribbon's Forms group opens the gallery of tab row and axis choices shown in Figure 15.60. When you click the Horizontal Tabs or Vertical Tabs, Left or Right option, in Design view a form opens with an empty Navigation Subform and a single Add New tab. Dragging a form or report from the Navigation pane to the Add New tab displays the form or report in the subform, replaces the Add New tab with the object name, ContactDetails for this example, and opens another Add New tab, as shown in Figure 15.61.

> **tip**
>
> You can make frmHRActionEntry safe for data entry operators by setting the Data Entry property of the form to Yes. Specifying Data Entry prevents operators from viewing existing records and only allows them to enter new records. In this case, you must change the Recordset Type property value of the subform to Dynaset, and set the AllowEdits, AllowDeletions, and AllowAdditions property values to Yes. Otherwise, the added record won't appear in the History subform.

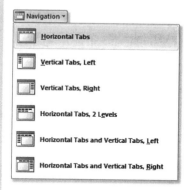

Figure 15.60
The Navigation control's gallery lets you choose horizontal, vertical or both tab axes and one or two rows of tabs.

Clicking the Create ribbon's Application Parts button in the Templates group opens a gallery of 10 basic Blank Form styles and five pre-built Quick Start forms (see Figure 15.62).

Figure 15.61
Dragging a ContactDetails form from the Navigation pane to the Add New tab adds the form as a Navigation Subform and generates another Add New tab in Layout view.

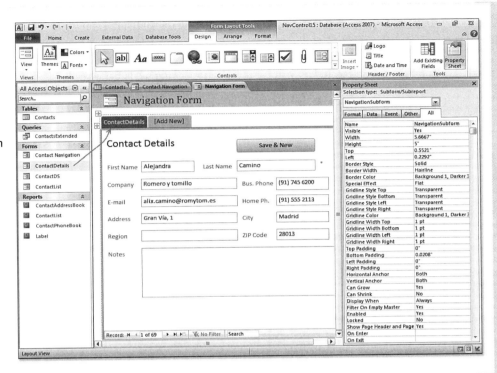

Figure 15.62
Clicking the Application Parts button opens a gallery of Blank Form styles and complete, pre-built Quick Start objects.

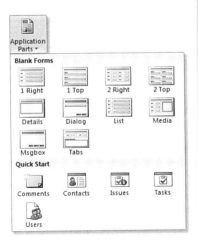

Application Parts generate individual Access objects rather than new databases, which templates generate. For example, following are descriptions of the 10 Blank Form styles:

1. 1 Right—Single-record, one column of labels for adding fields to the right

2. 1 Top—Single-record, one column of labels for adding fields below

3. 2 Right—Single-record, two columns of labels for adding fields to the right

4. 2 Top—Single-record, two columns of labels for adding fields below

5. Details—Single-record form with a subform

6. Dialog—Dialog form with Save and Save & Close buttons

7. List—List form with Add New, Edit and Delete buttons

8. Media—Single-record form with placeholders for media objects

9. MsgBox—Message box form with Yes, No and Cancel buttons

10. Tabs—Single-record form with labels for fields below and Tab control

Each of the five Quick Start forms generates a table and, except for Comments, one or more data entry forms for the table. The Contacts Quick Start generates an Outlook-compatible Contacts table, ContactDetails, ContactDS (datasheet), and ContactList forms, as well as ContactAddressBook, ContactList, ContactPhoneBook, and Label reports. The downloadable sample files' \Access2010\ Chaptr15 folder contains a NavControl15.accdb database with a Contacts table populated from an Outlook Contacts folder created from the Northwind sample database. The Contact Navigation form has a tabbed subform for each of the Contacts Quick Start's forms and reports, except Label (see Figure 15.63). Forms and reports have been realigned to better fit in Access's default tabbed window at 1,024x768 resolution. The Contacts table is prepopulated from the Outlook folder you created in the "Importing and Exporting Access Tables with Outlook 2010" section of Chapter 8, "Linking, Importing, and Exporting Data."

Figure 15.63
Clicking the Application Parts button opens a gallery of Blank Form styles and complete, pre-built Quick Start objects.

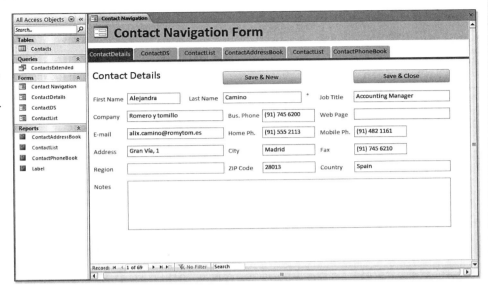

Using the Web Browser Control

Access 2010's new Web Browser control lets you display [X]HTML-encoded content in an Internet Explorer 8-compatible browser window. The Data Source for the control can be a web page URL or a *.htm[l], or other browser-compatible file. Alternatively, you can use a custom Expression Builder to generate the URL from field values of the table or query to which the form containing the Web Browser control is bound.

When you select the Web Browser control in the Form Design Tools—Design ribbon's Controls group and draw its initial size on a form, the Insert Hyperlink dialog opens. Clicking the Existing File or Web Page button enables entering a URL or file path and name in the Address text box (see Figure 15.64).

Figure 15.65 shows a post from the OakLeaf Systems blog in the Web Browser control. Text width adapts to the narrower display format, as illustrated by the text in the subtitle. The bitmapped diagram is 640 pixels wide and the left frame is 384 pixels wide, so the diagram's right side is cut off. The width of text below the graphic reduces to display correctly.

Chapter 25, "Importing and Exporting Web Pages," includes more examples of using the Web Browser control.

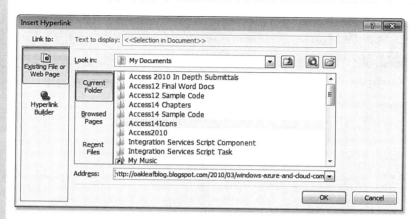

Figure 15.64
The Web Browser control can display HTML content from the a web URL, as shown here in the Insert Hyperlink dialog for the OakLeaf System blog, or other browser-compatible media types, such as graphic images.

Overriding the Field Properties of Tables

Access uses the table's property values assigned to the fields as defaults. The form or subform inherits these properties from the table or query on which the form is based. You can override the inherited properties, except for the Validation Rule property, by assigning a different set of values in the Property Sheet for the control. Properties of controls bound to fields of tables or queries that are inherited from the table's field properties are shown in the following list:

- Format

- Validation Rule

- Decimal Places

- Validation Text

- Status Bar Text

- Default Value

- Typeface characteristics (such as Font Name, Font Size, Font Bold, Font Italic, and Font Underline)

Values of field properties that you override with properties in a form apply only when the data is displayed and edited with the form. You can establish validation rules for controls bound to fields that differ from properties of the field established by the table, but you can only narrow the rule. The table-level validation rule for the content of the HRType field, for example, limits entries to the letters H, Q, Y, S, R, B, C, and T. The validation rule you establish in a form can't broaden the allowable entries; if you add F as a valid choice by editing the validation rule for the HRType field to `InS tr("HQYSRBCTF",[HRType])>0`, you receive an error when you type F.

Figure 15.65
The Web Browser control displays a typical page from the OakLeaf Systems blog with a 640-pixel wide graphic that's cut off because of the width limitation of the form.

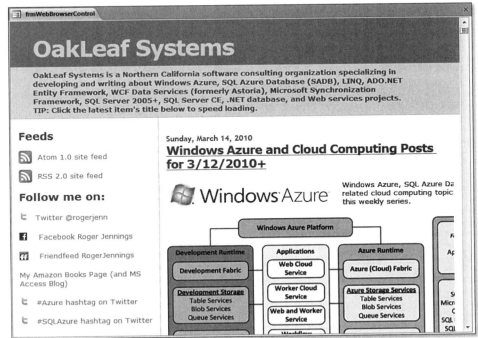

However, you can narrow the range of allowable entries by substituting `InStr("SQYB",[HRType])>0`. Notice that you can use expressions that refer to the field name as validation-rule expressions in forms; such expressions aren't permitted as field-level validation-rule expressions in Access 2010..

Adding Page Headers and Footers for Printing Forms

Access lets you add a separate pair of sections, Page Header and Page Footer, that appear only when the form prints. You add both of these sections to the form at once by choosing View, Page Header/Footer. The following list shows the purposes of Page Header and Footer sections:

- Page Header sections enable you to use a different title for the printed version. The depth of the page header can be adjusted to control the location where the Detail section of the form is printed on the page.

- Page Footer sections enable you to add dates and page numbers to the printed form.

PART

4

Page Header and Page Footer sections appear only in the printed form, not when you display the form onscreen in Form view. Figure 15.66 shows the frmHRActionEntry form in Design view with Page Header and Page Footer sections added.

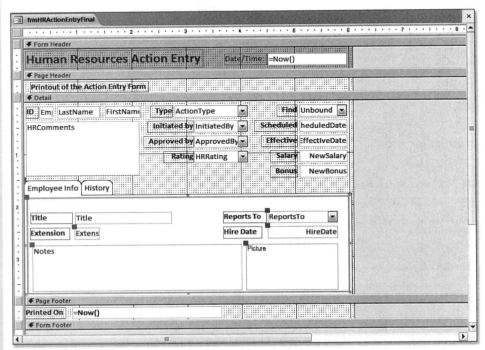

Figure 15.66
Page Header and Page Footer sections appear when you print the form, but not in Form view.

With the Display When (Format) property of the Property Sheet for the Form Header and Form Footer sections, you can control whether these sections appear in the printed form. In Figure 15.66, the Form Header section duplicates the information in the Page Header section (except for the Date/Time label and text box), so you might not want to print both. To control when a section of the form prints or is displayed, perform the following steps:

1. Double-click the title bar of whichever section of the form you want to change; this opens the related Property Sheet. (The Page Header and Page Footer sections don't have a Display When property; these sections appear only during printing.)

2. Click the Format tab if the formatting properties aren't already showing. Click to drop down the Display When list.

3. To display but not print this section in Form view, select Screen Only.

4. To print but not display this section, select Print Only.

WORKING WITH SIMPLE REPORTS AND MAILING LABELS

The final product of most database applications is a report. Access combines data from tables, queries, and—in some cases—forms to produce a report that you can print for people who need or request it. One of Access's major selling points is its capability to generate fully formatted reports easily and quickly. No other report generator application comes close to rivaling Access's flexible report-generation capabilities.

With the expansion of email and the growth of intranets and the Internet, it's becoming more common for people to read prebuilt reports online and, when necessary, post their own reports. Access offers the following methods of distributing paperless reports:

- Adobe Portable Document Format (.pdf) files, for viewing in or printing from Adobe Reader.

- Microsoft XML Paper Specification (.xps) files, for viewing in or printing with the XPS Viewer add-in for Internet Explorer. *Metro* was the code name for XPS during its development.

    > *For more information on sending reports as email attachments,* **see** *"Mailing Reports as Attachments,"* **p. 752.**

> **🔍 note**
>
> XPS is a Microsoft open format that's based on the Windows Presentation Foundation's (WPF's) Extensible Application Markup Language (XAML). According to Wikipedia, OpenXPS was standardized as an open standard document format on June 16, 2009.

> **🔍 note**
>
> SQL Server 2008 [R2] Reporting Services is an enterprise-grade, server-based report generator for SQL Server and Oracle databases. SQL Server 2008 R2 Express Edition with Advanced Services (SSXAS), which you can download from http://bit.ly/9HtmTh, includes a Reporting Services version that runs on the same computer as SSXAS. However, it's much easier and faster to create Access reports than Report Server reports.

- **2010 NEW** Access 2010 doesn't support Report Snapshots, which were self-contained .snp files that you could send as an email attachment with Outlook, Outlook Express, or any other Windows email program.

- **[W]** Rich Text Format (.rtf) files, for opening in and printing from Microsoft Word, primarily for backward compatibility.

- **[≣]** Text (.txt) files, for backward compatibility only.

- Static web reports, which apply an Extensible Stylesheet Language Transformations (XSLT) document to an Extensible Markup Language (XML) file to generate an HTML 4.0 simulation of the original report. You can export static—also called *snapshot*—web reports to a web server from conventional (Access) applications or Access data projects (ADPs). Recipients print the report from the browser.

- Live web reports, which are similar to static XSL/XML web reports, but deliver current data by executing an Active Server Pages (ASP) or HTML template query against SQL Server when opening the page in a browser.

> ➥ *To learn more about static and live web reports,* **see** *"Exporting Static Reports as XML and Web Pages,"* **p. 1070,** *and "Exporting Reports to HTML Tables,"* **p. 1031.**

Some reports consist of a single page, such as an order acknowledgment, invoice, graph, or chart. Multipage Access reports—typified by catalogs, general ledgers, and financial statements—are more common than the single-page variety. A multipage report is analogous to a read-only continuous form that has been optimized for printing.

Most methods of creating Access forms, which you learned about in Chapter 14, "Creating and Using Basic Access Forms," and Chapter 15, "Designing Custom Multitable Forms," also apply to reports. The following list details the principal differences between reports and forms:

- Reports are intended primarily for printing and, unlike forms, usually aren't designed for display in a window. When you view an 8 ½×11-inch report in the default Print Preview, its content might not be legible. In the zoomed (full-page) view, only a part of the report might be visible in the Print Preview or Layout Preview window, depending on your monitor's resolution.

- You can't change the value of the underlying data for a report with a control object from the toolbox like you can with forms. With reports, Access disregards user input from combo boxes, option buttons, check boxes, and the like. The primary controls you use on forms are labels and text boxes. You can use a check box to indicate the value of fields of the Yes/No (Boolean) data type.

  - **2007 NEW** Reports don't provide a Datasheet view. Only Print Preview, Report, Layout, and Design views are available. Report and Layout views were new in Access 2007.

- In multicolumn reports, the number of columns, the column width, and the column spacing are controlled by settings in the Printer Setup dialog, not by controls that you add or properties that you set in Design view.

Access reports share many characteristics of forms, including the following:

- *Basic reports* are generated by clicking the Create ribbon's Report button. The default basic report is a tabular list of all fields of all records in the table or query you select in the Navigation pane.

- *Report Wizards* create the three basic kinds of reports: single-column, groups/totals, and mailing labels. You can modify as necessary the reports that the Report Wizards create. The function of the Report Wizard is similar to that of the Form Wizard discussed in Chapter 14. The Label Wizard creates mailing labels for popular label brands and sizes.

- *Sections* include report headers and footers, which appear once at the beginning and at the end of the report, and page headers and footers, which print at the top and bottom of each page. The report footer often is used to print grand totals. Report sections correspond to similarly named form sections.

- *Group sections* of reports, as a whole, compose the equivalent of the Detail section of forms. Groups often are referred to as *bands*, and the process of grouping records is known as *banding*. You can add group headers that include a title for each group, and group footers to print group subtotals. You can place static (unbound) graphics in header and footer sections and bound graphics within group sections.

- *Controls* are added to reports from the Report Design Tools—Design ribbon's Controls group and then moved and sized with their handles. Reports support embedded bitmaps, attachments, OLE objects (such as graphs and charts you create with MSGraph.exe), and ActiveX controls (such as the PivotChart and PivotTable).

- *Subreports* can be incorporated into reports the same way you add subform controls within main forms.

Categorizing Types of Access Reports

Reports created by Access fall into six basic types, also called *layouts*, as detailed in the following list:

- **Tabular reports**—Provide a column for each field of the table or query and print the value of each field of the records in rows under the column header. If you have more columns than can fit on one page, additional pages print in sequence until all columns are printed; then the next page-length group of records is printed. The Create ribbon's Report button autogenerates a tabular report from the selected table or query. The AutoReport feature also can create a tabular report automatically.

- **Single-column reports**—List in one long column of text boxes the values of each field in each record of a table or query. A label indicates the name of a field, and a text box to the right of the label provides the values. Access's AutoReport feature can create a single-column report with a single click of the toolbar's AutoReport button. You seldom use single-column reports, because the format wastes paper.

- **Multicolumn reports**—Display single-column reports in multiple columns by using the "newspaper" or "snaking" column approach of desktop publishing and word processing applications. Information that doesn't fit in the first column flows to the top of the second column, and so on. The format of multicolumn reports wastes less paper than the single-column variety, but the uses of multicolumn reports are limited because the column alignment is unlikely to correspond with what you want.

- **Groups/totals reports**—The most common kind of report. Access groups/totals reports summarize data for groups of records and then add grand totals at the end of the report.

- **Mailing labels**—A special kind of multicolumn report that prints names and addresses (or other multifield data) in groups. The design of the stock adhesive label on which you print determines how many rows and columns are on a page.

- **Unbound reports**—Contain subreports based on unrelated data sources, such as tables or queries.

The first five types of reports use a table or query as the data source, as do forms. These kinds of reports are said to be bound to the data source. The main report of an unbound report isn't linked to a table or query as a data source. The subreports contained by an unbound report, however, must be bound to a data source.

Autogenerating a Simple Tabular Report

The process for autogenerating a tabular report from a table or query is dead simple. For example, following is the process for creating a Products report from the \Access2010\Chaptr16\Reports16.accdb database's qryInventory query:

1. Open the Reports16.accdb file from the downloadable sample files' \Access2010\Chaptr16 folder and select the qryInventory query in the Navigation pane.

2. Click the Create tab and its Report button to generate the qryInventory report in Layout view (see Figure 16.1).

Figure 16.1
The default
format of
autogenerated
reports is
very similar to
autogenerated
forms.

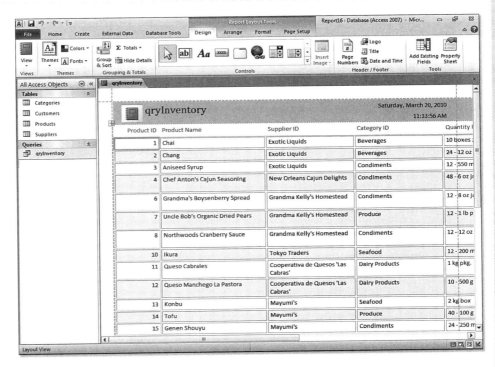

It's obvious that the default layout for autogenerated reports is much better suited to forms than reports. The 11-point font size is too large for ordinary reports (9-point is adequate), and row height and column width is excessive. Borders around field values aren't necessary and the default total value of the Unit Price column is meaningless. It's easy to adjust font sizes and column widths in Layout view, but Design view is more practical for making other adjustments. Figure 16.2 is a print preview of the rptInventory report's final version after the adjustments described have been made.

Figure 16.2
Modifying the layout of the autogenerated report shows all columns and their values across a single page and reduces the number of pages from eight to four.

rptInventory										

Inventory Report

Saturday, March 20, 2010
12:15:06 PM

Pro-duct ID	Product Name	Supplier	Category	Quantity Per Unit	Unit Price	Units In Stock	Units on Order	Reorder Level	Discon-tinued
3	Aniseed Syrup	Exotic Liquids	Condiments	12 - 550 ml bottles	$10.00	13	70	25	False
40	Boston Crab Meat	New England Seafood Cannery	Seafood	24 - 4 oz tins	$18.40	123	0	30	False
60	Camembert Pierrot	Gai pâturage	Dairy Products	15 - 300 g rounds	$34.00	19	0	0	False
18	Carnarvon Tigers	Pavlova, Ltd.	Seafood	16 kg pkg.	$62.50	42	0	0	False
1	Chai	Exotic Liquids	Beverages	10 boxes x 20 bags	$18.00	39	0	10	False
2	Chang	Exotic Liquids	Beverages	24 - 12 oz bottles	$19.00	17	40	25	False
39	Chartreuse verte	Aux joyeux ecclésiastiques	Beverages	750 cc per bottle	$18.00	69	0	5	False
4	Chef Anton's Cajun Seasoning	New Orleans Cajun Delights	Condiments	48 - 6 oz jars	$22.00	53	0	0	False
48	Chocolade	Zaanse Snoepfabriek	Confections	10 pkgs.	$12.75	15	70	25	False
92	Chu Hou Sauce	Zhongshan Sauces Co., Ltd.	Condiments	12 - 240 g jars	$12.25	5	0	10	False
38	Côte de Blaye	Aux joyeux ecclésiastiques	Beverages	12 - 75 cl bottles	$263.50	17	0	15	False

Page: 1 | No Filter

Creating a Grouped Report with the Report Wizard

This section shows you how to use the Report Wizard to create a grouped report based on data in the Products and Suppliers tables of the Northwind Traders sample database. (Like the Form Wizard, the Report Wizard lets you create reports that contain data from more than one table without first creating a query.) This report displays the quantity of each specialty food product in inventory, grouped by product category.

Creating an inventory report begins with modifying the basic report created by the Report Wizard. The process of creating a basic report with the Report Wizard is similar to the process that you used to create a form with a subform in Chapter 14. An advantage of using the Report Wizard to introduce the topic of designing Access reports is that the steps for this process are parallel to the steps you take when you start with a default blank report. Chapter 17, "Preparing Advanced Reports," explains how to start with a blank report and create more complex reports. Many of the adjustments you make to this report also apply to the sample autogenerated report in the preceding section.

> **note**
>
> The process of designing an Access data project (ADP) report is, for the most part, identical to that for conventional reports based on Access data sources. The difference is that ADP uses an SQL Server table, view, function, or stored procedure as the data source for the report. ADP doesn't support some Access features, such as domain aggregate functions, but the workarounds for ADP limitations are relatively simple. Chapter 28, "Upsizing Access Applications to Access Data Projects and SQL Azure," describes the principal workarounds required when migrating from Access applications to ADP.

To create an Inventory by Category report in \Access2010\Reports16.accdb, follow these steps:

1. Click the Create tab and then click the Report Wizard button to open the first Report Wizard dialog. Select Table: Products from the Tables/Queries list.

2. The fields that you select to display represent columns of the report. You want the report to print the product name and supplier so that users don't have to refer to another report to associate codes with names. The fields from the Products table that you need for this report are CategoryID, ProductID, ProductName, SupplierID, and UnitsInStock. With the > button, select these fields in sequence from the Available Fields list. As you add fields to the Selected Fields list, Access removes the field names from the Available Fields list. Alternatively, you can double-click the field name in the Available Fields list to move the field name to the Selected Fields list. The fields appear from left to right in the report, based on the top-to-bottom sequence in which the fields appear in the Selected Fields list.

> **💧 tip**
>
> You can retrace your steps to correct an error by clicking the Back button whenever it is enabled. The Finish button accepts all defaults and jumps to the end of the wizard, so you shouldn't use this button until you're familiar with the Report Wizard's default selections.

3. To demonstrate how the wizard deals with reports that bind to more than one table, add the CompanyName field from the Suppliers table. Open the Tables/ Queries drop-down list and select Table: Suppliers.

4. Instead of presenting the supplier name as the report's last field, you want the report's CompanyName column to follow the SupplierID report column. Select the SupplierID field in the Selected Fields list. Now select the CompanyName field from the Available Fields list and click the > button. Access moves the CompanyName field from the Available Fields list and inserts the field into the Selected Fields list (see Figure 16.3). Click Next.

Figure 16.3
After selecting the fields from the primary table, select the SupplierID field, and add the CompanyName field of the Suppliers table in the first Report Wizard dialog.

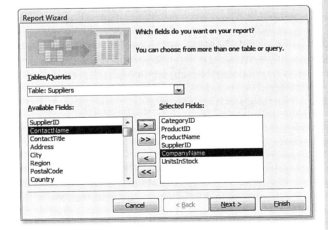

5. The Report Wizard asks how you want to view the data in the report, so select By Products, as shown in Figure 16.4.

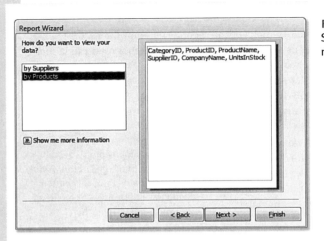

Figure 16.4
Select the Products table as the basis for your report in the second Report Wizard dialog.

6. Click Next to open the third Report Wizard dialog, which asks whether you want to add any grouping levels to the report. Select the CategoryID field in the list, and click the > button to establish the grouping by product category, as shown in Figure 16.5.

7. Click the Grouping Options button to open the Grouping Intervals dialog shown in Figure 16.6. By changing the grouping interval, you can affect how Access groups data in the report. For numeric fields, you can group items by units (Normal), 10s, 50s, 100s, and so on. For text fields, you can group items based on the first letter, the first three letters, and so on. The wizard checks the field data type and suggests appropriate grouping intervals.

 For additional methods of grouping data by characters in the field, **see** *"Grouping and Sorting Report Data,"* **p. 730.**

8. This report doesn't require any special grouping interval, so accept Normal in the Grouping Intervals list, click OK to return to the Report Wizard, and click Next.

 note

The purpose of adding the CompanyName field of the Suppliers table is to demonstrate how the wizard handles the design of reports based on more than one table. If you don't add the CompanyName field, the Report Wizard dialog of step 5 doesn't appear. The SupplierID field of the Products table is a lookup field, so CompanyName appears in lieu of the numeric SupplierID value. You remove the duplicate field when you modify the report later in the chapter.

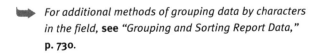 **tip**

If your application uses a text-coding scheme, such as BEVA for alcoholic beverages and BEVN for nonalcoholic beverages, you can combine all beverages in a single group by selecting *1st 3* Characters from the Grouping Intervals list. Access provides this option for fields of the Text data type.

Figure 16.5
Specify the field on which you want to group
your report in the third Report Wizard dialog.

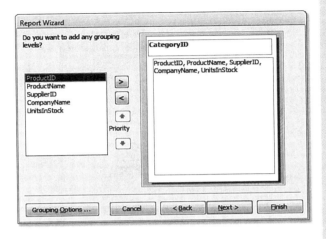

Figure 16.6
The Normal option groups numeric fields by individual
values. You also have the option to group numeric fields
by seven ranges of values.

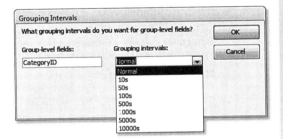

9. You can sort the records within groups by any field that
you select (see Figure 16.7), with up to four different sorted
fields. The dialog doesn't offer CategoryID as a choice
because the records already are grouped on this field, and
the field on which the grouping is based is sorted automatically by the table's primary key. Select ProductName in the
first drop-down list.

 note

By default, the sort order is ascending; if you want a descending sort
order, click the button to the right
of the drop-down list. (This button
is a toggle control; click it again to
return to an ascending sort.)

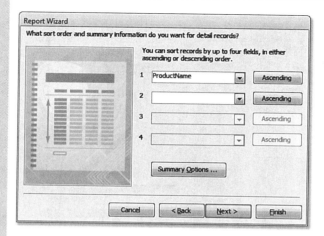

Figure 16.7
In the fourth Report Wizard dialog, select the field on which to sort records within the group you specified in the third dialog.

10. Click the Summary Options button to display the Summary Options dialog. If you want to add summary information to a report column, you set the options for that column in this dialog. The Report Wizard lists all the numeric fields on the report that aren't AutoNumber fields and offers you check boxes to select a Sum, Average, Minimum, and Maximum for that report column. Depending on the check boxes that you select, the Report Wizard adds those summary fields to the end of the report.

11. The Show option group lets you select whether the report shows the summary fields only or the full report with the summary fields added at the end of each group and at the end of the report. For this report, select the Sum and Avg check boxes for the UnitsInStock field, the Detail and Summary option, and the Calculate Percent of Total for Sums check box (see Figure 16.8). The Calculate Percent of Total for Sums check box displays the group's total as a percentage of the grand total for all groups. Click OK to return to the Report Wizard dialog, and click Next.

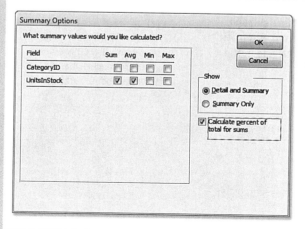

Figure 16.8
The Summary Options dialog lets you add to your report values based on calculations on numeric fields (other than AutoNumber fields).

12. The wizard asks you to select a layout for your report. The window on the left shows a preview of the layout style that you select; click each of the three Layout option buttons to check the layouts. For this report, select Stepped in the Layout option group (see Figure 16.9).

13. By default, the Report Wizard selects the Adjust the Field Width So All Fields Fit on a Page check box. As a rule, you should select this option to save paper and make reports with a few columns more legible. In the Orientation option group, you select the report's printing orientation. For this example, select the default Portrait option. Click Next to display the final Report Wizard dialog.

tip

When you restrict field widths to fit all fields on a page, fields with long lines of text often are truncated in the final report. You can adjust field widths in Report Design view to accommodate long text lines or change to multiline text boxes that expand automatically.

Figure 16.9
The Stepped report layout is the most common choice for reports with a few columns. You can increase the number of columns per page by choosing one of the Align Left layouts.

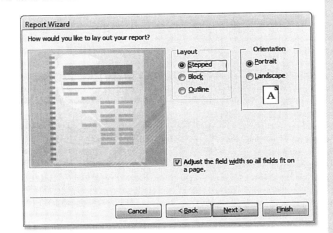

14. Type **rptInventoryByCategoryNew** as the title for the new report because the database contains a rptInventoryByCategory example. The Report Wizard uses this title as the name of the saved report it creates (see Figure 16.10). Accept the Preview the Report option, and click Finish to complete your report specification. The Report Wizard creates the report and displays it in Print Preview. Click the Close Print Preview button to show Report view.

Figure 16.11 shows in Report view the basic report that the Report Wizard creates, which has some major design deficiencies that you correct in the sections that follow. Use the vertical and horizontal scrollbars, if necessary, to position the preview as shown. When you're finished previewing the report, close it.

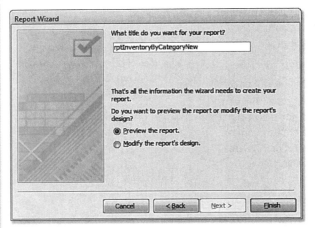

Figure 16.10
Type the name for your report in the last Report Wizard dialog. You change the report's caption to "Inventory by Category" later in the chapter.

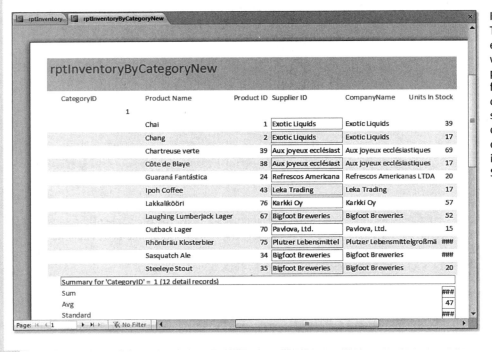

Figure 16.11
The report generated by the wizard doesn't provide sufficient space to display the full supplier names or the percent of total Units in Stock as the Standard value.

With a few design modifications, you can obtain a finished report with the information necessary to analyze Northwind's current inventory. The modifications correct obvious defects in the wizard-designed report, such as the excess width of the CategoryID column, cut-off names in the Product Name and CompanyName columns, duplication of the Supplier ID and CompanyName columns, and the truncated Standard value. You make these changes in the "Modifying a Basic Wizard Report" section later in this chapter.

Using Access's Report Ribbons

 Access 2010's updated Layout view for reports speeds the report layout process by enabling grouped controls in stacked or tabular styles and letting you manipulate individual controls or groups of controls with live data visible. Selecting Layout View in the Home or a ribbon's View gallery adds four ribbons to the UI: Report Layout Tools—Design, Layout Tools—Format, Report Layout Tools—Arrange, and Report Layout Tools—Page Layout. The following three sections describe these contextual ribbons' report-specific groups in detail.

> **tip**
>
> Unlike Access's record navigation text boxes, Print Preview's Page text box shows only the current report page. To obtain a page count, the Access report engine must paginate the report; pagination can take a considerable period of time for very long reports. To display the total number of report pages in the Pages text box, click the Last Page button (arrow and bar) at the bottom of the Print Preview window.

> **note**
>
> The following sections provide cross-references to tables that describe command buttons of groups that are identical for form and report ribbons.

The Report Design and Layout Tools—Design Ribbons

The Design ribbon has control button groups for specifying the current view: selecting an Office Theme, color scheme and fonts; setting grouping, sorting, totals, and Details section visibility; adding controls; configuring headers and footers; adding data fields; and opening the property sheet (see Figure 16.12).

Figure 16.12
The Report Design Tools—Design ribbon adds the Grouping & Totals group to the Form Design Tools—Design ribbon. The Report Layout Tools—Design ribbon is identical except for Tab Order and the three rightmost buttons.

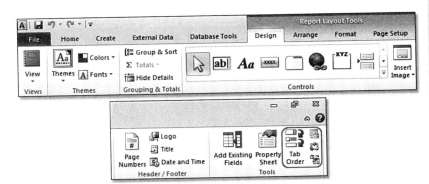

The Report Layout Tools—Design ribbon is identical to the Report Design Tools—Design ribbon except that the Tab Order, Subreport in New Window, View Code, and Convert Report's Macros to Visual Basic buttons are missing. The Report Layout Tools and Form Layout Tools—Design ribbons are identical except for the Controls complement (see Table 16.1).

Table 16.1 Icons, Command Buttons, KeyTip Shortcuts, and Command Button Actions for the Report Layout and Design Tools—Design Ribbon.

Icon	Command Button	Shortcut Alt+J,D,	Command Action
			Views Group W+
	Report View	R	Displays selected report in Form view
	Print Preview	V	Displays a print preview of the selected report
	Layout View	Y	Displays selected report in Layout view
	Design View	D	Displays selected report in Design view
			Groupings & Totals Group
	Group and Sort	HG	Opens the Group, Sort, and Total frame at the bottom of the report Layout view
Σ	Totals	HT	Opens a gallery to add one of the following aggregate values to a column: Sum, Average, Count Records, Count Values, Max, Min, Standard Deviation, or Variance
	Hide Details	HD	Toggles visibility of the Details section and its controls
			Controls Group, C+
	Select	S	Selects an object
ab|	Text Box	T	Enables drawing a text box with an associated label on the report
Aa	Label	L	Enables drawing a standalone label on the report
	Button	B	Enables drawing a control button on the report
	Tab Control	R	Enables drawing a tabbed container for other controls on a report
	Hyperlink	I	Opens the Insert Hyperlink dialog to add a button that opens an existing file or web page, a database object, or Outlook to author an email to the recipient
	Combo Box	C	Enables drawing a combo box on the form and starts the Combo Box Wizard*

Icon	Command Button	Shortcut Alt+J,D,	Command Action
	List Box	I	Enables drawing a list box on the form and starts the List Box Wizard*
	Check Box	K	Enables drawing a check box on the form to represent Boolean (Yes/No) values
	Option Button	U	Enables drawing an option button on the form to represent Boolean (Yes/No) values
	Attachment	A	Opens the Attachments dialog to add, modify, or delete a MIME attachment
	Image	M	Enables drawing a rectangle to display a static image from a variety of bitmap and vector image files
	Use Control Wizards	W	Specifies using wizards to design command buttons, combo boxes, list boxes and subreports
	ActiveX Control	O	Opens the Insert ActiveX Control dialog, which lets you select any ActiveX control registered on the local computer

➡ *To learn how to take advantage of the Group, Sort, and Total frame,* **see** *"Grouping and Sorting Report Data,"* **p. 730.**

➡ *To review icons, command names, KeyTips, and command actions for other Design ribbon groups* **see** *"The Form Design Tools—Design Ribbon,"* **p. 608.**

The Report Layout and Design Tools—Arrange Ribbon

The Report Layout Tools—Arrange and Report Design Tools—Arrange ribbons have identical groups for managing control groups, setting text margins and padding for controls, toggling the Snap to Grid layout feature, setting tab order, aligning and positioning controls, and displaying the Property Sheet. The Arrange ribbon is the same as the Form Layout Tools—Arrange ribbon except that the Positioning group's Anchoring button is missing (see Figure 16.13).

Figure 16.13
The same Arrange ribbon is present for the active Report Design Tools—Layout and Report Design Tools—Design tabs.

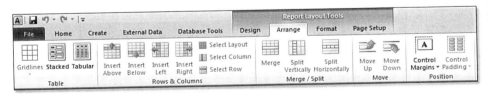

➡ *For descriptions of all groups and command buttons of the Report Layout Tools and Report Design Tools Arrange ribbon,* **see** *"The Form Layout Tools—Arrange Ribbon,"* **p. 572.**
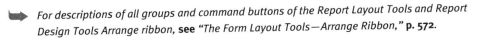

The Report Design and Layout Tools—Format Ribbon

The Format ribbon has control button groups for selecting objects, formatting text and numbers, adding background graphics, and control formatting. The Report Design and Layout Tools—Format ribbon and the Form Design and Layout Tools—Format ribbon are identical and serve the same purposes (see Figure 16.14).

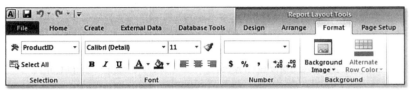

Figure 16.14
Report Layout view adds the Report Layout Tools— Formatting ribbon shown here; the Report Design Tools—Arrange ribbon are identical.

> *For descriptions of command buttons of the Selection, Font, Number, Background and Control Formatting groups,* **see** *"The Form Layout Tools—Format Ribbon,"* **p. 568.**

The Report Layout and Design Tools—Page Setup Ribbon

Like the Arrange ribbon, the Page Setup ribbon is present when either the Report Layout Tools or Report Design Tools tab is active (see Figure 16.15). The Page Setup contextual ribbon's controls duplicate many functions of the Page Setup dialog.

Figure 16.15
The Page Setup contextual ribbon's command buttons emulate those of the tabbed Page Setup dialog, which has only one group.

Table 16.2 lists the icon, name, KeyTips, and a brief description of each command button of the Report Layout Tools—Arrange and Report Design Tools—Arrange ribbons' groups. The keyboard shortcut to display KeyTips is Alt+S.

Table 16.2 Icons, Command Buttons, KeyTip Shortcuts, and Command Button Actions for the Report Layout Tools—Arrange and Report Layout Tools—Arrange Ribbons

Icon	Command Button	Shortcut Alt+J,P,	Command Action
		Page Size Group	
	Size	SZ	Opens a gallery of standard English and metric paper sizes.
	Margins	M	Opens a gallery of Normal (0.75"), Wide (1.00"), and Narrow (0.25", default) margins.
	Show Margins	I	Toggles margins' visibility in Layout view only.
	Print Data Only	D	Prints only data in bound text boxes; labels aren't printed.
		Page Layout Group	
	Portrait	R	Selects portrait orientation (default).
	Landscape	L	Selects landscape orientation.
	Columns	O	Opens the Page Setup dialog with the Columns page active.
	Page Setup	SP	Opens the Page Setup dialog with the Print Options page active.

➡ *To learn how to customize print settings with the Page Setup dialog,* **see** *"Adjusting Margins and Printing Conventional Reports,"* **p. 717.**

The Print Preview Ribbon

The Print Preview ribbon is common to most Office 2010 applications, but the command button collection and layout differs among Office members. Access 2010's ribbon incorporates the basic set of controls provided by the earlier Print Preview dialog the ribbon replaces. Figure 16.16 shows Access's Print Preview ribbon with a report selected.

Figure 16.16
The Print Preview ribbon's command buttons emulate those of the former Print Preview dialog.

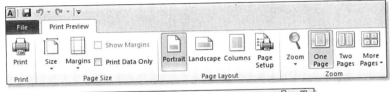

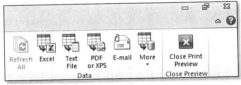

Table 16.3 shows the icon, name, KeyTips, and a brief description of each command button of the Print Preview ribbon's Print, Page Layout, Zoom, Data, and Close Preview groups. The keyboard shortcut to display KeyTips is Alt+P.

Table 16.3 Icons, Command Buttons, KeyTip Shortcuts and Command Button Actions for the Print Preview Ribbon

Icon	Command Button	Shortcut Alt+P,	Command Action
			Print Group
	Print	PD	
			Page Size Group
	Size	SZ	Opens a gallery of standard English and metric paper sizes.
	Margins	M	Opens a gallery of Normal (0.75"), Wide (1.00"), and Narrow (0.25", default) margins.
	Show Margins	I	Toggles margins' visibility in Layout view only.
	Print Data Only	D	Prints only data in bound text boxes; labels aren't printed.
			Page Layout Group
	Portrait	R	Selects portrait orientation (default).
	Landscape	L	Selects landscape orientation.
	Columns	O	Opens the Page Setup dialog with the Columns page active.
	Page Setup	SP	Opens the Page Setup dialog with the Print Options page active.
			Zoom Group
	Zoom	PZ	Toggles one page and 100% view.
	One Page	1	Show one page in window.
	Two Pages	2	Show two pages in window.
	More Pages	U	Opens a gallery of Four Pages, Eight Pages, and Twelve Pages choices.
			Data Group
	Refresh All	A	Refreshes the contents of all databound controls.

Icon	Command Button	Shortcut Alt+P,	Command Action
	Excel	X	Exports to Excel (disabled for reports).
	Text File	T	Saves as an ASCII text file (TXT).
	PDF or XPS	F	Saves as a Portable Document File or XML Paper Specification file.
	Email	N	Saves as an email message.
	More	G	Opens a gallery of Save As selections: Word and HTML Document are enabled for reports.
	Close Preview Group		
N/A	Close Print Preview	C	Closes Print Preview and returns to Report view.

Modifying a Basic Wizard Report

The Report Wizard tries to create the optimum final report in the first pass. Usually, the wizard comes close enough to a finished product that you spend far less time modifying a wizard-created basic report than creating a report from the default blank template.

In the following sections, you use Access's report design features to make the rptInventoryByCategory report more attractive and easier to read. In the process, you learn report design editing techniques in Access's new report Layout and Design views. Report Layout view makes many design changes much easier.

Deleting, Relocating, and Editing Existing Controls

The first step in modifying the wizard's report is to relocate the existing controls on the report. The Access 2010 Report Layout view makes relocating controls *much* easier. You don't need to align the labels and text boxes precisely during the initial modification; the "Aligning Controls Horizontally and Vertically" section later in this chapter covers control alignment.

This report is more useful if you include the unit cost of each product and its current inventory value, which is the product of unit cost and number of units on hand. To accommodate two additional columns, you must compress the horizontal space consumed by the current columns. To rename the report and start creating space for additional controls on the report, follow these steps:

> **note**
> SupplierID and CompanyName fields are added to demonstrate that the Wizard treats lookup fields inconsistently. ProductID is a lookup field for ProductName, CategoryID is a lookup field for CategoryName, and SupplierID is a lookup field for CompanyName. The ProductID and CategoryID columns show the expected numeric values, but the SupplierID column shows the unexpected CompanyName values.

1. Open rptInventoryByCategory in Report Layout view, if it's not already open, and click the Format tab.

2. Click outside the report's default margins to select the entire report, and press F4 to open the Properties Sheet.

3. Change the Format page's Caption property value to **Inventory by Category**.

4. Click the title label at the top of the page and make the same change.

5. The SupplierID and CompanyName columns are redundant in this report because the SupplierID column displays a lookup field. Select the Company Name label in the Page Header section, and press Delete to remove the stacked label and text box from the report. Click to select the Company Name column in the Details section and press Delete to remove it. Move the Units in Stock column to the left to occupy the vacated space.

6. Select the three small text boxes in the CategoryID Footer section and drag them to the left until their right side aligns with the right side of the Units in Stock text box. Drag the Grand Total text box to align with the three text boxes. Increase the width of all four text boxes and reduce the width of the Page 1 of # text box. (Look ahead to Figure 16.18 for approximate control dimensions).

7. CategoryID occupies a column, but you can display this column's content in the CategoryID footer (or header) without consuming the extra column space. Right-click the CategoryID text box and choose Layout, Remove to enable it to be moved, and then delete the CategoryID label.

8. For this report, you'll put the CategoryID text box in the footer section of the group. You can't cut and paste controls between sections in Layout view, so change to Design view. Select the CategoryID text box, press Ctrl+X, select the CategoryID Footer bar, and then press Ctrl+V to paste the text box. Drag the text box to a temporary location in the middle of the CategoryID Footer section.

9. Drag the Detail section bar upward to eliminate the space occupied by the now empty CategoryID Header, and drag the Page Header up to reduce the space below the report caption. Drag the ProductName label within one grid dot of the left margin.

10. Applying the sort on ProductName moved the ProductID column after the ProductName column. Most reports require IDs before names. Change to Layout view and drag the ProductID label to the report's left margin. To save space, change the label from Product ID to **ID** and reduce the width of the column. Change the Units in Stock label to **Units** and reduce the column width. Select all the labels and press Ctrl+B to apply the Bold attribute.

11. Increase the width of the Product Name and Supplier ID columns to accommodate the width of most items (about 2 inches), and change the Supplier ID label to **Supplier**. Click to select the Company Name text boxes and change the Border Style property from Solid to Transparent. Press Ctrl+A to select all controls and set their Fore Color property to black. Finally, drag the text boxes at the right of the CategoryID Footer, Page Footer, and Report Footer to align with the Units column's right edge. Your report now appears in Layout view as shown in Figure 16.17.

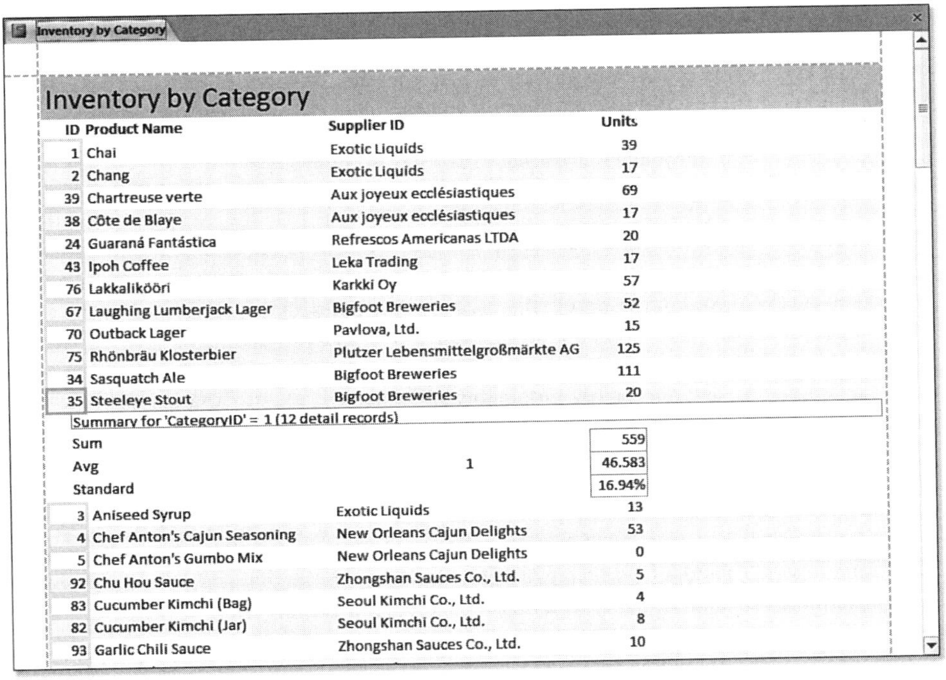

Figure 16.17
Layout view
shows the first
set of changes
to the report to
accommodate
new columns.

Inventory by Category

ID	Product Name	Supplier ID	Units
1	Chai	Exotic Liquids	39
2	Chang	Exotic Liquids	17
39	Chartreuse verte	Aux joyeux ecclésiastiques	69
38	Côte de Blaye	Aux joyeux ecclésiastiques	17
24	Guaraná Fantástica	Refrescos Americanas LTDA	20
43	Ipoh Coffee	Leka Trading	17
76	Lakkalikööri	Karkki Oy	57
67	Laughing Lumberjack Lager	Bigfoot Breweries	52
70	Outback Lager	Pavlova, Ltd.	15
75	Rhönbräu Klosterbier	Plutzer Lebensmittelgroßmärkte AG	125
34	Sasquatch Ale	Bigfoot Breweries	111
35	Steeleye Stout	Bigfoot Breweries	20

Summary for 'CategoryID' = 1 (12 detail records)

Sum			559
Avg		1	46.583
Standard			16.94%
3	Aniseed Syrup	Exotic Liquids	13
4	Chef Anton's Cajun Seasoning	New Orleans Cajun Delights	53
5	Chef Anton's Gumbo Mix	New Orleans Cajun Delights	0
92	Chu Hou Sauce	Zhongshan Sauces Co., Ltd.	5
83	Cucumber Kimchi (Bag)	Seoul Kimchi Co., Ltd.	4
82	Cucumber Kimchi (Jar)	Seoul Kimchi Co., Ltd.	8
93	Garlic Chili Sauce	Zhongshan Sauces Co., Ltd.	10

Printing the Lookup Fields of a Table

By default, the Report Wizard adds to the CategoryID Footer a calculated field that's visible in
Figure 16.17. The calculated field displays the group's field name (CategoryID) and value to help
identify the group footer's summary fields. For example, for CategoryID 1, the calculated field displays the following in Print Preview mode:

```
Summary for 'CategoryID' = 1 (12 detail records)
```

For this report, you want a more explicit description of the product category—more than just
the CategoryID number. You replace the Category ID Footer's calculated field that starts with
=`"Summary for"` in a later section with the category name. As usual, save your changes frequently.

Using the DLookUp Domain Aggregate Function for Lookups

Not every table that you use in your reports will have lookup fields, nor is it necessarily desirable
to create lookup fields for all numeric code fields (such as CategoryID and SupplierID). If you want
to display a looked-up value for a field that isn't defined as a lookup field, you use Access's domain

aggregate function, DLookUp, to find values from another table that correspond to a value in one of the report's fields. For example, to display both the actual CategoryID number and the CategoryName in the CategoryID Footer of the Inventory by Category report, you can use the DLookUp function to display the text of the CategoryName field from the Categories table, and a bound text field to display the CategoryID number from the Products table. The expression you use is

```
=DLookUp("[CategoryName]","Categories","[CategoryID] =
Report!CategoryID") & " Category"
```

[CategoryName] is the value that you want to return to the text box. Categories is the table that contains the CategoryName field. [CategoryID] = Report!CategoryID is the criterion that selects the record in the Categories table with a CategoryID value equal to the value in your report's CategoryID text box. The Report identifier is necessary to distinguish between the CategoryID field of the Categories table and a control object of the same name. (Report! is necessary in this example because Access has automatically named the report's CategoryID text box control as CategoryID.) Remember that the DLookUp function isn't available in ADP reports.

Taking Advantage of an Existing Lookup Field

CategoryID is a lookup field, but the wizard didn't take advantage of this feature when generating the report. To add a new field to display the CategoryName field in the CategoryID footer, and complete the redesign of the report, do the following in Design view:

1. Delete the ="Summary for " ... text box and the temporary CategoryID label you moved from the CategoryID Header section. For this report, the Avg field is unnecessary, so delete it and its label.

2. ▦ To add a bound text box to act as the label for the subtotal in the CategoryID Footer section, click the Design tab and the Add Existing Fields button, and select CategoryID from the Field List.

3. ▦ Drag the CategoryID field to the position of the text box you deleted. Because the CategoryID field is a lookup field, it displays as a drop-down list when you drag it from the Field List (see Figure 16.18). When printed or displayed in Print Preview, this field shows the CategoryName rather than the numeric code. Close the Field list.

Completing the Initial Report Modifications

Do the following to complete and review the report design prior to adding your own calculated controls to the report:

1. Drag the two calculated fields (=Now and ="Page...") in the Page Footer section until they are one grid mark away from the top of the Page Footer section. Drag the Report Footer bar upward to reduce the Page Footer's height.

 tip

To differentiate between calculated field text boxes that show only the first few characters of the expression, temporarily increase their width. Shift+F2 doesn't open the Zoom window for report text boxes, and there's no Zoom choice in the text boxes' context menu.

Figure 16.18
Replace the calculated field in the CategoryID Footer with the CategoryID lookup field.

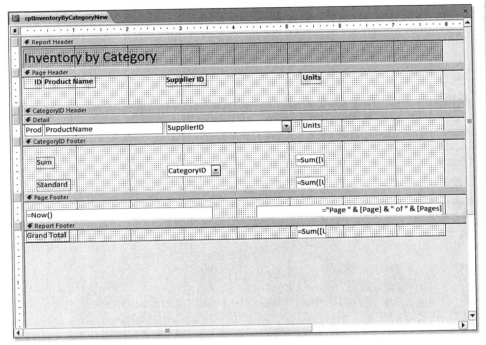

2. Click and drag the =Sum([UnitsInStock])/[UnitsInStock GrandTotal] text box from its present location below the =Sum([UnitsInStock]) text box to a position at the top of the CategoryID Footer, near the center of the page. Then drag the Standard label to the left of the text box you moved, and change its caption to **Percent Units** (look ahead to Figure 16.19).

3. Select the text box and Shift+click the Percent label. Then open the smart tag's list and select Associate Label## with Standard of UnitsInStock to associate the label with the text box.

4. Drag the =Sum([UnitsInStock]) field up to the bottom of the CategoryID footer and the Sum label to the left of the text box you moved, and change Sum to **Total Units**. Move the right edge of the text box to align with right edge of the UnitsInStock text box, if necessary. Move up the Page Footer divider bar to reduce the footer's depth (again, look ahead to Figure 16.20).

5. Repeat step 3 for the Total label and text box.

6. **B** To distinguish the category section breaks, select all controls in the CategoryID Footer section and press Ctrl+B to set them bold. Select the three text boxes and set the Border Style property value to Transparent.

7. ⊞ Underline the column headers by selecting the ID label, clicking the Format tab, and clicking Underline. Repeat this process for the Product Name, Supplier, and Units labels. Add spaces after the names to extend the underline.

8. Select the Grand Total label and text box in the Report Footer section and move the text box to align its right edge with the right edge of the text boxes above it. Your final report design appears as shown in Figure 16.19. Press Ctrl+S to save your report design.

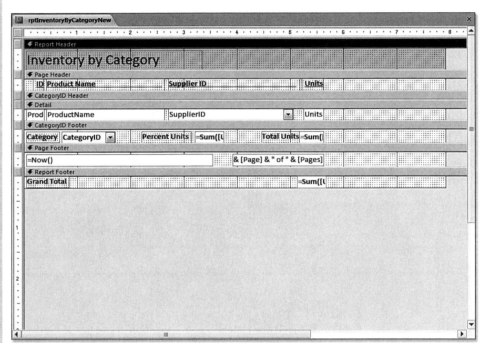

Figure 16.19
At this point, the initial redesign of the Inventory by Category report is ready for a test run.

Eliminating Empty Pages

Sometimes when you're previewing or printing a report, Access displays or prints a blank page after each page with data. This happens because the report's width has become greater than the net printable width (the paper width minus the sum of the left and right margins), so the number of report pages has doubled. Columns of fields that don't fit a page's width print on a second page, similar to the printing method used by spreadsheet applications. If you set your right margin beyond the right printing margin, or if the right edge of any control on the report extends past the right printing margin, the added pages often are blank. Change the printing margins or reduce the width of your report so that it conforms to the printable page width. (See the section "Adjusting Margins and Printing Conventional Reports" earlier in this chapter.)

To check the progress of your work, periodically click the Print Preview button to display the report prior to printing. Figure 16.20 shows your Inventory by Category report in Print Preview mode.

Figure 16.20
Report view
displays the
report design
of Figure
16.19 at the
equivalent of
Print Preview's
actual size
(100% zoom).

ID	Product Name	Supplier ID	Units
	Inventory by Category		
1	Chai	Exotic Liquids	39
2	Chang	Exotic Liquids	17
39	Chartreuse verte	Aux joyeux ecclésiastiques	69
38	Côte de Blaye	Aux joyeux ecclésiastiques	17
24	Guaraná Fantástica	Refrescos Americanas LTDA	20
43	Ipoh Coffee	Leka Trading	17
76	Lakkalikööri	Karkki Oy	57
67	Laughing Lumberjack Lager	Bigfoot Breweries	52
70	Outback Lager	Pavlova, Ltd.	15
75	Rhönbräu Klosterbier	Plutzer Lebensmittelgroßmärkte AG	125
34	Sasquatch Ale	Bigfoot Breweries	111
35	Steeleye Stout	Bigfoot Breweries	20

Category   Beverages   Percent Units   16.94%   **Total Units**   559

3	Aniseed Syrup	Exotic Liquids	13
4	Chef Anton's Cajun Seasoning	New Orleans Cajun Delights	53
5	Chef Anton's Gumbo Mix	New Orleans Cajun Delights	0
92	Chu Hou Sauce	Zhongshan Sauces Co., Ltd.	5
83	Cucumber Kimchi (Bag)	Seoul Kimchi Co., Ltd.	4
82	Cucumber Kimchi (Jar)	Seoul Kimchi Co., Ltd.	8
93	Garlic Chili Sauce	Zhongshan Sauces Co., Ltd.	10
15	Genen Shouyu	Mayumi's	39
6	Grandma's Boysenberry Spread	Grandma Kelly's Homestead	120
44	Gula Malacca	Leka Trading	27
91	Hoisin Garlic Sauce	Zhongshan Sauces Co., Ltd.	15
90	Hoisin Sauce	Xiamen Import & Export Co., Ltd.	12

Changing the Report's Record Source and Adding Calculated Controls

Calculated controls are very useful in reports. You use calculated controls to determine extended values, such as quantity times unit price or quantity times cost. Now you have enough space at the right of the report to add two columns: one for the Cost field, which is calculated as a percentage of UnitPrice, and one for the extended inventory value, which is UnitPrice multiplied by UnitsInStock. The following subsections explain how to provide the data for and add these controls.

Changing the Report's Record Source

You created the Inventory by Category report by selecting fields directly from the Products and Suppliers tables in the Report Wizard. Therefore, the Record Source property for the report as a whole is an SQL statement that selects only the fields that you chose initially in the Report Wizard. Although you can add

 tip

Alternatively, you can use the Filter and Filter On property values on the Data page of the report's Property Sheet to prevent discontinued products from inclusion in the report. Another approach would be to add a WHERE NOT Discontinued clause to the Record Source SQL statement. As a rule, however, it's easier to troubleshoot report problems if you apply constraints to the query that serves as the Record Source property of the report. Doing this lets you quickly preview the resultset on which your report is based.

fields to the report by creating unbound text box controls and using the Expression Builder to create an expression to retrieve the desired value, it's a more straightforward process to create a query to select the desired fields and then substitute the new query as the report's data source. You also can specify record-selection criteria in a query.

Following is the Access SQL statement generated by the Report Wizard:

```
SELECT Products.CategoryID, Products.ProductID,
    Products.ProductName, Products.SupplierID,
    Suppliers.CompanyName, Products.UnitsInStock
FROM Suppliers INNER JOIN Products
  ON Suppliers.SupplierID=Products.SupplierID;
```

Northwind.accdb's Products table includes some products that have been discontinued. Inventory reports shouldn't include counts and valuations of products that no longer are available for sale.

To create a query in the Reports16.accdb database that includes all fields and eliminates discontinued products from the resultset, follow these steps:

1. ![icon] Open a new query in Design view by clicking the Create tab's Query Design button to open the Show Table dialog.

2. Double-click the Products table in the Show Table dialog and then close the dialog.

3. Drag * from the field list to the first column of the query.

4. Drag the Discontinued field to the query grid's second column.

5. Clear the Show check box for the Discontinued field and then type **False** in the Discontinued field's first Criteria row.

6. If you want to list products alphabetically by product name, add the ProductName field, clear its Show check box, and select an ascending sort (see Figure 16.21). Alternatively, you can specify ProductName in the Order By list and set the Order By On property value to Yes.

7. Run the query to test your work, close the Query window, and save your changes using the name **qryInventoryNew** (Reports16.accdb contains a sample qryInventory).

> **◉ tip**
>
> You don't need to add the Suppliers table to the query because the SupplierID field of the Products table supplies the CompanyName lookup value to the table.

To change the report's Record Source property value to the new query, follow these steps:

1. ![icon] ![icon] Open the Inventory by Category report in Report Design view, and click the Select Report button to select the report.

Figure 16.21
This query prevents the Inventory by Category report from including discontinued products.

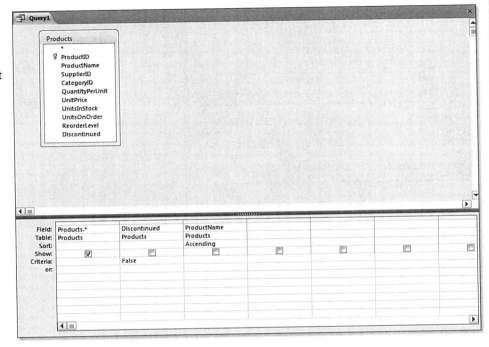

2. Click the Property Sheet button to open the report's Property Sheet and click the Data tab to display the report's data properties.

3. Click the Record Source text box and then use the drop-down list to select the qryInventory query as the report's new Record Source property (see Figure 16.22).

4. Check the report in Print Preview mode, and then save the changes to the report.

> **tip**
>
> A faster method of adding text boxes and labels is to select both the label and the text box and then press Ctrl+C and Ctrl+V to superimpose a copy that has an associated label over the existing controls. Drag the copy to its new location.

Adding the Calculated Controls

Now that you've changed the report's record source, you have easy access to the UnitPrice field, which you need for adding the calculated Cost and Value fields to the report. UnitPrice is the selling price of the product, not its cost to Northwind Traders. For this example, assume that Northwind Traders sells its goods at a uniform markup of 50%. In retailing terminology, this means that a product costing $1.00 sells for $1.50, and the inventory value is 66.7% of the UnitPrice value. Thus, the text box expression for the cost of the product is =[UnitPrice]*0.667 and the value is =[UnitsIn Stock]*[UnitPrice]*0.667.

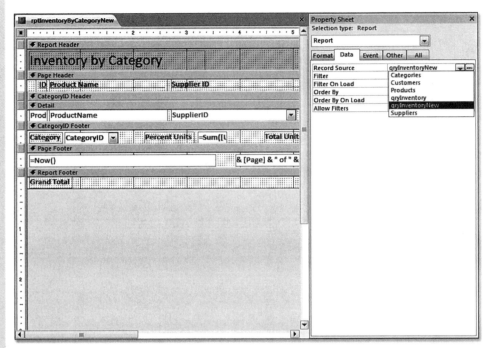

Figure 16.22
Replace
the wizard-
generated SQL
statement with
the new query
to serve as the
Record Source
property value
for the report.

To add the Cost and Value calculated fields to the report, follow these steps:

1. Return to Design view, and click the Report Design Tools—Design tab.

2. **Aa** Click the Label tool in the Controls group and draw a label to the right of the Units label in the Page Header section. Type **Cost** as the caption, click Ctrl+B to set it bold, click Ctrl+U to underline it; right-click it, select Fore Color, and set the text color to black.

3. **B** Add another label to the right of Cost and type **Value** as the caption. Then format the label as in step 2.

4. If necessary, change the font and size to match the other labels in the Page Header. For this example, click the Right Align button in the Home ribbon's Font group. (Access automatically sets the font name and size from the default Office Theme, but not bold, alignment, or other font attributes.)

5. **abl** Click the Text Box tool, and add two unbound text boxes in the Detail section under the new labels. Delete the attached labels, and align the right edge of the text boxes under the right edge of the Page Header labels.

> **⊛ tip**
>
> A good way to enter long, complex expressions is to click the Builder button to open the Expression Builder, which provides a larger text box in which to type the expression.

6. Click the Arrange tab, select the Cost text box and label, click the Control Layout group's Tabular button to associate the two controls, resize the width of the controls. Right-align the text, apply the black Fore Color, and use the Properties sheet to set the Border Style property value to Transparent.

7. ▦ Select the new Cost text box, open the Property Sheet, click the All tab, type **Cost** in the Name text box, select Currency as the format, and type **=[UnitPrice]*0.667** in the Control Source text box (see Figure 16.23).

Figure 16.23
Type as the
Data Source
property value
the expression
for the value
to print in the
calculated field
text box.

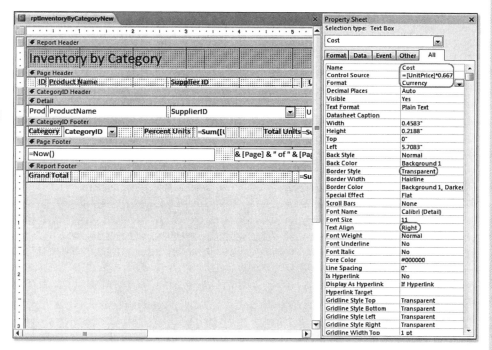

8. ▦ Select the Value text box, click the All tab, type **Value** in the Name text box, select Currency as the format, and type **=[UnitsInStock]*[UnitPrice]*0.667** as the expression. Change to Report view to check your work.

9. ▦ Return to Design view, drag the Percent label and text box to the left, and change the label caption to **% Units:**.

10. **B** | Calibri ▾ | 11 ▾ | Add a text box in the CategoryID Footer section under the Value label, but type **=Sum([UnitsInStock]*[UnitPrice]*0.667)** as the Control Source, type **CatValue** as the name, and select Currency as the format. Press Ctrl+B to set the Font Weight property to Bold, and select black as the Fore Color property value.

11. Repeat step 10 to create the grand total value text box with the **=Sum([UnitsInStock]*[UnitPr ice]*0.667)** expression as the control source in the Report Footer section, and set this text box's Name property to **TotalValue**. Set the Fore Color to black, Font Weight to Bold, and delete the associated label. Also apply the Bold attribute to the Grand Total label.

12. Add another unbound text box to the right of the % Units text box in the CategoryID Footer section. Type **=[CatValue]/[TotalValue]** as the value of the Control Source property, and set the Format property's value to Percent, the Fore Color to black, and the Font Weight to Bold. Change the label caption to **% Value** and conform the font.

13. Drag the form's right margin to within about one grid dot of the right edge of the text boxes. The report design at this point appears as shown in Figure 16.24. Press Ctrl+S to save your report.

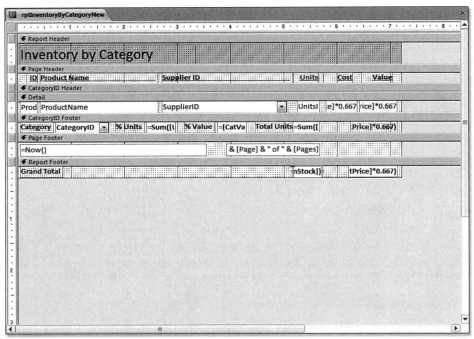

Figure 16.24
The enhanced report design with added Cost, Value, Cat(egory) Value, and Grand Total Value calculated fields.

Unexpected Parameters Dialogs

When a Parameters dialog appears when you've changed to report Preview mode, but the query to which the report is bound doesn't have parameter, you've misspelled one or more objects—usually text box or query field names—in expressions for text boxes or other controls that use calculated values. Click Cancel and verify that the expression in the Record Source property for each text box or other control on the report contains valid object names.

14. Click Print Preview to check the result of your additions. Use the vertical scrollbar, if necessary, to display the category subtotal. The next section describes how you can correct any values that are not aligned properly and the spacing of the Detail section's rows.

15. Click the Bottom of Report page selector button to display the grand totals for the report (see Figure 16.25). The record selector buttons become page selector buttons when you display reports in Print Preview mode.

Figure 16.25
The last page of the report displays grand totals for units and inventory values.

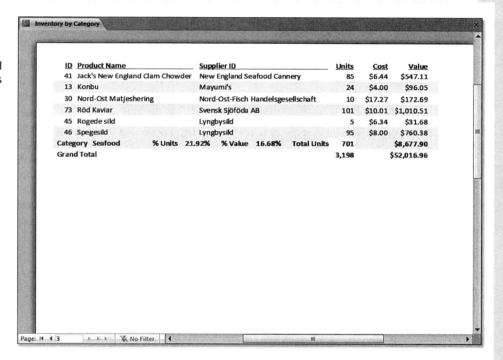

Aligning and Formatting Controls and Adjusting Line Spacing

The exact alignment of label and text box controls is more important on reports than it is on forms, because in the printed report, any misalignment is obvious. Formatting the controls further improves the report's appearance and readability.

The spacing of the report's rows in the Detail section is controlled by the section's depth. Likewise, you can control the white space above and below the headers and footers by adjusting the depth of their sections and the vertical position of the

> **note**
>
> The combination of the Report Wizard's accurate control placement and alignment assistance by the new Layout features minimizes the need to align controls for the preceding scenario. You probably won't see much change when you complete the following steps.

controls within the sections. To create a professional-looking report, you must adjust the controls' alignment and formatting as well as the sections' line spacing.

Aligning Controls Horizontally and Vertically

You align controls by first selecting the rows to align and then aligning the columns. Access provides several control-sizing and alignment options to make the process easier.

To size and align the controls that you created, follow these steps:

1. If you still have the Inventory by Category report open in Print Preview, click the Close button to return to Design view.

2. Select all labels in the Page Header sections and click the Control Alignment group's Align Top button. This process aligns the tops of each selected label with the uppermost selected label. Click a blank area of the report to deselect the labels.

3. Select all text boxes in the Detail section and repeat step 2 for the text boxes.

4. Select the labels and text boxes in the CategoryID Footer and Report Footer sections and repeat step 2.

5. Select all controls in the Units column and click the Align Right button so that Access aligns the column to the right edge of the text farthest to the right of the column. Then click the Font group's Align Right button to right-align the contents of the labels and text boxes. (The first part of this step aligns the controls themselves to the rightmost control, and the second part right-aligns the text or data displayed by the selected controls.)

6. Select all controls in the Cost column and repeat step 5.

7. Select all controls in the Values column (except the Page Footer text box) and repeat step 5.

8. Click Print Preview to display the report with the improved alignment of rows and columns.

Formatting Controls

You formatted the currency columns and percent fields as you added them in the preceding sections. However, following are typical changes you need to make to apply accounting-style numeric formats, underlines, and to align the header labels with currency columns:

1. In Design view, select the three text boxes related to the Units[inStock] column, press F4 to open the Property Sheet, and type **#,##0** as the Format template to add a thousands separator and display a 0 for null values.

2. The Value column's text box in the Details section is formatted for currency. Accountants prefer individual items to apply currency formatting only to the first item of a group. Access doesn't offer this formatting, but you can remove the currency symbol for all members of a group by specifying Standard format, which corresponds to a **#,##0.00** Format template. Select the Cost and Value text boxes in the Detail section and change the format from Currency to Standard.

3. Standard format doesn't reserve space for accounting-standard parentheses to indicate negative numbers. Therefore, you must move the CatValue and TotalValue text boxes to the right to realign their content with that of the Value items. (It's easier to do this in Layout view).

4. ✎ To apply subtotal and grand total lines above and below the appropriate text boxes, select the Line tool and draw lines above the Units and Value subtotal and grand total text boxes and add a pair of lines under the grand total text boxes. (Setting the Font Underline property to Yes adds only a single underline.)

5. Open the report in Report view and scroll to the last page to inspect your handiwork (see Figure 16.26).

Figure 16.26
The last page of the report in Report view displays the changes to item values and the formatting of subtotals/grand totals.

Inventory by Category				
57 Ravioli Angelo	Pasta Buttini s.r.l.	36	$13.01	$468.23
23 Tunnbröd	PB Knäckebröd AB	61	$6.00	$366.18
64 Wimmers gute Semmelknödel	Plutzer Lebensmittelgroßmärkte AG	22	$22.18	$487.91
Category Grains/Cereals % Units 8.82% % Value 6.71% Total Units		282		$3,488.74
55 Pâté chinois	Ma Maison	115	$16.01	$1,840.92
54 Tourtière	Ma Maison	21	$4.97	$104.35
Category Meat/Poultry % Units 4.25% % Value 3.74% Total Units		136		$1,945.27
74 Longlife Tofu	Tokyo Traders	4	$6.67	$26.68
51 Manjimup Dried Apples	G'day, Mate	20	$35.35	$707.02
14 Tofu	Mayumi's	35	$15.51	$542.77
7 Uncle Bob's Organic Dried Pears	Grandma Kelly's Homestead	15	$20.01	$300.15
Category Produce % Units 2.31% % Value 3.03% Total Units		74		$1,576.62
40 Boston Crab Meat	New England Seafood Cannery	123	$12.27	$1,509.55
18 Carnarvon Tigers	Pavlova, Ltd.	42	$41.69	$1,750.88
58 Escargots de Bourgogne	Escargots Nouveaux	62	$8.84	$547.94
37 Gravad lax	Svensk Sjöföda AB	11	$17.34	$190.76
10 Ikura	Tokyo Traders	31	$20.68	$640.99
36 Inlagd Sill	Svensk Sjöföda AB	112	$12.67	$1,419.38
41 Jack's New England Clam Chowder	New England Seafood Cannery	85	$6.44	$547.11
13 Konbu	Mayumi's	24	$4.00	$96.05
30 Nord-Ost Matjeshering	Nord-Ost-Fisch Handelsgesellschaft	10	$17.27	$172.69
73 Röd Kaviar	Svensk Sjöföda AB	101	$10.01	$1,010.51
45 Rogede sild	Lyngbysild	5	$6.34	$31.68
46 Spegesild	Lyngbysild	95	$8.00	$760.38
Category Seafood % Units 21.92% % Value 16.68% Total Units		701		$8,677.90
Grand Total		3,198		$52,016.96
Monday, March 22, 2010			Page 1 of 1	

Adjusting Line Spacing

The line spacing of the Inventory by Category report's sections is satisfactory, but you can also change this spacing. Minimizing line spacing allows you to print a report on fewer sheets of paper. You also can use the Can Grow property of text boxes to prevent truncation of long text items.

To change the spacing of the report's Page Header and Detail sections, follow these steps:

1. ⬗ Change to Report Design view.

2. Select all labels in the Page Header and move the group to the top of the section. The gridline moves with the labels.

3. Drag the CategoryID Footer section up to the bottom of the Detail section's text boxes.

4. A few ProductName and supplier CompanyName items exceed the width of their text boxes and are truncated. You can eliminate the truncation by setting the Can Grow property value for the text boxes to Yes. However, you have a substantial amount of free horizontal space, which allows widening the text boxes if you keep the printing margins within bounds.

5. Change to Report view to check the Page Header depth and line spacing of the Detail section. You can't reduce a section's line spacing to less than that required by the tallest text box or label by reducing the section's Height property in the Properties box. If you try this approach, Access rejects the entry and substitutes the prior value.

6. Select all controls in the Detail section and press F4 to open the Property Sheet. Change the Height property value to 0.18", which changes to 0.1799". Figure 16.27 illustrates the resulting truncation of text descenders.

> **note**
>
> You also can change the printing margins by clicking the Print Preview ribbon's Margins button and selecting Normal or Wide. However, these margins might not meet your requirements.

7. Attempting to change the Top property value from the default 0.0208" to 0" fails because the Top Padding property value is set to 0.0208". Change the Top Padding property value to 0" and try again. Drag the CategoryID footer up to the bottom of the text boxes.

Inventory by Category

ID	Product Name	Supplier ID	Units	Cost	Value
1	Chai	Exotic Liquids	39	$12.01	$468.23
2	Chang	Exotic Liquids	17	$12.67	$215.44
39	Chartreuse verte	Aux joyeux ecclésiastiques	69	$12.01	$828.41
38	Côte de Blaye	Aux joyeux ecclésiastiques	17	$175.75	$2,987.83
43	Ipoh Coffee	Leka Trading	17	$30.68	$521.59
76	Lakkalikööri	Karkki Oy	57	$12.01	$684.34
67	Laughing Lumberjack Lager	Bigfoot Breweries	52	$9.34	$485.58
70	Outback Lager	Pavlova, Ltd.	15	$10.01	$150.08
75	Rhönbräu Klosterbier	Plutzer Lebensmittelgroßmärkte AG	125	$5.17	$646.16
34	Sasquatch Ale	Bigfoot Breweries	111	$9.34	$1,036.52
35	Steeleye Stout	Bigfoot Breweries	20	$12.01	$240.12

Category	Beverages	% Units	16.85%	% Value	15.89%	Total Units	539		$8,264.30

3	Aniseed Syrup	Exotic Liquids	13	$6.67	$86.71
4	Chef Anton's Cajun Seasoning	New Orleans Cajun Delights	53	$14.67	$777.72
92	Chu Hou Sauce	Zhongshan Sauces Co., Ltd.	5	$8.17	$40.85
83	Cucumber Kimchi (Bag)	Seoul Kimchi Co., Ltd.	4	$150.08	$600.30
82	Cucumber Kimchi (Jar)	Seoul Kimchi Co., Ltd.	8	$28.35	$226.78
93	Garlic Chili Sauce	Zhongshan Sauces Co., Ltd.	10	$7.84	$78.37
15	Genen Shouyu	Mayumi's	39	$10.34	$403.20
6	Grandma's Boysenberry Spread	Grandma Kelly's Homestead	120	$16.68	$2,001.00
44	Gula Malacca	Leka Trading	27	$12.97	$350.28
91	Hoisin Garlic Sauce	Zhongshan Sauces Co., Ltd.	15	$7.00	$105.05
90	Hoisin Sauce	Xiamen Import & Export Co., Ltd.	12	$5.74	$68.83
79	Hot Cabbage Kimchi (Bag)	Incheon Food Trading Co., Ltd.	5	$83.38	$416.88
78	Hot Cabbage Kimchi (Jar)	Incheon Food Trading Co., Ltd.	5	$16.34	$81.71
87	Korean Hot Bean Paste	Incheon Food Trading Co., Ltd.	15	$35.02	$525.26
86	Korean Red Bean Paste	Incheon Food Trading Co., Ltd.	10	$32.02	$320.16
88	Korean Seasoned Bean Paste	Seoul Kimchi Co., Ltd.	10	$41.69	$416.88
89	Korean Traditional Bean Paste	Seoul Kimchi Co., Ltd.	20	$28.01	$560.28
65	Louisiana Fiery Hot Pepper Sauce	New Orleans Cajun Delights	76	$14.04	$1,067.07
66	Louisiana Hot Spiced Okra	New Orleans Cajun Delights	4	$11.34	$45.36

Figure 16.27
The report shows the effect of adjusting the depth of the Report Header, Page Header, and Detail sections, and reducing the Height of the Detail section's text boxes below about 0.185" (see the truncated letter "g" in Laughing and Big).

8. Change the Height property to 0.185", which Access changes to 0.1847", to eliminate the text truncation and then press Ctrl+S to save your changes.

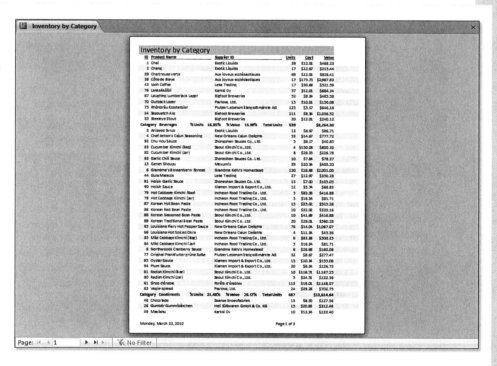 The Inventory by Category report, completed to this point, is included in the downloadable sample files in \Access2010\Chaptr16\Report16.accdb database.

Adjusting Margins and Printing Conventional Reports

Clicking the One Page button in Print Preview shows the report as it would print using Access 2010's default printing margins of 0.25" on the top, bottom, and sides of the report (see Figure 16.28). In the Print Preview's Print Setup dialog, you can adjust the printed version of the report. The procedure for printing a report applies to printing the data contained in tables and queries as well as single-record or continuous forms.

Figure 16.28
One Page view shows the report with the default 0.25" printing margins.

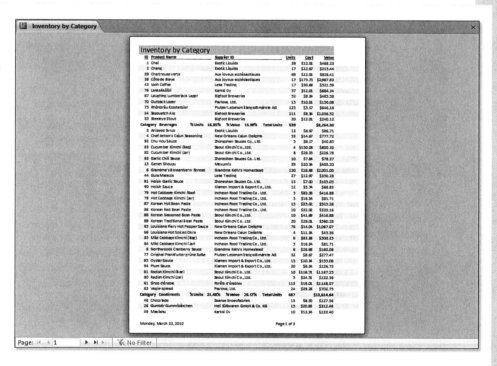

To change the printing margins for a report, follow these steps:

1. Open the report, click the File tab, click Print and Print Preview mode, and click the ribbon's Page Setup button to open the Page Setup dialog.

2. The Page Setup dialog is similar to the Print and Page Setup dialogs of other Windows applications, with a section for printing margins included. To increase the amount of information on a page, decrease the top and bottom margins. By selecting the Print Data Only check box, you can print only the data in the report; the Report and Page Headers and Footers don't print.

3. In the Left text box, type **1** to specify a 1.0" left margin for a three-hole punch. Type **0.5** in the Right text box. In the Top and Bottom text boxes, type **0.5** (see Figure 16.29). Click OK to see a One Page view of the report with the revised margins (see Figure 16.30).

Figure 16.29
The Page Setup dialog lets you set margins and other property values for printing reports, forms, datasheets, and other Access objects.

4. To print the report, click the Print button. The standard Print dialog appears for the printer specified in Windows as the default printer. Figure 16.31 shows, as an example, the Print dialog for a networked Brother laser printer. The Setup button opens the Page Setup dialog (refer to Figure 16.31).

5. You can print all or part of a report or print the report to a file for later printing. You can also select the number of copies to print. By clicking the Properties button, you can change the parameters that apply to the selected printer. Click OK to print the report.

> **tip**
>
> The printing margins that you establish for a report in the Page Setup dialog apply to the active report only; each report has a unique set of margins. When you save the report, Access saves its margin settings.

The Page Setup dialog includes a Columns page that allows you to establish specifications for printing mailing labels and other multiple-column reports. The "Printing Multicolumn Reports as Mailing Labels" section describes these specifications and how you set them.

Figure 16.30
The One Page preview shows the effect of applying the margin settings shown in Figure 16.30.

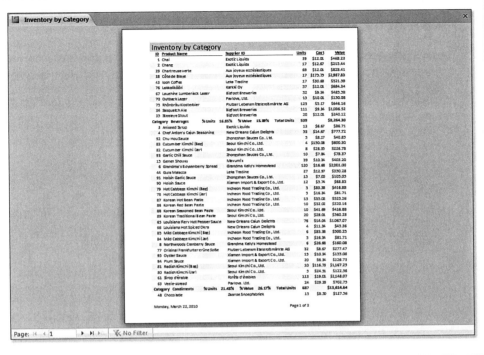

Figure 16.31
The Print dialog lets you select the printer, pages to print, the number of copies, and the collation sequence.

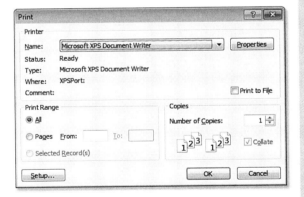

Preventing Widowed Records with the Group Keep Together Property

Access includes a property for groups, called Keep Together, that prevents widowed records from appearing at the bottom of the page. Depending on your report section depths, you might find that only a few records of the next group (called widowed records) appear at the bottom of the page. The report designs shown in Figures 16.28 and 16.30 have three and one widowed records at the bottom of the first report page, respectively.

You can force a page break when an entire group doesn't fit on a page by following these steps:

1. With the report in Design or Layout view, click the Group & Sort button to open the Group, Sort, and Total pane below the report Design window.

2. Select the group that you want to keep together. For this example, select CategoryID.

3. Click the More link to expand the grouping options, open the Do Not Keep Group Together on One Page option's list, and choose Keep Whole Group Together on One Page, as shown in Figure 16.32.

> **tip**
>
> 🖨 You can print the report on the default printer without displaying the Print dialog by clicking the File tab, Print, Quick Print.

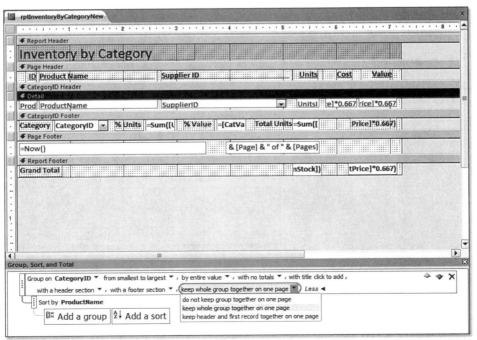

Figure 16.32
Select the group to keep together (CategoryID), and select Keep Whole Group Together on One Page.

4. [≣ 🔍 Click the Sort & Group button again to close the Group, Sort, and Total pane, and then select Print Preview to see the result of applying the group Keep Together property.

The Report Wizard makes the entries in the Sorting and Grouping dialog for you. The next chapter describes how to use the Group, Sort, and Total pane to design reports without the aid of the wizard.

Printing Multicolumn Reports as Mailing Labels

Access lets you print multicolumn reports. You can create a single-column report with the Report Wizard, for example, and then arrange the report to print values from the Detail section in a specified number of columns across the page. The most common application of multicolumn reports is the creation of mailing labels.

Creating a Mailing Label with the Label Wizard

You can create mailing lists with the Label Wizard, or you can start with a blank form. The Label Wizard's advantage is that it includes the dimensions of nearly every kind of adhesive label for inkjet and laser printers made by the Avery Commercial Products division and several other North American and overseas manufacturers. You select the product number of the label that you plan to use, and Access determines the number of columns, rows per page, and margins for the report's Detail section. You also can customize the Label Wizard for labels with unusual sizes or those produced by manufacturers who aren't included in the wizard's repertoire. Several label manufacturers include a note with their products that indicates the corresponding Avery label number.

To create mailing labels with the Label Wizard, using the Customers table for this example, do the following:

1. Select the Customers table in the Navigation pane.

2. 🖼 In the Create ribbon's Reports group, click the Labels button to start the Label Wizard.

3. If you're using Avery labels, select the product code (5160 for this example). Otherwise, select the manufacturer in the list, and select the product code for a three-across label. Accept the Sheet Feed option if you're using laser-printer labels (see Figure 16.33). Click Next.

4. In the second wizard dialog, select the font family, size, and weight for the label. The defaults— 8-point Arial light—make the labels hard to read. This example uses 9-point Courier New medium (see Figure 16.34). Click Next.

5. In the third wizard dialog, select the field of the record source for the label's first row—ContactName for this example—and click the > button to add it to the Prototype Label text box. Press Enter to add a new line.

> 🔍 **note**
>
> Although the Avery 5160 label has sufficient depth to add the Country field with 9-point type, the wizard doesn't let you add more than four lines.

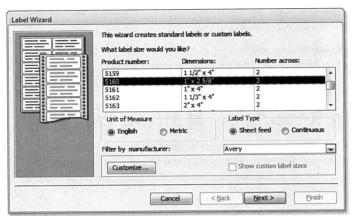

Figure 16.33
The first dialog of the Label Wizard lets you select a manufacturer and then a label size available from the manufacturer.

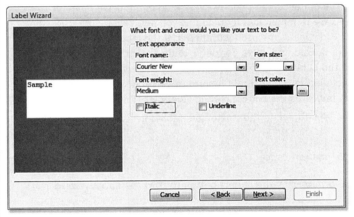

Figure 16.34
Specify the printer font and its attributes in the second Label Wizard dialog.

6. Repeat step 4 for the CompanyName and Address fields.

7. Select City, click >, and add a comma and a space.

8. Select Region, click >, add two spaces, select PostalCode, and click >. Your Prototype label appears as shown in Figure 16.35.

Figure 16.35
The Prototype Label text box displays the label design as you add fields from the Available Fields list.

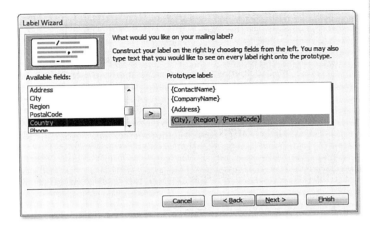

9. If the mailing is international, add an additional line for the Country field.

10. Click Next and specify the fields on which to sort the labels. Even if you didn't add the Country field, double-click Country in the Available fields list and then double-click PostalCode (see Figure 16.36). Click Next.

Figure 16.36
Specify the sort order for the labels in the fourth Label Wizard dialog.

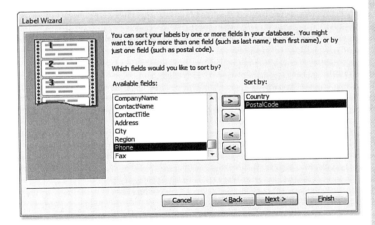

11. In the fifth wizard dialog, type a name for the report, such as **rptCustomerLabelsNew**, and click Finish to display the labels in Report view.

In many cases, you receive the error message shown in Figure 16.37 prior to opening the report in Report view or Print Preview. The error message for the preceding example is because of the wizard's miscalculation of column widths, which you correct in the next section. Click OK to dismiss the message and display the labels in Report view or Print Preview (see Figure 16.38).

 note

If the right margin is set to 0.25, you don't receive the error message shown in Figure 16.37. If you receive the message, choose File, Page Setup to open the Page Setup dialog, and set the right margin value to 0.25.

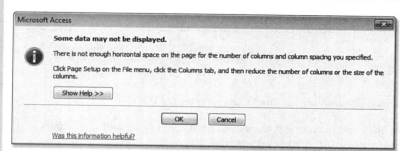

Figure 16.37
This error message occurs when using Avery 5160 labels, because the Label Wizard's page layout settings require a page width of 8.625 inches.

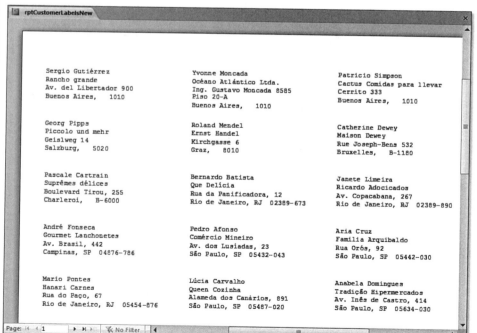

Figure 16.38
Print Preview with the Navigation pane hidden shows the first few labels in 1,024×768 resolution. Choose 75% in the Zoom button's gallery to check the top and side margins if your monitor is set to 800×600 resolution.

Modifying an Existing Mailing Label Report

The wizard doesn't let you add a line for Country, so you must alter the design of the report manually. To add the Country field to the label you created in the preceding section, do the following:

1. ![icon] Change to Report Design view, press Ctrl+A to select all the text boxes, and move them up within one grid dot of the bottom of the Detail section header.

2. Click outside the text boxes to deselect them, select the ContactName text box, and press Ctrl+C and Ctrl+V to add a copy of the text box to the Detail section.

3. Move the added text box directly under the `Trim([City]` text box.

4. ![icon] Right-click the added text box, choose Properties to open the Property Sheet, click the Data tab, and select Country in the Control Source list.

5. ![icon] If you didn't add Country as the first sorting field in the fourth wizard dialog, click the Sorting and Grouping button to open the dialog of the same name, select PostalCode, click Insert, and add Country above Postal Code in the Field/Expression list. Then close the dialog.

6. To prepare for fixing the wizard's column width miscalculation, press Ctrl+A to select the text boxes and move them one grid dot to the left.

7. ![icon] Click the Select Report button, click the Format tab of the Property Sheet, and replace the 2.625 Width property value with **2.583**. When you move the cursor to another text box, 2.583 becomes 2.5826. Your modified design appears as shown in Figure 16.39.

8. ![icon] Click Print Preview and zoom the report to 100% scale. Verify that label spacing is consistent. In this example, the label for Yvonne Moncada has an extra address line. The added line pushes down labels below the row with the extra line, which results in a print registration error (see Figure 16.40). Registration errors of this type are cumulative, so if more than one row of a label page has an extra line, the registration problem becomes serious.

9. ![icon] To correct the spacing problem, return to Design view, select the Details section's header bar, open the Property Sheet, click the Format tab, and set the Can Grow property value to No. Preventing the Detail section from expanding results in all rows having the same spacing (compare Figure 16.41 with Figure 16.40).

> **note**
>
> Following is the explanation of the 2.583-inch width for the label report: The Control Wizard calculates the required page width in inches as follows: 0.25 (left margin) + 3 * 2.625 (label width) + 2 * 0.125 (column spacing) + 0.25 (right margin) = 8.625. (In some cases, the right margin is 0.30, but you can change that to 0.25.) You need to reduce the width of the labels so the page width is 8.5 or less. Dividing 0.125 by 3, rounding up to 0.042, and subtracting from 2.625 results in a required width of 2.583.
>
> The result of the preceding calculation isn't perfect, because you need to take into account the reduced column width in setting the column spacing.

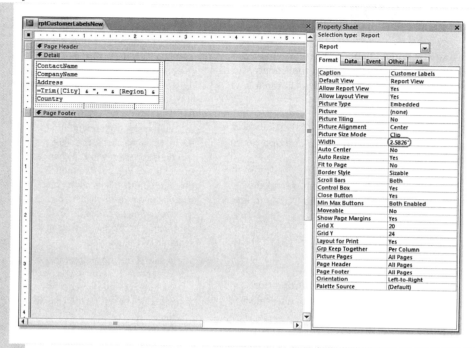

Figure 16.39
The modified label report design has the Country field added, text boxes relocated, and the width reduced.

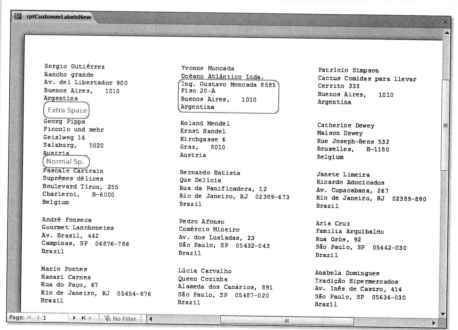

Figure 16.40
The increased space between the first and second lines of the labels is due to an extra line in the Address field of the label for Yvonne Moncada.

Figure 16.41
Setting the
Can Grow
property value
of the Detail
section of the
label report
prevents print
registration
problems. The
space for four-
line addresses
between
the first and
second rows
is now the
same as that
between other
rows.

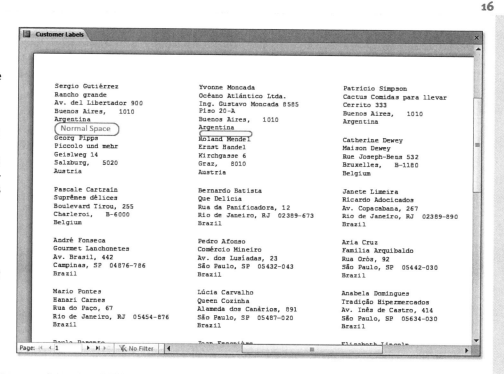

10. Press Ctrl+S to save your design changes, change to Print Preview, and print a sample of all pages on plain paper. If your labels appear to print correctly, print the first page on label stock for a test. If registration is correct, print the remaining pages.

The Page Setup dialog lets you tweak the wizard's settings and your adjustments to improve label printing registration. You specify the number of columns in a row and the number of rows on a page by selecting settings in the Columns page of the Page Setup dialog, as shown in Figure 16.42. This dialog opens when you choose File, Page Setup in either Print Preview or Report Design view. The Label Wizard sets these values for you automatically, and they change when you set new printing-related property values, but you might need to tweak them for the label stock or printer you use.

 note

Tests with Avery 5160 labels and a Brother HL-1440 laser printer demonstrate that the left, top, and bottom margins set by the wizard are satisfactory. You can fit six lines of 9-point type on a one-inch-deep label.

note

You might have to make minor alignment adjustments because the upper-left corner of the printer's image and the upper-left corner of the paper might not correspond exactly.

Figure 16.42
The Columns page of the Page Setup dialog lets you set the printing properties for reports using newspaper (snaking) columns. You also can change the column spacing and width, and the height (depth) of the labels.

The dialog's text boxes, check boxes, and option buttons let you set the following printing properties:

- The Number of Columns property sets the number of labels across the page. In this example, this property is set to 3, so the labels print three across.

- Row Spacing and the Height property determine the number of labels that fit vertically on a page and the vertical distance between successive labels. If you set Row Spacing to 0, the depth of your Detail section determines the vertical spacing of the labels.

- Column Spacing specifies the position of the left edge of columns to the right of the first column.

- The Width property in the Column Size group overrides the left margin, and the Height property overrides the bottom margin that you establish in Report Design view only if you clear the Same as Detail check box.

- The Down, Then Across option causes the labels to print in snaking column style. The first column is filled from top to bottom, then the second column is filled from top to bottom, and so on.

- The Across, Then Down option, the default for wizard-created labels, causes the labels to print in columns from left to right and then in rows from the top to the bottom of the page. This setting is preferred for mailing labels because it wastes less label stock when using continuous-feed printers to print on stock with more than one label across.

The rptCustomerLabels report is included in online sample files' \Access2010\Chaptr16\ Report16.accdb database.

17

PREPARING ADVANCED REPORTS

Access 2010's Report Wizard can create reports that you can use "as is" or modify to suit most of your database reporting requirements. In many cases, however, you must create reports that are more complex than or different from those offered by the Report Wizard. For example, you might have to apply special grouping and sorting methods to your reports. Including subreports within your reports requires that you start from a blank report form instead of using the Report Wizard. Like subforms, subreports use master-child relationships to provide detail information, such as the orders placed by each customer by year, quarter, or month.

Reports make extensive use of unbound fields having calculated values. To understand fully the process of designing advanced Access reports independently of the Report Wizard, you must be familiar with VBA and Access functions, which are two of the subjects of Chapter 10, "Understanding Access Operators and Expressions." You also must understand the methods that you use to create and design forms, which are covered in Chapter 14, "Creating and Using Access Forms," and Chapter 15, "Designing Custom Multitable Forms." Reports make extensive use of Access functions such as Sum() and VBA expressions such as ="Subtotal of" & [FieldName] & ":". If you skipped Chapters 10, 14, or 15,

 note

The report design techniques you learn in this chapter apply, for the most part, to Access data projects (ADPs). The queries on which you base reports in an ADP must conform to Transact-SQL syntax. For example, you can't use Access SQL's TRANSFORM...PIVOT statements to create ADP reports based on cross-tab queries. You also can't include Access-specific functions, such as DLookup(), that are provided by the Access expression service. Chapter 28, "Upsizing Access Applications to Access Data Projects," describes the workarounds you need to adapt Access-based reports to ADPs.

you might want to refer to the appropriate sections of those chapters whenever you encounter unfamiliar subjects or terminology in this chapter.

Grouping and Sorting Report Data

Most reports you create require that you organize the data into groups and subgroups in a style similar to the outline of a book. The Report Wizard lets you establish the initial grouping and sorting properties for your data, but you might want to rearrange your report's data after reviewing the Report Wizard's first draft.

The Group, Sort, and Total pane (see Figure 17.1) lets you modify these report properties in design mode. The sections that follow modify the Inventory by Category report that you created in the preceding chapter. The sorting and grouping methods described here, however, apply to any report that you create. To display the pane, open the report in Layout or Design view and click the Format or Design ribbon's Group & Sort button.

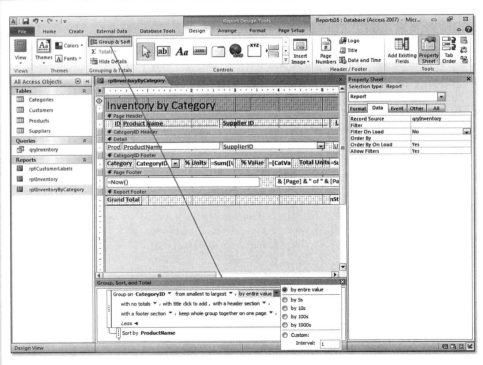

Figure 17.1
Use the Group, Sort, and Total pane to classify and sort your reports by numeric or alphabetic values.

Property values you set in the Group, Sort, and Total pane determine the fields or expressions on which Access is to group the products, up to a maximum of 10 fields or expressions. You can sort the groups and grouped data in ascending (from smallest to largest, or *A on top*) or descending (from largest to smallest, or *Z on top*) order, but you must select one or the other; "unsorted" isn't an option.

Grouping Data

The method that you use to group data depends on the type of data in the field you plan to group. You can group by categories, in which case a unique value must represent each category. You can group data by a range of values, which usually is numeric but also can be alphabetic. You can use the data in a field to group the report rows, or you can substitute an expression as the basis for the grouping.

 note

Apparently, the Access team wasn't confident Access users would understand the terms *ascending* and *descending order* for numeric and alphabetic values.

Grouping by Numeric Values

When you told the Report Wizard in the preceding chapter to use CategoryID as the field by which to group, you elected to group by a numeric value. You can alter the grouping sequence easily by using the Group, Sort, and Total pane. For example, you can group the inventory report by SupplierID to aid in comparing the inventory turnover rate of products from multiple suppliers. The report you create in the later "Working from a Blank Report" section provides some insight into inventory turnover by product category, not by supplier.

 note

Reports demonstrating the grouping examples in the following sections are included in the Reports17.accdb database in the \Access2010\Chaptr17 folder of the downloadable sample code.

➡ *To review the Report Wizard process,* **see** *"Creating a Grouped Report with the Report Wizard,"* **p. 688.**

To group the Inventory by Category report by SupplierID, do the following:

1. If you don't already have it open, open the rptInventoryByCategory report from \Access2010\Chaptr17\Reports17.accdb in Design view, and save the report as **rptInventoryBySupplier**. Change the title text box and report Caption property value to **Inventory by SupplierNew** (Reports17.accdb contains an Inventory by Supplier report).

2. ⌊≣ Click the Design tab and the Group & Sort button, open CategoryID's drop-down list in the Group, Sort, and Total pane, and select SupplierID as the first group field. When you change the group field, Access automatically renames the Group Header and Footer sections from CategoryID to SupplierID. Close the Group, Sort, and Total pane.

3. Delete the CategoryID label and lookup list in the SupplierID Footer section; CategoryID isn't appropriate to the new grouping.

4. 🖼 Click the Add Existing Fields button to open the Field List and drag the SupplierID field to the SupplierID Footer section. Then drop it in the position formerly occupied by CategoryID. SupplierID is a lookup field, so the new control for the field is a drop-down list.

5. **B** Delete the SupplierID label and position the SupplierID list at the top left of the Footer section. Remove the % Units label and text box to make room for the long CompanyName values displayed by the SupplierID list. Widen the SupplierID control to about 3 inches, and apply the Bold attribute (see Figure 17.2).

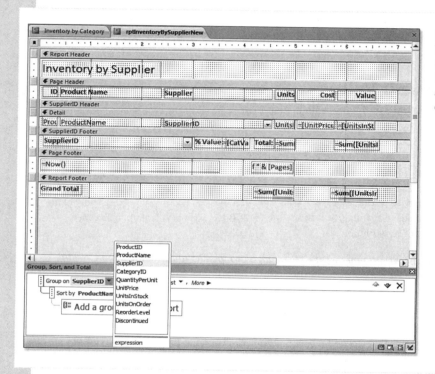

Figure 17.2
You can quickly repurpose an existing report by changing its Group By property value and making minor design changes to the new report.

6. Save your design changes, and open the report in Print Preview (see Figure 17.3).

Grouping by Alphabetic Code Characters

If you use a systematic code for grouping, you can group by the first five or fewer characters of the code field. With an expression, you can group by any set of characters within a field. To group by the second and third digits of a code, for example, use the following expression:

$=$**Mid**$([FieldName], 2, 2)$

Mid( )'s first numeric argument is the position of the starting character on which to group, and the second is the number of characters to use for grouping.

> ### note
> It only requires a bit more work to change the SupplierID field in the detail section to CategoryID, reduce the width of the list text box, move the field to the right, and increase the width of the Product Name column to display the entire names.

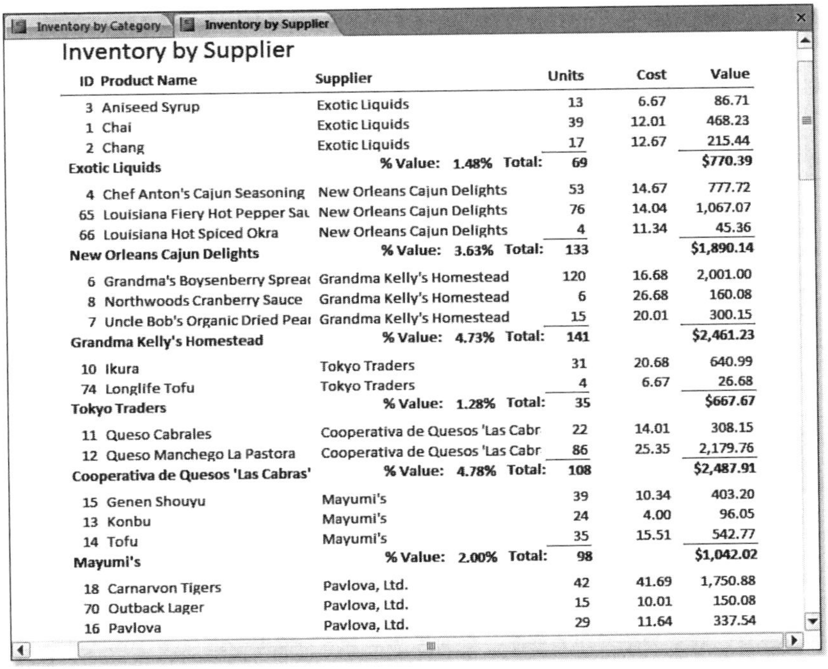

Inventory by Supplier

ID	Product Name	Supplier	Units	Cost	Value
3	Aniseed Syrup	Exotic Liquids	13	6.67	86.71
1	Chai	Exotic Liquids	39	12.01	468.23
2	Chang	Exotic Liquids	17	12.67	215.44
Exotic Liquids		% Value: 1.48% Total:	69		$770.39
4	Chef Anton's Cajun Seasoning	New Orleans Cajun Delights	53	14.67	777.72
65	Louisiana Fiery Hot Pepper Sau	New Orleans Cajun Delights	76	14.04	1,067.07
66	Louisiana Hot Spiced Okra	New Orleans Cajun Delights	4	11.34	45.36
New Orleans Cajun Delights		% Value: 3.63% Total:	133		$1,890.14
6	Grandma's Boysenberry Sprea	Grandma Kelly's Homestead	120	16.68	2,001.00
8	Northwoods Cranberry Sauce	Grandma Kelly's Homestead	6	26.68	160.08
7	Uncle Bob's Organic Dried Pear	Grandma Kelly's Homestead	15	20.01	300.15
Grandma Kelly's Homestead		% Value: 4.73% Total:	141		$2,461.23
10	Ikura	Tokyo Traders	31	20.68	640.99
74	Longlife Tofu	Tokyo Traders	4	6.67	26.68
Tokyo Traders		% Value: 1.28% Total:	35		$667.67
11	Queso Cabrales	Cooperativa de Quesos 'Las Cabr	22	14.01	308.15
12	Queso Manchego La Pastora	Cooperativa de Quesos 'Las Cabr	86	25.35	2,179.76
Cooperativa de Quesos 'Las Cabras'		% Value: 4.78% Total:	108		$2,487.91
15	Genen Shouyu	Mayumi's	39	10.34	403.20
13	Konbu	Mayumi's	24	4.00	96.05
14	Tofu	Mayumi's	35	15.51	542.77
Mayumi's		% Value: 2.00% Total:	98		$1,042.02
18	Carnarvon Tigers	Pavlova, Ltd.	42	41.69	1,750.88
70	Outback Lager	Pavlova, Ltd.	15	10.01	150.08
16	Pavlova	Pavlova, Ltd.	29	11.64	337.54

Figure 17.3
The Supplier column in the repurposed inventory report is redundant, but doesn't detract from the overall value of the report.

Grouping with Subgroups

If your table or query contains appropriate data, you can group reports by more than one level by creating subgroups. The Employee Sales by Country report (one of the Northwind Traders sample reports), for example, uses groups (Country) and subgroups (the employee's name—the actual group is a VBA expression that combines the FirstName and LastName fields) to organize orders received within a range of dates. Open the Employee Sales by Country report in Design view to view the additional section created by a subgroup. Change to Print Preview, and type **1/1/2006** and **12/31/2006** as the values of the Enter Beginning Date Parameter Value and Ending Date Enter Parameter Value dialogs to view all orders.

Using a Function to Group by Range

You often must sort reports by ranges of values. (If you opened the Employee Sales by Country report, close it and reopen the rptInventoryByCategory report in design mode.) If you want to divide the Inventory by Category report into a maximum of nine sections—each beginning with a three-letter group of the alphabet (*A* through *C*, *D* through *F*, and so on) based on the ProductName field—the entries in the Group, Sort, and Total pane should look like the entries in Figure 17.4.

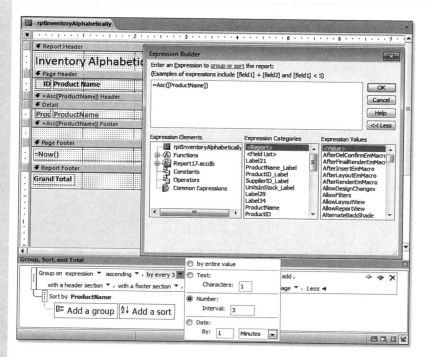

Figure 17.4
Set the Group By properties to those shown here to group product names by a three-initial-letter interval.

Alphabetic grouping demonstrates a grouping bug that has been present since Access 2.0. VBA's =Asc([ProductName]) function returns the ASCII (numeric) value of the first character of its string argument, the ProductName field. You set the Group On specification to Expression to open the Expression Builder, type =**Asc([ProductName])**, and then set the interval (by every) to 3. This setup *theoretically* groups the data into names beginning with *A* through *C*, *D* through *F*, and so on. You must add an ascending sort on ProductName to ensure alphabetic sorting within the group (see Figure 17.5). You can replace all text boxes in the Group Footer with a separation line because subtotals by alphabetic groups aren't significant. Although of limited value in this report, an alphabetic grouping often is useful for formatting long, alphabetized lists to assist readers in finding a particular record.

Grouping on Date and Time

If you group data on a field with a Date/Time data type, Access lets you set the Group, Sort, and Total pane's Group On property to Year, Qtr (quarter), Month, Week, Day, Hour, or Minute. To group records so that values of the same quarter for several years print in sequence, type the following in the Field/Expression column of the Sorting and Grouping dialog:

```
=DatePart("q",[FieldName])
```

 note

Requiring users to type an expression in a separate, unrelated dialog is an example of poor interface design. The single Sorting and Grouping dialog of Access 2003 and earlier versions is much more straightforward than this approach.

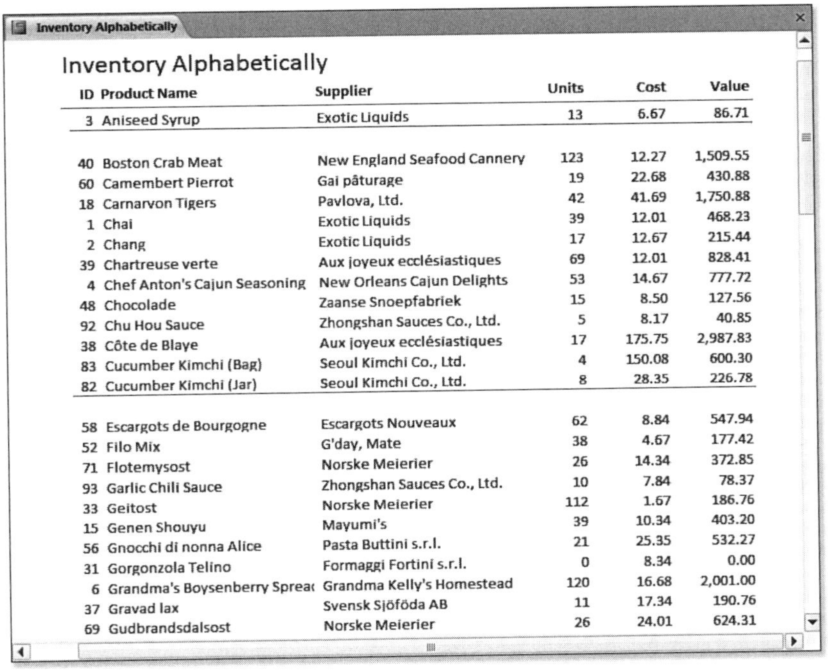

Figure 17.5
A bug in Access's interval grouping process when using a VBA expression causes grouping by *A, B* to *D, E* to *G*, and so on. This bug has been present since Access 2.0.

Inventory Alphabetically					
ID	Product Name	Supplier	Units	Cost	Value
3	Aniseed Syrup	Exotic Liquids	13	6.67	86.71
40	Boston Crab Meat	New England Seafood Cannery	123	12.27	1,509.55
60	Camembert Pierrot	Gai pâturage	19	22.68	430.88
18	Carnarvon Tigers	Pavlova, Ltd.	42	41.69	1,750.88
1	Chai	Exotic Liquids	39	12.01	468.23
2	Chang	Exotic Liquids	17	12.67	215.44
39	Chartreuse verte	Aux joyeux ecclésiastiques	69	12.01	828.41
4	Chef Anton's Cajun Seasoning	New Orleans Cajun Delights	53	14.67	777.72
48	Chocolade	Zaanse Snoepfabriek	15	8.50	127.56
92	Chu Hou Sauce	Zhongshan Sauces Co., Ltd.	5	8.17	40.85
38	Côte de Blaye	Aux joyeux ecclésiastiques	17	175.75	2,987.83
83	Cucumber Kimchi (Bag)	Seoul Kimchi Co., Ltd.	4	150.08	600.30
82	Cucumber Kimchi (Jar)	Seoul Kimchi Co., Ltd.	8	28.35	226.78
58	Escargots de Bourgogne	Escargots Nouveaux	62	8.84	547.94
52	Filo Mix	G'day, Mate	38	4.67	177.42
71	Flotemysost	Norske Meierier	26	14.34	372.85
93	Garlic Chili Sauce	Zhongshan Sauces Co., Ltd.	10	7.84	78.37
33	Geitost	Norske Meierier	112	1.67	186.76
15	Genen Shouyu	Mayumi's	39	10.34	403.20
56	Gnocchi di nonna Alice	Pasta Buttini s.r.l.	21	25.35	532.27
31	Gorgonzola Telino	Formaggi Fortini s.r.l.	0	8.34	0.00
6	Grandma's Boysenberry Spread	Grandma Kelly's Homestead	120	16.68	2,001.00
37	Gravad lax	Svensk Sjöföda AB	11	17.34	190.76
69	Gudbrandsdalsost	Norske Meierier	26	24.01	624.31

➡ For a full listing of ways you can sort by date or time, **see** "Functions for Date and Time," **p. 396**.

Sorting Data Groups

Although most data sorting within groups is based on the values contained in a field, you also can sort by expressions. When an inventory evaluation list is compiled based on the original Inventory by Category report, the products with the highest extended inventory value are the most important. The report's users might want these products listed first in a group. This decision requires sorting the records within groups on the expression =[UnitsInStock]*[UnitPrice], which is similar to the expression that calculates the report's Value column. (You don't need to account for the constant markup multiplier when sorting.) A descending sort is necessary to place the highest values at the top of the report. Figure 17.6 shows the required entries in the Expression Builder and the Group, Sort, and Total pane.

The descending sort on the inventory value expression results in the report shown in Figure 17.7. As expected, the products with the highest inventory value appear first in each category.

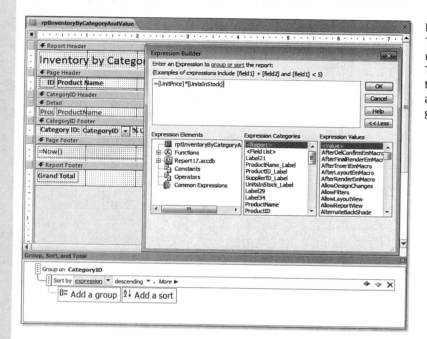

Figure 17.6
The expression in the second row of the Group, Sort, and Total pane places items with the largest inventory value at the top of each CategoryID group.

Figure 17.7
The grouping and sorting properties shown in Figure 17.6 result in a report that emphasizes the most important elements within a group.

Inventory by Category and Value

ID	Product Name	Supplier	Units	Cost	Value
38	Côte de Blaye	Aux joyeux ecclésiastiques	17	175.75	2,987.83
34	Sasquatch Ale	Bigfoot Breweries	111	9.34	1,036.52
39	Chartreuse verte	Aux joyeux ecclésiastiques	69	12.01	828.41
76	Lakkalikööri	Karkki Oy	57	12.01	684.34
75	Rhönbräu Klosterbier	Plutzer Lebensmittelgroßmärkte	125	5.17	646.16
43	Ipoh Coffee	Leka Trading	17	30.68	521.59
67	Laughing Lumberjack Lager	Bigfoot Breweries	52	9.34	485.58
1	Chai	Exotic Liquids	39	12.01	468.23
35	Steeleye Stout	Bigfoot Breweries	20	12.01	240.12
2	Chang	Exotic Liquids	17	12.67	215.44
70	Outback Lager	Pavlova, Ltd.	15	10.01	150.08
Category ID: Beverages	**% Units: 16.85% % Value: 15.89% Total:**		**539**		**$8,264.30**
61	Sirop d'érable	Forêts d'érables	113	19.01	2,148.07
6	Grandma's Boysenberry Spread	Grandma Kelly's Homestead	120	16.68	2,001.00
81	Radish Kimchi (Bag)	Seoul Kimchi Co., Ltd.	10	116.73	1,167.25
65	Louisiana Fiery Hot Pepper Sau	New Orleans Cajun Delights	76	14.04	1,067.07
4	Chef Anton's Cajun Seasoning	New Orleans Cajun Delights	53	14.67	777.72
63	Vegie-spread	Pavlova, Ltd.	24	29.28	702.75
83	Cucumber Kimchi (Bag)	Seoul Kimchi Co., Ltd.	4	150.08	600.30
89	Korean Traditional Bean Paste	Seoul Kimchi Co., Ltd.	20	28.01	560.28
87	Korean Hot Bean Paste	Incheon Food Trading Co., Ltd.	15	35.02	525.26
85	Mild Cabbage Kimchi (Bag)	Incheon Food Trading Co., Ltd.	6	83.38	500.25
79	Hot Cabbage Kimchi (Bag)	Incheon Food Trading Co., Ltd.	5	83.38	416.88
88	Korean Seasoned Bean Paste	Seoul Kimchi Co., Ltd.	10	41.69	416.88
15	Genen Shouyu	Mayumi's	39	10.34	403.20
44	Gula Malacca	Leka Trading	27	12.97	350.28

Working from a Blank Report

Usually, the fastest way to set up a report is to use the Report Wizard to create a basic report and then modify the basic report, as described in Chapter 16 and previous sections of this chapter. If you're creating a report style that the wizard can't handle or a report containing a subreport, however, modifying a standard report style created by the Report Wizard could take longer than creating a report by using the default blank report that Access provides.

Using a Report as a Subreport

The report you design in the following sections includes information about total monthly orders for products by category. Comparing the monthly orders to the inventory level of a category allows the report's user to estimate inventory turnover rates. This report serves two purposes—a primary report, and a subreport within another report. You add the Monthly Orders by Category report as a subreport of the Inventory by Category report in the "Incorporating Subreports" section, later in this chapter.

To create a report to use as the Monthly Orders by Category subreport (rpt2006MonthlyCategory-Orders) in the following section of this chapter, "Adding and Deleting Sections of Your Report," you need to base the subreport on a query (qry2006MonthlyProductOrdersCT) adapted for this purpose.

A copy of the qry2006MonthlyProductOrdersCT query is included in the Report17.accdb database in the \Access2010\Chaptr17 folder of the downloadable sample code.

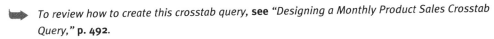

➡ *To review how to create this crosstab query,* **see** *"Designing a Monthly Product Sales Crosstab Query,"* **p. 492.**

To modify the query for this subreport, follow these steps:

1. From the Navigation pane, open the qry2006MonthlyProductOrdersCT query in Design view.

2. In the grid, change the first column's field name from ProductID to CategoryID by opening the Field drop-down list and clicking the CategoryID field name. You need the CategoryID field to link with the CategoryID field in the qryInventory query that the rptInventoryByCategory report uses as its data source.

3. Delete the ProductName column. The modified query appears as shown in Figure 17.8.

4. Click the Office button, choose Save As, Save Object As, and name the modified query **qry2006MonthlyCategoryOrdersCTNew** (Reports17.accdb contains a qry2006MonthlyCategory-OrdersCT report). Click Run to check the query. Your query resultset appears as shown in Figure 17.9.

5. Click the Create tab and the Report Design button to open a new report in Design view.

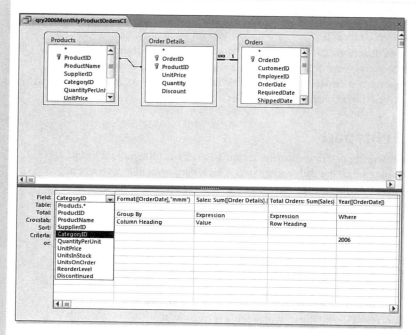

Figure 17.8
The query for inventory analysis uses RequiredDate rather than OrderDate to more accurately reflect the date on which an order became a sale.

qry2006MonthlyCategoryOrdersCTNew

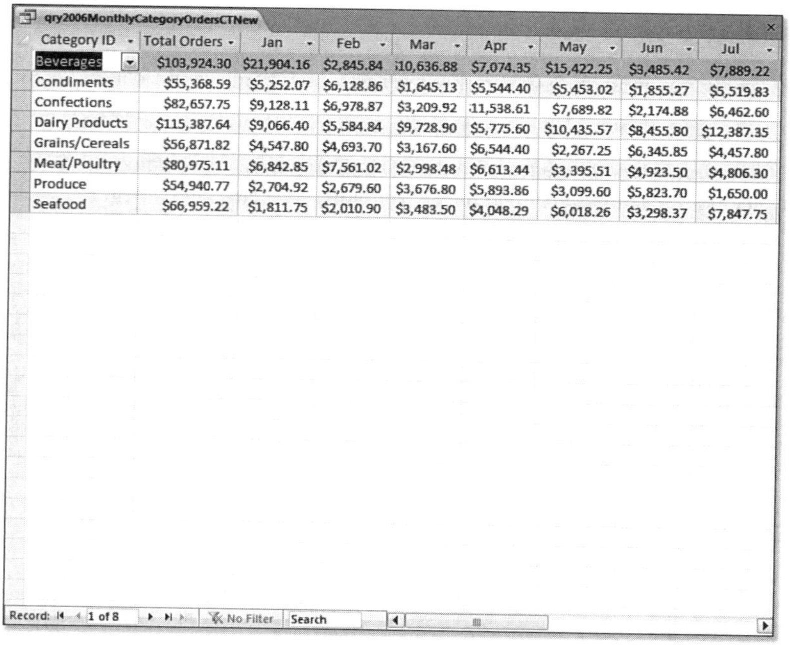

Category ID	Total Orders	Jan	Feb	Mar	Apr	May	Jun	Jul
Beverages	$103,924.30	$21,904.16	$2,845.84	;10,636.88	$7,074.35	$15,422.25	$3,485.42	$7,889.22
Condiments	$55,368.59	$5,252.07	$6,128.86	$1,645.13	$5,544.40	$5,453.02	$1,855.27	$5,519.83
Confections	$82,657.75	$9,128.11	$6,978.87	$3,209.92	:11,538.61	$7,689.82	$2,174.88	$6,462.60
Dairy Products	$115,387.64	$9,066.40	$5,584.84	$9,728.90	$5,775.60	$10,435.57	$8,455.80	$12,387.35
Grains/Cereals	$56,871.82	$4,547.80	$4,693.70	$3,167.60	$6,544.40	$2,267.25	$6,345.85	$4,457.80
Meat/Poultry	$80,975.11	$6,842.85	$7,561.02	$2,998.48	$6,613.44	$3,395.51	$4,923.50	$4,806.30
Produce	$54,940.77	$2,704.92	$2,679.60	$3,676.80	$5,893.86	$3,099.60	$5,823.70	$1,650.00
Seafood	$66,959.22	$1,811.75	$2,010.90	$3,483.50	$4,048.29	$6,018.26	$3,298.37	$7,847.75

Record: 1 of 8 No Filter Search

Figure 17.9
The query includes a Total Orders column that's useful for calculating average yearly inventory turns (total yearly sales divided by inventory value).

6. 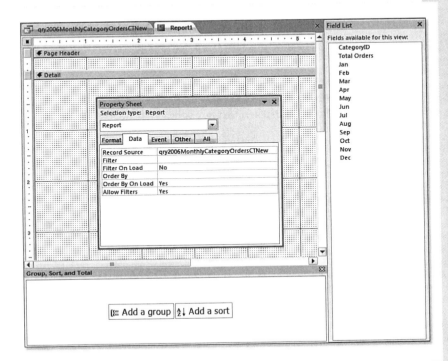 Press F4 to open the Property Sheet. Click the Data tab and select qry2006MonthlyCategoryOrdersCTNew as the Record Source property value (see Figure 17.10).

Figure 17.10
This blank report with qry2006MonthlyCategoryOrdersCTNew as the Record Source is the starting point for the subreport you add to the Inventory by Category report later in the chapter.

Creating the Monthly Sales by Category Report

The crosstab query that acts as the Monthly Sales by Category report's data source is closely related to a report, but the crosstab query doesn't include detail records. Each row of the query consists of subtotals of sales for a category for each month of the year. One row appears below the inventory value subtotal when you link the subreport (child) to the main (master) report, so this report needs only a Detail section. Each detail row, however, requires a header label to print the month. The CategoryID field is included so that you can verify that the data is linked correctly.

To complete the Monthly Sales by Category report (and later a subreport), follow these steps:

1. In the blank report you opened in the preceding section, remove the default Page Header and Page Footer sections by right-clicking the report and choosing Page Header/Footer to clear the toggle. This subreport requires only a Detail section.

2. Drag the right margin of the Detail section to the right so that the report is about 6 1/2-inches wide.

3. 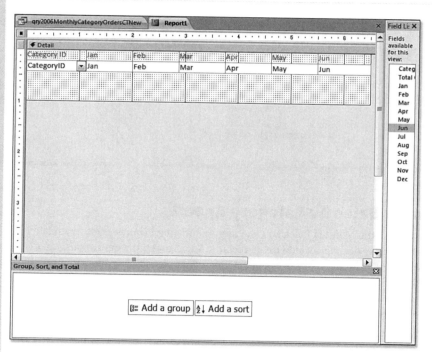 Click the Design ribbon's Add Existing Fields button, select CategoryID, and drag its field symbol to the Detail section.

4. Click the CategoryID label and relocate the label to the upper left of the Detail section directly over the CategoryID combo box. (CategoryID appears as a combo box, not a text box, in Report Design view because CategoryID is a lookup field.) Adjust the width of the label and text box to 1 1/8-inches. Edit the label's text to **Category**.

5. Click and drag the field list's Jan field to the right of the CategoryID field. Move the label to the top of the section, adjacent to the right border of the field to its left. Move the text box under the label. Adjust the label and text box width to 21 dots (7/8 inch).

6. Repeat step 5 for the month fields of Feb through Jun. The report design now appears as shown in Figure 17.11.

Figure 17.11
Start the report design by adding the CategoryID field and the Jan through Jun fields of the query to the first row of labels and text boxes.

7. Click each month label while holding down the Shift key so that you select all six month labels (but only the labels).

8. **B** ≡ Press Ctrl+B to apply the bold attribute to all month labels, right-click the label group, select Font/Fore Color and click Black. Then open the Properties group's Format page and set the Text Align property value to Center to center the labels' text above the text boxes.

9. Select the CategoryID text box and the label, and press Ctrl+B.

10. 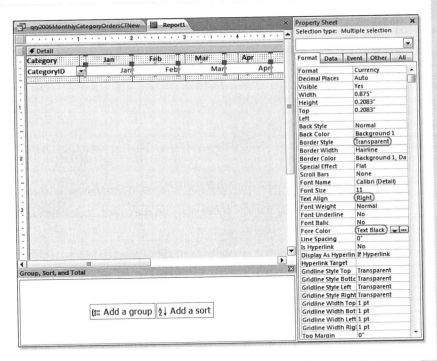 Select the six month text boxes, and set the Text Align property value to Right to right-align the dollar amounts, set the Border style property value to Transparent, and set the Fore Color property value to Text Black.

11. Click the Design tab's Line control and add a line at the top edge of the labels. Drag the line's right-end handle to the right edge of the Jun text box.

12. Repeat step 11 for another identical line, but add the new line under the text boxes.

13. Drag the Detail section's margins to within three dots of the bottom and right edges of the controls. The report's design appears as shown in Figure 17.12.

Figure 17.12
Format and align the labels, align the text boxes, and add two one-point lines to dress up the report.

14. Click Report View to verify the design (see Figure 17.13).

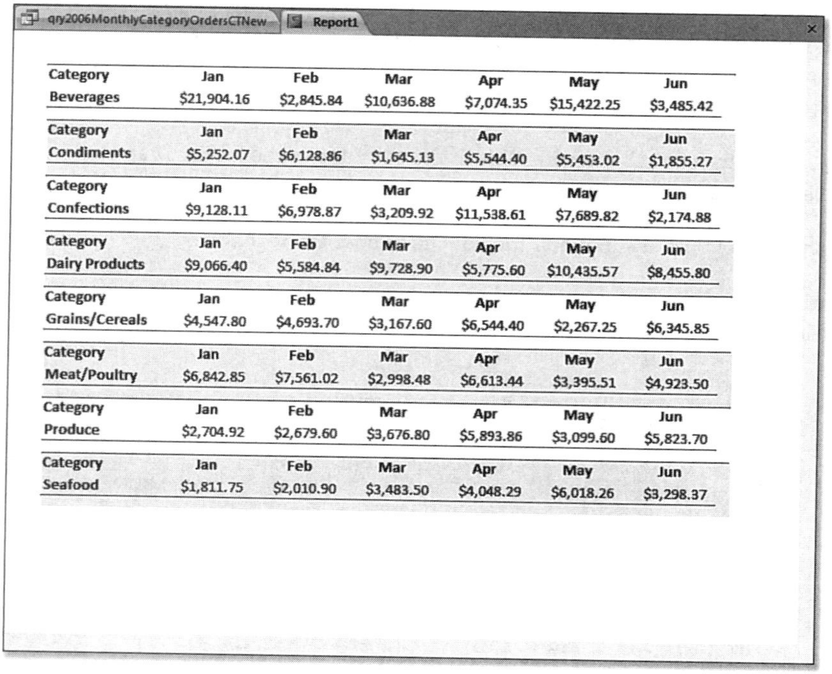

Category	Jan	Feb	Mar	Apr	May	Jun
Beverages	$21,904.16	$2,845.84	$10,636.88	$7,074.35	$15,422.25	$3,485.42
Condiments	$5,252.07	$6,128.86	$1,645.13	$5,544.40	$5,453.02	$1,855.27
Confections	$9,128.11	$6,978.87	$3,209.92	$11,538.61	$7,689.82	$2,174.88
Dairy Products	$9,066.40	$5,584.84	$9,728.90	$5,775.60	$10,435.57	$8,455.80
Grains/Cereals	$4,547.80	$4,693.70	$3,167.60	$6,544.40	$2,267.25	$6,345.85
Meat/Poultry	$6,842.85	$7,561.02	$2,998.48	$6,613.44	$3,395.51	$4,923.50
Produce	$2,704.92	$2,679.60	$3,676.80	$5,893.86	$3,099.60	$5,823.70
Seafood	$1,811.75	$2,010.90	$3,483.50	$4,048.29	$6,018.26	$3,298.37

Figure 17.13
Confirm the first phase of the report's design in Print Preview.

15. Press Ctrl+S and type **rpt2006MonthlyCategoryOrdersNew** as the report's name.

To add the remaining months of the year and the Grand Total field to your report, follow these steps:

1. 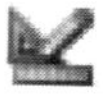 To accommodate another row of labels and text boxes, return to Design view and increase the depth of the Detail section by dragging the bottom margin down about 1 inch.
2. Shift+click each label and text box to select all the controls in the Detail section without selecting the two horizontal lines.
3. Press Ctrl+C to copy the labels, text boxes, and lines to the Clipboard.
4. Press Ctrl+V to paste a copy of the labels and text boxes to the Detail section.
5. Move this copy directly under the original labels and text boxes.
6. Click a blank area of the report to deselect the controls; then select and delete the new CategoryID text box. When you delete this text box, you also delete the associated label.
7. Edit both the labels and text boxes to display Jul through Dec. (Access automatically sets the text boxes' Control Source property to match the field name you type into the text box.)

8. 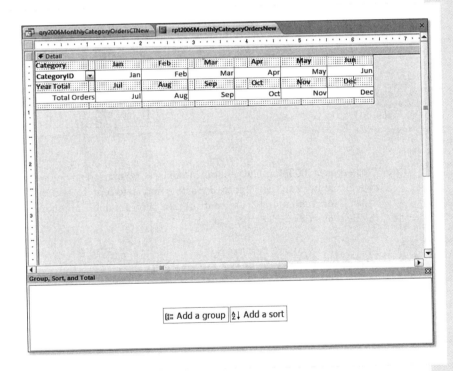 **B** Open the field list, if necessary, and add the Total Orders field and label in place of the second CategoryID field and label you deleted in step 6. Change the label caption to **Year Total**, select the label and text box, and apply the Bold attribute. Adjust the width of the label and text box to match the controls above.

9. Press Ctrl+A to select all the controls, and click the Arrange tab's Align to Grid button to correct any minor alignment discrepancies.

10. Move the line below the top text boxes to the bottom of the lower text boxes.

11. Drag the right side of the Jun and Dec text boxes to the right two dots, drag the right report margin to the edge of these two text boxes, and drag the bottom margin up to within two dots of the bottom of the text boxes in the second row. Figure 17.14 shows the final report design.

Figure 17.14
Copying the first row of controls to create a second row. Editing the labels and text boxes is faster than adding and adjusting another set of six control pairs.

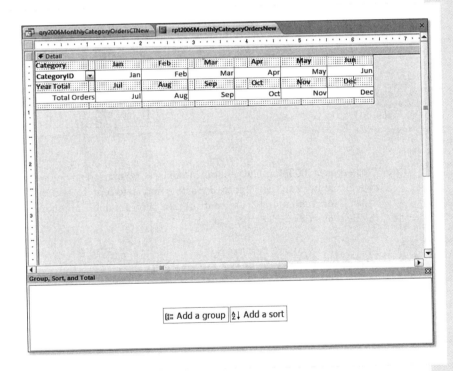

12. Click Report View to display the double-row report (see Figure 17.15).

Figure 17.15
Report view displays the report design of Figure 17.14.

Category	Jan	Feb	Mar	Apr	May	Jun
Beverages	$21,904.16	$2,845.84	$10,636.88	$7,074.35	$15,422.25	$3,485.42
Year Total	Jul	Aug	Sep	Oct	Nov	Dec
$103,924.30	$7,889.22	$5,836.92	$5,726.70	$8,374.90	$3,851.00	$10,876.65

Category	Jan	Feb	Mar	Apr	May	Jun
Condiments	$5,252.07	$6,128.86	$1,645.13	$5,544.40	$5,453.02	$1,855.27
Year Total	Jul	Aug	Sep	Oct	Nov	Dec
$55,368.59	$5,519.83	$4,220.02	$3,575.18	$6,565.91	$3,784.67	$5,824.20

Category	Jan	Feb	Mar	Apr	May	Jun
Confections	$9,128.11	$6,978.87	$3,209.92	$11,538.61	$7,689.82	$2,174.88
Year Total	Jul	Aug	Sep	Oct	Nov	Dec
$82,657.75	$6,462.60	$7,105.63	$6,708.59	$7,800.70	$5,081.85	$8,778.15

Category	Jan	Feb	Mar	Apr	May	Jun
Dairy Products	$9,066.40	$5,584.84	$9,728.90	$5,775.60	$10,435.57	$8,455.80
Year Total	Jul	Aug	Sep	Oct	Nov	Dec
$115,387.64	$12,387.35	$6,826.55	$11,420.30	$12,869.00	$12,992.47	$9,844.85

Category	Jan	Feb	Mar	Apr	May	Jun
Grains/Cereals	$4,547.80	$4,693.70	$3,167.60	$6,544.40	$2,267.25	$6,345.85
Year Total	Jul	Aug	Sep	Oct	Nov	Dec
$56,871.82	$4,457.80	$5,415.25	$5,371.47	$3,031.00	$5,787.35	$5,242.35

Category	Jan	Feb	Mar	Apr	May	Jun
Meat/Poultry	$6,842.85	$7,561.02	$2,998.48	$6,613.44	$3,395.51	$4,923.50
Year Total	Jul	Aug	Sep	Oct	Nov	Dec
$80,975.11	$4,806.30	$4,888.24	$10,945.97	$14,203.64	$1,029.00	$12,767.16

13. Close the rpt2006MonthlyCategoryOrdersNew report and save the changes.The technique of copying controls to the Clipboard, pasting copies to reports, and then editing the copies is often faster than creating duplicate controls that differ from one another only in the text of labels and the field names of bound text boxes.

Incorporating Subreports

Reports, like forms, can include subreports. Unlike the Form Wizard, however, the Report Wizard offers no option for automatically creating reports that include subreports. You can add subreports to reports that you create with the Report Wizard, or you can create subreports from blank reports, like you did in the earlier section "Working from a Blank Report."

Adding a Linked Subreport to a Bound Report

If a main report is bound to a table or query as a data source and the subreport's data source can be related to the main report's data source, you can link the subreport's data to the main report's data.

> **note**
>
> Alternatively, click the Builder button to open the Subreport Field linker dialog, and select CategoryID in the Master Fields and Child Fields lists, if necessary. Usually, these fields will be selected by default.

To add and link the rpt2006MonthlyCategoryOrdersNew report as a subreport to the Inventory by Category report, for example, follow these steps:

1. Open the rptInventoryByCategory report from Reports17.accdb in Design view.

2. Drag down the top of the Page Footer border to make room for the subreport in the CategoryID Footer section (about 7/8 inch).

3. 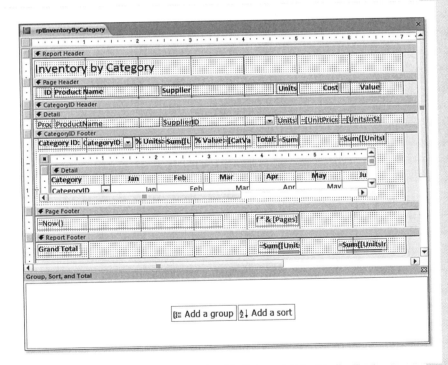 Click and drag the rpt2006MonthlyCategoryOrdersNew report from the Navigation pane to a location inside the CategoryID Footer section. Position the upper-right corner of the Report mouse pointer two dots to the right of the left margin and two dots below the bottom of the CategoryID text box.

4. When you release the right mouse button, Access adds a subreport control, which displays the subreport in Design view within a frame for in-site editing. Delete the subreport's label (see Figure 17.16).

Figure 17.16
Drag a report's icon to a section of another report and drop it to automatically add the subreport.

5. Adjust the CategoryID Footer's depth to provide about 0.1-inch margins above and below the section's controls.

6. 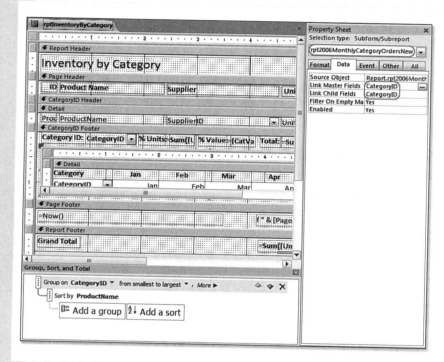 You need to link the data in the subreport to the data of the main report so that only the sales data corresponding to a specific group's CategoryID value appears in the CategoryID Footer section. Select the report and click the Property Sheet button to display the report's Property Sheet. Select the rpt2006MonthlyCategoryOrdersNew subreport in the object selection list, click the Data tab, and type **CategoryID** in the LinkChildFields and LinkMaster Fields text boxes (see Figure 17.17).

Figure 17.17
If you don't see the subreport's Design view in the subreport frame, type the Link Master Field and Link Child Field names in the Property Sheet.

7. Click the Report View button to display the report. The subreport appears as shown at the bottom of Figure 17.18. Scroll the report to confirm that the linkage is correct for all categories.

8. Save the modified report as rptInventoryByCategoryWith2006SalesNew. You can add and link several subreports to the main report if each subreport has a field in common with the main report's data source.

Figure 17.18
The appropriate rows of
the linked subreport print
below the text boxes in
the CategoryID Footer
section.

Inventory by Category with 2000 Sales New

Inventory by Category

ID	Product Name	Supplier	Units	Cost	Value
1	Chai	Exotic Liquids	39	12.01	468.23
2	Chang	Exotic Liquids	17	12.67	215.44
39	Chartreuse verte	Aux joyeux ecclésiastiques	69	12.01	828.41
38	Côte de Blaye	Aux joyeux ecclésiastiques	17	175.75	2,987.83
43	Ipoh Coffee	Leka Trading	17	30.68	521.59
76	Lakkalikööri	Karkki Oy	57	12.01	684.34
67	Laughing Lumberjack Lager	Bigfoot Breweries	52	9.34	485.58
70	Outback Lager	Pavlova, Ltd.	15	10.01	150.08
75	Rhönbräu Klosterbier	Plutzer Lebensmittelgroßmärkte	125	5.17	646.16
34	Sasquatch Ale	Bigfoot Breweries	111	9.34	1,036.52
35	Steeleye Stout	Bigfoot Breweries	20	12.01	240.12

Category ID: Beverages   % Units: 16.85% % Value: 15.89% Total: 539 $8,264.30

Category	Jan	Feb	Mar	Apr	May	Jun
Beverages	$21,904.16	$2,845.84	$10,636.88	$7,074.35	$15,422.25	$3,485.42
Year Total	Jul	Aug	Sep	Oct	Nov	Dec
$103,924.30	$7,889.22	$5,836.92	$5,726.70	$8,374.90	$3,851.00	$10,876.65

3	Aniseed Syrup	Exotic Liquids	13	6.67	86.71
4	Chef Anton's Cajun Seasoning	New Orleans Cajun Delights	53	14.67	777.72
92	Chu Hou Sauce	Zhongshan Sauces Co., Ltd.	5	8.17	40.85
83	Cucumber Kimchi (Bag)	Seoul Kimchi Co., Ltd.	4	150.08	600.30
82	Cucumber Kimchi (Jar)	Seoul Kimchi Co., Ltd.	8	28.35	226.78
93	Garlic Chili Sauce	Zhongshan Sauces Co., Ltd.	10	7.84	78.37
15	Genen Shouyu	Mayumi's	39	10.34	403.20

Link Expression Errors

When your attempt to create a link between the main report and subreport causes a Can't
Evaluate Expression error message, the most likely cause is that you are trying to create a
master-child (or, more properly, parent-child) link with an incompatible data type. Parent-
child linkages are similar to joins of queries that use the WHERE *SubreportName.FieldName* =
ReportName.FieldName criterion. As with joins, the data types of the linked fields of tables
or columns of queries must be identical. You can't, for example, link a field of the Text data
type with a field of the Integer data type, even if your text field contains only numbers. If you
use an expression to create the link, the data type that the expression returns must match
the field value. You can use the data type conversion functions described in Chapter 10 to
change the data type that the expression returns to that of the linked field. For example, you
can link a text field that contains numbers to a field of the Long Integer data type by entering
=**CLng**(TextField) as the linking value.

Using Unlinked Subreports and Unbound Reports

Most reports that you create use subreports that are linked to the main report's data source. You can, however, insert independent subreports within main reports. In this case, you don't enter values for the Link Child Fields and Link Master Fields properties. The subreport's data source can be related to or completely independent of the main report's data source.

Figure 17.19 illustrates the effect of including an unlinked subreport in a main report. The figure shows a part of page 1 of the rpt2006MonthlyCategoryOrdersNew subreport within the rptInventoryByCategoryWith2006Sales report after deleting the CategoryID values of the Link Child Fields and Link Master Fields properties, prior to saving the report with a new name. Notice that without the link, the subreport displays all records instead of just those records related to the particular category in which the subreport appears. You might need to set the CategoryID Footer section's Keep Together property to No to display the subform on the first page. The Keep Together property is one of the subjects of the "Controlling Page Breaks and Printing Page Headers and Footers" section later in the chapter.

tip

You can use calculated values to link main reports and subreports. Calculated values often are based on time: months, quarters, or years. To link main reports and subreports by calculated values, you must create queries for both the main report and subreport that include the calculated value in a field, such as Month or Year. You create the calculated field in each query by using the corresponding Access date function, Month or Year. To group by quarters, select Interval for the Group On property and set the value of the Group Interval property to 3. You can't use Qtr as the Group On property because the calculated value lacks the Date/Time field data type.

Inventory by Category with 2000 Sales New

75 Rhönbräu Klosterbier	Plutzer Lebensmittelgroßmärkte	125	5.17	646.16
34 Sasquatch Ale	Bigfoot Breweries	111	9.34	1,036.52
35 Steeleye Stout	Bigfoot Breweries	20	12.01	240.12
Category ID: Beverages	% Units: 16.85% % Value: 15.89% Total:	539		$8,264.30

Category	Jan	Feb	Mar	Apr	May	Jun
Beverages	$21,904.16	$2,845.84	$10,636.88	$7,074.35	$15,422.25	$3,485.42
Year Total	Jul	Aug	Sep	Oct	Nov	Dec
$103,924.30	$7,889.22	$5,836.92	$5,726.70	$8,374.90	$3,851.00	$10,876.65

Category	Jan	Feb	Mar	Apr	May	Jun
Condiments	$5,252.07	$6,128.86	$1,645.13	$5,544.40	$5,453.02	$1,855.27
Year Total	Jul	Aug	Sep	Oct	Nov	Dec
$55,368.59	$5,519.83	$4,220.02	$3,575.18	$6,565.91	$3,784.67	$5,824.20

Category	Jan	Feb	Mar	Apr	May	Jun
Confections	$9,128.11	$6,978.87	$3,209.92	$11,538.61	$7,689.82	$2,174.88
Year Total	Jul	Aug	Sep	Oct	Nov	Dec
$82,657.75	$6,462.60	$7,105.63	$6,708.59	$7,800.70	$5,081.85	$8,778.15

Category	Jan	Feb	Mar	Apr	May	Jun
Dairy Products	$9,066.40	$5,584.84	$9,728.90	$5,775.60	$10,435.57	$8,455.80
Year Total	Jul	Aug	Sep	Oct	Nov	Dec
$115,387.64	$12,387.35	$6,826.55	$11,420.30	$12,869.00	$12,992.47	$9,844.85

Category	Jan	Feb	Mar	Apr	May	Jun
Grains/Cereals	$4,547.80	$4,693.70	$3,167.60	$6,544.40	$2,267.25	$6,345.85
Year Total	Jul	Aug	Sep	Oct	Nov	Dec
$56,871.82	$4,457.80	$5,415.25	$5,371.47	$3,031.00	$5,787.35	$5,242.35

Category	Jan	Feb	Mar	Apr	May	Jun

Figure 17.19
Removing the link between the master and child fields causes each instance of the CategoryID Footer section to display all rows of the subreport.

You can add multiple subreports to an unbound report if all the subreports fit on one page of the report or across the page. In the latter case, you can use the landscape printing orientation to increase the available page width.

Customizing De Novo Reports

Most of the preceding examples in this chapter are based on a standard report structure and template you chose when creating the Inventory by Category report in Chapter 16. When you start a report from scratch, you must add sections required by your reports, set up printing parameters, and, if the number of records in the data source is large, consider limiting the number of detail rows to supply only the most significant information.

Adding and Deleting Sections of Your Report

When you create a report from a blank template or modify a report created by the Report Wizard, add new sections to the report by using the following guidelines:

- To add report headers and footers as a pair, right-click the report and choose Report Header/ Footer.

- To add page headers and footers as a pair, right-click the report and choose Page Header/Footer.

- To add a group header or footer to a report with a Group By value specified, click the Group & Sort button on the toolbar and set the Group Header or Group Footer property value, or both, to Yes.

Figure 17.20 shows a blank report in Design view, with the headers and footers for each section that you can include in a report. (Although Figure 17.20 shows only one group, you can add up to 10 group levels to your report.)

If you group the data in more than one level (group, subgroup, sub-subgroup), you can add a group header and footer for each level of grouping. This action adds to your report another pair of sections for each subgroup level.

You delete sections from reports by using methods similar to those that you use to create the sections. To delete unwanted sections, use the following guidelines:

> **tip**
>
> Page and report headers and footers that incorporate thin lines at the upper border of the header or footer can be difficult to delete individually. To make these lines visible, click Ctrl+A to add sizing anchors to the lines. Hold down the Shift key and click the controls you want to save to deselect these controls. Then press the Delete key to delete the remaining selected lines.

- To delete the Detail section or an individual Report Header, Report Footer, Page Header, or Page Footer section, delete all controls from the section, and then drag the divider bar up so that the section has no depth. To delete a Report Footer section, drag the report's bottom margin to the Report Footer border. These actions do not actually delete the sections, but sections with no depth do not print or affect the report's layout.

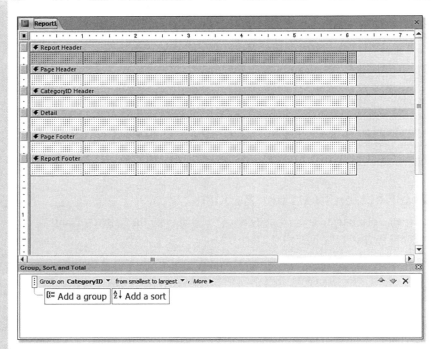

Figure 17.20
A report with a single Group By property value has a total of seven sections.

- To delete Report Header and Footer sections as a pair, right-click the report and choose Report Header/Footer. If the Report Header or Footer section includes a control, a message box warns that you will lose the controls in the deleted sections.

- To delete Page Header and Footer sections as a pair, right-click the report and choose Page Header/Footer. A warning message box appears if either section contains controls.

- To delete a Group Header or Footer section, click the Group & Sort button, click More, and change the properties to Without Header, Without Footer, or both.

Controlling Page Breaks and Printing Page Headers and Footers

The Force New Page and Keep Together properties of the report's Group Header, Detail, and Group Footer sections control manual page breaks. To set these properties, double-click the group's section header to display the section's Property Sheet. Force New Page causes an unconditional page break immediately before printing the section. If you set the Keep Together property to Yes and insufficient room is available on the current page to print the entire section, a page break occurs and the section prints on the next page.

To control whether Page Headers or Footers print on the first, last, or all pages of a report, press Ctrl+R or click the Select Report button, and then click the Properties button. You then select the Page Headers and Page Footers option in the Format page of the Property Sheet (see Figure 17.21).

Figure 17.21
Specify when page headers or page footers appear in the report in the Format page of the Report Property Sheet.

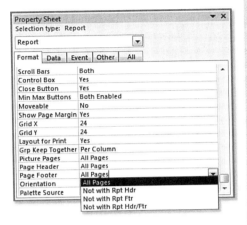

Adding Other Controls to Reports

Access places no limit on the native controls you can add to reports. So far, the controls that you've modified or added have been limited to labels, text boxes, lines, and the combo boxes that Access places automatically for fields configured as lookup fields. These four kinds of controls are likely to comprise more than 90% of the controls used in the reports you create. Controls that require user interaction, such as lists and combo boxes, can be used in a nonprinting section of the report, but practical use of these controls in reports is limited. The following list describes other controls that you might want to add to reports:

- *Bound object frames*—Print the contents of the OLE Object field data type, including bound charts you design in the next chapter. An OLE object can be a still or animated graphic, a video clip, CD audio track, or even MIDI music. Reports are designed only for printing, so animated graphics, video, and sound are inappropriate for reports.

- *Unbound object frames*—Display OLE objects created by OLE server applications, such as the Graph Wizard, Windows Paint, Microsoft Word, or Excel. Usually, you place unbound objects in the report's Form Header or Form Footer section, but you can add a logo to the top of each page by placing the image object in the Page Header section. A graph or chart created by the Chart Wizard is a special kind of unbound OLE object; you can't create a bound chart with the wizard.

> **note**
>
>
> **2007 NEW** Access 2007 added support for PDF and XPS files and removed Excel 5–7 and 97–2002 formats.
>
> **2010 NEW** Access 2010 returns support for Excel 97–2003 formats.

- *ActiveX controls*—Similar to objects within unbound object frames. You can add PivotTables and PivotCharts to reports, but you must establish the design parameters for the PivotTable or PivotChart before printing.

- *Lines and rectangles (also called shapes)*—Add graphic design elements to reports. Lines of varying widths can separate the sections of the report or emphasize a particular section.

- *Check boxes and option buttons*—Can be used to indicate the values of Yes/No fields or used within group frames to indicate multiple-choice selections. Group frames, option buttons, and check boxes used in reports indicate only the value of data cells and do not change the values. Reports seldom use option or toggle buttons.

Adding graphs in bound and unbound object frames and placing PivotTables and PivotCharts in reports are subjects covered in Chapter 18, "Adding Graphs, PivotCharts, and PivotTables."

Reducing the Length of Reports

A report's properties or controls don't limit the number of rows of detail data that a report presents. One way of minimizing detail data is to write a TOP *N* or TOP *N* PERCENT query using Access or Transact-SQL. Chapter 27, "Moving from Access Queries to Transact-SQL," has examples of the use of SELECT TOP *N* [PERCENT] statements. All rows of a table or query appear somewhere in the report's Detail section, if the report includes a Detail section with at least one control. To include only a selected range of dates in a report, for example, you must base the report on a query with the criteria necessary to select the Detail records or apply a filter to the report. If the user is to select the range of records to include in the report, use a parameter query as the report's data source.

Mailing Reports as Attachments

 Outlook or Outlook Express lets you send a report as an email attachment in several common formats: Excel 97 – Excel 2003 Workbook (.xls), HTMl (.html), Adobe Portable Document (.pdf), Rich Text (.rtf), Snapshot (.snp), Text (.txt), and XML Paper Specification (.xps).

Sending a Report with an Outlook Message

To send a report from Outlook as a PDF attachment to an email message, follow these steps:

1. Make sure that your email client (Outlook or Outlook Express) and current profile is operational. You must have a functioning email system to send a report.

2. In the Navigation Pane, select a report. You don't need to open the report to send it.

> **note**
>
> Microsoft released Report Snapshots (.snp) as an add-in for Access 97; the Report Snapshot feature is built in to later Access versions but is deprecated in Access 2010. The advantage of a Report Snapshot is that recipients don't need Access to view the reports. However, if recipients don't have the Snapshot viewer (Snapview.exe and Snapview.hlp) installed, they must obtain it from the Microsoft website: http://support.microsoft.com/support/kb/articles/q175/2/74.asp
>
> For widest usability, choose PDF format.

3. 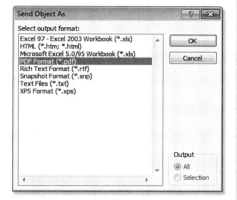 Click the E-mail icon in the External Data Ribbon's Export group button to open the Send Object As dialog.

4. Select PDF from the Select Output Format list (see Figure 17.22). Click OK to close the Send dialog. (You might be prompted to identify your email system at this point). Access creates the attachment file and opens your email application. The attachment icon appears in the body of the message.

Figure 17.22
Select the format you want in the Send Object As dialog, and click OK to generate the file and open your email application with the file as an attachment.

5. Complete the message and send it to the recipient. To test the attachment, send the message to yourself.

ADDING GRAPHS, PIVOTCHARTS, AND PIVOTTABLES

One of the primary factors leading to Microsoft Access's early success in the desktop PC database market was quick and easy *data visualization*— the capability to add to forms and reports attractive graphs and charts based on numeric data contained in tables or generated by queries. Data visualization is an element of *infographics*, which offer thought-provoking and insightful visual representations of information, data, or knowledge. Data visualization is vital when you must bring important information to the attention of busy executives who need to understand emerging trends or abrupt changes to manage effectively. Graphs and charts are the foundation of user interfaces for PC-based business information (BI) applications.

The chapter begins with sections devoted to creating bound and unbound graphs and charts with the traditional Chart control and Chart Wizard. Sections later in the chapter describe how to add bound and unbound PivotChart and PivotTable controls to Access- and SQL Server–based forms and reports.

Generating Graphs and Charts with Microsoft Graph

Microsoft Graph 14—called *MSGraph* in this book—is a 32-bit, OLE 2.0 miniserver application (Graph.exe), which originated as the charting component of Microsoft Excel 5.0. An OLE miniserver is an application that you can run only from within an OLE container application, such as Access 2010. Microsoft encourages use of the PivotChart control for new Access applications, but there's no "PivotChart Wizard" to lead you through the steps to design a PivotChart. The AutoForm: PivotChart option generates a data-bound form with a PivotChart that you must configure manually, as described in Chapter 12, "Working with PivotTable and PivotChart Views," and in more detail in the "Working with PivotChart Forms," section near the end of this chapter. The sections that follow describe how to use Access's Chart Wizard to add graphs and charts to conventional Access 2010 forms and reports. Access Data Projects (ADP) don't support the Chart Wizard, which generates an Access crosstab query to use as its final data source. As mentioned in Chapter 11, "Creating Multitable and Crosstab Queries," SQL Server doesn't support the Access SQL TRANSFORM and PIVOT keywords for crosstab queries. (PIVOT operator of SQL Server 2005 and later uses a different syntax to generate crosstabs.)

Creating the Query Data Source for the Graph

Most graphs required by management are the time-series type. Time-series graphs typically track the history of financial performance data, such as orders received, product sales, gross margin, and the like. Time-series graphs usually display date intervals (months, quarters, or years) on the horizontal x-axis—often called the *abscissa*—and numeric values on the vertical y-axis—also called the *ordinate*.

Choosing Data Sources for Summary Queries

note

The Developer, Standard, Enterprise, and Datacenter editions of Microsoft SQL Server 2008 [R2] include SQL Server Analysis Services (SSAS), formerly called *OLAP services*. OLAP is an acronym for online analytical processing, which manipulates multidimensional data from production databases. OLAP can operate directly on OLTP databases, but it's more common to roll up online data into OLAP data structures, often called *cubes*, and then perform analysis on the cubes. SSAS is one of Microsoft's primary BI applications and is responsible for much of SQL Server's recent success in the enterprise-level database market.

These editions incorporate Business Intelligence Management Studio (BIDS). BIDS, an acronym for an earlier product name (Business Intelligence Development Studio), is a Visual Studio 2010 add-in (shell) for creating OLAP roll-ups (cubes) from OLTP and historical databases.

In smaller firms, the numerical data for the y-axis comes from tables that store entries from the original documents (such as sales orders and invoices), which underlie the summary information. Queries sum the numerical data for each interval specified for the x-axis.

Detail data for individual orders or invoices, such as that found in the sample Order Details table, often is called a *line-item source*. Because a multibillion-dollar firm can accumulate millions of line-item records in a single year, larger firms usually store summaries of the line-item source data in tables; this technique improves the performance of queries. Summary data often is referred to as *rolled-up data* (or simply as *rollups*). Rollups of data on mainframe computers often are stored in client/server databases running under Windows Server 2003+ or various UNIX flavors to create data warehouses or data marts.

Although rolling up data from relational tables violates two of the guiding principles of relational theory—don't duplicate data in tables and don't store derived data in tables—databases consisting solely of rolled-up data are very common. As you move into the client/server realm with ADP and SQL Server, you're likely to encounter many rollup tables derived from production online transaction processing (OLTP) databases.

Designing a Query Based on OLTP Tables

Northwind Traders is a relatively small firm that receives very few orders, so it isn't necessary to roll up line-item data to obtain acceptable query performance on a reasonably fast PC. The Chart Wizard handles time-series grouping for you, so you don't need to base your chart on a crosstab query.

To create from the Northwind sample database a summary query designed specifically for use with the Chart Wizard, follow these steps:

1. Open the \Access2010\Chaptr18\Charts18.accdb database, click the Create tab and Query Design button to open a new query in Design view, and add the Categories, Products, Order Details, and Orders tables to the query.

2. Drag the CategoryName field of the Categories table to the first column.

3. Type the expression in the second column's Field row:

```
Amount: CCur([Order Details].[UnitPrice]*[Order Details].[Quantity]*

(1 -[Order Details].[Discount]))
```

4. Drag the ShippedDate field of the Orders table to the third column. Add an ascending sort on this column.

5. Add the criterion **Between #1/1/2006# And #12/31/2006#** to the ShippedDate column to include only orders shipped in 2006. This example uses the year 2006 instead of 2007 because data is available for all 12 months of 2006.

6. Save your query with the name **qry2006SalesChartNew** (see Figure 18.1).

7. Click the Run button to test your query (see Figure 18.2), and then close it.

The design of the qry2006SalesChart[New] query is a typical sample data source for time-series graphs and charts you generate with MSGraph as well as PivotCharts.

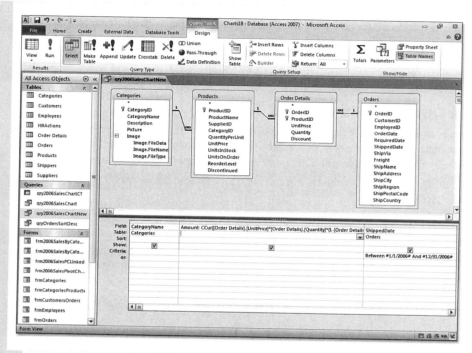

Figure 18.1
This query calculates the net value of all Northwind orders shipped in 2006 classified by product category and shipped date.

Category Name	Amount	Shipped Date
Seafood	$335.34	1/16/2006
Meat/Poultry	$471.60	1/16/2006
Dairy Products	$146.88	1/16/2006
Beverages	$360.00	1/16/2006
Dairy Products	$1,440.00	1/1/2006
Beverages	$285.00	1/3/2006
Produce	$585.90	1/3/2006
Confections	$58.80	1/3/2006
Confections	$1,307.25	1/3/2006
Dairy Products	$320.00	1/3/2006
Seafood	$48.00	1/3/2006
Confections	$394.00	1/3/2006
Seafood	$241.92	1/3/2006
Meat/Poultry	$1,650.60	1/3/2006
Dairy Products	$230.40	1/3/2006
Grains/Cereals	$288.00	1/6/2006
Dairy Products	$1,032.00	1/6/2006
Dairy Products	$583.80	1/6/2006
Confections	$68.00	1/2/2006
Produce	$648.72	1/2/2006
Beverages	$432.00	1/9/2006
Meat/Poultry	$2,073.60	1/9/2006
Confections	$600.00	1/8/2006
Dairy Products	$516.00	1/8/2006
Beverages	$504.00	1/8/2006
Condiments	$145.60	1/8/2006
Meat/Poultry	$2,079.00	1/16/2006

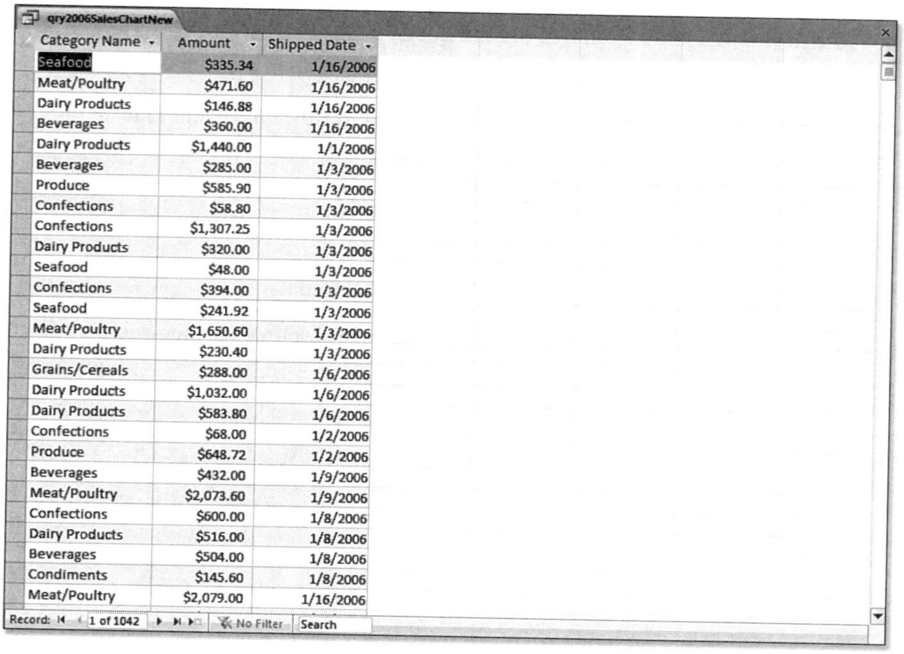

Figure 18.2
The query returns a row for each date on which an order was shipped and provides the total amount of the sale for the product categories.

Using the Chart Wizard to Create an Unlinked Graph

It's possible to create a graph or chart by choosing Insert, Object and selecting Microsoft Graph Chart in the Object Type list, but the Chart Wizard makes this process much simpler. You can use the Chart Wizard to create two different classes of graphs and charts:

- *Unlinked* (also called nonlinked) line graphs display a line for each row of the query. You can also create unlinked stacked column charts and multiple-area charts.

- *Linked* graphs or charts are bound to the current record of the form in which they are contained and display only a single set of values from one row of the table or query at a time.

This section shows you how to create an unlinked line graph based on a query. The "Changing the Graph to a Chart" section describes how to use MSGraph to display alternative presentations of your data in the form of bar and area charts. In the later section "Creating a Linked Graph from an Access Crosstab Query," you generate a graph that's linked to a specific record of a query resultset.

 note

The CCur VBA function is required to change the field data type to Currency when applying a discount calculation.

 tip

With the cursor in the Field row of the second column, press Shift+F2 to open the Zoom window to make entering the preceding expression easier.

To create an unlinked graph that displays the data from the qry2006SalesChart query, follow these steps:

1. Click the Create tab and the Form Design button to create an empty Form1 and display the Form Design Tools, Design ribbon.

2. Click the Controls group's Chart button, draw a frame about 7.5 inches wide and 5.25 inches deep on the form, and release the mouse to open the Chart Wizard's first dialog.

3. Select the Queries option and then select qry2006SalesChart or qry2006SalesChartNew in the list box (see Figure 18.3). Click Next.

Figure 18.3
Select the Queries option and then select the query for the graph or chart in the list box.

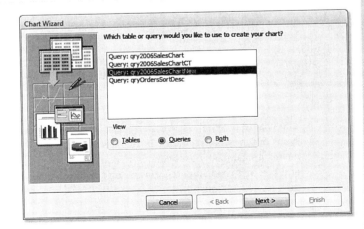

4. In the second wizard dialog, click the >> button to add all three fields to your graph (see Figure 18.4). Click Next to move to the third dialog.

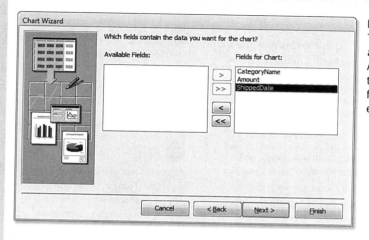

Figure 18.4
Time-series charts require at least date and value columns (ShippedDate and Amount, respectively). Creating a multiple-line chart requires a classification field (CategoryID) to provide the data for each line.

5. Click the Line Chart button, shown selected in Figure 18.5. Click Next.

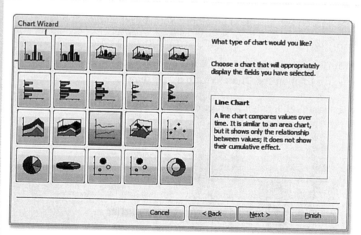

Figure 18.5
A line graph is the best initial choice for data presentation, because lines make it easy to determine whether the data meets reasonableness tests.

6. The wizard designs a crosstab query based on the data types of the query resultset. In this case, the Chart Wizard makes a mistake by assuming you want months in the legend box and product categories along the graph's horizontal x-axis (see Figure 18.6).

 note

This book uses the term *graph* when the presentation consists of lines, and *chart* for formats that use solid regions—such as bars, columns, or areas—to display the data.

Figure 18.6
Time-series graphs and charts almost always plot time on the horizontal axis, but the Chart Wizard's initial design puts classifications (CategoryName) on the x-axis.

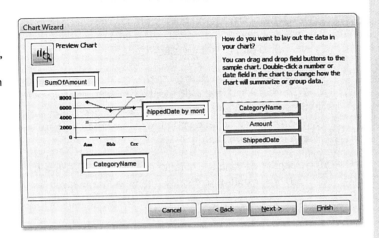

7. You want the categories in the legend and the months of 2006 across the x-axis. Drag the CategoryName button from the right side of the dialog to the drop box under the legend to the right of the chart, and drag the ShippedDate button to the drop box under the x-axis. The button title, partly obscured, is ShippedDate by Month (see Figure 18.7).

Figure 18.7
Drag the date column button from the right to the x-axis and the classification column button to the legend. The wizard's default time-series interval is month.

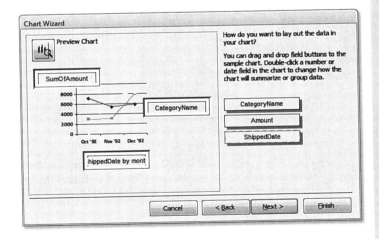

8. Click the Preview Chart button to display an expanded—but not full-size—view of your graph. The size relationship between objects in Chart Preview isn't representative of your final graph or chart. Click Close.

9. Click the Next button to go to the fourth and final Chart Wizard dialog. Type **2006 Monthly Sales by Category** in the text box to add a title to your graph. Accept the default Yes, Display a Legend option to display the Category legend (see Figure 18.8).

10. Accept the remaining default, and click Finish. Click the Form View button to display the initial graph layout (see Figure 18.9).

 tip

You can double-click the ShippedDate by Month button and select from a variety of GROUP BY date criteria, ranging from Year to Minute, and specify an optional range of dates. Marking the Use Date Between check box lets you add a WHERE *DateValue* BETWEEN *#StartDate#* AND *#EndDate#* clause to the crosstab query's SQL statement. You added this constraint to the source query, so it isn't required for this example.

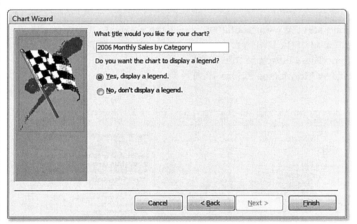

Figure 18.8
The last wizard dialog's default options are satisfactory for most graphs and charts. If your source query doesn't have a classification column, you don't need a legend.

11. Click the Design View button and increase the size of your graph to at least 7.5 inches wide by 5.25 inches high. Click the Properties button to display the Properties Sheet for the graph.

12. Scroll down the Properties sheet and verify that the Enabled property value of the unbound object frame (OLEUnbound0) is set to Yes and the Locked Property is set to No (the defaults). Set the Border Style property value to Transparent (see Figure 18.10).

 note

In the version of the graph illustrated by Figure 18.9, some month labels are missing and the legend crowds the graph without displaying the full category values. You fix these problems in the next section, "Modifying the Design Features of Your Graph."

Figure 18.9
The wizard makes a poor guess at the form, font, and the legend frame size needed to display the elements the wizard generates.

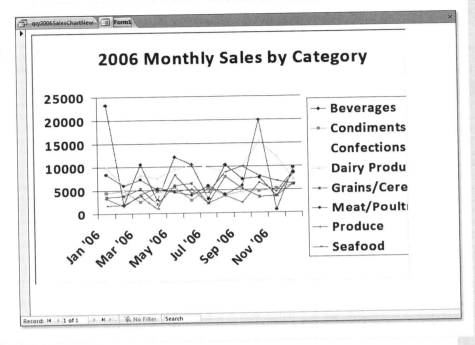

Figure 18.10
The All page of the unbound object frame that contains the chart lets you check the crosstab query's SQL statement and set the Enable and Locked properties. Graph. exe's version number is 14, but the Class version (8) hasn't changed since Office 97.

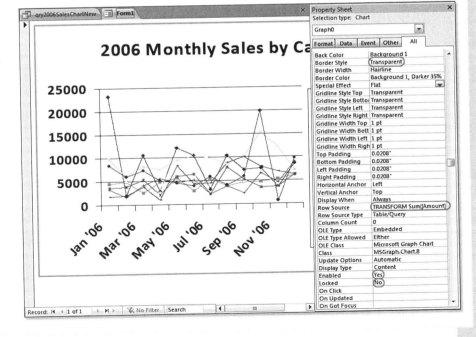

13. The chart is in an unbound object frame, so you don't need form adornments for record manipulation. Select Form in the Selection Type list, click the Format tab of the Properties window, and set the Scroll Bars property of the form to Neither, the Record Selectors property to No, and the Navigation Buttons property to No.

14. Use the sizing handles of the unbound object frame to create a 1/8-inch form border around the frame. Leaving a small form area around the object makes the activation process more evident.

15. Save your form with a descriptive name, such as **frm-2006SalesByCategoryChartNew**. Return to Form view in preparation for changing the size and type of your graph.

 note

The GROUP BY clause permits display of monthly data for multiple years, which isn't applicable to the sample query. The Format expression generates x-axis labels, such as Jan '06.

SQL Server's T-SQL doesn't support Access SQL's TRANSFORM...PIVOT statements, so you can't use the Chart Wizard with ADP. You can, however, write T-SQL statements to emulate a crosstab query, so it's possible to use the Insert Object approach to adding an MSGraph chart or graph to forms of ADP.

Access SQL

The wizard writes the following Access crosstab query to generate the data for the chart:

```
TRANSFORM Sum([Amount]) AS [SumOfAmount]
 SELECT (Format([ShippedDate],"MMM 'YY"))
 FROM [qry2006SalesChart]
 GROUP BY (Year([ShippedDate])*12 + Month([ShippedDate])-1),
(Format([ShippedDate],"MMM 'YY"))
PIVOT [CategoryName];
```

 For an example of the SQL Server equivalents of Access crosstab queries, **see** *"Emulating Access Crosstab Queries with T-SQL,"* **p. 1205.**

Modifying the Design Features of Your Graph

MSGraph (Graph.exe) is an OLE 2.0 miniserver, so you can activate MSGraph in place and modify the design of your graph. MSGraph also supports *Automation*, which lets you use VBA code to automate design changes. This section shows you how to use MSGraph to edit the design of the graph manually, as well as how to change the line graph to an area or column chart.

To activate your graph and change its design with MSGraph, follow these steps:

1. Display the form in Form view and then double-click the graph to activate MSGraph in place, which opens a Datasheet window that displays the values returned by the crosstab query (see Figure 18.11). A diagonally hashed border surrounds the graph; MSGraph's menus replace or supplement those of Access 2010. (The activation border is missing from the left and top of the object frame if you didn't create some additional space on the form around the object frame in step 12 of the preceding section.)

Figure 18.11 Activating the unbound object frame grafts MSGraph's menu commands to Access's menu bar and opens the Datasheet window.

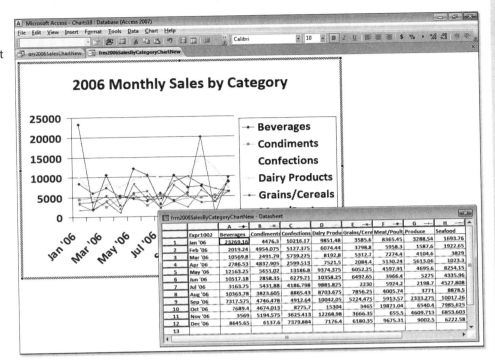

2. Change the type family and font size of your chart's labels and legend to better suit the size of the object. Double-click the graph title or right-click the title and select Format Chart Tile to open the Format Chart Title dialog. Click the Font tab, set the chart title's font size to 18 points, Bold (see Figure 18.12), clear the Auto Scale check box, and then click OK to close the dialog.

3. Double-click the legend to open the Format Legend dialog. Set the size of the legend font to 10-points, regular, and clear the Auto Scale check box.

4. The y-axis labels should be smaller and formatted as currency, so double-click one of the labels on the y-axis to display the Format Axis dialog. Set the font to 11-points, regular, and clear the Auto Scale check box.

5. Click the Number tab, select Currency in the Category list, and enter **0** in the Decimal Places text box (see Figure 18.13). Click OK to close the Format Axis dialog.

 tip

When you complete your design, set the value of the Enabled property for the form to No so that users of your application can't activate the graph and alter its design. It's also a good practice to set the values of the Allow Datasheet, PivotTable, and PivotChart View properties to No.

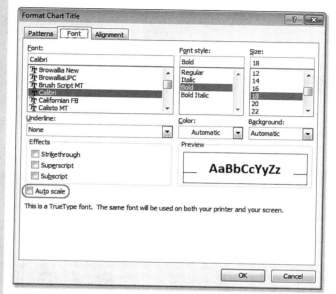

Figure 18.12
MSGraph has properties dialogs for most of its objects, including chart titles, legends, and axes. Reduce the font size of the Chart Title object to 18 points, and clear the Auto Scale check box to retain the font size regardless of the object frame's dimensions.

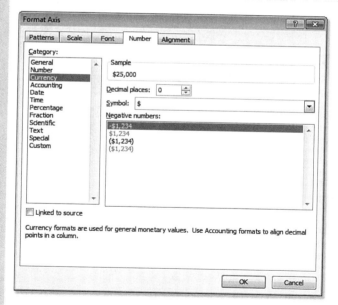

Figure 18.13
Reduce the font size of the y-axis labels to 11 points and apply currency formatting in the Format Axis dialog.

6. The default font size for axis labels at a graph size of 7.5x5.5 inches is 20 points, which causes MSGraph to label the x-axis diagonally. Double-click the x-axis and change its font size to 11 points, and also clear the Auto Scale check box. Click OK to close the dialog and apply the new format.

7. Resize the elements of the graph to take maximum advantage of the available area within the unbound object frame. Click the chart title and drag it to the top of the frame. Click an empty area in the graph to select the plot area, which adds a shaded rectangle around the region, and increase its size.

8. Click the form region outside the graph to deactivate MSGraph, and then save your changes. Your line graph now appears as shown in Figure 18.14.

Figure 18.14
The modified graph design corrects the poor choices the wizard made for the title, axis, and legend font sizes.

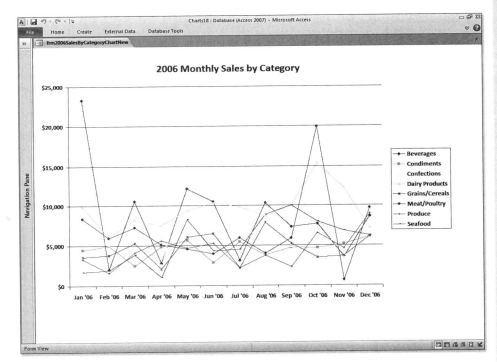

Depending on the use of the graph or chart, consider increasing its size to increase the accuracy of data interpretation for users. If you plan to print the chart, you can increase the width to about 8 inches without changing the default (Narrow) printing margins. You can save vertical space by deleting the chart title and changing the form's Caption property to that of the deleted title. The figures in the following sections reflect these design changes.

Changing the Graph to a Chart

You might want to change the line graph to some other type of chart (such as area or stacked column) for a specific purpose. Area charts, for example, are especially effective as a way to display the contribution of individual product categories to total sales. To change the line graph to another type of chart, follow these steps:

1. Double-click the graph to activate it and then choose Chart, Chart Type to open the Chart Type dialog with the Standard Types page active.

2. Select Area in the Chart Type list (see Figure 18.15).

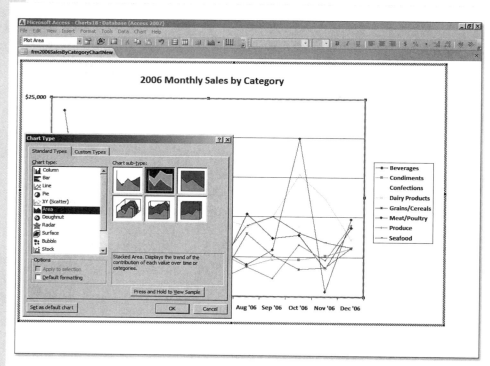

Figure 18.15
MSGraph's Chart Type dialog offers many more choices of chart and graph styles than the Chart Wizard.

3. Select the stacked area chart as the Chart Subtype setting (the middle chart in the first row—refer to Figure 18.15). Click OK to change your line graph into an area chart, as shown in Figure 18.16. The contribution of each category appears as an individually colored area, and the top line segment represents total sales.

 tip

You can preview your chart by clicking and holding down the left mouse button on the Press and Hold to View Sample button.

4. To convert the area chart into a stacked column chart, choose Chart, Chart Type to display the Standard Types page of the Chart Type dialog. Select Column in the Chart Type list, and then select as the chart subtype the stacked column chart shown (selected in Figure 18.17).

Figure 18.16
The stacked area chart shows the contribution of each category to total sales.

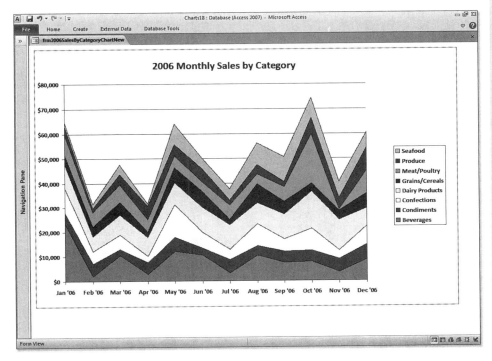

Figure 18.17
You can select a 3D stacked column chart, but conventional 2D column charts are easier to interpret.

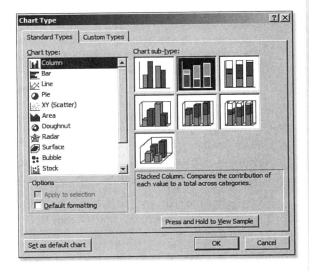

5. Click OK to close the Chart Type dialog. Your stacked column chart appears as shown in Figure 18.18.

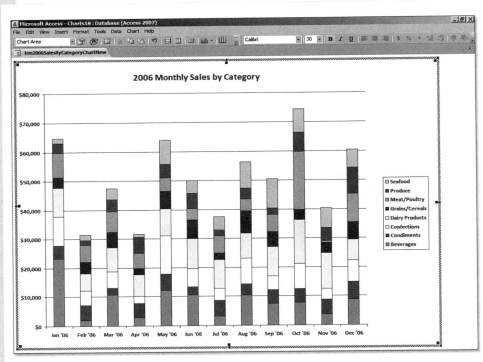

Figure 18.18
A stacked col-
umn chart is a
less-dramatic
alternative to
a stacked area
chart.

6. Another subtype of the area chart and stacked column chart is the percentage distribution chart. To create a distribution-of-sales graph, repeat steps 4 and 5 but select the 100% Stacked Column picture (the third thumbnail in the top row) with equal column heights as the Chart Subtype setting. Click OK to close the Chart Type dialog.

7. Because you previously set the format of the y-axis to eliminate the decimals, you need to change the format of the y-axis manually to Percentage. Double-click the y-axis to open the Format Axis dialog and click the Number page (refer to Figure 18.13). Select Percentage in the Category list, make sure that Decimal Places is set to 0, and then click OK to apply the format. Your chart appears as shown in Figure 18.19.

8. Change the chart type back to an area chart in preparation for copying it to a report's Header section in the next procedure. Change the y-axis format to Currency, click inside the form region outside the object frame to deactivate the graph, and then save your form.

Of the four types of charts demonstrated, most users find the area chart best for displaying time-series data for multiple values that have meaningful total values.

Figure 18.19
A 100% stacked
column shows
the distribution
of sales by cat-
egory.

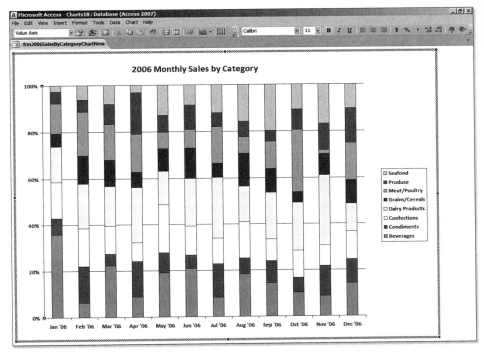

Printing Graphs or Charts in Reports

The process of adding an unbound MSGraph object to an Access report is identical to that for forms. Unless all your users have access to a color printer, you should select a line graph subtype that identifies data points with a different symbol for each category. For area and stacked column charts, a series of hatched patterns differentiate the product categories. The Custom Types page of the Chart Types dialog offers a selection of B&W chart types specifically designed for monochrome printers.

You can save a form created by the Chart Wizard to a report by choosing File, Save As, and selecting Report in the Save As dialog. It's almost as easy to create a new report and copy the form's unbound object frame to it, which also demonstrates how to add a graph to an existing report. Follow these steps:

1. Open the form with the graph or chart in Design view, select the unbound OLE object frame, and press Ctrl+C to copy the control to the Clipboard. For this example, copy frm2006SalesByCategory Chart[New]'s OLEUnbound0 object.

2. Click the Create tab and Blank Report button to open a new report in Layout view. Change to Report Design view.

3. Right-click the report and click the Report Header and Footer context menu item to add Report Header and Footer sections to the report. If you plan to add fields to the Detail section, you usually add the chart or graph to the report's Header or Footer section. Click the Page Header/Footer button to eliminate these default sections, close up the Detail and Report Footer sections of the report, and select the Report Header section.

4. Press Ctrl+V to paste the graph or chart to the selected Report Header section.

5. Adjust the height and width of the unbound object frame within the printing limits of the page. Optionally, move the object frame down, and add a label with a report title. Alternatively, you can add a chart title.

6. Double-click the object frame to activate the object, close the Datasheet window, and choose Chart, Chart Type to open the Chart Type dialog.

7. Click the Custom Types tab, and choose B&W Area to change the style to an area chart with hatching (see Figure 18.20).

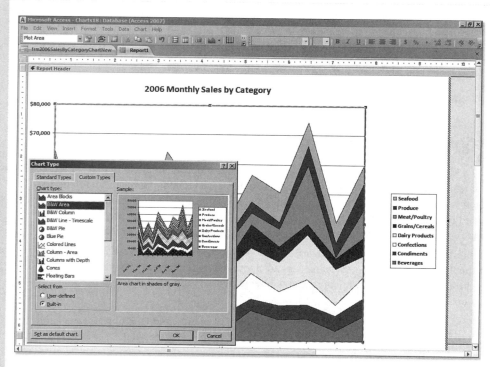

Figure 18.20
The B&W Area style is a better selection for printing (in most cases) than B&W Column, which includes a data table.

8. Click OK to apply the style. Click outside the graph to deselect it and display the monochrome chart, which has a gray background and unformatted y-axis labels, and change to Report view (see Figure 18.21).

Figure 18.21
Selecting a
different chart
style removes
much of the
formatting you
applied to the
copied chart.

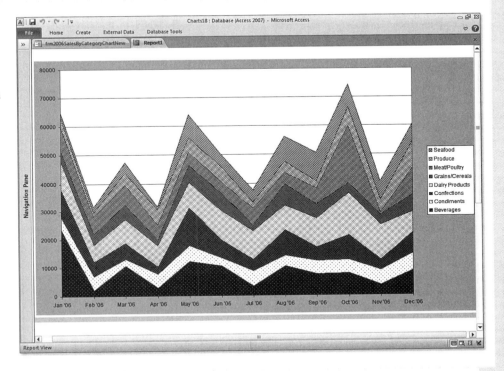

9. To remove the gray background, which consumes toner or ink but doesn't contribute to read-ability, change to Design view and double-click the object frame to activate it. Right-click the gray region, and choose Format Chart Area to open the dialog of the same name. On the Patterns page, select the None option in the Area frame to make the background transparent and then click OK.

10. Double-click the y-axis labels to open the Format Axis dialog, click the Number tab, select Currency, set Decimal Places to 0, and click OK.

11. Click the Report Header bar to deactivate the object; change to Design view, and open the Properties window for the object frame (OLEUnbound0 for this example).

12. Select the Report in the Selection Type list, and set the Caption property value to **2006 Monthly Sales by Category**.

13. Change to Report View to display your modified report design (see Figure 18.22).You can't acti-vate the chart object for editing in Report mode.

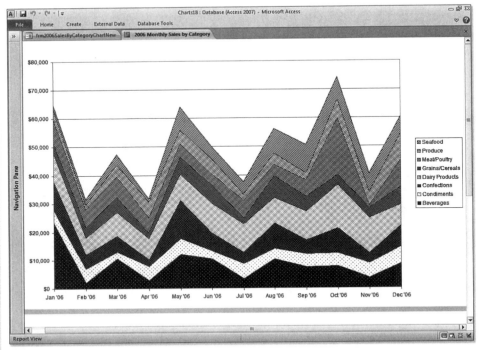

Figure 18.22
Monochrome reports use hatching and shading to differenti- ate areas by classification. Unfortunately, many laser printers don't distinguish dark regions, such as Confections and Beverages, in this example.

14. Save your report with a descriptive name, such as **rpt2006SalesByCategoryChartNew** for this example.

You can increase the printed width of the graph by returning to Design view and double-clicking the legend to open the Format Legend dialog. Click the Placement tab and select the Bottom option. Optionally, click the Format tab and select the None option in the Border frame. Figure 18.23 shows the report with the relocated legend.

Figure 18.23
Relocating the legend to the bottom of a report (or form) lets you increase the printed (or displayed) width of the chart.

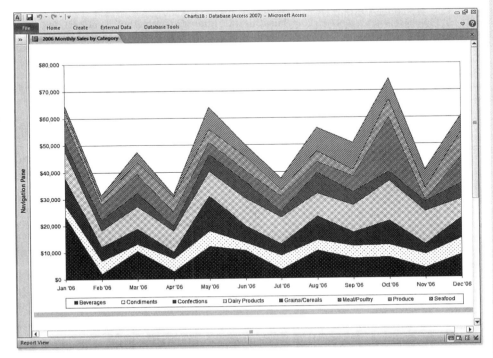

Creating a Linked Graph from an Access Crosstab Query

Access's Chart Wizard is quite parochial: It insists on creating a crosstab query for you. After you've created a chart with the Chart Wizard, however, you can change the graph's Row Source property value to specify a previously created crosstab query of your own design.

Linked graphs or charts display a succession of graphical representations of related data. Linked graphs are useful for delivering more detailed information than bar or area charts can impart. For example, it's difficult to interpret trends for sales of product categories in a stacked area chart. Linked graphs let you drill down into the data behind summary charts and add features to aid data interpretation—such as trendlines. Linked graphs are one of Access 2010's most powerful features.

For this linked graph example, you create the qry2006SalesChartCT crosstab query and use the query as the Row Source setting of the unbound object frame to complete the linked graph example in the following section. The linked graph example doesn't work with the crosstab query created by the Chart Wizard in the preceding steps, because its query resultset has months in rows and categories in columns. The linked graph needs categories in rows and months in columns, a process called *pivoting* the resultset.

Designing the Crosstab Query for the Graph

To create the pivoted qry2006SalesChartCT query from qry2006SalesChart, follow these steps:

1. Create a new query in Design view, add the qry2006SalesChart[New] query, and click the Query Types group's Crosstab button.

2. Drag the CategoryName field to the first column of the query and select Row Heading in the Crosstab row. Accept the default Group By value in the Total cell.

3. Alias the CategoryName field by typing **Categories:** at the beginning of the Field text box.

4. Type the expression **Month:Format([ShippedDate], "mmm")** into the second Fields cell to use three-letter month abbreviations. Then, select Column Heading in the Crosstab cell. Accept the default Group By value in the Total cell.

5. Drag the Amount field to the third column, set the Total cell to Sum, and set the Crosstab cell to Value (see Figure 18.24).

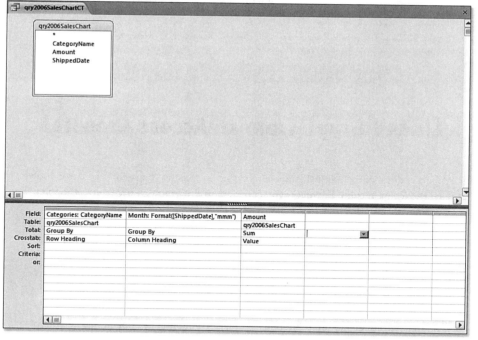

Figure 18.24
An Access crosstab query for a linked graph requires specifying Row Heading, Column Heading, and Value in the Crosstab row of the query design grid.

6. Click the Property Sheet button to open the query's property sheet. In the Column Headings text box, type the 12 month abbreviations (**Jan,...Dec**), separated by commas to arrange the columns in date, not alphabetic, sequence. Access adds the quotes around the month abbreviations for you (see Figure 18.25).

Figure 18.25
In the query's property sheet, add a comma-separated list of column headings that correspond to your crosstab query's Format expression for the Column Heading values.

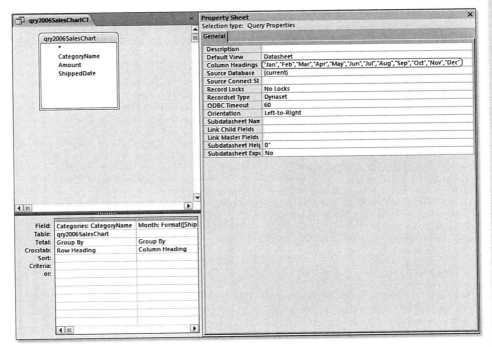

7. Save your query as **qry2006SalesChartCT**.

8. Click the Run button to check your query resultset (see Figure 18.26).

Access SQL

Using this technique, you create the link between the current record of the form and the row of the query that serves as the Row Source property of the graph (through the aliased Categories column of the query):

```
TRANSFORM Sum(qry2006SalesChart.Amount) AS
SumOfAmount
SELECT qry2006SalesChart.CategoryName AS Categories
FROM qry2006SalesChart
GROUP BY qry2006SalesChart.CategoryName
PIVOT Format([ShippedDate],"mmm")
  In ("Jan","Feb","Mar","Apr","May","Jun",
  "Jul","Aug","Sep","Oct","Nov","Dec");
```

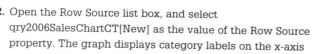

Assigning the Crosstab Query as the Graph's Row Source

The next stage in the process is to take advantage of your existing MSGraph design by changing its data source from the Chart Wizard's Access SQL statement to the new crosstab query. Do the following:

> **note**
>
> The primary difference between the two queries is the GROUP BY clause, which groups the data by the CategoryName column, rather than by a date expression. In this case, the In predicate is required to return the monthly data in date (instead of alphabetic) order.

1. Open frm2006SalesByCategoryChart[New] in Design view, select the chart's object frame (OLEUnbound0), and open its Property Sheet.

2. Open the Row Source list box, and select qry2006SalesChartCT[New] as the value of the Row Source property. The graph displays category labels on the x-axis and month labels in the legend.

3. Return to Form view, double-click to activate the graph, change the Chart Subtype to Line with Markers Displayed at Each Data Value, and click the toolbar's By Row button or choose Data, Series in Rows from the Chart menu. Verify that your line graph appears the same as the graph that the Chart Wizard created in the earlier section "Modifying the Design Features of Your Graph," with the exception that years don't appear in the X-axis labels (refer to Figure 18.14).

note

The crosstab query for the linked chart differs from that created by the Chart Wizard for an unlinked chart or graph. Following is the Access SQL statement for the linked chart's data source:

```
TRANSFORM Sum(qry2006SalesChart.Amount) AS SumOfAmount
SELECT qry2006SalesChart.CategoryName AS Categories
FROM qry2006SalesChart
GROUP BY qry2006SalesChart.CategoryName
PIVOT Format([ShippedDate],"mmm")
 In ("Jan","Feb","Mar","Apr","May","Jun",
 "Jul","Aug","Sep","Oct","Nov","Dec");
```

The primary difference between the two queries is the GROUP BY clause, which groups the data by the CategoryName col-umn, rather than by a date ex-pression. In this case, the In predicate is required to return the monthly data in date (in-stead of alphabetic) order.

 ### Reversing the X-Axis and Legend Labels

After the Row Source property of a chart is changed to the qry2006SalesChartCT crosstab query, the product categories appear in the chart as the x-axis labels, and the month abbrevia-tions appear in the legend. This happens because you didn't change to Series in Rows in step 3. Crosstab queries you design can have the legend values (representing a series of lines) as column headers or row headers. If your x-axis and legend labels are wrong, activate the chart, choose Data, and then choose either Series in Columns or Series in Rows to make the change.

Linking the Graph to a Single Record of a Table or Query

You create a linked graph or chart by setting the values of the MSGraph object's Link Child Fields and Link Master Fields properties. The link is similar to that between a form and subform. A linked graph displays the data series from the current row of the table or query that serves as the Record Source of the form. As you move the record pointer with the record navigation buttons, the graph is redrawn to reflect the data values in the selected row.

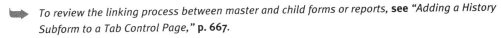 *To review the linking process between master and child forms or reports,* **see** *"Adding a History Subform to a Tab Control Page,"* **p. 667.**

To change the 2006frmSalesByCategoryChart form to accommodate a linked graph, follow these steps:

1. Change to Form Design view, select Form in the Selection Type list, and then click the Property Sheet button to open the Property Sheet for the form.

2. Click the Data tab, open the Record Source list box, and select qry2006SalesChartCT as the value of the Record Source property of the form, which binds the form to the crosstab query.

3. Your form needs record-navigation buttons for a linked graph or chart, so click the Format tab and set the value of the Navigation Buttons property to Yes.

4. Select the unbound object frame (OLEUnbound0) and then click the Data tab. Verify that qry-2006SalesChartCT is the Row Source for the chart. Type **Categories** as the value of the Link Child Fields and Link Master Fields properties (see Figure 18.27). Disregard any Can't Build a Link Between Unbound Forms error messages that might appear after typing the Link Child Fields value.

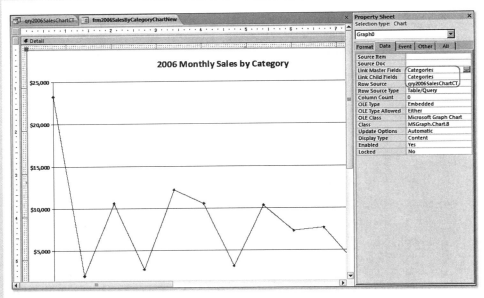

Figure 18.27
Type the column name of the field on which to link the graph and the form in the Link Master Fields and Link Child Fields text boxes. You can't use the Builder button to create the link; you receive an error message if you try.

5. To test your linked graph, click the Form View button. If (in the earlier "Changing the Graph to a Chart" section) you saved the line graph version of the form, your graph initially appears as shown in Figure 18.28.

6. The single line appears a bit anemic for a graph of this size, so double-click the graph to activate it in place. Right-click the line with all data points selected, and choose Format Data Series to display the Format Data Series dialog. Click the Patterns tab, select the Custom option, open the Weight drop-down list, and choose the thickest line it offers. Optionally, change the color from Automatic to a color from the pick list.

7. To change the data-point marker, select the Custom option, open the Style drop-down list, and select the square shape. Use the drop-down lists to set the Foreground and Background colors of the marker to Automatic to add solid markers of the line color. Optionally, increase the size of the markers by a couple of points (see Figure 18.29). Click OK to close the dialog and implement your design changes.

8. Double-click the legend box to open the Format Legend dialog. On the Patterns page, click the None option in the Border frame to remove the border from the legend. Click the Font tab, turn the Bold attribute on, and change the font size to 18 points. Click OK to close the dialog and apply your modification to the legend.

Figure 18.28
The linked graph displays a single line and legend entry for each of the eight product categories.

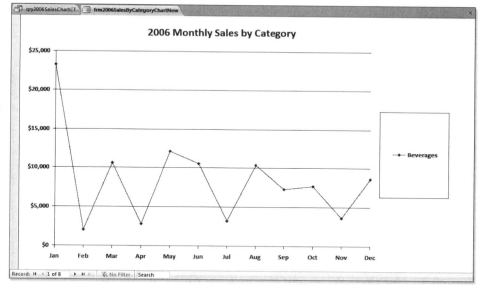

Figure 18.29
The Format Data Series dialog lets you change the thickness and color of the graph's line, add and format data markers, and change the line segment to a continuous curve between data points (called *smoothing*, which is shown later in Figure 8.31).

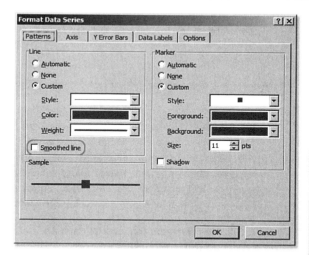

9. To use your enhanced legend as a title for the chart, delete the existing title, if present, and click and drag the legend to a location above the graph. Click the plot area to display the chart's sizing handles; drag the middle sizing handle to the right to increase the width of the plot area (see Figure 18.30).

10. Click the record navigation buttons to display a graph of the sales for each of the eight categories. As you change categories, notice that the y-axis scale changes. The maximum range for the Beverages category is $0 to $25,000, whereas that for Condiments is $0 to $7,000.

11. To add a trendline to your graph, activate the graph and choose Chart, Add Trendline to open the Add Trendline dialog. Accept the default Linear trendline on the Type page, and click the Options tab. Select the Custom option, type a legend for the trendline, such as **2006 Sales Trend**, and click OK.

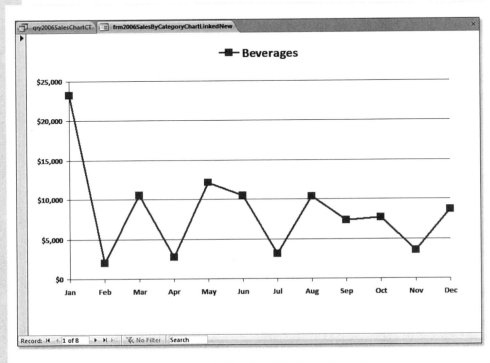

Figure 18.30
This graph is reformatted with increased line thickness, added data points, and a modified legend to act as the chart title.

12. To remove the sizing handles from the Form view of the deactivated object, change to Design view, select the object frame, and open the Property Sheet. Click the Data tab, and change the Enabled property value to No and Locked to Yes. (You can't change Locked to Yes in Form view.) Changing these two property values prevents users from activating the graph. With the Smoothed Line check box of the Data Series dialog marked, your modified graph appears in Form view as shown in Figure 18.31. Refer to Figure 18.29 for setting the Smoothed Line option.

13. Click the Office button, choose Save As, and then save your bound graph form with a new name, such as **frm2006SalesByCategoryChartLinkedNew**.

Figure 18.31
Adding a trendline to the graph aids in interpreting the data. Smoothing the data series line implies the existence of additional data points between those in the datasheet, such as the slower decline from May to June.

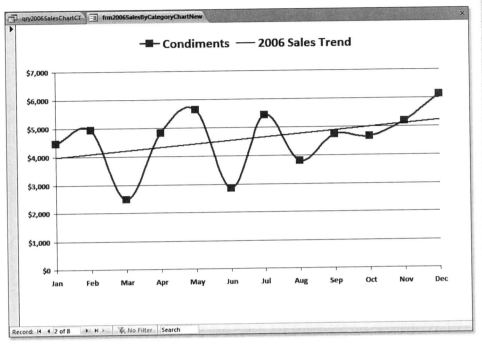

Working with PivotChart Forms

Microsoft promotes Office 2010 PivotCharts as a substitute for MSGraph OLE Objects for a good (marketing) reason: MSGraph requires a crosstab query (or equivalent) and, as mentioned earlier, SQL Server's T-SQL doesn't support crosstab queries directly. If you want to add graphs or charts to ADP, PivotCharts are the least-effort answer. The same is true if you anticipate upsizing your Access databases to SQL Server and upgrading conventional Access objects to ADP forms and reports.

The sections that follow describe how to use PivotCharts to emulate the unlinked and linked MSGraph objects you created in the preceding sections of this chapter. The sample PivotCharts use the qry2006SalesChart query, because the Access SQL and T-SQL versions of the query are identical. The PivotTable created from the query acts as the data source for the PivotChart by handling the data restructuring ordinarily accomplished by Access SQL PIVOT...TRANSFORM statements.

To review PivotChart design basics, **see** *"Formatting and Manipulating PivotCharts,"* **p. 528.**

Creating a PivotChart Form from a Query

PivotCharts don't have the formatting flexibility of MSGraph objects, but they let you duplicate most MSGraph chart types satisfactorily. To generate a stacked area PivotChart based on the qry-2006SalesChart query, do the following:

1. Select the qry2006SalesChart[New] query in the Navigation pane.

2. Click the Create tab, click the Forms group's More Forms button to open the gallery, and click the PivotChart button to open a PivotChart named qry2006SalesChart with the Field List super-imposed. (If the Field list isn't visible, click an empty area of the form.) Expand the Field List's ShippedDate by Month node to display period options (see Figure 18.32).

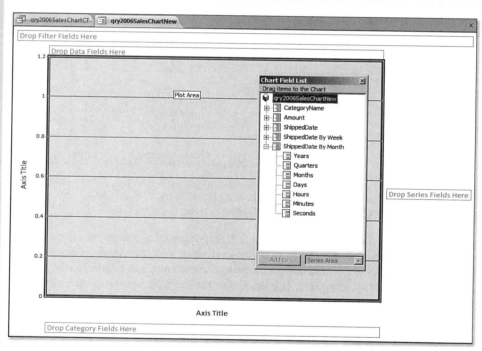

Figure 18.32
The quickest way to create a PivotChart form is to select a table or query and click the Create ribbon's PivotChart button.

3. Drag the Amount field from the Chart Field List to the Drop Data Fields Here zone and the CategoryName field to the Drop Series Fields Here zone. Each product category is a member of Series 1 of the PivotChart.

4. From the Field List's ShippedDate By Month node, drag the Months field to the Drop CategoryFields Here node. The default chart type is the conventional (not stacked) column version, so Months has one column for each of the eight product categories (see Figure 18.33).

note

The PivotChart detects the currency format of the Amount query column and applies standard currency formatting to the y-axis. Unlike with MSGraph, you can't remove the two digits after the decimal point without writing a considerable amount of VBA code.

Figure 18.33
Adding value,
category (clas-
sification), and
series fields
(columns) from
the qry2006-
SalesChart
query gen-
erates this
default multiple
column chart.

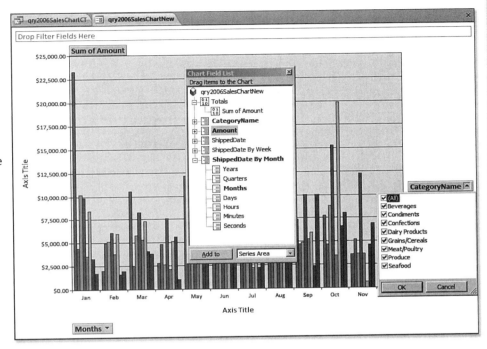

5. Click the PivotChart Tools, Design tab's Change Chart Type button to open the Type page of the Properties dialog. Select the Area chart type and click the Stacked Area subtype to emulate the MSGraph chart you created in the "Changing the Graph to a Chart" section early in the chapter (see Figure 18.34). (If the button is disabled, select the chart to enable it.)

6. Click the Property Sheet button to open the Properties dialog, click the Show/Hide tab, and clear all check boxes except Screen Tips and Commands and Options Dialog Box. Removing the field buttons prevents users from rearranging the chart.

7. With the Properties dialog open, click the y-axis line and then click the Format tab. Change the font size to 9 points, and apply the Bold attribute to the labels.

8. Repeat step 6 for the x-axis labels.

🔍 **note**

PivotCharts on forms don't have a fixed size in Form view. As you change the dimensions of the form, the PivotChart expands or contracts accordingly.

🔍 **note**

"Commands and Options" was the original name of the Properties dialog. Microsoft's developers overlooked changing the caption of the check box.

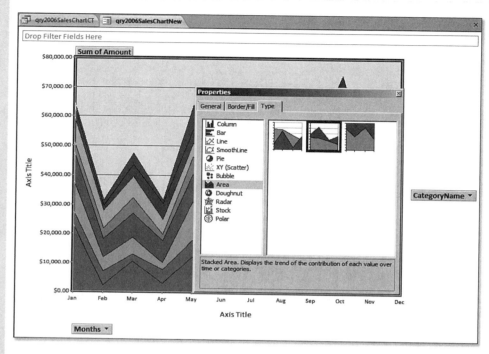

Figure 18.34
The PivotChart's Stacked Area chart type is almost identical to that of MSGraph's. Notice that the month abbreviations are centered under—instead of between—the x-axis value markers.

9. Select in the General page's list the Value Axis 1 Title, click the Format tab, and delete its Caption property value. Do the same for the Category Axis 1 Title. The form caption defines the axis titles adequately.

10. Optionally, select the legend and change the Position setting to Bottom. (If the legend isn't visible, click the Show/Hide group's Legend button.)

11. Change to Form Design view, click the Form Selector button, open the Form properties window, click the Format tab, and type **2006 Monthly Sales By Category** as the value of the Caption property. Your PivotChart in PivotChart view now appears as shown in Figure 18.35.

12. In Form Design view, open the form's Properties window again and set the Allow Form View, Allow Datasheet View, and Allow PivotTable View property values to No. Restricting the view of the form is important because it keeps users from being confused by extraneous views of non-meaningful data.

13. Save your form with a descriptive name, such as **sbf2006SalesPivotChart**, and close it. You apply the **sbf** prefix because you use the PivotChart form as a subform in the next section.

Figure 18.35
With the exception of the
two decimal
digits of the
y-axis labels,
this PivotChart
successfully
emulates the
MSGraph
stacked area
chart shown
earlier in Figure
18.16.

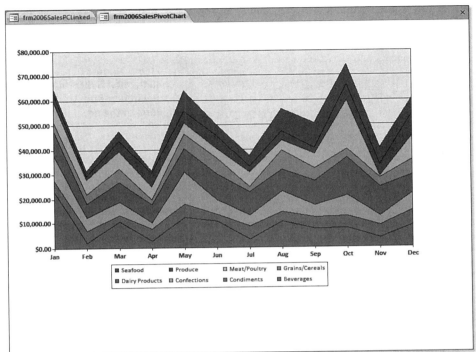

Using the PivotChart Form as a Subform

The PivotChart view of a form prevents you from altering the overall design of the form. For instance, you can't add a visible page header/footer or add extra space to the detail section in which to place a label for a chart title. To achieve form layout flexibility, use the PivotChart form as a subform by following these steps:

1. Click the Create tab; the Blank Form button to open a new empty form. Clicking the Add existing Fields button opens a Field list that displays a node for each table.

2. Change to Design view and expand the Detail section of the form to accommodate a chart or graph of reasonable size, approximately 7.5 inches wide by 4.5 inches deep for this example.

3. In the Form Design Tools, Design ribbon's Control group, make sure the Control Wizards button is selected.

4. Select the Subform/Subreport tool, and draw a subform container of moderate size. When you release the mouse, the SubForm Wizard opens.

5. In the first SubForm Wizard dialog, select the Use an Existing Form option, and select the PivotChart form to use as the subform. For this example, select the sbf2006SalesPivotChart or the form you created in the preceding section (see Figure 18.36). Click Next.

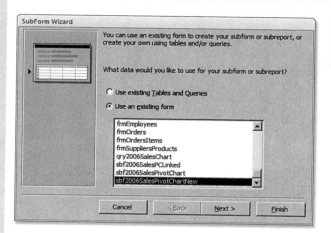

Figure 18.36

In the first SubForm Wizard dialog, select the PivotChart form you saved to serve as a subform of the new form you opened.

6. Accept the default name for the subform container and its label in the last wizard dialog, and click Finish to add the subform, which has a default size of about 8.5x1.5 inches. Reduce the width of the form to the original 7.5 inches. Disregard the appearance of the Form Header/Footer sections in Form Design view; PivotChart forms don't display these sections in Design or Form view.

7. Use the sizing handles to expand the subform to within about 3/8 inch from the top, and 1/8 inch or so from the left, right, and bottom edges of the form.

8. Change to Layout view to verify that the subform displays the PivotChart, and adjust the depth of the form to fit the available space (see Figure 18.37).

 note

If the subform opens in Form or Datasheet view, you forgot to disable all but PivotChart view in step 11 of the preceding section.

9. Return to Design view and open the form's property sheet. On the Format page, set the Caption property value to **2006 Monthly Sales By Category**, Allow Datasheet View to No, Allow PivotTable View to No, Allow PivotChart View to No, Scroll Bars to Neither, Record Selectors to No, and Navigation Buttons to No.

10. Add a **2006 Monthly Sales By Category PivotChart** Form label above the subform to serve as a chart title (see Figure 18.38).

Figure 18.37
Perform a quick
check of the
initial appear-
ance of your
PivotChart sub-
form to verify
that it opens
in PivotChart
view.

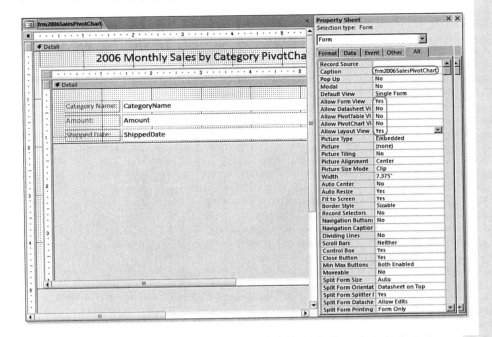

Figure 18.38
Here's the final
design of the
form/subform
combination
to display
the unlinked
PivotChart.

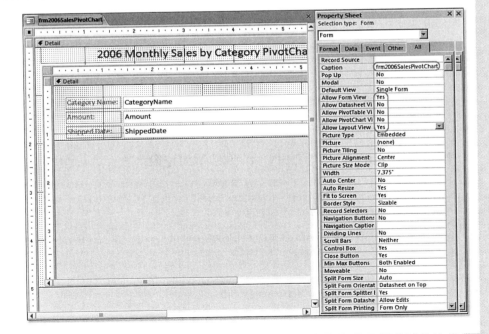

11. Select the subform, and set the Border Style property value to Transparent. Return to Form view, select an empty area of the form and click the Property Sheet button of the PivotChart Tools, Design ribbon's Tools group. Verify that Chart Workspace is selected on the General page, click the Border/Fill tab, open the Border group's Color picker, and click None. The form/subform combination appears as shown in Figure 18.39.

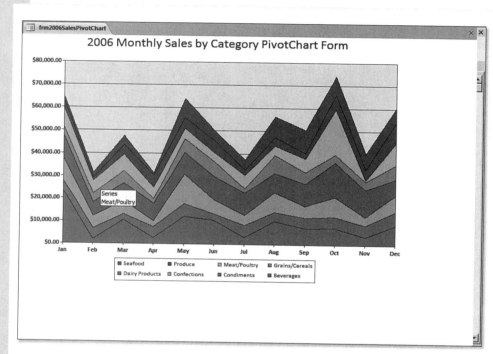

Figure 18.39
Adding the PivotChart form as a subform adds flexibility to the form layout and also enables conversion of the combination to a linked graph. Placing the mouse pointer on a data point shows a ScreenTip with the series name and value.

12. Save your form with the usual descriptive name (**frm2006SalesPivotChart** for this example) and close it.

Linking the PivotChart to the Main Form's Current Record

Creating a linked PivotChart isn't as simple as the method described in the earlier "Creating a Linked Graph from an Access Crosstab Query" section. The basic steps required to link a PivotChart form/subform combination are as follows:

1. Bind the form to a table or query that you can link to the query that provides the data source for the subform and its graph or chart.

2. Set the values of the Link Master Fields and Link Child Fields properties to the common fields of the main form and subform data sources.

3. Add Record Navigation buttons to the main form.

4. Modify the form and PivotChart design to take advantage of chart linking.

The following two sections describe how to modify copies of the form and PivotChart subform you created in the preceding two sections to link a graph to the Categories table.

Cloning a Linked PivotChart Form/Subform Pair

Take the following steps to create renamed copies of the form and subform, and link them:

1. Make a copy of the sbf2006SalesPivotChart[New] subform, and name it **sbf2006SalesPCLinkedNew**. (Select original subform in the Navigation pane and press Ctrl+C, Ctrl+V to quickly create the copy.)

2. Open the subform copy in Form view, click the Pivot Chart Tools, Design Change ribbon's Chart Type button, and select Line or Smoothline in the Chart Type Dialog's list. Click the first subtype, a standard line graph, and then close and save changes to the subform. Changing the chart to a graph verifies that you're using the correct subform when you make changes to the main form.

3. Make a copy of the frm2006SalesPivotChart as **frm-2006SalesPCLinkedNew**, and open the copy in Design view.

 tip

Use the design process described in this and the preceding section to create a report/subreport combination for printing. You can select a set of textures for the individual data series members of the PivotChart if your users need to print black-and-white reports.

You can print the form to color printers, but you might not be pleased with the initial aspect ratio of the chart. By default, the chart expands vertically to fill the entire printable area of the page. To retain the aspect ratio, set the Format page's Can Grow property value to No.

4. Open the Property Sheet for the form, click the Data tab, and set the Record Source property to the Categories table. The CategoryName field of the Categories table links to the CategoryName column of the subform's qry2006SalesChart data source.

5. Set the Allow Filters, Allow Edits, Allow Deletions, and Allow Additions property values to No to create a read-only (decision-support) form.

6. Click the Format tab and set the value of the Navigation Buttons property of the form to Yes.

7. Right-click the label at the top of the form and choose Change To, Text Box to replace it with a text box of the same size. Click the Data tab and set the Control Source property to =**"2006 Sales for" & [CategoryName]**, and the Locked property value to Yes.

8. To emulate a label with a text box, click the Format tab and set the text box's Back Style property value to Transparent.

9. Click the edge of the subform to select the subform container, click the Data tab, and select sbf-2006SalesPCLinked as the Source Object property value.

10. Click the Builder button of the Link Master Fields property text box to open the Subform Field Linker dialog. If CategoryName isn't selected in both the Master Fields and Child Fields lists, select that field (see Figure 18.40). Click OK.

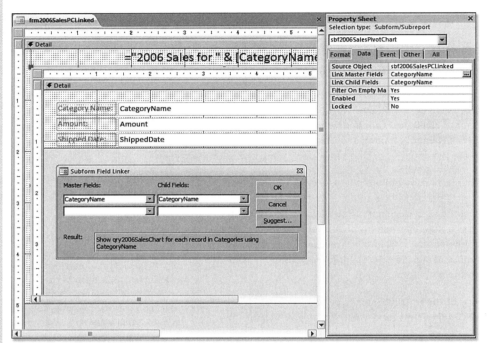

Figure 18.40
Use the Subform Field Linker to set the Link Master Fields and Link Child Fields property values.

11. Click Form view to display the linked line graph. Navigate the Recordset to verify that the category name in the caption and the legend track one another (see Figure 18.41). Close the form/subform combination, and save your changes.

Tweaking the Design of the PivotChart Subform

After you've verified that linking is working, you can delete the legend to devote more space on the form to the graph. Like with MSGraph objects, you can change the line (series member) formatting properties and add trendlines to PivotCharts. However, the process is much more tedious than that for linked MSGraph objects, because you must alter each member of the series.

To delete the legend, increase the line thickness, and add a trendline to a series member, do the following:

1. Open the sbf2006SalesPCLinked[New] form in PivotChart view. Then activate the PivotChart Tools, Design ribbon, right-click an empty area of the graph, and click Property Sheet to open the Properties dialog for the Chart Workspace. Be sure to open the subform, not the main form.

Figure 18.41
The linked
PivotChart sub-
form resembles
the linked
MSGraph
object shown
earlier in Figure
18.28.

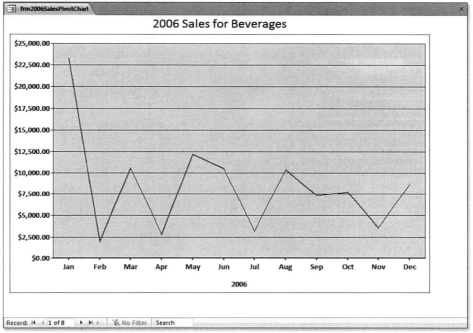

3. Open the Select list and choose Beverages to select the first series member. Click the Line/Marker tab, and set the Weight property to thick. On the General Page, click the Add Trendline button (the middle button below the Add line) to add a linear trendline to the graph.

4. Return to the General page, and select the added Beverages Trendline 1. Click the Line/Marker tab, and set the Weight property to thick.

5. Click the Trendline tab, and clear the Display Equation and Display R-squared Value check boxes.

6. Repeat steps 3–5 for the Condiments category.

7. Press Ctrl+S to save your final changes, and close the subform.

8. Open the frm2006SalesPCLinked form in Form view to check your design changes (see Figure 18.42).

 note

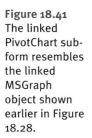 The final versions of the forms and subforms you create in this chapter are included in the Charts18. accdb sample database, which is included in the \Access2010\ Chaptr18 folder of the downloadable sample code.

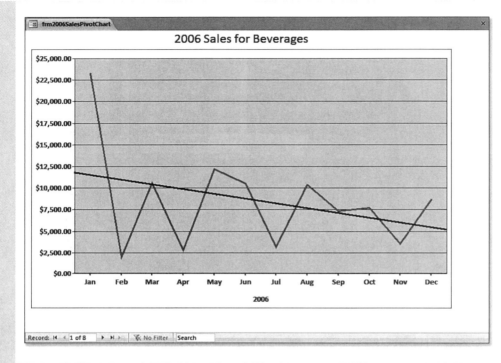

Figure 18.42
Thickening the
PivotChart's
series line
and adding
a trendline
duplicates the
final MSGraph
linked chart of
Figure 18.31,
except for the
data points and
line smoothing.

Persisting Linked PivotChart Properties with VBA Code

A defect in the PivotChart Web Component causes the PivotChart to lose the design changes you
made in the preceding section when you move the record pointer with the Navigation buttons.
This bug appeared in Access 2002 and persists in Access 2010. You must add VBA code to reapply
the properties for each category's graph. The code behind the frm2006SalesPCLinked form of the
Charts18.accdb sample database performs the following functions:

- Changes the number format of the y-axis labels from Currency to the custom $#,##0 format,
  which removes the unnecessary decimal digits.

- Sets the scale of all graphs to $25,000 so users aren't misled by scale changes when comparing
  results of categories with different maximum sales values for the year.

- Establishes a thick line weight.

- Adds a trendline and hides the equation and R-squared text.

- Changes the color of the trendline from black to red and the weight to thick.

Figure 18.43 shows the frm2006SalesPCLinked form of Charts18.accdb with formatting applied
by the Form_Current event handler. To view the VBA code, with the form open in Design view, click
the toolbar's Code button to open the VBA editor.

Figure 18.43
Code in the
Form_Current
event handler
of Charts18.
accdb's frm-
2006SalesP-
CLinked
form applies
the linked
PivotChart
formatting
changes shown
here.

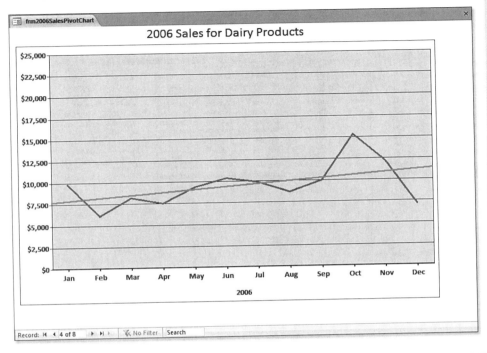

For the details on adding VBA formatting code for PivotCharts, **see** "Using the On Current Event to Set Linked PivotChart Properties," **p. 1312.**

Substituting or Adding a PivotTable in a Form

PivotCharts rely on an underlying PivotTable to supply data to the chart or graph. Thus, it's easy to alter a form or subform to display a PivotTable instead of a PivotChart. For example, you can open the sbf2006SalesPivotChart subform in Design view and change its AllowPivotChartView property value to No, AllowPivotTableView to Yes, and DefaultView to PivotTable.

When you open the modified sbf2006SalesPivotChart, the PivotTable appears as shown in Figure 18.44. Months are row headings and product categories are column headings, so you might want to pivot the table to correspond to the graph layout. In this case, you must mark the Field Buttons/Drop Zones check box on the PivotChart Property dialog's Show/Hide page to enable pivoting when you change to PivotTable view.

2006 Monthly Sales by Category

Drop Filter Fields Here

CategoryName ▾

Months ▾	Beverages	Condiments	Confections	Dairy Products	Grains/Cereals	Meat/Poultry	Produce	Seafood	Grand Total
	Sum of Amount	Sum of Amount	Sum of Amount	Sum of Amount	Sum of Amount	Sum of Amount	Sum of Amount	Sum of Amount	Sum of Amount
⊞ Jan	$23,269.16	$4,476.30	$10,216.17	$9,851.48	$3,585.60	$8,365.45	$3,288.54	$1,693.76	$64,746.46
⊞ Feb	$2,019.24	$4,954.08	$5,127.38	$6,074.44	$3,798.80	$5,958.30	$1,587.60	$1,922.65	$31,442.48
⊞ Mar	$10,569.80	$2,491.79	$5,739.23	$8,192.80	$5,312.70	$7,274.40	$4,104.60	$3,829.00	$47,514.32
⊞ Apr	$2,786.53	$4,837.91	$2,599.51	$7,521.50	$2,084.40	$5,130.24	$5,613.06	$1,023.30	$31,596.45
⊞ May	$12,163.25	$5,651.02	$13,186.80	$9,374.38	$6,052.25	$4,597.91	$4,695.60	$8,254.15	$63,975.36
⊞ Jun	$10,517.18	$2,858.35	$6,279.21	$10,358.25	$6,492.65	$3,966.40	$5,275.00	$4,335.96	$50,083.00
⊞ Jul	$3,163.75	$5,431.88	$4,186.80	$9,881.83	$2,230.00	$5,924.20	$2,198.70	$4,527.81	$37,544.96
⊞ Aug	$10,363.78	$3,823.61	$8,865.43	$8,703.68	$7,856.25	$4,005.74	$3,771.00	$8,878.50	$56,267.98
⊞ Sep	$7,317.58	$4,746.48	$4,912.64	$10,042.05	$5,224.48	$5,913.57	$2,333.28	$10,017.26	$50,507.32
⊞ Oct	$7,689.40	$4,674.01	$8,775.70	$15,304.00	$3,465.00	$19,871.04	$6,540.40	$7,985.63	$74,305.17
⊞ Nov	$3,569.00	$5,194.58	$3,625.41	$12,268.98	$3,666.35	$655.50	$4,609.71	$6,853.60	$40,443.13
⊞ Dec	$8,645.65	$6,137.60	$7,379.88	$7,176.40	$6,180.35	$9,675.31	$9,002.50	$6,222.58	$60,420.27
Grand Total	$102,074.31	$55,277.59	$80,894.15	$114,749.77	$55,948.83	$81,338.06	$53,019.99	$65,544.19	$608,846.88

Figure 18.44
To substitute this PivotTable for a Pi-votChart, change the Allow...View and Default View property values on the Format page of the Pi-votChart subform.

Another approach is to create individual PivotTable and PivotChart subforms. You can locate an additional PivotTable subform below the PivotChart. Alternatively, you can add a command button and VBA event-handling code to alternate between the two subforms as the Source Object property value of the subform container. The Access 2007 version of Northwind.mdb's sample Sales Analysis form uses this method to alternately display Sales Analysis Subform1 and Sales Analysis Subform2.

To examine the Sales Analysis approach, open Northwind.mdb from the \Access2010\Nwind folder, open the Sales Analysis form in Design view, and click the Code button to display the btnEdit_Click event handler's code.

19

AUTOMATING ACCESS APPLICATIONS WITH MACROS AND PROCEDURES

During Access's initial development, product management believed that Access 1.0's programming language—then called *Access Basic* and sometimes *Embedded Basic*—would be difficult for new users to master and would limit sales of Microsoft's fledgling desktop database application. Word for Windows 2.0 introduced WordBasic macros in 1991 and had gained at least a year of usage history before Access 1.0's November 1992 release.

Despite the popularity of Word 2.0 and its embedded programming language derived from the Dartmouth BASIC language, the Access team decided to develop a declarative programming methodology, which they originally called *scripts* and later referred to as *macros. Macros* is an abbreviation for macroinstructions, a term that means a collection of individual commands that issue many other (usually hidden) commands.

Bill Gates promoted WordBasic as a macro language, so Access Basic and, later, Visual Basic for Applications (VBA) became known as macro languages as well. This chapter deals almost exclusively with declarative macros, which are an alternative to using the procedural VBA language to automate Access applications. If you're not familiar with a Windows programming language, such as Visual Basic or VBA, you'll probably find defining simple declarative macros to be easier than adding programming code to a module, form, or report.

If the process you're automating is complex or involves row-by-row processing of the Recordset that serves as the Record Source for your form or report, you'll undoubtedly need to write VBA code. The four of the five chapters of Part VII, "Programming and Converting Access Applications," primarily cover VBA topics.

What Are Access Macros?

A macro is a list of actions to take in response to an event, a process often called "attaching a macro to an event." (In macro parlance, an *action* is a synonym for *command*.) Some events are occurrences of user actions, such as clicking a command button, opening or closing a form, or typing a value in a text box. Other events are generated by Access itself, such as starting up, beginning or completing the addition of a new row, or accepting or rejecting an edited value in an existing row. Chapter 21, "Emulating Table Triggers with Access Data Macros," covers Access 2010's new data macros, which respond to the BeforeUpdate, BeforeDelete, After Insert, AfterUpdate, AfterDelete events of Access tables.

Most macro actions have easily recognizable names, such as OpenForm, OpenReport, or Beep. Almost all actions require *arguments*. Arguments specify the object to which to apply the action, as well as how the action is to be applied. Two arguments for the OpenForm action, for example, are Form Name and View. You set these argument values to specify the name of the form to open and its view: Form, Layout or Design. In most cases, you select the action and argument value(s) from drop-down lists in a macro datasheet (usually abbreviated *macrosheet*) that you create in Access 2010's new Macro Builder. Figure 19.1 shows the Macro Builder with a macro that executes when you click the Collect Data via Email button (cmdCollectDataViaEmail) on the Tasks with Employees application's Task List form from Chapter 2, "Building Simple Tracking Applications."

note

Only the AutoExec (automatically executing) macro can respond to Access starting up, so almost everyone uses this macro to execute initialization code or other macro actions.

tip

Online help's "Macros and Programmability, Macro Actions" topic has a complete list of all 72 macro actions with brief descriptions and a list and explanation of their arguments. This list is useful for both macro and VBA programmers because VBA executes macro actions as methods of the Application or DoCmd object.

➥ To review the Tasks with Employees enhanced template application, **see** *"Integrating Objects from Other Template Databases,"* **p. 79**.

➥ For an example of collecting data with an Outlook HTML form, **see** *"Gathering Data by Email with HTML Forms,"* **p. 1044**.

Figure 19.1
Clicking the
Collect Data via
Email button
in the Task List
form's header
executes these
three macro
actions (macro
instructions) in
an embedded
macrosheet.

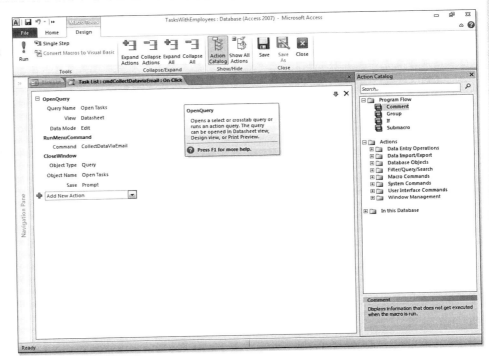

How Do I View a Macro's Actions?

Access 2007 introduced embedded macros, which are macros attached to forms. Embedded macros, sometimes called *macros behind forms*, correspond to VBA event-handling procedures embedded in form class modules, which often are referred to as *code behind forms* (CBF). Previous versions of Access offered standalone macros as database objects only. A standalone macro corresponds to VBA event-handling procedures in an Access module.

The Macro Builder is the same for embedded and standalone macros. To open the Macro Builder for an embedded macro, you must locate the event to which it's attached in the Property Sheet's Events page for its form or control object. For example, to open the macrosheet shown in Figure 19.1, do the following:

1. Open the Tasks with Employees.accdb database in the \Access2010\Chaptr02 folder.

2. Open the Task List form in Layout or Design view.

3. Right-click the Collect Data via Email button (cmdCollectDataviaEmail) in the Form Header section, and choose Properties to open the Property Sheet for the button (see Figure 19.2).

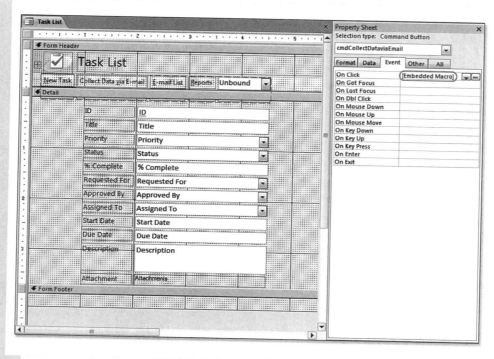

Figure 19.2
An event with an embedded macro displays [Embedded Macro] in the event-handler list and a builder button to the right of the list.

4. Click the builder button to open the Macro Builder with the macrosheet for the selected event.

Standalone macros, like other database objects, have names. To open the Macros Builder with a standalone macro, click its item in the Navigation pane.

The simple macro of Figure 19.1 executes the following three actions:

- `OpenQuery` executes the Open Tasks query, which is the Record Source for the Task List form in Datasheet view. You select Open Tasks from the Action Arguments pane's Query Name drop-down list of all Query objects in the application, select Datasheet as the View, and Edit as the Data Mode. This action refreshes the data behind the Task List form.

- `RunCommand`, which has a single argument (Command), performs the equivalent of clicking a ribbon's command button. In earlier Access versions, this action was called "executing a menu command." The Command drop-down list contains an entry for every native command, regardless of whether it is represented by a command button on a ribbon.

 tip

You'll find the description of the macro actions in the following list to be more useful if you open the builder and select each action in sequence.

 tip

It's quicker to right-click the control object and choose Build Event to open the Macro Builder directly. However, if the control doesn't have an event handler for its default event, the Choose Builder dialog opens.

- `Close` closes the Open Tasks query by specifying Query as the Object Type, and Open Tasks as the Object Name.

The other buttons and the Reports combo box in the Form Header execute macros of similar or greater complexity. The ID and New Datasheet cells also execute macros to open the Task Details form with the data for the selected record or an empty form for adding a new Tasks record.

Why Use Macros Instead of VBA?

Microsoft promotes macros in online help as a "simplified programming language" and claims that "most people find it easier to build a macro than to write VBA code." Simplicity often has shortcomings, and easier doesn't necessarily mean better. However, the Access team improved macros greatly in Access 2007. For example, embedded macros are an integral part of their containing form, so when you copy the form to the same or another database, the embedded macros copy with it. Access 2007 and later macros finally include error-handling with the `OnError` and `ClearMacroError` actions.

It's easier (and faster) to write macros for simple actions that don't involve complex conditional action execution. Conditional execution is controlled by VBA expressions in the `If` statement of an `If ...End If` block. Macros are a good choice for executing a single command that has built-in error handling, such as the Next and Previous record navigation actions described in the next section.

2010 NEW Conditions execute VBA expressions that return True or False. If True, the associated action (and the following actions within the `If ...End If` block, if any) execute. If a macro requires many actions and several conditions, the new conditional execution feature makes it easier to understand how the macros work and to de bug them by single-stepping through the actions. Access 2010 macros now support VBA's `If ...Else ...End If` and `If ...Else If ...End If` constructs

A disadvantage of macros is their proprietary nature; proprietary to Microsoft *and Access*. As mentioned in later chapters, learning VBA lets you leverage your Office programming skills to other Office members that use VBA, such as Word, Excel, Outlook, PowerPoint and Visio. Gaining VBA skills also readies you for advancement to programming with Visual Basic .NET for a wider range of data-intensive desktop and web-based projects.

 note

Web Databases that you export to SharePoint Server 2010 and run with Access Services won't execute VBA in the user's browser, so Access macros are required to program browser-based forms and reports. Chapter 24, "Sharing Web Databases with SharePoint Server 2010," covers modifications to conventional Access projects to Web-enable them.

Exploring Access 2010's Event Repertoire

When you interact with an Access object by using the keyboard or the mouse, you can change the object's state. The object's state is stored with the other data about the object. Access makes some of the changes in the object's state available as opportunities to interrupt normal processing. These special changes in an object's state are called *events*. An event is a change in the state of an object at which you can interrupt normal processing and define a response.

The best way to understand events is to categorize each by the type of action that causes the event to occur. There are 11 categories:

- *Mouse events* are triggered when you click form objects.

- *Keyboard events* are triggered by forms and form controls when you type or send keystrokes with the SendKeys action while the Form object has the focus.

- *Window events* are triggered by opening or closing forms or reports.

- *Focus events* are triggered when a form or form control gains or loses the focus or when a form or report becomes active or inactive.

- *Data events* are triggered by forms and form controls when you change data in controls or records, or by forms when the record pointer moves from one record to another. These data events aren't the same as those to which Access Data Macros respond.

- *Filter events* are triggered by forms when you apply or remove filters.

- *Print events* are triggered by reports and report sections when you print or preview a report.

- *Error events* are triggered by a form or report that has the focus when an error occurs.

- *Timing events* are triggered by forms when a specified time interval passes.

- *Class module* events fire when you open or close an instance of a VBA class. You use the With Events qualifier to intercept events from ActiveX Data Objects (ADO) and the RaiseEvent command to define custom events.

- *Reference events* fire when you add or remove a reference to an object or type library in the References collection.

Table 19.1 groups Access 2010's most commonly used events according to their source.

Table 19.1 Events Grouped by Cause

Event Category	Source	Events
Mouse actions	The user creating mouse DblClick MouseUp MouseWheel	Click MouseDown MouseMove
Keyboard or SendKeys sending keystrokes	The user typing on the keyboard KeyUp KeyPress	KeyDown
Window resizing a window	Opening, closing, or Load	Open Unload Close Resize
Focus focus, or a form or report becoming active or inactive	An object losing or gaining the GotFocus Exit LostFocus Activate Deactivate	Enter

Event Category	Source	Events
Data	Making changes to a control's data, displaying records in a form, or moving the focus from one record to another in a form	`Current` `BeforeInsert` `AfterInsert` `Delete` `BeforeDelConfirm` `AfterDelConfirm` `BeforeUpdate` `AfterUpdate` `Change` `Updated` `Dirty` `NotInList` `Undo`
Filter window, or applying or removing a filter	Opening or closing a filter `ApplyFilter`	`Filter`
Print for printing	Selecting or arranging data `Print`	`Format` `Retreat` `NoData` `Page`
Error	Generating an error	`Error`
Timing expiring	A specified period of time	`Timer`
Class Module	Opening a new instance of `Terminate`	`Initialize`
Class Module or terminating an instance of *Class Module*		
Reference	Adding or removing a reference to an object or type library	`ItemAdded` `ItemRemoved`

The `Dirty` event (and `Dirty` property) of bound forms and their controls is one of the most useful members of Access's event repertoire. The `Dirty` event fires and the `Dirty` property is set to `True` when you change underlying data by typing in a bound text box or combo box, or change a page by clicking a Tab control. The `Dirty` event doesn't fire if you change a value with code, nor does it fire for any action on an unbound form. The `Undo` event is the reverse of the `Dirty` event; returning data in the form to its original, unmodified state fires the `Undo` event.

Each event that an object triggers has a corresponding event property listed in a separate category of the object's Property Sheet. Usually the corresponding event property is the event name preceded by the word *On*. For example, the `Click` event triggered by a command button becomes the On Click property in the button's property sheet.

Figure 19.3 shows the Event page of the Property Sheet for a bound text box displaying the 17 events that the control can trigger. Notice that all event properties—except the Before Update and After Update data event properties—follow the pattern of preceding the event name with "On". A default drop-down list, which lets you select [Event Procedure] (but not [Embedded Macro]), and a builder button appear in the first event, unless another event has been assigned a VBA or macro event handler. Clicking the builder button for an empty event opens the Choose Builder dialog, which lets you open an empty Macro Builder macrosheet, Expression Builder dialog, or Code Builder (VBA Code Editor window) when you click OK.

Figure 19.3
Text boxes fire 17 different events. Clicking the builder button for an empty event opens the Choose Builder dialog.

Generating Embedded Macros with the Command Button Wizard

 The most common use for macros is handling the On Click event of buttons (called *Command Buttons* in earlier Access versions) to display objects or move the record pointer of the recordset to which the form is bound. When you add a Button control to a form with Control Wizards enabled, the Command Button Wizard's first dialog displays Categories and Actions lists. When you select a category, the most popular actions in that category appear in the Actions list.

For example, you can supplement the miniature VCR-style Navigation Buttons gadget at the bottom of the form with a set of four more-evident and easier-to-hit buttons in the form header of a split form. Figure 19.4 shows the result of adding four navigation buttons to the Details section of a split form.

To add a Previous Record navigation button with the Command Button Wizard, do the following:

1. Create a split form based on a table, such as Customers, and change to Design view.

> **note**
> Events are the same for embedded macros and VBA event procedures, which Access considers to be interchangeable event handlers.

2. 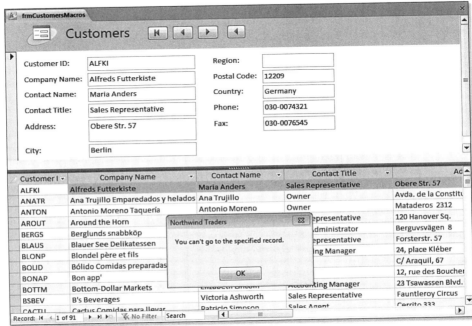 With the Use Control Wizards button of the Form Design Tools—Design ribbon activated, click the Button button and draw a button in the Header section of the form to open the first Command Button Wizard dialog.

3. With the default Record Navigation category selected, select Previous Record in the Actions list (see Figure 19.5).

Figure 19.4
Large record-navigation buttons are more evident than the small VCR versions in the Navigation Buttons object. Record navigation requires error handling; for example, the macro displays the message You Can't Go to the Specified Record when you click the previous button and the record pointer is on the first record.

Figure 19.5
Select the category and the action to perform when handling the On Click event of a button in the first Command Button Wizard dialog.

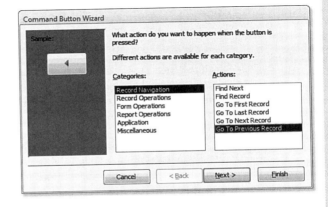

4. Click Next, accept the default Picture option, and mark the Show All Pictures check box to display a list of all bitmaps available to the wizard (see Figure 19.6).

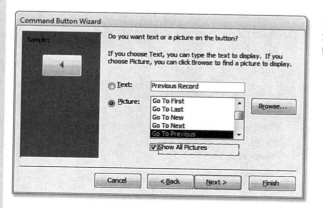

Figure 19.6
Select between a text caption or a bitmap icon for the action in the second wizard dialog.

5. Click Next and replace the default control name (Command#) with a more descriptive name, such as **btnPrevious** (see Figure 19.7).

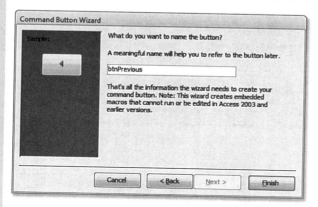

Figure 19.7
Add a descriptive name for the button, such as btnPrevious, to complete the wizard's task.

6. Click Finish to dismiss the wizard, click the Properties button to open the Properties Sheet, select the Auto_Header0 label in the Properties Sheet's list, change the Font Name to Calibri and the Font Size to 24 points, change the Caption property value to "Previous" and adjust the position and size of the added button to emulate the form header in Figure 19.4.

7. Select the button you added, change to the Form Design Tools—Format ribbon, click the Control Formatting group's Quick Styles button to open its gallery, click the Subtle Effect – Blue, Accent 1 (row 4, column 2) for this example. Click the Change Shape button and click the Rounded shape (row 1, column 3).

8. With the button selected, click the Property Sheet's Events tab and click the On Click event's Builder button to open the Macro Builder with the wizard-generated macrosheet (see Figure 19.8).

note

2010 NEW The Quick Styles and Change Shape buttons are new in Access 2010.

Figure 19.8
The wizard generates a macro with a condition that ignores the error caused by attempting to move the record pointer before the beginning of the file (BOF).

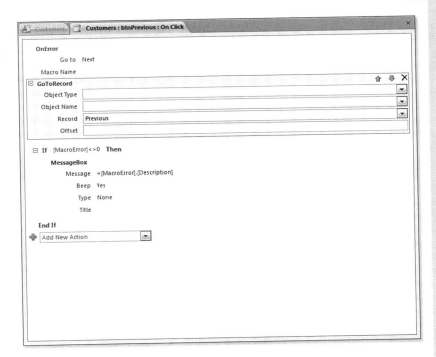

Control Wizards Don't Generate Embedded Macros

When events with builder buttons in the Events page of Property Sheets display [Event Procedure] instead of [Embedded Macro], the most likely cause of the error is that the Always Use Event Procedures check box is marked in the Access Options dialog's Object Designers page. To enforce the Access team's macros-over-VBA-code priority, marking this check box prevents the Control Wizards from generating VBA code. (The Control Wizards do generate VBA event-handling code for forms and reports in .mdb files.)

To solve this problem, do the following:

1. Click the Office Button and the Access Options link to open the Access Options dialog.

2. Click the Object Designers button and scroll to the Forms/Reports section.

Continues...

Continued

3. Mark the Always Use Event Procedures check box.

4. Close the dialog to return to your project.

The macrosheet for btnPrevious of Figure 19.8 demonstrates the most common method of error handling by macros:

1. Ignore errors initially by specifying `OnError` as the first action with `Next` (step) as its arguments. The other allowable argument values are `Macro Name` to execute a specified (named) macro and `Fail` (quit with an unrecoverable error).

2. Execute the action that might generate an error; in this case, `GoToRecord` with `, , Previous,` as its argument values. The three commas are placeholders for empty `Object Type`, `Object Name`, and `Offset` property values.

3. Detect whether an error occurred in the preceding step(s) by the `[MacroError]<>0` condition. Errors thrown by macro actions are identified by integer values. If the preceding step(s) succeed, continue. If there are no more steps, exit the macrosheet.

4. If an error occurred, display a message box with `=[MacroError].[Description], Yes, None,` argument values for `Message, Beep, Type,` and `Title`. If you select `Warning!` as the `Type`, and type **Previous Record Navigation Error** as the `Title`, the message box appears as shown in Figure 19.9.

The actions of the preceding macrosheet correspond to the following VBA event-handling subprocedure:

```
Private Sub btnPrevious_Click()
    On Error Resume Next

    DoCmd.GoToRecord , , acPrevious

    If Err.Number > 0 Then

        MsgBox Err.Description

    End If

End Sub
```

It's clear that creating the embedded macro with the Command Button Wizard will always be faster than writing the preceding code. However, the advantage of VBA code is that all procedures for a particular form or report are visible in a single page in the VBA Editor. The ability to scroll through all code behind the form, instead of opening individual macrosheets for each event handler, aids your understanding of programming structure and makes troubleshooting much quicker.

Figure 19.9
Compare this modified message box with that shown in Figure 19.4.

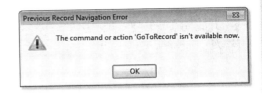

Empty `Object Type` and `Object Name` arguments in an embedded macro refer to the container (in this case, the form containing the macro).

The \Access2010\Chaptr19\Macros19.accdb sample database's frmCustomersMacros form incorporates the preceding embedded macro.

Table 19.2 lists the Command Button Wizard's action categories and their actions.

Table 19.2 Command Button Wizard Actions Grouped by Categories

Verified-SBD	
Category	Action
Record Navigation	Find Next
	Find Record
	Go To First Record
	Go To Last Record
	Go To Next Record
	Go To Previous Record
Record Operations	Add New Record
	Delete Record
	Duplicate Record
	Print Record
	Save Record
	Undo Record
Form Operations	Apply Form Filter
	Close Form
	Print a Form
	Print Current Form
	Refresh Form Data

Table 19.2   Command Button Wizard Actions Grouped by Categories

Verified-SBD	
Category	Action
Report Operations	Mail Report
	Open Report
	Preview Report
	Print Report
	Send Report to File
Application	Quit Application
Miscellaneous	Autodialer
	Print Table
	Run Macro
	Run Query

It's evident from the preceding table that most actions of wizard-based buttons substitute buttons on forms for command buttons on ribbons. The primary advantage of buttons on forms over buttons on ribbons is that macro arguments can specify a particular object as the target of the action.

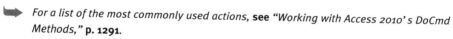   *For a list of the most commonly used actions,* **see** *"Working with Access 2010's DoCmd Methods,"* **p. 1291.**

Responding to Events from Combo and List Boxes

The most common application for combo boxes is to insert a value selected from a list into a data cell of the current record of the data source for a form. Combo boxes used to insert values in Recordsets are called "bound." An unbound combo box can pass its selected value to a macro that finds and displays a particular record or set of records. In most cases, you use the Combo Box Wizard to populate the combo box's list from a table or query.

Create a Category Combo Box with the Wizard

To add to a new split form an unbound combo box that ultimately selects the category of products to display, do the following:

1. In Northwind.accdb or your working database, select the Products table in the Navigation pane, click the Create tab, and click the Split Form button to generate a split form from the Products table.

2.  Change to Design view and, with the Control Wizards button active, draw a Combo Box control on to the Form Header section. When you release the mouse button, the Combo Box Wizard opens its first dialog.

3. Accept the default option (I Want the Combo Box to Look Up the Values in a Table or Query), and click Next.

4. With the default Tables option selected, select Categories in the list box and then click Next.

5. Click the >> button to add the CategoryID and CategoryName fields to the combo box's Selected Fields list, and click Next.

6. Optionally, apply an ascending sort on the CategoryID field, and click Next.

7. Double-click the right edge of the Category Name column to best fit the column width, verify that the Hide Key Column check box is marked (see Figure 19.10), and click Next.

8. Accept the default option (Remember the Value for Later Use) to create an unbound combo box, and click Next.

9. Type **Select Category** as the label name, and click Finish to dismiss the wizard.

10. Adjust the position of the combo box and its label, and optionally change the label text's size and color.

Figure 19.10
Setting the column width isn't important, but hiding the key field (CategoryID) prevents confusing users with more information than they need.

11. Right-click the combo box, choose Properties to open the Property Sheet, click the Other tab, and change the Name property value from Combo20 (or the like) to **cboCategory**. At this point, your Products form in Design view appears similar to Figure 19.11.

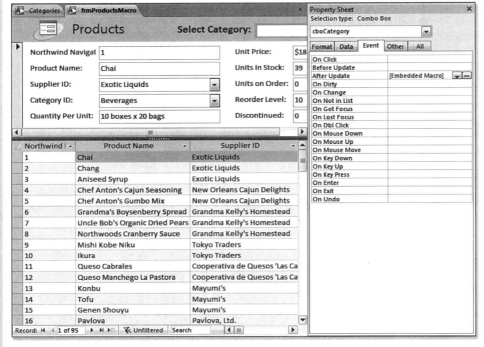

Figure 19.11
Give the
wizard-created
combo box a
meaningful
name by open-
ing its proper-
ties sheet and
clicking the
Other or All
tab. The cbo
prefix is an
abbreviation
for "Combo".

12. Save your form as **frmProductsMacros** or the like and
    remain in Design view with the cboCategory control's
    Property Sheet open.

Write and Test an Embedded ApplyFilter Macro

> **note**
> The help topic for the ApplyFilter
> macro has a note that's incorrect.
> Only ADPs support server filters, so
> the note doesn't apply to conven-
> tional .accdb database applications.

The final step is to write an embedded macro that applies an
appropriate filter to a form's record source (the Products table) depending on the CategoryName
value you select in the combo box. You can obtain online help with macro action syntax by selecting Developer Reference in the Search list, typing the action name in the Search text box, pressing
Enter, and clicking the *ActionName* Macro Action link. Figure 19.12 shows the online help topic for
the ApplyFilter macro action.

The help topic's sample macro uses Condition tests for the first letter of a company name. You can
use a similar approach to generate a filter for each of the eight CategoryID values. Table 19.3 is an
abbreviated list of the nine macrosheet entries.

Figure 19.12
Access's online help topic for the ApplyFilter macro has a sample macro at the bottom. The sample macro isn't shown here.

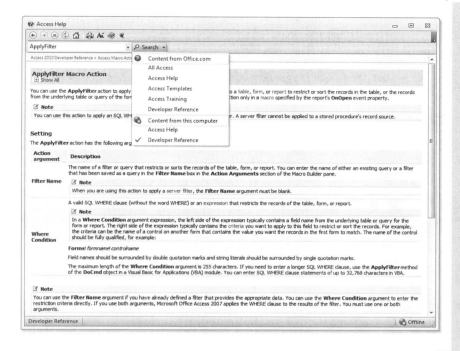

Table 19.3 Five of the Nine Macrosheet Entries for the frmProductsMacro Split Form

Where Condition	Action	Argument	Comment
(none)	ShowAllRecords	None	Clear a previous filter
[cboCategory]=1	ApplyFilter	, [CategoryID]=1,	Beverages
[cboCategory]=2	ApplyFilter	, [CategoryID]=2,	Condiments
	...		
[cboCategory]=7	ApplyFilter	, [CategoryID]=7,	Produce
[cboCategory]=8	ApplyFilter	, [CategoryID]=8,	Seafood

To open the macrosheet and add the nine required items, do the following:

1. Click the Property Sheet's Events tab, click the AfterUpdate builder button to open the Choose Builder dialog, select Macro Builder, and click OK to open an empty macrosheet.

2. In the first row, open the Add New Action list and choose ShowAllRecords. This action removes the filter applied previously, if any.

note

The preceding and trailing commas of the Arguments column entries represent unused Filter Name and Control Name argument values. This example and most ApplyFilter macros use the Where Condition argument only.

3. In the second row, select If in the New Action list, type [cboCategory]=1 as the If condition's argument, select ApplyFilter in the Add New Action list, and type [CategoryID]=1 in the Where Condition text box.

4. Repeat step 3 for each of the remaining seven categories, incrementing the two CategoryID numbers by 1. Your macrosheet appears as shown in Figure 19.13 when you're done.

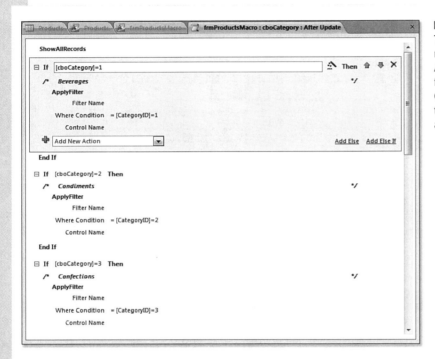

Figure 19.13
The completed macrosheet has a conditional ApplyFilter action for each of the eight CategoryID values. Only the first three conditional actions are shown here.

5. Click the Close button to close the macrosheet and save your changes.

6. Click the Property Sheet's Data tab, change the object list from cboCategory to Form, and verify that the form's Data Source property value is Products; otherwise, open the list and select Products.

7. Change to Form view and test the eight category choices in the combo box. Notice that the Filtered indicator is present at the bottom of the Datasheet and that you can remove and reapply the filter by clicking the Toggle Filter button (see Figure 19.14).

8. Close the form, save your changes, and then reopen the form and repeat step 7.

> **tip**
>
> Entry will go faster if you copy [cboCategory]= to the Clipboard, paste it seven times in the Condition column, and then add the number. Similarly, copy [CategoryID]= to the Clipboard and do the same for the Where Condition text box.

Figure 19.14
Selecting
a category
applies the
appropriate
filter and
positions the
record pointer
on the first
product record
in the cat-
egory.

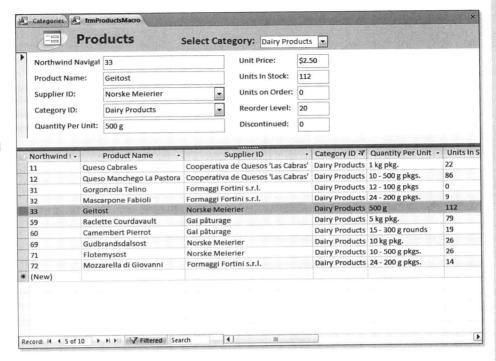

Form Is Filtered Before Selecting a Category

Sometimes you might open a form to which you've added a macro with ApplyFilter actions after saving it, and the Datasheet or form shows a selection you didn't make. When you make another filter selection, no rows appear in the Datasheet or the form shows the tentative append record instead of a record from the selection. What should you do?

When you saved the changes to the form after creating and testing the macrosheet with the ApplyFilter actions in it, the form's Data Source property value changed from the table you selected when you created the form to Select * From TableName Where ConditionColumn=[']CriterionValue[']. (Single quotes appear only for string criteria.) For this chapter's ApplyFilter example, the errant SQL statement is Select * From Products Where CategoryID = 1 or another number up to 8. This persistent filter doesn't turn on the form's Filtered indicator and prevents any other selection from displaying rows.

To solve the problem, open the form in Layout or Design view and change the form's Data Source property value to the original *TableName*. If the original Data Source property value was a query, remove the column that creates the permanent filter.

The \Access2010\Chaptr19\Macros19.accdb sample database's frmProductsMacro form incorporates the preceding embedded macro.

Exploring Access 2010's Macro-based Switchboard Manager

One of the Access team's goals in moving to tabbed documents and replacing the Database Window of earlier Access versions with the Navigation pane was to eliminate the need for switchboards. A *switchboard* usually is a hierarchical collection of relatively small forms with groups of command buttons to execute common tasks, such as opening closed forms, printing reports, or setting the focus to a form that has been overlaid by other forms, reports, or both. Figure 19.15 shows the default form (top) of a simple switchboard with buttons that open other switchboard forms (bottom)

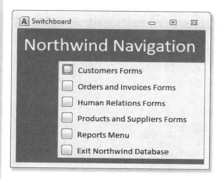

Figure 19.15
This simple switchboard created by Access's Switchboard Manager has a two-layer hierarchy. The first four buttons on the default form (top) open second-level forms that open forms and reports.

For an example of adding a group and buttons to Access's ribbon UI, **see** "Customizing Applications with RibbonX Objects," **p. 1294**.

2007 NEW Access 2010 includes a Switchboard Manager utility for creating standardized switchboards but doesn't expose a button to start it on the Database Tools or other ribbon. (The Access team omitted the button to discourage use of switchboards, which the Team doesn't consider to be a good user-experience feature.) The simplest solution is to add the Switchboard Manager button to the Quick Access Toolbar by following these steps:

1. Click the Quick Access Toolbar's rightmost Customize the Quick Access Toolbar (QAT) button and choose More Commands to open the Access Options dialog.

2. Select Commands Not in the Ribbon in the Choose Commands list.

3. Scroll to the bottom of the list, select Switchboard Manager, click Add to add it to the QAT, and click OK to close the dialog.

You create a new switchboard by clicking the Switchboard Manager button you added to open a message box that asks if you want to create a switchboard. (You can't add more than one switchboard to a database.) If you answer yes, the manager creates an empty default Switchboard form and a Switchboard Items table to hold button specifications, and opens the Switchboard Manager dialog. To add items to the Switchboard form with the Switchboard Manager, do the following:

1. With the Main Switchboard (Default) dialog open, click Edit to open the Edit Switchboard Page dialog.

2. Click the New button to open the Edit Switchboard Item dialog (see Figure 19.16).

3. Replace the default Text with the button's caption.

4. Select one of the eight items in the Command list and add the appropriate argument value in the bottom text box (see Table 19.4).

5. Click OK to close the Edit Switchboard Item dialog, add the command button to the form, and return to the Edit Switchboard page.

6. If you want to add another command button, repeat steps 2 through 5.Alternatively, click Close twice to return to the Switchboard Manager form, click New to generate a new form, and repeat steps 2 through 5 to add command buttons.

7. Click Close three times to exit the Switchboard Manager.

Table 19.4   Switchboard Button Actions and Arguments

Action (Command)	Argument
1 - Go To Switchboard	Switchboard Form Name
2 - Open Form in Add Mode	Form Name
3 - Open Form in Edit Mode	Form Name
4 - Open Report	Report Name
5 - Design Application	(none, opens Switchboard Manager)
6 - Exit Application	(none)
7 - Run Macro	Macro Name (standalone)
8 - Run Code	Function Name (in module)

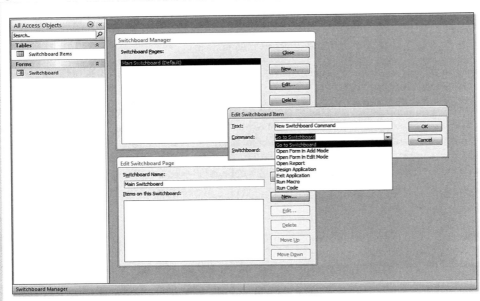

Figure 19.16
Switchboard buttons can initiate one of the eight actions you select from the drop-down list.

The original Switchboard Manager executed Access Basic or VBA event handlers in the form's class module to perform the specified actions. Apparently, the Access team believed that switchboards weren't fully obsolete, so they replaced earlier versions' VBA code with the embedded macro shown in Table 19.5, part of which is shown in Figure 19.17.

Table 19.5 Conditions, Actions, and Arguments for Switchboard Manager Options

Macro Name	Condition	Action	Arguments
		OnError	MacroName, ErrorHandler
Go To Switchboard	[Command]=1	SetTempVar	SwitchboardID, [Argument]
	...	Set Property	Label1, Caption, =DLookUp("ItemText", "Switchboard Items", "[SwitchboardID"))
	...	Set Property	Label2, Caption, =DLookUp("ItemTe xt","Switchboard Items","[SwitchboardID] = " & TempVars("SwitchboardID"))
	...	Requery	
	...	Stop Macro	

Macro Name	Condition	Action	Arguments
Open Form (Add)	[Command]=2 ...	OpenForm StopMacro	=[Argument], Form, , , Add, Normal
Open Form (Edit)	[Command]=3 ...	OpenForm StopMacro	=[Argument], Form, , , Add, Normal
Open Report	[Command]=4 ...	OpenReport StopMacro	=[Argument], Report, , , Normal
Design Application	[Command]=5 SwitchboardManager	RunCommand	SwitchboardManager
	...	SetTempVar	SwitchboardID, DLookUp("SwitchboardID", "Switchboard Items", "[ItemNumber] = 0 AND [Argument] = 'Default'")
	...	SetProperty	Label1, Caption, =DLo okUp("ItemText","S witchboard Items", "[SwitchboardID] = " & TempVars("SwitchboardID"))
	...	SetProperty	Label2, Caption, =DLookUp("ItemText", "Switchboard Items", "[SwitchboardID] = " & TempVars("SwitchboardID"))
	...	Requery	
	...	StopMacro	
Exit Application	[Command]=6 ...	CloseDatabase StopMacro	
Run Macro	[Command]=7 ...	RunMacro StopMacro	=[Argument], ,
Run Code	[Command]=8 ...	RunCode StopMacro	=[Argument] & "()"
Unknown Option		MsgBox	Unknown option., Yes, None,
ErrorHandler		MsgBox	

The \Access2010\Chaptr19\Macros19.accdb sample database's Switchboard form incorporates the preceding embedded macro, the initial few commands of which are shown in Figure 19.17.

2007 NEW Table 19.5 provides examples of commands for common macro operations, including domain lookup (DLookup) operations on table data to set temporary variables (TempVars), which were a new feature in Access 2007, and to deliver argument values to set Label captions.

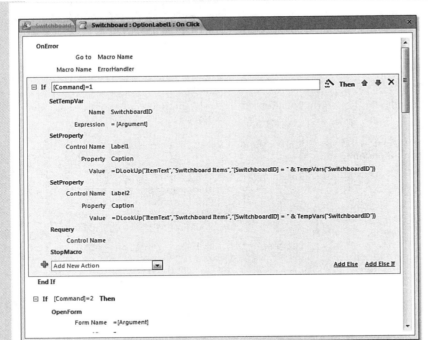

Figure 19.17
The ErrorHandling embedded macro opens a message box in the event of an error in the macro's execution.

 tip

Use the assignment operator (=) to simplify macrosheets that require only changes to argument values, not action types. For example, you can reduce the eight ApplyFilter actions in the macro of Table 19.3 to a single ApplyFilter action with =, "[cboCategory]=" & [cbo-Category, as the Where Condition argument.

EMULATING TABLE TRIGGERS WITH ACCESS DATA MACROS

2010 NEW Data macros are a new feature of Access 2010 that lets you extend the range of containers for embedded macros from forms and reports only to include Access tables. Data macros respond to events generated by Data Manipulation Language (DML) instructions, such as Access SQL INSERT, DELETE and UPDATE commands. In this respect, data macros are similar to SQL Server triggers, which are a special type of stored procedure. The first part of this chapter describes where to use and how to create event-driven data macros.

Unlike Access forms and reports, tables don't have event properties whose values you can set to embedded macros or VBA event-handling procedures. You create data macros by opening a table in Design view, selecting the Table Tools–Design tab, and clicking the Field, Record & Table Events group's Create Data Macros button to open its gallery of event-driven and named macro options, as shown in Figure 20.1. Items for data macros don't appear in the Navigation pane's Macros section because the table object stores the data macro.

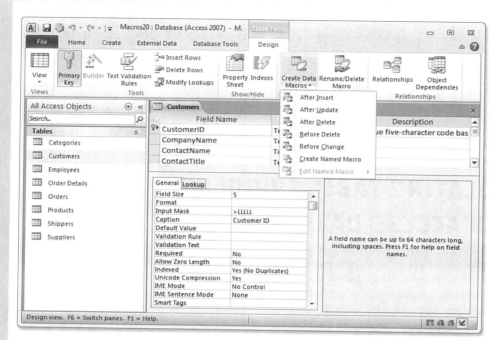

Figure 20.1
The Create Data Macros button's gallery lets you select a new event-driven data macro from five table-based events. The Edit Named Macro button is enabled only after you've created a named macro for the table.

 note

Before...events support the LookupRecord data block only.

The *current table* is the table you selected before clicking the Create Data Macros button.

The *current record* is the selected record in the *current table*.

A *domain* is a collection of records of a table or query specified by the In argument constrained by a Where clause. LookupRecord returns the first record of a domain having more than one record.

The current table, record or domain is called the *data context* of the data block.

Table 20.1 lists the five table-related events that invoke data macros.

Table 20.1   Table-Related Events That Drive Data Macros

Table-Related Event	Fires...
Before Change	After the INSERT or UPDATE operation has started but before the change to the record is committed to the table
Before Delete	After the DELETE operation has started but before the record is marked for deletion

Table-Related Event	Fires...
After Delete	After a record is marked for deletion
After Insert	After an INSERT operation has committed
After Update	After an UPDATE operation has committed

It's common to use event-driven data macros to validate the data in newly created and altered records to ensure consistency of table data. A significant advantage of event-based data macros over form-based macros for data validation and related tasks is that a single macro serves all forms for data entry to the table.

 note

You can prevent changes or deletions from committing in data macros invoked by Before Change or Before Delete events, respectively, with the RaiseError macro action, but you can't undo insertions, updates or deletions invoked by After... events.

 note

The USysApplicationLog table is hidden by default; to show it, do the following:

1. Click the File tab, click the Options button to open the Options dialog and click its Current Database tab.
2. In the Navigation section, click the Navigation Options button to open the dialog of the same name.
3. Click Show System Objects, and then click OK twice to return to Backstage.
4. Click OK to dismiss the message, and then close and reopen the database.

The USysApplicationLog table won't appear in the Navigation pane's Tables list until it contains at least one entry for a macro execution error or a LogEvent action.

Another application is adding records to transaction logs that specify who made what changes to a record and when the changes occurred. For example, After...event-driven or named data macros can use the LogEvent action to add a record to the USysApplicationLog system table for the condition(s) you specify.

Alternatively, you can create your own transaction log and add records to it with a CreateRecord data block. A custom transaction log table usually is preferable to the USysApplicationLog table because the LogEvent action only lets you specify the content of the Description field and doesn't support populating custom fields you add to that table.

Unlike event-driven data macros, *named macros* run in response to being called by the name from forms, reports or other macros. You assign the data macro name when you select Create Named Macro in the Create Data Macros gallery. The "Writing and Invoking Named Data Macros" section near the end of this chapter covers named data macros.

Designing Simple Event-Driven Data Macros

Writing event-driven data macros closely resembles the process of creating embedded macros (also called UI—user interface—macros) for handling form-based events of bound Recordsets. Program

Flow elements—Comment, Group and If...Then...Else—of data macros are the same as those for UI macros, except that Submacro isn't supported. However, the set of data actions available differs greatly from UI macro actions. Data macros that handle After ... events have a much more versatile array of data blocks and data actions from which to choose than those of Before ... events.

Table 20.2 lists and describes the data blocks available for After ... events.

Table 20.2   Data Blocks Available for After... Events

Data Block	Desctiption
CreateRecord	Creates a new record in the *current table* or at a table specified by an Alias string
EditRecord	Enables changing the values in the current record or a record specified by an Alias string
ForEachRecord	Applies a set of data actions to each record in a *domain*
LookupRecord	Applies a set of data actions to a single record in a *domain*

 note

Data actions marked with an asterisk (*) are available only to data macros.

Data macros for Before... events support only ClearError, OnError, RaiseError, SetField, SetLocalVar, and StopMacro actions.

Table 20.3 lists and describes the data actions available for After ... events.

Table 20.3   Data Actions Available for After... Events

Data Action	Desctiption
CancelRecordChange*	Cancels changes applied to a record in a CreateRecord or EditRecord data block before the changes are committed
ClearMacroError	Clears information about an error stored in the MacroError object
DeleteRecord	Marks a record for deletion
ExitForEachRecord*	Exits immediately from a ForEachRecord data block
LogEvent*	Adds a User entry to the USysApplicationLog table with a specified Description value
OnError	Lets you specify Next, a MacroName or Fail as the Go To argument value for a macro execution error
RaiseError*	Throws a macro execution error with Error Number and Error Description properties you specify
RunDataMacro	Runs the specified named data macro
SendEmail*	Sends a message you specify to one or more recipients
SetField*	Sets the value of the field you specify of a CreateRecord or EditRecord data context

Data Action	Desctiption
SetLocalVar	Names and sets the value of a local variable
StopAllMacros	Stops all currently running macros
Stop Macro	Stops the currently running macro

The following sections describe the process for creating and enhancing a simple macro that synchronizes a Tasks table's % Complete field value when users change the Status field values to Not Started (0%) or Completed (100%) in Table Datasheet view, the Task List and Task Details forms, and Tasks subform.

Writing a Simple Data Macro to Handle After Update Events

The built-in Access 2010 Tasks template generates Tasks.accdb with a Tasks table that the Task List and Task Details forms, and Tasks subform let you display and edit. The following sections show you how to use the EditRecord data block and SetFields data action to synchronize % Complete values with Not Started and Completed Status values and analyze macro execution errors written to the USysApplicationLog file.

Creating the Tasks.accdb Database

To create Tasks.accdb from the built-in Tasks template, do the following:

1. Click the File tab to open the Backstage window and click the New tab to display the Available Templates group.

2. Click the Samples button to display Access 2010's built-in templates.

3. Scroll to the bottom of the gallery; click the Tasks button to add Tasks.accdb to the File Name text box.

4. Click the Folder button and browse to the location to store the Tasks.accdb file, such as \ Access2010\Chaptr20 for this example, and click Create to generate the database.

5. If you exported Northwind contacts to Outlook in Chapter 8, "Linking, Importing and Exporting Data," or have other Outlook contacts to populate the Contacts table, open the Contact List form, and click the Add from Outlook button to open the Profile dialog. Otherwise, skip to the next section and enter a Contact record manually.

6. Select the profile you created in Chapter 8 or accept the default profile, and click OK to open the Select Names to Add–Contacts dialog.

7. Select Northwind or another Contacts folder in the Address Book list, select a few or all contacts, click Add to add them to the lower text box, and click OK to import them to the Contacts table.

8. Close the Select Names to Add: *FolderName* dialog.

Adding a Task and Selecting a Contact

A contact is required for each task. To add a contact manually, if necessary, and create a test task, do the following:

1. Open the Contact Details form. If you didn't import contacts from Outlook in the preceding section, complete an empty form as shown in Figure 20.2. Otherwise, go to step 3.

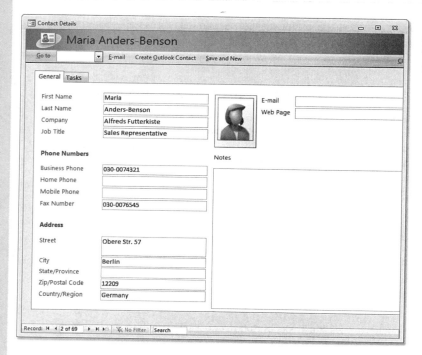

Figure 20.2
Create a contact manually if you didn't import contacts from Outlook.

2. Click the Save and New button to save your entry, close the Contact Details form, and open the Task Details form.

3. Add a Title, select a contact in the Assigned To list, accept the default values for Status, % Complete, Priority and Start Date, and optionally add a Due Date and Description, as shown in Figure 20.3.

4. Click Save and New and, optionally, add a second Tasks record with a different title for the same contact.

5. Close the Contact Details form.

Figure 20.3
Create a new Tasks record similar
to that shown here.

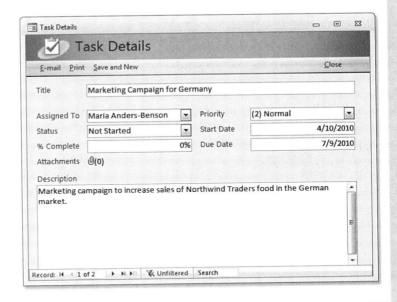

Creating the Completed Conditional Expression Block

Conforming the % Complete field value to 1, which corresponds to 100 %, for the Completed Status value and 0 for the Not Started value requires two conditional macro blocks. To create the first (Completed) macro block, do the following:

1. In the Navigation pane, right-click the Tasks table and select Design View to activate the Table Tools – Design ribbon.

2. Click the Fields, Records, and Table Events group's Create Data Macros button.

3. Click the After Update button to open the macro builder for the Tasks table.

4. Double-click the If icon of the Program Flow group to add an If conditional block to the builder.

5. Select the If block and click the Builder button to open the Expression Builder dialog.

6. Select the Tasks table icon in the Expression Builder's Expression Elements list to list its Expression Categories, double-click Status to add [Status] to the Builder's text box and append = **"Completed"** as shown in Figure 20.4.

> **note**
>
> If the selected table has one or more data macros, the gallery's Before... or After... icon(s) for the macro(s) will be highlighted. Selecting a highlighted icon will display the macro in the Macro Builder.

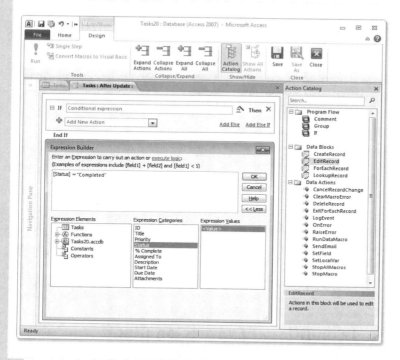

Figure 20.4
The Expression Builder will set the Conditional Expression to [Status] = Completed when you click the OK button.

7. Click OK to close the Expression Builder dialog and add the expression to and select the If block.

8. Open the Add New Action list to display the Actions applicable to the If conditional expression group, as shown in Figure 20.5.

9. You must edit the % Completed field of the current Tasks record, so select the Edit Record Data Block, which adds an Alias text box Add New Action list. Leave the Alias text box empty because the record to be edited is in the same (Tasks) table.

10. Open the Edit Record block's Add New Action list and select Set Field to enable editing the % Completed field, as shown in Figure 20.6.

 note

Data macros can't process fields of Attachment or multivalued data types.

Figure 20.5
The Add New Action list includes the Program Flow, Data Blocks, and Data Actions appropriate to the selected If conditional expression.

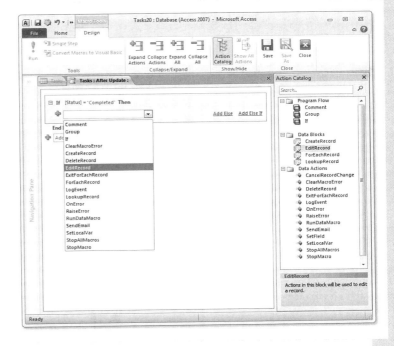

Figure 20.6
The Set Field Data Action is required to conform the % Complete value with the Status field's Complete and Not Started values.

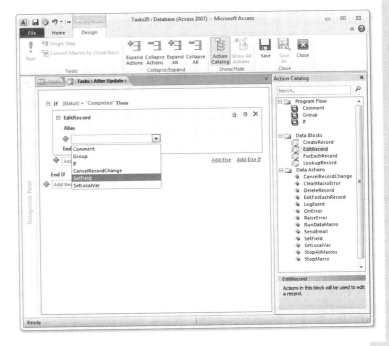

11. Use the Expression Builder to enter or type **[% Complete]** in the Name text box and **1** as the field value to set in the Value text box (see Figure 20.7).

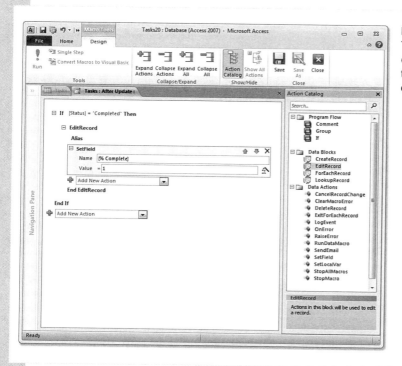

Figure 20.7
The Completed conditional expression's Edit Record block takes these Name and Value entries.

This completes the If conditional expression block for the first comparison.

Finishing with the Not Started Conditional Expression Block

Evaluating an Else If condition is slightly more efficient than a separate If block when multiple conditions are mutually exclusive, so following these steps to complete the macro with an Else If block:

1. Click to select the If condition block and click the Add Else If link to add an Else If block below the If condition block.

2. Repeat the preceding section's steps 5 and 6, except append = "Not Started in step 6."

3. Repeat steps 7 through 11, except set **0** as the field value to set in the Value text box as shown in Figure 20.8.

Figure 20.8
The second conditional expression for a Status value of Not Started is almost identical to that of the first expression for Completed.

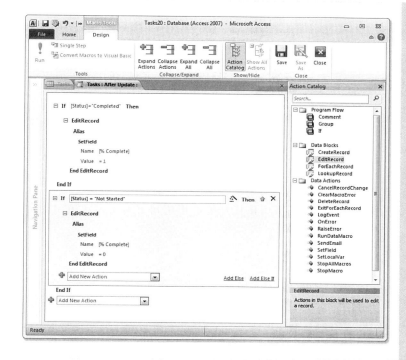

4. Right-click an empty area of the Macro Builder, press Ctrl+A to select all macro elements, press Ctrl+C, open Notepad and press Ctrl+V to paste the following XML representation of the data macro to Notepad for reuse:

```xml
<?xml version="1.0" encoding="UTF-16" standalone="no"?>
  <DataMacros xmlns="http://schemas.microsoft.com/office/accessservices/2009/11/applica-
  tion">
    <DataMacro Event="AfterUpdate">
      <Statements>
        <ConditionalBlock>
          <If>
            <Condition>[Status]="Completed"</Condition>
            <Statements>
              <EditRecord>
                <Data/>
                <Statements>
                  <Action Name="SetField">
                    <Argument Name="Field">[% Complete]</Argument>
                    <Argument Name="Value">1</Argument>
                  </Action>
```

```
            </Statements>
          </EditRecord>
        </Statements>
      </If>
      <ElseIf>
        <Condition>[Status]="Not Started"</Condition>
        <Statements>
          <EditRecord>
            <Data/>
            <Statements>
              <Action Name="SetField">
                <Argument Name="Field">[% Complete]</Argument>
                <Argument Name="Value">0</Argument>
              </Action>
            </Statements>
          </EditRecord>
        </Statements>
      </ElseIf>
    </ConditionalBlock>
  </Statements>
</DataMacro>
</DataMacros>
```

5. 🖫 ☒ Click Save and Close to close the Macro Builder and return to Table Design view.

6. ▦ Click Datasheet view, and click Yes when asked if you want to save the design changes.

> **⊷ tip**
>
> If you want to view the XML file formatted by Internet Explorers XML style sheet, change the XML declaration's encoding="UTF-16" attribute value to encoding="UTF-8" and save the file as **TasksDataMacro1.xml** with the UTF-8 file type. Otherwise save it with the Unicode file type. Before pasting file contents encoded as UTF-8 from Notepad into the Macro builder, change encoding="UTF-8" to encoding="UTF-16" temporarily.

Testing the Initial Data Macro Design

To verify that the new data macro behaves as expected, follow these steps:

1. ▤ Click the Home tab and open the Task Details form with one of the Tasks records you added earlier active, which should have the default Not Started Status value and 0 default % Complete value.

2. Open the Status list, select Completed, click the Next and Previous record navigation buttons to save the change and verify the % Complete value is 100. If you have the Home window's Status Bar visible, you see a "New Application Errors" message at the bottom of the window (see Figure 20.9).

3. Repeat step 2, but Select Not Started, and verify that the % Complete value is 0.

4. Close the Task Details form, click the File tab to open the Backstage window and click the Info tab, which displays a red Application Log message and a View Application Log Table button (see Figure 20.10).

Figure 20.9
The main form's status bar contains a "New Application Errors" message if an operation encounters a macro execution error.

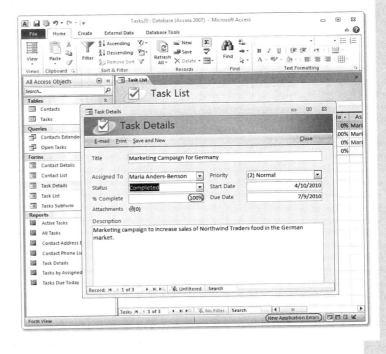

Figure 20.10
The Backstage window's Info page displays this Application Log message after the database's first macro execution error occurs.

5. Click the View Application Log Table button to display the USysApplicationLog file in Datasheet View, as shown in Figure 20.11.

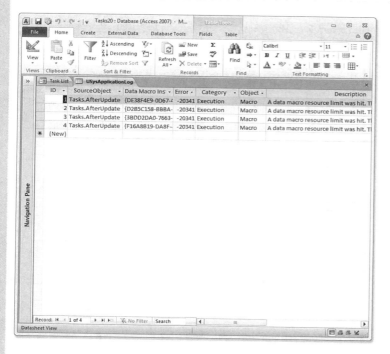

Figure 20.11
Each macro execution error adds a record to the USysApplicationLog file. The four records shown here are for two Status changes to two Tasks records.

The Description field explains Error Number -20341 in the EditRecord Context as follows:

A data macro resource limit was hit. This may be caused by a data macro recursively calling itself. The Updated(<Field>) function may be used to detect which field in a record has been updated to help prevent recursive calls.

In this case, recursion results from the data macro updating the % Complete field in response to an update of the Status field. The following sections describe how to use the Updated("*FieldName*") function to eliminate the error and how to log data macro actions in the USysApplicationLog file with the LogEvent data action.

 note

Data macros are limited to 10 levels of recursion.

This section's macro execution errors were created deliberately to create the USysApplicationLog table and display the Application Log message in the Backstage window's Info dialog.

Eliminating Macro Recursion Errors

Removing recursive updates requires adding an additional condition to the If and Else If conditional blocks that prevents executing the EditRecord data block for changes to fields other than Status.

Although you could nest another If Updated("Status")=True Then ... End If block within the two existing conditional blocks, the simpler approach is to add an And Updated("Status")=True condition to each. To create these two compound conditions, do the following:

1. Open the Tasks table in Design view, click the Table Tools–Design tab, click the Create Data Macros button and click the After Update icon to open the data macro in the Macro Builder.

2. Select the [Status]="Completed" condition and click the Builder button to open the Expression builder with [Status]="Completed" in its text box.

3. Click to expand the Functions node, click Built-In Functions to populate the Expression Categories list, and click Inspection to display its syntax below the list boxes.

4. Append **And Updated("Status")=True** to the original expression, as shown in Figure 20.12.

 note

Clicking the Updated(fieldname) link opens the Access Developer Help and How To page, not the expected help topic for the Updated() function. There's no mention that the fieldname argument must be enclosed in quotation marks.

 tip

Don't double-click the highlighted Updated item in the Expression Value list. Doing that adds «Expr» Updated(«fieldname») to the text box, which requires substantial editing.

Figure 20.12
It's easier to type the additional conditional statement than to add it from the Expression Values list and then edit it.

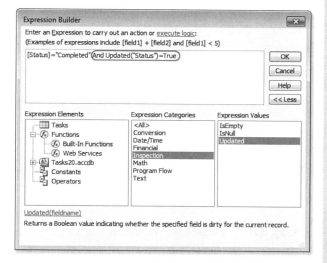

5. Repeat steps 2 through 4, except select [Status]="Not Started" condition in step 2. Alternatively, copy the added condition from the If condition and paste it into the Else If condition. Your Macro Builder appears as shown in Figure 20.13.

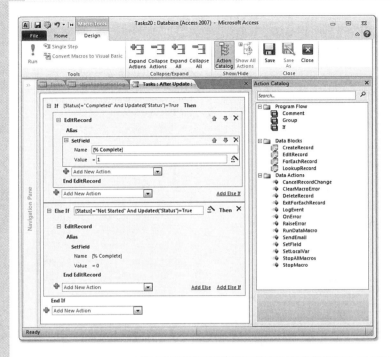

Figure 20.13
These changes to the condition arguments in the Macro Builder eliminate macro recursion errors.

5. Click Save and Close to close the Macro Builder and return to Table Design view.

6. Click Datasheet view, and click Yes when asked if you want to save the design changes.

7. Test the revised data macro with the technique described in the earlier "Testing the Initial Data Macro Design" section.

8. Verify that the "New Application Errors" message doesn't appear in the Status bar and the Backstage Info dialog displays the "Your Application Log has no new errors" message.

Logging Table Updates

As mentioned earlier in the chapter, logging table updates is essential for auditing data integrity. Data macros offer three options for logging changes to table field values:

1. Adding User records having a custom, static description String to the USysApplicationLog table with the LogEvent data action

2. Adding a dynamic description Variant value to the USysApplicationLog table

3. Creating a custom transaction log table with fields to hold before and after values and applying SetValue data actions to a CreateRecord data block.

 To review characteristics of the Variant *data type,* **see** *"The Variant Data Type in VBA,"* **p. 394.**

> **note**
>
> VBA's Variant data type is capable of holding data of any data type—such as String, Date, Time, Integer, Double and so on—and concatenating values of these data types to readable text.

Logging Static Updates to the USysApplicationLog Table

Typical string constants to describe operations performed by the data macro you created in the preceding sections might be:

- **If block**—"Tasks % Complete value changed to 100 for Status = Completed"

- **Else If block**—"Tasks % Complete value changed to 0 for Status = Not Started"

To add LogEvent data actions for the preceding, do the following:

1. Open the Tasks table in Design View, click the Table Tools – Design tab, and click the AfterUpdate button.

2. Click to select the If statement, open the Add New Action list below the End EditRecord line and select the LogEvent data action.

3. Type Tasks % Complete value changed to 100 for Status = Completed in the Description text box (see Figure 20.14).

4. Repeat steps 2 and 3, except select the End If statement in step 2 and change 100 to **0** and Completed to **Not Started** in step 3.

5. Click Save and Close to close the Macro Builder and return to Table Design view.

6. Click Datasheet view, and click Yes when asked if you want to save the design changes.

7. Test the revised data macro with the technique described in the earlier "Testing the Initial Data Macro Design" section.

8. Verify that the USysApplicationLog table contains the expected Description values with a Category field value of User (see Figure 20.15).

> **note**
>
> The [Old] identifier points to a temporary copy of the original value of the specified field, % Complete for this example. [Old] appears in IntelliSense but not in the Expression Builder lists.

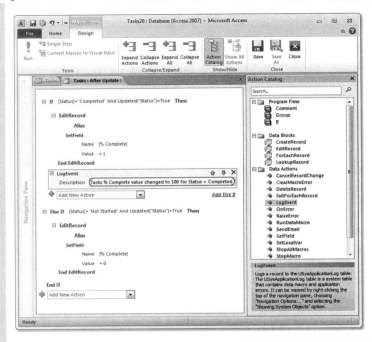

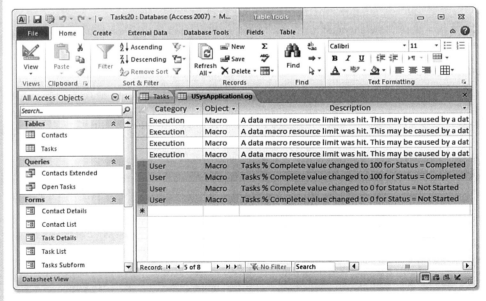

Changing to Dynamic Update Descriptions

An obvious defect with the preceding static string descriptions is failure to include the primary key value of updated record for its identification and lack of the original % Complete field value before the change. If your application requires users to log in and you save the currently logged-in UserID in a table, you should add the UserID value to the description with a reference to the appropriate field name.

Fortunately, you can substitute an expression for the Description text by typing = as the first character in the text box followed by the expression, which adds the Expression Builder icon to the control.

Replacing both instances of the LogError.Description property with ="Tasks ID " & [ID] & " % Complete value changed from " & [Old].[% Complete] & " to " & [% Complete] & " for Status = " & [Status] accomplishes the enhanced logging objectives (see Figure 20.16).

Figure 20.16
Typing = as the first character of the Description value enables using the Expression Builder to create the expression with IntelliSense.

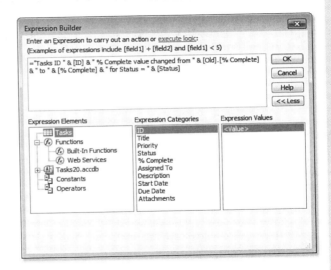

Figure 20.17 shows test results for the enhanced Description expression.

> **note**
> The data macro XML definition file for the preceding example is \Access2010\Chaptr20\ Tasks20DataMacro2.xml. Change UTF-8 to B before pasting the file's content to the Macro Builder.

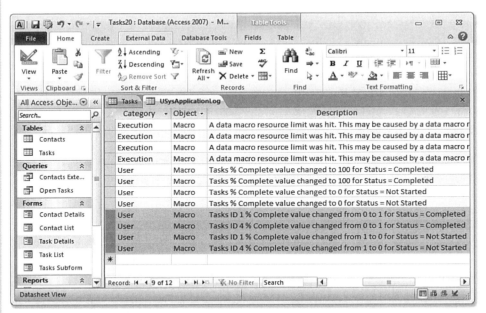

Logging Updates to a Custom Transaction Log

The alternative to narrative descriptions of table updates, as well as insertions and deletions, is to create a custom TransactionLog table with custom TableName, FieldName, UpdateType (Insert, Update or Delete), PreviousValue, NewValue, DateAndTime, and UserID (see Figure 20.18). In this case, you invoke the CreateRecord data block method to add a record to the transactions table and the SetField data action to set each field's value. All fields except DateAndTime use Access's Text data type and are required (with Allow Zero Length = No) except UserID. PreviousValue is "Null" for insertions and NewValue is "Null" for deletions.

> **note**
> The default name for a new data macro is DataMacro1. You can rename a data macro by Clicking the Save As button before the Close button.

You can invoke CreateRecord data block and the six or seven required SetField data actions within an AfterInsert, AfterUpdate, or AfterDelete data macro or run a parameterized named macro with the RunDataMacro action to execute the CreateRecord and SetField methods. Custom auditing macros are a good example of an application for named data macros, so the later "Writing a Parameterized Named Data Macro for Creating and Setting Custom Log Records" and "Invoking the Named Data Macro from an Event-Driven Data Macro" sections describe implementation of the auditing feature.

Figure 20.18
This simple
TransactionLog table
design contains the
basic information
required to audit
changes to a data-
base's tables, except
TransactionLog.

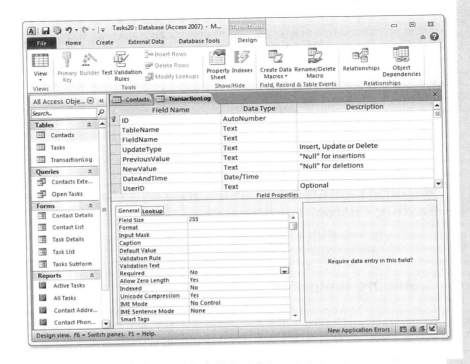

Writing and Invoking Named Data Macros

Named or "standalone" data macros are contained within and act on a specific table but not with
a specific event. You call named data macros by invoking the RunDataMacro action from any other
named or event-driven data macro or a traditional Access UI macro.

To create or edit a named data macro, do the following:

1. Open the table to contain the data macro in Design View.

2. Click the Create Data Macros button to open its gallery.

3. Click the Create Named Macro button to create a new named macro (see Figure 20.19, left)

4. Alternatively, if the Edit Named Macro button is enabled, click its right-facing arrow to display a list of existing named macros for the table and select the named macro to edit (see Figure
20.19, right).

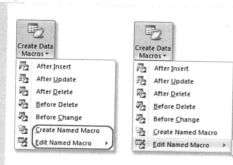

dmXactLog

Figure 20.19
Create a named macro by clicking the eponymous button (left). If the Edit Named Macro button is enabled, open its flyout submenu and select the named macro to edit (right).

Writing a Parameterized Named Data Macro for Creating and Setting Custom Log Records

Creating a named data macro involves two steps: Specifying the names and optional descriptions of input parameters and then defining the macro's programming logic.

Adding Input Parameters

In most cases, you define a set of input parameters to accept Variant data, including object references from UI macros, from the calling data or UI macro. The data can use parameter values in conditional statements or value calculations. The TransactionLog's CreateRecord statement requires definition of six input parameters. To add a parameter, do the following:

1. With the macro open in the Macro Builder window, click the Create Parameter button (link) to open Name and Description text boxes.

2. Type a parameter name, **prmTableName** for this example's first parameter of the TransactionLog's named CreateRecord macro.

3. Type optional text, **Name of table with changed field value (required)** for this example, in the Description text box (see Figure 20.20).

4. Repeat steps 1 through 3 for each parameter.

Refer to Figure 20.18 for the names of the remaining five input parameters.

> **note**
>
> **prm** is the most common prefix for macro parameters and is used for VBA parameters, also.

Figure 20.20
Name and describe the input parameters you need in the Parameters group.

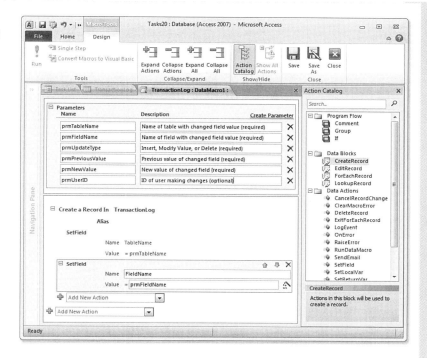

Adding the CreateRecord Data Block, SetField Actions, and Conditional Expression for the prmUserID Parameter

Completing the macro requires adding a CreateRecord Data Block to insert an empty record in the TransactionLog table, invoke the SetField action for each parameter/field value pair, and add an If ... Else If ... End If conditional expression to substitute a "Null" String value for Null-valued or zero-length prmUserID values. Follow these steps:

1. Open the Add New Action list below the Parameters group and select CreateRecord to add the Data Block to the macro.

2. Open the Create a Record In list, select TransactionLog, and leave the Alias text box empty.

3. Click the Add New Action list directly below the Create a Record In line and select the SetField action.

4. Type the field name, optionally surrounded by square brackets ([]), in the Field Name text box and the parameter name, which also takes optional square brackets, in the Value text box.

5. Repeat steps 1 through 4 for each parameter except prmUserID (see Figure 20.21).

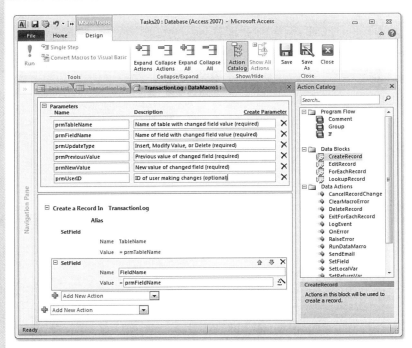

Figure 20.21
Add the second SetValue action for the FieldName field and prmFieldName parameter.

6. Click the Add New Action list directly below the SetField (NewValue, [prmNewValue]) line and select the SetField action.

7. Type **DateAndTime** in the Field Name text box and the Now() function, which returns the system date and time, in the Value text box (look ahead to Figure 20.22).

The calling macro may supply a Null or zero-length String value for the prmUserID parameter but the table design includes Required = Yes and Allow Zero Length = No constraints. Therefore, a conditional expression must supply a "Null" value for these two conditions and the prmUserID value otherwise. To add the conditional value, do the following:

Following the SetField action for the DateAndTime field, open the Add New Action list and select If.

1. Open the Expression Builder, expand the Functions node, select the Built-In Functions node, select Inspection in the Expression Categories list, double-click IsNull in the Expression Values list, and type **[prmUserID]** inside the parenthesis.

2. Add **= True** to the expression to complete the expression (see Figure 20.22), and click OK to close the dialog and return to the Macro Builder window.

3. Click the Add New Action list under the If expression and select the SetField action, type **[UserID]** in the Field Name text box and **"Null"** in the Value text box (include the parenthesis).

Figure 20.22
Add **[prmUserID]** as the value of the IsNull()
function's argument and **= True** to complete
the expression.

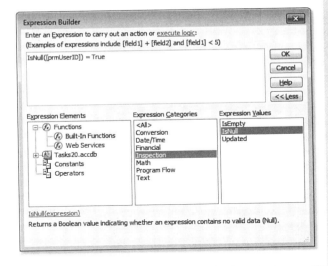

4. 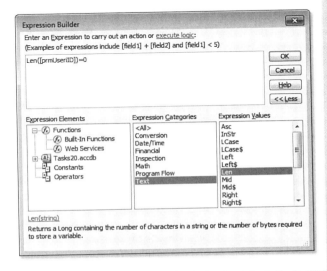 Click the Add Else If button (link), open the Expression Builder, expand the Functions node, select the Built-In functions node, select Text in the Expression Categories list, double-click Len in the Expression Values list, and type **[prmUserID]** inside the parenthesis.

5. Add **= 0** to the expression to complete the expression (see Figure 20.23), and click OK to close the dialog and return to the Macro Builder window.

Figure 20.23
Add Len([prmUseriID])=0 as the Else If condition.

6. Click the Add New Action list under the If expression and select the SetField action, type **[UserID]** in the Field Name text box and **"Null"** in the Value text box (include the parenthesis).

7. Click the Add Else button (link), click the Add New Action list under the Else expression and select the SetField action, type **[UserID]** in the Field Name text box and **[prmUserID]** in the Value text box (see Figure 20.24).

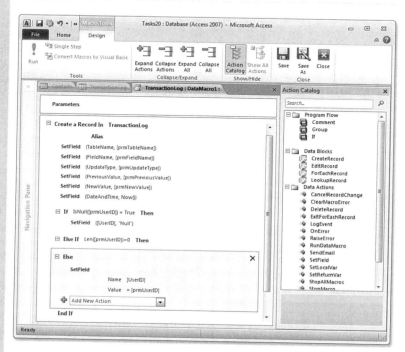

Figure 20.24
Complete the conditional expression with the Else condition for provided prmUserID value.

8. 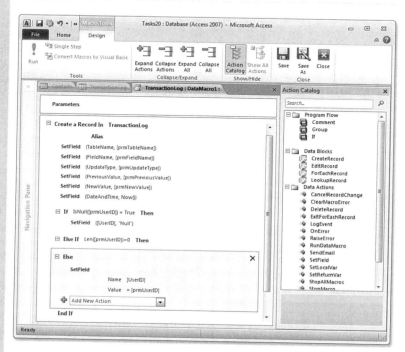 Click the Save As button to open the Save As dialog, name the macro **dmXactLog**, click OK to close the dialog, click the Close button, save changes, click the Datasheet View button, and save changes again.

Following is the XML representation of the dmXactLog:

```xml
<?xml version="1.0" encoding="UTF-16" standalone="no"?>
 <DataMacros xmlns="http://schemas.microsoft.com/office/accessservices/2009/11/applica-
tion">
   <DataMacro Name="dmXactLog">
     <Parameters>
       <Parameter Name="prmTableName"
                  Description="Name of table with changed field value (required)"/>
```

```
  <Parameter Name="prmFieldName"
            Description="Name of field with changed field value (required)"/>
  <Parameter Name="prmUpdateType"
            Description="Insert, Modify Value, or Delete (required)"/>
  <Parameter Name="prmPreviousValue"
            Description="Previous value of changed field (required)"/>
  <Parameter Name="prmNewValue"
            Description="New value of changed field (required)"/>
  <Parameter Name="prmUserID"
            Description="ID of user making changes (optional)"/>
</Parameters>
<Statements>
  <CreateRecord>
    <Data>
      <Reference>TransactionLog</Reference>
    </Data>
    <Statements>
      <Action Collapsed="true" Name="SetField">
        <Argument Name="Field">TableName</Argument>
        <Argument Name="Value">[prmTableName]</Argument>
      </Action>
      <Action Collapsed="true" Name="SetField">
        <Argument Name="Field">FieldName</Argument>
        <Argument Name="Value">[prmFieldName]</Argument>
      </Action>
      <Action Collapsed="true" Name="SetField">
        <Argument Name="Field">UpdateType</Argument>
        <Argument Name="Value">[prmUpdateType]</Argument>
      </Action>
      <Action Collapsed="true" Name="SetField">
        <Argument Name="Field">PreviousValue</Argument>
        <Argument Name="Value">[prmPreviousValue]</Argument>
      </Action>
      <Action Collapsed="true" Name="SetField">
        <Argument Name="Field">NewValue</Argument>
        <Argument Name="Value">[prmNewValue]</Argument>
      </Action><Action Collapsed="true" Name="SetField">
        <Argument Name="Field">DateAndTime</Argument>
        <Argument Name="Value">Now()</Argument>
      </Action>
      <ConditionalBlock>
        <If>
          <Condition>IsNull([prmUserID])</Condition>
          <Statements>
            <Action Collapsed="true" Name="SetField">
              <Argument Name="Field">[UserID]</Argument>
              <Argument Name="Value">"Null"</Argument>
            </Action>
          </Statements>
```

```
      </If>
      <ElseIf>
        <Condition>Len([prmUseriID])=0</Condition>
        <Statements>
          <Action Name="SetField">
            <Argument Name="Field">[UserID]</Argument>
            <Argument Name="Value">"Null"</Argument>
          </Action>
        </Statements>
      </ElseIf>
      <Else>
        <Statements>
          <Action Collapsed="true" Name="SetField">
            <Argument Name="Field">[UserID]</Argument>
            <Argument Name="Value">[prmUserID]</Argument>
          </Action>
        </Statements>
      </Else>
    </ConditionalBlock>
    </Statements>
    </CreateRecord>
    </Statements>
  </DataMacro>
</DataMacros>
```

Testing the dmXactLog macro requires invoking it with appropriate parameter values, which you perform in this chapter's final sections.

 note

The preceding XML data macro definition is available as \Access2010\Chaptr20\ XactLog20NamedDataMacro1.xml. Remember to change the UTF-16 attribute value to UTF-8 before opening the file in Internet Explorer.

Invoking the Named Data Macro from an Event-Driven Data Macro

The most straightforward approach to exercising the TransactionLog.dmXactLog named macro for updates is to create an If Updated([*FieldName*]) = True ... End If conditional expression for each field name. The If expression invokes a RunDataMacro action with the appropriate set of five or six output parameters. Although this approach creates a lengthy macro, you can copy, paste, and edit the required expressions quickly, as described in the next section.

Insertions and deletions affect all fields, so these data macros require unconditional execution of RunDataMacro actions for all fields.

 tip

A single After Update event can involve updates to several fields, which requires using a sequence of conditional If ... End If blocks rather than the If ...Else If...End If structures of the preceding examples. If you add Else If... conditional structures and the update contains more than one modified field, the macro logs only the change to the first modified field in the sequence.

All logging examples use the Tasks database's Contacts table as the invoking data macro's container. It's assumed that you previously populated this table from Outlook contacts from the Northwind Customers table or another source of compatible data. After testing the version for After Update events, you copy the macro instructions to newly created After Insert and After Delete event macros and edit the instructions as needed.

Copying, Pasting and Editing Conditional Blocks to Create the Test Data Macro

To run initial tests of the dmXactLog data macro with an After Update macro for a few Contacts table fields, do the following:

1. For this example, open the Customers table to contain the data macro in Design View.

2. Click the Create Data Macros button to open its gallery.

3. Click the After Update button to create a new event macro.

4. Double-click the If program flow element to add a conditional block.

5. Type **Updated("Company")=True** in the If condition text box for the first field.

6. Open the If statement's Add Macro Action list, select Run Data Macro, open the Macro Name list, which includes items for all macros in the database, and select TransactionLog.dmXactLog to open a Parameters group with items for each of the named macro's six parameters.

7. Type **"Contacts"** as the prmTableName value, **"Company"** as the prmFiledName value, **"Update"** as the prmUpdateType value, **[Old].[Company]** as the prmPreviousValue value, **[Company]** as the prmNewValue value and, optionally, your initials as the prmUserID value (see Figure 20.25).

8. Click Save, click Close, save your changes, click Datasheet view, and save changes to the Contacts table.

9. Make a change to one of the company names, such as Eastern Connection to Eastern Connection**s** and change the record pointer or click the Records group's Save button.

10. Open the TransactionLog table in Datasheet view, and press F5 or click the Records group's Refresh All button to display the added record (see Figure 20.26).

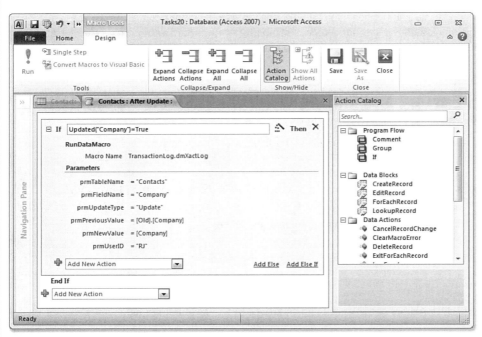

Figure 20.25
The initial (Company) field's conditional expression and template for the remaining fields' expressions.

Figure 20.26
Changing Eastern Connection's Companyname value to Eastern Connections adds this record to the TransactionLog table.

To clone the Company If block to a Last Name If block, as well as the other remaining fields, do the following:

1. Click the If button (link) and type **Updated("FieldName")=True** in the condition text box for the successive field.

2. Select the preceding RunDataMacro section and press Ctrl+C to copy its XML definition to the Clipboard.

3. Select the If section and press Ctrl+V to paste the cloned RunDataMacro section to the section.

4. Replace the value of prmFieldName with "FieldName", prmPreviousValue with **[Old].** [FieldName], and prmNewValue with [FieldName].

5. Repeat steps 1 through 4 for each remaining field (see Figure 20.27).

Figure 20.27
The first and part of the second clones—Last Name and First Name—of the Company RunDataMacro section.

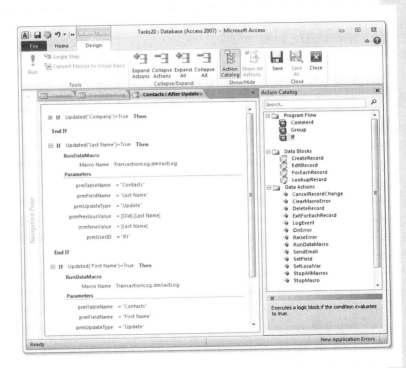

6. Test a change to the *FieldName* values with steps 8 and 9 of the previous procedure after adding changes to field values for each of the clones added (see Figure 20.28).

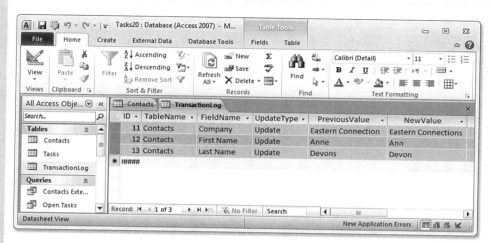

Figure 20.28
TransactionLog records for a single After Update action with changes to the Company, Last Name, and First Name fields.

Following is the XML definition file's content for a partially completed After Update data macro:

```xml
<?xml version="1.0" encoding="UTF-16" standalone="no"?>
<DataMacros xmlns="http://schemas.microsoft.com/office/accessservices/2009/11/applica-
tion">
  <DataMacro Event="AfterUpdate">
    <Statements>
      <ConditionalBlock>
        <If Collapsed="true">
          <Condition>Updated("Company")=True</Condition>
          <Statements>
            <Action Name="RunDataMacro">
              <Argument Name="MacroName">TransactionLog.dmXactLog</Argument>
              <Parameters>
                <Parameter Name="prmTableName"
                           Value="&quot;Contacts&quot;"/>
                <Parameter Name="prmFieldName"
                           Value="&quot;Company&quot;"/>
                <Parameter Name="prmUpdateType"
                           Value="&quot;Update&quot;"/>
                <Parameter Name="prmPreviousValue"
                           Value="[Old].[Company]"/>
                <Parameter Name="prmNewValue"
                           Value="[Company]"/>
                <Parameter Name="prmUserID"
                           Value="&quot;RJ&quot;"/>
```

```
          </Parameters>
        </Action>
      </Statements>
    </If>
</ConditionalBlock>
<ConditionalBlock>
  <If Collapsed="true">
    <Condition>Updated("Last Name")=True</Condition>
    <Statements>
      <Action Name="RunDataMacro">
        <Argument Name="MacroName">TransactionLog.dmXactLog</Argument>
        <Parameters>
          <Parameter Name="prmTableName"
                     Value="&quot;Contacts&quot;"/>
          <Parameter Name="prmFieldName"
                     Value="&quot;Last Name&quot;"/>
          <Parameter Name="prmUpdateType"
                     Value="&quot;Update&quot;"/>
          <Parameter Name="prmPreviousValue"
                     Value="[Old].[Last Name]"/>
          <Parameter Name="prmNewValue"
                     Value="[Last Name]"/>
          <Parameter Name="prmUserID"
                    Value="&quot;RJ&quot;"/>
        </Parameters>
      </Action>
    </Statements>
  </If>
</ConditionalBlock>
<ConditionalBlock>
  <If Collapsed="true">
    <Condition>Updated("First Name")=True</Condition>
    <Statements>
      <Action Name="RunDataMacro">
        <Argument Name="MacroName">TransactionLog.dmXactLog</Argument>
        <Parameters>
          <Parameter Name="prmTableName"
                     Value="&quot;Contacts&quot;"/>
          <Parameter Name="prmFieldName"
                     Value="&quot;First Name&quot;"/>
          <Parameter Name="prmUpdateType"
                     Value="&quot;Update&quot;"/>
          <Parameter Name="prmPreviousValue"
                     Value="[Old].[First Name]"/>
```

```
                    <Parameter Name="prmNewValue"
                                Value="[First Name]"/>
                    <Parameter Name="prmUserID"
                                Value="&quot;RJ&quot;"/>
                </Parameters>
            </Action>
        </Statements>
      </If>
    </ConditionalBlock>
    <Comment>Additional If ... End If blocks here</Comment>
  </Statements>
</DataMacro>
</DataMacros>
```

The preceding file is available as \Access2010\Chaptr20\Contacts20DataMacro1.xml.

Logging the Contacts Table's After Insert Event

The After Insert data macro is the same as the After Update data macro, except as follows:

- No If ... End If conditional blocks are used.
- The value of all UpdateType fields is ""Insert"".
- The value of all PreviousValue fields is ""Null""

Copying the individual RunDataMacro blocks from the After Update data macro to XML definition data in Notepad, pasting the XML to the After Insert data macro and editing the UpdateType and PreviousValue values is the fastest method for creating this macro.

 tip

Alternatively, edit the After Update event's complete XML definition file by removing `<ConditionalBlock>`, `</ConditionalBlock>`, `<If Collapsed="true">`, `</If>` and intermediate `<Statements>` and `</Statements>` elements. Then copy the edited content to an empty Macro Builder window.

If you have many fields, you can use Notepad's Edit, Replace feature to handle the UpdateType changes.

Change the `encoding` attribute value from UTF-16 to UTF-8 and open the edited file in Internet Explorer to confirm that the XML content remains well-formed after editing.

Figure 20.29 shows the first three RunDataMacro statements of the After Insert data macro XML definition file (\Access2010\Chaptr20\Contacts20DataMacro2.xml) open in Internet Explorer.

Figure 20.30 highlights the three field values logged for an After Insert operation.

Figure 20.29
The After Insert
data macro's
XML definition
field opened
in Internet
Explorer to
verify that it's
well-formed.

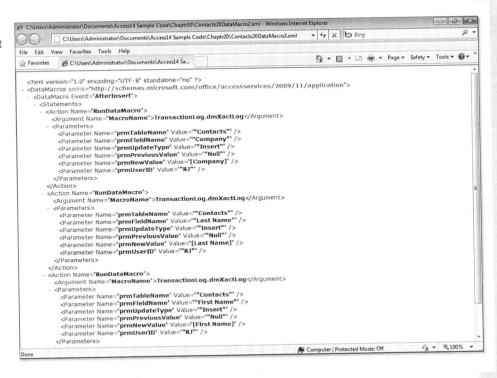

Figure 20.30
TransactionLog
records for a
single After
Insert action
with values for
the Company,
Last Name,
and First Name
fields only.

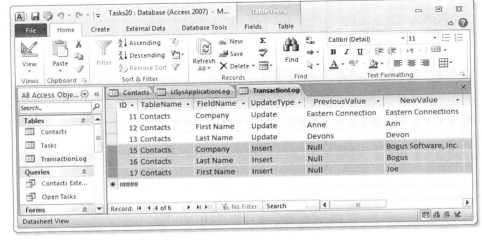

Logging the Contacts Table's After Delete Event

The After Delete data macro is the same as the After Update data macro, except as follows:

- No If ... End If conditional blocks are used.

- The value of all UpdateType fields is ""Delete"".

- The value of all NewValue fields is ""Null"".

Figure 20.31 shows the first three RunDataMacro statements of the After Delete data macro XML definition file (\Access2010\Chaptr20\Contacts20DataMacro3.xml) open in Internet Explorer.

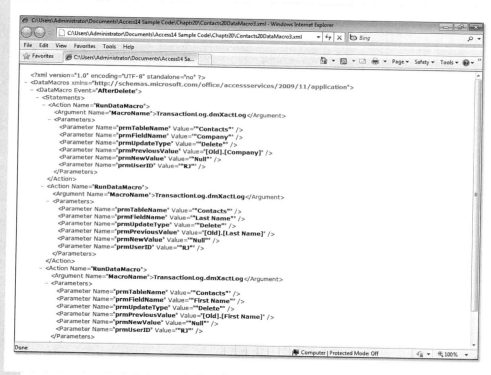

Figure 20.31
The After Delete data macro's XML definition field opened in Internet Explorer.

Figure 20.32 highlights the three field values logged for an After Delete operation.

Figure 20.32
TransactionLog
records for a
single After
Delete action
with values for
the Company,
Last Name,
and First Name
fields only.

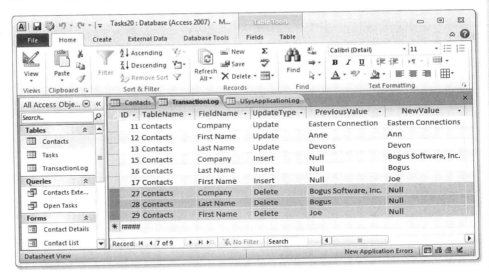

21

LINKING ACCESS FRONT ENDS TO ACCESS AND CLIENT/SERVER TABLES

A single .accdb file that contains Access *application objects* (forms, reports, macros, and VBA code modules) and Access *data objects* (tables and queries) is one of Access's strongest selling points. Other desktop database management applications—such as Visual FoxPro and Visual Basic—require multiple files for a single database application. The obvious advantage of a single .accdb file for a complete Access application is simplicity. You can deploy your application by copying its .accdb file to another computer that has Access 2010 installed.

Sharing your Access application with other users in a Windows XP/Vista/7 workgroup, or Windows Server 2003 or later domain, requires separating the application objects from database objects. It's *theoretically* possible for multiple users to simultaneously share a single .accdb application on a network or use the Terminal Services feature of Windows Server 2003 or later to run multiple instances of the application. In practice, however, application response time and network traffic issues make the single .accdb approach impractical for all but the simplest database projects. Another disadvantage of the single .accdb approach is that making changes to any Access query, form, or report object by opening it in design mode prevents all other users from interacting with the object.

 note

An SQL Server instance is simply an installation of the server software. A single computer can host multiple SQL Server instances, each of which has its own *named instance*. For example, the default instance name of an SSX named instance is *\ComputerName*\SQLEXPRESS in SQL Server 2005 and 2008, and \ComputerName\SQLExpress in SQL Server 2008 R2. Instance names aren't case-sensitive.

note

The following sections describe creating and securing back-end databases shared by a 32-bit or 64-bit Windows Server 2003 or later domain controller or member server. 64-bit Windows Server 2008 R2 is used for the examples because that operating system supports Windows SharePoint Foundation 2010 (WSF 2010, formerly Windows SharePoint Services, WSS, 3.0) and Windows SharePoint Server (WSS 2010, formerly Microsoft Office SharePoint Server, MOSS, 2007), which are likely to be accessible to users of Access 2010. The process for sharing files with a Windows Vista or XP Professional workgroup member is similar to that for an Active Directory domain, but the share and file security settings differ. The examples assume that you're familiar with creating file shares, have an administrative account for the server, and know how to manage Windows Vista/XP/7 users and security groups.

 note

Alternatives to separating Access application and database objects are exporting Access tables to SharePoint Foundation 2010 and linking them to the application objects or exporting all Access objects to a Web Database hosted by SharePoint Server 2010 with Access Services. Chapter 22, "Collaborating with SharePoint Foundation 2010," and Chapter 23, "Sharing Web Databases with SharePoint 2010 Server," cover these two approaches.

Separating Tables from Access Front-End Objects

Making your Access application accessible to more than one user at a time requires dividing the application into *front-end* and *back-end* components. For Access databases, the front end contains all application elements plus queries; the back end contains only Access tables. If you use the Upsizing Wizard and choose to link your Access application to the Microsoft SQL Server 2008 R2 or earlier Standard or Express Edition (SSX), SQL Server tables replace Access tables. The linking process for Access tables is similar to that for linking dBASE files; linking SSX tables uses the Open Database Connectivity (ODBC) driver.

 To review the table linking process for dBASE files, **see** *"Linking and Importing External ISAM Tables,"* **p. 324.**

 note

Sections later in the chapter cover linking to SQL Server 2008 [R2] Express, Developer, Workgroup, Standard, and Enterprise editions, Microsoft Desktop Engine (MSDE) 2000, and the four SQL Server 2000 editions—Personal, Developer, Standard, and Enterprise. This chapter uses *SQL Server* to refer to any SQL Server 2000 or later edition, except when discussing features that are specific to SSX.

Chapter 26, "Exploring Access Data Projects and SQL Server 2005," and Chapter 28, "Upsizing Access Applications to Access Data Projects," describe Access data projects (ADP). ADP connect directly to SQL Server tables, and Access queries become back-end SQL Server views, functions, or stored procedures.

Multiuser Access applications usually require that each user have a copy of the front-end .accdb file and network access to the back-end .accdb file or an SQL Server *instance*. Alternatively, users can run multiple front-end Terminal Server sessions. You can share Access back ends in a peer-to-peer Windows XP/Vista/7 workgroup environment or within a Windows Server 2003 or later Active

Directory domain. A single front end can link to multiple back ends. Providing network access to SSX in a Windows XP/Vista/7 workgroup environment requires modifying SSX's security settings. For workgroups, linked tables in Access back ends are simpler to implement.

Creating Linked Access Tables with the Database Splitter

You use the Database Splitter utility to create a conventional multiuser Access/Access application from a copy of the application's single .accdb file. The Database Splitter automatically creates a new .accdb file for the tables, moves the tables from the front-end to the back-end .accdb file, and creates individual table links between the two files.

Take the following steps to create and link the back-end database to the front-end application objects:

1. If the computer on which you're running Access 2010 has a network connection to a server or another workstation, create a share on the server or another workstation in your workgroup to store the back-end .accdb file. The server or other workstation doesn't need to have Office 2010 installed to share the back-end file. Otherwise, add a new folder to store the shared back-end .accdb file on your client machine.

2. If you're splitting a production database, create and use a copy of the database. This example uses a copy of the Northwind.accdb sample database named NWClient.accdb, which you'll find in the \Access2010\Chaptr21 folder.

3. Open the Access database to split, click the Database Tools tab, and click the Move Data group's Access Database button to open the utility's first and only dialog (see Figure 21.1).

Figure 21.1
The Database Splitter utility has only a single dialog.

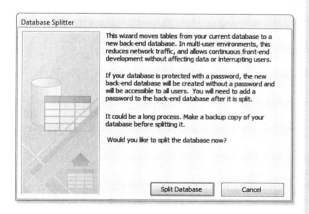

4. Click the Split Database button to open the Create Back-End Database dialog. The default name of the back-end .accdb is the front-end name with a _be suffix. Change the name to whatever you want; this example uses NWData.accdb as the name.

5. Navigate to the server share (or local folder, if you're not using a network server). This example uses the Northwind share on the WINSVR2008SP2VM Windows 2008 SP2 member server in the OAKLEAF domain (\\WINSVR2008SP2VM\Northwind), which also runs an SQL Server Express 2008 R2 instance and hosts SharePoint Foundation 2010 (see Figure 21.2).

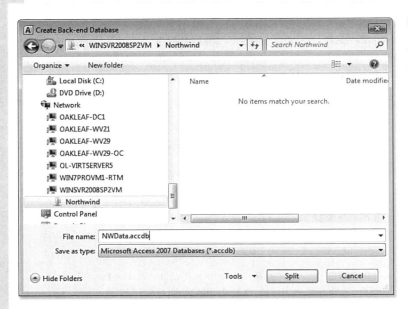

Figure 21.2
Specify a share on a workstation or server in your Windows Server 2003 or later domain or another workstation in your Windows XP/Vista/7 workgroup.

6. Click the Split Button to create the new back-end database and move the tables to it. Click OK to acknowledge the completion message. The links to the back-end tables appear in the front-end application, as shown in Figure 21.3.

7. Verify that the linked tables are operational by opening each table in sequence and navigating to the last record to ensure that the tables are updatable.

8. Open one of the tables in Design view. You receive a message that some properties of linked tables can't be modified in Design view. Click Yes and then click the Properties button to open the Table Properties window. The Description property value defines the link to the back-end .accdb file (see Figure 21.4).

9. Run a few queries, and open the forms and reports to verify that the application objects behave as expected with the linked tables.

tip

Assigning the Uniform Naming Convention (UNC) name—//*SERVERNAME*/*ShareName*—to connect to the server share is a better practice than allocating a local logical drive letter to the share. Users can delete or change the drive letter assignment. Converting the front end to the .accde format prevents users from changing the UNC link to the back-end file with the Linked Table Manager.

Figure 21.3
The table icons of the Database window gain an arrow to indicate that they're linked to the back-end .accdb file.

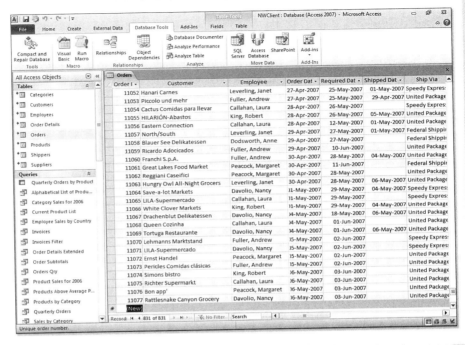

Figure 21.4
The Description property value of the linked table contains the linking information.

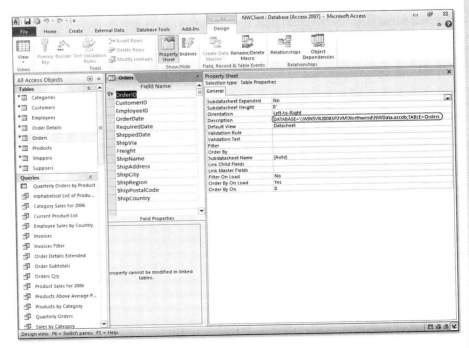

Establishing Network Share, Folder, and File Security for the Back End

The first step after you share a back-end database is to set share, folder, and file permissions on the .accdb file. If ordinary network users have Full Control permissions of the share and file, your back-end database is vulnerable to deletion, copying, or moving by any network user who has access to the server. Removal from Access 2010 of Access 2003 and earlier's user- and group-level security features means that network share, folder, and file-level security is your only defense against unauthorized users gaining access to your back-end database file, the data in the file, or both.

By default, the share, folder, and files you create as a network administrator inherit permissions assigned to the parent drive or folder. Windows 2000's default share permissions give the Everyone group Full Control; Windows Server 2003 domains assign Read share permissions to the Everyone group. This section's examples assume that the Everyone group has no default or inherited permissions for the share or the back-end .accdb file.

All users of your front-end application need Read permissions for the share, and Read, Write, Create, and Delete permissions for the folder. These permissions enable the first user to create the .laccdb locking file (NWData.laccdb for this example) when opening the .accdb file during login and the last user to delete the file when logging off the application.

 note

The locking file contains the computer name and Access security name—typically Admin—of each person who has an active link to the back-end .accdb file. This file can contain up to 255 records, which is Access's limit for concurrent database users.

You can assign permissions to security groups or users; this example assigns permissions to two security groups in the `oakleaf.org` Windows 2003 domain: NWReaders and NWWriters. You then assign an NWReader1 user to NWReaders and an NWWriter1 account to the NWReaders and NWWriters groups. Table 21.1 shows the permissions required by the NWReaders and NWWriters groups. You must remove the default Users and Domain Users security groups to prevent ordinary users from accessing the folder or its files.

Table 21.1 These Permissions Are Required to Authorize Security Groups to Enable Read or Read/Write Access to Back-End Data Files on a Windows Server 2003 Share

Group	Share	Folder	Back-End .accdb File
Domain Users	(Removed)	(Removed)	(Removed)
Users	(Removed)	(Removed)	(Removed)
NWReaders	Read	Read & Execute	Read
NWReaders	Change	Create Files / Write Data, Delete Subfolders and Files	
NWWriters			Write

Following are the steps required to secure the Northwind network share, Northwind folder, and the NWData.accdb file:

1. Log on to the server with an account that has Administrator privileges.

2. In Explorer, right-click the shared folder (Northwind) and choose properties to open the *FolderName* Properties dialog. Click the Sharing tab, and then click the Permissions button to open the Permissions for *ShareName* dialog.

3. If it's present, select the Everyone security group in the Name list and click Remove.

note

The following procedure assumes that you have or a domain administrator has used Active Directory Users and Computers to add the NWReaders security group and added the NWReader1 and NWReader1 account to it, as well as the NWWriters security group with the NWWriter1 account.

4. Click Add to open the Select Users, Computers, or Groups dialog, and type the name(s) of the users or groups to add in the text box, separated by semicolon, and click the Check Names button to verify your spelling (see Figure 21.5).

Figure 21.5
Type the groups or users to add in the Select Users, Computers, or Groups dialog. If the names (NWReaders and NWWriters groups for this example) are present in Active Directory, clicking the Check Names button underlines them.

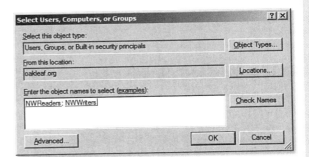

5. Click OK to add the groups or users to the Name list, and then grant them Read and Change permissions (see Figure 21.6). You need Change permissions for the share to enable all users in the designated groups to create and delete the .ldb file. Click OK to close the Permissions dialog.

6. Click the Security tab. If the Users group has been added to the Group or User Names list, click Advanced to open the Advanced Security Settings for *ShareName* dialog, clear the Allow Inherited Permissions from the Parent to This Object and All Child Objects check box, and click OK to open the Security message box (see Figure 21.7). Click Copy to copy all inherited Users permissions; then click OK again to close the dialog. On the Security page, select Users and click Remove.

7. Add the groups or users to the folder Permissions list and grant them Read & Execute permission, which enables List Folder Contents and Read permissions. Grant the read/write group or users Write permission (look ahead to Figure 21.9).

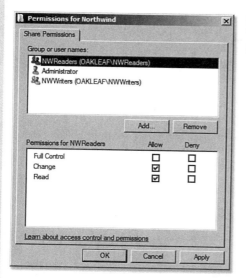

Figure 21.6
You must grant specific Access groups or users Read and Change permissions for the share.

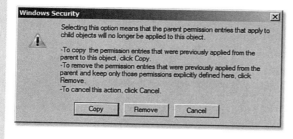

Figure 21.7
To prevent ordinary domain users from gaining access to the back-end database file, you must remove inherited permissions, if any, and then remove the Users group from the folder's Group or User Names list.

8. Click Advanced to open the Advanced Security Settings dialog, select the read-only group or user name in the list, and click Edit to open the Permission Entry for *GroupName* dialog and mark the Create Files/Write Data and Delete Subfolders and Files check boxes to enable the users or groups to open and close .laccdb files (see Figure 21.8). (Previous permission settings marked the other check boxes.)

9. Click OK twice to save your permission changes, close the Permission Entry for *ShareName* and Advanced Security Settings for *ShareName* dialogs, and return to the *ShareName* Properties dialog (see Figure 21.9).

Figure 21.8
Access users or groups must have Create Files/ Write Data and Delete Subfolders and Files permissions to add and delete the .laccdb locking file in the shared folder, even if they don't have Write permissions.

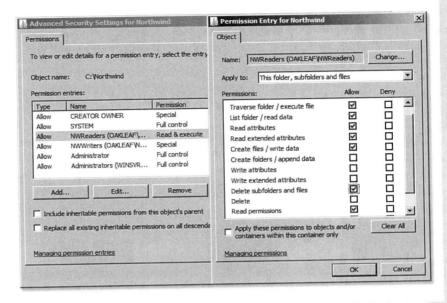

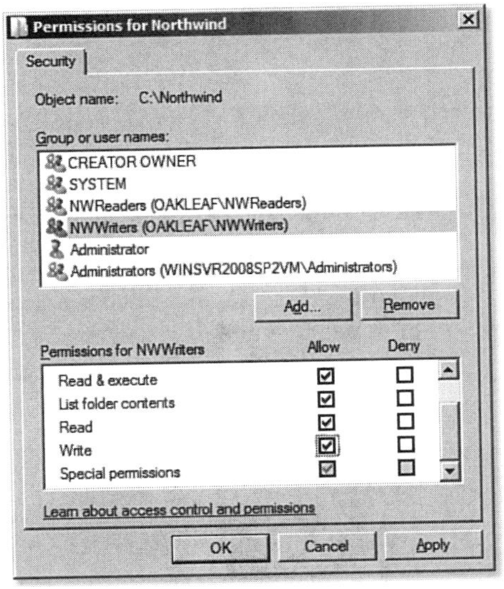

Figure 21.9
Read-write users or groups must have folder Write, as well as Read & Execute, List Folder Content, and Read permissions. For this example, in which read-write users are members of the NWReaders and NWWriters groups, it isn't necessary to add Read & Execute permissions for the NWWriters group.

10. Click OK to close the *ShareName* properties dialog, right-click the back-end data .accdb file, choose Properties to open the *FileName* Properties dialog, and click the Security tab. Verify that read-only users or groups have inherited the permissions Read & Execute, Read, and Special Permissions, and that read-write users or groups have these and Write permissions (see Figure 21.10).

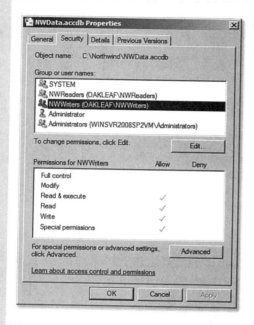

Figure 21.10
Users or groups inherit file permissions from the folder permissions you set.

11. Click OK to accept the file permissions and close the Security dialog.

Your back-end database files are now secured against access or updates by unauthorized users and inadvertent or intentional deletion or modification by non-administrators.

Verifying Back-End Database Network Security

It's a good practice to verify that your security settings work by following these steps:

> **note**
>
> The preceding steps may differ slightly, depending on the Windows Server version you use. However, the permissions shown in Figures 21.8 and 21.9 should be identical for Windows Server 2003 through 2008 R2.

1. Log off the server and log on to the client with the read/write account (NWWriter1 for this example), launch Access, and open the front-end .accdb file (NWClient.accdb).

2. Open a table and verify that the tentative append record is present, which verifies that the back-end database is read/write for this user (see Figure 21.11).

Figure 21.11
NWWriters members open the front-end .accdb file and see the Security Warning and Read-Only messages, as well as a tentative append record for tables they open.

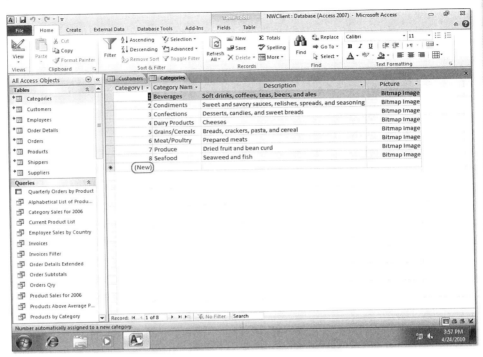

3. Log off and log on with the read-only account (NWReader1) and launch Access.

4. Open a table in the front-end client and verify that the tentative append record is missing, which confirms that back-end data isn't updatable. Attempts to edit table data also fail.

5. Finally, log off and log on with an account that's a member of the Domain Users or Users group but doesn't have permissions for the back-end share or file.

6. Attempt to open a table in the front-end client. You receive a message that the table is locked by another user or you need permission to view the data (see Figure 21.12).

Figure 21.12
Users who don't have read or write permissions for the back-end data field (NWData.accdb) receive this error message when they attempt to open a table.

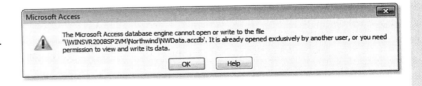

Shared Access back-end databases are satisfactory for Access multiuser applications that support up to about 25 concurrent users, with five or fewer making simultaneous data changes. In this case, you can skip the following sections about SQL Server and implement password security for your front end. If your application involves heavy-duty online transaction processing (OLTP) or the data is vital to the economic survival of your organization, you should consider linking to an SQL Server back end or migrating to Access data projects (ADP), which connect directly to SQL Server tables.

 caution

After you split a database, Access 2010's File, Save & Publish, Back Up Database button on the Backstage menu backs up the front end only. Unless you have automated nightly backup for the server or workstation that shares the back-end data, you must back up the data .accdb file manually. Backing up the .accdb file requires administrative access to the server or workstation.

Evaluating the Benefits of Migrating to Client/Server Databases

Modern client/server databases, typified by Microsoft SQL Server 2008 R2, provide a much more *reliable* and *scalable* data storage environment than shared-file databases, such as Access. The vast majority of production databases used by all but very small organizations follow the client/server model. Oracle currently claims the lion's share of the client/server relational database management system (RDBMS) business, but IBM, Microsoft, and Sybase each own significant market share. Several popular open-source RDBMSs also run under Windows—My SQL, PostgreSQL, and Firebird.

 tip

As an administrator, you can open the back-end data .accdb file in Access and take advantage of Access 2010's database backup and compact/repair utilities. For the preceding example, you would open \\WINSVR2008SP2VM\Northwind\ NWData.accdb.

 tip

One of the advantages of running SSX or other SQL Server 2008 R2 editions under Windows Server 2003 or later is the capability to manage the server from a Windows 7, Vista or XP Professional workstation by running Terminal Services in administrative mode.

You don't need to upgrade the Windows server to a domain controller to run SQL Server 2005 or later versions. If your network uses Active Directory, installing SSX on a member server, not a domain controller, devotes more of the server's available resources to database operation and management, and potentially improves performance.

Client/server technology ordinarily offloads much of the data-processing workload to the server. When an RDBMS client instructs the server to execute an SQL SELECT * statement having WHERE clause criteria, only those rows that meet the criteria pass over the network to the client. If you replace * with an explicit field list, the RDBMS only populates query columns that correspond to the specified fields. Minimizing the amount of data transmitted to the client saves costly network bandwidth and improves performance, especially for remote users who access the database over virtual private network (VPN) connections.

Another advantage of migrating from conventional multiuser Access applications to client/server back-end databases is elimination of routine compact/repair operations to remove deleted records from Access tables. When you delete records from a table, Access marks the records as deleted but doesn't remove them from the table. You must compact the database periodically to remove deleted records and regain the disk space they occupy. Using a client/server back end also eliminates the Access database locking problems that often occur after a power outage or unscheduled shutdown when users are in the process of making changes to Access tables.

Client/Server Reliability and Scalability Benefits

Reliability—also called *availability* in this context—is the most important property of a production database. The goal of most database administrators is to ensure that the database is available to users at least 99.99% of the time. 99.99% (called "four nines") availability means that the database has a maximum downtime of 45 minutes per month. Five nines, which is expected of banking, other financial, and national security databases reduces downtime to about five minutes per year. Achieving 99.999% or better database availability requires very costly server clusters, but it's reasonable to expect at least four nines from SQL Server 2005 or later running under Windows Server 2003 or later.

Database scalability primarily is hardware related. You can increase the number of concurrent users without suffering a performance slowdown by increasing the amount of RAM, CPU speed, and number of CPUs in the server(s). Unlimited-use licenses for most RDBMSs are based on the number of CPUs.

SQL Server 2008 R2 Express Edition Features and Limitations

SQL Server 2008 R2 Express Edition (called *SQL Express or SSX* when referring specifically to this version of SQL Server) running under Windows Server 2003 or later has the same level of reliability as SQL Server 2008 R2 Standard or Enterprise Edition running on a single server. You can achieve similar reliability when running SSX under Windows 7, Vista, or XP Professional, if you dedicate the machine to running SSX and don't use the machine to run desktop applications. The source code of SSX is identical to that of other SQL Server 2008 R2 editions; the scalability limitations applied to the freely distributable edition don't affect its reliability.

Microsoft limits the scalability of SSX by restricting it to using a single CPU, regardless of how many processors you plug into your multiprocessing server or workstation or how many cores each processor contains. Similarly, SSX will use a maximum of 1GB RAM, regardless of the amount of RAM on the machine, and the maximum database size is limited to 10GB. However, you can run up to 16 named instances (installations) of SSX on a single computer. SSX can't act as a replication publisher, which is unfortunate because Access 2007 and later no longer support replication. However, this limitation isn't likely to affect most Access users and developers.

Access 2003's lack of graphical RDBMS management tools for MSDE 2000 discouraged many Access power users and developers from migrating to linked or directly connected SQL Server databases. Several third-party tools became available for managing MSDE 2000 user logins and database security, but these GUI tools didn't measure up to the quality of SQL Server Enterprise Manager (EntMan) for SQL Server 2000 Developer Edition and later.

SSX offers SQL Server 2008 R2 Management Studio Express (SSMSX), a slightly restricted version of the full SQL Server 2008 R2 Management Studio that comes with SQL Server 2008 R2 Developer Edition and later. SSMSX is a full-featured graphical RDBMS management tool and query designer (see Figure 21.13).

 note

As mentioned earlier, shared Access databases have a fixed limit of 255 concurrent users. There's no limit on the number of Access clients simultaneously connected to SSX on a Windows server. However, Windows 7, Vista, and XP Professional have a fixed maximum of 10 inbound (client) connections, so the maximum number of simultaneous networked users connected to SSX running under either of these operating systems is 10.

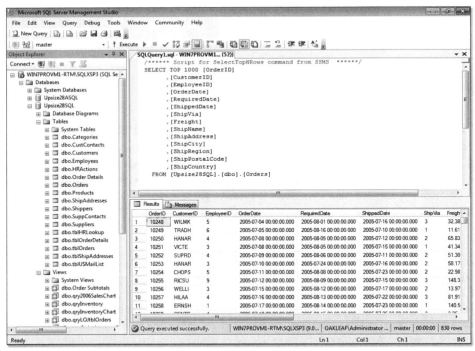

Figure 21.13 SQL Server 2008 R2 Management Studio Express (SSMSX) has almost all the bells and whistles of the version that comes with SQL Server 2008 R2 Standard, and Enterprise editions.

tip

SQL Server doesn't have data types that correspond to the Attachments and multivalued lookup field (MVLF) data types introduced by Access 2007. The Upsizing Wizard skips Attachments fields and upsizes MVLF fields to SQL Server's `ntext` (Unicode text) data type, which disables lookups.

If these data types are important to your application, but you want to take advantage of the benefits of client/server tables, you can elect to not update some tables during the upsizing process or rename and use the local table that the wizard leaves in the front-end .accdb file after completing its task.

Choosing a Client/Server Migration Strategy

Prior to the introduction of Access 2000, linking was the only method of migrating Access applications from Access tables to client/server databases. The primary advantage of linking client/server tables is that the Access 2010 database engine running on the client processes your Access SQL queries. Thus, crosstab queries continue to execute as expected, and you can use MSGraph objects in your forms and reports without reconstructing their Record Source property as an SQL Server 2005 or later `PIVOT` view.

Linked client/server tables let you take advantage of Access pass-through queries to send Transact-SQL (T-SQL) statements directly to SQL Server, PL/SQL to Oracle, or any other SQL dialect to your RDBMS. The downside of linking is that you lose the efficiency of server-side query processing, which is one of the most important features of client/server RDBMSs. The sections that follow describe Access 2010 options for moving to SQL Server databases.

 note

You can download SQL Server 2008 R2 RTM - Management Studio Express from http://bit.ly/d1gSU6 and run it under Windows 7/Vista/XP or Windows Server 2003 and later.

 To learn more about pass-through queries, **see** *"Writing and Executing Pass-through Queries,"* **p. 897.**

Migrating Access Applications to SQL Server with the Upsizing Wizard

Access 2010 supports the following three automated migration—called *upsizing*—scenarios from conventional Access applications to SQL Server:

- **Splitting, upsizing, and linking a single-user Access database**—If your .accdb file contains application objects (queries, forms, pages, reports, modules, macros, or any combination) and data objects (tables), you can split and upsize the tables, and link the application objects to the server tables in a single process. An example of this scenario is upsizing Northwind.accdb.

- **Upsizing and linking a multiuser Access application**—If you've used the Database Splitter utility to segregate application and data objects into front-end and back-end .accdb files, respectively, you upsize only the front-end .accdb file. Upsizing the back-end .accdb doesn't work directly; you receive a "Can't find *TableName*" error message when you attempt to open the upsized linked table in the front-end application's Datasheet view or in a form or report.

- **Upsizing an Access application to an Access data project**—This scenario moves your Access tables to SQL Server and attempts to update your queries to T-SQL stored procedures. Chapter 28, "Upsizing Access Applications to Access Data Projects," describes this upsizing method and how to overcome problems with Access queries that T-SQL can't handle.

You use the Access 2010 Upsizing Wizard—which works only with SQL Server 6.5 (having SP5 installed), 7.0, 2000 (including MSDE 2000), 2005, 2008 and 2008 R2 (including SSX)—for the preceding three scenarios, but this chapter focuses only on the first two. The client/server examples in this book use SSX as the server, but most examples also accommodate all SQL Server 2000 editions, including MSDE 2000. None of the examples have been tested with SQL Server 6.5 or 7.0, for which mainstream support ended on 1/1/2002 and 12/31/2005, respectively.

SQL Server enforces referential integrity by triggers or declarative referential integrity (DRI), if specified in the Relationships window for the Access tables. Access uses DRI, which conforms to ANSI-92 SQL syntax, and DRI is the preferred approach for SQL Server 2008 R2 and earlier databases. SQL Server 2005 and later also support Access's cascading updates and deletions; SQL Server 7.0 and earlier don't. No version of SQL Server has a field data type that corresponds to Access's Hyperlink data type, so the wizard converts Hyperlink fields to plain text.

 For a brief description of SQL Server 2008's feature set, see "SQL Server 2008 [R2] Express Edition SP2 Setup," **p. 35.**

 note

Access 2010 doesn't include SQL Server 2008 R2's Books Online documentation. Microsoft has published an online version of updated SQL Server 2008 R2 documentation at http://bit.ly/bEkY4j.

Exporting Tables to Other RDBMSs

Access uses the Open Database Connectivity application programming interface (ODBC API) to link conventional Access (.accdb) front ends to client/server RDBMSs. Office 2010 installs ODBC drivers for SQL Server and Oracle 8i or Access 2010 and earlier, and dBASE databases, as well as Excel worksheets. If you're using Oracle, IBM DB2, Sybase, Informix, or another RDBMS as your application's data source, you can't use the Upsizing Wizard to automate the table export and linking process; the Wizard supports SQL Server only. You must manually export (copy) your Access tables to the RDBMS and then link the RDBMS tables to your Access front end. You also must set up primary keys, relationships, and indexes for the tables manually.

Migrating tables and linking to databases other than SQL Server involve the following basic steps:

1. You or your organization's database administrator (DBA) must create the database, and you must have permissions to create, read, and write to objects in the database.

 note

Linking to databases of an RDBMS other than SQL Server, Access or dBASE requires a vendor-supplied or third-party ODBC driver. You can't use an OLE DB data provider to link client/server tables to Access front ends.

An alternative to linking tables in "foreign" databases to Access front ends is to use the *linked server* feature of SQL Server 2000 and later. Linking a server—]other than another SQL Server instance—requires an OLE DB data provider for the linked server. Linking servers to SQL Server 2005 and later is required to use ADP with other RDBMSs. Linking SQL Server to other RDBMSs is beyond the scope of this book.

2. Back up the Access database, and verify the integrity of the backup.

3. Use the External Data ribbon's More, ODBC Database button in the Export group to export the Access tables to the new database.

4. Use the RDBMS's management tools to designate primary keys, add indexes, default values, and validation rules, and to enforce referential integrity between the tables. Add cascading updates and deletions, if the RDBMS supports them (most do).

5. Rename the existing Access tables, and use the Import group's More, ODBC Database to establish links to the database tables.

6. Delete the existing Access tables after you confirm that the linked tables operate properly and have been backed up on the server.

Upsizing a Single-File Application to SQL Server 2005 or Later

If you've created a single-file Access application and want to make it available to your colleagues who have Access 2007 or 2010 installed, the Upsizing Wizard makes the process easy and fast. You must, of course, have downloaded and installed SSX from or have access to another version of SQL Server 200x before you can upsize your application. If your application is encrypted, you must decrypt it before upsizing. All examples of this chapter assume you are logged in to Windows 7, Vista, XP, or Server 2003+ as a member of the Administrators group.

 note

Chapter 27, "Moving from Access Queries to Transact-SQL," includes examples of T-SQL expressions you can use for default values and validation rules and shows you how to use SSMSX to change the property values of SQL Server tables and fields.

 For details about enabling remote user access to SSX, **see** *"Making SSX Accessible to Remote Users,"* **p. 41.**

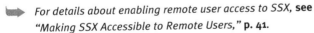 **tip**

For a production application, install SSX on the production server, if you don't intend to create the new database on an existing installation of SQL Server 2005 Workgroup, 200x Standard, or 200x Enterprise Edition. The network name of the server—called the SQL Server *instance name*—is embedded in the Description property value of each table. SSX named instances have a default \SQLEXPRESS suffix. You must enable client access to SSX running on a network server with the SQL Server Configuration manager to prevent errors when attempting to connect with the Upsizing Wizard.

If you specify the local instance of SSX installed on your client computer, you must change the property value—called the *ODBC connection string*—to reflect the NetBIOS name change when you move the database to a production server. Making this change isn't a simple process; you must update each link manually or use a VBA subprocedure to regenerate the links to the new server.

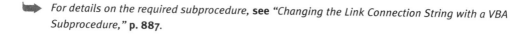*For details on the required subprocedure,* **see** *"Changing the Link Connection String with a VBA Subprocedure,"* **p. 887.**

Modifying Table Properties to Ensure Successful Upsizing

The Upsizing Wizard has several limitations, most of which are imposed by SQL Server 2005 or earlier. In some cases, the upsizing process fails silently, and the final upsizing report doesn't indicate the reason for the failure.

Following is a check list of modifications you must make to your tables—and a few other recommendations—to ensure upsizing success:

- **Validation rule and default value expressions**—T-SQL can't handle many Access-specific or VBA expressions that establish default field values, or table- or field-level validation rules. In such cases, the Upsizing Wizard might not create the SQL Server table. You must remove the offending expressions and run the Upsizing Wizard again to link only the missing tables. Then you must rewrite the expressions to comply with T-SQL syntax rules using SSMSX.

- **Hidden tables**—If you've applied the Hidden attribute to any of the tables you want to upsize, the wizard ignores the hidden tables during the upsizing process.

- **Fields added by Access replication**—If you've implemented Access replication, you must remove all replication system fields from the tables before upsizing. Tables with replication fields don't upsize.

- **Tables without unique indexes**—You can update an Access table that doesn't have a Unique Values Only index, but SQL Server tables require a unique index for updatability. Make sure all tables have a unique index. Add an AutoNumber field to the table if you can't create a unique index from the data in the table. (AutoNumber fields become `integer` fields with the `identity` property in SQL Server tables.) The unique index doesn't need to be a primary key.

- **Related fields with unequal Field Size property values**—Access lets you create relations on Text fields having different sizes, but SQL Server doesn't. The tables upsize, but the wizard doesn't establish the relationship between them. Make sure that the size of the primary- and foreign-key field pair is the same in both related tables. Specify the longer of the two size values to prevent inadvertently truncating data.

- **Very large tables**—During addition of data to an upsized table, SQL Server adds entries to the transaction log file. If you have a very large table and are short on disk space, the combination of the table and log file might exceed the free space on the destination disk. Make sure that the destination drive has free space greater than three times your .accdb file size.

 tip

Microsoft has published a whitepaper titled "Using the Access 2002 Upsizing Tools" that you can download from Microsoft's Knowledge Base article Q294407. The whitepaper hadn't been updated for Access 2010 when this book was written. Search the Knowledge Base at http://search.support.microsoft.com/search/ with Access 2010 as the product and **upsizing tools** as the text to find the updated version and other troubleshooting data. Search with Access 2007 or 2003 if you don't find the information you want for Access 2010.

Running the Upsizing Wizard

Following are the steps to upsize a simple, single-file Access application with the Upsizing Wizard:

1. Make a backup copy of the Access database to upsize, and verify that the backup copy works.

2. Open the original database file, but don't open any database objects. This example uses NwindSQL.accdb, a modified upgrade of the Access 2000 version of the Northwind.accdb database with images embedded in the Photo field of the Employees table and the Employees form imported from Access 2000's Northwind.accdb file.

 note
The NwindSQL.accdb database used for this example is included in the \Access2010\Chaptr21\Upsize folder of the downloadable sample code. NwindSQL.accdb includes the VBA subprocedure required to change the server name when you move the SQL Server database from one machine to another.

➡ *For an explanation of how to embed the EmpID#.bmp bitmap files in an OLE Object field,* **see** *"Dealing with Images in External Database Files,"* **p. 326.**

3. Click the Database Tools tab and click the Move Data group's SQL Server button to start the upsizing process.

4. Accept the default Create a New Database option in the first wizard dialog (see Figure 21.14) and then click Next.

Figure 21.14
The first Upsizing Wizard dialog lets you add your tables to an existing database or create a new database. You create a new SQL Server database unless you're running the wizard to upsize a table that wasn't upsized because of an error.

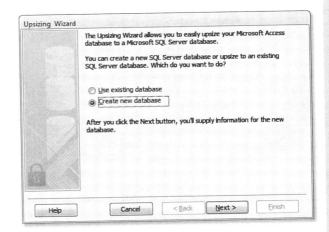

5. In the second wizard dialog, open the What SQL Server Would You Like list and select the name of a production server or peer workstation server that has SQL Server 2005 or SSX installed. This example uses SQL Server 2008

 note
If you're upsizing a sample database to become familiar with the process, you can select (local) or your computer's name. If you're using SSX, add an \SQLEXPRESS suffix.

R2 Express Edition installed on a Windows Server 2003 Standard Edition member server (WINSVR2008SP2VM\ SQLEXPRESS). The client computer (WIN7PROVM1-RTM) runs Office 2010 under Windows 7 Ultimate.

6. SQL Server 2008 R2 and SSX install by default with Windows authentication only enabled, which prevents use of the sa (system administrator) login and SQL Server–based security. Mark the Use Trusted Connection check box.

7. Accept the default database name, the name of your .accdb file with an "SQL" suffix, or change it to a name you like better (see Figure 21.15). Don't use spaces or punctuation symbols in the name; doing so violates generally accepted database naming practices. Click Next.

> **note**
>
> A trusted connection to SQL Server uses Windows integrated authentication for database connections, and is the *much* preferred method of managing client/server database security.
>
> Using Windows authentication requires your logon account to have at least **CREATE DATABASE** privileges for SQL Server. The Administrator member of the local Administrators group (BUILTIN\Administrators) of the machine running SQL Server has system administrator (sa) rights for the server and all databases by default.

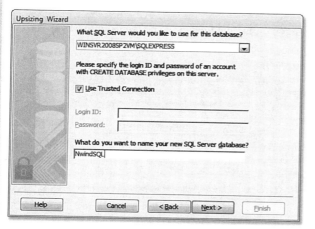

Figure 21.15
The second Upsizing Wizard dialog requires you to select the machine running SQL Server, specify the authentication method for your connection, and provide a name for the new database.

8. After a brief delay, the third wizard dialog opens with a list of the tables in the Access database in the Available Tables list. Click the >> button to export all the tables to SQL Server (see Figure 21.16). If you want to retain temporary or local tables on the client, select the table(s) and click the < button to move them from the Export to SQL Server list back to the Available Tables list. Click Next.

9. In the fourth wizard dialog, accept the default options except for the Add Timestamp Fields to Table? selection unless you have a specific reason for doing otherwise (see Figure 21.17). Click Next.

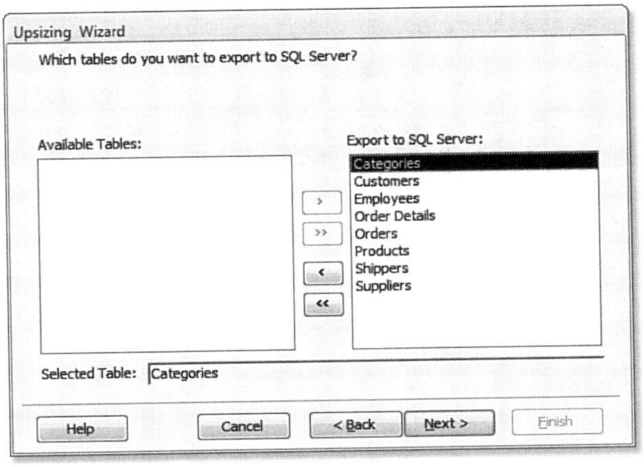

Figure 21.16
The only Access tables you should retain in the front-end application are temporary tables or local tables that you use to set user preferences.

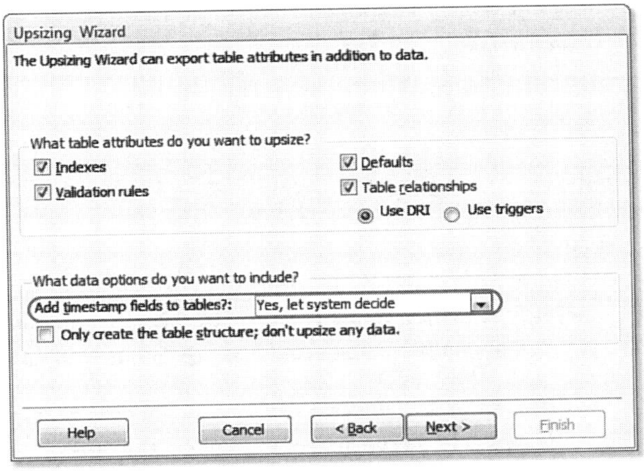

Figure 21.17
The fourth Upsizing Wizard dialog proposes the most common set of options for the upsizing process.

10. In the fifth wizard dialog, select the Link SQL Server Tables to Existing Application option (see Figure 21.18). If you accept the default No Application Changes option, you must manually link the tables to your database front-end application. Click Next to open the final wizard dialog and then click Finish to start the upsizing process.

note

As mentioned earlier in the chapter, SQL Server's DRI features are preferred over triggers to enforce referential integrity. Prior to SQL Server 7.0, triggers were the only method of enforcing referential integrity.

SQL Server can use optional timestamp fields to determine quickly whether large Memo fields (SQL Server `ntext` fields) and OLE Object fields (SQL Server `image` fields) have been updated. If your Access table includes lengthy Memo fields or if OLE Object fields contain large images or other data, accept the Yes, Let System Decide or Yes, Always choice in the Add Timestamp Fields to Tables list.

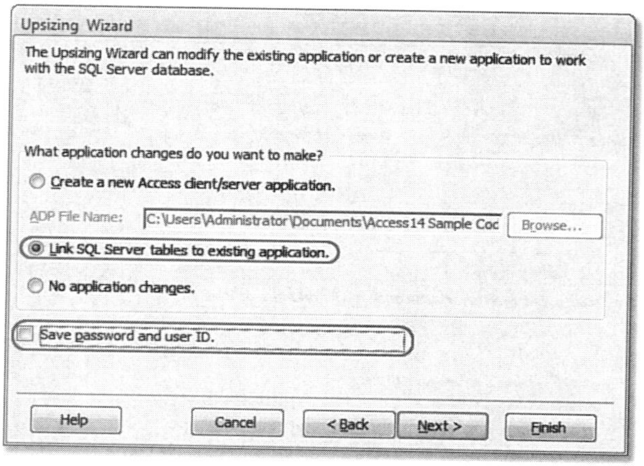

Figure 21.18
Be sure to select the Link SQL Server Tables to Existing Application option to have the Upsizing Wizard handle the table-linking process for you.

To learn how to pre-create SQL Server user accounts and add users to roles, before or after running the Upsizing Wizard, **see** *"Adding SQL Server User Logins with SQL Server Management Studio,"* **p. 900.**

11. A progress indicator dialog appears for a period that depends on the size of the tables, the speed of your computer and, if the database is remote, network and server performance. After the wizard completes its task, an Upsizing Wizard Report appears in Print Preview. Click the report to zoom to 100% scale and review its contents (see Figure 21.19).

12. Click the Data group's PDF or XPS button to save the report as an Adobe PDF or Microsoft XML Paper Specification (XPS) file. Print the report, if you want, and then close the Upsizing Wizard window. The wizard doesn't automatically save the report.

note

The Save Password and User ID check box applies only to SQL Server security, which isn't enabled by default. Even if you could save your administrative logon name and password, doing so would breach security rules—users would be able to impersonate your administrative account to gain full control over the SQL Server instance.

Figure 21.19
After the
Upsizing
Wizard updates
and links the
table, it gener-
ates a report
summarizing
the upsizing
process. Look
for errors and
"not upsized"
entries. (The
report for
upsizing
the sample
NwindSQL.
accdb tables is
15 pages long.)

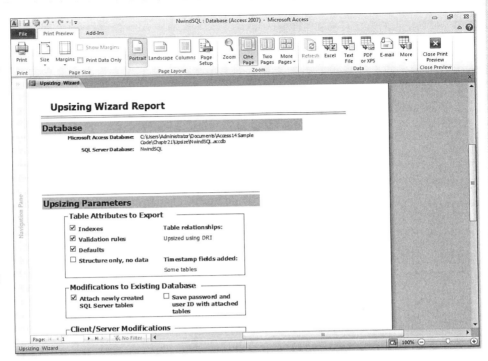

Verifying the Upsizing and Linking Process

The wizard renames your Access tables by adding a "_local" suffix to the table names and adds
links—identified by the ODBC symbol—to the SQL Server tables. The wizard creates a new Custom
Group 1 in the Navigation pane with tables as unassigned objects. Select Object Type and All
Access Objects to display the local and linked tables (see Figure 21.20). When you pass the mouse
pointer over a linked table item, a ScreenTip displays in a single line part of the ODBC connection
string for the database.

Access Tables Fail to Upsize

If you sometimes receive error messages during the upsizing process and some tables don't
upsize, the most common cause of failure is the presence of complex Access or VBA expressions in table or field validation rules. SQL Server has counterparts for many Access query
expressions, but only a few for VBA functions. SQL Server 2000's extended properties accommodate Access input masks, data display formatting, subdatasheets, and lookup fields. The
Upsizing Wizard, however, handles a surprisingly broad range of validation rules. For example,
you can upsize with no difficulty the Forms14.accdb application whose HRActions table has
several table and field validation rules.

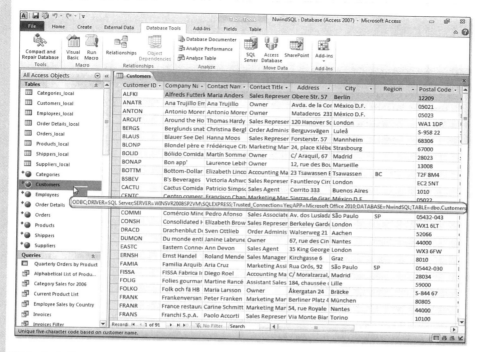

Figure 21.20
The Navigation pane displays linked tables with the original Access table names and the Access tables renamed with a "_local" suffix.

If you adhere to the recommendations in the "Modifying Table Properties to Ensure Successful Upsizing" section near the middle of this chapter, there's little probability of encountering table upsizing failures.

After you've verified that all required server tables have links, do the following to confirm that the tables are operable with your front end:

1. Open the front-end forms and reports to verify that the upsizing process completed satisfactorily.

2. Verify in Form or Table Datasheet view that default values, formats, input masks, field and table validation rules, and other special property values you've specified for tables have upsized successfully. SQL Server 7.0 doesn't support extended properties, so display formats, input masks, and other Access-specific properties aren't updated. Also, verify by the presence of the tentative append record that the tables are updatable.

3. If your tables have lookup fields, verify that these extended property features work as they did in the Access tables. Linked tables don't support subdatasheets because they cause a performance hit with tables that have a large number of rows.

4. Open the upsized tables in Design view, and acknowledge the message that warns you that you can't change some table properties. Check the data type of an Access Hyperlink field, which changes to an Access Memo field (see Figure 21.21). Access Memo fields upsize to SQL Server's `ntext` (Unicode text) data type. No version of SQL Server supports the Allow Zero Length property, so this value is No for all fields, regardless of your original setting. The upsize_ts field is the `timestamp` field added by the Upsizing Wizard.

Figure 21.21
Upsizing
Access
Hyperlink fields
results in a
change to the
SQL Server
data type
(ntext) that
corresponds
to an Access
Memo field.
Design view of
a linked SQL
Server data-
base displays
Access, not
SQL Server,
field data type
names.

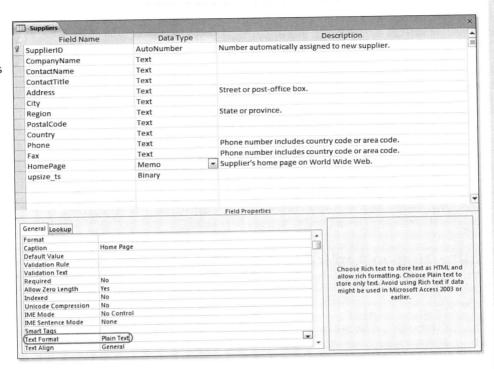

5. Right-click the Table Design view window, choose Properties to open the Table Properties dialog, and select the Description text box. Press Shift+F2 to open the Zoom dialog to view the full
   connection string for the table. Figure 21.22 shows the connection string for the Suppliers table
   with the Zoom dialog's font name changed to Calibri and size changed to 12 points, and newline
   characters added to format the string for readability.

Figure 21.22
The Zoom dialog displays a formatted
version of the ODBC connection string
for the Suppliers table.

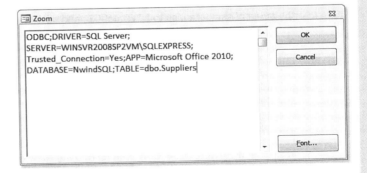

6. Execute every SELECT query to make sure the wizard hasn't modified the query and rendered it inoperable. Don't execute action queries that update table values. Some queries—such as Northwind.accdb's Sales by Year query—require entering parameter values.

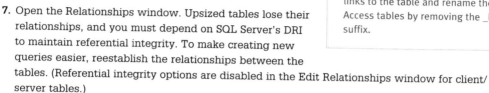

tip

To return a test application to its original condition, delete the links to the table and rename the Access tables by removing the _local suffix.

7. Open the Relationships window. Upsized tables lose their relationships, and you must depend on SQL Server's DRI to maintain referential integrity. To make creating new queries easier, reestablish the relationships between the tables. (Referential integrity options are disabled in the Edit Relationships window for client/server tables.)

After you've verified the success of the upsizing process, you can safely delete the ..._local tables, if you made a backup of your application. If not, export the ..._local tables to a new Access database and then delete them from the upsized front end.

Upsizing an Application with Linked Tables

As mentioned earlier in the chapter, the process for upsizing Access front ends with linked Access tables is identical to that for upsizing single-file applications. You run the Upsizing Wizard from the front-end .accdb. The wizard connects to the shared .accdb back end and generates the SQL Server tables from the linked Access database. This example uses the NWClient.accdb front end and NWData.accdb back end you created at the beginning of the chapter.

To create an SQL Server database on your local machine that you move to a production server later in the chapter, using the NWClient.accdb and NWData.accdb pair as an example, do the following:

1. Make backup copies of NWClient.accdb and NWData.accdb, if you haven't done this.

2. Open the NWClient.accdb front end, click the Database Tools tab, click the SQL Server button to start the Upsizing Wizard, accept the default Create New Database option in the first dialog, and click Next.

3. In the second wizard dialog, specify *ComputerName*/SQLEXPRESS as the SSX instance, change the name of the database to NWDataSQL, and click Next.

4. In the third dialog, select all tables, and in the fourth dialog, accept the defaults, except select Yes, Let the System Decide for timestamp fields.

5. In the fifth dialog, make sure to select the Link SQL Server Tables to Existing Application option and clear the Save Password and User ID check box, if it's marked.

6. Click Next and Finish to upsize the linked tables.

7. Verify the upsizing process with the methods described in the preceding section.

For detailed instructions about migrating Access 2010 applications to SQL Azure, **see** *"Linking Access Applications to SQL Azure Cloud Databases,"* **p. 1227**

Examining the ODBC Table Connection String

When you choose the Create a New Database option in the first Upsizing Wizard dialog, the ODBC connection string for each table contains all the information Access needs to connect to the server and link each table (refer to Figure 21.22). This type of ODBC connection doesn't require you to create a named ODBC user or system data source (user or system DSN) or a file data source to establish the connection. Using a DSN-less connection simplifies the process of making your linked-table application available to users, because they don't need a user or system DSN on their computer or a link to a file data source on the server.

A DSN-less ODBC connection string consists of the following elements, separated by semicolons:

- ODBC designates the connection as using the ODBC API.

- DRIVER=SQL Server specifies the version of the SQL Server ODBC driver to use. (SQL Native Client is the current version for SQL Server 2008 R2, but the Upsizing Wizard uses the preceding version for compatibility with SQL Server 2000 and earlier.)

- SERVER=SERVERNAME designates the computer name of the machine running the instance of SQL Server with the upsized database, followed by \SQLEXPRESS for SSX or a custom instance name for SQL 2000 or 2005. In a Windows 2003+ domain, the computer name often is called the *down-level* name of a computer. (The "up-level" name is the full *hostname.domainname.ext* of the computer—winsvr2008sp2vm.oakleaf.org for example.)

- UID=UserName (not shown in Figure 21.22) specifies the SQL Server logon name if you aren't using Windows integrated security.

- PWD=Password (not shown in Figure 21.22) is the SQL Server logon name if you aren't using Windows integrated security. Notice that the password is in clear text, which is a serious security violation. Using Windows authentication is recommended strongly, because it's integrated with Windows networking and is much more secure and easier to administer than SQL Server's username/password security approach.

- APP=Microsoft Office 2010 is for information only.

- WSID=COMPUTERNAME (not shown in Figure 21.22) is your computer name (workstation ID) and is for information only.

- DATABASE=DatabaseName designates the name of the upsized database.

- Trusted_Connection=Yes specifies use of Windows integrated authentication; No or a missing entry specifies SQL Server security and requires USR and PWD entries.

- TABLE=dbo.TableName specifies the SQL Server table and its owner prefix. (SQL Server 2005+ calls the owner prefix the *schema* name.) The default prefix is dbo, which is the abbreviation for the system administrator (sa) as the object's owner (database owner). When you log on to SQL Server with an administrative account, you are sa.

 note

The linked table's Description property value doesn't contain UID, PWD, or WSID values. The dbo.TableName element isn't present in the Connect property value of the link's TableDef object. (Access local or linked tables are members of the database's TableDefs collection). Access appends TABLE= and the SourceTableName property value of the TableDef to the Description property value.

If you select the Use an Existing Database option in the first Upsizing Wizard dialog, you must use an existing—or create a new—machine or file data source. If one of your tables won't upsize, you must run the wizard again to create the table and add the link to existing database. If you delete a link and must restore it, you must click More in the External Data ribbon's Import Data group, choose ODBC Database to open the Get External Data dialog, select the Link to the Data Source option, click OK to open the Select Data Source dialog, and select or create the DSN to use.

 note

When you use the Select Data Source dialog to link a table with ODBC, the link name gains a dbo_ prefix. Delete the prefix to enable existing Access objects to connect to the table.

 To learn how to create a temporary or permanent ODBC DSN, **see** *"Linking Client/Server Tables Manually,"* **p. 890.**

In either case, your tables end up with a combination of conventional and DSN-less convention strings. If you don't change the `Connect` property of the `TableDef` object to specify a DSN-less connection, all users of your application must add the ODBC DSN to their computer or have access to a server share holding a file data source.

The standard DSN for an SQL Server table replaces the `Driver=SQL Server` element with `DSN=DataSourceName`, and replaces the `SERVER=SERVERNAME` element with `Description=OptionalText` in the Description and `Connect` property values. Otherwise, the elements of the connection string are the same as in the preceding DSN-less connection list. The `ChangeServer` VBA subprocedure, which is described later in the "Changing the Link Connection String with a VBA Subprocedure" section, also changes DSN to DSN-less connections.

Moving the Upsized Database to Another Server

If you upsize the database to a local SSX instance and then decide to move the database to another server, be prepared to add a substantial amount of VBA code to your project to regenerate the links. There's no Access wizard or utility to automatically change the SERVER=SERVERNAME element of a DSN-less connection string for each linked table.

Moving or Copying the SQL Server Database Files

You can move or copy an SQL Server database from one machine to another by any of the following methods:

- Invoke the TransferSQLDatabase macro action or DoCmd.TransferSQLDatabase VBA method to move an SQL Server 7.0 or later .mdf and .ldf files from one specified computer to another.

 caution

Don't try to use the Linked Table Manager database utility to change the server name in a DSN-less connection string. The Linked Table Manager requires an ODBC user or system DSN, or a file data source, instead of modifying the current DSN-less connection string. If you use the Linked Table Manager to change the link, you must set up a machine DSN on each user's computer or create a file data source on the server and specify the Uniform Naming Convention (UNC) path to the file in the connection string.

> For an example of using the TransferSQLDatabase command to move an SQL Server database, **see** *"Transferring the Project's Database to a Server,"* **p. 1131.**

- Invoke the CopyDatabaseFile macro action or DoCmd.CopyDatabaseFile VBA method to copy the current SQL Server.mdf and .ldf files to another specified computer. This process leaves the original database intact.

- Close all connections to the database, use the source computer's SQL Server Configuration Manager to stop SQL Server on the source computer, and use Windows Explorer to copy *DatabaseName*.mdf (database) and *DatabaseName*.ldf (log file) from the \Program Files\ Microsoft SQL Server\MSSQL\Data folder to the same folder on the new server. After copying the files, create a temporary ADP and click Yes when asked if you want to connect to an existing database. In the DataLink Properties dialog, select the Attach a Database File as a Database Name option, specify the database name, and browse to the *DatabaseName*.mdf file, which must be on the same machine as the SQL Server instance you specify.

Changing the Link Connection String with a VBA Subprocedure

After you've moved the linked tables to the new server, you face the challenge of changing the SERVER=SERVERNAME element of the front end's DSN-less connection string to the new server name. Properties of linked table definitions, which Access calls TableDefs, are read-only. You can't persist changes to the Description property value of a linked table. If you alter the server name in the connection string of the Description property, and close and save your changes to the table design, the connection string doesn't change.

NwindSQL.accdb in the \Access2010\Chaptr21 folder of the downloadable sample files contains a modChangeServer module with a single VBA subprocedure: ChangeServers. You can use this procedure to change the connection string to point to the new server or change a DSN connection string to the DSN-less type. To add modChangeServer and its subprocedure to your front-end .accdb file, import the module from NwindSQL.accdb. The following example uses NWClientSQL.accdb, upsized to your local computer in the earlier "Upsizing an Application with Linked Tables" section. Running the example requires you to have a networked computer running SQL Server 2005+ or SSX.

> To review the process for working with VBA modules, **see** *"Using the Immediate Window,"* **p. 391.**

To run the ChangeServer subprocedure in an application that has tables linked to SQL Server and the modChangeServer module installed, do this:

1. Click the Modules shortcut in NWClient.accdb's Database window, and double-click modChangeServer to open the VBA editor with the ChangeServer subprocedure active.

2. Press Ctrl+G to open the Immediate window. Type **ChangeServer** "CurrentServerName", "NewServerName". For this example, the procedure call is **ChangeServer "WINSVR2008SP2VM\ SQLEXPRESS", "WIN7PROVM1-RTM\SQLEXPRESS"** (see Figure 21.23). If you haven't copied or moved the tables to another server, use the current workstation or server name as the value of both arguments.

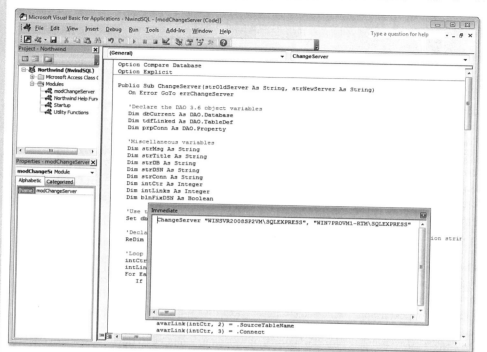

3. Press Enter to execute the procedure. The first stage of the procedure creates an array of the new connection data for each linked table and displays a message asking you to confirm the change (see Figure 21.24, top).

4. After a second or more, depending on the speed of your machine and the network, a `Debug.Print` statement confirms all new connection strings in the Immediate window (see Figure 21.25).

> **note**
>
> ChangeServer creates a test connection to the destination server to prevent deleting the first existing link. The properties of linked TableDef objects are read-only, so the existing link must be deleted before adding the new TableDef.

Figure 21.24
You see one of these two messages, depending on the validity of your source instance argument values.

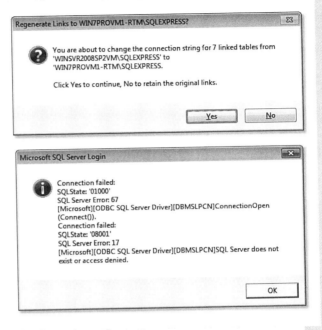

> **Regenerate Links to WIN7PROVM1-RTM\SQLEXPRESS?**
>
> You are about to change the connection string for 7 linked tables from 'WINSVR2008SP2VM\SQLEXPRESS' to 'WIN7PROVM1-RTM\SQLEXPRESS.
>
> Click Yes to continue, No to retain the original links.
>
> [Yes] [No]

> **Microsoft SQL Server Login**
>
> Connection failed:
> SQLState: '01000'
> SQL Server Error: 67
> [Microsoft][ODBC SQL Server Driver][DBMSLPCN]ConnectionOpen (Connect()).
> Connection failed:
> SQLState: '08001'
> SQL Server Error: 17
> [Microsoft][ODBC SQL Server Driver][DBMSLPCN]SQL Server does not exist or access denied.
>
> [OK]

Figure 21.25
The Immediate window displays the new connection strings for the links.

```
Immediate
ChangeServer "WINSVR2008SP2VM\SQLEXPRESS", "WIN7PROVM1-RTM\SQLEXPRESS"
Categories      ODBC;DRIVER=SQL Server;SERVER=WIN7PROVM1-RTM\SQLEXPRESS;UI
Customers       ODBC;DRIVER=SQL Server;SERVER=WIN7PROVM1-RTM\SQLEXPRESS;UI
Employees       ODBC;DRIVER=SQL Server;SERVER=WIN7PROVM1-RTM\SQLEXPRESS;UI
Order Details   ODBC;DRIVER=SQL Server;SERVER=WIN7PROVM1-RTM\SQLEXPRESS;UI
Orders          ODBC;DRIVER=SQL Server;SERVER=WIN7PROVM1-RTM\SQLEXPRESS;UI
Products        ODBC;DRIVER=SQL Server;SERVER=WIN7PROVM1-RTM\SQLEXPRESS;UI
Shippers        ODBC;DRIVER=SQL Server;SERVER=WIN7PROVM1-RTM\SQLEXPRESS;UI
Suppliers       ODBC;DRIVER=SQL Server;
SERVER=WIN7PROVM1-RTM\SQLEXPRESS;
UID=Administrator;
Trusted_Connection=Yes;
APP=Microsoft Office 2010;
DATABASE=NwindSQL
```

If you type a nonexistent server name as the second argument value, or the database isn't present on the destination server you specify, you receive the two error messages shown in Figure 21.26. The upper message from SQL Server appears after about 30 seconds of inactivity. Clicking OK opens an SQL Server Login dialog (see Figure 21.26, middle). Click Cancel to dismiss the dialog and display the procedure's error message (see Figure 21.26, bottom). Click OK to cancel execution and leave the connection strings unaffected.

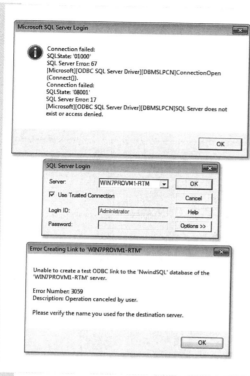

Figure 21.26
These three error messages appear in sequence if you type an invalid destination server name and don't correct it by clicking Cancel in the SQL Server Login dialog.

Linking Client/Server Tables Manually

As mentioned in the earlier section "Examining the ODBC Table Connection String," you must create an ODBC data source when you use the Upsizing Wizard with an existing SQL Server database. You also must create a DSN when you manually export Access tables to an RDBMS other than SQL Server, and then link the tables to your Access front end. The number and appearance of the dialogs varies according to the ODBC driver you use to make the connection to the existing database on the RDBMS.

After you create the DSN, you can use the Upsizing Wizard to add new tables to an SQL Server database. For other RDBMSs, you must manually export your Access tables to the database. You use the same DSN to export the data from and attach the tables to your Access front end.

Creating the ODBC Data Source

To create a DSN for any RDBMS for which you've installed an ODBC 2.x or 3.x driver, do the following:

1. Launch Control Panel's ODBC Data Source Administrator tool. Under Windows 7, Vista, XP, and Server 2003+, the Data Sources (ODBC) icon is in Control Panel's Administrative Tools subfolder. The Administrator opens with the User DSN page active.

note
If you select the Use Existing Database option in the first Upsizing Wizard dialog, the wizard opens the Select Data Source dialog.

2. If you're preparing a temporary data source for the addition of tables to an SQL Server database you created with the Upsizing Wizard, you can create a User or System DSN on your workstation. Otherwise, click the File DSN tab and navigate to a server share for which users of your application have at least read access.

3. Click the Add button to open the Create New Data Source dialog, and select the driver for the RDBMS with the database for your application (see Figure 21.27). This example uses the SQL Server Native Client 10.0 driver for SQL Server 2005+ installed by SQL Server 2008 R2 or SSX.

Figure 21.27
Select the ODBC driver for your RDBMS in the Create New Data Source dialog. Don't set Advanced properties, unless the driver vendor instructs otherwise.

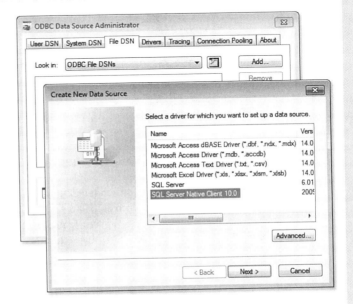

4. Click Next to open the second Create New Data Source dialog, and type the UNC path and name of the data source file (**\\WINSVR2008SP2VM\Northwind\NWindSQL.dsn** for this example). The standard extension for DSN files is, not surprisingly, *dsn*.

5. Click Next to confirm your initial settings and then click Finish to open the first driver-specific dialog: Create a New Data Source for SQL Server in this case.

6. Type a description of the DSN, and open the Server list to select the RDBMS server (OAKLEAF-DC1 for this example; see Figure 21.28).

 tip

The default location for a file DSN is the Documents or My Documents folder on the computer you use to create the DSN. The best location for the file DSN for an upsized multiuser application is the share in which you placed the original Access back-end database. Use UNC's \\ ServerName\ShareName network path format, not a mapped drive, to specify the file location.

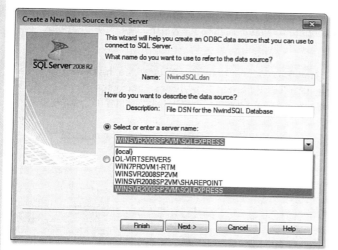

Figure 21.28
The first driver-specific dialog for the SQL Server driver lets you add a description of the DSN and specify the server name.

7. Click Next to open the second driver-specific dialog. For SQL Server, accept the default Windows NT Authentication option (see Figure 21.29). Alternatively, select With SQL Server Authentication, which requires a user account and password having at least CREATE DATABASE privileges.

 note

The Enter a Connection Plan option was intended to utilize the SQL Server Native Client's Connection Director. However, the SQL Server Connection Director was dropped from RTM (released to manufacturing) versions of SQL Server 2008 R2 and Visual Studio 2010.

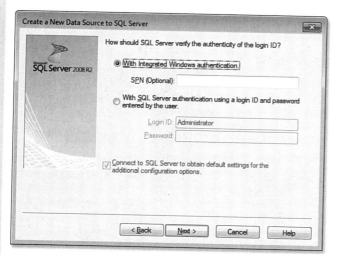

Figure 21.29
The SQL Server driver's second dialog lets you select the authentication method.

8. Click Next to make a temporary connection to the server. Mark the Change the Default Database To check box, open the drop-down list, and select the database name (NwindSQL for this example). Accept the default Use ANSI... settings (see Figure 21.30).

Figure 21.30
Select the default database for the DSN in the third SQL Server–specific dialog. SSX doesn't support SQL Server mirroring, so leave the Mirror Server text box empty.

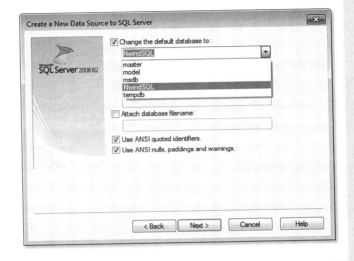

9. Click Next to open the fourth SQL Server dialog. The single default option, Perform Translation for Character Data, is satisfactory for most DSNs. Specify logging options only if you need to debug performance problems when using the DSN.

10. Click Finish to display a summary of your settings, and click Test Data Source to confirm connectivity to the database on the server (see Figure 21.31).

11. Click OK twice to save the file DSN, and then click OK to close the ODBC Administrator tool.

Exporting Access Table Data to the RDBMS

Manually exporting Access tables to an ODBC-connected client/server database is a straightforward process, but the manual export procedure creates only the basic table structure with a simple CREATE TABLE statement and then populates the table with an INSERT statement for each row. Unlike the Upsizing Wizard, exporting a table doesn't establish primary keys, add indexes, or enforce referential integrity with DRI. You or the DBA must handle these tasks after exporting all tables.

 note

If you use a temporary user or system DSN to add table(s) to a new SQL Server database you created with the Upsizing Wizard, run the ChangeServer subprocedure, described in the earlier section "Changing the Link Connection String with a VBA Subprocedure," to change to DSN-less connections for added tables.

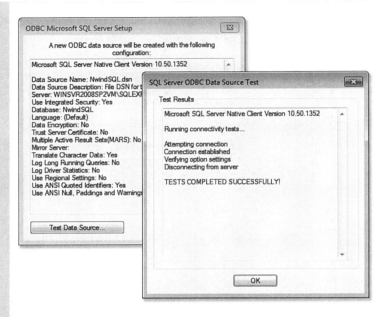

Figure 21.31
The final step when configuring an SQL Server ODBC data source is to test connectivity to the specified database.

Following are the steps to export Access tables to RDBMSs other than SQL Server:

1. Open the .accdb file containing the Access table(s) to export (Customers_local from NwindSQL. accdb for this example) and click the External Data tab.

2. Click the More button and choose ODBC Database to open the Export dialog with *TableName* in the Export *TableName* To text box (see Figure 21.32, top). Alternatively, right-click the table name in the Navigation pane and choose Export, ODBC Database.

3. Click OK to open the Select Data Source dialog with the File DSN page active. If you specified a default folder for file DNSs in step 3 of the preceding section, the file you created appears in the list. If not, navigate to the server share in which you stored the DSN. Select the file (see Figure 21.32, bottom), and click OK to close the dialog and start the export process.

4. Repeat steps 2 and 3 for each table to export. You don't need to wait for the export process to complete before selecting another table to export.

5. Use the RDBMS's toolset to specify primary key fields, add indexes, and establish referential integrity to emulate—as closely as possible—your original Access database.

Use SQL Server Management Studio to perform step 5's operations for SQL Server 2005+ databases or SSMSX for SSX instances. Alternatively, you can add SQL Server indexes and create relationships (called foreign-key constraints) by opening an Access data project for the database. The process for adding indexes and other table accouterments is tedious when upsizing many tables, so use the Upsizing Wizard for all Access export operations to SQL Server if possible.

Figure 21.32
When you select ODBC Databases in the Export group's More list, the Export dialog (top) opens with the selected table. Clicking OK opens the ODBC Administrator's Select Data Source dialog.

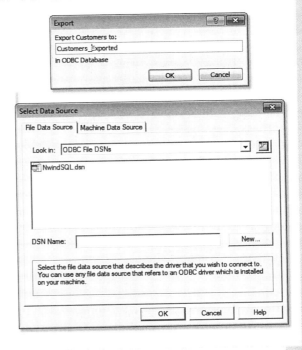

Attaching the Exported Tables

To attach the client/server tables you exported, do this:

1. Open the front-end .accdb, click the External Data tab, click the Imports Data group's More button, and choose ODBC Database to open the Get External Data–ODBC Database dialog.

2. Select the Link to the Data Source option to open the File DSN page of the Select Data Source dialog.

3. Type the path and name of the DSN file (**WINSVR2008SP2VM\Northwind\NWindSQL.dsn** for this example) or navigate to and double-click the *FileName*.dsn file to open the Link Tables dialog.

4. Multiselect the tables to attach to the front-end .accdb file. Figure 21.33 shows the seven upsized SQL Server Northwind tables and an imported HRActions table selected.

5. If you specified Windows authentication when you created the DSN, the Save Password check box should be cleared. Most Windows NT versions of client/server RDBMSs accommodate Windows authentication. For RDBMS-based security, you can mark the Save Password check box if you didn't use sa (or its equivalent) as the account when you created the DSN. Click OK to begin the linking process.

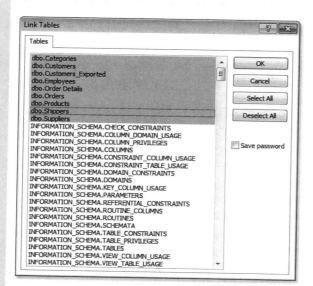

Figure 21.33
Select in the Link Tables dialog each exported table to attach to the front end.

6. If Access can't determine the primary key field(s) of linked tables, the Select Unique Record Identifier dialog opens for each table (see Figure 21.34). Select the key field(s) for the table; if you click Cancel, the table won't be updatable.

Figure 21.34
Specify the name(s) of the primary key field(s) if Access can't detect a table's primary key.

7. The prefix of the attached table names depends on the RDBMS's table naming conventions. As mentioned earlier in the chapter, SQL Server tables gain a dbo_ prefix. Temporarily rename the original tables or links, if any, and then rename the new ODBC links by removing the prefix.

8. Open the Relationships windows to verify all tables are present in the Show Table list. Add all tables to the Relationships window and verify that every table has key field(s) identified by a key symbol. Reestablish the relationships between the primary- and foreign-key fields of the tables.

9. Check all queries for proper execution and make sure your forms and reports operate as before.

After you've verified that all's well with the attached tables, you can delete the renamed Access tables or their links, if present.

Writing and Executing Pass-through Queries

The conventional approach to executing SQL commands against back-end, client/server databases is by opening persistent (stored) views, table-valued functions, and stored procedures. An alternative method is to send SQL statements as batch commands directly to the database server's query processor with *pass-through queries*. The term *pass-through* is apropos because the SQL statements pass through Access to the back-end server without touching the Access query engine.

For applications that have linked client/server tables, pass-through queries let you use the server's SQL dialect, rather than Access SQL. The server's dialect might offer capabilities that Access SQL can't match, such as SQL Server 2005 and later's T-SQL ranking functions—ROW_NUMBER, RANK, DENSE_RANK, and NTILE— or the UNPIVOT operator. Like row-returning stored procedures, all pass-through SELECT queries return read-only Recordsets.

To execute a pass-through query against linked SQL Server 2008 R2 tables using NwindSQL.accdb as the example, do the following:

 note

An explanation of T-SQL ranking functions is beyond the scope of this chapter, but ROW_NUMBER is obvious. This section's example includes a ROW_NUMBER (RowNumber) column ranked by average ShippedDate value for a quarter. For more information on these T-SQL keywords, type **ranking functions** in the SQL Server Books Online's Look In list.

1. Open the front-end database that has tables linked from a back-end SQL Server.

2. Click the Create tab, and click the Queries group's Query Design button to open the Query1 window with the Show Table dialog active. Click Close to close the dialog without adding a table.

3. In the Query Tools, Design ribbon, click the Query Type group's Pass-Through button to clear objects from the Query1 window, which becomes a large text box for writing SQL batches.

4. Click the Property Sheet button and select the ODBC Connect Str text box, which contains an ODBC—stub, to activate its builder button.

5. Click the Builder button to open the Select Data Source dialog with the File Data Source page active. Open the Look In list and navigate through My Network Places to the server share (//OAKLEAF-DC1/Northwind) that stores the file DSN (NWDataSQL.dsn), as shown in Figure 21.35.

note

You must navigate to My Network Places and then to server shares with the Look In list, because the Navigate Up button to the right of the Look In list stops at My Computer.

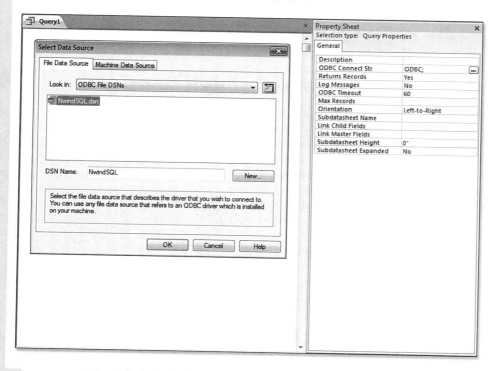

Figure 21.35
Navigate to and select the file DSN stored on a server share with the Look In list, unless the DSN is mapped to a local drive letter.

6. Select the file DSN and click OK to paste a DSN-less connection string as the ODBC Connect Str property value and close the Select Data Source dialog. Click No when asked if you want to store the password in the connection string.

7. Type the SQL batch statement to be executed by the server in the text box. If the batch statement is a select query, set the Returns Records property value to Yes; otherwise, set the value to No.

8. Click the Run button to execute the pass-through query and, if the query returns rows, fill the Datasheet (see Figure 21.36).

Figure 21.36
A complex query produces this resultset, which includes a RowNumber column whose values represent the rank of average ShippedDate values for products ordered in the quarter. A green globe identifies pass-through queries in the Navigation pane.

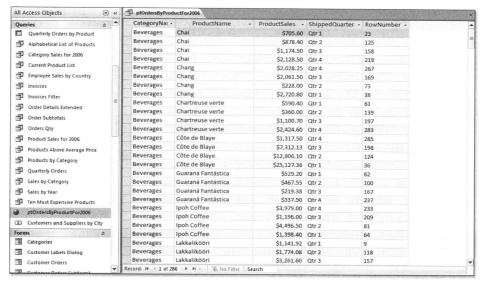

T-SQL

Here's the T-SQL Select statement for the ptOrdersByProductFor2006Select pass-through query that creates the resultset shown in Figure 21.36:

```
SELECT Categories. CategoryName, ProductName,
    SUM(CONVERT(money, ([Order Details].UnitPrice * Quantity)
    * (1 - Discount) / 100) * 100) AS ProductSales,
    'Qtr ' + CONVERT(char(1), DATEPART(q, ShippedDate)) AS ShippedQuarter,
    ROW_NUMBER() OVER(ORDER BY AVG(CONVERT(integer, ShippedDate)))
    AS RowNumber
FROM Categories INNER JOIN
    Products ON Categories.CategoryID = Products.CategoryID INNER JOIN
        Orders INNER JOIN [Order Details]
        ON Orders.OrderID = [Order Details].OrderID
            ON Products.ProductID = [Order Details].ProductID
WHERE (ShippedDate BETWEEN '1/1/2006' AND '12/31/2006')
GROUP BY Categories.CategoryName, ProductName,
    'Qtr ' + CONVERT(char(1), DATEPART(q, Orders.ShippedDate))
ORDER BY Categories.CategoryName, ProductName
```

UPDATE, INSERT, and DELETE pass-through queries execute without warning. If you don't set the Returns Records property value to No, you receive a "Pass-through query with ReturnsRecords property set to True did not return any rows" message.

Adding SQL Server User Logins with SQL Server Management Studio

caution

The ChangeServer VBA subprocedure, which is described in the earlier section "Changing the Link Connection String with a VBA Subprocedure," doesn't change the server for pass-through queries. You must change the SERVER= item manually.

It isn't practical to protect data in linked client/server tables with folder and file access to the back-end database. To restrict read and write access to a database or specific tables within a database, you must establish user logins for the database, grant permissions to these logins, and then add user accounts to the logins. Security features differ greatly between RDBMSs, so this section deals only with SQL Server 2008 R2 [Express] and its management toolset, SQL Server Management Studio 2008 R2 [Express]. There are no significant security differences between the Enterprise, Standard, and Express versions.

note

There are many aspects of SQL Server security, such as administrative security, file and folder encryption, and data protection, that this section doesn't cover because they're beyond the scope of this book. The purpose of this section is to show you how to set up SQL Server security for ordinary database users.

Two of SQL Server's security principals are *logins* to a server instance and *users* of individual databases. With Windows integrated security, logins correspond to Windows security groups and users as Windows users who are members of one or more of the login groups.

Installing SQL Server 2005 or later or SSX on a computer in an Active Directory domain creates the following logins for Windows groups and services (look ahead to Figure 21.37):

- **##MS_PolicyEventProcessingLogin##**—A SQL Server 2008 [R2]-only proxy login account mapped to the master and msdb databases with the Public role for those databases. This login is disabled by default.

- **##MS_PolicyEventProcessingLogin##**—A SQL Server 2008 [R2]-only proxy login account mapped to the msdb database with the Public role for that database only. This login is disabled by default.

- **BUILTIN\Administrators**—The local group containing the Administrator account, and the Domain Admins and Enterprise Admins security groups. Members have the System Administrator (sysadmin) role for all databases. Each member of this group has permissions to do *anything* to the SQL Server instance. Microsoft recommends that you create a new user login in the sysadmin role and then delete this login.

- **BUILTIN\Users**—The local group with default (public) database role for all Domain Users. The public role has no default access permissions to any objects.

- *COMPUTERNAME***SQLServer2005MSSQLUser$***COMPUTERNAME$-SQLEXPRESS**—A Domain Local user group with Log on as a Service, Log on as a Batch Job, and other permissions for SQL Server. This SQL Server 2005 only security group has explicit Read & Execute, List Folder Contents, and Read permissions on the SQL Server ...\MSSQL.1\MSSQL folder that contains the data and related files.

- *COMPUTERNAME***SQLServer2005MSFTEUser$***COMPUTERNAME$-SQLEXPRESS**—A SQL Server 2005-only Domain Local user group with the Log on as a Service right for the SQL Server Full Text [Search] Engine. Installing the Full Text Search service is an option when you set up SSX 2005 and SSMSX 2005 SP2 using the SQL Server 2005 Express with Advanced Features installer.

- *DOMAINNAME***Administrator**—The name of the user with administrative privileges who installed the SQL Server [Express] instance.

- **NT AUTHORITY\NETWORK SERVICE**—The default local service account under which SQL Server 2005 runs. Microsoft recommends that you create a domain user account with minimal privileges and run SQL Server 2005 under that account.

- **NT AUTHORITY\MSSQL$SQLEXPRESS**—The default local service account under which SQL Server 2008 [R2] Express runs.

- **NT AUTHORITY\SYSTEM**—The local service account that has access to all machine resources.

- **sa**—System Administrator (default). This account is added only if you selected the Mixed Authentication option during installation.

All security groups in the preceding list contain the Active Directory Administrator account if you used that account to install SSX. Otherwise, the SQLServer ...User group contains the account you used when installing SSX.

You take advantage of the NWReaders and NWWriters security groups and NWReader1 and NWWriter1 domain user accounts that you created in the earlier section "Establishing Network Share, Folder, and File Security for the Back End" to create SSX logins and NWDataSQL users in the next section.

Understanding Server and Database Roles

Roles simplify assigning privileges to logins or users. SQL Server provides the following two types of roles:

- **Server roles**—Roles for server-wide administrative permissions that you assign to logins, such as sysadmin, dbcreator, and securityadmin. Table 21.2 lists server roles and their permissions in approximate descending order of authority.

- **Database roles**—Roles for database-scoped data access, data entry, and administrative permissions that you assign to logins or users. Table 21.3 lists database roles and their permissions in approximate descending order of authority.

Table 21.2 SQL Server 2005+ Server Roles and Their Permissions

Server Role	Server-wide Permissions
sysadmin	Perform any server action.
dbcreator	CREATE, ALTER, DROP, and RESTORE any database.
securityadmin	GRANT, DENY, and REVOKE server-level and database-level permissions, and reset login passwords.
diskadmin	Manage SQL Server disk files.
serveradmin	Change serverwide configuration options and shut down the server.
processadmin	Terminate running processes of an SQL Server instance.
setupadmin	Add and remove linked servers, and also execute some system stored procedures.
bulkadmin	Execute the BULK INSERT statement.
Public	Read server metadata (VIEW ANY DATABASE).

Table 21.3 SQL Server 2005+ Database Roles and Their Permissions

Database Role	Permissions
db_owner	Perform all configuration and maintenance actions, including dropping the database.
db_ddladmin	Execute CREATE, ALTER, DROP, and any other Data Definition Language (DDL) command in the database.
db_accessadmin	GRANT or REVOKE database access by Windows logins or groups, or SQL Server logins.
db_backupoperator	Back up—but not restore—the database.
db_datareader	SELECT data from user tables.
db_datawriter	INSERT, UPDATE, and DELETE data in user tables.
db_denydatawriter	Deny INSERT, UPDATE, and DELETE operations on user tables.
db_denydatareader	Deny SELECT on user tables.

You must be in the securityadmin server role or db_owner database role to add logins and db_datareader and db_datawriter permissions. For this example, the NWReaders login requires db_datareader, and the NWWriters login requires db_datareader and db_datawriter roles for the NWindSQL database.

Creating the NWReader and NWWriter Logins with SSMSX

Most Access users who upsize single-file or front-end/back-end Access applications to linked SQL Server tables or Access data projects are members of an Active Directory (AD) domain. Thus, this procedure for creating SQL Server logins and granting permissions uses AD security principals—security groups and user accounts in the Domain Users group. You can emulate this process for workgroups or even a single computer by creating local groups for NWReaders and NWWriters, and local NWReader1 and NWWriter 1 user accounts that correspond to the AD accounts.

To create logins for the NWReaders and NWWriters security groups and assign the groups database roles, do the following:

1. If you didn't create the NWReaders and NWWriters groups with NWReader1 and NWWriter1 user accounts in your Active Directory domain in the earlier section "Establishing Network Share, Folder, and File Security for the Back End," do it now.

2. Log on with an administrative account to your local computer that has the NWClientSQL front end with tables linked to an SQL Server 2005 instance.

3. Open SSMSX and connect to the SQL Server 2005+ instance on your local machine or a remote server. This example uses the local WIN7PROVM1-RTM \SQLEXPRESS instance.

4. Expand the serverwide Security\Logins node that's below the last database node (see Figure 21.37).

Figure 21.37
SQL Server Management Studio Express displays the default Security\Logins node for an SQL Server Express 2008 R2 installation. BULTIN\Users, NTAUTHORITY\SYSTEM and NTSERVICE\MSSQL$ SQLEXPRESS Windows security groups.

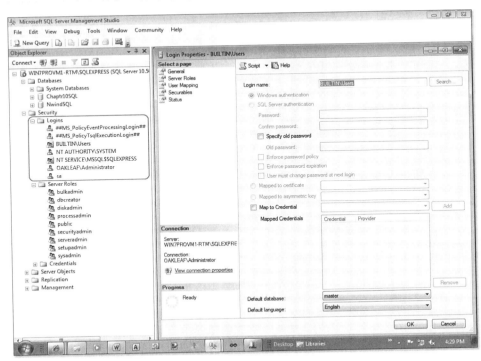

5. Right-click the Logins node and select New Logins to open the Login–New dialog with the General page active.

6. Click the Search button to the right of the Login Name text box to open the Add User or Group dialog, and click its Object Types dialog to open the Object Types dialog, which has Built-in Security Principals and Users selected by default.

7. Mark the Groups check box, click OK to return to the Select User or Group dialog, and click the Locations button to open the Locations dialog.

8. Expand the Entire Directory node, and select your domain (oakleaf.org for this example). If you're not a member of an AD domain, select your local computer name. Click OK to return to the Select User or Group dialog.

9. Type **NWReaders** in the text box, and click Test Names to verify that the group exists, indicated by an underline (see Figure 21.38). Click OK to close the dialog and return to the Login – New dialog.

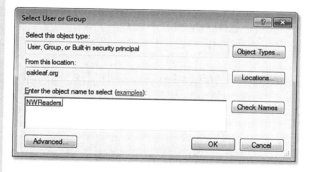

Figure 21.38
The Select User or Group Dialog lets you select a Windows group for a login from the entire directory, a specific domain, or a computer in a workgroup.

10. Open the Default Database list and select the database for the login—NwindSQL for this example (see Figure 21.39).

Figure 21.39
Specify the Windows security group and default database for the new login on the General page.

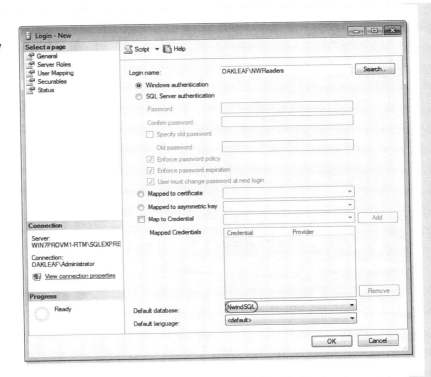

11. Select the User Mapping page, mark the Map check box adjacent to the default database (NwindSQL) to enable the Database Role Membership list, and mark the db_datareader role (see Figure 21.40). Click OK to close the dialog.

12. Repeat steps 5 through 11, but type **NWWriters** in step 8 and mark db_datareader and db_datawriter role check boxes in step 11.

13. The new logins appear in the Security\Logins list and under the Databases\NWDataSQL\Security\Users node (see Figure 21.41)

> **note**
>
> Specifying a Default Schema for a group login opens an error message. Only individual user logins can specify a Default Schema. (The default Default Schema is dbo.)

The NWReaders group's SELECT permissions enable members to open views, invoke inline table-valued functions, and execute SELECT pass-through queries. NWWriters members can execute pass-through queries that perform INSERT, UPDATE, or DELETE operations on tables.

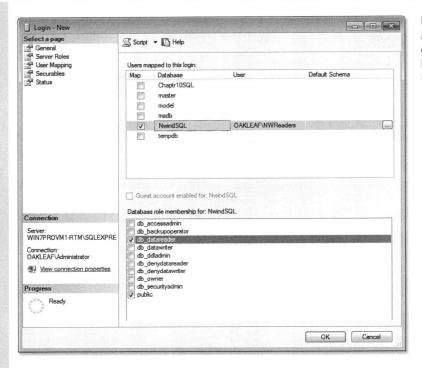

Figure 21.40
Map the login to the default database and assign database roles on the Mapping User page.

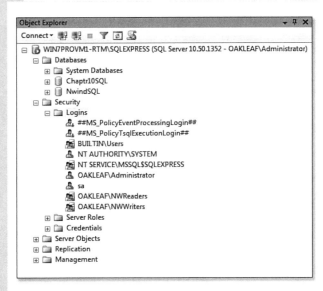

Figure 21.41
Adding logins to the server and mapping the logins to a database adds the group as a user to the mapped database.

Granting Execute Rights to Stored Procedures

Unfortunately, SQL Server 2005 doesn't have a db_executor database role that would enable a user or group to execute all user-defined stored procedures in the database. It's uncommon to execute stored procedures from front ends to linked client/server tables, but the requirement sometimes occurs. You use a pass-through query with EXEC[UTE] StoredProcedureName with added parameters, if necessary, as its query expression.

When you upsize Access databases to ADPs, the Upsizing Wizard creates stored procedures for several classes of SELECT queries and all action queries. ADP queries are the equivalent of pass-through queries, because their SQL statements execute directly against the back-end tables, rather than passing through the Access query processor.

T-SQL

The following T-SQL statements create a set of three user-stored procedures to test group and user permissions for UPDATE and SELECT queries:

```
CREATE PROCEDURE usp_AddThreeYearsUpdate
 AS
 BEGIN
     SET NOCOUNT ON;
     UPDATE dbo.Orders SET OrderDate = DATEADD(YEAR, 3, OrderDate),
                          RequiredDate = DATEADD(YEAR, 3, OrderDate)
     UPDATE dbo.Orders SET ShippedDate = DATEADD(YEAR, 3, OrderDate)
     WHERE ShippedDate IS NOT NULL
 END
 GO


 CREATE PROCEDURE usp_SubtractThreeYearsUpdate
 AS
 BEGIN
     SET NOCOUNT ON;
     UPDATE dbo.Orders SET OrderDate = DATEADD(YEAR, -3, OrderDate),
                          RequiredDate = DATEADD(YEAR, -3, OrderDate)
     UPDATE dbo.Orders SET ShippedDate = DATEADD(YEAR, -3, OrderDate)
     WHERE ShippedDate IS NOT NULL
 END
 GO


 CREATE PROCEDURE usp_2009OrdersSelect
 AS
 BEGIN
     SELECT * FROM dbo.Orders WHERE DATEPART(YEAR,OrderDate) = 2009
 END
 GO
```

Continues...

```
EXEC usp_AddThreeYearsUpdate
GO


EXEC usp_2009OrdersSelect
GO


EXEC usp_SubtractThreeYearsUpdate
GO
```

Executing the \Access2010\Chaptr21\UserStoredProcedures.sql T-SQL script creates and exe-cutes the preceding three stored procedures.

To execute the preceding script in SSMSX do the following:

1. Log in to your client machine as Administrator or another user that's a member of the BUILTIN\ Administrators group and open a SSMSX connection to the NWindSQL database.

2. Choose File, Open, File to open the File Open dialog, navigate to your \Access2010\Chaptr21 folder, and double-click UserStoredProcedures.sql to open its script in the Query window.

3. Click the Execute button to create and execute the three user-stored procedures, displaying Orders with OrderID values of 400 and higher in SSMSX's grid.

4. Expand the Programmability node, right-click its Stored Procedures subnode, and choose Refresh to display nodes for the three user-stored procedures (see Figure 21.42).

To enable members of login groups—NWReaders and NWWriters for this example—to execute a set of stored procedures with explicit permissions, do the following:

1. In SSMSX, double-click the \NWindSQL\Security\Users\NWReaders node to open the Database User–OAKLEAF\NWReaders dialog, and select the Securables page.

2. In SQL Server 2005 Management Studio, click the Add button to open the Add Objects dia-log, select the All Objects of the Types button, and click OK to open the Select Objects dia-log. Click the Object Types button to open the Select Object Types dialog and mark Stored Procedures.Alternatively, in SQL Server 2008+ Management Studio click the Search button to open the Add Objects dialog, select the All Objects Belonging to the Schema option, and select dbo in the Schema list (see Figure 21.43).

3. Click OK to return Database User dialog.

4. Scroll to the user-stored procedures in the Securables list—dbo.usp_2009OrdersSelect, dbo. spAddNineYearsUpdate, and dbo.spSubtractNineYearsUpdate for this example.

5. Only NWWriters should have execute permissions for the two ...Update procedures, so for SQL Server 2005 mark the check box for dbo.usp_2009OrdersSelect and click OK twice to return to the Database User–OAKLEAF\NWReaders' Securables page.

Figure 21.42
Creating and executing the stored procedures displays the first few Orders records for 2009 in the grid. Refreshing the Stored Procedures node displays nodes for each of newly added user stored procedures.

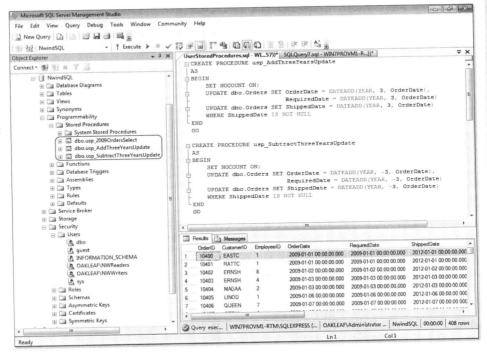

Figure 21.43
Creating and executing the stored procedures displays the first few Orders records for 2009 in the grid. Refreshing the Stored Procedures node displays nodes for each of newly added user stored procedures.

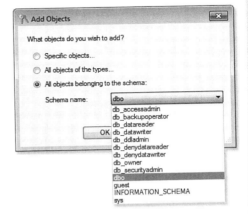

6. Mark the Execute and View Definition check boxes for the select stored procedure in the Grant column (see Figure 21.44). (With Grant, check boxes enable the user to grant the permission to other users.) Click OK to close the dialog.

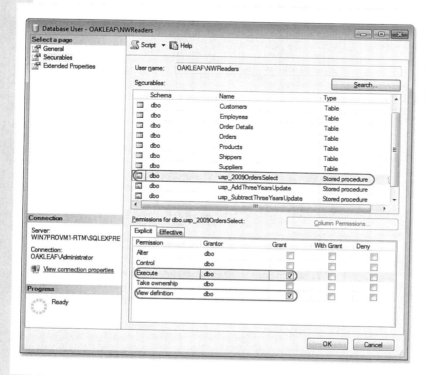

Figure 21.44
Select the stored procedure(s) to enable in the Securables list of the Database User–*Domain\ UserName* dialog.

7. Repeat steps 1 through 5 for the NWWriters user, but add all three stored procedures in step 4, and mark the Grant check boxes for each procedure in step 6.

Verifying Database Securables Protection

The process of verifying the SQL Server linked table permissions for members of the NWReaders and NWWriters Windows security groups is similar to—but more complex than—that for the linked Access tables scenario in the earlier section "Verifying Back-End Database Network Security." Here's the drill:

- Log on to the front-end computer as NWWriter1, and verify that you can read and update tables in Datasheet view, run Access queries, execute pass-through SELECT and UPDATE queries, and execute stored procedures.

- Log on as NWReader1 and verify that you read—but not update—tables, run Access SELECT but not UPDATE queries, and execute only SELECT pass-through queries and stored procedures.

Figure 21.45 shows typical error messages resulting from attempts to update tables and executing stored procedures without appropriate permissions.

Figure 21.45
These error messages occur when the NWReader1 user attempts to update a table (top) or execute a stored procedure without execute permissions (bottom).

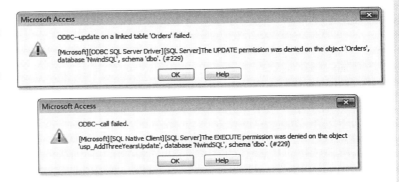

■ Log on as User1 and verify that you cannot open any linked table, run any Access or pass-through query, or execute any stored procedure (see Figure 21.46).

Figure 21.46
You receive this error message when a user with no permissions for database objects attempts to open or execute an object.

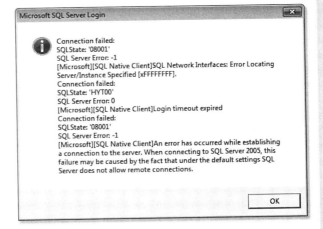

Password-Protecting and Encrypting Access Front Ends

All production database applications should have at least some level of security applied. The minimum level of security is password-protecting the front-end .accdb file. The problem with password protection is that users can copy the front-end .accdb file and then open any Access object—except password-protected VBA code—in Design view and make design changes.

The only method of preventing unauthorized design changes to a password-protected .accdb file is to distribute the front end as an ..accde file or supply a runtime version of your application. A runtime version requires the Access 2007 Developer Extensions' runtime version of MSAccess.exe, which was included with the Microsoft Office Developer Edition (MOD) for earlier Office versions. Creating an .mde version from a copy of your front-end .accdb file or use of runtime Access prevents users from opening any object in Design view.

As a general rule, don't password-protect or create.accde versions of back-end .accdb files. Instead, use share- and file-level security, as described in the earlier section "Establishing Network Share, Folder, and File Security for the Back End."

Providing your application's users with a password-protected .mde version of your front-end database is the simplest method to achieve nominal security. You set only the initial password for the .accdb precursor of the .mde file; users can change the password of an .mde file. This means that everyone running your front end can unset the password, which can compromise security. You or your network administrator can minimize security breaches by requiring network users to change their logon passwords periodically. Changing logon passwords doesn't require changes to file-based or SQL Server security parameters for the back end.

Adding a Database Password

To password-protect and encrypt a front-end .accdb file, do this:

1. Close the database if it's open, and store an unprotected backup copy of the front end on a secure medium, such as a recordable or rewritable CD or a floppy disk. Most front-end .accdb files will fit on a 1.44MB floppy disk. Use the backup copy if you forget the password. This copy also serves as the backup for an .mde version.

2. Click the File tab to open the Backstage view, and choose Open to display the Open dialog.

3. Select the file to protect, and click the arrow to the right of the Open button to display a list of Open options (see Figure 21.47). Choose Open Exclusive to open the file for exclusive use.

4. Click the Info tab and click Encrypt with Password to open the dialog of the same name. If you didn't open the file for exclusive use in step 3, you receive an error message.

5. Type and confirm the password in the two text boxes (see Figure 21.48), click OK, click OK to acknowledge the message that row-level locking will be ignored, and close the database.

6. Reopen the .accdb file, type the password in the Password Required dialog's Enter Database Password text (see Figure 21.49), and click OK.

 note

For maximum password security, use a combination of at least eight upper- and lowercase letters, numbers, and allowed punctuation characters. You can't use the following characters in a password: " \ [ ] : | ‹···· ····› + = ; , . ? *..

 note

The password used to encrypt the \Access2010\Chaptr21\ EncryptedWithPassword. accdb is "password" (without the quotation marks).

Figure 21.47
Use the Open button's list to open the .accdb file in exclusive mode. You need exclusive access to set the database password and encrypt the front end.

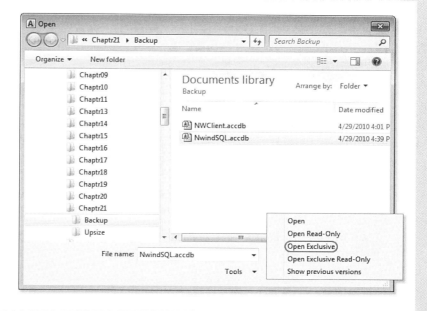

Figure 21.48
Type and confirm the front-end password in the Set Database Password text boxes (top) and confirm loss of row-level locking (bottom).

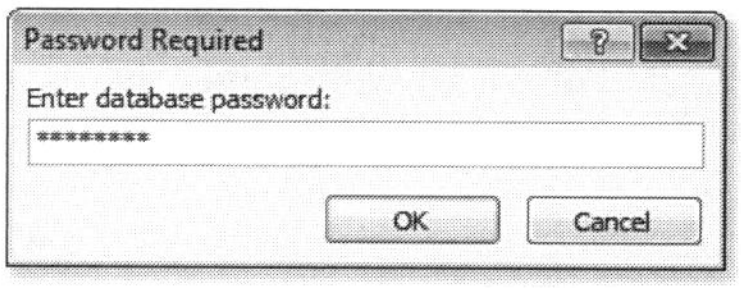

Figure 21.49
Users must type the database-specific password to open the front end. Password-protecting a front-end database doesn't prevent users from making design changes or other modifications to back-end database objects.

To remove the password, repeat steps 2–4, but click Decrypt Database in step 4. Type the password again in the text box and click OK.

Password-Protecting VBA Code

Access 2000 introduced password protection for VBA 6.0 code in conventional modules and Class Modules. You don't need to password-protect VBA code if you convert your front end to an.accde file, which compiles your source code and removes it from the .mde file. *Class Modules* (also called *Microsoft Access Class Objects*) hold the VBA code behind forms and reports. You might want to protect your VBA code against modification by users who have design privileges for the front end.

You can prevent users from viewing or modifying the VBA code in your entire front end by taking the following steps:

1. Open any module, or open a form or report in Design view, and click the Code button to open the VBA editor. Exclusive access isn't necessary to password-protect VBA code.

2. Choose Tools, *ProjectName* Properties to open the *ProjectName* Properties dialog, and click the Protection tab.

3. Mark the Lock Project for Viewing check box, and type and confirm a password in the two text boxes (see Figure 21.50). Click OK.

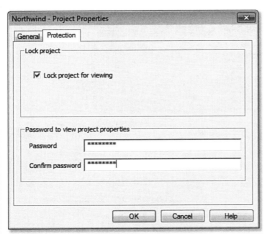

Figure 21.50
Prevent front-end users from viewing and modifying your VBA code behind forms and reports and in modules by password-protecting the code for the entire project.

4. Close and reopen the database, and then repeat step 1. Type the password in the *ProjectName* Password dialog, and click OK.

To remove the VBA code password, repeat steps 1 and 2, clear the Lock Project for Viewing check box, and click OK.

Creating and Testing an .accde Front End

As mentioned earlier, .accde files provide a quick way to protect your front ends from modification by users. Users can't add, delete, or view in design mode forms, reports, and modules. Users have unrestricted access to tables and queries, which means they can wreak havoc on their own copy of the program by deleting links to tables, rewriting queries, and performing other mischief. Applying user-level security is the only means of securing local and linked tables and preserving the integrity of queries and macros (if you use macros).

 Open your Access front-end .accdb file, click the File tab, and click the Make ACCDE button to open the Save As dialog. Accept the default *AccdbFileName*.accde or rename the file. Click Save to create the new .accde file. Open the .accde file and verify user restrictions for tables, forms (see Figure 21.51), reports, and modules. Users might be able to open the Visual Basic Editor but can't view source code, because creating the .mde file removes the source code.

> **tip**
>
> Don't use the same or a similar password for the VBA code and the database. The database password will be the first choice of curious users. More determined users will try variations on the database password, such as adding a numeric suffix.

Figure 21.51
The context menu for a form illustrates user restrictions by disabled choices. Unfortunately, there are no user restrictions for Design view of tables, queries, and macros.

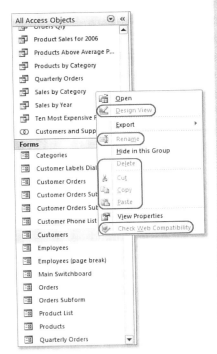

SQL Server Express Performance Problems

If your SSX back end appears to be running out of steam as you add more users, the first step is to optimize your queries to minimize the amount of data returned to the client. Revisit all queries with SELECT * statements to determine whether you need all columns returned. For example, don't include the shipping address fields of Northwind.accdb's Orders table in your query if you're interested only in order dates or customer billing information. Avoid Access-specific or VBA expressions in WHERE clause criteria, because the server must return all records for processing by the Access expression service. Both Access and SQL Server support SELECT TOP n [PERCENT] queries, but ODBC doesn't. Thus, the server must return all records to the client for TOP n processing by Access.

Try to design your form queries with WHERE clause criteria that return fewer than 100 rows. Such queries require only a single connection to the server.

After you've streamlined your queries, the next step is to add RAM. Minimum RAM for reasonable performance with five or fewer users is 512MB for Windows XP or 1GB for Windows Vista.

If some—but not all—users experience performance problems, check their client PCs for adequate RAM to run Office 2007 or the Access 2007 runtime version. The "System Requirements for Access 2007" section of the Introduction lists the RAM requirements for Office 2007. Network connectivity between the client and server also can be a problem; solving networking issues is beyond the scope of this book.

COLLABORATING WITH WINDOWS SHAREPOINT FOUNDATION 2010

Windows SharePoint Foundation (SPF, formerly Windows SharePoint Services, WSS) 2010 is a no-charge add-on to 64-bit Windows Server 2008 Service Pack (SP) 2 and R2 that provides an online, collaborative workspace with an ASP.NET Web-based interface. The most common applications for SPF 2010 are sharing documents from document libraries, managing lists, tracking tasks, handling workflows, displaying images from picture libraries, and enhancing team collaboration with calendars, blogs, wikis, discussions, and surveys.

You can integrate SPF 2010 and Access 2010 to improve the multiuser database experience and enable team members to collaborate in data entry and analysis or database application design. SPF 2010 shares data from SharePoint lists, which link to Access tables. Working with an Access front end enables customized data entry with forms and sophisticated data analysis with reports. The process of setting up data security for an SPF 2010 back end usually is simpler than securing an SQL Server database or the file share for an Access front-end/back-end application.

This chapter introduces you to SPF 2010 and shows you how to

 note

You can install SPF 2010 for development purposes on 64-bit Windows XP SP2 and Windows 7. Read the "Setting Up the Development Environment for SharePoint 2010 on Windows Vista, Windows 7, and Windows Server 2008" help topic (http://msdn.microsoft.com/en-us/library/ee554869(office.14).aspx) for OS-specific recommendations. Running production environments on client operating systems isn't supported and it won't be possible to upgrade deployments running on client versions of Windows to future versions of SharePoint. SPF and WSS 2010 won't install on 32-bit Windows operating systems.

substitute links to SharePoint lists for Access tables. This book uses the term *SharePoint* to include the SPF 2010 and Microsoft SharePoint Server (SPS) 2010 (formerly Microsoft Office SharePoint Services, MOSS) back ends, because list interaction with Access is almost identical for the two products. SPS 2010 is a set of enterprise-grade services that builds on the SPF 2010 foundation to deliver corporate portal capabilities, content management and search facilities, advanced workflow features, business intelligence (BI) capability, records management, and business process management (BPM). SPS 2010 replaces and upgrades MOSS 2007, SharePoint Portal Server (SPS) 2003 and Microsoft Content Management Server 2002.

 note

You can run this chapter's examples on SPF 2010 or either WSS 2010 edition. If you don't have Windows Server 2008 SP2 or R2 installed, you can obtain a 180-day trial version of 64-bit Windows Server 2008 R2 from www.microsoft.com/windowsserver2008/en/us/try-it.aspx.

SPS 2010 requires purchasing a server license and, for intranet users, Client Access Licenses (CALs). Microsoft licenses SPS 2010 in two editions: Standard and Enterprise. The Standard edition supports the following core capabilities:

- Sites

- Communities

- Content

- Search (excludes FAST Search)

- Composites (excludes Access Services and InfoPath Services

Each intranet (internal) user ordinarily requires a Standard CAL to connect to SPS 2010 and use the core capabilities.

The Enterprise Edition adds the following capabilities:

- FAST Search

- Access Services and InfoPath Services

- Insights: PerformancePoint Services, Excel Services, and Visio Services

Each intranet (internal) user ordinarily requires an additional Enterprise CAL to connect to SPS 2010 and use the Enterprise features. Access Services enable publishing Access projects as Web Databases, which are the subject of Chapter 23, "Sharing Web Databases with SharePoint Server 2010."

Microsoft licenses both SPS 2010 editions for two types of user groups: intranet (internal or employee users) and Internet (external or non-employee users). Each intranet user of SharePoint Server 2010 for Internet Sites requires a Standard CAL and, for the Enterprise edition, an Enterprise CAL, unless all the site's content is accessible to Internet (unauthenticated) users.

 tip

Reserve substitution of SharePoint lists for Access tables to applications that involve relatively simple data structures and no more than a few thousand rows (list items). Database tables created from Office Online's Access templates are good candidates for moving to SharePoint lists.

As you'll discover in this chapter's later topic, "Moving and Publishing an Existing Database to SharePoint," SharePoint doesn't maintain referential integrity, has a limited data type repertoire, and begins to exhibit performance problems with lists of 5,000 items or more.

Installing SPF 2010 Under 64-Bit Windows Server 2008

Follow these steps to install SPF 2010 under 64-bit Windows Server 2008 SP2+ or R2:

1. Go to http://technet.microsoft.com/en-us/sharepoint/ee263910.aspx, click the Download Microsoft SharePoint Foundation 2010 link, and download and save SharePointFoundation.exe (173 MB) to a temporary folder.

2. Double-click the saved copy of SharePointFoundation.exe to start the installation process and perform the three Prepare tasks (see Figure 22.1).

Figure 22.1
Running
SharePointFoundation.exe
opens this initial dialog.

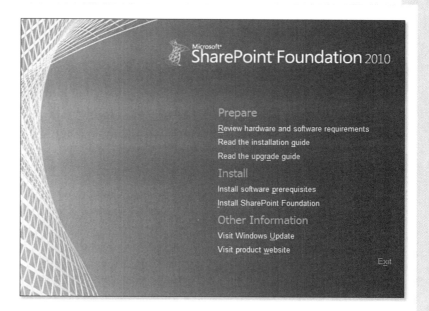

3. Click the Install Software Prerequisites link to open the Microsoft SharePoint 2010 Products Preparation Tool (see Figure 22.2).

4. Click Next, mark the I Accept the Terms of the License Agreements(s) check box, and click Next to begin installing the prerequesites.

5. After prerequisites installation completes, click Finish to close the Products Preparation Tool dialog, and click the Install SharePoint foundation link (refer to Figure 22.1) to open the Microsoft SharePoint Foundation 2010 dialog.

6. Mark the I Accept the Terms of This Agreement check box and click Continue to open the Choose the Installation You Want dialog.

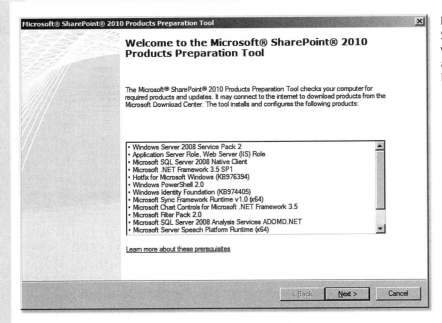

Figure 22.2
Software prerequisites
vary depending on other
applications you've added
before installing SPF.

7. Click the Standalone button to begin installation for testing and development, unless you want to customize a single-server or SharePoint server farm.

8. When installation completes and the Run Configuration Wizard dialog opens, accept the default Run the SharePoint Products Configuration Wizard Now option and click Close to start the Configuration Wizard.

9. In the Welcome to SharePoint Products dialog, click Next to start the wizard and click Yes to dismiss the message about stopping and starting services.

10. When the wizard completes its 10 tasks and displays the Configuration Successful dialog, click Finish to compile the default ASP.NET website and open its Home page.

11. Click Exit to close the main installation dialog (refer to Figure 22.1).

Getting Acquainted with SPF 2010

SPF 2010 creates and manages a collection of template-based websites in which lists and documents are the basic data storage mechanisms. Installing SPF 2010 under Windows Server 2008 SP2+ or R2 creates a default SharePoint site at http://*servername*/ and a mobile site at http://servername/?Mobile=1 and adds the Administrator account you used to log into Windows Server 2008 to the Owners group. The site's home page for PCs is at http://servername/SitePages/Home.aspx.

SPF 2010 stores site metadata and list data for standalone sites in a named instance (*ServerName*\ SHAREPOINT) of SQL Server 2008 Express Edition (SSX). Although you can connect to the SHAREPOINT instance in SQL Server 2008 and later Management Studio Express or other versions, manipulating the instance's data with tools other than SharePoint isn't recommended.

Standard SPF 2010 Site Types

SPF 2010 provides built-in templates for the following collaborative site types:

- Team sites provide basic collaboration features; this template is the default for new SPF 2010 sites. A Team site includes a default home page, Document Library, and empty Announcements, Calendar, Tasks, and Links lists, plus a Team Discussion Board.

- Document Workspace sites are a simplified version of a Team site that includes a Document Library as well as Tasks and Links lists.

- Blog sites provide basic posting and commenting capabilities.

- Group Work sites is a groupware solution that enables teams to create, organize, and share information quickly and easily. It includes Group Calendar, Circulation, Phone-Call Memo, the Document Library and the other basic lists.

- Blank sites have an empty home page and no default objects. You use a SharePoint-compatible web page designer—such as Microsoft SharePoint Designer—to add pages, lists, and other objects to the site.

 note

If you choose Edit in SharePoint Designer from the Site Actions menu and you don't have SharePoint Designer 2010 installed, a dialog opens for downloading its 32-bit or 64-bit version at no charge from the Microsoft website. Using the SharePoint Designer to edit lists is beyond the scope of this book.

 note

SPS 2010 offers a substantially wider variety of site types.

This chapter's examples start with Team sites that the default template creates. Figure 22.3 shows the home page of the default initial site with its name changed from Team Site to OakLeaf Systems, the Mission theme applied, the Microsoft Windows SharePoint Services logo replaced with the OakLeaf logo, and two subsites—Northwind Traders and Oakmont University—added. You add the Oakmont University subsite and customize it in the next two sections.

Add a New SPF 2010 Subsite

Microsoft designed SharePoint to make it easy for ordinary users to create, customize, and manage their own sites without the need to learn HTML or web page design and deployment techniques. Ease of use makes it practical for Access 2010 users to publish, move, link, and share their databases with SharePoint 2010.

To add a new subsite—Oakmont University for this example—to the initial (default) SPF 2010 site, do the following:

1. On the home page of the parent site, open the Site Actions menu list and select Site Settings to open the page of the same name (see Figure 22.4).

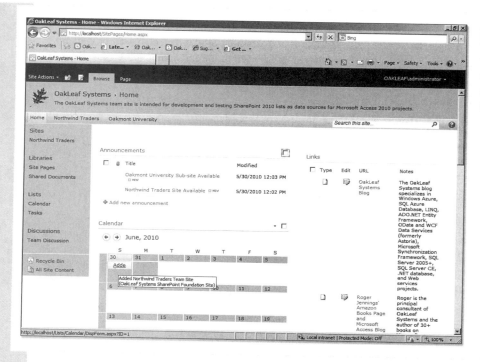

Figure 22.3
This initial WSS
Team site has been
customized with a
new title, logo, and
added subsites.

Figure 22.4
Selecting Site
Settings from the
Site Actions menu
list opens the Site
Settings page,
which contains
links to almost
all administration
pages for the par-
ent and subsites.

2. In the Site Administration group, click the Sites and Workspaces link to open the eponymous page (see Figure 22.5).

Figure 22.5
The Sites and
Workspaces
page lets you
add a new site
or workspace.

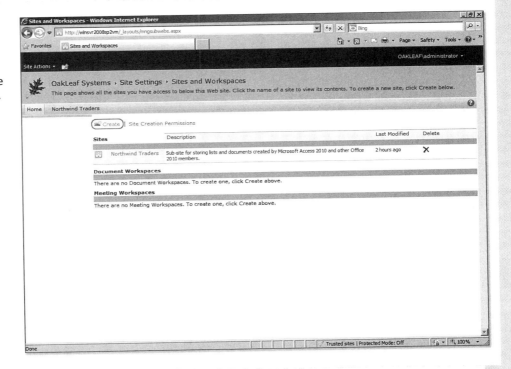

Figure 22.5
The Sites and
Workspaces
page lets you
add a new site
or workspace.

3. Click the Create link to open the New SharePoint Site page. Type the site's name in the Title text box, a brief explanation of the site's purpose in the Description text box, and the URL extension of the site (**oakmont**) in the URL text box. Accept the default permissions, inherited from the parent site (see Figure 22.6).

4. Accept most of the remaining Navigation, Navigation Inheritance, and Template Selection defaults, which add a link to the site on the parent site's Quick Launch pane and link bar, and use the Team Site template. Select the Yes option to Display This Site on the Quick Launch of the Parent Site and Use the Top Link Bar from the Parent Site (see Figure 22.7).

 note

Notice the similarity between the home page's Quick Launch pane and Access 2010's Navigation pane. Unlike the Navigation pane, you can't change the layout of the Quick Launch pane.

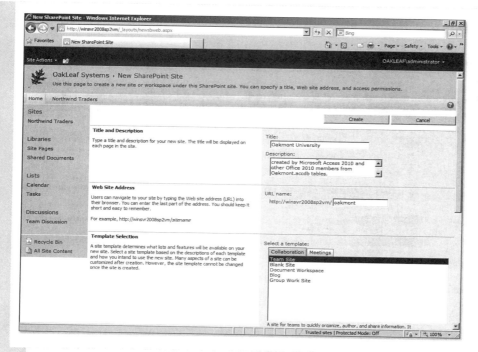

Figure 22.6
The top half of the New SharePoint Site page contains the required entries for the site.

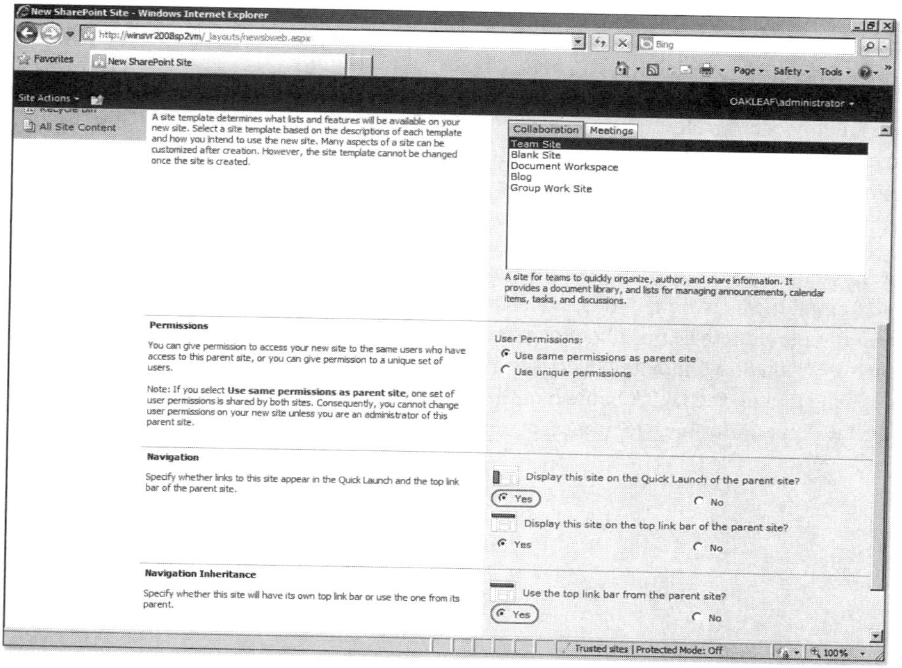

Figure 22.7
For most subsites, you can accept most of the defaults in the New SharePoint Site page's bottom half except those circled here.

5. Click the Create button at the bottom of the page to generate the new subsite's default home page whose URL is http://servername/oakmont/default.aspx (see Figure 22.8).

Figure 22.8
The default subsite contains Web Parts with a substantial amount of irrelevant content.

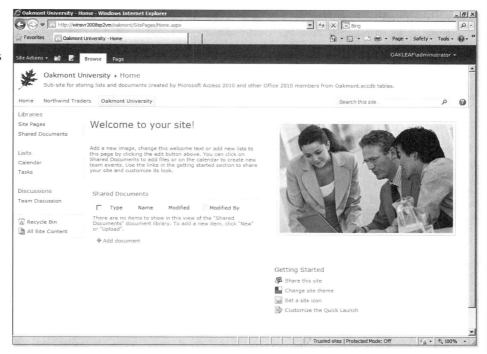

Configure the New Subsite

The default subsite's home page—illustrated by Figure 22.8 —is almost identical to that of the default parent site. Unlike WSS 3.0, it doesn't contain default SharePoint Web Parts for Announcements, Events (Calendar), Site Image (SharePoint Services logo), and Links. The only useful default Web Part is the Shared Documents list. *SharePoint Web Parts* are ASP.NET 2.0+ web controls with SharePoint-specific properties.

This section's step-by-step procedure demonstrates methods for adding and modifying lists, standalone Web Parts (without lists), and document libraries. These three activities are common when you create SharePoint sites that share Access 2010 databases with other users.

To start customizing the subsite by deleting the default Getting Started items and graphic image, changing the logo of the OakLeaf Systems parent site, and renaming the Shared Documents Web Part to Oakmont Databases, do the following:

1. On the Oakmont University home page, click the Quick Launch pane's View All Site Content link to open the All Site Content page (see Figure 22.9).

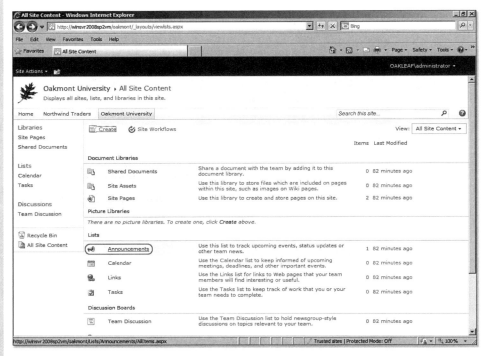

Figure 22.9
The All Site
Content page
has sections
for Document
Libraries,
Picture
Libraries, Lists,
and Discussion
Boards of
default sites.

2. Click the Announcements link to open the Announcements page, click the Get Started with Windows SharePoint Services! link to open the editing dialog, and choose Delete Item (see Figure 22.10).

3. Click OK to send the item to the Recycle Bin.

4. The site logo is in the home-page header in SharePoint 2010, but you can substitute logos for subsites, so click the Oakmont University breadcrumb above the Quick Launch pane to return to the Oakmont home page.

5. Open the Site Actions list and choose Site Settings to open the Site Settings page with the Web Parts in the Left and Right column containers for editing.

6. To change the name and image of the site icon, click the Title, Description, and Icon link (see Figure 22.11) to open the Site Image editing pane.

 note

You can add new items to lists with the home page's Web Parts, but you must open the list to edit or delete an item.

Figure 22.10
Items of lists have a dialog for viewing, editing, setting permissions, deleting, and alerting users about an item.

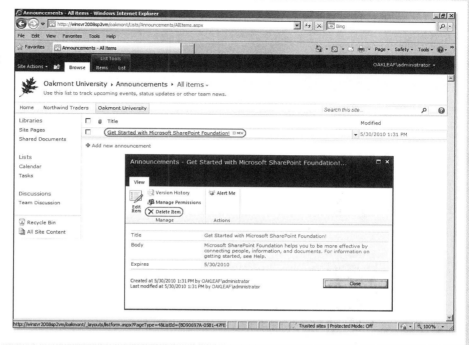

Figure 22.11
Clicking the Title, Description, and Icon link opens a dialog that lets you edit the site's title and description, as well as add the icon URL and alternative text (see Figure 22.12).

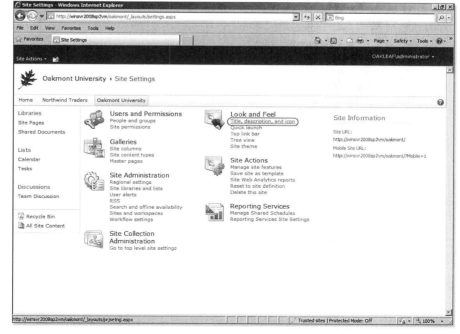

7. In the URL text box, copy and paste the logo's web URL, and click Test Link to open the image in a new page.

8. Type **Oakmont University Logo** in the Enter a Description text box (see Figure 22.12).

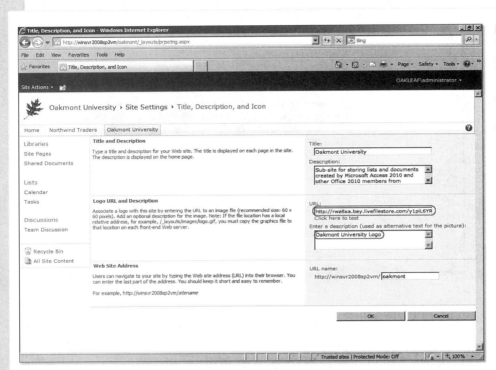

Figure 22.12
Using a web-accessible logo image eliminates the need to copy the graphics file to the /_layouts/images/ folder on each front-end web server of a multiserver production SharePoint site.

 note
The SkyDrive URL for the OakLeaf logo is http://rwz8xa.bay.livefilestore.com/y1piL6YRVibpQ52avRI5FOhUhdE_WkxqQ qwZRfNJZB4z6xAYfooXFXCeWASeowANmGxM4IKDMdojhb1h71t-zSm5LhQoLzite59/OakLeafLogo50px.gif. A shortened version is http://bit.ly/OakLeafLogo.

9. Click OK to save your changes and return to the Site Settings page.

10. In the Quick Launch pane, click the Shared Document item to open the page of the same name. Open the Settings menu list on the toolbar and choose Site Settings, click the Site Administration Group's Site Libraries and Lists link to open page of the same name, and click the Customize "Shared Documents" link to open the Document Library Settings page.

11. Click the Title, Description and Navigation link to open the Document Library Settings: General Settings page. Replace Shared Documents with **Oakmont Databases** in the Name text box, and add a brief description in the Description text box (see Figure 22.13).

Figure 22.13
Use the Document Library Settings: General Settings page to set the library's title, description, and navigation property values.

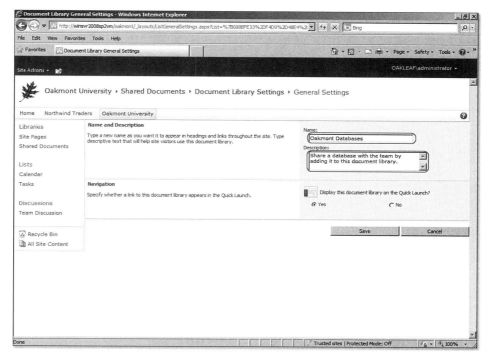

12. Accept the default Navigation option, and click Save to save your changes. Click the Oakmont University breadcrumb or tab to return to the home page and review your changes so far.

13. Choose Edit Page from the Site Actions to open the Oakmont home page in edit mode. Select the Welcome to Your Site! headline and replace it with Welcome to the OakLeaf **University** Site!, delete or replace the accompanying text, select the graphic image and the Getting Started items in the right column, and press Delete to clear this extraneous material from the page (see Figure 22.14).

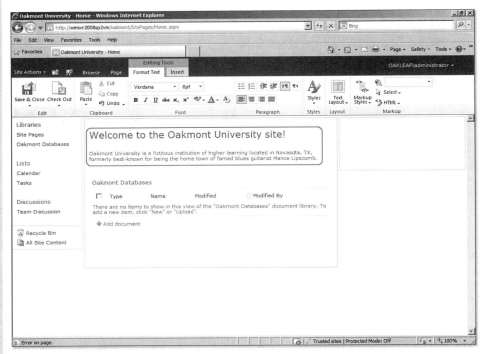

Figure 22.14
Your Oakmont University subsite is now ready to accept Access 2010 database publication, as described in the later "Creating a New Database from a Template and Moving It to SharePoint" section.

SPF 2010 Users and Security Groups

A site represents a security boundary. SPF 2010 has a relatively simple four-level, group-based permission hierarchy for designated SharePoint users. Following are SPF 2010's four default security groups:

- **Site Collection Administrators** have full control over all SharePoint sites in the site collection. The member of the Windows Administrators group who installs SPF 2010 becomes a Site Collection Administrators group member.

- **Site Owners** have full control permissions for the SharePoint site(s) they create. The initial Site Collection Administrator becomes an Owners group member for the default site.

- **Site Members** have read-write permissions, so they can contribute to lists, shared documents, and other site objects.

- **Site Visitors** have read-only permissions for the site.

You must be a member of the Site Collection Administrators group or the Site Owners group for a development site to complete this chapter's step-by-step examples.

Administrators add new sites; a site is a security boundary that can have its own set of users, groups, and permissions. A site contains lists and folders, and can contain a hierarchy of subsites. By default, subsites inherit user permissions assigned at the parent site level.

Create New Users and Assign Them to Groups

To assign permissions to three fictitious Windows Domain Users logins—SiteOwner, SiteMember, and SiteVisitor—to the OakLeaf Systems parent (default) site, do this:

1. Click the Home tab to open the initial site home page (OakLeaf Systems for this example), and choose Site Permissions from the Site Actions menu to open the Permission Tools page, which contains links to Team Site Members, Team Site Owners, and Team Site Visitors items. The Team Site Owners page displays the account used to install SPF 2010 and create the default website (see Figure 22.15).

Figure 22.15
The Team Site Owners page is one of three default pages that display a list of users in a SharePoint group. You also add users to groups, and edit and delete users on these pages.

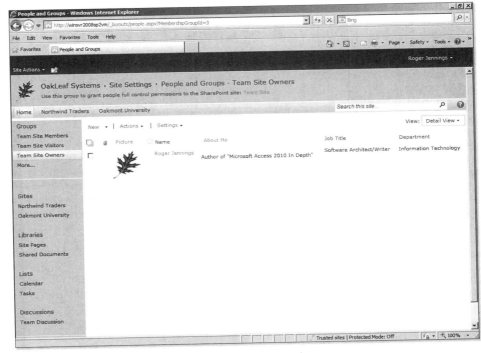

2. Click the Quick Access panel's Team Site Members link in the Groups group, open the New drop-down menu and choose Add Users to open the Grant Permissions dialog. Type the full user name for the Members group—**SharePoint SiteMember**—in the Users text box.

3. Click the Check Names button to test the account name. If the user name matches that of a local or domain account, your entry is underlined in black (see Figure 22.16). If not, a red "No exact match was found" message appears and the entry receives a wavy red underline.

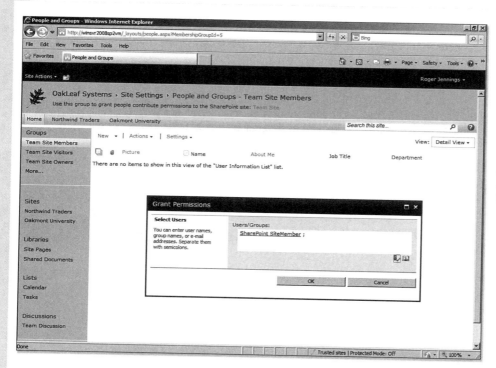

Figure 22.16
Adding a user to a SharePoint group requires typing and verifying the full user first and last names, not the user's logon ID. You can edit the user name later.

4. Click OK to add the user to the group and return to the People and Groups: Team Site Members page, which displays the added user in the list.

5. Click the Quick Launch pane's Team Site Visitors item and repeat steps 2, 3, and 4 for the SharePoint SiteVisitor user. Do the same for the Team Site Owners group and the SharePoint SiteOwner user.

6. Test each account by logging off with your administrative account and logging on with each of the three accounts you added in the preceding steps: *DOMAIN*/SiteMember, *DOMAIN*/SiteVisitor, *DOMAIN*/SiteOwner.

 tip

Add multiple users to a group by separating their user names with a semicolon.

 note

If you're not a member of an Active Directory domain or you created local user accounts, log on with one of those local accounts.

Edit User Information

You must assign user accounts by user name, but you can change the user name after you've created the account. You also can populate Picture (attachment), AboutMe (description), Job Title, and Department fields, which appear in the list's default view, plus E-Mail and SIP Address, which don't appear. The SharePoint account inherits corresponding values from the Active Directory Domain Users login.

To edit existing user data and add additional information about a user (SharePoint SiteOwner for this example), do the following:

1. In the People and Groups: Team Site Owners page, click the Name cell of the user whose data you want to edit. The User Information: *UserName - LogonID* page opens with only the Account and Name fields completed, unless you provided additional details when you created the Active Directory account.

2. Click the Edit item button on the toolbar to open an editable version of the page. Change the Name field entry, if you want; this example uses one of the Oakmont Outlook contacts, Eric Arthur, you create in the later "Working Offline and Synchronizing Lists" section.

3. Complete entries for the remaining text boxes, as illustrated by Figure 22.17.

 note

Microsoft Office Communication Server (MOCS) "14" uses the Session Initiation Protocol (SIP) address—also called the SIP URI (Universal Resource Identifier)—to provide presence information to clients. MOCS is one of Microsoft's Unified Communications offerings and was in the process of updating to version 14 when this book was written. For more about MOCS, go to www.microsoft.com/uc/.

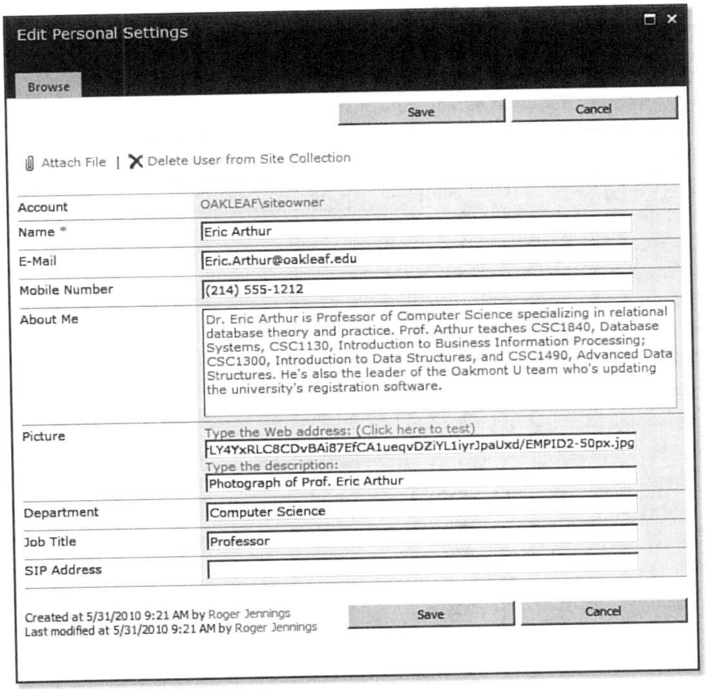

Figure 22.17
Add detailed information about and pictures of users in the User Information: - *User Name - LogonID* page.

4. Click Save to save your changes and return to the User Information: Eric Arthur – *DomainName*\siteowner page and review the user information you added. Click close to return to the People and Groups–Team Site Owners page (see Figure 22.18).

note

The three pages connect to the same list; each page presents a different view of the list.

Figure 22.18
The People and Groups: Team Site Owners and related pages display all fields except the user's email and SIP addresses. These entries appear in the Site Owners group in all People and Groups pages of the parent site and sub-sites.

5. Optionally, complete steps 1 through 4 for the SharePoint SiteMember (and SharePoint SiteVisitor users.

Managing Data with Access and SharePoint 2010

Access 2010 enables interaction with SharePoint 2010 in the following ways:

- **Save database as SharePoint**—Saving an Access 2010 database to a SharePoint 2010 site stores a copy of the database in a document library on the SPF or SPS server. Users can open a shared read-only master copy of the database or—with Site Member or Site Owner permissions—save a local read-write copy of the database to edit. Changes aren't saved to the master copy until the user republishes the local copy to the SharePoint server.

- **Move table data to SharePoint**—Moving (exporting) data to a SharePoint site creates lists that are linked as tables of your database. Access creates a new front-end application that contains the queries, forms, and reports, as well as the linked tables.

- **Create an Access database from a SharePoint site**—Users who want to take advantage of Access's editing and reporting capabilities can choose to open a list in a linked Access table and, if the database doesn't already exist, create a new database to hold the linked table(s) and added form(s) and report(s).

- **Export, import, or link a SharePoint list**—Access 2010 treats SharePoint lists like other data stores, such as Microsoft Excel, but linked SharePoint lists are editable.

The following sections describe how to perform each of the preceding Access-related tasks.

 note

The Export Tables to SharePoint Wizard automates the process of generating SharePoint lists from Access 2010 tables and then linking new tables in an Access 2010 database to the lists. You can then save the resulting database to a SharePoint document library when the move is complete.

 You start the Export Tables to SharePoint Wizard by clicking the Database Tools tab and the Move Data group's SharePoint button. The wizard creates a backup copy of the source database before performing the move operation.

Saving an Existing Access Database in a SharePoint Document Library

Sharing an existing Access 2010 database by publishing it to a SharePoint Document Library is a simple task. You don't need to link Access tables to SharePoint lists to publish the database, but linking eliminates the requirement to republish the local copy to save changes to its data. If you intend to link the tables, skip to the next section, "Moving Tables and Saving an Existing Database to SharePoint."

Do the following to publish an Access 2010 database to a SPF 2010 Document Library:

1. Open an existing database (\Access2010\Chaptr22\Nwind\ NwindPub.accdb for this example), click the File tab, and choose Save & Publish, Save Database As, Sharepoint to open the Save to Sharepoint dialog of the same name. If you haven't previously published a database, a list of computers on your network is present, along with other default icon(s).

   If you don't want to create the subsite, you can add the sample database to the root site's default "Shared Documents" Document Library. However, creating the Northwind Traders subsite is strongly recommended.When I open the File tab, I see a Publish to Access Services, or share as a Sharepoint. I don't see a Save and Publish choice. – SBD The choice is there (between Print and Help) with NwindPub.accdb.

note

You can use the NwindPub. accdb sample database in the \ Access2010\Chaptr22 folder to test saving a complete database. The following example assumes the existence of a Northwind Traders (http://*computername*/northwind) subsite, which you can add by the process described in the earlier "Add a New SPF 2010 Subsite" section.

2. Type http://*computername* and click Save to display the Document Libraries and Sites and Workspaces lists for the initial site. Continue to navigate by double-clicking icons until you reach the Document Library to store NwindPub.accdb, OakLeaf Systems/Northwind Traders/Shared Documents for this example (see Figure 22.19).

3. Click Publish to save the database in the Document Library, close the dialog, and open the database from the Document Library. Databases opened from a Document library display a Save Changes document action bar with a Save to SharePoint Site button for members of the Site Owners or Site Members group.

4. Click the Save to SharePoint Site button to open the Save to SharePoint dialog with the Northwind Traders Shared Document library selected (see Figure 22.20).

5. Click Save and click Yes to dismiss the Confirm Save As message box and save the current version of the database.

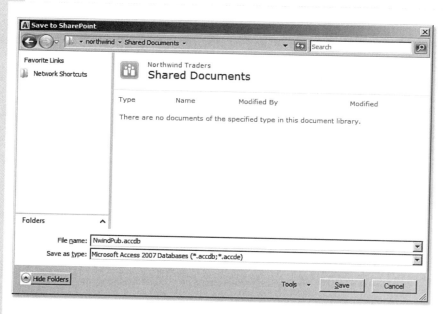

Figure 22.19
The Publish to Web Server dialog opens to the most recently used Document Library. If you haven't published an Access database to the site, you must double-click your way down the hierarchy to the desired Document Library.

6. Close the saved version of NwindPub.accdb, open the subsite at http:// *servername*/north-wind/, and click Shared Documents in the Quick Launch pane's Libraries section to open the All Documents list, which contains a new NwindPub item.

7. Click NwindPub to open a Microsoft Internet Explorer dialog, which lets users open the database in Read-Only or Edit mode (see Figure 22.21).

Figure 22.20
Clicking
the Save to
SharePoint
Site button
opens the Save
to SharePoint
dialog with
the destina-
tion docu-
ment library
selected.

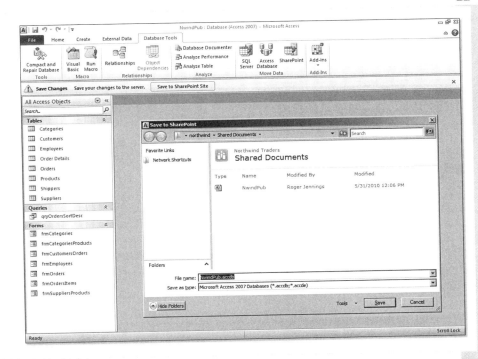

Figure 22.21
Site Members,
Site Owners, or
Site Collection
Administrators
have the choice
of opening
a published
database in
Read-Only or
Edit mode.
Site Visitors
are permitted
only Read-Only
access.

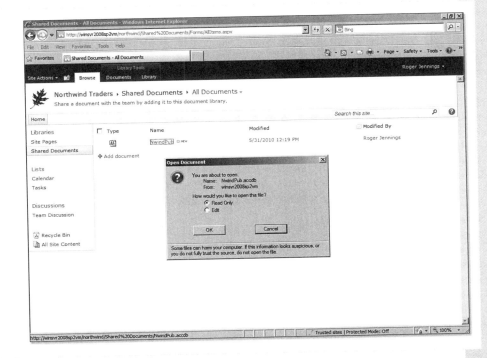

8. If you select Read-Only mode, SharePoint opens the shared database from the Document Library (see Figure 22.22). The Document Action Bar displays a Security Alert because the Document Library isn't a trusted location and a Read-Only notice. Verify that the data is read-only, and close Access to return to the Document Library page.

note

Members of the Site Visitors group see an Internet Explorer warning dialog that states, "You are opening the following file: File name: *FileName*.accdb From: *computername*."

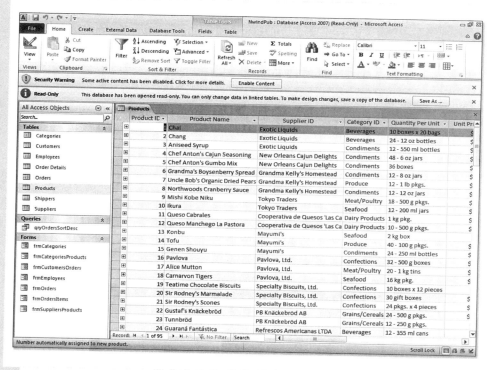

Figure 22.22
Shared databases opened in Read-Only mode from the Document Library include a Read-Only notice in the Document Action Bar.

9. If you select Edit mode, SharePoint opens the Save a Local Copy dialog to enable users to save a local copy of the database with a distinctive filename in a trusted location, ...\Documents\SharePoint for this example (see Figure 22.23).

10. Click Save to create the local copy and open in Access. The Document Action Bar displays the same Security Warning and Save to SharePoint Site button as when you selected Edit mode in step 8.

11. Click the Save to SharePoint Site button to open the Save to Web Server dialog (see Figure 22.24). Accept the default

note

You can add security for the source database by publishing an encrypted version of the file. Users are required to provide the password to read or create a local database copy. The local database copy is encrypted with the same password as the source database.

Document Library and filename, and click Publish to update the shared master database file, click Yes to acknowledge that you want to overwrite the file, and then close Access.

Figure 22.23
Users usually save local database copies for editing to trusted locations.

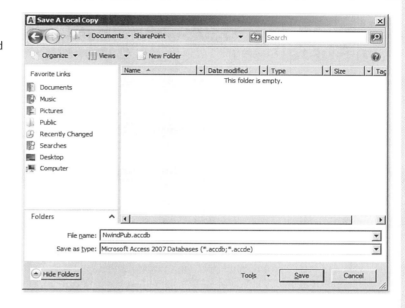

Figure 22.24
The Publish to Web Server dialog displays the default Document Library and filename for the republishing operation.

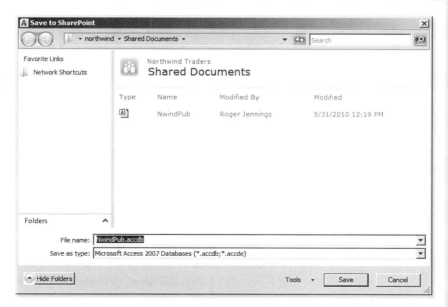

The obvious issue with the publishing and republishing scenario is the lack of concurrency protection. The last user to republish a local copy with changes overwrites any changes that other users make after the last user created the local database copy or republished changes.

Moving Tables and Saving an Existing Database to SharePoint

You can solve most data concurrency issues by moving an Access 2010 database's tables and their data to linked SharePoint lists. The process is similar to using the Database Splitter to create links to Access tables in a back-end database or upsizing Access tables to an SQL Server 2005 database. Changes to lists made by all SharePoint users are reflected in Access front ends and vice-versa.

SharePoint lists exhibit few characteristics of relational tables. For example, SharePoint lists don't maintain referential integrity, support cascading updates, enable validation rules other than required entry, accommodate multifield primary keys, or handle default value expressions much more complex than =Date(). Thus, the behavior of an Access application with linked SharePoint lists differs from that of conventional Access applications with linked or self-contained tables. You can work around most of these limitations by writing Data Macros for default values and validation rules.

 note

The Access AutoNumber data type becomes an ordinary SharePoint number, because all SharePoint lists have an autoincrementing ID field with a no-duplicates index. SharePoint supports only its own, auto-generated no-duplicates index.

SharePoint doesn't support Access's OLE Object fields, so they aren't moved to the SharePoint lists.

SharePoint List Data Types

SharePoint lists have data types that accommodate all Access data types except OLE Object. Table 22.1 lists the SharePoint list data types and their corresponding Access data types, with limitations where applicable.

Table 22.1 SharePoint Data Types That Correspond to Access Data Types

SharePoint Data Type	Access Data Type(s)	List Limitations
Single Line of Text	Text, AutoNumber as ReplicationID	Newline (CrLf) characters in Text data type values cause a change to the Multiple Lines of Text (Memo) Data Type.
Multiple Lines of Text	Memo	This data type has an Append-Only property for revision tracking.
Number	Number (all sizes except Replication ID), AutoNumber	Lists display a maximum of nine decimal places and display as a percentage if the Access Format property value is Percentage. Access AutoNumber fields lose their AutoIncrement property.

SharePoint Data Type	Access Data Type(s)	List Limitations
Date or Time	Date/Time	Lists display Date Only if the Access Format value is Short Date; the Access =Date() de fault value corresponds to Today's Date.
Currency	Currency	Access Currency fields import as Number and require changing the data type manually.
Yes/No	Yes/No	
Hyperlink	Hyperlink	
Attachment	Attachment	Lists support only one attachment field.
Lookup	Single-valued or multivalued Lookup fields	Other lists provide lookup data.
Choice	Single-valued or multivalued Lookup fields	Lists display literal lookup values separated by newline characters.

When you move an Access table to a SharePoint list, the Export Tables to SharePoint Wizard does a best-efforts job of matching table and list data types, transferring data from the table to the list, and regenerating Lookup or Choice field data. Access Text fields that contain newline (CrLf) characters move to Multiple Lines of Text (Memo) fields because Single Line of Text fields don't permit newline characters. Filter and Order By table properties don't propagate to the SharePoint list, and Text fields' Field Size properties don't propagate to Single Line of Text columns.

Customize SharePoint List Views

SPF 2010 displays only views of SharePoint lists; the default All Items view displays all significant list columns of exported tables in an Access Web Datasheet control by default. To display a list's default view, click the Quick Launch pane's View All Site Content item and then click the list name whose items you want to view. Figure 22.25 shows the first six columns of the Products list created by exporting the\Access2010\Chaptr22\Nwind\NwindMove. accdb's Products table.

Editing in Datasheet view follows the Access pattern. SupplierID is a multivalued Lookup field (MVLF), so opening this field's dropdown list displays a list with check boxes to specify multiple suppliers. CategoryID is a conventional (single-valued) Lookup field with a conventional dropdown list.

Users who don't have Office 2010 display and edit lists in standard view by default. To change to standard view, click the List Tools tab's List button to open the List ribbon and click the Standard View button.

 note

The Access Web Datasheet control is a component provided by Office 2010 and isn't installed by SharePoint. SharePoint users must have Office 2010installed to use the Access Web Datasheet control, also called the Office 2010 List Datasheet View 2010.

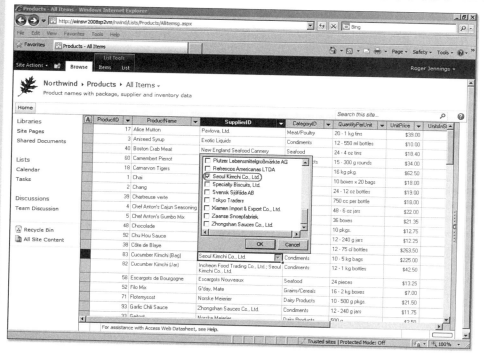

Figure 22.25
This partial All
Items view for
the SharePoint
list version of
the Northwind.
accdb data-
base's Products
table has a
column list
with the field
sequence of
the source
table.

To edit a single item, click the List Tools tab's Items button to enable selecting one or more items in the list, click the text in the ProductName column to add a marked check box to the row to be edited, and enable the Edit Item button in the ribbon's Manage group (see Figure 22.26).

Click the ribbon's Edit Item button in the Manage group to open the editing dialog (see Figure 22.27). Make your changes and scroll down to expose the dropdown list for the CategoryId value and the Save and Cancel buttons. Click Save to save your edits.

Figure 22.26
Clicking the ProductID or ProductName cell enables the row for editing or deletion. Clicking SupplierID or CategoryID opens an editing form for the selected supplier or category.

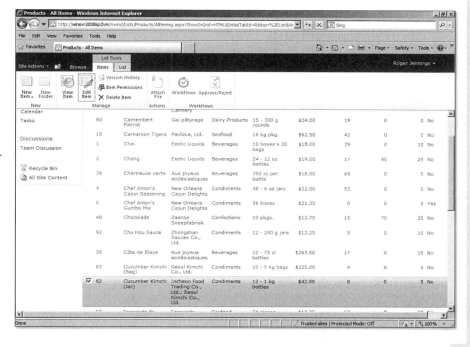

Figure 22.27
Editing an item with a multivalued Lookup field (SupplierID) adds a pair of list boxes for selecting multiple lookup values. The single-valued Lookup field (CategoryID), hidden below the dialog's bottom edge, has a drop-down list for selecting a single value.

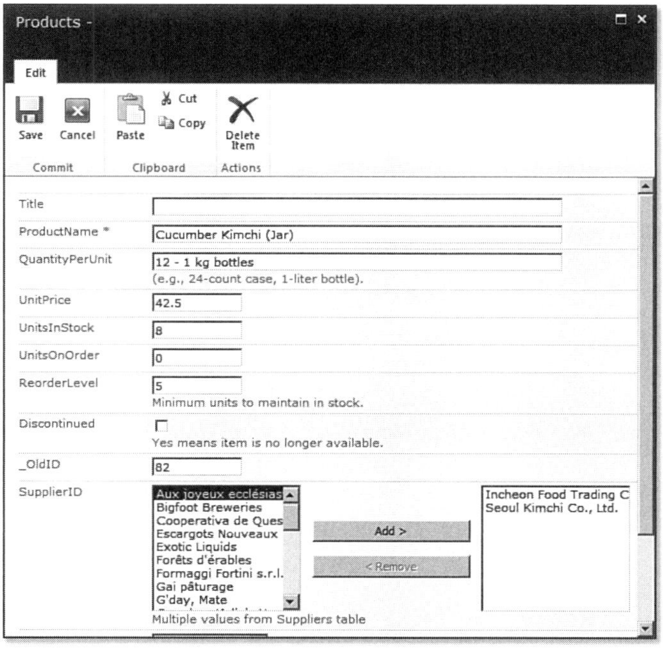

To change a view's name, web address, sort options, filter, totals, item limit or field sequence, click the List button in the List Tools tab, and click Modify View to open the *List Name* - List Settings - Edit Datasheet View page (see Figure 22.28). Change the list's column sequence by selecting a column's ordinal value with the associated dropdown list. The Edit View page also lets you sort and filter the view, as well as add aggregate values (Count, Sum, Average, Maximum, Minimum, Std Deviation or Variance) for numeric columns and Count for non-numeric columns.

Microsoft has adopted Really Simple Syndication (RSS) 2.0 XML files as an alternative method of interacting with SharePoint lists and related content types, such as blogs. Clicking the RSS symbol to the right of the web address text box for the view opens an RSS 2.0 full-text feed for the view in IE 8 (see Figure 22.29). Clicking the green arrow to the right of the author name opens the SharePoint Products: *ProductName* page for the selected product (Chu Hou Sauce for this example). You can edit or delete the item, as well as add a new item to list, manage user permissions, or request an alert when anyone edits the item. IE 8 lets users stay up to date with list data by subscribing to the view's RSS feed. The feed is compatible with all popular RSS readers.

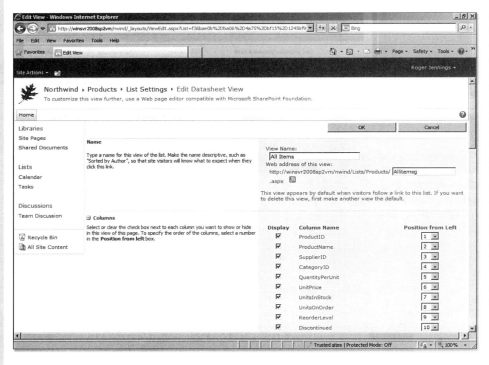

Figure 22.28
Change the view's name and column sequence in the Edit View: *ListName* page. Only the datasheet's 10 visible columns are shown here; the remaining 10 columns have cleared text boxes. Scroll down to expose Sort, Filters, Totals, Folders and Item Limit settings links.

Figure 22.29
RSS 2.0 transformations of SharePoint views let users subscribe to feeds with IE 7+ or third-party RSS readers. Each view is a channel that displays up to 100 recently edited items by default. (OldID is the ProductID value from the imported table.)

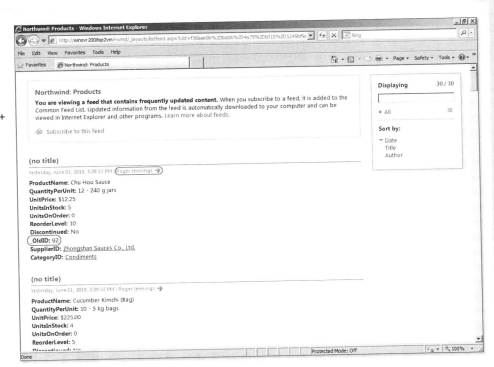

Following is a truncated version of the RSS document that generates an item similar to that shown in Figure 22.27:

```xml
<?xml version="1.0" encoding="UTF-8"?>
<!--RSS generated by Microsoft SharePoint Foundation RSS Generator on 6/2/2010
11:01:07 AM -->
<?xml-stylesheet type="text/xsl" href="/nwind/_layouts/RssXslt.aspx?List=f36bae0b-
ba06-4a75-bf15-1245bf9c4144" version="1.0"?>
<rss version="2.0">
  <channel>
    <title>Northwind: Products</title>
    <link>http://winsvr2008sp2vm/nwind/Lists/Products/Allitemsg.aspx</link>
    <description>RSS feed for the Products list.</description>
    <lastBuildDate>Wed, 02 Jun 2010 18:01:06 GMT</lastBuildDate>
    <generator>Microsoft SharePoint Foundation RSS Generator</generator>
    <ttl>60</ttl>
    <language>en-US</language>
    <image>
```

```
        <title>Northwind: Products</title>
        <url>http://winsvr2008sp2vm/nwind/_layouts/images/siteIcon.png</url>
        <link>http://winsvr2008sp2vm/nwind/Lists/Products/Allitemsg.aspx</link>
      </image>
      <item>
        <title>(no title)</title>
        <link>http://winsvr2008sp2vm/nwind/Lists/Products/DispForm.aspx?ID=17</link>
        <description><![CDATA[
          <div><b>ProductName:</b> Alice Mutton</div>
          <div><b>QuantityPerUnit:</b> 20 - 1 kg tins</div>
          <div><b>UnitPrice:</b> $39.00</div>
          <div><b>UnitsInStock:</b> 0</div>
          <div><b>UnitsOnOrder:</b> 0</div>
          <div><b>ReorderLevel:</b> 0</div>
          <div><b>Discontinued:</b> Yes</div>
          <div><b>_OldID:</b> 17</div>
          <div><b>SupplierID:</b> <a onclick="OpenPopUpPage(...)>Pavlova, Ltd.</a></div>
          <div><b>CategoryID:</b> <a onclick="OpenPopUpPage(...)>Meat/Poultry</a></
  div>]]>
        </description>
        <author>Roger Jennings</author>
        <pubDate>Tue, 01 Jun 2010 22:39:28 GMT</pubDate>
        <guid isPermaLink="true">
          http://winsvr2008sp2vm/nwind/Lists/Products/DispForm.aspx?ID=17
        </guid>
      </item>
    </channel>
</rss>
```

To change list data types, click the List ribbon's List Settings button to open the *ListName* List Settings page (see Figure 22.30), which also lets you add new columns, change read-write column order, and add duplicates-allowed indexes on the underlying SQL Server 2008 fields for most columns. You also can customize feeds by clicking the Communications column's RSS 2.0 Setting link to open the Modify List RSS Settings: *ListName* page. This page lets you specify the channel's title, description, and image, as well as the fields to display, maximum number of items or days to include.

Here are a few other SharePoint list characteristics that are useful to understand before you move Access tables or entire databases to a SharePoint site:

- All SharePoint lists have default Type (icon linked to document), Attachments, Title (linked to item with edit menu), Content Type, Created, Created By, Edit (linked to edit item), ID, Modified, Modified By, Title, Title (linked to item), and Version columns.

- The All Items (default) view displays only a few default fields. You must edit the All Items view to display the fields you need in the appropriate sequence. Alternatively, you can create another named view and make it the default.

Figure 22.30
The ListName
List Settings
page lets you
modify the
underlying list,
rather than a
view of the list.
The changes
you make on
this page affect
all the list's
views.

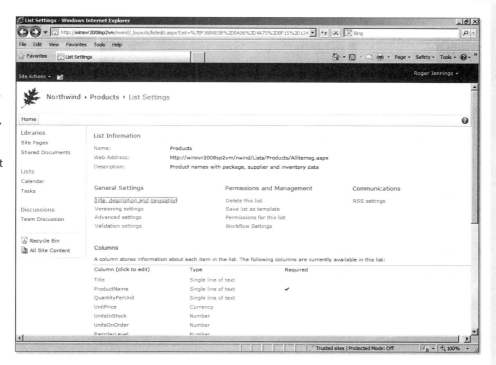

- All default fields except Attachments, Title (linked to item with edit menu), Created By, Modified By, and Title (linked to item) are read-only.

- You change list properties and field data types in the Customize *ListName* page. Change view properties in the Edit View: *ListName* page.

- When you import or move Access tables, the first required field (Categories.CategoryName, for example) or Text-type primary key (Customers.CustomerID, for example) replaces the Title column.

 note

The preceding list uses Northwind. accdb tables and fields as examples because—unlike tracking databases created from Office Online templates—this database and its table structure isn't optimized for SharePoint compatibility.

- In some cases, Access AutoNumber fields, such as Orders.OrderID, moved to list columns appear as _OldID values, which autoincrement.

- If a table has a multivalued field, such as Products.SupplierID, and another foreign key with a relationship specified, such as Products.CategoryID, you might be unable to export the table or move the database to SharePoint.

Moving and Saving the Northwind Database to SPF 2010

Order processing databases and related online transaction processing (OLTP) databases—such as Northwind.accdb—are much more complex than the simple Access tracking databases whose templates you download from Office Online. In the real world, you'd use SharePoint lists only for tracking very simple and infrequent transactions, such as block grants to a not-for-profit organization. However, moving a copy of Northwind.accdb to SPF 2010 is useful to demonstrate problems with multiple relationships, multivalued fields, a large number of rows, and conflicts with Access data types such as AutoNumber.

> **note**
>
> The NwindMove.accdb database in the \Access2010\Chaptr22\Nwind folder is intended for use as the source database to be moved to SharePoint in this example.

To move and save NwindMove.accdb to the a http://localhost/nwind/ SPF 2010 site that's similar to the Northwind site you created in the earlier "Saving an Existing Access Database to a SharePoint Document Library" section, do the following:

1. Open NwindMove.accdb, click the Database Tools tab, and click the Move Data group's SharePoint button to start the Export Tables to SharePoint Site Wizard.

2. Type the site address, **http://**_servername_**/nwind/** in the What SharePoint Site Do You Want To Use text box (see Figure 22.31).

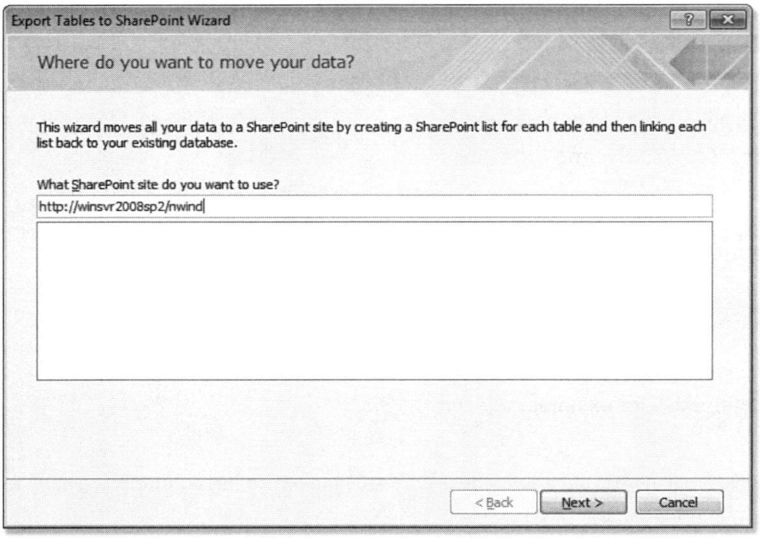

Export Tables to SharePoint Wizard

Where do you want to move your data?

This wizard moves all your data to a SharePoint site by creating a SharePoint list for each table and then linking each list back to your existing database.

What SharePoint site do you want to use?

`http://winsvr2008sp2/nwind`

[< Back]   [Next >]   [Cancel]

Figure 22.31
Specify the site and, if applicable, subsite address in the Move to SharePoint Site Wizard's first dialog.

3. Click Next to start the move and publish process, which displays a progress dialog (see Figure 22.32).

Figure 22.32
The Move to SharePoint Site Wizard's second dialog displays a progress bar for the move operation, which consists of several steps for each table.

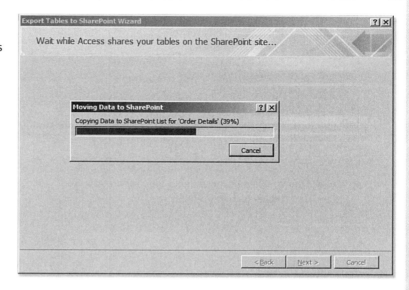

4. After a few minutes or longer, depending on your computer's CPU speed and amount of available RAM, the final Your Tables Have Been Successfully Shared dialog opens. Click the Show Details check box to display the result of the move and publish operations (see Figure 22.33).

Figure 22.33
The Details text box shows the lists created, the name and location of the backup database, and the URL for the published database.

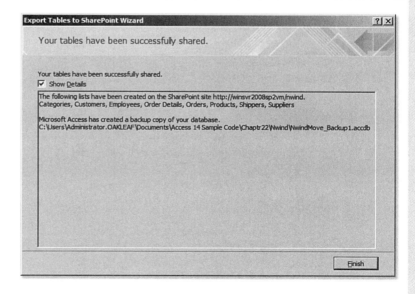

5. Click Finish to dismiss the Wizard and display the linked tables in the Navigation pane. Access creates a backup (NwindMove_Backup.accdb for this example) of the source database.

6. 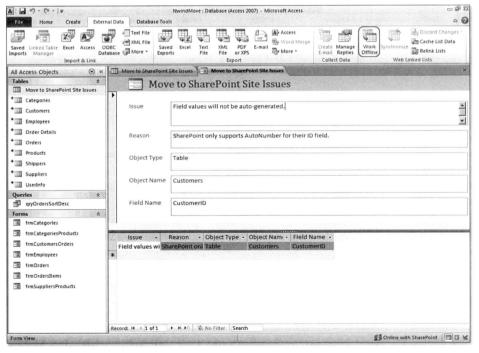 Open the Navigation pane, choose Object Type and All Access Objects, and open the Move to SharePoint Site Issues table. Optionally, click the Create tab, open the More Forms list and click Split Form to display the problem descriptions in form text boxes (see Figure 22.34).

7. Open the http://localhost/nwind subsite and click the Quick Access pane's Lists link to display the lists created from the Access tables (see Figure 22.35).

note

Notice in Figure 22.34 that the Web Linked Lists group's Work Offline button on the External Data Tab is enabled, which indicates that the data is linked to a SharePoint site. Users with a local copy of the database can work with the data when they can't connect to the SharePoint site and then update the site data when they reconnect. Working offline with SharePoint-hosted databases is the subject of the "Working Offline and Synchronizing Lists" section, later in this chapter.

Figure 22.34
A split form makes it easier to review rows of the Move to SharePoint Site Issues table.

Figure 22.35
The All Site Content view displays an item for each list generated by moving an Access table to the subsite. Default lists, such as Announcements and Tasks have been deleted.

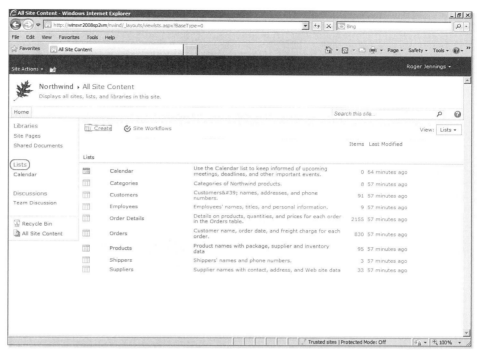

8. Open the default All Items view for each list and verify that it contains the content you expect and that the columns are in appropriate sequence. If not, modify the view as described in the earlier "Customize SharePoint List Views" section.

9. Activate Access and browse the linked SharePoint lists. You'll find that the structure of most linked lists differ substantially from that of the original table.

note
Access links to the SharePoint list, not a view of the list. Therefore, any design changes you make in the default All Items view don't propagate to the database.

The following section describes the changes to linked lists and how to work around some of the more problematic changes.

Fixing Up Lists to Resemble Source Tables

Despite its use of a SQL Server 2008 database as its data store, SharePoint lists aren't relational tables.

Following are the most important changes to source tables made by moving tables to SharePoint lists, examples, and possible workarounds:

- AutoNumber primary key fields are renumbered and hidden, unless the original TableID field value for the first row is 1.

  For example, the OrderID field of the Orders list is the AutoNumber primary key, but its seed (initial) value is 1, not 10248, and the last record is 830, not 11077. This issue isn't so evident with tables whose AutoNumber primary key starts with 1, but the values will differ if any table rows were deleted before the move. Renumbering of rows after the deleted rows is likely to be missed by casual inspection.

- When you move a database to a SharePoint list, the original AutoNumber primary key field values often appear in a hidden _OldID field, which you can unhide in Access with the Unhide Columns dialog.

  For example, the Orders table's original OrderID values are in a hidden _ID field. The Categories, Employees, Products, Shippers, and Suppliers tables also have *Table*ID primary key and a hidden _OldID field. These five tables export correctly because no rows have been deleted.

- You can't update fewer than all current links to a SharePoint list with the Choose the SharePoint Lists You Want to Link To dialog. If you clear check boxes to prevent re-creating the link by an import operation, the links are deleted. If you leave existing links checked, the links lose hidden primary key and _ID fields.

  If you want to add a new link and retain hidden or visible primary key and _ID fields for all existing lists, you must move the table from a single-table database, and then import the link from that database.

- Some fields lose lookup properties during the move to SharePoint list columns.

  For example, the Orders table shows the Customers list's CustomerID value in a text box rather than the expected CompanyName value in a lookup combo box. You can't fix this problem in Access because linked lists are read-only in Design view (except the Caption and Lookup properties). You can add a new CompanyName Lookup field in SharePoint's Customize *ListName* page, but you can't replace the CustomerID field with it, as you'll see in the later "Replacing a Missing Lookup Field" section.

- The length of all Single Line of Text columns is 255 characters, regardless of the Length property value set for the Access source field. You can change the maximum number of characters on the lists Change Column: *ColumnName* page.

  For example, the Customers table's CustomerID field is 255, not 5 characters. In this case, the Input Mask property limits the length to 5 characters. There is no protection from duplicate CustomerID values.

- Some lists gain unwanted/unnecessary Title fields when moved from Access tables, and all lists have Attachment fields.

The Order Details list's Title field values are missing, because Order Details has no required Text field. All linked tables have Attachments fields, unless you disable attachments on the List Advanced Settings page.

- You can't change a column's data type from Number or Single Line of Text to Lookup.

  The workaround for Single Line of Text data is to add a Lookup column to the list, and then populate the list by copying and pasting the data in SharePoint Datasheet view, as described in the "Replacing a Missing Lookup Field" section.

- Lookup or Choice list data types alter the list's column sequence. By default, the _OldID column follows the renamed Title column. You'll find Lookup or Choice columns after the last simple data type column.

  For example, the Orders list's _OldID column follows CustomerID, which is the renamed Title column, and EmployeeID and ShipVia columns follow ShipCountry. It's easy to change the column sequence by Datasheet view's drag-and-drop fields feature.

Figure 22.36 shows the Orders list's Datasheet view after hiding the OrderID column and changing the position of the _OldID, EmployeeID, and ShipVia columns.

Figure 22.36
This Orders list's Datasheet view has its OrderID and _ID columns unhidden and EmployeeID and ShipVia fields moved.

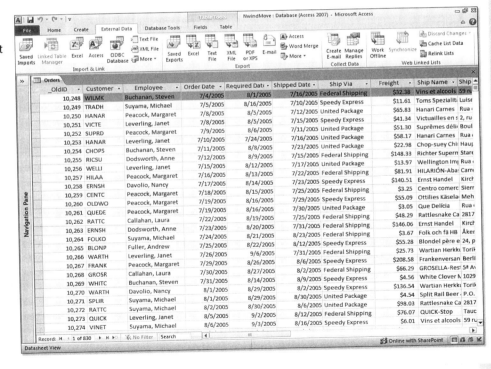

Figure 22.36's hidden _ID column has been unhidden by right-clicking the datasheet and choosing Unhide Columns to open the Unhide Columns dialog, and marking the _ID check box. The meaningless OrderID column is hidden (see Figure 22.37).

Figure 22.37
Use Access's Unhide Columns dialog to make the _OldID field visible in Datasheet view.

The following sections describe workarounds for most of the preceding list's issues.

Checking Out and Checking In a Database from a Document Library

The database file that displays the newly linked lists when the move operation completes is the source database—\Seua12\Chaptr22\Nwind\NwindMove.accdb for this example. Save the NwindMove.accdb database to the Northwind subsite's Shared Documents folder by the process described in the earlier "Saving an Existing Access Database in a SharePoint Document Library" section.

Users will make local copies of the source database copy of NwindMove in the Document Library—Shared Documents (or a new name you give it) in Northwind Databases. Therefore, you should make all Access database design modifications to the copy in the Document Library.

 tip

If you want the column order to survive synchronization and refresh operations, you must use SharePoint's Change Field Order: *ListName* page to set the sequence. Open this page by choosing Settings, List Settings and from the list's Datasheet view to open the Customize *ListName* page and clicking the Column Ordering link near the bottom of the page. However, you must unhide _OldID columns, even if you've renamed them, after each refresh or synchronization operation.

SharePoint includes a version control feature that requires checking out and checking in files stored in Document Libraries. While the file is checked out to a user, no one else can edit it. By default, your \[My]Documents\SharePoint Drafts folder holds checked-out documents.

To check out a database from a Document Library, do the following:

1. Open the Document Library from the Quick Launch menu.

2. Open the menu list for the database, and choose Check Out (see Figure 22.38).

Figure 22.38
SharePoint's document version control feature requires that you check out documents for editing.

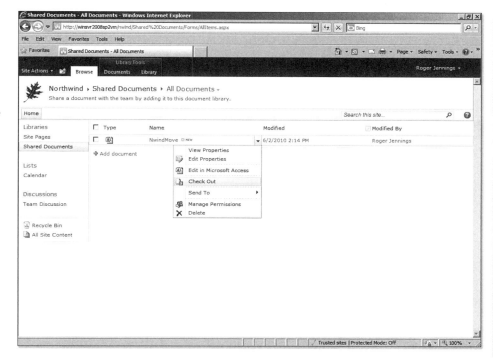

3. Accept the default Use My Local Drafts Folder option (see Figure 22.39), and click OK to create the copy in your \My Documents\SharePoint Drafts or \Documents\SharePoint Drafts folder.

Figure 22.39
This dialog lets you specify saving the edit copy in your \[My] Documents\SharePoint Drafts folder.

When you check out a database, the Access icon gains a green arrow symbol in its lower-right corner.

To check in the document, do this:

1. Open the Document Library from the Quick Launch menu.

2. Open the menu list for the database and choose Check In. Or, to cancel the check out operation or discard your changes, choose Discard Check Out.

3. In the Check In dialog, type a description of the changes you made in the Comments text box (see Figure 22.40), and click OK to check the database back in.

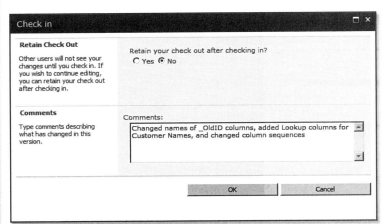

Figure 22.40
You make the changes described in the Comments text box in the next two sections.

4. Click Yes when notified that you're about to upload the .accdb file to the SharePoint site name.

Replacing a Missing Lookup Field

Lookup fields can aid in maintaining referential integrity by restricting entries in the SharePoint equivalent of foreign key columns to valid list items. For example, the NwindMove.accdb source database's Orders.CustomerID and Order Details.ProductID lookup lists prevent adding incorrect CustomerID and ProductID values to the Orders and Order Details tables.

The Access Orders table loses the lookup properties for the CustomerID field when you move or export the table to a SharePoint list. You can't change the data type of the CustomerID field from Single Line of Text to Lookup, but you can add a new Lookup column. However, populating the new Lookup column manually with 830 CustomerID values would be tedious, at best.

Fortunately, you can copy and paste in the data from the original column to a Lookup column's foreign key field, such as CustomerID, and then change the column design to show the display field, such as CompanyName. After you make this change in SharePoint, you must conform Access's Lookup properties to the SharePoint changes you made, because the Refresh Lists operation doesn't do this.

To create a CustomerID lookup list for the Orders list, do the following:

1. Open the Orders list from the Quick Access pane's Lists link, and the List and List Settings buttons to open the Northwind— Orders—List Settings page.

2. Click the CustomerID column to open the Change Column Orders page, and change its Column Name to Customer_ID. Click OK to return to the Customize Orders page.

3. Click the Create Column link below the column names list to open the Northwind – Orders – List Settings - Create Column page, type **CustomerID** as the Column Name value, and select the Lookup (Information Already on This Site) option.

4. Scroll to the Additional Column Settings section, type an optional description, accept the No defaults to temporarily not require data in the column or default values, and select Customers as the source table and, temporarily, CustomerID as the data source column (see Figure 22.41).

Figure 22.41
Specify the CustomerID Lookup column's name and data type at the top of the Create Column: Orders page and start completing the Additional Column Settings section.

5. Mark the Add to Default View and Enforce Relationship Behavior check boxes, and select the Restrict Delete option to prevent deleting the Customers table while the Orders table depends on the CustomerID values (see Figure 22.42).

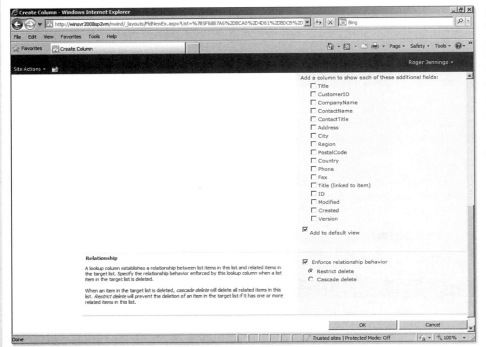

Figure 22.42
Complete the Additional Column Settings with the Default View and Enforce Relationship Behavior selections shown here.

6. Click OK to save your changes and click Yes to dismiss the message that you must index the column.

7. Click the Orders breadcrumb above the Orders caption to open the modified list in the Access Web Datasheet control. Click the Customer_ID column header to select all 830 cells (see Figure 22.43) and press Ctrl+C to copy the values to the Clipboard.

8. Scroll right to the last column (CustomerID), place the cursor in the first empty combo box, press Ctrl+V to copy the CustomerID values to the cells, and wait for the Pending Changes notice at the bottom of the Datasheet to disappear. (see Figure 22.44). Open the combo list to verify that it behaves as expected.

9. Click List, List Settings to return to the Northwind—Orders— List Settings page, click the CustomerID link to Northwind— Orders—List Settings—Change Column, change the In This Column selection to CompanyName, and click OK to return to the Customize Orders page.

10. Click the Column Ordering link near the bottom of the page to open the Change Field Order: Orders page. Set the Order ID field (renamed from _ID) to 1, Customer_ID column to 15, CustomerID to 2, EmployeeID to 3, and ShipVia to 7 (see Figure 22.45). Click OK to save the new column sequence.

Figure 22.43
The Access Web Datasheet ActiveX grid control lets you copy and paste multiple cell values.

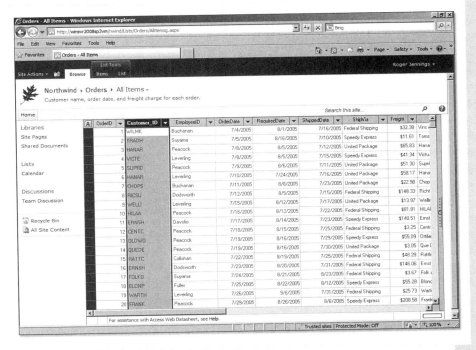

Figure 22.44
The CustomerID Lookup column has values pasted from the renamed Customer_ID field.

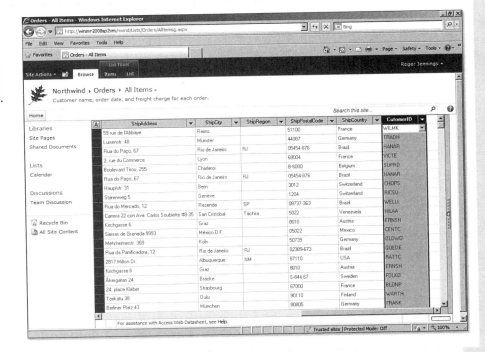

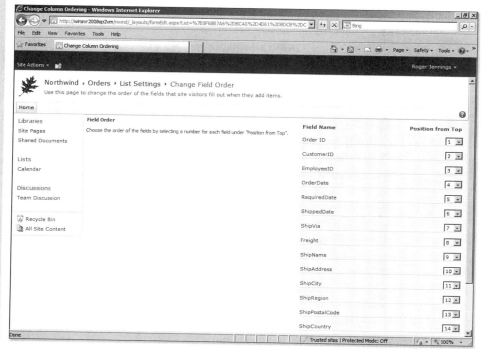

Figure 22.45
The Change
Field Order
page lets you
change the
order of the
list's columns
for new views,
not existing
views.

11. Return to the All Items view of the Orders list, and click All Items, Modify This View to open the Edit View: Orders page. Changing the list's column sequence doesn't change the All Items view's sequence.

12. Change the column sequence to match that of step 8. Optionally, change the sort order on OrderID to descending. Click OK to save the changes and verify the new All Items view (see Figure 22.46).

13. Open NwindMove.accdb in Access, right-click the Orders list in the Navigation pane, and choose More Options, Refresh List to synchronize the linked list design with the modified SharePoint version. The Customer column opens with numbers from the Customers list's ID column.

14. Change to Design view, select the CustomerID column, and click the Lookup tab. The Display Control is a combo box, but the Row Source property value is empty.

15. Click the builder button to open the Orders: Query Builder window, drag the CustomerID and CompanyName fields to the first two columns of the query grid (see Figure 22.47).

Figure 22.46
Here's the All Items view after making column sequence changes similar to those in Figure 22.46.

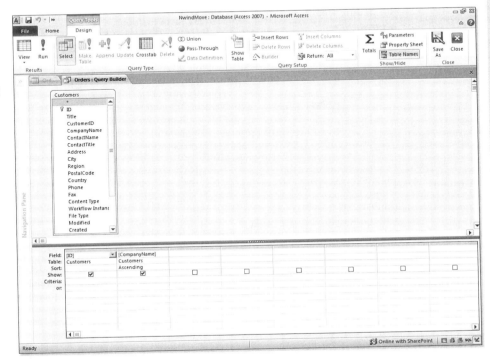

	Order ID	CustomerID	EmployeeID	OrderDate	RequiredDate	ShippedDate	ShipVia	Frei
A								
	10,248	Wilman Kala	Buchanan	7/4/2005	8/1/2005	7/16/2005	Federal Shipping	
	10,249	Tradição Hipermercados	Suyama	7/5/2005	8/16/2005	7/10/2005	Speedy Express	
	10,250	Hanari Carnes	Peacock	7/8/2005	8/5/2005	7/12/2005	United Package	
	10,251	Victuailles en stock	Leverling	7/8/2005	8/5/2005	7/15/2005	Speedy Express	
	10,252	Suprêmes délices	Peacock	7/9/2005	8/6/2005	7/11/2005	United Package	
	10,253	Hanari Carnes	Leverling	7/10/2005	7/24/2005	7/16/2005	United Package	
	10,254	Chop-suey Chinese	Buchanan	7/11/2005	8/8/2005	7/23/2005	United Package	
	10,255	Richter Supermarkt	Dodsworth	7/12/2005	8/9/2005	7/15/2005	Federal Shipping	1
	10,256	Wellington Importadora	Leverling	7/15/2005	8/12/2005	7/17/2005	United Package	
	10,257	HILARIÓN-Abastos	Peacock	7/16/2005	8/13/2005	7/22/2005	Federal Shipping	
	10,258	Ernst Handel	Davolio	7/17/2005	8/14/2005	7/23/2005	Speedy Express	1
	10,259	Centro comercial Moctezuma	Peacock	7/18/2005	8/15/2005	7/25/2005	Federal Shipping	
	10,260	Old World Delicatessen	Peacock	7/19/2005	8/16/2005	7/29/2005	Speedy Express	
	10,261	Que Delícia	Peacock	7/19/2005	8/16/2005	7/30/2005	United Package	
	10,262	Rattlesnake Canyon Grocery	Callahan	7/22/2005	8/19/2005	7/25/2005	Federal Shipping	
	10,263	Ernst Handel	Dodsworth	7/23/2005	8/20/2005	7/31/2005	Federal Shipping	1
	10,264	Folk och fä HB	Suyama	7/24/2005	8/21/2005	8/23/2005	Federal Shipping	
	10,265	Blondel père et fils	Fuller	7/25/2005	8/22/2005	8/12/2005	Speedy Express	
	10,266	Wartian Herkku	Leverling	7/26/2005	9/6/2005	7/31/2005	Federal Shipping	
	Total							

For assistance with Access Web Datasheet, see Help.

Figure 22.47
The key column of the Customers list is ID, which is the bound field for an Access single-valued lookup field.

16. Close the window and save your changes to the Row Source SQL statement: SELECT CustomerID, CompanyName FROM Customers;.

17. Change to Datasheet view, save your changes and expand the Customer column, which is aligned right because it's a Number field. Select the column and click Align Left to apply string formatting to the field.

18. Choose More, Unhide Columns from the Home ribbon's Records group, mark the Order ID check box, and close the dialog. Optionally, drag the Order_ID column from the Datasheet's far right to the right of the Customer column; alternatively, hide the Customer_ID column because it's no longer significant. Datasheet view appears as shown in Figure 22.48.

---

tip

You can create lookup fields in Access independently of SharePoint by following steps 11 through 15 of the preceding operation, but the Row Source property's SQL Statement disappears when you publish the change to SharePoint.

If the Orders table's EmployeeID field is empty, check to determine if the source data field of lookup control is Title or another empty column. If so, change the source data field to Last Name.

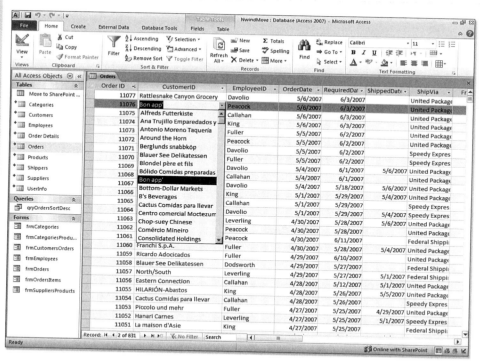

Figure 22.48
Conforming the appearance of the Orders table linked to a SharePoint list to the original Access Orders table requires a major effort.

19. Click the message pane's Save to SharePoint Site button and click Save to overwrite the existing NwindMove.accdb document.

Although the preceding procedure is specific to the CustomersID column of the Orders list, it works for most columns except ...ID fields, which don't appear in the Access Web Datasheet grid.

Using SharePoint-Specific Context Menus and Buttons

The Navigation pane's context menu and Table Tools, Datasheet ribbon's SharePoint List group for linked SharePoint lists offers several functions that don't apply to Access tables, as shown in Figure 22.49.

Figure 22.49
Linking tables to SharePoint lists adds this More Options submenu to the Navigation pane's context menu.

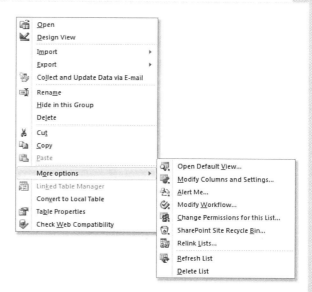

Following are brief descriptions of the action taken by each SharePoint List Options command button:

- *Open Default View*—Opens the default SharePoint view for the selected list in Datasheet or standard view.

- *Modify Columns and Settings*—Opens the Customize *ListName* page.

- *Alert Me*—Opens the New Alert page, which configures e-mail alerts that notify the user when there are changes to the specified item, document, list, or library.

- *Modify Workflow*—Opens the Change Workflow Settings: *ListName* page that lets you view or change the workflow settings for this list. Alternatively, you can add or remove workflows.

- *Change Permission for this List*—Opens the Permissions: *ListName* page that lets you modify the list's or its parent's permissions.

- *SharePoint Site Recycle Bin*—Opens the Recycle Bin from which you can restore deleted lists or items.

- *Relink Lists*—Opens the Relink Lists dialog in which you can select another SharePoint site from which to relink corresponding links.

- *Refresh List*—Synchronizes the Access linked list's design and contents with the SharePoint master.

- *Delete List*—Deletes the selected list.

Working Offline and Synchronizing Lists

The capability to work with shared data while offline— that is, not connected to the network—is an increasingly important feature of desktop applications. Taking the Access database offline creates local copies of all linked SharePoint lists. If the number and size of the lists are large, the disk space occupied by the offline version of the database grows substantially. When you reconnect, Access doesn't send the changes you made while offline to SharePoint until you click the Synchronize button.

> **note**
>
> Checking out a database to your \My Documents\SharePointDrafts folder is the equivalent of taking the file— but not the list data—offline.

To add items while disconnected from the SharePoint site to the Contacts and Issues list in the master copy of the Issues.accdb database that you open from the Document Library, do the following:

1. From SharePoint's Quick Launch menu, open the Shared Documents library's menu, select the NwindMove.accdb file, and choose Check Out to open IE's check out message box.

   ➥ *To review how to check out and check in an Access database in a Document Library,* **see** *"Checking Out and Checking In a Database from a Document Library,"* **p. 954.**

2. Mark the Use My Local Drafts Folder check box and click to save NwindMove.accdb to the SharePointDrafts folder and then open it in Access. Click the Enable Content button to close the warning message.

3. Click the External Data tab, and then click the Web Linked List's group's Work Offline button to temporarily disconnect the tables from the SharePoint site and cache the table data locally. The Navigation pane's linked table icons with a small SharePoint icon added behind the datasheet symbol replace the linked list icons (see Figure 22.50) and the Work Offline button's caption changes to Work Online.

Figure 22.50
Working offline results in table data being cached in the client PC's memory and links to SharePoint lists are severed, as indicated by the hybrid icons shown here.

4. Add a new entry to the Customers table. Added rows in the cache receive temporary negative ID values before they're committed to the linked sharepoint list (see Figure 22.51).

Figure 22.51
Access assigns temporary negative ID values to added cached rows while working offline.

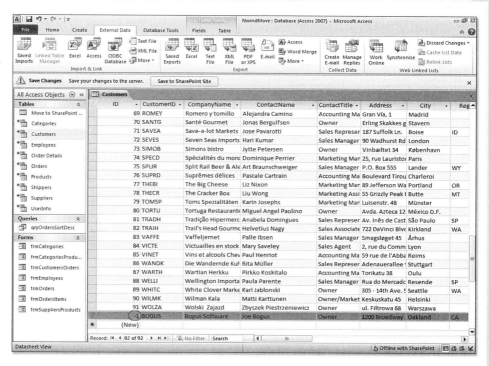

5. Open the SharePoint Customers list and verify that the contact you added while offline isn't present.

6. Return to Access, click the External Data tab, and click the Web Linked Lists group's Synchronize button to update the SharePoint lists and local table caches for changes that occurred after you severed the links. A message box opens with a progress bar opens and then closes, and the ID for the newly added Customer row changes from -1 to 92.

7. Return to SharePoint, open the Customers list, verify that the item for the newly added row is present after synchronization (see Figure 22.52), and make a minor edit to the row's data.

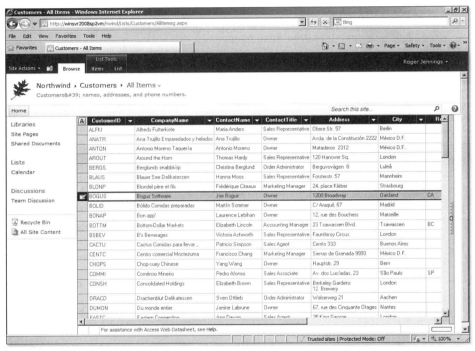

Figure 22.52
The newly added BOGUS customer entry appears in the Customers list grid, which is sorted by CustomerID values.

8. Return to Access, make a different edit to the added row, and click the Work Online button to reconnect to the list and update the SharePoint list. The changes made in both locations causes a concurrency conflict that opens the Resolve Conflicts dialog to show Other User's and Your Changes (see Figure 22.53).

Figure 22.53
The Resolve Conflicts dialog lets you resolve concurrency conflicts when two or more users edit the same record while one of them is offline.

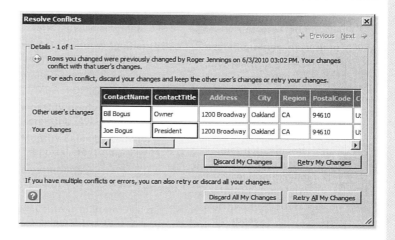

9. Resolve the conflict by retrying your changes and then return to SharePoint, press F5 to refresh the datasheet, and verify both users' changes appear, unless the changes were made to the same cell.

10. Close NwindMove.accdb and check it into the SharePoint Document Library to enable others to use it as the master copy.

Exporting Tables or Queries to a SharePoint List

The simplest interaction with SharePoint is exporting an Access table or query as a SPF list. In this case, there is only a momentary connection between the list and your Access database. Exporting doesn't create a link between the Access table or query and SharePoint list, but it does enable exporting query resultsets as lists. The most common use of Access's Export to SharePoint feature is as an intermediary for a format that SharePoint can't import directly.

To export a table—Northwind Products for this example—to the parent (OakLeaf) SPF 2010 site, do the following:

1. Open \Access2010\Chaptr22\Nwind\NwindPub.accdb, right-click the Products table entry, and choose Export, SharePoint List to open the Export Data to SharePoint List dialog.

2. Complete the URL to your SPF 2010 parent site (http://winsvr2008sp2vm/ for this example), and modify the default list name and description, if you want (see Figure 22.54).

3. With the Open This List When Finished check box marked, click OK to export the list. After a minute or so, the All Items view opens (see Figure 22.55).

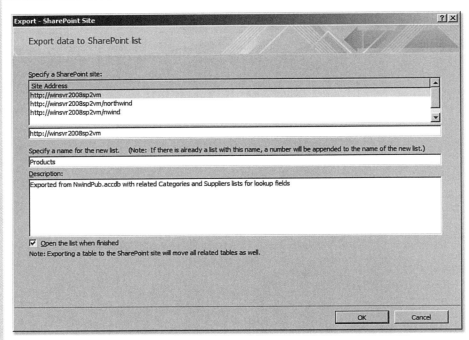

Figure 22.54
Select or type
the URL for
your SPF site
and give the
list a name and
description in
the Export Data
to SharePoint
List dialog.

4. Click the arrow at the right of the column name to open a column's drop-down list to sort or add a filter in datasheet view (refer to Figure 22.55).

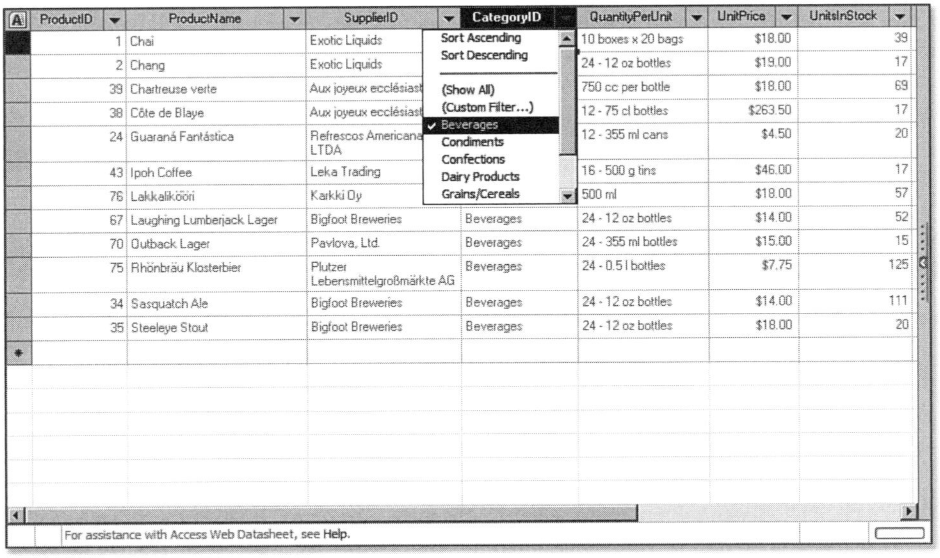

Figure 22.55
The exported
table opens
the All Items
view of the
Products list
in an Access
Web Datasheet.
Each column's
dropdown list
lets you sort,
filter, or both
on that column.

5. You can select Sort Ascending or Sort Descending, and then select an individual value or up to three custom filter conditions in the Custom Filter dialog (see Figure 22.56).

6. Open the list and select (Show All) to remove the filter. You can't remove the sort in this view; you're only choice is to sort on another column, such as the key field (ProductID).

note

The SupplierID and CategoryID columns shown in Figure 22.55 are Lookup columns based on values in the Suppliers and Categories tables. Exporting a table also exports the related tables to lists that might supply SharePoint Lookup column values.

Figure 22.56
The Custom Filter dialog lets you apply up to three WHERE clause criteria to the list column you specify (Category for this example).

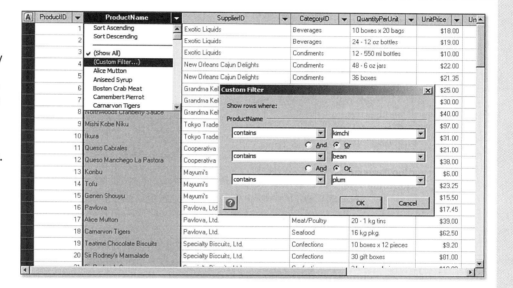

7. Click the List ribbon's List Settings button to open the List Settings page, and scroll to the Sort section, which lets you sort the list by a sequence of up to two columns (see Figure 22.57). You can remove the sort you applied in step by opening the drop-down list and selecting the empty choice for each field. You can remove all filters and sorting (except ProductID) by clicking the Remove Filter/Sort button.

note

You can't create a link from SharePoint to the SQL Server database of an Access Data Project. You receive a "Links can only be created between Microsoft Access database files" error message if you try.

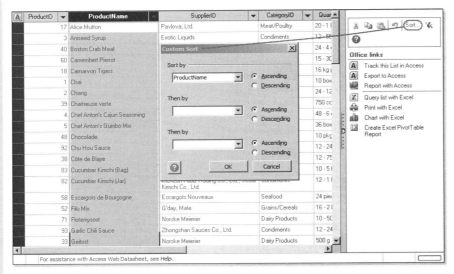

Figure 22.57
The Access Web Datasheet control's task pane enables sorting on up to three column values.

Table Column Name Conflicts with WSS Lists

Sometimes when you try to export an Access or SQL Server table to a WSS list, you might receive an error message, the list is missing some of the table columns, or both. The reason for these issues are that WSS lists have several internal columns for list management that don't appear in datasheet or standard view and tables having columns with the same names cause problems during the export process. The internal columns for list management are ID, Title, Modified, Created, Created By, Modified By, Attachments, and Edit. You must rename conflicting table columns or substitute a query with column name aliases to export the table data successfully. As an example, you should rename the Employees.Title table to Employees.JobTitle or the like before moving or exporting it to a SharePoint site.

Linking a SharePoint List to an Access Table

The most common reason to export Access data to a SharePoint list is to share it with others. You export the data when you don't want to move the source database's tables to SharePoint. However, you must manually update the Access, SharePoint, or both versions to maintain current data. Linking makes edits to the SharePoint list visible in both applications, which eliminates the need for manual updates. This capability lets you establish relationships between the list and other tables, and lets you use Access forms and VBA code to maintain the list.

Link or Export SharePoint Lists to Access Tables from Sharepoint

To link new Access tables to corresponding SharePoint lists using the Products list you created in the preceding section as an example, do the following:

1. Open the Products list in the Access Web Datasheet and click the List Tools' List button.

2. Click the Open with Access button (a stylized letter "A") to open the Open in Microsoft Access dialog. Accept or change the proposed database name, and accept the default Link to Data on the SharePoint Site option (see Figure 22.58).

Figure 22.58
The Open in Microsoft Access dialog lets you specify a new or existing database and whether to link or export the selected table and any related tables.

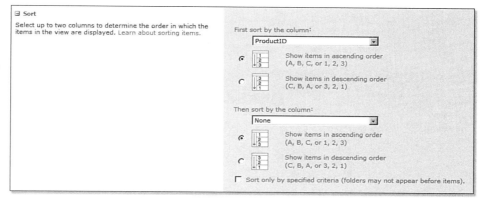

3. Click OK to to create and open the new database with three tables: Products, Categories, and Suppliers (see Figure 22.59).

Figure 22.59
Tracking the Products list with Access requires lookup values from the Categories and Suppliers lists so links to the related tables are created also.

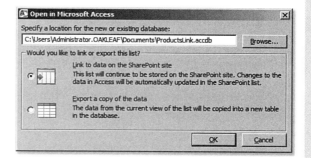

Link Access Tables to Sharepoint Lists from Access

Alternatively, you can create identical, individual links from an Access database by doing the following:

1. Click the External Data tab and the Import & Link group's More menu and SharePoint button to open the Get External Data - SharePoint site dialog.

> **note**
> Choosing the Export to Access link simply exports the Product list's data to a new Access table and doesn't create a link to the SharePoint Product list.

2. Select or type the site's address and accept the default Link to the Data Source by Creating a Linked Table option (see Figure 22.60), and click Next to open a list of lists in the selected site.

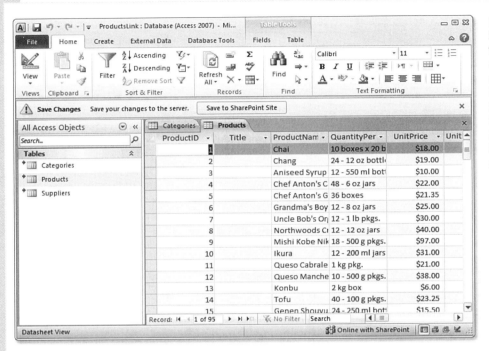

Figure 22.60
Select or type the SharePoint site's address and specify linking or importing in the first Get External Data - SharePoint site dialog.

3. Select the lists to link (see Figure 22.61) and click OK to generate the linked tables, which include tables related to those you choose (see Figure 22.62).

4. Click OK to add the links to your Access database.

Figure 22.61
Select the SharePoint site's address in the first Get External Data-SharePoint Site dialog.

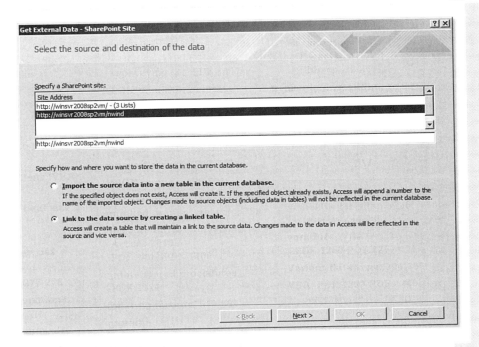

Figure 22.62
Select the SharePoint lists to link in the second Get External Data-SharePoint site dialog.

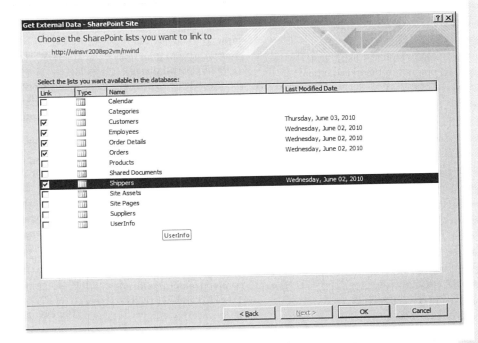

23

SHARING WEB DATABASES WITH SHAREPOINT SERVER 2010

Creating Access forms and reports that run in popular web browsers but emulate the behavior and performance of traditional Access objects running under a Windows operating system is a challenge. Enabling users to display and edit shared Access data in a browser eliminates their need to possess an Office Professional or higher license, or install databases packaged with the free Access runtime version. Running Access in a browser offers a user experience that's similar to Office Live Workspaces's Word, Excel, PowerPoint and One Note web applications.

Access 2000 introduced Data Access Pages (DAPs), which were data-bound web pages intended to enable intranet users to browse Access data in Internet Explorer 5.0 or later. DAPs added an ActiveX record navigation control and other Office Web Components (OWCs), Remote Data Service components, Page Wizard and Script Editor for VBScript and Jscript. DAPs suffered from poor performance compared with native Access forms and reports, page design difficulties, lack of Visual Basic for Applications (VBA) support, scripting languages unfamiliar to Access developers, and a complex approach to establishing Internet connectivity. As a result of these deficiencies, most Access developers and almost all ordinary users avoided creating DAPs. Microsoft subsequently deprecated this feature. Access 2007 could run but not create new or edit existing DAPs; Access 2010 won't even run them.

2010 NEW The Access team adopted SharePoint Server (SPS) 2010's Enterprise edition as the platform to bring improved web connectivity to Access 2010 with Access Services. Like Access, SharePoint emphasizes self-service design of sharable objects by teams or groups within small businesses to large enterprises. Publishing Access business applications to a SharePoint website enables IT management to secure and audit web databases, as well ensure availability by backing them up on a regular schedule. Users or developers perform all design work in Access 2010 and synchronize design changes with the SharePoint subsite. Access 2010 tables linked to SharePoint lists maintain data consistency between the two platforms automatically when connected. If an Access 2010 user is disconnected from the SharePoint site when making changes to data, the changes are reconciled when the user reconnects.

Licensing SharePoint Server 2010

Using the SharePoint platform to deliver Access forms and reports is a natural progression from Access 2003's initial version of an installable driver that provided connectivity to SharePoint Portal Server 2003's lists. Access 2007 added support for Windows SharePoint Services (WSS) 3.0 and Microsoft Office SharePoint Server (MOSS) 2007 and enabled users to take list data offline and then synchronize with the server when reconnecting. Access 2007 added new data engine features to provide parity with SharePoint data types, such as support for file attachments and multi-valued lookup columns. Access 2007's Fluent user interface simplified moving data to SharePoint lists and MOSS 2007/WSS 3.0 UI enabled storing Access applications in document libraries. Chapter 22, "Collaborating with SharePoint Foundation 2010," explains how to take advantage of these features with SharePoint Foundation 2010, a no-charge, downloadable add-on to Windows Server 2008 Service Pack (SP) 2 and 2008 R2.

Server, External Connector, and Client Access Licenses

Delivering Access 2010 forms and reports from SharePoint sites and enabling execution of Access macros requires SharePoint 2010 Products licenses, which are *not* free. SharePoint 2010 Products are available in two versions: SharePoint 2010 Server (SPS) for intranet use by licensed Windows Server users and SharePoint 2010 for Internet Sites (SPIS), which enables anonymous, browser-based access by users of the public Internet. Both versions require per-server licenses, which are the same for Standard and Enterprise editions (US$4,920). SPS requires a standard CAL for each connected user or device (US$94); the Enterprise edition also requires an Enterprise CAL (US$82). Enterprise CALs are additive to Standard CALs. Thus the licensing cost for a single SPS server supporting 100 users of the Enterprise edition is about US$22,520 or approximately US$225.20 each.

 note

SharePoint represents a remarkable success story: According to a Microsoft press release of October 19, 2009, "SharePoint Server is one of the fastest-growing products in Microsoft's history, with over $1.3 billion in revenue, representing over a 20 percent growth over the past year." A May 2010 presentation by Microsoft developer-evangelist Lynn Langit claims that there were 650,000 SharePoint developers and that more than 100 million SharePoint Client Access Licenses (CALs) had been sold at that time.

 note

Prices were those quoted by Microsoft-authorized Internet resellers when this book was written in mid-2010 for a minimum of five Open Business licenses and don't include the cost of Software Assurance. Microsoft Open Business licensing is for small to mid-sized organizations that have less than 250 desktop PCs and who order as few as five licenses. According to Microsoft, benefits of Open License include discounts off the retail price of software, the ability to track and manage licenses by using online tools, and the rights to create a standard image and deploy it on multiple machines, and rights to transfer licenses from one machine to another.

SPIS requires an SPS server license plus a Standard External Connector license (US$11,775) or Enterprise External Connector license (US$41,375). The licensee's employees can connect to SPS without CALs if all site content is open to the public; otherwise CALs are required.

SharePoint Server 2010's Enterprise license adds the following services to the Standard edition:

- **Access Services** let users edit, update, and create Access 2010 web databases, which users can view and manipulate in an Internet browser, the Access 2010 client application, or a linked HTML page.

- Business Connectivity Services (BCS) replaces MOSS 2007's Business Data Catalog and provides connectivity to external data, a symmetrical client and server runtime to interact with the data, and packaging for BCS solutions to be used with smart-client applications, such as web services for Access 2010.

- Excel Services enable users to publish and share Microsoft Excel client workbooks on SharePoint Server. Excel Services provide replacements for the OWCs, which are discontinued in SPS 2010: PivotChart, PivotTable and TrendChart options in the SharePoint Dashboard Designer.

- InfoPath Form Services lets you add InfoPath List forms, InfoPath document-based forms and InfoPath Web Parts to SharePoint sites.

- PerformancePoint Services replaces the earlier standalone PerformancePoint Server for business intelligence and lets users build dashboards, scorecards, reports, and key performance indicators (KPIs).

- PowerPivot for SharePoint extends SharePoint 2010 and Excel Services to deliver server-side processing, collaboration, and document management support for the PowerPivot workbooks that you publish to SharePoint.

- Visio Services perform data refresh and rendering on the server and deliver up-to-date diagrams in the browser. The diagram author no longer needs to repost the diagram every time the data changes, and diagram viewers no longer need the Visio client to see the diagram.

It's clear that you need the Enterprise edition to enable SharePoint to handle Access 2010 web databases.

Hosted SharePoint 2010 Enterprise Sites

The cost of licensing a significant number of new Access 2010 users for SharePoint Server 2010 Enterprise connectivity probably will preclude on-premises deployment of Azure web databases by most small and many medium-size organizations. Most large U.S. corporations already have MOSS 2007 Enterprise licenses; those that upgrade to SPS 2010 must replace 32-bit servers, if any, with 64-bit CPUs and operating systems. According to a May 2010 Directions on Microsoft research report, SPS 2010 Enterprise licenses and CALs cost 10% more than the MOSS 2007 versions.

SharePoint Server 2010 Enterprise edition's high entry cost for Internet sites will cause many potential producers of publicly accessible web databases to search for potential online sources of Access Services, such as Business Productivity Online Suite's SharePoint Online (www.microsoft.com/

online/sharepoint-online.mspx), which—as of mid-2010—offered MOSS 2007 Standard to a minimum of five users for US$5.25/ month each.

Microsoft was holding its SharePoint Online cards close to the vest when this book was written. In response to a "When will SharePoint 2010 be available online from Microsoft?" question posed during the May 12, 2010 Office/SharePoint 2010 Launch Event, a member of Microsoft's Online team replied, "It will be available to our larges[t] online customers this year, and we will continue rolling out the 2010 technology to our broad base of online customers, with updates coming every 90 days. You can expect to see a preview of these capabilities later this year." Asking "Will SharePoint 2010 Online offer the Enterprise Edition or at least Access Services to support web databases?" elicited

> **note**
>
> See the "Q&A with Microsoft about SharePoint 2010 OnLine with Access Services" post of May 14, 2010 on the OakLeaf Systems website (bit.ly/bX7CEP or oakleafblog.blogspot.com/2010/05/q-with-microsoft-about-sharepoint-2010.html) for more details about the forthcoming SharePoint Online upgrade and offline licensing.

this response: "We have not disclosed the specific features that will be available in SharePoint Online at this time, but you can expect most of the Enterprise Edition features to be available. Stay tuned for more details in the coming months." Microsoft's failure to mention SharePoint 2010's Online plans at the Launch Event drew derisive comments from a host of computer industry pundits and journalists. According to "All About Microsoft" blogger Mary Jo Foley, Microsoft disclosed in a pair of November 2009 PowerPoint slides entitled "SharePoint Online Detail Comparison" that Access Services will be included with SharePoint 2010 Online Dedicated (on-premises) and Standard (Microsoft-hosted) versions.

If you don't want to wait until the end of 2010 to find out if and when SharePoint 2010 Online with Access Services will be available from Microsoft, Access Hosting (www.accesshosting.com) offers a pay-as-you-go, cloud-based (hosted) alternative to deploying SPS 2010 Enterprise on-premises.

    To learn more about hosted SharePoint Server 2010 services, **see** *"Working with a Hosted SharePoint Site,"* **p. 998.**

SharePoint Trial Software

You can download Microsoft SharePoint Server Enterprise 2010 Trial software at bit.ly/9ljA6C or technet.microsoft.com/en-us/evalcenter/ee388573.aspx. The trial period is 180 days. You can convert to a licensed installation at any time during the trial or after the trial has expired by entering the appropriate product key. You can run the trial software under Windows 7, Windows Server 2008 R2, Windows Server 2008 Service Pack 2, Windows Vista Service Pack 1 and Windows Vista Service Pack 2 operating systems. See the later "Hardware and Software Requirements" section for installation prerequisites.

Understanding the Role of Access Services

In addition to storing tabular data from Access 2010 tables in lists, Access users can publish qualifying databases to SPS or SPIS 2010 Enterprise edition to create Access/SharePoint web databases. The later "Access Services Limitations and Restrictions" section describes what's required for an

Access 2007-format database to qualify as a web database candidate. When you publish a database to SPS, Access Services mediate all data access to the SharePoint lists of a web database, and enable caching to improve form performance.

Access Application Transfer Protocol (MS-AXL) and Windows Presentation Foundation's Extensible Application Markup Language (XAML) synchronize form design changes and generate ASP.NET pages that emulate Access forms.

Access Services process queries using AXL and Collaborative Application Markup Language (CAML). CAML is an arcane XML dialect that's supported by SharePoint Web Services and the SharePoint Client Object Model. Access Services implements conventional (UI) macros with JavaScript and data macros as SharePoint workflows.

 note

For more information about MS-AXL see the "[MS-AXL]: Access Application Transfer Protocol Structure Specification" at http://bit.ly/bKfZxF or msdn.microsoft.com/en-us/library/dd927584(office.12).aspx.

The Reporting Services 2008 R2 for SharePoint 2010 Add-in

Access Services use the SQL Server Reporting Services 2008 R2 for SharePoint 2010 Add-in to generate and synchronize reports, which deploy to the server with AXL and Report Definition Language (RDL). Access Services has two report deployment modes:

note

For more information about CAML and the SharePoint Client Object Model, see Eric White's "Using the SharePoint 2010 Managed Client Object Model – Using CAML to Query a List" blog post at http://bit.ly/9lellt or blogs.msdn.com/b/ericwhite/archive/2009/11/21/using-the-sharepoint-2010-managed-client-object-model-using-caml-to-query-a-list.aspx.

- **Connected mode:** Requires SharePoint 2010 Server, the same Reporting Services add-in and a SQL Server 2008 R2 Report Server deployment. You get server side features, such as setting up and managing subscriptions. If you have multiple web front-ends in your SharePoint farm, Microsoft recommends that you set up using Connected Mode. To set up connected mode, you will need SQL Server 2008 R2 Report Server and the Reporting Services Add-in.

- **Local mode:** You still install the add-in, but there is no actual report server deployed in this scenario. Reports from Microsoft Access 2010 and the new Reporting Services SharePoint list data extension can run locally from the SharePoint document library, without a connection to a Reporting Services server. If you are running a SharePoint farm with only one web front-end, you can set up Local Mode.

Access Services Limitations and Restrictions

Chapter 22, "Collaborating with SharePoint Foundation 2010," covers the process of moving Access tables to SharePoint Foundation 2010 lists and linking them to an Access 2010 application; the process of publishing tables to SharePoint Server 2010 is identical. Following is a summary of Access table features that SharePoint lists don't support:

- Tables linked to an external data source, such as SQL Server or a SharePoint list other than the publication target

- Tables with primary key data types other than Long Integer

- Tables with referential integrity specified in the Relationships window

- Table and field names that are the same as SharePoint reserved words or contain spaces or special characters

- Tables with composite indexes, such as the Northwind Order Details table

- Tables with more than one no-duplicate index

- Lookup fields whose source table field isn't a Long Integer primary key

- Lookup query definitions that include the DISTINCT or DISTINCTROW modifier

- Autonumber fields other than for the primary key

- Autonumber fields that start with a number other than 1, such as the Northwind Orders table

To review the details of data limitations and restrictions of SharePoint 2010 lists, **see** *"Moving Tables and Saving an Existing Database to SharePoint,"* **p. 940**.

Access 2010 includes a Web Compatibility Checker for table designs that you can run before publishing.

Access Services doesn't support VBA embedded in forms or reports or contained in modules. You must use conventional (UI) macros to respond to events on forms and reports and Data Macros to implement the equivalent of database triggers.

Installing SharePoint Server 2010

The process of installing SharePoint Server 2010 on Windows Server 2008 R2 is almost identical to that for installing SharePoint Foundation 2010 on Windows Server 2008 SP2 with the exception of minimum RAM requirements and the need to install the SQL Server 2008 R2 Reporting Services Add-In to support creating reports with Access Services.

 note

The Server2008R2VM4 virtual machine used for this chapter's examples has an Intel DQ45CB mother board with an Intel Core 2 Quad CPU Q9550 processor running at 2.83GHz with 8GB RAM (the maximum supported). The guest and host operating system is Windows Server 2008 R2 Standard Edition.

Hardware and Software Requirements

Table 23.1 lists Microsoft's minimum hardware required to run SharePoint Server Standard or Enterprise edition with a built-in SQL Server 2008 R2 database instance.

Table 23.1 Minimum Hardware Required to Run SharePoint Server Standard or Enterprise Edition

Component	Minimum Requirement
Processor	64-bit, 4 cores.
RAM	4GB for development or evaluation use 8GB for production use in a single server or multiple server farm.
Fixed Disk	80GB for system drive For production use, additional free disk space is needed for day-to-day operations. Maintain twice as much free space as you have RAM for production environments.

SPS 2010 Enterprise runs under the 64-bit edition of Windows Server 2008 R2 Standard, Enterprise, Data Center, or Web Server. Alternatively, you can use the 64-bit edition of Windows Server 2008 Standard, Enterprise, Data Center, or Web Server with SP2. If you are running Windows Server 2008 without SP2, the Microsoft SharePoint Products Preparation Tool installs Windows Server 2008 SP2 automatically. You can use 64-bit Windows 7, Windows Vista Service Pack 1, or Windows Vista Service Pack 2 operating systems for development on a single machine.

Starting Installation from a DVD

The preferred installation media for SharePoint Server 2010 is a DVD. If you download a SharePoint Server 2010 *.iso image, burn it to a DVD-R or DVD+R disc. You must have a valid 25-character product key for the Enterprise Edition; in most cases, the product key determines the edition.

Follow these steps to start the installation process under Windows Server 2008 SP2 or Windows Server 2008 R2 as a member of the built-in Administrators group:

1. If the DVD's Autorun.inf doesn't display the SharePoint Server 2010 splash screen (see Figure 23.1), run Default.hta (an HTML application file).

2. Verify that you have a live Internet connection. Setup downloads prerequisite software from the Microsoft website.

3. Optionally, read the Installation Guide.

4. Click the splash screen's Install Software Prerequisites link to run the Microsoft SharePoint 2010 Products Preparation Tool. SharePointServer.exe automatically runs the tool.

 note

The Microsoft SharePoint Products Preparation Tool doesn't install prerequisite software when run under Windows 7 or Windows Vista, so you must install required programs and hotfixes individually. The manual setup process is quite complex; see the "Setting Up the Development Environment for SharePoint 2010 on Windows Vista, Windows 7, and Windows Server 2008" white paper at http://msdn.microsoft.com/en-us/library/ee554869.aspx for the details.

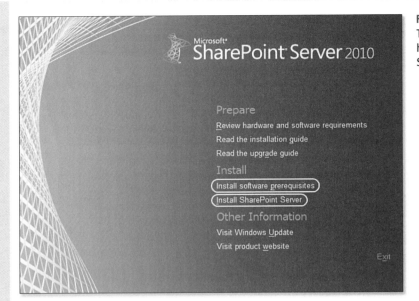

Figure 23.1
The Default.hta splash screen has links to local and online SharePoint 2010 content.

Installing the SQL Server 2008 R2 Reporting Services Add-In

Although the SSRS Add-in can be installed either before or after SharePoint Server is deployed, Microsoft strongly recommends that it be installed prior to installing SharePoint Server to avoid time-consuming manual configuration on a server-by-server basis:

- **If you install SSRS before SharePoint Server:** A deployment of Reporting Services integrates with a deployment of SharePoint at the farm level. No additional configuration or replication out to servers in the farm will be necessary. If you use the SharePoint prerequisite tool during SharePoint installation, the SSRS add-in will be automatically installed during that process (see Figure 23.2).

- **If you install SSRS after installing SharePoint Server:** If you choose to install SSRS after deploying SharePoint Server, the installation process will involve many more steps, especially if you have multiple web front-end servers. If you have multiple SharePoint web applications in a farm configuration, you must install the Reporting Services Add-in on each computer that has a front-end web.

You can tell if the SSRS Add-in is installed by looking for the SQL 2008 R2 Reporting Services SharePoint 2010 item in Control Panel's Programs and Features window. If you don't find it, do the following:

1. Download and run rsSharePoint.msi from http://go.microsoft.com/fwlink/?LinkID=186756.

2. Accept the license terms and continue with the installation.

Figure 23.2
The SQL 2008 R2
Reporting Services
SharePoint 2010 Add-In
is the last item in the
Microsoft SharePoint
2010 Products
Preparation Tool's list.

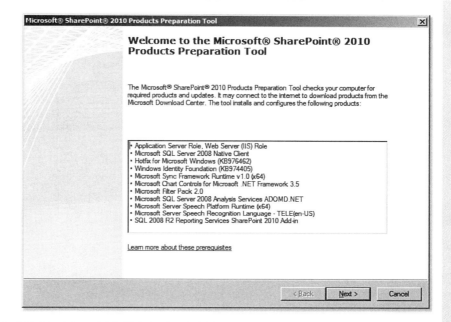

Figure 23.2
The SQL 2008 R2
Reporting Services
SharePoint 2010 Add-In
is the last item in the
Microsoft SharePoint
2010 Products
Preparation Tool's list.

3. Click the http://msdn.microsoft.com/en-us/library/cc281021.aspx link to open the "How Do I Learn About SharePoint Integrated Mode" help topic.

4. Read the help topic "How to: Install or Uninstall the Reporting Services Add-in."

If you're running the Microsoft SharePoint 2010 Products Preparation Tool at this point, click Next, accept the terms of the end-user license agreements, and click Next to run the Tool. Click Finish when the Installation Complete dialog appears.

Continuing the SharePoint Setup Process

Follow these steps after installing the prerequisite software:

1. Click the Install SharePoint Server link to start the installation process.

2. When the SharePoint Configuration Wizard starts, click the Standalone button.

3. When the Wizard completes its 10 tasks and displays the Configuration Successful dialog, click Finish to compile the default ASP.NET website and open its Template Selection page (see Figure 23.3).

4. Select the Collaboration tab's Team Site and click OK to apply the same template as that for Chapter 22's SharePoint Foundation 2010 example.

5. Accept the default Home Visitors, Home Members and Home Owners security groups, unless you want to change the names (see Figure 23.4).

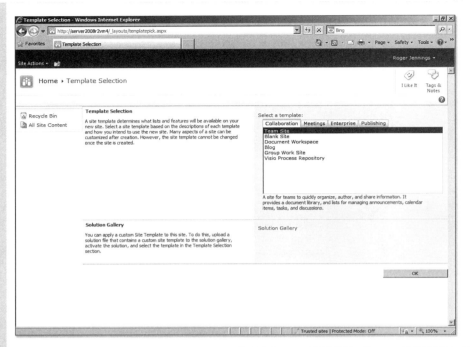

Figure 23.3
SharePoint Server 2010 offers pre-built templates for a wide range of standard site types in Collaboration, Meetings, Enterprise and Publishing categories.

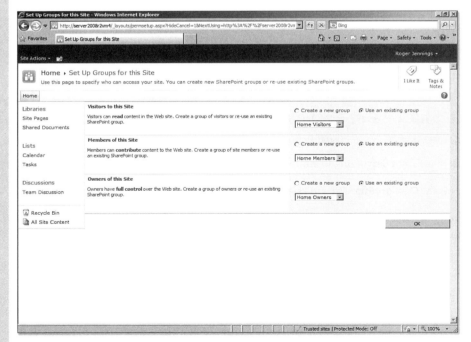

Figure 23.4
The Home – Set Up Groups for This Site page provides three default security group names with read-only (Visitors), read-write (Members) and full-control (Owners) privileges.

6. Click OK to open the site's default home page at http://*servername*/SitePages/Home.aspx.

7. Click Default.hta's Exit link to close the installation splash screen.

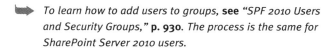 *To learn how to add users to groups,* **see** *"SPF 2010 Users and Security Groups,"* **p. 930.** *The process is the same for SharePoint Server 2010 users.*

> **note**
>
> Initial compilation might take a minute or two, depending on your computer's speed. If the Template Selection page doesn't appear, launch Internet Explorer 8, if necessary, and type **http://*servername*/_layouts/templatepick.aspx** in the Address text box to open the Template Selection page. The *servername* is Server2008R2VM4 for this chapter's examples.

Creating a Web Database from a Template

Selecting the New tab of the File tab's Backstage page opens links to local database templates, which include a Blank Web Database.

Clicking the Sample Templates button opens a gallery of local templates, which include pre-built Assets, Charitable Contributions, Contacts, Issues and Projects Web databases (see Figure 23.5).

Figure 23.5
Office setup installs these five local web database templates. This chapter's example is based on the Contacts Web Database template with data imported from Outlook 2010.

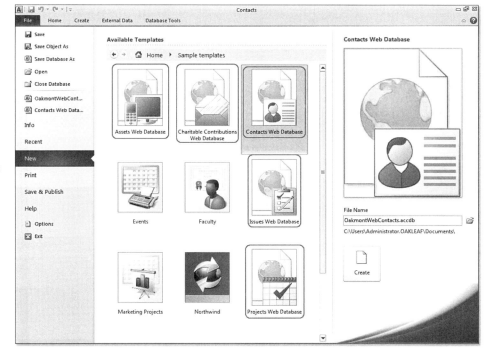

To publish OakmontWebContacts.accdb to a SharePoint subsite, do the following:

1. Open your test site's default home page at http://*servername*/SitePages/Home.aspx.

2. Open the OakmontWebContacts.accdb web database in Access.

3. Click the File tab to open the Backstage page, click its Info tab, and click the Publish to Access Services button to open the Access Services Overview pane.

4. Click the Run Compatibility Checker button to verify tables meet Access Services' requirements.

5. Click Yes to close open objects and dismiss the message box, if you have database objects open.

6. If you have compatibility issues, click the Web Compatibility Issues button to open the Move to SharePoint Site Issues, and review its contents. Otherwise, you see a "The database is compatible with the Web" message.

 tip

Start with a web database template—even the Blank Web Database template—if you plan to publish your database to SharePoint. Using a web database template limits table design features to those compatible with Access Services.

 note

The \Access2010\Chaptr23 folder contains OakmontWebContacts.accdb and OakmontWebBackup.accdb web databases with 91 Contact records imported from Outlook to the Contacts table.

7. Type the *servername* in the Server URL text box and the subsite name in the Site Name text box. For this example, the Full URL becomes http://server2008r2vm4/OakmontContacts (see Figure 23.6).

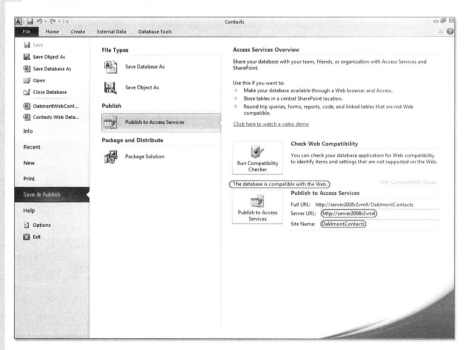

Figure 23.6
Specify the Server URL and Site URL to determine the Full URL of the publish subsite.

8. Click Publish to Access Services to start the publishing and synchronizing process, which displays a progress dialog (see Figure 23.7).

Figure 23.7
A progress dialog announces each step in the publishing and synchronizing process, which might take a minute or two for a large database running on a slow server.

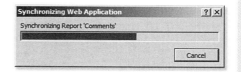

9. When the Publish Succeeded dialog appears (see Figure 23.8), click the link to open the default Address Book form in a Navigation control, which displays an error message: "This report failed to load because session state is not turned on. Contact your SharePoint farm administrator." (See Figure 23.9.)

Figure 23.8
Click the Publish Succeeded dialog's link to open the default Address Book page (form).

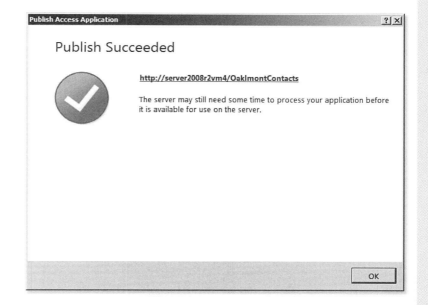

10. Click the Datasheet tab to display the web equivalent of a read-only Access datasheet, which isn't affected by the session-state problem (see Figure 23.10).

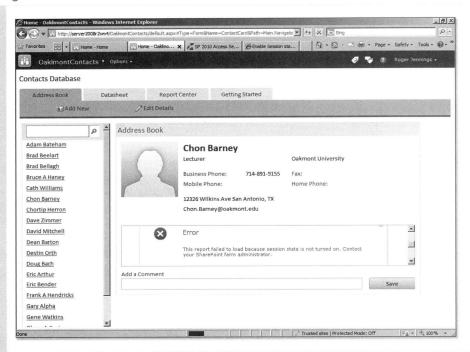

Figure 23.9
You must set up a session-state database to eliminate this error thrown by SSRS when attempting to open the web database report object that substitutes for a read-only subform.

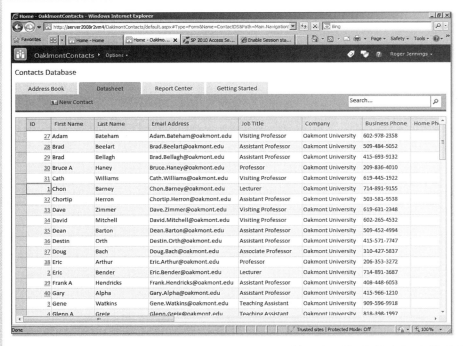

Figure 23.10
The read-only datasheet isn't affected by the session-state problem because it's a form, not a report.

11. Click one of the Datasheet grid's ID links to open the pop-up editing dialog, which also lets you edit the selected contact. This web form is almost identical to the corresponding client form opened in Access (see Figure 23.11).

 note

See the "Fixing the Session State Issue with the SharePoint 2010 Management Shell" section, which follows shortly, for instructions to fix the session-state problem. The SharePoint team might have fixed this problem by the time you follow this procedure.

Figure 23.11
This pop-up dialog enables editing and saving the selected con-tact's data.

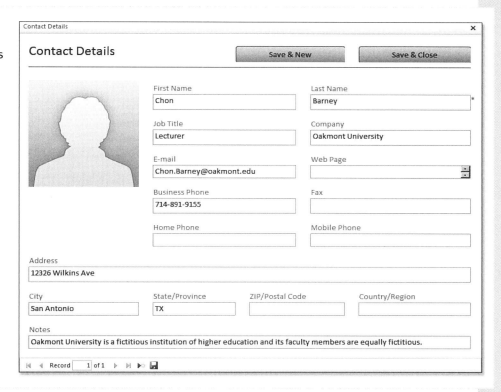

Fixing the Session State Issue with the SharePoint 2010 Management Shell

The preceding error message is due to failure of the Configuration Wizard to establish a session state database for Internet Information Server (IIS) when you select the Standalone configuration option during SharePoint setup. Fixing the error requires executing a PowerScript cmdlet to add the session state database to SPS 2010's SQL Server instance followed by an IISRESET command to restart IIS.

SharePoint administrators have traditionally used the Stsadm command-line tool to manage SharePoint sites. Microsoft describes Stsadm as follows:

> Stsadm provides access to operations not available by using the Central Administration site, such as changing the administration port. The command-line tool has a more streamlined interface than Central Administration, and it allows you to perform the same tasks. There are certain operations and certain parameters that are only available by using the Stsadm command-line tool.

The SharePoint team introduced the SharePoint 2010 Management Shell, which uses PowerShell and cmdlets. The MSDN Library's "Administering Service Applications Using the SharePoint 2010 Management Shell" topic at http://bit.ly/987ULq or http://msdn.microsoft.com/en-us/library/ee537913.aspx begins as follows:

> The SharePoint Management Shell in SharePoint Foundation 2010 provides an extensive set of Windows PowerShell cmdlets that make development, deployment, and administration of SharePoint 2010 easier and more efficient.

> The SharePoint Management Shell supersedes the Stsadm.exe administration tool. All current and future development of command-line tools and administrative files in Microsoft SharePoint Foundation 2010 should use this new scripting technology.

To turn on session state stored in an SQL Server database with the SharePoint Management Shell and the SPSessionStateService, do the following with the administrative account you used to install SharePoint Server 2010:

1. Choose Start, All Programs, Microsoft SharePoint 2010 Products, SharePoint 2010 Management Shell to open the command window with the C:\Users\YourAdministraterAccount folder active.

2. Execute a simple cmdlet to verify that SharePoint 2010 Management Shell cmdlets are registered, type **get-PSSnapin –Registered** at the command prompt and press Enter (see Figure 23.12).

note

SharePoint stores all Web database objects except tables—including queries, forms, reports and macros—in hidden lists. The Access team calls these Web database application objects *client objects*. When you open a form for viewing or to modify its design, Access retrieves the client objects and table data and caches them in memory. After the initial retrieval, only changes are exchanged between the Access application and SharePoint site.

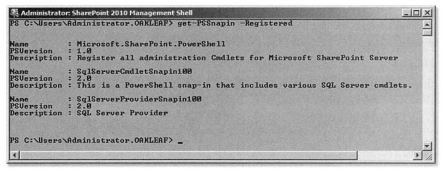

Figure 23.12
The SharePoint 2010 Management Shell uses a minor modification of the Command window. The get-PSSnapin cmdlet with the –Registered criterion returns a list of registered PowerShell Snapins with the SharePoint Snapin at the top.

3. Type **enable-SPSessionStateService** and press Enter to open a prompt for the database name.

4. Type any name you want at the DatabaseName: prompt (**SessionStateDB** for this example) and press enter. After a few seconds, the PowerScript prompt returns (see Figure 23.13), which indicates that the database has been completed.

Figure 23.13
Enabling the SPSessionStateServices requires executing the cmdlet and supplying an arbitrary database name.

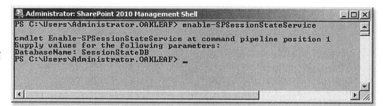

5. Choose Start, All Programs, Accessories, Command Prompt to open the Command window, type **IISReset /noforce** at the command prompt and press Enter to stop and restart IIS (see Figure 23.14).

Figure 23.14
It's a good practice to stop and restart IIS after initiating a new service.

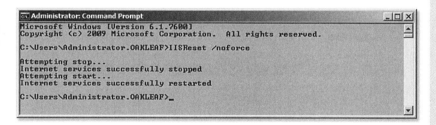

6. Return to IE, press F5 to refresh your SharePoint session and recompile the site, verify that there's no error message in the Address Book subform, and open a report in the Report Center page to verify that SharePoint session state is working correctly (see Figure 23.15).

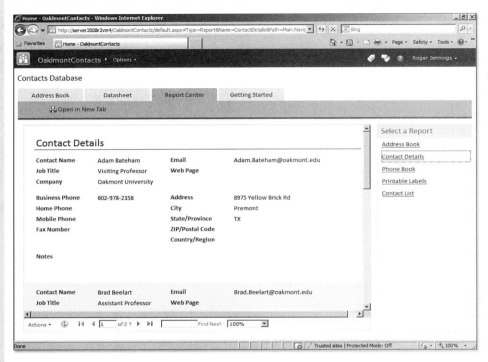

Figure 23.15
Opening a report indicates that you've successfully enabled saving SharePoint session state.

Making Design Changes to Web Databases

As mentioned earlier in the chapter, you make all design changes to client objects in the Access UI and publish them to or synchronize them with the web database after you've tested them in the Access UI. The following sections show you how to modify a Contacts web database and correct a deliberately induced synchronization issue.

Deleting the Getting Started Form from the Contacts Web Database

The Contacts template includes a Getting Started form that has a few non-functional links and isn't germane to SharePoint users. Follow these steps to delete it and generate a synchronization issue:

1. Open the OakmontContacts.accdb database that you published to SharePoint Server 2010 in the preceding sections in Access.

2. Select the Getting Started form in the Navigation pane and delete it.

 note

ContactsExtended is a datasheet with SharePoint-related fields—SharePointEditor (Text), SharePointAuthor(Text), SharePointModifiedDate (DateTime), SharePointCreatedDate (DateTime) and Searchable (a Text field that contains all column data for the row).

3. Click the Create tab, select the ContactsExtended query in the Navigation pane and click the Forms group's Datasheet (Web) button to create a Datasheet form (see Figure 23.16).

Figure 23.16
The web Datasheet form created with the ContactsExtended query as its datasource has five additional SharePoint-related fields.

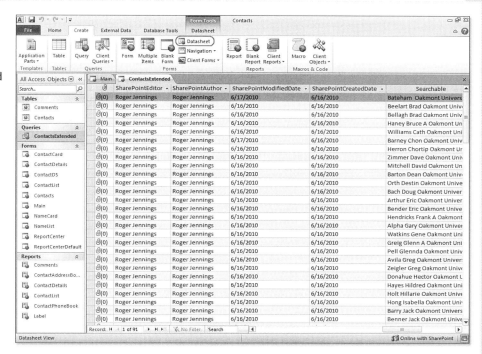

4. Right-click the Datasheet and choose Save to save the ContactsExtended form.

5. Select the Main form, change to Layout view, drag the ContactsExtended form to the right of the Navigation Control's Datasheet tab, and press Ctrl+S to save it.

6. Delete the Video Player and Default View forms from the Navigation pane (see Figure 23.17).

note

Notice that all icons in the Navigation pane as well as the Create ribbon's Query, Form, Multiple Items, Blank Form, Datasheet, Report, Blank Report and Macro buttons have gained a blue-green sphere (representing a globe) overlay to indicate that these objects are or will be created as web objects. Objects without the globe overlay will be created as Client objects, which won't be visible to SharePoint users.

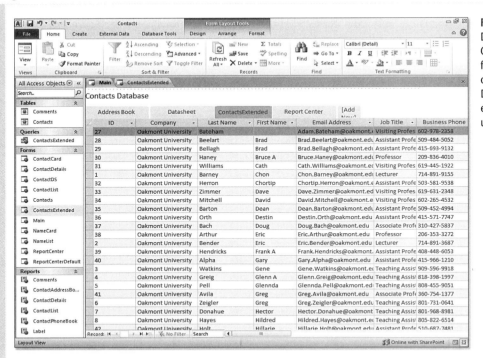

Figure 23.17
Drag the ContactsExtended form to the right of the Main form's Datasheet tab to enable SharePoint users to view it.

7. Open the http://*servername*/OaklmontContacts/ site if necessary, open the Address Book form, and press F5 to refresh the session. Notice that the Getting Started button is visible and the ContactsExtended button isn't, which demonstrates that the web database hasn't been updated in SharePoint.

8. Click the File tab to open the Backstage page, click the Info tab, and click the Check Sync Status button to update the Sync Status Last Checked label (see Figure 23.18).

9. Click the Sync All button to attempt to synchronize SharePoint's web database list with your changes.

10. After a few seconds you receive a Sync Failed message, which recommends opening the Web Compatibility Issues table (see Figure 23.19). Click OK to dismiss the dialog.

Figure 23.18
The Info page's Sync section receives a red background after you click the Check Sync Status button with unsynchronized changes to web objects.

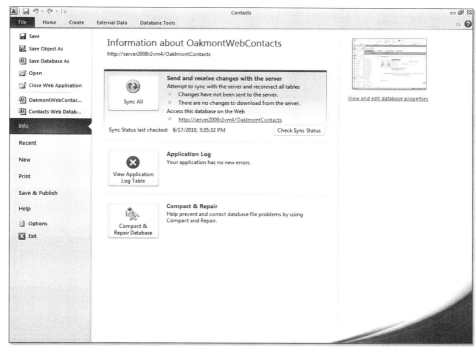

Figure 23.19
Appearance of the Sync Failed dialog indicates an incompatibility with web databases introduced by the design changes made in the preceding steps.

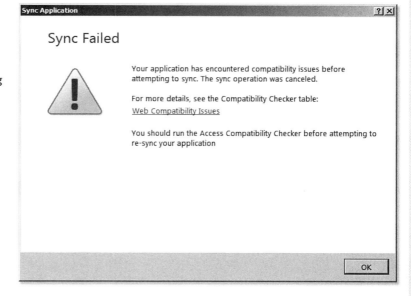

Investigating and Correcting Web Database Incompatibilities

1. Click the Create tab, select the Web Compatibility Issues table, click the Forms group's Client Forms button and choose Split Form to make the data easier to read (see Figure 23.20). The first issue relates to an On Load macro Em(bedded) in the ContactCard form that attempts to open the no-longer-existent GettingStarted form.

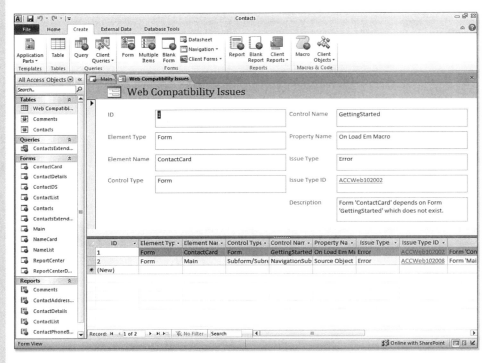

Figure 23.20
Opening the Web Compatibility Issues table in a Split form makes the rows easier to read.

2. Open the ContactCard form in Layout view, open its Property Sheet, select Form in the object list, and double-click the On Load event's builder button to open the Macro Editor.

3. Activate the BrowseTo action, open the ObjectName list, and replace GettingStarted with ContactsDS (see Figure 23.21).

Figure 23.21
Change the
BrowseTo
macro action
to display the
ContactsDS
form if the tmp-
FirstVisit and ID
values are null.

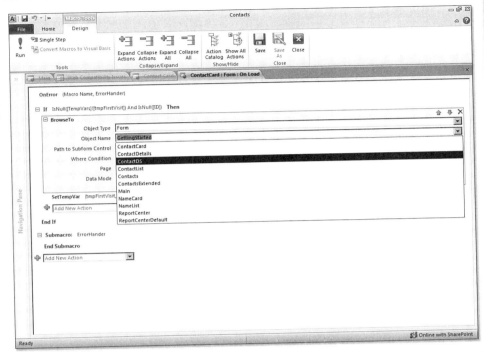

4. The second issue might be due to the first issue, so close the Macro Editor, save changes to the macro, click the File tab and the Sync All button, close all other changed objects, and save their changes. Synchronization completes without issues.

5. Return to http://*servername*/OaklmontContacts/, press F5 to refresh the page, click the ContactsExtended tab, and verify the presence of the SharePoint-related fields (see Figure 23.22).

Converting legacy Access applications that don't take advantage of pre-screening for web publishing and synchronizing issues by starting with a Blank Web Database template are likely to have many more issues that might be more difficult to diagnose than the preceding incompatibility.

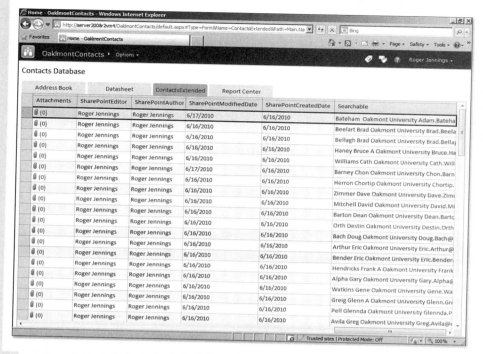

Figure 23.22
The ContactsExtended Web Datasheet closely resembles the Client object version in Access (refer to Figure 23.16).

Working with a Hosted SharePoint Site

As noted in this chapter's early "Hosted SharePoint 2010 Enterprise Sites" section, Access Hosting (www.accesshosting.com), a Microsoft Certified Hosting Partner, offers a web-accessible hosted version of SharePoint Server 2010 Enterprise Edition. Access Hosting offers a free 30-day trial with 25MB of data and one user account. The Microsoft Access team's Ryan McMinn announced this service in a "Free Access Services hosting trial for early adopters" blog post of January 4, 2010 (http://bit.ly/a79HTe or http://blogs.msdn.com/b/access/archive/2010/01/04/free-access-services-hosting-trial-for-early-adopters.aspx).

At rates between $19 (Developer edition) to $99 per month (Enterprise edition), Access Hosting provides an Internet-accessible SPS 2010 Enterprise implementation that has been specially tuned for publishing Access web databases. The monthly charge includes Standard and Enterprise CALs for the first user, deployment of from up to 1GB or 2GB of Access web databases, from 5 to 10 user accounts daily backup with three-set rotation, and FTP access to all backup sets.

Alternatively, Access Hosting's US$19 per month Developer Sandbox Hosting Plan offers 25MB storage and a single user account for testing and prototyping Access 2010 solutions without having to maintain your own SharePoint 2010/Access Services server.

Signing Up for and Testing a Trial Access Hosting Account

Smithbridge Technology Group, the owner of Access Hosting, provides a sign-up page for a 30-day free trial with a single user account at www.accesshosting.com/Free-Trial/Free-Access-2010-Hosting-Trial.htm. After you submit the Trial Account Request, Access hosting will assign you a http://companyname.accesshosting.com subsite, where companyname is the value you supply in the Preferred Site Name text box (see Figure 23.23). This chapter's hosted samples have http://oakleaf.accesshosting.com as their site name.

 note

The preceding hosting prices were valid when this book was written in mid-2010. The US$79 or US$799 per year introductory rates are valid until September 1, 2010 and will increase to US$99 per month or US$999 per year thereafter.

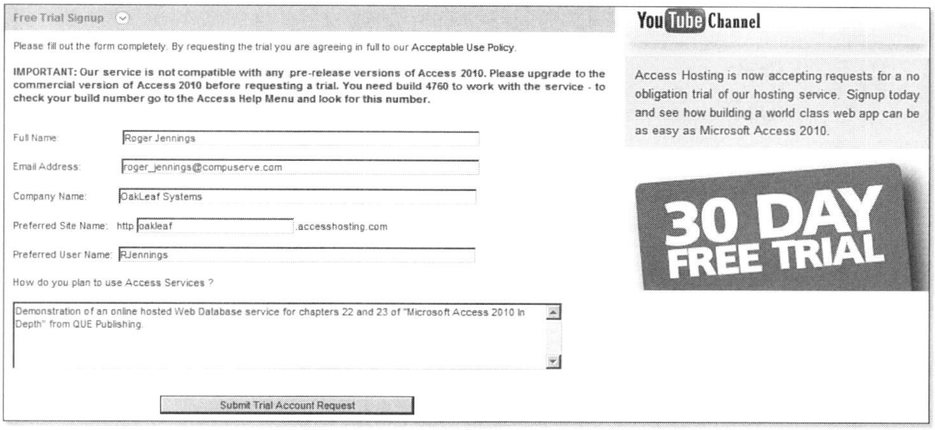

Figure 23.23
Access Hosting requires this information to grant you a 30-day free trial of their hosted SharePoint Server 2010 services for publishing web databases.

In a day or two, you'll receive an e-mail message confirming your site and user names and a pre-assigned password. Verify that you can connect to your main site by typing the site name in the address bar and typing the domain prefix, **AH**, assigned user name and password in the Windows Security dialog (see Figure 23.24).

Figure 23.24
When logging on to your site, http://oakleaf.access-hosting.com for this example, type the domain/user-name combination, AH\rjennings for this example, and password, mark the Remember My Credential check box, and click OK to log in.

The default landing page is the same as that for SharePoint Foundation 2010 and SharePoint Server 2010, if you choose the Team website option for the latter (see Figure 23.25).

Figure 23.25
Logging onto the site opens a landing page that's the same as that of an on-premise SharePoint Server 2010 Team site. Subsites you add by publishing web databases to the main multi-tenanted site don't get links on the landing page by default.

Publishing a Web Database to an Access Hosting Subsite

The only significant differences in publishing a web database to an on-premise SharePoint Server 2010 is the site address. The speed of synchronization, which varies with the client's Internet connection speed and database size, is noticeably slower than with an intranet connection. Access Services caches table, form and report data on the client for browser based rendition and PCs running an Access 2010 client, so repeated synchronizations only require sending changes from the Access client to the SharePoint server.

To generate and publish a Contacts web database to the Access Hosting site you created in the preceding section, do the following:

1. Create a ContactsAH web database from the Contacts Web Database template following the procedure described in the earlier "Creating a Web Database from a Template" section.

2. Click the File tab and save the database as OakmontContactsAH.accdb.

3. Click the Backstage page's Options link to open the Access Options dialog, click the Current Database button, change the Application Name to Contacts-Hosted (see Figure 23.26), accept the remaining defaults, and click OK to save the Application Name.

Figure 23.26
Add a –*Hosted* suffix to the Application name to identify the web database as hosted.

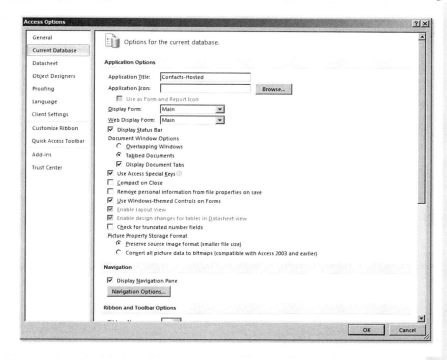

4. Click OK to acknowledge the message, and then close and reopen the database as instructed.

5. Click the File tab, Run Compatibility Checker button, and then click the Publish to Access Services button.

6. Click your assigned URL, http://oakleaf.accesshosting.com for this example, in the Recent Locations list or type it in the text box. The Application Name value becomes the Site Name (see Figure 23.27).

7. Click the Publish to Access Services button, type your password in the Windows Security dialog, mark the Remember My Credential check box, and click OK to connect to the Access Hosting site and synchronize the web objects. As mentioned previously, the synchronization time will depend on the upload speed of your Internet connection.

8. When the Publish Succeeded dialog appears with the link to your new subsite, click the link to open the web database's default Main form (see Figure 23.28).

9. Click OK to close the Publish Succeeded dialog and test the other forms, except Getting Started.

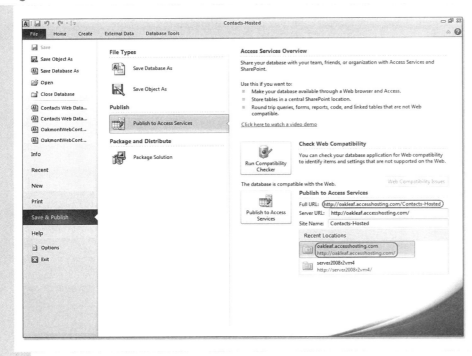

Figure 23.27
Use the site URL assigned to you by Access Hosting and the Application Name property value to create the full URL of your hosted site.

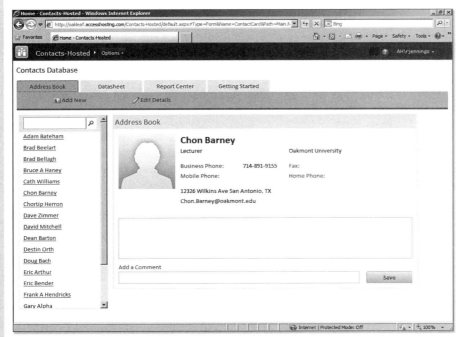

Figure 23.28
The default Main form opens in your hosted site after about 30 to 60 seconds for synchronizing the web objects with the local Client objects.

Working Around Time Zone Conflicts

AccessHosting.com servers are located in a data center in the (UTC – 5:00) Eastern Time (US & Canada) time zone. If you're computer's local time zone is other than Eastern, you'll probably receive this error message: "Your local machine time zone does not match your current SharePoint Regional Settings. Operations involving dates will not work correctly." To dismiss the message click the More Information link to open a Microsoft Support page. This page didn't provide more information about time zone conflicts when this book was written.

note

The full URL for the landing page of the new web database example is http://oakleaf.accesshosting.com/ Contacts-Hosted/default.aspx#Type= Form&Name=ContactCard&Path= Main.NavigationSubform.

To work around time zone conflicts, change the regional settings for your (and other users') account(s) by following these steps:

1. Open the user account menu by clicking the arrow at the right of the user name in the upper-right corner of the page (see Figure 23.29).

Figure 23.29
The user menu lets you change your user information, regional settings—time zone, in particular—and alerts, as well as that of other users if you're a member of the Owners group.

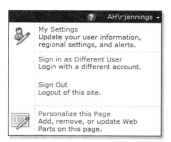

2. Click the My Settings link to open the User Information page and click its My Regional Settings link to open the Personal Settings–Regional Settings page, which has the Always Follow Web Settings check box marked by default (see Figure 23.30).

3. Clear the Always Follow Web Settings check box and select the appropriate local time zone—(UTC–08:00) Pacific Time (US & Canada) for this example—in the Time Zones list (see Figure 23.31).

note

All other controls are disabled (read-only) when Always Follow Web Settings is selected. The default Time Zone value matches that of AccessHosting.com— (UTC–05:00) Eastern Time (US & Canada). The client PC's local time zone is (UTC–08:00) Pacific Time (US & Canada) for this example.

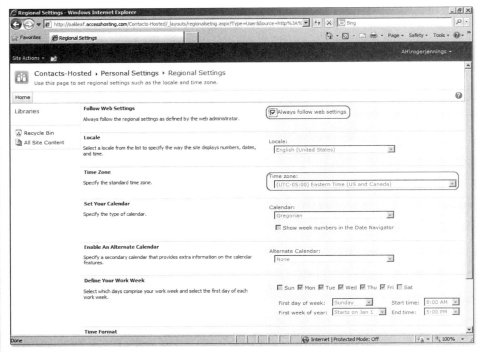

Figure 23.30
Set the time zone for user accounts on the Personal Settings – Regional Settings page.

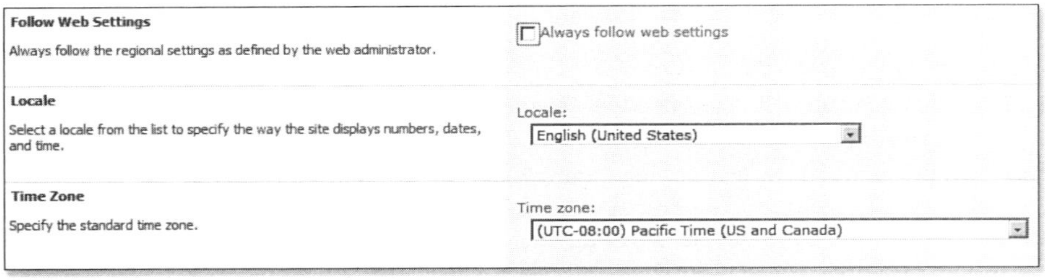

Figure 23.31
Enable selecting a time zone matching the user's local machine setting by clearing the Always Follow Web Settings check box.

4. Click OK to apply the setting and return to the Main form, close and reopen the landing pages to verify that the error message no longer appears.

Publishing Web Databases to Office 365 SharePoint Servers

Microsoft announced Office 365, the successor to Microsoft Business Productivity Online Services (BPOS) on October 19, 2010. Office 365 was about to enter the beta-testing stage when this book was written. The online suite includes Office Web Apps, together with SharePoint 2010 Online, Exchange Online and Lync Online in the cloud, (Microsoft Lync is the new name for products formerly known as Communications Server, Communications Online and Communicator, and it also now includes Lync Web App, and Lync Online.)

Office 365 for Small Business is priced at US$6.00 per month per user for up to 50 users and includes:

- Office Web Apps web productivity applications

- Exchange Online for email, mobile access, calendar, contacts , anti-virus, anti-spam

- SharePoint Online for team sites, Access services, and an easy-to-build public website

- Lync Online for instant messaging and online meetings

- 24x7 moderated community-based support

- Simplified setup and management

Exiting BPOS users can upgrade to Office 365 for Enterprises, which will cost US$10.00 per month per user and include:

- Exchange Online for email, mobile access, calendar, discovery, anti-virus, anti-spam

- SharePoint Online for advanced portals for collaboration

- Lync Online for IM and online meetings

- 24/7 IT-level phone support

- On-premises licenses

- Control and management features

New enterprice enhancements include:

- Single sign on

- New Outlook Web App

- Email archiving, retention and cross mailbox search

- View documents using Office Web Apps

- Increased SharePoint storage

- My Sites and other new team sites

- Site search capabilities

Basic Office 365 for Enterprises doesn't include Access, Excel, Forms or Visio services nor does it offer the full functionality of Exchange, SharePoint and Lync Online. Firms with more than 50 users must opt to include a subscription to Office 2010 Professional Plus, which increases the cost to US$24 per user per month. This version includes:

- Office Professional Plus desktop software

- Office Web Apps web productivity applications

- Exchange Online for email, mobile access, calendar, discovery, anti-virus, anti-spam, as well as advanced capabilities for voice mail, unified messaging, and compliance archiving

- SharePoint Online for advanced portals for collaboration and advanced capabilities including Forms, Access, Visio & Excel services

- Lync Online for IM and online meetings

- 24/7 IT-level phone support

- On-premises licenses

- Control and management features

Microsoft expects Office 365 to be generally available in the first half of 2011. Channel9's "Office 365: The power to think big and be small, to be big and act fast" video featuring John Betz, Microsoft's Director of Online Services at http://bit.ly/9bBmoB (http://channel9.msdn.com/posts/Office-365-The-power-to-think-big-and-be-small-to-be-big-and-act-fast) offers a preview of publishing an Access 2010 Web Database to SharePoint Online at 15:30. Check the Roger Jennings' Access Blog at http://accessindepth.blogspot.com/, which will include step-by-step instructions for publishing Access 2010 Web Databases to SharePoint 2010 Online after Office 365's release.

INDEX

A

.accdb files
   passwords, adding, 912
   properties, 183-185

.accde files, creating, 143-144

.accdr runtime files, creating, 144

Access 2007
   collaboration with SharePoint, PDF:1463-PDF:1464
   data types, PDF:1453-PDF:1454
   Datasheet view, PDF:1454-PDF:1457
   features, PDF:1424-PDF:1427
   forms, layouts, PDF:1459-PDF:1460
   macros, PDF:1462-PDF:1463
   Navigation Pane, PDF:1447-PDF:1452
   publishing to PDF documents, PDF:1461
   QAT, PDF:1439-PDF:1441
   ribbons, PDF:1429-PDF:1437
   SSX
      installing, PDF:1465-PDF:1470
      managing, PDF:1470-PDF:1472
   tabbed documents, PDF:1458
   templates, PDF:1458
   unsupported features, PDF:1464

Access 200x, upgrading to Access 2010, PDF:1412-PDF:1415

Access databases, creating from scratch, 181-183

Access Hosting, 998
   trial account, signing up for, 999-1004

Access Services
   limitations and restrictions, 979-980
   Reporting Services 2008 R2 for SharePoint 2010 Add-In, 979

Access SQL
   corresponding server data types, PDF:1202-PDF:1205
   DISTINCTROW keyword, PDF:1202
   reserved words not in ANSI SQL, PDF:1200-PDF:1202

action queries
   creating, 374-379
   make-table action query, 536-543
   records, appending to tables, 543-545
   records, deleting from tables, 546-549
   writing, PDF:1160-PDF:1165

actions (macros), viewing, 799-801

ActionType field, adding lookup list, 258-261

activating Property Options smart tag, 229-230

adding
   field-level validation rules, 255-256

   indexes to tables, 222-223
   records
      to HRActions table, 261-263
      to tables, 252-253
   tab controls to forms, 659-665
   table-level validation rules, 257-258
   text boxes to forms, 626-630

add-ins, 181

AddOrders.adp sample project, PDF:1398

.ade files, creating, PDF:1134

ADO
   AddOrders.adp sample project, PDF:1398
   Command object
      methods, PDF:1378
      properties, PDF:1374
   Connection object
      events, PDF:1373
      methods, PDF:1370-PDF:1372
      properties, PDF:1363-PDF:1366
   objects, comparing with DAO objects, PDF:1350
   objects, displaying with Object Browser, PDF:1360-PDF:1363
   Recordset object
      events, PDF:1396
      methods, PDF:1392
      properties, PDF:1384-PDF:1392
   Recordsets, creating, PDF:1352-PDF:1360

ADPs (Access Data Projects), 180, PDF:1089-PDF:1091
  benefits of, PDF:1092-PDF:1093
  database, transferring to a server, PDF:1131-PDF:1132
  NorthwindSQL sample project, PDF:1093-PDF:1095
  project designer, Table Design view, PDF:1097-PDF:1099
  projects, securing as .ade file, PDF:1134

advanced options, Import Text Wizard, 318-321

after update events, handling with data macros, 824-834

aggregate functions (SQL), PDF:1148-PDF:1152

aligning
  Form Design view controls to grid, 617
  report controls, 714

altering field names, 83-86

ANSI SQL, PDF:1140

ANSI-92 SQL standard
  conforming to, PDF:1183-PDF:1194
  DDL, creating tables with, PDF:1167-PDF:1169
  DISTINCT keyword, PDF:1202
  reserved words in Access SQL, PDF:1198-PDF:1200

append stored procedures, PDF:1119-PDF:1123

appending, records to tables, 543-545

Application Parts button (Create ribbon), 676-679

applications
  creating with templates, 46-59
  with linked tables, upsizing, 884
  linking to SQL Azure databases, PDF:1227-PDF:1237
  upsizing, PDF:1172-PDF:1173

ApplyFilter macro, writing, 812-816

applying CSS rules to HTML tables, PDF:1065-PDF:1067

arguments (VBA), PDF:1259-PDF:1260

arithmetic operators, 385

Arrange Ribbon (Form Design Tool), 612-613, 696

arrays, VBA, PDF:1254-PDF:1255

assignment operators, 386

attachment controls, adding to forms, 656-659

attributes, XML, PDF:1054

autogenerating
  tabular reports, 686-688
  transaction-processing forms, 566-568

automating communication with Outlook, 74-78

availability, 871

axes (PivotTables), interchanging, 519-520

Azure databases, linking to Access applications, PDF:1227-PDF:1237

B

back end
  security, 864-868

back end security, verifying, 868-870

backing up databases, PDF:1127-PDF:1131

Backstage view, 26-29

blank forms, creating, 621-623

bound reports, adding linked subreports, 744

broken links, re-linking, 330-331

C

calculated controls, adding to reports, 709-713

calculations
  based on all records of a table, 476-478
  based on selected data, 479-481

cascading deletions, 559-563
  testing, 562

cascading updates, testing, 562-563

CCL (Cursor Control Language), PDF:1139

charts
  creating from graphs, 768-771
  printing from reports, 771-775

class modules, 43, PDF:1280-PDF:1287

clean option (HTML Tidy), PDF:1038

Client Settings page, setting default options, 129-131

client\server RDBMSs, 158-159

client\server tables, linking manually, 890-897

Clipboard, copying controls to forms, 637-638

cloning PivotChart form\subform pair, 791-793

Codd, Dr. E.F., 157

code-signing databases, 31, PDF:1447

collaborating with Windows SharePoint Foundation 2010, 917-918

collecting data by email, 78-79

color of forms, customizing, 585-591

combining multiple resultsets, 495-499

Combo Box wizard, 640-644

combo boxes
adding to forms,
86-89, 640-644
converting to ADP project,
PDF:1340
creating, 809-812,
PDF:1318-PDF:1325
for finding specific records,
creating, 651-655
populating, 645-648
"Select All" option, adding,
PDF:1336-PDF:1340
with static values, creating,
647-650

**Command Button Wizard,
generating embedded
macros, 804-809**

Command object (ADO)
methods, PDF:1378
Parameter object,
PDF:1377-PDF:1378
parameter values, pass-
ing to stored procedures,
PDF:1381-PDF:1383
properties, PDF:1374

**communication, automating
with Outlook, 74-78**

compacting databases, 142

**comparing ADO and DAO
objects, PDF:1350**

compatibility
database compatibility levels, configuring, PDF:1419
with PC database files, 324

**compile errors,
troubleshooting, 143**

**composite filter criteria,
288-289**

**compound filter criteria,
286-289**

concatenation operators, 387

conditional formatting, 202

**conditional statements (VBA),
PDF:1261-PDF:1264**

**configuration files, HTML Tidy,
PDF:1028**

**configuring database compat-
ibility levels, PDF:1419**

confirming
back-end security, 868-870
validation rules, 264-266

**conforming to ANSI-92 SQL
standard, PDF:1183-PDF:1194**

**connecting to remote SQL
Server database, PDF:1133-
PDF:1134**

Connection object (ADO)
events, PDF:1373
methods,
PDF:1370-PDF:1372
properties,
PDF:1363-PDF:1366

contacts (Outlook)
exporting, 72-73
importing, 70-72

**context-specific table tools
ribbons, 110-117**

contextual ribbons, 24
in Access 2007,
PDF:1432-PDF:1437

**control error correction,
accepting/declining, 630-631**

controls
adding to reports, 751-752
attachment controls, adding
to forms, 656-659
copying to other forms,
637-638
data events, responding to,
PDF:1311-PDF:1316
grouping in Access 2007,
PDF:1461
Navigation control, 676-679
properties, modifying,
605-606
referring to with VBA,
PDF:1309-PDF:1311
for reports
aligning, 714
formatting, 714-715
SQL statements, upsizing,
PDF:1195-PDF:1197
Web Browser control, 679

converting
to Access 2007 format, 143
combo box forms to ADP
project, PDF:1340
data types, 226-227
field data types to Access
data types, 328-330
graphs to charts, 768-771
HTML 4.01 files to XHTML
1.0, PDF:1043-PDF:1044
macros to VBA, PDF:1280-
PDF:1283
macros to VBA callback
functions, PDF:1303-
PDF:1307
secure files to Access 2010,
PDF:1410-PDF:1411
unsecured files to Access
2010, PDF:1404-PDF:1409

copying and pasting
referential integrity,
troubleshooting, 266
tables, 232-235

**copying\pasting controls to
forms, 637-638**

Create ribbon, 118-119
Application Parts button,
676-679

creating
Access databases from
scratch, 181-183
combo boxes,
PDF:1318-PDF:1329
expressions, 404-419
for calculating field
values, 418-419
for query criteria, 405-414
for validating data, 405
HTML forms,
PDF:1045-PDF:1048
InfoPath forms,
PDF:1081-PDF:1084
Packaged Solutions, 150-154
queries
action queries, 374-379
crosstab queries, 485-497
multitable queries,
422-441

crossfooting crosstab queries, PDF:1221-PDF:1224

crosstab queries
creating, 485-497
crossfooting, PDF:1221-PDF:1224
emulating with T-SQL, PDF:1205-PDF:1221
fixed column headings, 493-497
linked graphs, creating, 775-783
monthly product sales query, creating, 492-493

Crosstab Query Wizard, 486-491

CSS code, generating with HTML Tidy, PDF:1041-PDF:1042

Current Database page, setting default options, 124-126

custom display formats, placeholders, 198

Customize Ribbons page, setting default options, 132

customizing
Office Themes, 579-585
PivotTable views, 519-520
SPF list views, 940-947
Table Datasheet view, 292-294

D

DAO
objects
comparing with ADO objects, PDF:1350
displaying with Object Browser, PDF:1360-PDF:1363
Recordsets, creating, PDF:1352-PDF:1360

data dictionaries, generating with Database Documenter, 240-243

data entry keys, 247-252

data entry options, setting, 246-248

data events, responding to, PDF:1311-PDF:1316

data macros
designing, 822-840
named data macros, writing, 841-857
table triggers, emulating, 820-822
table updates, logging, 836-840
after update events, handling, 824-834

data types
in Access 2007, PDF:1453-PDF:1454
changing, 226-227
conversion functions, 402
corresponding SQL server data types, PDF:1202-PDF:1205
selecting, 193-195
VBA, PDF:1248-PDF:1249

data validation rules, 172-173

database compatibility levels, configuring, PDF:1419

Database Documenter, generating data dictionaries, 240-243

Database Splitter, creating linked tables, 861-862

databases
history of, 156-159
MSDE, upgrading, PDF:1417-PDF:1418
repairing, 142
SQL Server 2008, backing up and restoring, PDF:1127-PDF:1131
transferring to a server, PDF:1131-PDF:1132

Datasheet page, setting default options, 126

Datasheet view
in Access 2007, PDF:1454-PDF:1457
tables, creating, 213

DCL (Data Control Language), PDF:1139

DDL (Data Definition Language), PDF:1139, PDF:1167-PDF:1169

default database folder, designating as trusted location, 53-54

default field values, setting, 213-215

default form layout, rearranging, 572-575

default options, setting
Client Settings page, 129-131
Current Database page, 124-126
Customize Ribbons page, 132
Datasheet page, 126
General page, 123
Language page, 129
Object Designers page, 126-128
Proofing page, 128-129
Quick Access Toolbar page, 132-134
Trust Center pages, 134-137

defining
functions, 95-98
operating modes, 98-99

deleting
Getting Started form from Contacts web database, 992-996
records, 254
records from tables, 546-549

design mode, 99

Design Ribbon (Form Design Tool), 608-612, 695-696

Design view, creating HRActions table, 208-212

designing
data macros, 822-840
HRActions table, 205-206
nested queries, 430
queries, parameter queries, 481-485

desktop RDBMSs, 158-159

diagramming table relationships, PDF:1125-PDF:1126

display components of tables, 103-105

display format, selecting, 196-202

display mode (forms), changing to modal popup window, 575-593

DISTINCT keyword (ANSI SQL), PDF:1202

DISTINCTROW keyword (Access SQL), PDF:1202

DML (Data Manipulation Language), PDF:1139

DocFiles, 180

DoCmd methods, PDF:1291-PDF:1294

Document Libraries (SPF 2010), publishing Access 2010 database, 935-940

documentation, RibbonX, PDF:1296-PDF:1298

downloading
    HTML Tidy,
        PDF:1026-PDF:1027
    SharePoint Server 2010 trial
        software, 978
    SSX, 35-41
    templates, 46-47

DQL (Data Query Language), PDF:1139

drill-down information, increasing in PivotTables, 517-518

drill-down list boxes, creating, PDF:1330-PDF:1334

E

editing
    data entry keys, 247-252
    HTML forms,
        PDF:1048-PDF:1051
    RibbonX documents,
        PDF:1299-PDF:1301

element-centric XML documents, PDF:1056

eliminating recursion errors, 834-836

email
    data, collecting, 78-79
    reports, mailing as
        attachments, 752-751

embedded macros, 46
    generating with Command
        Button Wizard, 804-809

emulating table triggers with data macros, 820-822

enabling object dependencies, 228-230

Enterprise External Connector license, 977

entity integrity, 172

error handling (VBA), PDF:1266-PDF:1268

evaluating benefits of migrating to client\server database, 870

events, 801-802
    Connection object (ADO),
        PDF:1373
    responding to with
        functions,
        PDF:1289-PDF:1291
    after update events,
        handling with data macros,
        824-834

examining
    class project module
        members with Object
        Browser,
        PDF:1287-PDF:1289
    ODBC connection string,
        885-886

Excel
    exporting PivotTables to, 523
    exporting tables to, 341-343
    worksheets
        importing, 299-306
        linking, 307-308

Exchange/Outlook wizard, 311-313

execute rights, granting to stored procedures, 907-910

exporting
    Access tables to HTML files,
        PDF:1028-PDF:1030
    contacts to Outlook, 72-73
    filtered data, 295
    PivotTables, to Excel, 523
    reports to HTML tables,
        PDF:1031
    tables, 341-343
        to RDBMSs, 874-875
        to SharePoint lists, 967
        as text files, 344
        to XML, PDF:1057

Expression Builder, adding table-level validation rules, 257-258

expressions, 382-384
    creating, 404-419
        for calculating field
            values, 418-419
        for query criteria, 405-414
        for validating data, 405

external database files, images, 326-328

F

field data types to Access data types
    converting to Access data
        types, 328-330

Field Size property, 193

field-level validation rules
    adding, 255-256

fields
    data types
        changing, 226-227
        selecting, 193-195
    default values, setting,
        213-215
    for HRActions table,
        selecting, 207
    Internet-based smart tags,
        adding, 231-232

lookup fields, 442-456
  foreign key drop-down list, adding, 443-447
matched values, replacing, 274
names, altering, 83-86
properties, 186-191
  overriding, 680-681
rearranging sequence of, 225
selecting in Query Design View, 356-359

fifth normal form, 169

files, linking, 298

filtering
composite criteria, 288-289
compound filter criteria, adding, 286-289
exporting filtered data, 295
by form, 278-283
menu-based filters, 284-285
PivotTable category values, 515-517
saving filters as queries, 291-292
by selection, 275-277
Text Filters option, 277-278

Find Duplicates Query Wizard, 371, PDF:1016-PDF:1018

Find Unmatched Query Wizard, 372-373

finding matching records, 271-274

first normal form, 164-165

fixed-value lookup list, adding to tables, 447-450

foreign key drop-down list, adding, 443-447

foreign keys, 160

Form Design Tool
Arrange Ribbon, 612-613
Design Ribbon, 608-612

Form Design view
controls
  aligning to grid, 617
  moving, 617-619
  multiple, aligning, 619
elements, selecting, 613-614

form letters, creating with Mail Merge Wizard, 332-339

Form wizard, creating master\ child forms, 594-601

Format Painter, 592-593

Format ribbon, 698

formatting
conditional formatting, 202
form text, 625-626
with query field property sheet, 472-474
report controls, 714-715

forms, 565-566
attachment controls, adding, 656-659
blank forms, creating, 621-623
color, customizing, 585-591
combo boxes
  adding, 640-644
  converting to ADP project, PDF:1340
  creating, 86-89, PDF:1318-PDF:1329
  for finding specific records, 651-655
  populating, 645-648
  with static values, creating, 647-650
control error correction, accepting/declining, 630-631
control objects, moving, 615-617
controls
  copying to other forms, 637-638
  Navigation control, 676-679
  tab controls, 659-665
  Web Browser control, 679
data events, responding to, PDF:1311-PDF:1316
default view, changing, 631-632
design, optimizing, 665-667
display mode, changing to modal popup window, 575-593

Format Painter, 592-593
group boxes, adding, 632-637
HTML forms, PDF:1044
InfoPath forms, PDF:1080
  creating, PDF:1081-PDF:1084
labels, adding to header, 624-625
layout, rearranging, 572-575
Layout view, 567-568
  ribbons, 568-573
list boxes, creating, PDF:1330-PDF:1334
master\child
  creating with Form wizard, 594-601
  generating, 567
opening
  with macros, 66-68
  from Navigation Pane, 62-64
Outlook HTML forms, collecting data by email, 78-79
Page Header/Footer sections, adding, 681-682
PivotChart view as subform, 787-790
properties, modifying, 605-606
referring to with VBA, PDF:1307-PDF:1308
resizing, 615
split forms, generating, 601-602
SQL statements, PDF:1169
  upsizing, PDF:1195-PDF:1197
tab controls, adding history subform, 667-673
Tabbed Document style, 58-59
text, formatting, 625-626
text boxes, creating, 626-630
transaction-processing forms, 566-568, 602-605

fourth normal form, 168

freezing table field display, 268

front end, adding passwords to .accdb files, 912

frozen columns, thawing, 270

function keys
global function keys, 121
shortcut key assignments, 121

functions, 384, 391-402, PDF:1245-PDF:1246
data type conversion functions, 402
defining, 93-98
events, responding to, PDF:1289-PDF:1291
SQL aggregate functions, 476
TempVars collection, 396
text manipulation functions, 398-402
Time and Date, 397-398
Variant data type, 394-396

G

General page, setting default options, 123

generating
CSS code with HTML Tidy, PDF:1041-PDF:1042
data dictionaries with Database Documenter, 240-243
self-signed digital certificates, 145-148
signed package files, 148
split forms, 601-602

Getting Started form, deleting from Contacts web database, 992-996

Getting Started window, downloading templates, 46-47

global function keys, 121

graphs
converting to charts, 768-771
data source, creating, 756-757
design features, modifying, 764-767

linked graphs, creating from crosstab query, 775-783
printing from reports, 771-775
unlinked, creating, 759

group boxes, adding to forms, 632-637

grouped reports, creating, 688-695

grouping
controls in Access 2007, PDF:1461
report data, 731-735

groups, Keep Together property, 720-721

GUIDs (Globally Unique Identifiers), 162

H

headers
adding to HTML tables, PDF:1067
XML, PDF:1055

help system
online help, 138-141
VBA, PDF:1270-PDF:1272

history of databases, 156-159

history subform, adding to tab control page, 667-673

Home ribbon, 106-109

hosted SharePoint sites, 998

HRActions table
adding to Northwind Traders sample database, 204-213
creating in Design view, 208-212
default field values, setting, 213-215
fields, selecting, 207
primary key, selecting, 221
records, adding, 261-263, 673-675
relationships, establishing, 215-220

HTML files
converting to XHTML 1.0, PDF:1043-PDF:1044
exporting to Access tables, PDF:1028-PDF:1030
templates, PDF:1035-PDF:1037

HTML forms, PDF:1044
creating, PDF:1045-PDF:1048
editing, PDF:1048-PDF:1051

HTML tables
CSS rules, applying, PDF:1065-PDF:1067
duplicate rows
finding,
PDF:1016-PDF:1018
removing,
PDF:1018-PDF:1020
headers, adding, PDF:1067
importing from web pages, PDF:1009
structure, analyzing, PDF:1009

HTML Tidy, PDF:1025-PDF:1028
clean option, PDF:1038
configuration files, PDF:1028
running from command prompt, PDF:1027

I

identifier operators, 387-388

identifiers, 384, 390

images, for external database files, 326-328

Import HTML Wizard, PDF:1020-PDF:1024

Import Text Wizard
advanced options, 318-321
text files, importing, 314-318

importing
Access tables with Outlook 2010, 308-311
Excel worksheets, 299-306
HTML tables from web pages, PDF:1009
missing objects, 80-83

Outlook contacts, 70-72
spreadsheets, 298-299
tables, ISAM, 324-326
text files, 313-321
XML to tables, PDF:1073

indexes, 172
adding to tables, 222-223

indirect relationships, creating queries, 433-438

InfoPath forms, PDF:1080

inline functions (SQL Server), PDF:1113-PDF:1116

input masks, 202-203

installing
SharePoint Server 2010, 980-985
SPF 2010 under 64-bit Windows Server 2008, 919-920
SQL Server 2000, PDF:1416-PDF:1417
SSX, 35-41, PDF:1465-PDF:1470

interchanging PivotTable axes, 519-520

Internet-based smart tags, adding to fields, 231-232

intrinsic constants, 403-404

invoking named data macros, 841-857

ISAM (indexed sequential access method), importing tables, 324-326

iterating list box items, PDF:1334-PDF:1335

J

Jet .mdb files, upgrading to Access .accdb files, 179-180

joins
multicolumn inner joins, creating, 438-441
outer joins, creating, 463-466
self-joins, creating, 466-467
SQL, PDF:1152-PDF:1155

tables, 422-441
theta joins, creating, 467-469

K

Keep Together property (groups), 720-721

keyboard, data entry keys, 247-252

L

Label Wizard, 721-725

labels, adding to form header, 624-625

Language page, setting default options, 129

layout mode, 99

Layout view (forms), ribbons, 568-573

libraries, 181

licensing, SharePoint Server 2010, 976-978

limitations
of Access Services, 979-980
of ADPs, PDF:1092-PDF:1093
of SSX, 871

line spacing
adjusting reports, 713, 715-717

linked graphs, creating from crosstab queries, 775-783

Linked Table Manager, 330-331

linked tables, creating with Database Splitter, 861-862

linking
applications to SQL Azure databases, PDF:1227-PDF:1237
client\server tables manually, 890-897
documents to CSS files, PDF:1042
Excel worksheets, 307-308

files, 298
PivotCharts to form's current record, 790-791
SharePoint lists to Access tables, 970

list boxes
creating, PDF:1330-PDF:1334
items, iterating, PDF:1334-PDF:1335
"Select All" option, adding, PDF:1336-PDF:1340

lists (SPF)
data types, 940
linking to Access tables, 970
as source tables, 951-964
synchronizing, 964-967
tables, exporting to, 967

literals, 384, 389-390

logical operators, 386-387

lookup fields, 442-456
foreign key drop-down list, adding, 443-447
multivalued lookup fields, creating, 450-456
printing, 703-705

lookup list, adding to ActionType field, 258-261

looping (VBA), PDF:1264-PDF:1266

M

Macro-to-VBA converter, PDF:1280-PDF:1283

macros, 33-34, 97, 798
in Access 2007, PDF:1462-PDF:1463
actions, viewing, 799-801
ApplyFilter, writing, 812-816
converting to VBA callback functions, PDF:1303-PDF:1307
data macros
designing, 822-840
logging table updates, 836-840
table triggers, emulating, 820-822

after update events,
handling, 824-834
embedded macros,
generating with Command
Button Wizard, 804-809
embedding in templates,
50-51
events, 801-802
forms, opening, 66-68
recursion errors, eliminating,
834-836
running in not-trusted
locations, 31
SwitchBoard Manager,
816-820
versus VBA, 801

Mail Merge Wizard, 331-340
form letters, creating,
332-339

**mailing labels, creating from
multicolumn reports, 721-728**

make-table action query
creating, 374-379
relationships, establishing,
540-542

**make-table stored procedure,
PDF:1117-PDF:1119**

**managing SSX, 41-43,
PDF:1470-PDF:1472**

**many-to-many relationships,
162**

**margins, adjusting on reports,
717-718**

**master/child forms, creating,
567, 594-601**

matching records
finding, 271-274
replacing, 274

menu-based filters, 284-285

**methods (VBA), DoCmd
methods, PDF:1291-PDF:1294**

**Microsoft Graph, creating
graph data source, 756-757**

**Microsoft Office Online,
creating databases, 55-57**

**migrating to client\server
database**
evaluating benefits of, 870
strategy, selecting, 873-875

**module window toolbar (VBA
editor), PDF:1269-PDF:1256**

modules, 97
VBA, PDF:1242-PDF:1246

**monthly product sales query,
creating, 492-493**

**Monthy Sales by Category
reports, creating, 739-744**

moving
control objects on forms,
615-617
controls in Form Design
view, 617-619
SQL Server database to
another server, 886-890

MSDE
databases, upgrading,
PDF:1417-PDF:1418
upgrading to SQL Server
2005, PDF:1415

**multicolumn inner joins,
creating, 438-441**

**multiple resultsets, combining,
495-499**

**multitable queries, creating,
422-441**

**multivalued lookup fields,
creating, 450-456**

N

Name AutoCorrect feature, 225

named constants, 402-404

**named data macros, writing,
841-857**

namespaces (XML), PDF:1056

**naming conventions, VBA,
PDF:1241-PDF:1242**

Navigation control, 676-679

Navigation Pane, 59-66
in Access 2007,
PDF:1447-PDF:1452

forms, opening, 62-64
object classification method,
selecting, 60-61
task records, adding, 64-66

nested queries, designing, 430

new features
in Access 2007,
PDF:1424-PDF:1427
in Access 2010, 18-22

normalization
fifth normal form, 169
first normal form, 164-165
fourth normal form, 168
second normal form, 166
third normal form, 167

**Northwind Traders sample
database**
HRActions table
adding, 204-213
default field values,
setting, 213-215
primary key, selecting,
221
records, adding, 261-263
relationships,
establishing, 215-220
moving to SPF 2010, 948-951
opening, 100-101
table, adding, 204

**NorthwindSQL sample project,
PDF:1093-PDF:1095**

null value, 198

numeric data
field size, selecting, 193-195
standard formats, 197

**NWReader security group,
creating logins, 902-905**

O

Object Browser
ADO objects, displaying,
PDF:1360-PDF:1363
class project module
members, examining,
PDF:1287-PDF:1289
DAO objects, displaying,
PDF:1360-PDF:1363

object classification method, selecting for Navigation Pane, 60-61

object dependencies, enabling, 228-230

Object Designers page, setting default options, 126-128

objects
DAO, comparing with ADO, PDF:1350
importing, 80-83
RibbonX, creating, PDF:1295

ODBC connection string, examining, 885-886

Office gallery, PDF:1442-PDF:1446

Office Themes, customizing, 579-585

OLE miniservers, 756

OLE Object field data type, 192

OLTP (online transaction processing), 173

one-to-many relationships, 161

one-to-one relationships, 161

online help, 138-141

opening
forms
with macros, 66-68
from Navigation Pane, 62-64
Northwind Traders sample database, 100-101

operating modes, defining, 98-99

operators, 384-389
arithmetic operators, 385
assignment operators, 386
identifier operators, 387-388
logical operators, 386-387

optimizing
form design, 665-667
PivotTable performance, 524-528

Option Group Wizard, adding group boxes to forms, 632-637

outer joins, creating, 463-466

Outlook
communication, automating, 74-78
contacts, importing, 70-72
data, collecting by email, 78-79
reports, mailing as attachments, 752-751

Outlook 2010, importing Access tables, 308-311

overriding field properties of tables, 680-681

P

Packaged Solutions, testing, 150-154

page breaks, controlling on reports, 750-751

Page Header/Footer sections, adding to forms, 681-682

Page Setup ribbon, 698-699

parameter queries, 481-485
data types, selecting, 484-485

parameterized inline functions (SQL Server), PDF:1113-PDF:1116

pass-through queries, writing, 897-900

passwords, adding to.accdb files, 912

PC database files, compatibility, 324

PDF documents, exporting tables to, 341-343

performance
of PivotTables, optimizing, 524-528
of SSX, troubleshooting, 915

permissions, roles, 901-902

persistent database objects, 291

persisting PivotCharts linked properties with VBA code, 794-795

PIVOT query syntax (SQL Server 2005), PDF:1216-PDF:1217

PivotCharts, 524-528
category presentation, changing, 530-532
chart type, changing, 532
creating from a query, 784-786
form\subform pair, cloning, 791-793
linked properties, persisting with VBA code, 794-795
linking to form's current record, 790-791

PivotTable views
category values, filtering, 515-517
display, customizing, 519-520
drill-down information, increasing, 517-518
queries, creating, 506-516

PivotTables
exporting, to Excel, 523
performance, optimizing, 524-528
property values, setting, 520-523
substituting in a form, 795-796

placeholders, 198
for input masks, 202-203

populating combo boxes, 645-648

preparing for application upsizing, PDF:1172-PDF:1173

preventing updates to query resultset (Query Design View), 362-363

primary keys, 160, 169-170

Print Preview ribbon, 699-701

printing
charts and graphs from reports, 771-775

lookup fields, 703-705
multicolumn reports as mailing labels, 721-728
queries as report, 367-369

program flow, controlling (VBA), PDF:1260-PDF:1266
conditional statements, PDF:1261-PDF:1264
looping, PDF:1264-PDF:1266

project designer, Table Design view, PDF:1097-PDF:1099

projects
default folder
changing, 48
upsized, securing, PDF:1225-PDF:1227

Proofing page, setting default options, 128-129

properties
of .accdb databases, 183-185
Command object (ADO), PDF:1374
of Connection object (ADO), PDF:1363-PDF:1366
of fields, 186-191
of forms, modifying, 605-606
of PivotTables, setting, 520-523
Recordset object (ADO), PDF:1384-PDF:1392

Property Options smart tag, activating, 229-230

publishing Access 2010 database to SPF 2010 Document Library, 935-940

Q

QAT (Quick Access Toolbar), PDF:1439-PDF:1441

QBE (query-by-example), Query Design View, 174-175

queries
action queries
creating, 374-379
records, appending to tables, 543-545
records, deleting from tables, 546-549
writing, PDF:1160-PDF:1165
constants, 402-404
creating
for PivotTable views, 506-516
from tables in other databases, 500-503
from tables with indirect relationships, 433-438
crosstab queries
creating, 485-497
crossfooting, PDF:1221-PDF:1224
emulating with T-SQL, PDF:1205-PDF:1221
fixed column headings, 493-497
linked graphs, creating, 775-783
exporting to SharePoint lists, 967
exporting to XML, PDF:1057
expressions, 382-384
fields, including all within table, 472-474
functions, 391-402
data type conversion functions, 402
TempVars collection, 396
text manipulation functions, 398-402
Time and Date functions, 397-398
identifiers, 390
literals, 389-390
multitable queries, creating, 422-441
nested queries
designing, 430
operators, 384-389
arithmetic operators, 385
assignment operators, 386
identifier operators, 387-388
logical operators, 386-387
parameter queries, 481-485

pass-through queries, writing, 897-900
PivotCharts, creating, 784-786
saved queries, applying as filter, 292-293
saving filters as, 291-292
SQL Server version, 414
table data, updating, 469-474
UNION queries, 495-501
writing, PDF:1155-PDF:1158

Query Design View, 174-175, 355-369
column headers, changing names of, 365-367
complex criteria, creating, 364-365
fields, selecting, 356-359
queries, printing as report, 367-369
query resultset, preventing updates to, 362-363
records, selecting by criteria, 360-362

Quick Access Toolbar page, setting default options, 132-134

R

RDBMSs, client/server, 158-159

rearranging
form layout, 572-575
sequence of fields in a table, 225

record-locking files, 180-181

records
adding
to HRActions table, 261-263, 673-675
to tables, 252-253
deleting, 254
filtering
composite criteria, 288-289
compound filter criteria, 286-289

by form, *278-283*
menu-based filters,
284-285
by selection, *275-277*
Text Filters option,
277-278
selecting, 254
updating values, 549-559

Recordset object (ADO)
events, PDF:1397
methods, PDF:1392
properties,
PDF:1384-PDF:1392

**recursion errors, eliminating,
834-836**

reducing length of reports, 752

referential integrity, 171-172

relational databases, 157
foreign keys, 160
GUIDs, 162
primary keys, 160
structure of, 159-164

relationships
changing between tables,
227-228
HRActions table,
establishing, 215-220
make-table action queries,
540-542

reliability, 871

re-linking tables, 330-331

**relocating report controls,
700-703**

removing
sections from reports,
749-750
table sort order, 270

repairing databases, 142

**replacing matched field
values, 274**

**Report Wizard, creating
grouped reports, 688-695**

reports, 683-685
bound reports, adding linked
subreports, 744
calculated controls, adding,
709-713

charts, printing, 771-775
controls
adding, *751-752*
aligning, *714*
formatting, *714-715*
relocating, *700-703*
exporting
to HTML tables,
PDF:1031
as XML, PDF:1070
graphs, printing, 771-775
grouped reports, creating,
688-695
grouping data, 731-735
line spacing, adjusting, 713,
715-717
mailing as attachments,
752-751
margins, adjusting, 717-718
modifications, completing,
704-707
Monthy Sales by Category
report, creating, 739-744
multicolumn, printing as
mailing labels, 721-728
page breaks, controlling,
750-751
record source, changing,
707-709
reducing length of, 752
sections, adding, 749-750
sorting data, 735-736
SQL statements, PDF:1169
*upsizing,
PDF:1195-PDF:1197*
subreports, 737-739
tabular reports,
autogenerating, 686-688
types of, 685-686
unbound, 748-749

**reserved ANSI-92 SQL words
in Access SQL,
PDF:1198-PDF:1200**

resizing forms, 615

**reviewing sample templates,
49-50**

ribbons, 22-25
in Access 2007,
PDF:1429-PDF:1437

Arrange ribbon, 696
context-specific table tools
ribbons, 110-117
contextual ribbons, 24
Create ribbon, 118-119
*Application Parts button,
676-679*
Design ribbon, 695-696
Format ribbon, 698
forms, Layout view, 568-573
Home ribbon, 106-109
Page Setup ribbon, 698-699
Print Preview ribbon,
699-701

RibbonX
documentation,
PDF:1296-PDF:1298
documents, editing,
PDF:1299-PDF:1301
objects, creating, PDF:1295

roles, 901-902

row fix-up feature, 471

run mode, 98

**runtime errors, handling
(VBA), PDF:1266-PDF:1268**

S

**sample templates, reviewing,
49-50**

saving filters as query, 291-292

schema (XML), PDF:1056
exporting, PDF:1078

second normal form, 166

**sections, adding\removing
from reports, 749-750**

**secure Access 9x files,
converting to Access 2010,
PDF:1410-PDF:1411**

**securing upsized projects,
PDF:1225-PDF:1227**

security
back-end security, 864-868
front-end, adding passwords
to .accdb files, 912
non-trusted locations,
running macros, 31

roles, 901-902

trusted locations, specifying, 31, PDF:1447

user logins, adding to SQL Server, 900-911

VBA code, PDF:1241

security groups (SPF 2010), 930-934

Select All option, adding to list and combo boxes, PDF:1336-PDF:1340

SELECT queries (SQL)

creating, 348-355

writing, PDF:1140

selecting

client\server database migration strategy, 873-875

display format, 196-202

fields, data types, 193-195

Form Design view elements, 613-614

primary key codes, 169-170

records, 254

self-joins, creating, 466-467

self-signed digital certificates, generating, 145-148

sequence of fields, rearranging, 225

session state issues (SharePoint Server 2010), troubleshooting, 989-991

setting

data entry options, 246-248

default field values, 213-215

PivotTable properties, 520-523

SharePoint Server 2010

enterprise sites, licensing, 976-978

installing, 980-985

interaction with Access 2010, 934-935

licensing, 976-978

session state issues, troubleshooting, 989-991

setup process, 983-985

trial software, downloading, 978

shortcut keys, 252

VBA editor, PDF:1270-PDF:1273

signed package files

generating, 148

testing, 148-149

Simple Query Wizard, 348-355

SELECT query, creating, 348-355

single-file Access applications, upsizing to SQL Server 2005 or later, 875-886

site types (SPF 2010), 921

smart tags

Internet-based, adding to fields, 231

Property Options smart tag, activating, 229-230

sorting

report data, 735-736

tables, 250-270

on multiple fields, 269-271

on single field, 268-270

source tables, SPF lists as, 951-964

SPF (SharePoint Foundation) 2010

Document Libraries, publishing Access 2010 database to, 935-940

installing under 64-bit Windows Server 2008, 919-920

lists

data types, 940

linking to Access tables, 970

as source tables, 951-964

synchronizing, 964-967

views, customizing, 940-947

security groups, 930-934

site types, 921

subsites, adding, 921-930

SPIS (SharePoint 2010 for Internet Sites), licensing, 976

split forms, generating, 601-602

spreadsheets

Excel worksheets

importing, 299-306

linking, 307-308

importing, 298-299

SQL, 157

aggregate functions, 476, PDF:1148-PDF:1152

joins, PDF:1152-PDF:1155

punctuation, PDF:1142-PDF:1143

SELECT queries, writing, PDF:1140

terminology, PDF:1138-PDF:1140

SQL Server

connecting to remotely, PDF:1133-PDF:1134

inline functions, PDF:1113-PDF:1116

other database tables, working with, PDF:1165-PDF:1167

tables, Table Properties dialog box, PDF:1099-PDF:1105

views, PDF:1106-PDF:1113, PDF:1144

SQL Server 2000, installing, PDF:1416-PDF:1417

SQL Server 2005, PIVOT query syntax, PDF:1216-PDF:1217

SQL Server database, moving to another server, 886-890

SQL Server editions, PDF:1092

SQL Server Management Studio, adding user logins to SQL Server, 900-911

SQL Server Migration Assistant, PDF:1230-PDF:1232

SSRS Add-in, installing, 982-983

SSX

features, 871

installing, 35-41,
PDF:1465-PDF:1470
managing, 41-43,
PDF:1470-PDF:1472
performance,
troubleshooting, 915

standard formats for numeric data, 197

standards, ANSI-92 SQL
conforming to,
PDF:1183-PDF:1194
reserved words in Access
SQL, PDF:1198-PDF:1200

startup mode, 98

**stored procedures,
PDF:1116-PDF:1125**
append, PDF:1119-PDF:1123
execute rights, granting,
907-910
make-table,
PDF:1117-PDF:1119
passing parameter values to,
PDF:1381-PDF:1383
update, PDF:1124
writing, PDF:1160-PDF:1165

**structure of relational
databases, 159-164**

subdatasheets, 456-463
query subdatasheets,
459-463
table properties, 185-186
table subdatasheets, 458-460

subforms
history subform, adding to
tab control page, 667-673
PivotChart view as, 787-790

subqueries, 499-501
UNION subqueries, 495-501

subreports, 737-739
linked subreports, adding to
bound reports, 744
unlinked, 748-749

**subsites (SPF 2010), adding,
921-930**

**substituting PivotTables in a
form, 795-796**

**summary calculations, SQL
aggregate functions, 476**

SwitchBoard Manager, 816-820

**symbolic constants (VBA),
PDF:1257-PDF:1259**

T

**tab controls, adding to forms,
659-665**

**Tabbed Document Style,
displaying forms, 58-59**

**tabbed documents, in Access
2007, PDF:1458**

**Table Analyzer Wizard,
235-239**

**Table Datasheet view,
customizing, 292-294**

**Table Design view (project
designer), PDF:1097-PDF:1099**

**table properties, of
subdatasheets, 185-186**

**table relationships,
diagramming,
PDF:1125-PDF:1126**

**table updates, logging with
data macros, 836-840**

**table-level validation rules,
adding, 257-258**

tables
adding to Northwind Traders
sample database, 204
copying and pasting,
232-235
creating in Datasheet view,
213
display components, 103-105
exporting, 341-343
as text files, 344
exporting to RDBMSs,
874-875
exporting to SharePoint lists,
967
exporting to XML, PDF:1057
fields
including all in queries,
472-474
properties, overriding,
680-681

sequence of, rearranging,
225
fixed-value lookup list,
adding, 447-450
General field properties,
188-190
HRActions table, adding
records, 673-675
indexes, adding, 222-223
ISAM, importing, 324-326
joining, 422-441
multicolumn inner joins,
438-441
lookup fields, 442-456
printing, 703-705
matching records, finding,
271-274
records
adding, 252-253
appending, 543-545
selecting, 254
updating values, 549-559
relationships, changing,
227-228
re-linking, 330-331
sorting, 250-270
on multiple fields,
269-271
on single field, 268-270
subdatasheets, adding,
456-463
XML, importing, PDF:1073

**tabular reports,
autogenerating, 686-688**

templates, 32
in Access 2007, PDF:1458
applications, creating, 46-59
customized template files,
creating, 137-138
downloading, 46-47
HTML, PDF:1035-PDF:1037
sample databases,
generating, 52
sample templates, review-
ing, 49-50
searching for, 51-52
Tabbed Document style,
displaying, 58-59
web database, creating,
985-992

TempVars collection, 396

testing
  cascading deletions, 562
  cascading updates, 562-563
  Packaged Solutions, 150-154
  signed package files, 148-149
  Upsizing wizard, PDF:1173-PDF:1179
  validation rules, 264-266

text boxes, adding to forms, 626-630

text comparison options (VBA), PDF:1278

text data, selecting field size, 193-195

text files
  exporting tables as, 344
  importing, 313-321

Text Filters option, 277-278

text manipulation functions, 398-402

thawing frozen columns, 270

theta joins, creating, 467-469

third normal form, 167

Time and Date functions, 397-398

TP (transaction processing), 173

TPL (Transaction Processing Language), PDF:1139

transaction-processing forms, 602-605
  autogenerating, 566-568

trial Access Hosting account, signing up for, 999-1004

troubleshooting
  compile errors, 143
  SharePoint Server 2010, session state issues, 989-991
  SSX performance, 915
  Upsizing wizard errors, PDF:1179-PDF:1183
  web database incompatibilities, 996-997

Trusted Center pages, setting default options, 134-137

trusted locations
  designating default database folder as, 53-54
  specifying, 31, PDF:1447

T-SQL, emulating crosstab queries, PDF:1205-PDF:1221

U

unbound reports, 748-749

UNION queries, 495-501
  writing, PDF:1155-PDF:1158

unlinked graphs, creating, 759

unsecured files, converting to Access 2010, PDF:1404-PDF:1409

update stored procedures, PDF:1124

updating records, 549-559

upgrading
  to Access 2010, PDF:1401
    secure files, converting, PDF:1410-PDF:1411
    unsecured files, converting, PDF:1404-PDF:1409
  Jet .mdb files to Access .accdb files, 179-180
  MSDE 1.0 to SQL Server 2005, PDF:1415
  MSDE databases, PDF:1417-PDF:1418

upsized project, securing, PDF:1225-PDF:1227

upsizing
  applications with linked tables, 884
  single-file applications to SQL Server 2005 or later, 875-886

Upsizing wizard, PDF:1171-PDF:1172
  errors, troubleshooting, PDF:1179-PDF:1183

second pass, running, PDF:1179
testing, PDF:1173-PDF:1179

user interface
  Backstage view, 26-29
  ribbons, 22-25

user logins, adding to SQL Server, 900-911

Utility Functions module (VBA), PDF:1273-PDF:1278

V

validation rules, 172-173
  field-level, adding, 255-256
  testing, 264-266

variables, VBA, PDF:1250-PDF:1257

Variant data type, 394-396

VBA, PDF:1239-PDF:1240
  Access objects, referring to
    controls, PDF:1309-PDF:1311
    forms, PDF:1307-PDF:1308
  arguments, PDF:1259-PDF:1260
  arrays, PDF:1254-PDF:1255
  class modules, PDF:1280-PDF:1287
  code, password protecting, 914
  converted code, testing, PDF:1283-PDF:1287
  data types, PDF:1248-PDF:1249
  DoCmd methods, PDF:1291-PDF:1294
  functions, 391-402, PDF:1245-PDF:1246
    events, responding to, PDF:1289-PDF:1291
    Variant data type, 394-396
  help system, PDF:1271-PDF:1272
  versus macros, 801

Macro-to-VBA converter,
PDF:1280-PDF:1283
modules,
PDF:1242-PDF:1244
  elements of,
    PDF:1244-PDF:1246
naming conventions,
PDF:1241
Object Browser, PDF:1247
program flow, controlling,
PDF:1260-PDF:1266
  conditional statements,
    PDF:1261-PDF:1264
  looping,
    PDF:1264-PDF:1266
references,
PDF:1246-PDF:1247
runtime errors, handling,
PDF:1266-PDF:1268
security issues, PDF:1241
symbolic constants,
PDF:1257-PDF:1259
text comparison options,
PDF:1278
Utility Functions module,
PDF:1273-PDF:1278
variables,
PDF:1250-PDF:1257
With...End With structure,
PDF:1257

**VBA editor,
PDF:1269-PDF:1272**
module window toolbar,
PDF:1269-PDF:1256
shortcut keys,
PDF:1270-PDF:1273

**verifying back-end security,
868-870**

**viewing macro actions,
799-801**

**views (SQL Server),
PDF:1106-PDF:1113**

**Visual Studio 2005, edit-
ing RibbonX documents,
PDF:1299-PDF:1301**

W

Web Browser control, 679

web databases
Contacts web database,
deleting Getting Started
form, 992-996
creating from templates,
985-992
incompatibilities,
troubleshooting, 996-997

web pages
HTML lists, importing to
Access tables,
PDF:1020-PDF:1024
HTML tables, importing,
PDF:1009

**websites, Microsoft Office
Online, 55-57**

**well-formed documents (XML),
PDF:1055**

**widowed records, preventing
with Keep Together property,
720-721**

**Windows Clipboard
operations, key
combinations, 249-252**

**Windows SharePoint
Foundation 2010,
collaborating with, 917-918**

**With...End With structure
(VBA), PDF:1257**

wizards
Combo Box wizard, 640-644
Command Button Wizard,
generating embedded
macros, 804-809
Crosstab Query Wizard,
486-491
Exchange/Outlook wizard,
311-313
Find Duplicates Query
Wizard, 371,
PDF:1016-PDF:1018

Find Unmatched Query
Wizard, 372-373
Form wizard, creating
master\child forms,
594-601
group boxes, adding to
forms, 632-637
Import HTML Wizard,
PDF:1020-PDF:1024
Import Text Wizard,
importing text files,
314-318
Label wizard, 721-725
Mail Merge Wizard, 331-340
  form letters, creating,
    332-339
Report Wizard, creating
grouped reports, 688-695
Simple Query Wizard,
348-355
  SELECT query, creating,
    348-355
Table Analyzer Wizard,
235-239
Upsizing wizard,
PDF:1171-PDF:1172

**Word, exporting tables to,
341-343**

writing
named data macros, 841-857
pass-through queries,
897-900
SELECT queries, PDF:1140
stored procedures,
PDF:1160-PDF:1165

**writing ApplyFilter macro,
812-816**

X

XML, PDF:1054-PDF:1057

    exported file sets,
      deploying to web server,
      PDF:1069

    exporting data in related
      tables, PDF:1077-PDF:1080

    exporting static reports as,
      PDF:1070

    headers, PDF:1055

    importing to tables,
      PDF:1073

    InfoPath forms, PDF:1080

    schema, PDF:1056

    well-formed documents,
      PDF:1055

**XPS files, exporting tables to,
341-343**

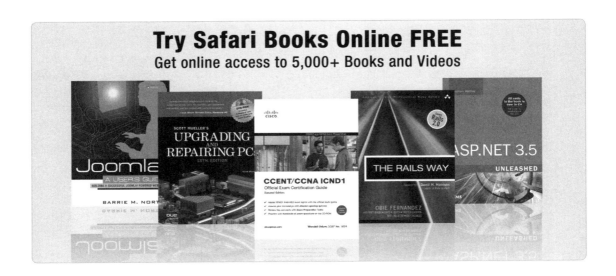